The Multicultural Student's
Guide to Colleges

THE MULTICULTURAL STUDENT'S GUIDE TO COLLEGES

What Every African-American, Asian-American, Hispanic, and
Native American Applicant Needs to Know about
America's Top Schools

ROBERT MITCHELL

THE NOONDAY PRESS · FARRAR, STRAUS AND GIROUX · NEW YORK

Library of Congress Cataloging-in-Publication Data
Mitchell, Robert.
The multicultural student's guide to colleges : what every African-American, Asian-American,
Hispanic, and Native American applicant needs to know about America's top schools / Robert
Mitchell.—1st ed.
p. cm.
1. Universities and colleges—United States—Directories. 2. Universities and colleges—United
States—Guidebooks. 3. Minorities—Education (Higher)—United States—Guidebooks. I. Title.
93-21749 CIP L901.M58 1993 378.73—dc20

For Mom and Dad
and
my students at
Chelsea High School

ACKNOWLEDGMENTS

In the course of writing this book, I relied on many people for advice, encouragement, and assistance, but none more so than the hundreds of college students I spoke with, all of whom took valuable time away from their studies and extracurricular activities to offer their perspectives about life at their schools. Without their help, this book could not have been written. In addition, I want to thank the admissions counselors and administrators at the colleges and universities included in these pages who responded to our lengthy admissions questionnaire.

There are dozens of friends and colleagues whose support and patience throughout has been invaluable. First, let me acknowledge the assistance of several of my former high school students who took time away from their studies at DePauw to help with research: Emilio Nieves, Carlos Ortiz, Joaquin Melo, Kevin Hibbert, and Allen Glover, I thank you. Georgette Wong, Bonita Chang, and Tanya Lieberman also provided much-appreciated research assistance.

On a day-to-day basis, there was no greater support than Martha Hanson. Her patience and encouraging words were as important and valuable to the completion of this book as any conversation I had with a college student. Likewise, Jan Scott was always there for me with her insights—often called into use at a moment's notice to read portions of the book's manuscript—and sense of humor. Caroline Lavelle, Susan Stark, Allen Scheuch, Carol Kleinert, and Hannah Hess were also supportive. I want to thank Charles Richardson, who helped shape the admissions questionnaire.

As always, my family, including my parents, Robert and Ruth Ann Mitchell, my sister Sydney Fox and my brother Todd Mitchell, have been among my most enthusiastic and constant sources of support. Thanks also to Mimi Mitchell and Dan Fox.

Super agent Jeremy Solomon of First Books/First Arts in Chicago was a believer in the project from the beginning, and I appreciate his hard work on its behalf and his friendship. I also want to express my gratitude to my editor, Elisabeth Dyssegaard, and her assistants, Angela Quilala and Joan Mathieu, at Farrar, Straus and Giroux.

Finally, I want to acknowledge an upcoming generation of college students, and give them all my love and best wishes, particularly Margot and Christopher Mitchell, Andrew and Meryl Fox, and Peter Scott Reyes.

CONTENTS

Introduction 3
How to Use This Book 5
The Application Process 9
The Financial Aid Search 18
On Choosing a Predominantly Black College 25

ALABAMA 27
University of Alabama 27
Auburn University 31

ARIZONA 35
University of Arizona 35
Arizona State University 39

ARKANSAS 44
University of Arkansas 44
Hendrix College 47

CALIFORNIA 50
University of California/Berkeley 50
University of California/Davis 54
University of California/Irvine 58
University of California/Los Angeles 61
University of California/Riverside 64
University of California/Santa Barbara 68
University of California/Santa Cruz 71

California Institute of Technology 74
Claremont/Claremont McKenna College 77
Claremont/Harvey Mudd College 80
Claremont/Pitzer College 83
Claremont/Pomona College 86
Claremont/Scripps College 89
Mills College 92
Occidental College 95
University of Redlands 99
University of Southern California 102
Stanford University 106

COLORADO 111
University of Colorado 111
Colorado College 114
Colorado School of Mines 118
United States Air Force Academy 121

CONNECTICUT 124
University of Connecticut 124
Connecticut College 127
Trinity College 130
Wesleyan University 134
Yale University 138

DELAWARE 142
University of Delaware 142

DISTRICT OF COLUMBIA 146
Catholic University of America 146
George Washington University 150
Georgetown University 153
Howard University 156

FLORIDA 161
University of Florida 161
Florida Institute of Technology 165
Florida State University 168

University of Miami 170
New College of the University of South Florida 174

GEORGIA 177
Agnes Scott College 177
Emory University 180
University of Georgia 183
Morehouse College 186
Oglethorpe University 190
Spelman College 193

IDAHO 196
University of Idaho 196

ILLINOIS 199
University of Chicago 199
De Paul University 202
University of Illinois/Urbana-Champaign 205
Illinois State University 211
Illinois Wesleyan University 214
Knox College 216
Loyola University 220
Northwestern University 223
Wheaton College 227

INDIANA 231
DePauw University 231
Earlham College 235
Indiana University 239
University of Notre Dame 241
Purdue University 244
Wabash Colleg 247

IOWA 251
Coe College 251
Cornell College 254
Grinnell College 257
University of Iowa 261
Iowa State University of Science and Technology 264

KANSAS 269
University of Kansas 269

KENTUCKY 273
Berea College 273
Centre College 276
University of Kentucky 279
University of Louisville 282

LOUISIANA 286
Louisiana State University and Agricultural and Mechanical
    College 286
Tulane University 289
Xavier University of Louisiana 292

MAINE 296
Bates College 296
Bowdoin College 300
Colby College 303

MARYLAND 308
Johns Hopkins University 308
University of Maryland 311
St. John's College 315
United States Naval Academy 318

MASSACHUSETTS 322
Amherst College 322
Babson College 326
Boston College 330
Boston University 333
Brandeis University 337
Clark University 339
Hampshire College 341
Harvard University 345
College of the Holy Cross 349
University of Massachusetts 353
Massachussetts Institute of Technology 357
Mount Holyoke College 361

Northeastern University 364
Smith College 368
Tufts University 372
Wellesley College 375
Wheaton College 379
Williams College 383
Worcester Polytechnic Institute 387

MICHIGAN 390
Albion College 390
GMI Engineering and Management Institute 393
Kalamazoo College 396
University of Michigan 399
Michigan State University 402

MINNESOTA 407
Carleton College 407
Gustavus Adolphus College 411
Hamline University 414
Macalester College 418
University of Minnesota 421
St. Olaf College 425

MISSISSIPPI 429
Millsaps College 429
University of Mississippi 432

MISSOURI 436
University of Missouri/Columbia 436
Washington University 438

MONTANA 442
University of Montana 442

NEBRASKA 445
Creighton University 445
University of Nebraska/Lincoln 448

NEW HAMPSHIRE 452
Dartmouth College 452
University of New Hampshire 455

NEW JERSEY 459
Drew University 459
Princeton University 462
Rutgers University 466
Seton Hall University 471
Trenton State University 474

NEW MEXICO 478
University of New Mexico 478
New Mexico Institute of Mining and Technology 481
St. John's College 484

NEW YORK 486
Adelphi University 486
Bard College 490
Barnard College of Columbia University 493
City University of New York/Brooklyn College 496
City University of New York/City College 500
City University of New York/Hunter College 503
City University of New York/Queens College 505
Colgate University 508
Columbia University/Columbia College 512
Cooper Union for the Advancement of Science and Art 516
Cornell University 519
Hamilton College 525
Hobart and William Smith Colleges 528
Hofstra University 531
Manhattan College 534
Manhattanville College 536
New York University 539
Rensselaer Polytechnic Institute 543
University of Rochester 546
Rochester Institute of Technology 550

St. Lawrence University 553
Sarah Lawrence College 555
Skidmore College 558
State University of New York/Albany 561
State University of New York/Binghamton 565
State University of New York/Buffalo 568
Union College 571
Vassar College 574
Wells College 577

NORTH CAROLINA 581
Davidson College 581
Duke University 584
Guilford College 589
University of North Carolina/Chapel Hill 592
North Carolina State University 595
Wake Forest University 599

NORTH DAKOTA 603
University of North Dakota 603

OHIO 607
Antioch College 607
Case Western Reserve University 609
Kenyon College 611
Miami University 614
Oberlin College 618
Ohio State University 621
Ohio Wesleyan University 625
Wittenberg University 628
College of Wooster 630

OKLAHOMA 634
University of Oklahoma 634
Oklahoma State University 639

OREGON 643
University of Oregon 643
Reed College 646
Williamette University 649

PENNSYLVANIA 653
Allegheny College 653
Bryn Mawr College 656
Bucknell University 659
Carnegie-Mellon University 662
Dickinson College 664
Franklin and Marshall College 668
Gettysburg College 671
Haverford College 673
Lafayette College 677
Lehigh University 679
Lincoln University 683
Muhlenburg College 686
University of Pennsylvania 688
Pennsylvania State University 691
Swarthmore College 694
Temple University 698
Villanova University 701

RHODE ISLAND 704
Brown University 704
Providence College 709
University of Rhode Island 711

SOUTH CAROLINA 714
Furman University 714
University of South Carolina 717
Wofford College 720

SOUTH DAKOTA 724
University of South Dakota 724

TENNESSEE 728
Rhodes College 728
University of Tennessee/Knoxville 731
Vanderbilt University 735

TEXAS 738
Rice University 738
Southern Methodist University 740
Southwestern University 743
University of Texas/Austin 746
Trinity University 750

UTAH 754
University of Utah 754

VERMONT 758
Bennington College 758
Middlebury College 761
University of Vermont 765

VIRGINIA 769
Hampden-Sydney College 769
Hollins College 772
Randolph-Macon College 776
Randolph-Macon Woman's College 778
University of Virginia 782
Virginia Military Institute 785
Virginia Polytechnic Institute and State University 788
Washington and Lee University 791
College of William and Mary 794

WASHINGTON 797
University of Puget Sound 797
University of Washington 800
Whitman College 804

WEST VIRGINIA 808
Shepherd College 808
West Virginia University 811

WISCONSIN 814
Beloit College 814
Lawrence University 817
Marquette University 820

Ripon College 824
University of Wisconsin/Madison 826

WYOMING 831
University of Wyoming 831

America's Predominantly Black Colleges and Universities . . . 835

The Multicultural Student's
Guide to Colleges

INTRODUCTION

America's college campuses are becoming more racially and culturally diverse. Yet the college guides currently available don't reflect or discuss these changes. At best, they mention the percentage of the school's student population that is "minority," but give little or no attention to the concerns of students of color? Yes, the other guides devote considerable space to issues of student life and academics, but what of the activities of an Asian-American club, or of the academic support services and financial aid opportunities offered to students of color? What about a school's strengths in African-American or Native American Studies?

As an English teacher at a public high school in New York City who frequently advises students about college, I became frustrated by the lack of information about these and other issues. I also became concerned that the voices heard from in these guides are rarely, if ever, those of students of color. *The Multicultural Student's Guide to Colleges,* which offers in-depth profiles of most of the country's top schools, seeks to fill the void left by the other guides by providing information that will allow students of color to make confident and wise college choices.

For generations, America's premier colleges and universities have served the country's white, and often male, elite. Today, however, many of these institutions seek to serve a broader spectrum of students and to have their student populations reflect more accurately the country's socioeconomic, racial, and cultural diversity. With increased recruiting and retention efforts, many schools are successfully doing so. Unfortunately, this is not yet true for all of the country's top schools.

Colleges are also making strides, often with student prodding, to diversify their curriculums. Despite a storm of controversy, led by William Bennett, the Secretary of Education in the Reagan Administration, Stanford was one of the country's first great universities to integrate non-Western studies into its core curriculum. Many schools are establishing or increasing their course offerings—some with full-fledged academic departments, others with majors and minors—in African-American, Native American, Hispanic, and Asian-American Studies. More than ever, college administrations and student organizations are hosting forums, lectures, and other programs to discuss issues related to cultural and racial diversity.

Issues of retaining and graduating students of color have also risen to the forefront at many of these schools, which have made serious commitments to their academic and non-academic support programs. At many of the predominantly white colleges included in these pages, students of color are being graduated at the same rates as their white counterparts, and in some instances, at even better rates. In recent years, colleges have also created their own financial aid opportunities—usually through private endowments—specifically for students of color.

Clearly, America's colleges are becoming more inviting to students of color. But all is not nirvana. Racism has reared its ugly head at many schools, even at some of our country's more liberal-minded campuses. PBS produced a show, entitled *Racism 101*, that depicted the racial tension at some of the nation's prominent colleges. Professors have been known to make jokes at the expense of "minority" groups. Slave auctions, racist graffiti, and other demeaning incidents have also occurred in recent years and serve to remind the campus community and the nation that there is still a great deal of work to be done when it comes to building better race relations.

Students also talk about the amount of self-segregation that takes place at their schools. Campuses have become more racially diverse, but often, other than in the classroom, there is little interaction among students from various backgrounds. Students point to all-white and all-black Greek systems, for instance, and to campus cafeterias where students of the same race tend to sit together at all-Asian or all-black dining tables.

Student activism, often relating to issues of racial and cultural diversity, has been on the upswing in recent years; since the 1991–92 school year, for example, students at numerous institutions of higher learning across the country have staged sit-ins and other forms of demonstration, demanding that their schools further diversify their faculty and staff, student body, and curriculum. At one university in the South, a student compared the race-related activism currently going on at her school to the antiwar demonstrations that went on there in the 1960s. Although such activism is viewed as vital by participants, more than one student pointed out that it takes valuable time away from what they're at college to do: to pursue an education.

Attending one of America's top colleges or universities isn't an inalienable right, as is the pursuit of happiness. However, the pursuit of happiness—particularly in terms of socioeconomic advancement and an increase in career options—is less difficult with a college degree. At many of these schools, you will compete academically with some of the country's most motivated and brightest students and have access to high-quality faculty and other resources. *The Multicultural Student's Guide to Colleges* will help you navigate your way through the myriad opportunities available at our country's best schools.

Robert Mitchell

HOW TO USE THIS BOOK

The information contained in *The Multicultural Student's Guide to Colleges* was supplied by those who know best: by the admissions offices and students at each of the more than 200 colleges and universities profiled in these pages. If schools were not able to supply us with information about a particular section, we indicated so with the abbreviation "na," for "not available."

The categories in this book are not an exact measure of diversity—indeed no category can be—but they do give a sense of whether a school puts a premium on creating a diverse community and intellectual life and to what extent they've succeeded. There might be some debate about how certain people fit into the categories. Hispanics, for example, can be white or black; but to the extent that they represent a tradition outside the mainstream, white European-American tradition, they contribute to the richness of multicultural life on campus. In the end, you must judge a school for yourself. You shouldn't make a decision based only on percentage points; but there is a difference between a school with 3 percent students of color and one with 15 percent.

THE STATISTICS SECTION

TUITION AND ROOM AND BOARD

The data for this section include the most current information available, but it is important to note that costs of tuition and room and board can increase annually and sometimes significantly. For public institutions, there are different tuition fees for in-state and out-of-state students, while private school costs are the same for in-state and out-of-state students. The dollar amount listed for room and board is generally for a double room with a full meal plan. Schools offer other dorm sizes and meal plans at various costs.

APPLICATION DEADLINE

A school's application deadline is the date by which students are expected to submit all of their application materials, including SAT scores, high school transcripts, and recommendations. The dates given here are for students applying for the fall semester. Schools with rolling admissions policies generally accept applications up to the first day of classes of a particular academic term and inform you of their admissions decision within a specified time period after receiving all of your application materials.

FINANCIAL AID APPLICATION DEADLINE

Perhaps the most important deadline to meet is the one for financial aid. Often, a school's financial aid and admissions application deadlines are similar, but students and parents are best advised to complete and return any financial aid forms well before their deadline. Frequently, financial assistance is given on a first-come, first-served basis, and schools are usually dealing with a limited amount of financial aid resources.

FRESHMAN ADMISSIONS

The information in this section should help you assess the admissions difficulty of a given college. Schools supplied us with some of the academic characteristics of a recently admitted first-year class, including high school class rank, SAT scores, and ACT scores.

ENROLLMENT FIGURES

All of the numbers given here reflect a school's undergraduate population, and do not include enrollment figures for schools' graduate programs.

NON-WHITE STUDENTS

These figures reveal the history, going back more than five years, of a college's enrollment of students of color. The figures represent the percentage of a school's total undergraduate enrollment who were African-American, Hispanic, Asian-American, and Native American in a given year. We included these figures to show the school's progress in diversifying its campus.

GEOGRAPHIC DISTRIBUTION

Many colleges work to have a geographically diverse student population, while others, usually because of limited resources, attract a more regional group of students. This section states what percentage of a school's undergraduate enrollment of students of color is from in-state and from the various regions of the country.

TOP MAJORS

The information contained here lists the most popular majors among a school's students of color.

RETENTION RATE OF NON-WHITE STUDENTS

The percentage of a school's first-year class that returns for the sophomore year is given here. Where indicated, we provide a school's graduation rate instead.

SCHOLARSHIPS EXCLUSIVELY FOR NON-WHITE STUDENTS

When available, we included information about scholarships offered specifically to students of color by individual schools. We asked schools to tell us the dollar value of the scholarships, the number of such scholarships awarded each year, whether the scholarships are need- or merit-based, and the criteria used for awarding these scholarships. If a school doesn't offer race-based awards, we indicated so with the word "None." It's important to note that all schools offer merit- and need-based scholarships to *all* students, regardless of race.

REMEDIATION PROGRAMS

In this section, we have listed the courses and programs a college offers students with special academic needs.

ACADEMIC SUPPORT SERVICES

This section includes a school's various academic support services, ranging from peer tutoring to special academic advising.

ETHNIC STUDIES PROGRAMS

Schools supplied us with information about their programs in African, African-American, Asian, Asian-American, Hispanic, and Native American Studies. Where possible, we included the number of students who were majoring or minoring in each of the areas, the year each of the programs was established on campus, and the number of tenured faculty who teach in the programs.

ETHNIC STUDIES COURSES

If a school doesn't offer a program in African, African-American, Asian, Asian-American, Hispanic, or Native American Studies, we listed related courses available in other departments.

ORGANIZATIONS FOR NON-WHITE STUDENTS

The organizations listed in this section include those that are recognized by a school's student government and/or student life office. Although the membership of each organization listed may reflect the ethnicity or culture implied in the group's name, most such groups include individuals from various backgrounds. In addition, in each of the narratives we focused on the cultural groups that are among the more active on a particular college campus. It's important to note, however, that the other groups listed in this section of a college profile also plan a variety of activities. When you visit colleges, be sure to find out what sort of activities the group or groups you're interested in joining have sponsored recently.

NOTABLE NON-WHITE ALUMNI

This section gives the names, graduation dates, undergraduate majors, and occupations of some of a school's more prominent multicultural graduates.

TENURED AND NON-TENURED FACULTY AND ADMINISTRATORS

Tenured professors are permanent members of a school's faculty. The percentage of a school's faculty and administration that is African-American, Hispanic, Asian-American, and Native American is given here.

STUDENT-FACULTY RATIO

The ratio of students to faculty is supplied to give you a rough idea of how many students you might expect in a typical class. But don't assume that a first-year English class will have only 17 students and one professor, if that is the ratio given by a school. Depending on the school, first-year classes can have hundreds of students. Use the ratios as approximations.

RECENT NON-WHITE SPEAKERS

At many schools, awareness about national and international issues is raised by guest lecturers, who are invited to campus to speak either by student organizations or by the colleges themselves. In this section, we have mentioned some of the speakers who have come to the schools within the past three years.

THE NARRATIVES

Each of the narratives includes information about a college's academics, cultural organizations, faculty and staff support, extracurricular activities, and location—to give you a sense of what you might expect should you decide to attend a particular institution. To obtain the information, we were basically reporters, asking students by phone and by mail—and we heard from hundreds of students—to comment on the particulars of their school's academic and non-academic life. We also visited dozens of colleges and universities throughout the country, meeting with students to discuss life at their colleges. We do not pretend to offer the definitive profile of any one school. An endeavor such as ours, in which we rely on the opinions and perspectives of individuals, is inherently subjective. In addition to the *Guide,* we recommend that prospective applicants rely on their own investigative work and visit colleges, read college catalogues thoroughly and critically, and talk to currently enrolled students.

HOW WE SELECTED THE COLLEGES

The *Guide* focuses on America's most prominent institutions of higher learning, ones that have traditionally appealed to the country's top students. It also includes a geographically varied group of schools, as well as schools with diverse characteristics of size, student body makeup, and personalities. Because of time and space limitations, we have not been able to include all of the schools worthy of close attention. But each of the schools in the *Guide* offers a rich variety of quality educational and social opportunities.

Finally, a word about our decision not to rank the colleges. We believe that such rankings—as used by many of the other college guidebooks and magazines that devote single issues to college ratings—can be extremely misleading, particularly to students of color, although we do rely on certain of these publications in several of our profiles, as they give a sense of a school's place in America's educational hierarchy. Such rankings, although they purport to be statistically based, are also subjective, relying on the perspectives of—often white—college presidents, admissions deans, and student respondents. Quality-of-life issues as they apply to students of color are not factored into these rankings. A college that is ranked number one by a majority of these individuals, for example, or that has four stars or mortarboards as symbols of high quality, may not appeal to every applicant. In the end, we trust that students are capable of creating a personal rating system that is most appropriate to their needs.

Despite repeated requests, some schools declined to respond to our admissions questionnaire. We have supplied the addresses, phone numbers, tuition costs, and application and financial aid deadlines for each of these schools' admissions offices, and information about their undergraduate enrollment figures, included in the narrative portion of the school's profile, was obtained from the U.S. Department of Education as reported in *The Chronicle of Higher Education.*

THE APPLICATION PROCESS

There are over 3,500 colleges and universities in the United States. Choosing a college can be an exciting challenge. The process of selecting a school will help you to learn more about yourself and your interests and to define your possible career goals.

Pursuing further education after high school is a proven means of increasing your knowledge and employment options. A college degree by itself cannot guarantee career success, but it can guarantee that more opportunities will become available to you. Post-secondary education is a means of self-empowerment—a means of creating a variety of new paths for career success.

TYPES OF POST-SECONDARY SCHOOLS

Primarily, post-secondary schools fall into two major categories: colleges and universities and vocational and career-related schools. A college offers educational instruction in a two-year (junior college) or a four-year (liberal arts college) program. A university offers undergraduate degrees in a variety of fields in addition to offering at least two graduate or professional degrees. The majority of colleges and universities emphasize a liberal arts curriculum of study in their undergraduate degree programs; that is, instruction is geared toward a broad base of disciplines.

Career and vocational schools are attractive options for students who believe that they have identified a particular area of study that they would like to pursue immediately after high school. This category of schools includes institutions such as trade and technical schools. These schools offer immediate employment training in fields such as the culinary arts, medical technology, plumbing, and clerical work. Some of these schools also offer a variety of degrees involving varying length of study in the areas of nursing and business.

Before you decide on the kind of school that you wish to apply to, there are some important issues to consider. First, if you pursue a program of study that is concentrated in its focus, you will probably be limited in the types of career or employment paths available to you. A two-year degree in secretarial work may prepare you only to pursue entry-level positions in the field of business. In contrast, the completion of a four-year liberal arts degree may make you eligible for a number of managerial trainee positions in business. In fact, a liberal arts degree would allow you to apply for further study in graduate school. As a general rule, the more comprehensive the educational program you select, the greater the number of opportunities you will have to choose from after you have completed the program.

THE COLLEGE SEARCH

There are many different types of colleges. When selecting a college, keep in mind the following criteria. The process of choosing the type of post-secondary institution to apply to begins with identifying your interests. The majority of students graduating from high school will not know exactly which particular academic major or field of study they wish to pursue. If you are undecided, you should consider a liberal arts college or university. At such schools you will be exposed to a wide variety of educational disciplines. Many post-secondary institutions expect most of their entering students to be undecided about their final career choices and are prepared to help students make these decisions.

Once you have decided on a general or specific area of study, there are several other factors to consider in identifying schools to which to apply:

LOCATION

Do you wish to be far from home or closer to home? Would you prefer to be in a rural area or a metropolitan area? Does the community surrounding the school offer acceptable social and cultural opportunities?

SIZE

Would you prefer to be in a small school (fewer than 2,000 students), a medium-sized school (2,000 to 3,500 students), or a large institution (3,500 or more students)? It is important to note that the size of the school will very often determine the size of the classes and the ratio of students to faculty. Some students like large, lecture-type classes, whereas others prefer smaller, more intimate discussion groups. So you should determine what type of class setting best suits your learning style and habits. Also, larger universities usually offer more academic programs and extracurricular opportunities from which to choose.

THE STUDENT BODY

The composition of a school's student body is an important consideration. There are single-sex and coeducational institutions, religiously affiliated schools, and historically black colleges. Schools also vary with regard to the geographic (regional vs. national), ethnic, cultural, and socioeconomic diversity of their student enrollment. Keep in mind that in choosing a school you are also choosing a community of potential friends and acquaintances.

SELECTIVITY

Post-secondary institutions have a wide range of admissions processes. Some institutions accept virtually all the students who apply, and other schools accept only a small percentage of their applicants. In choosing institutions, you should try to match your level of academic achievement with the level of a given institution's admission selectivity. But don't limit yourself. Also apply to schools that are more selective in admissions, should they offer programs that appeal to you. You may have what it takes to win acceptance, even if it's not high SAT scores or grade point average. To be on the safe side, you should also be sure to apply to schools that you're confident will accept you.

FINANCIAL AID

Should you be fortunate enough to win acceptance to more than one school, compare the financial awards offered to you by each institution. Although you shouldn't make a college choice based solely on a financial award, it is an important factor in deciding which school to attend. If a school that you're interested in attending doesn't offer you the aid you feel you're qualified for, contact its financial aid office and ask to speak to a counselor. He or she will be glad to discuss your concerns with you, and may make it financially possible for you to attend that school. Refer to the essay on page 18 for more information about the college financial aid application process.

SPECIAL FACTORS

Many people like to be exposed to new surroundings, opportunities, and people. However, many of us also like to have the comfort of knowing that there will be individuals who share our values, culture, ethnic heritage, or socioeconomic status when we enter a new community. When you choose a post-secondary school, the diversity of the student enrollment and the presence of support systems and role models can be important considerations for students of color.

If you are student of African descent, for example, and your ethnic and cultural heritage is important to you, you should consider the enrollment of students of African descent at the institutions you would ideally like to attend. Will you be one of a few at an institution, or will you one of many? Will you be comfortable with the ratio of students of color to white students?

As you have looked to your teachers, counselors, and administrators for advice and instruction in high school, you will also look for advice and instruction from their counterparts in college. This book provides you with information on the percentage of faculty and administrators of color at a number of institutions. The book also reports the percentage of faculty of color who have tenure at these institutions—that is, how many people of color are permanent members of their teaching staff. However, you should bear in mind that faculty and administrators of color may not necessarily be a primary source of support while attending college. So it is necessary for you to find out from students at a given college whether there is general, positive support given to students of color by all members of the community.

Graduating from some institutions of higher learning can be as challenging as gaining admission to them. One of the most important questions you should consider is an institution's graduation or retention rate of students—that is, what percentage of students finish their academic program in four or five years. If an institution has a high rate of retention, you can typically be assured that it has good academic, financial, social, and cultural support mechanisms in place for all its students. You may also wish to consider such factors as a school's athletic facilities, student organizations, library resources, and science facilities.

VISITING COLLEGES

All colleges have standard programs to welcome student visitors. Colleges may offer campus tours, interviews, information sessions, and opportunities to visit overnight on campus. You can determine what type of visitation program is available by contacting the college's admissions office. Many colleges and universities offer programs to bring you to their campuses for free or at discounted prices, either by bus or by plane. Such programs are usually offered to students who have demonstrated financial need and who have already applied for admission. Contact the school you're interested in to see if they have such programs.

The best time to visit a college is during the academic year when classes are in session. This is your opportunity to see the college functioning on a typical day. If it is not convenient for you to visit a college that you are interested in while it is in session, it is still better to visit the campus for a tour and to talk with admission officials than not to visit at all. Also, take advantage of any overnight visitation program that may be offered—such a program will give you a full sense of the residential and social atmosphere of the institution.

One of your best sources of information about a school are your conversations with students who are attending the school. When you are on a college campus, ask students about their social and academic experience, sit in on at least one class, and talk to professors and administrators—and to coaches if you are an athlete.

When you are choosing a college, you are also choosing a home for the next four years after high school. Once you have gained admission to a college, the name or the prestige of the institution will not be a factor in your day-to-day happiness on campus. What will be important will be the level of your social, academic, and cultural comfort. If you are happy at the institution, you will probably be successful there. So it is important to gather as much information as possible during your visits to college campuses.

WHAT DO COLLEGES LOOK FOR?

There is no single factor that determines a student's admission to a given college. Admissions officers at selective colleges take several factors into account in the admissions application process. Below are some of the important factors that are considered.

COURSES AND GRADES

The classes you take in high school and the grades you earn are the most important factors to prepare you for admission to college. Selective liberal arts colleges typically require four years of English, three years of a foreign language, three years of mathematics, two years of history and social science, three years of natural science (including one year of a laboratory science), and satisfaction of the art and physical education requirements of your high school.

Colleges will look at your selection of courses and academic performance from ninth grade through twelfth. In selecting courses each year, it is important to choose a program that ideally includes full-year courses in English, mathematics, science, a foreign language, and history or a social science. College admission officers prefer to see "academic solid" courses; that is, full-year courses in traditional academic disciplines. For example, do not take a course in accounting in place of a more challenging course in mathematics. You will have ample opportunity to take specialized courses in college. In high school, it is always best to take courses in the traditional academic areas.

Almost all high schools offer different levels or tracks of courses. A typical high school may offer English instruction at the advanced (very challenging), intermediate (challenging), and average (somewhat challenging) levels. It is important to know that college admissions counselors look at the level of challenge of your courses before they look at your grades in your courses. A college official will look more favorably upon a B grade earned in an advanced course than an A– grade earned in an average course. So try to choose the most challenging courses that you feel comfortable taking from among those that are available to you each year.

In preparing for college, remember that each of your four years in high school is important. College admission officers will look for any academic trends on your transcript. If your academic achievement is not strong in ninth or tenth grades, any significant academic improvement in your next two years will be looked upon quite favorably. However, a downward trend in your level of course choices or grade performance in your junior and senior years will not be to your advantage.

The higher the level of your academic achievement, the greater the control you will have over what college you ultimately attend.

STANDARDIZED TESTS

Most students place far too much importance on the role of standardized tests in the college admissions process. You should be firmly assured that standardized tests are only one component of the college application. Most colleges will not look at your scores on the Scholastic Aptitude Test (SAT), Achievement Test (ACH), or the American College Test (ACT) without first looking at your overall academic achievement in high school.

Colleges usually require a student to submit results from the SAT or ACT as part of their application for admission. Some colleges also require or recommend the submission of ACH results in one or more subject areas. A test such as the SAT may be one of the few standard academic measures used across the country, but it is widely recognized that such a test is not a perfect indicator of a student's potential for success in college. It is well known, for example, that there are variations in test performance for reasons of gender, geography, ethnic background, and socioeconomic status—reasons that have very little to do with a student's academic achievement in high school.

Most college admission officials believe that it is your selection of proper courses in high school and your academic achievement in them that are the best indicators for your success in college. College officials will look at your standardized test scores in the context of how you have performed academically in high school. If you have done well in your academic courses each year, average or below-average standardized test results will not prevent you from being a competitive college applicant. It cannot be emphasized enough that is it what you achieve in the classroom every day that is the most important factor in the college admissions process.

It is to your advantage to take the SAT or the ACT more than once; most students, however, take these exams no more than two or three times. You should take the SAT during your junior year, and again your senior year. If you take the SATs more than once, most colleges will only look at your highest verbal score and your highest mathematics score, even if these scores were earned on different test dates.

EXTRACURRICULAR ACTIVITIES

In addition to your academic performance, many colleges look at your activities outside the classroom. Your extracurricular activities may give college admission officials important information about your character, sense of responsibility, interests, and special talents. In building a college community, colleges look for students who will contribute to both the academic and the social atmosphere of their campuses. Admission officials believe that if you have been active in your high school or in your community, it is likely that you will be a positive contributor to student life at their institutions. Athletics, part-time employment, clubs, volunteer work, and involvement in the arts are all acceptable pursuits. The most important question is whether you use your time constructively after you leave your high school classes each day.

The depth and the quality of your involvement in activities is much more important than the number of your activities. Involvement in one activity for ten hours each week for each of your high school years is usually more meaningful than joining five clubs during your senior year for one hour each week.

RECOMMENDATIONS

Your teachers and counselors can be very helpful to you in the college application process. Most colleges request the submission of one or more letters of recommendation from them. Recognizing this, it is important that you build positive relationships with your high school counselor and a few of your teachers. If these individuals know you well, they can more accurately describe your strengths as a candidate for college admission.

In teacher recommendations, colleges look for an assessment of your writing, analytical, and quantitative skills, participation in class discussion, and your enthusiasm for learning. Are you quiet and attentive in class? Do you ask questions and show enthusiasm for the material that is being taught? In selecting teachers to write on your behalf, you should select people who will speak positively about your learning skills and academic achievement. It is also helpful to select people who know of your involvement and activities beyond the classroom. If you're not certain whether the teacher or counselor will write you a positive recommendation, ask him or her what they might include in the letter. A letter with negative comments about your abilities may mean not getting into the college of your choice, so speak candidly with the teacher or counselor about the letter's contents.

Recommendations from high school guidance personnel should describe you as an academic and social member of your high school, stating what you have achieved academically and what contributions you have made to your school and community.

It is important to identify and to approach teachers and counselors to write letters on your behalf by the end of your junior year. To assist them in describing your candidacy, you should make an appointment with each of them to discuss your achievements in high school and your college interests and plans.

THE COLLEGE ESSAY

Many colleges require that you submit one or more essays or personal statements with your college application. The first and perhaps foremost element that admission personnel look for in your essay(s) is your ability to communicate your thoughts clearly on paper. If you have taken challenging academic courses in high school, you should feel confident that you have the skills necessary to write an effective essay for your college application.

Colleges use your essay to find out more about you as a person. The questions that colleges ask you on their applications are essentially vehicles to get you to express yourself on paper. Rather than relying solely on grades and test scores, colleges wish to know more about you, how you think and how you feel.

The best advice on how to write a college essay is to be yourself—write in your own style, after giving your subject careful thought. Honest expression and clear writing are the two essential components to an effective college essay. There are several college guidebooks that encourage you to sound unique in your response to college essay questions. Other publications advise you to make your essay "glow in the dark" by taking creative risks. I believe it is important to listen to and to use your own voice. You should feel confident that your essays will be unique because no one like you has ever written them before! Just as with other elements of your college application, be sure to have a reliable person proofread your essay for possible errors you might have overlooked. You can never be too careful.

THE COLLEGE APPLICATION CALENDAR

Colleges usually require five different kinds of information about their candidates for admission. This includes the application for admission, standardized test scores, an official academic transcript, and recommendations from teachers and your high school counselor. In addition, schools require at least one financial aid statement from your family.

Since you must gather information from a number of different sources, organization is one of the most important factors in an effective college application. Since you are the person who is requesting information to be completed or submitted by other individuals on your behalf, outside of the application that you are completing, you must be sure that your requests are made in an orderly and timely fashion.

FRESHMAN THROUGH JUNIOR YEAR

It is never too early to start gathering information about colleges. As early as your freshman year in high school, you can start asking family members, friends, counselors, and teachers about the colleges they attended or have information about. Where did some of your favorite teachers attend college? Do you have an older brother, sister, or relative who has gone through the college application process? You should not hesitate to make an appointment with your school's college guidance counselor to learn more about college opportunities.

JUNIOR YEAR

Start writing to colleges to request admission information before or during your junior year. Some colleges will add your name to their mailing list as early as your sophomore year in high school. In addition, when you take the PSAT during your junior year, request that your scores be sent to any college that wants them—this will put you on the mailing list of many colleges that you may not have heard of but that may prove to be good college choices for you to consider.

At the beginning of your junior year, or earlier, you should speak to your college counselor. He or she will give you directions on how to get started in your college search. By the end of your junior year, you should have completed the PSAT, the SAT once (if possible), and one or more Achievement Tests (ACH), identified two or more teachers to write recommendations for you, and written to several colleges to request information and applications. Not all students will be able to complete all these tasks by the end of their junior year, but the more tasks you can accomplish, the easier your college search will be.

SENIOR YEAR

Most colleges publish new applications for admission annually. College applications are usually available to students during the summer between their junior and senior years. The deadlines for completion of applications for admission may vary from one institution to another. Some colleges are on a rolling admission policy and make decisions on applications as they receive them. Other institutions are on deadline admission and make decisions after specific dates during your senior year. Schools on deadline admission programs will typically request your completed application by the middle of your senior year, or sometimes even earlier. Schools indicate their application deadlines on the application forms; keep careful track of such deadlines.

COMPLETING THE COLLEGE APPLICATION

- No later than the beginning of your senior year, request and obtain all application materials for the colleges you're interested in attending.
- As it is essential that you are organized during the application process, keep a file and a deadline calendar for each of the colleges to which you are applying.
- Make sure that your teachers and counselors have blank recommendation forms well before the due date for their submission (at least a month).
- Keep a copy of all the completed forms that you submit to schools, for your records.
- Make sure that you have registered for or have taken all the appropriate standardized tests required by the institutions to which you are applying. Pay close attention to the deadline dates the schools have for taking the exams.
- Begin to write preliminary drafts of your college application essays during the summer before your senior year, or at the beginning of your senior year.

- Have a person whose opinion you trust review all your application materials, particularly your essay.
- Obtain and complete all the financial aid applications well before the deadline. As many schools and the federal and state governments have limited financial resources to award students, aid is sometimes given at some institutions on a first-come, first-served basis.
- Be certain that all the information you send to a college is legible and neat. It is not so important that you type your college application—what is important is that your application materials can be clearly read.

GET STARTED!

There are exciting years ahead of you after high school. You will be academically challenged and make new friends. In college, you will be empowered to take full charge and responsibility for your personal, social, and academic life. This guide provides an excellent resource for you in identifying college opportunities. In addition, you should feel confident about seeking out and creating your own sources of information. The more you know about the colleges that you are applying to, the more likely you are to be satisfied with the college you choose to attend.

Michael P. Whittingham
Associate Dean of Admission
Amherst College

THE FINANCIAL AID SEARCH

You *can* afford to go to college. *No matter what your and your parents' financial situation is, you should not use money as a reason not to pursue your higher education.* Billions of dollars are awarded to students each year—in the form of scholarships, grants, work-study opportunities, and loans—by federal and state governments, by the colleges themselves, and by various other community, church, and private resources.

Here are a few facts that should impress you:

FACT 1

Almost all of the colleges included in *The Multicultural Student's Guide to Colleges* provide at least 50 percent of their students with some sort of merit- and need-based financial aid, many with as much as half to full tuition. And much of this aid is in the form of scholarships and grants—which means you won't have to pay the money back.

FACT 2

You don't have to be a genius to receive merit-based awards. In addition to academic smarts as evidenced by high school class rank and SAT scores, colleges and universities award significant amounts of aid to students for demonstrated leadership abilities, geographic diversity, career and academic interests, talent, sports, etc.

FACT 3

As colleges are beginning to realize the importance of having racially and ethnically diverse student populations on their campuses, many award race-based merit scholarships through private endowments. When available, the *Guide* includes information about such scholarships in the statistics section of each college profile.

FACT 4

Often, private institutions have more scholarship and other financial aid opportunities available than public ones. Don't rule out a college just because it's private. After applying for financial aid, a student who had been accepted by both a public university in his home state of New York and a private school in the Midwest found that it was actually cheaper to attend the Indiana college because it had awarded him a merit-based scholarship.

FACT 5

Once you've been accepted, the college's financial aid office will try to work with you and your family to create a financial aid package that will enable you to attend their school. Your main concern should be getting into the college of your choice.

In short, there are plenty of opportunities to finance your college education—millions of students across the country take advantage of them each year—and, with planning, they can be made available to *you*. Here's how:

STEP 1

During the first term of your junior year in high school, establish a good rapport with your guidance counselor and your school's college adviser, if you haven't done so already. Let them know that you're interested in attending college and that you will need financial assistance in order to go. These individuals at your school regularly receive information about college scholarships and other financial aid opportunities. Check with them regularly to keep updated.

STEP 2

Also at the beginning of your junior year, get in touch with the colleges you're interested in attending. When you request application materials, be sure to ask for financial aid information. The financial aid information should answer the following important questions:

- What is the total cost—including tuition, room and board, travel, and books—of attending the college?
- What is the college's financial aid deadline?
- Does the institution have its own financial aid application form? If so, request it.
- Does the school have its own scholarship and loan opportunities? If so, what are they and how can you apply?

Colleges are more than willing to share such information with you, and the sooner you obtain it, the better prepared you will be when it comes time to fill out the necessary forms.

STEP 3

Start asking around now about financial aid opportunities other than those offered by individual colleges and the government. You'd be surprised at how many organizations and associations award scholarships to qualified students: fraternities and sororities, churches, professional organizations, corporations, unions, and your parents' employers are just some of the sources that often offer assistance to students looking for money to go to college.

Later in this section there is a list of publications with which you should become familiar. The books—available at most bookstores and libraries—provide information about scholarships, and they take you step by step through the financial aid application process.

STEP 4

As soon as possible after January 1 of your senior year of high school, obtain and complete a Financial Aid Form (FAF). It is the most important document you will need in order to obtain money for college. The information you include on the form—such as your and your parents' income for the previous year, the number of children in your household and in college, assets and liabilities, and much more—is what the federal government and the colleges rely on to award you financial assistance. Forms are available from your high school guidance counselor or college adviser; colleges also have FAFs readily available.

The following are some guidelines to assist you in filing a FAF:

* Complete and return the form to the College Scholarship Service (CSS) *as soon as possible after January 1.* An envelope addressed to the CSS is included with the FAF.
* Don't delay in filing the FAF, particularly as most scholarship opportunities, including those administered by colleges themselves and the government, are on a first-come, first-served basis.
* You are only able to file a FAF beginning in January of the year in which you plan to begin college; that is, if you're thinking of going to college in the fall of 1995, you should file the FAF only after January 1, 1995.
* The FAF requires that you include information from your W-2 form, which will be sent to you before the end of January, and data from your previous year's tax filings. You will want these forms handy as you complete the FAF.
* Although your high school college adviser or guidance counselor will not be familiar with your family's finances, he or she can usually answer any questions you may have during the application process.
* It's important that all of the information you include on the FAF be accurate and honest. Any errors or discrepancies will delay your filing, which could result in missed financial aid.

STEP 5

In March or April of your senior year, you will receive financial award letters from the colleges to which you have been accepted for admission. The letter will inform you of the amount of your financial need for a particular college, as demonstrated by the FAF, the financial aid awarded, and the amount you and your parents are expected to contribute to college expenses.

Once you receive the letter, review it carefully for any inaccuracies. Should you have any questions about the letter, or if your and your family's economic circumstances have changed since you filed (e.g., a divorce, loss of a job), don't hesitate to contact the school's financial aid office. Their counselors will be able to respond to any questions or concerns you may have.

TYPES OF FINANCIAL AID: NEED- AND MERIT-BASED

NEED-BASED AWARDS

The vast majority of financial aid awarded to students is based on a student's need, as assessed by the information on your FAF. Colleges and federal and state governments administer various need-based financial assistance programs, including grants, college work-study, and loans. To qualify for many of these awards, you will need to file an FAF.

Grants

The best part about grants is that they don't have to be paid back. The two major grant sources are the **Pell Grant** and the **Supplemental Educational Opportunity Grant** (SEOG). The Pell Grant, administered by the federal government, can be used to cover costs of tuition and other college expenses. The awards range from $250 to $2,400. The SEOG, also administered by the federal government, is available to students who must in addition take on certain self-help aid, such as college work-study or loans. A student who qualifies for an SEOG loan can borrow anywhere from $200 to $800 each year. You are automatically considered for the grants when you file your FAF.

State and local governments also administer their own grant programs.

College Work-Study

College work-study offers students the chance to defray expenses with on- or off-campus employment. The college pays 30 percent of a student's wages, while the federal government picks up the remaining 70 percent. Options for employment can include everything from working as a lifeguard at the college pool to assisting in the college library. Besides helping to cover expenses, work-study opportunities give you the chance to enhance your job résumé and to get out on campus and meet new and different people. As part of college work-study, students may work up to 12 hours per week, at pay that legally cannot go below minimum wage; often, however, salaries range up to $8.00 an hour. You are eligible for such positions by virtue of your demonstrated financial need on your FAF.

Loans

Federally funded loans, as opposed to grants, must be paid back, but not until after you graduate from college or leave school for any length of time. These loans are available at interest rates lower than those at commercial banks. There are four primary loan programs, the **Perkins Loan,** the **Robert T. Stafford Loan,** the **Supplemental Loans for Students** (SLS), and **Parent Loans for Undergraduate Students.**

The **Perkins Loan** allows you to borrow funds for college at 5 percent interest, and you don't have to begin repaying the borrowed amount until nine months after graduation. You have up to ten years to repay the loan, plus the interest. During your undergraduate enrollment, Perkins loans may not total more than $9,000, or more than $4,500 during your first two years. You are eligible for a Perkins Loan on the basis of the information on your FAF.

Stafford Loans, made by banks and savings and loan associations, are available at interest rates of 8 percent and may not exceed $17,000 during your years as an undergraduate. Repayment doesn't begin until six months after graduation, and you have ten years to repay the final amount. The federal government picks up the interest charges until repayment begins. Applications for Stafford loans are available at all banks and other lending institutions.

Supplemental Loans for Students are also administered by banks, where SLS applications are available. SLS loans are made to those students who are self-supporting and are not receiving financial assistance from parents. SLS interest payments—made quarterly—begin while you are still in college, but repayment of the principal doesn't begin until after you graduate. Should you qualify for an SLS, you may borrow up to $4,000 a year.

Parent Loans for Undergraduate Students, or PLUS, allow parents to borrow up to $4,000 a year for each independent child who is an undergraduate; $20,000 is the maximum. Repayment of the loan begins 60 days after it is granted, and the interest rate is approximately 9 percent.

When deciding to borrow funds for college, whether from the government, a bank, or the college itself, it's important to consider the amount of interest you are expected to pay. When at all possible, you should first consider the Perkins and Stafford loan options, as they have the lowest interest rates.

In addition, all 50 states offer their own loan programs, as do most colleges and many private organizations. Again, ask your high school guidance counselor and a college financial aid counselor about such loan opportunities.

Students and their parents rightly view college loans with some trepidation. Too often, students overburden themselves with indebtedness, making loan repayment difficult. Borrow only what is essential, and make borrowing a last resort. Finally, be sure you have exhausted all other financial aid options. Grants and additional awards, applied to your financial aid package, can diminish the amount of your loan.

MERIT-BASED AWARDS

Colleges and universities actively seek to recruit students who represent a broad range of achievements, interests, backgrounds, and talent. To attract such students to their campuses, colleges offer merit-based awards that are *not* based on need. Such awards can range from $100 to full tuition.

Academic achievement awards are the most common merit-based scholarships, and colleges automatically consider you for such awards when you apply. Academic achievement awards are based on your high school grade point average and class rank. SAT scores might also be taken into consideration. Check with the college to see what its eligibility requirements are for these awards. To continue to receive your academic achievement award, colleges require that you maintain a specified GPA while you're enrolled at their institution.

Colleges and universities, as well as other organizations and associations, also offer numerous merit-based scholarships unrelated to academic achievement. When you contact colleges, let them know about some of your talents and interests. They'll then inform you of any scholarships they may have available in these areas, which may include music, dance, athletics, and leadership potential. While these awards aren't typically as large in terms of dollars as those for academic achievement, they can help significantly.

PUBLICATIONS TO ASSIST YOU IN YOUR FINANCIAL AID SEARCH

The following publications offer extensive information about how to most effectively apply to colleges for financial aid. They offer step-by-step instructions on how to complete various financial aid forms, including the FAF, and list numerous scholarship opportunities. We've included the name of each book's author and publisher, so that if it is not available at a library or bookstore you can easily ask that it be ordered.

Financial Aid for Minorities (Garrett Park Press, Garrett Park, MD, 1989)

Bright Ideas: The Ins and Outs of Financing a College Education, by Donna Sammons (Simon & Schuster, 1992)

Fund Your Way Through College, by Debra Kirby (Visible Ink Press, 1992)

Free Money for College, by Laurie Blum (Facts on File, 1992)

Free Dollars from the Federal Government, by Laurie Blum (Prentice-Hall, 1991)

Winning Money for College, by Alan Deutschman (Peterson's, 1992)

Complete College Financing Guide, by Marguerite J. Dennis (Barron's, 1992)

The Scholarship Book, by Daniel J. Cassidy and Michael J. Alves (Prentice-Hall, 1990)

Paying Less for College (Peterson's, 1992)

College Financial Aid, by College Research Group Staff (Prentice-Hall, 1991)

The College Cost Book (The College Entrance Examination Board, 1991)

POINTS TO KEEP IN MIND WHEN APPLYING FOR FINANCIAL AID

- Applying to college and for financial aid is a task that requires a great deal of organization so that deadlines aren't missed. Record in a notebook the timetables of deadlines and names and addresses and phone numbers of individuals you've talked to about college and financial aid. You'll want easy access to such information as you begin the application process.
- Deadlines given by colleges and other scholarship resources represent the last possible date by which they will accept your financial aid application. Don't wait until the last minute to complete the necessary forms. Aim for at least a month in advance, so that if any problems arise you are still able to meet the deadline. Also, remember that a great deal of aid is on a first-come, first-served basis.
- Financial aid application processes can vary from college to college. Make sure you know what each institution's financial aid office requires from you.
- Talk to college advisers, guidance counselors, your parents, students currently enrolled in college, and anyone else you know who has gone to college. Ask them how they financed their educations. You'll be surprised at the array of scholarship opportunities taken advantage of by some of the individuals you'll talk to.
- Make copies of all the financial aid forms you will be completing. Treat the copies

as rough drafts. Ask someone whose opinion you respect, and who has the time, to review the draft for inaccuracies. Then transfer the revised material to the final version.

- Don't be afraid to ask questions of your teachers, parents, guidance counselors, or college advisers about college or the financial aid process. Most people will be more than glad to assist you. Often, you'll find they went through the same application process and turned to others for advice and assistance. Also, don't limit your questions to a few people at your school. Talk to a variety of teachers and counselors; the more input, the better.

- Become a regular visitor to your local and school libraries, if you're not already. There you will find college guides and publications that will offer you financial aid advice. Bring paper and a pen with you, as you will want to take careful notes.

- In many cities and towns across the country, there are agencies outside of your school that can provide college and career advice. Ask your guidance counselor and college adviser about such centers. The centers usually have a lot of information about the college and the financial aid application process, and have specially trained staff people to assist you.

- Take personal responsibility for finding financial aid resources. Don't leave it entirely up to others to find them for you. Although they are filled with good intentions, guidance counselors and college financial aid counselors are frequently overworked. Plan and be confident. The information—and the financial aid—is there for you.

Peter Johnson
Assistant Director of Admissions
Columbia University

ON CHOOSING A PREDOMINANTLY BLACK COLLEGE

Each year, many African-American high school students decide to continue their educations at historically black colleges and universities. Such institutions have graduated some of America's most respected civil rights leaders, politicians, artists, educators, doctors, and other professionals. Attending a historically black college or university isn't for everyone, however, and the decision to attend such a school—or any school, for that matter—should be made carefully. When deciding to attend a predominantly black or a predominantly white institution, consider the following:

- Look closely at what each school that you are considering offers, in terms of academic opportunities and support, location, costs, size, and extracurricular activities. Whether you decide to attend a predominantly white or a predominantly black college, if you are not satisfied with these criteria, then your college experience will be less than fulfilling.
- Ask yourself about the kind of student body that you would like to go to college with. Are you the type of person who would feel more comfortable with people who have similar racial backgrounds, or would you prefer to attend school with a broader racial mix of students? Answering such questions is a first step in helping you to decide about the kind of college you would like to attend.

There are numerous benefits to attending one of the country's historically black colleges and universities. Some of these benefits are:

- the opportunity to interact on a daily basis with African-American role models, both male and female, who are members of the faculty and administration;
- the chance to network professionally with recent alums and to follow in a long tradition of African-American graduates of the school, a tradition that can't be found at most of America's predominantly white colleges;
- attending classes, whether in the political science, sociology, history, English, or almost any other department, that incorporate Afrocentric themes;
- daily interaction with other motivated African-American students;
- a strong commitment to remedial programs in such areas as reading, writing, and math;
- the ability to learn in an environment in which the African-American student is the center of attention and which is relatively free of racism.

Despite the benefits, there are some drawbacks to attending a historically black college or university. Perhaps chief among them is that students don't have the opportunity to interact with a racially diverse group of students. In addition, with exceptions, historically black colleges and universities aren't as financially well-endowed as predominantly white colleges. Many of these institutions rely on state and federal subsidies for their day-to-day operations, and with today's economy and government cutbacks, predominantly black colleges are feeling the pinch. Without a significant endowment, it's difficult for colleges and universities to provide the necessary academic resources and facilities—particularly in the areas of engineering and medicine—to ensure that their students receive a top-flight education as preparation for today's competitive job market.

Attending a predominantly white college that's well endowed doesn't necessarily mean you will be better educated, however. Adjusting to a predominantly white campus may be difficult, particularly if you haven't ever been part of such an environment. Some students at predominantly white campuses complain of racism, which is most pervasive in the subtle forms, such as racist jokes. Such attitudes may affect your confidence and self-esteem. Should you decide to attend a predominantly white college or university, research the school's campus environment carefully by getting answers to the following questions:

- What sort of academic and emotional support services does the school offer to African-American students?
- How active and how large is the school's African-American student union?
- What percentage of the campus is African-American?
- What are the attitudes of the majority of the students at the school? Schools that have a more open-minded or progressive student population tend to be more tolerant of racial and cultural diversity.
- How large and how integral a part of the curriculum is the school's Black Studies courses or program?
- How quick is the administration when it comes to responding to incidents of racism on campus, and how effective and supportive is its response?

The Multicultural Student's Guide to Colleges answers such questions about the schools included in these pages; should your college search take you beyond these institutions, be sure to have such questions answered to your satisfaction.

The *Guide* includes profiles of five of the country's better-known historically black colleges and universities: Morehouse College and Spelman College in Atlanta, Howard University in Washington, DC, Xavier University in New Orleans, and Lincoln University in Pennsylvania. On page 835 ff. is a list of the names and addresses of the country's predominantly black colleges and universities, along with their addresses and phone numbers.

ALABAMA

UNIVERSITY OF ALABAMA

Address: P.O. Box 870132, Tuscaloosa, AL 35486-0132
Phone: (205) 348-5666 / (800) 933-BAMA
Director of Admissions: Dr. Roy C. Smith
Multicultural Student Recruiter: Claude Hutcherson
1992–93 tuition: $2,172 (in-state); $5,424 (out-of-state)
Room and board: $3,500
Application deadline: 8/1
Financial aid application deadline: 3/1
Non-white freshman admissions: Applicants for the class of '95: 721
Accepted: 69%
Accepted who enroll: 56%
Applicants accepted who rank in top 10% of high school class: na
Median SAT: na
Median ACT: 23
Full-time undergraduate enrollment: 15,360
Men: na
Women: na
Non-white students in
1988–89: 8.86%
1989–90: 8.74%
1990–91: 8.98%
1991–92: 9.1%
Geographic distribution of students: na
Top majors: 1. Criminal Justice 2. Social Work
Retention rate of non-white students: 72%
Scholarships exclusively for non-white students: National Achievement Scholarship: need- and non-need-based;

partial; dollar amount varies for each award.
Remediation programs: Remedial programs are offered in math and English.
Academic support services: Tutoring is available in various academic subjects.
Ethnic studies programs: The university offers an interdisciplinary minor in African-American Studies, which includes courses in history, literature, sociology, religion, social work, women's studies, criminal justice, and American Studies.
Ethnic studies courses: na
Organizations for non-white students: Afro-American Association, NAACP, Alpha Kappa Alpha, Delta Sigma Theta,

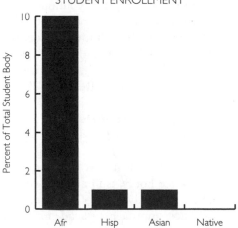

STUDENT ENROLLMENT

Alpha Phi Alpha, Kappa Alpha Psi, Phi Beta Sigma

Notable non-white alumni: Cedric Dent ('87; member of Take 6); Menyn Warren (member of Grammy-winning band Take 6); Lily Leatherwood ('88; social worker and Olympic medalist); Agnes Chappell ('73; Family Court judge); Dr. Everett McCorvey ('79; opera singer)

Tenured faculty: 569

Non-tenured faculty: 567

Student-faculty ratio: 19:1

Administrators: 124

   African-American: 0.81%

   Hispanic: 0

   Asian-American: 0.81%

   Native American: 0

Recent non-white speakers on campus: Dr. Na'im Akbar (clinical psychologist); KRS-One (rap artist and anti-drug lecturer); Yolanda King (civil rights activist and daughter of Martin Luther King, Jr.)

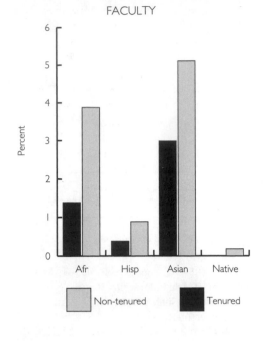

FACULTY

The University of Alabama is synonymous with football, thanks in large part to former coach Bear Bryant, who led the Crimsom Tide to 24 consecutive bowl games and who has been immortalized with two new recent campus additions—the Bear Bryant Museum and the Bear Bryant Conference Center.

Alabama has never really been known for its strong academics, however, as most students during football season are either getting ready for the game, going to the game, or attending a post-game party, usually at a fraternity. The university has sought to beef up its academic image by instituting an honors program and requiring all undergraduates to enroll in a core curriculum that emphasizes the liberal arts. But partying remains a priority among the majority of the school's students.

Decent academics can be had. Particularly strong programs are communications, history, and English, although students say the liberal arts generally take a back seat to the school's most popular department, business. Biology is also said to be good. The university's relatively new African-American Studies minor offers such respected courses as "The Black Religious Experience" and "Twentieth-Century Black History."

As at other state universities, class sizes tend to be large at Alabama, especially in introductory courses, but students say class sizes tend to shrink as a student progresses through his or her major. Gaining access to professors in entry-level courses can be a chore, but students say that with effort meeting a professor after class, usually during office hours, isn't an impossibility.

While the University of Alabama has long been synonymous with football and a laid-back approach to academics, the university has also been synonymous with segregation, which is pervasive throughout almost every aspect of campus life—from the social to the academic. "African-Americans have their own Greek organizations, as do the whites, and similar segregated situations exist in the football stadium at games and in the classrooms. The two populations rarely interact," says a student.

The lack of interaction among the races reached its breaking point in 1992, when two pledges of Kappa Delta, the school's oldest sorority, attended a party at a fraternity dressed in blackface, wigs with curlers, house slippers, and basketballs stuffed under their T-shirts. The theme of the party was "Who Rides the Bus?" The incident outraged the school's African-American students, who, along with other concerned students, conducted a silent march through Sorority Row, where the Kappa Delta house is located. The incident—and the march—received national media attention. But such racist incidents aren't the exception. The men of Kappa Alpha still celebrate Old South Day on campus, in which they glorify the days of the Confederacy, and hang the Confederate flag out of a fraternity window.

For support in such an environment, students join the Afro-American Association (AAA), but, according to one student, "the black community here isn't all that tight, except when we have to be, like after an incident like the one involving Kappa Delta. There's apathy among the black students, as there is among the campus at large, but, like I said, we do come together when we have to." Having a largely apathetic African-American community, adds the student, makes having an active AAA difficult. But the group is able to bring various prominent local and national speakers to campus each year, and to host picnics, including a back-to-school picnic designed to welcome new students to the university.

For the first time in school history, the AAA built a float for the 1992 Bama homecoming parade. "We figured that as black students we should be just as involved as the rest of the campus in such events," says a student leader. AAA also sponsors its Annual Greek Show, a step show put on by the school's Panhellenic Greek Council, an organization that consists of the school's historically black Greek organizations. The event draws a large audience—"more than a thousand people every year"—to the Bama Theater.

Alabama's black Greek organizations sponsor most of the social activities for the school's African-American students, which range from numerous parties and dances to community service projects. Several of the organizations—including Alpha Kappa Alpha, Delta Sigma Theta, Alpha Phi Alpha, and Kappa Alpha Psi—have their own residences.

While students say they can turn to the AAA and other organizations for support, they feel they get little, if any, real support from the university administration. "The administration says it's trying to improve the racial climate, but basically they always cop out," says a student. "Like after the incident with the Kappa Deltas, the university excused the sorority because they said it was free speech. But though the university apologized on behalf of the groups, we heard nothing from the sorority. After the incident, though, the university did sponsor a cultural awareness program, but it was a one-shot deal that didn't get much attention. Only when something happens, and the university looks bad in the media, does the administration do anything about the racism that goes on here."

In addition, the AAA's faculty adviser recently left the university for a job at another school, leaving the AAA with a temporary adviser. "There's really no one here on campus, or even an office on campus, who we feel we can turn to for assistance," says a student. "We mostly have to rely on each other and on the AAA for such support. In fact, although as students we contribute to the school's activity fund, there are no activities for students of color here. We're solely responsible for any programming in this area."

To understand why African-American programming is lacking when it comes to campus-wide events, one need only turn to the infamous Machine. The Machine, long a fixture of student politics at Bama, is a secret society consisting of leaders of several select all-white fraternities and sororities that controls much of the student programming and student government. None of the predominantly black Greek organizations are represented on the Machine, known more formally by the Greek letters Theta Nu Epsilon (ΘNE). Machine representatives meet secretly about once a week, and allegedly almost every campus organization comes under Machine influence, from fraternities and sororities to student government and honor societies, including Mortar Board. The Machine has been known to act viciously when it is crossed. Recently, a woman running for student body president against the Machine's wishes was beaten, allegedly by members of that organization. The incident received national media attention. "We've got a sick system here and it has got to be fixed," says university president Roger Sayers about the incident.

The Machine was the subject of a lengthy piece in the April 1992 issue of *Esquire* magazine: "The Machine today faces a crisis involving race. Though they lease university land, the Greek organizations are segregated. The blacks I saw inside the white Greek houses over ten days at Alabama were blowing on horns in the band at a fraternity party or carrying boxes of frozen vegetables to the kitchen. It's an embarrassing situation in a state that is more than 25 percent black. The university is trying to force integration, but it has met enormous resistance from [the Machine] and others who justify their segregation by invoking the great traditions of Greek life at Alabama." (As of this writing, according to a student, none of the white or black Greek organizations were integrated, except for Phi Beta Sigma, a predominantly black Greek fraternity that includes two white members.)

This "forced" integration is coming from the university's accreditation program, which requires the white Greek organizations to become integrated by an as yet unspecified date. If the white fraternities and sororities fail to become integrated, they risk their standing with the administration and will be forced to move off campus.

With such tension and attitudes, attending the University of Alabama can at times be trying for a student of color. Unfortunately, in-state African-American students are hard-pressed to find comparable educational quality at in-state prices. "Alabama provides a good education," says a student, "but earning that education can prove to be difficult, especially with so much that seems to be working against you here. I've liked the friends I've made through my fraternity and through the AAA, and I wouldn't trade those experiences for about anything, but there are days when I wish I'd gone elsewhere, a school where I might have been able to learn in a more supportive atmosphere."

AUBURN UNIVERSITY

Address: 202 Martin Hall, Auburn, AL 36849-5145
Phone: (205) 844-4080 / (800) 392-8051 (in-state)
Director of Admissions: Dr. Charles F. Reeder
Multicultural Student Recruiter: na
1992–93 tuition: $1,950 (in-state); $5,850 (out-of-state)
Room and board: $3,873
Application deadline: 9/1
Financial aid application deadline: 3/15
Non-white freshman admissions: Applicants for the class of '95: 563
  Accepted: 85.2%
  Accepted who enroll: 39.8%
  Applicants accepted who rank in top 10% of high school class: na
  Median SAT: na
  Median ACT: na

STUDENT ENROLLMENT

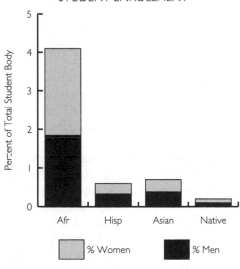

Full-time undergraduate enrollment: 16,926
  Men: 55%
  Women: 45%
Non-white students in
  1987–88: 4.4%
  1988–89: 4.6%

1989–90: 5.2%
1990–91: 5.6%

GEOGRAPHIC DISTRIBUTION OF STUDENTS

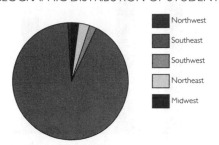

- Northwest
- Southeast
- Southwest
- Northeast
- Midwest

Students In-state: 69%
Top majors: 1. Liberal Arts 2. Engineering 3. Business
Retention rate of non-white students: na
Scholarships exclusively for non-white students: Presidential Opportunity Scholarship: merit-based; $1,500 each year; renewable; 25 awarded each year. Sonat Engineering: merit-based; available to a first-year African-American student planning to enroll in mechanical, civil, or electrical engineering; $2,000 each year; renewable; one awarded each year. E. I. Du Pont de Nemours: merit-based; $5,000; student must be enrolled in the College of Agriculture; one awarded each year.
Remediation programs: None
Academic support services: Tutoring is available in most academic subjects. Study resource rooms are also available for chemistry, engineering, and math. Mentor program.
Ethnic studies programs: The university offers a Latin American Studies minor.
Ethnic studies courses: na
Organizations for non-white students: Black Student Union, Gospel Choir, National Society of Black Engineers, Alpha Kappa Alpha, Delta Sigma Theta, Zeta Phi

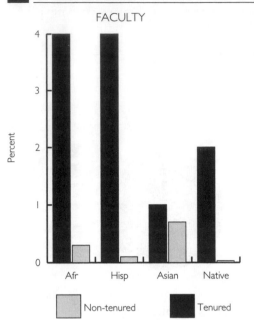

FACULTY

Non-tenured   Tenured

Beta, Alpha Phi Alpha, Kappa Alpha
Psi, Omega Psi Phi, Phi Beta Sigma
Notable non-white alumni: na
Tenured faculty: na
Non-tenured faculty: 372
Student-faculty ratio: 16:1
Administrators: na
  African-American: 3%
  Hispanic: 0
  Asian-American: 1%
  Native American: 0
Recent non-white speakers on campus: Dr.
Alvin Poussaint (professor, Harvard
Medical School)

Chartered in 1856, Auburn University was later established as a land-grant institution and today offers some of the best agricultural and technical programs in the South, including engineering and architecture. Pharmacy, veterinary medicine, and business are also popular and well regarded. In fact, such technical and pre-professional programs are the most popular on campus, and liberal arts majors at Auburn are a rare breed indeed.

Almost anything non-traditional or out of the ordinary is also a rare breed at Auburn. All dorms are single-sex; religious organizations, especially Campus Crusade for Christ, are among the more active student groups; fraternities and sororities dictate much of the campus social life; and ROTC membership is among the highest in the country.

This conservatism also translates into race relations on campus, and no more so than in recent differences between the Kappa Alpha fraternity, an all-white organization, and the Black Student Union. "Race relations on campus aren't exactly on the up-and-up, and have reached a sort of stalemate for the moment," says a student. "The problem was exacerbated by the Kappa Alpha fraternity, which for years has sponsored its Old South parade through one of the main streets of town. The fraternity members dress in gray uniforms from the Civil War and ride horses and the guys' dates walk along wearing their antebellum dresses. We [the BSU] tried to negotiate with them to get them to make it a little less offensive, like try to get them to move the parade to a different street, but they wouldn't meet with us. We could never hope for them to do away with the parade entirely. In negotiations with the student government association the KA's did give up carrying the Confederate flag in the parade. On this campus, that's progress."

As an alternative to the parade, the BSU and the Office of Special Programs for the past nine years has sponsored a Harmony Picnic on campus, which, according to a student, "gets bigger and better every year." Also to counter the parade, Students for Progress, a new student group, sponsored the campus's first New South parade in 1992, "where each participating group carried a banner that said something positive about themselves. The parade was basically an attempt to celebrate the diversity of the South now," comments a student leader. "The day after the parade, there was a festival where a lot of students had picnics and listened to bands on campus." Groups that participated in the event included the BSU, Amnesty International, the Auburn Gay and Lesbian Association (which the student senate has refused to grant a permanent charter), the National Society of Black Engineers, and others.

Much of the responsibility for cultural activity falls on the shoulders of the Black Student Union, with about 77 active members, and the Office of Special Programs. In a recent year, the BSU, which meets weekly, held a dance-a-thon to fight sickle-cell anemia, and for Black History Month held a semiformal dance, a fashion show, and a party. In 1991, the BSU was given an office with a computer in the student center. The Office of Special Programs "is like our backbone," says a BSU member. The Office, which oversees the activities of the BSU, the international student group, physically handicapped students, and students of non-traditional ages, also helps plan activities for Black History Month, such as forums and guest speakers. One campus leader reports that students are beginning to work to establish Latino and Native American student groups, but that there are no such official organizations yet on campus. Addine Woods and Vivien Larkin, Office of Special Programs administrators, are popular and well regarded by students. "They come to many of our meetings and most of our events. They're also good for just moral support," says the BSU member.

Auburn's historically black Greek organizations, says a student, are small and haven't been active in recent years; one of the fraternities—Alpha Phi Alpha—provides residence facilities for its members.

With slightly more than 1,000 African-American students on campus, a BSU member expresses disappointment that so few students are involved in the BSU. "But I can understand why," she adds. "They feel like the BSU can't really do any good here on this campus, so why bother. Their attitude is, until the administration decides we're important to this campus, why bother. Apathy is a big problem on this campus, and that applies to students of any color."

For social life off campus, Auburn's African-American students will head to some of the parties at nearby Tuskegee, a predominantly black university. "We definitely go there more than they come here," reports a student. The town of Auburn offers little in the way of an active nightlife, but Birmingham and Montgomery are just a couple of hours' drive away. Besides Greek life, most activity on campus focuses on the school's football team, especially when it comes to matches against state rival University of Alabama. Clashes have become so intense between Auburn and many of its opponents that the Auburn administration recently instituted Better Relations Days, in which campus leaders meet with leaders of other schools a week or so before game time in an attempt to ward off problems.

Positive race relations and awareness aren't exactly a hallmark at this Southern university. But with an increasingly active BSU and some fine academic programs, Auburn can be a worthwhile place to spend four years. "There are times when I wish I'd gone elsewhere, but when I graduate from here with my engineering degree I know I'm going to be employable."

A R I Z O N A

UNIVERSITY OF ARIZONA

Address: R. L. Nugent Building, First
Floor, Tucson, AZ 85721
Phone: (602) 621-3812
Director of Admissions: Loyd Bell
Multicultural Student Recruiter: Diane
Castro
1992–93 tuition: $1,840 (in-state); $7,396
(out-of-state)
Room and board: $2,000
Application deadline: 4/1
Financial aid application deadline: 3/1
Non-white freshman admissions: Applicants
for the class of '96: 2,547
Accepted: 82%
Accepted who enroll: 43%
Applicants accepted who rank in top
10% of high school class: 36%
In top 25%: 66%
Median SAT range: 420–430 V,
480–490 M
Median ACT: 21
Full-time undergraduate enrollment: 21,450
Men: 51.4%
Women: 48.6%
Non-white students in
1988–89: 12.8%
1989–90: 14.1%
1990–91: 15.7%
1991–92: 17.1%
1992–93: 17.8%
Students In-state: 63%
Top majors: 1. Liberal Arts
2. Business/Management 3. Engineering
Retention rate of non-white students: 71.1%

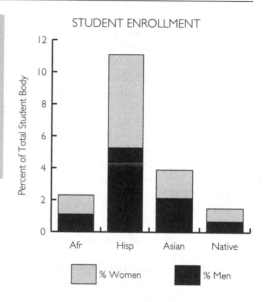

STUDENT ENROLLMENT

Percent of Total Student Body

Afr   Hisp   Asian   Native

□ % Women   ■ % Men

GEOGRAPHIC DISTRIBUTION OF STUDENTS

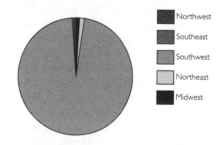

■ Northwest
■ Southeast
■ Southwest
□ Northeast
■ Midwest

**Scholarships exclusively for non-white
students:** The university offers dozens of

scholarships to minority students, based on both need and merit. Out-of-state tuition waivers are offered on a limited basis. Currently, minority students receive 18.5% of all aid available through the university.

Remediation programs: None

Academic support services: The Office of Minority Student Affairs offers a summer orientation program for incoming first-year students and peer tutoring in most subject areas. Three assistant deans for minority student affairs—Hispanic-American, African-American, and Native American—also assist students.

Ethnic studies programs: The Mexican-American Studies program, established in the mid-1970s, is interdisciplinary and has a faculty of 70. The university also offers minors in African-American Studies and American Indian Studies. The African-American Studies program, also interdisciplinary, was established in 1970 and includes four faculty members from political science, sociology, and women's studies. The American Indian program, established in 1971, includes 15 faculty members from linguistics, English, political science, sociology, education, law, and other departments.

Organizations for non-white students: Alpha Kappa Alpha, Kappa Alpha Psi, Delta Sigma Theta, Alpha Phi Alpha, Phi Beta Sigma, African-American Student Alliance, Amerind, De Colores (Photography Club), Minority Business Student Association, Minority Pre-law Student Association, Omega Delta Phi, National Society of Black Engineers, Minority Pre-med Club, Society of Hispanic Professional Engineers, Asian-American Cultural Association, American Indian Science and Engineering Society, Association of Minority Education Students, Minority Action Council, MECHA, Native American Business Organization

Notable non-white alumni: Rasheedah Ali

(director of public relations, Turner Broadcasting Systems); Thomas Aranda (former U.S. ambassador to Uruguay and general counsel to the Arizona state Republican party); Edith Auslander (human resources director, Tucson Newspapers, Inc.; former president of Arizona Board of Regents); Laura Banks (former president of Tucson Urban League); Raul Castro (former ambassador to El Salvador, Bolivia, and Argentina and former Arizona governor); Jaime Gutierrez (former Arizona state senator); Jose Galvez (Pulitzer Prize-winning photographer, *Los Angeles Times*); Ulysses Kay (professor of music, Lehman College, New York City); Geraldo Rivera (journalist and TV personality)

Tenured faculty: 1,077

Non-tenured faculty: 966

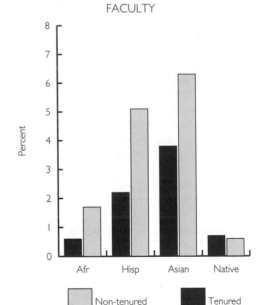

FACULTY

Student-faculty ratio: 14.7:1

Student-faculty ratio: 14.7:1

Administrators: 1,473

African-American: 2%

Hispanic: 5.4%

Asian-American: 8%

Native American: 1.2%

Recent non-white speakers on campus: Joe Clark (former high school principal and character for the film *Lean on Me*); Atallah Shabazz and Yolanda King (daughters of Malcolm X and Martin Luther King, Jr.); Dr. Billy Taylor (jazz musician and educator); Rosa Parks (civil rights leader); Lilly Francis (regional director, National Panhellenic Conference); Mario Martinez (artist); Mary Frances Berry (former U.S. representative and member of U.S. Civil Rights Commission); Cressworth Lander (director of Tucson's Community Service Department)

The University of Arizona, with a population of more than 35,000 undergraduates and graduate students, is a big place. But, according to students, that doesn't mean it has to be overwhelming.

Says a student: "I would strongly recommend the University of Arizona to a prospective minority student because there are so many opportunities for success. All a student needs to do is take advantage of the retention services the school offers, such as the New Start/Summer Bridge Program, Office of Minority Student Services Affairs tutoring, the Student Encouragement Program, and many more. A minority student also has a multitude of minority leaders in the faculty and administration to consult. Finally, there are several organizations, fraternities, and clubs for minority students. The university is not such a scary place for minority students as long as they take advantage of all that's set out in front of them. I admit that there is tension here, as many schools experience, but this school is definitely becoming aware of the voice of minority students."

One of the administrators students can look to for support is the university's newly appointed president, Manuel Pacheco, the highest-ranking Hispanic in American higher education. President Pacheco is a role model especially for those students from the lower socioeconomic strata. "Mr. Pacheco—who grew up in a small farmhouse with his parents and 11 siblings—has never been daunted by challenges," says an article in *The Chronicle of Higher Education* about his appointment. "When he left his family's New Mexico farm to attend college, he defied expectations. He also set an example for his mother and siblings, all of whom later earned college degrees." According to the president of the University of Arizona Board of Regents, Esther Capin, Pacheco impressed other board members because of his commitment to undergraduate education and minority access.

"There is a portion of our society that is not going to be successful unless they are a part of the educational mainstream," say Pacheco in the *Chronicle* article. "If we don't provide opportunities for them to succeed, we're not only going to affect their quality of life, but society as a whole will suffer."

One of the places that help students to succeed is the school's Office of Minority Student Affairs (OMSA), located in Old Main in the center of campus. "When I first came here I couldn't see myself graduating," says an education major. "I give OMSA a lot of credit for my still being here." The OMSA office oversees a great deal of the university's recruitment and retention of students of color, including coordinating peer and group tutoring sessions. One of the OMSA staff members who has been of assistance to students is Eddy Brown. "Every time I had a question I would go to Eddy, knowing full well that he could help me," says a media arts major. "I felt comfortable coming and talking to him." Diane Castro, an associate director of admissions, is also supportive.

The African-American Cultural Resource Center, the Native American Resource Center, and the Hispanic Student Resource Center provide career counseling, personal support, and academic tutoring for students. The centers also include meeting areas for student groups. Says a student of the school's academic support services: "There are many fine examples of minority faculty and administrators working hard to better the campus climate. Among them are Jesse Hargrove, director of the African-American Cultural Resource Center and assistant dean for African-American students; Salomon Baldenegro, assistant dean for Hispanic students; and Vivian Juan, assistant dean for Native American students. These three deans are creating cultural centers for students who may feel overwhelmed by the large undergraduate population here. In addition, I feel the Office of Admissions, headed by Jerry Lucido, has done an outstanding job of recruiting more quality minority students to campus. Diane Castro is at the root of these efforts to recruit minority students from all over the state. OMSA has done a good job providing services to get those minority students to their graduation day."

Shortage of academic opportunities certainly isn't a problem at Arizona. The university offers hundreds of programs in eight undergraduate colleges: business administration, nursing, pharmacy, architecture, agriculture, education, engineering and mines, and arts and sciences. Astronomy is one of the school's outstanding programs, especially as students have access to various telescopes around Tucson; the famous Kitt Peak National Observatory has offices on campus. The College of Engineering and Mines offers programs in 18 different areas, such as mechanical, chemical, electrical, and systems engineering. Within the College of Arts and Science, students say the journalism department is excellent, while English and history are also said to be standouts. The engineering and business schools offer the university's most popular majors.

Although the university billed 1988 as the Year of the Undergraduate—in which it attempted to focus less on research and more on undergraduate education—it is still rare for students to have full professors as teachers; teaching assistants are the norm in almost every introductory course, which can number into the hundreds. With careful planning, however, students say, meetings with professors can be scheduled.

The school's various cultural student groups—in particular the African-American Student Alliance, the Asian-American Cultural Association, and MECHA—sponsor numerous lectures, forums, film series, and social gatherings for the campus and members. The university also hosts numerous guest lectures on campus as part of cultural awareness programming; in a recent year, nearly 100 such speakers were brought to campus.

Despite the efforts of such groups, the university remains a largely racially segregated institution, at least when it comes to socializing, according to students. "Racial integration on the U of A campus is poor," says a student. "I often see a definite split in ethnic groups as far as daily campus activity goes. Minority students tend to spend leisure time with other students of the same ethnic background, which I believe is natural and comfortable. The campus Greek community is *very* white. The minority students on campus are forming fraternities and sororities of their own.

The African-American Greek system is gaining in popularity, and Hispanic students are even beginning to form their own Greek organizations." Says another student: "The only place I see racial integration is in the classroom."

Tucson (pop. 400,000), a city sixty miles north of the Mexico border, has a large Hispanic population, and offers a wide diversity of social and cultural activities, including movie theaters, restaurants, and concerts. Situated between three mountain ranges, the area around the university is spectacular.

On campus, sports—intramural and varsity—reign supreme among extracurricular activities, and the university's $15 million sports facility is a fitting tribute to a student body that prides itself on staying fit. Jogging is a popular outdoor activity. During a recent year, 14 of the school's 17 varsity teams ranked in the top 25 in the nation.

Arizona has earned a reputation—thanks in large part to its huge Greek system—as a party school. But the university has the academics and the support services to make almost any student's four years here a success. "To be a student of color at the U of A takes discipline and diligence," says a student. "There are many programs on campus to help those students through their first years as undergraduates. After that, it's up to them to build on what they've learned during their first two years. Opportunities abound for minority students at this school, but those students need to realize that and take full advantage of them."

ARIZONA STATE UNIVERSITY

Address: Tempe, AZ 85287-0112
Phone: (602) 965-2604 / (800) 252-2781
Director of Admissions: Susan Clouse
Multicultural Student Recruiter: Peggy
 Jordan
1992–93 tuition: $1,844 (in-state); $7,350
 (out-of-state)
Room and board: $3,968
Application deadline: 11/15
Financial aid application deadline: 3/1
Non-white freshman admissions: Applicants
 for the class of '95: na
 Applicants accepted who rank in top
 10% of high school class: na
 Median SAT: na
 Median ACT: na
Full-time undergraduate enrollment: 23,840
 Men: 52%
 Women: 48%
Non-white students in
 1987–88: 11.2%
 1988–89: 11.8%
 1989–90: 12.7%
 1990–91: 13.6%

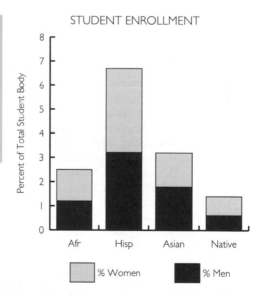

STUDENT ENROLLMENT

Percent of Total Student Body

Afr   Hisp   Asian   Native

% Women   % Men

Geographic distribution of students: na

Top majors: 1. Accounting 2. Management 3. Electrical Engineering

Retention rate of non-white students: 65%

Scholarships exclusively for non-white students: Maroon and Gold Scholarships: need-based; full tuition; 250 awarded each year. Community Coordinated Scholarships: need- and merit-based; full tuition; 204 awarded each year. Minority Support Scholarships: need- and merit-based; full tuition and room and board; 95 awarded each year.

Remediation programs: na

Academic support services: Tutoring is available in most academic subjects, as well as study skills workshops.

Ethnic studies programs: na

Ethnic studies courses: Available in sociology, women's studies, psychology, and anthropology.

Organizations for non-white students: Asian Students Association, Chinese Student Organization, Chinese Students and Scholars Friendship Association, Hong Kong Students Association, Japan Association, Korean Student Association, Singapore Students Association, Association of Minority Journalists, Hispanic Business Students Association, MECHA, Society of Hispanic Professional Engineers, American Indian Science and Engineering Society, Association of American Indian Business Students, Native American Media, Native American Students Association, Native Images, Alpha Kappa Alpha, Arizona Council of Black Engineers and Scientists, Black Business Student Association, Delta Sigma Theta, NAACP, Phi Beta Sigma

Notable non-white alumni: Cecil Patterson ('71; chief counsel, Arizona Attorney General's Office); Reggie Jackson ('69; professional baseball player); Vada Manager (former press secretary to the governor of Arizona and current press secretary to the mayor of Washington, D.C.); Joe Contreras ('55; judge, Arizona Court of Appeals); Peter Zah ('63; president, Navajo Tribe); Josiah Moore ('70; chair, Tohono ODham Tribal Council); Vernon Masayesva ('69; chair, Hopi Tribal Council); Billy Cypress ('72; chair, Miccosukee Business Committee, Miami); Rachel Rosales ('82; opera singer; Metropolitan Opera Company)

Tenured and non-tenured faculty: 1,765

Student-faculty ratio: 18.2:1

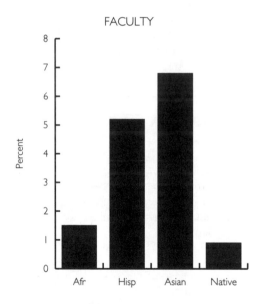

FACULTY

Administrators: 343

African-American: 5%

Hispanic: 10.5%

Asian-American: 1.5%

Native American: 1.8%

Recent non-white speakers on campus: na

It would be hard to find a resort community that could rival the facilities of Arizona State University, with its sports complexes, palm trees, fitness trails, bike paths, and, not far from campus, a man-made beach. And what's more, students can enjoy all this in weather that almost guarantees year-round sun.

With such an environment, it's no wonder studying often plays second fiddle for many Sun Devils. Already distracted by all of the above, students must also contend with the Old Town section, a row of bars, theaters, and nightclubs just off campus that is packed Thursday through Saturday nights. (*The New York Times* has ranked Tempe as one of the country's top ten college towns, and the city includes a Hispanic and a small African-American population.) Also distracting are varsity and intramural sports events.

When students do decide to hit the books, they are able to choose from more than 150 programs, which include everything from Wildlife Conservation Biology and math to aerospace engineering and English. By far the most popular programs are those offered by the College of Business. In fact, one in four degrees awarded to ASU students is in business. Majors are offered in accounting, the most popular and respected, computer information systems, economics, finance, and others. The School of Engineering, with nine different areas of study, is said to be strong. ASU's College of Architecture and Environmental Design received an added boost in 1989 with the completion of its new facility. Among the arts and sciences, English (especially creative writing), anthropology, geology (nearby Grand Canyon is a destination for many geology classes), and exercise science are sure bets. Students speak highly of the school's honors programs.

Academic support comes in many forms, including that of the Minority Engineering Program and the Minority Assistance Program, both of which provide academic and personal advising. At a school where an introductory course may have a class roster in the hundreds, it's no surprise that professors are remote. But with planning, students say, appointments with professors can be had.

Cultural awareness opportunities abound at the university, thanks in large measure to student groups, particularly the new coalitions that represent ASU's Hispanic, Asian-American, African-American, and Native American students. "The coalitions were established a few years ago after some racist incidents occurred on campus. The incidents spurred a lot of activity, rallies, and sit-ins." In addition to the formation of the four coalitions, the Council of Culturally Underrepresented Coalitions (CCUC) was established, which is composed of the coalitions. "CCUC is supposed to promote more cohesion between minority student groups, and people like to say there is more cohesion since the formation of the CCUC. But it really varies. We tend to have a problem in this area. For instance, each coalition is into their own issues, and any support from the others is more abstract and not too beneficial. For example, the African-American Student Coalition sponsored a rally in the Memorial Union demanding more black faculty and staff. But the African-American Student Coalition didn't notify any of the other coalitions about the rally, so it wasn't as if we could even help them out. But I approached members of the coalition and they said they didn't want the support of the other coalitions because they said it was a black thing. This is just one example of the divisiveness of the coalitions."

Coalition members were meant to come together at a mixer sponsored by the Chicano/Hispano Student Coalition, but it was mostly attended by Hispanic members. "We would like to have had a better turnout, and a better mix, but this was our first, so we hope this will be an ongoing thing." But students say that with time the coalitions may begin to work and socialize more together. "The coalitions were formed just two years ago. There are a lot of bright coalition activists who are doing a good job within their respective groups. It's up to us to make the coalitions work for all of us."

The African-American Student Coalition was successful in getting established on campus a residence hall—to be located in Ocotillo Hall—that would focus on Afro-centric issues. "The hall is going to be called Umoja Hall, and when it got approval it created a great deal of controversy on campus, among students and the administration who thought we were trying to segregate ourselves. They don't see it as necessary. But the truth is, all we're trying to do is help each other succeed. Black students at ASU don't have a high retention rate, and we believe the hall will foster a sense of community and help students with the adjustment of going to college."

When not staging rallies in the Memorial Union, the coalition, which includes about 50 active members, also sponsors various cultural activities, including a Tribute to Ethnic Women. The coalition also puts on plays, sponsors forums, and hosts art exhibits. The coalition also has its own peer mentoring program called Students Taking Action to Reach Success (STARS), which is overseen by Deborah Brouhard, a counselor in the Minority Assistance Program. Brouhard and coalition faculty adviser Toni Montgomery, an art department faculty member, are well regarded by students.

According to students, the African-American Student Coalition is a diverse group of students which "is like a history lesson in understanding our people. We have Pan-Africanists, we have People's Revolutionary Party members, and we have those in the mainstream of things. Working together can be difficult, but it's worth it. I know my experiences of working with people who have different viewpoints has enriched my experience here at ASU."

The Chicano/Hispano Student Coalition, which consists of six organizations, focuses much of its energies on their annual Cultural Week. "Each group from the coalition puts events together, including lectures and bands that play different types of dance music. Each day a group sponsors its own events, such as a Caribbean day, a Chicano day, and various Spanish themes." Coalition members, usually the heads of the different coalition groups, also attend an annual retreat to plan events for the next school year. The newest member of the coalition is a Puerto Rican student group, while the oldest and largest coalition member is MECHA, a predominantly Chicano student organization. Ed Delix, MECHA's adviser, "always comes to our events and is well liked by students," says a coalition member.

While organizations do their best to develop unity among members, students say the university's massive size—in terms of both undergraduate enrollment and acreage—gets in the way. "Our campus is so large. I'm active in the Chicano/Hispano Student Coalition, and I didn't even know about some of the activities that MECHA was sponsoring. You basically have to hang out at the Memorial Union to find out what's going on." Comments another student: "The black population here at ASU is small, about 1,000 students, and we're spread out all over campus, so it gets difficult to coordinate events and to get students active in events. It's especially difficult as many of our members are commuters. Umoja Hall should help matters, though."

Students say ASU's administration is making attempts to involve more students of color in the hiring of staff and policymaking. "The administration had a forum where there were some individuals who were applying for administrative jobs at the university," says a student leader. "At the forum, students were able to ask questions of the applicants. One of the administrators called us [coalition members] because they wanted to be sure we were involved in their decision."

Opportunities of almost every variety are available to ASU students, and many take advantage of them. But it's possible to just glide through four years here without much effort, either socially or academically. For the student who can bear down and take advantage of all that ASU offers, in addition to phenomenal recreational facilities, ASU has its rewards. "There's so much going on here. The university sponsors free screenings of good movies, and there are always good lectures going on somewhere. And the coalitions strive to include all interested students. But the hard part is getting the word out to all of the multicultural students about all the opportunities here. We are one of the biggest schools in the country."

ARKANSAS

UNIVERSITY OF ARKANSAS

Address: Administration Building 222,
Fayetteville, AR 72701
Phone: (501) 575-5346
Director of Admissions: Dr. Clyde Iglinsky
Multicultural Student Recruiter: Vikita Bell
1992–93 tuition: $1,732 (in-state); $4,608
(out-of-state)
Room and board: $3,100
Application deadline: 8/1
Financial aid application deadline: 4/1
Non-white freshman admissions: Applicants
for the class of '95: na
Applicants accepted who rank in top
10% of high school class: na
Median SAT: na
Median ACT: na
Full-time undergraduate enrollment: 11,667
Men: 54%
Women: 46%
Non-white students in
1987–88: 7%
1988–89: 8%
1989–90: 8%
1990–91: 8%
Geographic distribution of students: na
Top majors: na
Retention rate of non-white students: na
**Scholarships exclusively for non-white
students:** Minority Achievement Awards:
covers tuition; merit-based.
Remediation programs: Developmental
courses are provided in math, English,
and reading.

Academic support services: Tutoring is
available in most academic subjects.
Ethnic studies programs: The university
offers an interdisciplinary program in
Black Studies.
Ethnic studies courses: na
Organizations for non-white students: Alpha
Phi Alpha, Alpha Kappa Alpha, Delta
Sigma Theta, Kappa Alpha Psi, Phi Beta
Sigma, Zeta Phi Beta, Omega Psi Phi,
National Society of Black Engineers,
Inspirational Singers, Black Student
Association, Native American Student
Association
Notable non-white alumni: na
Tenured faculty: na

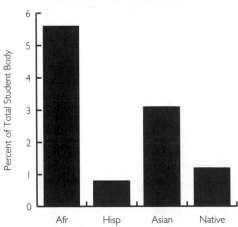

STUDENT ENROLLMENT

Non-tenured faculty: na

Student-faculty ratio: na

Administrators: na

Recent non-white speakers on campus: na

Should you decide to attend the University of Arkansas, chances are your roommate will be from Arkansas and he or she will be a Razorback football fanatic. During football season, the campus comes to life almost like New York City on New Year's Eve, and almost everyone sports Arkansas red and white, some even with paint on their faces.

Chances are also that your roommate may be a bit more academically oriented than students at the university in years past. Under the stewardship of Chancellor David Ferritor, Arkansas seeks to increase the school's academic reputation by stiffening admissions standards even for in-staters. In order to gain admittance, applicants must now have a 2.75 high school grade point average—an increase from the 2.5 that was required of applicants before the 1993 academic school year—and have completed necessary college preparatory course work. Students who don't meet any one of the requirements are admitted conditionally for one year.

While the University of Arkansas may not enjoy a stellar overall academic reputation, the university does have its share of outstanding departments and programs, most notably engineering, which can boast of the new state-of-the-art Bell Engineering Center. Founded as a land-grant institution, Arkansas also has strong programs in agriculture and home economics. Within the Fulbright College of Arts and Sciences, English, the natural sciences, chemistry, and physics enjoy the best reputations. The School of Architecture also enjoys a strong reputation, as do the popular colleges of business administration and education. "African-American History" and "Black Studies," a seminar-style course, are well regarded by students, as is the courses' professor, Nudie Williams.

Arkansas's head football coach, Jack Crowe, has become a popular figure among students lately. "His goal is to help improve the minority environment of the campus, and he seems very sincere. He says he'd feel like a hypocrite recruiting athletes to campus if the black students are having a hard time of it here. He comes to the Black Student Association meetings when he has a chance, and, probably because of his interest, we get athletes to come to our meetings."

Located in the Arkansas Union, the student center, the Office of Minority Affairs offers academic and non-academic support and provides assistance to cultural student organizations. Particularly successful is the university's Students Making It Lighter Everyday (SMILE), in which upperclass students are paired as mentors with first-year students. The director of the office, Lonnie Williams, is a favorite with students. "He openly gives help to all minority students. He's also very strong and respected by students." Also popular is Chauncey Brummer, a professor in Arkansas's law school, who is a frequent guest at Black Student Association events. In addition, Arkansas's chapter of the National Society of Black Engineers is a source of support for members.

For academic advice, students also turn to affirmative action officers in most of the university's undergraduate colleges. "We can go to them for scheduling, or if we're having trouble with a professor or just in class. They're an important resource for students," says a secondary education major. Naccaman Williams, in the College of Education, and Thomas Carter, in the College of Engineering, are some of the most effective counselors, according to students. The only schools which lack such officers are the schools of agriculture and business.

For peer support, Arkansas's Black Student Association (BSA), with about 250 active members, helps sponsor speakers on campus. Recent speakers have included Rev. Jesse Jackson and a Detroit minister who gave a talk entitled "The Crisis of the Black Male." The BSA also sponsors an annual Christmas banquet, held at the Fayetteville Hilton, and a banquet at the end of the school year honoring those students with a 3.0 GPA or better. At the beginning of each school year, the BSA hosts a picnic, usually held at nearby Lake Fayetteville, "for the freshmen to provide a sense of community for all members." The BSA also publishes a newsletter, *BSA Today,* that contains student opinion pieces and a list of events, and, as an added bonus, publishes the birthdays of BSA members.

The university's historically black fraternities and sororities are frequent party givers. Almost every weekend, the organizations hold dances, complete with a DJ, at the school's student union. "That's one of our main social outlets," says a member of one of the organizations. The student adds that there is little rivalry between the Greek organizations. "It's amazing that we all get along so well," he says. The organizations are also active in the community. Members of Alpha Kappa Alpha sorority, for example, help clean the homes of elderly area residents, and the Alpha Phi Alpha fraternity has adopted about a mile of highway, which it is responsible for keeping clean. A roadside sign marks the spot.

The most recent addition to the school's roster of cultural organizations is the Native American Student Association, formed during the 1992 school year. The group hosted the university's first powwow, in 1992. "Oklahoma, with a relatively large Native American population, is not far from campus at all, and tribes from there came to participate in the event." Members of the BSA have been working with Native American Student Association members to help structure their new organization.

Within the school's International Student Association (ISA) is the African Student Association. The group's biggest annual activity is African Week, a celebration that comes at the end of Black History Month. "The event consists of a fashion show, and we learn about African history through storytelling. We have also had a potluck dinner, where we served soul food and they served African dishes," says a BSA member. The ISA also includes Malaysian and Chinese student associations.

While students report that race relations are "sometimes good and sometimes not," most agree that there is little overt racism on campus. The difficulty comes, students say, not so much on campus as at some of the clubs in Fayetteville, especially Doc Murdoch's and Tremors. "You have to be a member to get in, and if you don't have your membership pass, especially as a black male, then they don't let you in. But I've seen them let in white students without a pass. That's one reason why the black Greek organizations have so many dances in the student union, because there's not that much for us to do in town." Fayetteville has other attractions, however, including movies and popular putt-putt courses, and the surrounding countryside—which includes the Ozark Mountains—offers ample opportunity for hiking, hunting, and camping. As many students come from Fayetteville, or just beyond, students say relations with the community are good.

While students say one of their biggest complaints about their school is the bureaucracy of the place—"registration is a huge hassle"—they nonetheless find the support they need to be successful. "The resources are definitely here. The people, like Lonnie Williams and others, and offices are there to see to it that you make it. You can be successful here. The key is just tapping into all the resources."

HENDRIX COLLEGE

Address: Conway, AR 72032
Phone: (501) 329-6811
Director of Admissions: Rudy Pollan
Multicultural Student Recruiter: Diana Arms
1993–94 tuition: $8,300
Room and board: $3,060
Application deadline: Rolling admissions
Financial aid application deadline: 4/1
Non-white freshman admissions: Applicants for the class of '95: na
  Applicants accepted who rank in top 10% of high school class: na
  Median SAT: na
  Median ACT: na
Full-time undergraduate enrollment: 1,006
  Men: 46%
  Women: 54%
Non-white students in
  1987–88: 7.2%
  1988–89: 7.6%

1989–90: 8.3%
1990–91: 9.3%
Geographic distribution of students: na
Top majors: na
Retention rate of non-white students: na
Scholarships exclusively for non-white students: None
Remediation programs: None
Academic support services: None
Ethnic studies programs: None
Ethnic studies courses: The college offers two history courses in Chinese Studies, and the English department offers "The African Novel."

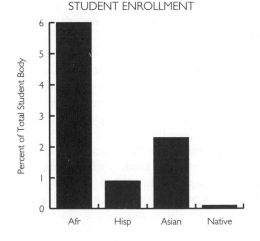

STUDENT ENROLLMENT

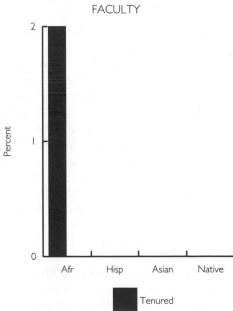

FACULTY

Organizations for non-white students:
  Students for Black Culture
Notable non-white alumni: na
Tenured faculty: 45

Non-tenured faculty: 55
Student-faculty ratio: 15:1
Administrators: na
Recent non-white speakers on campus: na

Hendrix College is regarded as Arkansas's best liberal arts school and continually attracts many of the state's brightest high school seniors, who find the 109-year-old school to be a welcome alternative to the state's large public universities.

Students say biology, chemistry, and English are among the school's most popular and respected majors, while pre-professional studies in law and medicine are also highly touted. Hendrix's economics and business program allows students to concentrate in accounting, computer studies, or economics, and the college's only Black Studies course, "The African Novel," earns high marks from students. Students would like to see the Spanish department become more diversified and include courses about Latin America. Because the average class size is only 19, close student-faculty interaction at Hendrix is common, and students comment that their professors are also good teachers.

Cultural programming at Hendrix hit a high note during the 1990–91 school year when its Murphy Programs in Literature and Language's theme was Africa. The programs, which focus on a new theme each year, brought to campus various distinguished African and African-American scholars, and included an African film series, an exhibition of French-African cultural artifacts, and stagings of two one-act plays written by Nigerian playwright Wole Soyinka.

The student organization Students for Black Culture (SBC) "is somewhat effective as a social vehicle, mainly for black students," says an SBC member, "but the level of its activity varies from year to year depending on its leaders." In recent years, SBC has worked to include more community and political activities in its programming, such as tutoring in a local elementary school and sponsoring and attending conferences dealing with African-American issues.

Alice Hines, SBC's adviser and an associate professor of English, "has always been open and available to help students," says a senior. "She has helped to push numerous minority-related issues. Many minority students seek advice from her." Allison Nicholas, director of career development, is also a source of support for students. "She has been a personal support for me and tries to keep abreast of minority-related issues within her department," says a student.

According to students, Hendrix's campus is relatively free of racist incidents, but an underground group calling itself the Society of Successful Rednecks has been stirring up controversy lately. "The group is anti-minority, anti-feminism, and homophobic," says a student. "This group was disbanded by our administration two years ago after some of its members were found guilty of harassing some students. The student reaction to the group varies. Some believe they are a joke and funny. Others, including me, are highly offended. The administration has threatened to expel any members if any other incidents occur. However," the student adds, "the mere presence of such mentalities adds to the air of tension at our school."

To avoid racial tension on campus, Hendrix president Joe B. Hatcher formed a panel on racial and ethnic concerns, but students are discouraged by its inability to effect change. "The group was formed in response to black student complaints of a lack of representation at the school—in the student senate, faculty, and administration," says a student. "Although this group has sponsored some helpful forums and solicited minority student concerns, I believe that it does not have the power to force change at Hendrix. After three years with this committee, we have not hired any more minority faculty or improved minority student retention."

While the primary activity of most students is their studies, Hendrix students also know how to let down their hair. There are no fraternities or sororities at Hendrix, so much of the partying takes place in dorms, and intramural activity, especially between the dorms, is spirited. Hendrix's Grove Physical Education Building offers impressive facilities, especially for such a small school. The student senate's Social Committee sponsors film screenings, picnics, and special events such as the "We Can Make You Laugh" comedy series.

The city of Conway, Arkansas, thirty miles northwest of Little Rock, offers the best of both worlds—close proximity to a major metropolitan center yet far enough away to let students take advantage of a number of outdoor activities. The Ozark Mountains are close and offer students opportunities for canoeing, backpacking, and sailing. Hendrix's Outdoor Activities and Recreation Program offers training and equipment for such excursions.

Although Conway includes a sizable African-American community, students say there is little interaction between the town and students. In an attempt to enhance town-gown relations, two African-American psychology majors recently founded Children Against Racism, an organization whose "goal is to provide local children with multicultural experiences." Hendrix students meet with the schoolchildren twice a month, on Saturdays. "The group wants to stop prejudice based on ignorance," says a student.

With its outstanding reputation in the state, a Hendrix degree is highly desirable. "The professors at Hendrix have encouraged me to excel in my classes simply by the enthusiasm they show for their particular disciplines. I always want to learn more about what is so exciting to them. Hendrix has more than met my expectations as an excellent liberal arts college in that it encourages excellence not only in one's major but in all aspects of the curriculum. For me, the quality of an institution is best judged by the quality of the people comprising it. Judging by its faculty and staff, Hendrix College gets top rating."

CALIFORNIA

UNIVERSITY OF CALIFORNIA/BERKELEY

Address: 110 Sproul Hall, Berkeley, CA
  94720
Phone: (510) 642-3175
Director of Admissions: André Bell
Multicultural Student Recruiter: na
1991–92 tuition: $2,678 (in-state); $10,377
  (out-of-state)
Room and board: $6,050
Application deadline: 11/30
Financial aid application deadline: 3/2

Non-white freshman admissions: Applicants
  for the class of '95: 10,337
  Accepted: 46%
  Accepted who enroll: 41%
  Applicants accepted who rank in top
  10% of high school class: 95%
  In top 25%: 99%
  Median SAT range: 490–640 V, 580–720 M
  Median ACT: na
Full-time undergraduate enrollment: 21,660
  Men: 53%
  Women: 47%
Non-white students in
  · 1987–88: 42.4%
  1988–89: 45.7%
  1989–90: 50.4%
  1990–91: 51.6%
Geographic distribution of students: na
Top majors: na
Retention rate of non-white students: 90%
**Scholarships exclusively for non-white
  students:** None
Remediation programs: The Summer Bridge
  program provides an introduction to the

university's academic and non-academic
programs.
Academic support services: Student
  Learning Center, Academic Achievement
  Division, Transfer Student Summer
  Institute, Transfer Student Orientation
  Courses, and Athletic Study Center
Ethnic studies programs: The university
  offers majors in Native American,
  Afro-American, Asian-American, and
  Chicano Studies. Each program includes
  at least five tenured faculty members.
Organizations for non-white students: Alpha
  Kappa Alpha, Alpha Phi Alpha,
  Afro-American House, Mexican/Chicano

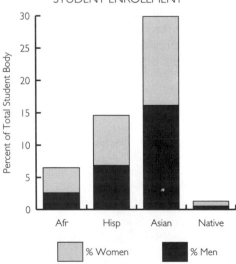

STUDENT ENROLLMENT

Theme House, Intertribal Students Council, Asian-American Students Association, MECHA, Hermanos Unidos (Chicano/Latino fraternity), as well as nearly 70 other student organizations

Notable non-white alumni: Allen Broussard ('50, '53; former justice of the California Supreme Court); Walter Gordon ('18; former governor of the Virgin Islands and first African-American to graduate from Berkeley's law school); Kevin Johnson ('87, Political Science; professional basketball player); Maxine Hong Kingston ('62, English; novelist); Wiley Manuel ('51, Economics; former justice of the California Supreme Court); Robert Matsui ('63, Political Science; U.S. representative); Ron Rivera ('89, Social Sciences; professional football player); Yori Wada ('40, Journalism; Regent of the University of California)

Tenured faculty: 1,434
Non-tenured faculty: 216
Student-faculty ratio: 12:1
Administrators: 120
  African-American: 12%
  Hispanic: 3%
  Asian-American: 9%
  Native American: 0

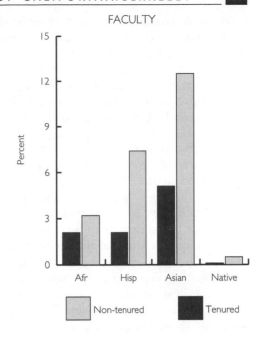

FACULTY

Recent non-white speakers on campus: David Dinkins (mayor of New York City); Robert Maynard (publisher, *Oakland Tribune*); Rev. Cecil Williams (Glide Memorial Church); Wallace Tashima (U.S. District Court judge, Los Angeles)

The University of California at Berkeley is truly one of America's great institutions of higher learning. It was recently the most highly ranked state-supported university in *U.S. News & World Report*'s annual survey of colleges, the school boasts some of the country's most outstanding undergraduate and graduate academic programs, and with nearly 52 percent of its students representing multicultural groups, the university is one of the most diverse campuses in the country—no one ethnic or racial group constitutes a majority at Berkeley.

Berkeley's academic programs are excellent, with English, history, engineering (particularly civil, mechanical, and chemical), the physical sciences, and math leading the way. Students also praise the school's programs in Native American, Afro-American, Asian-American, and Chicano studies. Wheeler Hall, a campus library, houses extensive library collections for each of these area studies.

Each of Berkeley's academic departments has its own graduation requirements, but no matter what major you plan to study, all students must take courses in English composition and literature. A newly instituted American Cultures requirement has won favor from students, and includes courses from various departments. According to a student: "Because the requirement is comparative, it is non-isolatory; because it is in all departments it is not segregated. All departments are having to make substantial new classes to suit the requirement in order to attract students, because the greater the number of students, the more funds a department receives. Thirty new courses have been added in a recent year, while 30 other such courses are expected to be added in a subsequent year. There is an American Cultures Office, which brings together professors in the ethnic studies departments and other departments in order to consult and advise other professors how to teach these topics and to develop new syllabi."

But Berkeley is not without its problems. A recent commission made up of 15 faculty members and students released a report that concluded, according to a *New York Times* article: "Life as an undergraduate at the University of California at Berkeley can be a hostile and alienating experience." The commission made 40 recommendations to the administration, which included smaller class sizes. "We found that the campus is so big and cold and unfriendly that it is discouraging not only to minority students but to everyone else as well," said commission member George Chang, an associate professor in the nutritional sciences, in the *Times* article.

The commission also noted that large lecture classes, which can have up to 400 students in some required courses, hamper student learning and is one reason cited by students for leaving Berkeley. Establishing a good rapport with faculty members—some of whom are Nobel Prize winners or just out-and-out geniuses—is akin to finding a needle in a haystack at a school with an undergraduate population of more than 21,000. The school is first and foremost a research university, and professors justifiably suffer from the "publish or perish" mentality. However, teaching assistants are helpful in leading class discussions and advising students, according to the report.

In addition, because of the school's tremendous diversity, there appears to be a growing separation between the school's various races and ethnicities, or as another *New York Times* headline described the situation: "Separate Ethnic Worlds Grow on Campus." In the article, the *Times* reporter described a Chicano student who lives in an off-campus apartment with Chicano roommates, is majoring in Chicano Studies, and will be participating in bilingual commencement exercises for Chicano and Latino students. "You could say that this campus is segregated for some reasons, but for me it was like family," says the student in the *Times* article. The *Times* article goes on to describe a typical day on Sproul Plaza, a favorite campus hangout: "At lunchtime, Sproul Plaza becomes an international bazaar: members of the Filipino-American Alliance are there, as are the members of the Vietnamese Students Association, the Chinese Student Association, the Asian Student Union, and Tonodach: The Japanese American Cultural Club."

One student sees the campus developing multiculturally as well as along ethnically separate lines. "We have begun to hear a lot about 'balkanization' on our campus, but I don't agree with most of the talk," he says. "I feel that most students are comfortable with students of other races, and most cafes and restaurants have integrated groups along with ethnic groups seated together. Still, many organizations tend to be ethnic-specific, and the social activities they plan are aimed at their respective racial groups. These activities have been labeled racist by some critics."

To address issues of diversity, the school's housing office sponsors Project DARE (Diversity Awareness through Resources and Education). Instituted four years ago by Edith Ng, Project DARE programming takes place in the freshman dorms during the first two weeks of school. "The program teaches about diversity, learning to tolerate, respect, and appreciate other cultures," says a student. "It teaches that there are other cultures inside each of us, some hidden, such as low socioeconomic status and dyslexia, and others not, such as Asian-American, African-American, and Chicano. DARE also teaches that culture applies to groupings outside of the racial/ethnic boundaries, including athlete, woman, gay and lesbian."

At Berkeley, there are nearly as many different student types as there are students. A favorite pastime is to people-watch from one of the many nearby coffeehouses and to hang out in Sproul Plaza. "Simply put, there's nearly everything to do here," exclaims one busy junior. Comments another student: "I think a big plus of Berkeley is that you can find real radical views and real conservative views here."

The university sponsors more than 200 student organizations, 70 of which are cultural groups, including groups as diverse as the Intertribal Students Council and Hermanos Unidos as well as the Asian-American Students Association and historically black fraternities and sororities. Almost all of the groups are quite active, sponsoring forums and dances, as well as providing academic and emotional support for members. An Afro-American House and a Mexican/Chicano Theme House, which both provide residence facilities, are popular with students. The school's Gay, Lesbian, and Bisexual Student Union is largely accepted and tolerated and sponsors some of the campus's best parties and dances. The group is pushing for a gay, lesbian, and bisexual studies program.

For those of you who paid attention to your high school history teacher when it came time to discuss the 1960s, you'll no doubt remember that Berkeley was at that time the center of much of the country's campus activism. Although students are decidedly more career-oriented than they were thirty years ago, vestiges of campus radicalism still remain. Long hair and tie-dyed T-shirts are the style of choice for many Berkeley students, and protest rallies, although not as frequent as in the 1960s, are still alive and well on the Berkeley campus. However, there has been an increase in recent years of Greek involvement; about 15 percent of the campus is Greek, and students report that there is tension between Greeks and non-Greeks. Students add, however, that the school's Greek organizations, including the Interfraternity Council, are reasonably well integrated.

According to a political science major, many Berkeley students are also committed to community service. "On the local level, Berkeley students have a great asset in a community that offers many opportunities for involvement. Berkeley, Oakland, and San Francisco social agencies, often founded by Berkeley alums, do everything from tutoring minority kids to taking care of injured animals. For students of color, work in many specific ethnic communities abounds. Diverse organizations, such as La Clínica de la Raza, Japanese-American Services of the East Bay, and the Association of Negro Business and Professional Women, give students a chance to be involved locally."

Adds the student: "Awareness of national and international issues is also high at Berkeley. Some students think we worry too much about the rest of the world, while ignoring more immediate issues, like students' access to computers. Up until three years ago, the Associate Students Senate often spent as much time debating international issues as campus issues. During the Gulf War, candlelight vigils for peace, teach-ins, teach-outs, rallies, and in-class discussions all took place, and I felt that most students supported discussion of the war, even if it took class time, as it had implications for almost any discipline."

For off-campus entertainment and diversion, Berkeley students are able to take advantage of myriad cultural activities in the Bay Area. There are bars, restaurants, and clubs galore. Bookstores and jazz clubs are favorite student haunts, and the San Francisco 49ers and many other professional sports teams are some of the city's other attractions. San Francisco's public transportation system, BART, is efficient and makes most points in the city—one of the most livable and culturally exciting in the country—easily accessible.

Berkeley's top-flight academics and culturally diverse student body make the campus a mecca for many a highly motivated student. Although Berkeley can't guarantee you an intimate learning environment, students say there are support groups and services that can make the school's sheer size a little less intimidating. Says a student: "At Berkeley, there's something for everyone. Personal development is important here and there are a lot of different resources, such as the Student Learning Center for tutoring, as well as the different campus organizations, study groups, and cultural organizations. There's always something going on."

UNIVERSITY OF CALIFORNIA/DAVIS

Address: 175 Mark Hall, Davis, CA 95616
Phone: (916) 752-2971
Director of Admissions: Gary Tudor
Multicultural Student Recruiter: Leslie Campbell
1993–94 tuition: $3,038 (in-state); $10,737 (out-of-state)
Room and board: $5,822
Application deadline: 11/1
Financial aid application deadline: 3/2
Non-white freshman admissions: Applicants for the class of '94: 7,520
  Accepted: 67%
  Accepted who enrolled: 34%
  Applicants accepted who rank in top 10% of high school class: na
  Median SAT range: 380–520 V, 480–630 M
  Median ACT: na
Full-time undergraduate enrollment: 18,395
  Men: 48.2%
  Women: 51.8%
Non-white students in
  1987–88: 30.7%
  1988–89: 33.4%

1989–90: 35.5%
1990–91: 36.5%

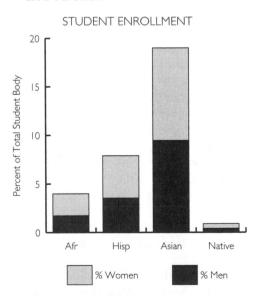

STUDENT ENROLLMENT

Percent of Total Student Body

□ % Women   ■ % Men

Geographic distribution of students: na
Students In-state: 97%

Top majors: 1. Biological Science
2. Psychology
3. Biochemistry

Retention rate of non-white students: 89%

Scholarships exclusively for non-white students: Chancellor's Achievement Award: need-based; amount of each award and number awarded varies each year. The Charles P. Gould Award is given to Native American students. The Pacific Telesis Scholarship is awarded to engineering students and is need-based. The Chevron Scholarship is awarded to engineering students.

Remediation Programs: UC/Davis has programs available in tutoring, English composition, and pre-calculus.

Academic support services: The university's Learning Skills Center offers skill-building workshops, peer, staff, and faculty advising, and several discipline-based academic support programs. UC/Davis also has a minority engineering program, and enrichment programs in economic-management-related majors and in math majors.

Ethnic studies programs: The university offers major and minor courses of study in Native American Studies, Afro-American Studies, and Chicano Studies. The university's Asian-American Studies program is offered as a minor course of study.

Organizations for non-white students: African-American Greek Letter Council, African-American Health Science Association, African-American Pre-law Association, African-American Students United, Alpha Kappa Alpha, Alpha Phi Alpha, American Indian Science and Engineering Society, Bible Christian Fellowship Gospel Choir, Black Engineers Association, Brothers and Sisters of Kemet, Casa Cuauhtemoc, Chicano & Latino Engineers & Scientists Society, Chicano Pride Productions, Chicano/Latino Student Media, Chicanos in Health Education, Delta Sigma Theta, Hermanos Machehual Fellowship, Kappa Alpha Psi, La Raza Pre-law Association, Lambda Sigma Gamma, MECHA, Minorities in Agricultural Natural Resources & Related Sciences, NAACP, Native American Student Union, Pan-African Student Association, The Sisterhood, Zeta Phi Beta

Notable non-white alumni: Elihu Harris (mayor of Oakland); Henry Gradellas (former principal, Garfield High School); Tilahun Yilma (professor of veterinary medicine, UC/Davis); George Blake (artist); Gus Lee (author)

Tenured faculty: 1,117

Non-tenured Faculty: 237

Student-faculty ratio: 19:1

Administrators: na

Recent non-white speakers on campus: Mary Frances Berry (Georgetown University law school professor); Derrick Bell (author); Cesar Chavez (head of the United Farm Workers); Gus Lee (author); Elizabeth Cook-Lynn (author)

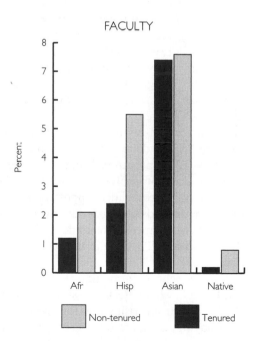

FACULTY

The University of California at Davis may not have the most cosmopolitan student population in the University of California system, but it does offer the variety of academic disciplines and extracurricular activities that should appeal to students with diverse interests.

UCD was established in 1909 as the state's agricultural school, and today the university's College of Agriculture and Environmental Sciences, which enrolls about a quarter of the undergraduate population, offers some of the best such programs in the world. The College of Agriculture's more than 35 majors range from environmental biology and resource sciences to food production and processing. UCD's College of Engineering, with about 2,200 undergraduates, offers six areas of study, such as chemical engineering, civil engineering, and electrical engineering, and the university's School of Veterinary Science is nationally known.

Students in the university's arts and sciences division, with offerings in more than 50 different programs, must complete requirements in a foreign language and English composition. Among the division's best programs are English, psychology, history, and political science. UCD has the only program in international affairs in California. "Survey of Ethnicity in the U.S." and "African-American Studies" rank as some of the school's best ethnic studies courses. Katrina Bell, an instructor in the Afro-American Studies program, is popular.

As at other large universities, UCD's faculty can be difficult to reach, especially in first- and even second-year courses, as many professors are very much into their own research. In addition to fine undergraduate programs, the university has several respected graduate school programs—in engineering and veterinary science, for example—that occupy many a professor's time and attention. With effort, however, students say, meetings with professors can be had, but by appointment. Nonetheless, studies at UCD can be intense. Not only do professors expect a lot from their students, but the university runs on the quarter system—10 weeks per quarter—which means final exams are given three times a year rather than the two times that a semester schedule permits. Academic competition is keenest among pre-vet, pre-law, and pre-med students.

Says a student about the school's academic support networks: "UCD genuinely wants to help students who are minorities to succeed. They have a strong EOP/SAA [Educational Opportunity Program/Student Affirmative Action] department with an excellent staff of professional and peer advisers." Gary Perkins, the program's coordinator, "is especially supportive of students," comments a junior. For additional assistance and advice, students also feel comfortable turning to Yvonne Marsh, an assistant vice-chancellor of student affairs, and Leslie Campbell, an associate director of admissions. "They make us feel as if there is always someone there for us," says a student.

With the school's agricultural history—the university was founded as the "University Farm," where Berkeley students came to learn the tricks of the agricultural trade—it's not surprising that the majority of UCD students aren't into politics. When not studying, most are into exercise—the university's physical fitness center is a hub of student activity and its jogging trails are like rush hour in certain large cities—rather than concerned with effecting change.

But for a small cadre of students—mostly students of color—1990 was the time for change. Petitions? Nah. That had been done. Rallies? Done, too. This small group of students—about four in all—vowed to fast on the steps of the university's administration building until all of their demands had been met, which included an on-campus ethnic and cultural center, investigations into alleged racism in the Spanish department, and the hiring of additional faculty to teach African-American, Chicano/Latino, Native American, and Asian-American studies. After five days of fasting and some negotiations, the university agreed to all of the demands. "This is just the beginning of the beginning. We have opened the door for action," says a sociology major in a *New York Times* article about the demonstration.

UCD's cultural student groups are far from inactive, especially in light of recent events such as the fast. "The minority organizations on campus are the least apathetic of any student group," says a campus leader. Each of the groups plans forums, community service projects, and lectures, and has regular meetings. *Third World Forum,* a campus weekly published by students, "deals with race relations around campus and in our nation." The Multi-Ethnic Building, which accommodates students from various racial and ethnic groups, is a popular student residence. "I lived there my sophomore year and I thought it was one of the best learning experiences—about different people and their cultures—that I'd had at UCD," reports a student.

The school's students of color have broadened their campus activity to involvement in student government. "The year 1991 marked history at UCD," proclaims a senior. "It was the first time that the majority of people on the executive council [UCD's student programming body], including the president and vice president, were students of color. *The Aggie* [the campus daily] ran an article entitled 'Council Gets an Ethnic Makeover,' alluding to the five African-Americans and one Chicana who made up the majority of the nine-member council board."

UCD's atmosphere is indeed "relaxed" and "small-town." The university is surrounded by some of the most expensive agricultural land in the state. The town of Davis (pop. 46,000), a predominantly white community, offers a wide assortment of off-campus diversions—restaurants, movies, and bars, as well as the more sedate opportunities available at the Davis Art Center. The town also has 18 city parks, contributing to the area's wide-open feel. Although Davis is a college town—college students account for about half of the city's population—students of color report mixed feelings about their relations with the community. "Three years ago, my friends and I were called names at a local restaurant. Since then, most of my social life takes place on campus. That event made me realize that I'm not part of the community." Sacramento is only 15 miles east, and San Francisco is about 72 miles southwest.

On campus, there's rarely a lack of things to do, even if it just means riding your bicycle—a must-have at UCD, as Davis is known as the City of Bicycles; more than 46 miles of bicycle paths crisscross the city. Frequent cultural activities take place on campus each year, from performances of the Joffrey Ballet to the Alvin Ailey American Dance Company. There is Black Family Week, in which alums and friends and relatives of students visit and attend events. Intramural sports—especially tennis, swimming, and Frisbee—are more popular than varsity sports, although the school's varsity football team has had some successful seasons recently.

While most students take full advantage of top-notch academics, the university also teaches students something else: self-reliance. "I would recommend Davis to any prospective minority student, but I would tell him or her to keep an open mind. Although Davis does reach out and look out for minority students, minorities must also be willing to look out for themselves. They cannot simply sit back and wait for someone to come get them. They must put in extra effort and get in contact with the right people."

UNIVERSITY OF CALIFORNIA/IRVINE

Address: 245 Administration Building Irvine, CA 92717	**1992–93 tuition:**$3,074.50 (in-state); $10,773 (out-of-state)
Phone: (714) 856-6703	**Room and board:** $6,300
Director of Admissions: James Dunning	**Application deadline:** 11/30
Multicultural Student Recruiter: na	**Financial aid application deadline:** 3/1

Don't decide to attend the University of California at Irvine just because it's near Disneyland and some of the best beaches in the country. Attend UCI because it is one of the fastest-rising stars in an already impressive University of California system.

Academic highlights at Irvine are its biological science programs, especially psychobiology and molecular biology; nearly 25 percent of UCI's student body is pre-med. Other notable departments include English, psychology, political science, and languages, and students say academics can be challenging and competitive, especially among pre-meds. However, don't expect to become close friends with your professors at UCI. It is primarily a research-oriented university, and UCI professors are often remote, especially during your first two years, when chances are you'll be placed in classes with more than a hundred of your classmates.

It's no wonder students say that UCI really means University under Construction Indefinitely. The university is constantly expanding and new buildings are popping up regularly. Although UCI is not of the overwhelming size that characterizes life at Berkeley or UCLA, students say that the school's various cultural organizations help create, in the words of one student, "a familylike atmosphere."

By far the largest of these organizations is the Asian Pacific Student Association. The group, along with nearly twenty other smaller Asian societies, sponsors an Asian Heritage Week, which includes traditional dancing, kick-boxing, and other entertainment. "The event is meant really to celebrate the cultural diversity of the Asian-American community at UCI," says a student. "Many people here tend to lump us into one group—Asian-American—but we're Chinese-American, Vietnamese-American, etc." The groups also sponsor the annual one-day Asian Pacific Awareness Conference, where speakers discuss such issues as establishing an Asian-American Studies program at UCI and the subject of Asian-Americans as "model minorities." Students can count on John Liu, a professor in the school's comparative culture department and a popular figure who contributes much of his time to the organization. Among the school's more active Asian groups are Tomo No Kai, a Japanese-American club, and the Korean-American Student Association.

MECHA, a Chicano and Latino student group, sponsors a variety of events and activities, including celebrations for Cinco de Mayo Week and the Day of the Dead. The Chicano/Latino Youth Conference, a MECHA-sponsored event, "is our outreach program to high school students in the area and in Los Angeles. We bring them to campus and talk to them about UCI and college in general and about Chicano/Latino culture," says a MECHA leader. The group also sponsors a lecture series every other week "where we try to expand the awareness of our culture for members. We usually bring in community leaders so they can discuss how they got to where they are in life, we talk about MECHA's situation here at UCI, and we also have people come in to discuss graduate school and the application process." Cesar Sereseres, dean of undergraduate studies at UCI, advises MECHA and is well respected by members.

The African-American Student Union (AASU) sponsors "good events all the time," says a member. For the Martin Luther King, Jr., celebration in January, the group sponsors a major walk through a nearby park, as well as events for Black History Month that include a lecture series and parties. The group also helps coordinate a Black Commencement each year, which is conducted at a Baptist church in Los Angeles.

A rift has been taking place between AASU and two other organizations, Black Students in Science and Black Students in the Social Sciences. "It's not that we're at war," says a Black Students in Science member. "It's just that the AASU takes it upon itself to speak for all black students on campus when it comes to different issues. Sometimes the other black student organizations aren't even contacted by the AASU to get our opinions about certain events or causes, and our names are sometimes used for events that we weren't even contacted for, which isn't right, because we're not meant to be political anyway."

UCI's four main cultural organizations, which include the American Indian Council, certainly show no rift when it comes to seeking to establish an ethnic studies program on campus. "All four groups are pushing for the program," says a senior. "Last year we spent time educating the community about the need for such a program, and this year we've actually been putting the structure of it together. Each cultural group has its own committee that is working to create their respective areas of concentration. Sometimes we get competitive because we're competing for faculty positions, and we end up fighting for just a few resources." According to a student in the proposed program, students will be able to major in ethnic studies and concentrate in African-American, Asian-American, Latino/Chicano, or Native American studies. Adds a student: "It's incredible that nearly 40 percent of the campus is Asian-American yet there are only three Asian-American courses offered. Three hundred students were recently enrolled in each class, and about a hundred students were on the waiting list to get in. There's obviously a big demand for such courses."

The Cross-Cultural Center, available to students of all backgrounds, is described by students as a "haven," "a place where we can feel comfortable," and as "a place where we know we can get support." Located on central campus, the center provides peer support services and academic counseling, and includes office space for numerous cultural organizations. With the help of the center's director, Corina Espinoza, and assistant director, Angela Calera, the center also sponsors events for Black History Month, Asian Week, Cinco de Mayo, as well as a faculty-student mentorship program.

While the center and the cultural groups work to create a family atmosphere on campus, there are those anonymous few at UCI who work against that. Recently, in an event that received national attention, racist epithets were scrawled on the walls and mirrors of a Latino student's dorm room because of her friendship with an African-American male. The two friends also had received more than a dozen threatening letters in the mail. The incidents took place in Sierra, a first-year multicultural hall, and occurred while the Rainbow Festival, a cultural awareness program sponsored by the center, was conducting a forum on crimes of hate. "I've talked to friends and family about UCI and I said we lived in a utopian type of place. When it hit close to home, I realized that I was wrong," said a junior studio arts major in a *New York Times* article about the incident. In the *Times* article, Sarah J. Johnson, the assistant dean of students, attributed the rise of such events to students' increased willingness to report them and to "these being meaner times."

UCI students usually tend to bypass Orange County for fun and cultural activity and head into Los Angeles, about forty miles north. "Orange County is a place where minorities are scrutinized every time they walk into a store. The area is very rich and very conservative." But, adds another student, "this doesn't translate into UCI campus life. The majority of students here are more apathetic about most issues of politics and race."

In addition to cultural activity and the famed LA nightlife, students also have easy access to the California Pacific coast—about five minutes away. Sports are also popular at UCI. Track and field, tennis, and water polo are some of the school's standout teams, and seventeen UCI graduates have competed in the Olympics.

UCI remains mostly a commuter campus, which results in a less than unified student body. But because of recent student activism, students are able to develop a camaraderie here that doesn't exist at some of the bigger schools in the state. "I knew I wanted to attend UCI because of its reputation, and because of the size, I knew I could make friends easily. Working to get the ethnic studies program has been a lot of work too, and it has been a huge learning experience, probably more than what I might have learned in the classroom. If the program works out, I can't imagine the feeling I will have knowing I helped leave that legacy."

UNIVERSITY OF CALIFORNIA/LOS ANGELES

Address: 1147 Murphy Hall, 405 Hilgard, Los Angeles, CA 90024
Phone: (213) 825-3101
Director of Admissions: Dr. Rae Lee Siporin
Multicultural Student Recruiter: na
1991–92 tuition: $2,337 (in-state); $10,035 (out-of-state)
Room and board: $4,530
Application deadline: 11/30
Financial aid application deadline: 3/2
Non-white freshman admissions: Applicants for the class of '95: 3,905
Accepted: 62.5%
Accepted who enrolled: 34.5%
Applicants accepted who rank in top 10% of high school class: na
Median SAT: 513 V, 612 M
Median ACT: na
Full-time undergraduate enrollment: 24,207
Men: 51.8%
Women: 48.2%

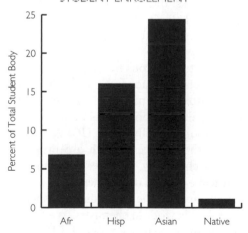

STUDENT ENROLLMENT

Non-white students 1987–91: na
Geographic distribution of students: na
Students In-state: 93.8%
Top majors: 1. Engineering 2. Psychology 3. Life Sciences
Retention rate of non-white students: 92%

Scholarships exclusively for non-white students: Bunche Scholarship: merit-based; award varies from $500 to $10,000; available only to first-year students. Ingle Scholarship: need-based; awards are valued at $600 to $1,200 each. Ortega Scholarship: need-based; awards are valued at $600 to $1,200 each; recipient must be a U.S. citizen of Mexican descent with a Spanish surname
Remediation programs: None
Academic support services: The university offers workshops in time management and study skills, as well as tutoring in most academic subjects.
Ethnic studies programs: The university offers majors in Chicano, Afro-American, and East Asian Studies, as well as African languages. Centers of study are available for each of these programs, including an American Indian Study Center.
Organizations for non-white students: Asian Pacific Coalition, African Student Union, MECHA, Retention of American Indians Now, Black Greek Letter Council, Phi Beta Sigma, Alpha Phi Alpha, and 32 organizations for Chicano/Latino students
Notable non-white alumni: Kareem Abdul-Jabbar (professional basketball player); Thomas Bradley (mayor, Los Angeles); Arthur Ashe (professional tennis player, first African-American male to win Wimbledon); Ralph Bunche (former United Nations diplomat and Nobel Peace Prize winner for his work in international affairs); Linda Alvarez (news anchorwoman)
Tenured faculty: na
Non-tenured faculty: na
Student-faculty ratio: 17:1
Administrators: na
Recent non-white speakers on campus: na

There is a great deal about UCLA that is impressive—its outstanding academics, especially in the sciences and the performance arts; its beautiful (and green!) campus, with the famous Royce Hall as a landmark; and, as anyone can attest who has stood in line on campus for almost anything from movie tickets to course registration, its sheer size. With about 34,400 undergraduates and graduate students, UCLA is the largest school in the University of California system. "Except for the people on my dorm floor, I'll go all day and not see anyone I know," says a student.

But there are ways to avoid the anonymity of such a large school. There is the College Honors, which gives qualified students the chance to learn in smaller classes; there are more than 500 clubs and organizations, among which fraternities and sororities are popular; and the school's academic advising system, which offers tutoring and other support programs, helps make surviving in the school's large introductory classes, which can number into the hundreds, a bit easier.

Many students find significance by joining one of the school's multitude of cultural organizations. "UCLA is a big campus, and it is easy to get lost and feel like a number and have a difficult time," says a student activist. "So you have to take advantage of the many resources here, such as tutoring or joining a student group. In them, you can find out about issues and meet people from your own background. I'm not saying that you should isolate yourself with those from the same background as yours, but just that the opportunity is there and that it's a good thing. The first year I became involved in the Asian Pacific Coalition was very enriching. Once you become involved, the campus becomes smaller and more personal."

On the other hand, many students don't mind the size of their school. Says a student: "I like bigger classes, like the ones they have here. The professors don't take roll every day, and if you don't show up for each class, then it's okay. You can also buy lecture notes, around eight dollars per quarter. I don't like to feel pressured by the professor, and if I know him or her personally, then I feel more pressure. I feel more on my own in bigger classes."

Another reason to revel in the school's size is the tremendous number of academic opportunities available, some of which are world-class. Among the school's liberal arts programs, students say economics, English, history, and philosophy are excellent, while communications, psychology, and urban planning are popular as well. As might be expected of a school located practically next door to Hollywood, UCLA's music and theater departments are top-notch. Among the sciences, which are primarily offered on the school's south campus, students say chemistry, biology, and computer science are strong. Engineering is also reputed to be a solid department.

Although many of the school's professors are among the most distinguished in their fields (Donald Cram, a Nobel Prize winner for his work in chemistry, is a faculty member here), students say getting to know them is nearly impossible. It is not surprising that the Academic Advancement Program, which provides peer counseling and tutoring, gets a lot of student use, and each of the school's main cultural organizations—MECHA, the Asian Pacific Coalition, and the African Student Union—offers similar services.

UCLA's Asian-American Research Center provides a variety of programs for students, publishes the highly regarded *Amerasia Journal,* and includes one of the most extensive collections of Asian-American research papers in the nation. One of the center's popular programs is the Leadership Project, "where we talk about self-determination, empowerment, things that have encouraged me to become an activist. The things I learned through the project are things I can apply to real life," says a student. The project, a two-quarter program, includes student outreach to area high schools. "I was involved in this as a high school student, and I came to UCLA as a result," says the student. The school's centers for African and Chicano studies offer services similar to those provided by the Asian-American Research Center, and students report that they're all well used.

The Asian Pacific Coalition is an umbrella organization that oversees 18 organizations "divided by ethnic, religious, and pre-professional interests," says a group organizer. "We try to be an advocate for all interests of the member groups and to educate Asian and Pacific Islander Americans and the general campus about Asian Pacific American issues. It's sometimes hard to come to a consensus, though, because we have so much diversity and potential within our large population. We try not to be a reactionary group, but a proaction group, and we try to eliminate problems before they come up." Some of the group's more recent activities include forums on the controversy surrounding the Broadway play *Miss Saigon* and affirmative action. The group also sponsored a forum on women's issues, such as domestic violence, the immigrant woman's experience, and lesbianism. In the spring, the group sponsors events for an Asian Pacific Heritage Month celebration, which recently included speakers, an Asian-American comedy night, and a Korean Cultural Night. The group also publishes *Pacific Ties,* a newspaper issued six times a year.

Through the Asian Pacific Coalition, Asian American students are also able to participate in an Asian Pacific graduation. "We talk about our experiences as Asian Pacific American college students, and it's much more personal than the regular graduation. Everyone gets a chance to speak. About ninety students come, and they generally thank their parents or whomever. Later, there are about six different types of Asian-American foods and usually there are some performers. When I graduated, there was a Filipino dance group," says a student. The graduation is optional, and students are able to participate in either the Asian Pacific or the general graduation ceremony, or both.

There are two Native American student organizations which serve "as a little family," says a student. The American Indian Student Association (AISA), which includes about 20 active members, sponsors annual powwows, and in 1991 sponsored a Repatriation Conference, which included rallies and guest speakers. A point of controversy for the school's Native American students is Haynes Hall, an anthropology building that Native American students refuse to enter because it holds the bones of Native Americans. AISA is also involved in political issues. Recently, the group sponsored an anti-Columbus Day celebration "where there was a march, drummers, American Indian flags, dancers, and a remembrance of those Native Americans who died when Columbus came to America," says a student.

Retention of American Indians Now (RAIN), established in the fall of 1990, is run by paid student workers, and includes tutoring services, run usually by volunteers, study halls, and a van service to and from home to campus.

As with many large universities, UCLA's diversity isn't only reflected ethnically and racially. It's reflected politically and socially as well. Almost every viewpoint on the political spectrum is represented on campus, from those of the radical to the more conservative bent. On the whole, students appear to be a bit more conservative here than their peers at Berkeley; economics is the school's most popular major. UCLA's Greek system even includes a gay fraternity and one of the country's first lesbian sororities.

While a great deal goes on on campus, there is also a plethora of activity offered off campus as well. Located south of campus, Westwood Village offers virtually anything for the happy coed, from record shops and bars to a variety of movie theaters and ethnic restaurants. Downtown Los Angeles is also a popular destination for students, but a car is essential.

UCLA offers a smorgasbord of activities and academic opportunities, and the successful student is one who is well focused and driven. Getting mired in all that's offered is easy to do, or as one student commented, "it's mostly sink or swim." For another student, there is more to his school than that. "I think UCLA is a great university because it is very ethnically diverse. There are people here of every nationality, and from almost every country imaginable. So it's not as if you're the only person of color among Anglo-Americans."

UNIVERSITY OF CALIFORNIA/RIVERSIDE

Address: 900 University Avenue, Riverside, CA 92521
Phone: (909) 787-1012
Director of Admissions: Eric V. Gravenberg
Multicultural Student Recruiter: Betty Benzor
1993–94 tuition: $4,113 (in-state); $11,812 (out-of-state)
Room and board: $5,430
Application deadline: 11/30
Financial aid application deadline: 3/2
Non-white freshman admissions: Applicants for the class of '95: na
  Accepted: na
  Accepted who enroll: na
  Applicants accepted who rank in top 10% of high school class: na
  Median SAT: 452 V, 548 M
  Median ACT: na
Full-time undergraduate enrollment: 7,217
  Men: 47%
  Women: 53%
Non-white students in
  1988–89: 38.3%
  1989–90: 40.3%

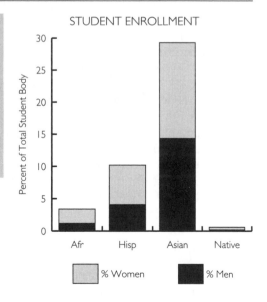

STUDENT ENROLLMENT

Percent of Total Student Body vs. Afr, Hisp, Asian, Native

% Women · % Men

  1990–91: 43.5%
  1991–92: 46.6%
Geographic distribution of students: na
Students In-state: 97%

Top majors: 1. Business Administration 2. Biology 3. Biomedical Sciences

Retention rate of non-white students: 91%

Scholarships exclusively for non-white students: UC/Riverside Foundation Academic Excellence: need-based; available to underrepresented minority students. UC Regents SAA Grants: need-based.

Remediation programs: The Learning Center provides study skills classes as well as academic tutoring.

Academic support services: In addition to the services offered as part of the Learning Center, the university offers programs through the Educational Opportunity Program/Student Affirmative Action, and through various programs targeted to specific groups of students of color, such as African Student Programs, Asian Pacific American Student Programs, Chicano/Latino Student Programs, and Native American Student Programs.

Ethnic studies programs: The university offers majors in Asian Studies, established in 1992, and in ethnic studies, an interdisciplinary program involving more than 40 courses from the sociology, anthropology, literature, and other departments. Within the program, students are able to emphasize Chicano or Black Studies and participate in courses in Native American Studies.

Organizations for non-white students: African Student Alliance, American Indian Science and Engineering, Asian-Americans in Law, Asian Pacific American Coalition, Asian Student Academic Peer Counseling Group, Asian-American Christian Fellowship, Chicanos Pre-law Student Association, Hispanic Business Society, Inter-Asian Club Council, Korean Students Association, MECHA, Native American Student Association, Women's Hispanic Organization

Notable non-white alumni: na

Non-tenured faculty: na

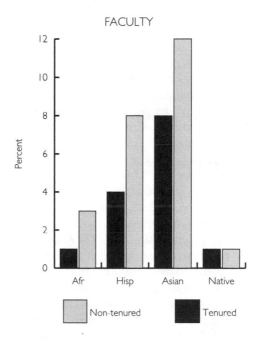

FACULTY

Tenured faculty: na

Student-faculty ratio: 14:1

Administrators: na

Recent non-white speakers on campus: na

The University of California at Riverside may not have the academic reputation of nearby UCLA, but it also doesn't have UCLA's overwhelming size. Students at UCR are treated to a respectable undergraduate education, and they don't have to wait in line for it.

UCR's best departments are in the liberal arts, particularly history and political science, as well as English, biology, psychology, entomology, and geology. The school boasts one of only two undergraduate business schools in the UC system, and students report the program is strong. Engineering, a relative newcomer on UCR's academic scene, is gaining respectability. Students are able to major in chemical, electrical, or environmental engineering. UCR's standout offering is its unique biomedical science program that allows qualified students the chance to study for four years at UCR and to finish up at UCLA medical school. The program is competitive, as only a lucky 24 of the more than 200 applicants are accepted each year.

To graduate, students must fulfill an ethnic studies requirement, and the school's new ethnic studies program has been greeted positively by students. "The department of ethnic studies has been very supportive of any and all students. The professors offer to help sponsor and co-sponsor student organization events or student programs." The school's Asian-American Studies program includes Edna Bonacich, a noted sociologist specializing in Asian-American issues. An ethnic studies staff member who is popular with students is Eufemia Moore. "She is helpful to everyone. If she doesn't know the answer to something, then she'll get on the phone and call right then and there for you. She is like a magnet for students—everyone comes to talk with her."

What makes UCR truly unique among UC schools is its faculty's commitment to undergraduate education. While professors at some of the better-known UC schools must publish or perish, professors at UCR have undergraduate education as their first priority. Students report that getting appointments to meet with faculty is relatively easy, and that professors have even been known to have lunch with students. With its relatively small size, registering for classes isn't the headache it is at some of the other UC schools. Students say that getting into first-choice classes is fairly easy. For additional academic support, the school's Learning Center is said by students to be effective.

Cultural organizations provide additional support for members, and plenty of on-campus programming. The Asian Pacific American Coalition, established in 1989, "is political, and seeks to get more ethnic studies classes and to diversify the faculty," according to an APAC organizer. The group is also seeking to have an East Asian Studies major or minor established. "It's amazing we don't have one, considering there are more than sixty courses offered in the area," says a student. UCR is also the only UC school to have an Asian-American film festival.

The Asian Pacific American Student Programs Office, established in 1988, does support work on behalf of 18 student organizations, including two fraternities, a radio show, a theater group, and *The Asian-American,* a newsletter. The office also sponsors a peer mentor program for incoming first-year students. Perhaps the driving force for much of the office's success is its director, Grace Yoo. "She does a fantastic job and is very outgoing and very committed to students," says a student.

Each year, APAC and the student program office sponsor Asian Pacific Heritage Month, which includes speakers, a food fair, and performances. In a recent year, the events included a performance by East West Players, a well-known Asian-American theater troupe in Southern California, and *Unfinished Business,* a film about the incarceration of Japanese-Americans during World War II.

The Native American Student Association is primarily a social organization. A recent association-sponsored event was the showing of a movie about reservation life "and how the culture differs on different reservations." Native American students are also able to take advantage of the services and programs of the Native American

Student Programs Office, which include the *Native American Student Association Newsletter,* and various activities, such as American Indian Education Week and Peace Day.

The African Students Programs Office publishes a newsletter as well as a semiannual journal, *Kokayi,* which includes essays and poems written by students. The office also sponsors two mentoring programs involving, respectively, staff members and upperclass students. The student group African Student Alliance works with the office in coordinating events for African History Month and African Women's Awareness Week.

The Chicano/Latino Student Programs Office provides counseling services and also works to coordinate events, such as a Chicano senior dinner, Cinco de Mayo programming, and leadership training.

The Multicultural Events Relations Committee has been active in creating programming on campus. "MERC consists of faculty, staff, administrators, and students. The group helps program multicultural events as well as providing essays for the school paper which attempt to educate the campus and to get beyond stereotypes," says a student. "MERC also targets the student who lives in the dorms. Recently, MERC sponsored two successful projects. The first was a movie and then a follow-up discussion about Native American scientists and researchers, which was meant to contrast the primitive view of Native Americans with the reality of their existence. The second was a comedy night, where black, Asian, and Chicano comedians were brought in to speak about negative stereotypes."

Social life is generally in the form of dorm parties, held religiously each weekend. The school's Barn is billed to be UCR's hottest nightspot, and regularly hosts comedy, open-mike nights, and some popular bands. Campus life isn't as hopping as it might be, however, as many UCR students are commuters. The city of Riverside, a predominantly white community, is a no-frills kind of place. But students are free to drive the fifty miles on Highway 60 to Los Angeles, where the nightlife is considerably more active.

UCR may not have the wealth of opportunities of some its larger UC brethren, but neither does it have many of their headaches. Students looking for a smaller-campus feel in one of the best state university systems in the country would do well to check out UCR.

UNIVERSITY OF CALIFORNIA/SANTA BARBARA

Address: Santa Barbara, CA 93106
Phone: (805) 893-2485 / (805) 893-3872
Director of Admissions: William J. Villa
Multicultural Student Recruiter: Mel
  Gregory
1993–94 tuition: $3,977 (in-state); $7,699
  (out-of-state)
Room and board: $5,816
Application deadline: 11/30
Financial aid application deadline: 3/2
Non-white freshman admissions: Applicants
  for the class of '95: 6,879
  Accepted: 69.3%
  Accepted who enrolled: 19.1%
  Applicants accepted who rank in top
  10% of high school class: na
  Median SAT range: 430–540 V, 520–630 M
  Median ACT: na
Full-time undergraduate enrollment: 16,176
  Men: 49.7%
  Women: 50.3%

STUDENT ENROLLMENT

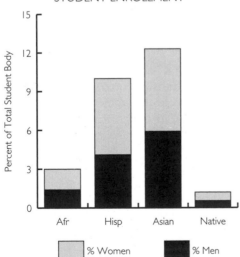

Non-white students in
  1987–88: 22.3%
  1988–89: 24.4%

1989–90: 26.7%
1990–91: 26.1%
Geographic distribution of students: na
Students In-state: 97%
Top majors: 1. Economics 2. Biological
  Sciences 3. Psychology
Retention rate of non-white students: 67%
**Scholarships exclusively for non-white
  students:** National Action Council of
  Minorities in Engineering: merit-based;
  $1,000 per year. Young Black Scholars:
  merit-based; $1,000 per year.
  Chancellor's Scholarship: merit-based;
  $1,500 per year
Remediation programs: The university's
  Campus Learning Assistance Services
  offer workshops in developing reading,
  writing, and studying skills, and provide
  individual tutoring services.
Academic support services: Academic
  advisers are available through the
  university's individual colleges, as well as
  through the Women's Center. Peer tutors
  also provide academic support in most
  subjects.
Ethnic studies programs: The university
  offers programs in Black Studies,
  Chicano Studies, Latin American Studies,
  and Asian Studies.
Organizations for non-white students: Alpha
  Kappa Alpha, Delta Sigma Theta,
  Kappa Alpha Psi, Alpha Phi Alpha,
  Omega Psi Phi, Sigma Phi Rho, Black
  Student Union, Hispanic Business
  Students Association, Black Business
  Association, National Society of Black
  Engineers, Akanke (African-American
  women's group), American Indian
  Student Association, Asian Culture
  Committee, Asian Student Coalition,
  Chinese Student Association, El
  Congreso/La Mesa, Korean Students
  Association, Greeks for Racial
  Awareness and Cultural Education,
  Black Greek Council
Notable non-white alumni: Lawrence R.

Baca (American History; senior trial attorney, U.S. Department of Justice); Richard Fajardo (Economics; attorney, Mexican-American Legal Defense and Education Fund); LeRoy Chiao (Chemical Engineering; astronaut); F. C. Richardson (Biology; president, State University of New York/ Buffalo); Richard Serra (English; sculptor)

Non-tenured faculty: 145
Tenured faculty: 580
Student-faculty ratio: 19:1
Administrators: 747
  African-American: 5%
  Hispanic: 8.6%
  Asian-American: 5.2%
  Native American: 0.66%

Recent non-white speakers on campus:
  Cesar Chavez (labor leader and head of United Farm Workers); Tritia Toyoto (anchorwoman, Los Angeles); Barbara Jordan; Toni Morrison

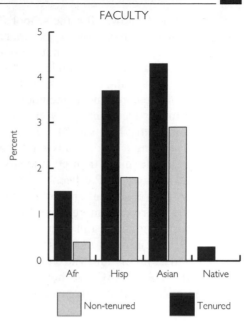

FACULTY

(Pulitzer Prize-winning novelist); Zak Vaz (vice president, Motown Records)

Situated on a cliff overlooking the Pacific Ocean and with the Santa Ynez Mountains behind it, UC/Santa Barbara arguably has the most spectacular campus in the country. Students are drawn to UCSB as much for the scenery as they are for the school's academics.

UCSB's academic departments certainly make use of the school's location; its aquatic biology program is one of the best in the country and its Marine Science Institute supports research projects of faculty and graduate students. The university's five engineering programs are chemical, electrical, mechanical, and nuclear engineering; and computer science. Mechanical engineering is said to be highly rated. Among offerings in its College of Letters and Science, students say religion, economics, communications, biology, and English are among the best. Unique to the University of California system is UCSB's College of Creative Studies, which allows its 150 students the opportunity to design their own course of study.

Courses in Chicano Studies earn praise from students. "Taking classes in the area gave me a good sense of who I am," says a student. "Women as Creators of Culture" is one of the program's more popular courses. The Asian Studies program "includes some of the toughest courses I've taken here," says a student. Sucheng Chan, director of the program, and Shirley Lim, a literature professor, are well regarded in the program.

UCSB students are treated to a student population that is somewhat manageable, especially when compared to the enrollments at UCLA and Berkeley. "I don't feel totally like a number here," says a student, "and I can usually walk along campus and see people I know." But the school's smaller size doesn't always translate into class enrollments, which can number more than 500 in an introductory course.

UCSB's Educational Opportunity Program (EOP), which provides academic and non-academic assistance to students, "is amazing," says a senior. EOP includes components for Asian-Americans, Native Americans, Latinos, and African-Americans; each of the components includes a director, counselors, student advisers, and different campus locations. "If you have roommate conflicts, academic problems, you can come here. The peer advisers and staff become your second family," says a student. Becoming a student adviser in the EOP office is no easy task; in a recent year, for example, more than 60 students applied for the five available positions in the Asian-American EOP office.

UCSB's cultural student groups are popular. The Asian Student Coalition (ASC) is large and represents more than 15 undergraduate and graduate organizations. ASC—a social, political, and cultural group—works each year to sponsor a Cultural Week, in May. The event includes various events and speakers. With the EOP office, ASC created an admissions video entitled "Making Waves: To Be an Asian-American Student at UCSB." ASC also hosted a conference that included all of the school's Asian-American student organizations, which "emphasized education and self-identity."

El Congreso, an umbrella organization representing the school's 13 Chicano/Latino student groups, "is a networking and support group, and a group where you can meet people who have the same interests," says a junior. El Centro, a building which houses the Chicano component of the EOP, is a popular meeting place for Chicano and Latino students. "There is a positive atmosphere there. It's not only a building but a home. A lot of us go there to relax or to meet up with friends," says a student. "There is a strong family atmosphere."

MUJER, which translates, according to a student, to Women United for Justice and Equality, is a support group for women "where we really help each other out by talking about problems and we also try to have a good time." La Escuelita (the Little School) is another Chicano student group, which provides tutoring to students at nearby junior high and high schools.

Each year the school's Chicano student groups sponsor commencement exercises, in which about 70 students participate. "We spend the year preparing for it," says a student. "During the first quarter we raise funds, since we don't receive any university funds. It's really nice because then you don't go through graduation with people that don't know you, and because it's done in English and Spanish, so that many parents can understand. Students can do either graduation, or both."

The American Indian Student Association (AISA) "is a very strong organization on campus, although we're the smallest minority group on campus," says an AISA leader. The group, with about 180 members, sponsors powwows, visits to reservations, conferences, and a tutoring program for high school and elementary students at nearby reservations. There is also an active AISA Women's Support Group, with more than 30 members.

The American Indian Culture Week, which is a focus of much of AISA's energies, "begins with a blessing at the UCSB Peace Tree, which was planted in 1985 by Jake Swamp of the Iroquois Sixth Nation." The week includes traditional dancing, arts and crafts, food, lectures, and panel discussions. Although the majority of AISA members are Cherokee, there are others from such tribes as Isleto Pueblo, the Pimas, and the Pomas.

UCSB's location—beaches are just a walk away—can be distracting, especially as a seat in the library includes a view of the ocean. In such environs, it's no wonder making time for studying is a challenge for many students. Parties are key to the social life, whether on the beach, at fraternities, or at any of the nearby bars on Del Playa Drive. The town of Santa Barbara is predominantly white and upper-middle-class—off-campus apartments are expensive—and students of color report that there is little interaction between them and town residents.

Almost any sort of outdoor activity is popular at UCSB. To get around, students rely on their bicycles. Varsity football made a comeback in 1984, and the school's men's varsity basketball and volleyball teams have had some recent successful seasons. Intramurals always brings the majority of students out to play.

A room with a view is certainly a reason to come to this school by the ocean. But strong academics is another. Says a junior: "The sun and the surf are great, but after a while you remember the reason you came here in the first place: to get a good education."

UNIVERSITY OF CALIFORNIA/SANTA CRUZ

Address: Santa Cruz, CA 95064
Phone: (408) 459-4008
Director of Admissions: Joseph Allen
Multicultural Student Recruiter: Allen Fields

1992–93 tuition: $3,129 (in-state); $10,828 (out-of-state)
Room and board: $5,931
Application deadline: 11/30
Financial aid application deadline: 3/1

University of California at Santa Cruz students are a concerned group. They're concerned about the environment, they're concerned about things spiritual, and they're concerned about their studies, in a laid-back sort of way. But Santa Cruz students are also becoming increasingly concerned about something that almost makes moot all of their other concerns: the identity of their school.

Santa Cruz was established in 1965 as an "alternative" school in the nine-member University of California system. Most courses were taught in seminar-style fashion, professors didn't give grades but written evaluations, and there never has been a varsity football team. While the university still retains many of its original charac-teristics— students still don't receive grades for most courses, and seminar-style classes are still par for the course—students are nonetheless worried that, with the university's plan to nearly double the student population in the next twenty years, the school will lose some of its appeal.

What students needn't concern themselves with, at least for now, is the school's commitment to academics. Graduate schools have also noted Santa Cruz's top-flight academics; more than 90 percent of those who apply to graduate school each year are accepted to graduate programs. Santa Cruz is the third most difficult of the UC schools to which to be admitted (behind Berkeley and UCLA), and the school is known for excellent programs in the social sciences, especially political science, as well as in marine biology, psychology, environmental studies, women's studies, physics, and biology. As the campus increases in size—and attracts a decidedly more conservative student population than in years past—some of the more conventional programs are becoming more popular, including computer science and business. To graduate, students must satisfy an ethnic studies requirement which was integrated into the curriculum after student demonstrations in the early 1980s.

Students say the school's American Studies program, in which various ethnic studies courses are offered, is good. Popular courses within the program are "Chicano History" and "Chicano Social Change." In addition, the Latin American Studies program is also said to be respectable. Other well-regarded ethnic studies courses include "Asian-American Experience" and "Asian-American Women," both taught by popular professor Judy Yung; "African Literature," "Black Experience," and "Culture and Ideology," the last taught by Angela Davis, the longtime political and civil rights activist.

In contrast to the other UC schools where faculty research reigns, professors at Santa Cruz are unusually accessible. It's not uncommon for students to refer to their professors by their first names, and faculty are easily available after class for continued discussion. As one student put it, "Professors are here for you and not vice versa." For students interested in majoring in the sciences, the school's Students of Color in the Sciences provides effective peer support.

Santa Cruz's cultural organizations are active. For Hispanic students, who make up nearly 7 percent of the student population, there's MECHA, composed of about 35 members, which meets every other week to plan its events. One of the group's biggest events is the Cinco de Mayo celebration, which in recent years has included dancing and a poetry reading by Francisco Alarcon, a Santa Cruz professor of Spanish literature. To celebrate Posada, traditionally a procession symbolizing Mary and Joseph's search for a place to stay, MECHA members sponsored a dinner-dance to benefit an off-campus health service. MECHA also sponsors an annual Parent Conference for high school students and their parents. "We have workshops on financial aid, we give tours of the campus, and we talk about college in general," says a student. "We had more than five hundred Chicano and Latino parents and their sons and daughters on campus."

Other active Chicano and Latino student groups include Teatro: La Raza, a theater group that presents a film festival and performs plays written by students, and Los Mexicas, a dance group. There is also a recently established Chicana/Latina sorority.

The Asian Pacific Islander Student Alliance (APISA), with about 50 to 75 active members, sponsors beach parties and culture nights, which consist of local talent. The group has an outreach committee which visits various San Jose and San Francisco high schools to talk to students about college. In addition, APISA publishes *Seaweed Soup,* a compilation of student poetry and prose. Other Asian student organizations are the Filipino Student Association and the Japanese Student Association. "One of the more unusual groups is the Hmong Student Association," one student notes. "There are only about ten Hmong on campus, and it's amazing that they were able to develop a support group and organize themselves with so few being on campus." Although Santa Cruz's Greek life is not very much of a force on campus, about 10 Asian-American men formed a fraternity on campus, called Lambda Phi Epsilon. At present, according to a student leader, there are about 800 Asian-American students on campus.

The African Black Student Alliance (ABSA) is in the process of working to get February's Black History Month celebrations changed to African Awareness Quarter, which would begin on Martin Luther King, Jr.'s birthday and end at the end of February. ABSA's recent Black History Month activities included a film series, poetry readings, and an HIV-positive panel discussion.

To help with programming and support, the university, after a student sit-in, established the position of assistant dean of African-American student life. Assistant dean Paula Powell "is great to have around. Even though she just finished her first year, she's been a help, especially when it came time to plan the statewide African Black Student Alliance meeting held here. She'll no doubt get even better with time," says a student. More than 300 students from around the state attended the African Black Student Alliance, held at Santa Cruz.

The Third World Coalition, composed of members of the school's cultural organizations, meets every week to discuss such issues as educational rights, according to a student. Recently, the coalition sponsored a comedy night, called Comedy in Color, for the school's Summer Bridge Program, part of Santa Cruz's Educational Opportunity Program/Student Affirmative Action. The event raised more than $3,000. "It was so successful we're probably going to make it a tradition," says an organizer. The coalition holds its meetings in the one-room Third World Lounge, located on the second floor of the student center.

Unique to Santa Cruz is its residential college system, which consists of eight autonomous residential areas that over the years have developed their own personalities. Students in each of the colleges take a course of study that is unique to that particular college, and students choose in which of the eight colleges they will live before they arrive on campus their first year. (Students are sent information about each of the colleges, including details about the colleges' core courses, during the summer before arriving on campus.) "Oakes and Merrill are the most popular for students of color, mostly because of their core courses," comments a senior. "Oakes's is 'Social Change in the Third World' and Merrill's is 'People of Color in the U.S.'"

Along with Berkeley, Santa Cruz has one of the UC system's more progressive student bodies, especially when it comes to environmental issues. And you'd be committed to the environment too if you ever visited the campus, one of the most beautiful in the nation. Surrounded by meadows and giant redwoods, the campus overlooks Monterey Bay.

Some of the country's most scenic beaches are within walking distance, as is a national forest, and San Jose and San Francisco are within easy driving distance. The town of Santa Cruz, predominantly white and known for being progressive, has a boardwalk and amusement park, much to the delight and distraction of some students.

Santa Cruz may have been too much of a good thing, and it was only a matter of time before the hordes discovered its riches and began applying in droves. Students are happy with their college choice, and many would do it over again. "I'm glad I came here instead of Berkeley because, although it's more diverse there, it's easier for me to get involved with my community here and to get political. There's very little administration support of students of color here at Santa Cruz, but the relative smallness of the place keeps it more personal." Well, at least for now.

CALIFORNIA INSTITUTE OF TECHNOLOGY

Address: Mailcode 55-63, 515 South Wilson Avenue, Pasadena, CA 91125
Phone: (818) 395-6341
Director of Admissions: Carole Snow
Multicultural Student Recruiter: na
1993–94 tuition: $15,800
Room and board: $6,135
Application deadline: 1/1
Financial aid application deadline: 2/1
Non-white freshman admissions: Applicants for the class of '97: 681
  Accepted: 198
  Applicants accepted who rank in top 10% of high school class: 97%
  Median SAT: na
  Median ACT: na
Full-time undergraduate enrollment: 900
  Men: 73%
  Women: 27%
Non-white students 1987–91: na
Geographic distribution of students: na
Top majors: 1. Engineering 2. Physics 3. Math
Retention rate of non-white students: 94%
Scholarships exclusively for non-white students: na
Remediation programs: None
Academic support services: Summer Bridge and Peer Tutoring programs
Ethnic studies programs: None
Ethnic studies courses: na
Organizations for non-white students: National Society of Black Engineers,

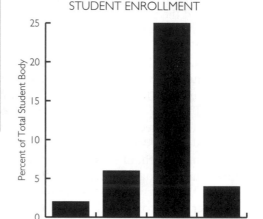

STUDENT ENROLLMENT

Society of Hispanic Professional Engineers, American Indian Society of Engineering Students
Notable non-white alumni: na
Tenured faculty: na
Non-tenured faculty: na
Student-faculty ratio: 3:1
Administrators: 20
Recent non-white speakers on campus: Nikki Giovanni (poet); Jerry Oliver (chief of police, Pasadena, CA); Alex Norman (professor emeritus of social planning, UCLA); Shirley Adams (director, Pasadena–Foothill Branch, L.A. Urban League)

It's ironic that the California Institute of Technology was established in 1891 as a small school of arts and crafts where students could study woodworking and cooking. Today, Caltech is, along with East Coast rival MIT, one of the world's most esteemed engineering and science schools, where students long ago dropped their chopping blocks and spatulas to study in such popular courses as "Quantum Physics" and "Engineering Design."

Don't attend Caltech if you're not willing to work hard. The school's academics are among the most rigorous in the nation. But the average Caltech student—who was more than likely his or her high school's math/science genius—is more than up to the challenge. The average SAT score at the school—1,420—is the highest in the nation, and virtually the entire student body graduated in the top 10 percent of their high school graduating class. At Caltech, a high school valedictorian is one of many, a disillusioning experience for those used to getting special treatment in high school.

Caltech is best known for its programs in physics and engineering, particularly electrical engineering. Chemistry, astronomy, and biology are also outstanding. In fact, all of Caltech's science programs are excellent. As you can imagine, the school's research facilities are as impressive as the professors and students who use them. The Mead Undergraduate Chemistry Laboratory boasts state-of-the-art equipment, the school's newest nuclear accelerator, nicknamed the "Yellow Submarine," is used to study the interior of stars, and the Palomar Observatory, with its five-meter telescope, is the nation's premier astronomical observing facility.

Humanities—and this should come as no surprise—play second fiddle at Caltech. To graduate, students must take at least a fifth of their courses in the area of humanities. "Most students just take these courses because they have to. The attitude here is, why come to Caltech to study social studies?" The most popular major in the humanities division, according to a student, is economics. Also popular within the division is "Latin American Literature in Translation" and "Films and Filmmaking."

While academics are undeniably intense (the average semester course load at Caltech is five, as compared with four at most other schools), there are a few things worth mentioning that may help deflect the intensity, if only a little. First, all grades during a student's first year are pass/fail. (Getting grades during the sophomore year is usually a shocker for some, especially when the student may have earned his or her first C ever.) With a 3:1 student-to-faculty ratio, professors are unusually accessible and, says a student, "actually good teachers." Students say professors and their teaching assistants are also more than willing to help when the going gets rough. The school's Honor Code system, which allows students to take their exams in their own dorm rooms and lets students feel comfortable leaving their rooms unlocked, is much appreciated and highly respected by students.

But perhaps the most effective source of academic support is a student's classmates. "No one here studies by himself. There are always study groups. Students are always willing to help each other, but you do have to ask for it. Upperclassmen are always willing to help out, too, even if they're busy." Academic tutoring, although available, isn't used as much as it perhaps should be, or at least when it should be. "The students are very proud here, and don't want to ask anyone for help, if they can help it. It's too bad, because it's usually not until after the student is in deep that he seeks help."

If you haven't noticed by now, most students at Caltech, when referring to their classmates, use the pronoun "he." As the ratio of men to women at the school is 4:1, the odds are he is referring to a he. At Caltech, which went coed in 1975, issues of diversity have focused more on gender than on race or ethnicity. "The women here have been asking for a women's center for ten years now, but they get a lot of flak for it. Now it looks as if they'll get an office, maybe next year," says a student, adding, "It's not so much an issue about whether or not women belong here at Caltech, it's more that people aren't aware of or don't care about women's concerns at such a predominantly male institution. Among the school's more than 200 faculty, for example, only 20 are women." The number of African-American female students at Caltech is equally dismal; in a recent year, the school enrolled only two.

Multicultural activity has emerged slightly on the Caltech campus. Within the last couple of years, the school has sponsored three engineering societies for non-white students—the Society of Hispanic Professional Engineers, the National Society of Black Engineers, and the American Indian Society of Engineering Students. Each of the societies sponsors trips for its members to regional and national conferences, and provides an important source of support for those involved. Members of the societies are working to create a tutoring program for area high school and elementary school students.

Certain Caltech students are working to establish a Cultural House, to be off campus. "It would include about seven residences of different backgrounds, but we haven't gotten approval for it yet," reports a student. "We recently took our five-page proposal for the house before the Interhouse Council, but they've put off making the decision whether we can have it. They say they want to put the idea of the house before the campus, which means certain of us will have to address house meetings of about sixty people and defend our reasons. I dread the questions, the same ones which will come over and over. 'What problems are minorities having here? I haven't seen any.' 'What constitutes a minority? The international students haven't asked for such a house, and aren't they minorities?'"

Adds another student about the proposal: "Most of the minority students here are for the idea, while the non-minorities seem to be willing to take a wait-and-see attitude. I took a formal mail poll of minorities about the house, and of the twenty responses, fifteen said they would support such a house and five said no. It was pretty even as to how many said they would and wouldn't live in the house. The non-minorities are worried that we will segregate ourselves, which wouldn't be the case at all."

Caltech has never been known for its social life. Working on nuclear reactors does have its demands, and the school's lopsided men-to-women ratio doesn't help matters. Much of the social life at Caltech centers on the school's seven coed houses, which in many ways resemble traditional fraternities. Intramural competition between the houses, which include about 70 residents each, is intense. Each week at least one of the houses has a party that usually includes a live band, and each of the houses develops its own distinct personality. Page House is known as the most athletic and least racially diverse house, Fleming House is known as "laid back" and the most racially diverse, and Blacker House is known as "the house where they like to build mechanical objects." According to a student, each of the houses, like Fleming, is culturally diverse. The student reports that typically each of the houses will include about two African-Americans and four Latinos, while Asian-Americans live in all of the houses.

First-year students decide on which house they will live in after a week of parties called Rotation, where students visit a different house each night of the week. It's a little like fraternity rush in that not only do the first-year students rank in order of preference the houses in which they'd like to live, but the upperclass students also make a preference list of those students they would like to live with.

For students who can find the time, nearby Los Angeles offers a world of culture and exciting nightlife. Pasadena offers little, by comparison, and is a predominantly white affluent community. "Across Highway 210, however, in North Pasadena, there's a black and Latino neighborhood that's mostly lower-middle-class but has neat houses," says a student, adding that there is little activity between Caltech students and the nearby communities.

At Caltech, for the student who can get in and then survive the rigors of the school's academics, there is one reward that makes it all worth it: a student with a Caltech diploma is a much-sought-after commodity. In 1989, the average starting salary for a graduating senior was $34,100, 12 percent more than the national average. "Caltech isn't famous for multicultural activity, but it is famous for its academics and its students' EP [earning potential]," says a student. "Little by little, the school is getting more diverse, but by and large the new students are coming here because of the school's academics." And those jobs.

CLAREMONT/CLAREMONT MCKENNA COLLEGE

Address: 890 Columbia Avenue, Claremont, CA 91711-6420

Phone: (909) 621-8088

Director of Admissions: Richard Vos

Multicultural Student Recruiter: na

1992–93 tuition: $14,810

Room and board: $5,180

Application deadline: Early decision: 12/1; regular decision: 2/1

Financial aid application deadline: 2/1

Non-white freshman admissions: Applicants for the class of '95: na
  Applicants accepted who rank in top 10% of high school class: na
  Median SAT: na
  Median ACT: na

Full-time undergraduate enrollment: 845
  Men: 61%
  Women: 39%

Non-white students 1987–91: na

Geographic distribution of students: na

Top majors: 1. Economics 2. Government 3. International Relations

Retention rate of non-white students: na

Scholarships exclusively for non-white students: None

Remediation programs: None

Academic support services: The college offers tutoring in most subjects, peer advising services, and a writing lab.

Ethnic studies programs: As part of the five-college Claremont system, students are able to study in the colleges' Asian, Black, and Chicano Studies programs.

Organizations for non-white students: Asian-American Mentor Program, Asian Student Association, *Harmony* (multicultural newspaper), Hawaiian Club, Korean Students Association

Ethnic studies courses: na

Notable non-white alumni: na

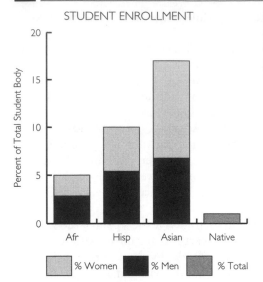

STUDENT ENROLLMENT

Percent of Total Student Body

Afr   Hisp   Asian   Native

% Women   % Men   % Total

Tenured faculty: na
Non-tenured faculty: na
Student-faculty ratio: 10:1
Administrators: na
Recent non-white speakers on campus: na

Claremont McKenna College emphasizes pre-professional training in business, government, and public policy, and tends to attract a conservative student body.

A CMC degree catches the attention of graduate schools. More than 80 percent of the school's graduates go on for further study within five years of graduation, usually in business or law and often at some of the country's top universities.

Economics is the school's most popular department, while government, literature, and international relations are also well regarded. To apply what they learn in the classroom, CMC students are able to take advantage of seven impressive research institutes located on campus: the Salvatori Center for the Study of Individual Freedom in the Modern World, the Rose Institute of State and Local Government, the Institute of Decision Science for Business and Public Policy, the Lowe Institute of Political Economy, the Keck Center for International and Strategic Studies, the Roberts Environmental Center, and the Family of Benjamin Z. Gould Center for Humanistic Studies.

Students interested in Black, Asian, and Chicano Studies are able to take courses at any of the five colleges in the Claremont system, and students looking to fine-tune their fine arts studies may want to head to Scripps or Pomona.

CMC professors are one of the college's best assets. Lunches with faculty members are common, and professors frequently give students their home telephone numbers. Classes are small, which ensures close faculty-student interaction in and out of the classroom. Academic support is also available through the Office of Black Student Affairs and the Chicano Studies Center. CMC's own Writing Resource Center is well regarded by students. As one CMC student describes the school's support services: "At CMC, help is available in every subject—from professors and from other students."

Students seeking cultural activity need to head to one of the organizations of the five-college Claremont system—MECHA, Asian Student Association, or the Pan-African American Student Association (PASA). In a recent year, PASA's president was a CMC student.

Students report there is some social interaction among the races on campus. Says a student: "I see a lot of the ethnic groups mingling. It's hard not to when we're such a small campus. None of the groups seem to consciously separate themselves from other ethnic groups or from white students. But there are white students who perceive it that way, especially when we tried to get an Asian-American Resource Center on campus. The students reacted like, there they go, separating themselves."

CMC is regarded by students of the other Claremont colleges as the most conservative campus in the system. During a recent demonstration against racial prejudice, for example, Claremont student activists were concerned about guiding the rally through the CMC campus. "We were afraid that the CMC students would get angry and that a fight would break out, which it did. We were lucky that the fight didn't escalate into something more." Another student agrees that the campus is conservative: "But it's due more to a reluctance to get involved, or just apathy, than to a political agenda."

For one student, the lack of multicultural programming on campus is perplexing. "It's amazing when you think about it. Our school's motto is 'Leaders in the Making,' yet many of the students don't have a clue about how to deal with people from other cultures, ethnicities, or backgrounds. There is little multicultural programming provided by the CMC administration."

Claremont, CMC's hometown, isn't exactly hopping at night, but for the adventurous Los Angeles is only an hour's drive away. Approximately half of the CMC student body own cars. Although having a car isn't essential, students say it makes it easier to head to the mountains for skiing, the beaches for sunning, or into the nightlife of Los Angeles, with its rich cultural and entertainment offerings. Parties, usually sponsored with Scripps women, are popular weekend activities.

If you are looking to a promising career in business or government, or impressive undergraduate credentials with which to apply for graduate study, a CMC degree may be your ticket to the big leagues. And for those looking for more multicultural opportunities than CMC provides, the facilities and the organizations are plentiful at the other colleges. Comments a student: "I would recommend CMC because, along with the other colleges, it serves as a good training ground for minority students, and provides an excellent education. We can learn here exactly what type of people we will be faced with throughout our lives, especially in the corporate world."

CLAREMONT/HARVEY MUDD COLLEGE

Address: Kingston Hall, Claremont, CA
  91711
Phone: (714) 621-8011
Director of Admissions: Jean
  Rutherford-Wall
Multicultural Student Recruiter: na
1991–92 tuition: $14,470
Room and board: $5,890
Application deadline: 2/1
Financial aid application deadline: 2/1

Non-white freshman admissions: Applicants
  for the class of '95: 363
  Accepted: 37%
  Accepted who enroll: 31%
  Applicants accepted who rank in top
  10% of high school class: 85%
  In top 25%: 90%
  Median SAT: 620 V, 740 M
  Median ACT: na
Full-time undergraduate enrollment: 615
  Men: 79%
  Women: 21%
Non-white students in
  1987–88: 25%
  1988–89: 25%

1989–90: 25%
1990–91: 26%
Geographic distribution of students: na
Students In-state: 50%
Top majors: 1. Engineering 2. Physics
  3. Chemistry
Retention rate of non-white students: 100%
**Scholarships exclusively for non-white
  students:** None
Remediation programs: None
Academic support services: The Chicano
  Studies Center, the Black Student Center,
  and the Asian Student Association,
  which are part of the five-college
  Claremont system, provide academic and
  non-academic support services.
Ethnic studies programs: Harvey Mudd
  students are able to enroll in Chicano
  Studies, Asian Studies, and Black Studies
  program courses, available as part of the
  five-college Claremont system.

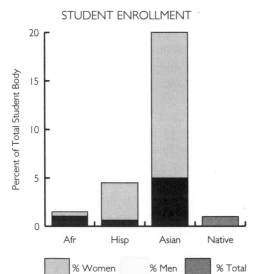

STUDENT ENROLLMENT

Percent of Total Student Body

% Women   % Men   % Total

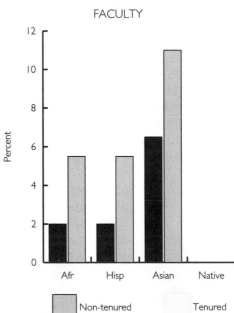

FACULTY

Percent

Non-tenured   Tenured

Organizations for non-white students: See
  Academic support services, above.
Notable non-white alumni: na
Tenured faculty: 46
Non-tenured faculty: 18
Student-faculty ratio: 8:1
Administrators: 37
  African-American: 2%
  Hispanic: 5%
  Asian-American: 2%
  Native American: 1%
Recent non-white speakers on campus: Judy
  Chu (mayor, Monterey Park, CA);
  Frances Fukuyama (Rand
  Corporation); Sergio Muñoz (editor,
  La Opinión); Julian Bond (former
  Georgia state senator and civil rights
  activist)

Established in 1955, Harvey Mudd College already ranks as one of the country's top engineering schools, and gives such powerhouses as Caltech and MIT a run for their money. The school offers intense academics in a supportive environment.

There is a great deal that makes Mudd unique among similar schools, but perhaps most obvious is its students, who are an eccentric—in that sciency sort of way—bunch. The unicycle is the mode of travel here, and juggling is a favorite pastime of many Mudders. Mudders are also smart. The school ranks among the country's top ten most selective colleges, and nearly a third of each entering class are National Merit Scholars. And the credentials of its graduates are nothing to sneeze at either. One out of every 66 U.S. citizens who earn Ph.D.s in chemistry, math, or physics is a Mudd graduate, 41 percent of all of its alumni earn Ph.D.s, and 11 percent are company presidents.

Harvey Mudd's curriculum is also unique. Not only are Mudders immersed in the school's engineering and science programs, they are also expected to complete 37 hours—nearly a third of their undergraduate careers—in the humanities and the social sciences, the most of any engineering college. While Mudd doesn't exactly offer a smorgasbord of such courses, students are able to take them at any of the four other Claremont colleges. Mudd students don't mind their school's liberal arts expectations. "It's one of the reasons I came here in the first place, so I could complement my engineering studies at schools as respected and intellectual as Pomona [another of the Claremont colleges]," says a senior.

Now let's talk about Harvey Mudd's raison d'être—which is clearly the sciences and math. In fact, the college offers only four majors: biology, chemistry, engineering, and math, which includes options in physics and computer science. Of these, students say chemistry is best, while engineering is most popular. Engineering students are able to study in the school's engineering clinics, co-sponsored by such companies as IBM and Kodak, where they receive real-world engineering experience.

Academics at Mudd are as intense as you'll find anywhere. Some have likened their school's academics to one constant final examination, or as another student observed: "It's more like a bucket of cold water tossed on you." But students praise their school's support network uniformly. "You're limited in the amount of support you receive by your own initiative. There's tons of it here." Students say interaction with faculty is excellent. Professors are frequent lunchtime companions of students at the dorms, and they are more than accessible at other times. Cooperative learning among students is also a Mudd hallmark. "We're able to work on projects and homework together, except there might be one starred homework question of twelve or so that we have to do ourselves. A student would have trouble lasting here if you don't co-op it. When I was a freshman, I'd just step outside my door and ask an upperclassman, usually a total stranger, for help. They were, and are always, willing to help. This is great, especially since we spend about 50 percent of our time here doing homework."

Students are able to take advantage of the support services of the five-college Chicano Studies Center and the Office of Black Student Affairs. Another source of support for students is Deren Finks, an admissions officer. "He's done more for me here than the Office of Black Student Affairs has," says a student. "He's a definite integral part of the campus." Mudd's African-American students were recently invited to Finks' house for dinner of the soul-food variety where they were given a "chance to meet each other in a comfortable environment. When we got to his house, Deren said that we were going to have a surprise visitor for dessert, and were we ever shocked when the president of the college and his wife walked through the door. It was a fantastic dinner. I got to meet new friends and talk to the college president. That just kind of typifies the kind of interaction that goes on at the school."

Students are not drawn to Mudd so they can address issues of multiculturalism. The school sponsors no cultural organizations of its own, although students do identify with some of the five-college organizations, such as the Pan-African Student Association, the Asian Student Alliance, and MECHA. The school is also the least diverse of the Claremont colleges. In a recent year, for example, the school enrolled only 5 African-Americans, 22 Hispanics, and 62 Asian-Americans.

Despite the relative low numbers, students report that there is a sense of camaraderie among students that makes their college experience less alienating. "There is definitely not a lot of bigotry," says a student. "Harvey Mudd has a welcoming attitude. Anyone who can make it in here is part of a family, no matter what the background or the race. It's almost as if Harvey Mudd is one big fraternity." Adds another student: "At first when students looked at me, they might have seen a black man. But as time goes on, students got to know me by name and by my ability, which is as it should be." In a recent year, the freshman class president was African-American.

Students also say that Mudd's administration is sensitive to multicultural student concerns. In addition to the efforts of Finks, one student remembers an incident when he was picked up by campus security for taking a Scripps College sign. "It was a prank, and we got caught, but I have to add that when the deans here at Mudd heard about it, the first thing they wanted to know was if I was harassed at all by the officers. I wasn't, but it was nice to see the concern of the deans."

For fun and excitement, Mudd students will often turn inward. "We like to study hard for six days a week, but we also party just as hard for that one night," says a student. Mudders, after their first year, are able to choose in which of the school's seven dorms they'd like to live. Over time, each dorm has developed its own distinct personality. West, North, and Atwood have been known traditionally as the rowdiest, and South, according to a student, "is where students are into jigsaw puzzles, fencing, and juggling." Another student says: "Living in the dorm you want develops a tremendous sense of unity among residents, even for minority students." Students report that the school's multicultural population is evenly divided among the dorms.

Students will also hit some of the parties at any of the other four colleges, especially at all-female Scripps. (The male-to-female ratio at HMC is heavily weighted toward men, but female students say there is no particular discrimination against them, in the classroom or socially.) Students rarely head into Los Angeles, just thirty-five minutes west, no doubt due to the school's overwhelming work load, and the city of Claremont offers little in the way of cultural or social diversion, except for Foster's, billed by students as the greatest doughnut shop in the world. Harvey Mudd's outdoor pool is popular with students from all the Claremont colleges, but Mudders aren't exactly into sunbathing.

To relieve stress—and also as a way to put some of their technical skills to use—Mudders are into pranks, big-time. Such antics range from filling a student's dorm with 1,000 Dixie cups full of water to figuring out how to get a Volkswagen into a dorm room or "borrowing" Caltech's 4,000-pound cannon.

Overworked and overstressed are no doubt feelings you'll encounter should you decide to attend this excellent engineering college. But if you have what it takes to get into Mudd in the first place, then you no doubt have what it takes to survive its rigors. "Mudd is certainly intense, but I have made close friends here. I also know that when I graduate, job prospects look a lot brighter armed with a degree from Harvey Mudd College."

CLAREMONT/PITZER COLLEGE

Address: 1050 North Mills Avenue,
  Claremont, CA 91711
Phone: (714) 621-8129
Director of Admissions: Lisa Meyers
Multicultural Student Recruiter: David Perez
1991–92 tuition: $14,992
Room and board: $5,002
Application deadline: 2/1
Financial aid application deadline: 2/15

Non-white freshman admissions: Applicants
  for the class of '94: 275
  Accepted: 61%
  Accepted who enrolled: 30%
  Applicants accepted who rank in top
  10% of high school class: 65%
  In top 25%: 70%
  Median SAT: 440 V, 490 M
  Median ACT: 23
Full-time undergraduate enrollment: 750
  Men: 40%
  Women: 60%
Non-white students in
  1987–88: 19.7%
  1988–89: 19.2%
  1989–90: 17.9%
  1990–91: 19.8%
Geographic distribution of students: na
Students In-state: 64%

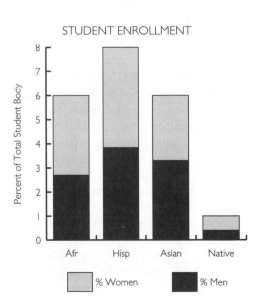

STUDENT ENROLLMENT

Percent of Total Student Body

Afr   Hisp   Asian   Native

☐ % Women   ■ % Men

Top majors: 1. Psychology
2. Organizational Studies 3. Sociology
Retention rate of non-white students: 82.2%
**Scholarships exclusively for non-white
students:** None
Remediation programs: None
Academic support services: Pitzer offers
academic support services through the
Chicano Studies Center, Black Student
Center, and Asian Student Association,
which are part of the five-college
Claremont system.
Ethnic studies programs: Pitzer's ethnic
studies program, established in 1969,
offers several courses from the
departments of history, English,
sociology, and others. As part of the
five-part college Claremont system, Pitzer
is able to offer major and minor courses
of study in Black, Chicano, and Asian
Studies.
Organizations for non-white students:
Chicano Studies Center, Black Student
Center, Asian Student Association, Pitzer
Promoting Asian-American Awareness
Notable non-white alumni: na
Tenured faculty: 50
Non-tenured faculty: 25
Student-faculty ratio: 9:1
Administrators: 35
African-American: 6%
Hispanic: 10%
Asian-American: 5%

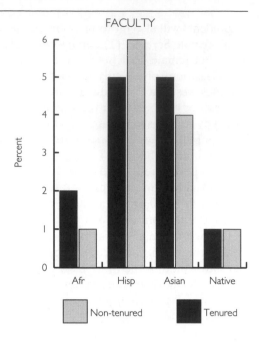

FACULTY

Native American: 1%
Recent non-white speakers on campus: Jesse
Jackson (former presidential candidate
and civil rights activist); Coretta Scott
King (civil rights activist and widow of
Martin Luther King, Jr.); Desmond Tutu
(Nobel Peace Prize winner and South
African civil rights activist); Cesar
Chavez (labor leader and head of United
Farm Workers)

The newest of the Claremont colleges, Pitzer is also the colleges' most iconoclastic. Interdisciplinary learning is not only encouraged, it's the norm; students have a say in all decisions that affect college life; they need only meet minimal general education requirements; and they design their own courses of study.

Pitzer is also among the colleges' most politically active campuses. "Our school is very active and aware of social and political issues," says a student. "We are a somewhat more progressive school, and protests are much more common here than at the other Claremont colleges. We protested against the Gulf War, and we were one of the first schools to divest from South Africa. We were also one of the first schools to get rid of the ROTC program because of the discrimination against gays."

While students are primarily attracted to the thirty-year-old college for its flexible academic programs and progressive-minded student body, once they're here they are pleased with their school's academic course offerings, which emphasize the social sciences. The school's strongest programs are sociology, political studies, and anthropology, while psychology, also strong, is the school's most popular. PACE (Program in American College English), which allows for intensive study of English, is popular with international students. Pitzer students are able to enroll in the Asian, Black, and Chicano Studies programs that are offered as part of the five-college consortium.

Perhaps reflecting the Southern California lifestyle, Pitzer's academics are not overly intense; in fact, students describe them as relaxed. Nonetheless, professors are accessible. Many students refer to them by their first names, and professors often give their home telephone numbers to students. For further academic support, the resources of the five-college Chicano Studies Center and the Office of Black Student Affairs are also available to Pitzer students.

In addition to the five-college student cultural groups, Pitzer has one organization specific to Pitzer, called Pitzer Promoting Asian-American Awareness. With about 15 active, primarily Asian-American members, the group "deals with issues that affect Asian-Americans. It's an exciting group to be in right now because most of the members are either freshmen or sophomores, which means the group can only get stronger," says a student. "This also means that the younger students are getting involved and dealing with these issues."

In a recent year, the group sponsored an Asian-American film series, trips to ethnic towns in Los Angeles, including Little Taipei and Little Japan, as well as frequent study breaks. The group is also working to establish a peer mentor program for its members. The group is beginning to become more political; it is lobbying the administration for more Asian-American Studies programs and faculty members. One student member says that the group has been so successful the student senate has increased its funding from $250 in 1991 to $900 in 1992. "It shows people appreciate us and that they see we're helping make people more aware."

Pitzer students also identify with the Pan-African Student Association, the Asian Student Association, and MECHA, which coordinate their own events and activities, although, apart from ASA, there are no such organizations specific to Pitzer.

Pitzer is one of the Claremont colleges' most racially diverse campuses. The diversity is reflected in the school's student senate. During a recent school year, the student senate convener and vice-convener were African-American, the secretary was Asian-American, and the treasurer was Latina. According to a student, 80 percent of the senate were students of color.

Students say that interaction between the various races and ethnicities at Pitzer is good. "I would like to think that if something happened in the African-American community, the Asian-American students would be there, and vice versa," says a senior.

While most students praise the school's progressive-minded student body, there are those who criticize the administration and faculty for its lack of diversity. "Pitzer tries to place itself as the more liberal Claremont college, but the administration isn't nearly as liberal or as diverse as the students," claims a student. "All of the top administrators, from the president to the dean, are white males and straight. There is one tenured woman of color, who is not involved in issues of multiculturalism at all. When it comes to its hiring practices, it seems as though the college is anti-multicultural."

As part of the Claremont cluster of schools, Pitzer students are able to take part in a variety of social activities on any one of the five campuses. You won't find any Greek organizations at Pitzer, where students pride themselves on their individuality. Students who grow tired of the social life at the college will drive the hour or so to Los Angeles to partake of its active nightlife. Students recommend that you bring a car, if you have one.

Pitzer is for the student who values his or her individuality and respects the same in others. Don't attend Pitzer if what you have is a narrow vision of the world. "I like Pitzer a lot," says a student activist. "Most of the people here are into the diversity movement. A lot of us care enough about this place to work hard for these causes. The people—everyone from students and professors to the staff—are wonderful. I'm a transfer student, and I can say I'm happier and more involved here than I ever have been."

CLAREMONT/POMONA COLLEGE

Address: 333 North College Way, Claremont, CA 91711
Phone: (909) 621-8134
Director of Admissions: Bruce Poch
Multicultural Student Recruiter: na
1992–93 tuition: $15,700
Room and board: $6,625
Application deadline: 1/15
Financial aid application deadline: 2/1

Non-white freshman admissions: Applicants for the class of '95: 1,061
Accepted: 38%
Applicants accepted who enroll: 32%
Applicants accepted who rank in top 10% of high school class: 77%
In top 25%: 90.5%
Median SAT range: 580–670 V, 640–730 M
Median ACT: na
Full-time undergraduate enrollment: 1,389
Men: 54%
Women: 46%
Non-white students in
1990–91: 29%
1992–93: 35%
Geographic distribution of students: na
Top majors: 1. Biology 2. Economics 3. Politics
Retention rate of non-white students: 99.2%
Scholarships exclusively for non-white students: None

Remediation programs: None
Academic support services: The Claremont colleges' Office of Black Student Affairs, Chicano Studies Center, and Asian Studies provide academic support.
Ethnic studies programs: Programs in Asian, Chicano, and Black Studies are open to all students attending one of the five Claremont colleges.
Organizations for non-white students: Pan-African Students Association,

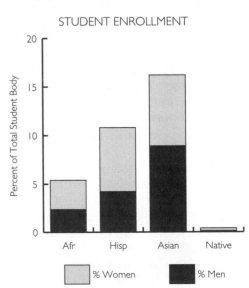

STUDENT ENROLLMENT

Percent of Total Student Body

□ % Women   ■ % Men

Korean Students Association, MECHA, Native American Students Association, Hui Laule'a, Asian Students Association, Asian Pacific Islanders, *Las Voces Unidas* (newspaper), Black Christian Leadership

Notable non-white alumni: George Wolfe ('76, Theater; playwright, *The Colored Museum*); Cruz Reynoso ('53, History; attorney and former California Supreme Court justice); Myrlie Evers ('68, Sociology; author, civil rights leader, and commissioner of Los Angeles County Public Works); Julian Nava ('51, History; former U.S. ambassador to Mexico); Larry Carroll ('73, Economics; broadcast journalist)

Tenured faculty: na

Non-tenured faculty: na

Student-faculty ratio: 9.5:1

Administrators: na

Recent non-white speakers on campus: George Takei (actor); Beulah Quo (actress); Lowell Gibbes (Stanford University professor)

Pomona College offers one of the most respected liberal arts educations in the West, or, some would say, in the country. Although the school doesn't have the name recognition of some of its East Coast counterparts, the 106-year-old college is every bit as good.

One of the keys to Pomona's success is its extremely accessible and bright faculty and staff. Says a student about the school's support network: "For minority students who come from a minority community, Pomona can be a case of major culture shock. However, we have the programs and professors that can help students with such culture shock. There are the Latino and black student organizations that assign incoming freshmen peer advisers. And there's all kinds of other support as well. For some students it takes longer to adjust than others, but the transition is possible and very much worth the effort."

Four faculty members who are especially supportive of Pomona students of color are Sidney Lemelle, a history and Black Studies professor; Agnes Jackson, an English professor; Sue Houchins, an associate professor of Black Studies; and Ruth Gilmore, an English professor. "These professors teach us not only the course material but also about their experiences," says a sophomore. "They are known to take students under their wings and mentor them throughout their time at Pomona."

As part of the five-college consortium, students also have access to the academic and social support services provided by the Office of Black Student Affairs and the Chicano Studies Center.

Pomona offers a rigorous and traditional liberal arts program, but it is best known for its offerings in the sciences, particularly chemistry and biology. Other academic standouts include English, international relations, music, psychology, and geology. Pomona students are able to take classes at any of the other schools in the Claremont system.

First-year students are required to enroll in a seminar course that is characterized by small class discussions—enrollment in each class is no more than 15 students—and interdisciplinary learning. Recent seminar topics have included "Environmental Issues" and "Liberals, Conservatives, and Radicals." To graduate, students must also complete course work in English, in a foreign language, and in the arts and the humanities, natural sciences, and social sciences.

The five-college departments of Chicano, Black, and Asian Studies feature well-regarded course offerings. "For the most part I have been impressed with these majors and feel these classes are an essential part of the Claremont curriculum," says a student. Among the Black Studies courses, students say "Race, Class, and Power" is one of the more popular. "Many students who have taken this class have come out of it with a new awareness," says a student. Harry Pachon, a Chicano Studies professor, is highly respected by students. "Because of his 'Latino Politics in the 1980s' course, I am on my way to pursuing a career in East Los Angeles politics," says a student. "Professor Pachon is terrific because he opened my eyes to all the work that needs to be done in our communities and he made us realize that we are the catalysts for that change." "Asian Traditions," "Arts of China," and "Asian-American Psychology" are among the best courses offered by the Asian Studies program.

For cultural activity, students are able to participate in any of the five colleges' organizations, including the Pan-African Students Association, MECHA, the Native American Students Association, and the Asian Students Association. There are no historically black fraternities or sororities at Pomona, although some students have been known to join these organizations at nearby California Polytechnic.

After a great deal of effort, students recently succeeded in getting the administration to fund an Asian-American Cultural Center on campus. Although the center is "still being formed," it already has a small library and a computer and publishes *Pacific Rim,* a student-written newsletter focusing on Pomona Asian and Asian-American student organizations and current affairs. The center, located in Oldenborg Center, will also establish a mentor program, matching freshmen with juniors and seniors. The director of the center, Ruth Gim, "is great," says a student. "She's an academic and sensitive to Asian-American issues. She also knows a network of other Asian-American scholars, which will be a resource for the center."

Pomona students are on the whole open-minded and interested in issues of diversity. "Due to our school's small size, members of some of the minority student groups often grow a little discouraged because of their modest numbers," says a student. "But overall I would have to say that this campus is politically and racially aware and addresses these issues. Students interested in these concerns would find more than enough opportunities to get involved." According to a junior, "Pomona students are in the middle politically when compared to the other Claremont schools. Pitzer is to the left of us, and Claremont McKenna is to the right."

Varsity sports are definitely déclassé here. Which isn't to say students don't like athletics. Intramurals are popular, and the school recently completed a new $15 million athletic center, the most impressive such facility on any of the five-college campuses.

On weekends, students hold their own parties, or attend parties at one of the other Claremont colleges. Students will also make the drive—a car is a must on this campus—into Los Angeles or, more specifically, to UCLA and Westwood. But most students bemoan the lack of a more active social life, thanks to their school's academic work load.

Pomona students seem happy with their college choice. "Pomona College is the best place for me to be," says a senior. "It has offered me so much. Not only have I gotten to know so many people from so many different social, cultural, and religious backgrounds, but I have also come to realize how important it is to go back to my community and change things. I want minority students to experience the liberal arts education that Pomona offers because the type of knowledge found here—both academically and personally—produces people who are aware of the issues of the day and who are willing to change things."

CLAREMONT/SCRIPPS COLLEGE

Women's college
Address: 1030 Columbia Avenue,
   Claremont, CA 91711
Phone: (714) 621-8149
Director of Admissions: Leslie A. Miles
Multicultural Student Recruiter: na
1991–92 tuition: $14,700
Room and board: $6,350
Application deadline: 2/1
Financial aid application deadline: 2/11
Non-white freshman admissions: Applicants
   for the class of '95: 263
   Accepted: 65%
   Accepted who enroll: 25%
   Applicants accepted who rank in top
   10% of high school class: 50%
   Median SAT range: 520–620 V, 540–640 M
   Median ACT range: 24–28
Full-time undergraduate enrollment: 622
Non-white students in
   1987–88: 21%
   1988–89: 23%

1989–90: 25%
1990–91: 26.5%

GEOGRAPHIC DISTRIBUTION OF STUDENTS

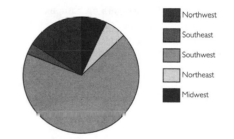

- Northwest
- Southeast
- Southwest
- Northeast
- Midwest

STUDENT ENROLLMENT

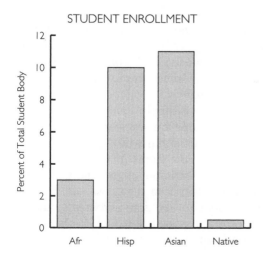

Students In-state: na
Top majors: 1. Psychology 2. English 3. Art
Retention rate of non-white students: 68%
**Scholarships exclusively for non-white
   students:** Martin Luther King
   Scholarship: need-based; $460 for each
   award. Academic Achievement:
   need-based; $5,500 for each award.
Remediation programs: na
Academic support services: As part of the
   five-college consortium, the Office of
   Black Student Affairs and the Chicano
   Student Affairs Center offer academic
   and non-academic support programs.
Ethnic studies programs: As part of the
   Claremont College system, students are
   able to enroll in programs in Black,
   Chicano, Hispanic, and Latin American
   Studies.

Organizations for non-white students:
Asian-American Student Association,
MECHA, Pan-African Student
Association, Scripps Association of
Latinas, AAWARE (Asian-American
Women as Resources for Each Other),
Wannawabe Weusi (an African-American
student group), Beautiful Black
Women

Notable non-white alumnae: na

Tenured faculty: 35

Non-tenured faculty: 24

Student-faculty ratio: 8:1

Administrators: 48
African-American: 6%
Hispanic: 2%
Asian-American: 4%
Native American: 0

Recent non-white speakers on campus:
Julian Bond (former Georgia state
senator and civil rights activist);
Johnnetta Cole (president, Spelman
College); Gloria Anzaldua (poet); Mario
Garcia (author and professor, University
of California/Santa Barbara); Antonia
Hernandez (attorney, Mexican-
American Legal Defense and Education
Fund)

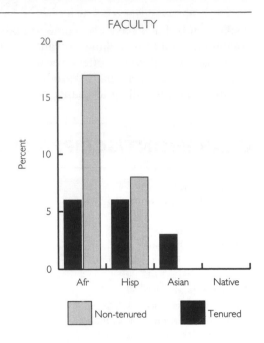

FACULTY

As the only all-women's college in the Claremont system and one of only three such colleges in the West, Scripps College provides its students with a quality education in an atmosphere supportive of women, while at the same time offering its students the coeducational opportunities—both of the social and academic variety—of the other Claremont schools.

Scripps's emphasis is on the humanities, and students say the school's best departments are history, languages, and psychology. Economics and English, while strong, are also among the more popular. Black, Chicano, and Asian Studies courses are available to Scripps women through the five-college consortium. A popular Black Studies course is "Introduction to African-American History," while "Hispanics in the U.S." is also well regarded. To graduate, students must take two multicultural studies courses which emphasize non-Western cultures.

At some women's colleges, men might be in scarce supply, but not at Scripps. "There are always men on campus. Although the dorms are supposedly all-women, each of the dorms has coed bathrooms, because we have this four-night rule where students are able to have guests for four nights in a row. Some of the women here will basically have their boyfriends live with them. After four nights, he will leave for a night, then he'll come back." Men are also plentiful in the classroom. Except for the school's required humanities program courses and some women's studies courses, according to students, most courses are integrated. "In fact, most of my classes are fifty-fifty, men to women," says a sophomore.

Again unlike other women's colleges, feminism is not on the front burner for most students. "If you say you're a feminist, that's weird here. Scripps is definitely not into feminism," says a student. But another student appreciates the school's approach to single-sex education. "I never thought I'd like going to an all-women's school. But it's really been helpful to me as a woman. There's an automatic bonding that goes on here between the students. You really get the sense that you're developing yourself as a woman."

Students differ on the receptivity of their classmates to issues of cultural diversity. "This place is really not diverse, and many of the students are not really open-minded when it comes to multiculturalism." Another student agrees, but adds: "It's hard at first coming to Scripps, especially when you'd like to be around people like yourself. But after a while, it's not as difficult. Scripps offers you so much that you tend to overlook this." According to students, the majority of Scripps women come from the upper middle and upper classes and, adds a history major, "have this attitude where they don't have to worry about getting a job because they've already got one lined up at their father's company."

Scripps women are able to participate in any of the five-college cultural organizations, but the college also sponsors three cultural organizations specific to Scripps. Perhaps the most vocal, and certainly the most political, is Revolutionary Union of Women of Color at Scripps (RUWOCAS), with about 15 members, who meet weekly. "We talk about how to bring about change. Since we have only one tenured faculty member of color on campus, we sent a letter to the administration demanding more minority faculty hiring. We had a meeting to discuss this and other issues with the president, and she lost her cool. She threatened some of the students with expulsion, just because she got so frustrated. We've had our share of heated confrontations with the administration." Adds another student: "There's a tag on us RUWOCAS members. If other students ever see more than three of us sitting together in the dining hall, they automatically wonder what we're going to protest. It's easy to look as if you're a revolutionary at Scripps." In a recent year, three of the group's members were Caucasian, while the majority of its members were Latinas.

The organization Wannawabe Weusi, which means Black Women in Swahili, "has died down in recent years. It's failed because we were seen as excluding non-African-Americans from our meetings," says a student. "But we were weren't trying to exclude anybody, but to bring us together. Students didn't feel as if they could come into our office. We're in the process of redesigning our structure." The organization has its own office in Frankel Hall, which includes a small library and a meeting space "where we can just have some discussions."

Scripps Association of Latinas (SAL) and Asian-American Women as Resources for Each Other (AAWARE) serve primarily as social organizations for their members. Each sponsors study breaks and other social functions for members.

Students say that on an individual basis, interaction between the different races and ethnicities represented at the college is good. "That's one of the things I like about coming to school here, that you can make friends with students of different backgrounds. It's hard not to, because the school is so small. You need to make friends, but that's nice because you're learning from them and they from you."

Socially, Scripps women tend to gravitate to the parties at Claremont McKenna College, located just across the street. Students mention a lack of activity on campus, although each of the school's seven dorms has been known to have its share of parties. Students will also go to the "drinking parties at the other schools." Most students remain on campus for the first year, but, for those with cars, many upperclass students will head into the nightlife and clubs of downtown LA.

Scripps students like their school because it's all-women yet it has all the diversions of a coed institution. "It's a good school, and I'm actually sad about leaving," says a senior. "I've gotten to know everyone, even faculty and administrators, on a first-name basis. I recognize there are problems here when it comes to multicultural issues, but things are changing, although slowly."

MILLS COLLEGE

Women's college
Address: 500 MacArthur Boulevard, Oakland, CA 94613
Phone: (510) 430-2135 / (800) 87-MILLS
Director of Admissions: Genevieve Flaherty
Multicultural Student Recruiter: Joan Jaffe
1993–95 tuition: $14,100
Room and board: $6,000
Application deadline: Rolling admissions
Financial aid application deadline: 2/15
Non-white freshman admissions: Applicants for the class of '96: 236
  Accepted: 77%
  Accepted who enroll: 31%
  Applicants who rank in top 10% of high school class: na
  Median SAT: 520 V, 520 M
  Median ACT: na
Full-time undergraduate enrollment: 774
Non-white students in
  1988–89: 21%
  1989–90: 20%
  1990–91: 21%
  1991–92: 21%
Geographic distribution of students: na
Students In-state: 69%
Top majors: 1. English 2. Psychology 3. Communications
Retention rate of non-white students: na
Scholarships exclusively for non-white students: None
Remediation programs: None

Academic support services: Mills offers Summer Academic Workshop, a summer program that introduces incoming first-year students to the academic and social life at the college. The college also offers the Computer Learning Studio, Minority Support/Advising, and tutoring in most academic subjects.

Ethnic studies programs: Mills offers a major and minor course of study in ethnic studies. The program, established in 1970, includes approximately 13 courses, which deal with ethnic topics.

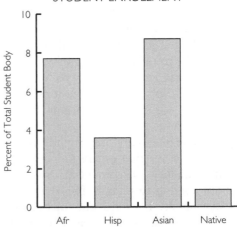

STUDENT ENROLLMENT

Percent of Total Student Body

Afr   Hisp   Asian   Native

Organizations for non-white students: Black Women's Collective, Asian Students Association, MECHA, Native American Council, Multicultural Alliance

Notable non-white alumnae: Bonnie Guiton ('74; director, California Department of Consumer Affairs); March Fong Eu ('47; California Secretary of State); Gwen Lewis ('68; dancer); Barbara Lee ('73; California state assemblywoman); Patricia Pineda ('74; general counsel, New United Motor Manufacturing Co.)

Tenured faculty: 42

Non-tenured faculty: 102

Student-faculty ratio: 10:1

Administrators: 80

    African-American: 14%

    Hispanic: 2%

    Asian-American: 0

    Native American: 0

Recent non-white speakers on campus: Ruby Dee (actress and writer); Angela Davis (civil rights activist); Susan Taylor (*Essence* magazine editor); Helen Zia

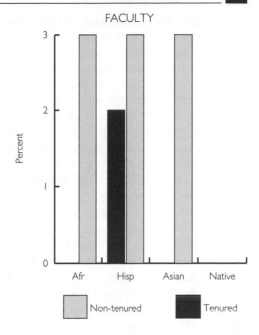

(*Ms.* magazine editor); Barbara Lee (California state assemblywoman)

All's quiet on the Mills College front, at least for now. Back in 1990, the decision of the Mills board of trustees to make the small women's college coeducational was met with such an uproar—from alums and students, especially—that the board rescinded its decision, temporarily. The college has until 1995 to prove to the board that it can remain viable, and to do so, it must raise student enrollment to about 1,000 and increase the endowment.

Whether the college will win the battle remains uncertain. Student enrollment in the fall of 1990 was 774, according to an article in *The Chronicle of Higher Education;* in the fall of 1991, there were just 745 enrolled. The article also claimed that, according to an administrator, "the college's $71.6 million endowment is slowly being eroded by a spending rate that is too high." But for those who find coeducation abhorrent, there is hope. A new energetic president—Janet Holmgren McKay—has arrived from Princeton University, alumni gift giving has increased, and students are actively involved in recruiting students from their home areas through a program called "Take Mills Home."

What is it about this small college that has friends so loyal? "You're never told you can't at Mills," says an economic and political analysis major. "You're always told 'you can.' In fact, the people here have often believed in me more than I've believed in myself." Adds a music major: "I've changed at Mills. I'm more confident and inquisitive. There's a can-do attitude at Mills, and it's contagious. My professors have encouraged me by their example to be strong and assertive. I feel more independent, more articulate, and more respected. I'm more open to cultural diversity, to different values and beliefs—things I'd never been exposed to before."

Mills offers strong academics in dance, English, history, French, and art, and women's studies and communication are popular. Those traditionally male-dominated fields, math and computer science, are solid.

Students say the Hispanic Studies program could include a greater diversity in course offerings ("The program deals mostly with the literature of Spain"), although the ethnic studies program is praised, as more than one student put it, as "excellent." Popular courses offered by both the Hispanic studies and ethnic studies programs are "Latinos in the U.S." and "Trends in the Latin American Migration to the U.S." Says a student about the ethnic studies program: "The program keeps getting stronger every semester. This is the first semester they've offered at least two courses in each group—African-American, Asian-American, and Latino. Usually, there's been a course or two in only one of these areas, but no more. This semester's schedule has set a precedent that we're confident will continue into the future."

But just when things appeared to be slowing down after the 1990 "Rather Dead Than Coed" controversy (as a popular T-shirt of the day summed it up), another controversy flared up on campus during the spring semester of 1992. It centered on the selection of a new provost, Faith Gabelnick, who assumed her position in the fall of 1992. "Things got pretty intense. We had a sit-in at the president's office, we wrote letters, staged marches, all because we wanted the new provost to be a person of color. There were no people of color involved in the selection process. So we wanted the selection process to be put off until the panel could get more diverse. But that didn't happen. The administration went ahead and selected a new provost anyway. Since then, it's gotten pretty heated and political here."

The controversy has had some positive results, according to a student. "Some of the students formed a White Woman's Coalition to discuss their own racism and to educate themselves about other cultures and races. A Woman of Color Coalition has also formed because we realized that we need to fight for our issues together." In the spring of 1992, the Woman of Color Coalition published its first literary magazine, *Womanist,* which includes poetry and short stories.

There is a great deal of multicultural interaction at Mills. "Students here are open to multiculturalism and accept and respect students from other cultures. We attend each other's events. We have a close line of communication. I can say in terms of interaction, this is the best place. There is no tension, and, when necessary, students organize quickly. The day after the Rodney King verdict, for example, I got a note slipped under my door to wear black, and most of the students on campus must have gotten the same note, as many were wearing black in mourning over the verdict."

The school's various cultural organizations plan their own respective activities as well. The Asian Students Association, with about 10 members, sponsors an Asian Woman's Awareness Week, which recently included a panel discussion about interracial dating, a dance, and a Japanese-American group that spoke about the internment of Japanese-Americans during World War II. MECHA, Mills's Latina student organization, also sponsors an awareness week, called La Raza. As part of their week's celebration, members brought to campus a Latina poet and a female Nicaraguan Sandinista leader, and sponsored a campus-wide picnic and movie night.

Mills's location is nothing to sneeze about. The weather, often compared to the Mediterranean weather, is nearly ideal, and the wealth of social and cultural activities available in San Francisco is overwhelming. A popular destination for students is the University of California at Berkeley and especially the fraternity parties there. The UC campus is just twenty minutes away by car. "Most of the social life here goes on off campus, but the best thing is that public transportation makes getting anywhere easy. A bus stop is located near the school, and the BART [subway] is near as well." The city of Oakland is one of the few American cities that do not have a racial or ethnic majority, and the city rivals New York City's Greenwich Village for the number of artists living in the area.

Whether Mills will remain as it is—albeit with an enlarged student population—is up to the present administration and faculty, student body, and, of course, the board of trustees. For one undergraduate, Mills has provided her the skills necessary to succeed in the world. "Here at Mills, we're expected to participate in the learning process, and it's nearly impossible to come here and not interact. There are always small group discussions going on. There are a lot of role models, in the administration and in the faculty. This place definitely provides a good environment for a woman to find her strengths and her own voice."

OCCIDENTAL COLLEGE

Address: Los Angeles, CA 90041
Phone: (213) 259-2500
Director of Admissions: Charlene Liebau
Multicultural Student Recruiter: na
1993–94 tuition: $15,855
Room and board: $5,325
Application deadline: 2/1
Financial aid application deadline: 2/1

Non-white freshman admissions: na
Full-time undergraduate enrollment: 1,575
Non-white students in 1988–92: 37%
Geographic distribution of students: na
Top majors: 1. English 2. Biology
Retention rate of non-white students: na
Scholarships exclusively for non-white students: None
Remediation Programs: None
Academic support services: The Learning Resource Center
Ethnic studies programs: Occidental offers an interdisciplinary program in Asian Studies, which includes courses in the history, anthropology, and religious studies departments. The program includes courses in Japanese- and Chinese-language studies.
Ethnic studies courses: The school's interdisciplinary American Studies program includes courses in "Afro-American Literature," "The

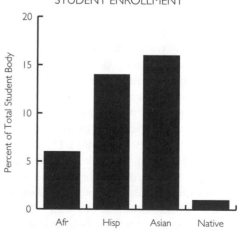

STUDENT ENROLLMENT

Percent of Total Student Body

Afr   Hisp   Asian   Native

Chicano Experience," "Ethnic America," and "African-American Religious Traditions." Occidental's history department includes courses in Asian, Latin American, and African and Middle Eastern Studies.

Organizations for non-white students: MECHA, Black Students Alliance, Asian Pacific Alliance, Chinese Culture Club, Korean Club, Native Hawaiians Club, Filipino Club, Japan Culture Club, Vietnamese Cultural Awareness League, Multicultural Hall

Notable non-white alumni: Michael Hernandez ('74; Los Angeles city council member); Joseph Duff ('68; president of the Los Angeles chapter of the NAACP); Elaine Woo ('76; writer, the *Los Angeles Times*)

Tenured and non-tenured faculty: 20% non-white

Student-faculty ratio: 10:1

Administrators: na

Recent non-white speakers on campus: na

Occidental, located near the heart of Los Angeles, is a 106-year-old college that provides students with an intimate learning environment that is challenging, diverse, and devoted to the liberal arts.

The college made history in 1988 when it became one of the country's first predominantly white institutions of higher learning to appoint an African-American to its presidency. Since his appointment, Robert Slaughter, the former chancellor of the University of Maryland's College Park campus, has won his share of fans. "He's the best as a role model," says a senior. "He gives us minority students hope that we can someday attain the positions that he has. He also gives multicultural issues more weight, I think, than another college president who might not have experienced racism. Dr. Slaughter does his job well. Students say hello to him on campus and they respect him."

Occidental attracts an open-minded student body that students say sincerely appreciates diversity of almost any sort. "It's hard not to make friends of different ethnicities at Occidental," says a student. "It's such a small campus, and very laid-back. You make friends at the oddest moments. There are no boundaries between people here. There's a lot of sharing. Before I came here, I hadn't been around blacks or Hispanics, but everyone's friendly. You find out quickly that all the stereotypes are wrong." Adds another student: "A large portion of the school is liberal and open-minded, and all the isms are always being discussed, from heterosexism and racism to sexism and whatever. The campus is definitely trying to deal with these issues." But the college isn't without its more conservative contingent. "Many students feel that they're having issues of multiculturalism shoved down their throats, and these issues are discussed a lot here. Many of the white students who come here are from Republican backgrounds and will eventually go back to voting Republican after they graduate, but while they're here, they're definitely more Democratic."

The Multicultural Institute, a summer orientation program available to qualified students of color as well as to white students, does a great deal to foster the campus's appreciation of diversity, and to make students who participate in it more comfortable at the college. Students say that campus organizations also do their part in raising the awareness about issues of cultural and racial diversity.

Perhaps the organization most familiar to Oxy students isn't an organization at all but a residence hall, commonly known on campus as the Multicultural Hall, a part of campus life since 1988. "There is nowhere else for me to live on campus, I like it here so much," says a student who has lived in the hall for three of his four years at the college. "In this hall, you have all your campus political leaders. This is known as the hotbed of radicals on campus, where we really get into tackling the issues." Adds another resident: "The people who tend to be drawn to the house are very supportive of one another and are very close-knit once they get here. You can also develop good leadership skills living here."

During a recent year, of the hall's approximately 100 residents, 10 were African-American, 20 were Chicano, 10 were Asian-American, 3 were Native American, 5 were white, and others were international students. The house reflects not only racial and ethnic diversity but also diversity based on sexual orientation, religion, and socioeconomic status. The house, which changes sites each year and is open to first-year students, usually co-sponsors events with the school's various cultural student groups. A recent discussion sponsored solely by hall residents, and which included professors, focused on the role of the white male in multiculturalism.

The Asian Pacific Alliance (APA) "sponsors a whole list of activities," according to a junior. Each year APA, along with the Asian student groups, sponsors an Asian Pacific American Heritage Week that in the past has included a karate demonstration, Filipino dances, a crafts fair, a Chinese calligraphy demonstration, and speakers. The college sponsors about seven Asian student groups, the most active of which are the Chinese Culture Club and the Filipino Club. The newest such organization is the Vietnamese Cultural Awareness League. "There are so many ethnicities in the Asian race here, and we all get along, but we're learning to be strong within our own ethnicities," says a student. "A lot of people think that the Asian Pacific Alliance is an umbrella organization for all the Asian groups, but it's not. We sponsor our own events. What we're going to do in the future is to get a president of one of the Asian groups to head APA each month. It's hard for any one person to be in charge because often the person is involved in two organizations."

MECHA/ALAS is the college's Chicano and Latino student group. "As far as I know, our organization is unique in the Los Angeles area. I should know, because I'm the person in charge of publicity and I interact with MECHAs at different schools, and I've yet to come across one like ours where Chicanos and Latino students are united. Our two groups merged two years ago for two reasons. First, because of our low numbers. We wanted to build unity and strength. Second, we realized that if the Chicano movement is going to survive we have to come together." But the two groups appear to be having adjustment problems. "The Chicano students are the predominant group in the organization, and sometimes the Latin American students feel we don't care for their concerns. We're trying." Of the organization's 40 active members, about 30 are of Mexican descent, and most of these are from the Los Angeles area.

MECHA/ALAS's main cultural focus is on Semana La Raza, a week of activities that in a recent year included a folk-dancing troupe, and speakers. According to one student leader, MECHA/ALAS "is beginning to work with the Black Students Alliance to discuss issues, such as stereotypes. We're beginning the process of communication between the two groups, and we're looking to bring the Asian students into the fold as well."

As a liberal arts college, Occidental requires students to satisfy one of two core curriculums to graduate. In Core I, called Culture and Society—by far the most popular—students study non-Western, European, and American cultures, as well as the fine arts. In Core II, called the Collegium, students participate in seminar-style courses that are interdisciplinary and focus on such topics as "Tradition and Change in the East and West" and "Revolutions." Students must also satisfy math, science, and foreign-language requirements, and, during their senior year, must pass a comprehensive examination.

In addition to the standard liberal arts fare, Occidental offers several unique interdisciplinary programs, such as cognitive science, geochemistry, diplomacy and world affairs, public policy, and psychobiology. With the purchase of the *R. V. Vantuna,* an 85-foot boat, the college was able to strengthen its marine biology program.

Occidental divides its school year into three eleven-week terms, making it easy for students to take advantage of the school's diverse course offerings. Students usually take three courses each term. But students say such a schedule only adds to the academic pressure on campus, which can get intense. However, professors are always accessible, even in introductory courses.

Occidental's campus, sitting atop a hill, is beautiful, full of well-manicured lawns and palm trees—and is self-contained. The area immediately surrounding the college, according to a student, is mostly middle-income Latino and African-American families. According to students, the majority of the school's African-American and Latino students are from the Los Angeles area, "or not far from here anyway," particularly Mexican-American students. While nearly a third of the campus comes from the Los Angeles area—and more than half are in-staters—the college also attracts students from almost every other state in the country, especially Arizona and the Northwest, as well as nearly two dozen foreign countries.

Los Angeles—LA's downtown is just ten minutes south—offers all the activity that only a large city can: museums, ethnic restaurants, professional sports teams, clubs and bars. Having a car is essential, according to students, especially if your destination is one of Southern California's famous beaches. The city's racial tensions have come onto campus, but mostly in the form of student speak-outs and rallies. "Many of us are from the area, so a lot of us went home to see how things were," says a student, referring to the time around the Rodney King verdict in the summer of 1992. "But a lot of us, even those of us from around here, were glad we were on campus away from it all."

Occidental has a great deal going for it, including size, committed faculty, and solid academics. Says a native Californian: "I'm glad I came to Oxy. I needed the individual attention the school offers, and I definitely get that here. It's also easy to get involved. And," he adds, "it's close to home."

UNIVERSITY OF REDLANDS

Address: 1200 East Colton Avenue, P.O. Box 3080, Redlands, CA 92373-0999
Phone: (909) 335-4074
Director of Admissions: Paul M. Driscoll
Multicultural Student Recruiter: na
1993–94 tuition: $15,760
Room and board: $6,000
Application deadline: 4/1
Financial aid application deadline: 2/1

Non-white freshman admissions: Applicants for the class of '96: 597
  Accepted: 80%
  Accepted who enroll: 29%
  Applicants accepted who rank in top 10% of high school class: na
  Median SAT: na
  Median ACT: na
Full-time undergraduate enrollment: 1,500
  Men: 48%
  Women: 52%

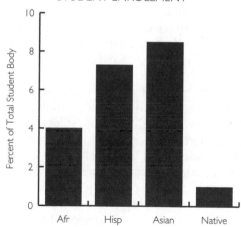

STUDENT ENROLLMENT

Percent of Total Student Body

Afr   Hisp   Asian   Native

Non-white students in
  1988–89: 13%
  1989–90: 16%
  1990–91: 15%
Geographic distribution of students: na
Top majors: 1. Liberal Arts 2. Business 3. Psychology

Retention rate of non-white students: na
Scholarships exclusively for non-white students: Bilingual/Bicultural Scholarship: $500–$2,500 per year; merit-based.
Remediation programs: None
Academic support services: The university provides tutoring in most academic subjects, labs in math and writing, and a study network.
Ethnic studies programs: Race and ethnic studies is an interdisciplinary program offered as a minor, involving courses in sociology, economics, philosophy, history, and education.
Organizations for non-white students: African-American Association, MECHA, Hawaii Club, Asian Studies Club
Notable non-white alumni: Dr. Margaret B. Wilkerson (director, Center for the Study of Education and the Advancement of Women); Gaddi Vasquez (Orange County Board of Supervisors and the highest elected Republican Latino in California); Garry Reaves (CBS news

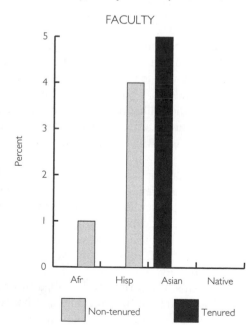

FACULTY

Percent

Afr   Hisp   Asian   Native

Non-tenured   Tenured

correspondent); Richard West (director, National Museum for the Native American)

Tenured faculty: 84
Non-tenured faculty: 32
Student-faculty ratio: 13:1
Administrators: 100
  African-American: 9%
  Hispanic: 3%
  Asian-American: 7%
  Native American: <1%

Recent non-white speakers on campus: Yolanda King (civil rights activist and daughter of Martin Luther King, Jr.); Atallah Shabazz (civil rights activist and daughter of Malcolm X); David Wong Louie (recipient of fellowships from National Endowment for the Arts); Helena Maria Viramontes (co-editor of *Chicana Creativity and Criticis*); Maya Angelou (poet)

The University of Redlands is characterized by personalized attention to education, a beautiful college campus, and an eclectic group of students, all in a rural setting just sixty miles east of Los Angeles.

Top-notch programs at Redlands include business and political science, as well as psychology and communicative disorders. English and economics are also respected departments. In an effort to enhance its offerings in the area, the university and students are currently in the process of a faculty search for a director of its race and ethnic studies program. The school's MacNair Asian Library is said by students to be more than adequate in providing research materials.

What sets the university apart from other small colleges in the region, indeed from many schools in the nation, is its Johnston Center for Individualized Learning, which enrolls about 10 percent of its students. The program, established in 1969, allows students to plan their own course of study, with assistance from professors, for their four years. There are no majors or core course requirements, students don't receive letter grades but extensive written evaluations, and students are expected to complete an off-campus cross-cultural studies program, usually fulfilled by participating in one of the school's study-abroad programs.

The Johnston participants include some of the school's most iconoclastic and progressive-minded students, especially when compared to the more traditional college students who populate the rest of the university. "Johnston students are definitely more liberal, almost radical, when compared to most of the other students here," observes an economics major. Johnston students publish a newspaper called *The Antithesis,* which, according to a student, "speaks out against war and abortion limits."

No matter whether students are enrolled in the Johnston program or not, they rave about the academic support they receive from professors. "Professors here are phenomenal when it comes to helping students. They want to assist anytime they can," says a student, although more than one student commented on the lack of faculty and administrative support when it comes to issues of race. "There really is no one on the faculty whom we can go to when we need this kind of assistance," says a student.

Redlands, California, is described by one student "as mostly a retirement community," although the area includes a movie theater and some bars. Students rarely head into town, however, as the university and student groups sponsor a wide range of activities and events. Currently, a little more than 10 percent of the campus belongs to one of the school's five local fraternities and four local sororities. Students report that the school's sororities are more integrated than the fraternities. While the university has no historically African-American fraternities, some black male students have recently affiliated with the Alpha Phi Alpha fraternity at the nearby University of California/Riverside campus. Students sometimes make the hour trek into Los Angeles. Intramural sports, thanks to nearly daily sunshine during the school year, are popular on-campus activities. The Willow Center, the school's student union, sponsors happy hours and comedy nights.

The cultural student groups are only somewhat active on the Redlands campus. The African-American Association recently changed its name from the Black Student Union "to encourage more student involvement," says a campus leader. During the 1991–92 school year, the group managed to host an art exhibit, a GospelFest that included area choirs, and a film series, "but the same few people worked to coordinate these events," says a student. Students are hopeful that the name change will encourage more participation; at the beginning of the 1992–93 school year, more than 25 students indicated their interest in joining the club. The Hawaii Club coordinates events for Hawaiian Culture Week, as well as a luau with song, dance, and food. MECHA, a Chicano student group, sponsors clothes drives, retreats, a film series, guest lectures, dances, and a recognition dinner for outstanding seniors and faculty members. The Asian Studies Club hosts the China Symposium/Convocation and Asian Studies Week programs each year.

Students of color on the Redlands campus have been active in student affairs; during a recent year, for example, African-American students served as president and vice president of the student government, while African-American and Latino students were in the student senate. An African-American student also headed the school's Inter-Fraternity council.

Although the university may not be as racially diverse as some of the nearby UC schools, students nonetheless appreciate the variety of students they go to school with. "There is no one prevailing attitude politically or socially here at the university," comments a student. "Everything is tolerated because there are so many different perspectives. The diversity of outlooks is what makes going to school here a great experience."

UNIVERSITY OF SOUTHERN CALIFORNIA

Address: University Park Campus, Los
 Angeles, CA 90089
Phone: (213) 740-8899
Director of Admissions: Duncan Murdoch
Multicultural Student Recruiter: Eric Abrams
1991–92 tuition: $15,435
Room and board: $6,040
Application deadline: 2/1
Financial aid application deadline: 2/15

Non-white freshman admissions: Applicants
 for the class of '95: 4,564
 Accepted: 70%
 Accepted who enroll: 24.1%
 Applicants accepted who rank in top
 10% of high school class: na
 In top 25%: 100%
 Median SAT range: 400–700 V, 400–700 M
 Median ACT: 24
Full-time undergraduate enrollment: 13,500
 Men: 55%
 Women: 45%

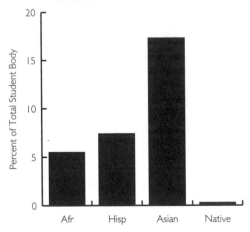

STUDENT ENROLLMENT

Percent of Total Student Body

Afr   Hisp   Asian   Native

Non-white students in
 1987–88: 25%
 1988–89: 26%
 1989–90: 26.5%
 1990–91: 28%

Geographic distribution of students: na
Students In-state: 65%
Top majors: 1. Letters, Arts, and Sciences
 2. Business 3. Engineering
Retention rate of non-white students: 85%
**Scholarships exclusively for non-white
 students:** Mexican-American Alumni
 Association: merit- and need-based;
 $400–$3,500 for each award. Black
 Alumni Association/Ebonics Support
 Group: merit- and need-based; amount
 for each award varies; 25 awarded
 each year. Asian Pacific American
 Support Group: need-based; amounts
 vary; 15 to 18 awards each year; must
 be U.S. citizen or permanent resident.
Remediation programs: None
Academic support services: The Learning
 Center, Minority Engineering Program,
 Letters, Arts, and Sciences (LAS)
 Advisement, Academic Initiative,
 Academic Relations, Joint Educational
 Program, LAS Publications, Program
 for Returning Students, Summer
 Honors Program, Summer Transfer
 Scholars Program, Urban Affairs
Ethnic studies programs: USC offers ethnic
 studies.
Ethnic studies courses: The university offers
 "Minority Cultures in the U.S.,"
 "Pan-African Literature," "Comparative
 Studies in Black Culture," "Introduction
 to Afro-American Literature,"
 "Ethnographic Field Methods and
 Practicum," and "The Afro-American
 Novel Since 1850."
Organizations for non-white students: The
 Latino Floor, Latino Business Student
 Association, MECHA, Latino Student
 Assembly, Department for Black
 Students, Brotherhood of African
 Men, Black Student Union, Evening
 of Soul, National Society of Black
 Engineers, Black Women's Caucus
Notable non-white alumni: John Singleton
 (writer/filmmaker); Mark Ridley-Thomas

(Los Angeles city councilman); Herb Alpert (founder, A&M Records); Linda Johnson-Rice (publisher, *Ebony* and *Jet* magazines)
Tenured faculty: na
Non-tenured faculty: na
Student-faculty ratio: 13:1

Administrators: na
Recent non-white speakers on campus: Maya Angelou (author and poet); Angela Davis (political activist); Cesar Chavez (labor leader and head of United Farm Workers)

At most schools, the Olympics are just something students watch on TV. But at the University of Southern California, students do more than that. They participate in the event. According to one estimate, more than 200 USC students have taken part in the Olympics, and the campus is just a short distance from many of the facilities of the 1984 summer games that were hosted in Los Angeles.

While many USC Olympians have earned the gold, so do several of USC's academic departments. USC's most famous program is its film school, reputed to be one of the best in the country, having graduated the likes of George Lucas, Steven Spielberg, and John Singleton. Music, drama, and journalism are also standouts, while pre-professional studies in law, engineering, and business are among the school's most popular programs. One goal of many Trojans is getting into USC's medical, law, or business school.

Students praise the school's "Pan-African Literature" and "Comparative Studies in Black Culture" courses. "The professor of both courses, Lloyd Brown, is excellent *and* difficult. The courses, especially the 'Black Culture' course, turned my life around and have made me want to get more involved in the black community politically," says a student.

According to students, professors try to make themselves available, despite the sometimes overcrowded classroom situations during students' first years. However, the Writing Center and the Learning and Support Services are said to be effective, and the director of LSS, Alonzo Anderson, is well regarded by students.

USC's cultural organizations add some spice to university life. MECHA, with about 30 members, is the political arm of USC's Chicano and Latino student community, but members would like to see more students get involved. "A lot of Chicano students don't like to get active in MECHA because they see us as radical. They've heard how we've gone to some protests and rallies in the area, but what they don't know is that all we're trying to do is help the community. Many of the students here are like, 'I'm here in school and if it doesn't help me get a job, then that's that,'" says a MECHA leader. MECHA is also spearheading efforts to get Chicano Studies integrated into the curriculum. "In the spring of '92 we presented a proposal, along with a curriculum, to the academic deans and to the vice president for a Chicano Studies program. We've been meeting with the administration on this, but nothing has been acted on as of yet."

Among some of the other active Chicano/Latino-centered organizations are Latino Unidas Para Soluciones, a women's support group, and Chicanos for Progressive Education, which, according to a student, "goes into area high schools and tries to show Chicano students that it's not enough to be happy with a high school diploma, and that college is a necessity."

A popular spot on campus for Chicano and Latino students is El Centro, located on the third floor of the United University Church on campus. "One of the nice things about the center is that students are always welcome here and they're welcomed not only by administrators but by other students as well. There is a staff of about twenty students that works here as student coordinators or as peer counselors," says a student. The director of the center is Abel Amaya, who is extremely popular with students. "He's not only active in the community here at USC, he's also active in the Chicano community here in Los Angeles."

The main purpose of El Centro, says a student, is student retention. To do this, the center sponsors a reception for parents before the school year begins at which they are introduced to administrators, older students, and the financial aid process and opportunities. During the first week of classes, the center also sponsors the Motivation Institute, a one-day event for incoming students. "That's where we bring all the Chicano student groups to the center so they can talk about their organizations to new students, and we also bring in alumni and present the new students with a calendar of events," says a student. There is also a Chicano/Latino commencement ceremony, and a mentor program that involves area professionals.

The Department for Black Students serves primarily as a support and advocacy group for USC's black students. The department sponsors leadership forums and tutoring for students. "But we're not nearly as active or as involved as El Centro," says a student. "Not nearly enough students have access to the director, Dr. Porter, but many of us do feel comfortable hanging out at the department." The largest black student group is the Black Student Union, which has about 50 active members. The group, which meets weekly, plans workshops and lectures about various topics, including black female/male relationships and the black/Korean conflict. "The BSU also throws dances twice a year—the informal 'let's dance until we sweat' type," says a student.

The Black Student Assembly, an umbrella organization that includes representatives of the school's black groups, has recently sponsored health fairs and the popular Evening of Soul, "which was entirely student produced, directed, and performed. We invited some big-name record producers this year, and one of the performers got approached by a record executive, which was, to say the least, quite impressive." Another active black student group is the Brotherhood of African Men, with about 20 members. Each year, the men of BAM sponsor a comedy night. The filmmaker John Singleton, class of '90, is credited with having revived the African-American Film Association. Singleton also served as the Black Student Union president during his tenure at USC.

Of special interest to anyone interested in African-American culture is the African-American History Museum, located on the edge of campus, which includes three galleries, one for historical documentation and the other two reserved for art. The museum also includes a resource library.

The Asian Pacific American Services Office is an active resource center for students and faculty which provides counseling and coordinates rap sessions. The office's director, Jeff Murakami, "is great. He's always open to students, and he cares as much for students as he does for the office's successes," comments a senior. The office also oversees all of the Asian-American student organizations, among which are the Asian-American Students Assembly, which allocates funds to student groups, and the Asian-American Tutorial Project, which works in the Chinatown and Korea Town communities. The Asian Pacific Service Organization, also active on campus, coordinates a canned food and clothes drive and makes and distributes lunches to the homeless. There are also three sororities and three fraternities for Asian women and men.

According to students, the USC administration, for budgetary reasons, is planning to consolidate the cultural centers, which has caused grumblings among students. "Because of this, we recently formed a coalition between the three major ethnic organizations on campus, called the United Students of Color, whose initials are like the university's. Some students protested the perceived action, and the administration was upset about the protest. We were under the impression that all the programs were going to be done away with. It's all being done so secretly, so we really don't know what's going on. The administrator in charge of most of this swore other administrators to secrecy. The head of our center knows what's going on, but he's not able to discuss it with us at all. We do know that he's not happy with what's going on. And what's amazing is that the administration is doing this without consulting at all with students. It makes us feel so powerless."

For many students, the size of USC, one of the largest private universities in the West, can be a bit intimidating. "The university is huge. Your adviser has probably zillions of advisees, many students don't go to any of the Minority Consortium offices [the umbrella term referring to El Centro, the Department for Black Students, and the Asian Pacific American Services Office] because they feel they're too segregated, and this place is physically sprawling. I think I can speak for the different minority groups here at USC when I say that all this brings up certain philosophical points, because how do you try to bring together a community of people when everyone is so spread out, especially when there are so few of us in the first place?"

Like students at other large Southern California private universities, many USC students come from affluent backgrounds, many from the LA area. "It's not uncommon for students to own BMWs and Mercedes-Benzes, or for me to hear of students going off to the Bahamas for three-day vacations," says a student. The predominantly white fraternities, located on the Row, and sororities are the site of much of this opulence, and students report that these organizations are not well integrated. "That's why we have minority-centered Greek organizations," says a student.

USC's campus is located near downtown Los Angeles, a common nighttime destination for students Thursday through Sunday. Westwood, UCLA turf, is also a popular area for its plethora of shops, restaurants, and people watching. On campus, fraternity parties, the center of much of the school's social life, keep things rocking. Football, however, turns out the fans like an unleashing of the Hoover Dam. In 1990 the Trojans were Rose Bowl champions, and they are always top national contenders.

You won't find any Nobel laureates at USC, but you will find plenty of job connections, as USC grads can be found in the upper echelons of most law firms, corporate offices, and businesses in Southern California. "I'm much stronger for having come here to USC. It's that sink-or-swim mentality. I decided I wasn't going to just swim, but to excel. I love it here because of that, and because I have a great job already lined up when I graduate."

STANFORD UNIVERSITY

Address: Stanford, CA 94305
Phone: (415) 723-2091
Director of Admissions: James Montoya
Multicultural Student Recruiter: na

1992–93 tuition: $16,536
Room and board: $6,314
Application deadline: 12/15
Financial aid application deadline: 2/15

Stanford University students have it all: a beautiful campus, excellent academics and support networks, athletic facilities even an Olympian would drool for, and all that wonderful Bay Area weather.

Stanford also features a diversity that many of the nation's top-flight schools can only envy. According to a 1992 study by *Money* magazine, the 108-year-old university is the country's fourth most racially diverse college campus. The university also has the academic support programs and organizations that, in the words of an undergraduate, "work and are truly here for the students."

One of the university's big successes is its Native American Cultural Center, which works to recruit and retain students, and rivals Dartmouth's and Cornell's as the country's best such program. According to one official, Stanford's program, which recently celebrated twenty years on campus, has an impressive 90 percent retention rate of Native American students.

The center also works with the school's Native American student groups, including the Stanford American Indian Organization (SAIO). The group, with about 50 active graduate and undergraduate members, is focusing much of its efforts on getting the administration to establish a Native American Studies program at Stanford. "We've got everything else but that," says a student. One of SAIO's most ambitious events, however, is its annual powwow, one of the largest on the West Coast. The event draws some 20,000 visitors to campus and includes tribes from as far as Iowa and Canada. The Native American Issues League brings speakers to campus to discuss such topics as American Indian education and environmental concerns. The group works to educate students at area high schools about Native American culture. The American Indian theme house, Muwekma-Ta-Ruk, is located on central campus and includes about 20 residents, about half of whom are Native American.

The university sponsors similar programs for other cultural groups on campus. El Centro Chicano, located in the basement of Old Union, includes office space for each of the school's Chicano and Latino student organizations and provides academic support services. Casa Zapata, a Chicano theme house, includes room for about 90 residents, about half of whom are Chicano or Latino.

MECHA, a cultural and political organization composed mostly of Chicano students, brings speakers to campus and celebrates Cinco de Mayo and the Day of the Dead, both traditional Mexican holidays. One of MECHA's more political tasks has been to organize on behalf of some of the school's custodial staff, called Justice for Janitors. "The university has been paying them about $6.30 an hour, and because of some budget cuts, they want to reduce their pay even more. To protest the cuts in wages we staged a one-day fast, but so far we haven't heard what is to happen to their pay."

Two years ago, students formed the Latino Student Association, "because there wasn't a group on campus that bridged American-born Latinos and international-born Latinos," says a student. "We're not political like MECHA, so we're not going to have rallies like they do. We have speakers who may be political, but we know that each side has a say. Our purpose is to celebrate the diversity of Latin American cultures with movie nights, parties, and dances, and we go to restaurants, sometimes here in the area or in San Jose or San Francisco, that serve almost any kind of ethnic food."

Barrio Assistance, also a Chicano and Latino student group, provides tutoring assistance to area schoolchildren. "Every Saturday a student volunteer works with a student, helping him or her with English or taking the student on field trips. It's very successful and popular with students," says a junior. The Stanford Society of Chicano and Latino Engineers and Scientists, which helps students form study groups and provides tutoring services for members, is the largest multicultural engineering society on campus. Group members participate in intramurals and attend job fairs and national meetings. Noe Lozano, associate dean of engineering and the group's adviser, is popular with members.

The Black Community Services Center, affectionately referred to by students as the Black House, "caters to the needs of black students," says a student. "It puts on programs and gives support to undergrads and grads, academically and socially. The Black Student Union sponsors Kwanzaa, a soul-food dinner, and a variety of events for Black History Month."

The Asian-American Activities Center, established in 1978, helps to create a "home away from home" environment by making available meeting spaces for student organizations and by providing resources through advising and community service opportunities.

The Asian-American Student Association (AASA), with nearly 200 active members, sponsors community activities, an all-campus semiformal dance, and a talent show. The group is also working to get an Asian-American Studies program established on campus. "We find it amazing at a school where nearly 25 percent of the student population is Asian-American that there is no Asian-American Studies program," says a student leader. "We've met with the administration to try to get more courses into the curriculum and more Asian-American professors."

Stanford's student organizations include more than 40 other Asian and Asian-American groups, the most active of which are the Undergraduate Chinese-American Student Association and the Korean-American Student Association, both social and cultural. More political is the Filipino-American Student Unity. "They're less social and growing a lot. They try to work with admissions to get more Filipinos into Stanford because they definitely feel underrepresented here. They also wrote a letter recently denouncing the Rodney King verdict that was read at a general meeting.

That's something the Undergraduate Chinese-American Student Association would never do, since we were founded for just social purposes." Two years ago about 15 Asian-American men formed the school's first Asian-American fraternity, Lambda Phi Epsilon, which today has about 30 members.

Don't be too quick to pigeonhole certain students in any of the abovementioned organizations. Two years ago, a small group of students formed Hapa, the Half-Asian People's Association, while another group formed Spectrum, for students of Korean and African heritage. Both groups made the national news when *The New York Times* reported on their formation.

Recently, student leaders formed the People's Platform, which includes representatives of MECHA, SAIO, the Black Student Union, and AASA. "The group was formed six years ago so that students of color on campus could have more of a say in how the campus is run," says a student. "Each of the four largest cultural student groups would run a candidate as part of the election slate, and for the first five years we had tremendous success. Each year our slate won. Last year was our first time to lose, and we lost to Students First, an all-white group that was formed in direct opposition to the People's Platform. Their attitude was that for the last five years the People's Platform had done nothing for white students, so they ran a slate." Stanford's student senate does include multicultural students. "The People's Platform didn't get a slate in the senate, but the platform does endorse individual candidates who are in the senate," says a student.

While Stanford's cultural organizations have formed a primarily political coalition, students say that some Caucasian students see such coalition building and the work of individual cultural groups as separatist. "Many of the students of color that come to Stanford wish to be active not only in the mainstream campus community but also within their own community. This is not understood by most white students, and the assumption is made that if you work with the black community you do not associate with other areas of Stanford."

Stanford's cultural theme houses have been a source of controversy. Says a student: "Stanford has four ethnic theme houses, and each house is required to be 50 percent not of the ethnicity of its theme. Many students at Stanford think that the theme houses are 100 percent the ethnicity of the respective group. They view them as separatist. Some have never been to a program in one of the houses or ever considered living in one of the houses. Debate over them has been ongoing. Many students still do not understand their purposes."

In addition to a plethora of student activity and support provided by the centers, Stanford students are afforded some of the best academics in the country. The university's strengths, as you might imagine with Silicon Valley located not too far from campus, are in the more technical and pre-professional fields, such as engineering (especially mechanical) and business. Students also rate highly the school's English, economics, philosophy, and political science departments.

To graduate, Stanford students must satisfy distribution requirements as well as a first-year sequence of courses called Cultures, Ideas, and Values (CIV). The sequence, which includes nine courses, introduces students to the history, literature, philosophy, and religions of European and non-Western cultures. Stanford was one of the first major universities to include a cultural diversity course in its core curriculum, which irked many conservatives, including William Bennett, the Secretary of Education in the Reagan administration. "At first students don't like having to take the courses, mostly because they don't want to be made to do anything. But once they take the courses, they're always glad they did and know they probably wouldn't get introduced to these topics elsewhere." But another student sees things differently. "Recently there's been a sort of backlash against the CIV courses. There was an article in the campus newspaper that talked about how the only reason the university integrated its requirements was because it gave in to student of color pressure. They think it gives the university a weaker image if it just bows to any sort of pressure from a group. But I do have to admit, some of the CIV courses are some of the worst courses I've ever taken here. They were absolutely boring courses. The Europe and the Americas sequence is supposed to be the best, and you read various multicultural perspectives of writers. But my track was philosophy and we read Aristotle and Plato and others, which was fine, but it was never integrated until the end of the course, after the final, when the professor gave us a piece of an essay written by Du Bois." She adds: "This is all discouraging because we feel the campus needs such requirements, but they don't have all that good of a reputation."

While the CIV requirement gets mixed reviews, students say the school's African-American Studies program is strong. "Many of the program's professors are lauded as the profs to take before you leave Stanford, not only by black students but by all students at Stanford. They are the tops in their respective fields, which range from English and law to Spanish and Portuguese," says a senior.

With all of the demands of classes, it's fortunate that students have the resources of the academic and cultural centers, as students say interaction with faculty could be better. "I went to one of the smaller Ivy League schools before I came here, and there professors were really into teaching at the undergraduate level. But here, the professors are too much into their own research and have little time for students," says a student.

However, the academic pressure doesn't seem to be as intense here as it is at other highly selective institutions. There are many alternatives to studying. "I love it here," says a student, echoing a sentiment expressed by other students. "I'm not just in my room the whole time. In fact, I hardly ever study. I'm in all sorts of activities, which makes the days go by so quickly." Says another student, "Sometimes it's difficult to remember why we're here."

Golfing, skiing, and jogging are popular, and while Stanford can't be described as a jock school, Stanford students won 11 medals in the 1988 Summer Olympics and school teams have brought home more national wins than any other school in the nation.

Like all great institutions, however, Stanford certainly isn't without its blemishes. The university had been under investigation by the federal government for misuses of federal funding that was meant to go for research. As an article in *The Chronicle of Higher Education* noted, the controversy, which led to the resignation of Stanford's president, Donald Kennedy, has affected alumni support, faculty morale, and students. "It's hard to believe the university is seeing the need to cut janitors' wages when it has been spending money on yachts at the same time," says a student activist. Another student says, "The controversy was a slap in the face to the minority students here at Stanford, especially when financial aid is being cut. But people didn't blame Kennedy. It was just the bureaucracy here. In fact, students are sad to see Kennedy go because he was interested in the students."

Students are concerned with the direction of the university after Kennedy's departure. "The new president is the former provost at the University of Chicago, a truly conservative institution where minority issues aren't exactly on the front burner. Gerhard Casper has already said he is going to review the university's need-blind admissions policy [in which an applicant's ability to pay is not taken into an admissions decision] to see if we actually need to keep it. If this is revoked, then it will definitely make it difficult for many minority students to attend here. I know I couldn't have afforded Stanford, and I still really can't." Recently the university named political science professor Condoleeza Rice to become provost, making her the first African-American in Stanford's history to have that position, which is the second-ranking post behind the president.

Stanford is one of the country's top universities, and with good reason. Students like the activities the school has to offer, as well as some of the nation's best academic programs, all offered in a relatively laid-back atmosphere. But one student adds that the most satisfied Stanford consumer is one who knows how to strike a balance and who seeks involvement in campus activities and clubs. "I would recommend Stanford to almost any applicant, but I would remind them that it is a predominantly white campus," says a student. "Because Stanford the institution has made a liberal move and placed multiculturalism as a priority for the next few years does not mean that the student population has. Once you get to Stanford, you are responsible for making it, no one else will assume that for you."

C O L O R A D O

UNIVERSITY OF COLORADO

Address: Regent Administrative Center,
  Boulder, CO 80309
Phone: (303) 492-6301
Director of Admissions: Bill Hathaway-Clark
Multicultural Student Recruiter: Ray
  Archibeque
1991–92 tuition: $2,400 (in-state); $10,330
  (out-of-state)
Room and board: $3,540
Application deadline: 2/15
Financial aid application deadline: 4/15
Non-white freshman admissions: Applicants
  for the class of '95: 1,912
  Accepted: 90%
  Accepted who enroll: 36%
  Applicants accepted who rank in top
  10% of high school class: na
  Median SAT: na
  Median ACT: na
Full-time undergraduate enrollment: 20,495
  Men: 54%
  Women: 46%
Non-white students in
  1990–91: 11.41%
Geographic distribution of students: na
Top majors: na
Retention rate of non-white students: na
**Scholarships exclusively for non-white
  students:** Arnold Opportunity
  Scholarship: approximately 40 awarded
  each year; each valued at about $1,000
  for Colorado residents and $2,000 for
  non-residents; merit-based. Hispanic
  Alumni Scholarship: number and value

of each award vary each year; merit- and
need-based. White Antelope Memorial
Scholarship: awarded to first-year
students who are Native American;
number of awards and amounts vary
each year from $50 to $5,000.
Remediation programs: None
Academic support services: The Learning
  Center offers academic tutoring, time
  management seminars, and study skills
  workshops. Minority Engineering
  Program aids underrepresented minority
  students pursuing engineering degrees.
Ethnic studies programs: The university
  offers programs of study in
  Afro-American, American Indian,
  Asian-American, and Chicano Studies.

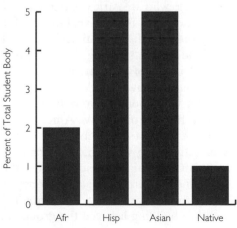

STUDENT ENROLLMENT

Organizations for non-white students: Asian Pacific American Coalition, Black Student Alliance, Cambodian Student Organization, Ethnic Women's Alliance, Korean Students Association, Hinou Association, Hmong Student Association, MECHA, Oyate Indian Club, United Mexican-American Students, Vietnamese Students at Boulder

Notable non-white alumni: na
Tenured faculty: na
Non-tenured faculty: na
Student-faculty ratio: 17:1
Administrators: na
Recent non-white speakers on campus: na

Set one foot on the University of Colorado's campus and you're sold on the place. Situated at the foot of the Rockies, CU's 600-acre campus is one of the most spectacular you'll find anywhere. And besides a great view, the university offers one of the best big-school educations in the region.

CU is divided into eight undergraduate colleges and schools: business administration, education, music, environmental design, engineering, journalism and mass communication, pharmacy, and arts and sciences. Psychology is one of CU's best-known departments, while the university's science departments, such as engineering and biology, also enjoy national reputations, as does the school's program in molecular biology. Also considered strong are business administration, history, and chemistry, whose faculty includes Thomas Cech, who won the 1989 Nobel Prize in chemistry. To graduate, students must now satisfy a gender or cultural diversity course requirement.

"Black Psychology" and "Chicano Women/Women of Color" are two of the school's more popular ethnic studies courses. Elisa Facio, a sociology professor who teaches the "Chicano Women" course, is a mentor to many of her students. "She's almost like a sister to many of us who seek her out," comments a student. Manning Marable, a prominent historian and political scientist, is also a faculty member. All of the school's ethnic studies courses come under the aegis of the Center for Studies of Ethnicity and Race, whose director is Evelyn Hu-Dehart. "She's one of the most truly multicultural persons on this campus. She knows four languages, is Asian, and did graduate work in Latin American Studies," says a recent graduate.

The Multicultural Center, located in Willard Hall, provides peer and staff counselors who are African-American, Native American, Chicano, and Asian-American. "The center is effective, but only for those students who know about its services. The problem is that the university doesn't advertise the center's programs very much."

In addition to studying, members of CU's cultural student organizations recently focused much of their attention on the events marking the 500th anniversary of Columbus' discovery of America. "All of the university's minority organizations are stronger than ever and we're fired up about the quincentenary," says a student. "In the fall, the school's Native American student group held a daylong rally, with guest speakers, against the celebration. UMAS [United Mexican-American Students] has been networking with Chicano organizations in Denver and Boulder, and members went to California's Mexican border during the height of the celebration to protest. All of the organizations saved money from fundraisers so they wouldn't be passive during the quincentenary. We weren't stagnant, that's for sure. In fact, I saw more coalition building between the groups than in all of my other years here."

While the groups have enjoyed recent strength through coalition building, each group is relatively weak on campus, with little influence over campus politics and events. With about 40 active members, the Black Student Alliance, for example, is in the process of reorganizing. "In the past, the group focused on the social and on having a good time. Now we want to become more politically active and culturally aware. One of the things we worked on recently was getting the university to diversify the history requirement of the school's core curriculum, which only included courses on European history. But mostly the BSA is planning to work on creating a more unified organization, and we plan to work more closely with other cultural organizations so we can all have our voices heard." The group, under the leadership of all new officers, is planning to create a mentor program that involves matching African-American professors and staff with students, as well as upperclass students with underclassmen.

The United Mexican American Students' main event is its annual Cinco de Mayo celebration, which, in a recent year, "focused on Chicano pride," according to a UMAS member. MECHA, a Chicano student group with a more political focus, was established four years ago as a result of infighting among UMAS members. "Now," says a student, "the groups get along completely and there's no conflict. In fact, some students are members of both organizations. But MECHA isn't very active and doesn't have many members. It never really got off the ground." In 1991, UMAS attempted—unsuccessfully—to halt the renaming of the school's Event Center as the Coors Event Center. "We believe the Coors company has been unfair to minorities in their hiring practices, and the way they've dealt with unions, so we didn't think the company should be honored," says a UMAS member.

To assist with additional cultural programming, CU's Third World Center, located in the University Memorial Center, provides space for cultural events and group meetings. The center's director, Valerie Embry, works closely with various student groups to provide cultural programming. UMAS holds its meetings in the center.

The Young Democrats Club is definitely the political club of choice at this mostly liberal campus. But issues of multiculturalism take a back seat with most CU students, according to BSA and UMAS members, as environmental and gay and lesbian issues are much more in the foreground. "If we don't include something in our events that have to do with the environment, or about the school's tuition increases, we get very little support from the white students here," says a BSA member. Adds another student: "Many of the white students here are very into the granola, sixties thing. Many of the more liberal students here are also among some of the school's richest. It gets to be sort of hypocritical after a while, but at least they're trying."

CU has been nicknamed Ski U, but the university promises more than just a day on the slopes. The university also provides a wide variety of extracurricular activities that appeal even to the non-outdoorsman, such as regular movies and concerts, thanks to the Program Council, one of the country's most active such councils. A walk along the Pearl Street Mall, with its numerous outdoor performers, is also a popular activity. Boulder is an ideal place for the lover of the outdoors, as opportunities for camping, skiing, and hiking abound nearby. Jogging and plain old walking are also favorite activities of this physically conscious student body, and the school's newly built gym facility gets frequent student use.

The University of Colorado may not provide a wealth of opportunity when it comes to multicultural awareness, but it does provide top-notch educational opportunities in a bucolic setting. "When I first came here, the multicultural student groups weren't very strong, but we're becoming stronger each year," says a senior. "I've become more confident since becoming a member of these groups—helping to program events and such—and I'm not sure I would have gotten to do these things if I'd gone to another school. I'm also confident that with a degree from here I will be more marketable when it comes time to enter the job market."

COLORADO COLLEGE

Address: 14 East Cache la Poudre, Colorado Springs, CO 80903
Phone: (719) 389-6344 / (800) 542-7214
Director of Admissions: Terrance K. Swenson
Multicultural Student Recruiter: Roberto A. Garcia
1991–92 tuition: $13,665
Room and board: $3,645
Application deadline: 2/1
Financial aid application deadline: 2/15
Non-white freshman admissions: Applicants for the class of '95: 309
Accepted: 61%
Accepted who enroll: 36%
Applicants accepted who rank in top 10% of high school class: na
Median SAT: na
Median ACT: na
Full-time undergraduate enrollment: 1,917
Men: 48%
Women: 52%
Non-white students in
1987–88: 8.32%
1988–89: 10.6%
1989–90: 10.6%
1990–91: 11.7%
Geographic distribution of students: na
Top majors: na
Retention rate of non-white students: na
Scholarships exclusively for non-white students: Faculty Minority Education Scholarship: need-based, $1,000–$1,500; renewable; two to four awarded each year. El Pomar Foundation Scholarship:

awarded to minority students; number and amounts vary each year.
Remediation programs: none
Academic support services: Peer tutoring is provided in various subjects, as well as assistance through the Writing Center.
Ethnic studies programs: Students are able to design their own major in East Asian languages, which includes Japanese and Chinese.
Ethnic studies courses: The English department includes four courses in African-American Literature, and the history department includes two courses in African History, six in Asian History, and four in Latin American History. The Political Science department offers

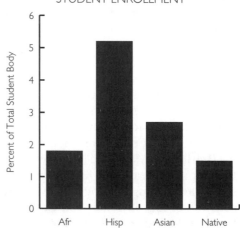

STUDENT ENROLLMENT

courses in Latin American and African Studies.

Organizations for non-white students: Black Student Union, MECHA, Native American Student Association, Association of Students Interested in Asia (ASIA)

Notable non-white alumni: na

Tenured faculty: 152

Non-tenured faculty: 108

Student-faculty ratio: 13:1

Administrators: 106

African-American: 1.9%

Hispanic: 2.8%

Asian-American: 1.9%

Native American: 0

Recent non-white speakers on campus: Sandra Cisneros (poet and short story writer); Gloria Anzaldua (Chicana lesbian/feminist poet); Evelyn Hu-Dehart (director of the Center for Studies of Ethnicity); Roce W. America (CSERA); Dinesh D'Souza (author); Gus Lee (writer); Henry Louis Gates, Jr. (professor, Harvard University); N. Scott Momaday (author and critic); Richard Boderquez (writer); Ntozake Shange (poet and playwright)

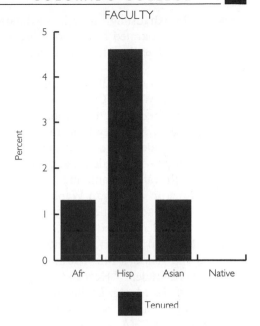

FACULTY

Tenured

Colorado College is regarded as one of the best liberal arts schools in the Rocky Mountain region and attracts students from all fifty states, not because of its almost idyllic location—majestic mountains and pristine air are part of this college's setting—but because of its unique academic schedule.

Called the Block Plan, this schedule divides the school year into eight three-and-a-half-week segments called blocks. Students take one course during each block, and each class has only about 15 to 25 students, which makes for close interaction with faculty. The classes meet usually in the morning for a couple of hours. Then students either pursue further research or continue class in discussion groups.

The Block Plan wins fans and allows for a great many off-campus opportunities. Geology and field biology classes, for example, go on expeditions to other parts of the area or country, and anthropology, archaeology, and Southwest Studies courses don't stay on campus at all. They meet at the college's Baca campus in southern Colorado and take day trips to dig sites or nearby Native American communities. Trips abroad are also common. The block also allows students to pursue a single course of study, in depth, without the distractions of having to attend to other courses that would be part of the standard semester schedule at most schools.

The plan does have its drawbacks. Although some courses meet for two blocks in a row, most don't, which can be frustrating for science and foreign-language students, who will lack continuity in their learning. In addition, students complain of burnout at the end of the four weeks. Studying a single subject every day of the week for four weeks can be exhausting—as well as exhilarating—according to students. Fortunately, each block is separated by four-day breaks, in which students use the time for some much-needed R & R, either on the ski slopes, on camping trips, or by simply staying put on campus.

In addition to unusually close interaction with their faculty, students have access to an effective Writing Center for academic support, which is fortunate, as much writing is required of students during the course of the school year.

The Office of Minority Student Life, located in Worner Center, "is a safe place for minority students to express themselves, their needs, problems, and complaints," but does not provide academic support. Established in 1990, the office assists student groups in cultural programming. Students have praise for the office's staff, Rochelle Mason, director, and Ryan Webb, assistant director. "They're the greatest people," says a student leader. "They're amazingly effective and hardworking." The office also publishes a student-edited paper called *Fight the Power*.

For additional support, students turn to Bruce Coriell, the school chaplain. "He supports the school's full divestment from South Africa, which the school hasn't done," says a student. "He's also a supporter of Black History Month and is a major organizer of the Martin Luther King, Jr., Day celebration."

The school's student organizations also sponsor a variety of cultural programming on campus. MECHA, a Chicano student organization, is one of CC's more active groups. Each year it "has a symposium, and it sponsors small parties and works hard to boost campus awareness of Hispanic culture," says a student. MECHA also sponsors Salsa Nights, evenings of dance and music. NASA, the Native American Student Association, sponsors various speakers and musicians in addition to a powwow in the spring. Recently, NASA brought a spirit healer to campus. The Black Student Union (BSU) focuses much of its energies on Black History Month activities, including speakers. Members of the BSU meet weekly, and, with the members of Kappa Sigma fraternity, sponsor Soul Night every Thursday, which includes refreshments and music. BSU also sponsors picnics and a mentor program where first-year students are paired with upperclass students.

Students would like to see the cultural events draw a more diverse crowd, however. "Usually when we're attracting people to our events, the same people come—ourselves and a small number of the same non-white students," says a student, adding, "Dining, parties, campus functions always look the same to me. If ethnic minorities are present, most likely they'll all be together."

An exception, however, is CC's Rainbow Jam, an outdoor food and music festival hosted by the school's cultural student groups that brings out almost the entire campus community. "This party is awesome and a huge amount of the campus showed up for it this year," reports a student organizer. "Traditional foods are set up at each group's table for any and all to sample. Traditional dances are performed in between the boogying down."

The college recently sponsored a multicultural theme house, called La Casa Raza. "It has been successful in providing a comfortable and familiar place for students to live," observes a student. In the dorms, students say integration is a "problem," however, "not because no one wants us, but because there aren't enough of us to go around. One non-white student on a wing in a dorm may be considered integrated, but I think the administration makes every effort to make sure that there is more diversity than that on all of the dorm floors."

The school's social life runs from the out-of-doors to fraternity parties, with emphasis on the out-of-doors, and, as one student says, "CC is a very busy place, not just limited to special interest groups." Skiing, bicycling, and camping are favorite outdoor activities of CC students, who tend to be on the more liberal side of the political spectrum. Clubs such as Colorado College Students for Environmental Action, the Feminist Collective, and Amnesty International are active on campus. Students also help operate KRCC-FM, a national public radio station located across the street from campus. Intramural sports, particularly ice hockey, softball, and basketball, are popular, and CC's women's varsity soccer team is consistently high-ranked in Division I play.

Colorado Springs, the home to CC and the U.S. Air Force Academy, provides various cultural and nightlife activities, but students say town-gown relations are strained. "Our school has a bad reputation in the community as a snooty school for rich, white, conceited, spoiled kids," says a student. "Unfortunately, CC students have a pretty ugly impression of the townies too." Adds the student: "There are small sections of the city where African-Americans and Hispanics live, but I rarely see them. The area is mostly white, lower-income families and there have been numerous racist statements shouted at minority students from townies."

Colorado College "is a place where your opinions will be heard and where you are responsible for making them heard, where independence and hard work are all challenged," says a student. "The Block Plan is here, so are special-interest groups as well as many other organizations. Resources and helpful people galore. Find out what you want and there will always be someone who cares to help."

COLORADO SCHOOL OF MINES

Address: Weaver Towers, 1811 Elm Street,
  Golden, CO 80401-1873
Phone: (303) 273-3220 / (800) 245-1060
  (in-state) / (800) 446-9488 (out-of-state)
Director of Admissions: Bill Young
Multicultural Student Recruiter: na
1992–93 tuition: $3,718 (in-state); $11,360
  (out-of-state)
Room and board: $4,100
Application deadline: 8/1
Financial aid application deadline: 3/1
Non-white freshman admissions: Applicants
  for the class of '97: 428
  Accepted: 82%
  Accepted who enroll: 45%
  Applicants accepted who rank in top
  10% of high school class: 40%
  In the top 25%: 90%
  Median SAT range: 470–600 V, 570–690 M
  Median ACT range: 24–28

STUDENT ENROLLMENT

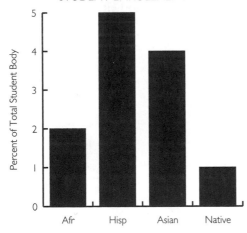

Full-time undergraduate enrollment: 2,100
  Men: 80%
  Women: 20%
Non-white students in
  1988–89: 10%

1989–90: 11%
1990–91: 12%
1991–92: 12%

GEOGRAPHIC DISTRIBUTION OF STUDENTS

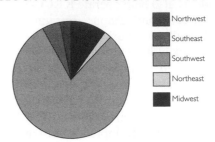

- Northwest
- Southeast
- Southwest
- Northeast
- Midwest

Students In-state: na
Top majors: 1. Engineering 2. Chemical
  Engineering 3. Petroleum Engineering
Retention rate of non-white students: 85%
**Scholarships exclusively for non-white
  students:** Scholarships for
  African-American and Native American
  Students: merit-based; full tuition;
  renewable.
Remediation programs: None
Academic support services: The college
  offers preparatory courses in chemistry
  and math.
Ethnic studies programs: None
Ethnic studies courses: None
Organizations for non-white students:
  American Indian Science and
  Engineering Society, Asian Student
  Association, National Society of Black
  Engineers, Society of Hispanic
  Professional Engineers
Notable non-white alumni: na
Tenured faculty: na
Non-tenured faculty: na
Student-faculty ratio: 13:1
Administrators: na
Recent non-white speakers on campus: na

Here's a paragraph pulled from the Colorado School of Mines' course catalogue: "The geophysical concentration is an interdisciplinary program between the Geophysics and Mathematical and Computer Sciences Departments. It is well suited for students interested in geophysical data analysis."

If you're the type of student who can appreciate what was just said, and are interested in this sort of study, then you would do well to consider attending 119-year-old Colorado School of Mines, a top-flight engineering school that has the respect and attention of many corporations and other employers. As CSM is a state-supported institution, a CSM education can also be had at a reasonable price, especially for Colorado residents.

All CSM students major in some sort of engineering program, many of which rank among the best in the country, including metallurgical and materials science, chemical engineering, petroleum refining, and mining engineering. Programs in math and computer science and geophysical engineering are also strong.

All first-year students follow the same course schedule, which includes chemistry, calculus, economics, and physical education, as well as a humanities course. Students must also complete a four-semester requirement titled EPICS, an acronym for Engineers Practical Introductory Course Sequence, which seeks to prepare students for more sophisticated engineering study. As part of EPICS, students work in groups of four or five to solve real-life problems provided by government agencies, such as the Department of Energy and county planning commissions. At the end of the program, students make a final presentation to the client. As part of EPICS, students also take courses in computing and graphics.

The academics at CSM are, to say the least, rigorous. But students say professors are accessible and are always willing to lend a hand with studies. Also an effective source of academic support is the Minority Engineering Program, established in 1989, which offers a variety of tutoring and support services for students. The coordinator of the program, Donald Velasquez, is a great supporter of students: "He takes care of so much, from recruiting students and going to meetings on our behalf with the administration, to attending all sorts of functions and ceremonies. He's accessible and easy to talk to about almost anything."

The program office includes a lounge area with computers and couches and a study room "where we can study and relax," says a student. The office is well used by students who live on and off campus, as the office includes locker space for commuters. Students complain, though, that because the office gets so much use it is outgrowing its space.

Support of CSM minority students doesn't stop at the Minority Engineering Program office, however. Students report that members of the administration are especially helpful and supportive of non-white student organizations. "The people in the administration are excited and happy to have the minority student organizations on campus, and these people provide us with a lot of help. There's Mary Vigil, in the admissions office and adviser to the NSBE (National Society of Black Engineers), who comes to many of our meetings and helps us to get organized and to cope with difficult professors. There's Harold Chevron, dean of students, who is helpful, fair, and supportive of all the students' endeavors. He's the one who encouraged members this year to go to various NSBE conferences. Attending the conferences was a first for us."

While students praise the intelligence of their professors, some say there are still those who don't think minority and female students belong in engineering sciences. "Sometimes professors assume that because you're a female and/or a minority your ticket is written for you for almost any opportunity," says a student. "Those are the white male professors who think that CSM should still be only for white males. But the minority students here are just as competitive as the white students, if not more so, because we have to compensate for this attitude and prove these people wrong."

No doubt due to the school's academic rigors, students say "CSM is definitely not a party school." The biggest event of the year is Engineers' Day, a three-day event held each spring that includes mining contests, softball games, a talent show and concert, and a fireworks display. For additional entertainment, students participate in the activities sponsored by the school's minority engineering societies, which sponsor regular meetings, films, and picnics, as well as professional workshops. "Most of the groups primarily want to serve as academic and emotional support for their members," says a student. Various professional associations, such as the American Association of Petroleum Geologists and the American Society of Civil Engineers, are also active. Fraternities, which are only reasonably integrated and include about 13 percent of the student body, provide much of the school's social life, as does the CSM student government, which brings to campus comedians and other events. Almost any athletic competition, especially football, against state rival Colorado College generates much student enthusiasm.

The town of Golden, Colorado, is conservative and predominantly white, and African-American students have complained of local police harassment. The town also offers little by way of entertainment. Denver, only fifteen miles to the west, is a more popular off-campus destination, as are the parties and cultural activities at the University of Colorado/Boulder. The dating scene at CSM is the blahs, according to a student, "especially with so many more men than women. Mostly, we just stay on campus and study on the weekends. We're certainly more academically minded than students at other schools I've visited, and that's no exaggeration."

The students at CSM, like many engineering students, are goal-oriented. "We definitely don't have any liberal arts majors confused about what they want to do in life," says a student. With high-paying corporations knocking at their doors, CSM students don't mind the rigors and the intensity of a CSM education. "I like it here, but it took a long time for me to feel this way," says a senior. "I've learned here that private industry is going to be very much like this place, but here, as opposed to industry, there are going to be people to support you and who will try to make things as equal as possible."

UNITED STATES AIR FORCE ACADEMY

Address: Colorado Springs, CO 80840
Phone: (719) 472-4219
Director of Admissions: Colonel Robert Y.
  Foerster
Multicultural Student Recruiter: Major Ray
  Barrows
1991–92 tuition: Free
Room and board: Free
Application deadline: 1/31
Financial aid application deadline: na
Non-white freshman admissions: Applicants
  for the class of '95: 1,406
  Accepted: 27%
  Accepted who enroll: 16%
  Applicants accepted who rank in top
  10% of high school class: 76.9%
  In top 25%: 95.5%
  Median SAT: 566 V, 655 M
  Median ACT: 28.5 English, 30.0 Math
Full-time undergraduate enrollment: 4,462
  Men: 88%
  Women: 12%

STUDENT ENROLLMENT

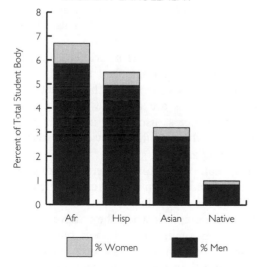

Percent of Total Student Body

Afr   Hisp   Asian   Native

% Women   % Men

Non-white students in
  1987–88: 14%
  1988–89: 14.4%

1989–90: 15.8%
1990–91: 16.4%

GEOGRAPHIC DISTRIBUTION OF STUDENTS

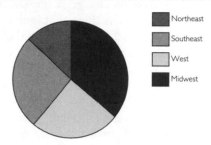

Northeast
Southeast
West
Midwest

Students In-state: na
Top majors: 1. Engineering Management
  2. International Affairs 3. Engineering
  Science
Retention rate of non-white students: 63.3%
**Scholarships exclusively for non-white
  students:** na
Remediation programs: None
Academic support services: Tutoring is
  available in most academic subjects.
Ethnic studies programs: None
Ethnic studies courses: na
Organizations for non-white students: Los
  Padrinos Club, Way of Life Committee
  (multicultural student group)
Notable non-white alumni: Frederick
  Gregory ('64; space shuttle *Challenger*
  pilot); Alonzo Babers ('83; two-time
  Olympic gold medal winner in track);
  Ernie Jennings ('71; first African-
  American All-American football player);
  George Keys ('70; Rhodes Scholar);
  Christopher Howard ('91; Rhodes
  Scholar); Micul Thompson ('91; Rhodes
  Scholar)
Tenured faculty: na
Non-tenured faculty: na
Student-faculty ratio: 8:1
Administrators:
  African-American: 10%
  Hispanic: 5%

Asian-American: 2%
Native American: 0

Recent non-white speakers on campus: na

The United States Air Force Academy is as challenging physically as it is emotionally and academically. The cadet who graduates having met the demands of the academy—and the demands are numerous and rigorous—has what's expected of him or her, say those in charge at the Defense Department, to serve as an officer in the U.S. Air Force. "The thing that ignites the initial spark in people who want to come here is the personal and professional challenge," says Joseph Richardson, one of the first African-Americans to serve as Cadet Wing Commander, a top honor at the academy. "The person who wants to come here must want to be here, to overcome or surpass these challenges, or they'll never make it through the first year, much less four years."

The academics are especially grueling at the academy. Cadets take seven courses a semester, nearly twice the amount of students at "civilian" schools. During a cadet's first and second years at the academy, he or she must satisfy the academy's core requirements, which leave no room for electives and include everything from "General Psychology" and "Modern World History" to "U.S. Defense Establishment" and "Flight Fundamentals." Electives come during a cadet's second class and first class.

Once the cadet has satisfied the core requirements, he or she may elect to choose from one of 24 programs in which to major. The school is famous for its engineering departments, and cadets can study aeronautical engineering, civil engineering, electrical engineering, and engineering mechanics, among other disciplines. Physics and biology are also well respected. The English and history departments are said to be good, but not as popular as most of the more "techie" majors at the academy. The academy's "African-American Literature" course is popular, but, says a student, "it is seldom offered."

Because academics can be especially rigorous, the academy offers various academic support services. The Air Officers Commanding (AOC), upperclass students who oversee squadrons of a hundred or so cadets, serve as support for their cadets, as well as the cadets' trainers and disciplinarians. AOCs are also the primary link between parents and cadets. Squadron faculty officers also offer academic and non-academic support services. The Curriculum and Scheduling Services personnel advise students on course selection and choosing of majors.

The cadet's Honor Code—"We will not lie, steal, or cheat, nor tolerate among us anyone who does"—is strictly enforced at the academy; in severe cases, such as cheating on an exam, dismissal from the academy is a possibility.

Academics are only half of the challenge greeting cadets when they arrive at the academy. All students must participate in a varsity or intramural sport during the four years they are at the academy, and at the end of each semester cadets must pass a fitness examination. The academy sponsors more than nine varsity sports for men and women, including a usually highly ranked football team (Notre Dame is the team's archrival), as well as numerous intramural sports activities, including boxing, rugby, and table tennis.

The academy also sponsors several extracurricular activities, including special-interest, religious, and musical groups. The two cultural student organizations on campus—the Los Padrinos Club, a Hispanic student group, and Way of Life Committee (WLC), an African-American student group—serve primarily social functions at the academy, according to members. "The WLC is involved in the local community," says a student. "We participate in Project A-OK, a mentorship program with high school kids, mainly minority kids, kind of like a big brother/big sister program." Says another WLC member: "WLC provides a sense of belonging for us. We help each other academically by setting up reviews before tests." WLC's adviser, Lt. Ronnie Hawkins, "always provides insights and encouragement for cadets," says a student.

Cadets say the academy is relatively free of the racial tension that sometimes can plague other campuses. "Race is not a big issue at the USAFA," reports a cadet. "We all try to think in terms of blue [the color of cadet uniforms], not black and white." Recently, however, an African-American cadet alleged racism when he was kicked out of the academy "for military deficiency," according to a cadet. In response, the commandant of the academy convened a special meeting with many of the African-American cadets on campus to discuss the discharged cadet's allegations. According to a student, "the panel found no significant racist attitudes existed in the administration or in the student body." Some of these cadets claim, in fact, that the system at the academy forces people to take into consideration aspects of cadets other than skin color. "The military is the closest thing to a meritocracy America has at this time," says an American politics major.

However, segregation along racial lines does occur socially, according to students. "As far as on-campus incidents go, racial relations are better than in the civilian world, simply because people tend to realize that racism cannot interfere with the military," observes a student. "But it is quite obvious that the minorities hang together just as much as the non-minorities do."

Despite the rules and regulations, cadets do manage to have a good time, first- and second-class cadets more than the "doolies." Older students are able to leave campus more frequently, and will head into Denver or Colorado Springs, easily accessible by car, for movies and dinner, or into the hills for some excellent skiing. On-campus socializing happens most often at Arnold Hall, the student center, where cadets can find a snack bar, a theater, and a disco.

For the student looking for access to multicultural student organizations and programs, the USAFA might not be for you. The school has relatively little of both. But for the student who wants top-flight academics and leadership training combined with a system that, in the words of a cadet, "emphasizes strength of character over skin color," then you might want to give the USAFA a close look. Adds a fourth-class cadet: "The academy provides an equal opportunity for each person to excel. Racial discrimination is not tolerated among the staff or the student body. The common good is to help each other through the curriculum of one of the most challenging undergraduate colleges in the nation."

CONNECTICUT

UNIVERSITY OF CONNECTICUT

Address: Storrs, CT 06269
Phone: (203) 486-3137
Director of Admissions: Dr. Ann L.
Huckenbeck
Multicultural Student Recruiter: Aida Silva
1993–94 tuition: $3,476 (in-state); $10,596
(out-of-state)
Room and board: $4,878
Application deadline: 4/1
Financial aid application deadline: 2/15
Non-white freshman admissions: Applicants
for the class of '96: 1,309
Accepted: 64%
Accepted who enroll: 33%
Applicants accepted who rank in top
10% of high school class: 29%
In top 25%: 69%
Median SAT: 452 V, 525 M
Median ACT: na
Full-time undergraduate enrollment: 14,167
Men: 49%
Women: 51%
Non-white students in
1987–88: 8.6%
1988–89: 9.3%
1989–90: 9.7%
1990–91: 10.3%
Geographic distribution of students: na
Top majors: 1. Biological Science
2. Psychology 3. Political Science
Retention rate of non-white students: 83.5%
**Scholarships exclusively for non-white
students:** Day of Pride Scholarships:
merit-based; covers tuition and room and

board; 15 awarded each year. In 1990,
$300,000 was allotted to the Admissions
Office for minority scholarships. The
awards ranged from $1,500 to $5,000.
Remediation programs: None
Academic support services: The Center for
Academic Programs, the Minority
Engineering Program, the Writing
Resource Center, the Reading Language
Arts Center, the Math Center, and the
Counseling Program for Intercollegiate
Athletes
Ethnic studies programs: The university
offers a Latin American Studies major,

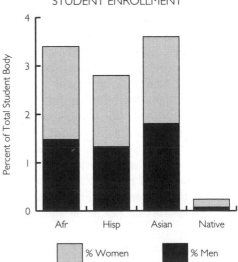

STUDENT ENROLLMENT

an interdisciplinary program, involving anthropology, history, political science, Latin American Studies, and Spanish.

Ethnic studies courses: The university offers about four courses in African-American Studies, involving history, English, and family studies. Other courses offered, such as "Ethnicity and Race," focus on racial and ethnic issues in America.

Organizations for non-white students: Minority Business Club, National Association of Black Accountants, National Society of Black Engineers, H. Fred Simons African-American Cultural Center, Puerto Rican and Latin American Cultural Center, Alpha Kappa Alpha, Kappa Alpha Psi, Omega Psi Phi, Phi Beta Sigma, Alpha Phi Alpha, Delta Sigma Theta, Black Students Association

Notable non-white alumni: Franklin Chang-Diaz (Engineering; astronaut); Eileen Baccus (president, Thames Valley Technical College); Les Payne (columnist, *New York Newsday*); Barbara Holmes (president, Milwaukee Area Technical College); James Lyons (president, Bowie State University)

Tenured faculty: 855
Non-tenured faculty: 318
Student-faculty ratio: na
Administrators: 1,062
African-American: 7.3%
Hispanic: 2%

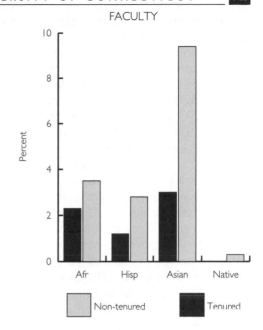

FACULTY

Non-tenured
Tenured

Asian-American: 2.9%
Native American: 0.1%
Recent non-white speakers on campus: William Julius Wilson (professor, University of Chicago); Dr. Jawanza Kunjufu (president, African-American Images); Maya Angelou (author and poet); Roy Brooks (professor, University of Minnesota); Thirman Milner (former mayor of Hartford, CT); Spike Lee (filmmaker)

Founded originally as the state's land-grant institution, the University of Connecticut today offers more than 100 majors in eleven different schools and colleges. UConn's relatively low price tag and solid academics haven't gone unnoticed; the university was ranked recently as one of the 100 best college buys by the editors at *Money* magazine.

UConn's strengths are in pre-professional studies, including business, pharmacy, physical therapy, economics, and accounting. Agriculture remains top-notch. The sciences are also strong, as are the school's engineering and psychology programs. Among the school's African-American and African Studies courses, students say "African-American Writers," taught by noted poet Marilyn Waniek, and "Precolonial Africa" are excellent.

The university offers a variety of academic support programs. The Minority Engineering Program (MEP), which includes a six-week Summer Bridge program on campus before classes start, offers services that include tutoring, advising, faculty mentoring, and internship and scholarship information. The Center for Academic Programs (CAP), which also starts with a six-week summer academic program on UConn's campus, provides tutoring and academic advising and counseling. Although UConn is a large university, students say professors are reasonably accessible, while their teaching assistants are even more so.

The H. Fred Simons African-American Cultural Center helps coordinate events and activities. "The center has sponsored a lot of recent programs," says a student. "We have forums, brown-bag lunches where we discuss issues facing the African-American community." During the 1992–93 school year, the center sponsored a year of discussions and activities for its Year of the Black Male program. During the previous school year, the center sponsored events for the Year of the Black Female, as part of the university's efforts to celebrate 100 years of women at UConn. During the Year of the Black Female, the center brought to campus the Queens Historical Society, an Atlanta-based organization that raises students' awareness about famous African queens. In the fall of 1993, a new director, Patricia Murdoch, will be appointed to the center. The selection of the new director was the result of a search that involved a student committee. "We interviewed her, and we're hopeful that she'll be a positive force for the center." Kent Butler, who was acting head of the center, will remain at the center.

UConn's historically black fraternities and sororities "are always sponsoring something in the center, usually dances," says a Greek. "The dances are always packed and include a DJ." The Greek organizations are also active in the community. "The Deltas [Delta Sigma Thetas] sponsored a storytelling program at a nearby hospital for mentally disturbed children, and we participated in a walk against leukemia. With the men of Omega Psi Phi, the Deltas also sponsored a forum discussion about black-on-black crime."

Other than the activities of the center and the Greek organizations, there is little cultural activity that focuses on or is sponsored by African-American organizations, largely because the school's Black Student Association recently disbanded. "There were a lot of power struggles between some of the members, so things just kind of fell apart. Now people are trying to build it up again. There's a big campaign now to try to get everyone involved."

The school's student association, the Student Union Board of Government (SUBOG), has recently started to diversify campus programming. As part of the school's Spring Weekend festivities, when the campus turns upside down with parties, SUBOG brought to campus such varied acts as the Indigo Girls, Leaders of the New School, and Spin Doctors. The Puerto Rican and Latin American Cultural Center hosts events for Hispanic Awareness Month, dances, concerts, and a variety of other activities.

Just because UConn is a large university, don't be too quick to assume that there's endless nightlife activity lined up for you just off campus. The city slicker may find Storrs a bit too isolated, but there are those students who find the quiet conducive to study. Storrs does offer a couple of bars, but the legal drinking age of twenty-one is strictly enforced. Most social life occurs on campus, but students will also travel the two hours to New York City or Boston. Hartford, the state capital, is also only a half-hour drive away. Until recently, UConn was justifiably known as a suitcase school—students tended to head for home most weekends—but the image is changing as the university constructs more dorms and provides more weekend meal plans.

What the University of Connecticut lacks in diversity of student population and cultural programming, it makes up for in academics—and, especially for an in-stater during these recessionary times, cost of tuition. Students find that with such a small multicultural enrollment there can be those isolating moments, but, as one student says, "when you come to UConn, come and get involved. That's what I did, and it's made me a stronger person."

CONNECTICUT COLLEGE

Address: 270 Mohegan Avenue, New London, CT 06320
Phone: (203) 439-2200
Director of Admissions: William H. Peck
Multicultural Student Recruiter: M. Ronnie Bernier
1993–94 tuition: $17,390
Room and board: $6,030
Application deadline: 1/15
Financial aid application deadline: 2/15

Non-white freshman admissions: Applicants for the class of '96: na
  Accepted: na
  Accepted who enroll: na
  Applicants accepted who rank in the top 10% of high school class: na
  Median SAT range: na
  Median ACT: na
Full-time undergraduate enrollment: 1,619
  Men: 49%
  Women: 51%
Non-white students in
  1988–89: 9%
  1989–90: 10%
  1990–91: 9.9%
  1991–92: 11%
Geographic distribution of students: na
Top majors: 1. Sociology
  2. Government/International Relations
  3. History
Retention rate of non-white students: 91%
Scholarships exclusively for non-white students: None

Remediation programs: None
Academic support services: The college offers tutoring in most academic subjects.
Ethnic studies programs: The college offers an interdisciplinary major in Hispanic Studies, which includes more than 25 courses, primarily focusing on Hispanic literature and language. The college's African Studies program is offered as a major course of study. Faculty: 4. The Asian Studies program includes more than seven courses focusing on the economics, art, and sociology of the area.

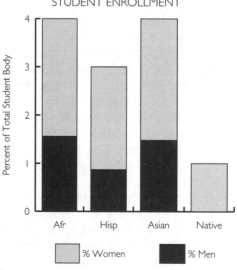

STUDENT ENROLLMENT

Percent of Total Student Body

% Women   % Men

Ethnic studies courses: The college offers courses in ethnic and racial relations, as well as a course in "Asian-American History and Culture."

Organizations for non-white students: Bridging Inter-Racial Difference, La Unidad, Society Organized Against Racism, Unity House, South African Scholarship Fund Committee, South African Support Committee, Connecticut College Asian/Asian-American Organization, Minority Student Steering Committee, Umoja (African-American student group), Diversity Committee

Notable non-white alumni: Anita DeFrantz (president, Amateur Athletics Association in California; only minority to serve on the International Olympic Committee)

Tenured faculty: 147 (total non-white: 7%)

Non-tenured faculty: na

Student-faculty ratio: 11:1

Administrators: 92 (total non-white: 7%)

Recent non-white speakers on campus: Maya Angelou (author and poet); Slow Turtle (executive director, Commission on Indian Affairs); Dr. Charles King (executive director, Urban Crisis League); Dr. Na'im Akbar (clinical psychologist); Andrew Billingsley (professor of family and community development, University of Maryland); Spike Lee (filmmaker)

Connecticut College was chartered in 1911 to educate women, according to school officials, when Wesleyan University's board of trustees "decided to admit men only to their university, thereby leaving the state of Connecticut with no educational institutions in which women could earn bachelor of arts degrees." Today, Conn, having started admitting men in 1969, is a fully coeducational liberal arts college that offers a personal approach to academics.

Connecticut College is strong in the arts, particularly dance, theater, and art. The school's Cummings Arts Center offers impressive facilities that include art studios, galleries, and an electronic music studio. During their junior year, theater majors are able to work as interns at New London's famed Eugene O'Neill Center. Asian Studies, economics, psychology, and English are also said to be excellent. Conn's Center for International Studies and the Liberal Arts is the first of its kind in the country. The certificate-granting program allows students to major in any area, from anthropology to zoology, while also studying a specific region's language—students can choose from seven foreign languages—art, politics, economics, and literature.

The school's "African-American Literature" course is popular with students—"It included great discussions"—as is its "Ethnic and Race Relations" course, offered by the sociology department. Robert Hampton, the professor of the "Ethnic and Race Relations" course, who also serves as dean of the college, "is a phenomenal professor," says a student. "He really urged us to participate in class. He's supportive of all students of color here. He acts as a liaison between us and the administration. He's easy for us to talk to about what's going on, even if we just need someone to talk to on a personal level."

Through a program funded by the Mellon Foundation, students are able to work with professors developing courses about traditionally underrepresented racial and ethnic groups. The program was featured in a recent *New York Times* article. "Minority Experience in Latin America," which focuses on the experiences of Africans, Asians, and Jews in the area, is one of the courses designed as part of the program. Others have focused on the religions of the Caribbean, Native American literature, and how the educational system affects students of color.

One of the pluses of Conn is the unusually close bonds that can develop between students and faculty. Students say it's not uncommon for professors to invite classes to their homes for discussions. "I definitely like the small-college atmosphere here," says a biology major. "If I'm having a problem in a class I can usually go up to my professor after class and talk to him about it."

Conn's Unity House, the college's multicultural student residence, is a popular on-campus meeting place. "I hang out there all the time," says a student. The house provides residence facilities for up to four students. In order to live in the house, students must submit to a rigorous application process and the decision is made by the executive board of the college's various multicultural student organizations. Renovated in 1989, the house has a small library, a large meeting room, and two administrative offices. Gisell Hodge, the director of the house, is "an effective and enthusiastic adviser to all the multicultural student groups on campus. She gives us advice, when we think we need it, on how to deal with students and faculty." Unity House also publishes a newsletter that contains student opinion and poetry.

The college's African-American student group, Umoja, has about "30 to 40 active student members," says a student leader. In a recent year, members of Umoja, a Swahili word meaning "unity," sponsored a workshop for members on the "relationships between African-American men and women on campus, but it turned into a rap session about our lives at Conn." Umoja also sponsors cultural dinners, usually held at Unity House. For Black History Month, campus events have included guest lectures and the production of a play entitled *Our Black Men are Dying and Nobody Seems to Care.*

La Unidad, the school's Latin American student group, has about 20 active members, who meet twice a month in Unity House. The group's primary activity is Latino Awareness Month, "which consists of about five to six events in which the whole campus is encouraged to participate," says a student. "This year, we invited a Peruvian band and a Puerto Rican storyteller to campus, and we also had an art exhibit." The group usually sponsors a trip for its members to New York City, about two hours away, "for dinner and a concert or a museum visit."

Students report that there is little trouble integrating socially. "I believe that racial integration on my campus is good," says a student. "For students of color, it is relatively easy to integrate at a party or sit wherever one would like in the dining halls. Dorms are well integrated as well."

Conn has no fraternities or sororities, a fact of life that doesn't prevent students from staging more than their share of keg parties, which are usually hosted by the dorms—all of which are coed—or student clubs. Florila Day, a spring festival, brings more than three bands and "a party-hearty atmosphere" to the campus each year. Most of the intramural activities are coed, and involve intense rivalries among the dorms. The college has impressive athletic facilities, including the Athletic Center, more than 20 acres of playing fields, and a nearby boathouse on the Thames River for crew and sailing.

New London, which has an African-American community, isn't a popular off-campus destination for students, although they will sometimes head to the area's movie theaters, bars, or restaurants. Students report there is little interaction between the college and New London communities, with the exception of Campus Outreach, "where students act as mentors in area elementary schools and junior and senior high schools." Beaches are just a few minutes' walk from campus. New York City and Boston are easily accessible by train.

As at many New England colleges, cultural and racial diversity is relatively new to Conn College. Many of its students are graduates of prep schools—more than 40 percent—and come from affluent suburbs around New England and the Middle Atlantic states. But with recently implemented programs, administrative support, and active student groups, Conn is becoming a more diverse institution. "I've gotten experience here I couldn't have gotten anywhere else, especially at a large school," says a student. "Student of color input is valued here, by the student community at large and by the administration. I know I'll be ready to deal with the outside world because of what I've learned here."

TRINITY COLLEGE

Address: 300 Summit Street, Hartford, CT 06106
Phone: (203) 297-2180
Director of Admissions: David Borus
Multicultural Student Recruiter: Angela Ringwood
1993–94 tuition: $17,950
Room and board: $3,370
Application deadline: 1/15
Financial aid application deadline: 2/1
Non-white freshman admissions: Applicants for the class of '95: 444
  Accepted: 60%
  Accepted who enroll: 23%
  Applicants accepted who rank in top 10% of high school class: na
  Median SAT: na
  Median ACT: na
Full-time undergraduate enrollment: 1,974
  Men: 50%
  Women: 50%
Non-white students in
  1988–89: 12.1%
  1989–90: 13.7%
  1990–91: 17%
  1991–92: 17%
Students In-state: 60%
Top majors: 1. Natural Science 2. Economics 3. English

Retention rate of non-white students: 85%
Scholarships exclusively for non-white students: None
Remediation programs: None
Academic support services: The college has a writing and math center. The Challenge Program introduces entering first-year students to the academic and non-academic programs at the college.
Ethnic studies programs: Within the Area Studies program, students may choose to concentrate in either Asian-American,

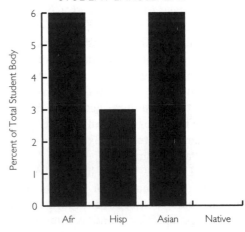

STUDENT ENROLLMENT

Percent of Total Student Body

Afr   Hisp   Asian   Native

GEOGRAPHIC DISTRIBUTION OF STUDENTS

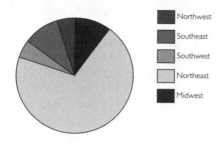

- Northwest
- Southeast
- Southwest
- Northeast
- Midwest

Latino-American, or African-American Studies.

Organizations for non-white students: Pan-African Alliance, Trinity College Black Women's Organization, La Voz Latina, Asian Students' International Alliance, Multicultural Society, Umoja House

Notable non-white alumni: Elizabeth L. Ross (opera singer); Frank Borges (Political Science; treasurer, state of Connecticut); Ousman Sallah (U.S. ambassador to Gambia); Donna Williams (press relations, PBS); Steven Newsome (director, Smithsonian Institute's Anacostia Museum of African-American Art)

Tenured faculty: 99
  Total African-American: 6
  Total Hispanic: 1
  Total Asian-American: 2
  Total Native American: 0
Non-tenured faculty: 115
  Total African-American: 4
  Total Hispanic: 7
  Total Asian-American: 13
  Total Native American: 0
Student-faculty ratio: 10:1
Administrators: 152
  Total African-American: 12
  Total Hispanic: 2
  Total Asian-American: 1
  Total Native American: 0
Recent non-white speakers on campus: Angela Davis (political activist); Mary Frances Berry (former U.S. representative and member of U.S. Civil Rights Commission); Gil Noble (journalist and TV producer); Dick Gregory (author and political activist); Charles Osgood (CBS News correspondent); June Jordan (writer and political activist)

Trinity College has been diversifying itself lately, in terms of everything from curriculum and student enrollment to activities. The 169-year-old college, long known as a haven for the New England prep school set, now has programs in African-American, Latin American, and Asian Studies and has nearly doubled its enrollment of students of color in the last several years.

What hasn't changed is Trinity's generations-old commitment to the liberal arts. Students say the college's best departments are English, political science, and history. Art, drama, and music students have access to the impressive facilities at the school's Austin Arts Center. Trinity's engineering program was strengthened in 1991 with the opening of its new $9 million Engineering, Mathematics, and Computing Science Building, which includes state-of-the-art research facilities and a twenty-four-hour computer center. Trinity is one of only a handful of liberal arts colleges in the country to offer a degree in engineering. With more than 800,000 volumes, Trinity has one of the finest small-college libraries in the country.

To graduate, students must take courses to show proficiency in math and composition, in addition to distribution requirements in the arts, humanities, natural sciences, numerical and symbolic reasoning, and social sciences. Students must also study one of nearly 30 interdisciplinary minors, in which students take six interrelated courses in an area of interest, such as marine sciences, legal studies, or performing arts. Minors are also offered in African Studies, Afro-American Studies, Asian Studies, and Latin American Studies.

First-year students are encouraged but not required to enroll in a Freshman Seminar, which seeks to prepare students for the rigors of a liberal education by focusing on students' critical thinking, speaking, and writing skills. Seminar classes are small and usually include no more than 15 students. A recent seminar topic was "The Legal History of Race Relations."

Students rate their school's program in African-American Studies highly. "The Afro-American Literary Traditions" and "Black Politics in Urban America" are two of the program's more popular courses. James Miller, who teaches "The Afro-American Literary Traditions," "is an excellent professor who gets his ideas across to students and encourages discussion," says a science major. Beyond the classroom, Miller is also considered a mentor to students. "He comes to all of the campus's cultural meetings and activities," says a student. Miller is also a faculty adviser to the Pan-African Alliance, Trinity's African-American student group. Professor Jerry Watts, who teaches "Black Politics in Urban America," is also well regarded. "He works closely not only with his own students but with all minority students," says a student. "He shows much compassion and is a role model for students and faculty."

To assist students with their studies, Trinity offers a math and writing center that is regarded as highly effective, and students say their professors are almost always accessible. Students also turn to Gail Woldu, an assistant dean of the faculty and a lecturer in music, who serves as an academic adviser. "She has been instrumental in guiding first-year students and in encouraging unity among the classes," says a student. "She is also key in finding job opportunities for students and in helping in any way she can with student-to-professor relations."

Trinity has four cultural student groups—the Pan-African Alliance, La Voz Latina, Multicultural Society, and the Asian Students' International Alliance—but students say these organizations are not as active now as they have been in the past. "The minority organizations reached a low point this year," reports a junior who has been active in the groups. La Voz Latina plans events to promote Hispanic awareness on campus. During a recent year, the group sponsored SALSA, a successful dance party in which students were treated to the various foods, dances, and music of Hispanic culture. "The party was great," says a student. "A professional dance group taught us some of their dances and we all ate too much." The group has also invited a Hispanic Hartford politician to speak to the campus community, and has hosted films and exhibitions of Hispanic art and music.

Trinity's Pan-African Alliance has about 40 active members. "The group was relatively inactive last year," says a student leader, but it did sponsor several dances that had good student turnout. Recently, the group brought Lenora Fulani, head of the New Alliance party, to campus for Black History Month.

The Black Women's Organization recently hosted a Black Women's Week, a series of panel discussions with professors about the role of African-American women in American society. "The group is primarily a place of support where we promote the awareness of the strength of black women," says a member. At the meetings, students are encouraged to share their poetry and essays.

The Umoja House, the black cultural center, is a popular meeting place on campus. "During my first year, the house was not used at all," says a senior. "Now, more and more the house is being used by students." The house has all of the amenities of off-campus living, as well as a library filled with books by black authors and a small museum that exhibits African and African-American art. Two African-American student "caretakers" live in the house each year, and are responsible for the upkeep of the house and the house's "schedule of events and meetings to make sure that nothing conflicts." The Pan-African Alliance and the Black Women's Organization hold their meetings at the Umoja House, and during Parents Weekend a reception is held there.

Students at Trinity have a variety of on-campus housing options, from dorms to fraternities. Students are also able to design their own theme houses that usually last for a semester or a school year. During a recent school year, the Multicultural Society successfully established a multicultural dorm on campus, which housed about 50 Asian-American, African-American, Hispanic, and white students.

Trinity's social life has long been dominated by its Greek system. Although less than 20 percent of the students belong to them, the fraternities host many of the school's weekend parties. But Trinity's social life has also become more diverse in recent years, thanks in large part to the Resident Life staff, which recently coordinated a "spring break" party during the winter (held at the school's newly revamped indoor pool), a jazz night, and a luau. Many students participate in sports, and the school's varsity men's basketball and track teams have been traditionally strong. Any athletic competition against Wesleyan University, Trinity's rival, brings out the crowds. The Ferris Athletic Center, with its swimming pool and squash courts, is especially well used. Students also congregate at the student center, which has a movie theater with screenings most nights of the week.

Trinity's campus is in a predominantly African-American and Hispanic community. The city of Hartford boasts art museums, ballet and symphony, and an NHL hockey team. Interaction with area residents comes mostly through the services of Community Outreach, a student volunteer organization that provides tutoring to schoolchildren in nearby schools. The city is also a rich resource for internships; according to the college, 60 percent of its students work as interns in companies or state or federal government agencies. The city is just a couple of hours' drive from New Haven, New York City, and Boston.

Trinity has done a great deal recently to create a learning environment that is more diverse, in the classroom and in student life. The college, however, still remains popular with many prep school students—in a recent year, nearly 40 percent of the student body attended private high schools—which explains some of the more conservative attitudes among many students. Students appreciate the direction their school is taking, its small size, and its location. "When I was thinking about a college, I looked for a liberal arts school because I wasn't sure what I wanted to do," says a recent graduate. "I like the fact that Trinity is small and students have so many opportunities to get involved. And Trinity is in between Boston, where my friends are, and New York, where my home is."

WESLEYAN UNIVERSITY

Address: Office of Admissions, Middletown,
CT 06457
Phone: (203) 344-7900
Director of Admissions: Barbara-Jan Wilson
Multicultural Student Recruiter: Clifford
Thornton
1992–93 tuition: $17,190
Room and board: $5,080
Application deadline: 1/15
Financial aid application deadline: 1/15
Non-white freshman admissions: Applicants
for the class of '96: 1,395
Accepted: 46%
Accepted who enroll: 35%
Applicants accepted who rank in top
10% of high school class: 54%
In top 25%: 87.5%
Median SAT range: 500–630 V, 560–700M
Median ACT: na
Full-time undergraduate enrollment: 2,800
Men: 49%
Women: 51%
Native Americans in student body: na
Non-white students in
1988–89: 19%
1989–90: 20%

1990–91: 21%
1991–92: 26%

GEOGRAPHIC DISTRIBUTION OF STUDENTS

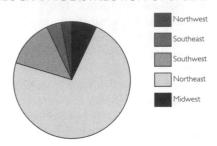

- Northwest
- Southeast
- Southwest
- Northeast
- Midwest

Students In-state: 6.3%
Top majors: 1. English 2. Biology
3. Economics/Government
Retention rate of non-white students: 87%
**Scholarships exclusively for non-white
students:** Charles B. Ray and
Gomez-Ibanez Scholarships: need-based;
$500 awarded during a student's first
year to help reduce loan aid.
Remediation programs: Workshops in
writing as well as peer tutoring
Academic support services: The Hughes
Program in the sciences and the Mellon
Program offer academic support. The
Office of Multicultural Affairs also
provides academic and non-academic
support services.
Ethnic studies programs: Wesleyan offers
three interdisciplinary programs in ethnic
studies, drawing courses from the history,
language, political science, religion,
economics, and other departments.
Minors and majors are offered in each
area. African-American Studies includes
more than 25 courses. Tenured faculty: 3.
East Asian Studies includes more than 30
courses, in addition to Chinese- and
Japanese-language study, which is offered
at all levels. Tenured faculty: 9. The
Latin American Studies curriculum
includes more than 25 courses.

STUDENT ENROLLMENT

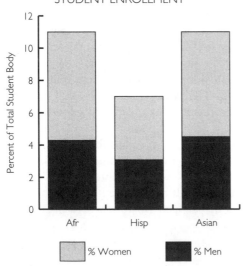

Percent of Total Student Body

Afr   Hisp   Asian

% Women   % Men

Organizations for non-white students:
Malcolm X House, Asia House, La Casa de Albizu Campos, Women of Color House, Ajua Campos (Latino Student Organization), Ujamaa (African-American student organization), Asian/Asian-American Student Alliance, Tri-Minority Council, Kappa Alpha Psi, Alpha Kappa Alpha, Delta Sigma Theta, Alpha Phi Alpha, Omega Psi Phi

Notable non-white alumni: Charles Stone (editor, *Philadelphia Inquirer*); Edgar Beckham (officer, Ford Foundation; commissioner, Connecticut Board of Education); Alberto Ibarguen (vice president, *Newsday*); Daphne Kwok (director, Organization of Chinese-Americans); Kim Wayans (Emmy Award-winning actress, *In Living Color*)

Tenured faculty: 294
Non-tenured faculty: 62
Student-faculty ratio: 11:1
Administrators: 24
African-American: 33%
Hispanic: 10%
Asian-American: 4%
Native American: 0
Recent non-white speakers on campus:

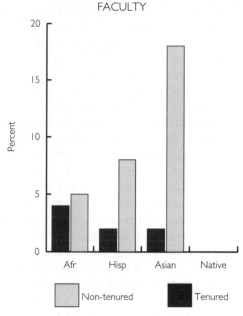

FACULTY

Non-tenured   Tenured

Desmond Tutu (Nobel Peace Prize winner and South African civil rights activist); Amiri Baraka (poet and activist); Gloria Anzaldua (writer and poet); Michael Manley (former prime minister of Jamaica)

Along with Amherst College and Williams College, Wesleyan University is one of the Little Ivies, small but every bit as competitive and scholarly as the much-lauded Ivy League. Wesleyan has the breadth and depth of studies and social opportunities, and the bright and independent-minded student body to take advantage of them, to place it in the ranks of the country's most prestigious small universities.

And as prestigious as Wesleyan is, it is also diverse, a word often used to describe almost any aspect of the campus—from curriculum and social opportunities to campus architecture and student mind-set. But unlike some other of the nation's elite liberal arts universities and colleges, Wesleyan is no stranger to issues of cultural and racial diversity. The university has long been committed to recruiting a diverse student body and offering diverse academic programs—Wesleyan's Afro-American Studies program was the first of its kind on the East Coast. "One of the reasons I came here was Wesleyan's very good academic name, but also it was a gut feeling. I knew there was a large percentage of minority students here, and that made me feel comfortable," says a member of the university's award-winning Ebony Singers chorus. "I learned a lot in my hall alone last year. It was very mixed, with Asian-Americans, Latinos, Russian, and Jewish students, and one biracial person. It's all a matter of understanding each person, being interested and understanding." And as a former member of Wesleyan's faculty says: "If you studied modern dance at Wesleyan, that meant black dance along with [George] Balanchine and others. If you studied American literature, it was [Richard] Wright along with Hemingway. It's a very special place."

Recently, however, there have been ripples in the Wesleyan waters, as some students and faculty have expressed doubts and frustration about the administration's commitment—under a relatively new president dealing with economic pressure—to multiculturalism on campus. As evidence, students and faculty point to the "dramatic exodus" since 1988 of six of the school's eleven African-American faculty members who either were tenured or were eligible for tenure. Wesleyan's president, William M. Chace, according to a *New York Times* article, said the professors left for offers at other, more prestigious universities. But Erness Bright Brody, head of the school's Afro-American Studies program, sees things differently. In an open letter signed by eight other African-American faculty members and published in the campus newspaper, *The Argus,* she wrote: "If the administration had a coherent policy to retain minority faculty, they might have remained."

Such issues came to a boiling point during the 1989–90 school year, when a firebomb was thrown into President Chace's closed and unoccupied office—the incident occurred at 4 a.m.—and racist graffiti was sprayed on a wall in Wesleyan's Malcolm X House, a residence and cultural facility for the school's African-American community. (No arrests have been made in connection with the crimes.) In response to the incidents, students sponsored a Unity Day at the end of the school year, which, according to a *Times* reporter, "was an attempt at catharsis." The day included student speakers, teach-ins, and group discussions.

While no school is free of racism, Wesleyan—particularly among students—is a school where such issues aren't ignored. Wesleyan students are politically and culturally aware in ways students at few other schools are. "Minority organizations are regarded as quite powerful and influential by the administration and other student groups," says a student. "Ujamaa, the black student organization, has been a successful voice of student concerns. Likewise, the Tri-Minority Council [a group made up of representatives of the school's primary African-American, Asian/Asian-American, and Latino student organizations] has gained much respect and recognition as the one organ of minority concerns." Adds another student: "We have engaged in anti-apartheid and divestment rallies, sit-ins, and we have built shanty towns. The students here are constantly engaging in political debates."

Besides being drawn to a school where students are known for being progressive-minded, students also come to Wesleyan because of its powerful academic reputation. This 152-year-old university offers an array of programs and departments that are the envy of schools twice its size—instruction is offered in 40 major fields of study through 30 departments and two centers and students may choose from more than 900 courses offered each year. Among some of the school's best-respected programs are economics, political science, art history, English, and history. Most of the science programs are also considered excellent, and students have access to the facilities of the school's state-of-the-art six-story Science Center. Wesleyan's film and women's studies programs are also well regarded. For theater majors, or just for those interested in the theater arts, the university's Center for the Arts is one of the most impressive on the East Coast; the eleven-building complex includes a cinema, theater, concert and rehearsal halls, and studios for theater, art, and dance. The center is host to a variety of performers, including concerts of West African drumming by Abraham Adzinyah, artist-in-residence in African music.

While the school's Afro-American Studies program, established in 1969, is undergoing a rebuilding stage—new professors are being recruited—it is nonetheless impressive, including a variety of courses about African-American and Caribbean experiences and cultures. In any given year, more than 1,000 students enroll in about 30 Afro-American Studies courses. "Peoples and Cultures of the Caribbean," "Afro-American Art," and "African Art and Religion" rank as some of the program's more popular courses. Erness Brody, head of the program, and Michael Harris, an associate professor of history, are well regarded by students. The resources of the school's Center for Afro-American Studies (CASS), established on campus in 1974, are also available, including the student-run W. E. B. Du Bois Library. Lectures, meetings, and concerts are also held in the CASS lounge. Off-campus study opportunities at any one of the country's top historically black colleges and universities, including Howard, Morehouse, and Spelman, are also offered.

Wesleyan's Latin American Studies program includes such noteworthy courses as "Survey of Latin America," a history course, and various courses in history and literature, although, as more than one student points out, "the program emphasizes only the cultures of Peru, Bolivia, and Central America and ignores Puerto Rico." Many Latin American Studies majors take advantage of one of the school's study-abroad programs in Mexico, Peru, Spain, and other countries. Carlos Alonso and Diana Goodrich, both associate professors of Romance languages and literature, are described by students as two of the program's outstanding faculty.

Academic intensity can run high at this university, where professors expect almost as much of students as students do of themselves. Wesleyan students are self-motivators, but the university sponsors a variety of academic and personal support services, particularly among individual staff and faculty, to assist even the brightest of them. Janina Montero, dean of studies at Wesleyan, "is extremely involved with minority concerns and concerned about the retention of our students," says a government major. Frank Tuitt, coordinator of multicultural affairs, Rick McLellan, director of career planning, and Clifford Thornton, an associate dean of admissions, are also cited by students as concerned staff members. "All have provided support emotionally and spiritually for many students of color," says a student. "They act as responsible family figures in paternal as well as brotherly situations. Their connections to the students run deep and they have a serious concern for the welfare of students."

Students have the option of living in any one of the school's cultural theme houses, including La Casa de Albizu Campos, which can house up to eight residents, and the Malcolm X House, which can house up to 30. Both houses serve as meeting places for students and student organizations, and residents sponsor their own cultural awareness programs and get-togethers.

Middletown (pop. 45,000) could hardly be described as your typical college town, but the largely blue-collar city, which includes African-American and Hispanic communities, offers a variety of churches, restaurants, and stores, all within walking distance. Students are heavily involved in the community, working as tutors at nearby elementary schools, serving as big brothers/big sisters, or work with Upward Bound, a joint Wesleyan-community educational project. For students looking to check out what's happening at other Connecticut schools, Yale University, Trinity College, and Connecticut College are all within a half hour drive from campus. Hartford, just fifteen miles north, and New York City and Boston, about two hours from campus, are popular destinations for students looking for the nightlife of bigger cities, although the latter two are not easily accessible by public transport.

More than 95 percent of Wesleyan's student body remains on campus during the weekends. Students are able to participate in more than 100 student-run organizations, including everything from fraternities and sororities to the Minority Pre-med Alliance and *The Ankh,* a student newspaper published by the African-American, Latino, and Asian-American communities. Varsity sporting events don't get a wide following, except when the opponents are archrivals Williams, Trinity, and Amherst. When not studying or in meetings, many students can be found at the school's new $22 million Freeman Athletic Center, which includes an indoor pool and an all-weather outdoor track.

Wesleyan University is a great many things to a great many people. The opportunities here are vast, sometimes to the point of being overwhelming. But no matter what niche you create for yourself, Wesleyan will help you do what you came here to do: "Wesleyan makes you evaluate yourself and your beliefs," says a student. "Whatever your thing is, you can find it. I'm glad I'm here."

YALE UNIVERSITY

Address: New Haven, CT 06520
Phone: (203) 432-1900
Director of Admissions: Margit Dahl
Multicultural Student Recruiter: Derek Gandy

1992–93 tuition: $17,500
Room and board: $6,200
Application deadline: 12/31
Financial aid application deadline: 1/15

The fact that liberal cartoonist Garry Trudeau (creator of "Doonesbury") and archconservative William F. Buckley, Jr., graduated from Yale University, one of the eight members of the illustrious Ivy League, isn't just coincidence. The country's third-oldest university has an incredible wealth of resources—both academic and extracurricular—that could please almost anyone.

However, Yalies tend to be liberal. In the most recent presidential election, for example, students voted overwhelmingly Democratic; Yale's gay and lesbian student group is active and largely accepted; and students are often volunteering their services through any number of New Haven or campus causes. And, according to a student, "Yale is a place where issues of race and multiculturalism are talked about, and most Yale students are open-minded people. This receptive attitude helps make Yale a very special place to go to school." Yale's admissions office did not respond to our questionnaire, but according to the U.S. Department of Education, of the university's

10,994 students in 1990, .3 percent were American Indian, 9.4 percent were Asian, 5.9 percent were black, and 4 percent were Hispanic.

As at some of the other Ivies, Yale is well known for its graduate school programs, 12 in all. But undergraduate education—Yale College—is at the heart of Yale University, and the emphasis here is on the arts and sciences. Full professors, many of whom are nationally recognized in their respective fields, teach first-year as well as upper-level courses, and teaching assistants teach only basic English and lab courses. "The good thing about Yale is that you can actually argue with professors, or have discussions with them over lunch or dinner," says a student.

Yale's Latin American Studies major is solid, and includes such popular courses as "Democracy in Latin America" and "U.S./Latin American Relations." American Studies' new program in ethnic studies has been winning praise from students. Although the school's two Asian-American Studies courses, a literature and a history course, are described by students as excellent, an Asian-American Student Task Force has been formed to encourage the university to include more Asian-American Studies courses in its curriculum and to hire more Asian-American faculty.

The academic challenges at Yale rival those at any of the country's highly selective schools. Although Yalies typically aren't the type to sit in the library twenty-four hours a day—there are all those group meetings and events to attend—Yale does require its undergraduates to satisfy 36 credits before graduating, slightly more than the 32 required of students at some of their peer institutions. But a weeklong reading period just before finals allows procrastinators some time to catch up.

But something is challenging Yale's corner on the education market. It's called the budget, a far more formidable challenger than Harvard ever was. "Like many other research universities across the country, Yale is slashing budgets, laying off staff members, and placing academic programs on the chopping block—all in the name of a leaner, meaner future," says an article in *The Chronicle of Higher Education.* Many of Yale's buildings are in sad need of repair. "I was met with an unusually explicit consensus from trustees, students, and alumni that Yale's facilities were in bad shape. It's not being driven by aesthetics," says former Yale president Benno Schmidt, Jr., in the *Chronicle.* As a result of Yale's budget predicament, the Commons dining hall has been closed, library hours have been cut, and numerous sports teams have been done away with.

While the university may be experiencing some belt tightening, the plethora of Yale's student groups and teams are as active as ever. Students can participate in any sort of on-campus activity imaginable, from Shades, a multicultural student a cappella singing group, to a variety of political, dramatic, and service organizations. And sports don't play second fiddle at Yale. Ron Darling, the major-league baseball pitcher, is a Yalie, and the Bulldogs' football, hockey, crew, women's gymnastics, and soccer teams have more than their fair share of fans and athletes.

Much of the campus activity centers on the university's residential college system. There are 12 residential colleges in all, each of which houses about 350 undergraduates. Each of the colleges is designed to reflect the cultural and racial diversity at Yale, so students are assigned to a particular college beginning their sophomore year. An ethnic counselor is also assigned to each of the colleges. In a recent year, there were two Puerto Rican counselors, two Chicanos, five Asian-Americans, and three African-Americans.

Intramural competition among the colleges is keen, and each of the colleges has its own master and dean, who provide academic and non-academic counseling. Each college also includes a library, a dining hall, and other facilities unique to that particular college. One college has a small theater, another has a photography lab, while another has squash courts.

For activity of the cultural sort, Yale sponsors three cultural centers for three major ethnic groups represented at the college: the Afro-American Cultural Center, the Asian and Mexican-American Cultural Center, and the Puerto Rican Cultural Center. "The centers are very helpful in that they provide a cultural home away from home, and the staff members are very comforting and understanding," comments a student. Each center has its own dean and assistant, and the school's various cultural student groups will have their meetings in their respective centers.

The Puerto Rican center, officially named the Julia de Burgos Culture Center for a member of the Nationalist party in Puerto Rico, has played host recently to two art exhibitions and a Christmas dinner to which area residents and administrators were invited. In addition to a library that focuses on Puerto Rican literature and economics, the center even includes an exercise room as well as a recently opened coffee shop "where people can come and study or be social," says a student. The center sponsors movie and domino nights, and an alumni conference was held in January 1993.

Yale's Puerto Rican student group, Despierta Boricua, sponsors a speaker series, which has included noted author Piri Thomas, and in September 1992 the first East Coast Puerto Rican Conference. "The conference is designed to focus on three main issues: community involvement, the high dropout rate among Puerto Rican college students, and Puerto Rican statehood," says one of the event's organizers. Students from various colleges and universities up and down the East Coast participated in the event. "We may be the smallest group on campus [according to one student, there were 72 Puerto Ricans enrolled at Yale in a recent year], but we pride ourselves on being one of the most active," says a student.

The Asian Student Association, according to one member, works primarily as an umbrella organization for the school's Asian and Asian-American student groups. According to a student, "the ASA just hands out money to the different groups and is relatively inactive, which, in a way, has its advantages because it brings the groups together." Among the more active of the Asian groups are the Korean-American and Japanese-American student organizations. With the ASA, the Japanese student group sponsored a forum to commemorate fifty years since the internment of Japanese-Americans. The three-day forum, titled "Undue Process: The Legacy of Japanese-Americans' Internment," included workshops led by World War II veterans, dance performances, and discussions with writers and filmmakers. About 100 people came to the workshops, says an organizer.

The Black Students Association at Yale (BSAY) is the most politically oriented of the African-American student groups, but according to students, it is "far from active. The group is crippled by its leadership and their inability to get people together." According to students, the African-American community-service-based groups, such as the Urban Improvement Corps and the work done by the historically black fraternities and sororities, are more active and effective.

The African-American Cultural Center, established at Yale in 1968, "is huge," says a student. The three-story facility includes a library, an art gallery, office space, a room for dances and meetings, and a TV lounge in the basement. But, according to one observer, the house is "underutilized by students because of the factions that have developed as a result of the BSAY leadership."

Students are hopeful that the center's new director will bring about a more unified BSAY and revitalize the center. However, there are those who express concern that students were not involved in the process for selecting the director. "There are no students who sit on the board of directors of the center, which makes students feel alienated from the whole process. The power definitely comes from above."

Students say there is little, if any interaction between the respective cultural student groups. "I've tried to get groups to talk about minority recruitment," says a student, "but people say they don't have the time or that they are too tired. But a big reason is that students are only concerned about the issues that face their own communities. People here don't like coalitions."

For another student, the campus social life seems less factionalized. "With respect to campus parties, I'd say they're usually fairly well integrated. Freshman year there was the issue of the 'black table' in Commons dining hall, but I think you'd find that kind of situation wherever you go—it also became less noticeable once we started eating in our residential colleges. Racial integration isn't much of an issue with the residential college system," she says. "Morse and Saybrook used to be called 'minority row' but I believe the housing committees began placing freshmen in such a way as to balance the racial makeup of all the colleges."

Another student sees campus social life differently. "Yale is very rarely racially integrated. There appears to be separate social lives for mainstream students and students of color. Very few students of color attend mainstream functions, such as dances, singing jams, and Caucasian fraternity parties."

New Haven has come to be a more inviting city into which to venture, according to students. A popular Harvard chant—"We may be losing the game, but at least we don't have to go back to New Haven"—doesn't quite have the sting that it once did. The city is well known for its pizzerias, and ethnic restaurants, bookstores, and bars are a short walk from campus. New Haven's theaters also play host to numerous shows before they hit Broadway, and its town green is the site of an annual Jazz Festival. Nonetheless, the city remains largely a poor community of African-Americans, and the contrasts between Yale and New Haven—architecturally, racially, and economically—are striking. Campus security has been a problem—a student was murdered recently just on the edge of the campus—but students say the situation has improved with a beefed-up campus security force and a student watch patrol. "It's strange walking outside of the Yale campus and being reminded of the city problems I thought I left behind," says a New Yorker. Yale is a short train ride away—about an hour and a half—from New York City, and Boston is easily accessible by train.

Yale academics and extracurriculars demand a great deal of students, and your typical Yalie is up to the challenge. In fact, he or she revels in all of the school's opportunities. "I would recommend Yale to a prospective student of color because Yale is one of the most ethnically and culturally diverse schools in the Ivy League, and many things are offered here for all students."

D E L A W A R E

UNIVERSITY OF DELAWARE

Address: Newark, DE 19716
Phone: (302) 831-8123
Director of Admissions: N. Bruce Walker
Multicultural Student Recruiter: Zenobia
  Hikes
1991–92 tuition: $3,390 (in-state); $9,050
  (out-of-state)
Room and board: $3,756
Application deadline: 3/15
Financial aid application deadline: 3/15
Non-white freshman admissions: Applicants
  for the class of '95: 609
  (African-American only)
  Accepted: 68%
  Accepted who enroll: 44%
  Applicants accepted who rank in the top
  10% of high school class: na
  Median SAT: 963 (total V and M)
  Median ACT: na
Full-time undergraduate enrollment: 13,398
  Men: 44%
  Women: 56%
Non-white students in
  1987–88: 6.1%
  1988–89: 6.6%
  1989–90: 6.9%
  1990–91: 7.2%
  1992–93: 7.9%
Students In-state: na
Top majors: 1. Psychology 2. Elem. Teacher
  Ed. 3. Business Administration
Retention rate of non-white students: 83%
**Scholarships exclusively for non-white
  students:** The University Scholarship

STUDENT ENROLLMENT

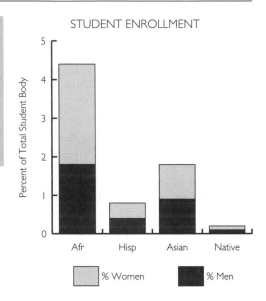

Committee may consider race or cultural
heritage and educational or economic
disadvantage as well as merit when

GEOGRAPHIC DISTRIBUTION OF STUDENTS

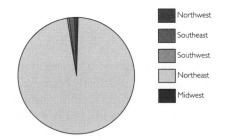

selecting scholarship recipients. University Merit Awards: merit-based; provides full out-of-state tuition; available to African-Americans who are not residents of Delaware. RISE Scholarships: merit-based; offers full room and board for non-white students majoring in engineering and participating in the RISE (Resources to Insure Successful Engineers) program.

Remediation programs: None

Academic support services: The university's Academic Advancement Office, Academic Studies Assistance Program, the Mathematical Sciences Teaching and Learning Center, and the Writing Center provide academic support.

Ethnic studies programs: Minors are offered in Black American Studies and East Asian Studies. Latin American Studies is offered as a major. Each program is interdisciplinary.

Ethnic studies courses: To satisfy the university's multicultural course requirement, students are able to enroll in courses offered by more than 20 academic departments.

Organizations for non-white students: Black Student Union, Alpha Kappa Alpha, Delta Sigma Theta, Sigma Gamma Rho, Zeta Phi Beta, Alpha Phi Alpha, Kappa Alpha Psi, Omega Psi Phi, Martin Luther King, Jr., House, Black Student Theatre

Notable non-white alumni: Rev. Lloyd S. Casson (French; canon and subdean, Cathedral of St. John the Divine, New York City); Leonard L. Williams (Political Science; attorney and retired Municipal Court judge); Linda Fitzgerald Winfield (Psychology; principal research

scientist, Johns Hopkins University); Elbert C. Wisner (Electrical Engineering; president and senior partner, SBS Consultants)

Tenured faculty: 544

Non-tenured faculty: 367

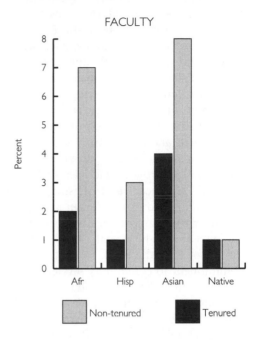

FACULTY

Student-faculty ratio: 17:1

Administrators: 724

  African-American: 9%

  Hispanic: 1%

  Asian-American: 3%

  Native American: 0

Recent non-white speakers on campus: Dick Gregory (author and political activist); Angela Davis (political activist); Charlayne Hunter-Gault (news correspondent, *MacNeil-Lehrer NewsHour*); Sonia Sanchez (poet)

Just off of Highway 95—a major thoroughfare that connects Boston, New York City, and Baltimore—sits the University of Delaware, an atypical typical state university. Atypical because it receives funding from both state and private sources, most notably the Du Ponts, and because more than half of its student body arrives on campus from states other than Delaware, mostly Pennsylvania, New Jersey, and Maryland.

Typical because, as at other state schools, UD offers a lively party scene as well as a variety of respectable academic programs.

Among the school's standout programs are those offered in its College of Engineering, which include chemical, civil, electrical, and mechanical engineering. The school boasts impressive retention rates for its minority engineering majors; in an average year, minority graduation rates equal or better rates of all other engineering students at the university. This is due in part to the school's RISE (Resources to Insure Successful Engineers) program, a support service for minority engineering students that includes scholarship opportunities as well as academic, career, and motivational support services. During the 1991–92 school year, about 133 students were enrolled in the RISE program. "RISE has helped me network," says an electrical engineering major. "It has also provided tutorial services and workshops on how to prepare yourself better for a position in industry."

UD also has impressive programs in business administration, economics, political science, art, and education. The honors program is also well regarded. The school's Black American Studies program, offered as a minor, is excellent, according to students. The program includes such popular courses as "Afrocentricity," "Rhetoric of Black America," and "History of Black America," as well as such well-noted professors as Howard Johnson and James Newton, the program's director.

The biggest sources of any sort of social life for the school's African-American students are the historically black sororities and fraternities. "They're a strong force on campus for the black students," says a senior, who points to the organizations' commitment to community service and to providing dances and parties for students. "Most of the students who have cars, however, head to Philadelphia or Baltimore," he adds. "Newark offers little to the minority student. There are the bars on Main Street, but few of us go to them."

The school's Center for Black Culture, built in 1976, also provides a social outlet for students. "The center is where students can go and feel at ease. It's kind of like a mini student center, with students always there. The director of the center, Vernese Edghill, has excellent rapport with students." The center is home to the school's Black Student Union and the African-American Programming Board, which sponsors lectures, plays, and an annual arts festival. The Center for Black Culture is centrally located, across the street from the main campus library and administration building.

With 12 officers, the Black Student Union, the school's primary African-American student group, was more political than ever, according to a BSU leader, during the 1991–92 school year. "It depends year to year what our focus will be, but this year we focused our energies on trying to make change occur on campus." The group was far from passive in how it went about alerting the campus and the region to these changes. "We sponsored three press conferences during the year. The first one had to do with the university never having divested its $27 million in stock shares from South African countries. The second was our attempt to get an education professor removed from office, as she used the classroom as a forum for her negative views of affirmative action policies. Our last press conference was about the University of Delaware's treatment of black students, the way they monitor our parties and always want to see our IDs."

In addition to political activism, the BSU has also sponsored a Welcome Back Dance, usually held in the student center, for returning and incoming students, and a program called Life After Graduation, which includes résumé-writing workshops. Perhaps BSU's most ambitious event is its African-American Consciousness Celebration, a weeklong affair that includes a lecture series and community service projects. During a recent celebration, the BSU worked with the men of Sigma Phi Epsilon and the women of Kappa Delta, both predominantly white Greek organizations, to sponsor a racial sensitivity workshop. A source of support for the BSU is Stuart Sharky, vice president for student affairs. "He's always a friend to the BSU," says a student.

Despite their efforts, BSU leaders complain of a general sense of apathy among the school's African-American student community: "One of the biggest things we fight is apathy." Another common complaint made by the BSU is the lack of reporting of BSU events by the school newspaper, *The Review*.

The majority of students at Delaware have the reputation of being conservative and middle-class, and the university enrolls a relatively small number of students of color—a combination that can create a somewhat alienating college experience for the unprepared student of color.

"The minority student who would be happiest here is one who will get actively involved in campus politics," says a student. "You can get a good education here, but I know I've been made stronger in my activism."

DISTRICT OF COLUMBIA

CATHOLIC UNIVERSITY OF AMERICA

Address: McManon Hall, 620 Michigan
Avenue N.E., Washington, DC 20064
Phone: (202) 319-5305 / (800) 673-2772
Director of Admissions: Dean David
Gibson
Multicultural Student Recruiter: Reginald
A. Taylor
1993–94 tuition: $13,184
Room and board: $6,116
Application deadline: Early action: 11/1;
regular decision: 2/15
Financial aid application deadline: 2/28
Non-white freshman admissions: Applicants
for the class of '95: 332
Accepted: 81%
Accepted who enroll: 36%
Applicants accepted who rank in top
10% of high school class: 19%
In top 25%: 36%
Median SAT: 447 V, 494 M
Median ACT: na
Full-time undergraduate enrollment: 2,681
Men: 43.3%
Women: 56.7%
Non-white students in
1987–88: 11.2%
1988–89: 14.2%
1989–90: 11.7%
1990–91: 11.8%
Geographic distribution of students: na
Students In-District: 20.2%
Top majors: 1. Architecture 2. Nursing
3. Politics
Retention rate of non-white students: na

**Scholarships exclusively for non-white
students:** The Baroni Scholarship:
need-based; 62 awarded each year, 18 to
first-year students; average award is
$7,800–$8,600. The Coca-Cola
Scholarships Awards: available to
students majoring in engineering or
education; students must have attended a
DC public high school; each scholarship,
which is matched by a gift from
Coca-Cola, is valued at $13,184; four
such scholarships were awarded in a
recent year.
Remediation programs: na
Academic support services: The university

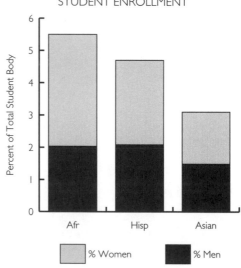

STUDENT ENROLLMENT

Percent of Total Student Body

Afr   Hisp   Asian

■ % Women   ■ % Men

has tutoring and writing centers, as well as a multicultural student adviser.

Ethnic studies programs: None

Ethnic studies courses: Courses include "Minority Relations" (sociology), "Urban Society" (sociology), "Latin American History" (history).

Organizations for non-white students: Black Organization of Students at Catholic University (BOSCUA), Hispanic Student Association, Korean Student Association, CUA Praise, Delta Sigma Theta, Gospel Jubilee, EASE Indian Student Association, Black Scholars

Notable non-white alumni: Martin Puryear ('63; sculptor); Harold Freeman (doctor); Carolyn Blackwell (vocalist)

Tenured faculty: 256

Non-tenured faculty: 155

Student-faculty ratio: 15:1

Administrators: 294
   African-American: 4%
   Hispanic: 1%
   Asian-American: 5%
   Native American: 0.3%

Recent non-white speakers on campus:

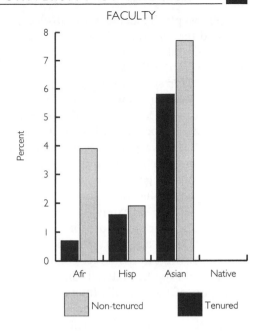

FACULTY

Yolanda King (civil rights activist and daughter of Martin Luther King, Jr.); Jacqueline Fleming (psychologist)

Catholic University in DC isn't just any old Catholic university in the country—it is *the* Catholic University of America, the Vatican's official university in the United States and the only university in the country to be established by the U.S. bishops.

Evidence of the school's Catholic roots are everywhere. The Basilica of the National Shrine of the Immaculate Conception, the largest Catholic church in the Western Hemisphere, sits on the edge of campus. Nearly 90 percent of the student body is Catholic. Dorms clear out on Sundays for Mass. Religious courses are required for graduation. No information about birth control is dispensed through the school's infirmary. And CUA gay students' attempt to become organized was recently turned down by the administration.

But don't be too quick to assume that all of one's experiences at CUA revolve around the Catholic Church. CUA has some well-regarded programs, most notably in the pre-professional areas, such as in engineering, architecture, and nursing. As might be expected, the university is best known for its programs in theology and philosophy. Students majoring in politics, the school's biggest program, are able to work as interns at various government agencies, with political parties, or in Congress. The School of Music offers outstanding programs in musical theater, piano, organ, conducting, and chamber music. "Highlights in African-American Literature," a course offered during the fall semester, is popular. In addition to courses in theology and philosophy, students must satisfy distribution requirements in language, humanities, and the natural and social sciences in order to graduate.

Second only to the student programming board when it comes to activities sponsored is the Black Organization of Students at Catholic University of America, BOSCUA for short. During a recent year, the group sponsored food and clothing drives, a fashion show, a "Night at the Apollo" talent show, and a dinner. "The twenty of us who come to BOSCUA meetings are a tight group, but there are a few others who will occasionally come to our meetings," says a student. "Usually we have meetings once every two weeks, but sometimes less frequently than that. Since we all know each other so well and see each other every day, we'll just meet informally at the student lounge. Also a popular spot for students is the BOSCUA office in St. Bonaventure. It has three rooms, including a library, a TV room, and an office, and come exam time we extend the hours of the office for study." BOSCUA upperclass students also work as tutors for first-year students. "We form a network to help each other out," says a senior. In addition, African-American students have no difficulty getting involved in the larger community of students; BOSCUA has two permanent positions on the legislative branch of CUA's student government.

As part of the school's Intercultural Week, members of CUA's Hispanic Student Association (HSA), with about 75 active members, help coordinate a Latino Festival, a daylong event that in a recent year included Salvadoran food and a Brazilian band. Members have also organized to tutor Salvadoran immigrants in English, even though a student leader says HSA meetings are infrequent.

Of particular interest to many students is the school's Intercultural Center, "where we relax and have fun. It's the only place on campus where there are Ping-Pong and pool tables." HSA and the International Student Association have their offices in the center.

Students say that, on the whole, the campus is accepting of racial and cultural diversity, with some exceptions. "The student government is open-minded in words and in theory, but they're usually reluctant to help fund BOSCUA or any of the other cultural student groups. It's not impossible for them to fund us, but every year it's an ordeal to get them to. It's mostly due to their conservative backgrounds and because they don't see the importance of such student groups. Every year we [BOSCUA] get money to fund a major speaker, but this year we didn't. All groups are having to deal with budget cuts, though. And it's also difficult for us to get other student groups to co-sponsor events. We've had groups who have wanted us to co-sponsor a conservative black speaker on campus, but we didn't do it. Just because the speaker was black didn't mean we had to sponsor him. During Black History Month we also don't get much cooperation from students. Most of the programming for the month is left up to BOSCUA."

During the 1991–92 school year, university president William Bryon established the school's first Black History Month Committee, a group of students and administrators responsible for creating programming for the month of February. The president awarded the committee $1,000 to fund speakers and other events. "But we don't know about the funding for next year," says a student committee member. "The president sent letters to all the department heads to encourage their office's participation, but there were few responses."

While students would like to see more collaboration among groups to support events, they can point to various administrators who are more than helpful. In the office of the dean of students, students say Karen Martin and Lorraine Krusa "help us with everything. If they can't help us, they'll tell us who can." Martin helped establish CUA's Black Scholars Program, which provides support for some of the school's African-American students.

Members of the Black Employees of CUA "have also been an active force in helping us coordinate events, xeroxing fliers, setting up speakers, you name it. The black faculty and staff here pretty much have an open-door policy for students." Two such staff members are John Scruggs and Michele Walker, both of the Office of Student Affairs. Beginning in the fall semester of 1993, the university will hire a minority student adviser to work with students in the school's arts and sciences division.

Although the CUA campus is self-contained—the only DC school to have grassy knolls and a "campusy feel to it"—the area surrounding it is a predominantly black and poor neighborhood that students say has a high incidence of crime. "At night we don't often venture far from campus," says a student. All of the cultural and nightlife activities of the nation's capital, however, are easily accessible via the Metro, the city's subway system, which has a station conveniently located on the east side of campus. The U.S. Capitol is just a walk away, as are numerous museums and other national treasures. However, students comment that most of the school's social life is focused either on campus or within two blocks of campus, where movie theaters and restaurants can be found.

Although CUA is distinctly Catholic, students say there's openness to religious diversity on campus. The majority of the students come from the East Coast, mostly New Jersey, but every other state in the country is also represented. The school also includes a large foreign student enrollment; in fact, 10 percent of its student population is international. According to one student, about 40 percent of the school's African-American students are Catholic.

Undoubtedly, most students choose to go to CUA because of its religious focus. But students of all religions attend school here, and Catholic and non-Catholic students express contentment with their college choice. "It's easy to get involved here, and for students who have sought support from the administration, the support has always been there." Adds a politics major: "CUA is a Catholic university, but there aren't all of those theological pressures that people associate with going to a school like ours. The school community is supportive of students, definitely more inclusive than exclusive."

GEORGE WASHINGTON UNIVERSITY

Address: 2121 I Street N.W., #201,
Washington, DC 20052
Phone: (202) 994-6040 / (800) 447-3765
Director of Admissions: George W. Stoner
Multicultural Student Recruiter: Sammie T.
Robinson
1993–94 tuition: $16,398
Room and board: $5,482
Application deadline: 2/1
Financial aid application deadline: 2/1
Non-white freshman admissions: Applicants
for the class of '95: 1,263
Accepted: 68%
Accepted who enroll: 25%
Applicants accepted who rank in top
10% of high school class: 38%
In top 25%: 73%
Median SAT range: 460–600 V, 520–650M
Median ACT range: 20–27
Full-time undergraduate enrollment: 5,593
Men: 49%
Women: 51%

STUDENT ENROLLMENT

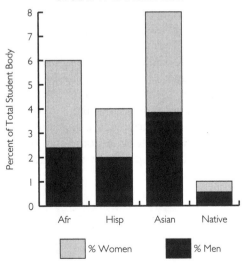

Non-white students in
1987–88: 13%
1988–89: 12%

1989–90: 15%
1990–91: 17%
Geographic distribution of students: na
Students In-District: 20%
Top majors: 1. Arts and Sciences
2. International Affairs 3. Business
Administration
Retention rate of non-white students: na
**Scholarships exclusively for non-white
students:** Eugene Ford Scholarship:
partial, need-based, provides cost of
room and board for Washington,
DC, area students; one awarded each
year.
Remediation programs: The university
offers a summer preparatory program
for entering freshmen known as PREP
(Pre-college Review and Evaluation
Program), available through the
Multicultural Student Services Center.
Academic support services: The Educational
Opportunity Program provides academic
and personal counseling, advising, and
tutorial services.
Ethnic studies programs: East Asian
languages
Ethnic studies courses: The university offers
seven courses in African Studies, four
courses in African-American Studies, and
various other courses in American race
and minority relations.
Organizations for non-white students: Alpha
Kappa Alpha, Delta Sigma Theta, Alpha
Phi Alpha, National Association of
Black Engineers, Black People's Union,
Caribbean Students Association,
Contemporary Gospel Ensemble
Notable non-white alumni: na
Tenured faculty: 659
Non-tenured faculty: 680
Student-faculty ratio: 14:1
Administrators: 149
African-American: 11%
Hispanic: 0
Asian-American: 1%
Native American: 0

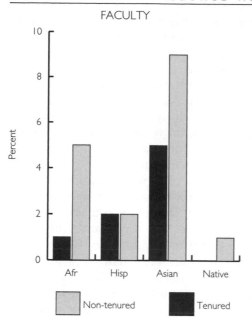

FACULTY

Percent

10
8
6
4
2
0

Afr   Hisp   Asian   Native

Non-tenured   Tenured

Recent non-white speakers on campus:
Vincent Reed (vice president for communications, *Washington Post*); Larry Echohawk (attorney general of Idaho); Randall Robinson (executive director, TransAfrica, Inc.); Odetta (folksinger); Craig Herndon (photojournalist, *Washington Post*); John Wilson (chairperson of the City Council, District of Columbia); Jesse Jackson (civil rights activist and former U.S. presidential candidate)

Located within walking distance of some of Washington, DC's most famous political and cultural landmarks, including the White House and the John F. Kennedy Center for the Performing Arts, George Washington University offers its undergraduates one of the best launching points for careers in politics, government, and business. Taking your studies to the lawn of the Lincoln Memorial is not uncommon here.

Not surprisingly, political science is one of the school's best departments, while history and international affairs are also standouts. Accounting, economics, art history, and biology are well regarded, and engineering, which allows for close interaction with faculty, also has its fans. While GWU is known for its large graduate school programs, which have nearly triple the enrollment of its undergraduate division, students say professors are accessible.

"African-American History," "Women of Color," and "Race and Minority Relations" are said to be some of the school's best—and among the few—ethnic studies courses offered by the university. Students are in the process of petitioning the administration to include more African-American Studies courses. "The administration keeps telling us that GWU doesn't need to offer these courses because we can take them at other area universities." As part of a ten-member consortium that allows students to take courses at such prominent DC schools as Georgetown and Howard, GWU students are able to significantly increase and diversify their class schedules. "I know two George Washington students who are majoring in African Studies at Howard, while they're still paying tuition here. In fact, they're in classes at Howard all day." George Washington's James Oliver, the professor of several of GWU's ethnic studies courses, is described by students as "excellent." GWU's Latin American Studies is said to be strong.

Although academics at GWU may not be as competitive as politics on Capitol Hill, students nonetheless find the resources of the school's Multicultural Student Services Center helpful. "The center offers every support you can imagine. It's kind of a cliché here, but a lot of us consider the center to be a home away from home," says a student. Center programs include tutorial services and the Buddy Program, which matches upperclass students with younger students. "The office is the first place that anyone should turn to, because there's always someone there to help, whether a student or an administrator. Valerie Epps, the center's director, and Janet Moore, the center's assistant director, are always here for students. Students are rarely out of their sight when it comes to academic assistance or advice."

The center is also a respite for students. "This is a place where minority students can come and share their experiences, talk freely among themselves, share each other's joys, obstacles, and to just seek help," says a student. During the course of a typical day, adds the student, as many as 70 students will make their way through the center.

Students say GWU's student government association provides little, if any cultural programming, so such events are left up to the school's cultural student organizations. The Black People's Union (BPU), established on campus in 1968, is the school's largest and most active cultural organization. "We're mostly a cultural and social organization. We're here to help African-American students who may need peer support or our services. Our aim is to strengthen our culture on campus." The BPU has invited speakers to campus to discuss a variety of issues, including such topics as Afrocentric studies. The organization's primary responsibility is scheduling the school's Black History Celebration. "We can't call it Black History Month because we have so many activities that we can't squeeze them all into one month. We start our activities in January, around MLK's birthday," says a BPU organizer. During a recent celebration, events included lectures about African marriage and courtship customs and African-American inventors. In 1992, the BPU also hosted its first trivia game that focused on Afrocentric questions. "Students from other schools in the area, like Howard and Georgetown, came. It was so successful we're going to host it again next year and probably make it an annual event. The game even got airtime on WPFW, a DC radio station."

The Latin American Student Association has parties and recently hosted a premiere of the movie *Mambo Kings,* and political organizations such as College Democrats and Republicans frequently bring visitors to campus. GWU's gay and lesbian student group is also visible on campus.

While GWU may compete in admissions with Georgetown and American University, the schools aren't competitors on the sports field. GWU has only a few varsity athletic teams, including a football squad. With not many opportunities to unite against a crosstown rival, students say there is little sense of campus unity, and in addition, the lack of a central campus is no doubt a contributor to the absence of school spirit. The university's men's basketball team, however, has had some recent successful seasons.

GWU is one of the least culturally and racially diverse campuses of the prominent DC schools, but students nonetheless find the cultural and academic opportunities available at the school worth staying for. "There are fewer blacks here at GWU than there are whites at Howard," says a student. "But because of the strong BPU, I'm glad I came here for school. The BPU has been a haven for many students, and has certainly helped make GWU worth coming to."

GEORGETOWN UNIVERSITY

Address: 37th and O Streets N.W., Washington, DC 20057-1002
Phone: (202) 687-3600
Director of Admissions: Charles A. Deacon
Multicultural Student Recruiter: na
1991–92 tuition: $15,510
Room and board: $6,084
Application deadline: Early decision: 11/1; regular decision: 1/10
Financial aid application deadline: 1/15
Non-white freshman admissions: Applicants for the class of '95: 2,357
Accepted: 32.4%
Accepted who enroll: 41%
Applicants accepted who rank in top 10% of high school class: na
Median SAT: na
Median ACT: na
Full-time undergraduate enrollment: 5,748
Men: 49.2%
Women: 50.8%

Non-white students in
1987–88: 15%
1988–89: 16.6%
1989–90: 18%
1990–91: 18.1%
Geographic distribution of students: na
Top majors: 1. International Politics 2. Government 3. Psychology
Retention rate of non-white students: 90%
Scholarships exclusively for non-white students: None
Remediation programs: None
Academic support services: The university provides a writing center and tutorial services, as well as the services of the Center for Minority Student Affairs, which sponsors a Peer Mentoring Program.
Ethnic studies programs: Programs include African, Asian, and Latin American Studies.
Organizations for non-white students: Black Theatre Ensemble, Minority Pre-health Club, Black Movements Dance Theater, Georgetown University Gospel Choir, Black Student Alliance (BSA), National Association for the Advancement of Colored People, Progressive Black Students, Coalition for the Advancement of Hispanic Americans, Hispanic Community, Sursum Corda, Baobab Club, Caribbean Culture Club, China Circle, Club Filipino, Cuban Students Association, Korean-American Students, Latin American Students Association, Puerto Rican Students Association, *The Blackboard* (literary publication by students of color), Students of Color Organized for Recruitment, Black Student House (meeting place and residence for several leaders of minority student organizations)

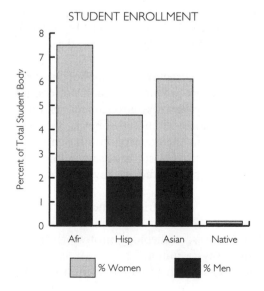

STUDENT ENROLLMENT

Percent of Total Student Body

Afr   Hisp   Asian   Native

☐ % Women   ■ % Men

Notable non-white alumni: Ronald Blaylock
  ('82; vice president, PaineWebber);
  Patrick Ewing (professional basketball
  player); Marcia Cooke ('75; U.S.
  Magistrate, U.S. District Court for the
  Eastern District of Michigan); Michael
  Dorris ('67; author)
Tenured faculty: na
Non-tenured faculty: 119
Student-faculty ratio: 17:1
Administrators: 146
  African-American: 4.8%
  Hispanic: 1.4%
  Asian-American: 1.4%
  Native American: 0
Recent non-white speakers on campus:
  Kenneth Mundy (attorney); Nikki
  Giovanni (poet); Spike Lee (filmmaker)

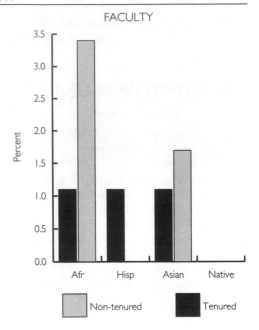

FACULTY

Non-tenured   Tenured

Georgetown University is one of the country's most competitive and cosmopolitan institutions of higher learning. Students come to the 205-year-old Jesuit university—attracted to its location in the nation's capital and its high-powered academics—from all fifty states and nearly a hundred foreign countries.

Georgetown is world-renowned for its School of Foreign Service, created in 1919, five years before the United States established its own Foreign Service. Graduates of Georgetown's Foreign Service program are required to show a proficiency in a foreign language, and students are encouraged to study abroad for a year or a semester; one undergraduate plans to study for a semester in Senegal, Africa, where "I will work to perfect my French and to acquire a working knowledge of Wolof, Senegal's second national language."

As do many of the school's academic programs, Georgetown's School of Business Administration, the university's newest and fastest-growing division, offers an international perspective. Students are able to study business-government relations and global-international management, as well as more traditional subjects. Georgetown is also one of the few prominent universities in the country with a School of Nursing. Among the school's arts and sciences departments, students say philosophy, religion, and English are outstanding, as are American Studies, government, and psychology.

Among the school's course offerings in African and African-American studies, students most highly recommend "Theology of the Black Experience," "African Politics," and "Liberation Theology." Diana Hayes, a theology professor, "is an excellent teacher and is well liked by students," says a junior.

Founded by Jesuits in 1788, Georgetown retains much of its religious flavor. All students are required to take two semesters of theology and philosophy, priests live in all of the dorms, and more than three-quarters of the student body identifies itself as Catholic. Mass is held at the university's Dahlgreen Chapel, located at the center of campus, every morning, noon, and night.

Academics at Georgetown are demanding—most undergraduates take five courses a semester—but students say professors are accessible, even in large introductory courses that can sometimes include more than 300 students. "The professors here advocate that we see them if we have any problems or concerns," says a student. Georgetown has an impressive faculty roster, which includes many DC movers and shakers, such as Jeane Kirkpatrick, a professor of government.

The Center for Minority Student Affairs helps students ease the transition from high school to the academic rigors at Georgetown. Services include tutoring and academic advising. "I wouldn't have succeeded at Georgetown if it hadn't been for the center," says a Foreign Service major. The director of the center, William Reid III, is "very much in touch with the students. He's not condescending, and he offers good advice. He's also a resource for student organizations." Lorraine Davis, an assistant at the center, "is also down-to-earth and helpful to students."

To raise the cultural awareness of Georgetown students, the Black Student Alliance, with about 30 to 40 active members, sponsors various activities on campus. The BSA, which meets regularly in the Intercultural Center, has formal and informal parties, but, says a member, "our main mission is the education of African-Americans and the community about African-American issues, regarding politics, history, and economics. Our organization is multifaceted." The school's NAACP chapter is also strong, and each year sponsors many of the activities surrounding Black History Month, particularly forums. Recent forums have included weekly presentations of *Roots* and discussions focusing on the relations between the Jewish and African-American communities.

One of Georgetown's biggest selling points is its location, close to the U.S. Capitol and other seats of power that so many Georgetown politicos aspire to work within. More precisely, Georgetown is located in a predominantly white residential neighborhood of the U.S. capital that includes cobblestone streets, movie theaters, shopping, clubs, and bars, all just a short walk from campus. Howard, a historically black university, is located in DC, but students report there is little structured activity between students at the two schools. Students add that there is little interaction between them and the city's African-American community. "Georgetown's location can make you forget there are other, less affluent parts of town," says a student.

Intramurals—often fielded at the state-of-the-art Yates Recreational Complex—are popular activities among Georgetown students, as is attending Hoya basketball games. There are no fraternities on campus, so most partying takes place in dorm rooms, in off-campus apartments, or at some of the area's more popular watering holes. The Basement, the school's popular on-campus pub, which serves beer, features live entertainment, although students complain that the entertainment "isn't exactly geared to a racially diverse crowd." The Leavey, the university's newest building, is the headquarters for more than 100 student clubs, and features restaurants, hotel accommodations, and conference rooms.

Georgetown students make time for volunteer service projects. The impressive Volunteer and Public Service Center oversees various programs that allow students to become active in the community. Among these programs is the Community Action Coalition, an organization of more than 500 students who work in area soup kitchens and homeless shelters, tutor children, and visit the elderly. Each year more than 100 students participate in the school's Spring Break in Appalachia program, in which they perform community service projects for residents of the rural areas.

Although Georgetown recruits students from every state in the Union and many countries, the typical Georgetown student is conservative and affluent. Expensive cars and clothes are often seen on campus. Georgetown students are also bright and focused; most know the careers they plan to pursue even before they arrive on campus. Rare is the bohemian student in search of himself or herself. The most controversial groups on campus are the school's gay and lesbian and pro-choice organizations, groups which espouse philosophies and lifestyles that are contrary to Catholic teaching.

Georgetown is one of America's most famous universities, both here and abroad, and offers top-flight academics to its job-conscious applicants. "I've been very happy here," says a senior from the South. "I've overcome my fear of public speaking, and I've immersed myself in a totally different environment. With a Georgetown degree, I also know I'm destined to get a good job, I hope with the Foreign Service."

HOWARD UNIVERSITY

Address: 2400 6th Street N.W., Washington, DC 20059
Phone: (202) 806-2752
Director of Admissions: Emmett R. Griffin, Jr.
Multicultural Student Recruiter: na
1991–92 tuition: $5,825
Room and board: $3,650
Application deadline: 4/1
Financial aid application deadline: 4/1
Non-white freshman admissions: Applicants
  for the class of '95: 5,200
  Accepted: 51%
  Accepted who enroll: na
  Applicants accepted who rank in top
  10% of high school class: na
  Median SAT: 430 V, 467 M
  Median ACT: 21
Full-time undergraduate enrollment: 9,276
  Men: 40%
  Women: 60%

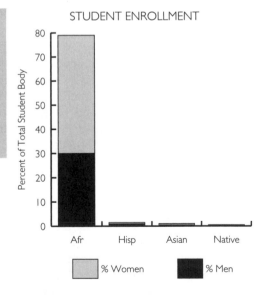

STUDENT ENROLLMENT

Percent of Total Student Body

□ % Women   ■ % Men

Non-white students in
  1987–88: 82%
  1988–89: 82%

GEOGRAPHIC DISTRIBUTION OF STUDENTS

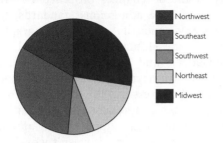

- Northwest
- Southeast
- Southwest
- Northeast
- Midwest

1989–90: 82%
1990–91: 82%

Students In-District: 16.5%

Top majors: 1. Accounting 2. Electrical Engineering 3. Computer-Based Information Systems

Retention rate of non-white students: 79%

Scholarships exclusively for non-white students: At this predominantly African-American university, all scholarships are available to non-white applicants.

Remediation programs: Remediation services are offered through the Center for Academic Reinforcement.

Academic support services: Tutoring is available in most subjects, as well as student study groups and computer-assisted instruction.

Ethnic studies programs: The university's Afro-American Studies program includes about 25 courses, while its African Studies program includes about 30. The university offers instruction in Arabic, Amharic, Yoruba, Wolof, Swahili, and other African languages.

Ethnic studies courses: Most courses include African-American perspectives and experiences.

Organizations for non-white students: Alpha Kappa Alpha, Delta Sigma Theta, Sigma Gamma Rho, Zeta Phi Beta, Alpha Phi Alpha, Phi Beta Sigma, and others

Notable non-white alumni: Phylicia Ayers-Allen Rashad (Fine Arts; actress); Toni Morrison (Pulitzer Prize-winning novelist); Andrew Young (Science; former UN ambassador and mayor of Atlanta)

Tenured faculty: na

Non-tenured faculty: na

Student-faculty ratio: 6:1

Administrators: na

Recent non-white speakers on campus: Dr. Clifton R. Wharton, Jr. (chairman and CEO, TIAA and CREF); Percy Sutton (president, Inner City Broadcasting); Delano Lewis (CEO, C&P Telephone); Dr. Billy Taylor (pianist and composer); Dr. Condoleeza Rice (former special assistant to the President for National Security Affairs)

What do former Supreme Court justice Thurgood Marshall, opera diva Jessye Norman, New York City mayor David Dinkins, and actress Phylicia Rashad have in common, besides being significant cultural and political figures? They each are members of the elite group of individuals who have earned diplomas from Howard University, long considered the country's most prominent historically black institution of higher learning.

But lately Howard has been losing ground as America's "black Harvard," especially as schools such as Morehouse and Spelman, also historically black colleges, continue to upgrade their facilities and attract talented students to their campuses. The average combined SAT score of Howard students was 897 in 1991, while the average scores of Morehouse and Spelman students were nearly 100 points higher. Much of the responsibility for regaining the university's preeminence has fallen on Franklyn Jenifer, Howard's new president, who quickly appointed a commission to "take a top-to-bottom look at the university," according to a recent *Wall Street Journal* article. The commission presented a 240-page report to Jenifer, says the *Journal* article, "which provided the basis for many of the 80 changes proposed by" the president. Among the changes are an attempt to raise admissions standards; the elimination of certain undergraduate departments, such as geology, geography, pharmacy, and teacher education; the closing of the Human Ecology School and dispersing its programs throughout the university; and the beginning of more aggressive fundraising efforts so the university will not have to be so heavily funded by the federal government. Howard, chartered by Congress in 1867 to educate freed slaves, receives about half of its operating budget from congressional appropriation.

For the most part, the changes have been greeted with support from alumni, students, and faculty. "We couldn't go back to where we were; it wasn't working," said R. Chester Redhead, president of Howard's alumni association. Adds a senior: "The fight is back. President Jenifer is a more visible president than the previous one. You can sometimes see him on campus or at football games waving and talking to students. His energy is definitely lifting morale here."

One of the characteristics of Howard that hasn't changed during the years, however, is its commitment to the liberal arts. Today, students praise the school's political science, psychology, and history departments, while engineering, especially electrical engineering, also earns high marks. As with students at other schools, the overriding sentiment at Howard is pre-professional, as the school's most popular majors are in the School of Business, which offers course work in nine areas, including accounting, business administration, finance, insurance, and hospitality management. The school's communications department is also outstanding and allows students to learn by using state-of-the-art equipment and to gain experience by working at Howard's cable channel 32. Howard also has a well-known medical school, and competition among undergraduate science majors is keen. Students say chemistry and zoology are among their school's best science programs. When students aren't able to find what they want to take at Howard, they are able to enroll in courses at other area universities as part of the DC Consortium of Universities, which includes such schools as Georgetown and George Washington University.

While the school offers a major in Afro-American Studies that students say is strong, they are quick to add that Afrocentric perspectives are integrated in most courses. "It just can't help but be so, as the classrooms are made up primarily of African-American students and the professors are more than likely also African-American."

The Greek organizations are some of the school's most active clubs, but students say you don't have to be in a fraternity or sorority to feel a part of the campus scene. "Howard University offers so many things that you don't have to be involved in a fraternity, and the Greeks here definitely are not cliquey. My roommate is in a fraternity and I'm not, but there's no difference between us when it comes to social life. The Greek life is also somewhat special here, as most of the black fraternities and sororities were founded here. The Greeks do throw a lot of parties and are involved in community programs. Each of the organizations has a week of its own, such as Delta [Sigma Theta] Week, when the Deltas brought various speakers to campus for an AIDS seminar. Other organizations have speakers here to discuss drug awareness, and to offer advice about graduate school applications."

Another student paints a slightly different picture of the Greek organizations.

"Every Greek unit has a spot on the yard, our quad. Each fraternity and sorority goes to one spot to hang out or to step. But when they step, they are respectful of one another and wait until the other is done before they begin. There gets to be some friendly competition between them. But everyone is truly interested in what the other group is doing, and is respectful of them as well."

For Greeks and non-Greeks, there are the popular state clubs, which include members who are from a given club's name state, the largest of which are the Wisconsin, California, Florida, Georgia, and Virginia clubs. The Detroit Club hosts a regular happy hour at a club off campus, while the Virginia Club was active during Douglas Wilder's campaign for governor. (Wilder, by the way, is yet another prominent Howard alum.) Student government associations, including the Howard University Student Association (HUSA), which manages a six-figure budget, and the General Assembly are also active on campus. In a recent year, HUSA sponsored study skills seminars and cultural awareness programs, among them an Awareness Series, which included such forum topics as African-American female/male relationships.

Also popular is the Campus Pals organization, which "helps incoming students make the transition to Howard. Not just to college life in general, but to Howard, because we think we're more special than that. Each Campus Pal is assigned about thirty-five to fifty new students, and we write the students handwritten letters during the summer before they arrive here. When the new students get here, we do more than take them on campus tours. We have ice-cream socials and we have roller-skating parties, and we also offer students advice and help with personal problems." To be a Campus Pal, you must survive a rigorous interview, as only 50 are chosen each year—and this is all on a volunteer basis!

And if you're anyone at Howard, you no doubt have an office at Power Hall, or at least hang out there. "It's our Wall Street and it's where all the deals are cut and made on campus," says a student leader. Located in the student center, the hall includes office space for HUSA, the Caribbean Student Association, the College of Arts and Sciences Student Council, the Undergraduate Student Assembly, and the Homecoming Committee.

According to one student, there is no one organization that deals specifically with African-American cultural awareness. "You'll find that everything we do directly meets the needs of black students, from the academics to the clubs. All of them deal with black issues. Our NAACP chapter is virtually nonexistent because we don't need that kind of support." Although Howard is predominantly a black institution, the university also enrolls students from other backgrounds and cultures. White students, most often enrolled in the university's graduate school programs, "are welcome here on campus. Almost all of our organizations are inclusive." The Young Republican Club, while small, is a presence on campus. But don't go looking for a Democratic Club. "Just about everyone here is a Democrat, so there's no real reason to have such a club," says a student.

Although the Howard campus offers an abundance of activities, students are known for getting off campus every so often and kicking up their feet at any one of the area clubs. The Ritz, Tacoma Station (especially on Thursday nights), and Chapter Three are some of the more popular nightspots. The DC area, besides being the seat of the nation's political power, is also home to a wealth of cultural opportunities, including those at the John F. Kennedy Center for the Performing Arts and numerous museums. The area immediately around Howard, however, isn't known for its glitz and glamour, as the area, like many parts of the nation's capital, has its share of crime and run-down city blocks. "Students usually don't venture off campus alone, but we learn to take precautions, just as you would in most urban settings." In fact, Howard's police officers recently staged a protest, saying they were understaffed and ill-equipped to protect the campus. They also urged the university president to hire more officers and purchase bulletproof vests for the officers. After meeting with the protesters, Jenifer has agreed to hire additional officers.

Geographically, Howard students are a diverse group. Students come from almost every state in the Union, as well as from more than a hundred different countries. The school also attracts a predominantly middle-class student body. "Howard has always been known as a bourgeois school. Doctors and lawyers send their kids here. But there are those working their way through. It's not uncommon to see BMWs or smaller Toyota Celicas or someone catching the bus," says a student.

With a new and energetic president, Howard University shows every sign of retaining its spot as one of the country's preeminent black universities. The university's academic programs, provided in a supportive atmosphere, continue to attract some of the country's most motivated African-American students. "I came to Howard looking for the black experience. It's been demanding, and sometimes I've wondered why I came here with all the work that's involved in getting my degree, but it has been great." He adds: "At my high school, I thought I knew just a few people who might be successful. Here, I feel that everyone will be. There are students going to Berkeley and Harvard graduate schools, and students sit around talking about global warming and politics. The atmosphere is so positive and reinforcing."

F L O R I D A

UNIVERSITY OF FLORIDA

Address: 201 Criser Hall, Gainesville, FL
  32611
Phone: (904) 392-1365
Director of Admissions: S. William Kolb
Multicultural Student Recruiters: Susie
  Neeley, John Boatwright
1991–92 tuition: $1,420 (in-state); $5,560
  (out-of-state)
Room and board: $3,790
Application deadline: 2/1
Financial aid application deadline: 4/15
Non-white freshman admissions: Applicants
  for the class of '95: 3,196
  Accepted: 89.7%
  Accepted who enroll: 27.5%
  Applicants accepted who rank in top
  10% of high school class: na
  Median SAT: na
  Median ACT: na
Full-time undergraduate enrollment: 23,236
  Men: 52.9%
  Women: 47.1%
Non-white students in
  1987–88: 13.3%
  1988–89: 13.9%
  1989–90: 14.3%
  1990–91: 15.1%
Geographic distribution of students: na
Top majors: na
Retention rate of non-white students: na
**Scholarships exclusively for non-white
  students:** na
Remediation programs: None
Academic support services: The university

offers tutoring in most academic subjects
as well as study skills workshops.
Ethnic studies programs: na
Ethnic studies courses: na
Organizations for non-white students:
  Association of Black Communicators,
  Alpha Phi Alpha, Alpha Sweets, Beta
  Eta Sigma, Black Student Union,
  Caribbean Student Association, Chinese
  Student Association, Club Creole, Delta
  Sigma Theta, Hispanic Engineering
  Students, Hispanic Student Association,
  Kappa Alpha Psi, Latinos En Acción,
  Minority Business Society, Minorities in
  the Institute of Food and Agricultural

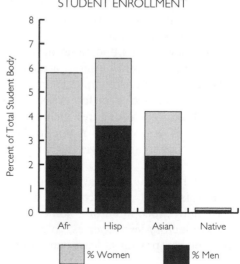

STUDENT ENROLLMENT

Sciences, Minority Preprofessional Service Association, NAACP, National Association of Minority Contractors, Omega Psi Phi, Presidential Scholars, Sigma Gamma Rho, Society for Black Student Engineers, University of Florida Gospel Choir, Zeta Phi Beta

Notable non-white alumni: na

Tenured faculty: 1,742

Non-tenured faculty: 1,449

Student-faculty ratio: 17:1

Administrators: 344

  African-American: 2.6%

  Hispanic: 0.6%

  Asian-American: 1.2%

  Native American: 0

Recent non-white speakers on campus: Dr. Na'im Akbar (clinical psychologist); Maya Angelou (author and poet); Alex Haley (author); Jesse Jackson (former U.S. presidential candidate and civil rights activist); Coretta Scott King (civil rights activist and widow of Martin Luther King, Jr.); Winnie Mandela (former wife of South African civil rights leader Nelson Mandela); Wilma Mankiller (chief, Cherokee Tribe of Oklahoma); William Raspberry (urban affairs columnist, *Washington Post*)

FACULTY

Should you decide to attend the University of Florida, you'll need more than just your Coppertone lotion and bathing suit. You'll also need to bring your academic smarts and motivation, as Florida is one of the South's most respected and demanding public universities.

Florida has almost every sort of academic program imaginable under the Florida sun. The university is well known for its nationally ranked School of Journalism, which gives students access to an electronic newsroom and hands-on experience with campus newspapers and radio and television stations. Also well regarded are the school's programs in business, accounting, engineering, and architecture.

Students aren't as complimentary about their school's African-American Studies program. "It's one of the few areas in which the university is lacking," says a student. "Usually, only two or three such courses are offered each semester, and I've taken all three. If you want to major in the area, be prepared for a lot of independent study." Students add, however, that the university is currently in the process of beefing up the program.

It's unfortunate, then, at a school with the quality of faculty that Florida has, that professors aren't more accessible. Classroom sizes can run into the hundreds, and learning by video monitor is sometimes the rule rather than the exception, especially in introductory-level courses. In addition, all students are required by state law to study on campus for at least one summer session. The second summer session seems to be the most popular, as many student groups, particularly the Black Student Union, use the time for meetings and to prepare for the school year ahead.

To individualize retention programs, each of the university's undergraduate divisions has its own Minority Affairs Program. "It's a comprehensive program, and is getting better, especially as the deans are listening more to student concerns than they were before," says a student. Willie Robertson, a Minority Affairs Program adviser in the School of Education, is highly praised by students. The Office for Minority Acceptance and Special Programs also works with student retention and earns the thumbs-up from students. "Although the office isn't as well used as it might be, it's definitely busy. The counselors there certainly aren't just sitting idly by twiddling their thumbs," says a student leader. The dean who heads the school's Student Service Program, Jim Scott, an African-American, is also well liked by students. His office oversees all student programming.

"A home away from home" for many of the school's African-American students is the university's impressive Institute of Black Culture. "Students hang out there and just talk and relax. A lot of the black student groups also have their own meetings there. I sell the place to new students as a place for black students to be themselves." William Simmons, director of the institute, "is always there for us to talk to," says a student. In addition to meeting rooms, the institute has the Heritage Room, a room that houses African and African-American art, a library, and an audiovisual center.

One of the student groups that make use of the institute is the Black Student Union, which meets every two weeks during the regular school year. "The membership is truly comprehensive and includes black members from Africa, Europe, Asia, all over," observes a student.

The events sponsored by the BSU include various activities for Black History Month. During a typical celebration, one student estimates, the group will spend up to $13,000 to bring speakers to campus and to sponsor forums. Recent forum topics focused on black-on-black crime, the school's attrition rate, and the betterment of study skills. The BSU also sponsors its own Cultural Festival, held in the spring, which features art displays and speeches by students. Kids Day has BSU members bringing area elementary school children to the Florida campus for a day of games. The group also sponsors events for Martin Luther King, Jr., Week and for Malcolm X Day. During the school year 1991–92, the BSU sponsored its first rally as part of Malcolm X Day, at which many students gave speeches.

Florida's predominantly black Greek organizations are also active in campus and community activities. Each year the organizations sponsor the state's largest step show, and in the spring of 1993 the group invited students from all Southeastern Conference schools to participate. The event was most recently held at O'Connell Center, with a seating capacity of 14,000.

The Hispanic Student Association, with about 100 members, "is very active and is more like a family," says a student. "Once a student chooses to join HSA, he or she is made to feel at home." To introduce HSA to prospective members, HSA hosts a meeting attended not only by student leaders but by the president of the university as well. HSA's primary activity has always been Hispanic Heritage Week, but because the group has experienced such success, the week has been expanded to a monthlong event. During a recent year, the event included a dance troupe, a food fair, an art exhibition, various performers and speakers, and the popular march of the flags of all the Latin American countries.

HSA also sponsors a pageant, for men and women. At the end of the evening, two lucky students are chosen to serve as that year's Mr. and Miss HSA. "But our contestants don't compete in bathing suits. The contest is based entirely on how well the contestants answer questions asked of them." The judges? Faculty, of course. Along with the Hispanic Faculty Association, HSA also sponsors an annual student-faculty picnic. As Gainesville has a small Hispanic community, HSA members sponsor food drives at a local church.

A big event for all student groups is the VISA Talent Show. "That's the event where all the cultural groups interact, and it packs the O'Connell Center. Each of the groups practices for three months, and it gets extremely competitive, in a friendly sort of way, because we're competing for trophies. It's very professional and well choreographed." During a recent year, HSA won the trophy for best visuals.

It's hard to separate the city of Gainesville, which recently elected an African-American mayor, from the university, as the town, says more than one student, "is the university." Students say they have met with no tension venturing into the stores or restaurants of the area. Gainesville's location provides easy access to the Sunshine State's famous beaches and no school year would be complete without at least one visit to Disney World, in Orlando.

Racial segregation doesn't seem to be as evident at UF as it is at other large Southern universities. Students say their classmates, with the usual exceptions, are accepting of diversity, but, adds a student, "the university is like the country, there's a lot of institutional racism." The most obvious examples, according to students, are older members of the faculty who "don't think minority students should be in their classrooms. But the university is attracting younger and more tolerant faculty who bring with them a more liberal attitude."

Outside the region, the University of Florida may be best known either for its athletic prowess or as a great suntanning locale. But the university is more than that. It's also one of the great public universities in the country and it offers a wealth of opportunity for its students. "The biggest drawback of going to Florida is its size," says a recent graduate. "It can be a little like finding your way through a city. But I got involved in campus events, and I grew a lot, both intellectually and socially. You can do a great deal at the university. The problem is choosing what and how much."

FLORIDA INSTITUTE OF TECHNOLOGY

Address: 150 West University Boulevard,
Melbourne, FL 32901-6988
Phone: (800) 888-4348
Director of Admissions: Louis Levy
Multicultural Student Recruiter: Judi Marino
1991–92 tuition: $11,400
Room and board: $3,465
Application deadline: Rolling admissions
Financial aid application deadline: 2/1
Non-white freshman admissions: Applicants
for the class of '96: 442
Accepted: 317
Accepted who enroll: 80%
Applicants accepted who rank in the top
10% of high school class: 8%
In the top 25%: 19%
Median SAT range: 450–499 V,
550–599 M
Median ACT range: na
Full-time undergraduate enrollment: 2,435
Men: 73%
Women: 27%

GEOGRAPHIC DISTRIBUTION OF STUDENTS

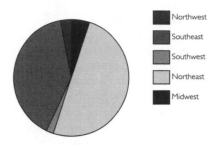

- Northwest
- Southeast
- Southwest
- Northeast
- Midwest

1989–90: 4%
1990–91: 11.3%
1991–92: 10%
Students In-state: 29%
Top majors: 1. Aeronautics 2. Marine
Biology 3. Aerospace Engineering
Retention rate of non-white students: na
**Scholarships exclusively for non-white
students:** Black Scholars: need- and
merit-based; covers 20% of tuition; five
awarded each year. Seminole Miccosukee
Indian Scholarship: need-based; amount

STUDENT ENROLLMENT

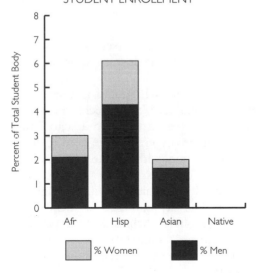

Non-white students in
1987–88: na
1988–89: 4%

FACULTY

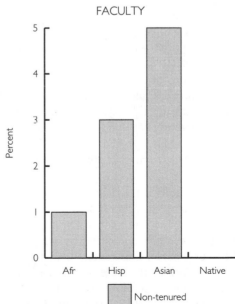

determined by students' respective tribes.

Remediation programs: None

Academic support services: The university offers tutoring in most academic subjects.

Ethnic studies programs: None

Ethnic studies courses: None

Organizations for non-white students: Spanish-Speaking Student Society, Caribbean Student Association

Notable non-white alumni: na

Tenured faculty: na

Non-tenured faculty: 222

Student-faculty ratio: 14:1

Administrators: 208
  African-American: .1%
  Hispanic: .1%
  Asian-American: 0
  Native American: .05%

Recent non-white speakers on campus: Sharin Tahir-Kheli (alternate U.S. delegate to UN); Jim Billy (Seminole chief); Paul Buster (Miccosukee chief)

Although the Florida Institute of Technology may be located in the Sunshine State, don't come here assuming the school's academics are a day at the beach. They're anything but. Successful FIT students are ones who place books ahead of the sand and surf.

FIT includes five colleges: the College of Engineering, the College of Science and Liberal Arts, the School of Psychology, the School of Aeronautics, and the School of Management. As might be expected, FIT's College of Engineering offers some of the school's best and most popular majors. The college's electrical and mechanical engineering programs are, in the words of one student, "very thorough and difficult." A recent graduate says the computer engineering program "is getting better every year." FIT students can also study oceanography and ocean engineering. The biology department, in the College of Science and Liberal Arts, also gets students' respect, and the School of Aeronautics' Aviation Center operates 50 aircraft and nine simulators in various phases of pilot training. The School of Management, however, is said to be FIT's weakest link.

In order to graduate, FIT students must take two years of courses that emphasize the humanities and writing skills, in addition to satisfying the degree requirements in their respective majors.

FIT does not offer any ethnic studies courses. Whether it should is a source of debate on campus. "I wanted to go to a college that emphasized the technical aspects of my education," says a senior. "I didn't necessarily need to go to a school that made us study race and ethnic relations." A classmate disagrees. "We need to study other cultures, as well as our own," she says. "At a school with so many nationalities represented we need to be taught about those other cultures."

Students have access to tutorial assistance in all academic subjects through the school's Individual Learning Center (ILC). Students say that ILC is "helpful" in introductory courses, especially calculus and physics, but less helpful in the upper-level courses. "When you get to the more advanced courses," comments one student who used the center frequently her first year on campus, "you need to turn either to some of your smarter classmates or to your professors."

The Caribbean Student Association (CSA) does its fair share of helping to make the student body more culturally and racially aware. In fact, CSA, with more than 65 members, is FIT's largest and most active student group. "The Caribbean Student

Association is the most popular organization on campus," reports a student member, "and we hold parties every year that are attended by all types of people." One of the parties is for graduating seniors.

CSA also brings cultural events to campus. Last year, CSA organized the school's first Black History Month activities, which included a lecture by a local black filmmaker and poet, an art display, and a panel discussion with two FIT students from Nigeria. The head of the Campus Community Board, the student activities organization, was so impressed with CSA's efforts during Black History Month that they have allotted CSA more funding for future programming. CSA members have also been known to take time out from their studies to be a part of the community's big brother/big sister program by tutoring young people at a neighborhood elementary school.

CSA's faculty adviser, Judy Marino, a counselor in charge of international admissions, is described by one student organizer as "very helpful. She helped us to reorganize recently so we could be more influential and get more students involved."

The majority of FIT's black students are from the Caribbean, especially Antigua and Jamaica. There is no student group specifically for African-Americans, although most of FIT's African-American students are CSA members.

FIT's Greek system encompasses about 15 percent of the student body and hosts many weekend parties, but fraternity and sorority life doesn't dominate the campus. Many parties can be found in off-campus apartments, which are welcome alternatives to the school's single-sex dorms. "The living conditions are better off campus," explains one student. "The apartments also give students more privacy and they are less expensive." For the men, social life is somewhat stymied by the fact that the male-to-female ratio is by far in the women's favor.

FIT's campus is just a few minutes' walk—or bicycle ride—to the beaches of the Atlantic coast. Orlando, where you'll find Disney World, and the Kennedy Space Center, where many students hope to someday land jobs, are both within an hour's drive. Movie theaters are the primary social outlet in the area, as are a few nearby bars.

Students are attracted to FIT because it provides respectable technical training in a less than cutthroat academic environment. "There isn't a lot of cultural awareness going on here, partly because there aren't many of us American minority students on campus to make things happen, so if that's what a student is looking for, then he or she might want to go to another school. I like FIT because I know I'm getting a good hands-on education in doing what I like to do, which is engineering."

FLORIDA STATE UNIVERSITY

Address: 216B William Johnston Building, Tallahassee, FL 32306-1009
Phone: (904) 644-6200
Director of Admissions: na
Multicultural Student Recruiter: David Moss
1993–94 tuition: $1,780 (in-state); $6,680 (out-of-state)
Room and board: $4,060
Application deadline: 3/1
Financial aid application deadline: 4/1
Non-white freshman admissions: Applicants for the class of '95: 2,828
  Accepted: 67%
  Accepted who enroll: 26%
  Applicants accepted who rank in top 10% of high school class: na
  Median SAT: 1,011
  Median ACT: 21
Full-time undergraduate enrollment: 18,602
  Men: 46%
  Women: 54%
Non-white students in
  1987–91: na
Geographic distribution of students: na
Students In-state: 85%
Top majors: na
Retention rate of non-white students: na
Scholarships exclusively for non-white students: na
Remediation programs: na
Academic support services: na

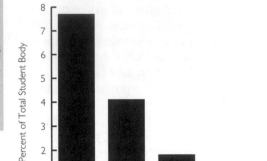

STUDENT ENROLLMENT

Ethnic studies programs: FSU offers programs in Black Studies, Latin American and Caribbean Studies, and Asian Studies.
Ethnic studies courses: na
Organizations for non-white students: Black Student Union, Hispanic Honor Society, United Latin Society
Notable non-white alumni: na
Tenured faculty: na
Non-tenured faculty: na
Student-faculty ratio: na
Administrators: na
Recent non-white speakers on campus: na

A day without sports at Florida State University is a day without sunshine, although that too is a rarity in the Sunshine State. Students live for football (a few years back MTV hosted the school's—and the world's—longest pep rally), especially against archrival University of Florida, and varsity baseball and basketball games are well attended. Intramurals of almost any sort are available to the students, and many students squeeze time in between their studies and social events to participate.

Although academics are said not to be high on many students' list of priorities, a good education is available to the industrious. Class sizes are large, and meetings with teaching assistants rather than professors are generally the rule. First-choice classes are also hard to come by. To help ease the transition to college, especially to a school the size of FSU, the university recently established the Multicultural Peer Facilitator Program. "It's kind of like a big brother/big sister program, where a first-year student is paired with an older student from his or her same racial background and with his or her academic interests. The mentor is supposed to help the new student adjust socially and academically, and we help the student get familiar with the campus and the support services, and just give him or her the lowdown about how to best succeed here at FSU, which can be an overwhelming place because it's so big." Although FSU is a big place, students say that meetings with professors can be had—although it depends a great deal on individual initiative.

Students consider the School of Criminology to be one of the university's best academic programs, but add that the school is "lacking in diversity of perspective because no minorities or women teach in the area." Students praise FSU's popular College of Business, as well as the departments of psychology and computer science. FSU also has solid programs in engineering and hotel and restaurant management. Because of the school's location in the state capital, students have opportunities to work as interns in state and local government offices.

The school's Black Studies program is described by one student minoring in the area as "excellent" because "it offers a totally new perspective." The director of the program, William Jones, "is a dynamic professor and person on campus. He gets us to look at history in a new way, and he teaches us how the history of oppression in this country affects all of us, not just African-Americans." Jones coordinated a recent panel discussion focusing on the political campaign of former Klansman David Duke.

Like many other state-supported institutions in the country, FSU has been affected by severe budget cuts in recent years. The most obvious cuts came in the form of fewer class offerings. "People who wanted to graduate during the summer won't be able to because the courses they need to take aren't being offered. The cuts should only be temporary," the student adds hopefully, "because of all the demonstrations that we've staged at the state capitol."

With about 500 active members, the Black Student Union is by far FSU's most active cultural student organization. For cultural awareness, the BSU sponsors regular seminars on campus. Recent seminars, which are led by African-American faculty members and students, have focused on African-American women and interracial dating. A popular BSU event is its annual Black Music Festival, a daylong event during which "music is played by a DJ to show how most of today's music, from blues to jazz, is linked back to Africa." An African drum group, from FSU's School of Music, also performs. The BSU sponsors a Goofy Olympics and regular barbecue parties. "The BSU always has something going on," comments a non-member, who participates in many of the group's activities.

Although there is no equivalent organization for the school's Latino students, there are two organizations—the United Latin Society and the recently established Hispanic Honor Society—that fill this void. "We formed the Hispanic Honor Society because we feel that many people here have negative images of what it means to be Hispanic. All too often they think only of migrant workers or people on welfare when they think of Hispanics. Our group is meant to correct that view," says one of the founders. Both groups provide tutoring for students at area schools, and the ULS organizes a food drive for migrant workers. The FSU music department recently helped sponsor a Music of the Americas Festival, "a sort of a Hispanic party that was held on the top floor of the capitol building."

To increase the enrollment of Latino students at the university, FSU's admissions office has Latino students contact prospectives to answer any questions they may have about life at FSU. "We accept a lot of our Hispanic applicants," says a student, "but very few of them end up attending. About half of the Hispanic students here are from Miami, and most who decide to go away to college will go to the University of Florida because it's closer to home, although not by much."

Diversity among students is not one of FSU's strong points. Only about 13 percent of the school's more than 20,000 undergraduates are non-white, and many of these students are from Florida. The second-largest FSU contingent hails from Georgia. A common student criticism isn't about the lack of non-white enrollment at the university, however, but the lack of interaction between the races on campus. "Except for sports, there's very little blending of the races here," says a student. "Hispanics hang out with each other, blacks hang out with each other, and whites hang out with each other. I don't like that fact of life here much, but I guess it's like that on most college campuses. There are no examples of blatant racism that I know of going on here. It's just that there's not a lot of mixing and learning of different cultures. Recently I tried to start a multicultural society, where we would include representatives from every single cultural group on campus. But it was dropped. The whole process was too complicated and there was a lot of disagreement about how such a group should be organized."

Going to football games isn't the only thing to do at FSU. The university recently built a new multimillion-dollar sports complex that keeps interested students in shape, and the school's intramural competition can be stiff, especially between dorms. The school's student union also brings films, concerts, and lectures to campus on a regular basis. Florida beaches along the Gulf of Mexico are just a thirty-minute drive from campus.

Florida State may not have the academic reputation of archrival University of Florida, but it does have its share of contented undergraduates. "FSU is certainly not a negative environment for minority students, but for almost any student it does have its drawbacks," says a student. "Mostly they have to deal with the school's sheer size. But I've been glad I've gone here because the people here are, on the whole, friendly and relaxed, and it has made me work a lot harder for the things I've gotten."

UNIVERSITY OF MIAMI

Address: P.O. Box 248025, Coral Gables, FL 33124
Phone: (305) 284-4323
Director of Admissions: Mary Conway
Multicultural Student Recruiter: Vivien Allen
1992–93 tuition: $14,080
Room and board: $5,575
Application deadline: 3/1
Financial aid application deadline: 3/1

Non-white freshman admissions: Applicants for the class of '95: na
Accepted: na
Applicants accepted who rank in top 10% of high school class: 38%
Median SAT range: na
Median ACT range: na

STUDENT ENROLLMENT

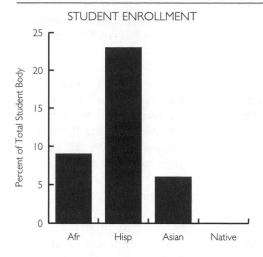

Full-time undergraduate enrollment: 8,638
   Men: 4,750
   Women: 4,164
Non-white students in
   1987–88: 26%
   1988–89: 25%
   1989–90: 25%
   1990–91: 29%

GEOGRAPHIC DISTRIBUTION OF STUDENTS

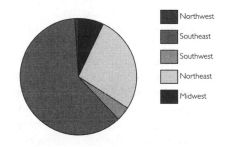

Students In-state: na
Top majors: 1. Business 2. Biology
   3. Psychology
Retention rate of non-white students: 84.9%
Scholarships exclusively for non-white
   students: na
Remediation programs: None
Academic support services: Freshman
   Success, Writing Center, Math Lab, and
   the Study Skills Center provide academic
   support.
Ethnic studies programs: Students can

minor in Caribbean, African, or
Afro-American Studies, which include
about 20 courses. Also offered is a Latin
American Studies major, with more than
25 courses.
Organizations for non-white students:
   United Black Students, Federation of
   Black Greeks, Caribbean Students
   Association, Organization of Jamaican
   Unity, Haitian Student Association,
   African Student Association
Notable non-white alumni: Freddy Berens
   ('64; vice president, Prudential Bache);
   Dawn Lewis ('82; actress); Marvis
   Martin ('77; opera singer); Gloria
   Estefan ('78; lead singer, Miami Sound
   Machine); Willie Waters ('73; artistic
   director, Greater Miami Opera)

FACULTY

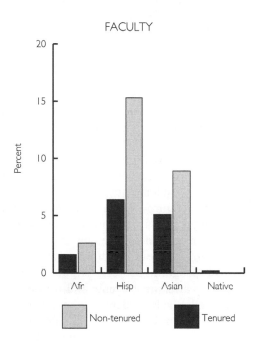

Tenured faculty: 826
Non-tenured faculty: 895
Student-faculty ratio: 8:1
Administrators: 1,061
   African-American: 8.6%
   Hispanic: 24%
   Asian-American: 2.6%
   Native American: 0.3%

Recent non-white speakers on campus: Maki Mandela (daughter of Nelson Mandela); Martin Luther King III (Georgia state representative and civil rights leader); John Amos (actor); Maya Angelou (poet and author)

Where beach wear is fashion de rigueur on campus, the University of Miami—with a double-sized pool at its center and Miami's famed beaches just minutes away—is perceived by many as Suntan U. But the 63-year-old university can no longer be described as a school only for students who want to work on their tans. The school has become increasingly recognized for its academics, and—as evidenced by SAT scores and high school class ranks—is attracting a brighter group of students every year.

Music is perhaps one of the university's standout departments, and includes courses in such areas as music engineering technology and media and industry, as well as in some of the more standard areas. The university has excellent programs in the sciences, and students report that the atmospheric studies and marine sciences programs are especially respected. Miami's medical school is one of the best in the country. The university's most popular majors are in the areas of business, particularly finance. The College of Arts and Sciences offers the Caribbean, African, and Afro-American studies program as a minor; currently students are working to have the program upgraded to a major course of study. Miami's Honors Programs are highly regarded and enable students to study with some of the university's best faculty members in seminar-style class settings.

For academic and non-academic support, students are able to turn to various faculty and staff members. "There are a large variety of student support organizations to become involved with and to voice your concerns through," says a finance major. "The minority faculty and administrators are also very concerned with and are supportive of minority students on campus. Overall, minority students have a positive relationship with the deans, vice-presidents, and president of the university." In particular, students turn to Jerry Houston, a dean in the student affairs office. "He is a father figure to many students, who look up to him because of his high morals and integrity," says a student. "You can always go to him with a problem and he is always interested in listening and helping you." Anna Price, an academic adviser, and Marvin Dawkins, director of the Caribbean, African, and African-American studies program, are also supportive of students and student organizations, often speaking at campus events and forums.

United Black Students, Miami's African-American student group, sponsors numerous cultural awareness activities, including events for Martin Luther King Week and Malcolm X Day, talent and fashion shows, and Black Student/Faculty Mixers. In addition to sponsoring events on campus, UBS interacts with the Miami-area community by sponsoring SAT prep courses for high school students, tutoring elementary school students, organizing food and clothing drives, and conducting fund raisers for the Miami chapter of the NAACP.

Nearly half of Miami's student body commute to campus, many from their family homes in nearby Dade, Broward, and Palm Beach counties. School spirit is never in short supply despite the relatively large commuter population, especially when it comes to football season. Miami's football team boasts frequent winning seasons, and is a usual Orange Bowl contender. The university's chief athletic rival is the University of Florida at Gainesville. Miami's baseball, swim, and basketball teams also fare well, and intramural sporting events are popular.

Other student activities are in abundance at Miami, from an active Greek social scene to participation in over 180 various art, debate, political, cultural, and social organizations. Hanging out at the pool located at the center of campus or at the "Rat," which includes various eating establishments and sponsors live entertainment, are also popular on-campus activities.

Coral Gables, the community in which the university is located, is affluent and predominantly white, and students say there is relatively little to do socially in the area. For off-campus entertainment, students usually head into greater Miami, for its ethnic restaurants, movie theaters, clubs, bars, and other cultural opportunities. Miami is home to large Hispanic and African-American communities and is easily accessible to students by public transportation.

Miami's student body includes an eclectic mix of students, with Hispanic students making up the largest non-white population at the university. Students say that there have been no overt racial incidents on campus in the last several years, and many attribute this to the university's culturally diverse student population. Students add that other than in the predominantly white fraternities and sororities the campus is reasonably well integrated. Miami's campus isn't a particularly politically active community of students, however. "Even though the campus is aware of national and local issues, we generally do very little in the area of protests, sit-ins, or other forms of demonstrations," says a student. "However, an occasional seminar, forum, or counseling session is held for those students, faculty, and staff members who are very interested in particular issues." With nearly 10 percent of the student body hailing from foreign countries, there is a certain cosmopolitan flavor to Miami's campus.

There are those students who still come to the University of Miami for the sunshine and beaches. But increasingly more are deciding to attend the university because of its recently enhanced academic reputation and varied programs, as well as for its cultural diversity. Says a student: "I am an unofficial recruiter for the university. I am a member of an organization that works directly with the admissions office, and I'm very active in seeking other minority youths to come to the university. I feel that this university is a true real world. It allows a minority student to experience other cultures and learn how to see the positive aspects of social and ethnic differences."

NEW COLLEGE OF THE UNIVERSITY OF SOUTH FLORIDA

Address: 5700 North Tamiami Trail,
  Sarasota, FL 34243-2197
Phone: (813) 359-4269
Director of Admissions: David L. Anderson
Multicultural Student Recruiter: na
1991–92 tuition: $1,675 (in-state), $6,690
  (out-of-state)
Room and board: $3,375
Application deadline: Rolling admissions
Financial aid application deadline: 2/15
Non-white freshman admissions: Applicants
  for the class of '95: 93
  Accepted: 27%
  Accepted who enroll: 68%
  Applicants accepted who rank in top
  10% of high school class: 40%
  In top 25%: 73%
  Median SAT: 570 V, 590 M
  Median ACT: 27
Full-time undergraduate enrollment: 522
  Men: 51%
  Women: 49%
Non-white students in
  1987–88: 4.6%
  1988–89: 6.9%
  1989–90: 7.9%
  1990–91: 9.4%
Geographic distribution of students: na
Students In-state: 70%
Top majors: na
Retention rate of non-white students: na
**Scholarships exclusively for non-white
  students:** Christiane Felsman Endowed
  Scholarship: awarded to a qualified
  African-American student; $4,500 each
  year; renewable; merit-based.
Remediation programs: None
Academic support services: Writing and
  mathematics tutorials are available, as is
  peer tutoring in most subject areas.
Ethnic studies programs: na

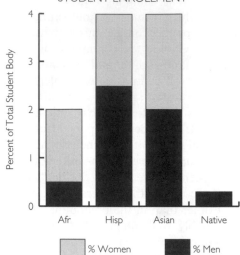

STUDENT ENROLLMENT

Percent of Total Student Body

Afr   Hisp   Asian   Native

☐ % Women   ■ % Men

Ethnic studies courses: na
Organizations for non-white students:
  Florida African-American Student
  Association
Notable non-white alumni: Anita L. Allen
  ('74, Philosophy; associate professor of
  law, Georgetown Law Center); David L.
  Smith ('74, American Literature;
  associate professor of English, Williams
  College)
Tenured faculty: 38
Non-tenured faculty: 12 (no non-tenured
  faculty of color)
Student-faculty ratio: 10:1
Non-white administrators: 2
  African-American: 50%
  Hispanic: 0
  Asian-American: 50%
  Native American: 0
Recent non-white speakers on campus: na

"I couldn't stand the idea of going to college in Florida," says a senior of her school, located on the shores of the Gulf of Mexico. "I'm not into the sun and tourism. But being able to design my own course of study and knowing that I would have close contact with professors made me want to come here."

If you haven't heard of this small elite school until now, then you're not alone. The New College, which functions as the honors college of the University of South Florida, does not actively market itself. Although the college may not have the name recognition of some of its better-known competitors, it has admissions statistics that would rival almost any other small, elite college in the country. In a recent year, the college accepted fewer than a third of its applicants, and the average SAT score of its students is about 1,160.

New College isn't for just any high school whiz with stellar SATs and an impressive list of extracurriculars. The applicant serious about attending New College must also be self-motivated. There are no distribution or core curriculum requirements as there are at most other schools; students design their own course of study, under the close supervision of faculty advisers; and instead of grades, students receive extensive written evaluations from professors. Much of the learning also goes on in one-on-one tutorials with professors, so falling behind in the course work is not acceptable.

Students says the school's best academic areas are in the humanities, particularly English and philosophy. Biology and chemistry are also said to be quite good. New College's fine arts offerings received an added boost recently with the completion of a new arts complex. The school's relatively new $6.1 million library is impressive.

There are no courses at New College that focus specifically on any particular ethnic or racial groups. "There isn't an African-American Studies program here, for example, but there are a lot of academic disciplines missing at a school that has only fifty faculty members," says a student. Latin American Studies, however, has become popular at the college. In order to major in the area, students need to enroll in courses at the University of South Florida campus, located across the street. Says a junior political science major: "You can major in whatever you make up here. Recently there has been a strong interest in Latin American Studies; several students will graduate in it this spring. There aren't really classes offered in the field, though; a student would take the regularly scheduled courses offered and heavily supplement them with tutorials, fieldwork, internships, and classes off campus. It can be done, but unless there are faculty members on campus who share your interest in a particular field, it's rather difficult."

New College seniors are required to complete a thesis and an oral exam, which students describe as especially intense—and rewarding. Often student theses are published in national academic journals or students present them at professional conferences. To allow students some real-world experience, New College students are required to complete three Independent Study Projects (ISPs) before graduation, which are planned with a faculty adviser. ISPs can involve library research, lab work, or fieldwork. Students complete their ISPs during the month of January.

Much of the learning here takes place in small seminar-style classrooms, and often in one-on-one tutorials. In fact, having the close contact with professors is one reason why many New College students chose to come here in the first place. "It was so strange to think that if I needed help on a project I could just knock on a professor's door and talk to him or her right there on the spot." Students commonly refer to their professors by their first names and often maintain relationships with them long after graduation.

Although the New College campus overlooks the Gulf of Mexico, students are more likely to be found at the school's library than on the beaches. Students here aren't particularly sports-conscious either (New College sponsors no formal athletic teams), but there are often spontaneous games of soccer, basketball, and volleyball on campus. With the work load expected of them, students say that it's hard to find the time to be involved in clubs or organizations and that the small size of the school makes sustaining interest in a group difficult. Says a student: "Minority organizations come and go, depending on who's here that semester and how motivated they are to start a group from scratch." Currently, there are no active cultural student organizations on campus.

Students who attend New College tend to be highly individualistic and progressive. Students say there is little, if any, racial tension on campus. "Everything is pretty integrated," says a campus leader. "It sort of has to be when only about 6 percent of your tiny student body is minority. We have no frat or sorority houses; all dorms are coed; most minority students live on campus and don't stick together, either by accident or by design. Everybody dates everybody else here, regardless of sex, race, or body odor; everyone eats at the same crowded cafeteria and there's no telling whose table you'll end up at." "Race is not a factor here at New College," adds another student. "I should mention that the minority students are in very low numbers, but generally a person is not seen in respect to his or her race."

The school's more popular campus organizations include Amnesty International and gay and lesbian student groups. The New College Student Alliance brings to campus guest artists, exhibitions, and lectures. Other student groups have organized and run a food cooperative, published a literary magazine, and sponsored foreign film festivals. The Hamilton Student Center, open twenty-four hours a day, has a game room, a cafeteria, and meeting and exhibition spaces.

The independence found at New College isn't for everyone, including some students at the school; each year a sizable percentage of students transfer to schools where they can earn an education in a more structured environment. But New College ranks as among the best—and most unique—small private colleges in the country. "New College is a total education," says a student. "It recognizes where you want to be and develops a plan to get there, a plan that focuses on the evaluation of everything you do—your class work, your activities, your writing, and your reading."

GEORGIA

AGNES SCOTT COLLEGE

Women's college
Address: Decatur, GA 30030
Phone: (404) 371-6000
Director of Recruitment: Jenifer Cooper
1993–94 tuition: $12,000
Room and board: $5,000
Application deadline: 2/1
Financial aid application deadline: 3/15
Non-white freshman admissions: Applicants
　for the class of '95: 122
　Accepted: 75%
　Accepted who enroll: 40%
　Applicants enrolled who rank in top 10%
　of high school class: 40%
　In top 25%: 60%
　Median SAT range: 430–490 V,
　430–550 M
　Median ACT: na
Full-time undergraduate enrollment: 544
Non-white students in
　1987–88: 10%
　1988–89: 11%
　1989–90: 11%
　1990–91: 14%
Geographic distribution of students: na
Students In-state: 84%
Top majors: 1. Psychology 2. Biology
　3. Art
Retention rate of non-white students: 50%
**Scholarships exclusively for non-white
　students:** None
Remediation programs: None
Academic support services: The college's
　Collaborative Learning Center and

Writing Workshop provide academic
support.
Ethnic studies programs: None
Ethnic studies courses: The college offers
　"African-American History," "Latin
　American Politics," "Minority Politics,"
　"Women in Latin America," and
　"Introduction to Latin America."
Organizations for non-white students:
　Witkaze (a multicultural student
　organization)
Notable non-white alumni: na
Tenured faculty: 39
Non-tenured faculty: 24
Student-faculty ratio: 8:1

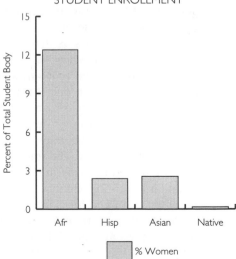

STUDENT ENROLLMENT

% Women

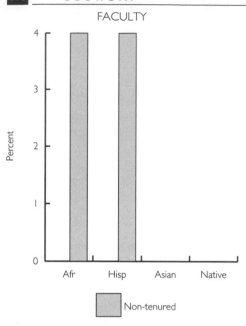

FACULTY

Non-tenured

Administrators: 40
  African-American: 10%
  Hispanic: 5%
  Asian-American: 0
  Native American: 0
Recent non-white speakers on campus:
  Johnnetta Cole (president, Spelman College); Gloria Scott (president, Bennett College); Brenda Hailiberton (director, Turner Center, Candler School of Theology); Rev. McKinley Young (pastor, Big Bethel AME Church); Rev. Deborah Austin (associate pastor, Ebenezer Baptist Church); Gloria Naylor (author); Rev. Bernice King (daughter of Martin Luther King, Jr.)

Located near the cosmopolitan city of Atlanta, Agnes Scott College is an all-women's liberal arts college devoted to providing students with a top-flight education that will prepare them for careers in an increasingly competitive job market.

With only about 550 students, Agnes Scott almost guarantees close interaction with faculty. "Professors are here to help the students. If I'm having a problem in a class, I know I can go to the professor and she'll help. The professor will also give us her home telephone number."

"She?" "Her?" Unlike at most coed schools, more than half of Agnes Scott's faculty are women, a fact that many students point to as one of the school's positive features. "Not to say that the male professors here aren't good, but it's refreshing to have female professors. It shows us that it's possible for women to be in control and to be successful, even in the sciences," comments a chemistry major.

Biology, psychology, and economics are most often said to be among the school's best departments, although one student adds that "all the academic programs here are rigorous and good." English and the sciences also enjoy good reputations, as does the school's pre-business program that offers internship possibilities. To graduate, students must satisfy distribution requirements in the humanities, math, natural sciences, a foreign language, and fine arts. As ASC is a Presbyterian-affiliated school, students are required to enroll in either a philosophy or a Bible study course, and to ensure that their writing ability is up to snuff, students must also take courses in English composition and literature.

As Agnes Scott is part of the Atlanta University system, its students are able to enroll in courses at other Atlanta schools such as Emory, Morehouse, Spelman, and Georgia Tech. "Until a year or two ago, cross-registering was not very popular, but now students learn about what is offered at the other schools," says a sophomore.

Agnes Scott's Honor Code, which requires students to uphold certain standards of academic and social behavior and to report those that don't, is adhered to—and appreciated by—students. "When it comes to academics, there's a lot less strain with the Honor Code. For instance, a professor is giving us a test on Friday. But we don't have to finish it then. We can take it to our dorm and complete it during any two-hour time period over the weekend. Because we sign a piece of paper stating we will abide by the code, the professor trusts us. I usually do better on my exams because I feel more relaxed while taking them."

Atlanta, just six miles from campus and easily accessible by MARTA (mass transit), is never short of providing things to do. "If we want to party on the weekends, we practically have to head off campus. The most popular places to go to are the clubs, but the club of choice varies from year to year. Sometimes we'll head to one of the colleges in the area, such as Morehouse or Spelman, for their parties. But just about anywhere in Atlanta is fun." If you haven't heard by now, Atlanta is the site for the 1996 Olympics. Hailed by many as the capital of the South, Atlanta offers a multitude of extracurricular activities to students, everything from shopping and dancing to theater and movies.

Back on campus, Witkaze, an African-American student group with about 20 members, provides activity of a more cultural and social sort. Although the membership of Witkaze is small, the group nonetheless works to plan a variety of events. Each year the group sponsors a convocation during Black History Month that includes singing, dancing, and poetry readings. Witkaze hosts and coordinates an annual banquet to which students, faculty, and administrators are invited. "We had a good crowd of about seventy people, of all races, at our last banquet," says a student. Witkaze also sponsors less formal parties primarily for members, although all parties are open to the entire campus. Witkaze's staff advisers—Ruby Perry-Ellis and Victor Wilson—"help us plan most of our events. We also know we can go and talk to them whenever we need to."

One of the newest student groups on campus is Racism-Free Zone, a group established in 1991 that seeks to raise the campus's race awareness. "After a speech by someone who talked about racist-free zones, some people and faculty here decided to start a Racism-Free Zone group on campus. At first there was a lot of controversy about the group, but it's a definite plus for the campus." Dr. Guthrie of the English department is an adviser to the group.

While students say many of the campus-wide activities don't cater to minority students, they say events are becoming more diverse. Recently, the student government association sponsored a Jamaican Me Crazy party and house parties. The college also has an impressive list of other groups and clubs that sponsor events and activities, such as a drama club, political organizations, religious organizations, an arts council, and a volunteer group. The Alston Campus Center is a happening place, with a snack bar, racquetball courts, and a popular aerobics room. The college fields four varsity sports, including basketball, cross-country, soccer, and tennis, as well as several intramural sports.

Agnes Scott can no longer be confused with a finishing school where the women are as concerned with getting a Mrs. degree as they are their diploma. The college's respected academics, provided in an unusually supportive environment, keeps alumni involved; the college's endowment, per student, is one of the nation's largest.

Students too are no less impressed by the quality of their education. "I'm glad I went to an all-women's school because it has given me the education and confidence to be successful after I graduate. But I like the personalization here the most. I know I can walk into the dean's office and she'll know my name. The other day I walked by the president of the college and she knew my name. I was shocked, but I shouldn't have been. That sort of thing happens here often. I know I won't get that kind of attention when I go to medical school."

EMORY UNIVERSITY

Address: 1380 South Oxford Road, Atlanta, GA 30322
Phone: (800) 727-6036
Director of Admissions: Daniel C. Walls
Multicultural Student Recruiter: na
1993–94 tuition: $16,820
Room and board: $5,010
Application deadline: Early decision: 11/1; regular decision: 2/1
Financial aid application deadline: 2/15
Non-white freshman admissions: Applicants for the class of '95: 1,071
Accepted: 72.5%
Accepted who enroll: 26%
Applicants accepted who rank in top 10% of high school class: na
Median SAT range: 470–590 V, 520–650 M
Median ACT range: 23–28
Full-time undergraduate enrollment: 4,795
Men: 47%
Women: 53%
Non-white students in
1987–88: 10.8%
1988–89: 11.3%
1989–90: 12%
1990–91: 15.7%
Students In-state: 38.8%
Top majors: 1. Psychology 2. Liberal Arts 3. Biology
Retention rate of non-white students: na
Scholarships exclusively for non-white students: None
Remediation programs: None

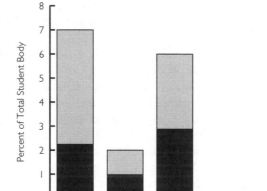

STUDENT ENROLLMENT

Percent of Total Student Body

□ % Women   ■ % Men

Academic support services: Tutoring is available in most academic subjects.

GEOGRAPHIC DISTRIBUTION OF STUDENTS

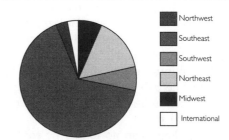

■ Northwest
■ Southeast
■ Southwest
□ Northeast
■ Midwest
□ International

Ethnic studies programs: Emory offers an interdisciplinary program in African-American and African Studies, involving 11 departments. One tenured faculty member teaches in the program as well as 17 professors from other departments.

Ethnic studies courses: na

Organizations for non-white students: Black Student Alliance, Alpha Kappa Alpha, Alpha Phi Alpha, Kappa Alpha Psi, Emory Chinese Student Union, Emory Chinese Students Association, Korean Students Association, African Students Association

Notable non-white alumni: Marvin Arrington (attorney and president, Atlanta City Council); Hamilton Holmes (medical director, Grady Memorial Hospital, Atlanta); Deborah Ann Robinson (U.S. Magistrate judge); Thelma Wyatt-Cummings (Superior Court judge); James B. O'Neal (director, Legal Outreach, New York City)

Tenured faculty: 330

Non-tenured faculty: 173

Student-faculty ratio: 9:1

Administrators: 58

    African-American: 12%

    Hispanic: 0

    Asian American: 0

    Native American: 0

Recent non-white speakers on campus: Desmond Tutu (Nobel Prize winner and

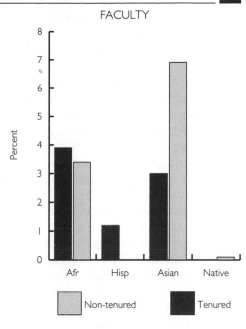

FACULTY

South African civil rights activist); Yvonne Brathwaite Burke (attorney and former legislator); Julius Chambers (director, NAACP Legal Defense and Educational Fund); Jewel Prestage (chairperson of the political science department, Southern University); Alton Hornsby, Jr. (chairperson of the history department, Morehouse College); Maya Angelou (author and poet)

Okay, it's your first day at Emory, and you're already lost. You want to know how to get to the Woodruff Physical Education Center, so you ask a friend who you know is smart because he's a Woodruff Scholar. To get to the center, he tells you, you must first walk by the Woodruff Library and the Woodruff School of Nursing. But, he warns, if you walk by the Woodruff Medical Center you've gone the wrong way. Easy enough.

By the time you get to the impressive center, you're wondering: Who is this man they call Woodruff? The answer: Robert W. Woodruff just happens to be the former head of Coca-Cola and he recently donated a cool $100 million to the university, helping to make Emory one of the best-endowed universities in the country. Emory's endowment has been used to attract first-rate faculty, to increase financial aid opportunities, and to provide outstanding facilities. Whereas Emory once traveled in the shadow of such prominent Southern schools as Vanderbilt and Duke, it is now one of their competitors.

The natural sciences (especially biology and chemistry), English, and psychology are among the school's best departments. The school offers nearly 40 other degree-granting programs, ranging from anthropology and film studies to philosophy and women's studies. With the approval of the dean of the college, students are able to supplement their school's courses at any of the other area colleges that are part of the University Center, encompassing the Atlanta University Center, which includes Morehouse and Spelman (historically black colleges), Agnes Scott College, and Georgia Institute of Technology. To graduate, students must complete extensive distribution requirements in science, English, math, history, social science, and physical education.

The school's African-American Studies program, which more than one student described as "solid," has a new director, Rudolph Byrd, as of the fall of 1992.

Although students may not have access to some of the best-known faculty at the university (former President Jimmy Carter teaches here), students say that on the whole professors are approachable. One student adds, however, that some of the professors in the African-American Studies program teach at other universities that are part of the Atlanta University system "and can't easily be reached for appointments." The school's Multicultural Learning Resource Center, located in Woodruff Library, provides tutors, who, comments one student, "act as big brothers or sisters to younger students who might need help in almost any subject." In addition to offering academic support services, the office helps coordinate cultural awareness programming.

Studies can be demanding, but Emory students make time for cultural activities as well. The Black Student Alliance, one of the school's most active cultural student groups, with about 60 members, "sponsors more events than I'll be able to mention here," says a BSA leader. The newest addition to the BSA's list of activities is the Banquet and Ball, a formal dinner that includes dancing. The banquet, the theme of which changes each year, also has an awards ceremony for outstanding students. In a recent year, more than 200 faculty and students attended the gala. BSA meetings are usually held in White Hall or the Geology Building every other Wednesday.

The BSA House, located near fraternity row on the edge of campus, provides residence facilities for up to five students. "Who lives in the house depends on a lottery," says an education major. "The house alternates each year between having two men and three women in the house, or three men and two women. The student must be a BSA member."

The BSA also sponsors rap sessions with members, usually held at the BSA House, but one student says the sessions aren't as regularly scheduled as they have been in years past. Sessions can gather up to 100 students. "We just sit on the floor and talk about whatever we decide is important. Sometimes there's not room enough to walk in the house." A BSA-supported newspaper, *The Fire Next Time,* is a popular on-campus publication.

Ngambika, a support group for African-American women, also has "rap sessions where the members can really get to know each other. They talk about the situation of black women on campus. Their weekly meetings provide a sort of sisterhood," says a student. The Brotherhood of Afrocentric Men, which meets in the BSA House, provides similar support for its members, although one student says the group "is not as stable as Ngambika because we meet irregularly." Historically black fraternities and sororities are also active on campus, sponsoring social gatherings and community service projects.

Students report that "Emory is in a state of transition" when it comes to campus race relations. "Multiculturalism is big, and people like to talk about it. There are still subtle signs of racism, but that is going to be the case at any predominantly white institution," says a senior. "As a member of a minority group, I feel as if I'm all too often called on to be the spokesperson for my entire race. It gets to be a big responsibility after a while." Communication among the races has increased in recent years, say students, who point to the school's annual Week of Awareness, which features cultural and ethnic awareness programming.

Much of the school's social life is supplied courtesy of Emory's predominantly white Greek organizations, to which nearly half of the campus belong. Most students find time to participate in intramural and varsity sports; in fact, according to the university, more than 80 percent of the student body participates in at least one organized sports activity. The school doesn't have a varsity football or baseball team, however, which, students complain, contributes to the lack of school spirit on campus.

Students say that one of the best aspects of attending Emory is getting to go to school in Atlanta. The city is home to numerous other colleges and universities, which students can visit, and it will soon play host to the 1996 Summer Olympics. Atlanta also offers the chance to attend professional basketball, baseball, and football games. For those more culturally inclined, the city has a ballet, a symphony, and clubs that feature most types of music—from rock and reggae to jazz and the blues. Underground Atlanta is also a popular off-campus destination.

With its huge endowment, Emory is looking to become a national university, and in a sense it already has. The 78-year-old school draws students from every region of the country, with particularly large contingents from the Northeast and Middle Atlantic states. More than a third of its students are from private high schools, which explains the air of affluence on campus.

Emory students are proud to be attending a school that is on the up and up. "My experiences at Emory have made me a stronger person. I feel confident that my education here has prepared me for the real world. Within the minority communities, there are many intelligent and diverse students, which has made the learning experience even more enriching."

UNIVERSITY OF GEORGIA

Address: Athens, GA 30602
Phone: (706) 542-2112
Director of Admissions: Claire Swan
Multicultural Student Recruiter: Jeff Cooper

1992–93 tuition: $2,175 (in-state); $5,757 (out-of-state)
Room and board: $1,485
Application deadline: 8/1
Financial aid application deadline: 3/1

The University of Georgia is the largest and oldest publicly funded institution of higher learning in the state. In fact, back in 1787, UGA was the first school in the Union to be chartered by a state legislature. Since then, the university has grown to encompass more than 22,000 undergraduates, 10 colleges, and more than 160 undergraduate degree-granting programs.

Some of the school's programs are nationally recognized, particularly journalism and agriculture. Other well-known and popular programs are business, pharmacy, veterinary science, history, and political science. The university's Institute of Ecology is renowned for having paved the way for much of today's scientific study of ecological systems, and UGA's libraries, with more than 2.9 million books and documents, rank among the top 25 research libraries in the nation. Computer labs, with personal and mainframe computers, are available for student use in numerous residence halls, classroom buildings, and libraries.

The African-American Studies program, offered as a minor, includes "wonderful instructors" and such respected courses as "African-American Folklore" and "African-American Rhetoric." But UGA students aren't content to have only a minor offered through the program. In conjunction with students at the 33 other state-supported institutions in Georgia, UGA students are working to get the Board of Regents—the administrative body of the university system—to establish African-American Studies departments on all of the state's campuses. "We're staging protests, rallies, and sending petitions to all of the university regents to get the departments established," says a student leader.

To help incoming first-year students get adjusted to university life, the Black Educational Support Team (BEST)—a sort of big brother/big sister program—links upperclass students with new students. "We take students on tours of the campus, help them find tutors, and just basically show them the ropes on how to be successful here at the university," says a student. "Supportive of all students" is how a student describes the Black Faculty and Staff Organization. "They come to many of our [Black Affairs Council] meetings, and help us with some funding. We also sponsor monthly lunches in the dining halls with them, and every year we all sponsor a huge picnic." When asked which African-American faculty are most helpful, the student adds: "I couldn't say, because all of them are and have been resources for students."

Located on the top floor of Memorial Hall, the African-American Cultural Center "is the hub of African-American student activity, and is the place for meetings, parties, plays, and it even has an art gallery," says a senior. "It's a nice place to host events, so the center is booked all the time, and not only by African-American student organizations."

The university's oldest and largest African-American student group is the Black Affairs Council (BAC), with about 120 active members. To help African-American students succeed in the classroom, the BAC has compiled a list of reliable tutors in most subjects and a test file. The organization, which meets twice a month at the cultural center, sponsors numerous events, usually in collaboration with other student groups. One such event is Reflections of Our Past, in which each of the school's African-American student organizations performs anything from skits and songs to poetry and dance routines. Where most schools celebrate Black History Month or

Day, UGA students schedule enough events for Black History Quarter, which features guest speakers and a variety of workshops on such topics as "Black/White Relations" and "What It Means to Be Black at the University of Georgia."

The BAC also sponsors tailgate parties before home football games. "At a typical game, you can expect thousands of people to come, and only a small percentage will be African-American. Before the game, we have a cookout and we usually get seats together. It's an informal gathering that gets a nice turnout."

Much of the social scene for African-American students, however, revolves around the school's predominantly black Greek organizations. "There's a party sponsored by one of the fraternities or sororities almost every weekend." Most dances and parties are held either at the Tate Student Center or at Memorial Hall. In addition, the women of Delta Sigma Theta sponsor a Miss Black University of Georgia pageant, the proceeds of which go to a scholarship fund. The men of Kappa Alpha Psi sponsor their own scholarship fundraiser when they host the well-attended Kappa Klassic, a step show that draws talent and spectators from across the state. "A couple of thousand people usually come each year to watch."

For social life off campus, African-American students say O'Malley's, the Club Mirage, and Dirty Harry's in Athens are popular clubs and bars. As many of the university's African-American students are from Atlanta, many head home for weekends, although they say more African-American students are sticking closer to campus as many of the school's student groups are providing more than enough reason to stay put. The university sponsors more than 350 student organizations, including everything from the Georgia Amateur Comedians Club to the Concert Choir.

The University of Georgia remains a largely segregated institution, with little interaction between the students of different races, whether in social or academic settings. In addition, it's not as if the school's student of color population has grown by leaps and bounds since the days when the school was forced, under orders from the federal government, to integrate in 1957. (Charlayne Hunter-Gault, a prominent broadcast journalist for the *MacNeil-Lehrer NewsHour,* and Hamilton Holmes were the first two African-Americans to enroll at the university.) In 1990, according to the U.S. Department of Education, the university's African-American population represented only about 5.3 percent of the school's more than 28,395 undergraduates (as opposed to 25 percent of the state's population), while the school's Hispanic and Asian-American populations accounted for another 2 percent. (The university did not respond to our questionnaire requesting enrollment statistics for students of color.)

But students say the atmosphere has become more supportive of African-American students in recent years. "Now there are certainly more diverse class offerings than when I was a freshman," says a senior. "And in housing there was always a lot of tension between black students and white resident advisers. But now there are more black resident advisers, and the Minority Assistance program, which works to smooth out any racial tensions in the dorms, is a good source of help for minority students." According to the student, there is about one Minority Assistance adviser per dorm. The student says there are also better relations between African-American non-Greeks and Greeks. "Before, it was as if you weren't anything if you weren't Greek, but the BAC has done its part to change much of that attitude."

With a relatively low enrollment of students of color, going to UGA, particularly for the unprepared student, can be a trying and lonely experience. But with the support of the Black Affairs Council and other student organizations, and especially with the support of faculty and staff, students say, the ultimate goal of earning a respected degree can be achieved. "I wouldn't have wanted to go anywhere else. It's what you make of it here. You can coast for four years here and just get that piece of paper in the end, but little else. If you choose to get involved, you can be a part of making some positive changes happen here at the university."

MOREHOUSE COLLEGE

Men's college
Address: 830 Westview Drive S.W., Atlanta, GA 30314
Phone: (404) 681-2800 / (800) 992-0642
Director of Admissions: Sterling H. Hudson III
Multicultural Student Recruiter: na
1991–92 tuition: $11,426 (room and board included)
Application deadline: 2/15
Financial aid application deadline: 4/1
Non-white freshman admissions: Applicants for the class of '95: 3,112
Accepted: 42%
Accepted who enroll: 51%
Applicants accepted who rank in top 10% of high school class: 28%
In top 25%: 76%
Median SAT: 483 V, 529 M
Median ACT: 23
Full-time undergraduate enrollment: 2,980
Non-white students in
1987–88: 100%
1988–89: 100%
1989–90: 100%
1990–91: 100%
Students In-state: na
Top majors: 1. Engineering 2. Biology 3. Business Administration
Retention rate of non-white students: 62%
Scholarships exclusively for non-white students: Academic Scholarships: merit-based; amount varies.
Remediation programs: Developmental

courses are offered in reading, math, and English.
Academic support services: na
Ethnic studies programs: Most humanities and social science courses at Morehouse integrate African-American-related issues. The college has an African-American Studies program, which involves more than 14 departments.
Ethnic studies courses: na
Organizations for non-white students: Omega Psi Phi, Alpha Phi Alpha, Phi Beta Sigma, Kappa Alpha Psi, Iota Phi Theta, and numerous other clubs

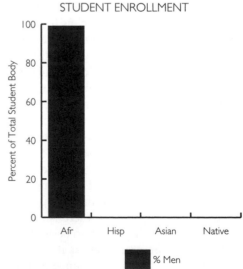

STUDENT ENROLLMENT

GEOGRAPHIC DISTRIBUTION OF STUDENTS

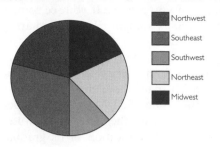

Northwest

Southeast

Southwest

Northeast

Midwest

African-American: 80%
Hispanic: na
Asian-American: na
Native American: na
Non-tenured faculty: 93
African-American: 78%
Hispanic: na
Asian-American: na
Native American: na
Student-faculty ratio: 19:1
Administrators: 50
African-American: 100%
Hispanic: 0
Asian-American: 0
Native American: 0

Notable non-white alumni: Martin Luther King, Jr. (Religion; Nobel Prize recipient, civil rights leader); Dr. Louis Sullivan (Pre-med; former U.S. Secretary of Health and Human Services); Lerone Bennett (English and History; editor of *Ebony* magazine and author); Spike Lee (Communications; filmmaker); Edwin Moses (Physics; track star and Olympic gold medalist)

Tenured faculty: 49

Recent non-white speakers on campus: John Bryant (bishop, AME Church, Liberia); Otis Moss (pastor, Olivet International Baptist Church); Maynard Jackson (mayor of Atlanta); Clayborne Carson (editor, King Papers Project); Henry Louis Gates, Jr. (professor, Harvard University)

Morehouse College is not only one of the country's premier black colleges; it is one of the country's more respectable colleges, period. In 1992, the editors of *U.S. News & World Report* ranked the 126-year-old institution of higher learning as one of the best regional liberal arts colleges in the South, and the college is one of only four Georgia colleges and three predominantly black colleges to have a chapter of Phi Beta Kappa, one of the country's most prestigious honor societies. Established in 1867 to educate freed slaves, Morehouse has since gone on to graduate some of the country's most significant political and cultural figures, including Martin Luther King, Jr., Atlanta mayor Maynard Jackson, and filmmaker Spike Lee.

But Morehouse College, the country's only black college for men, isn't just any school with an intimate campus atmosphere and loads of esprit de corps. "There's a popular saying here that goes: 'You can go through Morehouse, but Morehouse has to go through you,' which is basically true," says a history major. Adds another student: "The school pride is incredible here. There's the Morehouse mystique that expects you to be all you can be. Coming here is almost like a fraternity pledge process, and after you've gone through it, then you can call yourself a Morehouse man. A lot of it has to do with the history of the college."

There's also a sense of bonding here—of wanting to see classmates succeed—that is refreshing and sometimes uncommon at some of the country's more competitive colleges. "When I first came to Morehouse, I thought all the talk about 'brothers' was just that—talk," says a journalism major. "But the men at Morehouse care about each other. When they ask 'How are you doing?' they don't want to hear just 'fine,' they want to talk about your problems. I know that many of the friendships I've made here will last a lifetime." A sophomore agrees. "People genuinely care here. It's abnormal not to ask for help about anything, if you need it. If you see someone who needs help, you help him. It's not student versus student. We're all sharing a common goal: success."

Morehouse is a traditional liberal arts college with divisions of social science and humanities. Students say that among the school's best departments are political science, theology, and business administration, which enables students to concentrate in accounting, banking and finance, and insurance. Qualified Morehouse students are able to participate in a joint engineering program with the Georgia Institute of Technology, also in Atlanta. Morehouse has also had a tradition of its graduates going into the health professions—medicine, dentistry, and veterinary medicine, especially. In fact, more than 450 living Morehouse alumni are physicians or dentists, which represents about 7 percent of all African-American physicians and dentists nationally. Top pre-med students are also able to gain admittance to the college's own medical school.

By all accounts, the Morehouse faculty, many of whom are "House" graduates, is as supportive of students as students are of one another. Many give students their home telephone numbers and have offices with open-door policies. Students also see their faculty serving as role models. "You see a bit of yourself in your professors. Throughout my entire education before coming to Morehouse, I had three African-American teachers, two of whom were male. Then during my first year here, three of my professors were African-American," says a student. "It was a bit of a culture shock. The professors here want to see you do well, but they don't make it easy for you. Everyone here, from professors to other students, wants you to succeed. In other words, there's little cutthroat competition."

Morehouse is a member of the five-college Atlanta University Center, the largest consortium of black colleges in the world, which permits students to cross-register at Morris Brown College, Spelman College, Clark Atlanta University, Interdenominational Theological Center, and Morehouse School of Medicine. "It allows us to have the resources of a major university while we still attend a small college," says a student. Though each of the schools in the center maintains its own identity, the schools share a security force, a mental health clinic, and a placement service. Center-wide academic programs include fine arts, foreign language courses, and general science courses.

Although the college's curriculum is about as multicultural as you'll find anywhere, students say that it still needs some work in this area. "The curriculum is still very Eurocentric," says a student. "For example, the professor of the 'World Literature' course always has to supplement the text we use for the class with books he buys that are written by people of African descent. Even some of the history courses teach the history of civilization from the Western perspective. We start from Europe, and then it's like, 'Oh, by the way, these are the things that were going on in Africa and Asia during the time.' It's not so much the problem with the teachers; it's more with the textbooks."

Morehouse's closest Atlanta University contact—and that's putting it mildly—is with Spelman College, a prominent historically black college for women that's located across the street from the Morehouse campus. "It's not as if Morehouse is on some hill or in some rural area where we never see women," comments a sophomore. "Sometimes you have to be reminded that we're an all-men's campus." Contact with Spelman women comes in almost every shape and size—from the social to the academic. Coed classes are common, and the school's student government associations frequently work together for programming. In addition, at the beginning of a student's first year at Morehouse, each student is paired with a Spelman sister. "You basically hang out with her and talk to her. Rarely, but not never, these relationships develop into the more romantic kind. The relationship usually carries all the way through school," says a student. Morehouse's homecoming celebrations are also planned with Spelman. Spelman women are cheerleaders and majorettes for the festivities, and one lucky Spelman student is elected by Morehouse men to serve as the homecoming queen.

Morehouse men are able to participate in more than 50 organizations on campus. Some of the most active, which include about 10 percent of the student body, are the fraternities. The fraternities sponsor their fair share of parties, step shows, and formal dances, but all are involved in the community as well. The men of Kappa Alpha Psi, for example, help at a soup line at nearby St. Anthony's Church, and for Easter members sponsored an egg hunt for the children of a nearby housing project complex. "We also gave a hundred free haircuts, and the parents kept asking, 'What's the hitch?' We kept telling them that there was no hitch, and they finally believed us by the end of the day," remembers a student.

The fraternities haven't been without their problems. Alpha Phi Alpha was kicked off campus in 1989 when a pledge died in a hazing incident. Hazing practices have been notorious for the stringent demands placed on pledges. The Alpha tragedy forced many of the historically black fraternities to reevaluate hazing rituals. "Nationally, the hazing is supposed to have changed and filtered down to the local chapters. Hazing still goes on a little, but it's under control," comments a fraternity member.

State clubs, in which students link up with other students from their home states for parties and rides home, are also popular. There was recently a large party involving students from the states that had the final four basketball teams in the NCAA playoffs.

Although the campus is overwhelmingly Democratic, students say there is political diversity among students. "There's the whole spectrum here, from Republicans and Democrats to radicals. If you want to get into a political debate, you can find it here," says a student. But, adds the student, "there's more middle- and upper-middle-class students than lower-class." Student aspirations also tend to the pre-professional, such as law, medicine, teaching, and religion, perhaps reflecting the careers of most of their parents. Geographic diversity is also a plus at the school. Students hail from more than 35 states and numerous foreign countries.

Atlanta, the South's most cosmopolitan city, offers students a variety of nightlife and cultural activity that goes on virtually nonstop. Underground Atlanta, with its shops and restaurants, is popular with students, as are some area "hot spots," such as XS and 112. The city is also home to professional sports teams, museums, and theater companies and will play host to the Summer Olympics in 1996.

The Morehouse campus isn't known for its beauty, although one student comments that "the general appearance of the campus has gotten better these past two years." Students praise the president of the college, Leroy Keith, Jr., for his efforts in improving the campus, such as in the area of food services. The Kilgore Campus Center, the school's new student union, is a popular hangout and has a snack bar, student government offices, and "a beautiful water fountain in the back where we can study and talk." The air-conditioned Kilgore dormitory, a part of the campus center, houses upperclass students; first-year students live in the less appealing non-air-conditioned dorms. For 1996, Morehouse will get a new athletic facility that will be used by athletes during the Olympics. The facility is to include a swimming pool and gym. The college's present athletic facilities are less than desirable, according to students.

There are many reasons to attend Morehouse. Highly regarded academics and a small-campus environment are among them. But for one student, there's another, equally significant reason for attending the House. "During these days of the plight of the black male, it's good to see this many black men striving to succeed. It makes you want to do well yourself."

OGLETHORPE UNIVERSITY

Address: 4484 Peachtree Road, Atlanta, GA 30319
Phone: (404) 364-8307
Director of Admissions: Dennis Matthews
Multicultural Student Recruiter: Todd Shapiro
1993–94 tuition: $11,990
Room and board: $4,300
Application deadline: 8/1
Financial aid application deadline: 5/1

Non-white freshman admissions: Applicants for the class of '96: 203
Accepted: 68%
Accepted who enroll: 36%
Applicants accepted who rank in top 10% of high school class: 31%
Median SAT: na
Median ACT: na
Full-time undergraduate enrollment: 712
Men: 42%
Women: 58%
Non-white students in
1987–88: na
1988–89: 15%
1989–90: 13%
1990–91: 14%
1991–92: 15%

Geographic distribution of students: na
Students In-state: 65%
Top majors: 1. Business Administration 2. Biology 3. Psychology
Retention rate of non-white students: 65%
Scholarships exclusively for non-white students: None
Remediation programs: None

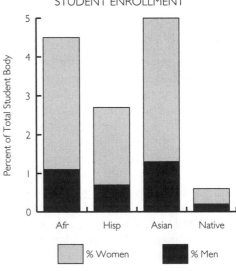

STUDENT ENROLLMENT

Percent of Total Student Body

Afr   Hisp   Asian   Native

□ % Women   ■ % Men

FACULTY

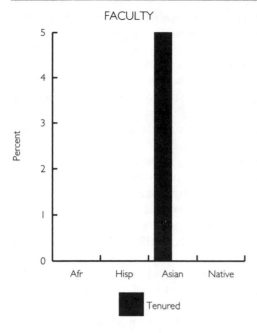

Tenured

Ethnic studies programs: None

Ethnic studies courses: "Minority Peoples," "Special Topics in Literature and Culture I," "Minority Voices," "Minorities in Media."

Organizations for non-white students: Black Student Caucus

Notable non-white alumni: Horace Shuman ('80; vice president, Bank South); Leslie Renee Jones ('80; assistant district attorney, New York City)

Tenured faculty: 28

Non-tenured faculty: 15

Student-faculty ratio: 14:1

Administrators: 30
African-American: 3%
Hispanic: na
Asian-American: na
Native American: na

Recent non-white speakers on campus: Bob Holmes (Georgia state representative); Julio Barragan (artist); Nieves Barragan (artist)

Academic support services: Tutoring in most academic subjects

For many students, the chance to attend a small school in Atlanta is reason enough to apply to Oglethorpe. Students also choose it because of its strengths in the liberal arts and pre-professional studies.

Despite its popular professional programs—particularly in accounting and business administration—one cannot graduate from Oglethorpe without a broad dose of the liberal arts. To graduate, students must complete a core curriculum that consists of 16 courses from various areas, including composition and communication, the humanities, the behavioral and social sciences, math, and the natural sciences.

Students say the school's best programs are education, political science, and English, as well as business administration and accounting. Students interested in going to medical school should know that Oglethorpe pre-med students have a 90 percent placement record in medical schools. In general, students give Oglethorpe's humanities programs low marks. "Most students will head to one of the other campuses in the Atlanta University system to take courses in the humanities, Emory being the most popular destination." (Oglethorpe students are able to enroll in courses at any of the 12 colleges and universities in the Atlanta area, which include Morehouse and Spelman.) "But students don't take advantage of the courses at other schools very often because it's a long and complicated process to get enrolled in them. Also, the administration doesn't advertise the program or the courses at the other schools very much."

"Minorities in Media," a recent addition to the Oglethorpe curriculum, is a popular course on campus. "The course is taught by a new professor who is African-American. Everyone ran over to take the course because they were looking forward to taking a class from a person of color. The class has not been a disappointment to any of us. Sara Lomax is very smart and for that reason she's a role model."

For academic support, a student comments, the school's peer tutoring program "can be helpful, but the program seems geared mostly to math and accounting courses." The school's small enrollment allows for small class sizes, with the average class having about 20 students. Students respect their professors' intelligence, but give the accessibility of the professors low marks.

The Black Student Caucus, which has about 15 active members, meets once a week in rooms at the school's student center. The group regularly brings gospel choirs to campus from various area churches. Recently, the group sponsored a poetry reading of African-American students' works. The BSC also sponsors book-review meetings, in which professors offer their perspectives on books about the African-American experience. For a recent Black History Month celebration, BSC activities included a film series that focused on the history of African-Americans in America, as well as "some films just for entertainment's sake." Primarily, however, the group provides peer support for members. "There are few black students here, so we spend a lot of our time trying to encourage each other and help each other out."

The BSC's two faculty advisers—Paul Hudson, a history professor, and James Bohart, head of the music department—are "extremely helpful in assisting the BSC to get organized and getting us started on different activities, such as inviting the gospel choirs onto campus. They're also very nice and accessible." Linda Taylor, an English professor, has also served as a resource for students. "She serves on the retention committee, which was formed lately to understand why students leave Oglethorpe, and she is very concerned about the minority student retention rate."

Much of the social life at Oglethorpe is supplied by the school's four fraternities and two sororities, all of which are national. In a recent year, according to one student, three African-American students were members of two of the Greek organizations. For nightlife, students seek out the fun and excitement offered in downtown Atlanta, just six miles from campus. "We frequently go to Underground Atlanta for entertainment. We'll also sometimes go to Morehouse [a historically black college for men in Atlanta] for parties, or just to movies." Students say that the lack of on-campus social activity, other than that of the Greek organizations, is due in part to the school's sizable commuter population. In a recent year, about 40 percent of the school's approximately 740 students lived off campus.

Atlanta is one of the South's fastest-growing cities and is the site of the 1996 Summer Olympics. Students praise their college's location and academics, but dream of a college with more in the way of social activity. "Oglethorpe's a good school. Other than its academics, though, I'm not happy here. The school's social life is lacking, especially for minority students."

SPELMAN COLLEGE

Women's college
Address: 350 Spelman Lane, Atlanta, GA
   30314
Phone: (404) 681-3643 / (800) 982-2411
Director of Admissions: Aline A.
   Rivers-Jones
Multicultural Student Recruiter: na
1991–92 tuition: $5,800
Room and board: $4,770
Application deadline: Early decision: 11/1;
   regulare decision: 2/1
Financial aid application deadline: 4/1
Non-white freshman admissions: Applicants
   for the class of '95: 3,319
   Accepted: na
   Accepted who enroll: na
   Applicants accepted who rank in the top
   10% of high school class: na
   Median SAT: 470 V, 490 M
   Median ACT: 22
Full-time undergraduate enrollment: 1,850
Non-white students in
   1987–88: 100%
   1988–89: 100%
   1989–90: 100%
   1990–91: 100%
Geographic distribution of students: na
Students In-state: 20%
Top majors: 1. English 2. Psychology
   3. Biology
Retention rate of non-white students: 80%
Scholarships exclusively for non-white
   students: Academic Scholarship: $2,000
   per year for each award; merit-based.
   Honors Scholarship: $3,000–$5,000 per
   year for each award; merit-based.
   National Merit Finalist Scholarships:

merit-based; recipient must be a National
   Merit finalist.
Remediation programs: None
Academic support services: Tutoring is
   available in most academic subjects.
Ethnic studies programs: As a traditionally
   African-American college, Spelman's
   departments and majors all address
   African-American-related issues.
Ethnic studies courses: na
Organizations for non-white students: Delta
   Sigma Theta, Alpha Kappa Alpha, Zeta
   Phi Beta, Sigma Gamma Rho,
   Drama/Dance Companies, Gospel Choir,
   Glee Club, State Clubs
Notable non-white alumnae: Aurelia Brazeal
   (ambassador, Federated States of
   Micronesia); Marian Wright Edelman
   (president, Children's Defense Fund);
   Varnette P. Honeywood (artist); Dr.
   Audrey Forbes Manley (Deputy
   Assistant Secretary for Health, U.S.
   Public Health Service); Marcelite J.
   Harris (first African-American woman
   Air Force brigadier general)
Tenured faculty: na
Non-tenured faculty: na
Student-faculty ratio: 16:1
Administrators: na
Recent non-white speakers on campus:
   Harry Belafonte (entertainer); Susan
   Taylor (editor-in-chief, *Essence*
   magazine); Toni Morrison (Pulitzer
   Prize-winning novelist); Angela Davis
   (political activist); Sonia Sanchez (poet);
   Mari Evans (poet); Haki Madhubuti
   (writer, educator, and publisher)

A lot has been happening lately at Spelman College, one of the country's preeminent
historically black colleges for women, not the least of which was a $20 million
donation in 1988 by actor/comedian Bill Cosby, a gift that ranks as one of the largest
contributions that has ever been awarded to a college. "I want [Spelman president]
Johnnetta Cole to understand the love that Camille and I have for this college, the
love for the women who, in spite of the odds against them, come to this school to

challenge themselves, to challenge the school, then to challenge what we call the outside world. This is for all those beautiful women," Cosby said of his gift.

In 1988, the 110-year-old college also inaugurated its first-ever African-American female president, Johnnetta Cole. Formerly the director of the Latin American and Caribbean Studies Program at Hunter College in New York City, Cole has fast become a popular and well-respected figure on campus. "Everyone loves her here. She is always accessible to students, and she stops to speak to students on campus. She's a truly beautiful woman," says a junior. Students are often heard to refer to her as Sister President.

Under Cole's leadership, Spelman has become an increasingly competitive school for admittance. The average SAT score of Spelman students now ranks as the highest of any historically black college—more than 70 points higher than the national average of students of all races—and the school continues to attract more applicants than it can possibly enroll. Besides having built a rapport with students, Cole has also established the Mentorship Program, in which students work as interns at some of Atlanta's most prominent corporations, among them First Atlanta Bank and Atlanta Life Insurance Company.

With almost the same enthusiasm they have for their college president, students are also enthusiastic about their school's academic course offerings. Students speak highly of the school's political science, biology, and computer science departments, while English and economics are also popular. Spelman students have the option of earning a 3-2 engineering degree by attending Spelman for three years and nearby Georgia Institute of Technology for two years. Established in 1981, Spelman's Women's Research and Resource Center, the first of its kind at a predominantly black college campus, has three components: curriculum development for women's studies, particularly black women's studies; research on black women; and community outreach to black women. To enhance their educational opportunities, Spelman women are able to enroll in courses in any of the five other area schools that are part of the Atlanta University Center (AUC), including neighboring Morehouse College. In addition to broad distributional requirements, students must take courses in African-American Studies or women's studies in order to graduate. With only about 1,850 students at the college, Spelman students enjoy close interaction with faculty members, and the average class size is small enough to allow students a chance to get to know professors in and out of the classroom.

An important component of the Spelman experience, according to students, is the school's commitment to community service. One student says that more than half of the college's students will participate in a volunteer program in the Atlanta area, from working in Grady Hospital to mentoring students in nearby elementary and high schools. "We students feel it's important to work in the community because we want to show the inner-city kids that we are real people who have been through some of what they're going through, and that they can someday get to where we are. We also perform the service to help ease the relations between the community and the campus. Sometimes there's resentment by the people in the area, who are mostly African-American, because they see us as more privileged, when the truth is, a lot of us have had to struggle to get to where we are too."

While Spelman is considered to be one of the safest schools in the AUC, students say the area around the school "isn't one where many of us feel safe." The campus is self-contained and has a security force, some of whose members, according to a student, are registered police officers. Men must be off campus by midnight during the week and by 2 a.m. on weekends.

Although Spelman is a women's college, there is never a shortage of men, except after hours. Spelman has a close relationship with Morehouse College, Spelman's unofficial brother school. The schools' student government associations work closely to sponsor parties and other events, and each year a Spelman woman is crowned queen of Morehouse's homecoming festivities. Students also frequently enroll in classes at Morehouse. The schools also have an official brother/sister program, in which first-year students from each of the schools are paired "to pal around with" an older student. "At times the relationship gets romantic, but that isn't encouraged. Usually students remain good friends with their brothers. When my brother was called to service in the Gulf War, we wrote to each other all the time."

Sororities, which were not part of the campus social scene until 1978, have become increasingly popular. Today, about 15 percent of the campus joins one of the school's two sororities, which sponsor dances, parties, and ice-cream socials and perform community service. Social life is also provided by Spelman's Student Government Association. One of the SGA's more successful activities is its Friday-afternoon festivities at Manley Center, the student union, where students listen to music courtesy of a DJ and where they are able to buy all sorts of Afrocentric wares from vendors, from T-shirts and jewelry to crafts and food. Also popular on campus are state clubs, in which students organize events with their home states as themes, and major clubs, for students interested in a particular course of study. The school's annual Health Fair is sponsored by the science department. Spelman's highly regarded Jazz Ensemble recently opened for Wynton Marsalis when he performed in Atlanta; the group traveled to Barcelona to perform at the Olympics.

As an alternative to the more social sorority, students recently established African Sisterhood (AST). "It's like a sorority, but it doesn't stress the social. Members concentrate on learning about their African heritage and stress community involvement. To become an AST member, students have to go through a period of pledging, during which they read about African history, wear African garb, and assume African names." Each year, approximately 15 women become AST members.

Off campus, students are able to take advantage of the South's most cosmopolitan city. Professional sports teams, high-caliber concerts, and ethnic restaurants are aplenty in the city. Popular destinations include Underground Atlanta, various shopping malls, as well as such clubs as Fat Tuesday's, the Texas Club, and XS.

Besides being a highly respected institution of higher learning among the black community, Spelman also is one of America's better liberal arts colleges. The school was ranked recently by the editors at *U.S. News & World Report* as one of the top regional liberal arts colleges in the country. Attending an institution with such credentials is indeed impressive, but no more so than the added bonus of attending a historically black institution for women. Says a student about her undergraduate experience: "Spelman can be summed up in one word: Sisterhood."

I D A H O

UNIVERSITY OF IDAHO

Address: University of Idaho, Moscow, ID
  83843
Phone: (208) 885-6326
Director of Admissions: Peter Brown
Multicultural Student Recruiter: Ben
  Coronado
Tuition: $1,236 (in-state); $3,746
  (out-of-state)
Room and board: $2,950
Application deadline: 2/1
Financial aid application deadline: 2/15
Non-white freshman admissions: Applicants
  for the class of '95: na
  Accepted: 141
  Accepted who enroll: 64
  Applicants accepted who rank in top
  10% of high school class: 23.4%
  Median SAT: 450 V, 500 M
  Median ACT: 21
Full-time undergraduate enrollment: 6,609
  Men: 59.9%
  Women: 40.1%
Non-white students in
  1987–88: 3.46%
  1988–89: 3.68%
  1989–90: 3.81%
  1990–91: 4.31%
Geographic distribution of students: na
Students In-state: 57.2%
Top majors: 1. General Studies
  2. Mechanical Engineering 3. Architecture
Retention rate of non-white students: 37.4%
Scholarships exclusively for non-white
  students: Louise L. Slade Scholarship:

average amount is $500; merit-based;
open to Native American or
Mexican-American students. Native
American Fund: average amount is $400;
merit-based; open to members of
recognized tribes of Idaho, Montana,
Wyoming, or Washington. Washington
Water Power: average amount of each
award is $1,000; merit-based. General
Minority Student Scholarship Fund:
merit-based; average amount for each
award is $1,000.
Remediation programs: The university offers
  remedial programs in math and English.
Academic support services: The university's

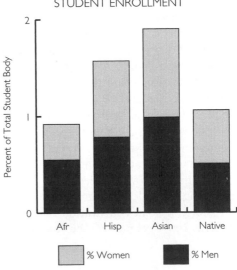

STUDENT ENROLLMENT

Percent of Total Student Body

% Women   % Men

Student Support Services Program provides tutoring and other academic assistance programs. The university is in the process of developing a faculty mentoring program.

Ethnic studies programs: None

Ethnic studies courses: na

Organizations for non-white students:
Recognizing African-American Concerns in Education, MECHA, Native American Student Association, American Indian Science and Education Society

Notable non-white alumni: na

Tenured faculty: na

Total African-American: 1
Total Hispanic: 2
Total Asian-American: 9
Total Native American: 3

Non-tenured faculty: na
Total African-American: 2
Total Hispanic: 2
Total Asian-American: 2
Total Native American: 2

Total faculty: 700

Student-faculty ratio: 17:1

Administrators: na

Recent non-white speakers on campus: na

Established in 1889, the University of Idaho is definitely not a city college. Some of its top programs are agricultural economics and rural sociology; animal and veterinary science; forest products; and plant, soil, and entomological sciences. Idaho is an outdoor person's dream school, as much for its academic programs as for its breathtaking surroundings—mountains and lakes are just a stone's throw from campus.

In addition to outdoor-oriented academic programs, Idaho has other strong programs in education, computer science, and engineering. The university also offers unique programs in resource recreation and tourism and landscape architecture, and students are able to take courses at Washington State University, located just eight miles across the border to the west.

Idaho is a relatively midsize state university, and students say professors are accessible. For additional academic support, students turn to the Office of Minority Advisory Services, which provides academic and personal support, as well as information about financial aid assistance and recruitment and retention programs. The director of the program, Diana Allen, is a source of support for students. "I went in to her and told her I had no idea what I was doing, and she got the ball rolling by giving me some scheduling advice and telling me where else to go on campus for help." The Student Support Services, which provides tutoring, among other assistance, is effective, say students, but limited in the number of students it can serve.

Much of the cultural programming is left up to the various organizations on campus. The newest organization, MECHA, a Chicano student group, was reestablished on campus during the fall of 1992. With only about 15 active members, the group recently participated in two fundraising events—a Mexican food sale at the International Fair and a Mexican pastry sale at the Siesta de Aztlan in Boise. The group has also sponsored a couple of small dances and instituted a telethon in which members phoned accepted Mexican-American students to welcome them to the university. The group also managed to send two members to a national MECHA conference held in New Mexico.

"It's been tough keeping the group going, especially when there are so many more Mexican-American students on campus who don't come to meetings or some of our events," says a MECHA leader. "But in the end it's always rewarding when you get to see an event that you sponsored covered by the school paper. I helped organize the group so that we can be recognized, heard, and seen on campus, and it's rewarding to be a part of that."

The Native American Student Association (NASA), which has about 25 active members, recently was given an office in the school's UCC building, a large classroom building located at the center of campus. "In the office, we post news items about our events and our powwows and job announcements. Since we have an American Indian Student Engineering Society, we also get notices of jobs and we post those," says a NASA leader. AISES was established on campus in the spring of 1991, and recently sent three members to the national AISES conference at the University of New Mexico.

Among recent NASA events were picnics and softball games against the Native American student group at Washington State. NASA also sponsored a powwow for graduating seniors. According to one student, "the community here is pretty close, especially as most American Indians are from reservations in the area and they've grown up together." The most popular major among Idaho's Native American students is the school's natural resource program, says a student.

Moscow isn't the source of a great deal of entertainment for students, although a mall and some bars aren't far from campus. Students with cars, or those with friends with cars, will usually head to Spokane, Washington, for more serious entertainment. Most of Moscow's surrounding countryside is just that—countryside. Not far from campus are the Palouse hills, and the mountains and lakes offer plenty of opportunities for skiing, boating, and hiking. For students interested in a cowboy lifestyle, the university sponsors regular rodeos on campus, and cowboy hats and boots are part of many students' wardrobes. The Student Union is a hub of activity and offers bowling alleys, music listening rooms, computer study rooms, and a snack bar. The Associated Student Union of Idaho regularly schedules speakers, films, dances, and other entertainment.

Cultural and ethnic diversity may not be one of Idaho's main strengths. But for students willing to overlook this, the combination of the school's academic programs and support services is almost enough to make up for the lack of diversity. "Coming here to school has definitely built up my character," says a senior. "I've learned a lot more than if I'd stayed in my neighborhood in Los Angeles, where people can also be pretty ignorant about other cultures, and I've liked being in such beautiful countryside. So, on the whole, coming here has been a positive if humbling experience, but I can do without all those rodeos and country music concerts."

I L L I N O I S

UNIVERSITY OF CHICAGO

Address: Chicago, IL 60637
Phone: (312) 702-8650
Director of Admissions: Theodore O'Neill
Multicultural Student Recruiter: na

1992–93 tuition: $17,061
Room and board: $5,940
Application deadline: 1/15
Financial aid application deadline: 2/1

The city of Chicago is more than just the home of the blues, the Cubs, and the world's tallest building. It is also home to one of the country's most outstanding private institutions of higher learning, the University of Chicago. Although the university's graduate school enrollment is more than twice that of the undergraduate division, Chicago is committed to undergraduate education.

At the heart of the undergraduate educational experience at Chicago is the common core, sometimes referred to by students as the "common chore." Of the courses a student needs to take in order to graduate, 21 are part of the core, and include courses in such areas as the humanities, math, natural sciences, physical education, and a foreign language. Students must also take a course in civilizational studies, which "provides an in-depth examination of the development and accomplishments of one of the world's great civilizations through direct encounters with some of its most significant documents and monuments." Civilization courses include courses in African, East Asian, South Asian, and Latin American Studies. "The Latin American civilization course was interesting, especially because it was about my own culture and taught me a lot that I didn't know before about the culture," says a student. "It took us back to the Aztecs and Mayans. It was very eye-opening."

Most of Chicago's academic departments are highly regarded, and many of its faculty members are world-renowned professors, some of whom have been awarded the Nobel Prize. Students say the sciences, economics, English, sociology, and history are among the school's best and most popular departments. The physics department allows for close interaction with faculty for research. The school's Summer Research Opportunity and Mellon Scholars programs, available to minority students, have also been a resource for students contemplating a career in higher education.

Chicago students are a bright and academically competitive group. "Students here don't like to tell each other the grades they got on papers or in class," says a senior.

"They sometimes won't even let you borrow their class notes if you weren't in class." Peer tutors are the most prevalent and popular form of academic support at Chicago. Each dorm is assigned tutors in almost every academic area, and the schedules and names of tutors are posted at the beginning of each quarter. The tutors are available four days a week. For commuter students, a writing tutor is available in the library. "The U of C has a lot of tutors who actually like to tutor, and they're always there," says a junior. Although the university has large graduate school programs, undergrads aren't lost in the shuffle. Even large lecture classes have discussion groups of about twenty-five students and are taught by full professors.

Attention to sports, a pervasive Greek life, and an active social life might characterize Northwestern University, Chicago's other highly ranked university, but such characteristics will never be attributed to U of C students. Ten percent of the student body are members of one of seven fraternities and two sororities, but students say the Greek units aren't popular and their events aren't well attended. In view of the demands of Chicago's academics, varsity sports aren't as popular as the less formal intramural sports teams and, again, aren't well attended. To unwind, students often seek out the nightlife of Chicago, which offers a plethora of ethnic restaurants, the Chicago Symphony Orchestra, and several outstanding theater companies. The university is located in Hyde Park, a Chicago neighborhood just fifteen minutes south of the Loop, as Chicago's downtown area is called. Hyde Park, a predominantly middle-class and African-American community, has restaurants and some neighborhood pubs. Students also report they'll head to parties at Loyola, De Paul, Northwestern, or the University of Illinois at Chicago. "It's essential to get off campus. This school can seem very small. After a while you see the same faces and attend the same parties. There's not a whole lot of variety," says a senior.

Perhaps one of the school's most frustrating points of concern for students, and some administrators, is the school's Coordinating Council for Minority Issues, which is charged with enhancing the quality of life for the U of C's minority students. "CCMI is focused only on African-American and Hispanic student concerns," says a member of the Organization of Black Students, a campus group. "They should change its name." Adds another student: "CCMI sponsors functions, such as speakers and panels, but it has trouble getting people to come. The panel discussions (a recent panel focused on minorities in education) and the participants usually aren't very interesting. Publicity for their events is also not well done." But perhaps the students' main complaint about the organization is its "secretive" ways. "Nobody ever knows what's going on at those meetings. It wasn't until 1991, after a lot of complaints, that students were even allowed to attend. Maybe I'm being too idealistic about democracy, but I think students should be able to take more of an active role on the committee." Since then, three students have been allowed to serve on the committee, but, as one student comments, "we come up with a lot of ideas, but not much ever gets done about them."

Students would also like to see the opening of a multicultural student center. "They have it at Stanford, and it would be nice to have it to open the eyes of the school's minority students about their own cultures, and, of course, the eyes of the white students as well."

The school's most active cultural student group is the Asian-American Students for Christ organization, which has about 90 active members—mainly Filipinos, Chinese, and Koreans. The group, which meets most Friday nights, sponsors weekly prayer meetings on Tuesdays and Thursdays and annual talent shows and square dances. Members also work in an area soup kitchen for the homeless. Due to the city of Chicago's frigid temperatures in the winter, group members stand outside on campus and distribute free cups of hot chocolate. "Students here say it's one of our group's most popular activities," says a student. "It certainly helps us to be visible on campus."

Less active is the school's Organization of Black Students, which has about 30 to 40 active members. "The OBS is not as active as it has been in the past. We used to do a lot more, like sponsor an intramural team, but we don't even do that anymore," says a senior. "The group has lost eight members, which is a lot, and which could have something to do with the apathy among the group." Activities the OBS has sponsored have included a potluck dinner, a Kwanzaa dinner, and parties. For support, students often turn to people in the school's admissions office, such as Tiffany Trent, a Chicago alum, and Deborah Basket. "Those are the people we go to a lot, maybe because they were the ones who convinced us to come here to school in the first place," says a student. A faculty member African-American students also rely on is Edward Epps, a professor of sociology. "He's helpful beyond belief. He's been an adviser for nearly every black student on campus. I think he sees it as his role to help minority students, especially black students."

The Hispanic Association for Cultural Expression and Recognition (HACER) "has been on campus for years, but it has a habit of dying," says a leader. "Since last year, we've been trying to rebuild it, and we've done pretty well." In 1992, HACER sponsored its First Annual Conference on Latino Education, a daylong event that featured panel discussions. Area high school students were invited to participate in discussions about the importance of going to college. One of the group's primary purposes is social activity. "We're trying to go on outings, so we can build bonds among our members, so that we can sometimes speak Spanish. Sometimes we schedule dinners, just time to ourselves," says an English major.

The school's Hispanic students are frustrated by a lack of Hispanic role models and a perceived lack of commitment to recruiting more Hispanic students. "We don't have anyone here. The people in the admissions office tell us to make ourselves at home in their offices, but there's really no one even there we can relate to. When we ask the university to hire someone of Spanish descent for admissions, they tell us they hired a Chicano before but she quit. Then they tell us that they're not going to hire someone just because they're Hispanic. But we're not asking them to be separatists. We're just asking them to hire someone who speaks Spanish."

Although the minority student resources that are available at many of the other prominent schools in the country aren't available at Chicago, Chicago's non-white students are pleased with the educational opportunities at their school. "The University of Chicago forces people to think and to challenge themselves," says a senior. "It's a real education that makes people grow." Adds a recent graduate: "One thing about Chicago is that they don't spoon-feed you at all. The curriculum sounds very rigid, but it's a good exercise in that it helps you decide what's important. And that promises intellectual freedom."

DE PAUL UNIVERSITY

Address: 25 East Jackson Boulevard,
  Chicago, IL 60604
Phone: (312) 362-8300 / (800) 4-DEPAUL
Director of Admissions: Lucy Leusch
Multicultural Student Recruiter: Carmita
  McCoy
1991–92 tuition: $9,300
Room and board: $3,500
Application deadline: 8/15
Financial aid application deadline: 3/1
Non-white freshman admissions: Applicants
  for the class of '95: 1,308
  Accepted: 62.5%
  Accepted who enroll: 24.4%
  Applicants accepted who rank in top
  10% of high school class: 26.2%
  In top 25%: 52.8%
  Median SAT: 440 V, 500 M
  Median ACT: 22
Full-time undergraduate enrollment: 9,757
  Men: 42.3%
  Women: 57.7%

STUDENT ENROLLMENT

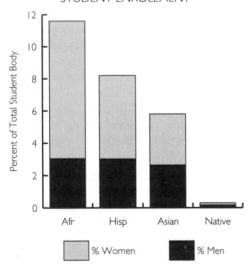

Non-white students in
  1987–88: 24.8%
  1988–89: 24.9%
  1989–90: 25.0%
  1990–91: 24.7%
Geographic distribution of students: na
Students In-state: 91.3%
Top majors: 1. Accounting 2. Computer
  Science
Retention rate of non-white students: 81.6%
**Scholarships exclusively for non-white
  students:** Scholarship for
  African-American students: merit-based;
  $2,000–$7,000 per year; renewable;
  approximately seven to ten awarded each
  year. Scholarship for Hispanic Students:
  merit-based; $2,000–$7,000 per year;
  approximately seven to ten awarded each
  year.
Remediation programs: Summer Bridge
  program
Academic support services: De Paul
  sponsors nine campus-wide academic
  support services ranging from biology
  and mathematics to writing. The Office
  of Multicultural Student Affairs provides
  tutoring and other academic and
  non-academic assistance services.
Ethnic studies programs: The school offers
  majors in Hispanic-American Studies,
  established in 1987, and Asian Studies,
  established in 1952. Programs also
  include Africana Studies, the American
  Indian program, Latin American Studies,
  and a Southeast Asia program.
Organizations for non-white students: Alpha
  Phi Alpha, Zeta Phi Beta,
  African-American Alliance, National
  Association of Black Accountants, Black
  Women's Professional Group, Gospel
  Choir, United Hispanics, Asian Cultural
  Exchange
Notable non-white alumni: Benjamin Hooks
  (former NAACP head)
Tenured faculty: 250
Non-tenured faculty: 220
Student-faculty ratio: 17:1
Administrators: 400
  African-American: 12%

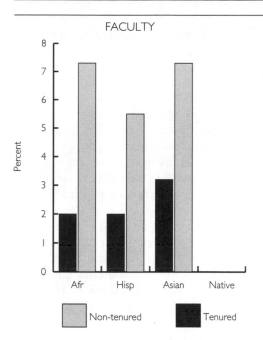

FACULTY

Percent

Afr   Hisp   Asian   Native

Non-tenured   Tenured

Hispanic: 4%
Asian-American: 1%
Native American: 0
Recent non-white speakers on campus: Jesse Jackson (civil rights activist and former U.S. presidential candidate); Maya Angelou (author and poet); Louis Farrakhan (head of the Nation of Islam); Roberto Durán (poet); Martin Luther King III (civil rights activist); Carol Moseley Braun (first African-American female U.S. Senator)

De Paul is a Catholic institution of higher learning that has come to be known nationally for its prowess on the basketball court. (The Blue Demons are usually top contenders for the national championship.) What people know locally is that the school also supplies its largely commuter student body with a practical and respectable education.

The 95-year-old university's Lincoln Park campus—which basically covers a four-block area—includes the College of Liberal Arts and Science, the School of Music and Fine Arts, the Theater School, and the School of Education. The downtown campus, located near Chicago's business district, houses De Paul's schools of law and commerce. Transportation between the campuses is relatively simple, thanks to Chicago's elevated train.

Best known among De Paul's schools is the College of Commerce, which has seven different degree-granting programs, including marketing, accounting, finance, and economics. The university also has a graduate school of business. De Paul's Theater School is nationally recognized, and has graduated the likes of Karl Malden and Mary Elizabeth Mastrantonio. Each year theater students produce more than 160 performances, which attract more than 55,000 people. The program includes concentrations in eight different areas, such as costume and lighting design and acting and production management. The school is host to an annual speaker series that brings well-known theater professionals to campus. De Paul's music department is also said to be excellent.

Students say the faculty is accessible, and that having lunch with professors is common. "Most professors give you their office phone numbers on the first day of class, and they encourage you to call them with any questions or problems," says a student. "Many of my professors have also given us their home telephone numbers." Students also say that the majority of their professors are good teachers.

De Paul is largely a commuter campus; only about 25 percent of its student body lives in one of the university's Lincoln Park dorms. Accommodations are reportedly good; three of the school's seven dorms were built in the past couple of years. Having such a large commuter population can get in the way of creating school unity, but students say that with hard work there are ways around that. "During my freshman year, people were always saying to me that if you commute you can't get as involved. I live about thirty minutes outside of the city, but I'm as involved in student activities as I'd be if I lived on campus. I'm president of an organization, and all of my executive officers are also commuters. In fact, I'd say most of the members of my organization are commuters. And we still get a lot done."

Of the students who do live on campus, many tend to get involved in at least one of the school's activities, whether it's working for the school newspaper, the *De Paulia,* or working for WDPU, the campus radio station. De Paul's Activities Board plans movies and concerts, usually with local bands. Attending Blue Demons basketball games is also a favorite student activity. De Paul's two gyms, Alumni Hall and Hayes-Healy, host a variety of other varsity and intramural sporting activities.

The Asian Cultural Exchange, with about 25 active members, is a source of unity for its members, who meet in the Stuart Center once every two weeks. "We're mostly social, and we don't limit our group just to Asians," says a member. "This year, about eight of our active members were non-Asian. We've had more, but with the United Hispanics organization starting recently, we lost some Hispanic students who used to come to our meetings. We try to make people who do come to our meetings feel as relaxed as possible, but right now the group is mostly Filipino and is not that diverse, especially with the Japanese, Koreans, and Chinese students starting their own clubs. We're hoping to sponsor future activities with the other clubs."

The city of Chicago offers a plethora of cultural and social activities for students, another obstacle to creating school spirit at De Paul. The clubs and bars of nearby Rush and Division streets are popular with students. Chicago is also home to famous blues clubs, the Chicago Symphony, and professional baseball (Cubs and White Sox), basketball (Bulls), and football (Bears) teams.

While De Paul students are a diverse group, some generalities can be made about them: the majority—about half, to be more exact—are Catholic, and about 80 percent of the student body is from the Chicago area. Many of the students also commute from home to school and are the first of their families to go to college. In addition, many hold down part-time jobs while earning their degrees; the university accommodates these students by offering many evening classes. With the completion of the new dorms, and plans to erect more, the university is beginning to attract more out-of-staters.

Like administrations at other Catholic universities, De Paul's is conservative. Although dorms are coed, intervisitation rules are many and strictly enforced. The school does not dispense birth control information, nor does it recognize a gay and lesbian student organization.

In Chicago, a De Paul degree is an impressive credential, particularly with the alumni connections in the area. De Paul students are able to earn the degree in small-class settings, while still having easy access to the resources of one of the country's great cities. "There are times I wish I'd gone to a school with more of a residential campus, but in light of the education I'm earning here, that desire almost comes second," says a student. "I know I couldn't have gotten a better education anywhere else, whether I lived on campus or not."

UNIVERSITY OF ILLINOIS/URBANA-CHAMPAIGN

Address: 10 Henry Administration, 506 South Wright Street, Urbana, IL 61801
Phone: (217) 333-0302
Director of Admissions: Patricia E. Askew
Multicultural Student Recruiters: Alicia Gilmore, Marianela Gonzalez
1993–94 tuition: $2,486 (in-state); $6,738 (out-of-state)
Room and board: $4,358
Application deadline: 1/1
Financial aid application deadline: 2/15
Non-white freshman admissions: Applicants for the class of '96: 4,230
Accepted: 71.5%
Accepted who enroll: 50%
Applicants accepted who rank in top 10% of high school class: 34.51%
In top 25%: 66.5%
Median SAT: na
Median ACT: na
Full-time undergraduate enrollment: 24,947
Men: 56%
Women: 44%
Non-white students in
1987–88: 14.6%
1988–89: 16.8%
1989–90: 19.1%
1990–91: 22%
Students In-state: 92.68%
Top majors: 1. Psychology 2. Finance 3. Accounting
Retention rate of non-white students: 97%
Scholarships exclusively for non-white students: President's Award Program: need-based; available to African-American and Hispanic students; number of awards varies from year to year. National Achievement Scholarship Program for Outstanding Negro

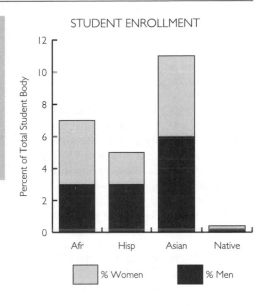

STUDENT ENROLLMENT

Percent of Total Student Body

Afr   Hisp   Asian   Native

% Women   % Men

Students: merit-based; $500–$2,000 for each award; renewable.
Remediation programs: Educational Opportunities Program provides academic support and tutoring through the school's Summer Bridge and Transition programs.

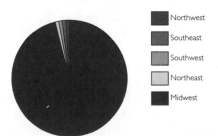

GEOGRAPHIC DISTRIBUTION OF STUDENTS

Northwest
Southeast
Southwest
Northeast
Midwest

Academic support services: Tutoring is available in all academic subjects. Academic support is also provided by the Office of Minority Student Affairs, as well as by nearly a dozen other offices on campus.

Ethnic studies programs: U of I offers an Afro-American Studies and research program, established in 1969, which includes courses in numerous social science and humanities departments. The program involves more than 40 faculty members.

Ethnic studies courses: na

Organizations for non-white students: Puerto Rican Student Association, Coalition for a New Tradition, Asian-American Association, Central Black Student Union, NAACP, La Colectiva Latina, La Raza, Alpha Kappa Alpha, Zeta Phi Beta, Delta Sigma Theta, Iota Phi Theta, Kappa Alpha Psi, Phi Beta Sigma, Sigma Gamma Rho, Omega Psi Phi, Alpha Psi Lambda

Notable non-white alumni: Roger Plummer (Engineering Mechanics; president and CEO, Ameritech); Robert Johnson (Political Science; president and CEO, Black Entertainment Network); Joyce Tucker (Psychology/Math; U.S. Equal Employment Opportunity Commission);

Dr. Nelvia Brady (Sociology; chancellor, City Colleges of Chicago)

Tenured faculty: 1,612
African-American: .8%
Hispanic: .7%
Asian-American: 3.5%
Native American: .1%

Non-tenured faculty: 1,482
African-American: 1.3%
Hispanic: 1.3%
Asian-American: 8%
Native-American: .4%

Student-faculty ratio: 12:1

Administrators: 2,021
African-American: 2.1%
Hispanic: 2%
Asian-American: 11.5%
Native American: .5%

Recent non-white speakers on campus: Dr. Tomas Arciniega (president, University of California/Bakersfield); Dr. Edgar Beckham (program coordinator, Ford Foundation); Tony Brown (host and producer, *Tony Brown's Journal*); Wilma Mankiller (chief, Cherokee Tribe of Oklahoma); Eleanor Holmes Norton (professor of law, Georgetown University); Marian Wright Edelman (Children's Defense Fund); Jesse Jackson (civil rights leader)

For the more than 25,000 undergraduates at the University of Illinois, it came as no surprise when the editors at *Money* magazine recently ranked the university as one of the best college buys in the country. With more than 25,000 undergraduates, 150 degree-granting programs, the country's third-largest university library (behind Harvard and Yale), and more than 700 student organizations on campus, the U of I is one of the country's most respected—and best-priced—mega-sized universities. The biggest challenge for many students may be deciding which activity (or activities) is right for him or her.

But it seems, oddly enough, that in-staters are about the only ones who know about the U of I's wealth of opportunities; nearly the entire student body—about 95 percent, to be exact—hail from the land of Lincoln, many from the suburbs of Chicago, while only about 1 percent are from foreign lands.

In addition to being from Illinois, the typical U of I student is also going to be pretty bright, as the university has some impressive admissions statistics, particularly for a state school. For a recent class, the average combined SAT score of all U of I students was more than 1,160, and more than 50 percent of the students graduated in the top 10 percent of their high school graduating classes. And although the student body is predominantly white, since 1985 the African-American enrollment has increased 60 percent and Hispanic enrollment 80 percent.

With such a bright crew, it's no wonder that academic competition can be intense, especially among the engineering and business majors, which are two of the school's more popular programs. The university offers a variety of other top-notch programs: political science, English, electrical engineering, psychology, physics, and the performing arts, to name just a few. Students say, however, that liberal arts programs on the whole are not as strong as those in more technical and pre-professional areas.

The U of I's Latin American and Caribbean Studies program "is excellent for what it offers," says a student, "but there's hardly ever anything offered about the Caribbean. The focus is mainly on Mexico, Peru, and Brazil, and places like Puerto Rico and elsewhere are pretty much left in the air." "People and Culture of South America" and "The Organization of Latin America" arc two of the program's more popular classes, although one major says, "I've liked them all." The director of the program, Enrique Meyer, a Peruvian, is also popular with students; he's a faculty adviser to the Hispanic fraternity, Sigma Lambda Beta.

In the spring of 1992, thc university granted its first undergraduate degree in African-American Studies to a student who, working with faculty advisers and a great deal of initiative, created his own course of study. "The student had to design his own major, and he was determined to study African-American culture and history, and he did it," says a student. "Afro-American Literature," "Black Chorus," and "Black Women in American History" are some of the area's best courses, while "Race and Politics," which focuses on present-day issues in Chicago politics, is also well attended.

Don't count on getting too close to many of your professors, should you decide to attend school here. Class sizes can run into the hundreds, and teaching assistants, who teach sections of these large courses to 20 to 30 students about once a week, are the norm for more than a quarter of all classes. However, the Office of Minority Student Affairs "is very well used" and "sees a lot of students because it offers almost anything students want—from financial assistance and advice to study sessions and tutoring. Students hear about the office by word of mouth, but they also get introduced to it during freshman orientation when they're taken on campus tours."

When talking about organizations at the U of I, it's hard not to acknowledge the vast extent of the school's Greek system, which encompasses more than 57 fraternities and 29 sororities. While the predominantly white Greek organizations are just that—predominantly white—there are those that are popular with students of color. "The minority fraternities and sororities, like mine, will sponsor an occasional party or two, but our primary focus is community involvement and cultural awareness programming," says a member of one of the school's Hispanic fraternities.

The U of I's predominantly black Greek organizations have an impressive history on campus. The country's second chapter of the Kappa Alpha Psi fraternity and the country's third chapter of the Alpha Kappa Alpha sorority were founded at the U of I. Most of the organizations have their own residences. But students comment that there is little interaction between the predominantly black and white organizations. "Each year Alpha Phi Alpha fraternity sponsors an Ebony to Ivory Week, which is an opportunity for black and white Greeks to come together. Each night a minority would be represented, and he or she would talk about their culture and how they feel about going to school here. But the event was attended only by students of color. The president of Alpha was pretty upset because each white organization could have sent at least one representative, but they didn't. It left a bad taste in a lot of people's mouths. Many of the white Greeks talk about wanting to diversify programming, but it seems to be all talk." While all of the U of I's black Greek organizations are represented on the school's Black Greek Council, only Kappa Alpha Psi is represented on the Interfraternity Council, composed of the school's predominantly white fraternities. No black sororities are represented on the U of I's Panhellenic Council.

When not planning cultural programming, many of the black Greek organizations are involved in community service. Every Sunday members of Omega Psi Phi volunteer their services in a nearby senior citizen home, while the men of Alpha Phi Alpha are involved in a nearby boys and girls club. At the beginning of each year, Alpha Phi Alpha and Delta Sigma Theta sponsor a forum in which race relations are discussed.

For non-Greeks, there's never a shortage of opportunities to interact with other African-American students, thanks in large part to the efforts of the highly organized Central Black Student Union (CBSU), an umbrella organization that represents seven smaller Black Student Unions (BSU) that are housed in the school's seven dorm areas. By the end of a school year, each of the BSUs takes on its own personality. "Salongo takes great pride in knowing they were the first BSU on campus, and they're a wonderful group and do a lot of wonderful programming," says a CBSU leader. "Last year, they did an AIDS awareness program and sponsored a Greek Talk, where representatives of each of the Greek organizations talked about their respective organizations. Salongo represents Pennsylvania Avenue Residence Hall and they won the BSU organization of the year last year. The BSU at Champaign Hall is wild. The hall is referred to as Six-Pack, if that tells you anything."

Students say having a decentralized BSU gives students a sense of family. "Even people who move out of the dorms and into apartments still identify with their BSU and feel welcome at their former residence halls," says a student. The works of each BSU are highlighted at the annual BSU Unity Week program, which includes skits, readings, and other performances.

The CBSU has many of its own programs, sponsored with the various BSUs. One of the most successful is the CBSU Buddy Program, which matches first-year students with upperclass students. "The older student writes to the new student over the summer, and when the new student arrives on campus, the older student takes him or her around campus and helps him with registration, which is a nightmare here. Basically, the buddy is the new student's first friend on campus. I don't know how I would have survived if it hadn't been for my buddy."

The CBSU, among a variety of other programs, recently sponsored its first Black Dad's Day Social and its annual Leadership Conference. Recently, group leaders visited four other schools, including Arizona State University and public universities in Illinois and Wisconsin, only to discover "we were so impressed by how structured and organized our system is," says a student. "It seems that the other schools are just getting their organizations off the ground." Cotton Club, another CBSU event held annually in Foellinger Hall, "is a huge variety show that has students reading poetry, dancing, and singing everything from classical and jazz music to rap and hip-hop. Last year, more than 8,000 people attended the event. It is getting so popular we're outgrowing the space."

The U of I's professional organizations for African-American students are also active. The school's black law and medical associations take members on tours of prominent law and medical schools, including Meharry and Howard. Established in 1990, If Not Now is one of the school's newest African-American organizations. "It's the most radical of the school's black groups," says a student. "They put together a book that listed all of the black businesses in the area, and they help out with freshman orientation. But they're mostly known for protests in favor of better retention of minority students and demanding more African-American professors and staff." Nia, a Swahili word meaning "purpose," is a student organization "dedicated to studying African history and philosophy. It's not political at all like If Not Now. It's solely devoted to study."

The Afro-American Cultural Center, known as the Afro House by students who frequent it, "is where we can go and relax between and after classes, watch TV, study, whatever." Located right off the school's main quad, the center is centrally situated, and is home to various student groups, including If Not Now; Omni Move, a dance troupe; *Griot,* a student newspaper; Black Chorus; WBLM, the only black radio station in central Illinois; and a theater company.

African-American students have also organized their own commencement exercises, held each year in Foellinger Hall. "The ceremony is so amazing, there's so much warmth that I can't even describe all the positive feelings I have," says a student about the event, which honors all undergraduate and graduate students receiving diplomas.

While smaller in numbers, the U of I's Latino students have been far from silent. "This past semester was quite a sight here on campus for Latino students," says a student leader. "We issued a set of demands to the administration, including better retention of Latino students and better recruitment of Puerto Rican students. While the school's Latino students have been politically active of late, students say they aren't as organized as the school's African-American student groups. "A lot of the Latino students bring with them their prejudices from their neighborhoods. The Puerto Ricans don't get along with the Mexicans, and vice versa. But some of the Latino student groups are working to break down some of these barriers," says a student. "Each year we sponsor Copacabana, held at the Illini Union, where students from all Latino backgrounds dance and read poems and literature—a kind of celebration of Latino culture."

Other organizations, including Hispanic fraternities and sororities, also work to unite the school's Latino students. "My fraternity alone has Hispanic students from Honduras, Guatemala, Puerto Rico, Peru, and Colombia," says a member of Sigma Lambda Beta, which has about 21 members.

La Casa, the school's Latino cultural center, is "a safe haven for Latinos to come together and to get to know each other." The center offers a living area with a TV, a piano, a dining room, a computer room that has five Macintoshes, and in the kitchen flags representing every Latin American country. Many of the school's Latino student groups, including the Puerto Rican and Mexican associations, have offices there.

The Asian-American Association, with about 80 active members, "does so much every year that I couldn't possibly explain all that we do," says an AAA leader. Perhaps the group's most ambitious project each year is playing host to the Midwest Asian-American Student Conference, a weekend-long event that recently featured workshops that focused on such topics as "Asian-American Women," "Asian-American Homosexuality," and "The Marginalization of Southeast Asia." As of now, the majority of AAA members are of Chinese descent, but there are also Thai, Filipino, and Indian members. Students representatives from more than two dozen universities attended the conference.

The Asian-American Programming Committee, a part of the Illini Board, sponsored its own share of workshops, among them "Asian-Americans in the Corporate World" and "Interracial Dating." Each year AAA also publishes its own calendar of events, as well as a newsletter. Unlike the Latino and African-American students, the Asian-American students do not have their own cultural center. "That's something we're working on," says an AAA leader. "Not until two years ago was there ever really a push to get one established on campus. We've been publicizing our efforts and have gotten numerous petitions signed, but we haven't made much headway."

Accord, a newly established Asian-American student organization, "is more political than AAA. It's more concerned with civil rights and freedoms. The group sponsored a rally on the quad on the fiftieth anniversary of the attack on Pearl Harbor. It was an open-mike event where students read poetry and other literature."

While there isn't much interaction, on a formal basis anyway, between the school's cultural organizations, these students have come together to rally against the school's mascot, Chief Illini. "As people of color, no matter whether we're Native American or not, we find Chief Illini offensive. But it looks as though there's no way we will get it changed, unlike similar offensive symbols which have been changed at Dartmouth and Stanford. Alums call in and say they will quit contributing to the university if the chief is done away with, and there's even a student group that fights to keep the chief in place." Before a recent football game against rival Ohio State University, students protested the use of the chief in front of the president's house.

The University of Illinois has the reputation of having a rather conservative student population, and being the only non-white student in a classroom of hundreds won't strike you as alienating after your first year or so. But once the adjustment is made, students come to love their university. "I've loved almost every minute of my stay here," says a senior. "I've grown a great deal, I've traveled a lot with my organization, and I've met many different types of people. It's been a wonderful experience, while at the same time allowing me the chance to deal with the real world at one of the best public universities in the country."

ILLINOIS STATE UNIVERSITY

Address: North and School Streets, Normal, IL 61761
Phone: (309) 438-2111 / (309) 438-2181
Director of Admissions: Dave Snyder
Multicultural Student Recruiter: Art Evans
1991–92 tuition: $2,430 (in-state)
Room and board: $2,648
Application deadline: Rolling admissions
Financial aid application deadline: 3/1
Non-white freshman admissions: Applicants for the class of '95: 2,060
   Accepted: 49%
   Accepted who enroll: 21%
   Applicants accepted who rank in top 10% of high school class: na
   In top 25%: 35%
   Median SAT: na
   Median ACT range: 18–20
Full-time undergraduate enrollment: 19,144
   Men: 45%
   Women: 55%

STUDENT ENROLLMENT

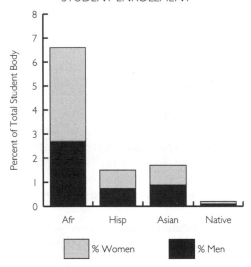

Non-white students in
   1987–88: 8.6%
   1988–89: 7.2%
   1989–90: 8.9%
   1990–91: 9.4%

Geographic distribution of students: na
Top majors: na
Retention rate of non-white students: 70%
Scholarships exclusively for non-white students: Women and Minorities in Educational Administration: merit-based; two awards each year; $737 each award; award based on race and/or gender, geographic location, and intended course of study. Minority Professional Opportunities: merit-based; 50 awarded each year; $700 each award. College of Applied Science and Technology: need-based; three awarded each year. ISU Associates Tuition Waivers: merit-based; 50 awarded each year; $1,740 each award.
Remediation programs: Developmental courses include "Basic Writing Skills," "Introduction to College Reading," and "Basic Algebra."
Academic support services: The Mathematical Assistance Center, the University Center for Learning Assistance, and the Academic Advisement Center provide academic support.
Ethnic studies programs: The university offers an ethnic and cultural studies minor, which allows students to focus on the experiences of Asian-Americans, Native Americans, Hispanic Americans, and African-Americans.
Ethnic studies courses: The courses "Cultural Awareness and Interracial Understanding" and "Introduction to Asian Cultures" are offered as part of the university's interdisciplinary studies program.
Organizations for non-white students: African Students Association, Association of Latin American Students, Black Action and Awareness Committee, Minority Professional Opportunities, Black Student Union, NAACP, Black Writers Forum, Student Association of

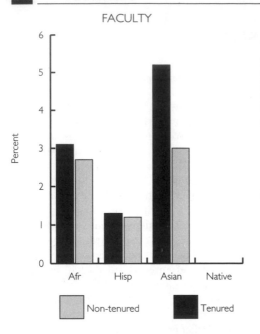

FACULTY

Non-tenured   Tenured

the Republic of China, Chinese Student Association, Thai Student Association, Third World Student Association
Notable non-white alumni: na
Tenured faculty: 712
Non-tenured faculty: 331
Student-faculty ratio: 21:1
Administrators: 392
   African-American: 9.9%
   Hispanic: 0.8%
   Asian-American: 4.3%
   Native American: 0
Recent non-white speakers on campus: na

To say that Illinois State University is far from the madding crowd is to put it mildly. Located in Normal, Illinois, a town of about 40,000-plus residents that's surrounded by cornfields, ISU offers solid academics in an atmosphere that's conducive to quiet study.

ISU is known throughout the state primarily for its teacher education programs, which allow students to serve as student teachers in nearby schools. ISU's College of Business, which offers accounting, management, finance, and marketing, is also popular. Students say the school's liberal arts programs play second fiddle to the other, more pre-professional courses.

Three years ago some faculty and students attempted to get an ethnic studies program implemented, but students say nothing happened because of what the administration said were budget constraints. "Afro-American History," taught by Brian Corpening, director of ISU's Multicultural Center, is one of ISU's more popular courses. "Students flock to it because there are so few ethnic studies courses offered," says a student. "Black Music" is also a well-attended course; Frank Scuggs, the course's professor, is highly respected by students.

While there are those students who attend ISU because of its academic programs, many choose to come here because of its location. "I'd say that about 90 percent of the black students here are from the Chicago area, which is only about two hours from campus," says a Black Student Union leader. "The students want to go to a school that's not too far from home, yet not too close either." This proximity can lead to a less than active weekend social calendar on campus. "You should see the Greyhound bus on Fridays. Many head home on the weekends to get their hair done, to go shopping, or just to be with family."

The exodus out of the city of Normal on weekends is no doubt also due to the lack of entertainment—outside of the mall and several movie theaters—in the area. After Hours, a black-owned dance club nearby, has become popular, particularly with ISU's black Greek organizations. These groups are active on campus, sponsoring various community service projects and parties. Alpha Phi Alpha fraternity and Delta Sigma Theta and Zeta Phi Beta sororities are among the most active.

To help keep students culturally entertained, the Black Student Union sponsors various events throughout the school year, including events for Black History Month, such as the Black Heritage Ball, the group's biggest and most popular event. "It's more or less a fashion show where we usually invite a guest speaker." The BSU also sponsors cultural dinners throughout the school year.

The group's big brother/big sister program is undergoing serious restructuring. "Older students worked with new students, but it didn't work very well. In fact, I'd say it was pretty ineffective. The older students didn't really have the time to help the new students, and the younger students usually didn't seek the older ones out. Everyone just kind of falls into his or her own clique and doesn't reach out. Now we're going to have it so the program reaches out to area minority students, where we work with students to encourage them to attend college and to do well in school. We want to work with the community more in this way."

The BSU's staff adviser, Floyd Carroll, from the school's High Potential Students Office, "has always been a friend to us," says a BSU member. "He's not just part of the administration."

The BSU, however, is not looked to as a source of strength by many students. "There's only been one time since I can remember when the president and the vice president of the BSU have been able to sustain their terms for the entire year. Many black students on campus don't have faith in the organization. This has led to a lot of disunity within the group. But the '92–'93 elected BSU officers are going to work to bring more unity within the BSU, first by staying in their positions for the entire year."

While the BSU is working to regroup, students say the school's Multicultural Center is less than effective. "For some reason, maybe because of location, the center is hardly used at all. The administration is thinking of closing it down. It's a beautiful house, where some students will go to relax, but it's so far off campus that most students don't even know it's there."

The BSU office has relocated to the campus's new Student Services Building. "The new building is located next door to the Boone Student Center, and the office is now really nice. We're centrally located. The BSU, hopefully, should become more active."

ISU may not have all the amenities of big-city life, but the student who comes here, especially from a larger urban center, usually knows that. It's a good place for quiet study and, for the motivated, a place where one can easily make connections with faculty and administration. "I've had a good experience here, and there are those who will surely disagree with me. But I made it my business to get to know the faculty and the administration, which has made getting around here easier. I think that's what it takes to graduate from ISU."

ILLINOIS WESLEYAN UNIVERSITY

Address: P.O. Box 2900, Bloomington, IL 61702-2900
Phone: (309) 556-3031/(800) 332-2498
Director of Admissions: James Ruoti
Multicultural Student Recruiter: Malik Jones
1991–92 tuition: $11,015
Room and board: $3,245
Application deadline: 3/1
Financial aid application deadline: 3/1
Non-white freshman admissions: Applicants for the class of '95: 255
  Accepted: na
  Applicants accepted who rank in top 10% of high school class: na
  Median SAT: na
  Median ACT: na
Full-time undergraduate enrollment: 1,743
  Men: 46%
  Women: 54%

Geographic distribution of students: na
Students In-state: 96.5%
Top majors: 1. Biology 2. Psychology 3. Math/Computer Science
Retention rate of non-white students: 80%
Scholarships exclusively for non-white students: None
Remediation programs: None
Academic support services: The Academic Skill Center, as well as student tutors in most subjects, provide academic support services.
Ethnic studies programs: None
Ethnic studies courses: Five courses are offered in African and African-American Studies, as well as about three courses in Latin American Studies and about two courses in Asian Studies.
Organizations for non-white students: Black Student Union, Council for Latin American Student Enrichment, Multicultural Center

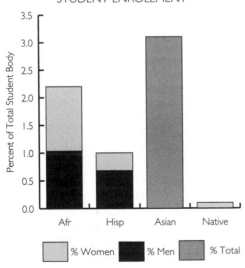

STUDENT ENROLLMENT

Percent of Total Student Body

% Women   % Men   % Total

Non-white students in
  1987–88: na
  1988–89: 5.3%
  1989–90: 5.6%
  1990–91: 5.6%

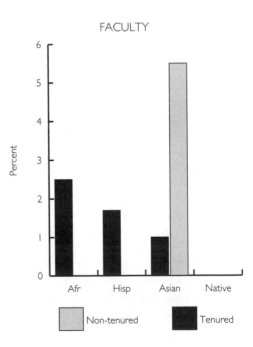

FACULTY

Percent

Non-tenured   Tenured

Notable non-white alumni: Frankie Faison (Theater; actor); Oliver Jackson (Art; artist); Barrington Coleman (Music; assistant professor of voice, Illinois Wesleyan)

Tenured faculty: 120

Non-tenured faculty: 18

Student-faculty ratio: 13:1

Administrators: na

African-American: na

Hispanic: 0

Asian-American: 0

Native American: 0

Recent non-white speakers on campus: Martin Luther King III (civil rights activist and Georgia state representative); Jesse Jackson (former U.S. presidential candidate and civil rights activist)

For three years running, Illinois Wesleyan University has earned accolades from the editors of *U.S. News & World Report* as the Midwest's top regional university. Even though IWU's reputation has not transcended statewide appeal—in a recent year, nearly 90 percent of its students were from Illinois—IWU offers a quality education that should appeal to students interested in a small-college experience in a laid-back atmosphere.

Although a university in name, IWU has the feel of a small liberal arts college. Interaction with faculty members is frequent and easy, and the school is committed to graduating a well-rounded individual. IWU has several notable academic programs, including nursing, biology, psychology, and business, and an impressive fine arts program, in which students are able to major in music, theater or theater dance. IWU's School of Music is outstanding and has impressive facilities.

Such courses as "African Politics," "Black Women Writers," and "Civil Rights" earn high marks from students. Paul Bushnell, an associate professor of history, who teaches the "Civil Rights" course, is supportive of IWU's minority students. "He has a respect for us that makes us respect him," observes a student.

IWU students are also able to take advantage of the school's 4-1-4 academic calendar, in which students earn credit by studying or working as interns on or off campus during the month of January. For a recent January term, George Kieh, an assistant professor of political science, who earned his degree at the University of Liberia, led a group of about 25 students to Nigeria. "The trip was designed for students to do independent research on almost any topic they wanted," says a student.

The Black Student Union (BSU), which has about 15 members, doesn't have much luck in getting students to show up for its forums. A discussion group about the Anita Hill/Clarence Thomas controversy generated little student interest. But the group's first all-campus dance was a hit. "We worked hard to make sure everyone knew that this event was for the whole campus, and not just for BSU members. Because of this, I think we were able to have such a good turnout." In conjunction with the Catholic Social Services agency in the area, the BSU also sponsors an annual African Cultural Experience program. "We have workshops for community children in which we teach them about African culture, such as jewelry making, folk tales, and cooking. It felt good to sponsor an activity that helped others." The Council for Latin American Student Enrichment (CLASE) also has an organization on campus, but because of the small number of Hispanic students on campus the group has a difficult time staying active.

The Multicultural Center, located on the west side of campus, houses the BSU office and has three computers and a printer for student use. The center also contains a small library of Hispanic, Native American, and African and African-American literature. While the center is used for some informal gatherings, "mostly we go there to study," says a student.

As at other small liberal arts colleges in the Midwest, much of the social life at IWU centers on the 11 traditionally white fraternities and sororities, to which about a third of the men and women on campus belong. As the Greek system is only nominally integrated, IWU's minority students rely on the activities of the BSU and other student groups for social and cultural outlets. Theater productions are popular, as are the school's numerous musical groups. The Student Education Association coordinates volunteer tutoring projects in the Bloomington/Normal area and the school's religious groups also enjoy strong memberships. Illinois State University, located just a few minutes' walk from campus, is also a source of much of students' social life, particularly when ISU's historically black fraternities host their parties.

The town of Bloomington, located in the middle of the state, is, for the most part, surrounded by cornfields, but, as one transplanted Chicagoan put it, "that just means the area's clean and safe." There is little variety to IWU's student body, either culturally or politically, and campus activism hasn't reared its head in this part of the state for years. For many students, attending school in just such a relaxed atmosphere is what they had in mind when they chose to come to IWU in the first place.

If what you're looking for is twenty-four-hour excitement—as well as a less homogeneous learning environment—then you may be disappointed at IWU. But if you're looking to gain a quality liberal arts education at a school with few distractions, then IWU's academics won't be disappointing. "This school has challenged me academically and has made me grow as a minority female," says a student. "I've learned a great deal about myself. Sometimes it takes being with people who are very different from you to make you see yourself most clearly."

KNOX COLLEGE

Address: Galesburg, IL 61401
Phone: (309) 343-0112 / (800) 678-KNOX
Director of Admissions: na
Multicultural Student Recruiter: Mary
   Crawford
1991–92 tuition: $12,609
Room and board: $3,411
Application deadline: 2/15
Financial aid application deadline: 3/1
Non-white freshman admissions: Applicants
   for the class of '94: 50
   Accepted: 80%
   Accepted who enroll: 34%
   Applicants accepted who rank in top

10% of high school class: 50%
In top 25%: 100%
Median SAT range: 440–490 V,
   500–550 M
Median ACT range: 20–25
Full-time undergraduate enrollment: 1,050
   Men: 50%
   Women: 50%
Non-white students in
   1987–88: 12%
   1988–89: 12%
   1989–90: 12%
   1990–91: 11.5%
Students In-state: na

STUDENT ENROLLMENT

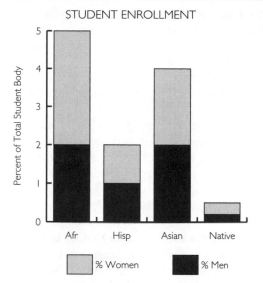

Percent of Total Student Body

Afr　Hisp　Asian　Native

■ % Women　　■ % Men

GEOGRAPHIC DISTRIBUTION OF STUDENTS

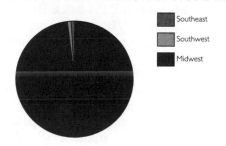

■ Southeast
■ Southwest
■ Midwest

Top majors: 1. Biology 2. Sociology 3. English

Retention rate of non-white students: 90%

Scholarships exclusively for non-white students: Barnabus Root Scholarship for African-Americans: merit-based; $3,000 awarded per scholarship; renewable.

Remediation programs: There is an Educational Development program.

Academic support services: Tutoring in most academic subjects is available.

Ethnic studies programs: Knox offers a Black Studies area of concentration, involving seven courses from four departments.

Ethnic studies courses: na

Organizations for non-white students: Allied Blacks for Liberty and Equality, Los Nuestros, Korean Club

Notable non-white alumni: Jerome Long (history professor, Connecticut Wesleyan); John Feemster (cardiologist)

Tenured faculty: 90

Non-tenured faculty: 90

FACULTY

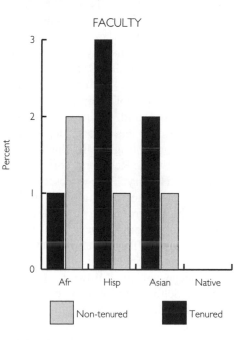

Percent

Afr　Hisp　Asian　Native

■ Non-tenured　　■ Tenured

Student-faculty ratio: 12:1

Administrators: 30
　African-American: 1%
　Hispanic: 0
　Asian American: 0
　Native American: 0

Recent non-white speakers on campus: Gwendolyn Brooks (Pulitzer Prize-winning poet); Julian Bond (former Georgia state senator and civil rights activist); Martin Luther King III (civil rights activist and Georgia state representative)

On the opening day of school every fall, Knox students can expect to participate in a ceremony dubbed "The Pump Handle," in which they will shake the hand of the college president and his wife. To those familiar with Knox, the event typifies the close interaction the students have with their administration and faculty.

In fact, it's this unusual accessibility to the faculty that brought many Knox students to school here in the first place. "The professors here have their phone numbers and addresses listed in a directory that students get, and on the first day of class, the professor always says we're welcome to call him or her almost anytime," says a senior.

Knox is a small college devoted to seeing that its students gain a well-rounded liberal arts education. To do this, students must pass at least two courses in three areas: math and the natural sciences, history and the social sciences, and humanities, including a foreign language. First-year students must participate in Freshman Preceptorials, seminar-style courses designed to improve students' analytical and critical thinking skills. Recent preceptorial topics have included "Perspectives on Being Human" and "Nature and Culture."

Despite the school's emphasis on the liberal arts, the most popular majors at Knox are economics and business administration, which also earns high marks from students. Knox has strong departments in chemistry, biology, political science, philosophy, and English. In Black Studies, two classes that are highly respected are "Race and Ethnic Relations," offered by the sociology department, and "Introduction to African History." The director of the Black Studies program, Frederick Hord, an associate professor of English, is well regarded by students. "He's the driving force behind the program," says a student. "He tries his best to get information about African culture out to the student body."

Knox also offers several specialized programs to qualified students, such as study-abroad opportunities in France and Spain. The college is also one of only two colleges in the Midwest to offer its freshmen qualified admission to Rush Medical School, and one of only 24 schools across the country to participate in the early admission plan with the University of Chicago's graduate school of business.

While many colleges and universities are just now exploring issues of cultural diversity on their campuses, Knox has been doing so for quite some time. In 1870, Knox was the first college in Illinois to award a college degree to an African-American, and the school's first Japanese student enrolled more than 100 years ago. But Knox is perhaps best remembered for having awarded Abraham Lincoln his first honorary degree, and in 1858 it was at Knox where Lincoln first declared his opposition to slavery on moral grounds.

Allied Blacks for Liberty and Equality (ABLE), founded in 1968 and having about 25 active members, "has been more active this year than in years past because there are more new black students on campus," says a student leader. ABLE works to bring various speakers to campus each year, and concentrates much of its energies on ABLE Week, held annually in March. "During ABLE Week we focus on a different topic each day," says a student member. "We'll have open forums and workshops. On one of the days, ABLE members put on Production Night, where students act out skits that deal with race issues on campus or on a more national level. The skits are meant to drive home a point, but we try to have everyone leave laughing."

ABLE's adviser, Quentin Johnson, is the director of Minority Student Affairs on campus. "Before Quentin came to campus in 1990, we only had ABLE to rely on," comments a student. "We were really the only voice on campus. But he now provides students with support on an everyday basis. He'll plead your cause to the administration. This frees up your time to do what we as students are meant to do in college."

ABLE members hold their meetings in the ABLE House, which provides residence facilities for up to six students. To live in the house, students "must be an active member of ABLE and be willing to go through the application process," says a student. "There are usually more than six students who want to live in the house each year." Although the house is open to any student at Knox, the student says that in the past four years only one non-black student, a Latin American, has lived in the house. The house has kitchen facilities and a large living area, as well as a library and art. "Dr. Hord has donated a lot of books to the library, and there's a sense among students that he'll do all he can do to make it a true center."

Extracurricular opportunities at Knox don't stop with ABLE, as Knox sponsors an impressive list of clubs and activities. The college's student-run literary magazine, *Catch,* has won recognition as one of the country's best college literary publications, and the Union Board regularly brings concerts and plays to campus each year. But the board is best known for sponsoring Flunk Day, a day when classes are canceled and students watch movies and participate in dunking and cart and buggy contests. Varsity sporting events are supported by students, and in a recent year 10 of the school's 11 men's teams had winning seasons. More than 50 percent of the campus participates in intramurals; a popular intramural group is the softball league, which includes a faculty team. About a third of the school's student body joins one or another of the school's predominantly white fraternities and sororities, but students say they in no way dominate campus social life.

Much of a student's social life is centered on campus, which is fortunate, as Galesburg (pop. 35,000) offers only minimal off-campus activity, including a mall, several restaurants, and a few cinemas. The city, which has African-American and Hispanic populations, is equidistant from St. Louis and Chicago, where a majority of the school's students are from. Students report there is little interaction with the community.

While the majority of Knox's students are from the Midwest, they don't embody the conservatism of the area. Whether they are drawn to Knox because of its progressive history—the school was a stop on the Underground Railroad for escaped slaves—or because of its quality academics, or both, students here are open-minded. "Students talk about issues here. They don't let things just fester," says a student.

LOYOLA UNIVERSITY

Address: 820 North Michigan Avenue,
   Chicago, IL 60611
Phone: (312) 915-6500 / (800) 262-2373
Director of Admissions: Dr. Allen V. Lentino
Multicultural Student Recruiter: na
1991–92 tuition: $9,210
Room and board: $4,760
Application deadline: 7/12
Financial aid application deadline: 4/1

Non-white freshman admissions: Applicants
   for the class of '95: 1,192
   Accepted: 66%
   Accepted who enroll: 42%
   Applicants accepted who rank in top
   10% of high school class: 25%
   In top 25%: 60%
   Median SAT: 500 V, 500 M
   Median ACT range: 21–25
Full-time undergraduate enrollment: 6,353
   Men: 40%
   Women: 60%

STUDENT ENROLLMENT

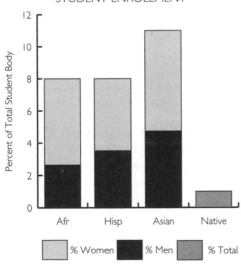

% Women   % Men   % Total

Non-white students in
   1987–88: 23%
   1988–89: 24%
   1989–90: 25%
   1990–91: 26%

GEOGRAPHIC DISTRIBUTION OF STUDENTS

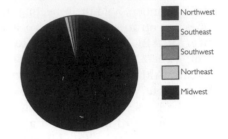

- Northwest
- Southeast
- Southwest
- Northeast
- Midwest

Students In-state: na
Top majors: 1. Business 2. Biology
   3. Communications
Retention rate of non-white students: 88%
**Scholarships exclusively for non-white
   students:** None
Remediation programs: None
Academic support services:
   African-American, Hispanic, and Asian
   American student advisers are available.
   Peer tutors are also available for most
   academic subjects.
Ethnic studies programs: Latin American
   Studies and African-American Studies
   programs are offered as minor courses of
   study.
Ethnic studies courses: na
Organizations for non-white students: Alpha
   Kappa Alpha, Alpha Phi Alpha, Loyola
   African-American Student Association,
   Vietnamese Student Association, Black
   Cultural Center, Black Student Council,
   Caribbean Literary Club, Chinese Club,
   Delta Sigma Theta, Filipino Club,
   Korean Club, Latin American Student
   Organization
Notable non-white alumni: Paula Banks
   (Psychology; president and executive
   director, Sears, Roebuck Foundation);
   Manuel Galvin (Political Science;
   editorial board, *Chicago Tribune*); Dr.
   William Bauta (Biology; research
   associate, University of Texas)
Tenured faculty: na

Non-tenured faculty: na
Student-faculty ratio: 10:1
Administrators: na
Recent non-white speakers on campus:
  Gwendolyn Brooks (Pulitzer
  Prize-winning poet); LeRoy Martin

(Chicago police superintendent); Fr.
George Clements (pastor, Holy Angels
Church, Chicago); Dr. Conrad Worrill
(director, Center for Inner-City Studies,
Northeastern University)

Ask students about their education at Loyola, and the first thing they'll tell you about is their core course requirement. "The core is intense." "It's like boot camp." "There are too many courses to take. I'll never graduate on time." Loyola's core course requirements are demanding and comprehensive and include courses in eight different areas, covering the humanities and the sciences. There are so many course requirements that graduating from Loyola in the usual four years is nearly impossible. "Summer school is practically required of most students, and many students just decide to go for an extra semester instead," says a psychology major.

While students may complain about the requirements, the core does appear to engender success. According to the administration, 10 percent of all Chicago doctors and lawyers are Loyola graduates, as are 50 percent of the city's dentists. Loyola's emphasis on community service—Loyola is a Jesuit institution—is also carried over into many students' career choices. Nearly a third of the city's social workers and public school principals are Loyola grads.

True to its traditions, Loyola's academic strengths are in theology and philosophy. Biology, education, clinical psychology, political science, drama, and nursing are also considered strong. The business administration program, well respected among Chicago area businesses, is huge, incorporating six different disciplines, including accounting, economics, and personnel management. Although Loyola is a midsize university, students say the school's professors are nonetheless accessible. Full professors teach all undergraduate courses.

The Multicultural Affairs Office, located in the Centennial Forum ("the closest thing we have to a student center"), "is open to everybody, and has African-American, Asian, and Latino counselors. It's nice to know you can go and talk to someone of your own race when you have problems. Basically, the office is a counseling service, and we go there whenever we need help with almost anything, such as problems with professors or we need references for tutors." Three of the school's cultural student groups the Black Cultural Center, the Council of Pan-Asian-Americans, and the Latin American Student Organization—have offices there, located in the Assisi Center.

Of the school's more than 6,300 undergraduates, only about 25 percent live on campus, a minus when it comes to developing school spirit. Although an increasing number of out-of-staters are coming to Loyola, most Loyola students hail from the Chicago area and commute to campus from home. "There isn't even a student center on campus where students can just hang out. We try to get commuters involved in activities, but it's almost impossible to do so. They're so quick to want to get home, and that makes it difficult to meet people unless they're in your class," says a campus leader.

One recent event that did bring much of the campus together was Unity in Diversity

Week. "All the multicultural student organizations got together and sponsored career forums, a poetry reading, an art exhibit, and workshops. The gay/lesbian/bisexual organization was also part of the events."

On campus, the school's various cultural student groups sponsor activities and events that draw campus-wide interest. "This is the first year that the Council of Pan-Asian-Americans (COPA) really hit big. It has a lot to do with COPA's new executive board. Before, the board never really sponsored much. But this year, we're doing tons to generate awareness about Asian culture and to say to the campus that we're proud about who we are." COPA sponsors career forums to which it invites Asians from the Chicago area to come and speak about their careers. In April, COPA sponsors activities for Asian-American Heritage Month. As part of the event's activities, COPA recently held an alumni reception "to increase networking and to get the alums involved in COPA" and an Asian dance festival. COPA also provides tutoring services to students at a nearby Southeast Asian Center.

In 1992, COPA hosted Chicago's first Asian-American conference, in which about 100 students from six area schools participated in a career forum and various workshops. "I can't believe there had never before been such a forum involving the area schools. We hope to have it again next year, but some of the schools, including the University of Chicago, didn't seem very interested. We got good response from most of the other schools, though."

Yvonne Lau, COPA's adviser and an assistant dean, is a popular figure on campus. "She keeps us in touch with what's going on politically when it comes to Asian issues. Through her we got to meet Illinois senator Paul Simon and his assistant Sandra Otaka, who is also an EPA lawyer. She's also phenomenal when it comes to one-on-one contact. She tells us how she feels about certain subjects, but never what to do."

The Black Cultural Center, with about 100 active members, "provides tutoring services for members, friendship, and guidance," says a BCC member. "We throw parties, have fashion shows and workshops about diversity, a film festival, and an annual African-American Student Ball. We do so many things that it's hard to remember them all. But the main activity is our rap group sessions, where we talk about anything, from our parents to classes."

Students report that there is little interaction among the races at Loyola but that certain student groups are working to change that. "Multiculturalism is a big thing here at Loyola. The student government recently printed up a T-shirt that said 'It's a Multicultural Thing: We Want You to Understand.' But there's still these major cliques. All the Filipinos hang together, as do the Hispanics, and most of the other ethnic groups on campus. At all of our COPA meetings we have people from different Asian backgrounds speak about their cultures, to try to build bridges among the school's Asian communities. Recently, after an Indian student spoke about his background and his experiences in this country, something really weird happened. A white student who happened to be at the meeting stood up and said, 'I've always been afraid to talk to some of the Asian students because you're always in groups, and, until now, I've never known what you go through in this country. What you said here has broken that barrier for me, and now I will feel more comfortable speaking with you when I see you on campus.' Even though what she said was weird, it was still kind of cool."

Besides the events sponsored by the cultural organizations, students have the opportunity to join any of the school's more than 100 clubs, which range from Volunteer Action and Amnesty International to student government and the socialists. The school also fields more than 40 intramural sporting events, including Ping-Pong, handball, and swimming. When it comes to varsity competition, men's cross-country and women's basketball are tops. Dating can be a major ordeal at Loyola, particularly as the women outnumber the men almost two to one. "It's great for the guys, but it's a bummer for us," says a disgruntled coed. Loyola students also interact with students from other area schools, including the University of Chicago and De Paul University.

But the biggest social and cultural diversions for Loyola students aren't on campus. These diversions can be found in the streets, in the restaurants, in the theaters, and in the clubs and bars of the Windy City, the Midwest's largest and most exciting city. Loyola students can also watch the Bears play in Soldier Field or view the latest art exhibit at the famed Art Institute of Chicago.

Although Loyola doesn't offer a great deal when it comes to school spirit, it does provide the sort of rigorous academic training that allows graduates to become members of Chicago's professional ranks. "It's hard getting to be friends with students who aren't in your classes," says a student. "But Loyola has made me more independent and has encouraged me to create a lot of my own social activities while I've been here. It's not just handed to you. My classes are good, and my professors are easy to get to know. So, yes, all in all, I'm glad I came to school here."

NORTHWESTERN UNIVERSITY

Address: 1801 Hinman Avenue, Evanston, IL 60208
Phone: (708) 491-7271
Director of Admissions: Carol Lunkenheimer
Multicultural Student Recruiter: Allison Gaines
1991–92 tuition: $14,370
Room and board: $4,873
Application deadline: Early decision: 11/1; regular decision: 1/1
Financial aid application deadline: 2/15
Non-white freshman admissions: Applicants for the class of '94: 2,900
Accepted: 43%
Accepted who enroll: 33%
Applicants accepted who rank in the top 10% of high school class: 81%
In the top 25%: 96%

Median SAT range: 530–640 V, 610–710 M
Median ACT range: 27–31
Full-time undergraduate enrollment: 7,402
Men: 50.3%
Women: 49.7%
Non-white students in
1987–88: 18.7%
1988–89: 19%
1989–90: 21%
1990–91: 22%
Geographic distribution of students: na
Top majors: 1. Engineering 2. Journalism 3. Economics
Retention rate of non-white students: 81%
Scholarships exclusively for non-white students: None
Remediation programs: None

STUDENT ENROLLMENT

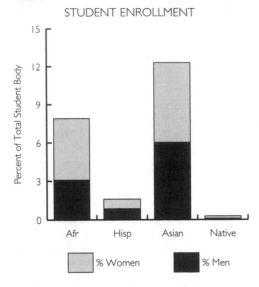

Undergraduate Law and Business Society, One Step Before (for pre-med students)

Notable non-white alumni: Daphne Maxwell Reid (actress); Irv Cross (sports commentator); Chico Freeman (jazz artist); Barbara Sizemore (classical languages professor, University of Pittsburgh)

FACULTY

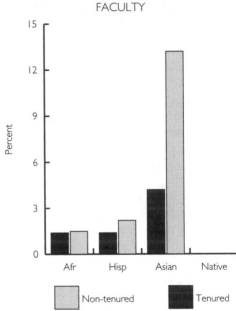

Academic support services: For incoming first-year students, Northwestern offers the Summer Academic Workshop and Minority Engineering Opportunity Program. Tutoring services are provided by the African-American Student Association and the Writing Place.

Ethnic studies programs: The university offers African-American studies (established in 1971), Asian Studies, East Asian Studies, and Latin American Studies.

Organizations for non-white students: National Society of Black Engineers, *Blackboard* (a quarterly publication), Chinese Students Association, Northwestern Community Ensemble, Asian-American Christian Fellowship, Filipino Student Association, Korean-American Student Association, Casa Hispana, For Members Only (African-American umbrella organization), Black Greek Council, Alpha Phi Alpha, Kappa Alpha Psi, Omega Psi Phi, Alpha Kappa Alpha, Delta Sigma Theta, Black Athletes United for Light, Blacks in Communication, Idele (tutorial program for children in the community), African-American Ensemble, Black

Tenured faculty: 1,035
Non-tenured faculty: 325
Student-faculty ratio: 8:1
Administrators: 1,078
  African-American: 1%
  Hispanic: 0.1%
  Asian-American: 1%
  Native American: 0
Recent non-white speakers on campus: Johnnetta Cole (president, Spelman College); Rev. C. T. Vivian (minister and civil rights activist); Haki Madhubuti (writer, educator, and publisher); Barbara Sizemore (professor, University of Pittsburgh); Charles Johnson (author); Vernon Jarrett (newspaper columnist and TV commentator); Vincent Harding (historian)

Sometimes it's hard to believe that Northwestern University, with an undergraduate population of just 7,400, is a member of the Big Ten, one of the toughest athletic conferences in the country, which includes mega-universities Indiana, Iowa, and Michigan. When it comes to major sports, such as football and basketball, Northwestern's teams usually fall at the bottom of the Big Ten heap. But when it comes to academics, the school is a powerhouse.

All of the university's six undergraduate schools are considered outstanding. Among the best known is the Medill School of Journalism, which has graduated 40 Pulitzer Prize winners and has about 600 undergrads. Students also praise NU's School of Music, while others comment that the university's seven-year honors pre-med program is especially intense. Among the arts and sciences, English and economics are strong. The School of Speech has excellent programs in communication sciences, radio/television/film, and theater. Accelerated degree programs are available in journalism, medicine, dentistry, and engineering.

The school's engineering program is also well regarded and has an impressive track record of graduating African-American students. According to the admissions office, in a recent year more than 15 percent of NU's engineering graduates were African-American, which makes NU one of the leading producers of African-American engineers in the Midwest.

Although total student enrollment at NU is small as compared with other Big Ten schools, first-year NU students are often placed in large introductory lecture courses that can be overwhelming. But students say some of these lecture professors have a flair for enlivening their material, and that professors make themselves available after class.

The African-American Studies program earns positive reviews from students. "The majority of the courses [in the program] are good ones and are not heavily biased toward European thought. The main problem I have with the African Studies courses here at Northwestern is that none of the African courses are taught by African professors, not even Swahili." Northwestern's extensive library collections include the impressive Melville J. Herskovits Library of African Studies, which has books in several languages, rare source materials from pre-colonial times to the present, and recordings of oral history.

For academic and personal support, students often turn to the resources of the Department of African-American Student Affairs, located in what is informally referred to as the Black House. "The Black House was established in 1968 to offer a haven for black students where they can congregate to study, meet, relax, or simply watch television," says a student. Comments another student: "All of the faculty and staff of the office are wonderful role models. There's the dean, Karla Spurlock; assistant deans Everne Saxton and Ulysses Jenkins; and our two secretaries, Jeree Michelin and Essie Williams. These adults substitute for our parents at times and we consult with them in times of social and academic need. Dr. Jenkins' office is frequently filled to capacity with students who want to learn more about the history of African people or how to cope in an environment that can be very hostile at times. With his advice comes recommendations of books that will broaden our scope on issues from history to health care." In addition to advising, the office helps sponsor numerous events, including forums, lectures, and the spring blues, jazz, and gospel festival.

When studies get too intense, students often seek off-campus diversions. Northwestern students have easy access to nearby downtown Chicago, with its numerous theaters, restaurants, and sports teams. Chicago, the birthplace of blues music, is also ethnically and racially diverse and provides many social and cultural outlets for students. However, living in an urban area—even in Evanston—has its disadvantages, and a consistent complaint made by students about their school has to do with the university's Department of Public Safety (DPS). Says a student: "Numbers and numbers of African-American men are stopped year-round on campus by DPS and are asked to show their identification. These male students have to go through a tremendous amount of humiliation and aggravation when encountering these situations."

For Members Only (FMO) is the umbrella organization for ten of Northwestern's African-American student groups, and is quite active. "FMO sponsors events featuring speakers that deal with African issues around the world. There are open forums wherein African-American students are kept abreast of issues that concern us within the realm of the university, and events such as Men's Day and Women's Day, when issues concerning the two are discussed and put into perspective to benefit future African-American relations." Says a student about FMO activities: "FMO is the reassurance that black students have a definable place in the NU community. Implicit in this reassurance is that freshmen feel welcomed and involved."

The black Greek organizations are never short of activities or enthusiasm. "The Greek system seems to ensure that students can let loose every weekend," comments a student. On the average, a black Greek party or step show was held once a week at NU during the 1990–91 school year."

Northwestern has often been referred to as the Midwest's answer to the Ivy League, but Northwestern, happily for its undergraduates, is lacking the competitiveness among students often seen in East Coast counterparts. There's a great deal to praise about NU. As one student notes: "In addition to being an excellent academic university, it is situated on a beautiful campus minutes away from Chicago. Although being a minority twice over, as an African-American and a female, has been difficult and challenging at times, I have learned to take advantage of the resources available to me. African-American students, faculty, and staff have also been a source of support for me."

WHEATON COLLEGE

Address: 501 East College Avenue,
Wheaton, IL 60187
Phone: (708) 752-5005 / (800) 222-2419
Director of Admissions: Daniel Crabtree
Multicultural Student Recruiter: Shawn
Leftwich
1992–93 tuition: $10,280
Room and board: $3,970
Application deadline: 2/15
Financial aid application deadline: 3/15
Non-white freshman admissions: Applicants
for the class of '95: 142
Accepted: 55%
Accepted who enroll: 58%
Applicants accepted who rank in top
10% of high school class: 32%
In top 25%: 53%
Median SAT range: 430–590 V, 520–650 M
Median ACT range: 20–25
Full-time undergraduate enrollment: 2,200
Men: 47%
Women: 53%

STUDENT ENROLLMENT

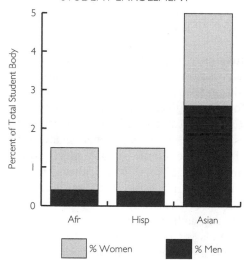

Non-white students in
1987–88: 6.2%
1988–89: 6.2%

GEOGRAPHIC DISTRIBUTION OF STUDENTS

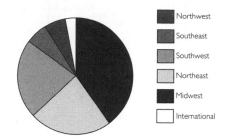

Northwest
Southeast
Southwest
Northeast
Midwest
International

1989–90: 6.2%
1990–91: 7.4%
Students In-state: 20%
Top majors: 1. Business 2. Communications
3. Education
Retention rate of non-white students: 85%
**Scholarships exclusively for non-white
students:** James E. Burr Minority
Scholarship: $800–$1,200; need-based;
ten awarded each year; renewable.
Allied-Signal Minority Scholarship for
Chemistry; merit-based; $2,000 awarded
each year; one each year.
Remediation programs: None
Academic support services: The college
offers study skills workshops as well as
tutoring in most academic subjects.
Ethnic studies programs: The college offers
a Gender/Ethnic studies minor,
established in 1992.
Ethnic studies courses: One course each in
African and Asian history and in African
and Asian religion. "The African-
American Experience" is offered as part
of the Urban Studies program. Three
courses on American race relations.
Anthropology curriculum includes
"Biculturalism."
Organizations for non-white students:
William Osborne Society (black student
organization), Asian Fellowship, Gospel
Choir, James Burr Scholarship
Committee, Literary Visions,

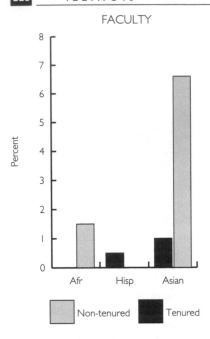

FACULTY

Non-tenured
Tenured

Korean-American Fellowship,
Hispanic-American Student Union

Notable non-white alumni: Dr. Rochunga Pudaite (founder and president, Bibles for the World); Dr. Ruth Bentley (director of academic counseling, University of Illinois at Chicago, and first vice president, National Black Evangelical Association)

Tenured faculty: 100

Non-tenured faculty: 52

Student-faculty ratio: 17:1

Administrators: 206
  African-American: 1%
  Hispanic: 0
  Asian-American: 0
  Native American: 0

Recent non-white speakers on campus: Sam Huddleston (executive director, Prison Ministries in Los Angeles); Tom Skinner (Tom Skinner Associates Ministry); Elward Ellis (Destiny Movement); Brenda Salter-McNeil (InterVarsity); Joyce Suber (director of counseling, Westminster School of Atlanta)

As might be expected on a campus that contains the Billy Graham (class of '43) Center, Christian teachings and ideals are central to campus life at Wheaton College. Bible study and prayer groups are among the most active and popular student organizations on campus, and two semesters of biblical studies are required before graduating.

But don't think that Wheaton College offers only religious studies. The 133-year-old college also makes sure its students receive a firm foundation in the liberal arts. Before graduating, Wheaton students, in addition to meeting course requirements for their major, must take courses in math, a foreign language, speech, and writing.

Wheaton also requires that students satisfy a cultural diversity requirement by enrolling in one of more than 30 courses offered in 18 departments, including anthropology, Bible and theology, biology, business/economics, and English. Course selections, which all have an international focus, range from "Multicultural Education" and "Third World Issues" to "Biculturalism" and "Latin American Peoples." On the whole, students report that the courses for the requirement receive mixed reviews. "Most of the Caucasians feel that they have learned from these classes, but most of my minority friends have found these classes boring because they teach us many of the things that we already know," says an elementary education major.

Communications and business/economics are Wheaton's largest majors, with about 200 students each. Literature and psychology are also popular. Wheaton's biblical studies department has about 85 majors, which makes it the school's tenth-largest major. The college also has a well-regarded conservatory of music, in which students emphasize composition, education, or performance. For music and non-music majors, the school has numerous performance groups, such as the concert and gospel choirs, a jazz ensemble, and the Women's Chorale. The science programs at Wheaton, especially chemistry and biology, are strong; students applying to medical school enjoy an 85 percent acceptance rate.

Students say their studies aren't overly rigorous, but they find the extremely accessible faculty useful nonetheless. Particularly helpful is Narl Hung, a chemistry professor. "She remembers you, even though you may have had her only once," says a student. "She has been very friendly and open to students." Alvaro Nieves, head of the sociology department, also works closely with students. "He is very visible on campus, and very willing to help, know, and associate with the Hispanic students," says a student. Students also think highly of Darlene Hannah, an assistant professor of psychology. "She is very personable, kind, and easy to relate to," says a student. Clarence Edwards, also known as C-Train, is a campus role model and adviser to the hockey club. "I think every student on campus knows who he is and many know him personally. Everyone loves him."

Students also turn to Rodney Sisco, head of the Office of Minority Affairs, for academic and personal assistance. Sisco, who invites students over to his house, keeps up with students' grades and performances and maintains close contact with professors. Sisco is also adviser to many of the school's cultural student groups.

Because of the relatively few students of color on campus, an education major reports, the school's "minority organizations are not influential or active." The William Osborne Society is the school's main African-American student organization. During a recent year, it sponsored two separate African-American Days, the first of which featured a gospel choir, a jazz group, and art displays. The second Day had a civil rights focus with a forum discussion. Literary Visions, a student-initiated reading group, focuses on African-American literature. The group, made up of both white and non-white students, meets once every two weeks to discuss works by such authors as James Baldwin, Frederick Douglass, and Richard Wright.

In conjunction with the Office of Minority Affairs, the organizations sponsor events for February's Cultural Awareness Week. During a recent year, the main attraction was a drama written by an African-American Wheaton alumnus, which addressed urban problems. There was also a panel discussion, headed by minority students and alumni, entitled "Racism in the Christian Community."

Wheaton is a dry campus, so all-out, let's-drink-until-we-get-drunk parties are out, not that students who choose to come here mind. The Office of Student Activities plans movies, concerts (Christian groups), and an annual Springfest, and a place to be seen is at the Stupe, a student-operated snack bar in the middle of campus. Varsity sports aren't slighted. Soccer, tennis, and swimming have had recent successful seasons.

The suburb of Wheaton is predominantly white, but students don't venture into the town much. Wheaton's campus is just twenty-five minutes outside of the Windy City, which is easily accessible by public transportation. Chicago offers all of the accoutrements of a large city: museums, opera, professional ball teams (Cubs, White Sox, Bulls, and Bears), and some of the world's best pizza.

Wheaton does not actively recruit students of color. According to one administrator, the school has a relatively large Asian-American population because of a conference of Asian clergy that took place fairly recently on Wheaton's campus. The clergy then went back to tell their communities and congregations about Wheaton. The school also doesn't recruit from the public high schools in Chicago, says the administrator. "The Chicago public school system is just not that good," she says. About the only diversity of any consequence to be found here is geographic. A little less than 25 percent of the student body is from Illinois; the state second in representation on campus is California, followed by Michigan, Minnesota, and Pennsylvania. Students are from almost every state in the country, as well as from nearly a dozen foreign countries. Most students are from evangelical Christian backgrounds.

For many of Wheaton's students of color, a lack of cultural diversity at the college is seen more as a challenge than as a reason not to attend. "If a student merely wants to hang out with his or her own ethnic group, then Wheaton would not be good, because there are very few Hispanics and African-Americans here," says a student. "There are plenty of Chinese and Koreans to hang out with. However, I would encourage minorities to come because their attendance will add to the campus." She adds: "Wheaton College also addresses issues that transcend race."

INDIANA

DEPAUW UNIVERSITY

Address: 313 South Locust Street,
Greencastle, IN 46135
Phone: (317) 658-4100 / (800) 447-2495
Director of Admissions: David C. Murray
Multicultural Student Recruiters: Morris
Price, Juan Mosquera
1993–94 tuition: $13,500
Room and board: $4,830
Application deadline: Early decision: 12/1;
regular decision: 2/15
Financial aid application deadline: 3/1
Non-white freshman admissions: Applicants
for the class of '95: 297
Accepted: 77%
Accepted who enroll: 30%
Applicants accepted who rank in top
10% of high school class: 42%
In top 25%: 75%
Median SAT range: 420–580 V, 430–580 M
Median ACT range: 21–26
Full-time undergraduate enrollment: 2,171
Men: 45%
Women: 55%
Non-white students in
1987–88: 4.5%
1988–89: 5.4%
1989–90: 7.7%
1990–91: 10%
Students In-state: 23.1%
Top majors: 1. Economics 2. English
Composition and Literature 3. Political
Science
Retention rate of non-white students: 90%
Scholarships exclusively for non-white

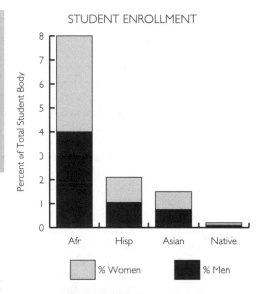

STUDENT ENROLLMENT

Percent of Total Student Body

□ % Women   ■ % Men

GEOGRAPHIC DISTRIBUTION OF STUDENTS

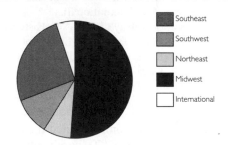

Southeast
Southwest
Northeast
Midwest
International

students: Alumni Achievement Awards:
available to all student applicants;
typically up to 25 are awarded each year
to African-American students and 12 to

Hispanic students; merit- and need-based; amount of each award varies from $5,000 to $17,000. Grady Scholarship: merit-based; full tuition, plus room and board; one awarded every four years; available to students of color.

Remediation programs: None

Academic support services: Centers for oral communication, quantitative reasoning, and writing. Tutoring available in most academic subjects.

Ethnic studies programs: DePauw offers interdisciplinary minors in African-American Studies and Asian Studies. Japanese- and Chinese-language study is offered at all levels.

Ethnic studies courses: The history department offers two courses about Latin America, while the Spanish department includes "Latin American Civilization" as well as courses about various Spanish and Hispanic authors.

Organizations for non-white students: Association of African-American Students, Kappa Alpha Psi, Alpha Kappa Alpha, Gospel Choir, Alpha Phi Alpha, Delta Sigma Theta, Ekabo (a multicultural theme house), Hispanic Student Association

Notable non-white alumni: Vernon Jordan ('57, Political Science; former president, Urban League, and current partner in DC law firm); Percy Julian ('20, Chemistry; founder of Julian Labs); Jerry Williams ('60, Pre-engineering; first African-American to head a Fortune 500 Company, AM International); Ambassador Tetsuya Endo ('60, History; director general, Japanese Ministry of Foreign Affairs); William Allison (vice president, Coca-Cola Company)

Tenured faculty: 112

Non-tenured faculty: 61

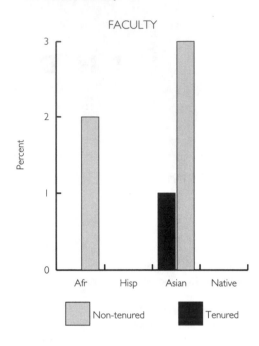

FACULTY

Student-faculty ratio: 12:1

Administrators: na

African-American: 5%

Hispanic: 1%

Asian-American: 0

Native American: 0

Recent non-white speakers on campus: Rev. James Forbes (Riverside Church, New York City); Toni Morrison (Pulitzer Prize-winning author); Franklyn Green Jenifer (president, Howard University); Rev. Richard Hicks (associate director, United Methodist Church Board of Higher Education); Gwendolyn Brooks (Pulitzer Prize-winning poet); Jesse Jackson (former U.S. presidential candidate and civil rights activist)

When Robert Bottoms assumed the presidency of DePauw University in 1986, he was a man with a mission. "To be educationally relevant and viable in the world community we have to courageously and seriously explore the issue of diversity in the student body, in the faculty, and in the curriculum," he said in his inaugural speech.

On most counts, the university that has graduated former Urban League head

Vernon Jordan and Percy Julian, a noted African-American chemist, is beginning to see the benefits of Bottoms's vision. DePauw has nearly tripled its enrollment of students of color—in 1986, the school enrolled just 80 such students, while today that figure is more than 200—the curriculum now allows students to minor in Black Studies and Asian Studies (which includes Chinese- and Japanese-language study), and the school's large Greek system has four historically black fraternities and sororities. In addition to an officer in charge of multicultural admissions, the university has a recruiter in charge of Hispanic admissions. A recent entering class of first-year students, for example, contained more than 30 Hispanic students, from such diverse cities as Bogota (Colombia), New York, and Chicago, more than double the amount at comparable institutions. In fact, the National Hispanic Chamber of Commerce recently chose DePauw as the one college to receive its prestigious Chairman's Award for its work with Hispanic youth.

DePauw has the academics and the facilities to rival many of the country's top liberal arts colleges. The school's best academic departments are also among its most popular: English, economics, and political science. DePauw also has a highly regarded school of music, which boasts a 5:1 student-to-faculty ratio and amazing performance facilities. Students say the Black Studies program is solid, and others comment that the Asian Studies program is "excellent with many diverse course offerings." Associate professor of Asian Studies Paul Watt and associate professor of history Yung-Chen Chiang are two of the program's noted faculty members. Women's studies was also recently added to the college curriculum. A popular course offered by the school's University Studies program is "Multiculturalism and Its Implications on Religion," which offers speakers and field trips.

While most schools are cutting back on new construction during these recessionary times, DePauw recently opened its doors to the new $6.6 million Center for Contemporary Media with state-of-the-art facilities for its budding print and broadcast journalists. The director of the center is Ken Bode, a well-known journalist who can be seen on CNN and who also regularly contributes news features to CNN via a computer at the center, often with student assistance. In the fall of 1993 DePauw is also set to open a new multimillion-dollar Olin biology center, and the school's library recently underwent major renovation.

Fortune magazine recently ranked the 156-year-old university eleventh in the nation, and first in the Midwest, in producing chief executive officers of Fortune 500 companies; one of those graduates is Jerry Williams, former head of AM International, the first African-American to head such a company. And, according to a study conducted by Franklin and Marshall, DePauw was among the top ten private liberal arts institutions in the country to produce Ph.D.s between the years 1920 and 1984.

As a break from the usual semester course schedule that most schools have, DePauw students are able to take advantage of their school's Winter Term. During the monthlong program in January, students take courses on campus—which range from "Gandhi" to "Advanced Calculus"—or study off campus or work as interns. First-year students are required to remain on campus for the month and study a single topic together; recent topics have focused on the environment and on China and Japan.

Studies at DePauw can be demanding, but professors are easily accessible. "Everything you've ever heard about a small-college atmosphere is true here. The professors expect you to do well, and if they see you on campus they always stop to speak to you or just say hi. If they find you're having difficulty, they will seek you out."

One of the professors students find especially helpful is John Dittmer, an associate professor of history. "He's good to talk to, and a lot of students will seek his advice about academics. He taught at Tougaloo College in Mississippi [a historically black college], and he really respects our views," comments a junior. Students also say that Dee Gardner, assistant dean of academic affairs, and Morris Price, an associate dean of admissions, are active in multicultural student life. "They come to many of the AAAS [Association of African-American Students] meetings and events. They're also helpful in getting things done and are always willing to listen." Alan Hill, DePauw's director of financial aid, hosts a picnic at his home each year to welcome new minority students. Several administrators and faculty members are also in attendance.

With about 50 active members, the Association of African-American Students plans various on- and off-campus programs. AAAS "does a lot of things, although we're looking to do even more in the near future," says an AAAS leader. The group's activities include an annual picnic for incoming first-year students, dinners and parties, tutoring, and a big sister/big brother program for members. AAAS also sponsors regular Black Issues Tables, in which students gather for informal discussions "about issues that face the community." Topics have been "Black Female/Male Relationships," "Black Men as an Endangered Species," and "Black Politics." At one recent gathering students read some of their favorite poetry written by prominent African-American authors. "We ordered ribs from a local barbecue restaurant, and we enjoyed each other's readings," comments a student. AAAS also sponsors a senior banquet for students about to graduate. At one such function, the president of the university and various administrators were in attendance. The school's Gospel Choir has received rave reviews.

The African-American community at DePauw is diverse, but no more so than geographically. Students hail from Atlanta, Florida, New York City, Colorado, the Caribbean, and elsewhere, making for an environment "where I can become familiar with people from all sorts of backgrounds and points of view, which means a lot to me," observes a student. African-Americans have no problem getting active in campus politics; during recent years, African-American students have served as president and vice president of the student body. DePauw's Hispanic students have traditionally identified with either AAAS or the International Student Organization, but students are in the process of forming a Hispanic student association.

DePauw is also diversifying its housing options for students. Anderson House, a new multicultural residence facility located next to the administration building, is home to "students from most backgrounds, black, white, and Hispanic," says a student. "There was a selection process, and more than thirty students live there." The house is known among students as Ekabo.

A popular hangout for students is the AAAS House, a non-residence facility centrally located on the school's north campus. The house, described as "cozy" by one student, provides a meeting space, a small library, a full kitchen, and test files.

DePauw's student body is predominantly Greek; more than 70 percent of the campus population are members of one or another of the school's 15 national fraternities and 11 national sororities. Students report, however, that the predominantly white Greek system is reasonably well integrated, with almost all organizations having multicultural students among their membership.

The school's black Greek organizations have grown more active of late. Community service is a focus of each of them. Members of Kappa Alpha Psi fraternity, for example, work with students at Indianapolis elementary schools, and Alpha Kappa Alpha sorority members recently sponsored a formal dance on campus.

No matter whether they're Greek or independent, DePauw students are into community service. In a recent year, students accumulated more than 150,000 hours of volunteer service, which equals about 65 hours of community service for each student. Students visited nursing homes and prisons, and built missions and school houses in such locales as Mississippi, Brazil, Honduras, and Guatemala.

Greencastle, DePauw's hometown, is not exactly a hub of activity, although most students don't mind, as studying is of prime importance. The town (pop. 9,000) has a small shopping area and some restaurants. Indianapolis, just an hour away, and Chicago, about three hours north, are popular destinations for the adventurous, but most students are content to remain on campus most weekends, as there is much activity—from lectures and concerts to fraternity parties—scheduled.

Especially for students who hail from outside the region, attending college in a rural section of Indiana may not be a dream come true. But for those students who do choose to attend school here, there are few regrets. "I'm definitely glad I came here. I look at my friends back home, and I see how far I've progressed. I now know how to present myself professionally, and I've gotten to assume a lot of leadership roles here that I wouldn't have been able to attain at a larger university. I've also gotten more into diversity here as I've reached out to students from different cultures and races."

EARLHAM COLLEGE

Address: Richmond, IN 47374
Phone: (800) EARLHAM
Director of Admissions: Bob de Veer
Multicultural Student Recruiter: Kyle
  Malone
1991–92 tuition: $14,130
Room and board: $3,894
Application deadline: 2/15
Financial aid application deadline: 2/15
Non-white freshman admissions: Applicants
  for the class of '95: 110
  Accepted: 80%
  Accepted who enroll: 30%
  Applicants accepted who rank in top
  10% of high school class: 5%
  In top 25%: 15%
  Median SAT: 450 V, 470 M
  Median ACT: 22

Full-time undergraduate enrollment: 1,150
  Men: 44%
  Women: 56%
Non-white students in
  1987–88: 10%
  1988–89: 11%
  1989–90: 11%
  1990–91: 10%
Students In-state: 22%
Top majors: 1. Biology 2. English
  3. Psychology
Retention rate of non-white students: 69%
Scholarships exclusively for non-white
  students: Cunningham Cultural
  Scholarship: merit-based; $5,000 for each
  award; ten scholarships awarded each
  year. Educational Enhancement Awards:
  need-based; replaces loans with grant

STUDENT ENROLLMENT

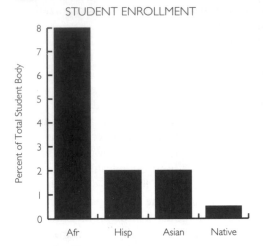

GEOGRAPHIC DISTRIBUTION OF STUDENTS

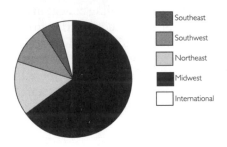

- Southeast
- Southwest
- Northeast
- Midwest
- International

dollars; available to African-American and Hispanic students who are Indiana residents.

Remediation programs: None

Academic support services: The Learning Center and the Office of Supportive Services provide academic assistance. The August Academic Term introduces first-year students to Earlham's academic and non-academic programs.

Ethnic studies programs: Interdisciplinary programs in Japanese Studies and African/African-American Studies are offered. Students are able to design their own Latin American Studies major.

Organizations for non-white students: Apartheid Action Coalition, Black Leadership Action Coalition, Committee Against Racism at Earlham, Committee in Solidarity with Latin America, Women of Color, Cunningham Cultural Center, Japanese House

Notable non-white alumni: Manning Marable ('71; director, Africana and Hispanic Studies, University of Colorado/Boulder); Linda Randall ('72; veterinarian and president, Ohio State Veterinary Medical Board)

FACULTY

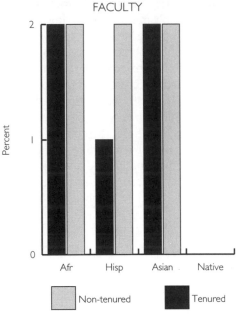

Tenured faculty: 55

Non-tenured faculty: 27

Student-faculty ratio: 12:1

Administrators: 90

African-American: 5%

Hispanic: 0

Asian-American: 0

Native American: 0

Recent non-white speakers on campus: James Cohn (professor, Union Theological Seminary); Margaret Avery (actress); Juan Williams (journalist)

Earlham may be in Indiana but it is far from being a Midwestern school. The college draws students from all parts of the country—only 13 percent are from the state;

international studies are an integral part of many of the school's academic programs; more than 80 percent of the students study abroad for at least a semester; and the school's progressive-minded students contrast with their more conservative Indiana neighbors.

Earlham was founded by Quakers in 1846, and the college "has preserved and reinterpreted the best of Quaker traditions to serve contemporary students." In the spirit of the school's founders, students are on a first-name basis with professors and school administrators; they are actively involved in formulating school policy; and all decisions—whether on the dorm floor or in campus-wide meetings—are arrived at by consensus.

Earlham's commitment to the liberal arts is reflected in the four-course humanities sequence required of students for graduation. The sequence, in which students read significant literary and historical texts that reflect different cultures, times, and traditions, has been praised by the National Endowment for the Humanities. Students must also satisfy distributional requirements in the study of a foreign language, fine arts, religion and philosophy, the social and the natural sciences, and physical education.

Earlham is well known for its interdisciplinary Japanese Studies program, which is complemented by the school's off-campus program at Waseda University in Tokyo. Biology, geology, philosophy, and English are also top-notch. Earlham's unique programs in Peace and Global Studies and Museum Studies are also well received by students. Management is becoming increasingly popular.

The school's African/African-American Studies (AAAS) program wins praise from students, but they say its offerings are "limited." The program's "African-American History" course, taught by Phyllis Boanes, director of the program, is well regarded. "Professor Boanes is one of the most focused African-American professors at Earlham. She's a good person," says a student.

As class sizes are small at Earlham, students say opportunities for interaction with faculty are many and the majority of the professors are good instructors. The school's Minority Affairs Office, which provides academic support, is effective, according to students, especially its director, Bonita Washington-Lacey. Kyle Malone, an assistant dean of admissions and adviser to the school's Black Leadership Action Coalition, is also said to be supportive.

The students at Earlham are politically and socially active in a way that is rare at most colleges these days. "Our campus responds well to major crisis; during the Gulf War there was a midnight vigil on the night it started," says a student. "The next day there was an all-student meeting and buses went to demonstrations in DC. The student activist groups are very involved." A cause of concern for students is the school's recent decision not to be need-blind in admissions, a decision that will no doubt make it more difficult to recruit economically disadvantaged students.

But the school's small size, says one student, can limit the life expectancy of some groups, and can burden some of the school's students of color. "It's not that Earlham students are apathetic," reports a student. "In fact, most Earlham students are supportive of the campus's cultural and social organizations. It's just that so few students are willing to give up their study time to keep things going. It always seems like it's the same students leading the groups." Adds another student: "At the beginning of the [1991–92] year, the Office of Student Development sponsored workshops that dealt with race issues. I was one of the few people of color to attend. I had the feeling that non-white students here are getting tired of explaining racism to white students. I can understand that, but I don't feel I can say it is an excuse for not trying to educate myself and others."

Earlham sponsors a variety of residence facilities, including dormitories and special theme houses; there is a Peace House, as well as the Cunningham Cultural Center (CCC), which focuses on African-American student concerns. The CCC, which has a library, provides living facilities for up to six students and is the site for various student organizational meetings.

The Multicultural Theme House, the school's newest housing option, had African-American, Asian-American, and white students as its first residents. "We did not all know each other before we moved in and many of us would never have become friends if we hadn't petitioned for this house," says a student. "It has been interesting getting to know the other sixteen residents."

The Black Leadership Action Coalition (BLAC), the school's African-American student group, provides academic and emotional support for members. "Two days a week we have study tables for our members. This is great because it allows us to help each other prosper in class. This type of help builds unity. The group also meets every Wednesday and we talk about a number of different things, mostly stressing the fact that we must lean on each other. The BLAC's support for students is directly related to the success of the school's African-American students."

Women of Color, a support group, gives members the opportunity to "talk about our concerns on campus, read each other's writing, and just try to help each other out," says a member.

Most of a student's social life takes place on campus, but students looking for off-campus cultural activity can find it at a performance of Richmond's symphony orchestra or civic theater troupe. The city of approximately 40,000 also is home to numerous fast-food restaurants and bars. Although Richmond has a small African-American community, students of color don't report the best relations with the area's largely blue-collar residents. "We get stares when we venture from campus," says a student.

There is rarely a shortage of things to do on campus, say students. Nearly all of the students participate in at least one of the school's intramural or varsity sports, and lectures and concerts are regularly featured. Students report that the Student Advisory Board has sponsored more diverse performers; recently the SAB hosted the school's first rap concert.

Earlham is a "friendly" campus, and students are pleased with the quality of their education and the small-school atmosphere. "The curriculum is tough, but it will make you give more of yourself than you've ever given in your life," says a psychology major. "I feel really prepared for graduate school. I was not afraid to come here, being black and being female. I felt that if I didn't try it, I would be cheating myself and not really giving myself a chance."

INDIANA UNIVERSITY

Address: Bloomington, IN 47405
Phone: (812) 855-0661
Director of Admissions: Bob Magee
Multicultural Student Recruiter: Lawrence
  Gonzalez

1992–93 tuition: $2,582 (in-state); $8,294
  (out-of-state)
Room and board: $3,565
Application deadline: 2/15
Financial aid application deadline: 3/1

Indiana University is about world-class basketball and world-class music programs, and almost everything in between. For generations, IU has been supplying Hoosiers and out-of-staters with the kind of academics that has earned the school a reputation as one of the country's more respectable public institutions of higher learning and one that also includes some of the country's top sports programs.

IU's music program ranks with New York's Juilliard School as one of the finest such schools in the country, and musical groups at the university represent everything from opera to jazz. Other top programs are journalism, physics, Russian, chemistry, East Asian Studies, political science, and theater and drama. IU's School of Business, also well regarded, offers specializations in nine different areas, such as accounting, finance, computer information systems, and marketing. Psychology, another top program, is popular with students, as are the school's interdisciplinary programs in Afro-American Studies and Chicano-Riqueño Studies. Within the Afro-American Studies program, students concentrate in either literature, art, or history. Well-regarded courses in the program are "Early Black Narrative" and "Contemporary African-American Literature." Fred McElroy and William Wiggins are among the program's top professors.

As IU is a large university, interaction with faculty can be limited, but students say that with perseverance it is possible, particularly in the upper-level courses, where class sizes tend to be smaller.

The Black Cultural Center, located on the south side of campus near the main library, houses the Afro-American Arts Institute, which features a choral ensemble, a dance troupe, and the IU Soul Review. The center offers a library, performance space for the groups, and tutorial services. "The center also contains a TV room, pianos, and pool tables, and original artwork by students," says a senior. "It's a place where students can hang out between classes or study. Just about anytime you walk in here you can hear people singing or playing the piano." The center was the site of a recent reception for graduating seniors and their families. "The center was packed for the event," says a student.

The director of the center, Frank Jones, "is always quick to talk to us. He asks us our opinions about issues and events, rather than telling us what to do. We all appreciate that."

But come 1995, the university will have completed construction of a new Black Cultural Center on the site of the present center. The $5 million center, to be named the Neal-Marshall Black Cultural Center in honor of IU's first African-American graduates, will house offices for the school's Afro-American Studies program and student organizations, including the historically black fraternities and sororities and the Black Film Archives.

The most politically active African-American student group is the Black Student Union, which meets every two weeks at the center. "The BSU presents the concerns of black students to the administration. We're more of a political group. We don't sponsor any parties, but we do organize a soul picnic each year around Little 500 [IU's annual bicycle race, made famous in the movie *Breaking Away*]. We have the picnic in Dunn Meadow, and we get a good turnout."

The responsibility for organized social activity within the African-American community falls primarily on the black Greek fraternities and sororities. "This year was a new high for these groups," according to a student. "They were all very involved on campus. For example, the men of Alpha Phi Alpha hosted a panel discussion about the Hill/Thomas hearing, and professors and students from IU's law school participated. Members of Alpha Kappa Alpha sorority had an evening where black students talked about what they're thankful for." Other than these groups, there is little organized social activity specifically for African-American students, although non-members do attend many of the Greek organizations' parties and other events.

Bloomington is a true college town, catering to almost all student needs. There are numerous bars, cafes, theaters, and clothing stores. Students who want to leave town occasionally head into Indianapolis, about forty-five miles northeast of Bloomington, or into Chicago, a few hours north. Students are most often content to stay put, however, even on weekends, as the university offers a plethora of social and cultural activities. And then, if you can get tickets, there's always the Hoosiers varsity basketball team, led by famous coach Bobby Knight.

IU is large—more than 35,000 undergraduates are enrolled—and students, if they are not careful, can get swallowed up by the school's sheer size. (Of those 35,000 in 1990, 0.2 percent of the campus was Native American, 2.3 percent Asian-American, 3.7 percent African-American, and 1.6 percent Hispanic, according to a U.S. Department of Education report. IU's admissions office declined to respond to our questionnaire.) But for students who can get used to the size of the school and the relatively small number of non-white students on campus, there's a great deal to like about the university. "I loved it here," says a recent graduate from a large Eastern city. "The campus is quiet and clean. You can walk almost anywhere, day or night, and feel safe. The professors are good, and there are so many resources. The key to doing well here is to get involved. IU definitely gives you a good education for your money."

UNIVERSITY OF NOTRE DAME

Address: Notre Dame, IN 46556
Phone: (219) 631-7505
Director of Admissions: Kevin M. Rooney
Multicultural Student Recruiter: Stephen D. Grissom
1993–94 tuition: $15,810
Room and board: $4,020
Application deadline: 1/6
Financial aid application deadline: 2/28
Non-white freshman admissions: Applicants for the class of '96: 1,091
Accepted: 58%
Accepted who enroll: 41%
Applicants accepted who rank in top 10% of high school class: 66%
In top 25%: 85%
Median SAT range: 450–550 V, 520–640 M
Median ACT: na
Full-time undergraduate enrollment: 7,600
Men: 59%
Women: 41%

STUDENT ENROLLMENT

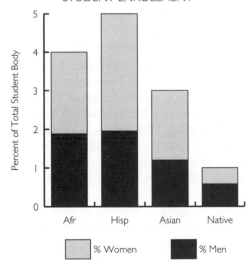

Y-axis: Percent of Total Student Body

Legend: % Women, % Men

Non-white students in
1988–89: 10%
1989–90: 11%

GEOGRAPHIC DISTRIBUTION OF STUDENTS

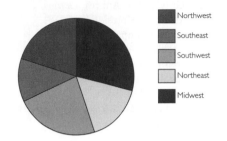

Legend: Northwest, Southeast, Southwest, Northeast, Midwest

1990–91: 13.1%
1991–92: 13.7%
Students In-state: 6%
Top majors: 1. Accountancy 2. Government 3. Science
Retention rate of non-white students: 85%
Scholarships exclusively for non-white students: Holy Cross Grants: need-based; more than 200 awarded each year; average award is $7,000.
Remediation programs: None
Academic support services: Freshman Year of Studies provides academic advising and tutoring. The Learning Resources Center also offers academic support.
Ethnic studies programs: The university offers an interdisciplinary African-American Studies program, established in 1970, involving anthropology, economics, English, government, history, and sociology. Students are also able to earn certificates in African, Asian, and Latin American Studies.
Organizations for non-white students: Multicultural Council, African-American Student Alliance, Black Cultural Arts Council, Asian American Association, Hispanic-American Organization, Native American Student Organization, LULAC, NAACP, Minority Science Club, League of Business Students, National Society of Black Engineers

Notable non-white alumni: Ignacio Lozano (Business; editor-in-chief, *La Opinión*); Ron Homer (Business; CEO, First Boston Bank); Dr. Percy Pierre (Engineering; vice president, Michigan State University); Aubrey Lewis (Education; vice president, F. W. Woolworth Company)

Tenured faculty: 446

Non-tenured faculty: 164

Student-faculty ratio: 12:1

Administrators: 336

    African-American: 3.2%

    Hispanic: 1.5%

    Asian-American: 1.2%

    Native American: 0

Recent non-white speakers on campus: Julian Bond (former Georgia state senator and civil rights activist); Spike Lee (filmmaker); Rosa Parks (civil rights activist); Maya Angelou (author and poet); Ignacio Lozano (editor-in-chief, *La Opinión*); Jesse Jackson (civil rights activist and former presidential candidate)

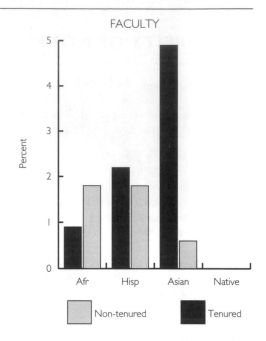

FACULTY — Non-tenured / Tenured

Almost everyone knows the Fighting Irish of the University of Notre Dame, that perennial contender for national football championships. But the 151-year-old university is also one of the country's top schools academically.

Students start off their first year at Notre Dame by participating in the Freshman Year of Studies, a program that ensures that they have been exposed to a wide spectrum of learning before declaring a major. Courses include composition, math, a foreign language, natural and social sciences, history, physical education, and a humanities seminar. The Freshman Learning Resources Center, which provides tutoring services, and the advising system are obviously effective; in a recent year, nearly the entire first-year class returned to Notre Dame for the sophomore year.

Following successful completion of the Freshman Year of Studies program, students move to one of the school's four undergraduate colleges: Arts and Letters, Business Administration, Engineering, or Science. Notre Dame's Colleges of Science and Engineering have the reputation of being the most academically demanding. Among the liberal arts, which enroll the majority of the school's students, English, government, history, and theology are said to be outstanding.

For additional academic assistance, the Office of Minority Student Affairs has proven to be a resource for students. Iris Outlaw, the director of the program, works closely with students. One of the office's more successful efforts is its Faculty-Mentor Program, established in 1989, which pairs students of color with various professors and staff members. Initially, the program was reserved for first-year African-American students, but since then it has been expanded to include Hispanic, Asian-American, and Native American students.

For additional peer support, students are able to join any number of on-campus cultural organizations, among them the Hispanic-American Council, the Native American Student Organization, and the Multicultural Council. According to students, these groups serve primarily as social organizations that also coordinate parties, lectures, and films.

Notre Dame is a distinctly Catholic institution of higher learning. More than 90 percent of its students are Catholic, and dorms clear out on Sundays for Mass. All campus dorms are single-sex, and visitation hours are strictly enforced. There is a Right-to-Life student group, but you won't find a Pro-Choice organization.

While such an atmosphere can be alienating for one not of that persuasion, it does foster a sense of community that is unusual at a school of this size. Although political activism is rare on this mostly conservative campus, students are socially aware and committed. There are dozens of do-good clubs and organizations, ranging from an Anti-Apartheid Network and Habitat for Humanity to FoodShare and Women United for Justice and Peace. One administrator estimates that nearly a third of Notre Dame's students are involved in at least one of these organizations.

A different type of student group has earned quite a few headlines in recent years. Called Students United for Respect (SUFR), it is demanding that the administration strengthen the school's African-American Studies and Latin American Studies programs, hire more faculty and administrators of color, recruit more students of color, and create a multicultural center. "Every year we (the students of color on campus) have become more of a cohesive group," says a SUFR member. As of now, students can declare African-American Studies as a second, and not as a first, major, and the Latin American Studies program is offered only as a concentration.

Notre Dame, Indiana, is a predominantly white community, but South Bend, which has a black population, is nearby. The university is about ninety miles east of Chicago, and Indianapolis is just a few hours south. Students rarely leave campus, however, as the university provides a great deal of cultural and social opportunities, from lectures and concerts to parties and intramural activity. Sports are truly a big deal here. It's estimated that nearly the entire campus participates in one intramural activity or another (intramural football is tackle here), and attending—or trying to get seats to attend—any home basketball or football game is on almost every student's weekend agenda.

Much of the on-campus social life occurs in the dorms, which more or less take the place of the banned fraternities and sororities. Intramural competition between the residence halls is keen, and each of the halls sponsors its own dances, parties, and other social gatherings. Students report, however, that there is little racial integration socially on campus. "The campus is not integrated very well, with parties and dining tables generally either black or white," says a student "but there is little overt tension." An on-campus dance club, Theodore's, is popular with students of color, according to a student, "because we don't like the keg parties that the other students attend."

Although the university has made significant strides in recruiting students of color, there is still the perception, says an admissions counselor in *Scholastic,* a student magazine, "that Notre Dame is a white male Catholic school and that it is not a place for minorities. That is tough in a lot of areas when it comes to recruiting minority students to attend Notre Dame." Adds a student: "As with women's issues, Notre Dame has a long way to go in addressing the needs of minorities. I think Notre Dame has started looking at some of the problems here, but it will be a while before this school truly is a place where minorities fit in."

The homogeneity of Notre Dame's student body will take some adjusting to, but the university has the academics—and the sports—to make four years here more than worth it. "If a minority student wants his or her concerns as a minority to be addressed, he or she would be better off at a historically black university," says a student. "However, if the student wants to go to a challenging school with a defined mission and which is working toward becoming a culturally diverse university, then I would recommend Notre Dame."

PURDUE UNIVERSITY

Address: West Lafayette, IN 47907
Phone: (317) 494-4600
Director of Admissions: William J. Murray
Multicultural Student Recruiter: Roger Blalock
1991–92 tuition: $7,440 (in-state)
Room and board: $3,610
Application deadline: Rolling admissions
Financial aid application deadline: 3/1
Non-white freshman admissions: Applicants for the class of '94: 3,295
Accepted: 50%
Accepted who enroll: 50%
Applicants accepted who rank in top 10% of high school class: 38%
Median SAT: na
Median ACT: na
Full-time undergraduate enrollment: 26,875
Men: 56.9%
Women: 43.1%
Non-white students in
1987–88: 6%
1988–89: 7%
1989–90: 8%
1990–91: 8%
Geographic distribution of students: na
Top majors: 1. Engineering 2. Liberal Arts 3. Science
Retention rate of non-white students:
African-American: 43%; Hispanic: 54%;

Asian-American: 73%; Native American: 44%
Scholarships exclusively for non-white students: CFS Minority Scholarship: merit-based; $1,000 per scholarship; renewable. Merit Award for Minorities in Engineering: merit-based; $500 to $3,000; renewable.
Remediation programs: None
Academic support services: The School of Liberal Arts Learning Center, the

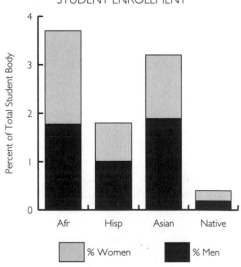

STUDENT ENROLLMENT

Percent of Total Student Body

Afr   Hisp   Asian   Native

% Women   % Men

Writing Lab, and the Chemistry Help Lab offer academic support.

Ethnic studies programs: Afro-American Studies, established in 1974, is interdisciplinary, involving sociology, history, psychology, anthropology, philosophy, and other departments.

Ethnic studies courses: na

Organizations for non-white students: Hermanos Hispanos, Purdue Asian-American Student Association, Alpha Kappa Alpha, Delta Sigma Theta, Association of Black Students, Black Greek Council, College Chapter of NAACP, Society of Hispanic Professional Engineers, Kappa Alpha Psi, Omega Psi Phi, Zeta Phi Beta

Notable non-white alumni: na

Tenured faculty: 1,254
Non-white: 7%

Non-tenured faculty: na
Non-white: 10%

Student-faculty ratio: 18:1

Administrators: na
Non-white: 11%

Recent non-white speakers on campus: Dick Gregory (author and political activist); Ossie Davis and Ruby Dee (actors)

In between Caltech and MIT, geographically speaking, there is Purdue University, one of the best-known and best-respected "techie" schools in the country. Famed aviator Amelia Earhart was a career consultant for women at Purdue in the 1930s; 19 Purdue graduates have flown in space (hence the university's nickname: the Mother of Astronauts); the first computer sciences department was established at this 124-year-old school; and one out of every 17 engineers in the country is a graduate of, you guessed it, Purdue.

Purdue's schools of agriculture and management are nationally recognized, and education and pharmacy are considered top-flight. For those overwhelmed by their engineering studies, students say the Minority Engineering Program, which provides tutoring and other academic support, is an effective resource. The program's Academic Challenge Grant, in which groups of 10 students each compete for academic prize money of up to $600 per student, is a favorite with students. "It's a team-oriented goal," says a student. "It means that we study together and we want to see each other succeed." Each of Purdue's undergraduate schools has counseling divisions for minority students.

Liberal arts programs are somewhat lacking, say students, particularly in comparison to the more technical research areas that generate tremendous amounts of revenue from federal grants and other sources. However, the school's Afro-American Studies program offers courses, according to one student, "that are very challenging and definitely not easy A's." Such courses as "The African-American Male," "The Minority Family," and literature are popular, as is Wallace McGlaughlin, a professor in the program.

As might be expected at such a "techie" school, some of Purdue's most active student groups—besides the university's incredibly large and active Greek organizations—are its professional associations. The National Society of Black Engineers, founded at Purdue, is one such organization. With about 200 active members, NSBE has 14 committees that cover the gamut from tutoring to professional development. *Echo,* published annually by NSBE members, contains information about professional conferences and other African-American student groups, and has a spotlight profile of an NSBE senior. Sidney Bryson, NSBE's adviser, is appreciated by students for his accessibility; Bryson is a graduate student at Purdue studying electrical engineering.

Cultural awareness at Purdue doesn't exactly generate the amount of support and enthusiasm that the professional societies have been able to. An exception to this, however, is the Black Cultural Center, located on the west side of campus near the armory. "It's a well-used social gathering place for students, especially between classes," says a senior. The center, which recently celebrated its twentieth anniversary on campus, has a library and sponsors the works of an African-American dance troupe and poetry workshops. The director of the center, Tony Zamora, "is someone we definitely feel comfortable with," comments a student; Zamora is a member of a jazz quartet on campus.

While the BCC sponsors its share of activities, the school's Association of Black Students has seen better days. According to students, ABS has been inactive due to ineffective student leadership. ABS's staff adviser, Jolyn DePriest, agrees. "I've been less than pleased with the way the ABS has gone," she says. But DePriest is more than busy with Purdue Cares, a multicultural student group with 10 white, African-American, Hispanic, Native American, and Asian members. The group meets weekly to discuss campus race issues.

Some of Purdue's historically black Greek organizations, especially Kappa Alpha Psi fraternity and Delta Sigma Theta and Alpha Kappa Alpha sororities, are more active on campus, sponsoring parties and community service projects.

Hermanos Hispanos, Purdue's largest Hispanic student group, is seeking to become more of a cultural than a social organization, according to members. "We sponsor regular activities every year," says a Hermanos Hispanos student leader. "The biggest is La Gran Fiesta in the spring, a festival with typical foods from Latin America," held in the Stewart Center. "And then that night we have a party to raise money for a scholarship fund. But next year we're going to start a peer tutoring program and go into area high schools to get more involved with the community. We definitely want to put more emphasis on academics in the group." Melba Martinez, Hermanos Hispanos' staff adviser, "is our main contact with the administration," says a student. "She's also a role model since she went to school here."

The newest Hispanic student group—this one for women only—is Delta Phi Mu, a sorority that during a recent year had 12 members. Members of the two-year-old organization have sponsored parties and a banquet, and have worked on a clothes drive for an area social service agency.

Purdue is one of the most conservative schools in the Big Ten athletic conference, and many students describe campus life as reminiscent of the 1950s. Purdue's Greek system is the second-largest in the nation; coed dorms aren't really coed, but the university likes to think they are; dorm rules—particularly those governing visiting hours—are strictly enforced; sports are the focus of much of the school's social life outside of fraternity and sorority rituals and parties; and political discourse of any sort is about as rare as finding Purdue's Stewart Center empty of students on any given Friday night.

"There are a lot of restrictions that other schools don't have," says a student. "For example, sexual awareness is just now being discussed openly, and the university is just now putting condom machines in some of the dorms. Purdue definitely has that country feel. You'd think that, being a part of the Big Ten, we might be more progressive, but we're not."

Students add that there is little interaction between students of different races, except among engineering students. "Most minority students stick with members of their own group. A lot of African-Americans like to hang out on the second floor of the student center, and Puerto Ricans usually can be seen in the Sweet Shop at the center," says a student. "But at the same time, with the intensity of the engineering program, I see integration among engineers. The main thing is to understand theories and technical problems. That's what gets students' respect in the program, not what race you are. Once you understand something, everyone respects you. I don't think it's like that in other academic areas, though."

Most of a student's social life takes place on campus, as West Lafayette offers little to the undergraduate no matter what his or her race or background, save a mall and the nearby strip of fast-food joints. Students with cars can head to Chicago, about three hours north, or Indianapolis, about two hours away by car. Macaw's, a club/bar in West Lafayette, is somewhat popular with African-American students—those who are at least 21 years old, that is, since Indiana drinking laws are strictly enforced. Purdue's Co-Recreational Center, "a huge gym," is a favorite spot on campus and offers almost any kind of athletic facility desired—from Ping-Pong tables to basketball courts.

With more than 26,000 undergraduates, Purdue ranks as one of the 25 biggest universities in the nation, so class sizes, especially in introductory-level courses, tend to be overwhelmingly large. Learning in such courses often takes place via a video screen and difficult-to-understand foreign teaching assistants are all too frequent in some courses. Finding your niche—socially and academically—can also take some doing. But students up for the challenge will find that Purdue is more than just about engineering. "There is an incredible amount of support here, whether from student organizations and friends or from staff," says a campus leader. "Getting involved in organizations makes the Purdue experience more personal, and it doesn't hurt to sit in the front row of a class, as sitting anywhere else in the huge classrooms can be intimidating."

WABASH COLLEGE

Men's college
Address: P.O. Box 352 Crawfordsville, IN 47933-0352
Phone: (800) 345-5385
Director of Admissions: Greg Birk
Multicultural Student Recruiter: Walter A. Blake
1991–92 tuition: $10,500
Room and board: $3,665
Application deadline: 2/1
Financial aid application deadline: 3/1

Non-white freshman admissions: Applicants for the class of '95: 89
Accepted: 88%
Accepted who enroll: 47%
Applicants accepted who rank in top 10% of high school class: 38
In top 25%: 59
Median SAT range: 410–530 V, 520–620 M
Median ACT: na
Full-time undergraduate enrollment: 817

STUDENT ENROLLMENT

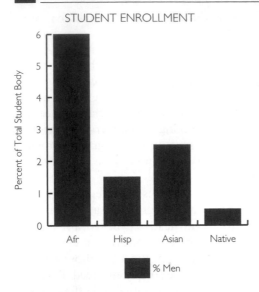

Percent of Total Student Body

Afr Hisp Asian Native

% Men

GEOGRAPHIC DISTRIBUTION OF STUDENTS

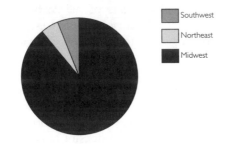

Southwest
Northeast
Midwest

Non-white students in
    1987–88: 4%
    1988–89: 6%
    1989–90: 7%
    1990–91: 7%
Students In-state: 65%
Top majors: 1. Biology 2. Political Science
    3. Psychology
Retention rate of non-white students: 70%
**Scholarships exclusively for non-white
    students:** President's Multicultural
    Scholarships: merit-based; unlimited
    number of scholarships awarded each
    year, which range from $2,500 to $7,000;
    renewable.
Remediation programs: None
Academic support services: The college
    provides a Study Skills Center and a
    Quantitative Skills Center.

Ethnic studies programs: None
Ethnic studies courses: Courses include
    "Native American Art," "Ethnic
    Literature in America," "Studies in
    African-American Literature,"
    "Afro-American History," and
    "American Indian Cultures." As part of
    a sophomore-year requirement, students
    must take "Cultures and Traditions,"
    which includes an African-American
    module.
Organizations for non-white students:
    Malcolm X Institute, Wabash Hispanics
Notable non-white alumni: Dr. Pramod K.
    Carpenter (Chemistry; chief of pathology
    and medical director of clinical
    laboratories, St. Mary's Hospital,
    Rochester, NY); Richard Cauthen
    (Spanish; attorney and Detroit "Teacher
    of the Year"); Dr. John Chambers
    (Psychology; psychology professor,
    Howard University, and government
    consultant for disbursement of federal
    funds to educational institutions);
    Reginald Meeks (History; alderman,
    Louisville, KY; helped create Kentucky
    museum of history and culture of ethnic
    peoples, and listed as one of *Ebony*'s top

FACULTY

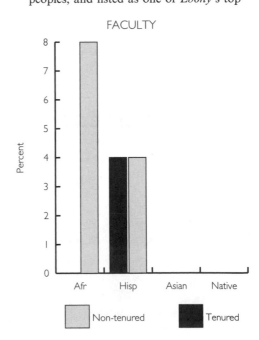

Percent

Afr Hisp Asian Native

Non-tenured   Tenured

50 young black leaders); Dr. Frank Starkey (administrator, Human Resources, GE Research and Development Center)
Tenured faculty: 50
Non-tenured faculty: 24
Student-faculty ratio: 11:1
Administrators: 25
  African-American: 8%

Hispanic: 0
Asian-American: 0
Native American: 0
Recent non-white speakers on campus: Dr. Ivan Van Sertima (author); Alexis DeVeaux (author, playwright, and features editor of *Essence* magazine); Dr. Valerie Lee (professor, Denison University); Turner Fair III (author)

Wabash, established in 1832, is a small, rigorous liberal arts college committed to the education of men, one of the last such schools in the nation. While most single-sex institutions of higher learning bit the bullet in the 1960s and 1970s and became coeducational to attract larger applicant pools, Wabash has held firm in its original mission to graduate the liberally educated male.

Although the faculty is said to be in favor of coeducation, the school's mission has certainly won fans among its students and alums. In terms of spending per student, Wabash's endowment is one of the healthiest in the country. With such a strong endowment, Wabash—in addition to awarding unusually generous financial aid packages—is able to turn down any federal assistance, and thus remain free from governmental regulations.

Wabash men are serious about their studies. Many are aiming to be lawyers and doctors, and many succeed at doing so. Acceptance rates to graduate schools—mostly professional ones—are consistently high. Among the school's best programs are political science, chemistry, history, psychology, and English. Biology is said to be the school's most cutthroat major.

The school's "Afro-American History" receives faint praise from students. "I really didn't learn anything new about my people," says a psychology major. "I felt like I was in the class to teach the other students." To increase the diversity of the faculty at Wabash, the college sponsors the Owen Dustin Program for visiting faculty. Last year, the program brought to campus Floyd Coleman, an art professor from Howard University, who taught a semester-long course on African art.

Studies are intense at Wabash. To graduate, students must take a Freshman Tutorial, take two "Cultures and Traditions" courses during their sophomore year, and satisfy distribution requirements in literature and the fine arts, behavioral science, and natural science and mathematics. Students must also show proficiency in a foreign language. Class sizes are small—usually fewer than a dozen students—so avoiding class participation is nearly impossible. Students say professors are supportive and genuinely want to see them succeed. The Writing and the Quantitative Skills centers are also "extremely helpful," says a student.

African-American students find the academic and non-academic support at the college's Malcolm X Institute beneficial. The institute, located across the street from campus, provides peer tutoring, a library of African and African-American literature, a test file, and professional and career workshops. In 1990, the institute celebrated its twentieth anniversary on campus, and alums set up a fund to help purchase computer equipment for the institute. The fund was named in honor of Jasmine

Robinson, a longtime Wabash employee and the school's first African-American staff member, who retired from the college in 1990. Since 1970, the men of the institute have hosted an annual Halloween party for Crawfordsville area children. In addition, institute men publish *The Malcolm X Institute of Black Studies Journal,* which contains opinion, news pieces, and poetry.

The director of the institute, Horace Turner, works a great deal behind the scenes to be supportive of students. "He always makes sure students are on top of things. He coordinates mentoring programs for upperclass students to work with freshmen, and he makes sure we are able to get to other schools so we can hear speakers and attend workshops. Recently, he sent us to a minority workshop at Indiana University Law School in Bloomington."

There is little racial integration on campus, according to students, and at times the relations between black and white students have reached, in the words of one student, "the boiling point." Students mention an incident involving members of a fraternity who yelled racist epithets at African-American students who were walking by their house. "The administration did nothing in response, even though we brought it to their attention," says a student. Such incidents have generated local media attention.

Studies take up a great deal of a Wabash student's time. But many make time to participate in any number of extracurricular activities—especially football. In fact, one out of every nine Wabash men is a member of the school's football team. Intramural competition, especially between fraternities, is heated, and most varsity sports are popular. Any athletic competition against archrival DePauw University brings out the crowds, especially when it comes to the Monon Bell game, the oldest football rivalry west of the Alleghenies. On a more cultural note, Wabash also sponsors an annual film series and several guest lectureships, and students put on four major stage productions each year.

For off-campus social diversions, students will often head to Indiana or Purdue universities, both of which are about an hour from Crawfordsville. Another popular destination is DePauw University, about thirty minutes south of campus. Indianapolis, about forty-five minutes away by car, and Chicago, about two hours north, are also popular. Crawfordsville (pop. 14,000) offers a variety of fast-food restaurants, but little else. Students say there are few, if any town-gown relations.

Cultural diversity is a relatively new concept at Wabash—"most of our minority alums are in their mid-thirties," says an administrator—but its brand of a top-quality liberal arts education isn't. "If the minority student is looking for a college where he can find himself, then I would not recommend Wabash to him," says a sophomore. "Wabash doesn't lie when it says it takes guts to come here. But if you are looking for a good education where you are challenged mentally and are able to go on to higher heights, then I would say Wabash is for you."

I O W A

COE COLLEGE

Address: 1220 First Avenue N.E., Cedar
Rapids, IA 52402
Phone: (319) 399-8500 / (800) 332-8404
Director of Admissions: Michael White
Multicultural Student Recruiter: na
1991–92 tuition: $10,280
Room and board: $3,940
Application deadline: Rolling admissions
Financial aid application deadline: 3/1

Non-white freshman admissions: Applicants
for the class of '95: 74
Accepted: 85%
Accepted who enroll: 25%
Applicants accepted who rank in top
10% of high school class: 1%
In top 25%: 4%
Median SAT: 460 V, 440 M
Median ACT: 22
Full-time undergraduate enrollment: 990
Men: 49%
Women: 51%
Non-white students in
1987–88: na
1988–89: na
1989–90: na
1990–91: 4.6%
Geographic distribution of students: na
Top majors: na
Retention rate of non-white students: na
**Scholarships exclusively for non-white
students:** None
Remediation programs: None
Academic support services: The college
offers tutoring in most academic subjects
as well as self-help workshops.
Ethnic studies programs: The college offers
interdisciplinary programs in
Afro-American Studies and Asian
Studies, which include courses from the
history, psychology, sociology, and
English departments. Japanese-language
study is available at the elementary level.
Organizations for non-white students: Black
Self-Education Organization, Black
Self-Education Organization House
Notable non-white alumni: Victor Taylor
(vice president and financial consultant,

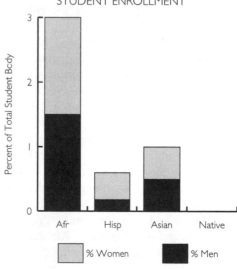

STUDENT ENROLLMENT

Merrill Lynch, Chicago); Dr. Darryl
Banks (deputy commissioner, New York
State Department of Environmental
Conservation)
Tenured faculty: na
Non-tenured faculty: na
Student-faculty ratio: 12:1

Administrators: na
Recent non-white speakers on campus:
Gwendolyn Brooks (Pulitzer
Prize-winning poet); Koko Taylor (blues
artist); Phil Hubbard (former dean of
academic affairs, University of Iowa);
Ray Young Bear (poet)

Located on eight city blocks in the heart of Cedar Rapids, Iowa's second-largest city, Coe is not like other liberal arts colleges in the state that can be found in more rural areas. The college has the resources of an urban environment, while still maintaining a small-college atmosphere.

The close interaction with faculty is one of the school's highlights. Students say they are just as likely to turn to professors for assistance as to any of the school's academic support services. "Professors here are available practically on a twenty-four-hour basis. You can call them anytime. We'll even have classes at a professor's home. Sometimes that means dealing with a screaming baby in the background, but that just kind of symbolizes the personal contact we have here with professors." Adds another student: "Professors here give a hundred percent. You definitely get attention from them."

Students say business administration, English, and psychology are the school's best departments. Also well regarded is the theater arts program. Students are able to design their own interdisciplinary majors, which have recently included marketing, public relations, and therapeutic recreation. Coe also has a 3-2 engineering and architecture program with Washington University in St. Louis. (Students study at Coe for three years before heading to Washington University for the next two.) First-year students must take Coe's "Ways of Knowing" course, an introduction to the liberal arts that has included readings and discussions about the Bible, the French Revolution, and the genius of Beethoven and Picasso. Coe also has a 4-1-4 academic calendar, in which students study on campus for the first and last four months of the school year and pursue independent study options or internships during the month of January.

Good writing isn't expected only of English majors here. Before graduation, all students must take four "writing emphasis" courses that ensure that they leave college as better writers. Writing emphasis courses are integrated into every department, including the sciences. Because of this emphasis on writing, the Writing Center is an important part of Coe's academic support services. "You don't go to the center to have the tutors correct your grammar and punctuation," says a senior. "The consultants look at your paper for ideas, and sometimes offer you perspectives that you didn't have before." Laura Kirkland-Clark, project counselor for the Educational Support Program, which provides academic support for students, is "straightforward, direct and open," observes a student, who says Kirkland-Clark also frequently attends Black Self-Education Organization (BSEO) events.

James Randall, an assistant professor of English, is credited by students with establishing a strong African-American Studies program at Coe. Randall, coordinator of the program, teaches the majority of the courses in the area and "does an excellent job with them," says a student. "For a winter term during January, we read the works of Ngui Wathongo. We just won't find these kinds of books anywhere else in the curriculum. Also, he's good to have on campus, not just for African-American students, but for white students as well." Randall serves as an adviser to the BSEO and regularly attends group meetings and activities.

Among the African-American Studies courses, "Black American Literature" is one of the best. "In the course we focus on works that we might not get in other English classes because the curriculum here is not as integrated as it might be," says one African-American Studies major. In a recent "Seminar in Black Literature" course, Pulitzer Prize-winning poet Gwendolyn Brooks came to campus to discuss her works.

Academic life at Coe received a boost recently with the $4.2 million renovation of the college's Stewart Memorial Library, located at the center of campus. New additions to the library include a computerized card catalogue, an on-line data base and interlibrary loan system which provides access to library collections around the world, and four art galleries.

The BSEO, which has about 15 active members, meets once a week in the Permanent Union Building on campus. The group sponsors social as well as cultural activities. In a recent year, the BSEO brought a step show to campus, and invited fraternities from various colleges and universities in the area to participate. The BSEO has also sponsored the Ebony Treasures exhibit on campus, a display of African art and artifacts. The organization hosts two parties each year that are open to the whole campus. The BSEO House, located just off campus, "serves as a haven where we can just hang out." Although the house is used primarily for social gatherings, it also provides residence facilities for four students active in the BSEO.

Although nearly a third of the campus is Greek, students say there is no pressure to rush and that there are always plenty of activities for independents. Available to Greeks and non-Greeks are various community service activities, including the Friends program, in which Coe students work with area elementary school children. Students also attend churches in the nearby area. Students can frequently be found at the recently completed K. Raymond Clark Racquet Center, a state-of-the-art athletic complex that offers an Olympic-size pool, indoor tennis and racquetball courts, and an indoor track.

Cedar Rapids has the laid-back pace of a Midwestern city. It has restaurants and theaters; it is also a resource for internships with area companies, law firms, and hospitals.

The college has a relatively large international student population, comprising nearly 9 percent of the school's 990 students. "The international students offer a great deal to the campus," says a student. "Some are from the Middle East, so it was especially interesting to talk to them about their experiences and their thoughts about the Gulf War."

Students are drawn to Coe because it virtually guarantees a small-college experience—close relations with faculty and other students. Now, with the completion of impressive new facilities, students have a second reason to come to school here. "When I first came here, the library was a shack," says a senior. "Now it's beautiful. When I first came here, there was no Racquet Center. Now there's the amazing Racquet Center. A lot of people who come here now do so because of these facilities.

I came here for another reason, a reason that still counts: the people here who are willing to be themselves."

CORNELL COLLEGE

Address: 600 First Street West, Mount Vernon, IA 52314
Phone: (319) 895-4000
Director of Admissions: Kevin Crockett
Multicultural Student Recruiter: na
1993–94 tuition: $14,103
Room and board: $4,197
Application deadline: 3/1
Financial aid application deadline: 3/1
Non-white freshman admissions: Applicants for the class of '95: 132
  Accepted: 93%
  Accepted who enroll: 29%
  Applicants accepted who rank in top 10% of high school class: 17%
  In top 25%: 45%
  Median SAT: 1,036 (total V and M)
  Median ACT: 24
Full-time undergraduate enrollment: 1,162
  Men: 45%
  Women: 55%
Non-white students in
  1988–89: 6.9%
  1989–90: 6.2%
  1990–91: 6%
  1991–92: 8%
Students In-state: 28%
Top majors: 1. English 2. Business 3. Psychology
Retention rate of non-white students: 82%
Scholarships exclusively for non-white students: None
Remediation programs: None
Academic support services: The Learning Skills Center provides writing, reading, and study skills assistance. Tutoring is also available in most academic subjects.
Ethnic studies programs: In 1991, the college established an Ethnic Studies program. In 1990, the college established a Latin American Studies interdepartmental major, involving the political science, religion, sociology, and Spanish departments.
Ethnic studies courses: The college offers "African Art," "African-American Literature," and two courses in African-American Studies.
Organizations for non-white students: Black Awareness Cultural Organization, Hispanic Student Association
Notable non-white alumni: Fred Castensen (French/Psychology; director, Minority Engineering Program, University of Connecticut); LeRoy Pony (Biology; pediatric dentist); Odell G. McGhee (Political Science/Education; attorney); Andrea Ashmore (English; corporate communications manager)
Tenured faculty: 44
Non-tenured faculty: 31
  (no faculty of color)
Student-faculty ratio: 14:1

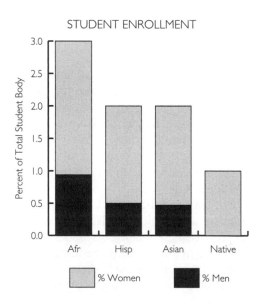

STUDENT ENROLLMENT

Percent of Total Student Body

Afr   Hisp   Asian   Native

% Women   % Men

GEOGRAPHIC DISTRIBUTION OF STUDENTS

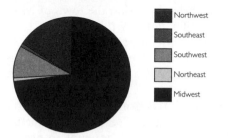

- ■ Northwest
- ▨ Southeast
- ▨ Southwest
- ▨ Northeast
- ■ Midwest

Administrators: na

Recent non-white speakers on campus: Floyd Jones (executive director, Civil Rights Commission, Cedar Rapids, IA); Jayne Cortez (poet); Mel Edwards (artist); Philip Jones (dean of students, University of Iowa)

Cornell College may not have the most diverse student population you'll find in our guide—only about 7 percent of its 1,162 students are non-white—but it certainly has one of the more interesting academic structures. Rather than requiring its students to take the usual four courses a semester as most schools do, Cornell asks that students take only one class at a time, with each class lasting three and a half weeks. Students must take these courses at least eight times a year and are expected to take a broad distribution of classes—including two years of a foreign language—that ensures that they're getting a liberal arts education, including courses in physical education, science, fine arts, and the humanities. (Don't forget, each of these courses, including physical education, is taken one at a time.)

The advantage of such a program is that subjects can be explored thoroughly, and, as only eight of the nine courses are required each year, students can plan vacations and jobs accordingly. The disadvantage is that continuity in learning, especially in the sciences and foreign languages, can be difficult to achieve. But students who make it through to graduation usually praise their educational experiences at Cornell; those who aren't fans right away usually end up transferring.

Students say that the school's best departments are math and science. Many of Cornell's liberal arts departments are also top-notch, including English, math, sociology, and philosophy. In 1990, Cornell spiced up its curriculum when it established a Latin American Studies program. Qualified Cornell students are able to apply for the school's 3-4 architecture program with Washington University in St. Louis, in which students study at Cornell for three years before heading to Washington University for the next four, or the school's 3-2 social service program with the University of Chicago.

"Afro-Americans in U.S. History," "African-American Literature," and "Civil Rights" rank among the school's best ethnic studies courses. Richard Martin, head of the English department and professor of the "African-American Literature" course, as well as a course on jazz, is well regarded by students. "Just through these classes he has raised awareness and consciousness of students about racial issues," says a junior. Students respect the work of Catherine Burroughs, an assistant professor of English, "because she is interested in challenging the classical canon and curriculum in the English department." Burroughs has also taught African-American and women's studies courses. Helen Damon-Moore, an instructor in the education department, "is a very sensitive, empathic person, and I went to her with problems

I had here," says a student. Damon-Moore is best known, however, for her community activism; according to a student, she helped petition the town of Mount Vernon so that the local theater would show the film *Boyz 'N the Hood.*

Students also turn to Guy Davis, Cornell's Multicultural Affairs adviser, for assistance because "he has a genuine interest in the minority students on campus," says a student. "He is well liked by the entire student body and is a redeeming factor in the administration."

The Black Awareness Cultural Organization (BACO) is Cornell's primary cultural student organization. "BACO is designed to provide a sense of security and sanctuary for Cornell's minority students," says a BACO member. "We attempt to organize events to bring cultural awareness and diversity to campus. Some years we are more effective than others. This year [1991–92] we have a lot of new minority students and they are excited about our group. We have planned a fashion show, films, radio shows, speakers, discussions, and a step show."

Cornell's Multicultural Affairs Task Force, made up of students and faculty, has become an integral part in diversifying the school's enrollment and programming. The task force "consists of four different committees: curriculum, programming, scholarship, and admissions," says a student. "The scholarship committee raised $2,500 in a phone-a-thon last spring. The admissions committee phoned prospective minority students last year. The curriculum committee developed a file on multicultural classes at Cornell, and worked on developing a multicultural/ethnic studies program. The programming committee got people to come and speak at Cornell and organized discussion groups on topics like interracial dating."

The Multicultural Affairs House ("the BACO House"), located on the south side of campus near the West Science Center, "can be used for studying, parties, or dinner (there is a kitchen). There is also a small library in the house which contains materials donated by various students and faculty," says a student. But students complain that the house isn't made more accessible. "Yes, there is a house that can be used for all these things. However, nobody uses it. BACO uses it for meetings but that's about it. Recently a group of students asked maintenance and the administration to have the house improved, since it's presently in poor condition." Adds another disgruntled student: "BACO has a house, but, unlike the other houses, students do not live there, so it is locked at the same time as the academic buildings on campus and BACO members are not given keys."

As far as interracial socializing goes, students say it's mixed. "There is a table in the dining hall where the majority of the black students sit," says a student. "It has four chairs. Just kidding. There is also a table where the majority of the Asian students sit. Sometimes white students sit at the table where many black students eat. There are so few minorities here that sometimes there aren't any at parties. Going to the town bars is a popular weekend activity, and you usually see a couple of black students together. I think that most black students are closest friends with other black students, but there are many interracial friendships and some romantic relationships too."

With only about 3,500 residents, the town of Mount Vernon is indeed small—and homogeneous. Students report that, except for a couple of students who tutor in area schools, there is little interaction between them and the mostly white community. As one student described town/gown relations: "They don't bother us, we don't bother them." There are a few pizza joints nearby, and a couple of other shops, but for off-campus diversions, students head to nearby Iowa City, the home of the University of Iowa, a much more active college town.

While the school doesn't have fraternities or sororities, it does have social groups, which amount to about the same thing. Students say these organizations are fairly well integrated, and throw their own parties and other events. For additional on-campus activities, the Performing Arts and Activities Council sponsors concerts, dances, and films. Cornell's varsity football team usually fares well, and almost any athletic event against state rival Coe College draws fans from all around.

Like the state in which it is located, Cornell College is far from being a diverse place. Students are mostly of the wholesome, Midwestern variety, with some international students thrown in. But for one student, the school's homogeneity isn't a reason not to go to the college. She sees it as a challenge. "I would only recommend coming to Cornell College if you are willing to help change it. The campus needs minority and non-minority students who are concerned about letting academically sound colleges such as this one slip further into homogeneity. I stuck with Cornell because I want to make a difference. If you just want an education, you could go anywhere. But if you want a challenge, I would recommend Cornell College."

GRINNELL COLLEGE

Address: P.O. Box 805, Grinnell, IA 50112
Phone: (515) 269-3600
Director of Admissions: Vince Cuseo
Multicultural Student Recruiter: Victoria Romero
1993–94 tuition: $15,048
Room and board: $4,386
Application deadline: 2/1
Financial aid application deadline: 2/1
Non-white freshman admissions: Applicants for the class of '95: 208
  Accepted: 61%
  Accepted who enroll: 37%
  Applicants accepted who rank in top 10% of high school class: na
  Median SAT: 549 V, 552 M
  Median ACT: 26
Full-time undergraduate enrollment: 1,291
  Men: 49%
  Women: 51%
Non-white students in
  1987–88: 6%
  1988–89: 8.2%
  1989–90: 8.8%
  1990–91: 10%

Geographic distribution of students: na
Top majors: 1. Biology 2. English 3. History
Retention rate of non-white students: na
Scholarships exclusively for non-white students: None
Remediation programs: None

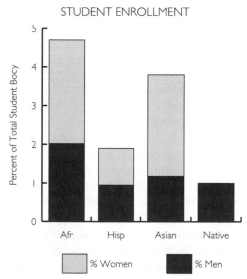

STUDENT ENROLLMENT

Percent of Total Student Body

Afr   Hisp   Asian   Native

☐ % Women   ■ % Men

FACULTY

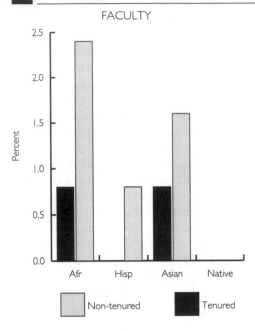

Non-tenured   Tenured

Academic support services: The college offers tutoring in most academic subjects, as well as labs in writing, math, and reading development.

Ethnic studies programs: Grinnell's Latin American Studies program includes more than 15 courses. The Afro-American Studies concentration includes nearly 20 courses and three faculty members who teach in the area. Students are also able to concentrate in Chinese Studies, which includes Chinese-language study and courses in the humanities and social studies.

Organizations for non-white students: Black Cultural Center, Concerned Black Students, Young, Gifted, and Black, Gospel Choir, Black Men's Support Group, Black Women's Support Group, African-American Programming Committee, Asian Students in Alliance, Student Organization of Latinos, Multi-Ethnic Coalition, Native American Interest Group

Notable non-white alumni: Alan Wheat (U.S. congressman, Missouri); Herbie Hancock (composer and musician); George Moose (U.S. ambassador to Senegal); Donald Stewart (president, College Board); Elizabeth Turner Beyene (U.S. State Department)

Tenured faculty: na
Non-tenured faculty: na
Student-faculty ratio: 10:1
Administrators: na
African-American: 3.3%
Hispanic: 0.08%
Asian-American: 0
Native American: 0

Recent non-white speakers on campus: Byllye Avery (executive director, National Black Women's Health Project); Johnnetta Cole (president, Spelman College); Cesar Chavez (labor leader and head of United Farm Workers); Marysa Navarro (history professor, Dartmouth College)

Grinnell College, founded by an abolitionist minister in 1846, is an anomaly in the state of Iowa. Its progressive-minded students and administration are a definite contrast to the more conservative area residents. But students aren't drawn to Grinnell because of its location. They come here because of the school's excellent academics and the personal attention given to them.

"This campus is more aware and involved with issues than the average American campus," says a student activist. "Students to End Apartheid, a student group, has been active for several years and has erected shanty towns, raised money for African student scholarships, and succeeded in getting the college to divest. We often have demonstrations for abortion rights and women's rights. A group recently formed to assist the Kurds, and several demonstrations against the Gulf War took place." While there is a great deal of activism on campus, students say that it sometimes stifles other than liberal points of view. "It should be noted that the attitude on campus is one of political correctness, and many students who may disagree with the demonstrations or more vocal liberal factions are afraid to say so," says another student. "This can lead to getting a one-dimensional perspective on campus."

This sort of global and national awareness fosters an appreciation for diversity that's uncommon at many of its peer institutions. "Grinnell's racial integration in terms of parties, dating, and dining situations is good," observes a student. "Most of the parties here are campus parties, meaning that everyone who would like to attend can, without restrictions of race. Interracial dating is quite acceptable on campus; it is not viewed as a problem. I have dated within my race and outside of my race. The dining situation is also very diverse. People usually eat with their closest friends, and they are not always with people of their own race." And students report that integration when it comes to campus living situations is comparable. "In all of the dorms on campus, I feel there is a variety of races and ethnic backgrounds living together," says a student. "All of the freshmen live on North Campus; thereafter, the college has nothing to do with placing students in the rooms. The students decide where they want to live for the rest of their remaining years at Grinnell, and they choose their roommates. Here too there is diversity."

While the campus is relatively integrated, both socially and in the dorms, a student adds: "There are too few people of color for us to isolate ourselves from our predominantly white classmates."

Grinnell's independent-minded student body is attracted to the college in large part because of its atypical approach to education. As opposed to most schools, Grinnell does not require students to satisfy core course or distributional requirements. Outside of satisfying course requirements for the major, the only course required of students is "Research and Writing Tutorial," a semester-long seminar course for first-year students that focuses on developing writing, reading, and research skills. Each year, more than 30 tutorials are offered to first-year students; recent tutorial topics have included "Visions of Utopia" and "Priorities in Ecological Decisions."

Grinnell has three divisions: humanities, social studies, and science. Among the humanities, students say literature and Chinese- and Russian-language study are strong, while theater and the classics are weaker. Among the social studies programs, anthropology, economics, history, and sociology are well regarded. And among the sciences, chemistry, psychology, and biology are top-notch. The college also offers interdisciplinary programs in gender and women's studies and environmental studies.

One of the Afro-American Studies program's more popular courses is "The Black Community," taught by Kelso Scott, an assistant professor of American Studies and sociology. "She is proud of her African-American heritage and is vocal about making sure African-American concerns are integrated in the curriculum," says a student. Another popular course in the program is "Tradition of Afro-American Literature," taught by Maria Mootry, an associate professor of English, who "is a true role model because she is a published author and because her lessons are always interesting and challenging," says a student. Keiko Yamanaka, an assistant professor of sociology, who teaches "Asian-Americans: Immigration and Assimilation," is respected by students as well.

Academics can be intense at Grinnell. Classes are small and professors expect a lot of their students. The Office of Multicultural Affairs is an effective resource, according to students, for those needing academic assistance. The director of the office, Eric Wynn, is supportive of students. "I view him as my father away from home," says a student. "I talk to him about everything socially and academically, very informal." Jodi Hester, assistant director and coordinator of minority admissions, and Kevin Ahuna, a residence hall adviser, are also supportive.

Grinnell's student activism is evident in campus organizations. "The most active cultural groups on campus are Asian Students in Alliance (ASIA) and Concerned Black Students," says a student. "They're influential in the sense that they encourage students to think about ethnic issues by sponsoring symposia, films, food sales, and other cultural events." Adds another student: "Money and administrative support exists for minority organizations, and the student body is very willing to learn about and to try to understand different ethnic groups." In a recent year, ASIA sponsored the school's first Asian-American Week, in which an Asian-American filmmaker and a law student were invited to campus for panel discussions. The weeklong event included an Asian-American film series. The Black Cultural Center, a non-residence facility, underwent recent renovation and includes a library and is the site of many parties and meetings.

Students have few complaints about their administration, but many were disappointed in its recent decision to discontinue its Preview Program, a summer orientation program designed to introduce incoming first-year students of color to the academic and social life of Grinnell. "I went to a mostly African-American high school, and I was glad that I had that introduction to Grinnell," says a senior. "If I hadn't gone through the program and met the people I did, I'm convinced I wouldn't have made it this far at Grinnell."

While *Newsweek* magazine may hail the town of Grinnell, Iowa, the students of color at the college certainly wouldn't. The town of "Grinnell is, for some of the people, not too particularly delighted with minorities," says a Chicagoan. "Everyone has been advised, when going into town, to always go with someone. I would not say there is a problem every time someone goes into town. The most one would usually get from a townie is a stare. As minorities being aware of the feelings toward us, we tend to ignore the stares or comments."

In an attempt to better town-gown relations, students founded the Community Service Center, which provides volunteer opportunities for students in the area, but, says a junior, "we still don't interact with the community much."

Aside from activities sponsored by the school's cultural organizations, the college offers a surprisingly wide variety of extracurricular opportunities on campus. During a typical year, more than 100 lecturers visited campus, and more than 60 concerts and recitals were performed by guests, students, and faculty. Recent events have included performances by the Alvin Ailey Repertory Ensemble and a northern Indian vocal concert. Popular hangouts on campus are Hector's, a student-run snack bar on the south side of campus, the Forum (known as "the campus living room"), and the Physical Athletic Complex. Grinnell students aren't big on varsity sports, although cross-country is somewhat popular. GORP (Grinnell Outdoor Recreation Program) organizes activities for students, including spelunking, sailing, and white-water canoeing, and has the appropriate equipment for students to borrow.

Grinnell isn't in a big city, but the myriad of on-campus opportunities and activities—both cultural and social—more than make up for what it's lacking in bright lights and traffic congestion. "I would recommend and I have recommended this college to prospective minorities," says a sophomore. "The people on this campus, I think, form a loving community with each other regardless of the color of a person's skin."

UNIVERSITY OF IOWA

Address: Iowa City, IA 52240-9977
Phone: (319) 335-3847 / (800) 553-IOWA
Director of Admissions: Michael Barron
Multicultural Student Recruiter: Kathryne Bassett
1991–92 tuition: $1,952 (in-state); $6,470 (out-of-state)
Room and board: $2,982
Application deadline: 5/15
Financial aid application deadline: 1/1
Non-white freshman admissions: Applicants for the class of '95: 841
  Accepted: 75%
  Accepted who enroll: 33%
  Applicants accepted who rank in top 10% of high school class: na
  Median SAT: na
  Median ACT: na
Full-time undergraduate enrollment: 15,977
  Men: 48%
  Women: 52%
Non-white students in
  1987–88: 5.6%
  1988–89: 5.8%
  1989–90: 6.3%
  1990–91: 7.8%
Geographic distribution of students: na
Top majors: 1. Business 2. Pre-med 3. Psychology
Retention rate of non-white students: 76%
Scholarships exclusively for non-white students: Opportunity at Iowa: amount ranges from full tuition to tuition and room and board; number awarded each year varies; merit-based. Iowa Black Alumni: merit-based; amount ranges from $500 to $1,500; up to three awarded each year; awarded to

sophomore, junior, or senior African-American students. Robert Vernon Family Memorial Fund Scholarship: up to resident tuition; merit-based; awarded to female minority student.
Remediation programs: None
Academic support services: Iowa offers workshops in developing study skills, a preparatory summer program, a transitional program for transfer students, and mentoring program. Tutoring is also available in most academic subjects.
Ethnic studies programs: The African-American World Studies program, established in 1969, is interdepartmental, involving American Studies, art, anthropology, English,

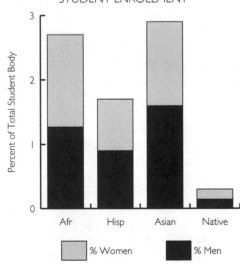

STUDENT ENROLLMENT

Percent of Total Student Body

Afr   Hisp   Asian   Native

% Women   % Men

political science, sociology, and women's studies. The university also offers major courses of study in Latin American Studies and Asian languages and literature.

Ethnic studies courses: Courses in American race relations are offered in sociology, social work, education, political science, and anthropology.

Organizations for non-white students: Afro-American Cultural Center, Chicano/Indian-American Cultural Center, Alpha Phi Alpha, Kappa Alpha Psi, Omega Psi Phi, Phi Beta Sigma, Alpha Kappa Alpha, Delta Sigma Theta, Sigma Gamma Rho, Zeta Phi Beta

Notable non-white alumni: Simon Estes ('86, Music; opera singer); Juanita Kidd Stout ('39, Music; U.S. District Court judge); Bruno Torres ('61, Journalism; photojournalist, UPI)

Tenured faculty: 1,705

Non-tenured faculty: na

Student-faculty ratio: 17:1

Administrators: 109
  African-American: 13%
  Hispanic: 7.3%
  Asian-American: 0.92%
  Native American: 0.92%

Recent non-white speakers on campus: Alex Haley (author); Gwendolyn Brooks (Pulitzer prize-winning poet); Spike Lee (filmmaker); Anne Medicine (assistant dean of graduate students, Stanford University); Deborah Horse Chief (national officer, American Indian Science and Engineering Society)

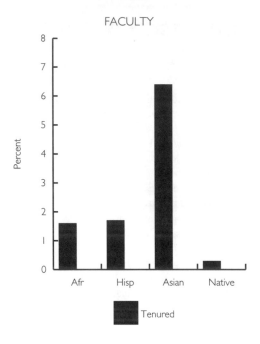

FACULTY

Tenured

Why attend college at the University of Iowa, located in the land of cornfields? Because the university offers a top-flight education with strengths in the liberal arts. Also, the University of Iowa has long been regarded, thanks in part to certain graduate school programs, as one of the more progressive universities in the Midwest. Iowa was the first public university in the country to open its doors to men and women on an equal footing, and the university attracts a geographically diverse group of students—only 73 percent are from the state, while others come from every state in the Union and more than 90 foreign countries. The gay and lesbian student union has enjoyed a relatively long history on campus and protests aren't uncommon over at Pentacrest, the twelve-acre parklike center of campus.

English (Iowa's Writer's Workshop, a graduate school program in creative writing, is world-famous), political science, journalism, psychology, astronomy, communications, and education are among the school's best and most popular programs. The school's pre-med programs are also strong, especially biology, as pre-med students are able to make use of Iowa's on-campus research hospital. Business and accounting are also popular, as are the school's engineering programs.

Students praise Iowa's African-American World Studies program, which includes such popular courses as "History of Black Music" and "Literature of the African Peoples." Students most often double-major in African-American World Studies and another subject, usually sociology. Peter Nazareth, of the English department, and Cherry Muhanji, a teaching assistant, are well-respected teachers in the African-American World Studies program.

The Black Student Union (BSU) wasn't as active during the 1991–92 school year as it has been in the past, but did manage to get a few events off the ground. "This year the Black Student Union focused mostly on educational issues," says a student leader. "We focused on apartheid issues, but we also had a talent show as part of homecoming, and we helped with the recruitment of African-American students by having panel discussions with prospective applicants." The BSU usually attracts between 50 and 75 students to its twice-monthly meetings, which are held in the school's Afro-American Cultural Center.

More active than the BSU, according to students, are the school's predominantly black Greek fraternities and sororities. At the beginning of each year, the Black Greek Caucus (BGC), an organization made up of representatives of each of the predominantly black Greek organizations on campus, sponsors a dance, usually held at the Masonic Temple in town, "as sort of an icebreaker for students to get reacquainted," says a student. Just before the dance, the BGC sponsors an event in which all of the Greek organizations are able to display information about themselves to first-year students. In addition to holding dances and parties almost every weekend, the organizations are actively involved in community service. The women of Alpha Kappa Alpha sorority, for example, sponsored a car wash for the American Cancer Society.

Located on the edge of campus near the law school, the Afro-American Cultural Center is frequented by students who just want to hang out or study. The center provides a library, meeting space, and African and African-American art. Says a student about the opportunities at the center: "It's a lively place where you can go and just be yourself." The director of the center, Billy Hawkins, is well liked by students.

The American Indian Student Association, with about 15 active members, sponsors an annual American Indian Education Conference; speakers are invited to campus to discuss such topics as education, history, and the law as it applies to American Indians. Perhaps the group's most ambitious event is its powwow, held annually in April, which attracts more than 3,500 participants and spectators from across the state and various parts of the country. The powwow is held in the school's recreation building. "We also sponsor get-togethers, usually at the Chicano/Indian-American Cultural Center, where we encourage each other," says a student.

The Chicano/Indian-American Cultural Center "is our home away from home," says an undergraduate. "It has a relaxing atmosphere; you can study or meet up with friends." The center has a living room, where the American Indian student group usually conducts its meetings, and dining and kitchen areas. The manager of the center is Sharon Bowers, who is "helpful, especially when you need information about minority affairs or how to get around campus."

Iowa City "offers few social outlets for students of color," says a student. "It's a small college town with some bars, restaurants, and movie theaters, but most students will make the trek to Cedar Rapids to go to the malls or for some alternative social opportunities when they feel the need to leave campus." But what the town lacks in social life it more than makes up for in the niceness of city residents. "In a big city, you'd be crazy to talk to someone you don't know. People here are open and friendly, so it's normal for someone you've never seen before to say, 'Hi, how's it going?'" Des Moines, Iowa's capital, is about 180 miles from campus.

As in the state in which it is located, racial and ethnic diversity aren't exactly hallmarks at the University of Iowa; only about 8 percent of the school's 16,000 undergraduates are students of color. But despite the low numbers, students say going to the University of Iowa "can be an affirming experience for students of color. The Office of Student Affairs embraces cultural diversity. The office makes minority students feel welcome. And the Office of Special Support Services [which works on the retention of the school's multicultural students] truly has their ears and hearts open to students. The advisers are like surrogate parents, especially the office's director, Roslyn Greene, an African-American woman admired by students." In addition, students praise university president Hunter Rawlings III, who comes to programs sponsored by the Office of Special Support Services and who regularly attends the school's annual Multicultural Graduation Banquet.

The image of Iowa as a land of cornfields is apt, but only up to a point. Students who come to the University of Iowa aren't disappointed. Says a biomedical engineering major from South Carolina: "When I told people at home that I was attending Iowa, I'd get responses like 'Really? . . . Iowa?' People thought I was leaving the country or something. They thought it was too far away and very much different from what I was used to. I'm happy with my choice. I think the function of college is to train a person to do something worth doing. You learn lessons here you can't learn anywhere else in so short a period of time."

IOWA STATE UNIVERSITY OF SCIENCE AND TECHNOLOGY

Address: 100 Alumni Hall, Ames, IA 50011
Phone: (800) 262-3810 (in-state) / (800) 247-3965 (out-of-state)
Director of Admissions: Karsten Smedal
Multicultural Student Recruiter: Dr. George Jackson
1991–92 tuition: $1,852 (in-state); $6,406 (out-of-state)
Room and board: $2,850
Application deadline: 8/26
Financial aid application deadline: 3/1
Non-white freshman admissions: Applicants for the class of '95: 719

Accepted: 82%
Accepted who enroll: 44%
Applicants accepted who rank in top 10% of high school class: 19%
In top 25%: 47%
Median SAT: na
Median ACT: 20.4
Full-time undergraduate enrollment: 20,855
Men: 58.1%
Women: 41.9%
Non-white students in
1987–88: 4%
1988–89: 5%

STUDENT ENROLLMENT

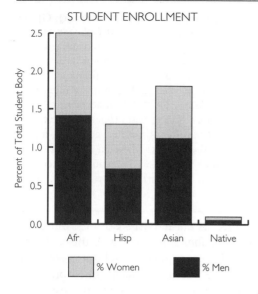

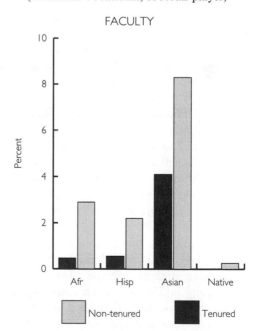

1989–90: 5%
1990–91: 5%

Geographic distribution of students: na

Students In-state: 50.3%

Top majors: 1. Pre-business 2. Liberal Arts and Sciences 3. Electrical Engineering

Retention rate of non-white students: na

Scholarships exclusively for non-white students: American Indian Scholarships: merit-based; available to first-year students who are at least one-quarter American Indian; amount of award varies. George Washington Carver Scholarships: merit-based; available to first-year African-American students who are National Achievement Scholarship finalists or semifinalists; amount of award varies. Hispanic Scholar Awards: same as George Washington Carver scholarships. Commended Scholars Awards: merit-based; covers tuition; available to first-year students as identified by the National Scholarship Competition. Iowa State Business and Engineering colleges also offer scholarships.

Remediation programs: None

Academic support services: The Student Counseling Center offers peer tutoring in addition to assistance for students with learning disabilities.

Ethnic studies programs: na

Ethnic studies courses: Six courses in African and African-American Studies are offered. "Introduction to Latin America" and "Ethnic and Race Relations" are also offered.

Organizations for non-white students: Alpha Kappa Alpha, Delta Sigma Theta, Zeta Phi Beta, Alpha Phi Alpha, Kappa Alpha Psi, Omega Psi Phi, Phi Beta Sigma, National Society of Black Engineers, United Native American Students Association, Hispanic-American Student Council, Black Student Government, Society of Hispanic Professional Engineers, American Indian Rights Organization, Mexican-American Achievers Society, American Indian Science and Society, Gospel Soul Innovators, Active Scholars of Puerto Rico, Society of Asian Engineers

Notable non-white alumni: George Washington Carver (1894, biologist); Vine Deloria (General Science; professor, University of Arizona); Keith Sims (Industrial Vocational; football player,

FACULTY

Miami Dolphins); Cecile Hoover Edwards (professor, Tuskegee Institute)

Tenured faculty: 1,074

Non-tenured faculty: 760

Student-faculty ratio: 12:1

Administrators: 508

African-American: 2.4%

Hispanic: 0

Asian-American: 2%

Native American: 0

Recent non-white speakers on campus: Jesse Jackson (former U.S. presidential candidate and civil rights activist); Gloria Scott (president, Bennett College); Henry Louis Gates, Jr. (professor, Harvard University); Shirley Malcolm (head of the Directorate for Education and Human Resources Programs, American Association for the Advancement of Science); Simon Estes (opera singer); Haki Madhubuti (writer, educator, and publisher); Maki Mandela (African women's rights activist and daughter of Nelson Mandela)

Iowa State University could hardly be described as an activist's campus, but at the 1992 celebration of VEISHEA (Veterinary Medicine, Engineering, Industrial Arts, Sciences, Home Economics, and Agriculture—ISU's original six schools)—billed as the country's largest outdoor party—more than 3,000 individuals rallied on behalf of more diverse cultural programming at the university. "It was the biggest media event of the year, and the protesters represented all ages, sizes, and colors of people," says a student organizer. "The demonstration started with just a couple of hundred people, but by the end of the march it had grown into the thousands."

Organizers demanded more ethnic studies programs, racial sensitivity training workshops for area store owners and police (although students report no particular problems with the police), and the immediate reporting of any racial harassment incidents that may occur on campus.

While Iowa State isn't exactly the Berkeley of the 1960s, there does appear to be developing on campus a sense of camaraderie among the school's students of color that wasn't always there in the recent past. In 1992, the Black Student Alliance rewrote its constitution to emphasize unity among members and more coalition building among the school's student of color organizations. A Hispanic-American Student council was recently established, an "active and outspoken" organization that seeks greater Hispanic student services and programs. And the school's American Indian Rights Organization seeks to address statewide issues that directly affect Iowa's Native American citizens.

"When I first came here as a freshman, most of the students were very cliquey," says a student describing the school's African-American community. "The athletes hung with each other, members of fraternities and sororities hung with each other, and so on. There was also more of a party, party, party atmosphere; that has changed too, just a little. But there's definitely a feeling among ourselves to strive for unity."

Until recently, the school's BSA wasn't terribly active. The annual Black Out Day, in which students attend various workshops, brought many of the school's African-American students together. Iowa State's chapter of the National Society of Black Engineers is also active on campus. Much of the school's social life for African-American students is furnished by the school's historically black Greek organizations, which also stress community involvement. The men of Omega Psi Phi fraternity are the most active when it comes to community involvement, sponsoring study tables and fundraising events for the local NAACP chapter.

ISU's United Native American Students Association has about 15 active members, about half of whom are white and international students. UNASA sponsors a yearlong tutoring project at the Mesquaki reservation, located about fifty miles from campus. Every spring, in conjunction with other student groups, UNASA also sponsors a four-day symposium featuring workshops, lectures, films, and panel discussions. Each year the symposium is built around a theme; recently, they have included education, alcohol awareness, and spirituality. UNASA's NAGS (Native American Group Support) dinners bring students to professors' homes for meals on various Sundays during the school year.

The American Indian Rights Organization (AIRO) is the political arm of the school's Native American student body, and focuses on such issues as fishing and mineral rights. Due to administrative rules governing the functions and funding of student organizations, UNASA is not able to co-sponsor politically focused events with AIRO. "It's very frustrating because we have to keep changing hats all the time. UNASA would like to reach people on various levels, but we can only focus on educational programming. If we sponsored any political activity, we would lose our funding. Some members get around this by joining both organizations."

When students hit the books, as they often do, the books usually have to do with education and business, two of the school's more popular majors. Iowa State is nationally known for its programs in science and technology, particularly engineering and design, as well as architecture. The school's programs in agriculture are excellent.

The African-American and African Studies programs have come under sharp student criticism of late for what students consider to be their Eurocentric points of view. Iowa State's American Indian Studies program fares better. When it came time to register for classes for the 1993 school year, more than 200 students had signed up for the program's introductory course, although it is designed for only 65. Special courses are popular, particularly "Treaty Rights." Well-regarded professors in the program include David Gradwhol, professor of anthropology; Stephen Pett, associate professor of English; and Jerry Stubben, assistant professor of political science.

Of particular importance—and accessibility—to Iowa State students is the school's Office of Minority Student Affairs, which provides a wide array of academic support services, including tutoring and counseling. Students and staff praise the work of the office's director, George Jackson. "Students love Dr. Jackson, and he loves his job. He's supposed to be primarily an administrator, but he's always spending time with students," says a counselor.

The Black Cultural Center, located on the edge of campus, is a popular destination for many of the school's African-American students. "It's a little house, really, but it's a place for students to get away and socialize." The center, which provides computer terminals, a library, and meeting space, has lately been the source of controversy among students. "Although the center is named the Black Cultural Center, Dr. Jackson's office is seeking to get it renamed the Multicultural Center. Right now only black students use the center, and other students want to broaden its uses to include other organizations."

While corn may thrive in Iowa, so do cultural opportunities. World-famous musical groups, such as the New York Philharmonic, have performed at Iowa State, as have entertainers such as the Rolling Stones and Stevie Wonder. Various student musical groups entertain on campus, and students can join any of the more than 500 clubs or other organizations. Intramural teams, which engage in such sports as pickleball and canoe racing, are popular. The dining facilities sponsor a "Favorites from Home" recipe competition; the winning recipe is then served in the dining halls. The Student Union—with a couple of restaurants and a non-alcoholic bar—is a popular hangout.

Ames isn't exactly a college town, although Campus Town, an area next to campus that has restaurants and watering holes, caters to ISU students. Most activities, however, are on campus. But Des Moines, Iowa's capital, is less than a half hour from town and offers a wider variety of shopping and social opportunities.

Iowa State, despite recruiting efforts, still remains a predominantly white university, reflecting the state's homogeneous white population. Only about 5 percent of the school's nearly 21,000 undergraduates are students of color. Many of the school's African-American students come from Chicago and St. Louis. Attending school in such a homogeneous environment can definitely be an eye-opening—if not alienating—experience, particularly for students coming to the nation's heartland from urban areas.

But students say the majority of Iowa Staters are open-minded, even though, they add, most come from small Iowa towns and probably have never interacted with a person of color before. In 1989–90, Iowa State students elected their first African-American student body president (who still attends the university as a master's degree candidate and BSU adviser). "There's a real community of people here," says a student leader. "Although you don't see a lot of minority students on campus, most of us are pretty close and are getting closer. We all say hi to each other on our way to classes. If anything, going to such a white school has only made us come together even more."

K A N S A S

UNIVERSITY OF KANSAS

Address: Lawrence, KS 66045
Phone: (913) 864-2700
Director of Admissions: Deborah Castrop
Multicultural Student Recruiter: na
1992–93 tuition: $1,456 (in-state); $5,628
  (out-of-state)
Room and board: $3,080
Application deadline: 2/1 (non-resident); 4/1
  (resident)
Financial aid application deadline: 3/1
Non-white freshman admissions: Applicants
  for the class of '96: na
  Applicants accepted who rank in top
  10% of high school class: na
  Median SAT: na
  Median ACT: 23
Full-time undergraduate enrollment: 19,287
  Men: 50%
  Women: 50%
Non-white students in
  1988–89: 6%
  1989–90: 6%
  1990–91: 7%
  1991–92: 8%
Geographic distribution of students: na
Top majors: 1. Psychology 2. Engineering
  3. Journalism
Retention rate of non-white students: 82%
**Scholarships exclusively for non-white
  students:** Minority Honors Scholarship:
  merit-based; $1,300 per year; unlimited
  number awarded each year; available to
  National Achievement and National
  Hispanic Scholars; renewable. Kansas

University Endowment Merit Program:
merit-based; 35 of the $1,000
scholarships are awarded each year;
renewable. Minority Engineering
Program Scholarship: merit-based; $500
to $1,000 awarded each year; renewable;
20 awarded each year.
Remediation programs: The university offers
  remedial courses in math.
Academic support services: The Student
  Assistance Center and the Office of
  Minority Affairs provide academic and
  non-academic support.
Ethnic studies programs: The African and
  African-American Studies program

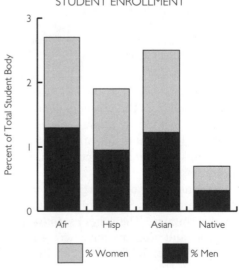

STUDENT ENROLLMENT

allows students to concentrate in either area. The program includes more than 50 courses, including language study in Swahili, Haitian, and Hausa. The Latin American Studies program is interdisciplinary, involving more than 12 departments. East Asian languages and cultures is also offered as a program.

Ethnic studies courses: The university offers various courses in Japanese and Chinese Studies.

Organizations for non-white students: Black Men of Today, Student Council for Recruiting, Motivating, and Educating Minority Engineers, Black Panhellenic Council, Black Student Union, Cross-Cultural Communications Network, Chinese Student Association, Hispanic-American Leadership Organization, Minority Business Student Council, Delta Sigma Theta, Zeta Phi Beta, Alpha Kappa Alpha, Sigma Gamma Rho, Native American Student Association, Society for East Asian Studies.

Notable non-white alumni: Lynette Woodard ('81; two-time Academic All-American basketball player, former member of the Olympic basketball team, and first female member of Harlem Globetrotters); Wilt Chamberlain ('58; former NBA basketball star); Etta M. Barnett ('31; Broadway and radio star of the 1930s; Gershwin wrote *Porgy and Bess* for her); Gale Sayers ('64; former NFL football star)

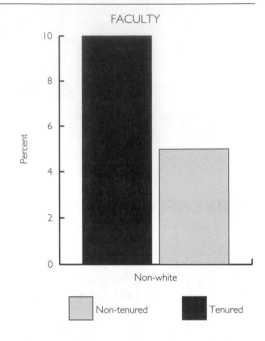

FACULTY

Tenured faculty: 1,407
Non-tenured faculty: 544
Student-faculty ratio: 16:1
Administrators: 560
  Non-white: 9%
Recent non-white speakers on campus: Emmanuel Cleaver (Kansas City, MO, mayor); Maya Angelou (author and poet); Constance Baker Motley (senior judge, U.S. District Court for the Southern District of New York); Angela Davis (political activist); Gene Chavez (Center for Intercultural Communication of El Centro de Servicios para Hispanos)

The University of Kansas in Lawrence is more than just your average Midwestern state university. There is actually an aura of sophistication to the campus, one that is complemented by a large international enrollment—more than 17 percent of the school's 19,000 students are from foreign countries (attracted to the graduate school programs in medicine and engineering)—and a myriad of outstanding academic programs.

In contrast to other large state universities, KU isn't a party school. Students do study here. KU's School of Journalism and Mass Communication is one of the finest in the country. The school's *University Daily Kansan* has won numerous national awards, and students have access to the facilities of KANU, KU's national public radio affiliate. KU's School of Engineering offers nine fields of study, including a highly regarded program in civil engineering. Among the school's more than 50 arts and science departments, students praise theater and film, Spanish, and English. Theater and dance students have enhanced opportunities in the school's recently constructed Lied Center for Performing Arts. Other noted programs include nursing, education, and pharmacy. Popular courses in the African and African-American Studies department are "West African History," "The Black Experience in the Americas," "Civil Rights," and "Black Leadership."

KU's Office of Minority Affairs provides more than ample academic and non-academic assistance. "The office is good for guidance for student organizations, and they also know and understands the struggles you go through as a student at KU," says a student. "They help build you up when you're down." Sherwood Thompson, the office's director, is "a very dynamic person," says a student leader. "He knows how to take your frustrations at KU and deliver them to the administration in to-the-point language. He's also good at helping you learn how to lead your organization. He's a good resource."

For additional academic support, students turn to the Supportive Educational Services, which provides peer tutoring in most academic subjects. "If you want to get a 4.0, get a tutor from SES at the beginning of the semester," says a journalism major. "The office will provide you with excellent tutors who seem to really care that you succeed." Students speak highly of Wendi Coleman, SES's director, who "is a funny and caring adviser," says a student. "She gets along with the students on our level. Her office is the chill-out place to get away from school and school politics."

For peer support, students are able to turn to various student organizations, including the Native American Student Association, the Hispanic American Leadership Organization (HALO), and the Black Student Union, which is an umbrella organization for two student groups, Black Men of Today and Ujima, a women's support group. Black Men of Today, established on campus in 1989, "speaks out about political and social issues on campus" by hosting forums and workshops. The group, which meets weekly, also hosts book-study sessions as well as lectures. Ujima has done community service work in the Lawrence area—for example, working with a local girls and boys club and a big sister/big brother program.

Students say they would like to see the African-American student groups become more active. "HALO seems to unify Hispanics more so than any other organization for minorities on campus," says a student. "There is some apathy. Some blacks think it is worthless to be involved in black organizations because they feel they don't do anything."

KU has a reputation for being one of the more progressive state universities in the Midwest. But, according to one student, this doesn't translate into a racially integrated campus. "The campus is very segregated," she says. "Blacks party with blacks. Whites party with whites. We have a black Greek system and we have a white-fraternities Greek system. There are few, very few, blacks in fraternities. And the organizations rarely do things together. Dorm life is not that bad, however. A lot of the dorms have students of all races and backgrounds."

The Greek system hasn't been without its controversy. One student reports that a member of the Sigma Alpha Epsilon fraternity yelled a racist epithet at an African-American pizza-delivery girl. "The black students at KU called for the expulsion of the fraternity house from the university, but it is still here. But the student who yelled at the delivery girl was immediately expelled from the university by the administration."

Much of the social life at KU revolves around the huge and predominantly white Greek system, which accounts for about 20 percent of the campus. But there's more to KU life than fraternity keggers. For example, you can go to a KU basketball game, or at least try to get tickets for one. The events are extremely popular. (James Naismith, the inventor of the game, coached at KU.) Football, particularly games against rivals Kansas State and Missouri, also draws crowds. The Student Union Activities Board sponsors everything from forums on the environment and college quiz bowls to movies six nights a week (and matinees every weekend) to the Day on the Hill, a free outdoor concert that features six bands.

Lawrence, with a population of more than 64,000, has numerous movie theaters, restaurants, and clubs. It is estimated that 15 percent of the city's residents are African-American and there is a sizable Asian and Asian-American community, but, according to one student, aside from minimal community service projects, there is little interaction between students and the people of Lawrence. Kansas City, just forty minutes away by car, is famous for jazz, barbecue, and Royals baseball and Chiefs football. Topeka, the state capital, is a twenty-five-minute drive west of campus.

The student of color population at KU, as in the state in which it is located, is relatively low. But with the support of the Office of Minority Affairs, students say, four years in Lawrence is not exactly like living in Oz but it can certainly come to be home. "If you want a relatively inexpensive but good education, come here," says a student. "KU is a big school, so there's a lot you can experience."

K E N T U C K Y

BEREA COLLEGE

Address: CPO 2344, Berea, KY 40404
Phone: (606) 986-9341
Director of Admissions: John S. Cook
Multicultural Student Recruiter: na
1993–94 tuition: free
Room and board: $2,457
Application deadline: Rolling admissions
Financial aid application deadline: 8/1
Non-white freshman admissions: Applicants
for the class of '96: 85
Accepted: 70%
Accepted who enroll: 81%
Applicants accepted who rank in top
10% of high school class: 10%
In top 25%: 50%
Median SAT range: 400–450 V, 425–475
M
Median ACT range: 18–22
Full-time undergraduate enrollment: 1,500
Men: 44%
Women: 56%
Non-white students in
1987–88: 9.5%
1988–89: 9.7%
1989–90: 11%
1990–91: 12.9%
Students In-state: 50%
Top majors: 1. Business 2. Education
3. Sociology
Retention rate of non-white students: 72%
**Scholarships exclusively for non-white
students:** All Berea students receive full
tuition grants valued at $10,800 a
year.

STUDENT ENROLLMENT

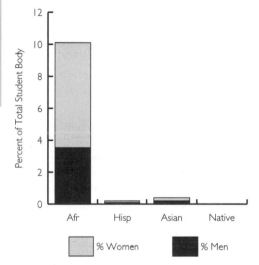

GEOGRAPHIC DISTRIBUTION OF STUDENTS

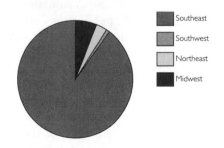

Remediation programs: Courses are
available in math and English.

Academic support services: Tutoring is available in math and English. Peer counselors are also available in most academic subjects.

Ethnic studies programs: None

Ethnic studies courses: The college offers six courses in African-American Studies, involving history, music, and English.

Organizations for non-white students: Black Student Union, Black Ensemble

Notable non-white alumni: na

Tenured faculty: 76

Non-tenured faculty: 38

Student-faculty ratio: 12.5:1

Administrators: 53

African-American: 1.9%

Hispanic: 0

Asian-American: 0

Native American: 0

Recent non-white speakers on campus: Jesse Jackson (former U.S. presidential candidate and civil rights activist); Giancarlo Esposito (actor); Nikki Giovanni (poet)

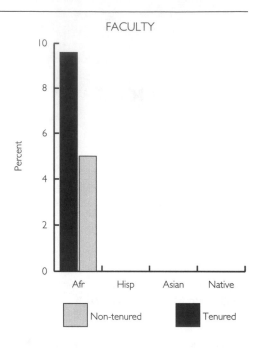

Berea is a small school with a big heart. This Christian school in central Kentucky is tuition-free and was founded in 1855 to educate students primarily from the southern Appalachian region "whose families would have a difficult time financing a college education without assistance." In order to be admitted to Berea, students must demonstrate financial need. Although 80 percent of the school's 1,500 students are from the southern Appalachian region, Berea also enrolls students from about 27 other states.

Berea's free education—students are responsible for only the cost of their books and other supplies—does come with one hitch. All students are required to work at least 10 hours a week in a job assigned by the college, while carrying a normal class load. The college attempts to assign students to areas of student interest. Students work in the school's publications office, at area hospitals, as computer programmers, and as audiovisual technicians. Students say they don't mind the work, and most appreciate the opportunity to beef up their résumé. "My interest in Berea College was sparked by its unique history and no-tuition policy, but its labor policy also heightened my curiosity," says a senior from Alabama. "As a freshman, I was assigned to work at the Boone Tavern Hotel. I had not had any experience with restaurant work and did not rate waiting tables high on my list of desirable jobs, but to my surprise, I liked some aspects of the job. I got to know many other students whom I might otherwise not have met. The labor program has taught me to respect all forms of work."

Berea has long been known for its education, philosophy, and religion departments.

Many students work as teachers or ministers in the region after graduation. Unique for a liberal arts college, Berea also offers majors in agriculture and in Appalachian Studies, which includes courses in Appalachian literature, music, and history. Berea's Black Studies minor is interdisciplinary and gets high marks from students. Says a biology major about the program: "The courses that are offered are very effective in teaching the history of African-Americans and relating it to students' present lifestyles." Adds another student: "Fortunately, students from several ethnic backgrounds enroll in the classes, which gives an opportunity for open discussion."

To graduate from the college, students must complete a core curriculum, which emphasizes skills in communication, and creative and critical thinking. Courses include: a laboratory and a behavioral science; math or computer science; Appalachian Studies, non-Western cultures, or a foreign language; physical education; and a senior-level course related to the topic "The Christian Faith in the Modern World."

Students report that academic support programs are accessible. "If a person needs help there is always someone or somewhere on campus to go to," says a student. Students say that the Black Cultural Center's peer counselors and teaching assistants provide a great deal of academic support. "On Berea's campus there is a peer counseling program aimed specifically at African-American freshmen and sophomores. Counselors, who are juniors and seniors, meet with their counselees on a one-to-one basis at least one hour a week. This time is used to discuss work problems, study or academic problems, or simply to determine whether the student is adjusting well to campus life. This program is one of the more effective ones on campus." Students report that teaching assistants are helpful. "There are teaching assistants for just about every class on campus," says a student.

Students mention various faculty and staff members who provide academic and non-academic support, among them Cora Newell-Withrow, chairperson of the nursing program; Cleo Charles of the history department; Janice Blythe, chairperson of the department of child and family services, and Betty Olinger, a nursing professor. "All of these instructors and others take an active interest in the welfare of students," says a student. "It is not uncommon for them to open their homes to students when they want to get away from campus for a while and be in a home setting." Andrew Baskin, director of the school's Black Cultural Center and a history professor, also wins student praise. "Mr. Baskin is a very straightforward but nice man. He is always encouraging the black students to work hard and do well," says a student. Professor Baskin was also responsible for creating the school's peer counseling program and "is always trying to put events together to improve the relations between all black students on campus, such as symposiums, student/faculty dinners, and special trips to help us learn more about our culture."

The town of Berea, "located on a ridge where the bluegrass of Kentucky meets the foothills of the Cumberland Mountains," isn't exactly a cultural or social mecca for most students, let alone for students of color, who, according to one student, "feel very uncomfortable anywhere in town except on campus." For shopping or other excursions, students head to Lexington, about forty miles north. Sports are an integral part of campus life. In the past few seasons, Berea's men's teams have won conference and district championships in basketball, soccer, swimming, golf, and track, and more than 75 percent of the men and 50 percent of the women participate in intramural sports, which range from Ping-Pong to swimming. Theater, music, and dancing groups are also popular.

Town/gown relations on the whole seem less than cordial, but various student groups sponsor activities that make leaving campus less essential. "One of the most active multicultural student groups on campus is the African Student Association," says a student. "The ASA sponsors African Awareness Week, which presents outside speakers, symposiums, cultural shows, documentary films, and an arts and crafts exhibit from Africa. All of these events are campus-wide. ASA also sponsors a graduation dinner at the end of the year for all Afro-American students." Berea's Black Ensemble, a gospel choir, sponsors annual fall and spring concerts, while the Black Student Union has a pageant and a children's Christmas party for community residents.

Students appreciate Berea's combination of a Christian environment, work requirements, academic quality—and free tuition. "As a senior, I am finding that I have excellent work experience that appeals to employers. I also have an outstanding education that will open doors when I apply to graduate schools." Comments another student: "Two of the reasons I chose Berea College were its size and its educational program. I didn't want to attend a larger university where I would be a number. At Berea I feel free to go to my professors whenever I have a problem. I also know I will get a good education. I'm glad I chose Berea. I'm already a more mature, responsible person."

CENTRE COLLEGE

Address: Danville, KY 40422
Phone: (606) 236-5211
Director of Admissions: na
Multicultural Student Recruiter: na
1991–92 tuition: $9,935
Room and board: $3,930
Application deadline: 3/1
Financial aid application deadline: 3/15
Non-white freshman admissions: Applicants
for the class of '95: na
Applicants accepted who rank in top
10% of high school class: 64%
In top 25%: 73%
Median SAT range: 380–610 V, 480–570 M
Median ACT range: 22–24
Full-time undergraduate enrollment: 875
Men: 49%
Women: 51%
Non-white students in
1987–88: 3%
1988–89: 3%
1989–90: 3%
1990–91: 4%

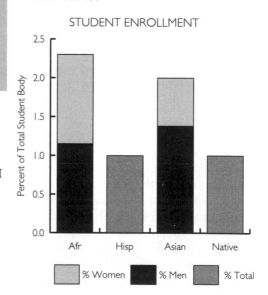

STUDENT ENROLLMENT

Geographic distribution of students: na

Students In-state: 55%

Top majors: na

Retention rate of non-white students: 85%

Scholarships exclusively for non-white students: Presidential Scholarship: merit-based; ten awarded each year; $5,000 for each award; renewable for four years.

Remediation programs: None

Academic support services: The college offers a non-credit study skills course, as well as tutoring in most academic subjects.

Ethnic studies programs: None

Ethnic studies courses: The college's Integrative Studies department offers "African-American History and Literature," while the anthropology/sociology department offers "Native Peoples of North America" and "Peoples of the Middle East and North Africa."

Organizations for non-white students: Black Student Union

Notable non-white alumni: Raymond Burse ('73; attorney, former Rhodes Scholar and former president of Kentucky State University)

Tenured faculty: 44

Non-tenured faculty: 31

Student-faculty ratio: 12:1

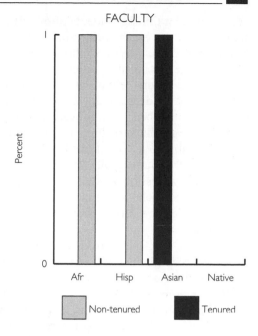

FACULTY

Percent

Afr   Hisp   Asian   Native

Non-tenured   Tenured

Administrators: 20

African-American: <1%

Hispanic: <1%

Asian-American: 0

Native American: 0

Recent non-white speakers on campus: Maya Angelou (author and poet); Dr. Betty Griffin (director of teaching training, Kentucky Department of Education)

Centre College offers one of the best liberal arts educations in the state of Kentucky. The college has graduated more Rhodes Scholars than any other college or university in the state, and it ranks first in the nation in the percentage of alumni who contribute annually to the college, ahead of such luminaries as Williams, Bowdoin, and Amherst.

Students say that the physical sciences and math are among Centre's more respected departments, as are the school's pre-med programs. The relatively new Franklin W. Olin Hall, which houses these departments as well as the computer science department, offers impressive facilities, particularly for a school of Centre's small size. Centre's music department, housed in the equally impressive Norton Center for the Arts, is well regarded on campus and regularly brings well-known performers to its stages. The college's history and government majors are also strong.

Two of the school's most successful academic support services are "Help Sessions" and close interaction with faculty. "Help Sessions assist those students who didn't understand what was going on in class," says a student. "Upperclass students teach the sessions, and in general they're helpful." Students also say that faculty members are effective in finding students tutors if the tutoring service on campus is unable to. In addition, "we get the professors' home phone numbers and their addresses on the first day of class," says a sophomore. "It's very easy to reach them when you need to. If they're not in their office, you're free to call them at home. Even outside of formal office hours, you are welcome to stop in."

The Black Student Union, with about 20 active members, serves primarily as peer support for members. "We're especially helpful to incoming freshmen," says a student. "We tell them what's really going on here on campus, and impress on them that it's not impossible to make it here. It's hard coming to a school that is so predominantly white, so our group is really important for its members." The BSU's adviser, Thomas McKune, is accessible to students. "When it comes to issues of family, financial aid concerns, and racial issues here on campus, Tom is easy to talk to," says a student. McKune, Centre's former dean of admissions, is currently assistant to the dean of the college.

Although the BSU provides its students primarily with emotional support, the group is becoming more political. "We are going to begin urging the college to integrate the curriculum more," says a student. Perhaps of more immediate concern to BSU members are certain campus-wide events. Recently, members of the BSU asked the college administration to discontinue the annual Freshman Auction, in which, according to a student, "freshmen are bought and sold like slaves. We here in the African-American community find the event offensive, as well as some of the humor that is made at our expense in connection with it." The actions of some other student groups have also raised the concern of BSU members and other students. "This year, a band playing at the Sigma Alpha Epsilon fraternity house and many fraternity members started chanting 'David Duke for President,'" says a student. "The three black students who were at the party, and a couple of the white students, left, saying they would never set foot in that fraternity house again." More recently, the same fraternity held a redneck party, at which a Confederate flag was used to help decorate the house. When African-American students took their concerns about these incidents to the administration, they felt "ignored. The administration keeps telling us that they'll schedule a meeting between the SAEs and us, but nothing ever comes of it. We're more than happy to meet with them, but the administration is just looking to sweep yet another such incident under the rug." Equally disturbing was an administration official's response to BSU members who had approached him with their concerns about the Confederate flag draped from the fraternity house window. "When we went to the administration, an official said he didn't know why we were so upset," says a student. "He said that when he sees the flag, he doesn't see a symbol of the old South. He said he is reminded instead of the *Dukes of Hazzard* TV show."

Danville, located in the exact center (hence Centre) of the state, is known as the city of firsts—the first U.S. post office in the West, the first Presbyterian church in the West, and the first college and law school in the West. Surrounded by the beautiful Kentucky countryside, Danville is not exactly the place for culture vultures or party animals. But Lexington, thirty miles north and home of the University of Kentucky, is, and students often make the trek. Lexington has a philharmonic orchestra, an opera, and a theater.

Back on campus, campus social life revolves around the Greek system, which encompasses nearly three-quarters of the student body. Some of the African-American women at Centre are seeking to establish a chapter of Alpha Kappa Alpha, a historically black sorority, "but we're only in the beginning stages of that," says a student. As there are no classes on Wednesdays, partiers get a couple of days' head start on the weekend. Basketball—both men's and women's—has had successful seasons, and football games always draw large crowds. Intramural competition is keen among the fraternities.

Intimacy comes in big doses at this small college. So if you're one who wants to be lost in a crowd while in school, look elsewhere. "In the long run, I'll be glad I came because I know I'm getting a good education that's respected in the region. It's sometimes difficult to see that, though, since there is so much to deal with now, especially with the fraternities."

UNIVERSITY OF KENTUCKY

Address: 100 W. D. Funkhouser Building, Lexington, KY 40506-0054
Phone: (606) 257-2000
Director of Admissions: Dr. Joseph L. Fink
Multicultural Student Recruiter: Emmett Burnam
1992–93 tuition: $1,988 (in-state); $5,348 (out-of-state)
Room and board: $2,934
Application deadline: 8/1
Financial aid application deadline: 4/1
Non-white freshman admissions: Applicants for the class of '96: 386 (African-American only)
Accepted: 70%
Accepted who enroll: 85%
Applicants accepted who rank in top 10% of high school class: 35%
In top 25%: 70%
Median SAT: 819 (total V and M)
Median ACT: 21
Full-time undergraduate enrollment: 17,500
Men: 49.5%
Women: 50.5%
Non-white students in
1987–88: 6%
1988–89: 6%
1989–90: 7%
1990–91: 8%
Geographic distribution of students: na
Students In-state: 80%

Top majors: 1. Business 2. Engineering
Retention rate of non-white students: 79%
Scholarships exclusively for non-white students: The university offers four-year renewable scholarships of $3,500 to incoming freshmen with composite ACT score of 28 and a cumulative GPA of 3.5; four-year renewable $2,500 scholarships available to incoming freshmen with a composite ACT score of 25 and a cumulative GPA of 3.0; and one-year scholarships of $2,000 may be awarded to incoming freshmen with a

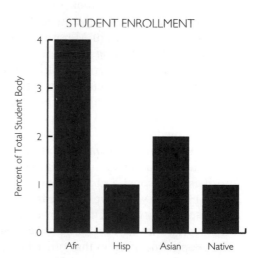

STUDENT ENROLLMENT

minimum composite ACT of 19–24 and a cumulative GPA of 2.5. Minority Student South Central Bell Honors Scholarship: full tuition. Minority Engineering Scholarships for incoming freshmen admitted to the College of Engineering. The awards are available to African-Americans who are Kentucky residents.

Remediation programs: na

Academic support services: The university's Office of Minority Student Affairs provides tutoring in most subjects and workshops in note taking, test taking, and writing.

Ethnic studies programs: None

Ethnic studies courses: The university offers ethnic studies courses in anthropology, English, geography, history, political science, and sociology.

Organizations for non-white students: Kappa Alpha Psi, Alpha Kappa Alpha, Alpha Phi Alpha, Delta Sigma Theta, Omega Psi Phi, Sigma Phi Epsilon, Phi Beta Sigma

Notable non-white alumni: Dr. George Wright (historian and vice provost, University of Texas); Kenny Walker (former NBA basketball player); Sam Bowie (NBA basketball player)

Tenured faculty: na

Non-tenured faculty: na

Student-faculty ratio: 15:1

Administrators: na

Recent non-white speakers on campus: Spike Lee (filmmaker); Dr. George Wright (vice-provost, University of Texas); Kwame Toure (political activist); KRS-One (rap artist and anti-drug lecturer)

The fact that the University of Kentucky has one of the country's largest basketball stadiums may tell you a bit about this public university founded in 1878. Students here are diehard basketball fans, even as the school comes off a recent three-year suspension for certain NCAA violations. But UK, a conservative, traditional university, offers a variety of academic and extracurricular opportunities that will satisfy even non-basketball fans.

The University of Kentucky, like other Southern universities, doesn't have the most impressive history when it comes to graduating minority students; the school didn't graduate its first African-American student until the early 1960s, and the first African-American to enroll, Lyman T. Johnson, was able to attend the university's law school only after he took the university to court in 1949. There are still rigid lines separating many of the students racially, but the university—largely through the efforts of the Office of Minority Student Affairs and various student groups—is becoming a more inviting place for students of color.

Greek organizations, particularly predominantly white Greek fraternities and sororities, have never been known for their progressive natures, but during a recent year, some of them, along with predominantly black Greek groups, attempted to bridge the school's racial barriers. The men of Kappa Alpha Psi and Phi Sigma Lambda, predominantly black and white fraternities, respectively, sponsored a football bash party that was well attended by members and friends, while the women of Alpha Kappa Alpha and Alpha Gamma Delta, predominantly black and white sororities, sponsored a chili dinner. "Although many of the Greek parties are still mostly black or white, we try not to be exclusionary," comments a senior.

Located in Patterson Office Tower, the Office of Minority Student Affairs, which focuses primarily on African-American students, "is outstanding," says a student. "The people who work in that office go beyond the call of duty. They don't just give you a pat on the back and tell you to be on your way. They really work with you, whether you're an organization, like the Black Student Union, or an individual. From the vice-chancellor of minority student affairs, Loretta Byars, to the dean of minority student affairs, Chester Gundy, this office is excellent." Emmett Burnham, head of the recruitment section, "also does an excellent job trying to get students here." The office has a great deal to be proud of; the university has the highest retention rate of African-American students of any of the state's public universities.

Students praise the Learning Services Center, which provides students with tutoring in most subjects. "I don't think I would have survived academically here if it hadn't been for that office," says one student.

There are nearly 20 active African-American organizations on campus. "There are tons of them and they're all doing things. You have your National Society of Black Engineers, which works with retention, sending members to conferences and helping them to get jobs, you have your Greek-letter organizations, you have your gospel choirs. I could go on and on." One of the newer African-American organizations to flourish on campus is Sima Elimeka. "It's three years old, and is primarily a discussion group where we read black authors, like Malcolm X," says a member.

The largest of these organizations, however, is the Black Student Union, with about 50 active members. Members work in the community, visiting nursing homes and holding blanket and clothing drives, among other activities. The BSU also hosts and co-hosts two annual events that get popular turnouts. The first is the All-Greek Formal, sponsored with the predominantly black Greek organizations. "There's always a good showing for that dance," says an event organizer. The BSU also sponsors the Lyman T. Johnson Banquet, "where we have awards for the accomplishments of African-American students and organizations," says a student about the event, which is usually held in the university's student center. Another award is named in honor of Doris Wilkenson, who began heading UK's African-American Studies program in the fall of 1992. In 1957, she was the first African-American to be admitted to the university as an undergraduate. Johnson is a frequent visitor to the UK campus and always attends the banquet.

Students report that on a day-to-day basis UK's African-American community isn't all that tight. "As in any place, cliques form," says a student. "But when we need to come together, we certainly do." An occasion for a united response was a date book put together by the Student Activities Board. "The book had the words of the original version of *My Old Kentucky Home,* which talks derogatorily about blacks," says a BSU leader. "But the BSU wouldn't tolerate it, especially when it was at the bookstore and hundreds had been printed up. We spoke to the university president, and the books were taken from the shelves and later given away free. We then drafted a resolution demanding a written and oral apology, which we got from the SAB president and its adviser. We also asked for a Black Studies director, which we also got. Although the effort was initiated by the BSU, the Office of Minority Student Affairs was also more than helpful."

The university has respectable programs in business and economics, journalism, engineering, and education. While it is not one of the country's larger state universities, students say that gaining access to professors can be achieved with a little effort. Classes for introductory courses tend to be large, some with more than

200 students, but once students enter upper-division courses they encounter more intimate class environments.

Academic competition isn't exactly intense at UK, where getting a ticket to a Wildcat basketball game is highest on many students' list of priorities. Nonetheless, the university does enjoy a good reputation in the state, which is important when it comes to finding jobs or internships.

The midsize city of Lexington is described by one student as "a small, wealthy horse town, with not very many social options for minority students." But there are certain downtown clubs, she says, that students like, among them Breedings (where else but in Kentucky, where Thoroughbred racing is king, would you find such a club name?), popular with African-American students on Tuesday nights, and Club 141 and Todd's, which draw racially mixed crowds.

UK has a way to go when it comes to breaking down some of the racial barriers that exist between students, but UK does have an active African-American community, and the good works of the Office of Minority Student Affairs, to make a student's four years here a pleasant—if not academically rewarding—experience. "The racial lines are strict, but I've matured a lot. I come from a background where I mixed with all sorts of people, and it was kind of a shock to come here and see how it is. But I know I'm getting a good education, and I'm glad I've stayed."

UNIVERSITY OF LOUISVILLE

Address: Houchens Building, Louisville, KY 40292
Phone: (502) 588-6531 / (800) 334-8635
Director of Admissions: Dr. Robert Parrent
Multicultural Student Recruiter: Reginald K. Meeks
1991–92 tuition: $1,800 (in-state)
Room and board: $1,500
Application deadline: Rolling admissions
Financial aid application deadline: 4/15
Non-white freshman admissions: Applicants for the class of '96: na
  Accepted: na
  Accepted who enroll: na
  Applicants accepted who rank in top 10% of high school class: na
  Median SAT: na
  Median ACT: na
Full-time undergraduate enrollment: 18,333
  Men: 47.5%
  Women: 52.5%
Non-white students in
  1987–88: 10.8%
  1988–89: 11.3%
  1989–90: 11.6%
  1990–91: 12.3%
Geographic distribution of students: na
Students In-state: 90.4%
Top majors: 1. Accounting 2. Biology 3. Chemistry

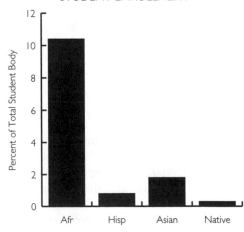

STUDENT ENROLLMENT

Percent of Total Student Body

Afr   Hisp   Asian   Native

Retention rate of non-white students: 72.1%

Scholarships exclusively for non-white students: Woodford R. Porter Scholarship: full tuition for four years; renewable; merit-based; 50 awarded each year. Woodford R. Porter Achiever Award: includes tuition and room and board; merit-based; renewable; eight awarded each year. Black Achiever Award: membership in YMCA Black Achievers program; 3.0 GPA required.

Remediation programs: na

Academic support services: The university's Center for Academic Achievement and Office of Minority Services provides academic and non-academic support programs.

Ethnic studies programs: The university offers Pan-African Studies.

Ethnic studies courses: na

Organizations for non-white students: Alpha Phi Alpha, *Louisville Messenger* (newspaper), Phi Beta Sigma, NAACP, Delta Sigma Theta, Society of Porter Scholars, Zeta Phi Beta, Alpha Kappa Alpha, Black Engineers and Technicians Association, Omega Psi Phi

Notable non-white alumni: na

Tenured faculty: 707

Non-tenured faculty: 460

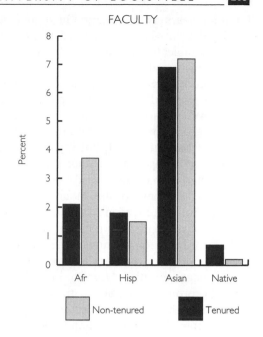

FACULTY

Non-tenured / Tenured

Student-faculty ratio: 19:1

Administrators: 227

  African-American: 9.7%

  Hispanic: 0.9%

  Asian-American: 0.4%

  Native American: 0

Recent non-white speakers on campus: na

Whoever said that schools don't give much back to their communities obviously wasn't thinking of the University of Louisville, a large public university that has supplied its home state of Kentucky with an impressive number of professionals. According to the university, 42 percent of the state's doctors are U of L graduates, as are 81 percent of the state's dentists, 34 percent of the state's lawyers, and 48 percent of the state's engineers.

These facts, however, aren't what impress most students at this sports-crazed school. Twice during the 1980s, Cardinal basketball teams won NCAA Division I championships; the school's football team won the 1990 Fiesta Bowl; and, a fact that hasn't gone unnoticed by most students, the school's cheerleading squad won national championships in 1986 and 1988. Now that's impressive.

Don't let them fool you, however; students here are also out to get a fine education. The university is divided into 11 schools and colleges, each of which has its own requirements and curriculum. The School of Business, located in a new complex, is popular and allows students to earn degrees in accountancy, equine administration, finance, or management. Qualified business students are able to participate in a program with the school's own graduate school of business in which students study for three years as an undergraduate and two years in the business school. Among the departments in the College of Arts and Sciences, students say chemistry, history, and communication are strong, while the Schools of Nursing, Music, and Engineering are also respected by students.

It should come as no surprise that classes at Kentucky's largest university tend to be large, especially during the first and second years. Students say, however, that upper-level courses decrease in size significantly. For academic support, students turn to the Center for Academic Achievement, which offers tutoring and other services. "A lot of students use it, but it gets to be a bit cliquey and social sometimes, so I had to stop going," says a student.

Although it no longer provides academic assistance, the Office of Minority Services is, as one student attests, "a home away from home. But," he adds, "a lot of African-American students on campus don't use it because they perceive it as being a place for militants. I'm not really sure why that is. But if the university worked to include it more in freshmen orientation, then it probably would become more popular." The office offers outreach to area high school students, and publishes a yearly magazine titled *Minority Voices,* which highlights students and events in the area. According to a student, the office also hosts afternoon mixers, usually about twice a month, as well as a lecture series during Black History Month. The school's gospel choir, the Black Diamond Choir, is also organized through the office. Carolyn Stephenson, director of the office, "is down-to-earth and tells it like it is," says a fan.

Other than the Office of Minority Services, the university student groups appear less than involved. "When I first got here, the Association of Black Students did a lot of things," says a senior. "Now we only have about fifteen active members, and we used to have more like fifty active members. Most students seem apathetic about the issues. I'm hoping that will change. Some of us are working to start a mentor program, informally with friends. The black Greek organizations also haven't been very active. Two years ago, the Deltas and the Alphas brought Malcolm X's daughter to campus, and that was reasonably successful. I think the black Greek organizations are sort of on a seven-year cycle; they hit peaks and valleys."

Outside of a recent production of the play *The Meeting,* the Minority Programming Committee and the Minority Project Fund Committee, both student-run organizations, also seem to have become dormant in recent years. "The MPC does sponsor a talent show." The historically black Greek organizations put on a twice-yearly step show at an off-campus theater.

The Multicultural Center, opened in 1991, is working to fill gaps left by some of the student groups. The center's director is Linda Wilson, who had been an associate director at the Center for Academic Achievement. The Multicultural Center serves mostly to provide cultural activities for students, and has worked recently with the school's women's and interfaith centers. The center recently co-sponsored an event with the Crane House, a Chinese cultural center in Louisville, as well as a powwow. But the center isn't looked upon favorably by the majority of the school's African-American students, who had earlier demanded that a Black Cultural Center be established on campus. "African-American students look down on students who go to the center," says a student.

Louisville offers a variety of activities, especially for those 21 and over. The famous

Kentucky Derby is held near the city, and there is also the Kentucky Center for the Arts. On campus, students can often be found at the school's new five-and-a-half-acre Student Activities Center.

Positive cultural interaction among students, alas, remains elusive for the most part at this state university. But the school's variety and depth of academic opportunities could make four years here worthwhile. Says a recent graduate: "I'm glad I came, because it's definitely the real world. Louisville was no bubble or fantasy world like I always thought it would be at college, but I'm confident I've earned a solid education."

LOUISIANA

LOUISIANA STATE UNIVERSITY AND AGRICULTURAL AND MECHANICAL COLLEGE

Address: Baton Rouge, LA 70803
Phone: (504) 388-1175
Director of Admissions: Lisa Harris
Multicultural Student Recruiter: na

1992–93 tuition: $2,376 (in-state); $4,026 (out-of-state)
Room and board: $1,690
Application deadline: 7/1
Financial aid application deadline: 3/1

Louisiana State University students have never let having a good time get in the way of their studies, but solid academics—which have prepared many a graduate for state politics and leadership positions—are there for the asking. The school has a respected honors program and the extracurriculars that only a large university could offer.

Located in the state capital, Louisiana State remains very Southern. Nearly 90 percent of the student body comes from Louisiana, most from small towns and cities. "I visited a friend who goes to Tulane in New Orleans [where out-of-state enrollment includes many New Yorkers and New Jerseyites] and that school seemed very Northern to me. I wasn't into that. I like it here because everyone always says hi to you. There's definitely that Cajun down-home feeling here."

The school's Southern identity manifests itself in other ways as well. Some of the facilities are named for famous Southern gentlemen, and General Sherman gave to the university the two cannons that sit in front of the Military and Aerospace Science Studies Building. Segregation along racial lines still permeates much of campus life, but that, says a student, "is being whittled away a little bit at a time."

As evidence, students point to the naming of a new classroom building after A. P. Turreaud, a prominent New Orleans civil rights lawyer who had successfully sued the state to integrate the university; Turreaud's son was the first African-American to enter the university as a student in the 1950s. The university also recently opened a new African-American Cultural Center, located across from the Student Union. The center, which will serve as a cultural resource for students and faculty, has a library and an art gallery and hosts forums and concerts.

As additional progress, students point to the house of Alpha Phi Alpha fraternity—a predominantly black Greek organization—on Greek row. "I have friends who are Kappa Alphas, who live across the street, and many of them resent us living on the row, but things are getting better," says an Alpha. "After a request from the Greek Council [which represents all of the school's Greek organizations], the KAs took down their Confederate flag, so now they only use it for their Old South Day [when the brothers glorify life before the Civil War]. The sorority row is very white, and it will probably take more time to integrate that area."

The student body also saw something new when they attended a recent Songfest, an annual event coordinated by the Greek Steering Committee, a 10-member committee that includes an African-American. "The Songfest is one of the biggest and oldest traditions at LSU. All the Greek organizations sing onstage, and it's always well attended. It's always been all-white, until last year, when Alpha Tau Omega, which is heavily black, was paired with a white sorority. Things are starting to change around here, that's for sure."

Free-Speech Alley offers a chance for students to vent their feelings about almost any topic, including racism. The event, which takes place every Wednesday at 6:30 p.m. "to whenever" is open to everyone and is kept organized by a moderator. "Free-Speech Alley always gets a large turnout and always focuses on heavy topics," says a student. "People preach, people talk about whatever's on their minds. Students have discussed everything from Malcolm X to the meaning of the Confederate flag. People respect the process, although many minds probably aren't changed by the speeches."

Nowhere is the campus more integrated than in the Student Government Association, which oversees the funding of all student activities and clubs. Of the 39 SGA officers, eight are African-American, including its vice president, and in 1990 the SGA president was African-American. "We've never had a Black Student Association at LSU. One reason is probably that we've always been so involved in different areas of the campus that we haven't felt the need for one," says a student leader.

A group of students did gather recently to draft a constitution for a Black Student Alliance, but the group has yet to get off the ground. "A lot of organizations do their part to promote black awareness," says a student. "The Black Culture Committee [part of the Student Union] sponsors art shows, speakers, and forums. A recent forum had to do with Malcolm X. And the black Greek organizations have a lot of dances and parties, at least one every weekend. Maybe it's been good we didn't have a central black student group, because perhaps then we wouldn't have gotten involved in the SGA and elsewhere the way we have."

None of the predominantly black Greek organizations are as active as Alpha Phi Alpha, which was named chapter of the year by the fraternity's national organization in 1990 and 1991. One of Alphas' most ambitious projects is to open their house, which can accommodate up to 13 students, for the summer to at-risk students from the area. "This is the first year we tried it. We invited eight high school students, aged thirteen to fifteen, to move into the house for the summer, and we [Alphas] served as counselors and we tutored them in English and math. We also did fun things with them, like take them swimming." The sororities aren't going to be outdone. The women of Delta Sigma Theta recently sponsored a forum as a salute to the achievements of African-American women.

Louisiana State offers plenty of opportunity in such disciplines as physics, chemistry, and accounting, which are among the school's toughest and most popular programs. Journalism, history, anthropology, and geography rank among the school's best liberal arts programs. Students who can't find what they want at Louisiana State are able to enroll in courses at Southern University, a predominantly black institution of higher learning located across town. (A fair amount of good-spirited competition exists between students at the schools as to which school provides the better education.)

"The Civil Rights Movement," "African-American History," and "Blacks in Politics" earn high marks from students as some of the school's best courses in these areas. The dean of the school's junior college, Carolyn Collins, is described by one student as "very intelligent and very down-to-earth." Collins is the first African-American to be an academic dean at LSU. Huel Perkins, executive assistant to Louisiana's chancellor, "is an esteemed educator, and will always speak at an event if we ask him. If you ever need to be uplifted, talk to him." "Like a mom," to many students, is Nona Mack, in the English department, who oversees the school's Summer Scholars program, an orientation for incoming students of color.

Perhaps the greatest source of support on campus is Gwyn Snearl, director of the school's Office of Minority Student Services and present head of Louisiana State's Black Faculty Caucus. "She helps us with everything, from getting tutors to programming events," says a student who relies on the office frequently. The office also oversees the publication of *Genesis,* a student-run newspaper.

Baton Rouge doesn't exactly provide a wealth of off-campus social opportunities, so most students tend to stay on campus for parties and other activities. "Baton Rouge has little culture," says a student. "The city is very laid-back, quiet, and filled mostly with yuppies." Students say race relations aren't a problem in the city. One popular nightspot for Louisiana State's African-American students is Onyx. New Orleans, about thirty minutes south, is a popular destination for the adventurous.

Louisiana State can't be called a hub of multicultural activity. But with the good works of several student groups, such as the Student Government Association, the school is more inclusive than other large Southern universities. If you are looking for a place where you can assume leadership positions, and be groomed for Louisiana politics (a common aspiration for many Louisiana State student leaders), Louisiana State deserves to be high on your list of college choices. "I've been happy during my time here, and sometimes I think of it as a four-year vacation," says a student. "There are times, though, when I think I should have gone to Southern University, but I wouldn't have had many of the opportunities I've had here, and the chance to meet different types of people, something I definitely need to learn, as I plan to serve in Louisiana state politics."

TULANE UNIVERSITY

Address: 6823 St. Charles, 210 Gibson Hall, New Orleans, LA 70118
Phone: (504) 865-5731
Director of Admissions: Richard Whiteside
Multicultural Student Recruiter: Robert Ruiz
1993–94 tuition: $18,500
Room and board: $5,780
Application deadline: 1/15
Financial aid application deadline: 2/1
Non-white freshman admissions: Applicants for the class of '96: 1,305
Accepted: 66%
Accepted who enroll: 25%
Applicants accepted who rank in top 10% of high school class: 47%
In top 25%: 75%
Median SAT: na
Median ACT: na
Full-time undergraduate enrollment: 6,762
Men: 50%
Women: 50%

STUDENT ENROLLMENT

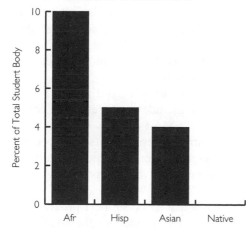

Non-white students in
1988–89: 15.6%
1989–90: 16.2%
1990–91: 16.7%
1991–92: 18%

Geographic distribution of students: na
Top majors: 1. English 2. Psychology 3. History
Retention rate of non-white students: 90%
Scholarships exclusively for non-white students: None
Remediation programs: None
Academic support services: The Educational Resource Center provides supplemental instruction, tutoring, and study skills workshops.
Ethnic studies programs: Tulane's Latin American Studies program is interdisciplinary and includes more than 150 courses taught by more than 80 faculty members from 17 departments.
Ethnic studies courses: The university's History department offers a minor in African-American Studies, and the English department includes a course in Chinese-American studies.
Organizations for non-white students: African-American Congress of Tulane, Alpha Kappa Alpha, Alpha Phi Alpha, Black Lawyers of Tomorrow, Black Social Workers Association, Caribbean Student Association, Delta Sigma Theta, National Society of Black Engineers, Tulane African Student Association, Tulane University Black Professional Association, People's Republic of China Organization, Taiwanese Student Organization, Tulane University Vietnamese Association, La Alianza del Derecho (Hispanic law organization), Latin American Student Association
Notable non-white alumnus: Harold Sylvester ('68; actor)
Tenured faculty: 6.2% (total non-white)
Non-tenured faculty: 13.7% (total non-white)
Student-faculty ratio: 13:1
Administrators: na
Recent non-white speakers on campus: Spike Lee (filmmaker); Jesse Jackson (former

U.S. presidential candidate and civil rights activist); Alfredo Cristiani (president of El Salvador); Gloria Naylor (author)

Tulane University offers outstanding opportunities for students interested in academic and social pursuits. For many, the biggest challenge of their four years here is finding the balance between the two.

Latin American Studies is one of Tulane's most respected programs and offers more than 150 courses taught by 82 faculty members from 17 departments. The Roger Thayer Stone Center for Latin American Studies, one of the three most comprehensive such centers in the country, includes more than 200,000 volumes about the region and coordinates summer research trips to various Latin American countries.

Other top programs include architecture and engineering, which received a boost recently with the dedication of the new Lindy Claiborne Boggs Center for Energy and Biotechnology. The school's undergraduate business school is also housed in impressive new facilities, Godring/Woldenberg Hall.

Tulane's liberal arts division includes the H. Sophie Newcomb Memorial College, for women, and the College of Arts and Sciences, for men. Both divisions share the same curriculum and faculty, but have different administrations. Within these colleges, students praise the biology, history, and psychology departments. The English department also gets positive reviews from students, particularly for recruiting a more racially diverse faculty. "The English faculty is always willing to listen to students, and it has worked the hardest to include multicultural themes and courses into its curriculum," says a student. As evidence, students point to "Southern Literature," a course that includes works of Zora Neale Hurston, Alice Walker, and Richard Wright. The course's professor, Rebecca Mark, "is accessible and very good in the classroom," comments a student. "If she can't help you, then she will refer you to someone who can." Felipe Smith, also an English professor, is well respected by students. "He's an excellent teacher. It's not what he has done for the students that earns him our respect. We respect him because he is so intelligent. He personifies intelligence." Ron Mason, a vice president of Tulane, and Francis Dodoo, a sociology professor, are also well regarded and helpful to students.

Tulane's African and African Diaspora program, established during the 1992–93 school year and offered as a minor course of study, includes such respected courses as "African Civilizations" and "Western Africa." Most of the courses in the program are from the English, History, and Sociology departments. The program is complemented by the university's Amistad Research Center, which contains the country's second largest collection of research materials and papers of African-Americans.

In the words of one student, "All of the school's academic support programs are helpful," particularly its Educational Resource Center, located in the Mechanical Engineering Building. "The center is especially good for tutoring and self-help workshops," says a student. The Office of Multicultural Affairs, in the University Center, also provides programs and support services to students. Some of the programs it has co-sponsored with student groups are a Black Arts Festival, International Week, and an Anti-Apartheid Week. The office's adviser, Carolyn Barber-Pierre, is "great, perfect," says a student. "She's a people person. She's understanding, and always willing to listen to students. I just wish the administration would give her more money so she could do more."

The African-American Congress at Tulane (ACT), a student group, includes about 140 active members. ACT members meet every other week, usually on Sundays, in the ACT lounge, located in the basement of the University Center. The lounge houses a small library of African-American literature and African art. The activities sponsored by ACT members include the annual Black Arts Festival, which lasts from January through April. A part of campus life for more than 25 years, the festival brings artists, authors, and musical groups to campus. Another popular event coordinated by ACT members is the annual Martin Luther King Week for Peace, in which Tulane students march with students from nearby Xavier, a historically black university, and Loyola, through the three campuses. Student forums and films are also part of the week-long festivities. "They are always well-received and hundreds march," says a student who has helped organize the events. "The events usually draw a racially and ethnically mixed crowd." ACT members also sponsor a Kwanzaa celebration each December, and an African Freedom Week, which includes speakers and films.

The school's Latin American Student Association sponsors a film series each year, as well as dances, conferences, musical performances, and speeches on Latin America. LASA sponsors some of these events in conjunction with the Stone Center.

The social life at Tulane is a little like the social life in New Orleans—hopping! Students say that on most any night of the week there are several major parties being held on campus, while Fridays are reserved for the campus-wide TGIF party, complete with live bands and plenty of beer. The university's predominantly white fraternities also sponsor numerous blockbuster parties throughout the school year, but students say that few students of color attend these events. "The minority students rarely mix with white students here, even in the bars off campus," says a student.

Students say that relations between the school's predominantly white Greek organizations and Tulane's students of color have been less than cordial. In 1987, Delta Kappa Epsilon, a predominantly white fraternity, was kicked off campus by the administration after members had marched around campus dressed in Ku Klux Klan outfits and black face, and in 1990 a cross was burned on the front lawn of the Delta Tau Delta fraternity allegedly because it had planned to pledge an African-American student. Members of the fraternity deny involvement in the incident.

When it comes to social events, racial integration has been slow coming to Tulane, adds a student. "Our school is multicultural, but we don't mix at all. This year things are changing, but just a little. We've [ACT] sponsored movies with TUCP (Tulane University Campus Programming), an organization we've had problems with in the past. TUCP has always acted as if they didn't want multicultural students on their committee. But different student groups have put pressure on TUCP to become more integrated and to diversify its offerings, so they've reached out more."

New Orleans offers plenty of off-campus social opportunities, especially when it comes to Mardi Gras, perhaps the country's biggest party. New Orleans, the birthplace of jazz, also has numerous well-known music clubs, bars, and theaters that are owned or managed by African-Americans. Other than some off-campus community service projects, students say there is little interaction with city residents, however.

New Orleans, which is predominantly African-American, is also one of the most racially segregated large cities in the south.

Tulane is not a politically active campus. According to an article in *The New York Times,* there was a stark contrast to the reactions to the Gulf War between the Xavier and Tulane campuses. At Tulane, the article says, "the war brought few protesters and no student editorials" in the campus newspaper. In reference to the Duke campaign, an ACT member says, "I felt people were disgusted and relieved when he ran and lost, but no one really protested against his campaign."

Attending school at Tulane can be "a difficult experience," says one student, pointing to the lack of integration in many aspects of campus life and the relatively few students of color on campus. Adds another student: "I've had a good experience here, especially since I've taken the opportunity to get involved in so many of Tulane's activities." One student summed up: "Tulane has a respectable academic reputation, and that's what I'm here for—the academics."

XAVIER UNIVERSITY OF LOUISIANA

Address: 7325 Palmetto Street, New Orleans, LA 70125

Phone: (504) 483-7577

Director of Admissions: Winston Brown

Multicultural Student Recruiter: Sondra Reine

1991–92 tuition: $5,800

Room and board: $3,200

Application deadline: 3/1

Financial aid application deadline: 5/1

Non-white freshman admissions: Applicants for the class of '95: 1,832

Accepted: 91%

Accepted who enroll: 37%

Applicants accepted who rank in top 10% of high school class: 36%

In the top 25%: 64%

Median SAT: 433 V, 464 M

Median ACT: 20.5

Full-time undergraduate enrollment: 3,071

Men: 32%

Women: 68%

Non-white students in

1987–88: 91.3%

1988–89: 91.5%

1989–90: 93%

1990–91: 91.4%

Geographic distribution of students: na

Students In-state: 64%

Top majors: 1. Pharmacy 2. Biology 3. Business Administration

Retention rate of non-white students: 77%–80%

Scholarships exclusively for non-white students: In a recent year, the university awarded 209 scholarships to incoming students. The average value of each award: $1,850.

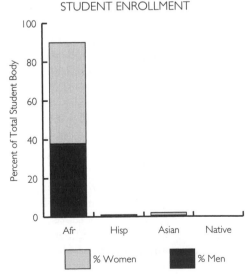

STUDENT ENROLLMENT

Percent of Total Student Body

Afr   Hisp   Asian   Native

% Women   % Men

Remediation programs: Non-credit courses in English, math, and reading are offered.

Academic support services: Tutoring is available in most academic subjects.

Ethnic studies programs: None

Ethnic studies courses: The college offers "Economics of Black America," "Afro-American Literature," "Afro-American Music," "Black Politics," "Survey of Africa," "The Black Family in Urban Society," and "Religion in Africa," although African-American perspectives are integrated into most courses.

Organizations for non-white students: Alpha Phi Alpha, Alpha Kappa Alpha, Omega Psi Phi, Zeta Phi Beta, Kappa Alpha Psi, Delta Sigma Theta, Phi Beta Sigma

Notable non-white alumni: Annabell Bernard ('56, Music; opera singer); Norman C. Francis ('52, Math; educator); Claude Organ ('47, Chemistry; surgeon); General Bernard Randolph ('51, Chemistry); John Scott ('62, Art; artist and educator)

Tenured faculty: 70

Non-tenured faculty: 122

Student-faculty ratio: 14:1

Administrators: 30
  African-American: 70%
  Hispanic: 3.3%
  Asian-American: 0
  Native American: 0

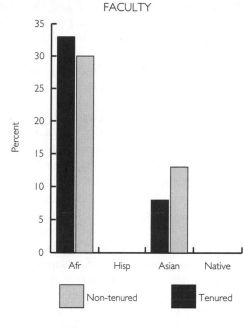

FACULTY

Recent non-white speakers on campus: Douglas Wilder (governor of Virginia); Barbara Fields (historian, Columbia University); Dr. Franklin Knight (historian, Johns Hopkins University); Margaret Washington (author); Portia Maultsby (ethnologist and chairperson of the black music department at Indiana State University)

It's no wonder a high percentage of Xavier University's alumni send their progeny to this small, historically black college in the heart of New Orleans. They want their sons and daughters to be treated to the same top-flight liberal arts education they had.

Perhaps they also have their eye on getting that son or daughter into medical school. The university has made national headlines in recent years for its excellent programs and its equally impressive record of getting students accepted into medical schools. In fact, Xavier ranks second only to the much larger Howard University—which has its own medical school—and ahead of such powerhouses as Harvard and Stanford in getting African-American students into medical school. The 68-year-old university also offers an outstanding pharmacy program. Nearly half of Xavier's graduates major in the sciences, while the national average at other colleges is just 7 percent.

What accounts for the school's success? In a *New York Times* article titled "Tiny

Black College Takes High Road in Sciences," a reporter writes: "A small group of determined professors, helped by several foundation grants they drummed up, designed a system combining introductory courses that build in remedial work with student tutoring and study groups, individual attention from faculty, and outreach to budding high school scientists." Or as J. W. Carmichael, a chemistry professor, explained in the same article: "The typical college faculty member sees his job as weeding out kids who come into science courses, in the interest of maintaining quality. I could always drop people from a helicopter into Lake Pontchartrain and see how many drown. But what we do is start from the shore and teach them how to swim." In 1990, Carmichael, who is responsible for much of the school's success, was named Professor of the Year by the Council for the Advancement and Support of Education.

Xavier boasts strengths outside of the sciences as well, in education, business administration, music, and political science. "A recent push by students has been to get an African-American Studies program here at Xavier," says a student. Popular African-American Studies courses are currently available in literature, religion, and psychology. Students say professors are accessible and friendly. One standout is John Scott, head of the art department. "He knows the history of Xavier, and of the civil rights movement, and a lot of students like to go to him and just sit and talk," says a student.

As the Western Hemisphere's only black Catholic institution of higher learning, Xavier "is only Catholic in certain ways so as not to make you feel inhibited," students say. However, all campus dorms are single-sex (there is no visitation allowed in the opposite sex's dorm), an invitation to have Louis Farrakhan, head of the Nation of Islam, speak was denied by the administration, and attending Mass is a Sunday-morning thing to do for many students. "But it's not a strict Mass; many students attend who are from a variety of religious backgrounds. The school's gospel choir performs and the whole congregation gets involved." Nearly half of the school's undergraduate population is Catholic.

Despite the university's relatively small size and close faculty-student interaction, Xavier graduates only 36 percent of its students within five years, as opposed to the usual 65 to 75 percent at other schools. Most often, students leave for financial reasons. However, the school's Freshman Program, which includes peer mentoring, is effective, say students, in large part because of the efforts of Denford Smith, freshman dean. "His motto is: 'Students first,' and you can always count on him to live up to it," says a student.

When not studying, Xavier students can often be found on the patio, an area on the side of the school's student center, where on most Friday afternoons there's a DJ or a reggae singing group. Within the Greek system, the Delta Sigma Thetas, the Alpha Phi Alphas, and the Alpha Kappa Alphas are particularly active. Twice during the year all the Greek organizations sponsor a step show, coordinated by the Panhellenic Council. The Student Government Association sponsors an assortment of activities, including a Dating Game. Student government members from the first-year class have their own executive board, and each year the class sponsors regular picnics, talent shows, and a Mr. Freshman contest, "a sort of Mr. Hunk contest," says a student.

For cultural activity, African-Americans With a Responsibility to Enlighten (AWARE), a student group, sponsors a Kwanzaa celebration featuring "a big expo in the gymnasium that has vendors selling all sorts of Afrocentric items, including T-shirts and jewelry. There's also entertainment provided, such as a reggae band," says a student. "A big issue this year on campus was a No [David] Duke Campaign. We worked with students from Dillard, Loyola, and Tulane universities. We went to each other's campuses for rallies just before the elections, and we walked people to the polls and made sure people voted," says a political science major.

While most students hail from Southern states, some are from places as distant as New York, Chicago, the Bahamas, and the Virgin Islands. Women have a tough time of it in the dating department at Xavier, since less than a third of the student body is of the male gender. "It's great for us, but not so for the women," says a male student. Students say that most of their classmates are liberal, but there is a small conservative population on campus.

With Mardi Gras and all sorts of bars and clubs, New Orleans is many a pre-college student's dream of a college town. "I was into it at first, but then you realize that it's all for the tourists, and that you've also got to study." The city offers a smorgasbord of cultural nightlife, with many fine restaurants, orchestras, and theaters.

While Xavier may lack the SAT scores of Morehouse and Spelman, also historically black colleges, there's no denying the success of Xavier graduates. Students also appreciate the opportunity to learn in an environment that is characterized by peer support and a tight-knit African-American community. "I'm glad I came here. I've learned to relate to a lot of different types of people within my own culture," says a student. "I've learned how to bond with people, and how to talk and to listen. Four years here really allows you to get your act together, helps instill in you a sense of pride and history. I don't think I could have gotten all of this at many other places."

M A I N E

BATES COLLEGE

Non-white freshman admissions: Applicants
  for the class of '95: 374
  Accepted: 44%
  Accepted who enroll: 25%
  Applicants accepted who rank in top
  10% of high school class: na
  Median SAT: na
  Median ACT: na
Full-time undergraduate enrollment: 1,500
  Men: 50%
  Women: 50%
Non-white students in
  1987–88: 5.7%
  1988–89: 6.5%
  1989–90: 7.2%
  1990–91: 10%
Students In-state: 2.3%
Top majors: 1. Political Science
  2. Psychology 3. Economics
Retention rate of non-white students: 82%
**Scholarships exclusively for non-white
  students:** Benjamin E. Mays Scholarships:
  need-based; amount varies; five to ten
  awarded each year; renewable;
  available to students of all races,

STUDENT ENROLLMENT

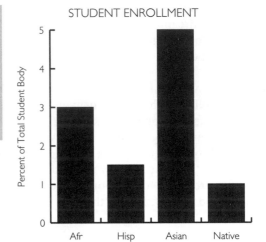

GEOGRAPHIC DISTRIBUTION OF STUDENTS

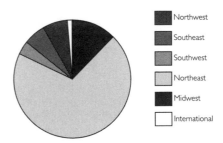

but preference given to students of
color.
Remediation programs: None
Academic support services: Tutoring is

available in most academic subjects, as well as writing workshops.

Ethnic studies programs: In 1991, Bates established a major course of study in African-American Studies.

Ethnic studies courses: Japanese-language instruction is offered at the elementary and intermediate levels. The history department offers three courses in Chinese Studies, four courses in Japanese Studies, and one course in Latin American Studies. Political science offers "Politics of Latin America." Other departments, such as philosophy and religion, offer East Asian Studies courses.

Organizations for non-white students: Bates Asian Society, Amandla! African-American Society, Hispanic-American Club

Notable non-white alumni: Dr. John A. Kenney, Jr. (Biology; dermatologist/physician); David O. Boone (Economics; president and CEO, Boone Young and Associates); Rev. Peter J. Gomes (History; professor, Harvard University); Karen Hastie Williams (Government; attorney); Bryant Gumbel (History; host, NBC's *Today*)

Tenured faculty: 66

Non-tenured faculty: 99

Student-faculty ratio: 12:1

Administrators: 92
   African-American: 6.5%
   Hispanic: 1%
   Asian-American: 0
   Native American: 0

Recent non-white speakers on campus:

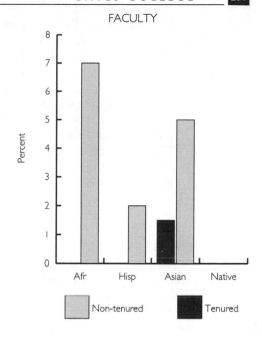

FACULTY

Beverly Guy Sheftall (director, Women's Research and Resource Center, Spelman College); Tony Harris (counselor); James Farmer (civil rights activist and co-founder of the Congress of Racial Equality); Angela Davis (political activist); Ruth Hsiao (lecturer in Asian-American literature, Tufts University); Byllye Avery (executive director, National Black Women's Health Project); Dith Pran (Cambodian journalist and refugee); Ntozake Shange (poet and playwright)

There aren't many colleges or universities that can boast of having been founded by abolitionists with a genuine sense of racial and religious tolerance, but Bates College can. Says the Bates catalogue: "The College was founded [in 1855] by people who felt strongly about human freedom, civil rights, and a higher education for all. . . . It was not by accident that Bates was the first coeducational college in New England; from its beginning the College admitted students without regard to race, religion, national origin, or sex."

The founders' spirit remains at Bates, as the Bates community seems to be truly that—a community. This communal spirit is most evident in the college's housing arrangements. You won't find any exclusive fraternities or sororities at Bates, nor are there select eating societies, as there are at other prominent New England colleges and universities. The living options range from traditional residence halls, which house about two-thirds of the campus population, to Victorian houses, each of which can accommodate about 10 to 30 usually upperclass students. No matter where students live, however, all eat together on the same meal plan in the Commons in Chase Hall.

Bates attracts a largely tolerant, progressive-minded student body. As one student describes a recent school year on campus: "The Bates campus is politically and racially aware. A large portion of the student body protested President Bush's decision in the Persian Gulf. The Democratic Socialists of America is the most active political group on campus, and Bates students definitely know what apartheid is." The student newspaper, *The Bates Student,* is known for its more liberal slant.

But students do complain that there tends to be little interaction between the various cultures on campus, even activities involving international students. "Ethnic groups stick together here, in dating, partying, and dining. In the Commons, you will always find a table with international students, and one with black students."

Bates is strictly a liberal arts college. There are no teaching assistants here, and class sizes are small, all of which can make for an intense learning experience. Students praise their professors for their knowledge of their subjects and their ability to teach. One such professor is Yang Ye, who teaches Chinese literature. "Rumor has it that he aided the student movement in China by faxing many documents to students," says a student. Other strong and supportive faculty members include Atsuko Hirai, a history professor; Peter Ngai-Sing Wong, an assistant math professor; Leslie Hill, a political science instructor; Patrick Nickoletti, an instructor in psychology; and Marcus Bruce, an assistant professor of religion.

For additional support, students are able to turn to James Alonzo Reese, an assistant dean of students, who works closely with students of color. "He is definitely the most popular dean on campus. He is always willing to listen, he will not patronize you, and he really cares about how you feel."

The most popular majors are political science, psychology, and economics, and students say these departments are also among the school's best. Philosophy and Asian Studies are also popular. The chemistry and biology departments, housed in the recently renovated Carnegie Science Hall and Dana Chemistry Hall, are said to be excellent. And Bates's Olin Arts Center provides impressive music and art studios for students.

In 1991, the school established its first majors in African-American and American Cultural Studies. Students report that courses in these areas are so popular that getting into them can be difficult. Some of the more respected courses are "Racism, Sexism, and Oppression," "Blacks in America," and "Slavery in America."

To graduate, Bates students must satisfy general education requirements (GERs), which include courses in the sciences, quantitative reasoning, the social sciences, the humanities, and physical education. To prove that they've learned the material, Bates seniors must take a comprehensive exam in their major field or write a senior thesis. Some students complain about the number of GERs—12 of the 32 courses required for graduation. But students find the school's innovative 4-4-1 academic calendar— which allows them to pursue independent study projects or internships on or off campus in May—adds diversity to the curriculum. Some recent on-campus Short

Term units, as the May program is called, have included environmental studies, "The Central American Crisis in Historical Perspective," and theater production, while off-campus Short Term internships have taken students to hospitals, state and local legislatures, and schools as student teachers. Students are also able to study overseas as part of the Short Term.

When it comes to cultural diversity, Bates, like other Maine colleges and universities, comes in on the more homogeneous side of the spectrum. But three cultural student groups—the African-American Society, the Hispanic-American Club, and the Bates Asian Society—work to provide campus awareness of their issues and to provide peer support. "The organizations are vocal and somewhat active, but it's hard to be influential with only a handful of people. But that is changing. Organizations have begun to involve themselves more in campus-wide activities and not just activities for members. That has helped tremendously to educate the campus and not only the minorities."

The Afro-Am, as the African-American Society is commonly referred to on campus, is the most active group, sponsoring a Black Arts Week, poetry readings, plays, a film series, dance ensembles, and lectures. In addition, "the group has always kept the Bates campus informed of racial incidents through the student newspaper and posters, and in my opinion the Bates community has welcomed such information," says a student. One such incident that drew campus-wide attention was the group's successful attempt to get the campus community to boycott a nearby liquor store for a perceived racist remark made to an African-American Bates student. "The Afro-Am issued a very strongly worded protest in *The Bates Student* about the incident and organized meetings. As a result, many students resolved to boycott the store."

Other extracurricular activities are popular at the college. The school's debate team is nationally ranked. The Modern Dance Company, a student group, sponsors about five major performances a year, while various musical performance groups are also active. There are numerous other organizations, such as an Outing Club for the lover of the outdoors, a Gay-Lesbian-Straight Alliance, and a jazz band.

Lewiston is described by one student as "a mostly white lower-middle-class town where the residents aren't accustomed to seeing minorities. There's some mild tension, but Lewiston residents sometimes tend to resent all Bates students." The town has movie theaters, golf courses, theaters, and shops, but not very much nightlife. The surrounding area is good for skiing—cross-country and downhill—and other outdoor activities, such as boating and swimming. Portland, about a half hour south, and Boston, 180 miles south, are easily accessible by Greyhound or car.

Despite Bates's remoteness and cold weather—it's fortunate that L. L. Bean with its warm parkas for sale is nearby—students appreciate the Bates experience as much for its academic programs as for its progressive-minded student body. "I would recommend Bates very strongly," says a biology major. "I have managed to fit in very well. It was hard at first, but I did it. In a strange way, the experience of being the 'odd' one at times has given me a stronger sense of respect for and love of my roots and my culture. One learns to be more tolerant here." Adds another student: "Bates does not have an environment where free speech is suppressed. Anyone may have any kind of view on anything, and the opinion will be respected by most. Bates is the best place. You really grow as a person here."

BOWDOIN COLLEGE

Address: College Street, Brunswick, ME
  04011
Phone: (207) 725-3100
Director of Admissions: Richard Steele
Multicultural Student Recruiter: Staci
  Williams
1993–94 tuition: $17,975
Room and board: $5,855
Application deadline: Early decision: 11/15;
  regular decision: 1/15
Financial aid application deadline: 3/1
Non-white freshman admissions: Applicants
  for the class of '95: 281
  Accepted: 53%
  Accepted who enroll: 35%
  Applicants accepted who rank in top
  10% of high school class: na
  Median SAT: na
  Median ACT: na
Full-time undergraduate enrollment: 1,375
  Men: 57%
  Women: 43%

STUDENT ENROLLMENT

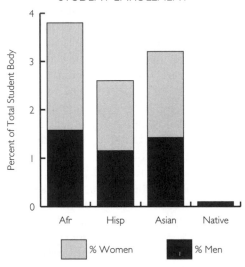

Non-white students in
  1987–88: 7%
  1988–89: 8%

GEOGRAPHIC DISTRIBUTION OF STUDENTS

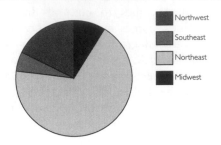

- Northwest
- Southeast
- Northeast
- Midwest

  1989–90: 9%
  1990–91: 9%
Students In-state: 5%
Top majors: 1. Government 2. Economics
  3. English
Retention rate of non-white students: 80%
**Scholarships exclusively for non-white
  students:** John B. Russwurm and
  Hispanic Scholarships: need-based;
  reduces loan portion of a student's
  financial aid package to $500 a year.
Remediation programs: None
Academic support services: The college
  offers tutoring in most subjects.
Ethnic studies programs: The college offers
  interdisciplinary programs in
  African-American Studies, Asian Studies,
  and Latin American Studies.
Organizations for non-white students:
  African-American Society, Latin
  American Student Organization, Asian
  Interest Group
Notable non-white alumni: Kenneth I.
  Chenault ('73; vice president, American
  Express); Dr. Cho Soon ('60; Deputy
  Prime Minister of the Republic of
  Korea); George H. Butcher ('72;
  Goldman, Sachs & Company); Michael
  Owens ('73; executive vice president and
  chief health officer, Watts Health
  Foundation)
Tenured faculty: 81
Non-tenured faculty: 38

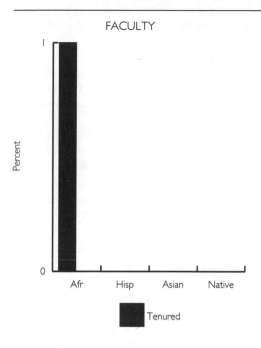

FACULTY

Percent

1

0

Afr   Hisp   Asian   Native

■ Tenured

Student-faculty ratio: 11:1
Administrators: na
  African-American: 4%
  Hispanic: 4%
  Asian-American: 0
  Native American: 0
Recent non-white speakers on campus:
  Ntozake Shange (poet and playwright);
  James Blackwell (emeritus sociology
  professor, University of
  Massachusetts/Boston); Byllye Avery
  (executive director, National Black
  Women's Health Project); Angela Davis
  (political activist); Kwame Toure
  (political activist)

Don't be too quick to overlook Bowdoin College, an excellent liberal arts college, just because of its location in rural Maine. True, the college *is* isolated and it's cold here much of the school year, but the academics and the beautiful surroundings rival those of almost any other prominent liberal arts college in the country.

The college, which will be celebrating its bicentennial in 1994, made news recently when its last all-male fraternity became coed. Bowdoin, which recognizes seven other fraternities, instituted the requirement in order to integrate women more into the college community. Bowdoin became coed in 1970, and currently about 43 percent of the school's 1,375 students are female. "You can't mandate equality in people's perceptions, but you can mandate equal treatment," says Jane Jervis, dean of the college, of the college's decision to have the fraternities become coed.

Academics at Bowdoin are competitive, and most students have a pre-professional bent, many wanting to become lawyers, doctors, and Wall Streeters. The college, however, has no set pre-professional programs and devotes itself solely to the liberal arts. Government and economics are the most popular majors, while students say the sciences—particularly chemistry and biology—are rigorous and top-notch. English and math are well regarded, and new programs in Asian and Arctic Studies win praise from students.

To graduate, students must satisfy distribution requirements in natural science and math, social and behavioral sciences, humanities and fine arts, and non-Eurocentric studies, which include courses in art, literature, religion, music, and politics. Courses in Afro-American and Native American Studies satisfy the requirement "when the emphasis is clearly on those cultures and their differences from the predominant culture of the United States." A first-year seminar must be completed; seminars have included such topics as Japanese mythology; computers, society, and thought; and the Vietnam War.

A committee of students and faculty is currently meeting to restructure the school's African-American Studies program. According to a student, most courses focus on African rather than African-American issues. "I took 'Political Economy of South Africa' my first year, which was offered as part of the African-American Studies program."

One of the benefits of attending such a small school is the chance to interact closely with faculty, many of whom students say are excellent teachers. Small class sizes are the norm, and students report it's not uncommon to be invited to a professor's home for dinner to continue class discussions. The dean of students office coordinates a tutoring program and helps to find tutors for students needing assistance. "The tutors are other students, so the effectiveness of the program depends on the knowledge of the student tutors," says a student.

The African-American Society, which has about 30 members, is the most "vocal" of Bowdoin's cultural student groups. "We sponsor dinners, dances, lectures, musical groups, dance troupes, films, and other types of performances that reflect positive, yet diverse, aspects of the African diaspora," reports a student member. Society members make use of the John Brown Russwurm African-American Center, named for the college's first African-American graduate, class of 1825. The center, known as the Am by students, has meeting rooms, an office for the director of the center, a reading room, and a 1,600-volume library of African and African-American materials. There are also living facilities in the center for two students.

The Latin American Student Organization sponsors films and guest speakers, including author Carlos Fuentes, as well as other cultural events. The Asian Interest Group, a new student group on campus, works with the admissions office to attract more Asian and Asian-American applicants, and also hosts biweekly dinner meetings, forums, and other social events.

Students would like to see the administration become more supportive of multicultural student groups. "The planning and execution of multicultural events rests solely with student of color organizations," says a student. Students voice disappointment in what they perceive as the administration's lack of commitment to issues of diversity on campus. "On November 2, 1990, the Coalition for Concerned Students—a multicultural group of students demanding more cultural programming—blockaded the administration's offices, and as a result the president, Robert Turner, established the Diversity Committee," says a student. "However, he has only come to one of our meetings. We've sent him memos requesting that he attend, and we've asked that his office come up with a professional plan to make the campus more diverse. But he hasn't responded to any of our requests." The Diversity Committee consists of students and faculty.

Students are able to find administrative support in Betty Thompson, in the college's counseling center. "She is very down-to-earth, yet spirited and full of energy," says a student. "She is active in many of the multicultural organizations. She has been at Bowdoin for only two years and I can truly say she is one of the most highly respected people on the campus—by the general student body, students of color, and the staff and administration." Dean of students Kenneth Lewellan is also considered a "personable" staff member. "He just doesn't sit in his office," says a student. "He keeps on top of things. He knows every student's first name, he eats lunch with students, and he approaches students for conversation." Faith Perry, a Bowdoin grad and the school's affirmative action officer and director of multicultural student affairs, "reaches out to students to see what it is we want. Although her office's budget is small, she always gets student input about what we would like to sponsor on campus."

Brunswick is a "bike ride away from the rocky shores and coves" of the Atlantic, and the city's Maine Street is lined with shops, restaurants, and galleries. It's about what you'd expect in a small town in Maine. Portland, just twenty-five miles south, offers a bit more excitement, and Boston is just two and a half hours south on I-95.

Maine schools—Colby College, Bates College, and the University of Maine among them—have a hard time when it comes to recruiting non-white students to their campuses, largely due to the state's small number of non-white residents, which limits cultural and social opportunities for students of color in the immediate area. To attend college in Maine, says a student, requires a high level of self-awareness. "I would recommend Bowdoin to students of color who have a strong sense of who they are and know what they want to get out of their education," says a campus leader. "Bowdoin provides many educational opportunities, but it offers very little for students of color beyond that. To survive at Bowdoin, persons of color really have to be comfortable with themselves. Bowdoin is not a place students of color can come to in order to find themselves."

COLBY COLLEGE

Address: Waterville, ME 04901
Phone: (202) 872-3168 / (800) 723-3032
Director of Admissions: Parker J. Beverage
Multicultural Student Recruiter: Roland M. Allen
1993–94 tuition: $17,840
Room and board: $5,540
Application deadline: 1/15
Financial aid application deadline: 1/15
Non-white freshman admissions: Applicants
  for the class of '96: 167
  Accepted: 67%
  Accepted who enroll: 27%
  Applicants accepted who rank in top
  10% of high school class: na
  In top 25%: na
  Median SAT: na
  Median ACT: na
Full-time undergraduate enrollment: 1,747
  Men: 48%

Women: 52%

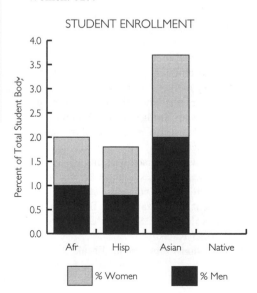

STUDENT ENROLLMENT

Percent of Total Student Body

% Women   % Men

Non-white students in
1988–89: 3.5%
1989–90: 4.7%
1990–91: 5.8%
1991–92: 7%
1992–93: 7.9%

GEOGRAPHIC DISTRIBUTION OF STUDENTS

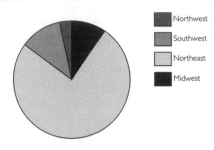

- Northwest
- Southwest
- Northeast
- Midwest

Students In-state: 13%
Top majors: 1. Government
2. Biology/Economics 3. English/Psychology
Retention rate of non-white students: 87%
**Scholarships exclusively for non-white
students:** Ralph J. Bunche Scholars
Program: need-based; 12 to 15 awarded
each year; $200 to $2,400 per each award.
Remediation programs: None
Academic support services: The college
offers tutoring in most academic subjects,
a Writing Center, and support for
students with learning disabilities.
Ethnic studies programs: Colby offers an
African-American Studies minor,
established in 1968, that is
interdisciplinary, involving more than 17
faculty members from various
departments. The college also offers an
East Asian Studies major. Minors are
also offered in Chinese and Japanese
languages.
Ethnic studies courses: Various Latin
American Studies courses are offered.
Organizations for non-white students:
Student Organization for Black and
Hispanic Unity, Students Organized
Against Racism
Notable non-white alumni: Frank O.

Apantaku ('70; surgeon, medical
director); Sebsibe M. Mamo ('78; former
Olympic athlete, Ethiopian relief worker);
William P. Mayaka ('73; deputy
secretary, Ministry of Agriculture,
Kenya); Henry J. Sockbeson III ('73;
directing attorney, Native American
Rights Fund); D. Omar Wynn ('74;
attorney); Lindsey Wynn ('75; IBM
executive)
Tenured faculty: 81
Non-tenured faculty: 57

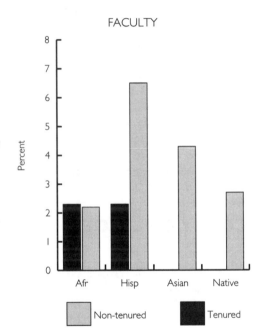

FACULTY

Student-faculty ratio: 10:1
Administrators: na
African-American: 4 total
Hispanic: 1 total
Asian-American: 1 total
Native American: 0
Recent non-white speakers on campus:
Maxine Hong Kingston (author); Sylvia
A. Boone (professor, Yale University);
Robert Franklin (professor, Emory
University); Christine Choy (filmmaker);
Bill Cosby; Lorene Cary (author)

To look at its L. L. Bean-clad, largely conservative student body, you would hardly know that Colby College has one of the more progressive histories in American higher education. The 180-year-old college was one of the first to establish an antislavery society, in 1871 it was among the first previously all-male schools in New England to admit women, and in 1961 it was the first to integrate a winter term course of study—which allows students to pursue on- or off-campus internships or research opportunities during the month of January—into its curriculum.

As part of its January Plan during a recent year, the college offered more than 80 courses, among them a seminar on William Faulkner, emergency medical training, Japanese- and German-language study, and off-campus study opportunities in Brazil, Russia, and London.

Students say that some of the school's best departments are English, economics, and government. Colby's Science Center has excellent teaching and research facilities for the study of biology, chemistry, geology, math, and physics. Psychology and foreign-language study are also said to be good. With over 500,000 volumes, Colby's Miller Library offers impressive resources, particularly for a school of its size.

The African-American Studies program is well thought of by students, who especially praise its "African-American Women Writers" course. "It's one of the school's more popular courses," reports a student. "It made me feel as if I was a teacher in the course because many of my classmates weren't aware of some of the issues that were discussed in class." "African-American Women and Social Change" is also popular. "We kept journals, talked about how we would solve problems," remembers a student. "There was something great about taking a course that was about you. It made me get into it more."

For academic support, students can rely on the Writing Center, located in Miller Library. To take full advantage of the center, students say, "it's best to make an appointment with one of the staff members or peer tutors." Colby's faculty are one of the college's best selling points. Faculty-student relations are extremely tight, and numerous faculty and staff members even live in the dorms and participate in dorm and campus functions. "Late-night conversations with a professor aren't uncommon," says a student. The Office of Intercultural Affairs, also designed to offer academic support, "is much less reliable," say students, who point to a perceived lack of commitment on that office's part to Colby's students of color.

Cheryl Townsend Gilkes, a sociology professor and director of the African-American Studies program, works closely with students. "She encourages students who are feeling the pressure of academia and helps students, other than just her advisees, to choose courses," says a student. Gilkes has also been active in coordinating events for recent Black History Month and Martin Luther King, Jr., celebrations. Each year at Colby, Black History Month activities usually focus on a particular theme. In a recent year, the theme was "Africa in the Americas" and featured Cuban, Panamanian, and Franco-African speakers, as well as a film festival. Jorge Olivares, head of the modern foreign language department, is also "easy to talk to and he encourages students to do well. He lives on campus, so students meet up with him frequently." Students also turn to Phyllis Rogers, professor of American Studies and anthropology.

For peer support, the Student Organization for Black and Hispanic Unity (SOBHU), established on campus in 1970, provides "activities and relationships that are important for students who don't feel they fit into Colby's social scene," says a student. SOBHU sponsors a big brother/big sister program, in which juniors and seniors mentor first-year students. One student says the program is effective with students because "it's nice to have someone to talk to who knows the ropes and," she adds, "who's going to remember your birthday." SOBHU members meet in the SOBHU Room in Mary Low, a dorm on campus. The room is actually two rooms that have a TV, a VCR, two computers, a fireplace—a must considering Maine's cold winters—and a library. "It's a tradition for seniors to donate their textbooks to the library," says a senior. The SOBHU Room "is nice for poetry readings, talk sessions, and just as a place to relax." There are currently about 25 active SOBHU members. Asian students were members of SOBHU, but, according to one student, in the late 1980s the Asian students left to form their own organization, the East Asian Cultural Club. However, because of lack of funds, the student reports, the club is no longer in existence and the Asian students are looking to SOBHU for peer support.

While many prominent New England colleges are just now figuring out how to deal with their pervasive Greek systems, Colby abolished its in 1984 when its board of trustees voted the school's eight fraternities and two sororities off campus for good, claiming they "were discriminatory against women and were exclusionary by nature." As an alternative to the Greek system, which supplied much of the housing for students, the college instituted its Commons Plan, which divides the campus into four areas, each with its own dining facilities, system of government, and residential faculty members. Students are encouraged to remain in their respective commons for more than a year "so that friendships can more easily be formed and sustained throughout the college years and afterward."

Students report that in large part because of the new residential living system the campus has become more scholarly and open-minded. "The majority of the minority students have very little difficulty enjoying and fitting into the Colby scene," says a senior. "Luckily there are small parties that suit many different styles of partying. It's not like it was before when most of the school's social life was at fraternity keggers, where minorities didn't feel particularly comfortable." Lovejoy Commons is named for Elijah Parish Lovejoy, a Colby graduate (class of 1826) "who became America's first martyr for the free press when he was killed by a proslavery mob in Illinois in 1837."

Despite, or maybe because of, the Maine weather, Colby students are into athletics. Ice hockey and downhill and cross-country skiing are popular, and any athletic competition against state rivals Bates and Bowdoin brings out almost the entire campus. Basketball also gets quite a following and the school has excellent athletic facilities.

Each day students and faculty are given a copy of *Moose Prints,* which lists the on-campus activities of the day, their times and locations, which on a typical day could include dozens of events such as a student art show or a handbell rehearsal. Before the start of school, all new Colby first-year students are invited to participate in COOT (Colby Outdoor Orientation Trip), which is designed to show students "aspects of Maine's wilderness," hiking Mount Katahdin, bicycling through Arcadia National Park, or shooting the rapids on the Penobscot River. Students are also able to participate in any number of club activities; theater and musical groups are the most popular.

Aside from a couple of bars and restaurants, the town of Waterville (pop. 20,000), a predominantly white community, doesn't offer many reasons to leave campus. Boston, about three hours away by car, and Portland, less than an hour away, do, however, and are popular weekend destinations for those needing an escape from small-college living. Other than some community service projects sponsored by students, students say, there is little interaction with Waterville residents.

Despite recruitment attempts to provide some diversity, Colby remains a racially homogeneous student body. This is no doubt due in part to the college's location in the state of Maine, one of the least racially diverse states in the country. But even within its majority population, students say there is little diversity, "except for pockets of liberals here and there. But even they usually come from affluent suburbs somewhere, usually outside of Boston."

Going to school in such an environment can be a culture shock, especially for the unprepared. But the school offers the small-school atmosphere, supportive faculty, and a picture-postcard setting that can make the shock less severe. Joining SOBHU, say members, is also important. SOBHU "helps me put reality into its proper perspective, providing me with the emotional strength and support to continue the fight against racism," says a student. "In this organization I've found exceptional, caring people."

M A R Y L A N D

JOHNS HOPKINS UNIVERSITY

Address: Baltimore, MD 21218	**1992–93 tuition:** $17,000
Phone: (410) 516-8171	**Room and board:** $6,300
Director of Admissions: Richard Fuller	**Application deadline:** 1/1
Multicultural Student Recruiter: Jody Hester	**Financial aid application deadline:** 1/15

The Johns Hopkins University is *the* university for studies in pre-medicine and the sciences, intense academics, and a ho-hum campus social atmosphere. Students who find contentment here aren't afraid of all-nighters, their own independence, and, as one student puts it, "a student body where everyone seems intensely pre-law, pre-medicine, or pre-engineering."

Hopkins is world-famous for its undergraduate and graduate programs in medicine, and more than a quarter of the students in a typical entering class declare themselves as pre-med majors—although, with the program's high demands, this number dwindles by senior year. Biology is the school's most popular pre-med major. Tucked away behind the pre-med programs are the school's equally respected programs in the arts and sciences, most notably English, art history, political science, and international relations, which is complemented by the school's Bologna Center in Italy and its School of Advanced International Studies in Washington, DC. For budding novelists, Hopkins offers a creative writing major, in which a fortunate few are able to study with the likes of noted authors Edward Albee and John Barth.

At present, the campus chapter of the NAACP is working with the administration to establish an African-American Studies program, but, as one frustrated student says, "we just got a women's studies program here, so it's not like we're holding our breath." One of the school's relatively few courses in Black Studies is "History of Africa," but students complain that it is taught from a Eurocentric perspective. Latin American Studies is reportedly strong.

Although Hopkins is well known for its graduate school programs—particularly medicine, international studies, and writing—students say professors, who are usually high in the ivory tower at research-oriented institutions, are accessible for academic help and can often be seen at student events. Academics at Hopkins are notoriously intense and overwhelming, or "throaty," as Hopkins students will sometimes refer to them, so having a friendly professor certainly can't hurt. In keeping with the image of lean and hungry pre-professionals in search of job offers and grad school acceptances, Hopkins students are an academically competitive bunch.

As opposed to other private universities, Hopkins is somewhat lacking in school spirit, no doubt due to the school's academic work load and its unique and limited housing system. First-year students are the only ones guaranteed on-campus housing, while the older students must move into either university-owned apartments off campus (in which approximately a third of the upperclassmen live, usually with three-year leases), fraternity houses, or Baltimore apartments, which are becoming less and less affordable as the city becomes increasingly more gentrified.

Hopkins' housing situation doesn't bother some, especially those who plan in advance. "After freshman year, everyone goes in their different directions," says a student. "It's hard sometimes to get everyone together, but by the time freshman year is over you pretty much know who your friends are and who you want to be with here at Hopkins." Should the first-year friend you met over lunch in the campus dining hall move to the other side of campus, there's a free shuttle van service that will take you to and from his or her place anytime between the hours of 5 p.m. and 3 a.m.—but your friend had better live within a mile of campus, as the service doesn't go any farther than that.

Despite the sometimes blasé social life at the Hop, the Black Student Union provides a unifying—although sometimes claustrophobic—support network for members that makes life at the school a bit more exciting and comfortable. "We're constantly having parties, but it's always the same people at them," says a student. The group sponsors primarily annual events, including a Martin Luther King, Jr., Lecture Series that recently featured Nikki Giovanni and a dinner for African Heritage Month festivities. The BSU, which has about 80 active members, also provides academic support by sponsoring a peer mentor program and study group sessions, most often in chemistry and physics.

In addition, the BSU publishes the newsletter *Perspective,* which comes out about twice a semester. A recent issue focused on Clarence Thomas' Senate confirmation hearings. Although there are no historically black fraternities or sororities on campus, Hopkins students are able to join any one of five citywide chapters of such Greek organizations.

The BSU Room, located in Alumni Memorial Residence Two, has study carrels and a small library of Afrocentric literature, but, according to one student, the room isn't used much.

According to a BSU member, the African-American community at Hopkins is fairly homogeneous, economically and geographically. "Most of the black students I know here are from the Northeast, and I know at least four black women who went to Choate and other expensive private high schools," she says. "I don't know any who aren't middle-class, except maybe two." Approximately 150 of the school's 2,900 undergraduates are African-American, according to a student. (Please note: Because the admissions office declined to be a part of our guide, all enrollment figures of American-born minority students were obtained from students.)

Olé, with about 25 active members, represents Hopkins' Latino student population, although one student says there isn't a great deal of unity among the Latino students.

"We really don't hang out together, because there are so few of us here at Hopkins, and there are also a lot of Hispanics here who don't identify with their culture," says a student, who adds that slightly less than 1 percent of the student body are Latinos. Olé members meet twice monthly, usually in a room in the student union conference center. In recent years, Olé has sponsored trips for its members to Washington, DC, area restaurants and clubs. Olé also seeks to interact with nearby colleges and universities, including Towson State and Loyola.

Hopkins is located in a residential section of Baltimore, which has recently undergone some renovation, especially at its harbor area. Students find a wealth of cultural and social activity in the city, although one student commented that there is no Latino population in Baltimore. The area immediately around the university leaves something to be desired. "The admissions office doesn't tell us this when we apply, but most areas around here aren't safe for anyone, but especially for blacks," observes a student. "Three blocks to the east of campus is an area called Hampden, inhabited by mostly poor white people who don't think too much of blacks at Hopkins. Three blocks to the west is Waverly, where mostly poor blacks live. When they see me with a Hopkins sweatshirt on, they automatically think I'm uppity. Then there's Roland Park, which is very posh and very white." During freshman orientation, student groups take the new students on a tour of the area.

According to a student, the majority of Hopkins' students "vote Republican, are from the East Coast, are most likely from New York City, and there's also a significant Jewish population here." Adds another student: "Hopkins is a place of extremes. We have the geeks and the reactionaries. In my sociology class, we did an anonymous economic study of the students in the class, and we found that no one came from below the middle classes," says a student. "Hopkins is more racially than economically diverse. I have friends here from Russia, Greece, Argentina, all over the globe."

The Johns Hopkins University is a tough place academically. Don't come here if you're looking to slide through four years of gut courses or to attend one big tailgate party. But if a student is able to survive the academic rigors at the Hop, he or she leaves knowing that almost anything else will be a piece of cake.

UNIVERSITY OF MARYLAND

Address: College Park, MD 20742-5235
Phone: (301) 314-8385
Director of Admissions: Dr. Linda M.
  Clement
Multicultural Student Recruiter: Dr. Patricia
  Thomas-Walton
1992–93 tuition: $3,179 (in-state); $8,783
  (out-of-state)
Room and board: $4,850
Application deadline: 4/30
Financial aid application deadline: 2/15
Non-white freshman admissions: Applicants
  for the class of '94: 3,812
  Accepted: 62%
  Accepted who enroll: 43%
  Applicants accepted who rank in top
  10% of high school class: na
  Median SAT range: 445–565 V, 525–660 M
  Median ACT: na
Full-time undergraduate enrollment: 21,543
  Men: 52%
  Women: 48%

1989–90: 23.7%
1990–91: 25.7%
Geographic distribution of students: na
Top majors: 1. Computer Science
  2. Electrical Engineering 3. Government
  and Politics
Retention rate of non-white students: 81%
**Scholarships exclusively for non-white
  students:** Benjamin Banneker Scholarship:
  merit-based; covers tuition, room and
  board, and mandatory fees;
  approximately 20 awarded each year.
Remediation programs: Development
  courses are offered in English
  composition and math.
Academic support services: Tutoring is
  available in most subjects, as well as
  workshops in study skills.
Ethnic studies programs: Maryland's
  Afro-American Studies program (two
  tenured faculty), established in 1968, is
  interdisciplinary and includes courses
  from the departments of political science,
  English, history, and others.

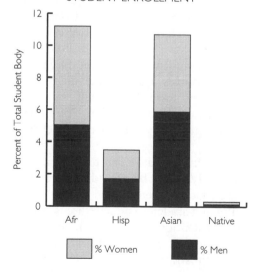

STUDENT ENROLLMENT

Non-white students in
  1987–88: 21%
  1988–89: 22%

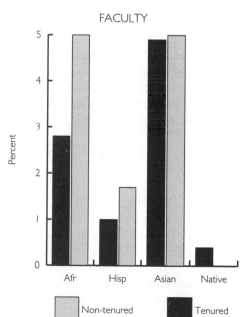

FACULTY

Ethnic studies courses: Courses in Asian Studies and Latin American Studies are offered.

Organizations for non-white students: African Students Association, Association for Development of Minority Scholars, Black Engineers Society, Black Student Union, Black Business Society, Black Women's Council, Caribbean Student Association, Chinese Culture Club, and others

Notable non-white alumni: Connie Chung ('69; news correspondent); Carmen Balthrop ('71; Metropolitan Opera singer); Len Elmore ('74; former professional basketball player, Harvard law school graduate, and NPR commentator)

Tenured faculty: 1,126

Non-tenured faculty: 1,505

Student-faculty ratio: 13:1

Administrators: 304
  African-American: 8.6%
  Hispanic: 0.3%
  Asian-American: 3%
  Native American: 0.3%

Recent non-white speakers on campus: Dr. Franklyn Green Jenifer (president, Howard University); Dr. Brunetta Wolfman (professor, George Washington University); Bill Cosby (comedian and civil rights activist)

University of Maryland graduates may not recognize the school they once attended—at least in terms of the quality of students who now go to the university. With a mandate from the Maryland state legislature, the university has embarked on programs, started in 1990, that seek to make the 134-year-old university into one of the country's top schools.

To do so, the university plans to decrease the size of undergraduate enrollment by about 20 percent, improve the student-faculty ratio, raise admissions standards, and strengthen the honors program and advising system. To date, much has already happened. The average SAT scores have markedly improved during the past ten years—up nearly 100 points during that time period—and a new language house (complete with direct satellite access to foreign-language broadcasts from Latin America, Japan, Russia, and Italy) and an honors dorm have been added to students' residential options.

There are still those headaches common to most students who attend large state universities: classes, especially in introductory-level courses, are overwhelmingly large, registering can be a pain, and getting to meet with professors is difficult. "You just have to plan carefully if you want to meet a professor," says a junior. "You might even have to cut a class because that's the only time the professor can meet with you."

Maryland's students praise their administration, an unusual thing to do at a large state university. "When we speak, we are definitely heard by the administration," says a student. "Two years ago, members of the Black Student Union had a summit on campus to which more than 350 black faculty and students came to discuss things particular to our campus, such as the problem of retention, the lack of minority role models in high positions in the administration, and the general atmosphere of the campus. We came up with a proposal for the administration on how to improve the quality of life for black students here. We also got more than 3,000 students from every race and nationality to sign a petition to back our proposal, and we even boycotted the student center. In our proposal, we requested a black activities center, more financial aid support, and an improvement in the retention rate of black students. There was some controversy among students about our proposal at first, especially when it came to our request for a black activities center. It was said we were being separatist, but we want a place where we can go when we come back as alums."

Students say that some of their requests have been met. "We're working closely with the vice president of student affairs, especially when it comes to the details of the activities center. We're not sure what will come of the plans, though, as Maryland is in a budget crunch and funding for new programs is slow in coming."

Maryland has some outstanding—and not so outstanding—academic departments. (The university's undergraduate division has 12 colleges.) Stellar departments include engineering, especially electrical, business, computer science, and math. Journalism and economics also get good marks from students. Biology and zoology are said to be so-so, as is the school's political science program. There are more than 100 degree-granting programs at the university, including certificate programs in Afro-American and East Asian Studies. One of the standout Afro-American Studies courses, say students, is "Black Culture in the United States." Sharon Harley, Otis Williams, and Rhonda Williams are some of the program's notable professors. During the 1989–90 school year, Maryland had the distinction of granting the second highest number of Ph.D.s to African-Americans.

Students say the Learning Assistance Service, which offers various academic support programs, is helpful. The university also provides academic and personal support through the Office of Minority Student Education (OMSE), which includes peer advising and tutoring. "OMSE sponsors everything for all minorities," says a junior. "For example, each year they invite twenty incoming black males to campus for a three-day orientation program that introduces them to different aspects of the campus and how to get along well here as a black male. The students are selected at random. The office also sponsors an annual Unity Picnic, usually held during the first couple of weeks after school starts, that bridges the gap between all the minorities on campus, including African-Americans, Asians, and Hispanics. Workshops and speakers are also sponsored by the center."

Adds another student: "Regarding academics, OMSE offers almost every kind of tutoring, from biology and math to chemistry and English. There's all kinds of stuff sponsored by the office. It gets a lot of respect and use by students."

Nyumburu Center, a place of special interest to multicultural students, coordinates many of the campus cultural programs, including student art shows and dramatic presentations, as well as jazz and gospel concerts. The co-directors of the center, Ann Carswell and Otis Williams, "work closely with students and the administration, which is definitely a help when it comes to planning events and activities," says a student. The Center for Minorities in Science and Engineering, which is judged by one user "as definitely a help," is home to such student groups as the Black Engineers Society, the Society of Minority Computer Science Students, and the Society of Hispanic Professional Engineers.

Students add that it's easy to meet students from different backgrounds outside the center as well. "Maryland's size attracted me because I'm from a large city. I meet people every day I've never seen before. It is a microcosm of the larger world, and that's what life is going to be about."

"Although we consider all black students to be members of the Black Student Union, there are really about 100 active members who come regularly to general meetings or who take an active role in planning events." The BSU, which meets monthly, recently established a mentor program with an elementary school and Northwestern High School in the area. The group also recently sponsored a revival that featured a local preacher and a choir. "The event obviously had a very Christian focus," says a student. The BSU usually draws a large crowd to its annual Cultural Festival. "It's more or less a block party; last year we had a steel band, a go-go band [a sound, says the student, that's particular to the DC area], and various rap groups. We have close relationships with local black businesses, and we invite them to be a part of the festival, where they sell T-shirts and cultural foods."

Located in the Stamp Union, the campus student center, the BSU office, which shares lounge space with the Jewish Student Union and the Student Government Association and other organizations, "has a definite homey feel to it," says a student. "For many of us, it's a home away from home. Many of us go there between classes to relax." The predominantly black fraternities and sororities have their share of parties and dances, say students, "but also do a lot of work in the community. Members of Zeta Phi Beta, for example, have worked with the homeless."

With more than 400 student groups, students are rarely wanting for things to do. When they do feel like leaving campus, however, the nation's capital, with its multitude of cultural and social activities, is close by. A popular destination for Maryland's African-American students is Howard University, a historically black institution, located fifteen minutes from College Park. However, with studying occupying an increasing amount of students' time, most undergraduates are content to stick close to campus during the week.

Maryland's academics and social life certainly please its share of students, while the university's size forces many to mature fast. "I've had good academic and social experiences, but going to school here also makes you grow up quickly. You learn a whole lot about yourself and what you're capable of. You have to work for a lot of what you get, and you have to work to not be a number. Nothing is going to be handed to you here, but isn't that kind of like life anyway?"

ST. JOHN'S COLLEGE

Address: P.O. Box 2800, Annapolis, MD 21404-2800

Phone: (410) 263-2371 / (800) 727-9238

Director of Admissions: John Christensen

Multicultural Student Recruiter: Dorcey Rose

1992–93 tuition: $16,150

Room and board: $5,450

Application deadline: Rolling admissions

Financial aid application deadline: 2/15

Non-white freshman admissions: Applicants for the class of '96: 24

Accepted: 90%

Accepted who enroll: 46%

Applicants accepted who rank in top 10% of high school class: na

Median SAT range: 540–650 V, 510–650 M

Median ACT: na

Full-time undergraduate enrollment: 408

Men: 58%

Women: 42%

Geographic districution of students: na

Students In-state: 16%

Top majors: na

Retention rate of non-white students: 80%

Scholarships exclusively for non-white students: None

Remediation programs: None

Academic support services: Academic assistance is offered in math, French, computers, and writing.

Ethnic studies programs: None

Ethnic studies courses: None

Organizations for non-white students: None

Notable non-white alumni: Ch'ao-Li Chi (Liberal Arts; actor); Charlotte King (Liberal Arts; chairman of the board, Catholic Archdiocese of Washington, DC); Robert George (Liberal Arts; Republican Eagles Communications Director); Theophus Smith (Liberal Arts; professor, Emory University)

Tenured faculty: 42

Non-tenured faculty: 19

Student-faculty ratio: 8:1

STUDENT ENROLLMENT

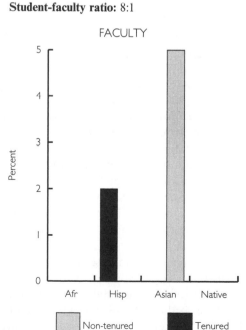

FACULTY

Non-white students in

1988–89: 7%

1989–90: 10%

1990–91: 11%

1991–92: 11%

There are many schools that consider themselves devoted to the liberal arts, but St. John's College, which has campuses in Annapolis, Maryland, and Santa Fe, New Mexico, is *the* liberal arts college.

There are no majors or academic departments at St. John's College. All students follow the same curriculum, called the Great Books Program, in which they study the works, in chronological order, that have helped shape Western civilization. Unlike at other colleges where students also study critical texts, St. John's students study only the works of the authors themselves. Secondary research material is usually out of the question, and students learn math by reading the works of Euclid and music by becoming familiar with the compositions of Mozart and Beethoven.

Students begin their first year by reading the literature of the ancient Greeks, including Homer and Plato; in their sophomore year, they progress to the Renaissance and read Shakespeare and Descartes. During junior year, students read seventeenth- and eighteenth-century authors, including Hobbes and Rousseau, and seniors read nineteenth- and twentieth-century authors, such as Goethe, Tocqueville, and Lincoln.

The emphasis seems to be on the philosophy of the ages, but students interested in music and the sciences aren't shortchanged. The music tutorial, taken during a student's sophomore year, focuses mostly on the compositions of musical greats rather than on performance, and the three-year laboratory program includes studies in biology, physics, genetics, and evolution.

There are no lecture halls at St. John's. Classes are typically taught in small seminars, in which professors, called tutors, serve to facilitate class discussion, not dictate it. Tutors begin the class with a question about the reading, and students take it from there. With only about 15 students per class, and fewer than 400 students on each campus, getting to know your professor is a relatively simple task. Students and tutors aren't on a first-name basis; in order to avoid titles and to place everyone on common ground, people refer to one another in class as Ms. So-and-so or Mr. So-and-so.

Although most Johnnies, as they affectionately refer to themselves, have nothing but praise for their education, some express concern about the school's exclusively Western focus. Students also point to the fact that the only work of a person of color taught is Frederick Douglass' "The Constitution and Slavery" and that fewer than half a dozen of the authors discussed are women. (Works by Jane Austen, Virginia Woolf, and Flannery O'Connor are read during a student's third and fourth years.) But these concerns don't seem to be much more than slight grumblings, as most agree with a third-year student, who writes: "The St. John's curriculum addresses the questions of existence and humanity, and transcends issues of race and gender."

More so than at most colleges, Johnnies seem genuinely interested in learning for learning's sake. Perhaps because of this attitude, there seems to be little racial tension on campus. "St. John's is completely integrated, perhaps because Johnnies are intellectuals who live and think on the conceptual level," says a student. "Johnnies are more apt to think of you as the 'nihilist' or 'Randian' rather than as black, Hispanic, or white. As for parties or the dining hall, no one feels pressure to sit anywhere or dance anywhere." Observes another student: "I have the sense that people here have no barriers in terms of race. We are all in the same happy pursuit of knowledge, so we have no time to waste on such matters."

Although there are no cultural student organizations, the college sponsors activities centered on Martin Luther King, Jr., Day and Black History Month. Activities include lectures and concerts. There are also no formal student clubs or theme houses on campus, and because of the school's small size, students say they consider themselves part of a single, rather close-knit community, instead of as members of subgroups or cliques. Consequently, the extracurricular life of the college tends to be informal and inclusive rather than structured by organizations with specific memberships.

Much of campus social life consists of dorm parties with plenty of beer and dancing. Conversations about books being discussed in class are common at even the most rambunctious room parties. Every Friday night the college sponsors guest lecturers who address various topics. The lectures get mixed turnouts, depending on the speaker and his or her topic.

Intramural activity—ranging from basketball and tennis to track and soccer—enjoys popular followings on each of the St. John's campuses. The exception to the Annapolis campus' 1939 ban on intercollegiate competition is the annual—and hotly contested—croquet match against the team from the U.S. Naval Academy, located nearby. Students on both campuses stage performances of popular or classical plays, and both campuses have film societies that screen foreign and domestic films each weekend. There are also waltz parties, rock parties, a Halloween costume party, and Reality Weekend, which features a talent show, a picnic, and athletic competition.

Aside from appearance, the two campuses are similar in academic quality and intensity, although it's said that the Annapolis campus enjoys a better academic reputation, perhaps because it's the older of the two campuses. It's also said that students at the Santa Fe campus are generally more laid-back than their peers at the Annapolis campus, no doubt due to the school's location, which is conducive to a great deal of outdoor recreation and reflection.

St. John's students, on the whole, are more academic than political. "There seems to be a small group of students who are aware of current racial and political issues," says a student. "There were small discussions on events like the police beating of a motorist in California, debates on the Gulf War. There have also been students who faithfully march in DC for the homeless. All in all, it is a very small group."

Students on both campuses have the opportunity to take advantage of the cultural activities offered in Santa Fe and Annapolis. St. John's in Santa Fe, an hour north of Albuquerque, is located just two miles from the center of the city's historic and trendy downtown area, and just a short bike ride from numerous art galleries, restaurants, and shops. Plentiful opportunities for shopping and moviegoing are nearby, as are the spectacular Sangre de Cristo Mountains. St. Johns' in Annapolis is located at the center of the city, near the U.S. Naval Academy. "Annapolis is a touristy state capital," says a student, and offers a variety of eating and drinking establishments not far from campus. Annapolis is just thirty-five miles east of Washington, DC, a popular destination for students.

Students come from all over the nation to partake of St. John's unique brand of education. It's certainly not for everyone, especially those looking for a highly structured, hierarchical social and academic life. Johnnies do not have the cultural programming and organizations students at other schools of its caliber have, but that seems to trouble few, if any. Says a third-year student: "St. John's does not specifically address the concerns of any group, whether white, women, Hispanic, or black. I would recommend St. John's to anyone who is looking for Truth and Beauty. A minority student will receive the assurance of his equality. The only judging done is on the correctness of ideas. Anyone who can survive the self-revealing application process and get admitted deserves our full attention as a worthy compatriot in our quest. And we give it to them."

UNITED STATES NAVAL ACADEMY

Address: Annapolis, MD 21402-5018
Phone: (301) 267-4361
Director of Admissions: J. W. Renard
Multicultural Student Recruiter: na
1991–92 tuition: Free
Room and board: Free
Application deadline: 3/1
Financial aid application deadline: na
Non-white freshman admissions: Applicants
   for the class of '95: 2,218
   Accepted: 11.9%
   Accepted who enroll: 10.2%
   Applicants accepted who rank in top
   10% of high school class: na
   In top 25%: 81%
   Median SAT range: 500–599 V, 600–699 M
   Median ACT range: 25–26 English,
   30–36 Math
Full-time undergraduate enrollment: 4,500
   Men: 90%
   Women: 10%
Non-white students in
   1987–88: 11.8%
   1988–89: 15.4%
   1989–90: 17.1%
   1990–91: 17.4%
Students In-state: na
Top majors: 1. General Science 2. General
   Engineering 3. Political Science

Retention rate of non-white students: 70%
Scholarships exclusively for non-white
   students: na
Remediation programs: The academy offers
   an Academic Intervention Program.
Academic support services: The academy
   offers the Writing Center and the
   Computer Services Showroom.
Ethnic studies programs: None
Ethnic studies courses: None

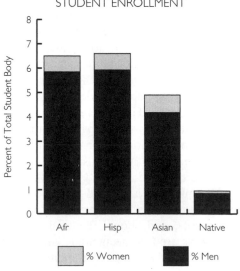

STUDENT ENROLLMENT

Percent of Total Student Body

Afr   Hisp   Asian   Native

□ % Women   ■ % Men

GEOGRAPHIC DISTRIBUTION OF STUDENTS

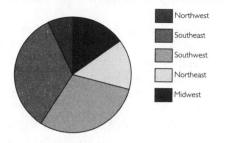

- Northwest
- Southeast
- Southwest
- Northeast
- Midwest

Organizations for non-white students: Black Studies Club, Hispanic Midshipmen Club, Filipino-American Midshipmen Club, Korean Club

Notable non-white alumni: Colonel Charles F. Bolden (Electrical Science; NASA space shuttle astronaut); David Robinson (Math; professional basketball player); Napoleon McCallum (Computer Science; profressional football player); Rear Admiral Benjamin Montoya (1989 Hispanic Engineer of the Year)

Tenured faculty: na

Non-tenured faculty: na

Student-faculty ratio: 10:1

Administrators: na

Recent non-white speakers on campus: Martin Luther King III, (civil rights activist and Georgia state representative); Colin Powell (chairman of the Joint Chiefs of Staff); Dr. Ronald Quincy (assistant president, Harvard University); Dr. Jawanza Kunjufu (president, African-American Images)

The weak of heart, mind, and body need not apply to the 128-year-old United States Naval Academy. There's only room here for those men and women who are bright and physically fit enough to handle the rigors of daily life at one of the country's most grueling undergraduate institutions of higher learning.

First-year students, or plebes, are introduced to life at the academy during the seven-week Plebe Summer that begins in July, during which they start their days "at dawn with an hour of rigorous exercise and end them long after sunset, wondering how [they] will make it through the next day." When the upperclass students return at the end of the Plebe Summer, the pressure continues for the plebes, who are at their mercy. Plebes are expected to have Navy rules memorized and be able to quote them should they be asked to by the older students, they must greet all upperclassmen when they pass by, and they must run almost everywhere.

One would never call life at the academy relaxed, as midshipmen perform a regular routine that becomes all too familiar by graduation time. Midshipment get up at 6:30 a.m. for personal fitness workouts and breakfast, followed by six class periods a day, with meals and extracurricular activities that also follow strict time schedules. For plebes, lights are out at 11 p.m.

Academics are just as intense as life outside of the classroom. Plebes must complete a core curriculum that includes courses in calculus, chemistry, computing, government, "American Naval Heritage," "Fundamentals of Naval Science," and "Rhetoric and Introduction to Literature I & II." In addition, physical fitness courses are required all four years, and during certain summer sessions midshipmen must take training cruises aboard naval submarines and ships.

Students must decide on their major course of study by the end of their first year, and are able to choose from 18 programs. The most popular programs are those in the fields of engineering, which include aerospace engineering, electrical engineering, general engineering, marine engineering, and naval engineering. Students are also able to concentrate in such areas as English and history, but relatively few choose to do so.

Although one student says, "This is not the place to come for ethnic studies," he does recommend such courses as "The History of Africa" and "African-American Literature." He adds that members of the Black Studies Committee, a student organization, "are trying to get more African-American Studies courses integrated into the curriculum, but there aren't many opportunities to take such courses because of the tightness of our academic schedules."

One of the best aspects of earning a degree from the Naval Academy, in addition to top-notch academic opportunities, is that it's free. The federal government picks up the tab. But graduates are required to serve in the Navy or Marines for five years. The desire to do well in class comes naturally to most of the school's midshipmen, but the school fosters competition with its order of merit, or academic class rankings. Midshipment with the highest class rank get first choice for postgraduate assignments. Joining the Seals, the Navy's diving unit, and joining the flight program are often top choices.

Midshipmen say that the academic support services are "excellent" at the academy. "The professors all really want us to succeed," says a student. "The Writing Center and Math Lab are also used frequently by midshipmen." Adds another student: "There's enough support here so that you can make it." Students say participating in sports is also a way to stay on top of studies. "It's a chance to unwind, a way to release some of the tension that comes with the academic work load that's expected of you here," says a midshipman. "I box, which gets rid of a lot of my frustration."

An additional source of support is the Black Studies Club; with more than 200 members, it is the largest and most active student organization on campus. The group has recently worked to bring military and civilian speakers, theater groups, and concerts to campus. George Bush hailed the club as one of his Thousand Points of Light. The group also works to provide peer support for members. "Upperclass students provide guidance to underclassmen. They advise students on academics and military performance," says a member. "Our goal is to see that 100 percent of our members graduate." Group members have also served as tutors in some of the schools in the Washington, DC, area. The Black Studies Club's staff adviser is Lt. David Welch, tenth-company officer, who "is helpful in almost every aspect of the club's activities," says a student. The Hispanic Midshipmen Club, says a midshipman, "provides mostly peer support for members."

Each midshipman is paired with an area sponsor, usually a family living nearby, "where midshipmen can go to have dinner, watch TV, and just get away from campus for an evening. All you have to do is phone your sponsor whenever you want and they will pick you up and drop you off back on campus. Many midshipmen are a long way from home, so it's nice to get some home cooking every once in a while." The midshipman adds that there is no particular effort made to match students with families of their own ethnicity or race. "If you want to be paired with an African-American family, you have to ask, which is usually no problem," he says.

Students say as much learning goes on inside the classroom as outside, or, as a midshipman says more bluntly: "Outside of the classroom, we run the school." The opportunities for leadership are almost limitless at the academy. The student body, called the Brigade, is divided into six battalions, each of which consists of six companies, for a total of thirty-six companies. Midshipmen head each of these units, and in a recent year three of the top positions, including the Brigade commander and two battalion commanders, were African-American. In addition, five of the company officers during a recent semester were African-American, two of whom were women.

For the most part, midshipmen's social life is confined to on-campus extracurricular activities, known on campus as ECAs. Participation on a varsity or intramural team is required during all four years. Finding one to be a part of is no problem, as the academy fields 32 varsity sports alone, ranging from football and soccer to tennis and swimming. The annual gridiron clash against archrival West Point brings out the troops from both campuses. Students also participate in numerous musical (gospel choir, Trident Band, among others), athletic (aerobics, bicycle racing), professional (drill team, flying club, small arms club), and recreational (amateur radio club, art and printing club, computer club) organizations. There are also numerous professional and religious clubs on campus.

It's fortunate that midshipmen have many choices when it comes to ECAs, as students are rarely granted permission to leave campus. Studies keep all students pretty much close to campus, but those in academic jeopardy are required to stay on campus to study. Plebes are rarely granted time away from campus, but upperclass students are often able to leave for weekends. Annapolis, according to one midshipmen, "is kind of like a small town," but the nearby area has cinemas, restaurants, and other reasons to leave campus, even for a Saturday afternoon. The city has African-American and Hispanic populations, but students report relatively little interaction between midshipmen and community residents. Washington, DC, and Baltimore, which are rich in cultural activities and home to numerous colleges and universities, are within thirty miles of campus, and are frequent destinations for those granted weekend leaves. With a lopsided male-to-female ratio, students comment that there is little to no dating on campus.

The emphasis at the Naval Academy, according to students, isn't so much on race or ethnicity as it is on one's ability to achieve. "I don't want to make it sound as if there's no racism here, because no place is free of such attitudes. But with all that's expected of us, and because of how we all start here on a level playing field, there doesn't seem to be the tension that there is at some of the schools where my friends are," says a student. "There are times when it can be tough," he adds, "especially because there's such a small percentage of us minority students here. But our small size helps foster a tight community, and we're all really here for each other."

MASSACHUSETTS

AMHERST COLLEGE

Address: Wilson Admission Center,
   Amherst, MA 01002
Phone: (413) 542-2328
Director of Admissions: Jane E. Reynolds
Multicultural Student Recruiter: Michael P.
   Whittingham
1993–94 tuition: $18,800
Room and board: $2,500
Application deadline: Early decision: 11/15;
   regular decision: 12/31
Financial aid application deadline: Early
   decision: 11/15; regular decision: 2/1
Non-white freshman admissions: Applicants
   for the class of '96: na
   Accepted: na
   Accepted who enroll: na
   Applicants accepted who rank in top
   10% of high school class: na
   In top 25%: na
   Median SAT: na
   Median ACT: na
Full-time undergraduate enrollment: 1,597
   Men: 54%
   Women: 46%
Non-white students in
   1987–88: 14%
   1988–89: 17%
   1989–90: 20%
   1990–91: 22%
Students In-state: 5%
Top majors: 1. Psychology 2. English
   3. Political Science
Retention rate of non-white students: 96%

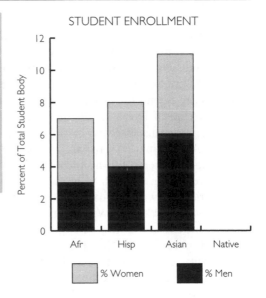

STUDENT ENROLLMENT

Percent of Total Student Body

% Women   % Men

GEOGRAPHIC DISTRIBUTION OF STUDENTS

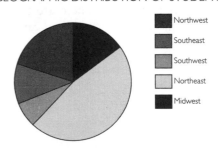

Northwest
Southeast
Southwest
Northeast
Midwest

**Scholarships exclusively for non-white
   students:** None

Remediation programs: None

Academic support services: Tutoring is available.

Ethnic studies programs: Amherst offers major courses of study in Black Studies and Asian languages and civilizations. As part of the five-college consortium in Amherst, the college offers programs in Latin American and Caribbean Studies and Native American Studies.

Organizations for non-white students: Black Student Union, Charles Drew Black Cultural House, Asian Student Association, Asian Cultural House, La Causa (Latino/Hispanic student group), Tri-Cultural Committee, Gospel Choir, Spectrum III (black and Asian student theater group), Asian-American Women's Group

Notable non-white alumni: Charles Drew ('26; first director of the First American Red Cross Blood Bank); Charles Hamilton Houston ('15; former special counsel to the NAACP, former dean of the Howard University Law School, and first African-American to be elected to the *Harvard Review*); Joseph Hardy Neesima (1870; first Japanese graduate of a Western college and founder of Doshisha University in Kyoto)

Tenured faculty: 115

Non-tenured faculty: 49

Student-faculty ratio: 10:1

Administrators: 105

African-American: 5.7%

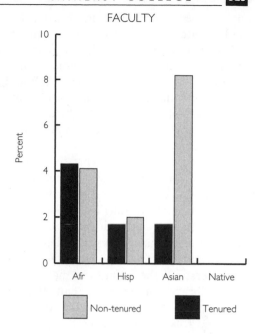

FACULTY

Hispanic: 2.9%

Asian-American: 3.8%

Native American: 0

Recent non-white speakers on campus: Rev. Silas Muhammad (Nation of Islam); Kwame Toure (political activist); Evelyn Hu-Dehart (educator); Ronald Takaki (author and professor of cultural diversity, University of California/ Berkeley); Toni Cade Bambara (author and poet); Julian Bond (former Georgia state senator and civil rights activist)

Amherst College is one of the country's premier liberal arts colleges. The editors at *U.S. News & World Report* consistently rank the 172-year-old college as one of the top three liberal arts colleges in the country; in 1991 the college earned top billing.

Amherst is devoted to the liberal arts. Students say that almost every academic department at the college is excellent, but most often they praise the English, history, and political science departments, as well as the departments of chemistry and physics. Although the college does not require its students to satisfy any set curriculum, with the exception of the requirements for the major, each first-year student must take "Introduction to Liberal Studies," a semester-long set of seminar-style courses team-taught by professors from different academic disciplines. Students choose from any number of such courses; recent ILS courses have included "Romanticism and the Enlightenment," "Decision Making and Uncertainty," and "Nuclear Weapons."

Students praise the college's Black Studies program, particularly its courses dealing with literature and history. Among the program's outstanding instructors, according to students, are David Blight, an assistant professor of history, C. Rhonda Cobham-Sander, an assistant professor of English, and Andrea Rushing, a professor of English. "Introduction to Black Studies," "Philosophy of Race and Racism," and "Religions of the Atlantic World" are some of the program's more popular courses.

Although Amherst students have the reputation of learning for its own sake, academics can nonetheless be intense. However, students say there are numerous support services and staff members who are helpful. "Jean Moss, associate dean of students, Charri Boykin-East, assistant dean/director of residential life, and Rebecca Lee, associate dean of students, are good role models because they are of a minority race and are female," says a student. "It is good to have minorities in positions of respect and a certain degree of power."

Amherst has the facilities to match its academic reputation. The college's Robert Frost Library contains more than 700,000 volumes, the school's Music Building has an electronic music and recording studio as well as impressive collections of classical, jazz, and folk music, and the Seeley G. Mudd Mathematics and Computer Science Building, completed in 1984, makes 65 terminals and microcomputers available to students twenty-four hours a day. Art and anthropology students, as well as the campus community at large, also make use of the school's Mead Art Museum, with a strong holding in eighteenth- and nineteenth-century American art, and the Pratt Museum of Natural History. Amherst also has its own observatory, with two major telescopes and a planetarium.

The pluses of attending Amherst don't stop there. Since Amherst is a member of the five-college consortium, students are able to take advantage of the resources—both educational and social—at the University of Massachusetts and Smith, Mount Holyoke, and Hampshire colleges. Amherst students may take courses for credit at any of the other colleges, and five-college programs include astronomy, Black Studies, East Asian languages, and peace and world security studies. A calendar of events at the five colleges is also published regularly, and a free and frequent shuttle van service escorts students to the other campuses.

Like other prominent colleges, Amherst has placed the recruitment of more diverse classes of students—cultural and socioeconomic—high on its list of priorities. Although the first African-American entered the college in 1826, it wasn't until the mid-1980s that the college started making strides in recruitment of students of color. The first-year class entering in 1987, for example, had 17 percent students of color, as compared with the 28.5 percent who entered with the class in 1991.

And students have noticed the change. "I can compare the current freshman class to my class and incredible differences show up," says a recent graduate. "The admissions office has worked very hard to bring together a more diverse class, both ethnically and socioeconomically, and the composition of all the classes has shown real change." She adds: "When I first came as a freshman, I found this to be very much the white finishing school. I just did not fit into that picture. But the school has changed and so have I. It was not easy, but Amherst made me discover and maintain both my self-confidence and my self-awareness."

But students aren't content to let the college rest on recent achievements in admissions. At the end of the 1991–92 school year, more than 300 Amherst and other five-college students staged a sit-in at Converse Hall, the school's administration building. The three-day demonstration, orchestrated by members of the college's Black Student Union (BSU) and La Causa, the school's Latino student group, sought to have the college hire a full-time affirmative action officer and to recruit and retain more of its faculty and staff of color. "The administration agreed to all of the demands, but we're going to have to be persistent in making sure they stick to them," says a student. As of this writing, students say the college is actively working to recruit a more diverse faculty, particularly in such departments as economics and theater. The student negotiators included five African-Americans, one Hispanic, and one Asian-American.

The college's cultural student organizations provide a variety of on-campus activities, as well as peer support for their members. "It's amazing all of the events and speakers the BSU sponsors every year," says a student. The Harlem Renaissance, sponsored annually by the BSU, offers "an evening of dance and lectures." BSU sponsors similar events as part of Black History Month celebrations. BSU members have also formed Project Recruitment and Retention, which seeks to recruit more faculty, staff, and students of color to Amherst. In a recent year, the group successfully lobbied the college's administration to provide Jean Moss, an associate dean of students, with an assistant. "She is a remarkable, warm, and genuine woman who listens well and who gives great strength with her compassion and her advice, and we are happy that she now has more time in her schedule to spend with students," says a member of Project Recruitment.

The Charles Drew House is a popular residence hall for up to 20 students of African and Caribbean descent, as well as for other interested students. At the house, named for Charles Drew, an Amherst alum who established America's first blood bank, students have access to peer support and tutoring, full kitchen facilities, and a library.

Amherst's Asian Student Association (ASA) brings to campus each year various dance groups, films, and lecturers. Recently, a student group was formed to encourage the Amherst administration to incorporate more Asian-American Studies courses into the curriculum. "I'm a part of a committee that pushed really hard this year to bring Asian-American studies to Amherst," says a sociology major. "So far, we're going to have a class next fall and then a lecture series in the spring semester. These, however, are temporary and no one has told us if they are going to be institutionalized, although in talks with the president he did hint toward this."

La Causa, with more than 30 active members, "has really gotten active in the last two years," says a student. "Before then, it was mostly the domain of international students and wasn't all that active, but ever since the admissions office has begun recruiting more Chicanos and other Latinos from the States it has gotten more so. Students now see it as a viable organization." Recently, La Causa sponsored a film series, a lecture series, dances, and a tutoring program for students at an area junior high school.

In addition to their smarts in the classroom (the college is among the top four undergraduate colleges in America in the number of graduates who have gone on to earn Ph.Ds), Amherst students are known for being athletically active. Nearly 85 percent of students participate in intramurals, while some varsity sports, especially basketball, are popularly attended events. The varsity football team has seen better days, but the water polo and basketball teams, on the other hand, have been at the top of their game in recent years. Almost any athletic competition against archrival Williams brings Amherst students out in full force.

The Campus Center, opened in 1987, is the hub of student socializing, and it has a coffeehouse, lounges, offices for student organizations, a movie theater, snack bar, and a TV/game room. The college has no fraternities—they were abolished in 1984 because the college said they were not inclusive—but more than 90 percent of its students live on campus in dorms or theme houses. Besides sports, Amherst students are involved in plays, musical groups, publications staffs, and professional associations. Outreach, a student volunteer group that has worked with Cambodian refugees and battered women in the area, has grown in popularity with students in recent years.

With its combination of high-powered academics and extracurriculars, Amherst is a first-choice college for many prospective students. The school's cultural student groups help alleviate—and make more enjoyable and worthwhile—a student's four years here. "I would recommend my school to a prospective minority student as a place that addresses his or her concerns," says a psychology major. "Though the genuineness of the politically correct attitude is sometimes questionable, students are willing to listen to other students' concerns. I feel that Amherst has a good mix of students, so that one does not have to feel alone. Though I have to admit there are times when I am frustrated with this campus, Amherst does, overall, provide a place where a minority student can feel safe to voice concerns. This student population is small and the faculty/administration is quite accessible. In addition, there are a good number of minority groups on campus where a student can seek support."

BABSON COLLEGE

Address: Babson Park, Wellesley, MA 02157
Phone: (800) 488-3696
Director of Admissions: Charles Nolan
Multicultural Student Recruiter: William Boyd
1993–94 tuition: $15,810
Room and board: $6,715
Application deadline: 2/1
Financial aid application deadline: 2/1
Non-white freshman admissions: Applicants for the class of '96: 241
  Accepted: 66%
  Accepted who enroll: 22%
  Applicants accepted who rank in top 10% of high school class: 29%

In top 25%: 66%
Median SAT: 400–540 V, 500–640 M
Median ACT: na
Full-time undergraduate enrollment: 1,679
  Men: 64%
  Women: 36%
Non-white students in 1987–91: 7%
Geographic distribution of students: na
In-state: 45%
Top majors: 1. Finance 2. Marketing 3. Accounting
Retention rate of non-white students: na
Scholarships exclusively for non-white students: Challenge Scholarship: need- and merit-based; the ten awards given

STUDENT ENROLLMENT

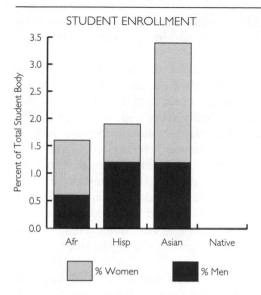

% Women   % Men

FACULTY

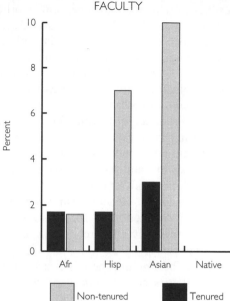

Non-tenured   Tenured

each year cover costs of tuition; renewable.

Remediation programs: None

Academic support services: The college offers Mathematics, Writing and Speech Resource Centers. Peer tutors are also available.

Ethnic studies programs: None

Ethnic studies courses: The college offers various courses in African, African-American, Chinese, Japanese, and Latin American history, politics, and literature.

Organizations for non-white students: Black Students Association, Babson Asian-American Association

Notable non-white alumni: Eric Johnson ('72, Management/Finance; president, Tri-Star Associates); Aaron Walton ('83; president, Aaron Walton Entertainment); Sharon Weeks ('74; marketing manager, IBM); Jeff Perry ('87, Quantitative Methods and Marketing; associate, BP Chemical)

Tenured faculty: 56

Non-tenured faculty: 60

Student-faculty ratio: 21:1

Administrators: 187
 African American: 2%
 Hispanic: 1%
 Asian-American: 1%
 Native American: 0

Recent non-white speakers on campus: Joe Clark (former high school principal, portrayed in the film *Lean on Me*); Dr. Dennis Watson (executive for the National Youth Black Leadership Council); Doris Leader Charge (actress); Ron Howard (president, Boston Bank of Commerce, only minority-owned bank in Boston); Ronke Okediji (purchasing agent, WGBH); Roland Smith (senior operations analyst, Keds Corp.); Rudges McKenney (senior programmer, Digital Equipment Corporation); M. David Lee (vice-president, Stull and Lee, largest minority-owned architectural firm in Boston); Melvin Benson (senior vice-president, Boston Bank of Commerce, only minority-owned bank in Boston)

Babson means business. Established in 1919 by financier and entrepreneur Roger Ward Babson, the college prepares students—at the undergraduate and graduate levels—for careers in the corporate world. The school does such a good job of it that the editors at *U.S. News & World Report* recently ranked it as the country's best school specializing in business education.

Although students aren't required to declare a major, they are able to major in one of 11 business-related areas. Marketing is the most popular, while finance and communications are regarded as two of the school's best departments. Accounting majors enjoy excellent job placement and consistently score high on national CPA exams. Students also can choose from eight interdisciplinary majors, such as accounting/management information systems and finance/investments.

To graduate, students must complete an extensive core curriculum that includes 11 courses in management, two in economics, and three in the liberal arts. In fact, nearly all of the first year is preordained; the student must take "Calculus," "English Composition," "General Management," "Probability and Statistics," "Business Law," "Introduction to Information Systems," "Speech Communications," and a liberal arts elective. The remaining core courses are completed over the student's next three years.

While the emphasis here is clearly on business, students nonetheless must complete a liberal arts concentration in an area such as classical traditions, creative arts, literature, and history. Students must also take courses in one of five areas: natural science, culture and values, behavioral science, history and politics, and literature and the arts.

While students in many undergraduate business school programs learn from professors trained in theory, Babson students have the benefit of learning from professors who have experience in the business world. Professors, nearly 94 percent of whom have their Ph.Ds, have served or are currently serving as business executives, consultants, and researchers in the private or public sector. The president of the college, William Glavin, earned an MBA from the Wharton School at the University of Pennsylvania, and is a former vice-chairman at the Xerox Corporation. Speakers from businesses in Boston and the nearby Route 128 technology belt are frequent in-class visitors. Publishing baron Rupert Murdoch and chicken magnate Frank Perdue have recently spoken on campus.

Class sizes are generally small, usually numbering no more than 30 students. Students say that the faculty is accessible, and that professors welcome interaction with students. As at the Harvard Business School, Babson students often learn by the case-study method, in which students, usually in groups, examine business problems and attempt to come up with solutions.

Among the faculty, students often turn to Geoffrey Kapenzi, an associate professor of sociology and author of numerous articles on inner-city problems. For additional support, students also rely on Bill Boyd, an assistant director of admissions, and Robyn Franklin Vaughn, a financial aid adviser. "They have dedicated much of their time to helping us structure the Black Students Association," says a student. "They have shown us how to prioritize our activities and coordinate events."

There is little diversity of any sort at Babson. Most of Babson's students are from middle-class families in the Northeast and are definitely politically conservative. Students here are looking to become part of corporate America, and many do just that, joining such firms as Pepsi-Cola, Ford, or their fathers' companies, places where challenging the system is hardly a matter of course. There is little integration socially on campus. "The majority of the African-Americans tend to sit together at mealtime, except for a few, the Asians sit together, and so do the white students," observes a student. "Recently, the Black Students Association threw a campus-wide party and no one came except for African-American students." The Greek system, which provides much of the school's social life on the weekends, is only minimally integrated. According to one student, during a recent year only one African-American student was a member of one of the school's two sororities.

Babson does attract a relatively large international student population—nearly 12 percent of its students are from foreign countries—and the school's Babson International Student Organization (BISO) is one of the more active cultural clubs on campus. Each year BISO hosts a fashion show, a semiformal dance, and numerous other events.

Until fairly recently, the school's BSA has been less than active. During the fall of 1991, however, the group resolved to become more visible on campus. "We've formed three committees that will enable us to do more and to keep us focused," says a BSA leader. "The advertising committee will contribute articles to the school paper about different issues, such as Kwanzaa and Malcolm X. The social committee will coordinate speaker visits, parties, and Black History Month activities. And the T-shirt committee will come up with designs for T-shirts that we will sell for fundraising purposes." Recently, as part of Black History Month, the BSA brought five African-American entrepreneurs to campus to discuss the business world.

Wellesley is home to Wellesley College, and other schools, such as Pine Manor Junior College, Regis College, and Brandeis University, are all within a twenty-minute drive from campus. Babson students are able to enroll in courses at these other schools. The town of Wellesley is a predominantly white upper-middle-class community that could hardly be described as a college town. Students report little interaction with community residents.

Although off-campus socializing is limited in the immediate area, there are more than ample supplies of such activity in nearby Boston. The city, home to numerous colleges and universities, offers a rich variety of restaurants, clubs, professional sports teams (the Red Sox and the Celtics, to name just two), symphonies, and museums. The "T," Boston's subway, is located two miles from campus, but students frequently rely on cars for transportation into Beantown and the surrounding area.

Babson fields varsity athletic teams in a variety of sports, including basketball, lacrosse, and swimming. The Athletic Complex offers impressive swimming, weight-lifting, and running facilities. A popular club on campus is the Babson Student Chamber of Commerce.

For the young entrepreneur, Babson is the answer to a dream, although he or she will have to do without strong programs in the liberal arts—including cultural studies—and a diverse student body. "I've always wanted to go into business, and I know I'm getting excellent job preparation here," says a student. "The professors care that you do well, and I like the school's small size. I've often wished I'd gone to a school that has students from more backgrounds. Babson doesn't encourage interaction among students of different races, because, besides the international students, there is little cultural diversity here. But by coming here, I'm learning to interact with many of the types of people I'll be dealing with in the business world."

BOSTON COLLEGE

Address: 140 Commonwealth Avenue,
Chestnut Hill, MA 02167
Phone: (617) 552-3100
Director of Admissions: John L. Mahoney
Multicultural Student Recruiter: Richard
Escobar
1991–92 tuition: $13,690
Room and board: $6,150
Application deadline: 1/25
Financial aid application deadline: 2/1

Non-white freshman admissions: Applicants
for the class of '95: na
Accepted: na
Accepted who enroll: na
Applicants accepted who rank in top
10% of high school class: na
Median SAT range: na
Median ACT: na
Full-time undergraduate enrollment: 8,806
Men: 45%
Women: 55%

STUDENT ENROLLMENT

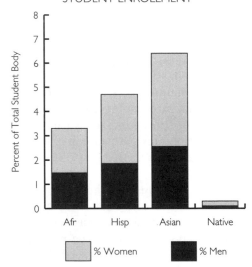

Percent of Total Student Body

Afr   Hisp   Asian   Native

☐ % Women   ■ % Men

Non-white students in
1987–88: 14.9%
1988–89: 16.2%

GEOGRAPHIC DISTRIBUTION OF STUDENTS

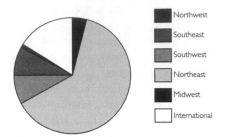

■ Northwest
■ Southeast
■ Southwest
☐ Northeast
■ Midwest
☐ International

1989–90: 16.5%
1990–91: 18.2%
Students In-state: 29%
Top majors: 1. Political Science
2. Communications 3. Finance
Retention rate of non-white students: 77%
**Scholarships exclusively for non-white
students:** None
Remediation programs: None
Academic support services: The AHANA
(African-American, Hispanic, Asian,
Native American) program provides
academic and non-academic support
services. Options Through Education
Transitional Summer Program, the
Academic Development Center, and the
Learning to Learn Program are also
available.
Ethnic studies programs: The college offers
a Black Studies minor and an Asian
Studies minor, both interdisciplinary.
Organizations for non-white students: Asian
Students Intercultural Association, Asian
Caucus, Chinese Student Association,
Korean Student Association, NAACP,
Organization of Latin American Affairs,
South African Task Force, Vietnamese
Student Association, Voices of Imani
Gospel Choir
Notable non-white alumni: Wayne A. Budd
(U.S. Attorney, District of
Massachusetts); Hon. David S. Nelson
(U.S. District judge); Blenda J. Wilson

(chancellor, University of Michigan at Dearborn); Dr. Sylvia Q. Simmons (senior vice president, Massachusetts Higher Education Assistance Corporation)

Tenured faculty: 381
Non-tenured faculty: 192
Student-faculty ratio: 13.6:1
Administrators: 326
  African-American: 3.7%
  Hispanic: 1.2%
  Asian-American: 2.2%
  Native American: 0.31%

Recent non-white speakers on campus: Mary Helen Washington (visiting professor of English, University of Maryland); Renose Makate (representative, African National Congress); Dr. Samuel Proctor (professor, Rutgers University); Barbara Ball (founder and director of Massachusetts Blacks for Life); Angela Davis (political activist); Dr. Ronald Takaki (author and professor of cultural diversity, University of California/Berkeley); Paula Gunn Allen (professor of Native American Studies at UCLA)

Boston College students—most anyway—are Catholic, sports-minded, and happy to be enrolled at this 130-year-old Jesuit institution. They are also treated to some outstanding educational opportunities, especially in the liberal arts and business.

Academics at BC have always been considered top-notch. BC students remain committed to their academics—especially after a good party. Degrees are awarded in four divisions at BC: the College of Arts and Science, whose best departments are English, theology, and philosophy; the highly selective Carroll School of Management, which allows students to concentrate in nine different areas, including accounting, computer science, human resources, and marketing; the School of Education, which offers a five-year program that enables students to earn their BA and MA degrees; and the School of Nursing, which also awards doctorates. The most popular division among BC's pre-professional-minded student body is the School of Management. Although BC is more like a midsize university than a college, students say they nonetheless enjoy close relations with their professors.

To graduate, all BC students must complete a core curriculum that includes two courses each in philosophy, theology, and English. Courses in European history are required of arts and science, education, and nursing students. The school is considering readjusting its core, however. An Intercultural Council, which consists of students, faculty, and administrators, including the president of the college, has recommended that a course on multiculturalism be integrated into the core. The final outcome is still pending. A course titled "Asian-American History and Identity," taught by a psychology professor of Korean descent, is popular with students.

As the city of Boston becomes more cosmopolitan and diverse, so does Boston College, although at a slightly slower pace. To improve the retention and recruitment of non-white students, BC instituted the innovative AHANA (African-American, Hispanic, Asian, Native-American) program, a support network for students that provides tutoring and counseling services and helps coordinate various cultural activities and events during the school year. AHANA also oversees 15 different cultural organizations.

The Asian Caucus, with more than 300 active members (in a recent year), is the school's largest cultural student group. It also serves as the umbrella organization for seven other Asian groups, the most active of which are the Chinese Student Association and the Korean Student Association. The Asian and Asian-American student populations at BC are the fastest-growing. According to one student, a recent graduating class had about 50 such students; by comparison, two recent entering classes each had more than 300.

"Our primary goal is to promote racial harmony, so we try to program events with other organizations," says an Asian Caucus leader. "The most recent and successful was Winter Jam, where we had Asian and African foods and performances by dance and rap groups. More than 600 people, from almost every culture you can imagine, attended the event. There have been rifts between the Asian-Americans and African-Americans on campus, but a lot of walls have been torn down lately. Before the jam, there wasn't much dialogue among our groups, but the dance has changed all that."

The Black Student Forum, whose 50 active members meet about once every three weeks, sponsors a Kwanzaa dinner and a film series throughout the school year. For Black History Month, forum members recently sponsored various workshops that dealt with police brutality in Boston and attending school at a predominantly white campus. A recent forum event held at O'Connell House was a party at which students wore African clothes. The Black Family Weekend is also popular with students and their families. Students, their parents, and alums attend various lectures and a performance of the school's gospel choir, which, according to one student, is diverse, with African-American, Caucasian, and Hispanic members.

Also of interest to African-American students is Umoja and Talented Tenth, support groups for women and men, respectively, that meet weekly.

BC student government is becoming more diverse. "For the second time ever, the student government president is African-American, and his cabinet is also finally diverse," observes a student. "Of the 46 cabinet members, 11 are AHANA students. When the dean of students gave out his awards for leadership, eight of the 20 or so went to AHANA students, whereas only one or two AHANA students received them in past years."

Despite the efforts of AHANA students and various cultural organizations, students say that the typical BC student is not aware of issues of diversity and that partying usually takes precedence over almost anything else. "Apathy is a huge problem here. The tendency is to go out drinking and to play Nintendo. And ever since the ban on kegs in 1990, students are now turning to hard alcohol."

AHANA students have experienced problems with campus security, but with a new chief of security who seems interested in building better relations with AHANA students, students are hopeful that such problems will be solved.

To develop a dialogue, various students and administrators sponsored a recent multicultural weekend retreat. "During the first phase of the retreat, we discussed our cultures and the pressures we feel here at BC," says a student. "Some of the non-AHANA students present started to feel uncomfortable when we talked, but we wanted them to understand what we feel like when we walk into an all-white classroom or party. The administrators were also surprised at the pressure we feel coming here. An African-American student got very emotional and angry, and told the academic vice president who was present that there is no real diversity in courses at BC."

Two ideas emerged from the retreat, according to a student. First, BC's Pride Workshops, which seek to sensitize participants to issues of prejudice, would be expanded to include members of the BC security staff. Second, plans were to be made for a similar retreat in the future.

BC is located just twenty minutes outside of Boston, the ultimate college town, but students say socializing with students at some of the schools in the city is infrequent. Easily accessible on the "T" subway system, Boston provides a wealth of cultural and social outlets—theaters, clubs and bars, concerts, just to name a few. But most of the campus's social life takes place on campus, either at dorm parties or through such annual events as Winter Carnival, Dorm Olympics, and World Fiesta Day. The school also has more than two dozen music and performance groups, including the popular Voices of Imani Gospel Choir, and the Flynn Student Recreation Complex ("the Plex") is any sports enthusiast's dream come true.

The racial and cultural homogeneity of Boston College may be trying for some students, but the school's location, academics, and support services make it a school worth checking out. Says a student: "Being a minority student has sometimes been a difficult experience, but with the support services of AHANA and some of the cultural student groups on campus, it's been less so. I've met some good friends here, and I'm confident I've also learned a great deal, about myself and cultures different from my own."

BOSTON UNIVERSITY

Address: 121 Bay State Road, Boston, MA 02215
Phone: (617) 353-2300
Director of Admissions: Thomas Rajala
Multicultural Student Recruiter: Arlene Cash
1991–92 tuition: $16,590
Room and board: $6,320
Application deadline: 1/15
Financial aid application deadline: 3/15
Non-white freshman admissions: Applicants
  for the class of '96: na
  Accepted: na
  Accepted who enroll: na
  Applicants accepted who rank in top
  10% of high school class: na
  Median SAT range: na
  Median ACT range: na
Full-time undergraduate enrollment: 13,663
  Men: 47%
  Women: 53%

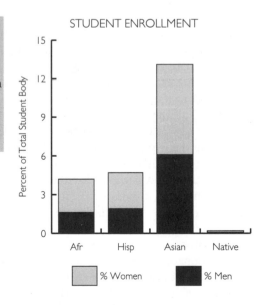

STUDENT ENROLLMENT

Percent of Total Student Body

Afr　Hisp　Asian　Native

☐ % Women　■ % Men

Non-white students in
   1987–88: 13.6%
   1988–89: 15.3%
   1989–90: 17.8%
   1990–91: 19.9%
Geographic distribution of students: na
Students In-state: 23.9%
Top majors: 1. Liberal Arts 2. Management
   3. Engineering
Retention rate of non-white students: na
**Scholarships exclusively for non-white
   students:** Lewis D. Apsley Scholarships:
   merit- and need-based; each award
   valued at $7,000; ten awarded each year;
   available to African-American applicants.
Remediation programs: None
Academic support services: The
   Undergraduate Resource Center, the
   Martin Luther King, Jr., Center, and the
   AHANA Peer Advising Center provide
   academic and non-academic support
   programs.
Ethnic studies programs: The university
   offers programs in African Studies,
   Hispanic and continental European
   literature, and Hispanic language and
   literature.
Ethnic studies courses: The College of
Liberal Arts offers various courses in
Asian Studies.
Organizations for non-white students:
   Minority Engineering Society, Minority
   Free Health Association, Black
   Investment Group, Latinos Unidos,
   NAACP, Society of Hispanic
   Professional Engineers, Alpha Phi Alpha,
   Delta Sigma Theta, Kappa Alpha Psi,
   Omega Psi Phi, Phi Beta Sigma, Alpha
   Kappa Alpha, Sigma Gamma Rho, Zeta
   Phi Beta, Asian Student Union, Umoja
   (African-American student group),
   Caribbean Club, National Collegiate
   Black Club, Chinese Student Club, Japan
   Culture Society, Korean Student
   Association, Black Students' Forum of
   the College of Basic Studies,
   Filipino-American Club, AHANA
   Pre-law Associates, Innerstrength Gospel
   Choir, United Association of Chinese
   Students of Boston University
Notable non-white alumni: na
Faculty: na
Student-faculty ratio: 15:1
Administrators: na
Recent non-white speakers on campus: na

Situated on the south side of the Charles River, Boston University is one of Boston's—and the country's—largest private institutions of higher learning. For some, BU can be overwhelming, but for others, and this includes the majority of BU undergraduates, the school is a wealth of academic and extracurricular activity.

But to focus only on the opportunities at BU and not the city of Boston would be to ignore half the reason why many students choose to come to school here in the first place. To say Boston is a college town would be putting it lightly. With more than 16 colleges and universities in the area, Boston caters to more student interests than almost any other city in the country. Students attend parties at any of the nearby campuses, many of them easily accessible either by foot or by public transit, and invite each other to one another's cultural and intellectual conferences. All kinds of bars, clubs, and restaurants are available in the area and are popular venues for students to meet with their peers.

And Boston University is very much a part of the city, as the campus is far from self-contained. A six-lane highway cuts a swath through the middle of campus, and fast-food restaurants and other shops are woven into the campus fabric, an atmosphere that pleases some. "There's always something to watch," comments a senior. "It's all part of what makes going here so exciting." Comments another student: "I like that it's not a closed campus. You get to feel the different atmospheres of a city."

Another aspect of what makes going here exciting is the myriad of organizations—283 in all—that are active on campus. Just about every kind of cultural, political, professional, and social group is offered to BU students, or, if it's not, says a junior, "then get some friends together and start your own."

Among the school's cultural organizations is Latinos Unidos, with about 100 active members, most of whom were born in other countries. "We have members from almost every Latin American country—Argentina, Cuba, Brazil, Ecuador, you name it," says a group leader. The organization is "very visible," according to the student, and sponsors lectures, movies, get-togethers, and poetry readings. One of the group's more successful efforts is the dance party it sponsors each year to raise money for its Latin American Scholarship Fund. Latinos Unidos members also tutor BU students who are studying Spanish, as well as young people at area community centers and high schools.

Umoja, BU's African-American student group, sponsors a Kwanzaa dinner each year, as well as a semiformal dance, a fashion show, and a Halloween party for eighth-grade students at a nearby middle school. Popular among BU's African-American students is Arlene Cash, an associate director of admissions, who also advises the Black Student Union. "She's like my mom. I can just call her anytime, at home or at the office. She also comes to most Umoja meetings and events."

BU's National Society of Black Engineers, which sponsors several workshops during the school year, recently received the NSBE zone chapter of the year.

One of the major focuses of the Asian Student Union in coming years is to unify BU's Asian community and student organizations. "In my opinion, the ASU lost its identity because there are always so many activities sponsored by the different Asian clubs that the events conflict with each other." He adds: "All Asian clubs have gone downhill. There aren't that many people participating. When I was a freshman, there was always lots going on with the groups. Now, they don't seem as popular. For example, we always get a lot of people to come to our first general meeting of the term, but then interest quickly drops off." However, several ASU parties are scheduled each year, as well as various workshops. Other active Asian clubs are the Chinese Student Club, the Japan Culture Society, and the Korean Student Association.

The university has the academic programs to satisfy even the most jaded of its undergraduate customers. The College of Communications is nationally recognized and popular, as is the College of Engineering. Archaeology, biology, business, and psychology are well regarded by students.

According to one student, BU's Latin American Studies program "is nothing yet to be proud of because it's only been around for a couple of years." But, he adds, the program does allow for some interesting programming. "In a course I took called 'Grass-Roots Development of Latin America,' we got to have phone conferences with officials of various Latin American countries while they were still in their countries."

Despite the school's vast size, students says professors do their best to make themselves available to students. For additional academic support, students say BU's Undergraduate Resource Center "really tries to help you out with tutoring and study skills workshops." The Office of Multicultural Affairs, located in the Martin Luther King, Jr., Center, "is good to go to for academic assistance and grad school and internship possibilities," says a student. The office also regularly publishes *Expressions of Color,* which contains interviews with faculty and staff, poems, and student profiles, as well as information about opportunities that might be of interest to its readers. The publication, usually about four pages long, is edited solely by students.

Although students say there is little racial tension, students are conflicted when they discuss race relations on campus. No doubt the differences in perception are due, at least in part, to the vast size of BU. "Whites at BU like learning about different cultures, and there is a lot of mixing here on campus. My roommates are Korean and Japanese, and I'm Latino, and there is no racial division between us. We're all good friends." Another student's experiences, however, are different. "The minorities here stay completely separate from one another. They all sponsor separate activities and events, and rarely, if ever, mix. Even within the Asian groups there is little intermingling. The Chinese students stay with the Chinese students, and the Koreans and Japanese stick with each other. The same can be said of the different black groups on campus. There are differences between Caribbeans and African-Americans."

In an attempt to encourage more multiculturalism, the Office of Multicultural Affairs has instituted an AHANA Empowerment Council. AHANA, an acronym which stands for African-American, Hispanic, Asian, and Native American, was developed at Boston College. Although the group is relatively new, it recently suffered a setback, according to a student, when the president of the university, John Silber, backed away at the last minute from a forum discussion on political correctness.

Silber has certainly made a name for himself at the university. Students call him controversial and reactionary. Many were hopeful he would win the Massachusetts gubernatorial race so they "wouldn't have to deal with his policies any longer." Others say he's put the university on the map, and is a well-regarded figure in academia. He is also one of the highest paid college presidents in the country. One of the more controversial of his policies, at least for students, was his 1989 ruling that no member of the opposite sex would be allowed in a dorm room after 1 a.m. "That means that parties end at 12:30, and when you're from New York City, as I am, where parties don't start until then, that's a bummer," says a student.

In short, there are three good reasons to attend "that other university" in Boston: respectable academics, never a shortage of things to do, and the city of Boston. The problem comes in knowing how to juggle it all. "I came here because I wanted to go to school in Boston, and I've liked the museums and being in a city and near the river," says a student. "And there's so much to do. BU certainly got me to broaden my horizons, in and out of the classroom."

BRANDEIS UNIVERSITY

Address: Waltham, MA 02254-9110
Phone: (617) 622-0622 / (800) 622-0622
(out-of-state)
Director of Admissions: Michael Kalafatas
Multicultural Student Recruiter: Betty Lloyd

1992–93 tuition: $17,320
Room and board: $6,505
Application deadline: 2/1
Financial aid application deadline: 2/15

In just 44 years of existence, Brandeis University has risen to become one of the country's more respected schools of higher education—a fact made even more noteworthy considering the plethora of generations-old colleges in the Boston area.

Brandeis is distinctive not only for its well-regarded academic programs but also because of its size. With only about 3,000 undergraduates, the university is able to provide students with the intimacy of a small liberal arts college while still providing the academic opportunities found at some of the country's larger research universities. (The university maintains a graduate school of arts and sciences and the Heller Graduate School for Advanced Studies in Social Welfare.)

Students say that pre- anything is good at the university, especially pre-law, pre-medicine, and pre-veterinary school. (Acceptance rates of Brandeis graduates into medical and law schools are indeed impressive—nearly 95 and 80 percent, respectively.) The school's Near Eastern and Judaic Studies program is said to be one of the best in the country; politics and economics are also strong, as are almost any programs in the sciences, including biochemistry, chemistry, physics, and biology. The university has instituted new programs in East Asian Studies and neuroscience. When students can't find what they want in the Brandeis curriculum, they're able to enroll in courses at any of the nearby colleges in Boston, including Boston College and Boston and Tufts universities. Academics are taken seriously by the typical Brandeis student; the school ranks 15th among all colleges and universities in the country in the number of graduates who go on to earn Ph.D.s.

Faculty and staff make themselves more than available to students. Todd Blake, an assistant director for student life, "has good rapport with minority students," comments a sophomore. "He serves as the main link between the administration and the minority students. He likes to be with students, and he hangs out with us. He genuinely cares that we do well here." Also a source of support for students is Elaine Wong, a dean of the college. "I was recommended to her by a friend as a woman I could talk to, and she was very helpful. She helped me clear up the problems I was having, and she listened to me. She's a good person."

When discussing the cultural atmosphere at Brandeis, one must first discuss the university's Jewish heritage. Brandeis was founded in 1948 by an American Jewish community to bring "to American higher education a unique cultural perspective reflecting Jewish traditions of scholarship and community service and the commitment to social justice personified by Louis Dembitz Brandeis, the distinguished

Supreme Court Justice for whom the University is named." Today, more than 60 percent of the university's student body is Jewish, and in 1987 the university's dining halls for the first time began serving kosher *and* non-kosher meals. Jewish religious organizations, such as Hillel, are also active.

But Brandeis' Jewish culture is by no means the only culture represented on campus. Brandeis was founded as a nonsectarian university and is under no religious organization's control; no religious courses are required and students and faculty of all backgrounds and beliefs are welcome. Catholic, Protestant, and Jewish houses of worship are on campus, and the gay and lesbian student organization has an active membership. In 1990, according to the Department of Education, 4.9 percent of the school's 3,791 students were Asian, 3.2 percent were African-American, 2.3 percent were Hispanic, and 0.1 percent were American Indian. (The admissions office declined to respond to our request for the most current statistics.)

Brandeis also succeeds in attracting a more progressive-minded student body, students who aren't averse to attending a protest march or demonstration or two—although the school's diversity does allow for a somewhat active Young Republican chapter on campus. Recently, an African-American was elected to serve as Brandeis' student body president.

The school's commitment to multiculturalism is evident in its new Intercultural Center, located near East Quad. The center, which one student described as "very student-oriented," has office space for various student groups, including the Black Student Association, the Korean Student Association, and AHORA, a Hispanic student group.

The Brandeis Asian-American Student Association (BAASA), however, has decided not to move from the student union to the Intercultural Center. "The BAASA already has a great office in the student union. Also, a BAASA tradition here at Brandeis is the Lunch Brunch, where students come up to the office to eat rather than in the cafeteria, which is located downstairs. It's nice to meet with students over lunch." The BAASA has about 30 active members.

With all of the attention given by students to their school work, campus social life suffers somewhat. Studying is a popular Friday-night activity. But new student clubs and organizations, including a theater group, a gospel choir, and a comic book and science fiction collective, work to provide social and cultural outlets. Brandeis also fields more than 40 sports teams and clubs, and its new Recreation Complex is one of the most impressive in the Northeast. Parties at colleges in Boston and Cambridge are easily accessible thanks to public transportation. Beantown, ten minutes from campus, provides a wealth of cultural and social activities—clubs, concerts, sporting events, to name a few. Waltham, Brandeis' hometown, offers little, however, to the student looking for off-campus diversions.

Brandeis is unique in American higher education, as much for its history as for the quality of its educational opportunities. Brandeis is a school for students who are bright and motivated and who don't mind rocking the boat. Says a philosophy major: "The students here have great opportunities to effect change at Brandeis. That ability to change Brandeis instills a certain pride—the pride of ownership. This more than anything makes Brandeis great: the fact that it is our university. I feel this is important training because we must also change our world when we leave here."

CLARK UNIVERSITY

Address: Worcester, MA 01610
Phone: (508) 793-7431
Director of Admissions: Richard Pierson
Multicultural Student Recruiter: Allan
  Brown

1992–93 tuition: $15,800
Room and board: $4,500
Application deadline: 2/15
Financial aid application deadline: 2/15

Clark University is not your typical prominent Northeastern university, where competition for grades is keen and business majors run rampant. Clarkies are highly iconoclastic, or, as one student aptly puts it: "Some of us were probably the kids in kindergarten who never worried about coloring inside—or outside—the lines."

Clark students most often fall on the more liberal part of the political spectrum. "If you're conservative when you come here you will definitely turn liberal by the time you graduate," comments a junior. One of the ways in which students express their social commitment is through various activities in and around the Worcester community. Popular among many Clark students are tutoring elementary school students, working at soup kitchens, and participating in big brother/big sister programs.

Although Clark students may not be concerned about staying inside the lines, they do care about academics. Clark's educational opportunities include some excellent academic departments. The school's geography department has graduated more Ph.D.s in geography than any other school in the country, and the psychology department is nationally recognized. (Clark was the only school in the country to award Sigmund Freud, the father of psychoanalysis, an honorary degree, and the school's first president, G. Stanley Hall, was a noted pioneer in the study of child development.) Other top-flight departments at Clark are management, English, biology, and history. Clarkies say study groups are popular and that professors are readily available for one-on-one assistance.

Among Clark's Asian Studies courses, students say the history department's "Modern Asia" is strong and challenging. The course's professor, Stephen Tanaka, is especially helpful, say students, when it comes time for research assistance. A Black Studies concentration is also offered; popular courses in the area are "African-American Women" and "Africa and the World." Clark students are also able to take courses at any one of the nine schools in the Worcester consortium, which includes Holy Cross and Worcester Polytechnic Institute.

Clark's campus, described by one student as "urban and beautiful," is located in the city of Worcester, which has attempted to overcome its rather nondescript image. The Worcester Centrum hosts such megastars as U2 and Bruce Springsteen, and a variety of outdoor cafes and ethnic restaurants are available in the area. Some students will make the 38-mile trek to Boston for additional nightlife and cultural activity.

Clark can by no means be described as a jock school. The fact that the university does not field a football team is a case in point. However, Clark's women's and men's basketball teams have been regular Division III top contenders in recent years. Women's field hockey also offers opponents some stiff competition.

Clark's various cultural student groups provide an assortment of activities. The Asian Society, which has about 40 active members, meets once a month, usually in a conference room in the university center. One of the society's more popular activities is the annual Asian Buffet. "People from different Asian cultures cook foods for the buffet, which is one of the big events of the school year. Students wait for it all year. This year we added entertainment, including Tae Kwon Do demonstrations and a song performed by three Indonesian students. An Indian dance was also performed," says a student. Although the Asians and Asian-Americans represent the largest non-white student population at Clark, one Asian Society member says there is little unity between the international and American-born Asian students.

Sunil Bahtil, the society's adviser, is, says a student, "very helpful in getting students motivated. We also feel comfortable going to her for emotional support."

The Black Student Union, with about 30 to 35 active members, "is the school's busiest cultural organization," according to a member, and is divided into three committees: social, political, and cultural. One of the group's biggest activities is its annual Student Solidarity Conference, in which representatives of black student organizations from various East Coast colleges and universities are invited to Clark to attend workshops. In a recent year, more than 30 schools, mostly from New York, were represented, involving more than 250 students. The BSU also sponsors an annual semiformal dance, also known as the Spring Cabaret. For Black History Month, in a recent year the BSU sponsored a movie night, poetry readings, and speakers and gospel singers from Boston. A Kwanzaa celebration was also held at an area church.

Perhaps the organization's most popular on-campus events are its parties—held at the university center—"which are usually packed," says a student. "The parties are always well publicized on and off campus, and we get one of the best turnouts at our parties in the city of Worcester."

Clark's Bethune Multicultural Center, located next to the admissions office, does not provide residence facilities but does offer a small multicultural library, a kitchen, and meeting space for the BSU. In the fall of 1992, members of the Asian Society began hosting their meetings in the center. However, students say the center is not used much. "When we decided to start using the house as a multicultural center, we didn't know that it was in such bad condition. Right now we're trying to get the student council to give us the money to paint the inside of the house."

Although Clark's admissions office did not participate in our guide, we were able to learn from school publications that 9 percent of a recent entering class of about 550 students was non-white. An additional 10 percent of the students were international, with more than 75 foreign countries represented in the student population of about 2,100. According to students, during a recent year approximately 5 percent of the campus were Asian or Asian-American, while 88 students were African-American, which amounts to about 4 percent of the student body. We were unable to obtain the exact figures for Native Americans and Latinos enrolled at the university. About half of Clark's student population comes from Massachusetts, New York State, and Connecticut.

Tolerance is one of the characteristics Clark students are most proud of in their campus community, and it's one reason why many people choose to become Clarkies. "When I came to Clark for the first time, I fell in love with the campus immediately. It's like it was today, a nice spring afternoon, when everyone just sits out in the quad studying and talking to friends. There's no other school more diverse than Clark. We have students from everywhere in the world. It's easy to fit in here."

HAMPSHIRE COLLEGE

Address: Amherst, MA 01002
Phone: (413) 549-4600
Director of Admissions: Audrey Smith
Multicultural Student Recruiter: Jarrett
  Saunders
1993–94 tuition: $19,490
Room and board: $5,160
Application deadline: 2/1
Financial aid application deadline: 2/15
Non-white freshman admissions: Applicants
  for the class of '96: 163
  Accepted: 55%
  Accepted who enroll: 31%
  Applicants accepted who rank in top
  10% of high school class: 35%
  In top 25%: 63%
  Median SAT: 550 V, 540 M
  Median ACT: na
Full-time undergraduate enrollment: 1,173
  Men: 41%
  Women: 59%
Non-white students in
  1987–88: 5%
  1988–89: 6%
  1989–90: 7%
  1990–91: 9%
Students In-state: 10%
Top majors: na
Retention rate of non-white students: na
Scholarships exclusively for non-white
  students: Arturo Schomburg Scholarship:
  merit- and need-based; $3,000–$5,000 for
  each award; ten awarded each year.
  Jean Flint Scholarship: need-based;
  recipient must have graduated from a
  public high school in Springfield,
  MA; two awarded each year; each
  award valued at between $3,000 and
  $5,000.

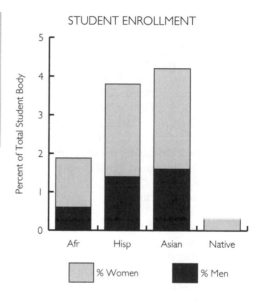

STUDENT ENROLLMENT

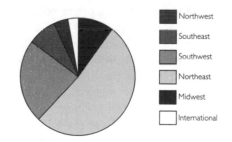

GEOGRAPHIC DISTRIBUTION OF STUDENTS

Remediation programs: None
Academic support services: Student Advising
  Center and the Third World Academic
  Advising Center offer academic and
  non-academic support services.
Ethnic studies programs: Students have the

ability to design their own programs of study.

Ethnic studies courses: "African Development," "Race in the United States," "Dynamics of Diversity," "The State of Third World Development," "Struggle for Democracy in the Third World," "African-American Poetry," and others.

Organizations for non-white students: Umoja (African-American student group), Raíces (Latino group), SOURCe (Students of Underrepresented Cultures), Black History Month Organization

Notable non-white alumni: Kevin Brown ('83, Theater; actor); Victoria Hernandez ('75, Education/Social Science; director, alumni affairs, Florida International University); Mary James ('76; professor); Walter Kyu-sung Lew ('78; professor); Matthew Patrick ('79; owner, director, producer, Panorama Productions)

Faculty: 99

Student-faculty ratio: 13:1

Administrators: 117
  African-American: 7 total
  Hispanic: 2%
  Asian-American: 0
  Native American: 0

Recent non-white speakers on campus: Johnnetta Cole (president, Spelman

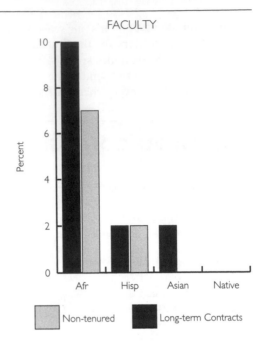

FACULTY

College); Barbara Sizemore (professor, University of Pittsburgh); Sheila Walker (professor of anthropology, College of William and Mary); Huri Kockiyama (political activist); John Edgar Wideman (author); Sister Souljah (rap artist, activist); Vanessa Gamble (professor of medicine, University of Wisconsin)

Founded in 1970, Hampshire offers one of the more innovative educational opportunities in the country. There are no distribution requirements at Hampshire, multidisciplinary learning is the norm, and students receive written evaluations from their professors at the end of the term rather than the standard letter grades.

Hampshire was the brainchild of a faculty committee appointed in 1958 by the presidents of the University of Massachusetts, and Amherst, Smith, and Mount Holyoke colleges to reevaluate liberal arts education. The committee's report, "The New College Plan," was essentially a blueprint for what would become Hampshire College.

Hampshire's courses of study are divided into only four areas: the School of Communications and Cognitive Science, the School of Humanities and Arts, the School of Natural Science, and the School of Social Science. Once at the college, students are not referred to as freshmen, sophomores, or juniors, but as students in Divisions I, II, or III.

In Division I, which usually lasts for the student's first three semesters, students study in each of the school's four areas. In Division II, which usually lasts for the next three semesters, students concentrate (i.e., major) in one of the four areas of Division I. As part of Division II, students draft a concentration statement that reflects the goals they expect to achieve over the next semesters. Students are able to move on to Division III only after successfully passing an examination, for which students submit the work completed during Division II. Before Division III, students are also expected to perform a community service project, which can range from college governance to volunteering to work with the developmentally disabled. In addition, students must satisfy a Third World Studies course requirement.

Hampshire offers various courses in African-American, Latin American, and Asian Studies, and students report they have been "eye-opening and educating." "They all got me to see a little bit of who I am and helped me see who I want to be," says a student who studies "Third World Feminism," "Race in the U.S.," and "Peasant Revolution in China." "These courses have taught me about racism, sexism, and all kinds of oppression that goes on in this world. Without these courses, I wouldn't be who I am today." Students can take additional courses in these areas at other schools in the Five-College Consortium.

Hampshire also offers several multidisciplinary programs, including business and society, civil liberties and public policy, computer studies, feminist studies, and Third World Studies.

Hampshire's curriculum is demanding and students are expected to be extremely self-motivated. Many incoming students aren't up to the task. Nearly 40 percent of almost any entering class transfers or drops out before graduating. To encourage more students to stick it out to graduation, the college's Office of Multicultural Affairs established the Third World Academic Advising Center, which provides four student tutors from the different multicultural groups.

The college recently established on campus the Le Bran-Wiggins-Pran Cultural Center. "Although the center is technically a building—a house, to be more exact—I think of it and refer to it as the embodiment of multicultural programming for Hampshire," says a campus leader. The center houses the Multicultural Affairs Office; the office of the coordinator of SOURCe, the umbrella organization for the college's four multicultural student groups; and the office of the affirmative action officer. The Multicultural Affairs Office, in conjunction with various student groups, sponsors speakers, symposiums, and lectures. "These events are usually extremely educational and informative," reports a fourth-year student. "I went to the Multicultural Affairs Office to apply for funding for the Multicultural Theater Collective production," says a student. "They gave us three hundred dollars of funding."

Until recently, SOURCe was the only multiracial student group on campus. Today, it serves as the umbrella organization for Raíces (the Latino student group), Umoja (the African-American student group), the Asian Pacific Students Association, and the Women of Color group. "Because students of different color have different interests, SOURCe couldn't meet them all," says a student. "Now each of the organizations gets separate funding from the student activities fund and does its own programming." One student, however, worries that the separation of the student groups will lead to conflicts. "Before dividing up SOURCe into separate groups, students of color were better friends. Now, politically, students must be involved with their own groups."

The Asian Pacific Students Association (ASPA) is Hampshire's newest cultural student group. "Before, Asian students would see each other on campus but wouldn't really speak to each other," says a student. "I didn't speak to a single Asian the first year I was at Hampshire. Now with ASPA we are trying to develop an Asian community. For those who find it useful, ASPA has been comforting. It helps first-year students adjust and develops an Asian kinship. This kinship is greatly appreciated by me since life can be lonely without Asian friends." Recent ASPA events have included a film series, a conference on the civil rights and liberties for Southeast Asians, a theater production of Frank Chin's *The Year of the Dragon,* and an anti-Asian violence workshop, as well as readings of Asian and Asian-American writers.

Raíces, which provides social and academic support, has brought various Central American speakers and movies to campus, and publishes a literary magazine, *La Fuerza.* Umoja activities have included an African-American Crafts Fair. Students have the option of living in the Umoja House or the Raíces House, for African-American and Hispanic students, respectively. Each house has room for eight students.

Students say the campus is "pretty integrated" socially. "Students of color as well as white students attend events sponsored by organizations of color," observes a student. "Everyone attends parties, especially if there is beer. I know a few students of color who mostly hang out with other students of color, but most students of color hang out with white students as well as students of color."

There is no shortage of activities in and around Amherst. The area is home to four other colleges and universities, and students often attend the events and parties at the other schools. Amherst, a diverse college community, also has an eclectic mixture of ethnic restaurants. Boston is less than two hours away, easily accessible by bus, and New York City is less than four hours away.

Hampshire's educational approach is not for the conformist, or one who needs a great deal of academic or social structure. For those who graduate from this non-traditional college, the education will have been as challenging as it is rewarding. "Here at Hampshire you face many problems as a person of color. You encounter problems with white students, other students of color, faculty/staff of color, administration, curriculum, and society," reflects a fourth-year student. "At Hampshire, you get to deal with all of them. And you deal with them in your own way. That's basically what one learns. In terms of having your concerns addressed, they will be addressed by your friends, your professors, books you read, movies you watch, plays you attend, and demonstrations in which you participate. Here at Hampshire you can address these issues every day, and there will be people doing so right along with you."

HARVARD UNIVERSITY

Address: Byerly Hall, 8 Garden Street, Cambridge, MA 02138
Phone: (617) 495-1551
Director of Admissions: Dr. Marlyn McGrath Lewis
Multicultural Student Recruiter: Jennifer Davis Carey
1991–92 tuition: $15,410
Room and board: $5,520
Application deadline: Early decision: 11/1; regular decision: 1/1
Financial aid application deadline: 1/1
Non-white freshman admissions: Applicants for the class of '96: na
  Accepted: na
  Accepted who enroll: na
  Applicants accepted who rank in top 10% of high school class: na
  Median SAT: na
  Median ACT: na
Full-time undergraduate enrollment: 6,622
  Men: 59%
  Women: 41%

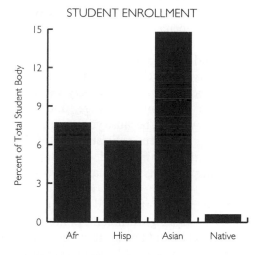

STUDENT ENROLLMENT

Percent of Total Student Body

Afr   Hisp   Asian   Native

Non-white students in 1987–91: na
Geographic distribution of students: na
Top majors: na
Retention rate of non-white students: na

Scholarships exclusively for non-white students: None
Remediation programs: None
Academic support services: The colleges offer a wide variety of non-credit study skills courses, as well as tutoring services.
Ethnic studies programs: Harvard's Afro-American Studies program, established in 1971, is interdisciplinary, involving courses in economics, English, government, history, music, religion, and sociology. The university offers a program in East Asian languages and civilizations which includes courses in Chinese, Japanese, Korean, and Vietnamese language, and a program in Latin American and Iberian Studies.
Organizations for non-white students: African Students Association, *Diaspora* (a journal), Afro-American Cultural Center, Forum on Hispanic Affairs, American Indians at Harvard, Asian-American Association, Koreans of Harvard/Radcliffe, Asian Theater Workshop, Kuumba Singers, Association of Black Radcliffe Women, Ngoma African Song/Dance Troupe, Ballet Folklórico de Aztlán, La Organización, Black Business Association, Philippine Forum, Black CAST (a theater company), South Asian Association, Black Cinema Society, Teatro Latino Estudiantil, Black Men's Forum, Radcliffe Asian Women's Group, Black Students Association, La Raza (a Latino student group), Caribbean Club, Vietnamese Association
Notable non-white alumni: na
Tenured faculty: 384
Non-tenured faculty: 231
Student-faculty ratio: 12:1
Administrators: 493
  African-American: 3.5%
  Hispanic: 1.2%
  Asian-American: 1.8%
  Native American: 0

FACULTY

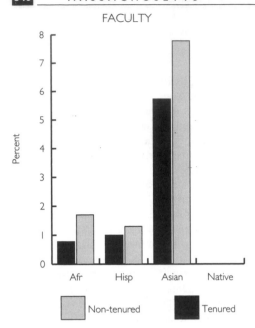

Non-tenured   Tenured

Recent non-white speakers on campus: Marian Wright Edelman (director, Children's Defense Fund); Sylvester Monroe (author and journalist); David Henry Hwang (playwright); Ali Mazrui (professor and author); Alex Haley (author); Louis Sullivan (former U.S. Secretary of Health and Human Services); Henry Hampton (producer); Carlos Romero Barcelo (former governor of Puerto Rico); Rafael Hernández Colón (governor of Puerto Rico); Arthur Ashe (tennis player and Wimbledon winner); Tony Brown (host and producer, *Tony Brown's Journal*)

Along with Cambridge and Oxford universities in England, Harvard University is one of the world's most famous—and best endowed—institutions of higher learning. Students flock to America's oldest university—the school is more than 350 years old—from every state in the country and many countries around the globe. And a letter of acceptance to Harvard isn't taken lightly by prospective students; nearly 75 percent of those accepted decide to attend, a higher percentage than at any other college or university in the nation.

In almost every respect—from politics to race and from geography to interests— Harvard is one of the most diverse schools in the Ivy League. "Harvard is proud of its diversity, and our president is always talking about the great diversity we have here," says a student leader. "It's also very in to be a minority here, and very comfortable. People don't expect you to act a certain way just because you're a certain color or because you're from a certain place." Adds a student activist: "One of the positives of this place is that I've made friends from all over the world, from all parts of the country, and from all backgrounds. The other students are in large part what makes it so exciting to go to school here."

Harvard's academics include some of the best programs of their kind in the nation. Among the best and most popular are English, economics, government, philosophy, and history. And to take anthropology with Stephen Jay Gould or to study economics with John Maynard Keynes is reason enough not to cut class. Although Harvard's faculty boasts some of the most famous and well-respected scholars in their respective areas, students do say gaining access to such stars can sometimes be difficult. "The faculty are geared to graduate schools and their research. You have to seek them out, but that process has only made me more independent. You need initiative, definitely." Teaching assistants, who usually lead smaller class discussions on days when professors aren't lecturing to large audiences, are said to be helpful and less intimidating than some of the faculty.

Harvard's East Asian Studies program is reputed to be one of the tops in the country, and the school's only Asian-American course, a literature course, is "outstanding and always packed," according to a student. The course, however, is taught by visiting professors, who, laments a student, "aren't able to advise theses." The university's African-American Studies program recently received a boost when it successfully recruited scholar Henry Louis Gates away from Duke University. Filmmaker Spike Lee had to turn students away when he taught "Contemporary African-American Cinema" during the spring semester of 1992.

A common quip is that it's harder to get into Harvard than it is to flunk out, or, as one student delicately puts it, "you don't have to cut your veins to survive academically here." While Harvard may not have the academic intensity of Yale University or Swarthmore College, there are those students who enjoy burning the midnight oil.

But what is most typical of Harvard students is their devotion to outside activities. "Everyone here is fairly academically oriented, but almost everyone has something they're interested in besides academics," says a senior. Harvard students have a wealth of activities from which to choose, everything from the famed Harvard *Crimson* and numerous other publications to a vast array of cultural, political, and social organizations. But here again is where some good old Harvard initiative—perhaps the same sort of stuff that got you into the school in the first place—is needed. "Getting on staff at one of the publications, like the *Crimson* or the *Lampoon*, for example, is nearly as competitive as getting into Harvard. The same can be said of trying to be a leader of a lot of the groups here," observes a junior.

With a new administration, Harvard's Asian-American Association has set a new agenda. "In the past, AAA has been lax. We've always been social and had our share of parties, forums, and meetings, but now we're looking to be more political. As a group, we plan to push the administration to increase Asian-American course offerings, and we want to increase the number of women and minority faculty members on staff," says an AAA leader. "At a recent general meeting, we drew up a three-point plan. First we decided that *East Wind,* a magazine formerly on campus, would be reinstituted, which will educate the Harvard community about Asian-American concerns. Second, the group will develop a more political focus. And third, we plan to establish a political chair."

With about 200 active members, AAA is Harvard's largest cultural student group. The group publishes its own monthly newsletter—*SAAAVY*—that highlights activities and events on campus. Many of the group's activities are held during Asian-American Cultural Month, in December. Activities include lectures, food festivals, and film series. The events are co-sponsored with the school's various Asian student groups, the most active of which, according to a student, are the Chinese Student Association and the Korean Student Association. General AAA meetings occasionally focus on specific issues, including, recently, interracial dating and dealing with stereotypes.

The Black Students Association, which has approximately 175 active members, "is stronger and more committed this year than in recent years," according to a BSA leader. The association is committed to making sure that the African-American community succeeds academically at the university. "We try to do a lot for ourselves. I want to make sure my friend graduates, and vice versa—this is the common idea of the BSA. We share textbooks, resources, and help each other with paper topics," says a student. The BSA's Academic Committee coordinates study groups and assists first-year students in planning course schedules. The BSA also sponsors its own successful big brother/big sister program. "I'm still friends with my big brother, who's now at Harvard Law School. Not only are big brothers a help when they're on campus as students, but they're also someone to network with."

BSA events include parties, faculty-student receptions, as well as forums, which have featured such recent topics as "Afrocentricity in the 1990s," "Politics in the BSA," and "Race Relations." The BSA also publishes *BlackWatch,* a monthly four-page magazine that contains listings of activities and resources of interest to members. The BSA office is located in Memorial Hall.

The Freshman Black Table serves to help make the transition from high school to life at Harvard a bit easier. "The Freshman Black Table is its own organization and has its own office and officers," says a student. "Members get together once a week to discuss a topic. It's very informal, and we talk about anything—black-Jewish relations, interracial relationships. It provides an atmosphere for freshmen to get to know each other."

BSA members are also committed to community involvement. Members frequently tutor Boston and Cambridge area students, as well as participate in events such as the annual Walk for Hunger. "We're very committed to the progress of our race. We're not just committed to our academics," comments a student.

According to a student active in the BSA, the African-American community is diverse. "Not everyone is from the inner city, or from all-white or all-black neighborhoods. We're from all over the country and from all parts of the political spectrum."

With about 45 active members, La Organización Estudiantio Boricua, Harvard's Puerto Rican student group, brings in live bands each fall semester for its Latin Rhythms Festival, as well as for occasional parties. The student group Native Americans at Harvard and Radcliffe, with eight active members, sponsors an annual weeklong film festival, as well as informal dinners three times a semester for its members. "We're mostly a support network for our members," says a student. The Council of Native American Students at Harvard, a graduate school group, is more active and some of its members are from the undergraduate student group. The council sponsors regular poetry readings and lectures. More recently, the council helped sponsor a teach-in at North Quincy High School, in which members attempted to persuade the school not to use the Indian as its sports teams' mascot.

Harvard's multicultural students, however, do have their complaints about the school, which focus mostly on the *Crimson,* the school's daily newspaper. "With all of the multicultural activity going on on campus, the *Crimson* has only one beat reporter assigned to cover all the events that the different groups sponsor," says a student. Another student says: *"Crimson* reporters and editors focus only on those of our speakers who might be controversial, but when we do things that are positive, we receive very little coverage." The *Crimson* also failed to report on a recent East Coast Asian Student Union meeting that was held on campus and which included students from numerous schools on the East Coast.

Some of the school's most successful multicultural programming events are sponsored by the Harvard Foundation, whose 20-member student advisory committee is drawn from the five major cultural student groups on campus and also has representatives from each living zone, the Radcliffe Union of Students, and ten undergraduates who are elected by the student body. The foundation sponsors a Cultural Rhythms Festival, conducted each year in Sanders Hall, in which performers from all of Harvard's cultural groups put on song and dance routines. The festival is usually followed by a food festival that offers cuisine from a multitude of cultures. The foundation also "brings to campus speakers who represent a whole range of topics and ethnic groups," says a student.

Harvard's Minority Student Alliance "is completely student-run, and is the organization most likely to stage rallies," says a student. "It started about four years ago when the big issue on campus was to put pressure on the administration to hire more women and minority faculty. But the group is not as visible as it used to be."

There is no shortage of off-campus activities—from restaurants to theaters—in the Boston area, easily accessible by the "T" subway system. A popular Boston hangout, especially for Latino students, is M-80, which sponsors a weekly merengue music and dance night. Back home in Cambridge, there are numerous ethnic restaurants and shops, but students complain that shopping and eating in the area gets expensive fast. Students also report that, with a diverse community, Cambridge is a comfortable place for multicultural students. Boston, however, has earned a reputation, particularly with some reported police brutality incidents, as being less so.

Harvard is a diverse community of doers and scholars. "To come and be happy here, you need to bring initiative. I came here and I grew, and I can't believe it's almost over," says a senior. "I love it here. They're going to take me out of here kicking and screaming."

COLLEGE OF THE HOLY CROSS

Address: One College Hill, Worcester, MA 01610
Phone: (508) 793-2443
Director of Admissions: William Mason
Multicultural Student Recruiter: Thomas Stokes
1993–94 tuition: $17,200
Room and board: $6,300
Application deadline: 2/1
Financial aid application deadline: Early decision I: 11/1; early decision II: 1/15; regular decision: 2/1

Non-white freshman admissions: Applicants for the class of '96: 332
Accepted: 19.8%
Accepted who enroll: 56%
Applicants accepted who rank in top 10% of high school class: na
Median SAT: na
Median ACT: na
Full-time undergraduate enrollment: 2,700
Men: 50%
Women: 50%
Non-white students in 1987–88: 6%

STUDENT ENROLLMENT

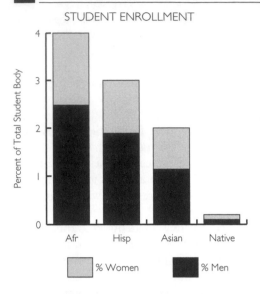

Ethnic studies programs: The college's African-American Studies concentration, established in 1990, is interdisciplinary and involves the departments of literature, history, and others. Other concentrations available include Latin American Studies and Asian Studies, both established in 1985.

Organizations for non-white students: Black Student Union, Hispanic Club, Asian Awareness Group, Multicultural Awareness Club

Notable non-white alumni: Stanley Grayson (former deputy mayor, finance, New York City); Timothy Porter (vice president, AT&T); Clarence Thomas (U.S. Supreme Court Justice); Theodore Wells (attorney)

Tenured faculty: 130

Non-tenured faculty: 56

GEOGRAPHIC DISTRIBUTION OF STUDENTS

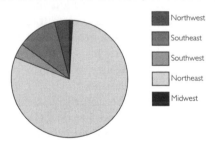

1988–89: 8%
1989–90: 10%
1990–91: 10%

Students In-state: na

Top majors: 1. History 2. Biology 3. Political Science

Retention rate of non-white students: 96%

Scholarships exclusively for non-white students: Martin Luther King, Jr., Scholarship for Black Students: need-based. Fr. Pedro Arrupe Scholarship: need-based; available to admitted Hispanic students who are first generation to attend college.

Remediation programs: None

Academic support services: The college offers writing and calculus workshops, as well as tutoring in all subjects.

FACULTY

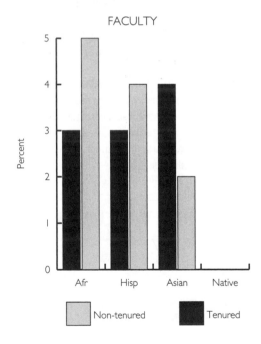

Student-faculty ratio: 14:1

Administrators: 180
African-American: 7 total
Hispanic: 1%
Asian-American: 4 total
Native American: 0

Recent non-white speakers on campus: Dick Gregory (author and political activist); Dorothy Cotton (civil rights activist); Susan Taylor (editor-in-chief, *Essence* magazine)

Supreme Court Justice Clarence Thomas would see a slightly different Holy Cross campus today than the one he graduated from. The college is now coeducational, Jesuit control of the living units has loosened considerably, and the campus is more racially and ethnically diverse. Holy Cross's curriculum has also become more diverse and includes courses in women's studies, African-American Studies, Latin American Studies, and Asian Studies. Two aspects of college life at the Jesuit institution have remained the same, however: excellent academics and a predominantly conservative, Catholic student body.

Students say that classics, English, and history are among the school's outstanding departments; economics also gets high marks. Holy Cross's science departments have earned the respect not only of students but of outside scholars; the college is one of 48 members of the Oberlin Group, a consortium of liberal arts colleges noted for their excellence in undergraduate science education. The college also offers unique programs in peace and conflict studies and international studies, which includes concentrations in Middle Eastern Studies, Russian Studies, Latin American Studies, and Asian Studies. When students can't find what they want at the Cross, they're able to enroll in courses at any of six area schools, including Worcester Polytechnic Institute and Clark University.

To graduate, Cross students must take ten courses from six areas: the arts, language and literature; religious and philosophical studies; historical studies; social science; natural and mathematical sciences; and cross-cultural studies, as well as courses in a foreign language. The cross-cultural studies course may be satisfied by taking a course in the art, literature, politics, or religion of another region, including Asia, Africa, or India. "African-American History," "Urban Politics," "The Black Experience," and "Asian Religion" rank among the school's top-rated cultures courses.

"Holy Cross offers very effective and useful academic support services," says a student, pointing to such programs as the school's writing and calculus workshops. No doubt students also find comfort in the college's relatively low student-to-faculty ratio of 14 to 1; professors are accessible and often are willing to assist students outside of the classroom. In particular, students find B. Eugene McCarthy, who teaches "American Black Literature," and Matthew Toth, director of the counseling center, helpful.

To increase the cultural and political awareness of its students, Holy Cross sponsors an annual Social Concerns Week, which offers student panels on "Understanding Cultural Diversity," as well as speakers on homelessness and poverty. During the spring semester, there is an African-American Experience Week. Last year, the film *Eyes on the Prize* was shown and African-American students held a panel discussion on their experiences at Holy Cross.

The most active cultural group on campus is the Black Student Union (BSU), which helps coordinate African-American Experience Week, events to observe Martin Luther King, Jr.'s birthday, and speakers and forums during Black History Month.

BSU adviser Thomas Stokes, who is also a Cross alum, works closely with students "and he is a mentor to all of us in the BSU," says a student. The Multicultural Awareness Club sponsors dinners, informal discussions with students and teaching assistants from abroad, and forums about discrimination. The club also co-sponsors events with the BSU.

Students say there is not much racial integration in the campus's social life, although there is little tension between the races either. "When it comes to housing, our campus is integrated as well as it can be with so few minorities," says a student. "The keg parties aren't attended much by African-Americans because most of us don't like that scene. As far as dining goes, integration is fine, although a lot of blacks typically sit at a certain table."

Although Holy Cross is a relatively small school, there is never a shortage of things to do. SPUD (Student Program for Urban Development) is the campus's largest organization, which usually has nearly 500 students in its numerous off-campus volunteer activities, such as participating in a big brother/big sister program, helping prepare meals for the homeless, and tutoring area school students. Other popular activities are working for WCHC-FM, the campus radio station, and intramurals. Varsity sports have a huge following here; football and basketball enjoy the biggest student turnouts. The Hart Athletic Center offers impressive facilities. For the majority of students, drinking, particularly at the on-campus Pub, remains one of the most popular extracurricular activities.

The city of Worcester (pop. 150,000), which has sizable African-American and Hispanic populations, offers a variety off-campus diversions for students needing to unwind from the academic rigors at the Cross. Restaurants, movie theaters, and shopping opportunities are plentiful, and students also attend concerts at the Centrum, which has hosted everyone from Dolly Parton and Lionel Richie to the Grateful Dead. Other than the activities sponsored through SPUD, however, students report little interaction between the campus and the minority community.

The majority of students who decide to attend the Cross are attracted to its religious foundation and its small size. While students of color bemoan the lack of much of a social life at the Cross, they are confident that they're earning the kind of respected degree that only a small school with a supportive faculty can provide. "Socially, it's easy for a minority student to come here and be disappointed," says a student, "but academically Holy Cross is great."

UNIVERSITY OF MASSACHUSETTS

Address: Admissions Center, Amherst, MA
01003
Phone: (413) 545-0222
Director of Admissions: Timm Rinehart
Multicultural Student Recruiters:
Aguila-Ayana McCants, Juan Caban
1991–92 tuition: $4,863 (in-state); $10,731
(out-of-state)
Room and board: $3,587
Application deadline: 2/15
Financial aid application deadline: 3/1
Non-white freshman admissions: Applicants
for the class of '94: 2,042
Accepted: 69%
Accepted who enroll: 18%
Applicants accepted who rank in top
10% of high school class: na
Median SAT range: 420–530 V, 470–600 M
Median ACT: na
Full-time undergraduate enrollment: 16,883
Men: 49%
Women: 51%

STUDENT ENROLLMENT

Non-white students in
1987–88: 7%
1988–89: 7.4%

1989–90: 7.7%
1990–91: 8%
Geographic distribution of students: na
Students In-state: 67%
Top majors: 1. Engineering 2. Management
3. Psychology
Retention rate of non-white students: 37%
**Scholarships exclusively for non-white
students:** None
Remediation programs: Courses are offered
in basic writing and elementary algebra.
Academic support services: Tutoring is
available in most academic subjects.
Ethnic studies programs: The university
offers major courses of study in
Afro-American Studies and Asian
languages and literatures.
Ethnic studies courses: na
Organizations for non-white students:
African Student Association, American
Indian Association, Asian-American
Student Association, Chinese Student
Club, Japan American Club, Korean
Student Association, South Asian Club,
Vietnamese Student Association, Honor
Society (African-American and Latino
student organization), Black Mass
Communication Project, Concepto
Latino Organization, Nummo News,
New World Theater, Central American
Solidarity Association, Alpha Phi Alpha,
Delta Sigma Theta, Omega Psi Phi, Phi
Beta Sigma, Zeta Phi Beta, Alpha Kappa
Alpha, Kappa Alpha Psi
Notable non-white alumni: Natalie Cole
(singer); Taj Mahal (musician); Julius
Irving (former professional basketball
player); Buffy St. Marie (singer)
Tenured faculty: 1,024
Non-tenured faculty: 277
Student-faculty ratio: 17:1
Administrators: na
Recent non-white speakers on campus: na

"These are the best of times and the worst of times" should perhaps be the University of Massachusetts' new motto. In a state well known for top-quality liberal arts colleges and universities, UMass is able to hold its own by offering a diverse array of social and academic opportunities. But, due to state funding cuts, the university has fallen on hard times that have led to the canceling of certain programs and the defections of numerous high-ranking administrators and professors. The university has also had its share of media attention resulting from some recent racial incidents that have occurred on campus.

Despite the funding cuts and the incidents, students say that, if anything, the university's cultural organizations have gotten more, not less active. The Black Student Union—an umbrella organization representing all of the school's black student groups—was established on campus in the spring of 1991, the university's five cultural centers (located in the various residence hall areas) have become increasingly more active, and the school's Afro-American Studies program has added several new courses, including the eagerly anticipated "Malcolm and Martin."

"The students are definitely looking forward to this school year, as far as cultural activities go. There's been a revitalization of the minority communities on campus," says a campus leader. Adds another student: "When it comes to student activism, we're a small Berkeley." Students point to certain recent national events, as well as student initiative, as reasons for the increase in cultural activity.

Among the more unique aspects of cultural education at UMass are the university's student-run cultural centers, each of which has its own personality. The Malcolm X Culture Center, located in the southwest residential area, for example, sponsors social and academic events and is governed by African-American students. The Sylvan Cultural Center is the smallest center and "sponsors an arsenal of educational, recreational, and academic opportunities," says a student. The Anna Kowanna Center, located in central campus, focuses primarily on Caribbean cultural awareness, while the Martin Luther King Cultural Center concentrates on African culture. A recent MLK center event featured a food festival. The Dr. Josephine White Eagle Cultural Center is run by Native American students and raises awareness about Native American concerns.

While most of the cultural centers are experiencing a resurgence in activity, there's one—the United Asian Cultural Center—that isn't as fortunate. Students, as a result of several rallies, decided to have the funding for the center transferred to the United Asian Learning Resource Center "so it could be stronger," says a student. The center provides academic support for students, and thanks to the additional funding, the center has two new counselors, four new computers, and a laser jet printer. "Even though the UALRC is located in a dungeon [in Knowlton Hall], we are definitely more visible than we were before," says a student. The center, which is frequented by bilingual students, also isn't without its amenities, including popular tutors. UALRC director Lucy Ng is praised by students for her organization and accessibility.

The Asian-American Student Association, with nearly 90 members, has been more active in recent years. "Thanks to a great executive board," says an AASA leader. One of the group's new activities will be the preparation of a packet of materials that will be sent to incoming students during the summer before they arrive on campus. The packet will include personal experience pieces written by currently enrolled Asian-American students. An annual AASA focus is its Asian Night, which includes professional acts. During a recent year, Asian Night presented a Korean traditional drumming group, Vietnamese performers, and a fashion show. According to one student, the event, held in the campus center auditorium, drew more than 900 spectators, among them students of all races. During the school year, the AASA sponsors a film series called "Learning Culture Through Film."

AASA certainly doesn't shortchange social activity. The group sponsors volleyball tournaments, dances, coffee hours, and informal get-togethers. The Korean Student Association, which sponsors its own culture night, is one of the more active Asian student groups.

The formation of the Black Student Union "has been an idea that's been kicked around for quite some time. For years we've had traditionally black fraternities and sororities and professional organizations. But we needed some type of gluing together to help us be more cohesive. The BSU seeks to promote cooperative financing with other black student groups so events won't go underfunded. It's taken a lot of time to get the BSU off the ground, and we're still working on the fine tuning. We're not leaving anything to chance. All of our events are designed to promote unity, such as a major reception to greet new black students to campus. We're going to be stressing the social as well as the educational because we think that's important for building a foundation. The black student groups have been hurting recently in terms of membership and funding, but with the BSU the black community is now more unified, and we're excited."

Despite the work of the cultural centers and student organizations, the campus has experienced its share of racial strife in recent years. In the fall of 1992, for example, an African-American student living in Washington Tower, a 22-story dormitory on campus, was punched and human feces were spread outside his dorm room in a bias-related incident. The assailant was a visiting guest of a UMass student. Students of color, claiming the administration wasn't taking quick enough action against the incident, blocked a road and raided the dormitory. The situation became so heated that officials from the United States Justice Department mediation team were brought in by the administration to help resolve the conflict. In response to these events, the chancellor of the university, Richard O'Brien, agreed to increase security in the dorms and to set aside $100,000 for multicultural events.

Academics have been hurt significantly by the state's budget cuts. Courses have been dropped, and reports of students having to take classes that don't interest them just to satisfy a graduation requirement have appeared in the media. *The New York Times* published a lengthy piece about the effects of the cuts on the campus under the headline "U. of Massachusetts Is Losing Money and Morale." UMass is the second most expensive state school in the country, behind the University of Vermont. "A lot of us feel like we are paying more and getting less," said a student in the *Times* article.

One program that has been meeting with success is the school's Minority Engineering Program, which was also the subject of a recent *Times* article. MEP offers almost any kind of academic assistance, as well as emergency loan assistance.

The office "helped me tremendously," said a recent UMass graduate in the *Times* piece. "If it wasn't for the program, I emphatically say I would not have graduated as an engineer. What the program did for me was to give people I could talk to, people who gave me a lot of support. They made it easier by setting up study groups, they hired tutors and helped students get together with other students. Some people say to me that having an MEP was unfair. If life was fair, there would be no need for the program."

UMass's engineering program is one of the school's toughest, while management is also considered top-notch. Highly respected programs in the College of Arts and Sciences are political science, art, economics, languages, English, and women's studies. Afro-American Studies is well regarded by students, who especially praise the program's approachable faculty, including John Bracey and Michael Thelwell, both of whom teach the popular "History of the Civil Rights Movement." William Strickland, another popular Afro-American Studies professor, will be teaching the "Malcolm and Martin" course. Social thought and political economy attracts many of UMass's more progressive-minded students. The university's schools of nursing and education also earn praise from students.

An added advantage to attending UMass is its participation in the five-college program, which includes some of the country's top liberal arts colleges: Amherst, Mount Holyoke, Smith, and Hampshire. Students are able to take courses at any of these nearby schools, allowing UMass students to reap the benefits of a small liberal arts community while paying state tuition costs. A free bus system connects the schools. Cultural organizations at the schools are closely linked and co-sponsor parties and speakers.

The highly successful Committee for the Collegiate Education of Black and other Minority Students (CCEBMS) provides a great deal of academic support for students. "CCEBMS is well known on campus and all of the counselors in the office are also well known and accessible. Students get to know their counselors on a first-name basis. The office's director, Floyd Martin, is very friendly. He even knows me by my first name."

CCEBMS, along with offices for the black Greek organizations and the BSU, are housed in the New Africa House, a popular meeting place on campus. "It's where we go to feel safe and comfortable," says a student. "There's a historical reason why we consider it home. In 1988 some students took over the house because they wanted some sort of center. Because it was obtained as the result of a struggle, it makes us all appreciate it more." The house, located in central campus, has state-of-the-art computer equipment for student use.

Also home to UMass students is Amherst, Massachusetts, which offers a wealth of eating establishments, from Indian to Caribbean, and theaters and small clubs. The town, as well as the area that includes Northampton, is known for being progressive and tolerant of cultural diversity. "I've never felt uncomfortable going into any of the shops in town," comments a BSU member. "The area also has a great deal of gay and lesbian activism. You really can't talk about cultural diversity at UMass or in Amherst period without discussing their contributions. I think it has been good for students to be exposed to gay and lesbian issues, as it's taught us that there is more diversity—and discrimination—out there than just what's based on race."

While the UMass administration may have to contend with some financial woes, students seem to take little notice. They are happy that their university is getting more active culturally and politically, despite some difficulties about course cancellations and large class sizes.

"I love UMass," says one student. "I've learned so many things. This place is a melting pot of ideas. I've come to know a vast amount about my own heritage, by getting the BSU off the ground and meeting other minority students from all sorts of different backgrounds. There's a full spectrum of ideas here that I'm glad I've been exposed to; even the negatives I've been able to turn into positive experiences."

MASSACHUSETTS INSTITUTE OF TECHNOLOGY

Address: 77 Massachusetts Avenue, Room 3-108, Cambridge, MA 02139-4307
Phone: (617) 253-4791
Director of Admissions: Michael C. Behnke
Multicultural Student Recruiter: John B. Hammond
1991–92 tuition: $16,900
Room and board: $5,330
Application deadline: Early decision: 11/1; regular decision: 1/1
Financial aid application deadline: 2/1
Non-white freshman admissions: Applicants for the class of '95: 504 (Asian-Americans not included)
Accepted: 60%
Accepted who enroll: 58%
Applicants accepted who rank in top 10% of high school class: 90%
In top 25%: 95%
Median SAT range: 560–650 V, 630–730 M
Median ACT range: 26–31
Full-time undergraduate enrollment: 4,389
Men: 66%
Women: 34%
Non-white students in 1987–91: na
Geographic distribution of students: na
Top majors: 1. Electrical Engineering 2. Chemical Engineering 3. Mechanical Engineering
Retention rate of non-white students: 80%
Scholarships exclusively for non-white students: None
Remediation programs: None
Academic support services: Undergraduate

Academic Support Office, Office of Minority Education, Office of the Dean of Student Affairs, Pre-professional Advisory, Student Assistance Services. Others include dormitory residence tutors and individual class tutorials.
Ethnic studies programs: na
Ethnic studies courses: na
Organizations for non-white students: Association of Puerto Rican Students, Alpha Phi Alpha, Alpha Kappa Alpha, Delta Sigma Theta, Kappa Alpha Psi, Black Student Union, Society of Hispanic Professional Engineers, LUCHA (Mexican-American Student Organization), American Indian Society of Engineering Students, Native American Student Association, National

STUDENT ENROLLMENT

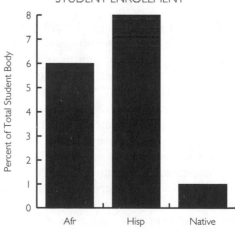

FACULTY

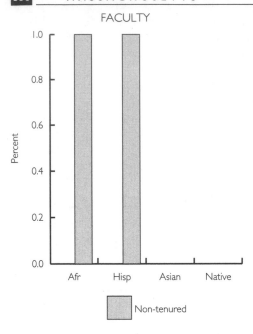

Percent

Non-tenured

Society of Black Engineers, Black Christian Fellowship, Black Mechanical Engineers at MIT

Notable non-white alumni: Dr. Shirley Jackson ('68; first African-American woman in the U.S. to earn a Ph.D. in Physics); Dr. Jennie Patrick ('79; first African-American woman in the U.S. to earn an Sc.D. in chemical engineering); Dr. Henry Hill ('42; first African-American to serve as president of the American Chemical Society)

Tenured faculty: 800

Non-tenured faculty: 300

Student-faculty ratio: 4:1

Administrators: na

Recent non-white speakers on campus: Toni Morrison (Pulitzer Prize-winning author); William Gray (director, United Negro College Fund and former U.S. Congressman)

The Massachusetts Institute of Technology is arguably the world's most famous engineering and science-related school, and MIT graduates and professors have certainly made their marks in these and other fields. MIT scholars have helped decipher the genetic code, develop a comprehensive picture of the universe, reshape the contours of architecture, and create new technology.

MIT's civil and electrical engineering programs are said to be among the best in the country, and its excellent computer science program enrolls nearly two-thirds of the student body. Biology, physics, and mechanical, biomedical, and chemical engineering are also MIT standouts. And teaching these courses aren't medicore minds; MIT faculty include Nobel laureates, MacArthur Fellows, and Pulitzer Prize winners.

But what sets MIT apart from many of the country's other best-known "techie" schools is that it offers impressive programs in other areas, which makes for a more academically diverse group of students. The 132-year-old school has well-regarded programs in urban studies, management, economics, linguistics, and environmental studies. Noted linguist Noam Chomsky teaches here, as does Paul Samuelson and other well-known economists. In addition, MIT students are assured a well-rounded education. To graduate, students must satisfy distribution requirements in the humanities (eight courses), in the sciences (two courses), and laboratory science (two courses), as well as in writing and physical education.

Academics at MIT, and professors' expectations of students, are indeed demanding. To help alleviate the stress, grades for first-year students are strictly pass/fail (a C is necessary to pass). "This really helps in the transition from high school to college," says a student. "It makes us definitely more relaxed during the first year, but sophomore year can be a kind of shock when it comes time to compete for grades." MIT's January term, in which students participate in a variety of non-credit courses or pursue on- or off-campus research possibilities or internships, is no doubt a welcome respite for students.

For academic support, students are able to turn to the services of the Office of Minority Education. "The office provides tutoring services and monitors a student's progress, and does a reasonably good job at both," says a student. "The tutors have improved a great deal. After a lot of student complaints, most of the tutors are now graduate students."

More than one student expressed disappointment in the office. "It has changed a lot in the four years since I've been here," says a student. "There's been a lot of turnover in the staff. Now, the office provides strictly academic assistance. Students no longer feel as if they can go there for emotional support, whereas before we could. In fact, they discourage it. They say if we need that kind of support we should go to Student Assistance Services. But sometimes that's not too helpful because it's nice to know that if you need a counselor, you will have one who's a minority. Students rarely stop by the office just to say hi anymore."

The most important sources of academic and social support for students are other students. "When the place gets to be a little overwhelming, that's when older students tell us to hang in there. I also know that if I need to, I can call any member of SHPE [Society of Hispanic Professional Engineers], even if I don't know him or her very well. We're all friends, and we all want all of us to graduate." Adds another student: "If there's one thing I want to stress, it's the importance of the multicultural student organizations in students' lives at MIT. They provide much of the support we need, and we all know that we're there for each other."

Indeed, a mixer between three of MIT's professional societies—the American Indian Society of Engineering Students, the National Society of Black Engineers, and the Society of Hispanic Professional Engineers—was so successful that students who were in attendance have said future mixers are definitely in the planning. Each organization is also instrumental in helping its members find summer jobs in engineering fields. "One summer I worked in California, and last summer I worked in Rochester, New York, all because of the contacts I made through SHPE," says a student.

The American Indian Society of Engineering Students (AISES), with about 25 to 30 active members, has been at MIT for four years and "owes a great deal to Donna Marie Horse Grant," the group's adviser and a director of urban studies and planning. "When I got here, there wasn't an organization for Native Americans, and now there is," says a student. "She got on the ball and started the group. Her battles with the admissions office have been somewhat successful. Largely due to her efforts, the institute now recruits students from reservations, particularly Navajo reservations in New Mexico. She's very visible, and some of us consider her a mother figure." In 1992, AISES sent 20 members to the national chapter's annual conference, held in Albuquerque, New Mexico, and the group works closely with the admissions office in recruiting Native American students. AISES members usually meet twice monthly in one of the school's classrooms, "depending on what's happening on campus and what we're planning."

The National Society of Black Engineers (NSBE) is perhaps the school's most successful professional society. MIT's NSBE chapter has won the country's most outstanding chapter award two years in a row. The Society of Hispanic Professional Engineers, the only such chapter in Massachusetts other than at the University of Massachusetts at Amherst, has about 30 to 40 active members. "We mostly sponsor workshops on a biweekly basis," says a student member. "Some of our more recent topics were 'The Attack on Affirmative Action,' 'The Graduate School Application Process,' and 'The Hiring of Minorities.'" SHPE members also sponsor a tutoring program at a nearby high school in Cambridge.

Of particular assistance to students and student groups is Ann Davis Shaw, a counselor in the Career Services Office. "Whenever any of us need help, she lets us know her door is always open. SHPE hosted a regional conference here recently, and she was instrumental in helping us to get the money—nearly $25,000—for it." Comments another student: "She's a very fair administrator. Although she's an adviser to NSBE, she gives equal attention to each of the three multicultural professional organizations."

The Black Student Union offers more of a social outlet for members. The BSU, with about 50 to 100 active members, has sponsored a Kwanzaa celebration, a dinner to greet incoming first-year students, and a quiz bowl to celebrate Black History Month. BSU members meet in the BSU Lounge, located in Walker Memorial, usually once every two weeks, on Sundays. The lounge, most popular at lunchtime, has couches, a TV and VCR, and two computers.

The African-American student community at MIT, according to one student, "is tight and supportive of one another. The black and Hispanic students are stronger than I've seen at other schools I've been to. Everybody knows everybody, and there aren't the elite groups among the black students that there seem to be at other schools." For at least a decade, a section of New House, a dorm on campus, has become so popular among African-American male students that it is now officially recognized as Chocolate City and has it own governing board and budget.

Undoubtedly, most students' time is spent with the books. But students nonetheless find time to participate in any number of student clubs devoted to automobiles, art, bridge, chess, dance, film, or Frisbee. MIT's intramural program is huge. It involves more than 1,150 students annually who compete in more than a dozen sports—billiards, rugby, and tennis, among them.

Cambridge and Boston, just a short commute away, offer a plethora of social activities, although students say taking advantage of the cities' nightlife can be difficult given the academic demands of their school. The area has numerous colleges and universities—including Harvard and Boston universities—whose campuses, according to one report, enroll more than 100,000 students. The sports enthusiast is able to attend professional games almost any time of the year; Boston is home to the Red Sox baseball team, the Bruins hockey team, and the Celtics basketball team. Numerous art museums, including the famous Museum of Fine Arts, are also easily accessible. Boston's "T" subway line makes getting to these spots easy.

Although MIT has never really been known for student activism, recently the school came to be known for its professorial activism. James Williams, a mechanical engineering professor, sat outside the office of the president of the institute every

Wednesday and fasted, "from morning to night," to draw attention to the need for more faculty of color. For a day, more than 100 sympathetic students joined in his demonstration. "The demonstration opened people's eyes." According to the school newspaper, the president of MIT has instructed heads of departments to look for more minority faculty members, and his office will provide financial help for the search.

The MIT degree isn't easily earned, but for those up to the challenge, excellent job prospects loom on the horizon. "I'm happy here. MIT has good student groups. I feel at home, which is important in view of the intensity of the place. You can make a lot of friends here, and a lot of job contacts."

MOUNT HOLYOKE COLLEGE

Women's college
Address: College Street, South Hadley, MA 01075
Phone: (413) 538-2023
Director of Admissions: Anita Smith
Multicultural Student Recruiter: Terri Davis
1993–94 tuition: $17,980
Room and board: $5,520
Application deadline: 2/1
Financial aid application deadline: 2/1
Non-white freshman admissions: Applicants for the class of '96: 364
 Accepted: 89%
 Accepted who enroll: 40%
 Applicants accepted who rank in top 10% of high school class: 45%
 Median SAT: 1,156 (M, V)
 Median ACT: 27
Full-time undergraduate enrollment: 1,850
Non-white students in
 1988–89: 11%
 1989–90: 12%
 1990–91: 12%
 1991–92: 13%
Geographic distribution of students: na
Students In-state: 13%
Top majors: 1. English 2. Political Science 3. Biology
Retention rate of non-white students: 97%
Scholarships exclusively for non-white students: None
Remediation programs: None
Academic support services: The college offers a writing center and tutoring services in most academic subjects.
Ethnic studies programs: The college offers programs in African-American, Latin American, and Asian American Studies.
Organizations for non-white students: Betty Shabazz House (African-American residence), Association of Pan-African Unity, Korean-American Organization, La Unidad, Minority Pre-health Society, Voices of Faith Gospel Choir Ensemble, New World Theater, Asian Student Association, ASIA, African and Caribbean Student Association
Notable non-white alumnae: na
Tenured faculty: na

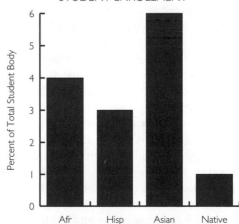

STUDENT ENROLLMENT

Non-tenured faculty: na   **Administrators:** na
Student-faculty ratio: 9:1   **Recent non-white speakers on campus:** na

Mount Holyoke is a college that is truly—and singularly—committed to the education of women. The college "made me aware of and played an important role in developing my academic abilities, discipline, and determination to succeed in my chosen field," says a recent graduate. "You have to be disciplined and ready for a rigorous academic experience in order to get the most out of Mount Holyoke. My experience there proved to me that being a woman, and being African-American, made it a greater, but by no means unattainable challenge to succeed."

Mount Holyoke is part of the Five-College Consortium that includes well-regarded Smith, Amherst, Hampshire, and the University of Massachusetts. Students are able to take courses or participate in activities at any of the member schools. In a recent year, for example, Mount Holyoke students enrolled in 773 courses at the other four schools, and students from the other schools enrolled in 827 Mount Holyoke courses.

Students say the school's strongest departments are English, international relations, and the sciences, especially biology and chemistry, which has graduated more women who have gone on to earn their Ph.D.s in chemistry than any other school in the country. The school also has some of the most impressive facilities for the study of chemistry of any of the country's four-year undergraduate colleges. Dance, theater, and art students also have access to outstanding facilities. Students rate the school's history and political science departments highly. Mount Holyoke's library recently underwent extensive renovation and expansion, and now contains all of the college's main library collections.

Students are happy that numerous academic departments at their school are diversifying their course offerings. They point to the politics department's courses in "Urban Politics" and "Racial Stratification" as evidence. The theater department's "Black Women in Theater" course, taught by a visiting professor from Spelman College, is popular, and "Spirituals and the Blues," a religion course taught by Professor John Grayson, is also well received. "The departments are diversifying a lot because of student pressure and because the administration is willing to listen to student concerns," says a senior.

Although Mount Holyoke offers a degree in Latin American Studies, students say that most of the courses in the area are offered at one of the other four colleges. One of Mount Holyoke's courses in the area that earns high marks from students is "Latino Literature in the United States." "I liked the course so much that it made me switch my major from psychology to Latin American Studies," says a student.

To graduate, students must satisfy a Third World course requirement by taking courses such as "Comparative Caribbean History," "African-American Literature," or "Introduction to Latin American Economics." "Most students are pleased to have to take the course," says a junior. "It's opened a lot of people's eyes to things they wouldn't otherwise know or have the chance to learn about." In addition, students must take a total of seven courses distributed among the humanities, the sciences and mathematics, and the social sciences. Students must also show a proficiency in a foreign language and satisfy a physical education requirement.

The school's January Term, a welcome break in the rigors of the school's two-semester schedule, allows students to study a single topic on or off campus for the month, or to pursue off-campus internship or research opportunities. Qualified students are even able to teach a course themselves.

Mount Holyoke is definitely not a party school. "It's not as if the social life here is going to jump up and bite you," says a student. "If you search for it, though, you can usually find something to do. We spend a lot of time together, but we also go off campus, usually to [multicultural student] parties in Amherst, but mostly at UMass." The Five-College van service is "reliable and always there," says a student.

The Association of Pan-African Unity meets once every two weeks in the school's Betty Shabazz House. (Shabazz, the wife of slain civil rights activist Malcolm X, is a UMass graduate.) The house has African-American artwork, a full kitchen, and a computer room, and students are currently collecting books for a house library. APAU events include an annual dinner with African-American members of the college staff and faculty. For Black History Month in 1992, the group sponsored its first Africa Day festivities, which featured a variety show, skits about African life, dance, and poetry readings.

La Unidad, which has about 15 active members, meets regularly in Wilder Hall. La Unidad's main activity is La Unidad Week, in April. "The events change from year to year," says a student. In a recent year, the group sponsored a talent show, a pool party, and a trip to Boston. The group has also sponsored a Five-College Reception at the college for Hispanic students.

Rochelle Calhoune, an assistant dean of students and one of the founders of the APAU, is well liked by students. "When any of the school's multicultural student groups has a problem, she's the one they go to," says a student. "She's a Mount Holyoke grad, and she knows the place well. She'll know how to solve the problem, if one comes up, and she's also very dynamic."

The Commons, in the town of South Hadley, across the street from campus, contains a well-known area bookstore, which sponsors readings and book signings, a movie theater, restaurants, and shopping opportunities. Students are more likely to be found at the school's relatively new Blanchard Student Center, however, which has a game room, lounge areas, and a cafeteria. Mount Holyoke students like sports, and volleyball, riding, and basketball are the most popular.

A great deal of the school's social life takes place off campus, at parties or cultural events sponsored by the other colleges in the area, which are all easily accessible by bus. Boston, about ninety miles east, or Northampton are also popular weekend destinations.

The college attracts students from almost every state in the country and nearly as many foreign countries. Although the students cover the gamut politically and socially, most are liberal. The school's lesbian student group is active and largely accepted, and feminist issues play an important part in a typical Mount Holyoke student's life.

Students who come to Mount Holyoke for college do so because of its well-regarded liberal arts curriculum and its devotion to the education of women. "I have really grown as a [multicultural] woman and a woman in general," says a student. "I realize it's quite sheltered here and that it's a warm community of students. But I know I'm stronger for having attended school here, and I know what I'm capable of and what my potential is." Adds another student: "I was very aware that the black population [at Mount Holyoke] was small. And for a student like me, who comes from a big city, a place where she's surrounded by people in her own community, it can be a real culture shock to find herself in South Hadley. Organizations like the Association of Pan-African Unity, the Asian Students Association, and La Unidad help you keep in touch with your own community, but I knew that it wouldn't always be easy for me at Mount Holyoke. I wanted to come here *because* I knew it would be a challenge."

NORTHEASTERN UNIVERSITY

Address: 150 Richards Hall, 360 Huntington Avenue, Boston, MA 02115
Phone: (617) 437-2200
Director of Admissions: Humberto Goncalves
Multicultural Student Recruiter: na
1991–92 tuition: $10,523
Room and board: $6,690
Application deadline: Rolling admissions
Financial aid application deadline: 3/1

Non-white freshman admissions: Applicants for the class of '95: 1,807
Accepted: 1,342
Accepted who enroll: 469
Applicants accepted who rank in top 10% of high school class: 7%
In top 25%: 23%
Median SAT: na
Median ACT: na
Full-time undergraduate enrollment: 12,429
Men: 7,431
Women: 4,998
Non-white students in
1987–88: 8%
1988–89: 8.6%
1989–90: 9.6%
1990–91: 10%
Geographic distribution of students: na
Top majors: 1. Criminal Justice 2. Accounting 3. Electrical Engineering
Retention rate of non-white students: na

Scholarships exclusively for non-white students: Ralph Bunche Scholarship: merit-based; provides full tuition for the first year and half tuition during a student's sophomore through senior years. National Fund Minority Engineering Student Scholarship: merit-based; number and amount of award vary each year; $500–$2,000 each. R. G. Vanderwell Scholarship: need-based; amount and number of awards vary each year; available to

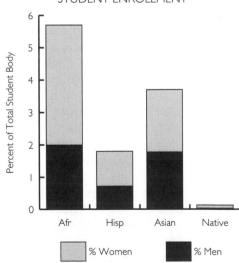

STUDENT ENROLLMENT

Percent of Total Student Body

□ % Women   ■ % Men

full-time minority engineering students from Boston.

Remediation programs: na

Academic support services: Services are provided by Northeastern's Academic Assistance Center, African-American Institute, Counseling and Testing Center, English Language Center, Northeastern University Progress in Minorities in Engineering program, and the Office of Minority Affairs.

Ethnic studies programs: The university offers a program in African-American Studies.

Ethnic studies courses: na

Organizations for non-white students: African Student Association, Asian-American Student Association, Cambodian Student Association, Caribbean Student Organization, Chinese Student Club, Haitian Student Unity, Hellenic Association, Indian Culture Group, International Students Forum, Japanese Club, Latin American Student Organization, Northeastern Black Student Association, Republic of China Student Association, Vietnamese Students Club, Future Black Lawyers Club, Black Business Student Association, Black Engineering Student Society.

Notable non-white alumni: na

Tenured faculty: 498

Non-tenured faculty: 337

Student-faculty ratio: 11:1

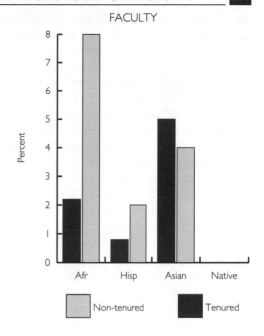

FACULTY

Percent

Afr   Hisp   Asian   Native

Non-tenured   Tenured

Administrators: na

Recent non-white speakers on campus: Maya Angelou (author and poet); Derrick Bell (professor, New York University Law School); Dr. Horace Boyer (curator, Smithsonian Institution); Martin Luther King III (civil rights activist); Nathie Marbury (activist and educator); Eusi Kwayana (member, Guyana Parliament); Dessima Williams (former Grenadan ambassador to the UN)

Does the idea of making about $35,100 over five years while still earning college credit appeal to you? That's the average salary of a co-op student at Northeastern University, where the chance to work with almost any sort of company or laboratory—for pay—is an integral part of all co-op students' education. The co-op program, which attracts more than three-quarters of Northeastern's students, is one of the university's biggest drawing cards—that and its location in the hometown of colleges—Boston.

And co-op opportunities aren't flipping burgers at a local fast-food joint. With the help of the university's co-op staff, students are able to line up jobs in areas that usually are related to their major field of study. The money students earn generally goes back to the university to defray a student's educational expenses. Some recent co-ops have been at the *Boston Globe,* General Foods, IBM, and any number of banks, government agencies, and other corporations. Each year about 7,800 under-graduates work with more than 2,100 employers, both in this country and abroad.

Co-op students spend their first year on campus. Thereafter, they spend every other quarter—the school year is divided into quarters and includes summers—at North-eastern. Usually, students spend seven or eight quarters on campus, including the last one of their senior year. Due to their co-op experiences, it takes students five years to graduate, but most students don't mind, as about a third of the school's graduates take jobs with one of their previous co-op employers.

The on-again, off-again campus atmosphere isn't picture perfect. Students say friendships often last only as long as any two or more students are on campus, and if a student organization leader leaves for a quarter or more, staying organized can be difficult. Northeastern's lack of dorm space—it says it can accommodate only 67 percent of its first-year students—also contributes to the feeling of fragmentation on campus; nearly two-thirds of its students are commuters. But, as Northeastern is one of the nation's largest private universities, it's not as if these criticisms dissuade too many from attending school here. In fact, in a recent year the school accepted only slightly less than half of its applicants.

Northeastern's best departments are, as you might expect at a school where students are avowedly pre-professional, business, engineering (especially electrical), and criminal justice. The College of Computer Science is also highly regarded. Among the university's arts and science programs—generally regarded as the school's weakest link—students say African-American Studies is excellent. "Foundations of Black Culture" and "The Black Family" are two of the program's most popular courses, while Leonard Brown and Maryemma Graham are among its most respected professors. All students, no matter which undergraduate division they choose, must satisfy a writing proficiency requirement.

Students say the intensity of their school's academic atmosphere varies depending on a student's major, but seeking professor input can be a chore. Classes, especially in the lower division, are huge, and getting into first-choice courses can be a challenge, as even required classes fill up quickly.

One of the school's most effective academic support systems, according to students, is the African-American Institute, a three-story facility located on the south side of campus. The institute provides tutoring, a game room and a library, staff offices, and a conference room. "I can honestly say that if it wasn't for the institute I wouldn't have survived here," says a junior. Dean Keith Motley and staffers Lula Petty and Karen Johnson are well respected by students. "But everyone who works in the building is so popular and positive and do so much that it's difficult to point to any one person as most outstanding. We all do work for each other in the institute—students, faculty, and staff," says a senior.

The Northeastern Black Student Association (NBSA), which meets weekly at the institute, sponsors an annual fashion show and an occasional party, and in conjunction with the institute sponsors a Martin Luther King Convocation, which features a guest speaker and a candlelight vigil. In conjunction with the institute, the NBSA sponsors Unity Week, a seven-day affair "that has a different event each day," says a Unity Week organizer. One of Unity Week's events is a Cultural Extravaganza, held in the Ell Ballroom, to which various cultural organizations are invited. At a recent celebration a member of the Latin American Student Organization read poems and a Boston dance troupe performed.

"But the program that's very important to many of us is the new Ignacio St. Rose Scholarship Fund. It started in September 1992, and it's named for a deceased Northeastern student. The fund is for any student of color who is having difficulty financially. If a student needs assistance, he or she must apply for aid. Requirements to get aid include an essay, a 2.5 grade point average, and he or she must be active in at least one student organization." To raise funds for the scholarship, students organized a mini-marathon. "The participation was really great; it was a lot of fun. We raised a couple of thousand dollars. Not bad for our first year for the fund."

There are more colleges and universities per square foot in Boston than in any other city in the country, although the city is considered one of the country's most segregated. The city provides students with a myriad of opportunities to interact with students from other schools, and is easily accessible, as a "T" subway stop is on the south side of campus. Northeastern's town rival, especially in athletics, is Boston University. The city also offers a variety of cultural and nightlife opportunities, and the renowned Boston Museum of Fine Arts and the New England Conservatory of Music are located on the edge of Northeastern's campus. Northeastern Red Sox fans are pleased to note that Fenway Park is just a hop, skip, and jump away. Northeastern's campus is, to say the least, compact. In fact, with more than 30,000 graduate and undergraduate students crammed into 55 acres that contain some not very pretty campus architecture—the buildings look more functional than collegiate—the place can get downright claustrophobic.

Northeastern's size and location can intimidate those looking for a small-school experience, and the school's co-op program definitely detracts from creating school spirit. But students who choose to attend school here aren't doing so because they want a typical college experience. They come here because they want to get an education that's practical and will help them get that all-important job. "I'm pleased and very happy I came to school here. The co-op has been an incredible experience for me. The university also has a good reputation with employers, so I'm definitely glad I came here for school."

SMITH COLLEGE

Women's college
Address: Garrison Hall, Northampton, MA 01063
Phone: (413) 585-2500
Director of Admission: Juliet Brigham
Multicultural Student Recruiter: Terran Whittingham
1992–93 tuition: $17,980
Room and board: $6,100
Application deadline: 1/15
Financial aid application deadline: 1/15

Non-white freshman admissions: Applicants for the class of '95: 538
Accepted: na
Accepted who enroll: 25.5%
Applicants accepted who rank in top 10% of high school class: 45%
In top 25%: 79%
Median SAT range: 500–610 V, 530–640 M
Median ACT: na

Full-time undergraduate enrollment: 2,607

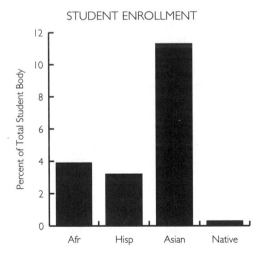

STUDENT ENROLLMENT

Percent of Total Student Body

Afr Hisp Asian Native

Non-white students in
1987–88: 12.7%
1988–89: 13.5%
1989–90: 15.2%
1990–91: 18.3%

Geographic distribution of students:
Midwest: 11.2%
Southeast: 0
Northeast: 13.3%
Northwest: 0
Southwest: 4.3%
South: 9.8%
West: 24.9%
Middle Atlantic: 31.3%
Students In-state: 8.2%
Top majors: 1. Government 2. Economics 3. Psychology
Retention rate of non-white students: 91%
Scholarships exclusively for non-white students: None
Remediation programs: None
Academic support services: The Center for Academic Development offers programs in developing writing and quantitative reasoning skills. The college also offers peer tutoring.
Ethnic studies programs: The college offers major courses of study in Afro-American, East Asian Studies, and Latin American Studies. The college offers minor courses of study in East Asian languages and literatures and Third World Development Studies.
Ethnic studies courses: Smith's curriculum includes nearly 20 courses in Native American and Hispanic American Studies.
Organizations for non-white students: Asian Students Association, Black Student Alliance, South Asian Students Organization, Korean-American Students of Smith, Nosotras (Latina student group), Smith African Students Association, Indigenous Americans at Smith, South African Students Association
Notable non-white alumnae: Yolanda King ('76; civil rights activist, daughter of Martin Luther King, Jr.); Carol Thompson Cole ('73, Government; city administrator, Washington, DC); Glenda Copes Reed ('66, American Studies;

assistant vice president, Aetna); Ng'endo Mwangi ('61, Pre-med; first woman physician in Kenya); Adelaid Cromwell ('40, Sociology; professor and director of Afro-American Studies [retired] Boston University, taught the first Afro-American Studies courses at Hunter College and developed first Afro-American Studies program at Boston University)

Tenured faculty: 174
Non-tenured faculty: 95
Student-faculty ratio: 10:1
Administrators: 411
  African-American: 2%
  Hispanic: 1.7%
  Asian-American: 2.9%
  Native American: 0
Recent non-white speakers on campus: Carol Thompson (city administrator, Washington, DC); Anita de Frantz (president, Amateur Athletics Foundation of Los Angeles); Carrie Saxon Perry (mayor, Hartford, CT, and the first African-American mayor of a Northeastern city); Eleanor Holmes Norton (law professor, Georgetown University); Sonia Sanchez (poet)

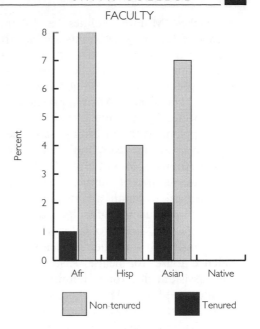

FACULTY

"At Smith," says a student, "there is bound to be your kind of person. There are the preps, the sixties types, those who always wear black, and the jocks. You're bound to be able to relate to someone." Smith students do, however, have several qualities in common, among them motivation, intelligence, and gender. The 118-year-old college is the country's largest independent women's institution of higher learning, and also one of the most respected. Students come to Smith from every state in the Union and numerous foreign countries.

Smith has long been known for its high-quality liberal arts programs. Art history is well regarded and popular, and students studying the subject have access to the rich resources of the Smith College Museum of Art, one of the outstanding university museums in the country. More than a quarter of Smith's students—a phenomenal number especially when compared with the number of women who major in these areas at coed institutions—major in the sciences, in the impressive Clark Science Center. The college's Center for Foreign Languages and Cultures' state-of-the-art facilities include an electronic classroom and interactive digital audio and video for individualized study. Government, English, East Asian Studies, and history are among the school's stellar departments.

Students say that the Latin American Studies program is "solid"; it offers such well-regarded courses as "Colonial Latin American History" and "Latinos in the Political System," a seminar class. Velma Garcia, an assistant professor of government who teaches "Minority Politics," and Ann Zulaski, an assistant professor of history, are two of the program's outstanding professors. Students say the school's Afro-American Studies program's strengths are in literature and history, although one student commented on its wide variety of courses, among them "Psychology of the Black Experience" and "Major Black Writers: Fiction." Louis Wilson, a history professor, and Brenda Allen, a psychology professor, who teach in the program, are well respected by students.

To supplement their learning—and their social lives—Smith students are able to take courses at the area schools that are part of the Five-College Consortium, which includes Amherst, Mount Holyoke, UMass, and Hampshire. A shuttle bus regularly takes students, free of charge, to the various campuses.

Academics at Smith are demanding, but students say that with the school's relatively low student-to-faculty ratio of 10 to 1, professors are especially accessible and supportive. "Professors almost always make themselves available for after-class discussions, and want their students to learn," says a senior. "Many come to the residence houses for meals." Also supportive of students are Terran Whittingham, a senior assistant director of admission, and Marjorie Richardson, the assistant dean of minority affairs. The school's recently established Student Forums, in which members of the college community gather to discuss specific topics, should strengthen the ties between the administration and students.

One of the unique qualities of the Smith experience is the college's housing system. Rather than requiring students to live in high-rise dorms (there are none at Smith), all students—except for the tiny minority who live off campus—reside in one of the school's 43 houses, the largest of which accommodates about 100 students, the smallest about 36. Each house has its own governing system and its own constitution. Students say that many of the houses have women of color as officers. Each house also has in place a Managing Diversity Plan, a set of guidelines designed to discourage racism. For breaking any of the rules, disciplinary action can be taken, such as requiring violators to attend race sensitivity workshops. Students say that housing at the college is well integrated.

There is no shortage of extracurricular activities at Smith, although, with the absence of men, students say the campus is relatively quiet during the week. Especially popular are sports. The college fields 14 varsity teams—among the most offered for women at any school in the nation. Swimming, crew, field hockey, and tennis are among the school's more successful sports.

There are also more than 70 student organizations on campus, including numerous cultural groups such as the Asian Students Association and South Asian Students Organization. Nosotras, the Latina student organization, has about 40 active members and meets twice a month to plan such events as Latina Week and an annual Fall Symposium with lectures and workshops. Members also regularly attend meetings of the East Coast Chicano Student Forum, which includes the Ivy League and other schools; Smith recently hosted a meeting of the association. Nosotras sponsors a big sister/little sister program, in which seniors help first-year students adjust to the academic and social life at Smith. The departments of Latin American Studies and Spanish/Portuguese frequently help fund Nosotras events.

The Black Student Alliance (BSA), with about 80 members, plans numerous annual events, including the weeklong Black Arts Festival and the New England Black Student Association conference. The conference draws students from numerous East Coast schools to a weekend of workshops facilitated by Smith students, faculty, and staff. A highlight of the year, particularly for seniors, is the Black Graduation Ceremony, which features a dinner to honor the graduates and their families. An active component of the BSA is its big sister/little sister program. The group also hosts a Jazz Night with a soul food dinner and live music, a Kwanzaa celebration, and an annual trip to the homecoming festivities at Howard, a historically black university in Washington, DC. Although there are no sororities at Smith, students are able to join one of the historically black sororities with chapters in the area. Sorority meetings have occasionally taken place on campus at the M'Wangi Cultural Center, located in Lily Hall. The center, which has two study rooms, a TV lounge, a kitchen, a library, and numerous artworks, "is where 99.5 percent of the BSA's activities take place," says a member.

Students make frequent use of Smith's Unity House, home to the school's cultural student groups. The non-residence facility has two living rooms, one of which has a TV and VCR, a kitchen, and a study room with cubicles and computers.

Smith students are known for their concern for feminist causes, and most describe themselves as moderate to liberal when it comes to politics, although there is a smattering of conservatives on campus. Smith's active lesbian student community is largely, but not entirely, accepted. The college hasn't been without its racist incidents. During a recent year, racist remarks were made to African-American students, and someone left a racist note at a "black [dining] table" in one of the school's residence houses. Although it was never discovered who had written the note, the students who made the remarks were found guilty by Smith's judicial board, a student-run committee, of making "inappropriate comments that were racist in nature," according to a student. As part of their punishment, the students had to publicly apologize to the students and their classmates in the residence hall, where the incident occurred, and they had to write a paper on a design for diversity.

The college's decision to reverse its need-blind admissions policy (under which it admitted students without considering their ability to pay tuition) has particularly affected the recruitment of African-American women, according to a student leader. During the 1991–92 school year, she says, the first-year class had 34 African-American students; the first-year class that entered a year later—after the policy change—had just 20 African-Americans.

To raise students' awareness about racial and cultural differences, the college sponsors a day of workshops named in honor of Otelia Cromwell, the first African-American to graduate from Smith, in 1900. "During the workshops, which get decent turnouts, we discuss almost all of the isms you can imagine, heterosexism, racism, ageism, sizeism, you name it," says a student.

Northampton, affectionately dubbed NoHo, is home to a rather cosmopolitan community, and has small Hispanic and African-American communities. The town has sidewalk cafes, three movie theaters, and many restaurants, and the Northampton Center for the Arts hosts numerous plays and musical and dance performances. Students also volunteer at the town's Casa Latina, a community support service that provides tutoring and other programs for area Hispanic residents.

Northampton is only 18 miles from Springfield, a city with a large African-American population, and Boston and New York City are 93 and 156 miles away, respectively. Students sometimes make the trek to Hartford, Connecticut. Each of these destinations is accessible by bus, but students say traveling is easier—and cheaper—with a car. Smith students regularly attend parties and other social events at the five area colleges, which have a combined enrollment of nearly 30,000 students.

Attending a women's college may not appeal to everyone, but by the time students graduate from Smith, they feel it has almost been a dream come true. "If I'd gone to a coed school, there's no way I would have had the opportunities I've had here," says a sophomore. "Women support one another in a way they don't at a coed institution, where they are forced to be more competitive with each other. I've also been a campus leader, something I would never have attempted if men were around. The focus is on women here, and because of what I've learned about being a woman, I feel more confident about going to graduate school."

TUFTS UNIVERSITY

Address: Bendetson Hall, Medford, MA 02155
Phone: (617) 627-3170
Director of Admissions: David D. Cuttino
Multicultural Student Recruiter: Donna M. Walker
1993–94 tuition: $18,793
Room and board: $5,693
Application deadline: Part I: 1/1; Part II: 1/10
Financial aid application deadline: 2/1
Non-white freshman admissions: Applicants for the class of '95: 1,464
  Accepted: 59%
  Accepted who enroll: 30%
  Applicants accepted who rank in top 10% of high school class: na
  Median SAT: na
  Median ACT: 28
Full-time undergraduate enrollment: 4,301
  Men: 52%
  Women: 48%
Non-white students in
  1988–89: 12%
  1989–90: 14%
  1990–91: 15%
  1991–92: 19%
  1992–93: 22%
Geographic distribution of students: na
Students In-state: 25%

Top majors: na
Retention rate of non-white students: 87%
Scholarships exclusively for non-white students: na
Remediation programs: None
Academic support services: Tutoring is available in most academic subjects.
Ethnic studies programs: The university offers programs in African and New World Studies, Asian Studies, and Latin

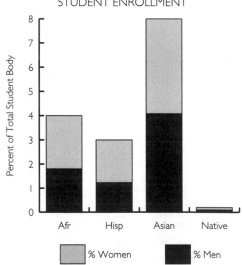

STUDENT ENROLLMENT

Percent of Total Student Body

Afr　Hisp　Asian　Native

☐ % Women　■ % Men

American Studies. More than 25 courses are offered in each of the areas.

Organizations for non-white students: Pan-African Alliance, Tufts Asian-American Society, Hispanic-American Society, Caribbean Club, Chinese Culture Club, Korean Students Association, Indian Subcontinent Association, Vietnamese Students Club, Third Day Gospel Choir, Black Theater Company, Alpha Kappa Alpha, Delta Sigma Theta, Kappa Alpha Psi, Alpha Sigma

Notable non-white alumni: Jester Hairston ('29; actor); Tracy Chapman ('85; musician and songwriter); Bette Bao Lord ('59; author)

Tenured faculty: 279

Non-tenured faculty: 286

Student-faculty ratio: 13:1

Administrators: 892

  African-American: 3%

  Hispanic: 1%

  Asian-American: 6%

  Native American: 0

Recent non-white speakers on campus: KRS-One (rap artist and anti-drug lecturer); Paule Marshall (author);

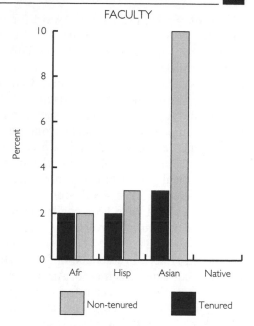

FACULTY

Kwame Toure (political activist); Angela Davis (political activist); Chinua Achebe (Nigerian author); Amiri Baraka (author and poet)

Tufts is a top-flight university that competes with the best of them. The 141-year-old school has the academic programs, the talented student body, and the facilities to rival some of America's best schools.

The university has an incredible wealth of academic opportunities. Liberal arts majors and minors are offered in nearly 60 different areas, ranging from English to history and environmental studies to linguistics. Students say that most of the school's academic programs are outstanding, particularly courses in biology, art history, English, international relations, and its unique child study program. Minor courses of study in peace and justice studies and urban and environmental policy earn high marks from students. Students are able to create their own course of study under the Plan of Study program. Recent plans of study have included Black Studies, "Aspects of Dance," and bilingual education. Tufts also has one of the few veterinary schools in New England.

Tufts is both a research university and an intense undergraduate institution of higher learning. Students can enroll in graduate courses in the school's internationally renowned Fletcher School of Law and Diplomacy and in the recently developed School of Nutrition.

"Tufts offers an amazing breadth of classes and is one of the leaders in offering Asian-American Studies on the East Coast," says a student. "Asian-American Literature" is one of the more popular Asian-American Studies courses. Li-li Ch'en, winner of the National Book Award for her translation of *Master Tung's Western Chamber of Romance,* is a professor of Chinese at Tufts.

Academic competition is tough at Tufts. To assist students with their studies, the university offers an abundance of effective academic and non-academic support programs. The Academic Resource Center, which provides peer tutoring services, "offers a lot of one-on-one assistance." Students also find the Counseling Center beneficial. "If there's a problem, the center is there. It is conveniently situated at one edge of campus, just two blocks from the campus center. It is staffed with people of color, which is a plus if there is a preference."

Tufts faculty—some of whom are nationally recognized in their respective fields—can be difficult to reach; many introductory courses have up to a couple of hundred students. But for upper-level courses, classes may have fewer than a dozen students. "Academically, I have been challenged by professors who are conscious enough to encourage a culturally diverse atmosphere," says an English major.

For additional support, Tufts sponsors centers on campus for African-American and Asian-American students. In fact, Tufts is one of the few universities on the East Coast to have such a center for Asian-American students. Called the Asian-American Center, it provides a peer tutoring program for freshman and advises on personal, academic, and career concerns. The center is a source for educational and cultural programming, including films, discussions, and lectures. Linell Yugawa, director of the center, works closely with students and keeps track of the academic performances of all Asian-American first-year students.

Tufts's African-American Center provides academic, career, and personal support for African-American students and also serves as a meeting place for African-American student organizations. The center hosts lectures, exhibits, and other cultural presentations. The director of the center, Anita Howard, is "extremely supportive of students," according to a junior.

The campus's three largest cultural student groups—the Asian Student Club, the Black Student Union, and the Hispanic-American Society—"are essential to bringing awareness to the whole community as well as providing a support network for students of color." In addition to social gatherings, the groups sponsor forums, films, and lectures.

A variety of on-campus housing options are offered at Tufts, including the traditional residence halls as well as theme houses, such as an Environmental House, language houses, and a crafts house. Students also have the option of living in one of the school's cultural theme houses. The Start House, located across the street from the Mayer Campus Center, is of special interest to Asian-American students. Currently, the house provides living facilities for eight students of Asian descent and serves as a meeting place for leaders of the school's eight Asian and Asian-American student groups. The house has a small library of Asian-American authors. The African-American House provides living facilities for about thirty students and sponsors various activities, including speakers, art, and song and dance programs.

Although students praise the cultural theme houses, they would like to see a more diverse group of students take advantage of the facilities. Says a student: "All houses welcome students from different groups, but few accept the invitation, because of the stigma and stereotypes associated with the groups and their houses."

The Asian Student Club sponsors "cultural and political events, like coalition-building events with other groups for students of color." The organization also brings speakers to campus. The Hispanic-American Society, the campus's newest cultural student group, recently hosted a basketball fundraising event, as well as parties "on or off campus, including a Caribbean/Hispanic-American Jam and a Harvard/Tufts Hispanic Night." The Black Student Union also sponsors speakers, social gatherings, and forums.

Social life definitely plays second fiddle to academics here. For weekend fun, students will throw the occasional dorm party and the fraternities have their share of bashes. The town of Medford isn't much of a stopping-off point for students looking for a good time, as most will make the short trek into Boston (via the "T" subway line) for some of that city's cultural and nightlife activities. Popular destinations are the parties at Harvard and MIT. To unwind, students are active in the school's varsity and intramural sports programs; sailing, men's crew, football, and hockey have had some recent successful seasons. Known as the "living room" of the university, the Mayer Campus Center offers the Hotung Cafe and the Rez, both popular eating establishments, as well as lounges and meeting and study rooms.

Although Tufts may lack some of the tradition and clout of its competitor in Cambridge, for one New York City transplant, attending the university has none-theless proven to be a rewarding experience. "In addition to never having been separated from my father in my life, and missing home, my friends, and my neighborhood as most college students initially do, when I arrived at Tufts University I had an overwhelming feeling of not belonging here," she says. "How long ago that seems. Tufts has become 'my' university during the past four years, as I have grown, learned, participated, and worked. I am literally not the same young woman I was four years ago. Then I was shy, but now I am aggressive; then I was afraid to speak out, but now I am assertive; then I felt different and inferior, but now I feel equal and worthwhile."

WELLESLEY COLLEGE

Women's college
Address: Wellesley, MA 02181
Phone: (617) 235-0320
Director of Admissions: Kelly A. Walter
Multicultural Student Recruiter: Terri James
1991–92 tuition: $15,966
Room and board: $5,656
Application deadline: 2/1
Financial aid application deadline: 2/1
Non-white freshman admissions: Applicants
  for the class of '94: 710
  Accepted: 60%

Accepted who enroll: 27%
Applicants accepted who rank in top
10% of high school class: 71%
In top 25%: 89%
Median SAT: na
Median ACT: na
Full-time undergraduate enrollment: 2,279
Non-white students in
  1987–88: 22.5%
  1988–89: 25.8%
  1989–90: 27.9%
  1990–91: 31%
Students In-state: na

STUDENT ENROLLMENT

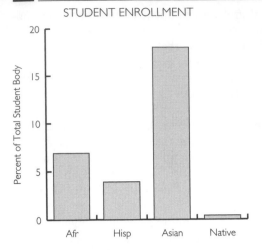

GEOGRAPHIC DISTRIBUTION OF STUDENTS

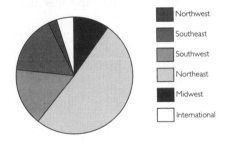

Northwest
Southeast
Southwest
Northeast
Midwest
International

Top majors: 1. Economics 2. Political Science 3. English

Retention rate of non-white students: 85%

Scholarships exclusively for non-white students: None

Remediation programs: None

Academic support services: Wellesley offers APluss (peer tutoring), summer enrichment program for first-year students, and the services of the Department of Academic Assistance.

Ethnic studies programs: Wellesley offers a major and minor course of study in Black Studies, established in 1973. Faculty: 4. The college also offers programs in Japanese and Chinese Studies.

Ethnic studies courses: na

Organizations for non-white students: Alianza, Mezcla (a Puerto Rican and Chicano student group), Asian Society, Alpha Kappa Alpha, Ethos (an African-American student group)

Notable non-white alumnae: Wendy Lee Gramm (Economics; chair, Commodity Futures Trading Commission); Amalya L. Kearse (Spanish; judge, 2nd Circuit Court of Appeals); Claudine B. Malone (Philosophy; president, Financial & Management Consulting Inc.); Genevieve L. Young (Political Science; editor-in-chief, Doubleday & Co., The Literary Guild); Shirley Young (Economics; vice president, Consumer Marketing Division, General Motors)

Tenured faculty: 149

Non-tenured faculty: 183

FACULTY

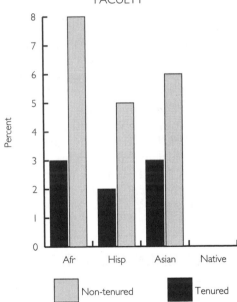

Non-tenured   Tenured

Student-faculty ratio: 10:1

Administrators: 858

    African-American: 6%

    Hispanic: 4%

    Asian-American: 2%

    Native American: 0

Recent non-white speakers on campus: Bishop Barbara Harris (first African-American woman to be an Episcopal bishop); Diane Abbot (member of the British Parliament); Nien Cheng (author)

You will no doubt have to engage in many debates about the role of women in today's society should you choose to attend all-female Wellesley, one of the top liberal arts colleges in the country. Wellesley, like other prominent women's colleges, is committed to the education of women for the boardroom and other positions of power. Each year, a high percentage of students are accepted at some of the country's top medical, law, business, and graduate schools. The typical Wellesley woman also seems to be more confident than her peers at coed institutions. "There's a kind of joke around here, which is that you can always tell a Wellesley student from an MIT woman because the Wellesley women are always the ones doing the talking during class," says a junior.

Wellesley's academics and facilities are excellent. The school's Science Center, which has undergone recent renovations, provides state-of-the-art equipment for the study of biology, chemistry, and other sciences. The center's library contains more than 95,000 volumes. Art and drama students are able to take advantage of the facilities at the impressive Jewett Arts Center, as well as those at the Wellesley College Museum. The Black Studies program is praised by students. According to a sophomore, two of the program's more popular courses are "African-American Music" and "Black Women Writers."

A popular and innovative First-Year Cluster program is available to students on a first-come, first-served basis. Students who elect to participate in the interdepartmental program live in the same dorm for a year and take the same courses. Each year, the program is centered on a single topic. In 1991–92, the topic was "A Nation of Minorities: Race and Ethnicity in Contemporary America." In 1992–93, the topic was "Gendered Selves: Biology, Culture, and Ethnicity."

In order to graduate, Wellesley students must satisfy a one-credit multicultural issues course requirement, adopted into the curriculum in 1990; the college offers more than 100 such courses from various departments. For those looking to supplement their education, especially in the sciences, Wellesley students can cross-register at MIT. A free bus drives students to MIT's Cambridge campus in about forty minutes.

Academics at Wellesley are competitive, although students say "they're not cutthroat. It's not like students are competitive with each other but more with themselves." Adds another: "I think everyone really takes pride in being stressed out here. There's a real superwoman image here."

Fear not, however, as Wellesley has an impressive support system, for both academic and non-academic needs. "It's close to impossible to fall between the cracks here. People are always looking out for you, from administrators to your peers," comments a junior. Wellesley's deans top most students' lists as the best source of support. "I worship the deans. They're not just here for academics, although they will certainly talk to a professor if for some reason you're having trouble in her class. The deans also know your name and your major," says an English major. Students stay with the same dean during their sophomore, junior, and senior years; first-year students have a separate dean. Students say that their professors, many of whom are nationally recognized scholars in their fields, are unusually accessible and that it's not uncommon to be on a first-name basis with professors; classes also tend to be small, usually averaging around 20.

For support closer to home, each of Wellesley's dorms has what the school refers to as a head of house, a woman "who's also there for us for emotional support." The college's peer tutoring programs are effective, say students. Wellesley's Honor Code, which allows students to schedule exams themselves, helps alleviate the academic stress at the college.

Interaction among students of different races seems more extensive than at other colleges. "There is zero overt racism here. People have friends within their own racial or ethnic groups, but we don't limit ourselves to those groups at all. A lot of us cross race boundaries regularly," says an English major. Observes another student: "Students here recognize their own ignorance and try to overcome it."

Students especially like to cross these boundaries at on-campus parties sponsored by Ethos, Wellesley's African-American student group, and the Asian Society. "Everyone knows the Asian Society has some of the best parties on campus, so almost everyone comes to them, and Ethos parties, which take place at the student center, have great DJs and get a fair mix of students."

Wellesley's student-run Intercultural Awareness Now (I CAN) student organization also seeks to alert students to cultural diversity issues. I CAN members sponsor a daylong workshop during orientation for incoming students in which new students discuss issues of anti-Semitism, racism, and homophobia. In 1991, two I CAN members organized Dare Today, during which Wellesley students, on a volunteer basis, attended one or another of 30 to 40 workshops dealing with multicultural issues. Classes were canceled for the day, and, according to one student, more than 600 students, faculty, administrators, and trustees were in attendance. I CAN is a vital part of campus governance; each dorm has an I CAN member, and I CAN has a representative in the college government.

Wellesley also sponsors several cultural student organizations. Ethos's "purpose is to pool the resources of African-American women on and off campus on matters of concern to the African-American community. We're mostly a support group, but we are also academic, in that we have our own study groups." Ethos, which meets once every other week at Harambee House, the African-American cultural awareness house on campus, also sponsors various activities for Black History Month, referred to at Wellesley as Quintessence. During the month, the group brings dance ensembles and speakers to campus. Ethos also has a representative on the student senate.

Although Harambee House does not provide residence facilities for students, "it is a popular place for us to hang out and relax." The house has a kitchen, a living area used for meetings and study, and a library, and offices for Ethos and *Ethos Woman,* a literary magazine. The director of the house, whose office is located there, is Wynn Holmes, a popular figure on campus.

Mezcla, a Puerto Rican and Chicano student group, "is a politically aware group concerned with the U.S. situation and the treatment of Latinos and Latinas in America," according to a student. One of its primary activities is Mezcla Week, in which it seeks to raise the cultural awareness of the campus with respect to Latino/Latina culture, presenting a food and dance festival, lectures, and other events. Mezcla members are also active in attending area conferences. Recently, members participated in a weekend conference at Columbia University in New York City. As of this writing, a similar conference to be held on Wellesley's campus is in the planning stages.

Issues of sexuality are also addressed on campus. Members of Straight Talk, a student group, visit each of the dorms during the school year to discuss their experiences as lesbians, and the Wellesley Organization of Lesbian Friends (WOLF) also sponsors programming.

The dry town of Wellesley doesn't offer much in the way of excitement. It's a predominantly white affluent suburb of Boston that doesn't provide any of the activities usually associated with college towns; there are no movie theaters or bookstores or even clubs. The nightlife of Boston, however, is just a free bus ride away, which will take students to MIT and Harvard Square, a popular spot for many a Wellesley woman on the weekends. Boston is just twelve miles east of campus.

There is really no consensus on what defines the typical Wellesley woman, although "academically inclined" and "hardworking" are words that come up often. Students who survive the four years here are more than pleased. "Wellesley has made me aware of my identity as a woman in the world and what that means to me and society," says a student. "Students leave here knowing what they want to do. They want to be CEOs, doctors, or teachers. There's a tremendous sense of clarity one has after graduating."

WHEATON COLLEGE

Address: Norton, MA 02766
Phone: (508) 285-7722 / (800) 394-6003
Director of Admissions: Gail Berson
Multicultural Student Recruiter: Lynne Stack
1993–94 tuition: $17,670
Room and board: $6,050
Application deadline: 2/1
Financial aid application deadline: 2/1
Non-white freshman admissions: Applicants
for the class of '96: 220
Accepted: 83%
Accepted who enroll: 26%
Applicants accepted who rank in top
10% of high school class: 26%
In top 25%: 53%
Median SAT: 480 V, 510 M
Median ACT: na
Full-time undergraduate enrollment: 1,283
Men: 33%
Women: 67%
Non-white students in
1988–89: 11%

1989–90: 12%
1990–91: 12%
1991–92: 12%
Students In-state: 39%
Top majors: 1. Economics 2. International
Relations 3. Social Psychology
Retention rate of non-white students: 88%
**Scholarships exclusively for non-white
students:** Balfour Minority Scholarship:
need-based; the college makes available
each year about $30,000 to qualified
minority students to replace the loan
portion of the students' financial aid
package. First-Savitt Scholarship:
need-based; one awarded each year;
value of the award varies, depending on
the fund's earnings. Trudy Villars
Memorial Scholarship: need-based; one
scholarship awarded each year to a
female minority student studying in the
field of science.
Remediation programs: None

STUDENT ENROLLMENT

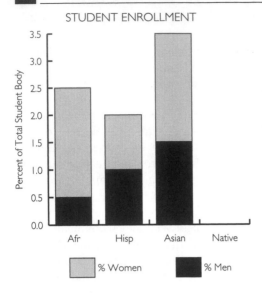

American Student Organization, Multicultural Network Program

Notable non-white alumni: Ruth Ann Steward ('63, Biology; senior specialist, arts and humanities, Library of Congress); Patricia Cross King ('63, Religion and Philosophy; professor, Georgetown University Law School); Giovinella Gonthier ('72, History; president, Gonthier International, and former ambassador of the Seychelles to the UN); Alice Gloster Burnette ('64, Sociology; Smithsonian Institution)

Tenured faculty: 54
Non-tenured faculty: 34

GEOGRAPHIC DISTRIBUTION OF STUDENTS

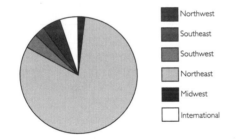

FACULTY

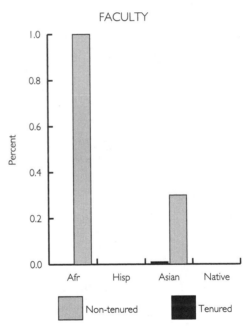

Academic support services: Peer tutoring is available in most academic subjects.

Ethnic studies programs: Wheaton offers an interdisciplinary program in Asian Studies. Students are also able to minor in African Studies.

Ethnic studies courses: The college offers "Indians of Latin America: The Non-Western Experience," "Multicultural Education," "Minorities in Education," and "Race and Ethnicity."

Organizations for non-white students: Wheaton Asian Students Association, Black Students Association, Society Organized Against Racism, Latin

Student-faculty ratio: 13:1
Administrators: na
  African-American: 0.78%
  Hispanic: 0
  Asian-American: 2.3%
  Native American: 0
Recent non-white speakers on campus: John Edgar Wideman (author)

In 1988, Wheaton College began accepting male students. Although the transition to coeducation has been less than ideal, students at the 158-year-old school are still treated to a quality education in an intimate environment.

Students also have easy access to "faculty who really like to help." Says another student: "You could be a student in a class at Wheaton, get your grades, and you would learn a lot. But not as much as if you participate. If you ask questions, and show some interest in the subject, the faculty really respond. I developed a good relationship with Dr. Tong in the biology department. He was more of a friend and mentor than a teacher, and after two years of working closely together, sometimes we would just sit in his office all afternoon talking about things that had nothing to do with research or academics."

Students praise almost all of the school's academic departments, particularly English, biology, and political science. Although Wheaton is a liberal arts college, it does offer minor programs of study in such pre-professional areas as legal studies, urban studies, computer studies, and education. The women's studies program, offered as a minor, is outstanding, with nearly 30 courses that include "Women in Africa," "Feminist Criticism," and "Women in Asia: Past and Present." To complement course work, Wheaton's Filene Center for Work and Learning, established in 1986, helps students find internships, community service activities, and fieldwork opportunities.

To graduate, students must complete a general education curriculum that includes a Freshman Seminar and courses in a foreign language, math, arts and the humanities, natural and social sciences, and Western history. In addition, students are required to enroll in a course in non-Western studies and a course that focuses on cultural diversity in the United States.

Wheaton's ideal location near almost every worthwhile port of call in New England—including numerous colleges and universities—has long been a mixed blessing. Students are able to take advantage of the social and other extracurricular activities that can be found in Providence, about fifteen minutes west, particularly at Brown University, or in Boston, about thirty minutes north. But with all of these opportunities, students usually clear out on the weekends, although they say this is changing somewhat with the advent of men on campus. "This is not a real social school," says a student who heads to Worcester Polytechnic Institute to visit friends most weekends. "Even if you don't go away for the entire weekend, you will at least go in to Boston, even just for the night."

The administration is hoping that the school's Balfour-Hood Campus Center, which offers everything from meeting and study lounges to Nautilus equipment and a snack bar, will keep students on campus, even on the weekends. The Loft, an on-campus bar, serves beverages of the alcoholic variety, but only to those 21 years of age or older.

The three-year-old Latin American Student Organization (LASO), with about 15 active members, provides social outlets for students. LASO meetings usually take place every other week at the Multicultural House on campus or in a lounge in the library. "LASO is geared to fundraising for children affected by cholera in Latin America. We sponsor dinners, speakers, and parties with a cover charge, and then send the proceeds to UNICEF. This year we've raised about $500 for the cause." LASO has also served to raise students' awareness of Latin American culture. "Some people thought, when I first came here, that we didn't have running water and electricity," says a student from Colombia. "But now I think people are understanding more about the region because of the work LASO and other students have done."

Hector Medina, LASO's faculty adviser and a Spanish professor, is "a wonderful person," comments a student. "He's enthusiastic about Latin American affairs, and is very accessible. He helped us to organize a Latin American movie festival on campus."

Established in 1987, the Wheaton Asian Students Association (WASA), which has about 100 active members, celebrates the Chinese New Year, coordinates fashion shows and dinners, and sponsors informal get-togethers. The Black Students Association also schedules lectures and informal gatherings.

Wheaton's cultural student groups make use of the facilities at the Multicultural House. "It's our base," says a LASO member. The house does not have residence facilities, but it does have a small library with books by multicultural authors, a huge kitchen, and offices for three multicultural student groups.

The town of Norton has few fans. "About all it has is a diner and a couple of stores," says a student. Students also report strained town-gown relations. "The Norton townies just don't like Wheaton students period," says a student, "no matter what color or race you are." The recently completed Great Woods Performing Arts Center, located just ten minutes from campus, has brought some culture to town.

The big news here, however, is coeducation, and many of the women aren't yet keen on the idea. Some of the more sedate and studious of them complain of too many late-night parties and the lack of all-female dorm floors (there's only one on campus). "A lot of the women here are regretting the school's decision to go coed," says a student.

Although the judgment is still out for many students about Wheaton's having gone coed, one male student is content with his school choice. "My first days at Wheaton were at an orientation meeting for minority and international students," he says. "We had people here from Bangladesh and London. Wheaton is not just diverse in where people come from or the shade of their skin. It's diverse in the way people think. It's diverse in opinions and living styles, in people respect. They respect you for who you are."

WILLIAMS COLLEGE

Address: P.O. Box 487, Williamstown, MA
  01267
Phone: (413) 597-2211
Director of Admissions: Thomas H. Parker
Multicultural Student Recruiter: Kristina M.
  Broadhurst
1993–94 tuition: $18,640
Room and board: $5,595
Application deadline: 1/1
Financial aid application deadline: 1/1
Non-white freshman admissions: Applicants
  for the class of '95: 703
  Accepted: 53.6%
  Accepted who enroll: 38.5%
  Applicants accepted who rank in top
  10% of high school class: na
  Median SAT: na
  Median ACT: na
Full-time undergraduate enrollment: 2,036
  Men: 52%
  Women: 48%

STUDENT ENROLLMENT

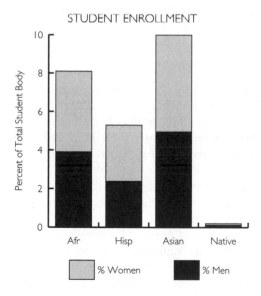

Percent of Total Student Body

Afr   Hisp   Asian   Native

% Women   % Men

Non-white students in
  1989–90: 19.8%
  1990–91: 21%

GEOGRAPHIC DISTRIBUTION OF STUDENTS

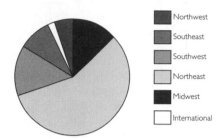

- Northwest
- Southeast
- Southwest
- Northeast
- Midwest
- International

  1991–92: 24%
  1992–93: 25%
Students In-state: 12%
Top majors: 1. History 2. English
  3. Political Science
Retention rate of non-white students: 87%
**Scholarships exclusively for non-white
  students:** Opportunity Scholarships:
  need-based; four awarded each year;
  recipients do not have to assume campus
  employment during their first year and
  portions of their student loans are
  forgiven.
Remediation programs: None
Academic support services: Tutoring in most
  academic subjects is available.
Ethnic studies programs: Williams offers an
  Asian Studies program, as well as an
  African-American Studies concentration.
Ethnic studies courses: na
Organizations for non-white students:
  Multicultural Center, Asian-American
  Students in Action, Chinese Student
  Organization, Koreans of Williams,
  VISTA (Hispanic student support
  group), Black Student Union, Harrison
  Morgan Brown Pre-med Society, Gospel
  Choir, Williams African Ensemble,
  Students of Mixed Heritage
Notable non-white alumni: Rayford W.
  Logan (chairperson, department of
  history, Stanford University); Allison

FACULTY

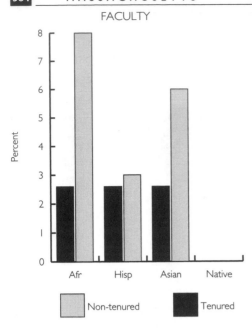

Non-tenured **Tenured**

Davis (sociology professor, University of Chicago); Sterling Brown (poet)
Tenured faculty: 114
Non-tenured faculty: 116
Student-faculty ratio: 11:1
Administrators: 120
  African-American: 7%
  Hispanic: 3%
  Asian-American: 2.5%
  Native American: 0
Recent non-white speakers on campus:
  Ronald Takaki (historian); Arnold Rampersad (author and head of American Studies program, Princeton University); Amilton Costa (Candomblé priest); Maya Ranchod (coordinator of Open Society Scholars Fund Project, a project of the University of Cape Town scholarship fund); Dr. Jesse Vasquez (professor, Queens College); Dr. Beverly Tatum (professor, Mount Holyoke College); Dr. Joseph Fernandez (former chancellor, New York City public school system)

There are those who consider Williams to be America's best liberal arts college, and they're not just students and alums. They're also the editors at *U.S. News & World Report,* who in 1993 gave the 200-year-old college top billing in their annual ranking of schools.

Williams can be described as a powerhouse liberal arts college, and students here take their studies seriously. Across the board, the school's programs are excellent, from art history and economics to biology and political science. The Williams Museum of Art is one of the finest college museums in the country and each year stages dozens of exhibitions. The Bronfman Science Center's facilities are also exceptional and allow students a great deal of hands-on research opportunities with sophisticated equipment.

To graduate, students must satisfy distribution requirements in three divisions: languages and the arts, social studies, and sciences and mathematics; students must also satisfy a non-Western studies course requirement.

Williams' academic climate is intense—the library, open 113 hours a week, is usually filled—but students say the pressure is more self-generated and is not the result of competition among peers. Students praise their faculty—some of whom are nationally recognized in their fields—for their intelligence and for their accessibility. It's not uncommon for professors to give out their home phone numbers or to host class discussions at their houses.

Williams' Winter Study Program, which allows students to study or pursue research or internship possibilities on or off campus during the month of January, is a welcome break for many of the grade-conscious. First-year students must stay on campus, however, and choose from a variety of seminar-style course topics for study; recent topics have included "The Harlem Renaissance," "New England and the Sea," and "The Idea of the Modern in the Arts."

Students say they're also able to find additional academic and non-academic support from a variety of professors and staff members. "Robin Powell, who is the new assistant director of alumni relations, is a role model because she is young, intelligent, gregarious, helpful, and accessible," says a student. "She tries to bridge the gap between alumni and students. There is also Shanti Singham, a history professor, who has gotten very involved with the Black Student Union since her arrival in 1987. David Sheppard, assistant professor of physical education, is known to most black students as someone who is 'deep.' He helps many students through any number of personal problems. Preston Smith, associate dean of the college, is another role model. He hosts dinners at his house and is very involved with students." Monica Martinez, an assistant dean of the college, also works closely with students. "She too is young, intelligent, and successful," observes a student.

Students find additional support at the college's Multicultural Center, which contains a large meeting area, a kitchen, a library, and organizational offices for most of the school's cultural student organizations. The center, established on campus in 1989 as a result of a student sit-in during the 1987–88 school year, brings to campus various film series, theater and dance groups, and lecturers, and sponsors prejudice reduction workshops. The center is headed by Nura Dualeh, a Williams alum, who, according to one student, is "like a comrade."

Williams, long known for being a bastion of preppiness and affluence, has been on the fast track when it comes to diversifying its student body, racially and socioeconomically. "There is no denying the diversity here," says a first-year student. "It is a truly wonderful thing, even though the school tends to pat itself on the back about it a little much." Students of color now account for more than a quarter of the student body—a recent entering class had nearly a third—and financial aid awards are designed to attract a more diverse socioeconomic student body. For a recent entering class, the average aid award was nearly $13,000, compared with the $4,500 average award given to students in 1979.

To diversify its faculty, in 1985 the college established the Gaius Charles Bolin Fellowship, named in honor of its first African-American graduate (class of 1889), which enables two "minority" graduate students to teach at Williams. Students praise Scott Wong, who teaches Asian-American history. "He is a tenured-track professor who was hired without any student activism or prompting the way they've had to do at other schools," says a student.

The college's various cultural student groups are reportedly quite active. According to a history major: "The Black Student Union, VISTA, Asian Students in Action, and Bharat (an Indian group) are all busy groups. All of them sponsor social/cultural events such as parties, theme movies, and theme food nights. Also, there is Black History Month (February), Asian Awareness Month (November), and Latino/a Awareness Month (April). During these theme months there are many lectures, roundtable discussions, and literature sponsored by the groups and the college. We also have debates on topics such as affirmative action and these groups go on retreats in order to foster a sense of community, understanding, and cooperation."

Asian Students in Action (ASiA) has about 40 active student members and attracts about 200 students, faculty, staff, and area residents to its activities. Some of ASiA's more popular events have been the Annual Lunar New Year Dinner, a Chinese Youth Goodwill Dance and Group performance, as well as lectures.

VISTA, Williams' Hispanic student organization, provides emotional and academic support, according to students. VISTA's approximately 80 members include students from the United States, Puerto Rico, Mexico, Spain, Uruguay, and Peru.

The Black Student Union, which has about 50 active members, sponsors a big sister/big brother program, a tutoring program that matches upperclassmen with first-year students. Other BSU events are "Apollo at Williams," a talent show, and Project Life, a community outreach program in Pittsfield, a predominantly black city south of the campus.

By most accounts, the transition to a more racially integrated Williams campus has been relatively smooth. Says a student: "Overt racial tensions do not exist on campus, but there have been some comments about how the racial groups—blacks, Asians, and Hispanics—tend to stick together. This is particularly evident in the dining halls, where one finds an all-black, all-Asian, or all-Hispanic table. I don't know if the situation is any different at other colleges, but most people at Williams don't seem to have a problem with this. I occasionally join the all-Asian tables, but that's because I'm friends with them, and if there's a white person at the table, nobody pays attention to the fact that he or she is white. We're all friends." A sophomore says: "The campus doesn't break down on racial lines as much as according to who is interested in what. All parties on campus are open. When the Black Student Union throws a party everyone comes and everyone is open. The team sports are all pretty evenly integrated." A senior sees the situation as slightly different. "Campus parties are interesting," he says. "The pure keg parties are overwhelmingly populated by white students. Other parties, where dance is offered, are pretty well integrated. However, if the Black Student Union has a party many white students feel uncomfortable going, especially by themselves. This has become so due to the many rumors circulated about the BSU, both merited and unmerited (e.g., we're prejudiced, separatist, etc.)."

Sports are an important part of the Williams experience, especially as a vast majority of students participate on one of the school's varsity or intramural teams. The football season has had some recent successful seasons—and any season would be considered successful as long as archrivals Wesleyan and Amherst are defeated—as have the ski, soccer, and squash teams. The college offers a variety of on-campus and well-used sports facilities, from a golf course to a skating rink.

Theater, dance, and community service projects are also popular group activities, but don't go looking to join any fraternities here—they were banned in 1962. Parties are usually held in the residential houses, while campus-wide parties with student bands are common on the weekends. Weekend trips to Boston and New York City, both about three hours away by car, are sometimes popular.

Williamstown (pop. 8,542) is a small picture-postcard New England town. Each year its famed Williamstown Theatre Festival brings in more than 55,000 spectators and presents numerous celebrity performers. Students report, however, that town-gown relations are sometimes strained. "There are many class tensions between the campus and the townspeople who are in the immediate vicinity," says a student. "Thus, the racial tensions which exist are in many ways an extension of the class dynamics. There are more people of color here at Williams than ever. This is unsettling to many of the townspeople. There have been several instances of racial slurs, staring, you name it."

Williams has long been known for its academics, and more recently it has deservedly come to be known for its diversity. "The people of Williams for the very most part do seem to be trying to achieve 'racial harmony,' to dust off a cliché. And more importantly, in the process of trying to find that harmony, there is still relatively little patronization and more respect than I have seen anywhere else. I would definitely recommend Williams to any student who is of color or not and who wants a diverse and intelligent environment in which to go to college."

WORCESTER POLYTECHNIC INSTITUTE

Address: Worcester, MA 01609
Phone: (508) 831-5286
Director of Admissions: Kay Dietrick
Multicultural Student Recruiter: na

1992–93 tuition: $14,555
Room and board: $4,820
Application deadline: 2/15
Financial aid application deadline: 3/1

At most engineering- and science-centered institutions, students learn in an academic vacuum. They rarely, if ever, are exposed to liberal studies, let alone the impact their inventions and technology will have on society. But not at Worcester Polytechnic Institute, the nation's third-oldest college of science and engineering. Ever since the school established the WPI Plan in 1972, WPI has distinguished itself as one of the more unusual "techie" schools in the country, and to this day the plan remains one of the school's main drawing cards.

The WPI Plan involves three graduation requirements. The Interactive Qualifying Project (IQP) offers students, under the tutelage of a humanities and science professor, the opportunity to study the relationship between society and technology. Recent IQPs have included analyzing the ability of solar energy to power a mass transit system in Malaysia and identifying future rationales for manned space flight beyond the earth's orbit. The Major Qualifying Project (MQP), completed during the senior year, allows students to apply what they learned in the classroom to the real world. For his MQP, one senior designed and constructed a solar-powered racing car to be entered in a national competition. The final component of the WPI Plan is Sufficiency, which requires students to enroll in at least five humanities courses and to complete a project in the student's chosen area.

If you're wondering whether or not the WPI Plan is successful, then wonder no more. In a typical year, 90 percent of those graduating from the institute had jobs or had been accepted to graduate school programs, while 80 percent of the school's science graduates had entered graduate school immediately following graduation.

Clearly the school's academic strengths are in the fields of engineering, which include civil, biomedical, chemical, electrical, and mechanical engineering. Chemistry and biology are also considered strong. Although the school requires its students to enroll in at least five humanities courses, students say offerings in the area are comparatively weak and limited. To enhance their school's academic offerings, WPI students are able to take courses at any one of the ten schools in the Worcester consortium; a free shuttle takes students to and from the various campuses, which include Clark University and Holy Cross College. However, students say that due to red tape and the inconvenience of course scheduling, taking courses at other colleges is not popular.

Faculty-student interaction at WPI is unusually close, especially for a research-centered institution. Students often work one-on-one with faculty on projects. In an attempt to get the faculty even more involved with students, a system has now been established in which a professor serves as an adviser to students in a residence hall. In a recent year, even WPI's president, John Strauss, advised dorm residents.

WPI's racial and geographic diversity is less impressive. In 1990, according to the U.S. Department of Education, of the school's 3,911 students, 4.8 percent were Asian, 0.1 percent were Native American, 0.6 percent were African-American, and 0.8 percent were Hispanic. To improve racial and ethnic diversity on campus, WPI's administration has created the Multicultural Advisory Board, which includes an MIT administrator, corporate bigwigs, and WPI faculty and administrators. The board proposed Project Strive, which brings in area high school students for a summer's worth of engineering and science study. To enhance the school's already impressive international student enrollment, which accounted for 7.9 percent of the student body in 1990, the admissions office has been conducting focus groups with already enrolled international students to discuss ways to better recruit such students.

Campus social life is far from hopping, particularly with the absence of a student center. As a result, much of the social activity centers on the school's active Greek system, to which about 45 percent of the men and 40 percent of the women belong. The school's male-to-female ratio—about four to one—is also wanting, depending, that is, on your point of view. "For men, it's a nightmare, but for women it's a virtual smorgasbord," says a student. To alleviate some of the imbalance, students—both male and female—socialize with students at nearby Becker and Assumption colleges, or any one of the other colleges in the immediate area.

With about 70 active members, the Hispanic Student Association "works to get a culturally diverse group of students at our events," says an HSA leader. "Last year we held a dance at Clark, and an hour before the dance we gave merengue and salsa dance lessons to students." Although HSA had about eight non-Hispanic students in its organization in a recent year, most of the group's members are foreign-born, primarily from Venezuela, Mexico, Costa Rica, and Spain.

"The Hispanic students at WPI are very united," says a student. "We party together, usually in a club in Boston or in an off-campus apartment. We like our music and we get together to talk Spanish. We know each other well." Tau Kappa

Epsilon, one of WPI's fraternities, is also popular with Hispanic students; in a recent year, 13 of the chapter's members were Hispanic.

WPI's Asian Student Club, like HSA, is composed primarily of foreign-born students, mostly from Indonesia, China, Thailand, and Taiwan. The club, which has about 100 members, sponsors an annual trip to Montreal during the school's fall break. Back on campus, the club also sponsors an annual dinner buffet, which in a recent year served Thai cuisine. According to a club member, more than 100 students and faculty attended the event, which was held on the Lower Wedge, an extension of the dining hall.

The African-American Cultural Society has about 15 members and recently sponsored a consortium-wide party held on campus at Gompeii's Place, an on-campus hall. The society also coordinates displays in the library that focus on African-American history. As an alternative to the usual residence facility, WPI sponsors the World House, which can accommodate up to 25 students. The house is popular with African-American students; in a recent year, about 80 percent of its residents were African-American. "It's a place where African-American students can feel really comfortable. There we can listen to the music we want to and hang out with friends."

As at most "techie" schools, WPI students are, if anything, politically and socially apathetic. "There is no prejudice on our campus, but there is at the same time little awareness about issues of diversity," says a student. Adds another student: "The students at WPI are very open-minded, even in the fraternities. They want to know what it's like in Central America. Some didn't know we had electricity there. It's nice to discuss cultural differences."

To enhance multicultural awareness on campus, WPI recently hired its first director of multicultural affairs, Ron Macon. One student says Macon is too new on campus to judge his effectiveness. Another student comments that Macon is "very open. Recently he hosted a barbecue for African-American students and faculty where we students were able to rub shoulders with administrators. He did it to build a sense of community, and it worked."

Also successful in building "a sense of community" among students is Tom Thompson, an associate dean of students. "Tom is accessible to all students and will help us with any questions we have," says a campus leader. "He knows a lot about budgeting, and he comes to many of the cultural groups' meetings and events. Recently, he won an award for being the school's best adviser."

Off-campus social and cultural opportunities exist primarily at the other area colleges, as students say that heading into Worcester isn't a popular activity, except for going to some of the concerts at the Centrum, a major entertainment center in the area. Recent Centrum performers have included Janet Jackson and Sting. Boston is less than an hour's drive from campus.

While WPI may lack the cachet of MIT or Caltech, it also lacks the cutthroat competition that characterizes an education at those other schools. And that's just fine with WPI students, who are proud of their school's efforts to develop "technological humanists." "I wanted a small-campus community, where I felt people would help each other. A lot of colleges emphasize competition. At WPI, everybody helps each other. We learn together here."

M I C H I G A N

ALBION COLLEGE

Address: 616 Michigan Avenue, Albion, MI 49224
Phone: (517) 629-0321 / (800) 858-6770
Director of Admissions: Dr. Frank Bonta
Multicultural Student Recruiter: T. Annette Washington
1993–94 tuition: $13,556
Room and board: $4,588
Application deadline: 4/1
Financial aid application deadline: 2/15
Non-white freshman admissions: Applicants for the class of '97: 100
  Accepted: 75%
  Accepted who enroll: na
  Applicants accepted who rank in top 10% of high school class: na
  Median SAT: na
  Median ACT: na
Full-time undergraduate enrollment: 1,650
Non-white students in 1987–91: na
Geographic distribution of students:
  Midwest: 95%
  Southeast: na
  Northeast: na
  Northwest: na
  Southwest: na
Students In-state: na
Top majors: 1. Music 2. Political Science 3. History
Retention rate of non-white students: 71%
Scholarships exclusively for non-white students: Diversity Awards for African-Americans
Remediation programs: None

Academic support services: Albion's Developing Skills Center assists students with their writing, provides tutors, and sponsors time management workshops.
Ethnic studies programs: None
Ethnic studies courses: Courses include "People and Cultures of Africa," "Racial and Cultural Minorities," "African-American Literature," "Race and Nationality in American Life," "Modern Africa," and "Asian and African Leaders."
Organizations for non-white students: Black Student Alliance, Asian Awareness Group
Notable non-white alumni: John Joyner (neurosurgeon); Daniel Boggan (vice-chancellor, University of

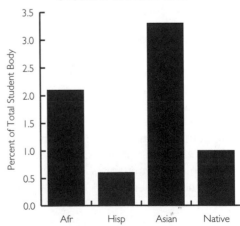

STUDENT ENROLLMENT

California/Berkeley); John Porter (former president, Eastern Michigan University, and superintendent of Detroit public schools); Milton Barnes (Michigan Coach of the Year; assistant basketball coach, University of Minnesota); Dr. James Curtis (director of psychiatry, Harlem Hospital Center)

Tenured faculty: 108
  African-American: 0
  Hispanic: 0
  Asian-American: 0
  Native American: 0
Non-tenured faculty: 23
  African-American: 0
  Hispanic: 1 total
  Asian-American: 1 total

  Native American: 0
Student-faculty ratio: 14:1
Administrators: 121
  African-American: 3%
  Hispanic: 0
  Asian-American: 0
  Native American: 0
Recent non-white speakers on campus: Judy F. Richardson (associate director of the PBS series *Eyes on the Prize*); Naomi Long-Midgett (historical researcher); Linda Ammons (assistant law professor, Cleveland Marshall College of Law); Serena Williams (assistant law professor, Howard University); Gloria Naylor (author); Roger Wilkins (author and poet)

For generations, Albion has been regarded as one of Michigan's best liberal arts colleges. It was the first private college in the state to secure a Phi Beta Kappa chapter, and the college's small size ensures that students work closely with professors.

Albion has several well-respected academic programs, including history, music, and English. Business students take advantage of the school's competitive Gerstacker Program in Professional Management, which offers internship possibilities and requires students to complete a summer program of study. Students are selected for the program on the basis of their academic record and their potential for leadership, as evidenced by prior leadership experience. Albion's Gerald R. Ford Institute for Public Service, also a selective program, "assures qualified students a broad liberal arts education with concentrated study in the areas of government and public service." Members of each entering first-year class are required to participate in the Common Reading Experience, in which students must read a text recommended by the college before arriving on campus. A recent text was *Their Eyes Were Watching God,* a novel by African-American author Zora Neale Hurston. Students discuss the work more formally when they arrive on campus as part of the orientation program.

With only 1,700 undergraduates, Albion students are able to work closely with faculty. "The faculty is very accessible here. There isn't one professor that I don't feel as if I can get in touch with." The college also has the "Take a Faculty Member to Lunch" program, in which students are able to take a faculty member of their choice for lunch at Baldwin Hall, the campus's main dining hall. "All you have to do is show your ID and your meal and your professor's meal are paid for," notes a student. Preston Hicks, director of multicultural affairs, works closely with students. "His policy is to always have an open door. His line is: 'If you're in the neighborhood, stop by and talk.'" Through Hicks's efforts, the college recently established an on-campus chapter of the NAACP.

Although the Black Student Alliance (BSA) has only about 15 active student members, the organization is one of the campus's most active student groups. In conjunction with two other student groups, the BSA is sponsoring activities for

Albion's Peace Through Equality Week. During the course of the school year, the BSA sponsors Nights of Culture. The most popular Nights of Culture activities are student-performed skits. "Our skits are usually about college life here at Albion," says a student. "We try to depict things that we think should be changed on campus. The events are always well attended. A lot of students show up, and so do the college president and his wife." Recent Nights of Culture shows have presented traditional African as well as modern dance. The BSA also sponsors the Gospel Extravaganza, in which various churches from the area are invited to sing on campus.

BSA meetings are usually conducted in the BSA Lodge, located on the east side of campus on Erie Street. The lodge is currently undergoing extensive remodeling. When completed, it will have two study lounges upstairs, a student office, and a guest room.

The city of Albion has a large African-American community. According to students, relations between the city and the college could be better. In an effort to better town-gown relations, the BSA, with Hicks's assistance, has set up a tutoring program in the area for junior high school students. Students also attend the area's churches, a popular Sunday activity for Albion students. Otherwise, the city of Albion offers little culturally or socially, but students have been known to seek outlets in such larger cities as Lansing and Ann Arbor, homes to Michigan State University and the University of Michigan.

Other popular activities for students can be found at the school's Lomas Fieldhouse, a sports enthusiast's dream that has everything from tennis courts to basketball courts. The men's intramural athletic program fields more than 25 activities and sports—including football and Ping-Pong—and all of the men's residences, especially the fraternities, compete. Greek life is pervasive at the college, and many of the weekend parties are held at one or another of the school's six fraternities. Sororities do not have residence facilities. Religious groups, particularly Campus Crusade for Christ, enjoy large memberships. The Union Board also sponsors movies, concerts, and plays.

Albion's reputation is outstanding in a state where large universities predominate, but the school has primarily a regional appeal; more than 80 percent of its student body hails from Michigan, including nearly all of the school's non-white students, and almost all students come from the Great Lakes region, which tends to create a more homogeneous atmosphere.

While diversity isn't exactly a hallmark at this small liberal arts college, an excellent regional reputation is. Says a junior: "I was drawn to the college because I wanted to go to a school where I knew I could get to know my professors and where I wouldn't feel like a number. I've been challenged academically and socially here, and I think I'm a stronger person than when I first arrived."

GMI ENGINEERING & MANAGEMENT INSTITUTE

Address: 1700 West Third Avenue, Flint, MI 48504-4898
Phone: (313) 762-7865 / (800) 955-4464
Director of Admissions: R. Thomas Cerny
Multicultural Student Recruiter: na
1991–92 tuition: $9,400
Room and board: $2,840
Application deadline: Rolling admissions
Financial aid application deadline: Rolling
Non-white freshman admissions: Applicants for the class of '95: 411
  Accepted: 59%
  Accepted who enroll: 40%
  Applicants accepted who rank in top 10% of high school class: 50%
  In top 25%: 88%
  Median SAT range: 430–540 V, 570–660 M
  Median ACT range: 23–26
Full-time undergraduate enrollment: 2,400
  Men: 79%
  Women: 21%

1989–90: 12.9%
1990–91: 15%
Geographic distribution of students: na
Top majors: 1. Engineering 2. Management
Retention rate of non-white students: 70%
Scholarships exclusively for non-white students: None
Remediation programs: None
Academic support services: The university offers student survival skill programs, as well as leadership development training seminars.
Ethnic studies programs: None
Ethnic studies courses: "Culture and Personality" is offered by the social science department, and "Issues, Art, and Ideas of Africa and the Diaspora" is a humanities elective.
Organizations for non-white students: Black Unity Congress, Hispanic Leadership Committee, Delta Sigma Theta, Omega Psi Phi, National Society of Black Engineers, Alpha Kappa Alpha, Kappa Alpha Psi, Alpha Phi Alpha

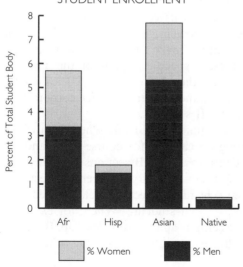

STUDENT ENROLLMENT

Non-white students in
1987–88: 11.3%
1988–89: 12.3%

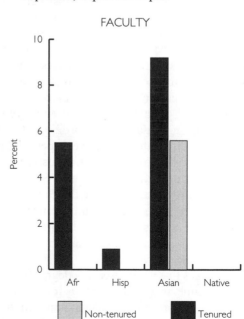

FACULTY

Notable non-white alumni: Ronald Pirtle ('77; executive, General Motors Corporate Strategic Planning Group); Steven D. Pettiford (plant manager, General Motors); Barbara Whittaker (director of production control, General Motors)
Tenured faculty: 109
Non-tenured faculty: 18
Student-faculty ratio: 13:1
Administrators: 78
  African-American: 10%
  Hispanic: 1.3%
  Asian-American: 0
  Native American: 0

Recent non-white speakers on campus: Joe Anderson (director, Exterior Systems, General Motors); Dr. Erice Doss (professor, Tennessee State University); Dr. Paul Shang (director, education department, Colorado State University); Dr. Blandina Cardenas Ramirez (director of minority concerns, American Council of Education); Dr. Samuel Betances (sociology professor, Northeastern University); Yolanda King (civil rights activist and daughter of Martin Luther King, Jr.)

GMI, located sixty miles north of the Motor City, offers well-regarded programs in engineering and business. The school, once affiliated with General Motors, "isn't for students who are uncertain about what they want to do," says a mechanical engineering major. "Everyone who comes here is focused and has definite and clear career goals."

The institute has two divisions: business and engineering and environmental design. Business programs include accounting, marketing, business administration, information systems, and management. Engineering programs include computer engineering, electrical engineering, and industrial engineering. GMI's major in manufacturing systems engineering is the first such program in the country; electrical and mechanical engineering are the school's most popular programs.

What sets GMI apart from most other schools is its co-op program, one of the largest in the nation. All students are required to participate in the program—one of the main reasons they chose to attend the institute in the first place. Students plan their co-ops with work managers, who represent specific regions of the country. Students can also specify in which type of industry they'd like to work. UPS, General Motors, including its Saturn plant in Tennessee, and numerous other corporations around the country are regular employers of GMI students.

To accommodate such a program, GMI has a unique academic schedule in which students alternate, for 12-week periods, being on campus for course work and off campus for their co-ops. Students are divided into A and B sections and only one section is on campus at a time. Students say there is rivalry between the sections, although they rarely interact because of their schedules. "Sections get annoyed with each other, especially within the fraternities," says a student. "When, for example, A section throws a big party before they leave campus and doesn't clean up, B section gets angry and might do the same thing. Also, each section thinks the other has a better time on campus."

It takes five years to earn a degree from GMI, as opposed to the usual four, because of the time away from campus for co-ops. But with all the work experience gained as part of the program, students don't mind at all. To graduate, students must complete course work in math, chemistry, physics, history, communications, and economics.

Academics at GMI are rigorous; those who enjoy math and science do well here. Students say professors are accessible and more than willing to help.

The most active student organizations on campus are fraternities and sororities, to which about 60 percent of the students belong. The fraternities are the center of many of the school's weekend social activities. There are also three historically black Greek organizations on campus—the Alpha Kappa Alpha sorority and the Alpha Phi Alpha and Omega Psi Phi fraternities—which sponsor parties and community service projects.

The National Society of Black Engineers provides peer tutoring for members. The Black Unity Congress, a student group, "does fun things," says a member. Recently, the group sponsored a trip to Wayne State University in Detroit, where they attended an African art exhibit.

The Hispanic Student Organization has grown in recent years. The group, which has about 25 members, brings speakers to campus each year and conducts weekly meetings. "We mostly have meetings so we can keep in touch and help each other when needed," says a member. The group recently scheduled a dinner excursion to a section of Detroit known as Mexican Village. Students give a lot of credit to Edith Whitney, a staff member in the dean of student development's office, for her support of the organization. "She shows a lot of interest in the students and attends many of our events and meetings," says a student. "She also helped me improve my grades by seeing to it that I got tutoring." Students are currently working to have a chapter of the Society of Hispanic Professional Engineers on campus.

Students say that the campus is relatively well integrated, although the majority of African-American students live in the upperclassmen floors of Thompson Hall. According to one student, this is because these students don't choose to join one of the campus's residential fraternities.

GMI is located in Flint, "a city that seems more like a town," says a student. The city's downtown area recently underwent a sort of renaissance, but students say the area doesn't offer much of interest to city residents or students. Flint has African-American and Hispanic populations. Members of the Black Unity Congress help tutor at a church in the city. Detroit is a popular destination for students looking to get away from the campus's occasional feeling of smallness; the school has only three buildings—the campus center, which houses the cafeteria and administrative offices, a residence hall, and an academic building.

With all of that work experience under their belts, GMI students are content with their college choice. "There are times when I wish I had gone to a larger school that was more social and that had more activities," says one student. "But the co-op part of this school is amazing. I'm confident that with what I've done here I'll be able to find a job."

KALAMAZOO COLLEGE

Address: 1200 Academy Street, Kalamazoo, MI 49007-3295

Phone: (800) 253-3602

Director of Admissions: Michael Donahue

Multicultural Student Recruiter: Tony Dennis

1991–92 tuition: $12,669

Room and board: $4,053

Application deadline: 3/1

Financial aid application deadline: 3/1

Non-white freshman admissions: Applicants for the class of '95: 174

Accepted: 78%

Accepted who enroll: 28%

Applicants accepted who rank in top 10% of high school class: 50%

In top 25%: 80%

Median SAT range: 470–570 V, 520–640 M

Median ACT range: 24–29

Full-time undergraduate enrollment: 1,250

Men: 48%

Women: 52%

GEOGRAPHIC DISTRIBUTION OF STUDENTS

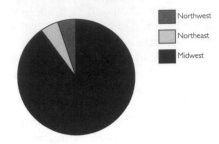

Northwest
Northeast
Midwest

Students In-state: 76%

Top majors: na

Retention rate of non-white students: 71%

Scholarships exclusively for non-white students: John T. Williamson Scholarships: merit-based; $1,000 to $6,000; eight to ten awarded each year.

Remediation programs: None

Academic support services: The college provides tutors in most academic subjects and a writing center.

Ethnic studies programs: None

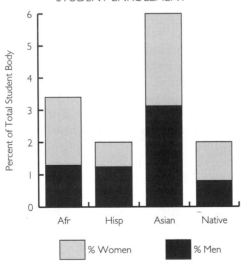

STUDENT ENROLLMENT

Percent of Total Student Body

Afr   Hisp   Asian   Native

% Women   % Men

Non-white students in

1987–88: 6.9%

1988–89: 7.3%

1989–90: 8.1%

1990–91: 9%

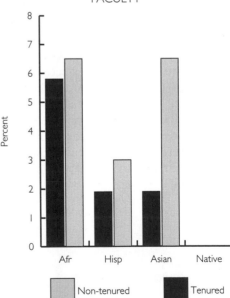

FACULTY

Percent

Afr   Hisp   Asian   Native

Non-tenured   Tenured

Ethnic studies courses: The college offers more than 15 courses in African-American studies and other ethnic studies.

Organizations for non-white students: Black Student Organization

Notable non-white alumni: na

Tenured faculty: 52

Non-tenured faculty: 31

Student-faculty ratio: 12:1

Administrators: 79

    African-American: 26%

Hispanic: 0

Asian-American: 0

Native American: 0

Recent non-white speakers on campus: Steven Pettiford (plant manager, General Motors); Sidney Williams (attorney); Carolyn Williams (judge, Kalamazoo County Juvenile Court); Lyle Logan (senior director, Continental Bank); Dr. Roy Hudson (vice president, Upjohn Company)

At quick glance, Kalamazoo College looks like a lot of other top-flight liberal arts schools—small, committed to educating well-rounded students, close interaction with faculty—but there is a difference. The college's K-Plan, an innovative alternative to the usual grind of semester-long courses that's found at most schools, is what sets this 160-year-old school apart from all of the others.

The K-Plan divides the school year into 10-week quarters and includes a Career Development Program, foreign study, and an individualized senior project. The Career Development Program, usually taken during the spring quarter of a student's sophomore year, allows students to work off campus at any one of 900 possible internships the college has on file in its Career Development Center. During a student's junior year, the college encourages study in a foreign country, all at Kalamazoo's regular tuition costs. More than 90 percent of the school's student body studies in any one of its 14 centers abroad or through programs sponsored by the Great Lakes College Association. Finally, seniors are required to complete an individualized project, which they themselves design based on their academic needs and career interests.

For many students, the K-Plan provides opportunities of a lifetime. "I spent three months as a political intern in Washington, DC, eight months studying in Italy, and, in my senior year, I did a three-month study in Kenya," says a recent graduate. For other students, however, the K-Plan can make for a disjointed college experience, particularly as more than 200 students will be off campus during a typical quarter. "My girlfriend was in Europe when I was on campus for one of the quarters, and when she came back it was my turn to do my off-campus internship. But we were able to get together over the summer."

The K-Plan, while stressing career opportunities, does not lose sight of the school's liberal arts mission. The K-Plan is Kalamazoo's attempt to graduate a well-rounded professional. With such emphasis on developing the career interests of students, it's no wonder the majority of Kalamazoo students are decidedly pre-professional—business and pre-med majors abound.

Kalamazoo's English, economics, and math departments rank as some of the school's best. Two African-American Studies courses—"South Africa and the American South," a history course taught by a graduate student from nearby Michigan State, and "Sisters of the Spirit"—are popular.

The Black Student Organization (BSO) sponsors two events during the school year. Each February, as part of Black History Month, the BSO coordinates a dinner that features a guest speaker. The BSO also helps to coordinate a vigil each January as part of Martin Luther King, Jr., Day, and students have staged performances based on various King speeches. The BSO, which has about 16 active members, usually meets in the Black Student Organization room in the student union building on campus. The room contains a TV, African and African-American art, and a small library with textbooks and books by and about African-Americans.

BSO adviser and director of minority affairs Jeanne Baraka-Love "is like a mother to us. I know I can talk to her about anything. She always makes herself available when she can, and she'll come to us if we're having any problems. She also always helps us with our activities and comes to our events."

Kalamazoo's social life gets exciting when it comes time for Monte Carlo Night, a campus-wide formal dance, and K-Derby, festivities on the same Saturday as the Kentucky Derby. There are also a number of special-interest and religious clubs, and the school's Weekly Forum brings several prominent speakers to campus each year.

Kalamazoo (pop. 200,000) has numerous theaters and restaurants, and concerts usually come to the area. With Western Michigan University located across the street from Kalamazoo, students get a chance to attend big-time parties and to use the school's gym and library. For those with cars, Detroit and Chicago are only about two and a half and three hours away, respectively. The beaches of Lake Michigan, just a half hour away, are also popular destinations, especially for those few who stay on campus for the summer quarter.

If you want to plant your roots in one spot for the next four years, then Kalamazoo isn't for you. But if you're looking for a school that will help you broaden your career opportunities while you earn a liberal arts degree, then Kalamazoo just may interest you. "There are times when I would rather have attended a larger school, or even a school with more diversity in the student body and in activities. But I came here for one reason: to get an education. And Kalamazoo is helping me to get that. I've learned a lot of leadership skills through the different organizations I've participated in, and Kalamazoo is definitely the place to come to find job and internship experience."

UNIVERSITY OF MICHIGAN

Address: 1200 SAB, Ann Arbor, MI
48109-1316
Phone: (313) 764-7433
Director of Admissions: Richard Shaw, Jr.
Multicultural Student Recruiter: na
1992–93 tuition: $4,100 (in-state); $14,396
(out-of-state)
Room and board: $4,285
Application deadline: 2/1
Financial aid application deadline: 2/15
Non-white freshman admissions: Applicants
for the class of '95: 4,283
Accepted: 70%
Accepted who enroll: 44%
Applicants accepted who rank in top
10% of high school class: 64%
Median SAT range: 420–520 V, 460–570 M
Median ACT range: 21–25
Full-time undergraduate enrollment: 19,641
Men: 53%
Women: 47%

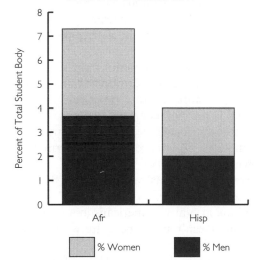

STUDENT ENROLLMENT

Percent of Total Student Body

□ % Women   ■ % Men

Non-white students in
1988–89: 15%
1989–90: 16.4%

1990–91: 18.2%
1991–92: 19%
Geographic distribution of students: na
Top majors: 1. Psychology 2. English
3. Mechanical Engineering
Retention rate of non-white students: 90%
**Scholarships exclusively for non-white
students:** Michigan Scholar Award:
merit-based; each award is $3,000;
available to non-Michigan residents; 300
to 370 awarded each year; renewable.
Scholar Recognition Award: merit-based;
covers cost of tuition; approximately 100
awarded each year; available to Michigan
residents; renewable. Michigan
Achievement Award: merit-based; $1,500
for each award; available to Michigan
residents; 150 to 200 awarded each year;
renewability depends on need.
Remediation programs: None
Academic support services: The university
offers the services of the Comprehensive
Studies Program, as well as tutoring in
most academic subjects.
Ethnic studies programs: The university
offers the Afro-American and African
Studies program, established in 1971.
Ethnic studies courses: na
Organizations for non-white students: Black
Student Union, Labor of Love
Fellowship, Black Theater Workshop,
Sister, Gospel Chorale, Omega Psi Phi,
Bursley Family, Alpha Kappa Alpha,
Delta Sigma Theta, Alpha Phi Alpha,
Kappa Alpha Psi, Zeta Phi Beta,
Asian-American Association, University
of Michigan Asian-American Student
Coalition, Native American Student
Association
Notable non-white alumni: James Earl Jones
('53; actor); Jessye Norman ('69; opera
singer); Ben Carson (neurosurgeon); Jesse
Hill (Business; CEO Insurance); Cazzie
Russell (professional basketball player)
Tenured and non-tenured faculty: na
African-American: 3.9%

Hispanic: 1.6%
Asian-American: 5.6%
Native American: 0.1%
Student-faculty ratio: 12:1
Administrators: na

African-American: 11%
Hispanic: 2.3%
Asian-American: 6.8%
Native American: 0.4%
Recent non-white speakers on campus: na

The University of Michigan is known for its athletic prowess. The Wolverines have been in the Rose Bowl thirteen times and the basketball team is always a top contender in the Big Ten. But as strong as its athletic programs are, the university's academic programs are just as strong, and in some areas—especially engineering—maybe even stronger. It's this powerful combination of athletics and academics—and a plethora of social activities—that continues to attract bright and talented students to the Ann Arbor campus.

Michigan isn't just a school for in-staters; in fact, the university has one of the most geographically diverse student populations of any state school in the country. It attracts more than 30 percent of its students from out of state, most notably the Midwest and the Northeast, and dozens of foreign countries. Each undergraduate division—there are 17 in all—has its own admissions selection criteria, but for out-of-state applicants, the competition is heated. Michigan's colleges of liberal arts and engineering are the most competitive, and often compete for students with some of the Ivy League schools.

Nearly every department at Michigan is top-flight and boasts internationally recognized scholars in their respective fields. Engineering offers the university's most popular and most respected programs, and among the liberal arts and sciences students especially recommend the history, biology, political science, and foreign-language programs. The new five-story chemistry building on campus has upgraded that department's offerings and research capabilities. Michigan's college of business administration is equally outstanding, and students praise their school's health-related programs.

Courses in Asian-American Studies are also available at the university. Students point to "The Asian-American Experience" and "Asian-American Literature" as the area's best courses. Visiting professor Gail Nomura of the American culture department and English professor Steven Sumida are popular with students. "Both are always open to conversation and are easily approachable," reports a student. "Their extensive knowledge of the Asian-American experience is quite informative to students who are still developing their own Asian identity."

One of the Native American Studies courses that students rank highly is "Native Peoples of America," an anthropology course. "The professor is excellent," says a student. "She's good at getting everybody to look at Native Americans in a different light. She treats the culture with respect, but doesn't treat the culture as if it's something exotic."

Beginning with the class that entered the university in the fall of 1992, all first-year students in the literature, science, and arts divisions must satisfy a one-course cultural diversity requirement. Although each undergraduate college has its own graduation requirements, most include a foreign language and English composition.

Having all these academic—and extracurricular opportunities—doesn't come without its headaches, however. Course registration is a pain, sitting in introductory-level classrooms with 300 other students is common, getting to know your professors, who are often involved in their own research, is a little like getting an appointment to meet with the President, and obtaining a dorm room in a choice location is just as difficult.

The university has academic and social support services that can help make attending school here a more inviting experience. First and foremost is the Office of Minority Student Services, which maintains full-time staff advisers, individuals of various racial and ethnic descents "whom we can approach if we have any ideas or opinions about campus activities or incidents," says a student.

For additional support, the Trotter House, located near central campus, is also geared to undergraduate student needs. The house "serves as a meeting place, office space, and mailbox for minority student groups on campus," reports a student. "It is staffed by full-time university employees as well as live-in student staff members who are of color." The house, which one student described as "very, very active," sponsors cultural events and assists student groups with their activities.

According to one student, the Asian-American Association (AAA) and the University of Michigan Asian-American Student Coalition (UMAASC) "complement each other. The AAA serves more a social agenda while the UMAASC provides activities of a more political nature. These two groups do not encompass all the Asian-American student groups, but they do try to include Asians of varying ethnicities." He adds: "The AAA hosts dances and semiformals every term and a banquet every year to celebrate Lunar New Year. They also sponsor a big sib/little sib program where new members can meet older members and get to know the organization. Biweekly workshops provide members with the chance to expose themselves to cultural and current topics. The UMAASC hosts an annual AA film series and art show, as well as workshops and speakers on various topics. Recently, we hosted a commemoration of the Japanese internment during World War II."

The Native American Student Association, with about 35 active members, works to coordinate the country's largest annual indoor powwow, which draws tribes and organizations from Arizona, Washington, and Canada. The event, open to the campus community, regularly brings spectators from around the country. The organization also provides social and academic support for its members. "Because some of us in the group didn't grow up with close links to our heritage, we spend time talking and learning about our heritage," says a student leader of the group. "Also, since there aren't many Native American Studies courses here we often find that we are in the same classes together, so we help each other with our studies."

The Black Student Union is also active, sponsoring forums, speakers, and social functions for members and the campus community.

Students are able to join any of the school's more than 800 student organizations and clubs. There are the religious, political, and gay and lesbian groups, and there are the feminist, professional, and sports clubs. "There are so many ways in which students can express themselves here," says a student. With its lounges, travel agency, game rooms, and numerous eating establishments, the Michigan Union is a hub of activity. But attending sporting events, especially against archrival Ohio State, remains *the* student activity of choice, eclipsing almost all others.

Ann Arbor, said by some to be the cultural mecca of the state, is a diverse community of students, university staff and faculty, and community residents. The city has numerous theaters, restaurants, clubs, and cultural events that can cater to almost any student's desire. Ann Arbor is just a couple of hours from Chicago and Detroit, but with the wealth of opportunities available on campus, students are usually content to stay close to campus.

The University of Michigan is indeed huge, and feeling overwhelmed by the immensity of the place is standard for many students. To avoid feelings of alienation, finding your niche—most likely at the Trotter House or in one or another of the student groups on campus—is essential. "I came from a big high school, but I never experienced anything like this before," says a junior. "Getting around socially and academically was difficult at first, and sometimes it still is, but I don't think I could have made it without being involved in my cultural student group. It was important for me that I could feel part of a family."

MICHIGAN STATE UNIVERSITY

Address: East Lansing, MI 48824
Phone: (517) 355-1855
Director of Admissions: William H. Turner
Multicultural Student Recruiter: na
1991–92 tuition: $3,474 (in-state); $6,063 (out-of-state)
Room and board: $3,375
Application deadline: 30 days prior to beginning of each term
Financial aid application deadline: 4/1
Non-white freshman admissions: Applicants for the class of '94: 3,111
  Accepted: 75%
  Accepted who enroll: 30%
  Applicants accepted who rank in top 10% of high school class: na
  Median SAT: na
  Median ACT: na
Full-time undergraduate enrollment: 34,634
  Men: 48.1%
  Women: 51.9%
Non-white students in
  1987–88: 9.5%
  1988–89: 10.4%
  1989–90: 11.1%
  1990–91: 11.8%
Students In-state: 89.9%
Top majors: 1. Business 2. Engineering 3. Social Science

Retention rate of non-white students: 70%
Scholarships exclusively for non-white students: Distinguished Freshman Minority Scholarship: full tuition; merit-based. Michigan State National Achievement: need- and merit-based; $750 to $1,000 for each award. National Hispanic Scholarship: need- and merit-based; $1,500 from the national organization and $1,500 from MSU.

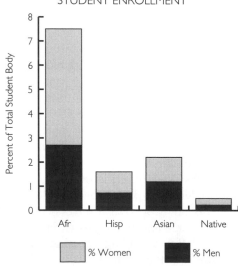

STUDENT ENROLLMENT

Percent of Total Student Body

Afr Hisp Asian Native

% Women % Men

GEOGRAPHIC DISTRIBUTION OF STUDENTS

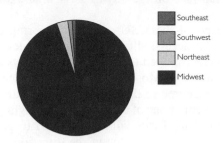

- Southeast
- Southwest
- Northeast
- Midwest

FACULTY

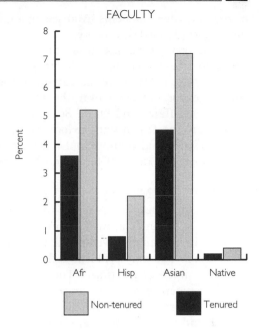

Remediation programs: The Office of Supportive Services provides academic support programs.

Academic support services: The Service Learning Center provides academic support in most subjects. Several colleges within the university offer academic support services especially targeted at minority students. The offices of Minority Programs and Minority Affairs also provide academic support services.

Ethnic studies programs: MSU offers programs of study in African, Asian, and Latin American and Caribbean Studies.

Organizations for non-white students: Delta Sigma Theta, Kappa Alpha Psi, Alpha Kappa Alpha, Alpha Phi Alpha, Minority Progressive Student Affairs, North American Indian Student Organization, Coalition of Hispanic Students for Progressive Change, Black Student Alliance, Asian-Pacific-American Student Organization

Notable non-white alumni: Rick Inatome (chairman, InaCom Corp.); Magic Johnson (professional basketball player); Bubba Smith (actor and former football star, Baltimore Colts)

Tenured faculty: 1,765

Non-tenured faculty: 919

Student-faculty ratio: na

Administrators: 326

African-American: 10%

Hispanic: 0.9%

Asian-American: 1.8%

Native American: 0.9%

Recent non-white speakers on campus: Asa Hilliard (professor, Georgia State University); Sara Melendez (vice-provost and dean, University of Bridgeport); Norbert Hill, Jr. (executive director, American Indian Science and Engineering Society); Maria Molina (director, Women's Resource and Action Center, University of Iowa); Ronald Takaki (historian); Roger Wilkins (professor of history and American culture, George Mason University); Manning Marable (author)

Look up the word "immense" in the dictionary, and you might almost find the words "Michigan State University." The 132-year-old institution has more than 34,000 undergraduates, 125 academic majors, nearly 350 student organizations, and a 5,200-acre campus.

The school's size *can* present a problem. Getting from one end of the campus to the other requires a bicycle or a moped. Classes, especially introductory ones, can have hundreds of students. And seeing a familiar face on the way to class, unless the meeting is planned, is a rarity.

But students are quick to say there are aspects of the MSU campus that bring it down to size—somewhat. First, they praise the accessibility of certain high-level administrators. "Many of the administrators here are open to student needs," says a student leader. Gordon Geyer, the university president, Moses Turner, vice president for student affairs, and David Scott, the provost, come to the events of the cultural student groups. It's amazing to look up and see them at one of our functions, mingling with students. I also know that if I have a problem, I can call any of them to get help, which I've done. If they can't help me, then they point me in the direction of who can."

The Office of Minority Student Affairs, located in the Student Services Building, has African-American, Native American, Asian-Pacific-American, and Hispanic counselors. "They're a great help to all of the students, and a lot of us go to them to get help in planning events and academic counseling. They are a definite resource on campus. The only problem is that they are all overworked, and it gets stressful for them much of the time." The counselors also work closely with several of the cultural student groups on campus.

MSU's dorms, which accommodate about half of the student body (mostly first- and second-year students), are divided into complexes—of which there are five on campus—made up of four residence halls each. Each of the halls has a Minority Aide, an upperclass student who acts as an adviser to students in his or her dorm. "Students can go and talk to their advisers about almost anything, from academic or social problems to finding directions to someplace on campus," says a student.

The university was founded as a land-grant institution that stressed agricultural programs, and while agricultural studies are still an MSU strength, it now offers areas of study in almost anything imaginable. MSU standouts are hotel, restaurant and institutional management, engineering, communications, pre-veterinary science, and psychology. Students also praise their school's programs in urban studies, accounting, and education.

Among the research facilities at the university are centers for African, Asian, and Latin American and Caribbean Studies. Students say the school's Black Studies programs are, according to a senior, "impressive," and are taught by numerous outstanding faculty members, such as Curtis Stokes, a political science professor, Geneva Smithermann, an English professor recently voted as one of the university's distinguished professors, Richard Thomas, a history professor, and June Thomas, a professor of urban planning.

More than sixty student groups focus on cultural matters, and students say there is a growing amount of interaction among them. "Most of the students at Michigan State are friendly, not cold or distant," observes a student. "People try to work together. Many of us are now working to put together a retreat for women of color as a way to start a student group for us. We also frequently sponsor programs and forums together. We've realized that we all have the same concerns on campus." Groups such as the Council of Racial and Ethnic Students and the Council of Progressive Students try to promote this sort of interaction, according to students, with forums and social gatherings.

Members of the Black Student Alliance (BSA) are working to put together a proposal to have the university establish an African-American cultural center on campus "where we can be more social and more unified," says a student. "We traveled to several Big Ten universities to find out what they had, and we talked to students and administrators at those schools to find out how they went about getting their centers established and how effective and active they are on their campuses." According to a member, the BSA serves as a central resource for the school's 41 other African-American student groups, a place "where they can come for funding, ideas for programming, and co-sponsorships." Murray Edwards, the adviser to the group, is also the African-American counselor in the Office of Minority Student Services. "He helps us in any way he can; we go to him often," says a student.

Historically black Greek fraternities and sororities are active. Each year members of the Alpha Phi Alpha fraternity mentor students at area high schools, while members of Alpha Kappa Alpha sorority work to develop retention programs for the campus's African-American community. As One, primarily a cultural and social organization, is also active, inviting speakers to campus and hosting weekly meetings. During the 1991–92 school year, several groups hosted a step show and speakers at East Complex, a residential hall area. "We had booked a space for about 400, but more than 500 showed up. It was one of the best events we've had since I've been here as a student." Unity Icebreakers were popular on campus, but because "they got out of hand, thanks to students," they were canceled by the university administration. The BSA is looking to reestablish the social events.

The North American Indian Student Organization (NAISO) sponsors an annual powwow, usually held in the winter, that attracts participants and visitors from the region. NAISO, the Asian-Pacific-American Student Organization, and the Coalition of Hispanic Students for Progressive Change also sponsor numerous forums, lectures, and parties during the school year.

East Lansing is a predominantly white city, although the nearby city of Lansing has a larger African-American community. Other than community service projects, students say there is little interaction between these communities and students. A short walk from campus are several popular bars. The university is about eighty miles west of Detroit, home to many MSU students.

A new multimillion-dollar student center is a source of a great deal of campus activity, and dorm rooms and off-campus apartments, as well as fraternities, are frequent sites for parties. Organizations range from the political to the religious, and are often active. Dances, movies, and concerts are regular events on campus.

The vast majority of Spartans hail from the Midwest, more than 90 percent from Michigan. But every other state in the Union is represented, as well as numerous foreign countries. Students say the political attitudes on campus cover the gamut; others add, however, that national political and social issues don't get much attention. Students say race relations on campus are "decent," but that there's a definite hostile and overt homophobia at MSU; recently, a leader of one of the school's gay student organizations received hate mail, and anti-gay graffiti is common. The school's gay, lesbian, and bisexual student group is active.

Students are pleased with the school's decision, beginning with the 1992–93 school year, to go from the quarter to the semester system. "Now we only have two finals to study for," says a student. But numerous students we spoke to say the switch made it difficult, for financial reasons, for many multicultural students to return to campus. "When they went to the new schedule," says a student, "the summer before the new school year was made significantly shorter, which meant that students didn't have much time to get summer jobs or to make money. The administration also recently jacked up tuition by 9 percent, and they're going to raise it another 3 percent soon. It's made it difficult to afford to go to school, which explains why there was a poor retention of students this year."

The school's size doesn't discourage students. Most like attending one of North America's largest institutions of higher learning, particularly because of its less pretentious atmosphere. "I'm definitely glad I've gone here," says a student. "There's so much to do and see. I almost went to the University of Michigan in Ann Arbor, but I'm glad I didn't. I've been there numerous times and I have friends who go there, and it seems so much more socially competitive and less friendly there than at MSU."

CARLETON COLLEGE

Address: 100 South College Street,
  Northfield, MN 55057
Phone: (507) 663-4190 / (800) 995-2275
Director of Admissions: Paul Thiboutot
Multicultural Student Recruiter: Miguel
  Cordova
1992–93 tuition: $18,279
Room and board: $3,750
Application deadline: 2/1
Financial aid application deadline: 3/1
Non-white freshman admissions: Applicants
  for the class of '95: 434
  Accepted: 66.8%
  Accepted who enroll: 20.3%
  Applicants accepted who rank in top
  10% of high school class: na
  Median SAT: na
  Median ACT: na
Full-time undergraduate enrollment: 1,842
  Men: 50.8%
  Women: 49.2%
Non-white students in
  1989–90: 13%
  1990–91: 14.5%
  1991–92: 15%
  1992–93: 16%
Geographic distribution of students: na
Top majors: 1. Political Science 2. English
  3. Economics
Retention rate of non-white students: 74%
**Scholarships exclusively for non-white
  students:** Donald Cowling Scholarships:
  need-based; amount of award varies.
  McKnight Foundation Scholarship:

need-based; amount of award varies.
Carolyn Foundation Scholarship:
need-based; amount of award varies.
Alice Bean Fraser Scholarship Fund:
need-based; amount of award varies.
League of United Latin American
Citizens Scholarships: need-based;
available to Hispanic students. National
Bar Association Scholarships:
need-based; amount of award varies;
available to African-American students.
Japanese-American Citizens Alliance
Scholarships: need-based; amount of
awards varies. Carleton National
Medical Association Scholarships:
need-based; amount of award varies;
available to African-American students.

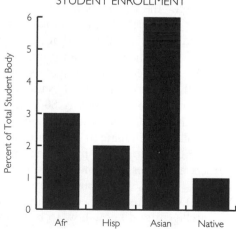

STUDENT ENROLLMENT

Carleton Korean-American Scholarships: need-based; amount of award varies.

Remediation programs: None

Academic support services: The college offers the Write Place, the Math Skills Center, and a tutoring program.

Ethnic studies programs: Carleton offers four interdisciplinary programs of ethnic studies: African/African-American Studies, Asian Languages and Literatures, Asian Studies, and Latin American Studies.

Organizations for non-white students: Students Organized for Unity and Liberation, Latin American Student Organization, Asian Students in America, American Native People's Organization, Latin American Interest House, African-American Awareness House, Multicultural Center

Notable non-white alumni: Rev. Earl A. Neil ('57; executive, Episcopal Church Center, New York City); Joyce Hughes ('61; professor, Northwestern University Law School); Kiyoaki Murata ('46; former editor, *Japanese Times*)

Tenured faculty: 102

Non-tenured faculty: 58

Student-faculty ratio: 11:1

Administrators: 93

African-American: 6%

Hispanic: 2%

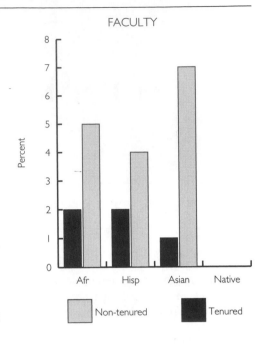

FACULTY

Asian-American: 1%

Native American: 0

Recent non-white speakers on campus: Ruby Dee (actress); Julian Bond (former Georgia state senator and civil rights activist); Maya Angelou (author and poet); Rev. Ben Chavis (Executive Director, NAACP)

Carleton College, located in rural and often frigid Minnesota, provides its students with one of the finest liberal arts educations in the country. Students come to the 127-year-old college from every state in the Union and numerous foreign countries, and some have even been known to bypass the Ivies for Carleton's brand of intimate—and rigorous—education.

Carleton students are as bright as they are motivated. The school regularly enrolls one of the highest number of National Merit scholars of any four-year liberal arts college in the country; nearly 80 percent of its students were from the top fifth of their high school graduating classes; and more than three-quarters of its graduates are enrolled in graduate or professional school within five years of graduation, usually at some of the country's preeminent institutions of higher learning. The school also attracts a progressive-minded, and socioeconomically diverse, student body. Says a student, "every sort of opinion is represented here. We have Young Republicans and Young Democrats, and we have pro-choice and pro-life students. All of the students are intelligent and know how to back up their opinions with facts."

Almost all of the school's academic departments shine, but some of the brightest are English, history, chemistry, biology, geology, and economics. To graduate, students must take courses in arts and literature; history, philosophy, and religions; social science; and math and science. Students must also enroll in English composition, foreign-language, and physical education courses.

Students describe the school's African-American Studies department as "fine" and "excellent," pointing to such professors as Kofi Owusu, who teaches African and Caribbean literature, Harry Williams, who teaches courses in African-American history, and Mary Williams, the head of the department, who offers instruction in African and other forms of dance. Students say Carleton's Latin American Studies program is small but "decent and could be made stronger if it offered courses in U.S. Hispanic studies."

The school's quarter system, which divides the school year into three terms, contributes to the school's academic intensity. Students say the winter term is the most trying, particularly, says a student, as "the days are short, the nights are long, the air is cold, and there's a lot of work to be done." Students praise their faculty for their intelligence, but one student says they can sometimes be difficult to reach. "Even though the professors have office hours, many of them live in Minneapolis or St. Paul [about an hour from Carleton] and commute to campus. So many of them don't get the chance to attend student functions, or to get to know students on a less formal basis. Some live in the area, though, and those who do are truly dedicated to students." Hudlin Wagner, an associate dean of students, and Clem Shearer, dean of budget and planning, are staff members students turn to frequently for support. "They come to some of our [cultural group] meetings and to our activities."

The Multicultural Affairs Office provides additional academic support, and is available to students who are physically disabled, financially in need, as well as to students of color. The office offers peer counseling and book lending services, among other programs. The office gets frequent student use because, says a peer counselor, "the college advertises it well and upperclass students make sure the new students know about it."

With Carleton's demanding work load, there's often time for little else, let alone student activism. But during the spring semester of the 1991–92 school year, "we [Carleton's student of color community] really got active and demanded that the administration change some things." Students, who staged sit-ins and rallies to voice their concerns, had been especially disappointed in the way the school's Multicultural Affairs Office had been run, and they complained that too much time had been given by its administrators to obtaining funding for cultural programming and too little for student support. "The office did a terrific job at what it was doing," says a student, "but it wasn't doing enough."

As a result of student demands, according to campus leaders, the college hired a new associate dean of students, Chi-Ling Chen, to work closely with students of color. "We're excited to have her here," says a student. "She's young, vibrant, and smart, and she's going to help students get organized. She's also very supportive." In addition, a Multicultural Advisory Board, composed of students and administrators, has been established, which will "oversee what happens in the Multicultural Affairs Office," according to a student. The meetings of the board are open to anyone who wants to attend, and students who do so, whether they're on the board or not, are able to vote on issues addressed by members.

With a larger student of color community on campus, students say the school's cultural groups have recently gotten more active. The 20-year-old Latin American Student Organization (LASO) regularly brings guest speakers to campus, who have addressed such topics as education and migrant workers. LASO, which has about 20 members, the majority of whom are Mexican and Mexican-American, also sponsors dances and dinners with Hispanic themes.

Students Organized for Unity and Liberation (SOUL), Carleton's African-American student group, has brought to campus speakers, drum ensembles, and gospel choirs. SOUL members conduct their meetings during brunch on Sundays. Asian Students in America "isn't as active as the other groups," says a student, "probably because there are so many Asian students on campus that they don't have the need for peer support like members of SOUL and LASO do." Students also observe that there is a great deal of cultural diversity among the Asian and Asian-American communities on campus, with students hailing from numerous regions and countries. The school's American Native People's Organization meets regularly and serves mostly as a source of peer support for members.

The emphasis of the Coalition of Women of Color "is purely on peer support," says a member of the group, which reflects the diversity on campus, with members from the school's Asian, Hispanic, Native American, and African-American communities. "We discuss women's issues, we have slumber parties, and we are working to get a women's center established on campus. We don't focus on any one particular issue. The group meets once a week and has dinner together, and we'll also invite speakers to campus."

Among the students of color on campus, students say that women outnumber men almost four to one. With such numbers, one student describes the dating scene "as sometimes a problem."

The Multicultural Center provides coed residence facilities for up to seven students; in a recent year, six students—two African-American, two Asian-American, and two Latino students—lived in the house, which has meeting rooms, cooking facilities, and a TV room.

Northfield (pop. 12,000) is located in rural central Minnesota. The town is predominantly white, but has a growing Hispanic population, although students say there is little interaction between students and community residents. Carleton shares the town with St. Olaf College, just a mile or so away on the other side of town. There is also little interaction between the two campuses, except in varsity sports competition. Northfield offers a few watering holes and shopping opportunities, as well as a movie theater. Students sometimes make the hour or so drive to Minneapolis–St. Paul, which offers a wealth of social and cultural opportunities. The cities are home to famed museums, concert halls, colleges and universities, and professional sports teams.

Varsity sports don't receive much attention on campus, although more than a third of the school's students participate in at least one such activity. Carleton's soccer, tennis, cross-country, and volleyball teams usually enjoy successful seasons. Many students are involved in intramurals, yet the most popular sport on campus remains

Frisbee tossing. Annual events such as the Reggae Fest, Spring Concert, and homecoming are popular. Co-op coordinates many of the campus-wide dances, free movie nights, and other well-received events. Weekend dorm parties are common, according to students.

One of the few drawbacks to a Carleton education is Minnesota's harsh winters, which can last up to four freezing months. But the high quality of the school's academics and a tight network of students more than compensate for the cold and snow. Says a student: "I would recommend that minority students come to Carleton because it is able to address concerns of individuals. Students are never numbers, and the administration is always willing to listen."

GUSTAVUS ADOLPHUS COLLEGE

Address: 800 West College Avenue, St. Peter, MN 56082
Phone: (507) 933-7676 / (800) GUSTAVUS
Director of Admissions: Mark Anderson
Multicultural Student Recruiter: Christyanna Egun
1991–92 tuition: $11,900
Room and board: $2,800
Application deadline: 4/15
Financial aid application deadline: 4/15
Non-white freshman admissions: Applicants for the class of '95: 65
Accepted: 91%
Accepted who enroll: 48%
Applicants accepted who rank in top 10% of high school class: 36%
In top 25%: 78%
Median SAT: na
Median ACT range: 21–26
Full-time undergraduate enrollment: 2,255
Men: 46%
Women: 54%
Non-white students in
1987–88: 2%
1988–89: 2%
1989–90: 2%
1990–91: 2.9%
Geographic distribution of students: na
Students In-state: 55%
Top majors: 1. Management 2. Communications 3. Political Science
Retention rate of non-white students: 85%

Scholarships exclusively for non-white students: Paul Rucker Minority Scholarship: need-based; each award is worth up to $5,000; renewable; 25 to 30 awarded each year.
Remediation programs: None
Academic support services: The college offers tutoring in most academic subjects as well as writing labs.
Ethnic studies programs: None
Ethnic studies courses: Art courses include "Art Before Cortez." English courses: "The Arts of Equatorial Africa" and "Afro-American Literature." History

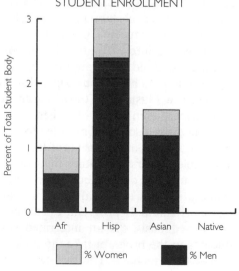

STUDENT ENROLLMENT

Percent of Total Student Body

Afr   Hisp   Asian   Native

% Women   % Men

course: "Afro-American History."
Spanish course: "Reading in Latin
American Culture." Music course:
"Muslim Cultures."
Anthropology/sociology course: "Native
North Americans."

Organizations for non-white students: Black
Student Organization

**Nationally/internationally acclaimed
non-white alumni:** Dr. Talmadge King, Jr.
('69, Biology/Psychology; medical
director, Cohn Clinic, and professor of
medicine at the University of Colorado);
Dr. Doris McCully ('69, Biology; medical
director, Provident Medical Center in
Chicago, and first to establish a medical
clinic in the Chicago public schools);
Chester Fuller ('72, English; assistant
managing editor, *Atlanta Constitution,*
and author)

Tenured faculty: 94
Non-tenured faculty: 50
Student-faculty ratio: 14:1
Administrators: 87
  African-American: 2%
  Hispanic: 1%

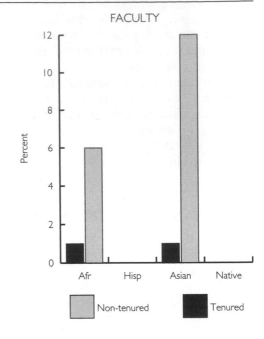

FACULTY

Asian-American: 0
Native American: 0
Recent non-white speakers on campus: na

It would be hard to ignore the role religion—and in particular the Lutheran religion—plays in campus life at Gustavus Adolphus College. Standing tall at the center of campus is Christ Chapel, which can seat 1,200 congregants; more than 60 percent of Gustavus' 2,200 students identify themselves as Lutheran; and a course in religion that "is substantially in the Christian tradition" is required of all students.

According to students, Gustavus is a friendly place to go to school, which students say translates into a comfortable atmosphere for students of color. "The students here are interested in one another, and are always saying hi to each other on campus," says a senior. "The campus has had no blatant racial incidents that I know of since I've been at Gustavus. Students seem to be supportive of students of color, even though there aren't a lot of us here."

Gustavus is a school committed to the liberal arts, and to ensure that students are exposed to a broad spectrum of learning, the 131-year-old college requires students to complete courses in either the Curriculum I or the Curriculum II program. The Curriculum I program includes courses in areas as diverse as the arts, religion, quantitative and empirical reasoning, and human behavior and social institutions. The Curriculum II program, open only to 60 students each year on a first-come, first-served basis, "is an integrated studies approach to general education." All students in the program take the same sequence of courses, spread over four years. Course titles include "The Biblical Tradition," "The Individual and Morality," and

"The Natural World." Gustavus' Writing Across the Curriculum program, which requires that students take three courses that stress writing, is nationally recognized. Courses in the program are taught in almost all of the college's departments.

Gustavus' best departments include psychology, physics, biology, and music. The college's science programs were enhanced with the recent completion of the multimillion-dollar Olin Hall. Gustavus also offers numerous pre-professional programs in law, the ministry, architecture, medicine, dentistry, engineering, and pharmacy. As befitting a school founded by Swedes, Gustavus has a strong program in Scandinavian Studies. The school's Japanese Area Studies program includes the well-regarded "Intercultural Communication" course, which focuses on issues of communication between countries. "It is a great class that opened my eyes to a whole different world," says a student. Japanese Area Studies majors have the option of studying in the college's overseas program in Japan. Other strong programs include Russian Area and women's studies.

Philip Bryant, who teaches creative writing and the "African-American Literature" course, is a professor "all of the students warm up to because he's got a fun personality and he respects us," says a student. "He's also very helpful, whether assisting with financial aid problems or with more personal problems."

The school's January Term enables students to study off campus for the month in a foreign country or almost anywhere in the United States. During the month, students are also able to pursue on- or off-campus research or internship possibilities.

Although the majority of students are Lutheran, many other religions are represented on the Gustavus campus. However, racial diversity is not as common; Minnesota's relative homogeneity doesn't help matters when it comes to recruiting. Students say there isn't much political diversity or activism at Gustavus, which leads to a "conformist" attitude on campus. The Black Student Organization and the International Student Organization are the school's most active cultural groups, sponsoring theme nights, guest lectures, and social gatherings. But, says a student, "I would guess that nearly a third of the campus doesn't know what the BSO or the ISO is." Students at Gustavus are environmentally concerned, and the Greens are a prominent student organization. The campus is surrounded by some of the most beautiful countryside in the upper Midwest, and students no doubt want to preserve their area's spectacular scenery.

In sports, Gustavus is best known for ice hockey and women's tennis; each team has had several successful seasons recently. Students at the school are extremely sports-conscious; more than 80 percent of the campus participates in at least one intramural or varsity activity. Gustavus' Lund Center for Physical Education and Health provides excellent facilities for a host of sports.

The College Activities Board (CAB) each year sponsors a film series, concerts, dances, and special events such as homecoming. The Dive, a non-alcoholic pub located in the school's recently renovated Johnson Student Union, hosts regular entertainment, coordinated by CAB. Students also find time to participate in the school's more than 20 musical groups. Once a thriving fraternity system existed here, but in the late 1980s the administration banned their chapters on campus. Students say, however, that several such organizations still exist, but have been forced to go underground.

Other than gorgeous scenery and a couple of bars and restaurants, the predominantly white town of St. Peter (pop. 9,000) offers few off-campus diversions. The famed twin cities of Minneapolis and St. Paul, however, are only an hour's drive from campus, and offer a wealth of educational, cultural, and entertainment activities. The cities are home to several colleges and universities, as well as to professional sports teams, the Walker Art Center, the Guthrie Theater, and movie theaters, comedy clubs, and restaurants. The college offers a free weekend shuttle service to the cities.

Evidence of the college's Swedish heritage is almost everywhere on campus, from the names of certain buildings and scholarships to the predominantly blond and blue-eyed student body. While the school doesn't offer much in the way of racial diversity, it certainly does provide a close-knit academic community. "Gustavus has been perfect for me," says a senior. "Its size has allowed me to get a lot of personal attention from professors, which I would never have gotten at a larger school. I plan to go to dental school when I graduate, and I'm convinced Gustavus has more than prepared me to be successful when I get there."

HAMLINE UNIVERSITY

Address: 1536 Hewitt Avenue, St. Paul, MN 55104-1284
Phone: (612) 641-2207 / (800) 753-9753
Director of Admissions: Scott Friedhoff
Multicultural Student Recruiter: Darryl Stanton
1992–93 tuition: $12,190
Room and board: $3,895
Application deadline: Rolling admissions
Financial aid application deadline: 4/15
Non-white freshman admissions: Applicants for the class of '96: 119
　Accepted: 83%
　Accepted who enroll: 41%
　Applicants accepted who rank in top 10% of high school class: 23%
　In top 25%: 53%
　Median SAT: 460 V, 520 M
　Median ACT: 22
Full-time undergraduate enrollment: 1,335
　Men: 45%
　Women: 55%
Non-white students in 1992–93: 9%
Students In-state: 73%
Top majors: 1. Psychology 2. Management 3. English
Retention rate of non-white students: 87%

Scholarships exclusively for non-white students: Engquist Scholarship: available to Native American students. Minority Student Grant: merit-based; $1,000 awarded each year.
Remediation programs: None
Academic support services: The college provides a Multicultural Affairs office, Study Resource Center, a Writing Center, and tutoring in most subjects.

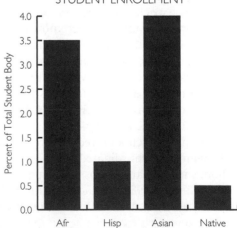

STUDENT ENROLLMENT

Percent of Total Student Body

Afr — Hisp — Asian — Native

GEOGRAPHIC DISTRIBUTION OF STUDENTS

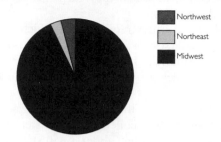

- Northwest
- Northeast
- Midwest

FACULTY

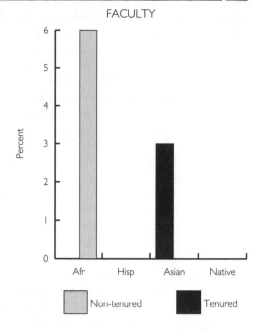

Non-tenured   Tenured

Ethnic studies programs: Hamline offers East Asian and Latin American studies programs.

Ethnic studies courses: Hamline's courses include "Racial and Cultural Minorities" and "Education and Cultural Diversity."

Organizations for non-white students: PRIDE (living unit), Hamline Asian-American Student Union, Hamline Open Organization for Diversity

Notable non-white alumni: Anna Arnold Hedgeman ('22, Education; first woman to run for mayor of New York City)

Tenured faculty: 60

Non-tenured faculty: 33

Student-faculty ratio: 14:1

Administrators: 108
  African-American: 8 total
  Hispanic: 1 total
  Asian-American: 1 total
  Native American: na

Recent non-white speakers on campus: Mary Frances Berry (former U.S. representative and member of U.S. Civil Rights Commission); Jesse Jackson, Jr. (law student); Marian Wright Edelman (president, Children's Defense Fund); Barbara Christian (educator and writer); Nilo Cayagueyo (member of the Mapuche Indian tribe); Anita Hill (University of Oklahoma law professor)

Newsweek magazine describes Hamline University's hometown of St. Paul "as one of the best places to live and work in America today." St. Paul, one of the famous twin cities with Minneapolis, offers the tourist—and the student—a myriad of social and cultural activities, from professional baseball (the Twins) and football (the Vikings) to the renowned Walker Art Center in Minneapolis. The Hamline campus offers plenty of activity as well, of both the academic and the social variety.

Hamline is a liberal arts college, with a small law school. All entering first-year students must complete a Freshman Seminar, an interdisciplinary course that serves to introduce students to college life and academics. Recent seminar topics have included "The History of Freedom in America," "This Is Your Life," and "Faith and Fiction." Students say the school's best departments are chemistry, foreign languages, business management, and English. Although math is well regarded, students comment that some of the department's professors "don't know how to give their information to the student." Qualified Hamline undergraduates are able to take advantage of the 3-3 program with the law school, in which they earn their B.A. degree in three years and their law degree in three years.

In order to graduate, students must complete a cultures requirement, which can be satisfied by enrolling in foreign-language courses or courses from various departments. The English department's "African-American Literature" course, newly integrated into the curriculum during the 1991–92 school year, is one such course that can be used to satisfy the requirement.

As a member of the Associated Colleges of the Twin Cities, Hamline allows its students to enroll in courses at any of the four nearby colleges: Macalester, St. Catherine, St. Thomas, and Augsburg. During each semester, about 1,450 students from the five colleges cross-register. An hourly shuttle service takes students to the campuses during class hours. Socially, however, interaction between the campuses is minimal. "Hamline's student activities board is trying to increase the communication between the campuses," says a student.

Attending a school of Hamline's size has its advantages, especially when it comes to establishing a rapport with professors. "My Freshman Seminar professor practically became a friend. She would have the class over to her house for dinner, and she would call us on the phone to see how we were doing in our other classes. I don't think I would be able to get this kind of attention at a larger school." Although students say the academics at Hamline are only moderately difficult, they nonetheless say the school's Study Resource Center—featuring tutoring and study skills workshops—comes in handy.

Additional support can be found at the Office of Multicultural Affairs, located in the student center. The director of the office, Starletta Poindexter, is "responsive to students' concerns. If you're having a problem with a teacher, she's always able to listen and to give suggestions about how to deal with a situation," says a student. Poindexter has initiated two mentoring programs for students, the Professional Mentor Program, in which a professional in the community is paired with a student, and the Student Mentor Program, in which upperclass students work with first-year students. "My professional mentor is an African-American woman at the law school, since I am interested in going to law school. I meet with her at least once a month for dinner, or I attend some lectures at the law school with her. It's a help to have a role model like her," reports one student.

PRIDE, the school's multicultural student group, has about 15 to 20 members. For Black History Month, members of PRIDE brought guest speakers to campus, hosted a gospel night that presented choirs from the area, sponsored African dance lessons, and hosted a dance. As part of the festivities, PRIDE also organized a panel discussion titled "Students of Color in a White-Collar World." "PRIDE is undergoing some restructuring," according to a student. "Although we're supposed to be a multicultural group, we are perceived to be, and in reality are, an African-American group. We're working on how to best be able to integrate the group more, especially with Hispanic students."

The PRIDE Culture House, which provides residence facilities for three students, is located across the street from the Norton football stadium. "This year, there are three African-American women in the house, and last year, three guys lived here, but it can be a coed residence house," says a student. Each of the rooms in the two-story house is a single, and there is a large front room where PRIDE members hold their meetings.

The most recently established cultural student group is Hamline Asian-American Student Union (HAASU), which in 1992 was in its second year on campus. In a recent year, the group had five active members, including two Asian-Americans, two whites, and a Native American. For Chinese New Year, HAASU invited various performers to campus. "When it comes to multicultural issues, it seems that they really only talk about African-Americans and Hispanics here, and never about Asians and Asian-Americans. It's as if we're always on the sidelines. We established ourselves so that we can make the campus, and ourselves, more aware of the contributions of Asians and Asian-Americans to American culture," says a student.

The Hamline Open Organization for Diversity, commonly referred to as HOOD, is the umbrella organization for the school's various multicultural student groups, as well as the school's gay, lesbian, and bisexual organization. In a recent year, HOOD, which had only one non-white student, addressed the issue of homophobia on campus.

Hamline offers an impressive array of other activities as well. The Hamline University Theater presents three to five productions a year, and students are able to join numerous musical groups, including a well-regarded jazz ensemble. Students can also play an informal game of volleyball in the sandpit outside Manor Residence Hall, and intramural events generate friendly competition between dorms. The Get Into Volunteering program provides Hamline student tutors to area schools, and voter registration drives are common.

Although Hamline is not as diverse as some other colleges of its caliber, students report that the typical Hamline student is open-minded and accepting of racial and ethnic diversity. In response to a recent racist incident at the law school—a hate letter was mailed to a student—the campus community, including faculty, administration, and students, held a candlelight vigil in front of the law school building. "It was freezing outside, but the vigil was packed. We had an open microphone, and anyone could speak if they wanted to, and many people did, including the president of the student body, who was African-American, and the president of PRIDE, and a lot of others," says a student. Minnesota's relative lack of racial diversity is reflected in the relative homogeneity of the campus.

For some, being one of only a few students of color on a predominantly white campus can be taxing. "I have a joke with a friend of mine that between the two of us we have served on almost every student organization. Whenever the university or a student group needs a student of color to do something, they call either him or me. Sometimes it gets exhausting feeling as if you're the only representative of the entire black race on the campus."

MACALESTER COLLEGE

Address: 1600 Grand Avenue, St. Paul, MN
55105
Phone: (612) 696-6357 / (800) 231-7974
Director of Admissions: William M. Shain
Multicultural Student Recruiter: Karen Dye
1991–92 tuition: $13,230
Room and board: $3,970
Application deadline: Early decision: 12/1,
1/15; regular decision 2/1
Financial aid application deadline: 3/1
Non-white freshman admissions: Applicants
for the class of '95: 288
Accepted: 72%
Accepted who enroll: 27%
Applicants accepted who rank in top
10% of high school class: na
Median SAT: na
Median ACT: na
Full-time undergraduate enrollment: 1,735
Men: 47%
Women: 53%
Non-white students in
1987–88: 7%
1988–89: 7.8%
1989–90: 8.7%
1990–91: 10%

GEOGRAPHIC DISTRIBUTION OF STUDENTS

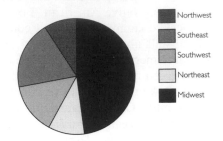

- Northwest
- Southeast
- Southwest
- Northeast
- Midwest

Students In-state: 27%
Top majors: 1. Political Science 2. History
3. International Studies
Retention rate of non-white students: 87%
**Scholarships exclusively for non-white
students:** Catharine Lealtad Scholarships:
merit-based; minimum award: $2,000.
Remediation programs: None
Academic support services: The
Multicultural Affairs Office and the
Learning Skills Center provide academic
and non-academic support services.
Ethnic studies programs: The college offers
a major course of study in East Asian
Studies. Macalester students are also able
to design their own course of study in
Latin American Studies, although no set
curriculum is established in the area.
Ethnic studies courses: Macalester offers
three courses in African and
African-American Studies and a "Native
American Literature" course.
Organizations for non-white students: Black
Liberation Affairs Committee, Adelante
(Latin student organization), Proud
Indigenous People for Education, Asian
Student Association, Cultural House
Notable non-white alumni: Carl Lumbly
(actor); Edythe Ellis (TV anchorwoman);
Warren Simmons (associate director,
New Standards Program with National
Center on Education and the Economy);
Dr. Charles Cambridge (management
professor, California State University)

STUDENT ENROLLMENT

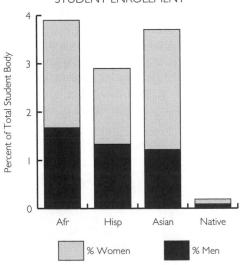

Percent of Total Student Body

Afr   Hisp   Asian   Native

☐ % Women   ■ % Men

Tenured faculty: 81
Non-tenured faculty: 43
Student-faculty ratio: 12:1
Administrators: 14
   African-American: 4%
   Hispanic: 2%
   Asian-American: 2%
   Native American: 1%
Recent non-white speakers on campus: Jewell
   Plummer Cobb (retired president,
   California State University/Fullerton);
   Max Roach (jazz drummer and music
   professor, University of Massachusetts);
   Rayna Greene (director of the American
   Indian Program, Smithsonian
   Institution); Cornell West (professor,
   Princeton University); John Nobuyta
   Tsuchida (director of minority and
   special events, University of Minnesota);
   Nircisco Aleman (Hispanic Studies
   professor, University of Minnesota)

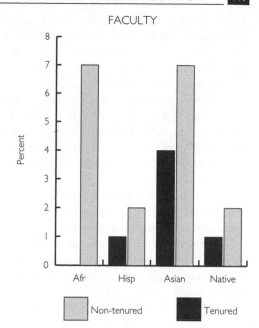

FACULTY

Macalester is one of America's most worldly small colleges. Ten percent of its students are from more than 80 foreign countries—including places as varied as Argentina, Botswana, Laos, Norway, and Tanzania; about half of its students study abroad for a semester or a year; and almost all of its academic departments offer international studies courses.

The 138-year-old institution of higher learning is also one of the country's finer liberal arts colleges. Self-designed and interdisciplinary majors are common; they are available in such areas as environmental studies, East Asian Studies, and Japan Studies. Political science, history, geography, and anthropology are among the school's best departments, while history and international studies are also popular and well regarded. In the sciences, students say chemistry and biology are top-notch. As part of the Associated Colleges of the Twin Cities, Macalester students are able to enroll in courses at Hamline, St. Catherine, St. Thomas, and Augsburg.

"Native American Literature" and "Native American History" win praise from students, as do the professors of the courses, respectively Diane Glancy, an assistant professor of English, and Jack Weatherford, an associate professor of anthropology.

The faculty is one of the college's greatest assets, many making themselves available beyond their regular office hours. Small class sizes—which facilitate interaction with faculty—also make the school's demanding work load less daunting.

The Multicultural Affairs Office (MCA) provides academic retention services, including a peer counseling service, which, says a senior, "is a crucial support group especially for first-year students of multicultural backgrounds. Eight upperclass students serve as mentors to the freshmen. It is a fairly effective program, and it has improved dramatically in the last two years." The MCA also offers financial aid guidance and it supports the campus's cultural student organizations. "The office is a great place to find out how to go about meeting your different needs, whether it be academic or social," says a student. A popular MCA staff member is Laurel Young, who helps advise the school's cultural groups.

Adelante, a Hispanic student group, sponsors events for two Latino Weeks, one during the fall semester and the other in the spring. The weeks feature speakers, movie nights, and dinners. During a recent year, the spring festival presented an Andean Ensemble, a dance with live music provided by a group called Latin Sounds, and a Market Plaza, in which vendors, usually with a Hispanic focus, sold jewelry, books, and food.

The Proud Indigenous People for Education (PIPE), a Native American student group that meets twice a month, coordinates events as part of Native American Awareness Week, usually held in April. Recent awareness weeks have included speakers, dances, powwows, exhibitions, and, to protest Columbus Day, bonfires. "We're a small but active group," says a member. "We're all good friends." The Native American community at Macalester is made up of students from the upper Midwest states and the Southwest.

The Black Liberation Affairs Committee and the Asian Student Association are also active campus organizations, sponsoring speakers, gatherings, and other well-attended events and activities.

The Cultural House, which provides residence facilities for two coordinators of special events, "is a hangout for all the students of color." The house has a TV and two kitchens and is a meeting place for the school's cultural student groups. Recent events held at the house included an Indian Taco Night, at which members of Adelante and PIPE prepared that evening's dinner.

Macalester's campus is situated in a relatively affluent and predominantly white section of St. Paul. The city is culturally rich, with large Native American, Latin, Asian and African-American populations. Native American students take advantage of the resources of the American Indian Movement, an activist group centered in the city, and powwows are sponsored during the year in various parts of the city and surrounding area. Recently, Adelante members decorated a van and participated in the Latino community's Cinco de Mayo parade, on the west side of the city. Students also head to that part of town to shop and eat out. Near campus, students also have easy access to many restaurants, movie theaters, clubs, and bars.

Minneapolis and St. Paul have in recent years come to be known for some of their other cultural resources, such as the Guthrie Theater, the Walker Art Center, and other theaters, galleries, and shopping plazas. The area is also home to various professional sports teams, including the Minnesota Vikings and the Minnesota Twins.

Back on campus, Macalester students never complain of a lack of things to do. Activities range from intramural sports—water polo on inner tubes is a unique school event—to participation in drama and musical groups. There are no fraternities or sororities at Macalester, which is just fine with the majority of the students, who have little tolerance for such exclusive organizations. Students also participate in numerous volunteer activities in the cities, such as helping to build homes for Habitat Humanity, and dorm parties are popular.

Macalester has traditionally attracted a politically left-leaning student body, as evidenced by the school's most popular on-campus activity: political demonstrations. "Students here will protest almost anything," says a student, who adds that "a lot of the Macalester students are very hippyish and into the late sixties early seventies way of dress, with tie-died T-shirts, bell-bottom jeans, and, for the men, long hair." The gay and lesbian student group is well supported and their lifestyle is largely accepted. The school isn't without its conservative faction, however, as evidenced in the campus's Macalester College Conservative Organization, a small group of students that recently invited a white supremacist from the University of Minnesota to campus to participate in a panel discussion. There was such an outcry from the student of color community on campus in response to the invitation that he ended up not coming.

Macalester is a school that combines the friendliness of many small Midwestern liberal arts colleges with an international twist. "Although the school can tend to be too small sometimes—it seems everyone knows everybody's business—and Minnesota winters can be brutal, I think Macalester has been the best school for me," says a student. "The teachers here are fantastic, and the chance to meet people from all over the world makes Macalester an exciting place to be."

UNIVERSITY OF MINNESOTA

Address: 240 Williamson Hall, 231 Pillsbury Drive S.E., Minneapolis, MN 55455
Phone: (612) 625-2008 / (800) 752-1000
Director of Admissions: Wayne Sigler
Multicultural Student Recruiter: Linda G. Johnston
1993–94 tuition: $3,160 (in-state); $9,480 (out-of-state)
Room and board: $3,300
Application deadline: 2/15
Financial aid application deadline: 3/1
Non-white freshman admissions: Applicants for the class of '96: 1,300
  Accepted: 67.4%
  Accepted who enroll: 60.6%
  Applicants accepted who rank in top 10% of high school class: 51.8%
  In top 20%: 52.3%
  Median SAT: na
  Median ACT: na
Full-time undergraduate enrollment: 24,352
  Men: 51%
  Women: 49%
Non-white students in
  1988–89: 7.7%
  1989–90: 7.9%
  1990–91: 8.5%
  1991–92: 9%
Geographic distribution of students: na
Students In-state: 77%
Top majors: na
Retention rate of non-white students: na

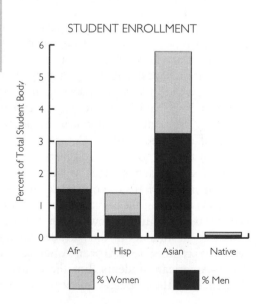

STUDENT ENROLLMENT

Scholarships exclusively for non-white students: None

Remediation programs: The Office for Students with Disabilities offers academic and non-academic support to students with learning disabilities, and the university's General College program offers support to students.

Academic support services: The university's Office of Minority and Special Student Affairs, Project Technology Power, the School of Management Advantage Program, and the Liberal Arts' MLK program offer academic support services. Support is also available to students through the university's ethnic learning resource centers.

Ethnic studies programs: Minnesota offers major courses of study in Afro-American, American Indian, East Asian, and Chicano Studies.

Organizations for non-white students: American Indian Science and Engineering Society, La Raza, Business Association for Minorities, Sovereign Native Dakota-Lakota Language Society, American People's Project, ESL Club, La Rama, La Raza Legal Alliance, Minorities in Institute of Technology, National Society of Black Engineers, Ojibwe Language Society, African Students Cultural Center, All-African Student Alliance, American Indian Student Association and Cultural Center, Asian-American Student Cultural Center, and numerous others

Notable non-white alumni: Allen Page (attorney and University of Minnesota Regent); Hattie Koufman (CBS news correspondent)

Faculty: 2,939 total tenured and non-tenured

Student-faculty ratio: 15:1

Administrators: na

Recent non-white speakers on campus: na

As one of the country's largest universities, the University of Minnesota can be—and is—a lot of things to a lot of different people. But there is one adjective that all undergraduates will agree to use when describing their school: immense. The university enrolls more than 40,000 undergraduate and graduate students, occupies more than 2,000 acres, and the school's 19 undergraduate colleges offer more than 200 majors, which range from computer science and costume design to film studies and forest resources.

With such a variety of course offerings—more than 4,700 are offered each year—the university is able to provide strong programs in ethnic and other area studies. Students praise the university's Afro-American Studies program, and are hard pressed to name the program's best courses. But they point to such outstanding program faculty members as John Taborn, associate professor of psychology; John Wright, professor of psychology; and Rose Brewer, director of the program and associate professor of sociology. Students say American Indian Studies is outstanding, particularly courses in tribal arts and culture. Collins Oakgrove and Gary Cavender are two of the program's most popular instructors.

Other strong departments at Minnesota are engineering, especially electrical and mechanical, journalism, political science, history, math, economics, and geography. Large class sizes at the university are the norm in introductory courses, but upper-level courses usually number fewer than 35 students per class.

To assist students in their academic endeavors, the university sponsors learning resource centers for African-American, American Indian, Chicano/Latino, and Asian-American students, but the centers receive different reviews from students. Students say the African-American Learning Resource Center is weak, as it focuses primarily on recruitment. The American Indian Learning Resource Center, however, "is like a family atmosphere," says a student. "If this place wasn't here, many first-year students wouldn't survive school. The peer counselors let you know you're not alone." The Asian-American Learning Resource Center is also said to be strong, and students praise the work of its director, Carolyn Nayematsu. In addition, the support services of the Martin Luther King Program—such as tutoring and academic advising—receive high marks from students.

The university sponsors four cultural centers, one for each of the school's largest non-white student groups. All of the centers, except for the American Indian Cultural Center in Jones Hall, are located in Coffman Memorial Union on the East Bank. "The centers are places where students can hang out and be with friends who come from similar backgrounds and have had some similar experiences going to school here," says a student. Each of the centers has offices for various student groups and they each sponsor their own cultural awareness and educational programs.

The Asian-American Student Cultural Center, which provides a kitchen, a lounge, and computers, helps sponsor a New Year's celebration with some of the other, smaller Asian student groups. The center also sponsors an annual three-day workshop for students from area colleges and universities. Each of the workshops focuses on a theme; a recent subject was "Evolution of Asian-American Identity." According to one student leader, most of the students using the center during a recent year were first-generation Americans, while in the previous year they were second- and third-generation Americans. "This changes every year, but no matter what, we are a very tight community of students," he adds.

The African-American Student Cultural Center, according to one student, "has sole responsibility for programming the university's Africana History Month activities. The center is also a gathering place for us and it's where we can come and listen to music and talk with friends. Students also come in to use our computers and laser printer. The university charges students thirty-five dollars a quarter to use their computers, but ours are free." For Africana History Month, the group focuses primarily on bringing prominent speakers to campus. The center also sponsors a two-day workshop for area high school students to learn more about the university and its application process.

Center activities draw a great deal of support from residents of the St. Paul–Minneapolis area. "It's kind of a tradition, especially as a lot of our students come from the area," says a student. "Also because many of our students go to church around here, mostly the Zion Baptist Church in Minneapolis, and because a lot of us have jobs in the area. So we invite people we know and meet to our events. In fact, usually most of the people who come to our events are from the community. Some of our choices of speakers have generated controversy on campus, but we've always had strong support from the community."

Students involved at the African-American Cultural Center complain that their events are inadequately reported in the campus newspaper. "Either the paper doesn't send anyone to cover the event, or when they do they don't really understand the events they're reporting on," says a student. Another student would like to see more students use the center. "The African-American students here aren't really that tight or close. I suppose this is so because everyone is so spread out on campus, or because they commute from home. If you want to see someone you almost have to make an appointment. Also, the university has the African-American Studies program on the West Bank campus and our cultural center is on the East Bank, which separates us from two of our important resources."

The American Indian Student Cultural Center is primarily a place for peer support, says a student. "There are more than 40,000 students at Minnesota and it's easy for us to get swallowed up by the mainstream. So a lot of us come to the center to meet with friends and just for support." Adds another student: "The center is a nice, quiet, and relaxing place that many of us consider our home away from home." The center, which has lockers for commuter students and computers and a kitchen area, sponsors activities for Indian Month, which presents a powwow and speakers. In December, the center sponsors a popular storytelling event involving numerous elders.

Minnesota is basically a commuter school—only 10 percent of its student population lives on campus—so school spirit isn't overwhelming and some students describe the campus atmosphere as fragmented. However, a unifying event occurred during the 1991–92 school year with student reaction to the formation of a White Student Union, a now defunct student group. "Over a hundred student organizations protested against the new group," says a student. "We had to, as the administration didn't do anything about it. The four cultural centers on campus [African-American, Asian-American, Chicano/Latino, and American Indian] were the central places of organization and action. At first the White Student Union said it was going to focus on American culture, but then they began to write articles in the *Minnesota Daily* in which they expressed their ideology, which was basically racist. There was a lot of minority bashing, and while all this controversy was going on, a student hung the Nazi flag out of his dorm window. The administration didn't do anything about it because they said it was freedom of expression. In a way, though, the controversy was a good experience for us because for the first time that any of us can remember we were all unified." The event also generated considerable media attention.

On the whole, however, students say there is little racial tension on campus, and, according to one student, "most students are just here to get their diplomas and graduate." The Twin Cities of Minneapolis and St. Paul, which have become famous for their livability, offer a variety of social and cultural outlets for students. Each year, for example, the American Indian Center in Minneapolis, a city with a relatively large American Indian population, hosts a banquet for American Indian graduates of all of the area colleges. The area also has a rich variety of restaurants and theaters, as well as professional sports teams, such as the Vikings and the Twins. The Walker Art Center in Minneapolis is also world-class, and famous performers from opera diva Kathleen Battle to pop star Janet Jackson regularly appear in area concert halls and auditoriums.

Determination and the ability to focus are two qualities you'll want to bring with you should you decide to attend Minnesota. The university is huge, an environment that can swallow you up. And, like the state in which it is located, the university has a small population of students of color. But for the determined and focused who do attend school here, four years here will certainly be no waste of time. "Minnesota can have a lot to offer its students, and it gives you plenty of room to grow," says a sociology major. "But you have to be determined to get your degree, no matter what."

ST. OLAF COLLEGE

Address: 1520 St. Olaf Avenue, Northfield,
MN 55057-1098
Phone: (507) 663-3025
Director of Admissions: John Ruohoniemi
Multicultural Student Recruiter: Bill Green
1991–92 tuition: $12,080
Room and board: $3,345
Application deadline: Rolling admissions
Financial aid application deadline: 3/1
Non-white freshman admissions: Applicants
for the class of '95: 140
Accepted: 73%
Accepted who enroll: 46%
Applicants accepted who rank in top
10% of high school class: na
Median SAT: na
Median ACT: na
Full-time undergraduate enrollment: 3,010
Men: 47%
Women: 53%

GEOGRAPHIC DISTRIBUTION OF STUDENTS

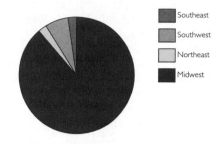

Top majors: 1. Biology 2. Chemistry
3. English/Psychology
Retention rate of non-white students: 87%
**Scholarships exclusively for non-white
students:** Hoeft Endowed Scholarship:
need-based; number and value of awards
vary from year to year. Dr. Martin
Luther King, Jr., Endowed Scholarship:
need-based; number and value of awards
vary from year to year.
Remediation programs: None
Academic support services: Tutoring in most
academic subjects is available, as well as
a Writing Center.
Ethnic studies programs: St. Olaf offers
interdisciplinary majors in Asian Studies,
American Race and Multicultural
Studies, African-American Studies, and
Hispanic Studies.
Organizations for non-white students: Asian
Concerns Groups, Harambe, Presente!,
Southern African Concerns, Students
Against Racism, Zebra Patch,
Multicultural House, Afro-American
Women's Support Group
Notable non-white alumni: Anton
Armstrong ('78, Music; conductor, St.
Olaf Choir); Mikal Baissa ('73, Art;
senior editor, Voice of America); Samuel
B. Ho ('78, Chemistry/Religion; research
physician, University of Minnesota);
Sandra Scheffler Littlejohn ('82, Nursing;
director of nursing services, Cedar Pines
Health Care Facility, Minneapolis);

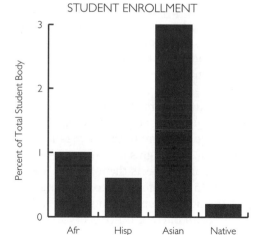

STUDENT ENROLLMENT

Non-white students in
1987–88: na
1988–89: na
1989–90: 5.4%
1990–91: 6.8%
Students In-state: 66%

Ronald McKinley ('71, Political Science; executive director, Minnesota Minority Education Partnership); David Wallace ('79, Music; horn player, Chicago Civic Orchestra); Carl Warren ('72, Political Science; professor, University of Minnesota Law School); Donnie Watson ('78, Religion; assistant professor of psychiatry and pediatrics, Morehouse School of Medicine); Rene Whiterabbit ('85, Religion; AIDS project coordinator, Indian Health Board of Minneapolis)

Tenured faculty: 183
Non-tenured faculty: 220
Student-faculty ratio: 12.5:1
Administrators: 147
    African-American: 4%
    Hispanic: 0
    Asian-American: 2%
    Native American: 0
Recent non-white speakers on campus: Joe Clark (former high school principal, portrayed in the film *Lean on Me*)

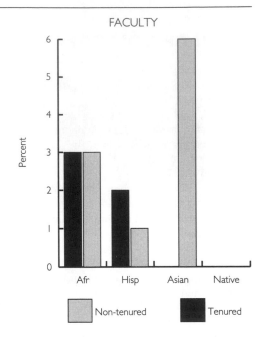

FACULTY

St. Olaf's Uncle Mel is not the school's mascot or a favorite residence hall adviser. Uncle Mel, as the students sometimes refer to him, is the president of the 119-year-old college, one whom students praise for his commitment to students and to issues of multiculturalism. Melvin D. George, the president's full name, sits on a panel on multiculturalism that he himself created. Says a student: "It's easy to get to know him as a personal friend. If the multicultural students have a problem on campus, we just go to him."

Needless to say, interaction with faculty and administrators is the rule rather than the exception at St. Olaf. Dinners at professors' houses are not uncommon. Leona Collins, head of the Multicultural Affairs Office, also lends more than her fair share of support to students. "She certainly knows her job. Although she's African-American, she knows a great deal about various cultures, and respects them all. She's also a great trainer of student leaders, and she's a big help when it comes to planning our annual Harambee conference here on campus. It's not uncommon to see her in her office until ten or eleven at night, and if you don't drop into her office every so often, she'll send you a note asking you why."

St. Olaf has gradually gained national prominence for its respected academics at affordable prices. A recent issue of *Money* magazine's *Money College Guide* referred to St. Olaf as "one of America's best college buys," the only Minnesota college to earn such an honor.

The college is best known for its music program, and also has well-respected departments of chemistry, biology, English, and math. Religion and economics are well regarded, while Asian Studies is popular with economics students, who often choose to major in both areas. Students say the school's program in American Race and Multicultural Studies is strong. Reflecting the school's Lutheran heritage, in order to graduate students must enroll in at least two Christian studies courses, and a third course that may be in either Christian or non-Christian studies. St. Olaf students are also able to take courses at Carleton College, located on the other side of town.

For those not into the traditional way of learning things in college, St. Olaf offers two slightly alternative degree-seeking routes. The Paracollege is based on interdisciplinary seminars and British-style tutorials that allow students to design their own majors. Students in the two-year Great Conversation program read the Western classics in chronological order, from the works of Homer to those of Darwin and Dostoevski; however, none of the program's courses include works of non-white or female authors.

The school's cultural student organizations, which are open to students of all races and ethnicities, "basically educate the campus by using the shock method," says a junior, "because so many of the issues we bring up haven't been discussed before. We're usually subtle in our approach, but not always." The student points to a recent activity sponsored by the campus group Students Against Racism. "That group uses guerrilla warfare. Recently in the student cafeteria, a white student jumped on a table and started shouting all these politically incorrect remarks, like 'Look at all these minority students. They only got into St. Olaf because of their race.' Then another member of the group, a female at the other end of the room, started teaching him that they earned the right to be here just as much as any one else in the room." It's a start.

With about 50 active members, Harambee, the school's multicultural student organization, "is sort of St. Olaf's version of the melting pot," comments a junior. One of Harambee's major activities is its annual conference, in which it invites students from various area colleges to participate. In a recent year, more than 100 students participated in the three-day affair, titled "Beyond the Melting Pot," which included student and guest panelists from the Minneapolis–St. Paul area. Harambee members meet weekly in the Cube in Yterbol Building, which has an office and kitchen area. "But more than anything," says a Harambee member, "the members of Harambee support one another."

For additional social life on campus, students say the various multicultural student groups have parties. Harambee sponsors an annual "retreat" in the college's gymnasium. The Intercultural House can also be socially active. The house has residence facilities for ten students of the same sex, which changes from year to year. Leona Collins also helps coordinate trips to Minneapolis–St. Paul churches on non-consecutive Sundays. "There's never a dull moment on campus," says a student, which is fortunate, as the local town, Northfield, offers little to students. Students with cars will make the drive north to the Twin Cities, which have a wide variety of cultural and social activities.

On campus, the most popular activities are those that have to do with music. The St. Olaf Choir was one of five international choirs to perform in 1988 at the Seoul Olympics, and the annual St. Olaf Christmas Festival, which features performances of five St. Olaf choirs and the school's orchestra, was telecast nationwide in 1989 by the Public Broadcasting System. Numerous intramural sports opportunities exist, from basketball to hockey. The Olaf Lesbian and Gay Alliance received funding from the Student Activities Committee during a recent school year.

There is much that is uniquely Norwegian at St. Olaf College, which has a largely blond, blue-eyed, and Lutheran student body. Norse immigrants founded the college back in 1874, naming it for Norway's patron saint. Students can major in Norwegian Studies, and there are the buildings with Norse-sounding names, such as Rolvaag Memorial Library, Skoglund Athletic Center, and Steensland Hall. Then, of course, there are the seemingly endless winters, when "brrrrr" is as common a refrain as any you'll hear from the famed St. Olaf Choir.

St. Olaf's multicultural student population *is* small. In fact, it's miniscule. But what the students lack in numbers they more than make up for in camaraderie. "The multicultural students here, and some of the concerned Caucasian students, are tight and provide a lot of support for one another. When I first visited this campus, it was something I noticed and it was one factor that got me to enroll here," says a sophomore. "Each class of us multicultural students tries to help out the class behind him or her so that coming here won't be as much of a shock as it was for us."

MISSISSIPPI

MILLSAPS COLLEGE

Address: 1701 North State, Jackson, MS 39210
Phone: (601) 974-1050 / (800) 352-1050
Director of Admissions: Florence W. Hines
Multicultural Student Recruiter: John Leach
1993–94 tuition: $10,686
Room and board: $4,250
Application deadline: 3/1
Financial aid application deadline: 3/1
Non-white freshman admissions: Applicants for the class of '95: na
  Median SAT: na
  Median ACT range: 24-28
Full-time undergraduate enrollment: 1,089
  Men: 51%
  Women: 49%
Non-white students in
  1987–88: 5%–6%
  1988–89: 5%–7%
  1989–90: 5%–7%
  1990–91: 7%
  1991–92: 7%
Geographic distribution of students: na
Students In-state: 54%
Top majors: 1. Business 2. English 3. Biology
Retention rate of non-white students: 90%
Scholarships exclusively for non-white students: Minority Student Scholarship: need-based; amount varies.
Remediation programs: None
Academic support services: Millsaps offers centers for writing and math in addition to tutoring in most subjects. The Counseling and Career Planning and Placement Center also provides support.
Ethnic studies programs: None
Ethnic studies courses: The college offers "Cross-Cultural American Heritage" and "Ethnic American Literatures."
Organizations for non-white students: Black Student Association, Cross-Cultural Connection, Alpha Kappa Alpha, Alpha Phi Alpha, Campus Ministry Team, Delta Sigma Theta
Notable non-white alumni: Randall Pinkston ('73; CBS News White House correspondent)
Tenured faculty: 52

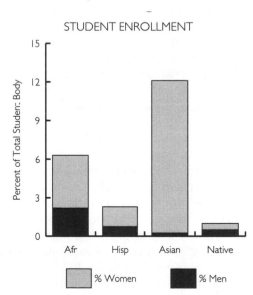

STUDENT ENROLLMENT

Percent of Total Student Body

% Women % Men

Non-tenured faculty: 35
Student-faculty ratio: 14:1
Administrators: 30
  Non-white: 3.3%

Recent non-white speakers on campus:
Randall Pinkston (Millsaps alumnus and
CBS News White House correspondent);
Jocelyn Elders (surgeon general designate)

Millsaps has long been known as one of Mississippi's best colleges and has traditionally attracted some of the state's brightest high school students. Although the school is a relative unknown outside the South, Millsaps graduates enjoy the respect and attention of employers and graduate schools. Over a 10-year period, for example, 98 percent of its law school applicants and 81 percent of its medical school applicants were accepted.

By far the most popular major among Millsaps students is business administration, one of the school's strongest departments. Nearly half of a recent graduating class were Business Administration majors. Qualified Millsaps graduates are able to take advantage of a program with the school's graduate school of business in which students can earn a B.A. and an M.B.A. degree in five years. Students say the school's pre-med program is solid, particularly with the completion in 1988 of the Olin Hall of Science, which houses the biology and chemistry departments, and the school's music department is also considered to be among the school's best departments. Students speak highly of the history department's "Afro-American Experience" course, but express regret that the course, the school's only African-American studies course, is just offered during alternate years. Although Millsaps' strengths are in preprofessional studies, Millsaps students can't graduate without having studied the liberal arts. To satisfy some of their graduation requirements, many first-year students enroll in the popular Heritage Program, an interdisciplinary humanities program that includes courses in history, fine arts, and religion. Students comment that interaction with faculty members is frequent and comfortable.

For academic and non-academic support, students most often praise the work of Jeanne Forsythe, head of the education department and a Millsaps alum. She "serves as a role model because she is a black woman who has managed to prosper professionally," observes a student. Formerly an adviser to the BSA, Forsythe, according to one student, wasn't able to continue in that position since she assumed her responsibilities as head of the education department. "She still helps us in planning some of our activities and is always there to talk to us."

Although Millsaps was the first college in Mississippi to voluntarily have an open-door admissions policy for students of color, the college is just now beginning to be more responsive to those students' concerns. The school recently established the Multicultural Studies Room, in Chimneyville, the student life center. The Multicultural Studies Room includes art displays and serves primarily as a study and meeting room for student organizations. The school has also recently created the full-time position of Minority Affairs Coordinator, which previously was only a part-time position. The present coordinator, Sandy Carter, has been busy coordinating various events, including Black History Month and Cultural Awareness Week activities. "Sandy really cares about students and has worked closely with us in helping to get these events organized."

The most active support group for students is the Black Student Association. "The

BSA not only serves as a support service but also provides cultural programs to make the community aware of minorities. The BSA is very effective in trying to improve the environment for black students," reports a junior. Each year, the BSA sponsors Cultural Awareness Week and Black History Month activities, which have included speakers, films, and gospel choirs.

One student expressed disappointment at how few African-American students participate in BSA events. "At our first meeting, about 55 students were signed up to be involved in the BSA, but now there are only about 25 students involved." The student blames the lack of student involvement on "student apathy and academics." Students would also like to see more diversity within the African-American student population at the college; in a recent year, all but one of the college's African-American students were from Mississippi, and the majority of them were from Jackson, which, says a student, "can get a little boring hanging out with people who are all from the same area."

Much of the campus social life is centered on the Greek system, in which more than two-thirds of the students participate. "Anyone who is anyone is a member of one of the fraternities or sororities," reports a student, although, she adds that relatively few students of color tend to join the organizations. Each of the fraternities has its own special eating area in the school's dining hall. Millsaps' Greek system also includes a fraternity and sororities that are traditionally black—Alpha Phi Alpha, Alpha Kappa Alpha, and Delta Sigma Theta—which, say students, have become more active in recent years. Recently, Alpha Kappa Alpha sponsored a holiday formal dance, the first to be sponsored by a black sorority or fraternity at Millsaps.

Campus social life is far from integrated. "As far as integration is concerned, that is nice and pretty on paper, but in reality it is not in existence here. Minorities, most specifically blacks, are very much in the minority. Other minorities are able to assimilate, but blacks aren't. Campus parties, for the most part, are all one-sided the majority of the time. The same is true in the cafeteria, where all the blacks sit together at one table." Despite the lack of interaction, one student comments that "relations among students appear good when we're around each other. I don't know of any evidence to prove otherwise."

Millsaps has the benefit of being located near the center of downtown Jackson, a city of 400,000 that offers students a variety of off-campus social and cultural activities. In fact, the city is so rich with activity, says a student, that, "basically, we're at Millsaps just to go to school. We leave campus for most of our social activities and go to Jackson State University and Tougaloo," a historically black college. Activities at those colleges include step shows and parties.

There is very little at this small college that can be considered progressive, not least the dorm situation. All but one of the dorms are co-ed, and rules governing visiting hours are strictly enforced. Most of the school's African-American juniors and seniors live in the north wing of Bacot Hall. "The dorms are not very integrated," says a student. "This is mainly upon request, though, because we would feel uncomfortable otherwise."

Millsaps students are also on the more conservative side of the political spectrum, but a student observes this is more due to apathy than any real political conviction. "You're not going to see any shanties protesting South African apartheid," comments the student.

Although Millsaps may not have the national appeal of some of its Southern competitors, the college does provide an intimate college experience that students find rewarding. But despite the work of administrators and students, when it comes to multicultural concerns, Millsaps can prove to be a disappointing experience. "If a prospective minority sought my opinion about Millsaps, I would tell him or her that if they are looking for a good liberal arts education only, Millsaps is the right choice. As far as a social life is concerned, there is none. As a black student, I feel as if I have sacrificed my social life for a good education. However, I have been working with the Associate Dean of Student Affairs. He is working to improve life for minorities by getting the administration involved, recruiting more minority students, bringing more black sororities and fraternities to the campus, and getting more ethnic studies courses added to the curriculum. Until these matters are addressed, the campus can not be considered truly integrated."

UNIVERSITY OF MISSISSIPPI

Address: Lyceum Building, University, MS 38677
Phone: (601) 232-7226
Director of Admissions: Beckett Howorth
Multicultural Student Recruiter: Kylia Carter
1991–92 tuition: $2,434 (in-state); $4,294 (out-of-state)
Room and board: $2,660
Application deadline: 7/28
Financial aid application deadline: 3/1
Non-white freshman admissions: na
   Applicants for the class of '95: na
   Median SAT: na
   Median ACT: na
Full-time undergraduate enrollment: 8,221
   Men: 50%
   Women: 50%
Non-white students in
   1987–88: 7%
   1988–89: 7%
   1989–90: 8%
   1990–91: 8%
Geographic distribution of students: na
Students In-state: 85%
Top majors: 1. General Business
   2. Accountancy 3. Elementary Education
Retention rate of non-white students: 83%
Scholarships exclusively for non-white students: Afro-American/Black Student Scholarship: one awarded each year to

an applicant who scores between 25 and 27 on his or her ACT; the award is valued at $1,500. Gannett Scholarship: merit-based; available to an African-American student planning to major in journalism; amount of each award varies; renewable. Sunburst Bank Scholarship: merit-based; one $10,000 award given each year to an African-American student planning to major in banking. Neel Schaffer

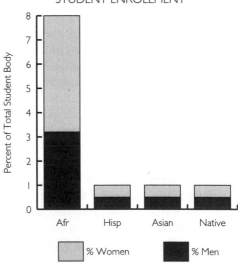

STUDENT ENROLLMENT

Percent of Total Student Body

Afr   Hisp   Asian   Native

   % Women   % Men

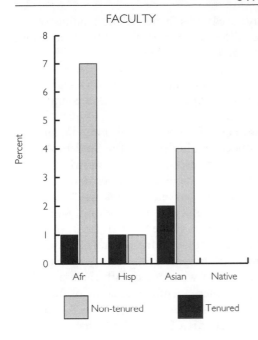

FACULTY

Scholarship: merit-based; available to African-American students planning to major in engineering; one $12,000 award given each year.

Remediation programs: Offered are developmental courses in English, math, and reading, as well as courses in English as a second language.

Academic support services: The university offers tutoring in most subjects, as well as study skills workshops.

Ethnic studies programs: None

Ethnic studies courses: The university offers various courses in African-American Studies.

Organizations for non-white students: Black Student Union, Zeta Phi Beta, Kappa Alpha Psi, Blacks in Engineering, Omega Psi Phi, Alpha Kappa Alpha, Phi Beta Sigma, Delta Sigma Theta, Alpha Phi Alpha

Notable non-white alumni: na

Tenured faculty: 257

Non-tenured faculty: 382

Student-faculty ratio: 17:1

Administrators: 466

   African-American: 7%

   Hispanic: 1%

   Asian-American: 3%

   Native American: 0

Recent non-white speakers on campus: na

The University of Mississippi, which boasts some solid academic programs, has an image problem. Like the state in which it is located, Ole Miss has been labeled by outsiders, and by some insiders, as a segregated institution. And where waving the Confederate flag is one of the high points for many students at football games and where the school's sports teams are named the Rebels, one must admit there is some reality to the perception.

But things are beginning to change at Ole Miss as the university and various student groups are working to bridge the gaps that have long existed between the races. (The first African-American graduated from the university in 1966.) "Although the school is far from perfect, the university has improved a lot in this regard since my freshman year, particularly when it comes to campus events and programming," says a recent graduate. "It used to be where the events catered only to white students, and if you went, all you would see were white students. But now that the Student Programming Board is more racially diverse, some of the campus programming has also become more diverse. Now if you go to an event you'll see students of all races, which is important because it causes students to talk and to be together. That's where real learning about each other takes place."

Even the issue of Confederate flag waving at football games has been pushed to the forefront by students. "The entire senior class of '91 got together and came up with a new university flag, because they knew that the old one—the Confederate flag—was offensive to black students," says a campus leader. "The administration approved the class's proposal to ban the use of the Confederate flag at football games, and the university divorced itself from the flag. The senior class came up with a new flag, called the Battle M flag, that is more appropriate. Although there are still students who wave the Confederate flag at football games, that will change soon, with the new flag and with the administration's disapproval of the Confederate flag at the games."

When it comes to campus social life, things are also getting a bit more integrated. Each year, for example, Ole Miss's Black Student Union (BSU), the Student Affairs Office, and the Student Programming Board sponsor Afrolympics, which pairs predominantly white fraternities with predominantly black fraternities to compete in various athletic contests, including a tug-of-war and basketball dunking. "The event was designed to promote diversity and racial harmony, and it is working. As part of the Afrolympics, there's also a step show, and members of the black fraternities taught members of the white fraternities how to step. At first it was frustrating because some of the white fraternity students didn't want to participate because they didn't think they had the rhythm that black students have. But we worked with them and they picked it up fast. We all had a great time. Since then, members of some of the white fraternities we were paired up with have invited us over to their houses for dinner, and we now talk to each other on campus. That sort of thing didn't happen much before the Afrolympics."

In a recent year, the winning Afrolympics team included the men of Phi Beta Sigma, a historically black fraternity, Delta Psi, Sigma Nu, and Sigma Chi. "Kappa Alpha fraternity was supposed to be a part of the event but their members voted not to be a part of it. We tried to talk them into being with us, but their president kept saying that his membership wouldn't have any part of it." According to the student, race relations have never been a focus of some of the members of KA, whose symbol, the Confederate flag, frequently hangs from a fraternity house window. According to a student, the Afrolympics is the brainchild of Thomas Wallace, an assistant vice-chancellor. "He encourages the BSU to plan programs that will appeal to a wide spectrum of students. He doesn't want us to be separatist, and we don't want to be," says a BSU member. As adviser to the BSU and to Old Miss's gospel choir, Valeria Harmon, an executive secretary to another vice-chancellor, also works closely with students. "Words haven't been invented to describe how important she is to us," says a student.

In addition, the university sponsors the Cultural Awareness Program, an annual event that presents a play and student-read poems. Held in Fulton Chapel on campus, "the event was well attended by a diverse group of students and faculty—black and white," says a student.

Students say dorm life at Ole Miss also promotes a better sense of racial understanding among undergraduates. "Each dorm has a resident adviser, and they're a diverse group of students, including foreign students. Each semester, each resident adviser is required to host five programs that appeal to a broad range of interests. This gets students to being social and learning about different perspectives and cultures," says a student who has attended numerous such programs.

A sign of the changing times also occurred in 1991 when an African-American student won for the first time the title of Miss Ole Miss. "Our representative was up against a member of Delta Delta Delta, a white sorority that practically runs the campus. But we campaigned and campaigned and won," says a BSU member. "The victory made national news."

The BSU also does its share of raising campus awareness. With about 200 active members, the organization hosts guest speakers, sponsors workshops, and holds regular NAACP membership drives. The university's gospel choir, which has about 55 members, regularly sings at community churches and performs at an annual concert on campus. During a recent year, three of the gospel choir singers were white students. The school's predominantly black fraternities and sororities are also active in the community. The women of Alpha Kappa Alpha, for example, work in a women's shelter and coordinate a canned-food drive. AKA and Phi Beta Sigma are the only two predominantly black Greek organizations to have houses on campus.

Although a great deal has been done to ease racial tension, students still describe a campus that is largely segregated. Racism has also manifested itself on campus; in 1988, unidentified vandals set fire to the fraternity house of Phi Beta Sigma, a historically black Greek organization.

Ole Miss's curriculum, however, doesn't stress diversity the way some of campus programming tends to. But students are able to study a wide array of subjects; some of the more respected are pharmacy, forensics, history, physics, and business administration. While there are few Black Studies courses at Ole Miss, students nonetheless praise the school's "Afro-American History" and "Afro-American Literature" courses. Although Ole Miss's academic atmosphere has a reputation of being more lax than intense, the admissions office is quick to point out that the school has graduated 23 Rhodes Scholars.

Ole Miss provides one of the best public educations in the state, and with the continued improvement of race relations on campus, the university is increasingly becoming a more hospitable place for students of color. "I learned a lot during my four years at Ole Miss," says a recent graduate. "Some people feel you lose a sense of your black identity by going to Ole Miss because of some of the things that have gone on here, and they think that you can only keep that identity by going to a black college. But in light of my experience here, I'm not sure that's true. In addition to the experience gained outside the classroom, I also feel I'm able to compete with the Harvard grad because of what I've learned in the classroom."

MISSOURI

UNIVERSITY OF MISSOURI/COLUMBIA

Address: Columbia, MO 65211
Phone: (314) 882-7651 / (800) 225-6075
  (in-state)
Director of Admissions: Georgeann Porter
Multicultural Student Recruiter: Tracy
  Ellis-Ward

1992–93 tuition: $2,642
Room and board: $3,200
Application deadline: 5/15
Financial aid application deadline: 2/15

To out-of-staters, the University of Missouri is best known for its School of Journalism, the oldest and, some consider, best such program in the nation. For in-staters, the university offers other top-flight academics that can be had at reasonable prices.

Should you come to "Mizzou" to study journalism, you won't leave disappointed. Students have a variety of hands-on opportunities, including work on a daily newspaper, a national public radio station, and an NBC network television station. The School of Journalism also has a Minority Student Development Program, which seeks to recruit more minority students into the program, as well as a Multicultural Management Program, established in 1986, that seeks, through training workshops, to encourage more multicultural students to become media managers.

Other strong programs are education, agriculture, and business, particularly accounting, as well as engineering, especially civil engineering. The school's Black Studies program "is great because the professors let you shine in your own way," remarks a junior. Students praise the program for its breadth of study as well as for its faculty, especially Sundiata Cha-Jua, the program's director, and K. C. Morrison, who also serves as a vice-provost for minority affairs.

While the educational opportunities are certainly among Mizzou's strong points— the university has been ranked by the Carnegie Foundation for the Advancement of Teaching as one of the top research universities in the country—the social opportunities for minority students pale in comparison. "The education I'm earning here is great, but there are times when I wish I'd gone to a school where there are more social outlets for students of color," says a member of the Legion of Black Collegians,

Mizzou's largest African-American student group, echoing the concerns of other minority students.

Students complain of the lopsided ratio of black women to black men—one student estimates it's almost two to one—that creates, in the words of one female student, "fierce competition for men." The city of Columbia, although said by the writers of *Newsweek* magazine to be one of the country's most livable cities, also offers little socially—outside of movies and shopping and skating rinks—to the student of color. Nearby Lou's Lounge, a bar, attracts some African-American students from Mizzou, but is primarily a place for "older" locals, and Doc 'n' Eddy's, a dance club, is popular with students only "every so often." Concerning the weekend social life for the students of color on campus a student says: "A lot of us go home on weekends, as there isn't that much for us to do, and because most of us are from St. Louis or Kansas City, both within a few hours' drive from campus."

The minority community at Mizzou is tiny. Of the school's more than 25,000 undergraduates, according to a 1990 U.S. Department of Education report printed in *The Chronicle of Higher Education,* only 0.3 percent were American Indian, 1.6 percent Asian, 4 percent black, and 0.9 percent Hispanic. (Current figures were unavailable, as the university's admissions office declined to complete our questionnaire.)

Historically black Greek organizations have been known to throw parties and are quite active. Members of the Alpha Phi Alpha fraternity sponsored their first Alpha Academy on campus during the summer of 1992, in which at-risk students from public high schools were invited to campus for part of the summer to attend classes, to live in the dorms, and, says a student, "to just get a sense of what it's like going to college." Members of Delta Sigma Theta sorority sponsor clothes drives and work in a soup kitchen. The Greek organizations serve another purpose as well: "Most students join because they can feel part of a family. Sometimes it can be cliquey, but it's a way to feel that you belong somewhere."

The Black Culture Center, located near the center of campus on Virginia Avenue, "is basically a place where black students stressed out at being at such a predominantly white campus can come and relax," says a student. "At the center we celebrate Kwanzaa, arrange study groups, but mostly we gather to talk about issues that concern the African-American community both locally and nationally. The center is rarely used for social purposes, but more for discussion of important issues. These types of discussions are what make coming to the center exciting." The center is also the site of a black faculty lecture series.

The Legion of Black Collegians (LBC) sponsors various social events throughout the school year, including a Fall Fest, "which is basically a big picnic where any minority student attends to make contacts with minority professors and friends." In the past, the event has been held on McKee Field, but the group is looking to bring it to the lawn of the school's Black Cultural Center. The LBC hasn't been as active during recent years, however, due to infighting among members, according to campus leaders. Some members say the LBC leadership is ineffective when dealing with the administration, while others claim the leadership is doing all that it can.

A recent incident that generated much attention and controversy on campus took place at a party in Greek Town, a section of campus dominated by white fraternities and sororities, in which, according to students, African-American youths were beaten by white fraternity members. The fraternity members allegedly attacked the youths because the youths "were wandering where they weren't supposed to, in the all-white section of town," says a student, who added, "The boys were pretty badly beaten." Students say the administration's response to the incident was "limited. They put the fraternity on probation and made it undergo some racial sensitivity workshops, but the fraternity got around it by just making its pledge class undergo the workshop. The university was more concerned with the number of people who were at the party and the amount of alcohol that was consumed." Says a student about Greek Town: "The word around here is not to go walking there. It's not that all the Greeks are going to fight, but you never know." Adds a particularly cynical undergraduate: "They don't call this place Little Dixie for nothing." Students report that Jewish students have also been the victims of certain bias attacks in on-campus dorms.

Although the university enjoys a national reputation—thanks in part to its journalism program—it has a primarily regional appeal. More than 80 percent of its students are from in-state, and, according to one report, 10 percent of Missouri high school graduates end up attending the university. Mizzou's large and pervasive Greek system also does its share to perpetuate the school's conservative image.

To be socially and academically successful at Mizzou, according to students, requires getting involved in campus activities and joining organizations, which can make the big campus more manageable. Success can also be found in the classrooms and offices around campus. "I can tell you this. If you want to be successful here, you have to learn to network with the black faculty and staff. They are all there for you, no matter what. They are a network of mentors who will help you with academic advising or just friendly support. You will not graduate from here if you don't get to know them, so get to know these people right away if you come here. I'm convinced that's how I made it through."

WASHINGTON UNIVERSITY

Address: Campus Box 1089, One Brookings Drive, St. Louis, MO 63130
Phone: (314) 935-6000 / (800) 638-0700
Dean of Admissions: Harold Wingood
Multicultural Student Recruiter: Brent Reeves
1993–94 tuition: $17,600
Room and board: $5,731
Application deadline: 1/15
Financial aid application deadline: 2/15
Non-white freshman admissions: Applicants
   for the class of '95: na
   Accepted: na
   Accepted who enroll: na
   Applicants accepted who rank in top
   10% of high school class: na

Median SAT: na
Median ACT: na
Full-time undergraduate enrollment: 4,896
   Men: 52%
   Women: 48%
Non-white students in
   1987–88: 13.6%
   1988–89: 13.4%
   1989–90: 14.8%
   1990–91: 16.9%
Geographic distribution of students: na
Students In-state: 13%
Top majors: 1. Engineering 2. Business
   3. Psychology
Retention rate of non-white students: na

STUDENT ENROLLMENT

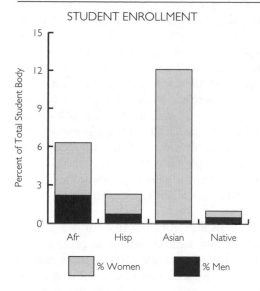

Percent of Total Student Body

% Women   % Men

Scholarships exclusively for non-white students: John B. Ervin Scholarship Program for African-American Students: merit-based; renewable; full scholarship plus $2,500 stipend.

Remediation programs: None

Academic support services: Student Educational Service provides tutoring, study skills workshops, and career and personal counseling.

Ethnic studies programs: African and African-American Studies, Asian Studies, and Latin American Studies are offered.

Organizations for non-white students: Association of Black Students, Asian Student Association, Association of Latin American Students, Korean Students Association, Hawaii Club

Notable non-white alumni: Kenneth J. Cooper (national correspondent and Pulitzer Prize winner, *Washington Post*); Walter E. Massey (director, National Science Foundation); Chia-Wei Woo (president, Hong Kong University)

Tenured faculty: na

Non-Tenured Faculty: na

Student-faculty ratio: 6:1

Administrators: na

Recent non-white speakers on campus: Jesse Jackson (former U.S. presidential candidate and civil rights activist); John Singleton (writer and director); Wole Soyinka (author); Jamaica Kincaid (author); Marian Wright Edelman (president, Children's Defense Fund); Yolanda King (civil rights activist and daughter of Martin Luther King, Jr.)

Washington University has come into its own as one of the country's more prominent institutions of higher learning, and only the relatively unenlightened would confuse it with a school in the state of Washington or in DC. The 140-year-old university has tough admissions standards, top-flight academic programs, and a bright and motivated student body.

Wash U, with one of the country's best-known medical centers, has long attracted pre-med majors to its campus; in a recent year, nearly 20 percent of the student body declared itself pre-med. Biology, chemistry, and physics, all of which offer extensive research opportunities, are said to be the school's best departments for those destined for medical school. The school of business, with about 550 undergraduates, is housed in impressive new facilities, thanks to a $15 million grant from the John M. Olin Foundation of New York City. (Olin had been a Wash U trustee for more than 40 years.) The School of Engineering and Applied Science, with 1,000 students, is demanding, but one student says, "The engineering faculty care that we do well." Among the departments in the College of Arts and Sciences, students say economics, history, and languages are good. Cooperation among Wash U's graduate schools of business, medicine, and social work allows students to take advantage of a variety of additional programs.

Students are now able to major in African-American Studies, which had previously been only a minor course of study. "From the courses I've taken, on a scale of one to ten, I would give the program a nine," says a student. "The program has a lot of good professors who know their subjects, and there's always a variety of courses offered, from African-American history courses to a course on black psychology." Robert Williams, a noted psychologist, teaches the "Black Psychology" course. "Dr. Williams is an excellent professor. He's the former president of an organization of black psychologists, so he brings in a wealth of experience to the classroom." The Asian Studies program, which offers both undergraduate and graduate degree programs, "is tough and involves a lot of research and reading." Students have access to the school's impressive East Asian Library.

Getting through Wash U isn't easy. Students usually enroll in five courses a term, and with all of the engineers and pre-med students around, academic pressure can be intense. To satisfy distributional requirements, students must enroll in three courses in the physical and life sciences, three courses in the social and behavioral sciences, three courses in literature and history, and three courses in two additional areas: language study, art forms, aesthetic and ethical values, or modes of reasoning. Students must also satisfy English composition and quantitative reasoning course requirements.

It's no wonder, then, that one of the primary activities of many undergrads is, in the words of a student, "basically, drinking a lot." On Thursdays, the Rat [a bar at the student center] has happy hour with beer, and on Friday and Saturday nights most of the social life goes on on fraternity row, where students drink to get drunk." About a third of the campus pledges one or another of the school's 13 fraternities and seven sororities. In a recent year, about eight African-Americans were members of the school's predominantly white Greek organizations; approximately 20 students have affiliated with citywide chapters of historically black fraternities and sororities.

The Asian Student Association (ASA) is said to have some of the best parties, not counting the ones at the fraternities. With about 50 active members, ASA meets once every two weeks and sponsors an annual Asian Awareness Week, which holds a charity luncheon, with the raised money going to a local Vietnamese center. The week also consists of a martial arts demonstration, an Indian dance night, and a variety show that includes a fashion show with traditional Asian garb. ASA also coordinates an annual semiformal dance and celebrations for Chinese New Year and the Moon Festival.

"The ASA membership is very diverse," observes a member. "We have students from Taiwan, Japan, Korea, India, and Thailand. Most, however, are Asian-Americans from the East Coast and Hawaii. We even have Asians here who were raised in England. It makes for some interesting conversations." Says another student: "The ASA is like one big family. When you have problems, there's always someone to turn to in the ASA, for academic and social problems."

The Association of Black Students, which has been on campus since 1968, has about 75 to 100 active members and meets regularly in the MLK Lounge in the Women's Center. The lounge, sometimes referred to as the ABS Lounge, has areas for study, as well as a TV and couches. One of ABS's primary activities is its annual Black Arts and Science Festival, a weeklong event that includes a semiformal dinner and guest speakers. John Singleton, director of *Boyz 'N the Hood,* was a recent keynote speaker for the festival. ABS also sponsors an annual MLK Forum, "which is the political arm of the ABS. We've had Shirley Chisholm, a former presidential candidate, speak, as well as a South African exiled speaker." For the symposium, ABS also brings local African-American entrepreneurs to speak to students, and sponsors a two-day forum on the relations between African-American men and women.

The city of St. Louis, the Gateway to the West, is a rich resource of cultural activity, with everything from restaurants and theater to professional baseball (the Cardinals) and the Black Repertory Theater Company. "But socially," says a student, "we don't go into the city much. We're always told here that the campus has almost everything we need, and, for the most part, it does. But when you want to go off campus, almost all bars and clubs are geared to those 21 and older." Forest Park, 1,300 acres "of grass, trees, hills, and lakes," is just across Wash U's campus and is a common destination for more than just the sun worshipper. Other than community service activities, students say there is relatively little interaction with the Richmond Hills community, a predominantly white suburb of St. Louis where the university is actually located.

On-campus cultural and social opportunities abound. The Filmboard sponsors four different movies each week, and every week the school's Assembly Series brings noted speakers to campus, among them Jimmy Carter and Alex Haley. During Engineers' Weekend, engineering students compete in the infamous "egg drop" from Shepley Hall, and each year Foreign Language Week attracts students to plays, exhibitions, speakers, and movies sponsored by the language departments. Intramural sports, which range from flag football to inner-tube water polo, are popular. The school's Lopata Basketball Classic, "the Brain Bowl," brings teams from such powerhouse schools as MIT and Amherst to campus for some competition. The women's volleyball team is always a standout, having won the NCAA Division III title in 1989.

With one of the richest endowments in the country, the university not only has been able to attract a more than able faculty; it has also been able to recruit students from every state in the nation and more than 30 foreign countries. However, Wash U remains a school with a much more laid-back, less competitive edge to it than other schools of its caliber. The person given credit for much of the school's friendly atmosphere is its president, William Danforth. "Everyone likes him, and he's a common sight on campus," says a student. "We even refer to him as Uncle Bill."

"Here, you can learn a lot about your own culture and about the cultures of others." Adds another student: "You're exposed to a lot of different people here, and it was a good decision for me to come here. Wash U is not too big, and the people are friendly."

M O N T A N A

UNIVERSITY OF MONTANA

Address: Missoula, MT 59812
Phone: (406) 243-4277
Director of Admissions: Michael Akin
Multicultural Student Recruiter: na
1992–93 tuition: $1,800 (in-state); $5,400 (out-of-state)
Room and board: $3,500
Application deadline: 7/1
Financial aid application deadline: 2/1
Non-white freshman admissions: Applicants for the class of '95: na
Applicants accepted who rank in top 10% of high school class: 10%
In top 25%: 25%
Median SAT: na
Median ACT: 22
Full-time undergraduate enrollment: 10,614
Men: 50%
Women: 50%
Non-white students in
1987–88: 4.47%
1988–89: na
1989–90: na
1990–91: 4.8%
Geographic distribution of students: na
Students In-state: 75%
Top majors: 1. Social Work 2. Psychology 3. Interpersonal Communications
Retention rate of non-white students: na
Scholarships exclusively for non-white students: The university sponsors seven merit-based scholarships for non-white applicants.
Remediation programs: Remedial courses are offered in math and writing.
Academic support services: A writing lab and a mentor program, and an additional mentor program for Native American students.
Ethnic studies programs: The university offers a major course of study in African-American Studies and minors in Asian and Native American Studies.
Organizations for non-white students: Native American Student Association, Black Student Union
Notable non-white alumni: na
Tenured faculty: na
Non-tenured faculty: na
Student-faculty ratio: 19:1
Administrators: na
Recent non-white speakers on campus: na

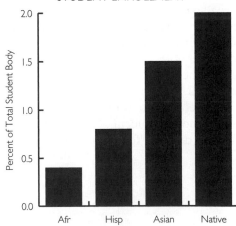

STUDENT ENROLLMENT

Percent of Total Student Body

The University of Montana is the outdoor student's dream school. Within 100 miles of campus lie some of the country's most scenic spots and recreation areas, from millions of acres of wilderness area perfect for camping to Yellowstone and Glacier national parks. With some of the best slopes around, skiing is also a favorite pastime of many Montana students.

Back indoors, the university also offers some solid academic programs, many with a decided emphasis on the out-of-doors, including resource conservation, wildlife biology, and forestry. The university owns a 29,000-acre teaching and research forest and a freshwater biological research station on nearby Flathead Lake. Montana also offers respectable programs in journalism and business. Students say that professors are easily accessible and encourage students to call on them during office hours.

The Native American Studies program "is good because it offers a wide variety of courses, especially because we get a lot of visiting professors in the area who offer us diverse viewpoints," says a student minoring in the program, which includes such well-regarded courses as "Contemporary Issues in Indian Lifestyles" and "Indian Education." Richmond Crow is one of the program's more popular professors. Students are able to turn to the resources of the Native American Studies program house, which has a peer mentor program. Bonnie Heavy Runner Craig, the house's director, and Woody Kipp, its counselor, are frequently relied on by students.

"All of the classes offered by the African-American Studies program are outstanding," reports a student. Course highlights include "Gandhi and King" and "Racism and Sexism." "The courses are so popular that there's always a waiting list to get in. People always have to sit on the floor, that's how crowded it gets." Ulysses Doss, the professor of these courses, "is excellent. He participated in all of the civil rights demonstrations back in the sixties, and he really knows his history," says a student.

Montana students can have their cultural awareness raised outside the classroom as well. "One of the biggest events we had last year was Speak Out Against Racism, held in the university center. It was an open-mike event, and we tried to have people with various perspectives speak. We had an African-American woman talk about what it's been like for her to grow up in Missoula, where her father's a professor. Then a student talked about his mixed heritage. And a woman then talked about her interracial marriage. More than 300 people showed up, many more than we expected."

The Black Student Union, with about 45 active members, sponsors various cultural activities for members and the campus community, and had prime responsibility for the Speak Out Against Racism event. During Black History Month, the group set up a tabling area in the university center and invited all of the minority student groups to display literature about their organizations. There was also a screening of the PBS film *Eyes on the Prize.*

KYI-YO, the school's Native American student group, has a Thanksgiving dinner, an annual powwow, as well as bake sales and other fundraisers for group-sponsored conferences. "At the last conference, lawyers, doctors, and teachers, all on a volunteer basis, came and talked about various issues, such as health, AIDS, drinking and drugs, and the centennial." KYI-YO has about 50 active members.

Missoula will never be confused with Los Angeles or New York City, which is just fine with most of the students who choose to attend school here. "I'm from the Bay

Area of California, and where I grew up it's really diverse. I know that a lot of people think of Montana as a place of rednecks, but I want any applicant to know that I've done things here that I never would have done had I stayed in the city. Since I've lived here I've learned to fly-fish, and next week I'm going up to Glacier National Park. I've also gotten to meet friends of all different races and backgrounds, people I know I'll keep as friends for a lifetime. I definitely like it here."

NEBRASKA

CREIGHTON UNIVERSITY

Address: 24th and California Street, Omaha, NE 68178
Phone: (402) 280-2703
Director of Admissions: Howard J. Bachman
Multicultural Student Recruiter: Henderson Gines, Jr.
1993–94 tuition: $9,932
Room and board: $4,180
Application deadline: 7/15
Financial aid application deadline: 4/1

Non-white freshman admissions: Applicants for the class of '96: 280
Accepted: 247
Accepted who enroll: 42%
Applicants accepted who rank in top 10% of high school class: 28.6%
In top 25%: 60.1%
Median SAT: na
Median ACT: 22.6

Full-time undergraduate enrollment: 3,883
Men: 40.7%
Women: 59.3%

Non-white students in
1988–89: 9.6%
1989–90: 9.8%
1990–91: 10.4%
1991–92: 11.2%

Students In-state: 47%

Top majors: 1. Biology 2. Psychology 3. Finance

Retention rate of non-white students: 84.9%

Scholarships exclusively for non-white students: Creighton Scholarship for Minority Scholars: merit-based; amount

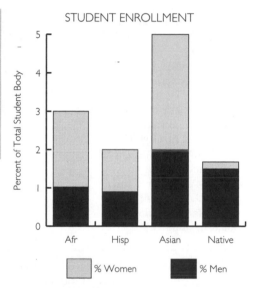

STUDENT ENROLLMENT

Percent of Total Student Body

□ % Women   ■ % Men

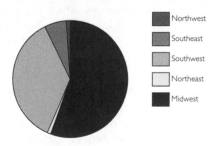

GEOGRAPHIC DISTRIBUTION OF STUDENTS

Northwest
Southeast
Southwest
Northeast
Midwest

of award and number of awards vary from year to year.

Remediation programs: The university provides workshops in reading, writing, math, and developing study skills.

Academic support services: Creighton offers workshops in stress management, time management, as well as tutoring in most academic subjects.

Ethnic studies programs: None

Ethnic studies courses: Seventeen courses in Black Studies are offered through the history, English, political science, and sociology departments.

Organizations for non-white students: Creighton University African-American Student Association, Latino Student Association

Notable non-white alumni: J. Clay Smith, Jr. (professor, Howard University School of Law)

Tenured faculty: 134
   African-American: 1 total
   Hispanic: 1 total
   Asian-American: 7 total
   Native American: 0

Non-tenured faculty: 97
   African-American: 2 total
   Hispanic: 1 total
   Asian-American: 3 total
   Native American: 2 total

Student-faculty ratio: 14:1

Administrators: 203

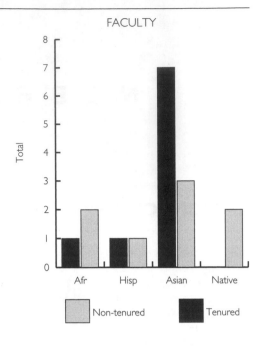

FACULTY

African-American: 3.9%
Hispanic: 0.98%
Asian-American: 0
Native American: 0

Recent non-white speakers on campus: Maya Angelou (author and poet); Dr. Jacqueline Fleming (psychologist)

Creighton has fine professional schools of nursing, pharmacy, dentistry, law, and medicine, and, for many students, the school's Jesuit, Catholic orientation is an important part of campus life.

Students say philosophy and religion are among Creighton's best departments. The College of Business Administration offers major areas of study in eight different areas, including accounting, finance, and marketing. Psychology is one of the school's more popular majors. The School of Nursing, which enrolls about 250 students, allows students to gain practical experience at St. Joseph Hospital, located on campus. One of the school's more popular courses in the Black Studies program is "The History of the African-American Church," offered by the theology department.

Academic competition, especially among the pre-professional students looking to get a foot in the door of one of Creighton's graduate schools, can be keen. For academic support, students praise the school's Student Support Services Program, located in Markoe Hall. "I have found this program to be very helpful through its tutoring assistance and personal counseling," says a junior about the federally funded program. Various Creighton staff members also work to advance students academically and socially. "Personally, I'd have to list Joel Scherling, director of Student Services, John Pierce, director of affirmative action, and Lloyd Beasley, Creighton University African-American Student Association's (CUASA) counselor, as being the most supportive individuals on this campus who are geared toward the advancement of minorities here at Creighton," says a student. "They all take an active part in CUASA activities and offer critical advice."

After being a relatively dormant organization during the past few years, CUASA has recently become a more important source of academic and non-academic support. "CUASA is the one organization on campus designed to meet the needs of the African-American and other minority students on campus. It provides an outlet for people to come and enjoy themselves through community service commitments, parties, fundraisers, and other activities geared to satisfy the wants and needs of its members. This organization is the most influential factor I can note in regard to my being satisfied at Creighton."

CUASA members are active within the Omaha community. "CUASA carries out community service projects to help those in need. For example, for Thanksgiving each year we give baskets to needy families. We also get involved with community churches in helping with their youth membership. CUASA volunteers at the Children's Museum during Septemberfest, which happens to be one of Omaha's biggest attractions."

CUASA was also influential in establishing contact with campus security, which, according to various students on campus, had been harassing African-American male students. "We understand that public safety has an obligation to secure the campus. However, we also believe they have a duty to distinguish a student from an on-campus visitor who warrants a check. We brought the occurrences to the attention of the public safety director, who immediately showed concern by attending the next CUASA meeting, where he took complaints and answered questions from the members present. Since these incidents, which occurred in the fall of 1991, we've facilitated better lines of communication with public safety."

For entertainment, students have easy access to downtown Omaha (pop. 500,000), a predominantly white city with a relatively small African-American community, two miles from campus. The city has a rich diversity of restaurants: Mexican, Italian, Chinese, to name a few. The Omaha Community Playhouse and the Civic Auditorium bring out the local, and some better known, talent. The city is home to more than sixty movie theaters. A few blocks from campus is the Central Park Mall, with plenty of space for Frisbee throwing and picnicking.

For fun on campus, students will frequent the fraternity parties, which are only reasonably integrated. The school's Kiewit Physical Fitness Center is one of the finest such facilities in the Midwest. Varsity sports, particularly football and basketball, are popular attractions.

Like the state in which it is located, Creighton is a racially homogeneous and politically and socially conservative school. Rare is the campus demonstration, as most students seem content with the status quo. Nearly two-thirds of the campus is Catholic, and more than half are from Nebraska, primarily the immediate area.

Students come here to gain a good education in the Catholic tradition. "Creighton University is a fine institution," says a student. "However, I believe a minority person must give careful thought to the decision to attend Creighton. The school has many programs designed to help the minority student academically, but not as a person who has other needs besides acquiring an education. I recommend Creighton to the individual who has the desire to be a leader and to bring his people together so that they may grow educationally and spiritually."

UNIVERSITY OF NEBRASKA/LINCOLN

Address: 12 Administration Building, Lincoln, NE 68588-0415
Phone: (402) 472-3620 / (800) 742-8800
Director of Admissions: John Beacon
Multicultural Student Recruiter: Traci M. Fields
1992–93 tuition: $1,845 (in-state); $5,021 (out-of-state)
Room and board: $2,915
Application deadline: 8/15
Financial aid application deadline: 3/1
Non-white freshman admissions: Applicants for the class of '95: na
  Median SAT: na
  Median ACT: na
Full-time undergraduate enrollment: 16,830
  Men: 55%
  Women: 45%

Non-white students in
  1987–88: 3.6%
  1988–89: 3.5%
  1989–90: 3.7%
  1990–91: 4.1%
Geographic distribution of students: na
Top majors: 1. Psychology 2. Business Administration 3. Pre-med
Retention rate of non-white students: na
Scholarships exclusively for non-white students: Davis Scholarship: minimum award $1,500 per year; renewable. Larsen Scholarship: ten awarded each year; renewable; each award valued at $4,000. David Scholarship: 15 to 20 awarded each year; each award is valued at up to $4,000; renewable. Gupta Scholarship: two to three awarded each year; covers cost of room and board; renewable.
Remediation programs: None
Academic support services: The university offers tutoring in most subjects, as well as workshops in developing skills in note taking, test taking, and studying. Also offered is intensive academic advising for at-risk students, as well as self-paced and slower-paced courses for these students.
Ethnic studies programs: The university's Institute for Ethnic Studies offers minors in Ethnic Studies, Chicano Studies, American Indian Studies, and Black Studies.
Organizations for non-white students: African People's Union, Zeta Phi Beta, Mexican-American Student Association, Alpha Phi Alpha, Vietnamese Student Association, UNITE (University of Nebraska Inter-Tribal Exchange), Black Poets Society

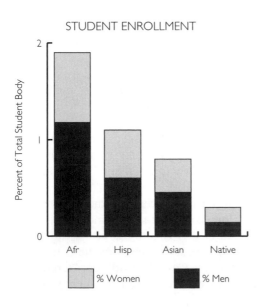

STUDENT ENROLLMENT
Percent of Total Student Body
Afr   Hisp   Asian   Native
% Women   % Men

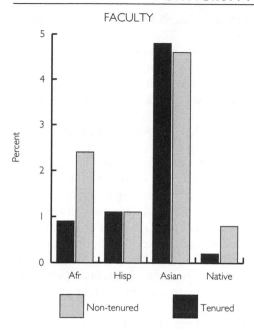

FACULTY

Percent

Afr Hisp Asian Native

Non-tenured Tenured

Notable non-white alumni: Barbara Hendricks (chemistry; opera singer); Dr. Michael Koehler (counselor, educator, and author); Roger Craig (professional football player); Michael Fultz (former professional football player and educator); Ray Shepard (publisher, author, and educational consultant)

Tenured faculty: 1,144
Non-tenured faculty: 370
Student-faculty ratio: 17.5:1
Administrators: 116
  African-American: 1.7%
  Hispanic: 0
  Asian-American: 0
  Native American: 0
Recent non-white speakers on campus: Henry Cisneros (former mayor of San Antonio); Cesar Chavez (labor leader and head of the United Farm Workers); Dr. Na'im Akbar (clinical psychologist); John Singleton (filmmaker); Dr. Jawanza Kunjufu (author and educator)

Nationally, the University of Nebraska at Lincoln is known for its powerhouse football, basketball, and gymnastic teams. Within the state's borders the school is also known for strong programs in agriculture and engineering.

Established in 1869 as the state's land-grant institution, the university has graduated many of the state's agriculture majors. Since then, it has expanded to include seven other divisions: architecture, engineering, arts and sciences, business administration, home economics, journalism, and education. Among the top majors in the College of Arts and Sciences, students point to psychology, English, history, and sociology. "Chicano Literature" is one of the more respected courses offered in the area. Music and art students have access to the impressive facilities of the school's Lied Center for Performing Arts and the Sheldon Memorial Art Gallery. The university's journalism program allows students to study advertising, broadcasting, and news and editorial writing. With nine different program areas, the College of Business Administration offers the school's most popular majors and is selective in admissions.

For academic support, students turn to the office of Multi-Cultural Affairs (MCA). "MCA is a great resource, whether a student is looking for academic assistance or just for someone to talk to," says a math major. "The atmosphere is very relaxed and it's a place where students can just come to visit. MCA provides free tutoring, counseling on financial aid, and use of its facilities, which include a career information library." Students also rely on Lisa Schmidt, an admissions officer, for support. "She has become a great friend," says a psychology major. "She helped me get organized long before school even started. She is extremely helpful and truly a wonderful person."

For other out-of-the-classroom diversions, students are able to turn to a variety of cultural activities and organizations. One of the more popular sites for gathering is the Culture Center, which has meeting rooms, study lounges, a typing room, a television room, and a fully equipped kitchen. "The center is like a home for many of us," says a student.

The Mexican-American Student Association (MASA) has grown in popularity in recent years. "MASA helps to make the transition to college life easier for Mexican students who are used to being around people of their own ethnic background," reports a student member. "MASA is like a big family; it's there for moral support and for students to feel like part of the university." The Chicano Special Events (CSE) coordinates activities "that provide a better understanding of Chicano culture to the entire university population," says a CSE leader. The group's biggest event, Chicano Awareness Week, is usually held during the second week in April, and offers speakers, cultural presentations, art shows, and Mexican dancers. Comments a sophomore CSE organizer: "Chicano Awareness Week tries to bring the university community together with the local community to help them relate and understand each other better, and to create a good atmosphere."

The University of Nebraska Inter-Tribal Exchange (UNITE) is also an active student group. "Through speakers and special events such as the annual powwow held in September, UNITE brings history back to the Native Americans in the surrounding community, as well as educating the rest of the community on the beliefs and customs of the Native American culture," says a UNITE leader. The African People's Union (APU), an African-American student group, sponsors various social activities each year, including a Dating Game, a semiformal dance, and parties.

To increase racial understanding, the university has established a Racial Pluralism Action Team (RPAT), which acts as an advisory committee to the vice-chancellor of student affairs. The committee, made up of 16 members, includes students, faculty, and administrators. RPAT publishes a newsletter listing information about campus activities, meeting times of cultural student organizations, and advice on how to deal with diversity. Recently, RPAT sponsored a retreat to a camp in Milord, Nebraska; about 40 students and five staff members attended to discuss diversity issues on the Nebraska campus.

Weekends are for football and parties at the predominantly white fraternities and sororities. Native Nebraskans live and breathe the sport, especially against archrival Oklahoma. Home football games draw people by the thousands—students, alums, and locals—and road trips to away games are common. Nearly a quarter of the men and women join the Greek organizations, which are the center of much of the campus social life. There is one historically black fraternity, Alpha Phi Alpha, and one historically black sorority, Zeta Phi Beta, on campus; they sponsor dances and community service projects.

Lincoln, like the state itself, is predominantly white. The city has movie theaters, restaurants, and numerous shops. Students don't report feeling any particular discomfort going into town, "except for some stares when I go to the mall with some of my white girlfriends," says a male student. Most of the cultural and social outlets a student might want can be found on campus.

Attending school at Nebraska for the student of color will definitely involve a period of adjustment, particularly as more than 95 percent of the university's student body is white. But students praise the work of various administrators and offices, especially the Office of Multi-Cultural Affairs, for making the adjustment less overwhelming. Says a student: "Nebraska is a good school. The support groups they have are excellent, and all you have to do is look for them and they will help you."

DARTMOUTH COLLEGE

Address: McNutt Hall, Hanover, NH 03755
Phone: (603) 646-3360
Director of Admissions: Karl M. Furstenberg
Multicultural Student Recruiter: Lorna J. Hunter
1991–92 tuition: $23,289 (room and board included)
Application deadline: 1/1
Financial aid application deadline: 2/15
Non-white freshman admissions: Applicants for the class of '95: 1,415
Accepted: 40%
Accepted who enroll: 50%
Applicants accepted who rank in top 10% of high school class: 85%
In top 25%: 99%
Median SAT: na
Median ACT: na
Full-time undergraduate enrollment: 4,275
Men: 55%
Women: 45%
Non-white students in
1987–88: 22.6%
1988–89: 17.5%
1989–90: 18.2%
1990–91: 20%
Geographic distribution of students: na
Students In-state: <1%
Top majors: na
Retention rate of non-white students: 89%
Scholarships exclusively for non-white students: None
Remediation programs: None
Academic support services: Dartmouth's Intensive Academic Support provides assistance in English, math, and science. Also offered is a writing lab and the support services of the Academic Skills Center.
Ethnic studies programs: Dartmouth offers programs in African and African-American Studies, Asian Studies, Latin American Studies, and Native American Studies.
Organizations for non-white students: Native Americans at Dartmouth, Alpha Phi Alpha, Afro-American Society, Kappa Alpha Psi, La Alianza Latina, Alpha

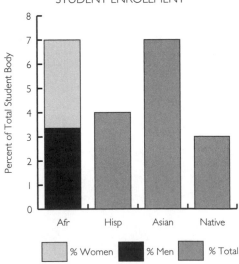

STUDENT ENROLLMENT

Percent of Total Student Body

Afr   Hisp   Asian   Native

% Women   % Men   % Total

Kappa Alpha, Korean Student Union,　**Non-tenured faculty:** na
Delta Sigma Theta, Asian Students Union　**Student-faculty ratio:** 11:1
Notable non-white alumni: na　**Administrators:** na
Tenured faculty: na　**Recent non-white speakers on campus:** na

---

Unlike some of its counterparts in the prestigious Ivy League, Dartmouth College directs its main focus on the undergraduate. Therefore, with all of the resources of a major university available to them, Dartmouth students receive one of the finest educations in America.

Despite its educational opportunities, however, Dartmouth has an image problem that has made recruiting students of color to the college difficult. African-American students who apply under Dartmouth's early decision plan, for example, have decreased in recent years. In large part, the creator of this negative image has been the *Dartmouth Review,* which has received national attention by way of the Phil Donahue show and other media for its offensive and often hostile attitudes toward women, gays, affirmative action, and people of color. One recent article parodied the teaching style of an African-American professor. The publication, which does not receive administration support, puts many of the college's more open-minded students on the defensive when called on to describe the merits of their school.

"Dartmouth College is a place that is incredibly aware of both racial and political issues," says a campus leader. "Our campus is so politically aware largely because of the presence of the *Dartmouth Review,* a right-wing, off-campus, non-college-affiliated newspaper that has found itself at the center of national controversy. Because Dartmouth is so often in the national headlines, our campus is almost politically energized. I want to stress that the *Dartmouth Review* receives almost no support from the student body. It survives because it has the backing of such prominent conservatives as William F. Buckley, Patrick Buchanan, and William Simon." Adds another student: "Precisely because Dartmouth has dealt with many of the problems resulting from diversity in an explosive and public manner, it is very sensitive to political and racial issues. In fact, some students would complain that Dartmouth students are overly sensitized. Additionally, they would complain that the administration wastes all its time trying to make special-interest groups comfortable here and ignores the vast majority of students. Dartmouth's administration and student leadership is often attacked as being politically correct for the reason that both groups champion minority issues and work to bring them to the fore of campus life."

The image of the typical Dartmouth student has traditionally been the beer-drinking, preppy jock who values a good beer as much as a good book. The Greek system, which includes more than half of the student population at Dartmouth, does its fair share to perpetuate that image. The fraternity parties dominate the weekend social scene; beer pong, which involves sinking a Ping-Pong ball into a cup of beer, is a popular fraternity activity. It's no coincidence that the writers of the screenplay for *Animal House* are Dartmouth alums, who loosely based their movie on their undergrad experiences. Multicultural students don't tend to frequent the fraternity parties, however. "There's usually enough going on around campus so that some of us don't feel the need to just stand around and drink," comments a senior.

In addition to being actively Greek, some members of Dartmouth's campus are actively political. "We have protested Dartmouth's investments in South Africa through shanties, rallies, sit-ins, and demonstrations and successfully lobbied the trustees to divest all funds," says a senior. "We have protested the CIA's presence on campus for recruiting purposes as well as the existence of ROTC on our campus. A student group organized on campus to oppose the Gulf War had a membership of over 250 at its height. This fall, over 2,500 students out of 3,300 enrolled went to a Dartmouth United Against Hate rally after the insertion of a quote from Hitler into the masthead of the *Review*. Aside from the rally, a petition disassociating the college from the paper was circulated. This petition received 2,200 signatures."

Dartmouth's academics are top-notch, and some of the school's facilities are among the best you'll find anywhere. The Romance-language departments are highly regarded, as are the departments of government, history, and English. The engineering and computer science programs also enjoy strong reputations. Opportunities for foreign study are plentiful; more than 65 percent of the student body studies off campus at one time or another.

A unique aspect of the college's system is the Dartmouth Plan, more informally referred to as the D-Plan. The D-Plan divides the academic year into four ten-week academic terms, including a summer term. Although first- and fourth-year students are required to remain on campus during the fall, spring, and winter terms, students are otherwise able to plan which terms they'd rather be on campus. Students use their off-campus terms for foreign study or for employment or internship experiences. Dartmouth students, who are on the whole pre-professionally oriented, like the D-Plan for its résumé-building capabilities. A common criticism of the D-Plan, however, is that friendships are often interrupted, and careful planning is in order if relationships of the more romantic sort are to be maintained.

Students praise the school's Native American Studies program, arguably one of the best such programs in the country and certainly the most extensive among the Ivy League universities. "I would have gone to Dartmouth for its Native American studies courses and programs alone," says a student double-majoring in anthropology and Native American Studies. Dartmouth was established, in the 1700s, in part to educate the Native Americans of the region. After much protesting and student complaining, the Dartmouth mascot, a Native American, was recently changed.

Native American students are able to take advantage of the Native American Studies program office, which has a counselor and an assistant. "The office is extremely accessible and friendly," reports a junior. "Colleen Larimore [the program's director], who is part Comanche, is there for us at any time. I've never seen her angry. She's helped to organize weekly discussions for us. The topics cover a wide range of issues, from what I did last summer to what it's like to be a Native American here at Dartmouth." The Native Americans also have the option of living in a theme house, located on the edge of campus. Referred to as the NAD house, it houses up to eight students and has a kitchen and a small library filled mostly with used textbooks. The house has also been used recently for informal gatherings in which students are able to meet professors interviewing for jobs within the Native American Studies program.

Faculty and staff members make themselves available for academic and emotional support. "The minority faculty and administrators are extremely involved in student life, as advisers, resource people, allies and friends," says a student. "They serve as advisers for organizations, attend or participate in many student-sponsored events, and are very supportive of Dartmouth students. Among these, the associate dean of the college, Ngina Lythcott, as well as professors William Cook, Raymond Hall, Deborah King, and Bruce Nelson come immediately to mind as advocates and role models for students who are very involved."

Despite Dartmouth's jock-school image and the inflammatory *Dartmouth Review,* there are those who are making attempts to bridge cultural and racial differences. "This winter, the student government sponsored a speaker series, keynoted by Harvey Gantt [an African-American who unsuccessfully challenged Jesse Helms for the Senate seat in North Carolina], that dealt with issues of diversity, affirmative action, and free speech on college campuses," says a student. "One of my friends, a senior, was initially hesitant to go to the reception the Afro-American Society had after Gantt's speech, as my friend had no idea where the AM [a residence facility focusing on African and African-American cultures] was. I dragged him over, and when the reception ended, he thanked me because he would have graduated without having ever been in the AM, and was grateful for the people he met and the conversations he had."

UNIVERSITY OF NEW HAMPSHIRE

Address: 4 Garrison Avenue, Durham, NH 03824
Phone: (603) 862-1360
Director of Admissions: David Kraus
Multicultural Student Recruiter: na
1993–94 tuition: $3,844 (in-state); $11,467 (out-of-state)
Room and board: $3,914
Application deadline: Early decision: 12/1; regular decision: 2/1
Financial aid application deadline: 2/15
Non-white freshman admissions: Applicants for the class of '96: 369
  Accepted: 79%
  Accepted who enroll: 29%
  Applicants accepted who rank in top 10% of high school class: na
  Median SAT: na
  Median ACT: na
Full-time undergraduate enrollment: 10,704
  Men: 45%
  Women: 55%

Non-white students in
  1988–89: 1.7%
  1989–90: 1.7%

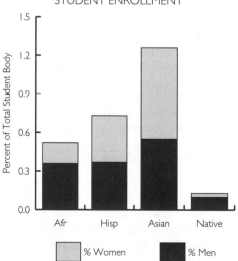

STUDENT ENROLLMENT

% Women   % Men

1990–91: 1.71%
1991–92: 2.2%

Geographic distribution of students: na

Top majors: na

Retention rate of non-white students: na

Scholarships exclusively for non-white students: Andrew Young Scholarships: need-based; value and number of awards vary each year. Sojurner Truth Scholarships: need-based; available to in-state applicants; value and number awarded each year vary. Melbourne Cummings Scholarships: value and number of awards vary each year; available to students outside of New Hampshire and Massachusetts.

Remediation programs: None

Academic support services: The university's Training in Academic Skills Center provides study skills instruction as well as peer support and workshops. The Student Support Services includes tutoring and writing and reading assistance.

Ethnic studies programs: None

Ethnic studies courses: UNH offers five courses in African-American and African Studies. UNH's history department offers "Native Peoples of the Americas." Several courses in Latin American and Asian Studies are offered.

Organizations for non-white students: African-American Student Alliance, Native American/Hispanic Student Association, UNH/New Hampshire African-American Partnership Council, Multicultural Center, Native American Cultural Association, Latin-American Student Association, Chinese Student Friendship Association, Women of Color Support Group

Notable non-white alumni: na

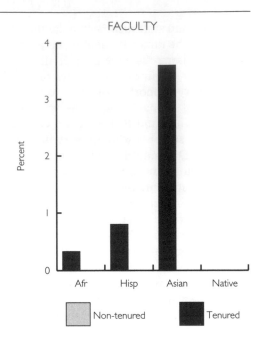

FACULTY

Tenured faculty: 442

Non-tenured faculty: 165

Student-faculty ratio: 17:1

Administrators: 135

African-American: 0.7%

Hispanic: 0

Asian-American: 0.7%

Native American: 0

Recent non-white speakers on campus: Spike Lee (filmmaker); Ishmael Reed (poet); Henry Louis Gates, Jr. (professor, Harvard University); Lemuel Johnson (Center for Afro-American Studies, University of Michigan); Trudier Harris (English professor, University of North Carolina); Paule Marshall (author); Carmen Fields (newscaster); Julianne Malveaux (social researcher and syndicated columnist)

The residents of the state of New Hampshire have more to gloat about than their beautiful views and mountains. They also have a highly respected public university within their borders. This is by no means an easy achievement, particularly as the Northeast is home to a myriad of outstanding public and private institutions of higher learning.

UNH is unusual among public universities in that more than 40 percent of its students are from out of state, from every state in the Union, although mostly from the region. What draws students to Durham? Excellent academic facilities, a midsize student body that makes getting lost in the crowd difficult, and a pastoral college campus make the 127-year old university very appealing.

UNH is organized into five colleges, including the popular Whittemore School of Business and Economics, which offers programs in economics, business administration, and hotel administration. The university's College of Engineering and Physical Sciences recently upgraded its offerings with the construction of impressive new facilities. Located just a short distance from the Atlantic Ocean, UNH also has excellent programs in marine sciences. Students say that most of the school's liberal arts departments are strong, particularly English, history, journalism, and communications.

To graduate, students must now satisfy a diversity course requirement, which has met with some controversy. "While there has been a lot of talk about increasing awareness of diversity on campus, the actions do not reflect the talk," says a student. "The administration put through the requirement without even asking any of the student minority groups what they thought of either the proposal or the classes that were selected as fulfilling the requirement. Personally, I think some of these classes are less than helpful. We've been trying for months to get the academic senate to talk with us about this, but they still have not called us back. The student body has had a mixed response to all of this. Many students truly support broadening their horizons and affirmative action. Others are indifferent or resistant to some changes."

Recently, the university established an Office of Multicultural Affairs (OMSA) on campus. One student reports that the office's staff members, particularly the director, Carmen Buford, are "quite helpful and motivated and will go out of their way to assist minority students." Says a student of Buford's efforts on behalf of the students: "Despite limited funds, annoying administrators, and uncaring students, Carmen has put together excellent programming and a major start toward serious support for students of color." Another helpful OMSA staff member is Joan Rodriguez. "Joan has been terrific at getting good coordination and cooperation between the different minority student groups on campus."

For social outlets, students turn to cultural student organizations. The Native American Cultural Association "provides monthly programming of Native American speakers, as well as an annual powwow, usually held in October. We try to provide other support, including information and establishing connections with tribes in New England and communicating with Native American organizations in the area." Paul Tamburro and Dennis Seavey, both grad students at UNH, are especially supportive of the association. "They are the real backbone of support for Native Americans, despite being students themselves."

The African-American Student Alliance "is quite active and provides both social support and activities," says a student. Recent AASA events have included African-American comedy nights as well as guest speakers.

As might be expected of a school in a state that is one of the least racially diverse in the country, UNH has a tiny student of color population. And it's generally, and correctly, assumed that a significant number of the black men enrolled on campus are athletes. In fact, UNH was one of about 100 schools singled out by a study conducted by *The Chronicle of Higher Education* as a university where "at least one of every five full-time black male students in the academic year 1990–91 was an athlete."

Students say that within the majority white population, there is a great deal of political and socioeconomic diversity. "There are the preppies who drive their Saabs, but there are also your deadheads, your granola types, and those who fall in between," says a student. "Many progressive-minded people on campus try to welcome minority students, but often to the point of making them feel singled out," says a student, who nonetheless points to several recent racist incidents on campus, including racial slurs.

Main Street, Durham's commercial strip, located just a ten-minute walk from campus, offers shops, restaurants, and bars. The larger and more culturally diverse town of Portsmouth, on the seacoast, is nearby, and Boston is only an hour's drive away. A university bus service takes students to towns in the area, including Newington, which has a mall. More than a dozen such trips are scheduled each day. Skiing in the nearby White Mountains is a popular activity, as is rock climbing and camping.

The Memorial Union Building, a hot spot of activity on campus, has a movie theater, lounges, bowling alleys, and rooms with video games and pool tables. MUB has hosted several well-known musical performers, such as Inxs, Elvis Costello, and R.E.M. Fraternities and sororities—to which about 20 percent of the students belong—throw many of the weekend parties. The women's varsity field hockey team is one of the school's more popular teams, while football and baseball also draw crowds. The men's and women's nationally ranked lacrosse teams, however, are the school's most successful.

For students of color, much of the school's social life takes place off campus. Says a student: "I would recommend that prospective minority applicants consider living off campus, for two reasons: one, they do not need to worry about being the only minority student in a 400-person dorm, and two, there is a great deal of social life off campus—parties, get-togethers, etc.—while on campus it is virtually nonexistent." First-year students are required to live on campus; upperclass students can take advantage of the off-campus housing options, which are plentiful and not exorbitantly priced.

Despite its lack of cultural and racial diversity, students recommend their school to prospective applicants, but with a reservation. Says a student: "I would gladly recommend this institution to a student of color, but only as long as he or she is well aware that the minority population at UNH *is* small. The professors tend to be top-notch and minority student organizations do a lot with what they have."

NEW JERSEY

DREW UNIVERSITY

Address: College Admissions House,
  Madison, NJ 07940
Phone: (201) 408-DREW
Director of Admissions: Roberto Noya
Multicultural Student Recruiter: Sheila
  Jackson-Tillman
1991–92 tuition: $16,104
Room and board: $4,850
Application deadline: 2/15
Financial aid application deadline: 3/1
Non-white freshman admissions: Applicants
  for the class of '95: 321
  Accepted: 66%
  Accepted who enroll: 24%
  Applicants accepted who rank in top
  10% of high school class: na
  Median SAT: na
  Median ACT: na
Full-time undergraduate enrollment: 1,435
  Men: 43%
  Women: 57%
Non-white students in
  1987–88: 9%
  1988–89: 11%
  1989–90: 11%
  1990–91: 10.1%
Students In-state: 70%
Top majors: 1. Political Science
  2. Psychology 3. Sociology
Retention rate of non-white students: 77%
**Scholarships exclusively for non-white
  students:** Thomas H. Kean Scholarship:
  merit-based; $1,000 to $10,000 awarded
  per year.

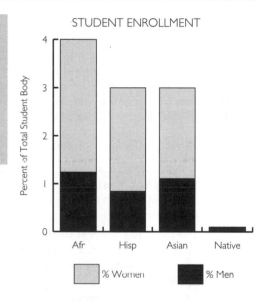

STUDENT ENROLLMENT

Percent of Total Student Body

Afr   Hisp   Asian   Native

% Women   % Men

GEOGRAPHIC DISTRIBUTION OF STUDENTS

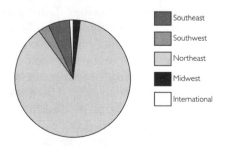

Southeast
Southwest
Northeast
Midwest
International

Remediation programs: None
Academic support services: Drew offers
  tutoring services in most academic

subjects, a writing center, and academic support groups conducted by counseling and psychological services campus.

Ethnic studies programs: None

Ethnic studies courses: na

Organizations for non-white students: Black Student Union, Hispanic Student Union, Ujamaa (theme house), La Casa de España, Asian Student Union

Notable non-white alumni: na

Tenured faculty: 69

Non-tenured faculty: 100

Student-faculty ratio: 12:1

Administrators: 147

   African-American: 10%

   Hispanic: 0.7%

   Asian-American: 2.7%

   Native American: 0

Recent non-white speakers on campus: Randall Robinson (executive director, Trans-Africa); Tony Brown (host and producer, *Tony Brown's Journal*); Dr. John Herrick-Clarke (historian and lecturer); Dr. Molefi Asante (professor of African-American Studies, Temple University)

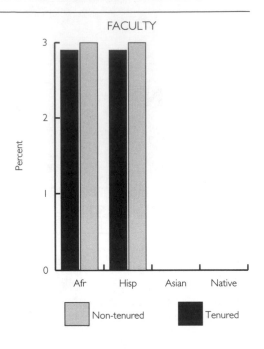

FACULTY

Percent

Non-tenured   Tenured

Drew University may be the only college in the country that can boast of a former governor as president. In 1990, Tom Kean, former governor of New Jersey, assumed the leadership of the 121-year-old university.

Drew also has solid academics. Students say that political science is the school's best and most popular major, and students take advantage of the internship possibilities in nearby New York City. Drama and the natural science departments are said to be strong. The school's Hall of Sciences, which houses its biology, chemistry, mathematics, computer science, and physics departments, offers impressive research facilities. Undergraduates can also take courses in Drew's highly regarded graduate school of theology. During the past ten years, the school's library complex has undergone more than $10 million worth of renovations.

Although the school offers no majors or programs in ethnic studies, the university does have several courses in these areas. "The Hispanic classes are very strong," comments a student. "There are many of them and the professors teaching them are great." Unfortunately, the African-American courses don't fare as well. "To my knowledge, only one class, 'Modern Africa,' was offered in the area last year and it was awful," comments a student.

In 1984, Drew became the first comprehensive liberal arts college in the country to issue a personal computer to every member of its freshman class. (The cost is built into a student's tuition.) It is therefore no surprise that Drew's Academic Computing Center provides worthwhile computer support. Says a student: "Since computers are a vital part of our everyday campus life, it is important that we are offered some type of assistance with them."

Drew's writing center is effective, according to students, as is the school's peer tutoring program, coordinated by the dean of academics office. The most effective sources of academic support, however, are professors. "They always want to make sure you're doing well," says a student. "Classes are usually small, so asking a professor for help after class isn't a big effort."

The Educational Opportunity Scholars (EOS) program, a state-funded program that provides additional academic and non-academic support, is described by more than one student as "wonderful." EOS requires its students to participate in a seven-week summer college prep course on campus. Throughout the year, EOS students also have access to tutoring, study skill training, personal and academic counseling, and financial aid assistance. One student observes that, in part because of the EOS program, first-year housing is not as integrated as it might be. "Most minority students come to this school through the EOS program, and have a chance to meet each other before the semester begins. These students usually room together, leaving out any students of color that come in through regular admissions. Thus, integration within the rooming selection is rare in the first year."

Although there are no fraternities or sororities at Drew, various student groups organize events and activities on campus. "The most active cultural groups on campus are Ariel, which is the Hispanic cultural society, and Hyera, which is the African/African-American/Caribbean group," says a student. "Ariel sponsors a month dedicated to their heritage and culture in November, as well as other events throughout the year. Hyera sponsors many speakers and workshops throughout the year. In addition, Black History Month is filled with events such as fashion shows and the African Emphasis Weekend."

Other activities can be found at the school's athletic center, which has recently been expanded, and at the Other End, a non-alcoholic cafe on campus. The University Center Board sponsors various campus-wide events, including a picnic to greet incoming students. Drew's on-campus radio station, WMNJ-FM, which runs twenty-four hours a day, is popular.

Drew provides its students with alternatives to the more conventional dorm living. Says one student: "The multicultural theme houses on campus, the Ujaama-African Studies House and La Casa de España, serve a very important purpose. In these houses a community is built and concerns and issues are raised and hopefully solved. Through networking, programming, and workshops, the houses communicate their culture and concerns to the rest of the campus."

According to students, there is little, if any interaction between the students and the residents of the mostly affluent town of Madison. "Other than going to the supermarket, CVS, or to the takeout restaurants, students of color remain on campus or go home on weekends," says a student. New York City, forty minutes east of campus, and Newark are easily accessible by public transportation and are popular destinations for students looking for exciting nightlife and cultural activities.

Drew students are confident they are getting a solid liberal arts background, but many concede they would like to see the school become more diverse racially and ethnically. "I would recommend this school to prospective students of color," says a student. "Although there are not many things this school can offer them in terms of learning about their heritage, we do need more students. If the number of students of color was increased, then all of our voices together would effect change."

PRINCETON UNIVERSITY

Address: P.O. Box 430, Princeton, NJ 08544
Phone: (609) 258-3060
Director of Admissions: Fred A. Hargadon
Multicultural Student Recruiter: John M. Templeton
1991–92 tuition: $16,570
Room and board: $5,311
Application deadline: Early decision: 11/1; regular decision 1/2
Financial aid application deadline: 2/1
Non-white freshman admissions: Applicants for the class of '95: 3,636
   Accepted: 16.4%
   Accepted who enroll: 44.8%
   Applicants accepted who rank in top 10% of high school class: na
   Median SAT: na
   Median ACT: na
Full-time undergraduate enrollment: 4,538
   Men: 58%
   Women: 42%

Non-white students in
   1987–88: 21%
   1988–89: 20%
   1989–90: 24%
   1990–91: 24%
Geographic distribution of students: na
Students In-state: 16.6%
Top majors: 1. Woodrow Wilson School 2. Economics 3. Molecular Biology
Retention rate of non-white students: 95.2%
Scholarships exclusively for non-white students: None
Remediation programs: None
Academic support services: First-Year Student Orientation Program, a writing center, tutoring services, departmental study sessions, and residential college review sessions
Ethnic studies programs: East Asian Studies, Afro-American Studies, and Latin American Studies are offered.
Organizations for non-white students: Acción Puertorriqueña y Amigos, Chicano Caucus, Hermanas, NAACP, Onyx, Organization of Black Unity, United Strong, West Indian Students Association, Latino Men's Group, Latino Task Force, Native Americans at Princeton, Taiwanese Students Association, Asian-American Students Association, South Asian Students Association, Vietnamese Students Association, Third World Center, Hawaiian Students Association
Notable non-white alumni: na
Tenured faculty: 455
Non-tenured faculty: 200
Student-faculty ratio: 7:1
Administrators: 705
   African-American: 6%
   Hispanic: 0.5%

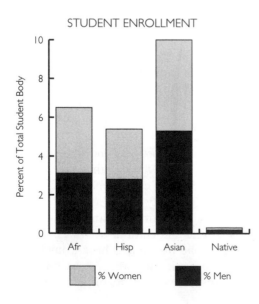

STUDENT ENROLLMENT

Percent of Total Student Body

10
8
6
4
2
0

Afr   Hisp   Asian   Native

☐ % Women   ■ % Men

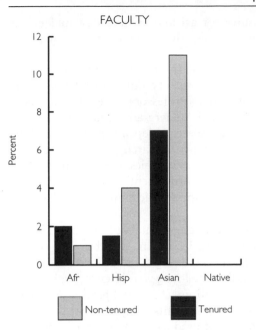

FACULTY

Percent (y-axis: 0, 2, 4, 6, 8, 10, 12)

x-axis: Afr, Hisp, Asian, Native

Non-tenured · Tenured

Asian-American: 2%
Native American: 0

Recent non-white speakers on campus:
Chang-Lin Tien (chancellor, University of California); Mario Garcia (professor, Yale University); Paul Robeson, Jr. (founder and president, Paul Robeson Archives); Paula Giddings (professor, Spelman College); Haki Madhubuti (writer, educator, and publisher); Randall Kennedy (professor, Harvard Law School)

Princeton is the most selective school in the Ivy League. Students apply to this elite university because of its world-class academics, the attention given to the undergraduate, and its outstanding facilities and faculty.

For the class of 1996, Princeton, as opposed to Harvard and Yale, did not have to draw from its wait list of students, according to an article in the *The Daily Princetonian*. Women comprised 45 percent of those admitted, but the number of Asian-American, African-American, and Hispanic students who decided to accept admission to the university—the school's matriculation rate—decreased from the previous year, according to the article. Says Dean of Admission Fred Hargadon about the decrease in enrollment: "We're not in a metropolitan area and we're so small that any minority group is not going to be as large as Harvard's, for example."

Princeton's academic strengths cover the spectrum. Its liberal arts and engineering programs are nationally recognized. The university's programs in architecture are excellent, and for aspiring diplomats its Woodrow Wilson School of Public and International Affairs rivals Georgetown University's public policy program as one of the nation's best. Established in 1969, Princeton's interdisciplinary Afro-American Studies program, which is headed by noted scholar Cornel West and in which Pulitzer Prize-winning novelist Toni Morrison teaches, is nationally recognized, as is the school's East Asian Studies program. The Latin American Studies and sociology programs, however, are considered weaker by students.

Princeton's Firestone Library is one of the largest open-stack libraries in the world, and for special research projects students have access to the papers of Woodrow Wilson (class of 1879), Ernest Hemingway, and F. Scott Fitzgerald, among other prominent figures, as well as to the materials of the Gest Oriental Library. The

Princeton University Art Museum, a resource for art and archaeology students, is nationally recognized for its collections, and has been the site of several major recent exhibitions.

The emphasis at Princeton is on the undergraduate. In the Ivy League, Dartmouth is the only school that is smaller, and Princeton faculty don't spend their time absorbed in research or with graduate students. Professors here, among them numerous world-renowned scholars, actually teach undergrads, and, according to students, do a good job of it. Princeton also emphasizes independent research by its students. To graduate, juniors must write at least two research papers and seniors must complete a thesis. Recent senior research thesis topics have included "An Examination of the Emergence of the Black Power Movement" and "From Agreement to Implementation: Winset, Japanese Domestic Politics, and the U.S.-Japan Security Relationship."

Students say the school's academic support services—including those provided by the Third World Center, established on campus in 1971—are effective. The center, located on Prospect Street near the engineering quadrangle and Princeton's famed eating clubs, provides a computer cluster, a library, lounges, a kitchen, and a large meeting room. Student groups also use the center for meetings and parties. Although Princeton's splendid campus is relatively compact, students complain that the center is "too far of a walk for most students, so it's not used as often as it could be."

The center's director, Michael Rodriguez, also a Princeton alum, is "really helpful" to students. "He's in touch with what students want and need." Paula Chow, an assistant director at the center, is also frequently turned to by students. "She's extremely friendly, and a lot of us know her on a first-name basis. She helps us keep continuity in the Asian-American Students Association, and she helps us organize the Asian-Pacific-American Heritage month," held annually in April.

To establish more of a sense of community among first- and second-year students, underclassmen live in one of five residential colleges, each of which develops its own distinct personality. Each college has about 400 to 500 students. For their first two years students live in the same dorm and eat in the same dining hall. Each residential college has three Minority Affairs Advisers, "who try to make the students' first years more comfortable. When I was a first-year student, I needed my MAA, and I try to be there for the new students. Basically, we try to be students' friends," says a current MAA. As this system can tend to alienate underclassmen from juniors and seniors, the university has established Minority Liaison Advisers, "upperclass students who get to know the younger ones and help them get used to Princeton."

Although Princeton's academics offer a plethora of opportunities, the school's social life is not as diverse, particularly for those who choose not to join one of the school's eating clubs, which are basically social clubs. Nearly half of the students join one of the school's clubs, which have all recently gone coed. Three of them are called bicker clubs, in which students participate in a sort of rush system. The others are not competitive. Students report that most of the eating clubs are reasonably well integrated, although one student says: "I got into the Cottage Club, but I was one of only three women of color in the club, so I felt I had to leave. The eating clubs are also very expensive, and when you don't have much money, staying in one can be difficult. I still go there, and to the other clubs, though. You can do meal exchanges, and I have a friend from a club here to my college to eat, and I'll go to one of the clubs with a friend." Among the Asian-American students, Campus, Quadrangle, and Tower are the most popular.

Although fraternities have not been officially recognized by Princeton since 1875, the campus does have a Latino-oriented fraternity, Lambda Psi Lambda, which in a recent year had five members. The fraternity also has chapters at the University of Pennsylvania, Rutgers, and Yale. Princeton also has chapters of Kappa Alpha Psi, Alpha Phi Alpha, Delta Sigma Theta, and Alpha Kappa Alpha, all historically black Greek organizations.

Princeton's cultural student clubs are not as active socially or politically as similar organizations are at the other Ivies. The school's most active cultural student group is the Asian-American Students Association, which has about 60 to 70 active members. AASA publishes a monthly newsletter and sponsors biannual banquets and a Little Sibling program for younger students. The AASA executive committee meets weekly, while the general membership meets monthly, usually in Whig Lounge. "Right now we're most active in intramural sports, such as volleyball, softball, and bridge," says a student leader. "We're strong socially and athletically, but not that active politically. We're going to try to get more involved in admissions."

The Chicano Caucus, with about 180 members on its mailing list, sponsors dances with Latino music, as well as twice-monthly study breaks "where we can just chill with friends and eat and have drinks" (of the non-alcoholic variety). At the beginning of each school year, caucus members also sponsor a picnic for incoming first-year students. In 1992, Princeton played host to the East Coast Chicano Student Forum, a consortium of Chicano student groups from Ivy league schools and others. Meetings of the association generally take place during Thanksgiving break.

The Organization of Black Unity is perhaps the school's least active cultural student group. "I really don't know why we aren't more active," says a student. "There are a lot of conservative and moderate blacks who don't think that OBU responds to their concerns, especially considering some of the speakers we've invited to campus, such as Kwame Toure. Also, many of us have independent projects due, which makes getting to meetings difficult. But that doesn't explain why more freshmen and sophomores don't go."

In the past, OBU has sponsored forums. Recent forum topics have included, according to a student, "'Black Love,' about the lack of black romantic relationships at Princeton, and 'Black Conservatism,' where we talked about the Clarence Thomas hearings." Onyx and United Strong are emotional support groups for African-American women and men, respectively.

In an attempt to improve race relations and awareness on campus, university president Shapiro asked provost Ruth Simmons to review the campus environment in these areas. Her 49-page report, released in March 1993, "reflects the widespread sense of uneasiness among minority students who feel pressure from white students to justify their presence on campus," says a *Princetonian* article. To relieve some of this "uneasiness," the report urges Shapiro, among other improvements, to create programs that will heighten race awareness and to construct a student center that will appeal to a diverse crowd. According to the article, Simmons hopes such a center will provide an alternative to the eating clubs, which, she says, are a "particular manifestation of selectivity that excludes" students of color. Shapiro, according to the article, will pledge the necessary funds to implement Simmons' recommendations.

Princeton (pop. 30,000) is a predominantly white, affluent community which offers relatively few diversions for students save a few bars, restaurants, and cinemas, as well as the busy McCarter Theater, a regional performing arts center. Students of color have complained of discrimination in some of the nearby stores on Nassau Street, but meetings with administrators and area merchants have taken place in an attempt to resolve these problems. When heading off campus, students will go to New York City or Philadelphia, which are both about an hour away by train.

Among Ivy League schools, Princeton is the most homogenous. Nearly half of its students are graduates of private high schools. "I have this model of the typical Princeton student. He is upper-class and has a strong Republican view and has a lot of interests, usually of the social sort," says a student. Says another student: "When some of the students here first get to know me and know I'm in the Ivy Club [an exclusive eating club], they think I'm cool and seem to want to get to know me. But when they find out I'm active in OBU and that I'm a Kappa [Alpha Psi], they automatically think I'm a radical black militant."

For the iconoclast, attending Princeton may be a lonely experience. But for students looking to "belong," Princeton provides excellent educational and social opportunities. "I've done more here than I ever would have done had I gone to another school. I've been challenged a great deal, and I've been to all sorts of places over breaks, from Harvard and Duke to Rome." Adds another student: "When I first came here, the homogeneity of the place was alienating. But once I found my niche and got involved in a multicultural student group, I got more confident. Most minority students, especially those who grew up in minority neighborhoods, will have some adjustment problems. But once he or she finds a niche, it gets much better."

RUTGERS UNIVERSITY

Address: P.O. Box 2101, New Brunswick, NJ 08903-2101
Phone: (908) 932-3770
Director of Admissions: Dr. Elizabeth Mitchell
Multicultural Student Recruiter: Barbara McNeil-Wright
1993–94 tuition: $3,417 (in-state); $6,955 (out-of-state)
Room and board: $4,454
Application deadline: 1/15
Financial aid application deadline: 3/1
Non-white freshman admissions: Applicants for the class of '95: 6,056
  Accepted: 55%
  Accepted who enroll: 39%

Applicants accepted who rank in top 10% of high school class: 34%
In top 25%: 69%
Median SAT range: 410–540 V, 490–640 M
Median ACT: na
Full-time undergraduate enrollment: 28,543
  Men: 48%
  Women: 52%
Non-white students in
  1987–88: 24.2%
  1988–89: 25.6%
  1989–90: 26.1%
  1990–91: 27.8%
Geographic distribution of students: na
Students In-state: 92%
Top majors: na

STUDENT ENROLLMENT

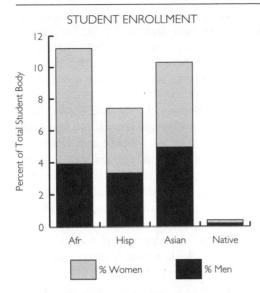

Percent of Total Student Body (y-axis, 0 to 12)

Afr, Hisp, Asian, Native (x-axis)

□ % Women ■ % Men

Retention rate of non-white students: 86.6%
Scholarships exclusively for non-white students: Amelia T. C. Watkins Award: available to African-American applicants and based on merit and community service. Bishop Tutu Award: student must be nominated by the Bishop Tutu Foundation for South African Refugees. Hispanic Scholarship Fund: available based on merit and community service. James A. Bryan Fund: available to African-American applicants from the greater New Brunswick area. James Dickson Carr Award: available to African-American and Hispanic applicants and based on merit. Maria & Louis Caballero Award: merit-based; available to Hispanic engineering majors. National Action Council for Minority Engineers: merit-based; available to engineering majors. N.J. Cable TV Award: merit-based; awarded to qualified African-American applicants. Victoria Caballero Van Allan Award: merit-based; awarded to qualified nursing majors.
Remediation programs: The university offers programs in assisting students to develop basic academic skills.
Academic support services: The university offers a Learning Resource Center, as well as an Academic Resource Center and a writing center.
Ethnic studies programs: na
Ethnic studies courses: na
Organizations for non-white students: na
Notable non-white alumni: Paul Robeson ('19; actor and civil rights activist); Avery Brooks ('73; actor); Herbert Tate, Sr. ('33; diplomat); Yolanda Jones ('53; director of health services, Temple University); Ricardo Kahn ('73; co-founder, Crossroads Theater)
Tenured faculty: 1,552
Non-tenured faculty: 861

FACULTY

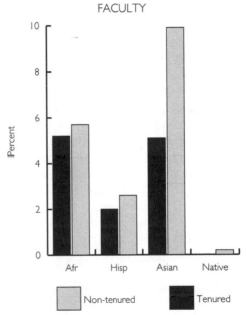

Percent (y-axis, 0 to 10)

Afr, Hisp, Asian, Native (x-axis)

□ Non-tenured ■ Tenured

Student-faculty ratio: 16:1
Administrators: 399
  African-American: 11.8%
  Hispanic: 1.5%
  Asian-American: 1.5%
  Native American: 0
Recent non-white speakers on campus: Spike Lee (filmmaker); Paul Mphela Makgava (South African actor and activist); Marshini Shatazz (director of the African People's Freedom Movement); Sonia Sanchez (poet); Gwendolyn Brooks (Pulitzer Prize-winning poet)

Established in 1766, ten years before Thomas Jefferson drafted the Declaration of Independence, Rutgers University offers one of the best public educations on the East Coast. With fourteen undergraduate divisions spread out over three different cities—New Brunswick, Camden, and Newark—Rutgers offers students a wealth of academic and extracurricular activities.

The heart of the university system lies in New Brunswick, the home of four of Rutgers' undergraduate residential colleges: Rutgers College, the oldest and most prestigious of the schools; Douglass College, exclusively for women; and Cook and Livingston colleges. Except for Cook, a land-grant institution with specialties in the sciences and agriculture, the schools offer strong programs in the arts and sciences. New Brunswick is also home to University College, an undergraduate division for adults that offers evening courses, as well as the relatively young School of Business, the Mason Gross School of the Arts, the College of Pharmacy, and the College of Engineering. Students at any one of the New Brunswick campuses may take courses at any of the others, and a shuttle service takes students to the various campuses. Rutgers also maintains commuter campuses in Newark and Camden.

Rutgers' strengths are many and varied, and include such programs as history, English, political science, women's studies, math, computer science, psychology, and economics. Rutgers' Africana Studies program is held in high esteem by students and offers such popular courses as "The Black Experience in America," "The Black Woman," and the program's introductory course. Cheryl Wall, a scholar in black and minority literature, is one of the program's popular professors.

During the summer of 1992, the university offered one of its first multicultural studies courses, titled "Introduction to American Cultures." "The administration is watching to see if the course is strong and worthwhile enough to make it a requirement for all first-year students," says a student. The course, offered by the Educational Opportunity Fund, includes master lectures by Rutgers faculty members that address such topics as conflict in the cities, immigration, and racial stereotyping. Classes then break down into smaller groups for the remainder of the week to discuss that week's lecture.

Rutgers' academic opportunities are no more varied—and numerous—than its student body. More than 90 percent of its students are from the Garden State, and the student body reflects the diversity—ethnic, racial, socioeconomic, and religious— of the state. "Although most of my friends are from New Jersey, I sometimes feel they're from other parts of the country and the world because they're all so different," says a junior. The university is also huge. More than 30,000 students populate its campuses, and getting in required classes can sometimes be tough. First- and second-year courses are also usually overwhelmingly large, and students say getting to talk to professors in such courses is almost impossible. But upper-level course enrollments are more manageable and some have small seminar-style classes.

Students say that administrative support has increased lately. "Rutgers has changed in the four years since I've been here," says a student. "There are a lot more student services. Actually, I don't know if there are more, but they are all advertised better. All of the students know there is someone to talk to and to get help from—any sort of help, from emotional support to academic support."

High on students' list of such places is the office of the dean of minority affairs, George Ganges. "Although the office works mostly with student groups in their programming, everyone knows that Dean Ganges is a person we can trust and turn to when we need help."

For the student looking to find a niche, there's hardly a shortage of activities. A list of more than 200 organizations, ranging from fraternities and political groups to religious and professional societies, is available at the New Brunswick campuses. Rutgers' cultural student groups are also active.

The Rutgers Asian-American Coalition for Equality (RACE) has become more active than ever. "We're coming of age, politically speaking," says a RACE member. RACE's recent "Call for Action" forum explored such topics as Japan bashing, gender issues, and the Asian-American lesbian and gay community.

RACE is actually an umbrella organization representing 13 smaller Asian and Asian-American groups, including Korean and Chinese student groups, each of which has its own peer mentoring programs and sponsors various activities. "When I first came here four years ago, it used to be that the Koreans hung out with the Koreans, and the Chinese hung out with the Chinese, but that doesn't seem to be the case anymore. All Asian and Asian-American students seem to realize that it's important that we work together to promote a more united front," says a recent graduate. "But, as with other student groups, apathy is ridiculously high among Asian-American students. The racist incidents got us active and more unified." Asian and Asian-American students have complained of blatant racism on campus, including slurs and physical assaults. Their attempt to organize against such discrimination resulted in the formation of RACE.

RACE members publish the impressive *Common Interest,* a newspaper started by a South Asian student in 1991. The sixteen-page paper, issued once every other week, includes articles about Asian-American history, a calendar of events, and articles about RACE and student events that don't make it into *The Targum,* the campus daily newspaper. "We have a widespread readership, and not just among the Asian-American community," says a *Common Interest* contributor. "This past year, with some of the incidents that have happened on campus, we really established ourselves as a legitimate paper."

One of RACE's community service projects didn't take place in New Brunswick, or even in New Jersey, but in the Far East. Group members sponsored six needy Far Eastern children. RACE's faculty adviser, Peter Li, a professor of Asian Studies, is highly respected by students, both for his scholarly work and for his involvement with RACE.

Good news for students is the recently completed $1.1 million Paul Robeson Cultural Center, designed to meet the needs of the school's African-American students. Located next to the Busch Campus Center, the new cultural center provides office space for fourteen student organizations, two conference rooms, a computer room, reading and lounge areas, and a suite for the staff of the center's *Black Voice/Carta Boricua,* a sixteen-page newspaper issued every Wednesday that contains national and local news articles, columns written by national contributors, poetry and special-events sections, and a popularly read "Speak Out" column, to which students submit letters. The paper provides valuable experience for many of the staff members who are journalism majors.

Students and staff members are also working to get a statue of Paul Robeson erected in front of the new center. Robeson was a Rutgers alum and was the nation's first African-American All-American football player and a prominent actor and singer. The Paul Robeson Special Interest Section, located on the third floor of Mettler Hall, provides living facilities for up to 58 male and female students. In order to live in the section, students—from freshmen to seniors—must submit an application to the Residence Hall office. Then upperclass section residents make the final recommendations. While the floor is open to students of all races, in a recent year it had only two Asian students; the rest were African-American. The section sponsors some of its own activities for Black History Month, including speakers, and students say older students act as big brothers and big sisters to the younger students.

The Paul Robeson Club, the school's most active African-American student group, focuses most of its attention on, you guessed it, Paul Robeson Week, held during the week of his birthday, April 9. Events include workshops and a musical performance. The club, which meets every Sunday evening, has about 50 active members. It brings about 30 to 40 high school students to campus for a week to check out the college experience. Students attend classes and workshops about financial aid and the college application process and live in the Paul Robeson Special Interest Section. Wallie Torian, an assistant director in the Equal Opportunity Fund office and the club's adviser, "is known on campus for being there for help of almost any kind," says a student.

Rutgers' black Greek organizations also sponsor a variety of on-campus parties and dances and are active in the New Brunswick community. The fraternities and sororities are organized under the Minority Greek Council.

The Latino Student Council, like RACE, is an umbrella organization, representing 16 different Latino organizations. "We meet once every two weeks, basically to exchange information about community service projects, such as a blood drive," says an LSC leader. One of LSC's more active groups is the Latin American Women's Organization, "the only women's cultural organization at Rutgers," says a student. "The group was founded by two Puerto Rican students in 1969, and we sponsor walkathons for a Hispanic scholarship fund and help out in soup kitchens. One of biggest concerns now is the exploitation of migrant Mexican workers." Kathryn Nieto-Boccher, the group's adviser, works closely with students. "She's always there for us."

Many of the Latino student groups hold meetings in the school's Latino Center for Arts and Culture. "This is our house. It's a really important part of many of our lives," says a student. "We do everything here. We even recently held an art exhibit of prominent Latino artists." The director of the center and the LSC adviser, Isabel Nazario, is well liked by students.

Little interaction takes place between the various cultural groups, with the notable exception of the annual Unity Day picnic, held on the first Saturday of May before final exams. The picnic, held in a nearby park, brings faculty, students, and staff together, for a day of fun, games, and music. The event is sponsored by the Paul Robeson Club, the Latino Student Council, the African Student Congress Programming Board, and other groups. "It takes a lot of planning and collaboration, and the event attracts a more diverse crowd each year," says an organizer. "It used to just attract African-American students. Now more Latino students, but few Asian students attend."

While New Brunswick provides most of the amenities—such as restaurants and movie theaters—an undergraduate could want, students say the university itself is so large and offers so much that "Rutgers is like a city in a city. Students don't go into New Brunswick much, except maybe to shop. But New Brunswick is diverse and it's a wonderful place to live. It's very culturally balanced. There are three theaters downtown, including Crossroads, a famous black theater." The city includes African-American and Hispanic communities. The wonders of New York City are a short train ride away on the New Jersey Transit.

As Rutgers is a large institution, getting lost—metaphorically speaking—is a definite possibility. So, should you decide to attend school here, the best advice students have is to get involved, and stay involved, in campus activities and organizations. "Rutgers isn't without its racial tensions, but it is a very good school. There is support, and the student organizations help out so much, not just socially, but also academically. We look out for each other, by having study sessions and cultural programs. Students here are really here for one another."

SETON HALL UNIVERSITY

Address: 400 South Orange Avenue, South Orange, NJ 07079
Phone: (201) 761-9332 / (800) THE-HALL
Director of Admissions: Patricia L. Burgh
Multicultural Student Recruiter: Pamela Nazareth
1992–93 tuition: $11,552
Room and board: $6,254
Application deadline: 3/1
Financial aid application deadline: 4/15
Non-white freshman admissions: Applicants for the class of '96: 1,488
  Accepted: 57%
  Accepted who enroll: 32%
  Applicants accepted who rank in top 10% of high school class: na
  Median SAT: 456 V, 508 M
  Median ACT: na
Full-time undergraduate enrollment: 4,434
  Men: 50%
  Women: 50%
Non-white students in
  1988–89: 17%
  1989–90: 18.3%
  1990–91: 19.6%
  1991–92: 23%

Geographic distribution of students: na
Students in-state: 80%
Top majors: 1. Communication 2. Business 3. Social Science
Retention rate of non-white students: 88%

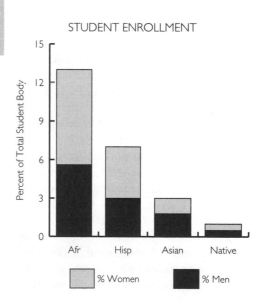

STUDENT ENROLLMENT

Percent of Total Student Body

Afr   Hisp   Asian   Native

% Women   % Men

Scholarships exclusively for non-white students: Martin Luther King, Jr., Scholarship: merit-based; ten awarded each year; covers cost of tuition.

Remediation programs: Developmental courses in math and English are available.

Academic support services: The university offers tutoring in most academic subjects, the Freshman Studies Program, and the Educational Opportunity Program, which includes a seven-week summer program for entering first-year students.

Ethnic studies programs: Major courses of study are offered in African-American and Asian Studies.

Ethnic studies courses: na

Organizations for non-white students: Adelante, Black Student Union, Caribe, Chinese Students Association, Filipino League, MLK Scholars, Lambda Theta Phi, Omega Psi Phi, Lambda Theta Alpha

Notable non-white alumni: Donald Payne ('57; Congressman); Andrew Valmon ('87; Olympic gold medalist, track); Dr. Delores Cross ('63; president, Chicago State University)

Tenured and non-tenured faculty: na
African-American: 6%
Hispanic: 3%
Asian-American: 10%
Native American: 0

Student-faculty ratio: 17:1

Administrators: na
African-American: 10%
Hispanic: 6%
Asian-American: 2%
Native American: 0

Recent non-white speakers on campus: Betty Shabazz (civil rights activist and former wife of Malcolm X); Lucille Clifton (poet)

Until recently, Seton Hall University was known by New Jerseyites as the state's primary Catholic institution. But ever since the Pirates almost clinched the Division I NCAA basketball championship three years ago, the largely commuter school has come to be known by those beyond the Garden State's borders. The university has some strong academic programs and the facilities to make it transcend statewide appeal.

For now, however, the university draws the majority of its students from the area. In fact, about 50 percent of the student body commutes to campus, which can get in the way of planning activities and maintaining school spirit—outside of Pirates sporting events, that is. "The commuting throws a big monkey wrench into our events," says a Black Student Union organizer. "But we've begun to really try to get more commuters involved in BSU activities, especially as the majority of African-American students commute to campus. We've started putting fliers up about our events in the game room in the student center, where a lot of the commuters hang out between classes, and we approach them on a one-on-one basis to tell them about our events. Since we've been doing that we've gotten a lot more students to come to our lectures and other events."

The BSU has also worked in recent years to make the African-American community on campus more cohesive. "During my freshman year, the BSU organized a Love Week, where black students were encouraged to give a brother or sister a hug," says a junior. "Ever since then, the black students have started talking more to each other. It wasn't always like that."

Lest things get too social, however, the Black Student Union, under a new administration, has changed its direction. "In years past, we were always more social, having parties and such to bring the African-American students together. But we've decided we should educate our community here at Seton Hall, so we focus most on inviting guest speakers to campus. We still have a couple of parties, but our thrust is definitely on education and cultural awareness."

One of those speakers invited to campus by the BSU was Leonard Jeffries, the controversial City College of New York professor. "We had invited him to speak because he is a voice in the black community, but the university administration wouldn't allow him to speak on campus because they thought he went against the mission of the university. That decision created an uproar on campus, and students really came together. The Student Government Association, the Chinese organization, and almost all of the groups except for the Young Republicans were in favor of his coming. They thought that if one voice was stifled, then when would the next one be stifled? Jeffries ended up speaking at a small church near campus, but it was touching the way the students came together to protest the administration's decision. We even had a speak-out on the green, which generated some local media attention, where presidents of some of the organizations, including the SGA, spoke out about how their organizations felt about the decision."

The BSU, with about 50 active members, sponsors an annual Kwanzaa celebration, some parties, and as part of Kwanzaa brings children from a nearby Newark orphanage to campus. The BSU also has an informal peer mentoring program and textbook exchange. Several African-American students have recently served on the Student Government Association.

Students say racial tension on campus can sometimes be tense. "There have been several recent racist incidents on campus, such as some graffiti sprayed on a black student's dorm door. The chancellor of Seton Hall spoke out against it, and there was an investigation, but whoever did it was never caught. That's the way it usually is. It seems that incidents happen, but then nothing is really done to stop it in the long run." Controversy was also stirred recently when the BSU wanted an African-American flag flown on campus during Black History Month.

South Orange, New Jersey, a predominantly white middle-class city, doesn't offer much of an alternative to campus life. "There's absolutely no social outlets for minority students in town. City police have also been known to give black male students a hard time. Students looking for fun off campus usually head to Newark or one of the schools in the area, like Upsala, New Jersey Institute of Technology, or Rutgers/Newark. Newark has some spots that are popular, like Club America, Zanzibar, and the Mirage. Newark is cheap and easy to get to. In fact, you can walk there in just a few minutes." The Hall is a short PATH train ride away from New York City.

Communications, computer science, business, chemistry, and education are some of the school's more respected departments, while Asian Studies and religion are also said to be strong. The school's African-American Studies program is respected, according to students, who praise its "African Civilizations" course, taught by Patrick Caulker, an assistant professor of history. As might be expected at a Catholic institution, students are required to take three religion courses for graduation.

Other than the religion courses, students say Seton Hall is not "all that Catholic. Back during the Jeffries controversy, we went around and asked students what the mission of the university was, and no one really seemed to know. The only way you get to feel this is a Catholic school is by seeing the priests in robes walking around campus." Nearly all of the students who attend the Hall are Catholic, but only a small percentage of the faculty are priests.

Seton Hall students and the school's fans tend to be conservative. During the Gulf War, when a Seton Hall basketball player from Italy refused to wear an American flag patch on his uniform, the athlete was heckled and booed into leaving the team. "False patriots do not see things the Constitution's way. They harassed Mr. Lokar on the basketball court and threatened his family relentlessly by telephone," said an editorial in *The New York Times*. "Fearful for his own safety and that of his wife and the unborn child she carries, he quit Seton Hall and announced that he was taking his wife back to Trieste," in Italy.

Seton Hall is more than a basketball powerhouse, but thanks in large part to the sport, the university has gained name recognition. "I'm glad I came here for the academics. There are times when I feel I'm missing out on some social opportunities by not having attended an all-black college, but I definitely feel I'm getting a good education, and I've learned how to get along with all sorts of people, which is why I decided to come to school here."

TRENTON STATE COLLEGE

Address: Hillwood Lakes CN 4700, Trenton, NJ 08650-4700
Phone: (609) 771-2131 / (609) 771-3101
Director of Admissions: John Iacovelli
Multicultural Student Recruiter: David Morales
1992–93 tuition: $2,964 (in-state); $4,566 (out-of-state)
Room and board: $5,027
Application deadline: 3/1
Financial aid application deadline: 3/1
Non-white freshman admissions: Applicants for the class of '95: 500
  Accepted: na
  Applicants accepted who rank in top 10% of high school class: na
  Median SAT: 500 V, 500 M
  Median ACT: na
Full-time undergraduate enrollment: 5,176
  Men: 37%
  Women: 63%
Non-white students in
  1987–88: 10%
  1988–89: 13%
  1989–90: 14%
  1990–91: 15.7%
Students In-state: 90%

Top majors: 1. Elementary Education 2. Biology 3. English
Retention rate of non-white students: 80%
Scholarships exclusively for non-white students: Presidential Scholarships I, II, and III: merit-based.
Remediation programs: The Division of Academic Support offers peer tutoring and the services of the Educational Opportunity Fund.

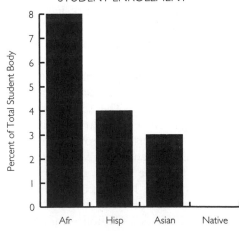

STUDENT ENROLLMENT

Percent of Total Student Body (y-axis: 0–8)

Afr: 8, Hisp: 4, Asian: 3, Native: 0

GEOGRAPHIC DISTRIBUTION OF STUDENTS

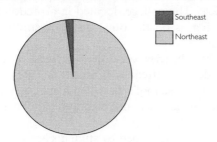

Southeast
Northeast

FACULTY

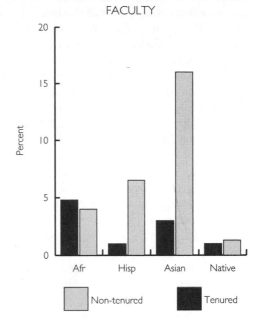

Academic support services: In addition to the services provided by the Office of Academic Advising, the university offers a one-credit course designed to introduce students to the academic resources at TSC.

Ethnic studies programs: TSC offers a minor in African-American Studies. Faculty: 3

Ethnic studies courses: na

Organizations for non-white students: Asian Community of TSC, Black Student Union, Caribbean Student Association Gospel Choir, Langston Hughes Players, African-American History Month Committee, NAACP Minority Student Coalition, *Utimme Umana/La Voz Oculta* (literary magazine), National Association of Black Engineers, Unión Latina, Alpha Phi Alpha, Kappa Alpha Psi, Lambda Theta Phi, Omega Psi Phi, Phi Beta Sigma, Alpha Kappa Alpha, Delta Sigma Theta, Lambda Theta Alpha, Zeta Phi Beta

Notable non-white alumni: William W. Cook ('54, English; poet and professor of English, Rutgers University)

Tenured faculty: 233
Non-tenured faculty: 83
Student-faculty ratio: 15:1
Administrators: 165
  African-American: 22%
  Hispanic: 3%
  Asian-American: 2%
  Native American: <1%
Recent non-white speakers on campus: Kwame Toure (civil rights activist); Toni Morrison (Pulitzer Prize-winning novelist); Ntozake Shange (poet and playwright); Danny Glover (actor)

In a little more than ten years, Trenton State has transformed itself from a teachers college that served primarily the Trenton area to a quality liberal arts college that attracts some of the Garden State's brightest high school students. The 138-year-old school has been hailed by *Money* magazine as one of the country's best college buys.

But TSC's transformation has not gone smoothly, as faculty and administration don't seem to agree on the school's direction. "There's no question that there's bad blood between the president [Harold Eickhoff] and many of the faculty members here," says Joseph Ellis, president of the faculty senate, in an article in *The Chronicle of Higher Education* about the rift.

Part of the conflict is over how well the college is serving its immediate community. The faculty is "concerned that Trenton's high admission standards deny good, but not excellent, students from the local community the chance to attend their region's state college," according to the *Chronicle* article. The college, located in a predominantly white middle-class township called Ewing, is on the outskirts of Trenton, a city with a large African-American population.

While the library isn't on a par with the libraries of other colleges of its caliber—another faculty complaint—the academics often are. Students rate the business and engineering programs as among their school's best departments, and say that nursing is outstanding. Criminal justice, education, and communications are highly regarded.

The school's African-American Studies program is described by students as "small, but excellent." Students say Don Evans and Gloria Dickinson, the program's director, are among the program's best professors. "They take a personal interest in minority students and freely offer career guidance and advice about TSC," says a sophomore.

To get students prepared for the academics at TSC, the college requires incoming students to complete a summer reading assignment, which changes each year. A recent assignment was Maya Angelou's *I Know Why the Caged Bird Sings.* Once on campus, students participate in seminar-style classroom discussions about the readings.

TSC is unique as a public college in that no teaching assistants lead undergraduate courses, thanks in part to the school's relatively small size. (In its drive to better the school's quality of education, the administration cut enrollment significantly. At its height, enrollment exceeded more than 12,000; today it's less than 5,500.) Students say their professors are extremely accessible, even in introductory-level courses.

TSC's Office of Minority Mentoring is an effective academic support network, according to students. David Morales, the program's director, "is always willing to listen to student concerns and he is a hard worker on our behalf," says a law and justice major. The Educational Opportunity Fund (EOF), which has one of the best retention records among New Jersey's state schools, has been on campus for more than twenty years. James Boatwright, EOF's director, is supportive of students, as is Joyce Perkins, EOF's assistant director. Joanna Lee, director of affirmative action at TSC, also works closely with students. "She is truly concerned about the welfare of minority students on campus," says a business administration student. Lee also advises the college president about multicultural issues at TSC.

Students say that Trenton State "is an integrated school, but not an integrated campus." One student adds: "What I mean is that there are minorities as well as whites who attend this school, but there is a definite line drawn to a certain extent. Part of the reason is that there are a lot of black and Latino students who come from urban areas and have never had a lot of contact with anyone but other blacks and Latinos. When they get here, human nature takes over and they tend to stick with the people that are familiar to them. This situation also applies to the school's white students."

Trenton State has long been known as The Suitcase College, a play on its TSC initials. But as the school attracts students from farther away, this image is changing somewhat and students are staying on campus and participating in events sponsored by the college and student organizations. The Rathskeller, also known as the Rat, is a popular hangout that offers beer, music, and theme nights, such as football and jazz parties. Music and theater groups sponsor shows, and the student center has movie nights. Many of the school's students participate in intramural competition, including football, volleyball, and baseball. TSC's varsity football, basketball, and wrestling teams can also brag about some recent successful seasons. The school also sponsors a Multicultural Lecture Series, which brings several noteworthy speakers to campus each year.

Some of the school's cultural student organizations, particularly Unión Latina and the Black Student Union, host social gatherings for members, invite speakers to campus, and conduct workshops. *Utimme Umana/La Voz Occulta,* a popular literary magazine put out by Latino and African-American students, contains short stories, articles, poems, and artwork done by TSC students; it also publishes information each year about Latin Awareness Week and Black History Month activities.

According to one student, the relations with the communities around the campus are "positive. Students usually involve themselves in projects which give back to the surrounding communities, such as big brother/big sister programs." Trenton and its environs, where the majority of the school's students of color are from, offer a variety of off-campus diversions, including shopping malls, clubs, bars, and restaurants. New York City and Philadelphia are each about an hour away from campus and are easily accessible by train.

While many students appreciate the school's improved reputation, which can't help but impress future employers, they also value their school for other, more immediate reasons. "I'd recommend this school to a prospective minority student because, although this place isn't perfect, there are plenty of home bases to which the student is able to turn," says a student. "The minority faculty and staff at TSC are very helpful and always ready and willing to look out for their students."

UNIVERSITY OF NEW MEXICO

Address: Albuquerque, NM 87131
Phone: (505) 277-0111
Director of Admissions: Cynthia Stuart
Multicultural Student Recruiter: na
1991–92 tuition: $1,554 (in-state); $5,520
  (out-of-state)
Room and board: $3,274
Application deadline: 7/24
Financial aid application deadline: 3/1
Non-white freshman admissions: Applicants
  for the class of '95: 1,456
  Accepted: 82.5%
  Accepted who enroll: 51.9%
  Applicants accepted who rank in top
  10% of high school class: na
  Median SAT: na
  Median ACT: na
Full-time undergraduate enrollment: 12,379
  Men: 46.1%
  Women: 53.9%
Non-white students in
  1987–88: 29%
  1988–89: 28%
  1989–90: 28%
  1990–91: 28%
Students In-state: 91.2%
Top majors: 1. University Studies
  2. Electrical Engineering 3. Elementary
  Education
Retention rate of non-white students: 72.1%
Scholarships exclusively for non-white
  students: The university, with outside
  agencies and corporations, sponsors
  several scholarships, including: Zia

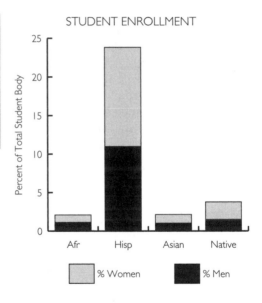

STUDENT ENROLLMENT

Percent of Total Student Body

Afr   Hisp   Asian   Native

☐ % Women   ■ % Men

GEOGRAPHIC DISTRIBUTION OF STUDENTS

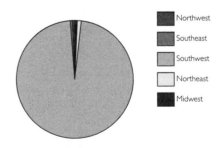

Northwest
Southeast
Southwest
Northeast
Midwest

Scholarship: merit-based; $200–$1,000;
non-renewable. Zia Transfer Scholarship:
merit-based; $1,000 each year; renewable;

must have a GPA of at least 3.25 with 30 hours from transferring college.

Remediation programs: The university offers skills courses in English, reading, math, and natural sciences.

Academic support services: The Center for Academic Programs provides tutoring in all course subjects.

Ethnic studies programs: Interdisciplinary majors are offered in African-American, Native American, and Chicano Studies.

Organizations for non-white students: Black Student Union, Chinese Student Association, Korean Student Association, MECHA, Mexican Student Association, Minority Student Coalition, Southwest Indian Student Coalition, United Mexican-American Students, Alpha Phi Alpha

Notable non-white alumni: na

Tenured faculty: na

Non-tenured faculty: na

Student-faculty ratio: 16:1

Administrators: na

Recent non-white speakers on campus: Carlos Fuentes (author and diplomat); Maya Angelou (author and poet); Paula Gunn Allen (author)

The University of New Mexico is unlike any school in the Northeast, or anywhere else in the country, for that matter. You are surrounded by Spanish- and Pueblo-inspired architecture, the sky—and there's a lot of it, as there are no buildings on campus taller than four stories—is seemingly always blue, and from almost any vantage point on campus you have dramatic views of mountains.

There's also a hushed quality to the campus, even at midday, that strikes the visitor at once as odd—where's the music?—and refreshing. The campus, in short, is beautiful and laid-back.

The campus's relaxed atmosphere, however, also reflects many students' approach to their studies. Typically, only 13 percent of the student body graduates in under five years, as opposed to the 60 or 70 percent of most other schools. This is no doubt due to the school's large part-time population and to its minimal admissions standards.

The campus wasn't so quiet during the summer of 1992, however, after the administration announced plans to consolidate the school's three cultural student support centers, one each for African-American, Native American, and Hispanic students. Under the proposed plan, the new Multicultural Center was to provide assistance to financially needy students of any race and ethnicity as well. "We were shocked and outraged," says a student. "The university says the centers haven't been doing their jobs well enough, and they also cite budgetary concerns. But the administration also didn't think that the various cultural groups would come together as we did. We've made the local papers because of our reaction. And because each of the directors is a woman, we encouraged the school's women's groups to join in our demonstration." Because of the demonstrations against the decision staged by students and numerous members of the faculty, university president Richard Peck rescinded the decision, and the three centers remain separate.

On a more subdued note, the school's cultural student organizations are only somewhat active in supplying the school with diverse programming. The most active cultural club, the Kiva Club, a Native American student group, performs community service by visiting inmates at an area correctional facility every Wednesday. Kiva's biggest activity is its Nizhoni Week, in April, that presents speakers, singers, poets, and films. The week is followed by a powwow. "In the past we've gotten about 500 to 700 spectators and participants to come," says a student organizer, "and we usually had the event in a relatively small ballroom on campus. But this year [1992] we generated a lot of publicity and had a huge turnout. It was held at Johnson Gym on campus, which is a four-court basketball arena. We're going to have it there in years to come because it was so successful." Kiva's powwow is followed by another powwow that is not sponsored by Kiva or the university but is billed as the world's largest such event and is held annually at the Pit, the university's sports arena.

The Black Student Union "hasn't done much lately," according to a member. "There was internal disagreement about the agenda and direction of the organization, so there's been less activity this year than in years past." Every two years, the group sponsors a fashion show. The predominantly black fraternities are a bit more active and host their share of dances. "But when there's a problem, as with the service centers, the African-American students will come together."

When it comes to academics, most UNM students will gain a respectable education. Programs offered as part of the Anderson School of Management are popular, as are anthropology, history, and art, among the school's arts and science programs. UNM's programs in Latin American Studies, environmental studies, and photography are highly regarded, and courses such as "Black Politics," "African History," and "The Civil Rights Movement" are described by students as excellent. Students say that faculty support is there for the asking, but the Office of Minority Retention and Support, which is designed to provide academic assistance to students, is considered weak. The National Society of Black Engineers and the American Indian Science and Engineering Society provide peer support for members.

Albuquerque has a wealth of restaurants, and the city is the setting for many cultural activities. Backpacking, skiing, fishing, swimming, and hang gliding are also popular off-campus activities.

But the controversy surrounding the multicultural centers is still foremost in many students' minds. "With the administration's announcement that it intends to close the centers, UNM's multicultural student groups are more involved with each other than we've ever been," says a student.

Another student praises her school: "I came here from California because I wanted to learn to appreciate a different environment and meet different kinds of people. I've found a lot of what I was looking for when I decided to come to UNM. It's a beautiful place with a lot of nice people."

NEW MEXICO INSTITUTE OF MINING AND TECHNOLOGY

Address: Campus Station, Socorro, NM 87801
Phone: (505) 835-5333 / (800) 428-TECH
Director of Admissions: Louise E. Chamberlin
Multicultural Student Recruiter: na
1993–94 tuition, room and board, and fees: $9,532 (in-state); $13,994 (out-of-state)
Application deadline: 8/11
Financial aid application deadline: 3/1
Non-white freshman admissions: Applicants for the class of '95: na
  Applicants accepted who rank in top 10% of high school class: na
  Median SAT: na
  Median ACT: na
Full-time undergraduate enrollment: 1,311
  Men: 61%
  Women: 39%

Top major: Computer Science
Retention rate of non-white students: 70%
Scholarships exclusively for non-white students: None
Remediation programs: Development courses are available in English and math.
Academic support services: Tutoring is available in all academic subjects.
Ethnic studies programs: None
Ethnic studies courses: None
Organizations for non-white students: Society for Hispanic Professional Engineers, American Indian Science and Engineering Society, Black Awareness Association
Notable non-white alumni: na
Tenured faculty: 101
Non-tenured faculty: na

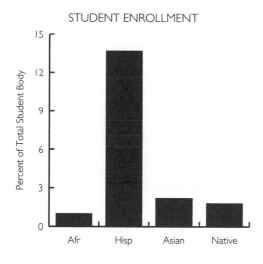

STUDENT ENROLLMENT

Non-white students in
  1987–88: 13.4%
  1988–89: 18.3%
  1989–90: 18.1%
  1990–91: 18.2%
Geographic distribution of students: na
Students In-state: 60%

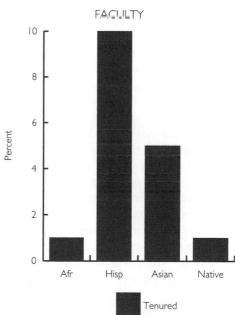

FACULTY

Student-faculty ratio: 13:1
Administrators: na
Recent non-white speakers on campus: na

The New Mexico Institute of Mining and Technology is characterized by its commitment to the sciences and engineering and to the education of undergraduates. With fewer than 1,350 students and small class sizes, New Mexico Tech offers a top-quality—and rigorous—education in a supportive atmosphere.

New Mexico Tech offers undergraduate degrees in nearly 20 different areas, many of which are nationally recognized, such as geology, petroleum engineering, and mining engineering. Students in these programs are able to participate in numerous field and laboratory work experiences, and many such courses are conducted in Tech's fully equipped underground facility, the Waldo Mine. Tech's programs in geo-science—geology, geophysics, and hydrology—are excellent, and state-of-the-art research equipment is available to students to use in their studies. Tech's computer science program, one of the first in the country, offers impressive facilities that are open twenty-four hours a day. The school's biology and chemistry majors enjoy high placement rates in medical schools.

Unlike other technically oriented schools, Tech lets students get hands-on research experience during their first years on campus. More than half of the students have jobs on campus; in fact, 54 percent of the school's students are employed in an academic, laboratory, or research position, including nearly a quarter of the first-year students. The school says that with the amount of experience students obtain in these positions, they will have earned the equivalent of seven months of full-time laboratory experience. In such an environment, it's not surprising, then, that student-to-faculty interaction is close.

You won't find any liberal arts majors walking around campus here. What you will find are students working to complete numerous distribution requirements that ensure they're versed in other than just the most technical aspects of life. Students must take courses in the social sciences, literature, philosophy, and the arts, in addition to courses in the physical sciences and mathematics.

Academics at Tech are intense—only 55 percent of a typical entering class remains to graduate in four years. To assist students with their studies, the school's Academic Support and Assistance Program (ASAP) provides them with student tutoring in all academic subjects and offers workshops each semester on improving study skills.

Additional assistance is available from the school's professional student associations, which provide peer support, as well as social activities for the campus and their members. The Society for Hispanic Professional Engineers (SHPE) is the campus's largest cultural student organization. "We meet regularly to support each other, and we invite in recruiters from big companies," says a materials engineering major. The American Indian Science and Engineering Society (AISES) is also an active and "very influential" student group on campus. According to an engineering science and mining engineering major, AISES "takes incoming freshmen under its wings and advises them on matters such as which classes to take and how to study for finals." The group also sponsors an annual leadership forum.

For a recent Black History Month, Tech's Black Awareness Association (BAA) invited to campus Shiame Okumar, a professor of African-American Studies at the University of New Mexico. BAA also organized an art exhibit titled "Black Women: Achievements Against All Odds."

Tech students come from all 50 states and 42 foreign countries, mostly various Arabic and South American countries. Thirteen percent of Tech's students are international. According to one student, "there is a lot of interaction between the different cultures on campus. Students here tend to be friends because they're in the same class together or because they're from the same area of the country. But the parties can be a different story. I go to parties that are sometimes all white or all minority and sometimes mixed racially." Another student adds that the residence halls are reasonably integrated. "Most students choose to live with friends here, regardless of ethnicity or cultural background." Tech offers various housing options, including single-sex and coed dorms. Baca, a coed residence hall, offers 24-hour quiet. About 40 percent of all students live on campus.

Socorro, with a population of about 9,200 that includes sizable Hispanic and Native American communities, will never be mistaken for New York City, or even nearby Albuquerque. The town does offer activities such as fairs, rodeos, and trade shows, but students report little interaction with community residents. The surrounding countryside has the wide-open spaces one usually associates with the Southwest desert. Albuquerque, seventy-five miles north on Highway 25, provides some additional cultural and social life.

Studies demand a great deal of a student's time at Tech, which is fortunate as there's not a great deal else to do on campus. There are no varsity sports teams, although there are club sports, such as soccer, volleyball, Frisbee, and rugby, that take students to various campuses. The dating scene for men isn't a Tech bright spot; they outnumber the women almost two to one. There is an on-campus eighteen-hole golf course, and the school sponsors an annual musical festival that features jazz bands and vocal ensembles. Tech's physical recreation program helps students take advantage of the area's temperate climate by offering courses such as mountain biking and rock climbing. The school's sports facilities also are well used.

With its provision of early research opportunities in a close-knit academic community, New Mexico Tech is a viable alternative to some of the country's more competitive "techie" schools. "I would tell a prospective minority applicant that Tech itself doesn't really do anything to directly address the needs of minority students," says a student. "However, if you're a hard worker, you can get things done by bringing speakers to campus and arranging other events. I would also tell the applicant that Tech provides an excellent education, and employers are extremely impressed with a Tech degree."

ST. JOHN'S COLLEGE

Address: 1160 Camino Cruz, Santa Fe, NM 87501
Phone: (505) 982-3691 / (800) 331-5232
Director of Admissions: Larry Clendenin
Multicultural Student Recruiter: na
1991–92 tuition: $15,400
Room and board: $5,200
Application deadline: 3/1
Financial aid application deadline: 2/15
Non-white freshman admissions: Applicants
    for the class of '95: na
    Applicants accepted who rank in top
    10% of high school class: na
    Median SAT: na
    Median ACT: na
Full-time undergraduate enrollment: 407
    Men: 55%
    Women: 45%

GEOGRAPHIC DISTRIBUTION OF STUDENTS

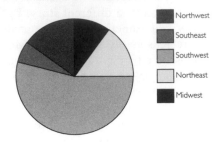

- Northwest
- Southeast
- Southwest
- Northeast
- Midwest

Top majors: na
Retention rate of non-white students: 80%
**Scholarships exclusively for non-white
    students:** None
Remediation programs: None
Academic support services: na
Ethnic studies programs: None
Ethnic studies courses: None
Organizations for non-white students: None
Notable non-white alumni: na
Tenured faculty: 27
Non-tenured faculty: 27

STUDENT ENROLLMENT

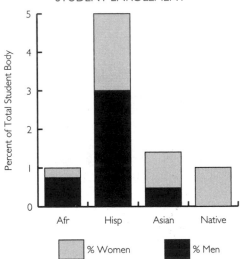

% Women   % Men

Non-white students in
    1987–88: 7%
    1988–89: 8%
    1989–90: 10%
    1990–91: 8.4%
Students In-State: na

FACULTY

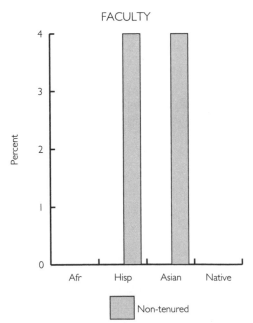

Non-tenured

Student-faculty ratio: 8:1
Administrators: 27
  African-American: 0
  Hispanic: 33%
  Asian-American: 4%
  Native American: 0

Recent non-white speakers on campus:
  Manuel Morales (scholar in residence,
  National Institute of Health); N. Scott
  Momaday (author)

See page 315 for more information.

NEW YORK

ADELPHI UNIVERSITY

Address: South Avenue, Garden City, NY
  11530
Phone: (516) 877-3050
Director of Admissions: Dr. John E. Russel
Multicultural Student Recruiter: Lance
  Gumbs
1991–92 tuition: $8,800
Room and board: $4,920
Application deadline: Rolling admissions
Financial aid application deadline: 5/1
Non-white freshman admissions: Applicants
  for the class of '95: 576
  Accepted: 55.7%
  Accepted who enroll: 53.2%
  Applicants accepted who rank in top
  10% of high school class: 22.2%
  In top 25%: 49.3%
  Median SAT: 450 V, 490 M
  Median ACT: na
Full-time undergraduate enrollment: 3,262
  Men: 36%
  Women: 64%
Non-white students in
  1987–88: na
  1988–89: 16%
  1989–90: 16%
  1990–91: 16%
Geographic distribution of students: na
Students In-state: 85%
Top majors: 1. Business Management
  2. Social Work 3. Nursing
Retention rate of non-white students: na
**Scholarships exclusively for non-white
  students:** None

Remediation programs: None
Academic support services: The Learning
  Center offers workshops in reading,
  critical thinking, research, writing, and
  enhancing study skills.
Ethnic studies programs: Adelphi offers an
  interdisciplinary major in Latin American
  Studies, established in 1970, involving
  anthropology, economics, history,
  political studies, sociology, and Spanish.
  The university also offers an
  interdisciplinary minor in
  African-American Studies, which includes
  more than ten courses in three
  departments.

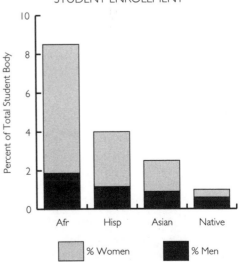

STUDENT ENROLLMENT

Percent of Total Student Body

% Women   % Men

Organizations for non-white students:
African People's Organization, Caribbean Cultural Awareness Club, La Unión Latina, Alpha Kappa Alpha, Delta Sigma Theta, Asian-American Students Association, Alpha Phi Alpha, Kappa Alpha Psi

Notable non-white alumni: Hazel Dukes (Social Sciences; former president, NAACP)

Tenured faculty: 233

Non-tenured faculty: 64

Student-faculty ratio: 13:1

Administrators: 266
African-American: 5%
Hispanic: 3%
Asian-American: 3%
Native American: 1%

Recent non-white speakers on campus: Tony Brown (host and producer, *Tony Brown's Journal*); Spike Lee (filmmaker); Arthur Mitchell (artistic director, Dance Theatre of Harlem); Heberto Padilla (Cuban dissident writer)

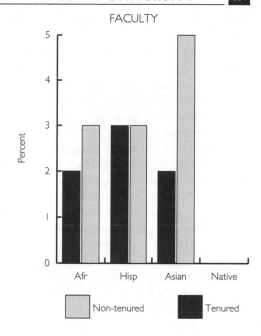

FACULTY

Adelphi was established in 1896 as Long Island's first liberal arts institution of higher education, and after emphasizing pre-professional studies for much of that time, the university is now returning to basics. Beginning with the class of '94, all first-year students must satisfy a core curriculum that includes a composition and a senior seminar course, as well as courses in such categories as the origins of the modern condition and modes and versions of knowledge. The National Endowment for the Humanities thinks so highly of the new core curriculum that it awarded a grant to the university.

Despite the new emphasis, the university remains best known for its pre-professional programs in business, nursing, communications, education, and social work. Chemistry and biology are also considered strong. Students say the school's African-American Studies program is top-notch, particularly such popular courses as "Black Drama Workshop" and "Ethnic Dance," which is regularly oversubscribed. Linda Day, Alven Makapela, and Frances Rhymes are three of the program's well-liked professors.

What makes Adelphi unique among many of Long Island's universities is its relatively small size, which not only almost guarantees small class sizes but also allows a sense of camaraderie to develop among students that is sometimes difficult to achieve at larger schools. "I have been to every school on Long Island, and I can say Adelphi has the closest bonds among the students of color on any of the campuses. There's a small enrollment of students here, and a decent number of African-American, Asian-American, Latino, and Native American students. And even though this is a mostly commuter campus, a lot of us do live on campus. There's not one person that we don't know by name. That's one of the most important reasons to come here."

The administration gets less favorable reviews. "The administration does not see things as we do," states a student. "The Office of Minority Affairs is set up as a place for us to go to if we're having difficulty with the administration or a professor. Although the office has a good staff, they're often put into compromising positions because they can't go as far as we students would like. We have some radical and aggressive members of some of our cultural student groups, and we've stood up to events we thought needed standing up to."

One of the events that elicited a great deal of student emotion but little action was the closing, in the spring of '91, of the school's Higher Education Opportunity Program (HEOP), which offered tutoring and financial aid assistance. "The HEOP created a family, a bond for students of color on campus. The office was the headquarters for everything. At the time, there were about a hundred HEOP students at Adelphi, mostly students of color. So you can imagine the disappointment and frustration of students when the office was closed. The HEOP director and his two counselors were also friends of students, so we hated to see them go. But because the director didn't want us to take any action, we didn't stage any rallies or protests."

Students say the school's general studies program is designed to take the place of the HEOP program, although it offers no financial assistance. "The general studies is 98 percent white, and instead of HEOP money, students of color received good scholarships from the administration that allowed them to continue to go to school here. But who knows what's going to happen to scholarship money in the future. Nothing has been said about that." The student adds, however, that despite the loss of the HEOP office, the enrollment figures of African-American and Hispanic students have remained steady.

Students also complain not so much about the university as about the surrounding community of Garden City, a predominantly white affluent suburb just thirty minutes from New York City. "The area is really nothing but houses, big beautiful houses, in which no Jews or blacks live," says a student. "And what makes it seem even more affluent is its proximity to Hempstead, a predominantly black poor community." Students complain that a walk through Garden City to Hempstead, where some clubs and fast-food restaurants are located, will usually elicit a reaction from area police. One student estimates that a black male student walking to Hempstead might be stopped by police at least three times. Hempstead does have a couple of spots worth getting to, however, in particular Roosevelt Field, a major area mall, and Nagasaki, a West Indian club and restaurant popular with African-American students.

But the most popular destination—besides weekend trips home, as most Adelphi students are from Long Island and the five boroughs of New York City—is Manhattan, the cultural mecca of the world. Students often take advantage of day trips into the city to visit restaurants, clubs, and museums. The Long Island Rail Road, which runs along the north side of campus, offers convenient service to the city.

Students also enjoy the activities of some of the school's student organizations. Perhaps Adelphi's most active political group is the African People's Organization (APO), which has African-American, Hispanic, and Native American student members.

APO events include Fall Fest, "a barbecue we have as a way for all student cultural organizations to come together for good food and music. We mostly have it as a way to greet incoming students of color," a student says of the event, which is held annually on the Earle Hall quad. In November, APO sponsors an impressive list of events for Black Solidarity Day, "where all the people of color wear black and we pass out ribbons to other students as a sign of solidarity. We gather at seven a.m. to sing 'Lift Every Voice and Sing.' Then we attend guest lectures and forums, hear videotapes, and watch Professor Rhymes's own dance company perform. The day ends with a candlelight vigil by the dorms."

Other APO events include a Kwanzaa celebration, held at the University Center, and Black History Month festivities, offering three to four guest speakers and events sponsored by each of the school's black Greek organizations. Adelphi's black Greek organizations are also active in the community during the school year; the Delta Sigma Theta sorority recently sponsored programs for an AIDS awareness day, while the Kappa Alpha Psi fraternity has established a $500 scholarship, awarded to an African-American, Hispanic, or Native American male student from an area high school with the highest grade point average. The groups also host their own parties, held at the Harley University Center, primarily for fundraising purposes, and students report that each of the school's black Greek organizations are supportive of one another's events. The organizations have established close bonds with brother and sister organizations at other area schools, especially SUNY/Stony Brook, Hofstra, St. John's, and C. W. Post.

La Unión Latina, better known on campus as LUL, "is definitely a tight group of students," says an LUL leader. "We all do a lot together even during the summers. Our meetings are fun because we have them informally over lunch." LUL's biggest event of the year is its Parents Night, held in April in the University Center ballroom, "where we honor our parents with a semiformal dinner and dance." The evening culminates with a dance extravaganza, choreographed by an Adelphi alum who was active in the group, put on by LUL members.

A second major event of the group is its International Hispanic Celebration, held in November. "Everybody cooks food from their native country, and we have a banquet with music in the University Center ballroom. We invite other minority student groups at Adelphi and other Latino student groups from area schools," says a student. "It's a party of awareness." The group's faculty adviser, Jerome Fischman, an associate professor of history, "is great," adds the student. "He's especially helpful when it comes to recruiting more students for the group."

With about 10 active members, Cause to Achieve Leadership, Independence, Brotherhood, Excellence, and Respect (CALIBER) was established in 1984 by students to promote multicultural awareness. The coed group, which holds meetings throughout the school year, sponsors an annual fashion and talent show, usually in February, and is, according to one student, "primarily social without being like a fraternity or sorority." The student adds that most CALIBER students are members of other student groups, such as APO and LUL. Students also report that there is a great deal of interaction among the school's various cultural student groups. "If APO throws a party, we're there," says an LUL member, "and vice versa."

It's rare that one can pick up a local or national publication and not see an advertisement for Adelphi. One recent ad that appeared in an issue of the highbrow *Atlantic* pictures Madame Curie, the famed chemist, who is not, by the way, an Adelphi alum. Adelphi is obviously looking to enhance its image as a quality university that has strengths not only in pre-professional studies but also in the liberal arts—especially in light of its new core curriculum.

Despite these changes, for many students there is a better reason to attend Adelphi: friendships. "If there's one reason why I tell students to come here, it's because of all the friends he or she will meet. My friends are going to be the biggest reason why I'm going to hate graduating."

BARD COLLEGE

Address: Annandale-on-Hudson, NY 12504
Phone: (914) 758-7472
Director of Admissions: Mary Inga Backlund
Multicultural Student Recruiter: na
1993–94 tuition: $18,674
Room and board: $6,030
Application deadline: 2/15
Financial aid application deadline: 2/15

Non-white freshman admissions: Applicants
for the class of '94: 136
Accepted: 77.6%
Accepted who enroll: 36%
Applicants accepted who rank in top
10% of high school class: na
Median SAT: na
Median ACT: na
Full-time undergraduate enrollment: 1,023
Men: 48%
Women: 52%
Non-white students in
1987–88: na
1988–89: na
1989–90: 15%
1990–91: 13%
Geographic distribution of students: na
Students In-state: 56%
Top majors: 1. Political Studies
2. History/American Studies
3. Drama/Dance
Retention rate of non-white students: 60%
**Scholarships exclusively for non-white
students:** None
Remediation programs: The college offers

the academic support of the Higher Education Opportunity Program.
Academic support services: Peer tutors are available in most academic subjects.
Ethnic studies programs: The college offers a program in multicultural and ethnic studies, established in 1990, and Asian Studies, established in 1989, with two tenured faculty.
Organizations for non-white students: Bard Black Student Organization, Latin American Student Organization, Asian Student Association

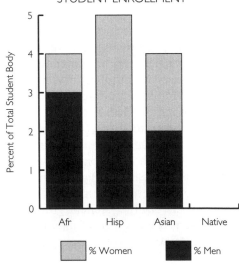

STUDENT ENROLLMENT

Percent of Total Student Body

% Women   % Men

Notable non-white alumni: Jewell Jackson McCabe (president, National Coalition of 100 Black Women); Dr. Jin H. Kinoshita (Biology; Vision Research); Arthur Aviles and Bill T. Jones (Drama/Dance; Arnie Zane Dance Co.); Vine Deloria (former archdeacon of South Dakota and missionary among the Sioux)

Tenured faculty: 87

Non-tenured faculty: 43

Student-faculty ratio: 10:1

Administrators: 27

    African-American: 11%

    Hispanic: 0

    Asian-American: 4%

    Native American: 0

Recent non-white speakers on campus: For the past three years Bard has sponsored a minority studies seminar in which eight speakers are invited to campus to speak on minority-related issues. Recent speakers have included: Dr. James Washington (professor, Union Theological Seminary); Dr. Marilyn Jimnez (chairperson, Africana Studies department, Hobart and William Smith College); Dr. Jose Piedra (professor, Cornell University); Dr. Portia Maultsby (chairperson, department of Afro-American Studies and ethnomusicologist, Indiana University)

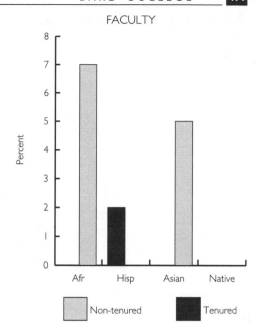

FACULTY

To those who know Bard—a truly liberal liberal arts college—it's not surprising that the school has innovative admissions procedures. First there's the fact that SATs aren't required with your application. Then there's the school's one-day Immediate Decision Plan, in which students submit their application materials in the morning or prior to arriving on campus and, after an interview with an admissions officer, are told whether or not they've been admitted. Finally, for selected students who graduate among the top ten in their public high school classes, Bard expects them to pay only what it would cost to attend a public institution in their home state.

Bard's unique approach to education is reflected in its atypical, cosmopolitan student body. Tie-dyed T-shirts are in, as is dressing in all black. "Bard is known to be liberal and progressive," says a student. "Everyone thinks they're politically correct. And to an extent, people are. Most people are welcoming to students of color."

In addition to attracting a usually left-of-center student body, Bard appeals to students who want the independence a Bard education fosters. There are few distributional requirements to hem students in, and self-designed majors are popular. Among Bard's few course requirements, all first-year students participate in the three-week Workshop on Learning and Thinking, a sort of academic and social orientation to Bard. Sophomores must "moderate," which means students work closely with professors to discuss the student's past and future careers at Bard. The student must submit papers as part of the moderation, and, once the student passes, he or she then goes on to the upper division of the college.

Bard's offerings in the humanities and the arts are outstanding and include the school's most popular courses of study. The school's film studies program is nationally renowned. Students say that math and the sciences, although less popular, are becoming stronger, particularly with the recent addition to the science building. Beginning in the fall of 1992, Bard's first African-American literature course became part of the curriculum. "This year the school has offered many more courses in ethnic studies areas than they have in the past, such as a course in Kenyan politics, African dance, and modern South Africa." In addition, each year Bard hosts a minority studies seminar in which at least eight speakers are brought to campus to discuss various issues. During the 1991–92 school year, the college held a symposium to recognize the work of Chinua Achebe, a noted novelist and a Bard professor.

As at most schools, the academics at Bard are what you make of them, but students say professors do expect a lot of their students. The greatest source of academic support on campus, says a student, is the school's Higher Education Opportunity Program office. "Donna Ford, director of the HEOP office, and Alex McKnight, the assistant, are always there for the students," says a student. "Mary Lemming, HEOP's financial aid counselor, is also someone we can talk to. If it wasn't for the resources of the office, I'm sure many of us wouldn't be here today. The Beehive, as we call it, is part of the HEOP office, and it has a couple of computers, which we use a lot."

Bard does not have an office of multicultural affairs, a point of frustration for many students. "The HEOP office is really about it," says a student. "The Bard Black Student Organization is working on a proposal to get a multicultural affairs director established on campus. Many of the students here, and not just the minority students, definitely feel the need for it."

Myra Young-Armstead, a professor of history, is also regarded as a source of support for students. "She's the only black woman faculty member on campus, and she understands what we're going through, especially since she graduated from predominantly white institutions as well. She's a good resource for BBSO. Her "Broken Vessel" course, about ethnic conflict in urban cities, is popular on campus." Leo Smith, a visiting professor and a prominent jazz musician, is also well liked by students. "Basically, he's rehired by the administration every couple of years or so, and we [the BBSO] are working to get him a permanent position here."

The BBSO, which has about 15 active members, sponsors video showings and annual events during Black History Month and April. According to a student, the majority of the school's African-American students are from New York City.

Despite the activities of the BBSO, students say Bard "is definitely not oriented to students of color. Although the school and groups have been making an effort, the bands and events that are brought here aren't geared to us much." To escape the relative smallness of Bard—and with only about 1,000 students, Bard is indeed small—students will head to Albany, about forty-five minutes north, although New York City, about two hours south, is by far the most popular destination. "Bard is in the boondocks. A lot of us go to New York City at least twice a month. Being able to go to NYC has made going to Bard survivable for students." The town of

Annandale-on-Hudson is small, and aside from some coffee shops, isn't much of a college town.

On-campus activities focus mostly on the arts—poetry readings and theater, musical, and dance performances—and on dorm room parties, "where we like to talk about everything from world and political issues to what we think of a show we just saw." The student center is also host to numerous films, lectures, and dances throughout the year, and Winter Carnival and Spring Fling are two popular campus-wide events.

Individuals—and we mean the real thing here—find Bard an excellent place to attend school. "Bard has outstanding academics, and it's small, so you can get to know your professors well," says a sophomore. "I know this is going to sound corny, but it's also a great place to grow as an individual. You really have to depend on yourself to succeed and to be happy here."

BARNARD COLLEGE OF COLUMBIA UNIVERSITY

Women's college
Address: 3009 Broadway, 111 Milbank Hall, New York, NY 10027-6598
Phone: (212) 854-2014
Director of Admissions: Doris Davis
Multicultural Student Recruiter: Karen N. Jean-Louis
1993–94 tuition: $17,756
Room and board: $7,736
Application deadline: 1/15
Financial aid application deadline: 1/15
Non-white freshman admissions: Applicants for the class of '97: 1,158
Accepted: 48%
Accepted who enroll: 42%
Applicants accepted who rank in top 10% of high school class: na
Median SAT: na
Median ACT: na
Full-time undergraduate enrollment: 2,200
Non-white students in
1988–89: na
1989–90: na
1990–91: 33%
1991–92: 38%
Geographic distribution of students: na
Top majors: na
Retention rate of non-white students: na
Scholarships exclusively for non-white students: None

Remediation programs: None
Academic support services: The services of the Higher Education Opportunity Program and the National Opportunity Program are offered. Tutoring is also available.
Ethnic studies programs: The college offers East Asian Studies, foreign studies programs, and Pan-African Studies.
Ethnic studies courses: Such courses are available in English, political science, sociology, anthropology, and Spanish.

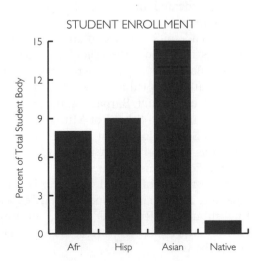

STUDENT ENROLLMENT
Percent of Total Student Body
Afr   Hisp   Asian   Native

Organizations for non-white students:
Barnard Organization of Black Women, Acción Boricua, Alianza Latina, Asian Student Union, Black Students Organization, National Society of Black Engineers, Black Theatre and Performing Arts Ensemble, Caribbean Students Association, Chicano Caucus, Club Zamana, Unidad Hispana

Notable non-white alumnae: Zora Neale Hurston ('27; author); Ntozake Shange ('70; poet and playwright); Jackie Fleming (psychology professor, Barnard College); Thulani Davis (author)

Tenured faculty: 65

Non-tenured faculty: 90

Student-faculty ratio: 10:1

Administrators: na

Recent non-white speakers on campus:
Julian Bond (former Georgia state senator and civil rights activist); Maya Angelou (author and poet); Gwendolyn Brooks (Pulitzer Prize-winning poet); Madeleine Gardiner (novelist and critic); Alexis Massol (engineer and environmentalist); Faye Wattleton (former president, Planned Parenthood)

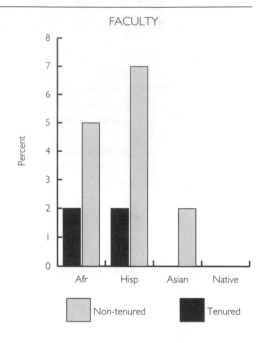

FACULTY

(Bar chart showing Percent on the y-axis from 0 to 8, with categories Afr, Hisp, Asian, Native. Non-tenured: Afr 5, Hisp 7, Asian 2, Native 0. Tenured: Afr 2, Hisp 2, Asian 0, Native 0.)

Non-tenured   Tenured

Barnard graduates always seem to be doing interesting things. Either they're off to law or medical school, choreographing new dances, pursuing Ph.D.s, or doing field research in places like Asia or Africa. It's no wonder. As undergraduates, the women of Barnard have the opportunity to study at one of the country's premier liberal arts colleges, located in one of the most exciting and diverse cities in the Western Hemisphere.

The academics at Barnard are top-notch, and students take their studies seriously. Students rave about the school's English, political science, and art history departments. Barnard's science departments are also well regarded, and students are consistently accepted at some of the country's leading medical schools. Psychology is said to be difficult. Barnard students interested in music are able to enroll in courses at the Manhattan School of Music, just two blocks north, and at the world-famous Juilliard School, located at Lincoln Center—a short subway ride away. Dual-degree programs with Columbia University, across the street, are offered in law, engineering, and public administration.

"Explorations of Black Literature" is popular and rigorous. The course's professor, Quandra Prettyman is respected and "expects a great deal of her students," says an English major. Robert O'Meally, an English professor and teacher of various African-American literature courses, "is into the material he teaches and he wants you to be too."

Barnard is part of Columbia, which means students are able to take advantage of the resources of one of the country's major universities. Barnard women use Columbia's libraries, dormitories, dining halls, and gym. Although there is a great deal of interaction between the two schools, Barnard women maintain their own identity and are content not to be coeds at the much larger and, according to some, less personal Columbia. There also seems to be a bit of competition between the two campuses. "A lot of us don't like going over to Columbia," says an English major. "Columbia may only be across the street, but it might as well be across town. Columbia is a less friendly place than Barnard. Students over there actually seem to growl at you if you ask them the simplest question." A recent Barnard graduate believes the differences between Barnard women and Columbia women can be summed up easily: "CC women are much preppier than the women at Barnard."

Barnard has always attracted students who are politically left of center. Although there is a small pro-life contingent, for example, the campus is predominantly pro-choice, and most students would identify themselves as feminists. Observes a student: "If you have problems with feminist issues, then you won't like it here." Barnard has also always appealed to a cosmopolitan, sophisticated student, one who is aware of global and national issues, which are often discussed over dinner or in dorm rooms. Students come to the northern part of Manhattan for their education from all fifty states and more than fifty foreign countries.

A favorite human resource on Barnard's campus is Gloria Gadsen, associate director of the school's Higher Education Opportunity Program and a Barnard graduate. "She treats you as an adult," comments a student. "She never tries to tell you what to do, but she gives you advice on just about everything, from personal relationships to helping you deal with difficult professors." Another resource for Barnard women is Francesca Cuevas, director of HEOP and a Barnard graduate. "She's extremely caring and loving," a student says. "She's a hug therapist. No matter what she's doing she's there to offer advice, whether it's about your boyfriend, parents, or classes." Cuevas has also compiled a directory of African-American alums who are interested in mentoring students, which students find useful.

The Barnard Organization of Black Women (BOBW) has about 15 to 20 members and meets regularly in the Zora Neale Hurston Room in Reed Hall. The room has a small library, "couches with Kinta cloth, and a large Keith Haring poster depicting the oppression that exists in South Africa," reports a student. The Asian Student Union, the Chicano Caucus, and the Alianza Latinoamericana also sponsor cultural events.

School spirit, in the sense of football rallies and cheerleading squads, has never been part of the social scene at Barnard. Rather than staying close to campus on weekend nights, students head for the nightlife of New York City for their entertainment and cultural activities. The Metropolitan Museum of Art, Lincoln Center, and Central Park are all just a subway ride away, as are a myriad of clubs, bars, and theaters. Barnard is located on the edge of Harlem, a culturally rich section of Manhattan that contains the Schomburg Center for Research in Black Culture, the Apollo Theatre, and a plethora of restaurants.

While the area around the college is rich in things to do, there's certainly no shortage of on-campus activities. There are more than 70 student groups, ranging from cultural and political organizations to theater and musical clubs. The McIntosh Center is the hub of a great deal of student life, and offers a snack bar, lounges, music practice rooms, a pottery studio, bowling alleys, and a mail room. Barnard women participate in Division I athletic competition in basketball, cross-country, soccer, and numerous other sports. Barnard athletic facilities include a swimming pool, a running track, and a gym, and students are able to make use of the impressive Dodge Fitness Center at Columbia. Riverside Park, just a block west of campus, has tennis courts and jogging areas available to students.

Barnard women are happy with their choice of school. They can have the small-college experience while living in New York City. The student looking for a strong community of women will certainly find it here. "Come here if you're strong-willed and strong-minded," says a student. "This place will make you challenge your basic views of life."

CITY UNIVERSITY OF NEW YORK/ BROOKLYN COLLEGE

Address: Bedford Avenue and Avenue H, Brooklyn, NY 11210
Phone: (718) 780-5485
Director of Admissions: Glenn N. Sklarin
Multicultural Student Recruiter: na
1991–92 tuition: $1,850 (in-state)
Room and board: na
Application deadline: Rolling admissions
Financial aid application deadline: 5/1
Non-white freshman admissions: Applicants for the class of '95: na
Applicants accepted who rank in top 10% of high school class: na
Median SAT: na
Median ACT: na
Full-time undergraduate enrollment: 12,000
Men: 43%
Women: 57%
Non-white students in 1987–91: na
Geographic distribution of students: na
Top majors: na
Retention rate of non-white students: na
Scholarships exclusively for non-white students: None
Remediation programs: Development courses in English and math are available, as well as courses in English as a second language.
Academic support services: Brooklyn College's Tutorial Center, Reading Lab, and Writing Center provide academic support services.
Ethnic studies programs: The university offers a major and minor in Africana and Puerto Rican Studies. As part of an area studies program, the university offers concentrations in East Asian, Middle Eastern and North African, Latin American, and Sub-Saharan African Studies.
Organizations for non-white students: Phi Beta Sigma, Black Student Union,

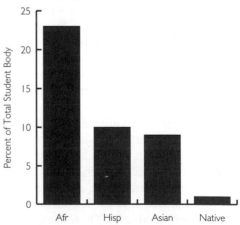

STUDENT ENROLLMENT

Percent of Total Student Body

Chinese Language/Culture Club, Hispanic Society, National Association of Black Accountants, National Black Science Student Organization, Korean Culture Club, Asian Students Alliance, Latin Women's Group

Notable non-white alumni: Jimmy Smits (Theater; actor); Barbara Greaves (Education; general manager, Earl Greaves, Ltd.); Isaura Santiago (Education; president, Hostos Community College); Benjamin Ward (Sociology; former NYC police commissioner).

Tenured faculty: 583

Non-tenured faculty: 73

Student-faculty ratio: 16:1

Administrators: 165

    African-American: 15%

    Hispanic: 2%

    Asian-American: 2%

    Native American: 0

Recent non-white speakers on campus:

    Pyong Gap Min (assistant professor of sociology, Queens College); Dr. Rosemay Latortue (physician, University Community Hospital); Madeleine Gardiner (novelist and critic); Sheng-Yen (Buddhist master)

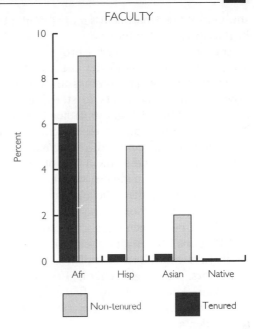

FACULTY

Brooklyn College, located at the end of the IRT subway line in Brooklyn, is not your typical city college. First there's the campus, which features grassy knolls and red brick buildings similar to those at any New England liberal arts college. Then there's the high-powered faculty, which includes a host of nationally and internationally recognized professors. And finally there are the school's often stellar academic programs.

The jewel of Brooklyn College's academic program is its core curriculum, which ensures that students are exposed to the liberal arts. For the core, students must complete courses in ten different topic areas, including music and art; people, power, and politics; the shaping of the modern world; landmarks of literature; philosophy; science; and math. Students must also take a course in African, Asian, or Latin American Studies. "Knowing about politics, art, and science gives you a competitive edge. I have friends who graduated from other colleges, started work, and found that they had to read up on history, diverse cultures, or world affairs to become well-rounded professionals," says a recent graduate in praise of the core.

Also noteworthy is the school's Africana Studies program, which more than one student praised as excellent. Students were hard pressed to name the program's best courses, but say courses in African and African-American history and drama are well regarded. Linda Day and Regine Latortue, head of the department, are two of the program's best professors. Students also praise the school's Puerto Rican Studies department, particularly the efforts of Anthony Stevens-Arroyo, an associate professor. One of the department's more popular courses is "Spiritism and African Religions in Puerto Rican Culture."

English, which includes a program of study in creative writing, and theater and art are also top departments at the college. Among the sciences, chemistry, biology, computer science, and physics are highly rated. Students interested in engineering now have the opportunity of studying for two years at Brooklyn College and then for two additional years at either CUNY/City College or Polytechnic Institute of New York. Pre-professional programs in business, especially accounting, are also becoming popular and well respected. The college has impressive rates of graduates getting into law and medical schools, and the school ranks eleventh in the nation in the number of its graduates who have gone on to earn their Ph.D.s.

The quality of the college's faculty is indeed impressive, and its roster includes such impressive scholars and figures as actor F. Murray Abraham (star of the film *Amadeus*), poet Allen Ginsberg, physicist Hans Trefousse, violinist Itzhak Perlman, and Philippa Strum, a political science professor and vice president of the American Civil Liberties Union. Students report a great deal of interaction with their professors. "In high school, I was definitely a number. But here, all of my professors know me by my first name and are a great help. Class sizes are usually small, with fewer than twenty-five people, and one of my English classes had only ten students."

Recent budget cuts—which did away with all of the school's athletic programs—have affected morale on campus. "Tuition is out of control. We pay more but get less. Every time they raise tuition, there are fewer minorities in school here. It also means that it's going to take many of us longer to get through school."

Like the city in which it is located—more specifically, like the borough in which it is located—Brooklyn College is a diverse campus community. Nearly a third of the students are Jewish, while about another third are students of color. The college's diversity, according to students, is both positive and negative. "Our campus is very rich, very diverse culturally and racially," observes a student. "You can walk down campus and hear people speaking Chinese, Creole, German, or Yiddish. The diversity is fantastic. But it is also a disadvantage, as there is no unified Brooklyn College feel or spirit. It's too fragmented, and rarely do the cultures come together." The area in which the college is located—a residential community with some large high schools—is also diverse. "Nearby there are some predominantly black and white neighborhoods. You have to deal with different cultures on and off campus."

For another student, this diversity, even the fragmented student body, is an exercise, he feels, "in dealing with the real world. I didn't want to go to a black college because in my opinion they coddle students too much and make them feel that the world is going to be that nurturing. But the world isn't. Here you learn how to deal with students from diverse backgrounds. This campus reflects society and going here definitely prepares students for what's to come after graduation." Nearly 85 percent of the school's students call Brooklyn home.

While students may feel that there is a lack of interaction between students of various cultures—and Brooklyn's commuter campus environment doesn't help matters much—students point to a recent successful forum sponsored by Hillel, a

Jewish student organization, and the Black Student Union as progress in bridging some of the differences between these two groups. The forum was held in response to recent tragic events that occurred in the not too distant Crown Heights section of Brooklyn involving the area's African-American and Jewish communities. "There was a definite need for the forum, as students from the different groups don't know each other well, if at all," says a BSU leader. "It was an open forum and almost anyone was allowed to speak about what was on their mind. Although no solutions were arrived at, it was good that the dialogue had been started."

The Black Student Union is one of the school's most active cultural organizations. "We try to meet the needs of everyone in the group," says a BSU member. "We deal with both national and local problems. One of our big messages within the group is the importance of voting, so we have a voter registration drive each year. We believe that in order to effect change, students must vote. Too many of us feel that we're not part of the system, so we don't vote. But we're trying to change that attitude. We try to help each other with the day-to-day issues of just going to school: getting textbooks to students who can't afford them and advising each other about what classes and professors to take and not to take." In addition, the BSU, which has an office in James Hall, hosts weekly forums and coordinates a mentor program with Brooklyn College Academy, a predominantly black high school on campus, and events for Kwanzaa and Black Solidarity Day.

But, a BSU member is quick to point out, "the BSU is not all about business." As a way to attract more interest in the group—students say apathy is pervasive on campus—the BSU also sponsors parties and informal gatherings. "People don't always want to talk about issues, or about the state of the economy, or about how blacks have suffered in this country, although that's what the BSU officers would like to address," says a student. Of particular assistance to the BSU is Lenora Peterson, an assistant in the Africana Studies department. "She helps tremendously when it comes to planning BSU events. If there's a speaker we'd like to have, she always knows who to call and just like that we've got the speaker."

The Caribbean Student Union (CSU) sponsors a weeklong series of activities during Caribbean Awareness Week, which offers foods, performers, speakers, and a fashion show. "There's a vast world in the Caribbean," says a CSU member, "and by the end of the week we have gotten to know each other's music, food, cultures, races, and backgrounds. But the thing is, the Caribbean takes in both Spanish- and English-speaking countries, and usually only English-speaking students come to CSU meetings. Most of the Spanish-speaking students go to meetings at Spanish clubs, like the Puerto Rican Alliance," whose activities include Christmas and Thanksgiving parties. The CSU also sponsors its own peer tutoring workshop for members.

For students content to stay close to home while earning a college degree, Brooklyn College provides academic opportunities similar to those of many of the country's more notable liberal arts colleges and universities, along with all the pluses and minuses of the city in which it is located. Says a transfer student from an upstate college: "By coming to school here and taking courses in the Africana and Puerto Rican Studies programs, I truly got to know myself in ways that I couldn't have at the school I first attended. And the college has good facilities and people who want you to succeed. With a Brooklyn College degree, I feel confident that I will be able to face a lot of the challenges after college with confidence and intelligence."

CITY UNIVERSITY OF NEW YORK/CITY COLLEGE

Address: 138th Street and Convent Avenue, New York, NY 10031
Phone: (212) 650-6977
Director of Admissions: Nancy P. Campbell
Multicultural Student Recruiter: na
1992–93 tuition: $2,450 (in-state); $5,050 (out-of-state)
Room and board: na
Application deadline: 1/15
Financial aid application deadline: 1/15
Non-white freshman admissions: Applicants for the class of '95: na
　Median SAT: na
　Median ACT: na
Full-time undergraduate enrollment: 11,448
　Men: 54.6%
　Women: 45.4%

Geographic distribution of students: na
Students In-state: 85%
Top majors: 1. Electrical Engineering
　2. Computer Science
Retention rate of non-white students: na
Scholarships exclusively for non-white students: None
Remediation programs: The college offers numerous remediation programs.
Academic support services: The university provides counseling services through special programs, including research programs, engineering support programs, as well as math, writing, and English-as-a-second-language labs.
Ethnic studies programs: Offered are Puerto Rican Studies, Asian Studies, Afro American Studies, and Latin and Caribbean Studies.

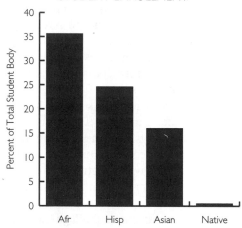

STUDENT ENROLLMENT

Non-white students in
　1987–88: 85.3%
　1988–89: na
　1989–90: 85.9%
　1990–91: 85.5%

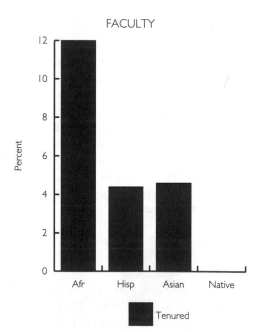

FACULTY

■ Tenured

Organizations for non-white students: na

Notable non-white alumni: Colin Powell (chairman, Joint Chiefs of Staff); A. Philip Randolph (labor leader); Herman Badillo (former Manhattan borough president)

Tenured faculty: na

Non-tenured faculty: na

Student-faculty ratio: 15:1

Administrators: na

African-American: 39%

Hispanic: 26%

Asian-American: 16%

Native American: 4%

Recent non-white speakers on campus: na

For generations, City College has been known as the "workingman's Harvard." The 146-year-old institution of higher learning has graduated more Nobel Prize winners than any other school in the country, and it has impressive numbers of students who go on to earn their Ph.D.s.

Among the seven schools in the CUNY system, City College is best known for its outstanding engineering and science programs. The School of Engineering offers majors in civil, electrical, and mechanical engineering, urban design, and others. The engineering facilities are presently undergoing renovation and should be available for student use in 1994. Architecture is also highly regarded, while computer science is one of the school's more popular departments. City College's rigorous Sophie Davis School of Biomedical Education enables qualified students to earn their bachelor's and medical degrees in seven years; after completing the program, students agree to serve in an underprivileged area of the city. The school's nursing program earns favorable reviews. Among the sciences, students say physics and biology are top-notch, and among the humanities, English, history, political science, and psychology are well respected.

African-American Studies courses "include a lot of class discussion, with many varied points of view," says a student. Courses such as "Malcolm X," "African Dance," "Black Women," and "African-American Literature" generate a great deal of student enthusiasm. The department has such notable instructors as Sister Yarboro, a professor of dance, and Leonard Jeffries, its controversial former chairperson; Jeffries, amidst a great deal of media focus, was removed from the post after he made remarks that were perceived to be anti-Semitic.

City College's core curriculum requires students to take courses in world civilizations, world arts, U.S. society, computer literacy, and a foreign language. Writing is emphasized in each course.

As at other city universities in New York, state budget cuts have significantly affected the quality of life at City College. In addition to tuition hikes, library hours have been reduced, subscriptions to some periodicals have been cut, and numerous academic programs have been merged or moved off campus; for example, the school's technology department, once part of the School of Engineering, moved to New York Technical College in Brooklyn.

Students also complain that the amount and quality of academic advising suffered with the budget cuts, but they add that the college's Office of Academic Advising is "somewhat" effective. "The staff there is overworked," says a student. "The advice I would give an incoming freshman is check the information about your major requirements as listed in the course catalogue. Otherwise, you might miss out on some of your requirements, or even opportunities."

Two organizations that provide academic support and job contacts for members are the Society of Hispanic Professional Engineers (SHPE) and the National Society of Black Engineers (NSBE). "SHPE is one of the most active organizations at City, and has about a hundred members," says a student. "Members attend regional conferences, tutor high school students and each other, and visit area high schools to talk about engineering and City College. And when they want to get something done, they do it. One day, they sponsored a successful résumé drive for a conference where there were going to be employers." NSBE members attend local and national conferences and often present academic support programs; they particularly try to help members develop time-management skills.

A definite plus of attending City College is its racial and cultural diversity. Dozens of foreign languages can be heard in the school's cafeteria at lunchtime, and students come to the college from more than 50 foreign countries. "I like to meet different types of people, which is easy to do at City College," says an engineering student. "On campus, you can meet Greeks, blacks from all over the world, Puerto Ricans, Dominicans, and Chinese. I believe being a part of this diversity has made me a more well-rounded person."

There are several student organizations on campus that promote interaction among the races represented on campus, as well as groups that foster awareness about their respective cultures, such as a Hispanic student group that plans trips, has parties, and sponsors study skills workshops. The City College campus is located in the Harlem section of Manhattan, a predominantly African-American and Hispanic community. Numerous inexpensive restaurants and pizza parlors are nearby, but students don't tend to socialize much off campus; the majority of students congregate in the cafeteria or on the first floor of the North Academic Center building. Various subway stations and bus stops are located on or near campus.

As the City College campus is 100 percent commuter, establishing school spirit is difficult. "The average age of students is twenty-six, and most go to school part-time because they have jobs and families," says a campus leader. "It takes most students more than four years to complete their education. Students are mostly here to get their degrees, and that's it. They don't have time to go to club meetings, to hear guest lectures, or to attend organization parties." A recent exception—and a notable one—was the student takeover of certain academic buildings to protest tuition hikes in 1992; City College students, and in particular members of the group Students for Educational Rights, paved the way for students at other city universities to stage similar protests.

Despite its financial woes, City College remains one of the city's best buys for the education dollar. Its strengths are its diverse student enrollment and numerous top-flight academic programs; students also like the school for its flexible academic schedule, which allows students to pursue their education while also holding down a job. "City College is a rich place, not so much financially as culturally," says a student. "Students study and eat together, no matter what race, culture, or creed. It's been a pleasure to come here to school."

CITY UNIVERSITY OF NEW YORK/ HUNTER COLLEGE

Address: 695 Park Avenue, New York, NY 10021
Phone: (212) 772-4490
Director of Admissions: William Zlata
Multicultural Student Recruiter: na
1991–92 tuition: $1,850 (in-state); $4,450 (out-of-state)
Room and board: $1,600
Application deadline: 1/15
Financial aid application deadline: 5/13
Student-faculty ratio: 18:1
Non-white freshman admissions: Applicants for the class of '95:
Accepted: na
Applicants accepted who rank in top 10% of high school class: na
Median SAT: na
Median ACT: na
Full-time undergraduate enrollment: 14,866
Men: 27%
Women: 73%
Non-white students in 1987–91: na
Geographic distribution of students: na
Top majors: na
Retention rate of non-white students: na
Scholarships exclusively for non-white students: None

Remediation programs: Hunter offers remedial programs in science, math, and English, as well as services of various state and federally funded programs.
Academic support services: The college offers counseling and tutoring programs and an Academic Resource Center, which offers assistance in time management, study skills, and math anxiety.
Ethnic studies programs: Hunter has programs in Black and Puerto Rican Studies, Chinese language and literature, and Latin American and Caribbean Studies.
Organizations for non-white students: na
Notable non-white alumni: na
Tenured faculty: na
Non-tenured faculty: na
Student-faculty ratio: 18:1
Administrators: na
Recent non-white speakers on campus: Jesse Jackson (civil rights activist and former U.S. presidential candidate); Louis Farrakhan (leader, Nation of Islam); Rev. Al Sharpton (civil rights activist)

Established in 1870 as the female coordinate of what was at the time the all-male City College of New York, Hunter is today one of the Big Apple's most highly ranked city colleges. Its programs in liberal arts and nursing attract top-notch faculty as well as bright and motivated students.

English, economics, French, biological sciences, chemistry, and political science are among the school's standout departments. Hunter's education programs are also well regarded. The college also offers pre-professional studies in such areas as engineering, law, medicine, and social work, and the school's Honors Curriculum, which has seen numerous graduates go on to law, medical, and other graduate school programs, offers students individualized courses of study and small-class settings.

Hunter's Black and Puerto Rican Studies program "is very responsive to students' needs, especially in terms of course offerings," says a student. "All of the faculty in the program are outstanding, and very knowledgeable." Popular courses in the program include "African-American Literature," "Caribbean Literature," "African

History," and "Prison Issues," which explores aspects of civil liberties. The college's Latin American and Caribbean Studies program also gets positive reviews.

Hunter offers numerous special programs, including Education for Public Service. Qualified students enroll in intensive seminar classes on campus while also interning at high levels in the government. Students wanting to experience life on a smaller campus are able to enroll in courses, with departmental approval, at Marymount-Manhattan College. Qualified students are also able to participate in the college's Minority Access to Research Careers Program and the Minority Biomedical Research Support Program, which encourages students, with stipends and other incentives, to pursue careers in the health and medical fields. Music majors can take courses at the Mannes College of Music, located in Manhattan.

Like other city colleges, Hunter has been forced to do its share of financial belt tightening. The budget cuts have not only hiked tuition costs significantly; they have also led to increased class sizes and fewer course offerings. The academic tutoring service is no longer offered to all students but only to those with demonstrated financial need. In addition, one of the school's buildings, Roosevelt House, which had space for student organizations and lectures, was forced to close. One student feels the budget cuts have had a serious impact. "The retention of students isn't as good as it used to be, and the character of the school is changing. It's no longer going to be a school that's diverse economically, racially, and in terms of perspectives."

Various student groups, including the student government association and the Black Student Union, have started offering tutoring services to members and to the campus community.

The Black Student Union meets regularly to plan such events as food drives and study groups. The BSU also hosts a Political and Historical Education Study Group that focuses on "different works relevant to the political and social issues of underrepresented peoples," says a BSU member. "We might read books about America, but we also read about China and its fight for democracy, and about Vietnam and South America." He adds: "A lot of the group's socializing goes on at our events. For instance, we sponsor monthly arts events, such as the 'Poetry Explosion,' and dance and musical performances. Students, faculty, and guests all perform." The group also brings guest speakers to campus, including, recently, several well-known New York City civil rights activists.

The Asian-Pacific Island Student Alliance, another active group on campus, sponsors forums and other cultural awareness programming, such as dances and readings.

According to students, the groups tend to work independently of faculty and staff advisers, although many of them will, says a BSU member, "help out when we need them." Students say they would be more likely to seek assistance from Hunter staff but "there's always a lot of infighting going on among the faculty, so we don't want to be used as a pawn in someone's power game. We've found we're more successful when we act independently."

Like the other city colleges, Hunter is a commuter campus, although there is a dorm for nursing students in downtown Manhattan. There are two active under-graduate student government associations, one for evening and the other for daytime students. Other popular campus groups include a concert band, a musical theater group, and drama and choral groups. Hunter has an impressive multilevel sports complex right on campus, which explains the popularity of many of the school's intercollegiate teams, such as in diving, fencing, gymnastics, and soccer. Club sports in swimming, tennis, and weight training are also popular. Hunter students have the opportunity to join the college's numerous performance, cultural, political, and religious organizations.

Hunter is located in one of the city's high-rent districts, and many of the school's students commute to school via the subway, which has a station right on campus. The area immediately around the school, which is well maintained, has some expensive restaurants, as well as bookstores and movie theaters. However, students say the college's dining service is more than adequate.

Cultural and ethnic diversity and top-flight educational opportunities are Hunter's strengths. "I transferred here from another school, and I'm glad I did," says a student. "At Hunter, more so than at many other colleges, there's a lot of mixing of people from different races and backgrounds. You see it in the lunchroom and on the skybridges. I don't know if this level of interaction occurs because there aren't a lot of places to go on campus since it's so small. But at Hunter we learn to deal with each other, and because of that I feel that I've definitely been enriched by coming here."

CITY UNIVERSITY OF NEW YORK/ QUEENS COLLEGE

Address: 65-30 Kissena Boulevard, Flushing, NY 11367
Phone: (718) 997-5600
Director of Admissions: Susan Reantillo
Multicultural Student Recruiter: Diane Warmsley
1991–92 tuition: $1,850 (in-state); $4,450 (out-of-state)
Room and board: na
Application deadline: Rolling admissions
Financial aid application deadline: 5/1
Non-white freshman admissions: Applicants for the class of '95: na
  Applicants accepted who rank in top 10% of high school class: na
  Median SAT: na
  Median ACT: na
Full-time undergraduate enrollment: 14,704
  Men: 40%
  Women: 60%
Non-white students in
  1987–88: na

  1988–89: 34%
  1989–90: 37%
  1990–91: 36%

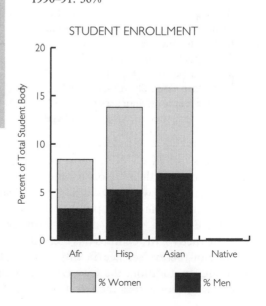

STUDENT ENROLLMENT

Percent of Total Student Body

% Women   % Men

Students In-state: 100%

Top majors: na

Retention rate of non-white students: na

**Scholarships exclusively for non-white
students:** Dr. Pearl D. Foster Scholarship:
one $500 award offered each semester to
a junior minority student majoring in the
biological sciences. Ivan C. Daly, Jr.,
Scholarship: one $500 award offered each
semester to an African-American junior
majoring in the physical sciences.

Remediation programs: The Search for
Education, Elevation, and Knowledge
program offers developmental courses
and support. The university also offers a
program in English as a second language.

Academic support services: The Academic
Skills and Resource Center offers
tutoring in writing, math, and reading.

Ethnic studies programs: The university
offers majors in Africana, Latin
American, Puerto Rican, and East Asian
Studies.

Organizations for non-white students: Black
Student Union, Caribbean Student
Association, Council of Latin American
Organizations, Future Black Lawyers,
Haitian Club, National Association of
Black Accountants, National Society of
Black Engineers, Science Organization of
Minority Students, SEEK Association,
Third World Alliance, Phi Beta Sigma

Notable non-white alumni: Reri Grist
(Metropolitan Opera singer); Toni Cade
Bambara (author); Helen Marshall (New
York state assemblywoman); Andrea
Wallace Benton (chairperson, Black
Studies department, Amherst College)

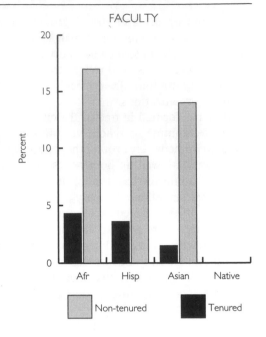

FACULTY

Percent

Afr   Hisp   Asian   Native

Non-tenured   Tenured

Tenured faculty: 600

Non-tenured faculty: 107

Student-faculty ratio: 18:1

Administrators: 90

African-American: 19%

Hispanic: 1.1%

Asian-American: 3.3%

Native American: 0

Recent non-white speakers on campus: Dr.
Leonard Jeffries (professor, Africana
Studies department, CUNY/City
College); Hazel Dukes (former national
president, NAACP); James Forman
(former SNCC member); Gil Noble (TV
host); Adelaide Sanford (regent, New
York State Education Department)

Queens is one of CUNY's most academically competitive colleges, and its students
are as proud of their school's campus as they are of its fine academics. With green
grass, numerous walkways, and a great deal of open space, Queens is unique among
the city universities. "Just put some dorms on campus and it would look like a college
in New England," says a student. Although the buildings themselves aren't particularly attractive, the campus has erected several new facilities in recent years, including
a state-of-the-art science facility, an outstanding library, and a top-notch music
building. In addition, the City University of New York has established its relatively
new law school across the street from the Queens College campus.

Academically, Queens has numerous well-respected programs in the liberal arts and sciences, especially in English, political science, anthropology, biology, and chemistry. The Aaron Copland School of Music is highly regarded and offers a four-and-a-half-year BA/MA program to qualified students. Education majors are able to student-teach at a well-regarded high school located near campus. Outstanding students are able to participate in one or another of the school's special sequences, including Honors in the Western Tradition, Honors in Mathematical and Natural Sciences, and Business and Liberal Arts Studies.

Students say the school's interdisciplinary Africana Studies program is strong, and praise such courses as "Introduction to Black Culture," "African Civilizations," and "Social Framework of Black Cultures." Puerto Rican Studies also earns high marks from students. The college's Asian-American Center provides a rich variety of resources about the Asian-American experience.

To graduate, students must complete a rigorous program of study called Liberal Arts and Science Area Requirements, or LASAR for short. As part of the program, students take courses in the humanities, physical and biological sciences, scientific methodology and quantitative reasoning, social sciences, and pre-industrial/non-Western civilization.

As at other relatively large universities, accessibility to professors can be difficult in introductory classes at Queens College, but in upper-level courses professors are readily available. Such classes rarely have more than 35 students. Students speak highly of many of their professors, whom they praise for their intelligence and effective teaching.

As a 100 percent commuter college, there isn't much in the way of school unity on the Queens campus. A great deal of student activity takes place at the student union, located on the south side of campus. The union has a restaurant, a game room, meeting rooms, and offices for student clubs and student government.

One of the campus's more active cultural student organizations is the Black Student Union, which has an office in the union. The BSU meets twice a month and works to bring speakers to campus regularly. The BSU also sponsors an annual fashion show and participates in the school's Cultural Night, held in the union, for which various groups prepare foods and sponsor musical entertainment. The BSU office is a popular hangout for members. "It's a place where we can be together and get to know each other," says a student. "We listen to music, study, and have impromptu discussions about important national and local issues." The BSU leadership is working to establish a more formal peer mentor program in which upperclass students work with incoming freshmen.

Two historically black Greek organizations, the Alpha Kappa Alpha sorority and the Phi Beta Sigma fraternity, are on campus, although the Queens College administration doesn't officially recognize any Greek associations. The Greek organizations sponsor dances and numerous community service projects.

The Fitzgerald Gym provides excellent facilities for those students who are athletically inclined, including an Olympic-size pool and Nautilus equipment. Nearby are numerous tennis courts and outdoor athletic fields. The college's student government is active, sponsoring numerous annual events, such as parties, concerts, and dances.

To say that the Queens College student population is diverse would be an understatement. More than 60 foreign languages are spoken on campus, a third of the student enrollment is Jewish, and students, all of whom are commuters, come to the college from the counties of Long Island and the boroughs of New York City. Students say that although there isn't much racial tension on campus, there is little integration. "There really isn't very much unity among the students," says a political science major. "Most people seem to stick with their own race. For example, most of the minority students congregate in the student union, while it seems that most of the whites are in the cafeteria. There are exceptions to this, of course."

Compared with the expensive private colleges and universities in the area, Queens College offers a top-quality education for the money. "Queens is a great college. Its facilities are excellent and you get to meet all sorts of people," says a student. "It's also a place where the minority student can come and not feel isolated, where he or she can learn and grow."

COLGATE UNIVERSITY

Address: 13 Oak Drive, Hamilton, NY 13346
Phone: (315) 824-7401
Director of Admissions: Thomas S. Anthony
Multicultural Student Recruiter: Veronica McFall
1991–92 tuition: $16,012
Room and board: $5,070
Application deadline: 1/15
Financial aid application deadline: 2/1
Non-white freshman admissions: Applicants for the class of '95: 795
  Accepted: 55%
  Accepted who enroll: 25%
  Applicants accepted who rank in top 10% of high school class: 60%
  In top 25%: 90%
  Median SAT: na
  Median ACT: na
Full-time undergraduate enrollment: 2,700
  Men: 53%
  Women: 47%
Non-white students in
  1987–88: 13%
  1988–89: 14%
  1989–90: 15%
  1990–91: 15%
Students In-state: 50%
Top majors: na

Retention rate of non-white students: 80%
Scholarships exclusively for non-white students: None
Remediation programs: None
Academic support services: Peer and departmental tutoring is offered in almost all academic subjects, as are writing workshops. The Office of Undergraduate Studies offers academic support.

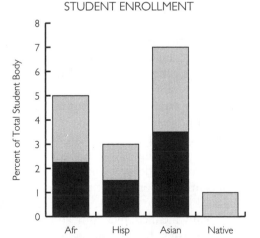

STUDENT ENROLLMENT

GEOGRAPHIC DISTRIBUTION OF STUDENTS

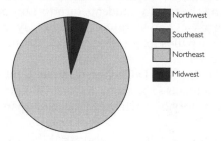

- Northwest
- Southeast
- Northeast
- Midwest

Notable non-white alumni: na
Tenured faculty: 112
Non-tenured faculty: 85

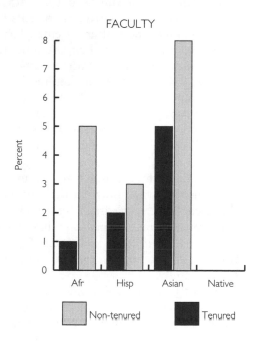

FACULTY

Percent

Afr   Hisp   Asian   Native

Non-tenured   Tenured

Ethnic studies programs: Latin American Studies, offered as a major and minor, includes courses in history, language, and social studies. African Studies, offered as a minor, includes courses in religion, philosophy, English, and political science. The university's African-American Studies program, offered as a minor, includes more than 20 courses that focus on African-American themes. Native American Studies, also offered as a minor, includes courses that focus on the experiences of Native Americans of North, Central, and South America. Colgate also offers programs in Asian Studies and East Asian languages and literature.

Organizations for non-white students: African-American Student Alliance, Asian Society, Caribbean Student Association, Korean Club, Unidad, Harlem Renaissance Center, Latin American Student Organization, La Casa Pan-Latina Americana, Sojourners (a gospel choir)

Student-faculty ratio: 11.5:1
Administrators: na
  Total African-American: 8
  Hispanic: 0
  Asian-American: 0
  Native American: 0
Recent non-white speakers on campus: na

Students who attend Colgate University know how to balance an active social life with a rigorous academic schedule. There's an abundance of both at this 174-year-old private university located in rural upstate New York.

Colgate offers numerous excellent departments—philosophy, English, religion, and history among them—but one of its outstanding features is its relative small size, which almost guarantees students easy accessibility to professors. Classes usually number no more than two dozen students, usually less, and freshmen are required to enroll in small seminar-style classes that foster interdisciplinary learning. The Olin Life Science Building recently underwent extensive renovation and offers top-flight research opportunities, particularly in the areas of biology and chemistry.

In Colgate's cultural studies program, students give high marks to "Theological Themes in Black History." For support among the faculty, students turn to Lourdes Rojas, an associate professor of Romance languages and literature. Students say that Jerome Balmuth and Ann Ashbaugh, both of the philosophy and religion department, are also especially supportive of students of color.

Built in 1988, the Cultural Center, located near the O'Connor Campus Center, provides social and cultural opportunities for students. The center has a small library with resources in the art, literature, music, and history of African-American, Hispanic, Asian, and Native American cultures.

While students say dorm living is more than adequate, they also speak highly of the school's eight theme houses, each of which accommodates anywhere from 15 to 80 students. Houses range from the Bolton House, which focuses on women's issues, to the Creative Arts House, for students interested in the arts. La Residencia Hispanica and the Harlem Renaissance Center are other housing options. Says a student about the cultural theme houses: "At first I lived in Cutten, which is a predominantly white dorm at the bottom of the hill. Now I live in La Residencia Hispanica. You can learn a lot about the Latino culture living there, and it's a completely different feeling to go into a house as opposed to going back to a dorm. You have a room to sit and watch TV in, a kitchen, and you also have your own room. There is an option for you to be alone when you need to, but there is also a sense of family."

Most of Colgate's social life takes place on campus, particularly as the town of Hamilton doesn't offer a lot of diversions. Hamilton is home to 2,500 residents—Colgate's student enrollment is slightly bigger—and a couple of bars and shops. Utica and Syracuse are both within an hour's drive of campus. According to students, there are pluses and minuses to Colgate's rural setting. "I thought about the fact that it was seven hours from home, an hour from the airport, half an hour from the train station. I spent more money traveling than I had anticipated," says a student from Washington, DC, about his early days on campus. Adds another student: "The rural setting helped me. There are lots of places to escape to on campus if you want to be by yourself or just go for a walk. I am easily distracted, so I chose a school with an environment with limited distractions." Colgate, which sits on 1,100 acres and has a pond, is one of the most beautiful and spacious campuses around. Numerous students comment that seeing the campus was a factor in their decision to attend Colgate.

The college hosts numerous lectures, films, and concerts throughout the school year. Many of the school's cultural activities are sponsored by one or another of the more than a dozen student organizations, including the Asian Society, the African-American Student Alliance, the Latin American Student Organization, and the Caribbean Student Association. Each of the groups plans social gatherings, offers peer support, and sponsors cultural events, such as films, guest speakers, and forums. "Granted Colgate is isolated. In Hamilton, we don't have the clubs New York City offers, or the wealth of people of color that Detroit and Washington, D.C., have, but we do have We Funk, which offers alternative music; we have the Sojourners—they are a gospel choir with the black church experience. We have the Korean Society, Asian Society, Latin American Dance, and LASO. There are a lot of opportunities to get involved."

Thanks to the Cultural Center and the student groups, a student of color community has evolved on campus. "I think there is definitely a community of color, but within that community there are also people with differences," says a student. "For instance, West Indian students have different needs and different cultures from African-American students, and sometimes they may step on each other's toes. But you find that everywhere you go. I do think that within this community of color we are able to respect each other's differences—more so than people outside of the community do." Comments another student: "I was involved in a [predominantly white] sorority in my freshman year, but eventually I realized that when it came down to it on issues that were important to me, the sisterhood that I had joined did not meet my needs. I'd say toward the end of my freshman year I found out just what a support group the community of color could be and still is."

Sports are an important part of many students' extracurricular lives. One recent graduate estimates that almost every student participates in at least one varsity, club, or intramural activity. Varsity swimming, ice hockey, and football are among the school's best teams. Colgate's multimillion-dollar athletic complex is the site of many athletic—and social—activities. The school's predominantly white fraternities—to which about half of the school's men belong—are popular weekend social venues. Beer is never in short supply on Colgate's campus, thanks in large part to the fraternities. Colgate students also participate in numerous other activities, ranging from music and dance clubs to religious organizations. The *Colgate Maroon* is the country's oldest college weekly newspaper.

Colgate is regarded as one of the Northeast's better respected liberal arts universities, and it attracts students who are bright and motivated, although usually not when it comes to political activism, which is in relative short supply at this largely conservative and affluent campus. The school's most politically active students reside in the Ralph Bunche House, known as the center of political activism on campus. The majority of Colgate's students are from the suburbs of New York, Connecticut, and Massachusetts, as well as from more than thirty other states and numerous foreign countries.

Although Colgate's location may not have the possibilities or the diversity of a large city, the school has the academic and non-academic programs and resources to make four years here an enlightening experience. "These are the years of your development, the time when you will find out who you are," says a student about her time at Colgate. "Find three or four people you respect, students or faculty, who are willing to help you and be supportive. You will have a wonderful experience—you will be ready to go out and extend yourself to the rest of the community. You will be willing to be a resident adviser, get involved in the Student Affairs Board, have friends, face any obstacles that come before you. I really believe that."

COLUMBIA UNIVERSITY/COLUMBIA COLLEGE

Address: 212 Hamilton Hall, New York, NY 10027
Phone: (212) 854-2522
Director of Admissions: Lawrence W. Momo
Multicultural Student Recruiter: Peter V. Johnson
1991–92 tuition: $15,823
Room and board: $6,122
Application deadline: 11/15
Financial aid application deadline: 1/15
Non-white freshman admissions: Applicants for the class of '95: 2,220
  Accepted: 35.5%
  Accepted who enroll: 43%
  Applicants accepted who rank in top 10% of high school class: 80%
  In top 25%: 95%
  Median SAT range: 536–641 V, 577–675 M
  Median ACT: na
Full-time undergraduate enrollment: 3,146
  Men: 51%
  Women: 49%

STUDENT ENROLLMENT

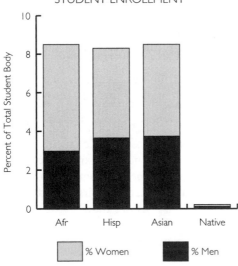

Non-white students in
  1987–88: 24%
  1988–89: 35%

1989–90: 35%
1990–91: 40%
Geographic distribution of students: na
Students In-state: 15%
Top majors: 1. Political Science 2. English 3. History
Retention rate of non-white students: 90%
Scholarships exclusively for non-white students: Kluge Scholars Program: need- and merit-based; 16 awarded each year; available to African-American or Hispanic Columbia graduate with plans to pursue a Ph.D. Any Columbia graduate who earns a Ph.D. will have the undergraduate loan reduced by one-half if the doctorate is earned at an accredited university. If the doctorate is earned at Columbia, the loan will be reduced by three-quarters.
Remediation programs: None
Academic support services: The school has a Learning Center and a Tutorial Center.
Ethnic studies programs: Columbia offers programs in African-American Studies and Asian Studies.
Ethnic studies courses: In addition to the courses offered through the African-American and Asian Studies programs, the university offers numerous courses in Latin American Studies.
Organizations for non-white students: Black Student Organization, Haitian Student Association, Caribbean Student Association, Black Theatre Production Association, Gospel Choir, Charles Hamilton Pre-law Society, National Society of Black Engineers, Charles Drew Pre-medical Society, Delta Sigma Theta, Alpha Phi Alpha, Omega Psi Phi, Alpha Kappa Alpha, *Black Heights* (literary magazine), Chicano Caucus, Alianza Latino Americano, Acción Boricua, Korean Students Association, Club Zamana, Chinese Students Club, Asian Women's Coalition, Asian Student Union

Notable non-white alumni: Dr. Alvin F.
  Poussaint ('56; professor, Harvard
  Medical School); Pixley Seme ('06;
  founder of African National Congress);
  Franklin Thomas ('56; president, Ford
  Foundation)
Tenured faculty: na
Non-tenured faculty: na

Student-faculty ratio: 8:1
Administrators: na
Recent non-white speakers on campus:
  Antonia Hernandez (president,
  Mexican-American Legal Defense and
  Education Fund); Jose Torres (writer and
  journalist); Nikki Giovanni (poet); Maya
  Angelou (poet and author)

Combine the educational resources of Columbia University with all of the cultural and social opportunities of New York City and what have you got? One of the most stimulating and rewarding educational experiences in the Ivy League. Each year students from every state in the nation and from more than two dozen foreign countries are drawn to Columbia's unique educational blend, a blend the university has been serving up for more than 250 years.

What most distinguishes Columbia from its peers—besides location—is the core curriculum it requires of all of its first- and second-year students. The core is taught by some of the college's most distinguished faculty members and not in large lecture halls but in small seminar-style settings of no more than 24 students each. The core includes four required courses that span a student's first two years at Columbia, "Contemporary Civilization," "Literature Humanities," "Masterpieces of the Fine Arts," and "Masterpieces of Music." Dialogue and debate characterize core course discussions.

There is an incredible array of academic opportunities at Columbia. Each year more than 3,100 courses are offered to the undergraduate, including instruction in 39 foreign languages. Columbia's nationally known School of Engineering, the first in the nation, has 17 different degree programs, while the school's arts and sciences division has more than 50. And the school's faculty features an impressive list of distinguished scholars, including numerous winners of Nobel Prizes and National Medals of Science. Some of the university's graduate school programs, particularly business, education, law, and engineering, are ranked among the best in the country.

Most of Columbia's arts and sciences departments are nationally known, and political science, English, Russian, history, and psychology enjoy especially good reputations. Columbia's East Asian Studies department is among the most respected in the country, and chemistry and physics are also considered top-notch.

Columbia students are no less enthusiastic about their school's ethnic studies programs and course offerings. "I've taken a number of ethnic classes, and they are very good and well taught," says a student. "The courses are taken by non-minorities as well as minority students and there are always heated debates and really interesting and pertinent issues." One of the more popular courses is "Race and Racism."

Columbia also enjoys a unique relationship with Barnard College, a prestigious women's college located across the street on Broadway. Columbia students frequently take courses at Barnard, and students of both schools share dining halls and dormitory facilities.

Academic competition is stiff here, especially among Columbia's pre-med, pre-business, and pre-med majors, who account for nearly half of the school's undergraduate enrollment. Their hard work pays off; in a recent year 95 percent of those who applied to medical school or law school from Columbia were accepted, and nearly all of those who applied to business school were accepted.

Columbia students are an extremely aware group, perhaps partly because of their campus's location. "Everything that happens in the world reverberates on campus, mostly because we are in New York City, the capital of all that's newsworthy and controversial," says an English major. The campus is politically liberal, and many of the campus's publications, including *The Spectator,* reflect this sentiment. "When Coors was under the spotlight for racial discrimination in their hiring practices, no one drank or bought it," says a student. "This campus is extremely politically correct. It's very liberal, so the conservatives tend to stay undercover as much as possible."

The extracurricular opportunities available on campus almost rival those of the university's hometown. Each year the university brings to campus a list of national and international figures that has included the President of the Russian Federated Republic, Boris Yeltsin; former Japanese Prime Minister Noboru Takeshita; film-maker Martin Scorsese; and former Nicaraguan President Daniel Ortega.

Then there are the activities of the school's numerous student associations, all of which are completely student-run. "Columbia's organizations live or die entirely on student initiative, since there are no faculty advisers, and elected students hold the purse strings." Students perform in the school's varied and numerous musical groups—jazz, rock, or classical—or join the chess club or the student government. Columbia is famous for its student publications, such as *The Spectator,* the second-oldest student daily in the country. WKCR, Columbia's radio station, is no less impressive. The station reaches three states and its presentation of jazz and new music rival those of professional broadcasts. The station plays reggae, bluegrass, folk, Latin, and Chinese music and has festival presentations in honor of musical greats; recently the station held a three-day Charlie Parker festival.

Cultural student groups are no less active, especially the Black Student Organization (BSO) and the Chinese Students Club. "The BSO is one of the most powerful organizations on campus because it's well organized and very vocal about its issues," says a student. "The Chinese Students Club is also very influential, and it has close to 400 members. During the Tiananmen Square incident, the CSC was able to bring one of the exiled student leaders to campus to speak on human rights and communism."

The BSO publishes *Black Heights,* an annual literary magazine, and the school's eight traditionally black fraternities and sororities are "well structured, exclusive, and very tight," says a student. "They're most visible during rush week. They're the ones that you see marching stoically across College Walk in threes, in matching somber uniforms and a painted face. They're not even allowed to speak to anyone during the initiation period." Columbia's chapter of the National Society of Black Engineers is said to be well organized, and publishes a résumé book that employers can refer to when seniors are job hunting.

The Alianza Latino Americano, an umbrella organization for various Latino student groups, sponsors field trips, films, and workshops. The Chicano Caucus, the Mexican-American student organization, provides peer counseling and sponsors various social events. The Asian Student Union organizes an annual Asian Cultural

Weekend and a Chinese New Year celebration and publishes an annual literary magazine. Each year the United Minorities Board, which is composed of all campus minority groups, sponsors a Third World Weekend, which introduces applicants to Columbia and campus activities.

According to students, the campus social life is relatively integrated. Interracial dating is "completely free and open," says a student. "However, we still have editorials or publicly arranged discussions on the issue." Students say the dining and living situations are also integrated. "The campus's residence halls are extremely well integrated. Given the ratio of minority versus Caucasians on campus, the mixture seems right. No one dorm gets more or less of a race than the next."

Columbia may be a city college, but it is unique among city colleges in that it is a primarily residential community of students. Nearly 95 percent of the students live in campus residence halls, fraternity houses, or special-interest "houses." (The African House, located in a dorm on the college's East Campus, is one such option.) A block from campus is Riverside Park, with more than 320 acres of jogging trails and grass, and just off campus are numerous ethnic restaurants, bookstores, a popular jazz and comedy club, and six other, unrelated universities, among them the City College of New York and the Manhattan School of Music.

The IRT subway station is located on the edge of campus, and the subway can take students from the northern tip of Manhattan to Wall Street and the World Trade Center. The Schomburg Center for Research in Black Culture, on 135th Street not far from campus, is nationally known for its resources.

Columbia and its environs offer almost anything imaginable under the sun—culturally, socially, and academically. For some, all of the excitement may be a bit much. But for those looking to have it all, Columbia just about fills the bill. Columbia is also the most racially and ethnically diverse college in the Ivy League, a fact that makes many Columbia students proud. "Our school is the most open and liberal of those schools, and we are confident enough to deal with all racial issues," says a junior. "Neither the administration nor the students are closed or secretive. Minorities are powerful on campus, and concerns are never ignored or stifled. We definitely have a voice on campus, and if you're the kind of person who demands to be recognized but not pampered for being a minority, Columbia is the school for you."

COOPER UNION FOR THE ADVANCEMENT OF SCIENCE AND ART

Address: 41 Cooper Square, New York, NY 10003
Phone: (212) 353-4120
Director of Admissions: Richard Bory
Multicultural Student Recruiter: na
1991–92 tuition: free
Room and board: $4,500
Application deadline: Art: 1/10; Architecture: 1/1; Engineering: 2/1
Financial aid application deadline: 5/1
Non-white freshman admissions: Applicants for the class of '95: na
Median SAT range: 500–620 V, 650–740 M (Engineering only)
Median ACT: na
Full-time undergraduate enrollment: 1,005
Men: 70%
Women: 30%

Geographic distribution of students: na
Top majors: 1. Art 2. Architecture 3. Engineering
Retention rate of non-white students: 94%
Scholarships exclusively for non-white students: All students at Cooper Union receive full-tuition scholarships.
Remediation programs: None
Academic support services: Tutorials, a mentor system, and a writing center are offered.
Ethnic studies programs: None
Ethnic studies courses: Cooper Union's department of humanities and social sciences offers about 12 ethnic studies courses, including "Native America" and "Contemporary Chinese Society," as well as courses in African, Chinese, and Japanese art.
Organizations for non-white students: Onyx (an African-American student group), Korean Student Association, National Society of Black Engineers; Filipino

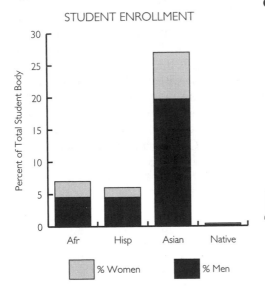

STUDENT ENROLLMENT

Percent of Total Student Body

% Women   % Men

Non-white students in
1987–88: 27%
1988–89: 33%
1989–90: 33%
1990–91: 38%

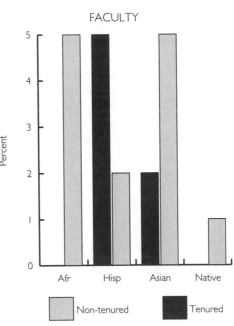

FACULTY

Percent

Non-tenured   Tenured

Student Group, Unión (a Latino student group), Hong Kong Student Association, Society of Hispanic Professional Engineers, Chinese Student Association

Notable non-white alumni: Annie Walker (1895; painter); Augusta Savage ('20; sculptress); Ashley Bryan ('46; children's book writer and illustrator); Donald Miller ('49; painter); Reynold Ruffin ('51; a founder of the Pushpin Studio in New York in the 1950s); Palmer Hayden ('20; painter)

Tenured faculty: 43
Non-tenured faculty: 167
Student-faculty ratio: 7:1
Administrators: 22
  African-American: 5%
  Hispanic: 0
  Asian-American: 0
  Native American: 0
Recent non-white speakers on campus:
  Charlayne Hunter-Gault (broadcast journalist, *MacNeil-Lehrer NewsHour*); Ed Love (professor of art, Florida State University)

Cooper Union—one of the country's best schools for engineering, art, and architecture—is located in the funky and lively East Village section of Manhattan. Academics at Cooper are rigorous and intense, and the school attracts a student body that is as motivated academically as it is focused on careers.

Besides top-notch academics, Cooper has something else going for it: thanks to wise investments and generous alums, it's tuition-free. All that students have to pay is an annual $300 activities fee. But there is one hitch. Because the school has dorm space for only about 80 students—at about $400 a month, not including food—students are responsible for finding their own housing accommodations. And what you've heard about New York real estate is true: rents in the East Village can be high and apartments can be hard to come by. Cooper has a housing office that can help locate apartments, but most students tend to find places in New Jersey or one of the nearby New York City boroughs or to commute from their parents' homes.

Cooper is best known for its engineering programs, which include chemical, civil, electrical, and mechanical engineering. Engineering students have the option of participating in summer projects with Kings College and Imperial College, both located in London, England. Cooper offers a master's degree program in engineering. The school's five-year architecture program boasts many outstanding faculty members, and the city of New York provides a virtual laboratory for the architecture student. The bachelor of arts degree offers concentrations in drawing, graphic design, painting, photography, printmaking, and sculpture. Courses are also available in film, video, and calligraphy. The art student has access to some of the world's greatest art museums and trendy SoHo and East Village art galleries are nearby. Students are able to supplement Cooper's offerings in the humanities by enrolling in courses at New York University, just a few blocks west.

To graduate, all students must take courses in general studies and Western civilization, which students complain are devoted solely to European studies. Members of different cultural student groups have met with the administration to try to get a multicultural perspective integrated in these required courses. Students praise such courses as "Black Literature" and "Black Artists," both taught by James Wylie, a popular associate professor of the humanities.

The academic work load at Cooper is heavy. Students say that their professors are easily accessible and that class sizes, except for a few of the introductory courses, are usually small. Pamela Jones, administrative associate of engineering students, works closely with students. "She's got a personality that's a combination of mother and best friend," says a student. "She gets along with everybody and everyone trusts her."

Numerous professional associations, including the National Society of Black Engineers (NSBE) and the Society of Hispanic Professional Engineers (SHPE), provide a great deal of academic support for members. During the fall semester of 1992, NSBE members hosted a daylong symposium in which NSBE alums conducted workshops on corporate etiquette and other job-getting techniques. "Our biggest goal is to see to it that our members strive to achieve academic excellence," says an NSBE member. "We have an informal big brother/big sister program where older students counsel new students who are in their respective schools. It's a way for us to talk to one another and help each other out, such as giving advice about what courses to take and what professors to take and to avoid." NSBE members also attend regional NSBE conferences and work with the admissions office in recruiting more African-American students to the school. SHPE members also bring speakers to campus and provide academic support for students.

According to a student, Onyx, Cooper's African-American student union, "is getting stronger each year." The group's biggest annual event is its Black Student Show, in which students from Cooper's art, architecture, and engineering schools display their works. The event is held in the school's Houghton Gallery, located in the Foundation Building, a registered national historic landmark. It was in the Foundation Building that Abraham Lincoln delivered one of his most famous campaign speeches before he was elected President.

New York City is Cooper Union's campus, and all of the pluses and minuses of going to school in the city that never sleeps are nearby. Cooper's campus—actually only three buildings situated between well-traveled Second and Third avenues in Manhattan—is a stone's throw from the nightclubs, bars, and restaurants of the East Village and Greenwich Village. Chinatown and Little Italy are just a few blocks south. The midtown and Wall Street business districts are only a few subway stops from Cooper Union; a subway station is located across the street from campus.

With such opportunities, combined with the fact that the school doesn't have a student center, Cooper Union is short of esprit de corps. According to undergraduates, there is little interaction among students in the different schools. The engineering students tend to be more conservative politically, particularly compared to the more liberal art students. "Everyone is into their own world here," says a student. "You really have to make an effort if you're an engineering student and want to make friends in the art school. Few people try to bridge that gap. Mostly it's because of the academic work load we're expected to carry."

Cooper Union's students come from more than a dozen states and half as many foreign countries. Many of its students hail from the New York City region and attended some of the city's most prestigious public high schools, such as Bronx High School of Science, Brooklyn Tech, and Stuyvesant.

In terms of cost, Cooper Union is tough to beat. In its annual rankings of America's best college buys, *Money* magazine puts the school in a category all its own, and the editors at *U.S. News & World Report* single it out for the same reason. But matching the educational opportunities available at the prestigious Cooper Union would also be difficult. "Looking back, I'm glad I came here for school," says a student. "It's been a trade-off, though. There are times when I wish the school had more of a social life, and during my freshman year I even thought of transferring schools for that reason. But I'm glad I didn't. The price of tuition is definitely right. But I also know that with a degree from here I am ready for the real world."

CORNELL UNIVERSITY

Address: 410 Thurston Avenue, Ithaca, NY 14850-2488
Phone: (607) 255-5241
Director of Admissions: Nancy Hargrave Meislahn
Multicultural Student Recruiter: na
1991–92 tuition: Private schools (Arts and Sciences; Architecture, Art and Planning; Engineering): $17,276
Public schools (Agriculture and Life Science; Human Ecology; Industrial and Labor Relations): $7,000 (in-state); $13,250 (out-of-state)
Room and board: $5,676
Application deadline: 1/1
Financial aid application deadline: 2/15
Non-white freshman admissions: Applicants for the class of '95: 5,786
Accepted: 34%
Accepted who enroll: 44%
Applicants accepted who rank in top 10% of high school class: 75%
In top 25%: 95%
Median SAT: na
Median ACT: na
Full-time undergraduate enrollment: 12,585
Men: 57%
Women: 43%
Non-white students in
1987–88: 19.4%
1988–89: 19.9%
1989–90: 21.2%
1990–91: 22.5%
Geographic distribution of students: na
Students In-state: 39.5%
Top majors: 1. Biological Sciences
2. Architecture 3. Electrical Engineering

Retention rate of non-white students: na
Scholarships exclusively for non-white students: na
Remediation programs: None
Academic support services: The Office of Minority Educational Affairs provides academic and non-academic services. In addition, there are nine campus-wide academic support services, ranging from biology and math to writing.
Ethnic studies programs: Hispanic-American Studies, Asian Studies, Africana Studies, American Indian Studies, Latin American Studies, and Southeast Asia Studies.
Organizations for non-white students: Cornell sponsors more than 50 cultural organizations, including Asociación

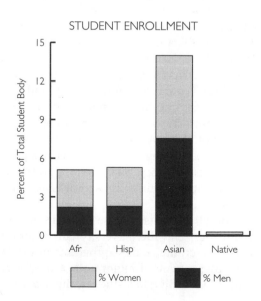

STUDENT ENROLLMENT

Percent of Total Student Body

□ % Women   ■ % Men

Latina, Black Students United, Students
United for Cultural and Racial
Awareness, Alpha Kappa Alpha, Alpha
Phi Alpha

Notable non-white alumni: Jerome Holland
('39, '41; former U.S. ambassador to
Sweden); Derrick Harmon ('84; former
professional football player); Leah
Sears-Collins ('76; Superior Court judge,
Fulton County, GA)

Non-tenured faculty: 347

Tenured faculty: 1,245

Student-faculty ratio: 8:1

Administrators: 819

   African-American: 3.2%

   Hispanic: 0.4%

   Asian-American: 0.7%

   Native American: 0.1%

Recent non-white speakers on campus: Jesse
Jackson (former U.S. presidential
candidate and civil rights activist); Maya
Angelou (author and poet); Louis
Farrakhan (leader, Nation of Islam);
Roberto Durán (poet)

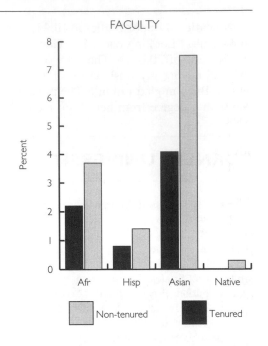

FACULTY

Ezra Cornell, whose statue graces the center of Cornell University's campus, would be proud of the university he helped found in 1865. Cornell, the largest and youngest school in the Ivy League, is the embodiment of the school its founder envisioned "where any person can find instruction in any study."

To this day, the "any study" is reflected in the university's vast array of academic challenges. Cornell, New York State's land-grant institution, has long been considered an anomaly among Ivy League schools, as the university is a part-public and part-private institution. Three of the school's seven academic divisions are state-funded (agriculture and life sciences, human ecology, and industrial and labor relations) while the others (arts and sciences; architecture, art, and planning; engineering; and hotel administration) are privately funded.

Students say each of the programs is strong. With about 700 undergraduates, the School of Hotel Administration, the first of its kind in the country, is internationally renowned. Among the arts and science programs, Cornell's largest division, students say English, history, philosophy, government, and most of the sciences are excellent. Engineering, architecture, and industrial and labor relations are also considered tops in the country.

Cornell students are also given ample opportunity to explore various cultures and ethnicities, and the university curriculum includes some of the strongest and most extensive ethnic studies programs in the Ivy League. The school's Asian-American Studies program, a minor course of study, is the only one of its kind on the East Coast. According to a student, the program usually offers about two to three courses a semester. The introductory course and the course "Asian-American Personal Identity" are among the more popular. "When the program first started a couple of years ago, the intro course would have only about 10 students. Last semester, there were 25. The 'Asian-American Personal Identity' course had 50 people. The professor had to turn more than 20 away." Cornell's Asian Studies program is also highly regarded. Courses in Japanese- and Chinese-language study are especially well respected.

To enhance the Asian-American Studies course offerings, students are able to take advantage of the materials in the student-run Asian-American Resource Center, established in 1991. Located in Caldwell Hall, the center offers a small library, stocked with periodicals as well as posters of museum showings and Asian-American documentaries. The Asian-American Program office, next to the resource center, helps bring speakers to campus, and recently sponsored a symposium about Asian-American Studies in which representatives from various East Coast schools participated.

Lee C. Lee, director of the program and a professor in the department of human ecology, is "very supportive of us and our endeavors," comments a junior. "She's the one who got the Asian-American Studies program off the ground, and the resource center was her idea."

Cornell's Africana Studies program, which comprises the study of blacks in Africa, America, and the Caribbean, is no less impressive. "The program has some amazing scholars who are also phenomenal teachers," says a senior. "There's Dr. James Turner, Dr. William Cross, Dr. Anne Adams, and Dr. L. Edmondson, all of whom challenge you to think critically." Among the program's more popular classes is "Black Politics." Students are also able to study Swahili through to the advanced level. The Africana Studies and Research Center, whose staff coordinates the program, has a library and brings guest speakers to campus.

The school's eleven-year-old American Indian Studies program is reported to be strong. "It's a good program. You can go to the program office and just hang out and visit with people. They're always there for you, and they go all out to help." The program received a boost recently with the completion of what is considered to be the first American Indian residence hall. The building, called Akwe:kon, a Mohawk term meaning "all of us," "was designed with a unique American Indian character," reports *The Chronicle of Higher Education.* According to the article, about 35 students will live in the new facility, about half of whom are American Indian and are enrolled in the school's American Indian program. Ron LaFrance, a Mohawk, will direct the house, which will provide students with academic counseling and other activities.

The fact that Cornell has the largest undergraduate division of any in the Ivy League does have its disadvantages—although a rich variety of course offerings certainly isn't one of them. Students complain that classes, particularly at the introductory level, can be overwhelmingly large. An introductory course in psychology, for example, reportedly can have up to 1,000 undergraduates, while a beginning-level writing class may have more than 200 students. Although class sizes dwindle come senior year, students find the large lecture halls of their first years alienating. Nonetheless, professors attempt to be as accessible as possible, while teaching assistants are also worth turning to. "I didn't learn much from the professor who taught my writing course, but the TA for the course helped make me a more confident writer," says an economics major.

For additional academic support, students say the services provided by the Learning Skills Center—such as supplemental instruction in core courses, and tutoring and study sessions—and the services of the Committee on Special Educational Projects—such as academic and personal counseling—are helpful. The school's library services are also impressive.

Although Cornell's campus is one of the most Greek of the Ivies, students report that it's possible to have fun without going Greek. Much of the responsibility for providing outlets falls on the shoulders of the school's cultural student organizations. Black Students United (BSU), which has about 100 active members, "attempts to network with all of the school's more than 20 black organizations to promote unity," reports a BSU leader. "The BSU is primarily an educational and cultural organization, so it doesn't sponsor parties, mostly because there are parties going on everywhere on campus." Each year, the BSU sponsors a Kwanzaa celebration and tutors young people at the Greater Ithaca Activities Center, where members also teach younger students how to cook African and Caribbean cuisine. During the spring semester of '92, the BSU also sponsored a Black Truth Conference, a weekend-long meeting that featured workshops and speakers, such as Maulana Karenga, a California State University professor and founder of the Kwanzaa celebration. More than 200 students, a few from area schools such as SUNY/Albany, attended the conference. BSU also interacts with the African-American student group at nearby Ithaca College.

BSU has been known for being political, particularly since some of its members took over the university's main administration building in 1969. Although the BSU may not be as militant as it was fifteen years ago, the group has certainly been exercising its political arm of late. During a recent school year, the group staged a sit-in at Day Hall. "We weren't getting enough financial aid, and the university didn't want to deal with the problem, although it's something we've been telling them about for a while now. The protest worked. The administration promised that we would all get the necessary aid that would enable us to return for the following semester. I honestly believe that 100 of us black students—and there are only 500 of us here—wouldn't have been able to return if we hadn't drawn attention to the problem."

Along with students from other cultural student organizations, including the Asian-American Coalition, the BSU is fighting the university's proposed random housing policy, which is supposed to go into effect during the fall of '94. Currently, students, including freshmen, are able to select the living unit in which they want to live. Students are concerned that if the policy is enacted, the fate of the Ujamaa Residential College, a multicultural facility used primarily by African-American undergraduates, lies in the balance. "The proposed new policy will ruin the Ujamaa House. Some trustees and students complained that the house segregates the campus, so they want us to be housed on other parts of campus as well. But there has been an increase in black and Latino students living on the west campus (the house is on the north campus), so they can't tell us that we're segregated. Our point is that if they want us to be integrated, they should do it educationally, not by playing with our housing options. There are certain things that happened to me my first year here, and I honestly believe that if I hadn't had my friends at Ujamaa I wouldn't be here today." According to another student, Cornell students were, in a survey conducted on campus after elections for the student assembly, overwhelmingly in favor of eliminating the proposed random housing plan. At present, about 70 percent of the Ujamaa House's 165 residents are first-year students, while other African-American students choose to live in residence facilities near the house.

The Asian-American Coalition (AAC), with only about 30 active members, is the school's smallest Asian student group. The largest Asian groups—the Chinese Students Association, with 400 members; the Cornell Korean Society and the Hong Kong Students Association, each with about 300 members—"are very social and state in their constitutions that they are not political organizations. They have parties and sponsor cultural events, which mostly focus on Asian topics," says a student.

The AAC is the more political and educational Asian student group on campus, although there isn't much activity in that regard, say students. "We try to keep in touch with the BSU, but we're not that active. We're working with the BSU to fight the random housing policy, and we sponsor trips to East Coast Asian Student Union meetings. We used to be more active in bringing speakers to campus and educating the public about Asian and Asian-American concerns, but a lot of that is now taken up by the Asian-American Studies program office."

According to the student: "The Asian-American community here has the reputation of being apathetic. I'm not really sure why that is, and I'm just guessing here, but most Asian-American students at Cornell are from the middle and upper classes and so they don't identify with being people of color." The student speculates further that much of what politicizes Asian-American student groups at other schools—Harvard and Yale, for example—is the demand for more Asian-American Studies courses, a program Cornell already has.

While Cornell may have a diverse academic program, the university cannot boast equally of the geographic diversity of its students. Cornell has one of the least geographically diverse student bodies in the Ivy League, with nearly half of the students hailing from New York State, especially New York City and Long Island. One student reports that many of the school's Asian-American students are from these areas, while another student says that the school's African-American students hail from places "as far away as Chicago, Los Angeles, and rural towns and cities." But, adds the student, "students tend to come more from rural areas and are less politically minded."

Students say the campus has experienced its share of racial tension. According to one student, the Cornell *Review,* which "is anti-black, anti-gay, anti-anything except for whatever it is they stand for," is responsible for fueling some of the racial tension on campus. A student describes a recent situation in which the president of the student finance commission, the board which oversees the allocation of student funding, denied funding to 11 of the school's 21 black student organizations. "It's no coincidence that the guy was also an editor for the *Review.*"

One student reports that there have been isolated cases of "anti-Asianism, but they aren't prevalent and most of the ones that do occur go unreported. The administration and public safety are working to try to get them reported more. Recently, there were some anti-Asian and anti-Semitic posters hung up on campus, which were up only for a very short while, but the university said they weren't hung by Cornell students. I still don't know to this day how they were able to know that students weren't involved," says a student activist.

Formal interaction among the school's cultural student groups is getting off the ground with the formation of a new student group "that is supposed to promote unity. We need to be fighting together." The group, which as of this writing has yet to be named, will sponsor workshops designed to sensitize members of the various student groups to the concerns and issues facing members of other cultural organizations. The new group will be made up of the coordinators of the different cultural student groups on campus.

Ithaca, in upstate New York, is a winter athlete's dream school location. Skiing opportunities—of both the downhill and the cross-country variety—are nearby. The city has an African-American population, although interaction with the university, except for the BSU service activity, is limited. Ithaca is home to an opera company, a ballet company, as well as theaters, orchestras, and outstanding jazz performances. Cornell's 700-acre campus is breathtakingly beautiful and surrounded by rolling hills and ravines and gorges. The campus sits on the edge of Cayuga, the largest of the five Finger Lakes.

Cornell may be surrounded by great beauty, but it is far from any major city. New York City and Philadelphia are each a half day's drive away; Boston and Toronto are even farther. While the winter and the relative isolation may prove claustrophobic to those used to big-city environs, students say there's more than enough social and cultural activity on campus to keep a person distracted.

The educational opportunities at Cornell are vast and famous. A Cornell degree is a plus in the job market, and graduate schools are no less impressed with a Cornell diploma. For one student, much of her education at Cornell has taken place outside of the classroom. "You really learn about life here and about all you'll have to deal with in the real world. If I'd gone to an all-black school, I would have been too sheltered. I'm glad I came here because now I know what to expect." Another student feels that "a large part of my experience here has been a minority experience. Living at Ujamaa has made the transition to Cornell easier. You can kick off your shoes and feel at home, feel that you're part of the family."

HAMILTON COLLEGE

Address: 198 College Hill Road, Clinton, NY 13323
Phone: (315) 859-4421 / (800) 843-2655
Director of Admissions: Douglas C. Thompson
Multicultural Student Recruiter: Vicki D. Green
1991–92 tuition: $16,650
Room and board: $4,550
Application deadline: 1/15
Financial aid application deadline: 1/15

Non-white freshman admissions: Applicants for the class of '95: 402
Accepted: 251
Accepted who enroll: 20%
Applicants accepted who rank in top 10% of high school class: na
Median SAT range: 460–580 V, 540–630 M
Median ACT: na
Full-time undergraduate enrollment: 1,691
Men: 54.4%
Women: 45.6%

STUDENT ENROLLMENT

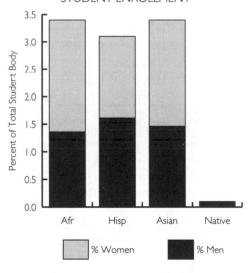

Percent of Total Student Body

Afr   Hisp   Asian   Native

☐ % Women   ■ % Men

Non-white students in
1987–88: na
1988–89: 7.1%

1989–90: 8.7%
1990–91: 9.8%
Geographic distribution of students: na
Students In-state: 62%
Top majors: 1. Sociology 2. Philosophy 3. Psychology
Retention rate of non-white students: na
Scholarships exclusively for non-white students: George I. Alden Scholarship. William and Ethel Marran Scholarship: awarded to a female minority student. Jules L. Rubinson Memorial Scholarship: awarded to women and minority students who at the end of their sophomore year have been identified as strong candidates for medical school. Hilde Surlemont Sanders Memorial Scholarship: need-based. All scholarships are need-based and the number and amount of each award vary.
Remediation programs: None
Academic support services: English as a second language; New York State Higher Education Opportunity Program, which provides tutoring in various academic subject areas.
Ethnic studies programs: Programs are offered in Asian Studies, interdisciplinary minors in African Studies, Latin American Studies, and East Asian languages and literature.
Organizations for non-white students: Asian Cultural Society, Black and Latin Student Union, La Vanguardia, Kappa Alpha Psi, Hamilton College Gospel Choir, Sisters in Support of South Africa, Afro-Latin Cultural Center, *As I Am* (Asian Cultural Society publication)
Notable non-white alumni: na
Non-tenured faculty: 111
Tenured faculty: 90
Student-faculty ratio: 11:1
Administrators: 98
African-American: 5.1%
Hispanic: 1%

FACULTY

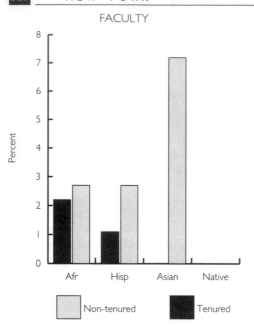

Asian-American: 0
Native American: 0
Recent non-white speakers on campus: Rev. Tyrone Cryder (former executive director, Operation Push); Dr. Bruce Hare (African-American Studies professor, Syracuse University); Dr. Alvin Poussaint (professor, Harvard Medical School); Hector Velez (associate professor of sociology, Ithaca College and Cornell University); Irene Fornes (Cuban-American playwright)

When Hamilton's admissions office tells you the college is located in the "village of Clinton," they truly mean a village. Clinton offers a couple of bars and a pizza restaurant and miles of beautiful countryside. Although some may find the small size stifling, to others it is the ideal environment in which to take advantage of Hamilton's well-regarded programs in the liberal arts and sciences.

Chartered as a men's school in 1812, Hamilton became coed in 1978, when the college merged with all-female Kirkland College, located "across the road." Kirkland's programs in the performing and studio arts, comparative literature, and sociology complemented the offerings at Hamilton. Hamilton has long been strong in the sciences, government, history, and English. The college, which has excellent library facilities, also offers impressive programs in public policy, biochemistry/molecular biology, Russian Studies, and world politics. "Race and Ethnicity," a sociology course, "African-American Literature," and "Africana Women," a women's studies course, earn high marks from students.

One of the college's strengths is its small size and the easy accessibility of professors. After-class conversations are common, and students say many of their professors actually like to teach and do it well.

Hamilton's graduation requirements are extensive and demanding. Students must satisfy distribution requirements in four areas: sciences and mathematics, historical studies and social sciences, the humanities, and the arts. Seniors must complete a project in their major. Beginning with the class of '93, students are also required to take three writing-intensive courses, available from any number of departments. "It's impossible to graduate from this school and not be a better writer," says a student. One of the courses must be from outside the student's major area.

Because of Hamilton's writing requirement, students make good use of the college's Writing Center. The Study Skills Center, which offers the assistance of tutors, is also rated as "very good" by students. For additional support, students turn to Christine Johnson, director of the college's Higher Education Opportunity Program. "She's a powerful woman on campus," says a student. "She has earned a lot of respect from students and faculty. She bends over backwards to help students with just about anything we need, such as tutoring, financial aid advice, and personal assistance."

Karen Green, Hamilton's new Director of Multicultural Affairs, has also proved to be a tremendous resource for students. "I can't find the words to describe her importance to us here," says a student, "that's how good she is. She's very accessible, and if you have a problem, she's there." Green has previously served at Spelman College, a historically black college for women in Atlanta, and Agnes Scott College, another women's college, also in Georgia. One of Green's achievements, say students, was the Leadership Training program she coordinated recently for heads of the school's cultural student groups. They were brought back to campus a week before other students and participated in workshops on how to delegate and mediate conflict and on group dynamics.

The Black and Latin Student Union (BLSU) sponsors lectures, plays, and dance groups, which in a recent year performed traditional African and Latino dances. "We were different this year," says a student leader. "Instead of focusing all of our events in February, we sponsored African-American awareness activities throughout the spring semester." Among the offerings were movies, student panels, bands, and guest lecturers. The group's primary focus, says a student, is to "serve as a support system for members. We try to educate each other about our common culture because we aren't able to get much of that kind of an education in the classroom here. As growing individuals, we need to remind ourselves about where we came from. In trying to do so, we also try to build the self-esteem of our group members."

Three students are able to live at the Afro-Latin Cultural Center, located at the center of campus. The center has a small library, artwork donated or created by alums, and a meeting area, where BLSU meetings are usually conducted.

According to students, members of the school's cultural student groups, as well as other students, have recently become more political. In response to a racial slur made by a student recently, about 50 students, dressed in black, marched up the football stadium's steps during Parents Weekend to draw attention to the incident. "We wanted to let the parents know what was going on here," says a participant. The next day, according to the participant, nearly 250 students, administrators, and faculty, as well as "parents who were still here that day," marched through the school's dining halls to demonstrate against the incident.

Much of Hamilton's social life centers on the Greek system, to which about 45 percent of the men and 15 percent of the women belong. In a recent year, the school's traditionally black fraternity, Kappa Alpha Psi, had only about two members, "and next year they're graduating," says a student. For a small fee, the school's Outing Club offers a variety of ways to explore the Adirondack countryside. Varsity sports, especially basketball, have more than enough fans, especially when the opponent is rival Colgate. The women's volleyball and men's golf teams have had some successful seasons recently.

For off-campus fun in the winter, students will often hit the slopes, as downhill skiing is popular. Utica, a city with an African-American community, is about twenty minutes away by car, and the Jitney, a van that takes students to an area mall on weekends, provides some sort of an escape from campus, but, as one student comments, "I get tired of going to the mall all the time."

The majority of Hamilton's students hail from the Northeast, and students of color aren't well represented, although the college is working to increase their enrollment. Hamilton students, with the exception of those drawn to some of the school's more "artsy" programs, are conservative, but students say that not a great deal of political activity takes place on campus.

In the words of one student, Hamilton is located in the "boondocks and away from civilization." But for those who are prepared for such relative isolation, and who don't mind attending college in a homogeneous environment, Hamilton will provide the rest: a solid and respected liberal arts education.

HOBART AND WILLIAM SMITH COLLEGES

Address: Geneva, NY 14456
Phone: (315) 789-5550
    Hobart: (800) 852-2256; William Smith:
    (800) 245-0100
Directors of Admissions: Mara O'Laughlin
    and Leonard Wood

Multicultural Student Recruiter: na
1992–93 tuition: $16,992
Room and board: $5,358
Application deadline: 2/15
Financial aid application deadline: 2/15

Hobart and William Smith Colleges, located across the street from each other in Geneva, New York, started as single-sex institutions, Hobart (established in 1822) for men and William Smith (established in 1906) for women. In 1941, the colleges merged, sort of. Each still has separate deans, admissions offices, athletic programs, and student governments. But they share a board of trustees, a president and central administration, faculty, curriculum, and various other academic and non-academic support services. Coed housing is available, although on a limited basis; most of the schools' residence halls remain single-sex.

Hobart and William Smith Colleges (it would be a mistake to refer to just one of the colleges) are solely undergraduate institutions geared to the liberal arts. One of the hallmarks of an HWS education is the rapport students are able to establish with faculty. "I have friends at other, larger schools who have never talked to their professors on a one-on-one basis. I've not only talked to many of mine after class, but I've also gone to some of their houses for dinner."

Political science and economics are strengths, as are the school's pre-med programs, most notably chemistry and biology. The schools also offer programs in urban studies, women's studies, and environmental studies. Gulick Hall, which houses the school's psychology department, and Smith Hall, which houses the language and dance departments, have undergone recent renovation. The schools sponsor joint-degree programs in engineering, architecture, and business with various other universities, including Columbia, Washington University in St. Louis, and Clarkson. HWS actively encourages students to study off campus during their junior year.

The colleges' Africana and Latino program is staffed with "good faculty who are enthusiastic and who know what they're talking about," says a student. "Most of the courses in the program are literature courses, which are very good, especially 'Third World Women's Text.'" To complete this interdisciplinary studies program, a student must get approval from the Individual Majors Committee, which involves an application process one student describes "as complicated and a lot of red tape."

To graduate, students must satisfy distribution requirements by taking two courses in each of three divisions: humanities, social science, and natural science. Because of the stipulations of a major bequest, students must also pass a swimming test. During their first year at the college, students also participate in a seminar course that introduces them to learning in a liberal arts context. Each first-year seminar has no more than 15 students, so establishing a good relationship with a professor is easy. Some recent seminar topics have included "Philadelphia: 1787," "The Making of the Atomic Bomb," and "Prejudice, Discrimination, Responsibility."

The Third World Cultural Center, located near the campus's main dining hall, "is well used by students, especially around exam time, and it gets a cross section of students of color." The two-story center, established on campus in 1991, has computers and a lounge area. Classes are also held in the center.

The Intercultural Affairs Office, which provides academic and non-academic advising, is also a popular resource on campus. Students report that the office's staff is hardworking and cares a great deal for students. "Allison Upshaw, a counselor in the office, works primarily with first-year students, and keeps in constant contact with them about their social lives and their academics," says a student. "She also helps coordinate the peer advising system where upperclass students work with freshmen. Edith Hunt, the office's assistant director, works mostly with upperclass students, and she is very accessible. People stop in the office just to chat with Edith and Allyson. That shows the kind of rapport students have with them." The associate dean of the office, Edward Blackwell, "also works hard for the students, but he's so busy with the administration and other activities that it's necessary to make an appointment with him if you want to see him. He's always working on ways to get students financial aid."

Richard Mason, a professor of sociology and education, and Richard Heaton, a professor of religious studies, are "both very sensitive to the needs of minority students," says a junior. "They're incredibly open-minded. You never fear you'll be criticized in their classes for what you say."

The Latin American Student Organization and the African-American Student Coalition are the colleges' most active cultural student groups. "We keep in constant contact with each other," says a coalition member. "We co-sponsor an annual cookout that serves hamburgers and hot dogs as well as ethnic foods from Latin America and the Caribbean."

With approximately 25 active members, the African-American Student Coalition, which meets twice a month in Coxe Hall, sponsors several events annually, such as Kwanzaa ("in November because we're not in session in December") and Caribbean

Week, which features foods and music from the area. According to a student leader, half of the coalition's membership are students from the Caribbean, especially Jamaica. Students also come from Africa. "It's a diverse group, and it's interesting to learn about different cultures within a single race," comments a student.

The social life pretty much focuses on the parties thrown most weekends by the campus's eight fraternities (there are no sororities at William Smith). In a recent year, one Latino student was a member of a fraternity, while no African-Americans were. The Scandling Center, which houses the Cafe and the Creedon Room, is a popular on-campus hangout. The center also shows movies during the week.

Geneva, a small, predominantly white community, offers little in the way of social or cultural life, so when students need to leave campus for fun, most head to Rochester, Syracuse, and Cornell, each about an hour away by car.

To say that sports are popular at the colleges is an understatement, especially when it comes to lacrosse; Hobart's team has won 11 consecutive NCAA Division III championships since 1980, while William Smith's team is also a tough national contender. In addition, William Smith's soccer team recently won the Division III nationals. In 1989, the school opened an impressive Sport and Recreation Center.

Students at the colleges tend to be conservative and are primarily from the Northeast, mostly Connecticut and New York State, although William Smith students have the reputation of being slightly more cerebral and diverse in terms of perspectives and backgrounds than their counterparts at Hobart. "I'd like to think that the students here are more liberal and open-minded than they are, but they aren't," says a student. "There are some white students who come to our marches, but you see the same few faces at each event."

Hobart and William Smith has a beautiful campus setting and an accessible faculty and staff. "I'm getting a good education here," says a student, adding, "The colleges are a microcosm of the real world. This place gives you a taste of what you can expect once you graduate. It's a shock to come here, especially for those from predominantly minority high schools. I'm lucky. I came from a predominantly white school where I learned early on how to deal with these issues."

HOFSTRA UNIVERSITY

Address: Holland House, Hempstead, New York 11550
Phone: (516) 463-6700
Director of Admissions: Joan Isaac-Mohr
Multicultural Student Recruiter: Darren Morton
1991–92 tuition: $9,240
Room and board: $5,366
Application deadline: Rolling admissions
Financial aid application deadline: 3/1
Non-white freshman admissions: Applicants for the class of '95: na
  Median SAT: na
  Median ACT: na
Full-time undergraduate enrollment: 6,802
  Men: 46%
  Women: 54%

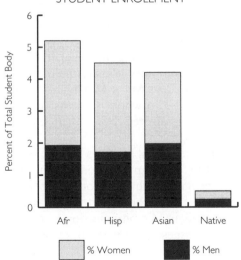

STUDENT ENROLLMENT

☐ % Women   ■ % Men

Non-white students in 1987–91: na
Geographic distribution of students: na
Top majors: na
Retention rate of non-white students: na
Scholarships exclusively for non-white students: None

Remediation programs: na
Academic support services: The university's New Opportunities at Hofstra (NOAH) program provides academic and non-academic support, including reading, writing, math, and social science assistance. Counselors and tutors are also available.
Ethnic studies programs: Asian Studies and Africana Studies are offered.
Ethnic studies courses: na
Organizations for non-white students: African People's Organization, Imani Dance Group, African/Caribbean Society, Joel Rector Science Club, African and Latino Students Interested in Communication Arts, Hispanic Organization of Latin America, National Association of Black Accountants
Notable non-white alumni: na
Non-tenured faculty: 703
Tenured faculty: 278
Student-faculty ratio: 17:1

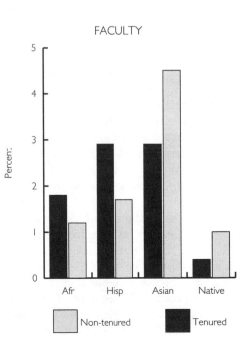

FACULTY

☐ Non-tenured   ■ Tenured

Administrators: 409
  African-American: 7.3%
  Hispanic: 2%

Asian-American: 1.2%
Native American: 1.5%
Recent non-white speakers on campus: na

Hofstra University is working hard to change its image from that of a largely commuter school with above-average academic programs. Recent ads in various area papers, most notably *The New York Times,* show kids playing the violin or flying model airplanes in the spirit of innovation. With financial strength and an increase in enrollment—and the completion of several new dorms—Hofstra shows signs of transcending its largely local appeal.

And as the university's academic reputation increases, so do the opportunities for the school's students of color. "There's a lot going on here, and it has definitely gotten better since I first arrived on campus," says a senior. "There's the new African and Latino Students Interested in Communication Arts; there's Common Ground, a new multicultural student organization; and the African People's Organization and Hispanic Organization of Latin America have gotten more active."

Hofstra's biggest academic draws include accounting and computer science, and the 82-year-old university's undergraduate and graduate degree programs in business are the only accredited programs of their kind on Long Island. The drama department wins rave reviews from students, and students say the school's engineering programs are improving. Hofstra's new $5 million state-of-the-art Television Institute has four studios and a mobile van with cameras. In the humanities, political science, history, sociology, English, and communications rank among the school's best offerings. Hofstra's Africana Studies program is relatively small, but the "Literature of Black America" course draws numerous students.

To graduate, students must satisfy some stiff distributional requirements, including courses in the humanities, natural sciences and math/computer science, and the social sciences. Joyce Toney, an assistant history professor, and Mary McKnight-Taylor, an associate professor of counseling, are among those to whom students turn for advice and who frequently show up for events sponsored by student cultural organizations.

Although class sizes can be large, especially for freshmen, students say professors are genuinely concerned that they succeed. "I'm a communications major, and there aren't a lot of minority students in the program, which is too bad because the school has such good facilities," says a student. "So the department started a group, African and Latino Students Interested in Communication Arts, an organization that gets us together to talk about issues and to try to get more of us interested in the area."

For most of the school's students of color, much of the social life takes place off campus, usually at area colleges, such as Adelphi, C. W. Post, or SUNY/Old Westbury. "We spend a lot of time traveling from school to school. If we hear that a black student group is having a party at a nearby school, we get in our cars and go. Or if one of our black groups is having a party, we let other schools know so they can come. There's a lot of social networking that goes on between the schools," says a party chaser. New York City, just forty minutes on the Long Island Rail Road, is a popular destination, but most students are content to stay on the Island. Students tend to ignore Hempstead, Long Island, for social life. "There's Roosevelt Field [a mall] and a couple of bars, but it's mostly a run-down neighborhood without much going on."

Hofstra's cultural groups sponsor their own on-campus activities. The Hispanic Organization of Latin America, with more than 75 members, "is very active and members are tight with one another," says an HOLA member. A popular hangout spot on campus for Hofstra's Hispanic students is the HOLA office in the student center. "There's always someone in the office between the hours of nine to five. Commuters also think of the office as a home, and a lot of students stop by just to relax between classes. A lot of us eat our lunches in the office."

Recently HOLA sponsored a conference on campus to which Hispanic organization members from area colleges were invited to discuss issues relevant to Hispanic clubs, but students were disappointed in the low turnout. Members vow to keep the conference an annual event, hoping that it will become more popular through word of mouth. HOLA also sponsors a fashion and talent show and activities for Latin Week, held during the spring semester. Part of the week features Parents Dinner Night, with a live band, and an Extravaganza Night, which presents a play and poetry readings. HOLA hosts two parties each year, and members have been known to head into New York City to eat at Hispanic restaurants. HOLA members visit area high schools to discuss with students the transition from high school to college. Students are also working to get established on campus a chapter of Sigma Iota Alpha, a Hispanic sorority.

Issues of multiculturalism are addressed in the always exciting weekly forums of Common Ground. "Each week Common Ground members post fliers around campus that pose questions that are to be the focus of discussion at the next meeting." During a recent year, Common Ground sponsored a banquet in which the school's cultural organizations participated.

The African People's Organization (APO) sponsors a Kwanzaa celebration, a spring picnic, and theater and dance companies. Speakers are also brought to campus courtesy of the APO, which has office space on the second floor of the student center. Recently, students broke away from the APO to form the African/Caribbean Society, which threw its own on-campus Spring Fete in 1991 that offered dinner and dancing.

Each of the school's black Greek organizations sponsors its own community service and social activities. Members of Kappa Alpha Psi fraternity, for example, recently mounted an AIDS awareness campaign and have also adopted a Brooklyn, New York, elementary school as a tutoring site. The group is currently in the process of planning a step show in which all Long Island colleges and universities will be invited to participate.

Members of APO and the black Greek organizations have had their differences lately, according to students. "Students active in APO don't agree with the ideas of the Greek organizations," says a fraternity member. "They think that by becoming Greek we forget our Africanness, but we don't. People think the APO is mostly for cultural events, while the fraternities and sororities are more social."

To bridge the gap between the Greeks and the non-Greeks, the African Fraternity/Sorority Alliance, a recently formed governing body representing the black Greek organizations on campus, plans to establish a big brother/big sister program in which upperclass students will work with first-year students. An added benefit of the program, says a member of a Greek organization, is that it will help maintain the visibility of the Greek system, particularly since the national organizations have discontinued the pledging rituals of local chapters.

For other social activities, Hofstra students take advantage of the school's excellent athletic facilities, regularly scheduled movie nights, and the Entertainment Center, an on-campus hangout that draws students to its game room and restaurants. The Nassau Coliseum, home to the Islanders ice hockey team, is near campus, and the beaches of Long Island are minutes away. Most Hofstra students tend to head home during the weekends, however, so much of the school's social life happens during the week.

Hofstra's increasing academic reputation is no doubt one of the reasons many students choose to attend the university that has graduated the likes of Francis Ford Coppola, the director of *The Godfather*. Location is another. "I'm glad I came here. Hofstra has opened my mind to a lot of different cultures and opportunities. I'm from New York City, and it's definitely better living here. Things are safer and better economically. It's made me see there's more to the world than my old neighborhood."

MANHATTAN COLLEGE

Address: New York, NY 10471	**1992–93 tuition:** $10,800
Phone: (212) 920-0200	**Room and board:** $3,125
Director of Admissions: John Brennan, Jr.	**Application deadline:** 3/1
Multicultural Student Recruiter: na	**Financial aid application deadline:** 2/1

Located just twelve miles north of the heart of New York City, Manhattan College, founded as a Catholic institution in 1853, retains the qualities of a small liberal arts college while offering its students the opportunities of one of the world's most exciting and diverse cities. Manhattan College's 47-acre campus, situated on a hill overlooking Van Cortlandt Park, is self-contained and is in a quiet residential section of the Bronx.

Manhattan College students are decidedly pre-professional. In a recent year, 900 of the school's approximately 3,000 undergraduates majored in business, while nearly as many majored in engineering. The business program offers majors in seven different areas, including accounting, economics, finance, and computer information systems. Manhattan College's well-respected School of Engineering allows students to major in chemical, civil, electrical, or mechanical engineering. Unlike students at other "techie" schools, Manhattan College engineering students are expected to complete 12 credits in humanities and social science courses, which must include at least one history and one philosophy course. Among the programs in the School of Arts and Science, students praise English, philosophy, and religious studies. Education is also a popular major. Students are also able to enroll in courses at Mount St. Vincent, a college located near campus.

Grade competition is not overly intense, and professors are readily available to students. More often than not they give out their home telephone numbers—as well as their office hours—on the first day of classes. "Sometimes freshmen are afraid to seek help, but when sophomore year comes around, students feel more comfortable and don't mind going to their professors," says a junior.

By far the most active student group at the college (and "no doubt about it," says a student) is the Minority Student Union (MSU), with about 30 active members. According to an MSU leader, "the organization has African-American, Caribbean, Asian, Italian, and Greek members, although Latinos account for about three-quarters."

MSU sponsors various activities for the school's Latino Festival, usually held in October. A dinner with dancing and a DJ who plays Spanish music concludes the month of festivities and programming. For African Heritage Month, MSU recently sponsored a forum that drew attention to the influence of African architecture, art, and religion on the West, although, according to one student "only about 15 people came." As a finale to the month, the MSU held a reggae dance party at Plato's Cave, a dry pub on campus. MSU also sponsors an annual fashion show. Each year the proceeds from the group's first party in the fall go toward establishing a $300 book scholarship for an MSU member.

Perhaps the most effective event sponsored by the MSU was its recent Stereotype Forum, in which "we broke down stereotypes of Hispanics, Italians, African-Americans, every type person," says a student. "We had a good turnout of faculty and staff. The event included a panel discussion with a total of eight students and faculty—African-Americans, Latinos, Asian-Americans, and European-Americans. A man and a woman represented each race and ethnicity. Many people who were there want us to do it again next year."

The MSU adviser, Winsome Downie, "is involved in more things on campus than even the MSU," says a student, "but no matter how busy she is, she always has time for students. She comes to all of our MSU events, and she was even a judge for our talent show." Downie is head of the college's government and politics department. Arlene Hunter, dean of students, has also been supportive of MSU events. "We have a new student activities director this year, which can be frustrating, especially since the director is not familiar yet with how the campus and the MSU run. But Arlene knows she can count on the MSU to do what is right and that we can stand on our own two feet," says a student.

Although only about 10 percent of the students are part of the Greek system, according to one student, it is getting more popular with non-white students, particularly with the introduction of two new Greek organizations on campus, both of which are oriented toward non-white students. Beta Phi Gamma, a sorority established at Manhattan College in the spring of '92, already has 32 members. Established on campus in the spring of '91, Gamma Alpha Sigma, a Latino-centered fraternity, has about 18 members. None of the Greek organizations at Manhattan College provide living facilities for members. Cornerstone, a student religious organization, is popular.

MSU members feel frustrated about the lack of a multicultural affairs staff person on campus. "We [multicultural students] get a lot of support from the administration, but the MSU is pushing for a multicultural affairs director," says an MSU leader.

While approximately 20 percent of the student body is non-white, the majority of Manhattan College's students are "Irish- or Italian-American, Catholic and conservative," says a student. "There's a students-for-life group on campus, but there's definitely not a pro-choice group. It's not that there aren't any pro-choice students here, it's just that no one has really tried to establish a pro-choice organization. This is also definitely a drinking school. Students are forever getting drunk at some bar or pub on Broadway. There's no one here on campus on St. Patrick's Day, for example. They're all at the parade in the city."

Located in the city that never sleeps, Manhattan College lets students take advantage of the city's plethora of cultural and social activities. The famed Lincoln Center is just a subway ride away, as are Chinatown and Little Italy. Latino restaurants are also within a stone's throw of campus, as is Harlem, with its wealth of Afrocentric activities and restaurants.

Manhattan College promises a good education—particularly in pre-professional studies—to those willing to work hard. With a variety of extracurricular activities in which to take part, there is never a shortage of things to do on or off campus. "I'm glad I came here," says a student who hails from Puerto Rico. "I wanted to be in a large city, but I knew I would need a small college, especially since I was used to a small-school atmosphere in high school. There's a lot to do here, and it's easy to get carried away with MSU events because the group is so active. But during the week I make myself study."

MANHATTANVILLE COLLEGE

Address: 125 Purchase Street, Purchase, NY 10577
Phone: (914) 694-2200
Director of Admissions: Jane Raley
Multicultural Student Recruiter: David Wright
1991–92 tuition: $12,400
Room and board: $5,625
Application deadline: 3/1
Financial aid application deadline: 3/1
Student-faculty ratio: 12:1
Non-white freshman admissions: Applicants
　for the class of '94: 218
　Accepted: 65%
　Accepted who enroll: 23%
　Applicants accepted who rank in top
　10% of high school class: na
　Median SAT: na
　Median ACT: na
Full-time undergraduate enrollment: 1,005
　Men: 36%
　Women: 64%

Non-white students in
　1987–88: 14%
　1988–89: 16%
　1989–90: 17%
　1990–91: 17.9%
Geographic distribution of students: na
Top majors: na

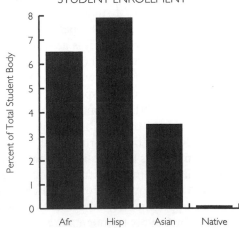

STUDENT ENROLLMENT

Retention rate of non-white students: na

Scholarships exclusively for non-white students: None

Remediation programs: The college offers the services of the Higher Educational Learning Program and the Higher Educational Opportunity Program.

Academic support services: The Academic and Resource Center provides tutoring services. The English Language Institute also offers support.

Ethnic studies programs: None

Ethnic studies courses: na

Organizations for non-white students: Black Student Union, Latin American Student Organization, Asian-Pacific Student Alliance

Notable non-white alumni: Josie Cruz Natori (president, Natori Company); Sila Calderón (former secretary of state, Commonwealth of Puerto Rico); Anita Florio (justice of the New York State Supreme Court and president of the New York State Association of Women Judges); Sylvia Quarles Simmons (senior vice president, Massachussetts Higher Education Assistance Program)

Tenured faculty: na

Non-tenured faculty: na

Student-faculty ratio: 12:1

Administrators: na

Recent non-white speakers on campus: Alton Maddox (political activist and attorney); Billy Demby (Du Pont spokesperson); Kris Parker (musician); Lenora Fulani (chairperson, National Alliance Party); Dr. Lenworth Gunther (president, EdMedia Associates)

Students at the 152-year-old Manhattanville College are treated to a fine education that is as challenging as it is diverse, while enjoying close proximity to all the excitement and diversity of the Big Apple.

At the heart of Manhattanville's academic curriculum is the portfolio system, which requires that students put into their respective portfolios papers and other course material completed during their four years at the college. Each student's portfolio, which is kept in the Advising Office, also includes a four-year study plan, developed by the student and his or her faculty adviser. Portfolios are reviewed by faculty members four times during the student's tenure at the college. In addition to broad distributional requirements, Manhattanville College students are expected to complete global perspectives courses; this program ensures that students study Western and non-Western civilizations.

Popular and respected majors at Manhattanville include management and economics, art and art history, English, and psychology. Asian Studies also enjoys a good reputation; among Manhattanville's graduates is an associate curator of Asian Art at New York City's Metropolitan Museum of Art. Students say that academic competition at the college is not overly intense, although, as more than one student pointed out, it's what you make of it. For the school's many career-oriented students, internships are plentiful at nearby Nestlé and IBM.

Beginning in the fall of '92, the college will offer a major and minor course of study in African-American Studies, thanks in large part to student initiative. "People had been attempting to get such a program implemented here for years," says a student. "Three years ago, at one of our Quad Jams [the school's biggest campus-wide party), several students staged a sit-in that prevented the bands from performing. More recently, students made a presentation speech at a faculty meeting, where the faculty voted unanimously to create a full-fledged African Studies program. Until then, we were able to major in the area, but doing so involved a lot of red tape and many students didn't bother." Among the school's presently offered courses in the area, students say the history department's "Black Nationalism" and the sociology department's "Culture and Sex Roles in Africa" are popular.

Professors, according to students, are readily available for academic assistance and are often in attendance at student-sponsored events. "The faculty here is so accessible that you have to run and hide from them if you cut their class, especially since many of them live on or near campus," says a student, "and you always see them walking around campus or at the de Ville," an on-campus student hangout.

To further improve the school's cultural programming, Manhattanville's Black Student Union "offers tons of activities," according to a student leader. With about 25 to 30 active members, the BSU works to involve a diverse group of students in its events and activities. "This year we were definitely more inclusive than in years past," comments a student. "Most of our events had an Afrocentric theme, but we're open to the whole campus. During freshman orientation week we requested that we have a time slot to introduce the BSU to interested students. We got a huge turnout; about 80 percent of those who came were black." In a recent year, about five of the group's members were Hispanic, among them the group's social vice president. A recent president of the BSU was given the Student Leader of the Year award in '92 for her work on her organization's behalf.

To attract a bigger and more diverse group to its parties, the BSU has adopted some aggressive advertising tactics. "We used to pretty much rely on word of mouth, but now we mass-produce fliers and stuff them under every student's door. We do this when we're having speakers, parties, or events for African Heritage Month." The group's monthly parties "are important because they bring us together."

For African Heritage Month, BSU events included a Haitian folk art exhibit. According to one student, the majority of Manhattanville's black students are from the Caribbean or are of Caribbean descent. "We want to reflect the diversity among the blacks on campus," says a student about the exhibit.

What Manhattanville's multicultural students have at their school is definite and obvious support on the part of the administration. "I know the president of the college [Marcia Savage] almost personally," says a student. "The president constantly states she will not tolerate racism or sexism on campus. For example, our head of security called the police department when the BSU was having what he considered a controversial speaker on campus. The police came and kept watch. When the president heard of this, she ordered the cops off campus."

The school's dean of intercultural and community advancement is equally supportive. "She coaches us on the political reality of how to do things on an institutional level and on a predominantly white campus. She also helps with some of our BSU activities." Other involved faculty include religion professor Jimmy Jones and sociology professor Bruce Haynes.

In the way of cultural and nightlife activities, the town of Purchase offers relatively little, particularly when compared with the variety of things to do in New York City, a popular weekend destination for students and just forty-five minutes away by train.

Despite the school's stress on multiculturalism, the typical Manhattanville student can best be described, in the words of one student, as someone "from an affluent Catholic or WASP background who has led a very sheltered life and who knows very little about people of color. Many students drive around in Range Rovers and BMWs."

But for one student, the school's academics and the opportunity to meet students from the world over is reason enough to keep her at Manhattanville. "I'm from the Bronx, and all you see there are blacks and Hispanics. The United States is not made up of only those people. So it's been great to come to a school where I've gotten to meet people from all over, including Russia, Colombia, and the Middle East. The quality of education here is also . . . wow!"

NEW YORK UNIVERSITY

Address: 22 Washington Square North, New York, NY 10011
Phone: (212) 998-4500
Director of Admissions: David Finney
Multicultural Student Recruiter: Victor M. Singletary
1991–92 tuition: $14,470
Room and board: $6,650
Application deadline: 2/1
Financial aid application deadline: 2/15
Student-faculty ratio: 13:1
Non-white freshman admissions: Applicants for the class of '94: 4,901
　Accepted: 51%
　Accepted who enroll: 41%
　Applicants accepted who rank in top 10% of high school class: na
　Median SAT: na
　Median ACT: na
Full-time undergraduate enrollment: 12,000
　Men: 43.5%
　Women: 56.5%
Non-white students in
　1987–88: 19%
　1988–89: 31.4%
　1989–90: 34.1%
　1990–91: 34.9%
Geographic distribution of students: na
Top majors: na
Retention rate of non-white students: na
Scholarships exclusively for non-white students: None
Remediation programs: None
Academic support services: The office of African-American Student Services

offers academic and non-academic support.
Ethnic studies programs: The university offers African-American Studies, an interdisciplinary program, involving anthropology, comparative literature, economics, English, fine arts, history, journalism, politics, psychology, sociology, and music. The university's East Asian Studies department offers more than 30 courses, including Chinese-, Japanese-, and Korean-language study. Students can major in Latin American Studies, an interdisciplinary program, involving history, anthropology, Spanish, politics, fine arts, and cinema studies.
Organizations for non-white students: Aesculapian League, African Student Congress, Asia Society, Asian-American

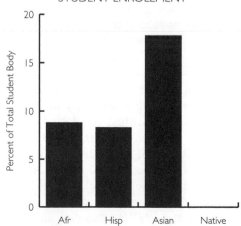

STUDENT ENROLLMENT

Council, Asian Cultural Union, AWAMU, Black Business Student Association, Black Science Students Organization, Black Student Services Center, Caribbean Student Association, Chinese Christian Fellowship, Chinese Students Society, El Club Hispano, Haitian Cultural Society, Hispanic Graduate Students Organization, International Association of Filipino-Americans, Korean Christian Fellowship, Korean Students Association, LUCHA, Minority Journalists, National Association of Black Accountants, Organization of Black Women, United Artists of Color, Vietnamese Student Organization

Notable non-white alumni: Fernando Ferrer (Bronx borough president); Gladys Carrion (New York City commissioner, Community Development Agency); Constance Baker Motley (judge, District Court of New York); Fritz W. Alexander II (judge, New York Court of Appeals); Countee Cullen (poet); Dr. Lorraine Hale (CEO, Hale House Center, New York City); Stephen J. Wright (former president, Fisk University)

Tenured faculty: 734
Non-tenured faculty: 3,645
Student-faculty ratio: 13:1
Administrators: 1,333
  African-American: 9%
  Hispanic: 3.8%
  Asian-American: 3.2%
  Native American: 0
Recent non-white speakers on campus: Dr. Lee Brown (former commissioner, New

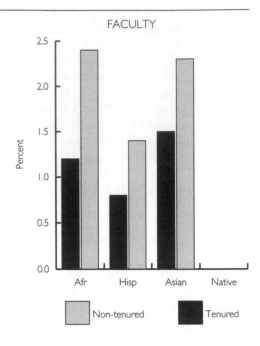

FACULTY

York City police department); William Gray III (former U.S. representative and minority whip, current head of the United Negro College Fund); Lee Bertram (owner, Denver Nuggets professional basketball team); Clarence Smith (publisher, *Essence* magazine); Lely Hayslip (author); Margaret Chin (New York State Democratic Party committeewoman); Bill Chong (president, Asian Americans for Equality); Charles Pei Wang (vice president, U.S. Civil Rights Commission); Marta Moreno Vega (president, Caribbean Cultural Center)

For much of its existence, New York University has suffered from the image of being that "other" private university in New York City (other than Columbia University uptown, that is). Most of its students were commuters and many of its academic programs were more or less second-rate. But since the early 1980s, NYU has become more visible as it strengthens and establishes innovative academic programs that continue to attract a more than motivated student body.

But before one can talk about NYU's academics, one must acknowledge the university's unique campus environment. Located in the Greenwich Village section of Manhattan, NYU embodies all of the pluses and minuses of the big city. Just outside of almost any one of NYU's dorms, students have easy access to a potpourri of expensive and inexpensive restaurants, hip clubs, bars, and just about any other sort of nighttime entertainment imaginable. On the way to the library or out for dinner, however, students will also witness the underside of urban living: the homeless and drugs. The intensity of living in New York City is one reason many students choose to attend school here in the first place. Says a student: "I can't imagine going to a school in the middle of nowhere, or where I'd have to drive just to get to a club or a restaurant. NYU has it all. How absolutely boring it must be to attend school anywhere else."

Students also choose to come here because of its academics, some of which are absolutely stellar. A standout is the Tisch School of the Arts, which has nationally recognized programs in the performing arts and film and television. (Spike Lee earned his master's degree in film studies here.) NYU's Gallatin Division allows students to design their own programs of study, with close faculty supervision. The Stern School of Business includes one of the country's most respected undergraduate business programs and features an outstanding accounting program. NYU's School of Education, Health, Nursing, and Arts Professions also offers some top-notch programs, particularly physical therapy and occupational therapy. While NYU's College of Arts and Sciences (CAS) doesn't rate as high as some of the school's other divisions, students consider English, journalism, math, and French among CAS's better departments.

With much prodding from students, particularly members of the African Student Congress, the university is now in the planning stages of establishing an Africana Studies department, which will allow students to major in Caribbean, African, or African-American Studies. According to students, NYU's East Asian Studies department is solid.

Although NYU has a large undergraduate enrollment, students say that professors are accessible, particularly once you are beyond the introductory-level courses that can sometimes have hundreds of students. A favorite figure on campus is the school's new president, Jay Oliva. "He lives in the penthouse apartment of Hayden House, one of the dorms here on campus, because he wants to live near the students. Every year he has a Halloween party to which he invites students, and there are always prizes given to the person with the best costume." According to the student, Oliva is also frequently seen at many of the events sponsored by student clubs.

NYU is primarily a commuter campus, although in recent years the school, after completing and renovating new dorms, is now able to offer housing to all first-year students. Still, nearly two-thirds of the students commute to campus, many from the outer boroughs, which contributes to a less than unified campus environment. Students say the commuting situation can be a problem when it comes to sponsoring late-night events. But various student organizations and activities seek to create more of a bond between students.

The League of Unified Cooperation of Hispanic Americans (LUCHA), which has about 150 active members, "helps to create a family environment for members," says a LUCHA leader. To help create this "family" feel, LUCHA held a party for first-year students in the Ultraviolet, which doubles as a nightclub on weekends. More than

150 first-year students showed up, along with more than 100 upperclass students. With the student activities office, LUCHA recently sponsored a variety of events for Latin Heritage Month, among them lectures and a Latin American music concert held in Loeb Student Center. Two of LUCHA's biggest events were a talent show and a food festival. LUCHA, according to a student, is a diverse group and represents students from most Latin American countries, as well as members who are Asian, African-American, and European-American. Students recently formed the school's first Latina-centered sorority, Tau Sigma Phi, with about 25 members.

The African Student Congress "is incredibly organized and motivated," says an observer. Besides working to get the university to establish an Africana Studies program, ASC, an umbrella organization for the school's black student groups, holds annual events for African Heritage Month, such as Carnival Africa, which features vendors who sell Afrocentric food, jewelry, books, and clothing. The ASC was established three years ago "to allow students to have a stronger voice on campus, and to help us plan our activities so that no conflicts would arise among some of the black student groups," says a business major. One of the more active black student groups is the Black Business Student Association, with about 50 members, which brings area business leaders to campus to discuss career options, and also sponsors a talent and fashion show. Proceeds from the events usually go to charity. Another organization is the Black Student Services Center, a student-run group that "is more politically oriented." One of the group's main activities is the annual Black Solidarity Day celebration, an all-day event that offers movies, dancing, and guest lecturers.

After years of ASC urging, LUCHA finally decided to join the ASC. "The new relationship has really been working out," says a student. "If either group sponsors an event, the other group attends. By having the two groups work together, we can be more supportive of one another and try to bring about change, like the creation of the Africana Studies program. The two organizations have the same goals: to be recognized by NYU and the campus community."

Socially, almost anything goes at NYU. Students cover the political spectrum, and experimentation with one's sexuality and hair color is not unusual. And why not? NYU is located in the one of the funkiest sections of the country. "Standing on one corner will be rappers and on another will be punkers, and on another will be people with green and blue hair with spikes covering much of the leather goods they're wearing. It's quite an amazing sight." The Greek system is somewhat active, and accounts for about 5 percent of the student body; perhaps the most diverse such organization is Tau Kappa Epsilon, a fraternity; half its membership is Latino. The school's gay and lesbian student organization is the largest on campus.

Attending college in New York City, particularly in Greenwich Village, can be intimidating and can prove to be an overwhelming experience. The ability to be focused, mature, and motivated is a quality you will want to bring with you should you decide to attend this university. Although the school is urban and many of the pluses of attending a small rural college are elusive here, NYU students, with perseverance, are able to find their niche. "I'm shocked by all the organizations and activities I've been involved in here. When I came here, I was a shy, mostly Catholic-educated student. Now I am head of two organizations, and I'm not afraid to meet people. I think this has a lot to do with the nature of NYU. You're able to form any type of club or organization you want to here. Except when it comes time to pay tuition, I can definitely say that NYU exists for you, and not you for it."

RENSSELAER POLYTECHNIC INSTITUTE

Address: Admission and Financial Aid Building, Troy, NY 12180-3590
Phone: (518) 276-6216 / (800) 448-6562
Director of Admissions: Conrad Sharrow
Multicultural Student Recruiter: Tyrone Jordon
1991–92 tuition: $15,150
Room and board: $5,468
Application deadline: 1/15
Financial aid application deadline: 2/15
Student-faculty ratio: 11:1
Non-white freshman admissions:
   (These figures reflect only African-American and Hispanic students.)
   Applicants for the class of '94: 493
   Accepted: 80%
   Accepted who enroll: 55%
   Applicants accepted who rank in top 10% of high school class: 40%
   In top 25%: 80%
   Median SAT range: 400–600 V, 500–710 M
   Median ACT range: 24–29
Full-time undergraduate enrollment: 4,422
   Men: 80%
   Women: 20%
Non-white students in
   1987–88: 17%
   1988–89: 19%
   1989–90: 22%
   1990–91: 20.4%
Students In-state: na
Top majors: 1. Electrical Engineering 2. Mechanical Engineering 3. Computer and Systems Engineering
Retention rate of non-white students: 60%
Scholarships exclusively for non-white students: NACME Scholarship for Engineers: a minimum of $2,000 per award. Garnet Baltimore Scholarship: available to minority transfer students; $5,000 per award.

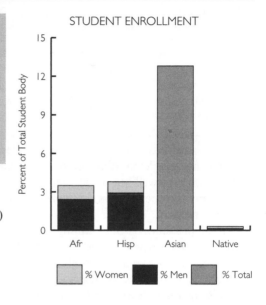

STUDENT ENROLLMENT

Percent of Total Student Body

% Women   % Men   % Total

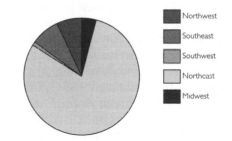

GEOGRAPHIC DISTRIBUTION OF STUDENTS

Northwest
Southeast
Southwest
Northeast
Midwest

Remediation programs: na
Academic support services: The university's Writing Center and Learning Center and the Higher Education Opportunity Program provide tutoring and academic support.
Ethnic studies programs: RPI has a minor in African-American literature, which offers three courses.

Ethnic studies courses: na

Organizations for non-white students: Rensselaer Society of Black Engineers, Society of Hispanic Professional Engineers, Black Student Alliance, Latin Student Association, Alpha Phi Alpha, Kappa Alpha Psi, Omega Psi Phi, Delta Sigma Theta, Phi Iota Alpha, Black Cultural Center

Notable non-white alumni: Dr. Raymond Parker ('77, Physics; attorney, Johnson & Johnson Worldwide Headquarters); Dr. Janet Rutledge ('83, Electrical Engineering; professor, Northwestern University); Gregory Shepard ('83, Electrical Engineering; president, Shepard, Patterson & Associates); Kathryn Tyler-Prigmore ('78, Architecture; architect, Segreti Tepper Architects); Dr. Ronald Sheppard ('61, Physics; director, Continuing Education and Business Development, College of Staten Island)

Tenured faculty: na

Non-tenured faculty: na

Student-faculty ratio: 11:1

Administrators: na

Recent non-white speakers on campus: Dr. Johnnetta Cole (president, Spelman College); Jawanza Kunjufu (author and educator)

Students are drawn to Rensselaer Polytechnic Institute because of the school's outstanding and demanding programs in engineering, architecture, and the sciences. Although not as well known as their peers at MIT or Caltech, RPI graduates are hot job prospects, especially as the world comes to rely increasingly on engineering and technical services.

One of the school's outstanding features is its Office of Minority Student Affairs (OMSA), which was founded in 1979. "If it wasn't for OMSA, I wouldn't be here anymore," says an engineering student. The office provides peer tutoring, counseling, and science and professional development workshops. OMSA has been so successful in retaining students at RPI that it was featured in a 1988 *Christian Science Monitor* article. "The prescription [for keeping students here] isn't fancy," says the *Monitor* reporter. "It's characterized by hard work, modest gains, and constant shepherding of students by a staff that 'doesn't talk failure.'" The program's director, Norman Burnett, "is more of an adviser to us than someone who tells us what we've got to do. He doesn't push his advice on us. He also makes sure we're kept abreast of the activities on other college campuses in terms of multicultural events. He's a great resource." In addition to Burnett, first- and second-year students find support in upperclass students who work in OMSA as counselors. "If you have any questions, they can help you," says a student. "They know what it's like to come here and struggle. They give good advice because they know how competitive this place can be."

According to students, RPI's toughest programs are nuclear and aeronautical engineering. Although popular, mechanical, industrial, and civil engineering are not as rigorous. RPI's School of Management, which also offers a graduate degree program, is said to be solid. To ensure that students aren't graduating only with knowledge about theorems and computer networks, RPI students are required to take four courses each in the humanities and the social sciences. "Although it's hard to find a humanities major here, people usually don't mind taking these courses," says an aeronautical engineering major.

Various cultural organizations offer a change of pace from the school's academic grind. The Latin Student Association (LSA), with about 50 active members, "is basically concerned with social functions and cultural events," says a student. LSA sponsors dances and Spanish food sales. Phi Iota Alpha, a Latin-oriented fraternity, has about 22 men, with about 15 living in the house. "We don't sponsor many activities. We mainly serve to help each other achieve our goals," says a leader of the fraternity, among whose members are the presidents of LSA and the Society of Hispanic Professional Engineers.

In a recent year, for Black History Month the Black Student Association sponsored jazz and fashion shows, a soul food night, and Wednesday-afternoon workshops. One of the workshops, according to a student, focused on campus racial tension, which one student says "has risen to new heights this year." She points to the controversy surrounding the school's new Office of Multicultural Affairs. The office, which opened in the fall of 1991 to help coordinate campus cultural events, was criticized in an editorial in the campus newspaper. "We've pretty much given up on the campus paper. The only time they ever mention the BSA is when there's some controversy involving us, like when we had Stokely Carmichael here. They never mention any of the many programs we sponsor. We've met with the editorial board to discuss this, but they never seem to change." As a result of their frustration with the paper, African-American students have started their own newspaper, *The Rising Voice.* "The paper was actually in existence back in the eighties but it sort of died out until last year. This year, it's gotten to be even more successful. We publish once every month or so and each issue has about twelve pages. The next issue, for April–March, will focus on women's issues for Women's History Month."

The ratio of men to women at RPI is nearly four to one. "For many men, that's an incredible source of frustration, but for us it's great," comments a coed. RPI men will often visit Russell Sage, a women's college, located "just three blocks from here." RPI's multicultural students also interact with students from Siena and Union colleges, as well as SUNY/Albany, which are all within driving distance.

The predominantly white fraternities are a big deal at RPI, and much of the school's social life revolves around them, especially on weekends. "A lot of drinking goes on here in the frats," reports a student. About a third of RPI's men belong to one or another of the school's 27 fraternities and about a quarter of the school's women are members of one or another of three sororities. The three historically black fraternities on campus have anywhere from two to seven members. "We don't really rely on them for any kind of social outlet. They primarily rely on their brothers at SUNY/Albany or Union for parties and other support."

One of the school's sororities was founded in the late 1980s as a multicultural sorority and "includes whites, blacks, Asians, and Indians. Each year they sponsor an amazing event, called the International Festival, when all of the groups sponsor booths at the union building. The event really unifies the cultural groups." The sorority, Psi Beta Nu, has a residence facility for about 20 women.

For RPI students, there are plenty of social outlets. As one student observes: "Everyone is able to find their own niche here. There's always something to do." For many, adjusting to the school's rigorous academic demands is tougher. But with the assistance of OMSA, an education at well-regarded RPI is less an impossibility than a challenge. "I wanted to make it here because I wanted to prove to myself that I could," says a senior. "I want a degree with the Rensselaer name. But I also came here because I knew this was a place where I could make a difference, and I wanted to go to a school where I could feel that the changes I might make would be around even after I graduated. And, in looking back on my four years here, I feel I've helped open the dialogue on racial issues here on campus. No longer is it all kept in the closet."

UNIVERSITY OF ROCHESTER

Address: Wilson Boulevard, Rochester, NY 14627
Phone: (716) 275-3221
Director of Admissions: Dr. B. Ann Wright
Multicultural Student Recruiter: Mary Gilbert
1991–92 tuition: $21,270 (room and board included)
Application deadline: 1/15
Financial aid application deadline: 2/1
Non-white freshman admissions: Applicants for the class of '94: 1,535
Accepted: 58%
Accepted who enroll: 25%
Applicants accepted who rank in top 10% of high school class: 59%
In top 25%: 90%
Median SAT range: 420–550 V, 470–610 M
Median ACT range: 21–27
Full-time undergraduate enrollment: 4,823
Men: 55%
Women: 45%
Non-white students in
1987–88: 14%
1988–89: 15%
1989–90: 16%
1990–91: 18.2%
Students In-state: na
Top majors: 1. Biology 2. Psychology 3. Economics
Retention rate of non-white students: 70%
Scholarships exclusively for non-white students: AHORA: need-based; $2,500 per year; five awarded each year; must be nominated by a Hispanic organization or school officials in Rochester or Puerto Rico. Urban League: non-need-based;

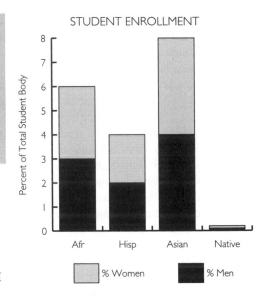

STUDENT ENROLLMENT

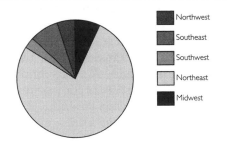

GEOGRAPHIC DISTRIBUTION OF STUDENTS

$2,500 per year; 30 to 45 awarded per year; must be nominated by local Urban League chapter.
Remediation programs: None
Academic support services: The Office of Minority Student Affairs and the Center

for Academic Support provide academic support services. Tutoring is available in most academic subjects. The Early Connection Orientation program introduces students to the academic and non-academic opportunities available at the university.

Ethnic studies programs: The university offers an interdisciplinary course of study in African and African-American Studies, established in 1985, involving anthropology, economics, history, English-language study, political science, women's studies, and religion. More than 30 courses are taught as part of the program. Faculty: 6. Rochester also offers a program in Asian Studies, which includes more than 30 courses from 10 departments. Chinese- and Japanese-language study is offered at all levels. Faculty: 15. The university's Latin American Studies program, offered as a minor, includes 12 courses from 4 departments.

Organizations for non-white students: Asian-American Association, Black and Hispanic Women's Alliance, Black Student Union, Chinese Students Association, Korean Students Association, Spanish and Latin Students Association, Vietnamese Students Association, Association of Black Drama and the Arts, Association of Minority Engineers, Black Greek Council, Alpha Phi Alpha, Kappa Alpha Psi, Omega Psi Phi, Alpha Kappa Alpha, Delta Sigma Theta, Zeta Phi Beta

Notable non-white alumni: Joan Mitchell Salmon Campbell (director, Presbyterian Church); Mary Frances Winters (president, Winters Group); William Warfield (performer, baritone); Deborah

Flemister Mullen (associate dean, McCormick Theological Seminary); Leslie Byron Dunner (director, Detroit Symphony Civic Orchestra and director of Dearborn Symphony)

Tenured faculty: 548
Non-tenured faculty: 673

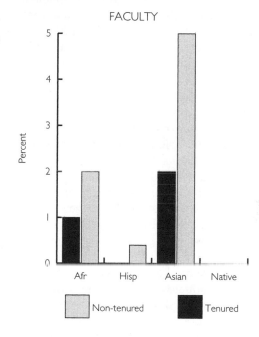

FACULTY

Student-faculty ratio: 12:1
Administrators: 719
   African-American: 5%
   Hispanic: 1%
   Asian-American: 0.6%
   Native American: 0
Recent non-white speakers on campus: Spike Lee (filmmaker); Barbara Fields (historian, Columbia University); Alex Haley (author); Sonia Sanchez (poet); James Evans (president, Colgate Rochester Divinity School)

The University of Rochester, contrary to common belief, is not a large public university. Located ten minutes from downtown Rochester, it is actually a midsize, private institution that offers top academics in pleasant surroundings.

The university's facilities are outstanding. The Wilson Commons, designed by world-renowned architect I. M. Pei (he also designed the new addition to the Louvre in Paris), is said to be one of the best student centers in the nation and houses an art gallery and student organization offices, and is the site of many student activities and events. The school's biochemistry and psychology buildings offer state-of-the-art equipment; its observatory, located in Bristol Hills forty miles south, is the highest observatory in the eastern half of the country; the university's $8 million Zornow Sports Center is ideal for any athlete, from the tennis player to the weight lifter, and the school's computer facilities are equally impressive, with 29 minicomputers and 250 microcomputers that are available to students twenty-four hours a day.

Students believe that the education they're getting is as outstanding as the school's facilities. The university's Institute of Optics is well regarded and is one of the few such programs in the country. (Kodak is located nearby and is a big recruiter of Rochester grads.) English, political science, and economics are among Rochester's best programs in the humanities. The school's engineering program is rigorous; students apply to the program only after sophomore year. The nursing program is also said to be good. The university's Eastman School of Music, located two miles from campus in downtown Rochester, is world-renowned. Students, even philosophy majors, are able to earn a certificate in management.

The school's Frederick Douglass Institute for African and African-American Studies is expanding its course offerings. "Black Intellectuals and the Crisis of the Twentieth Century" is one student favorite.

While students say the academic intensity of the university is what you make of it, they nonetheless are thankful for the school's innovative Ventures program, in which first-year grades do not appear on your transcript. This not only creates a more relaxed first year but also encourages students to take courses that they might otherwise have shied away from. Students also say that the professors, who teach all undergraduate courses in line with school policy, are easily accessible.

The university's Office of Minority Student Affairs, housed in Morey Hall, has recently been reorganized with the arrival in the fall of '91 of the new director, ErVin Gross. "The office is just now coming out of turmoil. We didn't have a director for a year. Last year was Dr. ErVin's year to get the office back on track," says a student. According to a senior, ErVin "has been very helpful with obtaining funds to support groups' activities. He's always willing to support students—for example, helping students buy tickets to events with discretionary funds from his office's budget. The office still has its problems—there have been some conflicts among the staff members—but it certainly is better than it was."

The Black Student Union, with about 35 to 65 active members, "has lost momentum since the class of '95 came in," reports a student. "Students just don't seem to want to get involved." Although not as active as in the past, the BSU still manages to sponsor various activities throughout the school year. Its most ambitious project is the Pan-African Exposition, held each February to celebrate Black History Month. The exposition "is a celebration of all heritages that have descended from Africa, including Latin America. It's an all-day event, and no other organization sponsors activities that day on campus. In addition to art displays, there are workshops, panel discussions, a banquet, and a party." The events take place in Wilson Commons. Other events sponsored by BSU are a Kwanzaa dinner each December and a semiformal dance, usually held in April, to pay tribute to the graduating seniors. Traditionally the event has been held at the commons, but in a recent year the group chartered a boat. The BSU has its office in the Wilson Commons, and meets every other Sunday. It shares its office with two other organizations, the Black and Hispanic Women's Alliance and the Association of Black Drama and the Arts.

A common complaint made by African-American students at the university, particularly among the male students, is the almost predictable harassment by the campus's security. "My freshman year I got asked twenty or thirty times if I go to school here by a security officer," says a senior. "Just the other day my roommate was walking across the new pedestrian bridge that connects the campus to the Nineteenth Ward, and he was asked by one of the security people if he was a student here. He even had his book bag over his shoulder. My roommate took the officer's badge number and called the security chief about the incident, but all the chief did was apologize. Three articles have appeared in the campus newspaper about this type of harassment, but it never seems to change."

The Black and Hispanic Women's Alliance, which holds meetings on Sundays alternating with the BSU meetings, "has had trouble keeping up a membership, but they do things on a smaller scale than the BSU, such as sponsoring forums and speakers on feminism and relationships," says a senior.

With the BSU, the Spanish and Latin Students Association (SALSA) sponsors Harambee La Parranda, a daylong orientation for incoming first-year and transfer students. "A representative from the different minority organizations speaks to the new minority students about the functions and activities of each group. Also present are representatives from financial aid, career services, and the Center for Academic Support," says a student. Although the orientation is targeted at all minority students, in recent years only Hispanic and African-American students have attended. SALSA also sponsors Tropicana, an event similar to the BSU's exposition, "but on a smaller scale," which features guest speakers, a dance, and movies.

To ensure that there are no scheduling conflicts among the various multicultural student groups on campus, students recently established the Minority Student Advisory Board, which meets Wednesday evenings. "The board is an umbrella organization consisting of the president and vice president of each minority student group. At the meetings we discuss the future events of the groups represented, and we also sponsor leadership conferences for future board members."

Wilson Commons and the Zornow Sports Center are the hubs of student activity at Rochester. Students have the opportunity to participate in more than 100 student clubs and organizations, including pre-professional societies, social service organizations, religious groups, and fraternities and sororities. Yellowjacket Day and Dandelion Day (hailed by *Newsweek* magazine as one of the best 15 college parties) and Winter Carnival are popular annual events. As part of University Days, students and faculty attend lectures and seminars sponsored every Wednesday, although students have been known to use the afternoon to catch up on their sleep or studies.

Downtown Rochester, just a ten-minute (free) bus ride from campus, is home to more than twenty malls, as well as numerous restaurants, dance clubs, movie theaters, and art galleries, all of which are popular destinations for students. Free concerts at the Eastman School are given almost daily. The city has African-American, Asian-American, and Hispanic communities, but other than visiting local restaurants and participating in community service projects, students say there is little interaction with them.

The city of Rochester and its environs may be cold much of the school year, especially during the winters, when heavy snowfall is a fact of life. But the University of Rochester, with a tight academic community and demanding studies, offers a great deal to do indoors. Says a senior: "I think of Rochester as a microcosm of society. For minority students, the issues are pretty much the same here as they are out there. You can come here and initiate change. You can have an impact."

ROCHESTER INSTITUTE OF TECHNOLOGY

Address: One Lomb Memorial Drive, Rochester, NY 14623
Phone: (716) 475-6631
Director of Admissions: Daniel R. Shelley
Multicultural Student Recruiter: Joy Houck
1992–93 tuition: $12,238
Room and board: $5,100
Application deadline: 3/1
Financial aid application deadline: 3/1
Student-faculty ratio: 14:1
Non-white freshman admissions:
Applications for the class of 95: 500
Accepted: 65%
Accepted who enroll: 49%
Applicants accepted who rank in top 10% of high school class: na
Median SAT range: na
Median ACT range: na
Full-time undergraduate enrollment: 9,000
Men: 68%
Women: 32%
Non-white students in
1987–88: 8.2%
1988–89: 8.6%
1989–90: 9.4%
1990–91: 10%
Geographic distribution of students: na
Students In-state: 68%
Top majors: 1. Engineering 2. Imaging Arts and Sciences 3. Applied Sciences and Technology
Retention rate of non-white students: na
Scholarships exclusively for non-white students: RIT Urban League Scholarship: $2,500 for each award. RIT Puerto Rican Youth Development and Ibero-American Action League Scholarship: merit- and need-based; $2,500 for each award. RIT Minority Transfer Scholarship: $2,500 awards; merit- and need-based.
Remediation programs: The university has a Higher Educational Opportunity Program and the University Program, available only to New York State residents.
Academic support services: Tutoring is available in most subjects, as well as labs in writing and math and for students diagnosed with learning disabilities or who are first-generation college students.

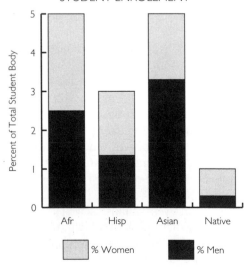

STUDENT ENROLLMENT

Percent of Total Student Body

Afr   Hisp   Asian   Native

□ % Women   ■ % Men

Special academic support services are also available.

Ethnic studies programs: None

Ethnic studies courses: Approximately six courses in African-American and African Studies.

Organizations for non-white students: Black Awareness Coordinating Committee, Hispanic Student Association, B'Strong, Native American Student Association, Society of African-American Business Students, Black Sisters Together Reaching Out for New Goals, Unity House (special-interest floor in a residence hall), Alpha Kappa Alpha, Omega Psi Phi, Delta Sigma Theta, Alpha Phi Alpha, Kappa Alpha Psi, Zeta Phi Beta, Phi Beta Sigma, Sigma Gamma Rho

Notable non-white alumni: na

Tenured faculty: 433

Non-tenured faculty: 128

Student-faculty ratio: 14:1

Administrators: na

Recent non-white speakers on campus: Rev. C. T. Vivian (civil rights activist); Atallah Shabazz (civil rights activist and daughter of Malcolm X); Dr. Na'im

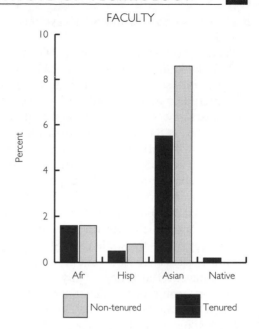

FACULTY

Akbar (clinical psychologist); Dr. Juanita Pitts (coordinator, Rochester's Frederick Douglass Organization); Susan Taylor (editor, *Essence* magazine); Ruby Dee (actress)

Technical training is at the heart of an education at the Rochester Institute of Technology. RIT students don't mind all the hours they put into their studies—the school is on a quarter system that keeps things busy—as employers are knocking on most students' doors come graduation.

RIT offers an incredible array of academic opportunities, ranging from social work and imaging science to printing management and international business management. The school is best known for its nationally recognized programs in photography, printing, and computer science. RIT's engineering programs—electrical, computer, industrial, mechanical, and microelectronic—are also outstanding. The school's recently built Center for Imaging Science and its new computer engineering center offer state-of-the art facilities for research in those areas. Among the school's liberal arts offerings, students say the "Black Literature" course is excellent.

A popular option at RIT is its co-op program, the fifth-largest such program in the country. The school's Office for Cooperative Education and Placement helps hook up juniors and seniors with more than 1,300 employers from all across the country. Employers include engineering firms, small businesses, government agencies, or local companies such Bausch & Lomb and Kodak. Says a student about her co-op experience: "When it comes down to the application of what you've learned, RIT has other schools beat. Co-op gave me the luxury of being able to learn from my mistakes."

Whether they want to or not, RIT students must take courses in the liberal arts. Although requirements vary from school to school, all students take courses in English composition, science, the humanities, and social science.

The studies at RIT don't tax a student's intellect as much as his or her time. Professors pile on the work, and with four quarters a year, finals come all too frequently. As RIT is a research-oriented school, professors are oftentimes engrossed in their own work, which has negative and positive aspects. The negative is that professors are inaccessible, particularly in lower-level courses, although class sizes diminish considerably in the upper-level courses. The positive is that students are frequently able to work on original research tasks with professors.

RIT's Higher Education Opportunity Program assists students with their academic and non-academic concerns. The director of the program, Arlette-Miller Smith, is highly regarded by students. "She always encourages the minority women on campus," says a student. "She tells us and shows us that we can make it and that we should never let anything or anybody pull us down." Smith is adviser to B' Strong, a support group for female students of color at RIT.

The Office of Minority Student Affairs (OMSA) also provides support. Each year OMSA sponsors racial awareness workshops, leadership development opportunities, annual tributes to Dr. Martin Luther King, Jr., and minority students' fall orientation. The orientation wins high marks from students. "As part of the program, we had discussions about being culturally aware, interracial relationships, how to adjust to college life, how to study, and dorm life." Mike Arroya, OMSA's director, "has helped to set up a book fund for minority students and makes sure that the minority students are aware of all the scholarships that we are eligible for," says a student. Vernon Grier, a professor of social work, works closely with students. "He always encourages the minority students to work hard so that he can be proud of us."

Some of the more active cultural student groups at RIT are the Black Awareness Coordinating Committee, which sponsors activities each year for Black Awareness Week in April, and the Hispanic Student Association. The Unity House, which occupies a floor in one of the campus's dorms, is a popular residence for the school's African-American students and helps coordinate Black Awareness Week activities.

Women on campus are able to find support through Women's Network. "This group brings women of all races together, which is very much needed," says a student. "This unification is strong and ongoing." Men at RIT outnumber the women more than two to one.

Students say there is little racial integration socially on campus. "The white students have their parties and the minority students have their parties. Rarely, if ever, will students mingle at parties held by other races." Likewise, students say there is little integration when it comes to campus dining. "If black and white students sit and eat together here, they are looked at by their peers as being different," says a student.

RIT is located in a suburb of Rochester, and students report that "we have a good relationship with the nearby black community. They support our functions and donate money for some of our special projects." For off-campus entertainment, students will venture into the city, just about seven miles north. Rochester is the third-largest city in New York State, and 25 percent of its population is African-American. Rochester is also home to the University of Rochester. Syracuse, Albany, and Buffalo are within easy driving distance.

Parties, mostly in the residence halls, are popular, as is attending men's varsity ice hockey games. Most students are more active pursuing their studies, however, than engaging in extracurricular activities.

RIT is for the student with clear career goals in the practical fields of engineering and other technical areas. Students looking for a great deal of cultural enlightenment may be disappointed. But, as one student says, "RIT may not teach me a lot about other cultures, but the degree will prepare me to get a good job."

ST. LAWRENCE UNIVERSITY

Address: Canton, NY 13617
Phone: (315) 379-5261
Director of Admissions: Joel Wincowski
Multicultural Student Recruiter: Carlos Arias

1992–93 tuition: $16,700
Room and board: $5,300
Application deadline: 2/1
Financial aid application deadline: 2/15

St. Lawrence is New York State's oldest coed university. It is also one of the state's northernmost. Located just a few miles south of the Canadian border, the 137-year-old university offers a respectable liberal arts and sciences education in what one student describes as a "warm and supportive atmosphere."

This is fortunate, as the winters here can be long. But academics, which have grown more rigorous in recent years, provide more than enough reason to brave the cold. Courses in government, English, foreign languages, and history are regarded as among the school's best. Other top departments are computer science and sociology. The school's Caribbean and Latin American Studies program is praised by students, but they say the African-American Studies program is limited because of its relatively few course offerings. The university's programs in Canadian Studies, gender studies, and environmental studies are well respected. Students praise their professors for the amount of individual attention they receive.

To graduate, first-year students must complete the Freshman Program, entitled "The Human Condition: Nature, Self, and Society," in which they attend classes and share dorms with the other 47 students in their respective sections. The program is interdisciplinary and each section is team-taught by three professors from different departments. The program stresses writing and analytical and critical thinking skills.

St. Lawrence has active study-abroad programs in ten different foreign countries, including Canada, Austria, Denmark, and Kenya. St. Lawrence also has cooperative-degree programs with several major universities, including Rensselaer Polytechnic for engineering and Columbia University and the University of Rochester for nursing.

St. Lawrence's course offerings are certainly more diverse than its student body. The university continues to attract conservative white students, mostly from the suburbs of Connecticut and New York, who have a laid-back approach to academics.

(Many of these students are pleased to note the university's golf course on the edge of campus.) There is very little deviation from the norm, and issues of race relations aren't talked about much, except maybe in rare classroom situations. "I remember in my Freshman Program course we discussed racial discrimination," says a senior. "I was the only minority student in the class, and when I discussed these issues, no one could believe all the experiences I've been through. But that was that. No one likes to talk about such things outside of the classroom. People here just don't want to rock the boat."

Such issues are discussed, however, in the school's cultural organizations. Ahora, St. Lawrence's Hispanic student organization, "had difficulty getting established on campus two years ago," says a student. "The student government officers wondered why such a group needed to be formed. They were worried that all we were going to do was speak Spanish and cut ourselves off from the rest of the campus. So what we've done is to try to initially make the activities less festive and more academic, and we've attempted to include white students." In a recent year, about five of Ahora's 20 active members were white, says a student. Recently, Ahora hosted its first all-day workshop on campus, titled "The Latino Student Today," which featured a Mexican-American keynote speaker. "The hard part is getting even Hispanics to come to the event," says an organizer. The majority of the school's Hispanic students are from New York City.

The Black Student Union, with about 30 active members, is made up of students from the Caribbean and Africa, as well as African-Americans, most of whom are from the New York City area. In a recent year, the BSU, which meets regularly in the university center, sponsored a three-day conference entitled "Reunification of the Black Community: Mind, Body, and Soul," which offered a panel discussion, workshops, and a dance. "But the events drew little attention on campus," says a student. "This year we have an apathetic student body. I think, and hope, we'll be more active next year, because people are getting tired of letting opportunities slip through their fingers." To commemorate Martin Luther King's birthday, students staged a daylong teach-in on campus.

Alternatives to living in the dorms include the Black Cultural Center, which has a reading room and sitting rooms and kitchen facilities. The two-story center provides living facilities for six African-American female students. African-American men have the option of living in the Louis Ray House of Brotherhood. The house, named for a St. Lawrence graduate, accommodates about six men in single and double rooms.

The bulk of the social life at St. Lawrence is courtesy of the Greek system. Nearly half of the school's students belong to the school's predominantly white fraternities and sororities; in a recent year, approximately nine African-American and Latino students were members of these organizations. Additional on-campus activity is found at the field house, which provides an indoor track, a pool, a weight room, and tennis courts. Cross-country and downhill skiing are popular, and are even offered as intramural sports activities. The men's varsity ice hockey team is *the* team to watch.

The village of Canton, a predominantly white community of about 7,000 residents, has a movie theater and some restaurants, but little else. For social life off campus, St. Lawrence's non-white students will head to parties at nearby Canton State or Potsdam, about five and twenty minutes away by car, respectively. New York City,

Boston, and Philadelphia are each about six and a half hours away, also by car. Public transportation to any of these spots is limited.

St. Lawrence University may not provide the most rigorous educational experience in upstate New York, but it does offer one that is every bit as supportive as the other schools in the area. Says a New Yorker: "When I first came here, I wanted to leave. I never found a clique to hang with. But ever since I've gotten involved with Ahora, I've liked it more. Being involved with the group made me feel as if I belonged here, and it has made the transition from home to college easier."

SARAH LAWRENCE COLLEGE

Address: Bronxville, NY 10708
Phone: (914) 395-2510 / (800) 888-2858
Director of Admissions: Robin Mamlet
Multicultural Student Recruiter: Beverly Fox
1991–92 tuition: $16,400
Room and board: $6,400
Application deadline: Early decision: 1/1;
    regular decision: 2/1
Financial aid application deadline: 2/1
Non-white freshman admissions: Applicants
    for the class of '95: 313
    Accepted: 56%
    Accepted who enroll: 19%
    Applicants accepted who rank in top
    10% of high school class: 30%
    In top 25%: 75%
    Median SAT range: 490–540 V,
    460–540 M
    Median ACT range: 24–27
Full-time undergraduate enrollment: 1,000
    Men: 30%
    Women: 70%
Non-white students in
    1987–88: 11%
    1988–89: 16%
    1989–90: 21%
    1990–91: 24%
Students In-state: 15%
Top majors: 1. Writing 2. Literature
    3. Psychology
Retention rate of non-white students: 80%
**Scholarships exclusively for non-white
    students:** None
Remediation programs: None
Academic support services: Each student is

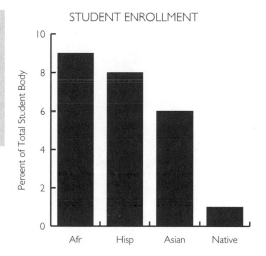

STUDENT ENROLLMENT

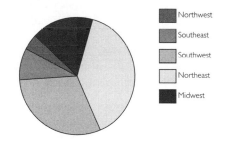

GEOGRAPHIC DISTRIBUTION OF STUDENTS

Northwest
Southeast
Southwest
Northeast
Midwest

assigned a faculty don for four years. Tutoring in writing is available.
Ethnic studies programs: There are no majors at Sarah Lawrence. Students construct their own curriculums with the assistance of their dons.

Ethnic studies courses: More than 20 courses in ethnic studies. Courses in Japanese and Chinese are offered, as are five courses in African and African-American Studies, and the course "Native American Societies in the Twentieth-Century."

Organizations for non-white students: Harambe, Asian Student Union, Unidad!, Concerned Students of Color, Students of Coloring

Notable non-white alumni: Alice Walker (Pulitzer Prize-winning author); Renee Pouissant (news anchor, WJLA, ABC-TV); Holly Robinson (actress); Yoko Ono (artist); Robin Givens (actress)

Tenured faculty: 65

Non-tenured faculty: 87

Student-faculty ratio: 6:1

Administrators: 55
  African-American: 13%
  Hispanic: 2%
  Asian-American: 4%
  Native American: 0

Recent non-white speakers on campus: Jamaica Kincaid (author); Alton Maddox (political activist and attorney);

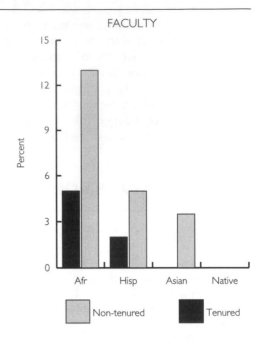

FACULTY

James Miller (professor, Trinity College); Milyoung Cho (Committee Against Anti-Asian Violence); Sonia Sanchez (poet); Charles Barron (activist)

In its commitment to top-quality education and its relatively small size, Sarah Lawrence resembles many other liberal arts colleges in the Northeast. But in almost every other respect—from the type of student it attracts to its academic programs—the 67-year-old school is its own unique place.

Beginning with a student's academic program, Sarah Lawrence stresses individualism. With the close supervision of a faculty member, known as a don, students design their own major course of study, which not only eliminates academic competition between students but also allows students to study what interests them most. The only requirements for graduation are that students take at least one course in three of the school's four academic areas: creative arts, the humanities, the natural sciences and math, and history and the social sciences.

Sarah Lawrence is well known for being an "artsy" school whose academic strengths are in such areas as the visual and performing arts. Writing is one of the school's most highly rated programs; on its faculty is noted author Lindsey Abrams, one of the school's more popular professors. Literature is also well regarded. Psychology students have the benefit of studying in the school's Early Childhood Center, which allows them to observe and teach pre-school children. Pre-med students enjoy high placement rates in medical schools. Other top programs at Sarah Lawrence are film history and filmmaking and philosophy.

Interaction with faculty members is one of the truly outstanding features of an education at Sarah Lawrence. Professors and students are on a first-name basis, and a student's don serves as his or her academic and personal counselor for the four years he or she is enrolled at the college. At other schools long lines are inevitable at registration time, but students at Sarah Lawrence actually have the chance to interview professors about their respective courses before registering, asking them about course content, expectations, and perspectives. In addition, professors don't give out letter grades—although grades are kept on file should a student need them for graduate school applications or for employment purposes—but provide extensive written evaluations.

Some of the professors who work closely with students are Tamara Floyd, dean of residential life; Daphne Dumas, assistant dean of studies and dean of international students; Komozi Woodard, a history professor; Horatio Williams, a political science professor; Chi Ogunyemi, a literature professor; and Pilar Rotella, a Spanish professor. "All these people have attended Harambe and Unidad! meetings," writes a student. "They have worked with and encouraged students of color politically and have been available and supportive on a personal level." Regina Arnold, a professor of sociology, is also supportive of students and has led several racism workshops on campus in recent years.

As unique as Sarah Lawrence's educational programs are, so are the school's students, whose commitment to nonconformity is about all any two students have in common. Well, that and dressing in black, which is de rigueur for many students. Students are also on the whole progressive-minded, socially and politically. But, says a student, "in general, the awareness of any political issues is based on individual experiences. There is no general campus consciousness. Anyone planning to attend Sarah Lawrence should be aware of this. At times the individualist atmosphere makes it difficult to come together for group action. However, because of the close proximity to New York City, many students are involved with national and local organizations there, which leads to the creation of campus political organizations and political action by individuals. Examples of this are Sarah Lawrence's homeless task force and the midnight runs into New York City with food and clothing, women organizing an escort service for women's health-care facilities, and the Animal Liberation Organization, where students participate in rallies against the wearing of fur."

According to another student, however, "the closest Sarah Lawrence has come to achieving a complete campus awareness on an issue was during the spring semester of 1989, when a series of events culminated in a sit-in and a virtual shutdown of the school for one week. Harambe, the African-American student association, submitted a proposal to the administration requesting more courses in African and African-American history and culture and the reevaluation of health services and security in order for the offices to be more sensitive to the needs of students of color." Students have complained about campus security harassing African-American males visiting friends on campus. Also during the spring semester of '89, students organized under the group name Concerned Students of Color staged a sit-in, demanding that the college diversify its curriculum and recruit more faculty of color.

Sarah Lawrence's gay and lesbian student group is largely accepted and tolerated. "Most cultural education on campus comes from actions taken by student groups," says a student. "Recently many speakers sponsored by Harambe, Unidad!, and the Asian Student Union have come to campus." During the 1990–91 school year, the school sponsored activities for its first Asian-American Awareness Month, in April, and its first Latino poetry series. Except for pre-med students, Sarah Lawrence students are also characterized by a lack of pre-professionalism.

Although the college is actually located in Yonkers, it borders Bronxville, a posh and predominantly white residential section of the Bronx that offers some shopping and dining opportunities. Students don't report the best relations with their neighbors, who complain of loud music and the weird dress of the students. For additional off-campus diversions, students will frequently make the half-hour trek, either by train or by car, to Manhattan, with its wealth of cultural and social activities.

Sarah Lawrence is a rare breed in American higher education, especially in the pragmatic and career-conscious '90's. But the college says applications are increasing each year, so it is obviously doing something right. No doubt its draws include close personal attention to the individual student and well-regarded academics. "I had thought about going to one of the SUNY schools, but once I visited Sarah Lawrence, I knew this was where I wanted to come," says a recent graduate. "I could tell that the students here were their own people and that the professors were friendly and really cared."

SKIDMORE COLLEGE

Address: North Broadway, Saratoga Springs, NY 12866
Phone: (518) 587-7569
Director of Admissions: Mary Lou W. Bates
Multicultural Student Recruiter: Kevin Brown
1991–92 tuition: $15,785
Room and board: $5,090
Application deadline: 2/1
Financial aid application deadline: 2/1
Non-white freshman admissions: Applicants for the class of '95: 582
Accepted: 68%
Accepted who enroll: 19.7%
Applicants accepted who rank in top 10% of high school class: 25%
In top 25%: 61%
Median SAT: 460 V, 500 M
Median ACT: 23.5
Full-time undergraduate enrollment: 2,156
Men: 43.2%
Women: 56.3%

Non-white students in
1987–88: 7.6%
1988–89: 7.6%

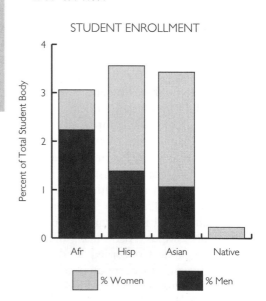

STUDENT ENROLLMENT

Percent of Total Student Body

Afr   Hisp   Asian   Native

☐ % Women   ■ % Men

1989–90: 9.0%

1990–91: 9.1%

Geographic distribution of students: na

Students In-state: 71.4%

Top majors: 1. Business
2. Biology/Chemistry 3. Art

Retention rate of non-white students: 90.4%

Scholarships exclusively for non-white students: None

Remediation programs: None

Academic support services: Skidmore's Office of Academic Advising Services and the Higher Education Opportunity Program provide academic and non-academic support. The college also provides programs in writing, math, and foreign languages, as well as peer tutors.

Ethnic studies programs: None

Ethnic studies courses: Offered are "African-American Literature," "Afro-American Music," "Southwest Indians," "North American Indians," "Race Relations and Minority Groups," "Arts of Africa, Oceania, and the Americas," "History of Jazz in America," "African Arts from the Old World to the New," "Race and Politics Since 1928," and "The Psychology of Prejudice."

Organizations for non-white students: Asia Club, Students Organized Against Racism, Black Action Movement, Latino Cultural Society, RISEN (a student organization focusing on diversifying the college's curriculum)

Notable non-white alumni: na

Tenured faculty: 102

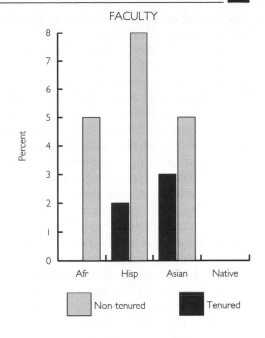

FACULTY

Non-tenured   Tenured

Non-tenured faculty: 39

Student-faculty ratio: 11:1

Administrators: 190

African-American: 4%

Hispanic: 5%

Asian-American: 0

Native American: 0

Recent non-white speakers on campus: Chinua Achebe (author); Martin Luther King III (Georgia state representative and civil rights activist); Maya Angelou (author and poet); Amiri Baraka (author and civil rights activist)

Once a women's school with strengths in the arts and a reputation as a school for debutantes, Skidmore College is today a fully coeducational institution of higher learning committed to the liberal arts and sciences.

Skidmore's liberal studies program—which involves interdisciplinary learning and team teaching—is testament to the school's mission to graduate well-rounded students. Integrated into the curriculum in 1985, the program requires students to enroll in courses in four different areas of learning: human experience, cultural traditions and social change, artistic forms and critical concepts, and science, society, and human values. But that's not all. Students are also expected to complete courses in a foreign language, non-Western cultures, a laboratory science, and visual and performing arts. Students find that the many course requirements can be stifling, as they leave less room for electives, but most agree the quality of the courses is excellent.

Two of the school's best departments are government and English. The college recently revamped its business program, which offers some of the school's most popular majors. Students are now able to combine a major in business or economics with a major in a variety of disciplines, such as a foreign language, government, or even physical education. The school's theater and already highly respected music programs were enhanced with the recent completion of a new fine arts center, that boasts an impressive theater and set design studio. Skidmore also offers several joint-degree programs with numerous other schools, such as engineering at Dartmouth College or education at Union College.

In an attempt to introduce more culturally diverse courses into the Skidmore curriculum, a student group called RISEN (Reforms in Student Education Now) donated $600 to the college's board of trustees "as a first installment of a fund to expand the multicultural aspects of faculty research," said a recent *New York Times* article about the donation. David Porter, Skidmore's president, matched the contribution with college funds. Additional funds will come from fundraisers, including a benefit concert and donations from student organizations. According to a letter that accompanied the check, RISEN members requested that the money be used for "summer and faculty development programs that will enable interested faculty members to learn how to incorporate into their classes issues of race, ethnicity, and gender, as well as a more diverse pool of authors and contributors within their respective fields." One of the school's more popular cultural courses currently offered is "History of African-American Music."

Professors at Skidmore, as is typical at schools committed to undergraduate education, are highly accessible. "I've taken advantage of the peer tutors in math and foreign languages here at Skidmore," says a student. "But most students think interaction with professors is better and easier. I can telephone my professors at home and call them by their first names. Calling on a professor doesn't always have to be done during his or her office hours. I wouldn't change a small-college education for anything."

Skidmore's Office of Multicultural Affairs is undergoing a period of adjustment, according to students. Recently the director's position had gone unfilled for a school year, but Rene Montenegro, its new director, "has many great ideas and he's been meeting with student leaders," says a student. "But it's going to take time for anything much to change. The office has been mostly inactive since I've been here." One of the programs instituted by Montenegro that has won praise from students is a yearlong film series that focuses on various ethnic and racial themes.

The Latino Cultural Society, a student group, has about 25 active members and, says a member, "works to educate the Skidmore community about the Latino influence in the United States." The group, which meets twice a month, sponsors movies, lectures, a talent show, and, in the fall semester, Hispanic Heritage Month, which features a dinner and a dance. According to a student, Hispanic Heritage Month activities are "well attended by the community" at and around the college. The organization also interacts with Latino student groups from SUNY/Albany and SUNY/New Paltz. Each year, the group heads to the Albany campus to attend the

Latino Collegiate Conference, at which numerous workshops are scheduled. The event is sponsored by Hispanic groups at Albany.

The Black Action Movement (BAM), with about 15 active members, meets once every two weeks, usually in one of the college's dorm lounges. BAM regularly sponsors discussion groups, forums, and, comments a student, "our share of parties." BAM members also work closely with the Latino Cultural Society.

The Student Government Association at Skidmore is active, overseeing a budget of nearly $350,000 that is distributed to more than 80 clubs and organizations on campus. There's rarely, if ever, a shortage of activity on the Skidmore campus—and all without fraternities or sororities. The Outing Club takes members hiking and camping in the nearby Adirondacks, and WSPN, the popular campus radio station, is listened to in the community. Intramurals, especially football, continue to attract more participants each year, and the school's varsity tennis, soccer, and golf teams ("the country club sports") usually have successful seasons. Annual celebrations that bring the campus out in droves are the school's Winter Carnival, Spring Fling, and Oktoberfest.

Saratoga Springs, famous for having the most bars per square inch in the state of New York, is also well known for its horse racing, restaurants, galleries, and museums. Students frequently visit the available attractions—particularly the watering holes—on most weekends, which for many start on Thursday nights. Albany is about thirty minutes away by car, while New York City and Boston are both about three and a half hours away.

Skidmore students tend to be politically conservative, if not apathetic, and affluent; they are proud of their school's usually winning varsity polo team (the sport of royalty) and of their mascot, a thoroughbred. But the college has come a long way since its days as an all-women's arts school for debutantes, and today it offers a more diverse curriculum, as well as a nearly 50-50 female-to-male ratio, and concerned faculty. "I'm glad I came to a small school, especially after having gone to a large high school in a large city," says a student. "There are a lot of rich students who go here who can't relate to what it might be like to be of color, but on the whole they are interested and nice."

STATE UNIVERSITY OF NEW YORK/ALBANY

Address: 1400 Washington Avenue, Albany, NY 12222
Phone: (518) 442-5435
Director of Admissions: Dr. Michelean Treadwell
Multicultural Student Recruiter: na
1991–92 tuition: $2,150 (in-state); $5,750 (out-of-state)
Room and board: $3,666
Application deadline: 2/15
Financial aid application deadline: 2/15

Non-white freshman admissions: Applicants for the class of '94: 3,848
Accepted: 47%
Accepted who enroll: 28%
Applicants accepted who rank in top 10% of high school class: 34%
In top 25%: 68%
Median SAT: 480 V, 580 M
Median ACT: na
Full-time undergraduate enrollment: 10,731
Men: 56%
Women: 44%

STUDENT ENROLLMENT

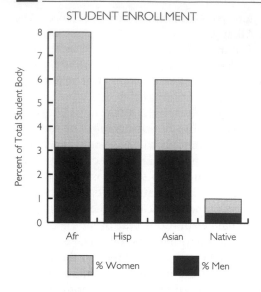

Percent of Total Student Body

☐ % Women   ■ % Men

Non-white students in
  1987–88: 13%
  1988–89: 15%
  1989–90: 17%
  1990–91: 18%
Students In-state: 99%
Top majors: 1. English 2. Psychology
  3. Political Science
Retention rate of non-white students: na
**Scholarships exclusively for non-white
  students:** None
Remediation programs: The university's
  Educational Opportunities Program
  includes tutoring and counseling.
Academic support services: Tutoring is
  available in most academic subjects.
Ethnic studies programs: The university
  offers East Asian Studies, Chinese
  Studies, Hispanic and Italian Studies,
  African and African-American Studies.
Ethnic studies courses: The university
  requires students to enroll in a

three-credit human diversity course,
which in a recent year allowed students
to select from 18 courses from various
departments.
Organizations for non-white students:
  Albany State University Black Alliance,
  Fuerza Latina
Notable non-white alumni: na
Tenured faculty: 484
Non-tenured faculty: 417

FACULTY

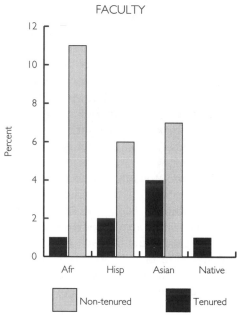

Percent

☐ Non-tenured   ■ Tenured

Student-faculty ratio: 18:1
Administrators: 411
  African-American: 9%
  Hispanic: 2%
  Asian-American: 2%
  Native American: 1%
Recent non-white speakers on campus: na

The State University of New York system has long been known for providing an
excellent education, and SUNY/Albany, located in the state's capital, is one of the
system's brightest stars. Although 97 percent of its students are from New York,
Albany's campus reflects much of the racial and ethnic diversity of the state, which
encompasses everything from New York City to rural upstate.

The university made news in 1991 when it appointed H. Patrick Swygert as its president, the first African-American to achieve such a position in the SUNY system. President Swygert earned his undergraduate and law degrees from Howard, a historically black university in Washington, D.C.

Albany offers a vast array of majors, more than 50 in all. Standouts include most of the science programs, especially biology and chemistry. The criminal justice program enjoys a national reputation. Students in the program are able to take advantage of internship possibilities in government agencies. The school recently scored a coup when it hired Pulitzer Prize-winning author William Kennedy to oversee its New York State Writers Institute. Among the school's humanities offerings, psychology, English, and political science are top-notch. Albany's School of Business is extremely competitive for admissions—students are accepted after their first year at Albany—and is rigorous academically. Students can earn degrees in either accounting or business administration. The university's programs in computer science, atmospheric studies, and education also win student praise.

Albany students are required to complete general education course requirements, in which they must earn six credits in six different areas, ranging from natural and social science to literature and the fine arts. In addition, students must complete a human diversity course requirement, in which students may choose from more than 20 courses. Some recent offerings were "Hispanic Cultures in the United States," "History of the Civil Rights Movement," and "Classism, Racism, and Sexism."

Albany's African and African-American Studies major is highly regarded. "I have taken three Africana Studies classes, and I have learned a lot from excellent professors," says a senior.

Academics at Albany can be rigorous. The university sponsors a summer orientation program for students that participants have said is excellent. It offers a cultural awareness section called "Just Community." Orientation also includes a Minority Student Luncheon, in which entering students get to meet faculty, residential life staff, and other students.

Orientation is also available for potential science majors. "C/STEP [Collegiate Science and Technology Entry Program] sponsors a workshop on helping students figure out their first-year course schedule," says a C/STEP student adviser. "A lot of freshmen come in as science majors and then drop out because of poor grades or because they took on too heavy a work load. We are trying to prevent that." During the school year, C/STEP, which is available to non-white students enrolled in courses or programs in the sciences, technical and health-related fields, or economics, also sponsors tutoring and peer advising services. Anthony Torres, director of C/STEP, works closely with students. "Mr. Torres is very influential with his students," says a science major. "He is understanding and his drive for excellence and achievement sets a model for students to follow."

In addition to the services of C/STEP, Albany students are able to take advantage of the academic and non-academic support services provided by the Minority Student Development Office, which offers individual and group counseling, tutoring, and information about internships. Jerome Hutson, director of the office, "always extends himself beyond the realm of his job," says a student. Carl Martin, the assistant director, "is always willing to provide any assistance he can to our students," says a senior. "He works with many student associations on campus. His office also conducts workshops for students of color. Mr. Martin is very influential with students and strives to enhance our skills and knowledge."

"Fuerza Latina, the Albany State University Black Association, Pan Caribbean, and the African-American and Latino Pre-professional Association are some of the more active multicultural student groups on campus," reports a senior business administration major. "These associations sponsor annual career fairs, lectures, conferences, parties, and dinners." According to a senior biology major: "The Minority Science Club sponsors trips to medical schools and conferences to try to get minority students into medical and graduate schools." The groups also sponsor Christmas parties and toy drives for underprivileged children in the area.

Students say their campus isn't as integrated socially as they'd like it to be. "Sometimes I look around and see the segregation that goes on here and I just don't understand it. I see it from both sides because I have friends from different ethnic and racial backgrounds, so I have a somewhat broader perspective. No one really tries to talk to one another. They're all set in their ways and that's the way they like it. I think that students could try a lot harder to get along." Students report that the most integrated residence halls on campus are Dutch and Indian, while the least integrated are State and Colonial.

The social life at Albany centers on the main fountain at the center of campus, where you'll find sunbathers, Frisbee tossers, and students perfecting the art of socializing. The student center plays host to numerous movies, concerts, and other student functions during the school year. The Performance Art Center also hosts a variety of events each year.

Albany, the state's capital, has sizable African-American and Hispanic communities, and offers many of the advantages of a midsize city: movie theaters, restaurants, clubs, and a myriad of cultural opportunities. Students of color report that they feel comfortable taking advantage of the city's off-campus diversions.

Albany's strong support network, combined with its outstanding academic programs, makes it one of the top universities in the SUNY system, and with its reasonable price tag, a good investment. "My time and experiences here have made me a more well-rounded person, ready to face the realities of the outside world," says a senior. "Therefore, I would suggest that any student of color attend Albany and seek out opportunity."

STATE UNIVERSITY OF
NEW YORK / BINGHAMTON

Address: Binghamton, NY 13902-6001
Phone: (607) 777-2171
Director of Admissions: Geoffrey Gould
Multicultural Student Recruiter: Sharon
  Williams

1992–93 tuition: $2,650 (in-state); $6,550
  (out-of-state)
Room and board: $4,800
Application deadline: 1/15
Financial aid application deadline: 2/15

In just forty-seven years of existence, SUNY/Binghamton has grown to become one of the most respected schools in New York's already outstanding state university system. The university has been hailed by *The New York Times* and other publications as a public Ivy, and, indeed, it does compete with those older schools in many ways except one: its relatively low cost of tuition.

While SUNY/Binghamton does not boast the admissions statistics of the Ivies, the university is doing all it can to put itself in the same league. The cover of its admissions literature reads "Genus Varium Hederae" (A Different Breed of Ivy), and in a recent move that was a surprise to students, the university reanointed itself the University of Binghamton. "The administration is trying to make the university sound more prestigious, more like a private school, so it is distancing itself from the SUNY name," says a student.

As with the Ivies, Binghamton's strengths are in the arts and sciences. Students in Harpur College, Binghamton's liberal arts division, must take two courses in each of three divisions to graduate: the humanities, science and mathematics, and the social sciences. Even engineering majors can't get away from the liberal arts at SUNY/Binghamton, as they must take courses in communications and the humanities or the social sciences.

Political science, English, biology, and psychology are some of the best programs in Harpur College, and students brag about their school's African-American Studies program, particularly such classes as "Black Women Writers in the Twentieth Century," "Race, Slavery, and Gender," and "African History." One of the program's more respected professors, Darryl Thomas, also serves as the adviser to the school's Black Student Union. Other noteworthy professors in the program are Carole Boyce-Davies, an associate professor of English, and Akbar Muhammad and David McBride, associate professors of history. The school's program in Latin American and Caribbean Area Studies is also strong, according to students, and includes such popular courses as "Women in Latin America" and "History of the English-Speaking Caribbean." The temporary head of the program, Randy McGuire, "is doing an excellent job," says a student.

Binghamton's Watson School of Engineering, established in 1983, offers programs in computer science, engineering technology, electrical engineering, and mechanical engineering, and is said to be getting stronger each year. The university's School of

Management offers programs in accounting and management, as well as unique concentrations in East Asian Studies and management studies.

Academics at Binghamton rank among the most difficult in the SUNY system, but students trying to get to know their professors in introductory courses will have a tough time of it. Teaching assistants lead smaller class discussions in some of these courses, and students say they're usually more than willing to lend a hand. Class sizes get more manageable in upper-level courses. The school's rigors and academic programs must be working; in a recent year, 80 percent of its graduates who applied to medical school were accepted and 99 percent were accepted to law school.

Binghamton's cultural groups do a great deal to raise the campus's cultural awareness. The Intercultural Awareness Committee, which is made up of representatives from 14 different organizations, "brings the groups together to establish a working relationship and to let each other know about events and to talk about co-sponsoring events," says a student. "We publish a newsletter about the groups and their events for the campus." One of the events the committee coordinates is the Festival Weekend, held in November, which features forums and music.

The Black Student Union, the oldest student of color organization on campus, established in 1968, annually hosts Black Solidarity Day events, which have presented an African dance troupe, a jazz band, and speakers. Other events are a Kwanzaa celebration, a Pan-African Festival, which features a cabaret and displays of African clothing and art, and Black History Month speakers. Binghamton's historically black Greek organizations sponsor events during the month. The BSU also publishes the popularly read *Vanguard,* a four- to six-page publication issued about six times a school year that contains articles about events on campus and national and local issues.

The Latin American Student Union, with about 80 active members, "is growing slowly," says a LASU leader. One of the group's biggest events is Latino Weekend, held in the fall, complete with food, music, and performances by students. The weekend isn't without its serious side, however; during the day, group members sponsor workshops on such topics as campus activism and making the transition from high school to college. The group's Latin Heritage Month offers a dance-a-thon, as well as a film series and various conferences. The group also publishes *Latin Voices,* a newsmagazine released three times a semester, and sponsors its own peer mentoring program called Uni.

One of LASU's biggest events is the Afro-Latin Cultural Festival, "which seeks to show the common heritages of African-Americans and Latinos," says a student. The event includes art exhibits, a banquet, speakers, and music. During the fall semester of 1992, LASU also sponsored a two-day Columbus Day Conference that included speakers and art exhibits. Steve Durante, an Educational Opportunity Program counselor, is supportive of students and attends LASU meetings and events.

Recently established on campus is Pi Delta Epsilon, a sorority that stresses issues of multiculturalism. As of this writing, the sorority had 16 members, including African-American, Latino, and Jewish students. The school's Latino and African-American fraternities and sororities are also active on campus, sponsoring community services projects, food and clothes drives, and events with other cultural student groups.

The director of the Educational Opportunity Program, Michael Boyd, a Binghamton graduate, is never too busy to meet with students and student groups. "He's instrumental in helping us get a lot of things done," says a BSU member.

The university did not respond to our admissions questionnaire, but according to the U.S. Department of Education, in 1990, of the school's 12,202 students, 4.9 percent were African-American, 6.6 were Asian-American, 4.1 percent were Hispanic, and 0.1 percent were Native American.

Relations between Binghamton's cultural groups and its Student Association, the university-wide student government system, have improved markedly in recent years, according to students. "This year, it's been different than in years past, but it's taken some effort to get it to this point," says a campus leader. "Last year, we [students-of-color organizations] tried unsuccessfully to get the association's academic vice president impeached because of her condescending attitude toward multicultural students. We also unsuccessfully tried to censure some remarks of the association president. But, like I said, this year is different. The association is now half white and half student of color. We recruited students of color heavily to run for office, and convinced them of the importance of being involved. We plan to stay as involved as we were last year." The Student Association maintains a permanent position for a Minority Affairs Coordinator, who, according to a student, "acts as the liaison between the association and the cultural groups."

On a day-to-day basis, however, students say, there is little interaction among students of different backgrounds. "The segregation has gotten worse here since the affluent eighties bottomed out," says a student. "I look at Binghamton as having two distinct societies. There's the ghetto society, with their music and way of dress. Then there's the mainstream society, and the two rarely meet. But it's not all bad, I guess, because it's possible to have Latino and black cultures distinct from the mainstream."

The town of Binghamton offers little in the way of social outlets for students of color, and most students confine their activity to campus. New York City, from where the majority of the school's students of color hail, is about 200 miles to the southeast; other cities—Ithaca and Syracuse—are considerably closer. In addition to the activities of the cultural groups, there's a variety of on-campus activities that range from intramural football to theater groups. In fact, there are more than 200 active student organizations on campus. The music department and the Anderson Center for the Arts, one of the finest facilities in the area, regularly bring culture and the arts to campus.

Students who venture to Binghamton aren't disappointed with their college choice. For one transplanted New Yorker, going to Binghamton has more advantages than just a top-quality education at state-supported prices. "I'm glad I'm out of the city. It's good to be away from home because I've learned to be more independent. Binghamton is very relaxing and quiet, which makes it easier to study, as the professors expect a lot of their students."

STATE UNIVERSITY OF NEW YORK/BUFFALO

Address: Hayes Annex A, Buffalo, NY 14214

Phone: (716) 831-2111 / (716) 831-2333

Director of Admissions: Kevin M. Durkin

Multicultural Student Recruiter: Carmela Thompson

1991–92 tuition: $2,150 (in-state); $5,750 (out-of-state)

Room and board: $4,108

Application deadline: 1/5

Financial aid application deadline: 3/15

Non-white freshman admissions: Applicants for the class of '95: 4,566
Accepted: 41.2%
Accepted who enroll: 11.1%
Applicants accepted who rank in top 10% of high school class: 21.3%
In top 25%: 51.6%
Median SAT range: 330–510 V, 430–640 M
Median ACT range: 17–25

Full-time undergraduate enrollment: 13,238
Men: 58.7%
Women: 41.3%

1989–90: 14.4%
1990–91: 15.6%

Geographic distribution of students: na

Top majors: 1. Engineering 2. Business 3. Social Science

Retention rate of non-white students: na

Scholarships exclusively for non-white students: na

Remediation programs: The Educational Opportunity Program and the Special Services Project provide support.

Academic support services: The Methods of Inquiry Program, the Collegiate Science and Technology Program, and the Liberty Partnership provide academic and non-academic support.

Ethnic studies programs: The university offers African-American Studies, and within the university's American Studies program students may concentrate in Puerto Rican and Native American Studies.

Organizations for non-white students: Alpha Kappa Alpha, Alpha Phi Alpha, Delta

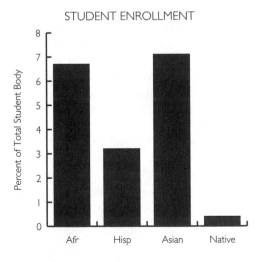

STUDENT ENROLLMENT

Non-white students in
1987–88: 13.1%
1988–89: 14%

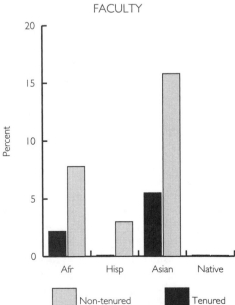

FACULTY

Sigma Theta, Kappa Alpha Psi, Omega Psi Phi, Phi Beta Sigma, Sigma Gamma Rho, Zeta Phi Beta, African Student Association, Anti-Apartheid Solidarity Committee, Asian-American Student Union, Black Student Union, Blacks in Health-Related Professions, Caribbean Student Association, Chinese Student Association, Korean Student Association, Latin American Student Association, Minority Management Association, Minority Nursing Student Association, National Society of Black Engineers, Native American People's Alliance, Nigerian Student Association, PODER: Latinos Unidos, Southeast Asian Studies Association, UB Gospel Choir

Notable non-white alumni: na
Tenured faculty: 942
Non-tenured faculty: 1,051
Student-faculty ratio: 20:1
Administrators: 663
  African-American: 10%
  Hispanic: 2.3%
  Asian-American: 1.5%
  Native American: 0.6%
Recent non-white speakers on campus: na

Each flu season, Buffalo, New York, is the location of choice for Madison Avenue advertising execs looking for scenery to advertise their clients' flu and cold products. But the city's overabundance of snow in no way gets in the way of students who have come here to take advantage of top-flight academics at reasonable prices.

Buffalo is the state system's largest and most comprehensive university, occupying two campuses, located about five miles apart. The more modern, I. M. Pei-designed campus, in Amherst, a Buffalo suburb, is the site of most of the school's undergraduate activity, while the older Buffalo campus is home to some of the university's well-known graduate programs, including medicine and dentistry. A shuttle system connects the campuses.

Academic strengths at Buffalo are primarily in the pre-professional fields, such as engineering, business, and pre-med. Buffalo has impressive law and medical schools to which achievers can apply. The English and art departments are also considered strong. The school's impressive African-American Studies program boasts such faculty members as Endesha Mae Holland, author of *From the Mississippi Delta,* a play nominated in 1988 for the Pulitzer Prize. "Blacks in Film" and "Introduction to African-American Studies" are popular with students, as are professors James Pappas and Y. GM Lulat. Students say the American Studies department's program in Puerto Rican Studies is weak. The university's Native American Studies program, part of the American Studies program, is well regarded, as is its director, Oren Lyons. The program's course "Indian Image on Film" is especially popular.

For minority applicants with high grades, Buffalo has a Minority Academic Achievement Program, which guarantees students peer mentors, $200 per year for books, special academic advising, and housing in dorms conducive to studying. To qualify, applicants must rank in the top 20 percent of their high school graduating class, have a combined SAT score of 1,000, and have had a high school GPA of at least a 90.

For other students, academic advising and counseling gets mixed reviews. Professors, as is common at large research universities, can be difficult to reach. Class sizes also tend to be large, but students say the school's professors are good teachers.

As goes the classroom situation, so goes much of the campus life. The university, with more than 25,000 undergraduates, is a big place. To bring the school down to scale, students participate in a variety of on-campus activities, including cultural student organizations.

With about 50 active members, the Black Student Union brings speakers to campus and sponsors picnics and skating parties. The group also recently sponsored a trip to an amusement park in Canada. One of the group's more ambitious events was a rap concert that featured Black Sheep and other popular rap artists. The school's predominantly black Greek organizations "are always throwing parties," says a fraternity member, usually at the student union or a local club.

PODER: Latinos Unidos, a student organization, "is looked to as a leader in the western New York State Hispanic community," says a student. The group, established on campus in 1967, primarily focuses on the school's Hispanic Heritage Festival, an annual event that's been ongoing for more than six years. The festival, held at the Father Belle Center in Buffalo, draws more than 10,000 to the two-day affair, which offers food booths, dancers, a five-kilometer race, and a fashion show. "It's a truly beautiful thing," says an organizer. In October, the group hosts Día Latino, a ceremony in which PODER members and those who've helped the group during the year are presented with awards. The event, held at the Buffalo Convention Center, provides a night of dinner and dance for the 300 people who usually attend.

In addition, the group sponsors annual picnics, tours of the campus for prospective applicants, and speakers. "Every week we bring someone in to speak to members about job opportunities and graduate schools," says an organizer.

But one of PODER's most popular events is its annual dance, held in the spring, at which Hispanic groups, usually from New York City, are invited to campus to perform. The event is usually held at the Marriott or the convention center downtown. As a community service project, PODER brings more than 100 Hispanic high school students to campus each year to introduce them to college. Prospectives participate in workshops that deal with financial aid and career planning, and the day is topped off with a dance.

The city of Buffalo, the state's second-largest city, offers numerous off-campus diversions. Nearly a third of the city's residents are either African-American, Hispanic, or Native American. Niagara Falls is just a twenty-minute drive away, and New York City, from which more than two-thirds of the school's minority students hail, is about eight hours away by car. But students tend to stay close to campus, as the university and student organizations play host to lectures, sporting events, and concerts.

Students at Buffalo tend to be liberal, although more than one student comments that when it comes to issues other than tuition hikes, the student body is generally apathetic. This is no doubt due to the university's large commuter population; nearly half of its students live off campus, either at home or in an off-campus apartment. But with a new athletic facility and the university's entry into Division I athletic competition, students see school spirit on the rise. As at the other SUNY schools, the student population is overwhelmingly—more than 95 percent—from New York State.

Buffalo is a good school, so don't let some cold weather freeze you out of attending.

The key to survival here, in addition to a parka, is to get involved. "I've liked it here a lot," says a senior. "I think that has a lot to do with the clubs I've gotten involved in. Otherwise it's easy to get apathetic and lost."

UNION COLLEGE

Address: Schenectady, NY 12308
Phone: (518) 370-6112
Director of Admissions: Daniel Lundquist
Multicultural Student Recruiter: Darryl Tiggle
1993–94 tuition: $16,578
Room and board: $5,722
Application deadline: 2/1
Financial aid application deadline: 2/1
Non-white freshman admissions: Applicants
for the class of '97: 685
Accepted: 58%
Accepted who enroll: 23%
Applicants accepted who rank in top 10% of high school class: 54%
In top 25%: 80%
Median SAT: na
Median ACT: 27
Full-time undergraduate enrollment: 1,989
Men: 55%
Women: 45%

Non-white students in
1987–88: 9.1%
1988–89: 9.9%
1989–90: 10.4%
1990–91: 10.7%
Students In-state: 79.4%

GEOGRAPHIC DISTRIBUTION OF STUDENTS

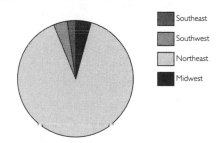

Southeast
Southwest
Northeast
Midwest

Top majors: 1. Biology 2. Civil Engineering 3. Economics
Retention rate of non-white students: 73%
Scholarships exclusively for non-white students: IBM Scholarship: need-based; $6,000 awarded per year to women and/or minority students majoring in engineering; one to three awarded each year.
Remediation programs: None
Academic support services: The college offers academic support in the areas of writing, calculus, biology, chemistry, electrical engineering, and computer science, as well as the services of the Higher Education Program.
Ethnic studies programs: Union's Latin American Studies program, established in 1970, is interdisciplinary, involving the economics, sociology, and Spanish departments. The college's East Asian

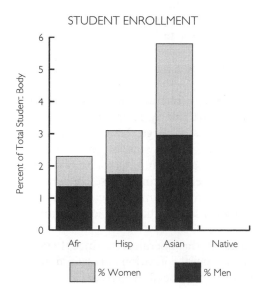

STUDENT ENROLLMENT

Percent of Total Student Body

Afr   Hisp   Asian   Native

% Women   % Men

Studies program, also interdisciplinary, was established in 1989, and draws on the resources of the economics, history, philosophy, and political science departments. Japanese- and Chinese-language study at the elementary and intermediate levels is also offered.

Ethnic studies courses: The college offers about three courses in African Studies, and other courses are offered focusing on American minority groups.

Organizations for non-white students: African and Latino Alliance of Students, Union College Gospel Choir, Asian Student Union, Alpha Phi Alpha, THE MASS (community service), National Society of Black Engineers

Notable non-white alumni: na

Tenured faculty: 82

Non-tenured faculty: 94

Student-faculty ratio: 12:1

Administrators: 140
  African-American: 3%
  Hispanic: 1%
  Asian-American: 1%
  Native American: 0

Recent non-white speakers on campus: Kwame Toure (political activist); Dr.

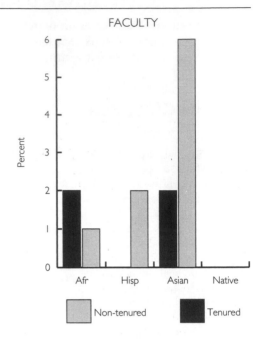

FACULTY

Ron Walters (Jesse Jackson's campaign manager); Dr. Lenora Fulani (chairperson, National Alliance Party); John Amos (actor)

Union College is one of a handful of prominent colleges and universities around the country that have made taking the SAT optional for admission. "We are convinced that the SAT cannot escape cultural bias," said Union's president, John Morris, in 1987, when the university made the decision to make the test optional. "The evidence is quite clear that the SAT handicaps certain groups—women and minority students being the prime examples. We believe that making the SAT optional will encourage applications from students in those groups."

Union College, founded nearly 200 years ago as a liberal arts college, has long been known for its pre-professional programs, particularly in medicine, law, and engineering. In conjunction with the Albany Medical College, Union has a unique and rigorous seven-year medical degree program. Union students can also take advantage of a five-year JD program with Albany Law School. Union, in 1845, was the first liberal arts college in the nation to offer an engineering course, and students can now study civil engineering, electrical engineering, and mechanical engineering. Among the school's liberal arts programs, students say political science, economics, and math are tops.

To ensure that students are getting a taste of the liberal arts, since 1989 the administration has required students to satisfy a general education curriculum, which includes courses in history, literature, and civilization; social or behavioral sciences;

mathematics and natural sciences; and other languages or other cultures, offering a foreign language or a non-Western studies track.

Union students are able to turn to various offices on campus, including the dean of students office, for academic and non-academic support. "Our dean of students office has proven to be helpful, in my opinion," comments a student. "We have one dean and two assistant deans. They are all good people who sincerely care about the success of the minority students on campus." In particular, dean of students Joseph Mammola "is sensitive to the minority student community. He fought to establish our Cultural Unity Center and he is supportive of our minority organizations. He also helped us get our National Society of Black Engineers [NSBE] chapter started and maintain its name. The student government objected to both of these. In the first case they felt we were segregating ourselves and in the second case they did not like the word 'black' in NSBE. In both cases he was on our side."

Union's assistant dean of students, Patricia Williams, is also a support for students. "She is the only black person in the administration here," says a student. "Unfortunately, with this being the case, anything concerning minority students is put in her lap, no matter what it concerns." Adds another student: "She's always willing to listen to us, and she has an open-door policy."

Union students recently formed an NSBE chapter, which "is geared toward recruiting, retaining, and graduating minority students in the field of engineering, sciences, and technology," reports a member. "We have organized test files and study sessions. We send our members to conferences where they attend workshops designed to help them succeed in their field of study. In my opinion, this is a fantastic organization. Students have been able to get internships, co-ops, and permanent jobs through the NSBE."

The recently established Cultural Unity Center, which provides residence facilities for about 12 students, also serves as a place of support for the school's non-white students. According to one student, most of the residents are African-American and Latino, "although it is open to all students." Comments a biology major about the center: "This is where we students draw our strength and find solace." All African and Latino Alliance of Students meetings are held at the Cultural Unity Center.

Union has a very active Greek system (17 fraternities and three sororities), which includes a historically black fraternity on campus, Alpha Phi Alpha. The chapter sponsors speakers, step shows, and parties. The Gospel Choir sponsors concerts each year. "The choir invites community choirs to participate in its gospel festivals," reports a choir member. "The choir holds a small service every year for Dr. Martin Luther King, Jr.'s birthday."

Despite the efforts of these organizations, and in part because of the school's tiny student of color enrollment, Union remains largely segregated when it comes to the school's social life. "The students of color basically stay to themselves," says a student. "We have some Caucasian friends we associate with, but on the whole it is 'us' and 'them.' In the dining halls there is the black and Latino table, and we usually don't go to the fraternity parties because we are not into the drinking scene every night. If we do go out it is to black fraternity/sorority parties off campus [in Albany] or Alpha Phi Alpha parties on campus."

Schenectady isn't exactly a hub of cultural activity, say students. "There really isn't a lot to do in the city. If it were not for the school and General Electric [which has a large office nearby] the place would be a ghost town." Students also say there is a great deal of tension between the college and the community. "The students of color don't get along well with the Schenectady community," says a student. "The blacks here feel the black students are sellouts and rich kids, and the whites think we think we're better than them." Students looking for a taste of urban—and a more accommodating—nightlife will usually make the trek to Albany, about forty-five minutes by car, where there are any number of colleges and universities, including SUNY/Albany. The majority of the school's students of color come from the New York City area, according to a student.

Union lags behind many other New York State schools when it comes to quality-of-life issues for its students of color. But the college provides well-respected academics that could brighten many a student's job prospects. Says a student: "In all fairness to Union, it is a good school and it has all of the accreditations and it turns out top-of-the-line individuals. As far as minority students are concerned, I know they could do a lot worse than Union."

VASSAR COLLEGE

Address: Raymond Avenue, Poughkeepsie, NY 12601
Phone: (914) 437-7300
Director of Admissions: Thomas A. Matos
Multicultural Student Recruiter: Robyn Brady
1991–92 tuition: $16,250
Room and board: $5,260
Application deadline: 1/15
Financial aid application deadline: 3/1
Non-white freshman admissions: Applicants for the class of '95: na
   Accepted: na
   Accepted who enroll: na
   Applicants accepted who rank in top 10% of high school class: na
   Median SAT: na
   Median ACT: na
Full-time undergraduate enrollment: 2,250
   Men: 44%
   Women: 56%
Non-white students in
   1987–88: 15.6%
   1988–89: 17.4%
   1989–90: 18.8%
   1990–91: 19.7%

Geographic distribution of students: na
Students In-state: 37%
Top majors: 1. English 2. Political Science 3. Psychology
Retention rate of non-white students: 80%
Scholarships exclusively for non-white students: None

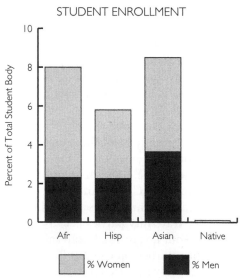

STUDENT ENROLLMENT

Remediation programs: None

Academic support services: The college provides the services of the Academic Resource Center and the Academic Computing Center.

Ethnic studies programs: The African Studies interdisciplinary program includes more than 50 courses and is offered as a major and a minor. The Asian Studies program includes more than 15 courses, in addition to Chinese- and Japanese-language study, which is offered at all levels. The Hispanic Studies program offers more than 15 courses, including Spanish language study. Courses focus primarily on Latin American and Spanish Studies.

Organizations for non-white students: Asian Student Association, Black Student Union, Ebony Theatre Ensemble, Gospel Choir, Intercultural Center, SALSA (Hispanic student organization)

Notable non-white alumni: Billie Davis Gaines ('58; president, Horizon Productions); Dr. June Jackson Christmas ('45; physician); Josephine A. V. Allen ('68; first tenured African-American woman professor, Cornell University); Iris Mack ('78; first African-American faculty member of the mathematics department at MIT); Marian Grady Secundy ('60; associate professor of medicine, Howard University); Sandra Wilson ('75; first ordained African-American priest in the Episcopal Diocese of New York and the fourth in the nation); Keith John ('81;

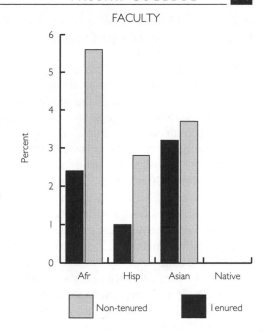

FACULTY

Non-tenured   Tenured

first African-American staff attorney at the Legal Aid Society of Northeastern New York)

Tenured faculty: 123

Non-tenured faculty: 107

Student-faculty ratio: 11:1

Administrators: 143

  African-American: 0.02%

  Hispanic: 0.01%

  Asian-American: 0.01%

  Native American: 0

Recent non-white speakers on campus: Jesse Jackson (former U.S. presidential candidate and civil rights activist)

For most of its existence, Vassar was known as one of the elite Seven Sisters colleges, the alternatives to the all-male Ivy League. But since 1968, the 132-year-old college has been coed.

Students are attracted to Vassar because of its individualized approach to education. Most classes are small—usually with enrollments of no more than 10 to 15—allowing students to develop close relationships with professors; by the end of the term, students are often on a first-name basis with many of their professors. Students point to David Wong Louie, an assistant professor of English, as being especially supportive of students. "He is one of the few people on our campus who are knowledgeable about Asian-American issues, history, and literature," says a student. Students also look to Steven Moore, an assistant professor of English, Diane Harriford, an assistant professor of sociology, and Gretchen Gerzina, an assistant professor of English.

The art history and English departments have traditionally been among the college's best. Art history students have access to the school's renowned Vassar College Art Gallery, one of the oldest museums in the country. Each of the college's physical science departments—chemistry, geology/geography, physics/astronomy—is housed in impressive facilities, and the school's program in cognitive science is one of the few such programs in the country at an undergraduate institution. The college also offers well-regarded programs in women's studies, international studies, and drama (Meryl Streep is a Vassar graduate). Vassar's library contains more than 650,000 volumes, an impressive number for a small college.

Although the school's Asian Studies program gets mixed reviews from students— "It's small and needs a more diverse teaching staff"—it does include one of the faculty's more respected members, Yin-Lien Chin, a professor of Chinese. "She is very close to the Chinese community at Vassar," says a student. "Over her years here she has become a sort of mother figure to many students. She is famous for her barbecues and social events. She is also very knowledgeable about the history of Asian women."

"African Studies has some very good courses," says a student, pointing to such classes as "Race and American Law" and "The Civil Rights Movement in America." Obika Gray, director of the program and a professor of political science, is especially well regarded by students, as is Lawrence Mamiya, a professor of religion. "There are students who basically major in Professor Mamiya," says a junior.

Academics at Vassar are demanding. For additional support, students rely on Edward Pittman, a Vassar alum and director of the college's Office of Multicultural Affairs. "He has constant and very close contact with the minority communities at Vassar," says a junior. "He is loved by all the minority students on campus. He works hard at his job and is not just a tool of the administration. He is here to make real changes and he has gained a great deal of respect from the Vassar community."

Vassar students of color are active participants in campus affairs and politics. During a recent school year, for example, the presidents of both the senior class and the student government were African-American, the junior class president was Asian-American, and the sophomore class president was Hispanic. The school's three largest cultural student groups—the Black Student Union, the Asian Student Association, and SALSA, the Hispanic student group—sponsor a variety of cultural awareness activities on campus, including films, social gatherings, forums, and guest lectures.

Vassar has long been known as a school that welcomes innovation, a characteristic that took on a new dimension in 1991, when a group of three African-American students broke away from the commencement committee to form their own, after feeling that their ideas weren't being acknowledged. Their commencement event included gospel choirs and the traditional "daisy chain"—a select group of sophomores chosen by the senior class to assist in the ceremonies—was joined by a separate group of African-American students calling themselves African Violets.

Vassar students are usually characterized as politically liberal, and dressing in black is popular with the school's more "artsy" crowd. Students are commonly described as New York chic, which makes sense as the campus is only a two-hour train ride away from the clubs, shops, and restaurants of New York City. Many of the school's students of color come from the boroughs of the city, so getting home is easy. The town of Poughkeepsie, an economically poor community that has African-American, Hispanic, and Asian populations, offers little socially or culturally to students, except for a few bars and restaurants. Asian students frequently attend the services of a local Korean church in town, however, and other students participate in tutoring and other volunteer service projects in the area.

The Campus Center, the site of a great deal of on-campus activity, offers the Retreat, a popular snack bar, Matthew's Mug, a pub, student organization offices, the campus radio station, and an art gallery. Student groups often sponsor weekend concerts, plays, and films. There's rarely a dull moment on the Vassar campus.

Things got particularly heated in 1990, when 75 students occupied the campus's main administration building for 35 hours to protest an award that was to go to Daniel Patrick Moynihan, one of New York's U.S. senators, who had allegedly made a racist remark to a local government official. The sit-in was successful, according to students. Senator Moynihan did not come to campus, and he returned his speaking fee. "The minority community felt very empowered and there was a new sense of unity. Externally, people saw that Vassar was not just a school for rich girls. It became known for what it is: a community of people with ideas, a vision, and a voice."

WELLS COLLEGE

Women's college
Address: Aurora, NY 13026
Phone: (315) 364-3264
Director of Admissions: Mary Ann Kalbaugh
Multicultural Student Recruiter: Constance M. Blake
1991–92 tuition: $12,500
Room and board: $4,600
Application deadline: 3/1
Financial aid application deadline: 2/15
Non-white freshman admissions: Applicants for the class of '95: 76
  Accepted: 69.7%
  Accepted who enroll: 34%
  Applicants accepted who rank in top 10% of high school class: 46%
  In top 25%: 92.3%
  Median SAT: na
  Median ACT: na
Full-time undergraduate enrollment: 400

Non-white students in
  1987–88: na
  1988–89: 5.6%

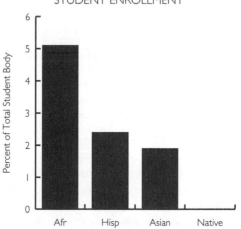

STUDENT ENROLLMENT

GEOGRAPHIC DISTRIBUTION OF STUDENTS

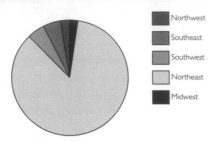

- Northwest
- Southeast
- Southwest
- Northeast
- Midwest

FACULTY

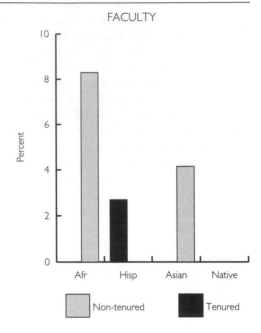

Non-tenured   Tenured

1989–90: 6.4%
1990–91: 9.4%

Students In-state: 63.4%

Top majors: 1. English 2. Political Science 3. History

Retention rate of non-white students: 84.6%

Scholarships exclusively for non-white students: Anonymous Grant: need-based; $50,000 awarded annually to African-American students; each award ranges from $500 to $6,000. Caroline Spooner Award: merit-based; one awarded each year; $4,000 for each award; awarded to an African-American or Native American student.

Remediation programs: Tutoring and study groups are provided to enhance students' math and writing skills. A basic math course is also available.

Academic support services: The college offers peer tutoring in most academic subjects and workshops on study skills and time management.

Ethnic studies programs: None

Ethnic studies courses: The college offers two history courses in African-American Studies, "History of Black Women in White America" and "Afro-American History"; two sociology courses, "Social Inequality: Class and Ethnicity" and "Understanding the Americas"; and an anthropology course, "North American Indians."

Organizations for non-white students: United Women of Color, Radical Alliance at Wells

Notable non-white alumnae: na

Tenured faculty: 36

Non-tenured faculty: 24

Student-faculty ratio: 8:1

Administrators: 33
African-American: 0.03%
Hispanic: 0.03%
Asian-American: 0
Native American: 0

Recent non-white speakers on campus: James Farmer (former director and founder of CORE); Dorothy Cotton (former education director, Southern Christian Leadership Conference)

Tiny Wells College in upstate New York isn't so small in scale when it comes to academics. Wells students are provided a quality education in a beautiful college setting.

As might be expected, the Wells faculty are no strangers to their students. "The faculty are definitely here for you. Once when I was absent from class, a professor sent me a note to see if anything was wrong. Nothing was, but it showed me he cared." The average class size of about 12 students also means that ducking work can be difficult, if not impossible. "Sitting in a small class, you'd better have done the work, because you're going to be called on to discuss it. One time I missed a class because I hadn't done the work, and later I saw my professor in the mail room. That was so embarrassing."

Wells is a liberal arts college, and in order to graduate students must satisfy core courses in the humanities, social sciences, writing, formal reasoning, a foreign language, and physical education. Students say the school's science departments are good, especially computer science, as are English, art, and history. During the January term, students are able to pursue further studies on or off campus, in places as close as Albany and as far as Greece.

The school's "African-American Studies" course, which covers two semesters, "is great." The school's Multicultural Interests Group, a committee composed of students, faculty, and administrators, is "working now to get the curriculum more diversified," reports a student.

Wells students are happy with their choice of attending a women's college. "In high school, I was very shy in my classes, especially in my science classes, and I think it had a lot to do with the guys in class. I felt like a second-class citizen. Now I raise my hand all the time. It's a confidence boost to attend an all-women's college."

To add to the diversity of college programming, the school's United Women of Color organization, with about 14 active members, "sponsors a variety of things," says a member. The group's main focus is the annual Minority Awareness Week, during which we "show the campus and even our members the importance of issues of cultural diversity. This year, we had an African drummer perform, Johnnetta Cole (president of Spelman College) spoke, and we had a Heritage Night when group members cooked foods from their own cultures." UWC members meet weekly in the UWC office in Smith Hall.

Being one of only a handful of non-white students can be frustrating for some. "We end up being the teachers or spokespeople for all minority issues on campus. After a while, it gets tiring. The school has been increasing its diversity, which helps this situation. When I first started there were only ten of us. This year, there are twenty-four. I know some people might not think that's a lot more, but to us it is."

UWC members have a new adviser, Elysie Torres, a staff person in the school's library. "She's been involved in UWC for years and years. We've traditionally had people come in from off campus to advise us, but for various reasons it never worked out. We should have thought of Ms. Torres a long time ago. She'd do anything for UWC because she knows how important it is to have an organization like ours on the Wells campus."

For many students, the social life at Wells leaves a little to be desired. "The parties here don't cater to non-white students too much. We can only listen to so much Top 40. You have to make your own fun here, or head off campus." Nearly half of the students leave campus on weekends, often heading to either Hobart and William Smith Colleges or Cornell University. A van service transports Wells women to and from these schools, "but the last van from Cornell leaves at one-fifteen. This being the nineties, parties don't really start going until after eleven, so it can be a drag having to leave so early. Ideally, you need to find a friend with a car." Popular on-campus activities include numerous musical groups, foreign-language clubs, and a current events forum. Intramural competition is sponsored in tennis, bowling, and swimming. The college sits on the edge of beautiful Cayuga Lake, which offers opportunities for fishing and boating.

The town of Aurora is beautiful and quaint, but provides little in the form of nightlife. During those slow-paced nights, students at Wells rely on the good old-fashioned art of conversation. "Socially, we just talk and talk and have fun, and it's possible to make really good friends here, friends I know I'll keep forever." According to one student, the typical Wells student is from a small town in upstate New York where she hasn't interacted with non-whites. The majority of the non-white students, the senior adds, are from cities, particularly New York City.

Wells, founded in 1868, is a school with more than its share of tradition. Tea is still served every afternoon in the Art Exhibit Room in Macmillan, "though long dresses and china cups have long since disappeared," and the school's elaborate Commencement Weekend festivities include a huge picnic, a party, and a concert. On the morning of the ceremony, graduating seniors and their families get to ride in the original Wells, Fargo stagecoach. (Wells was established by Wells, Fargo founder Henry Wells.)

Men and an active nightlife are in short supply at Wells, but students who choose to spend four years here don't usually seem to mind, although there are grumblings every once in a while. "Coming here, I've gotten a lot academically. Wells is great for the liberal arts, and I knew I would get all the skills I would need in order to survive in a male-dominated world. But, I have to admit, I've missed being with more minority students during college. It's a trade-off."

DAVIDSON COLLEGE

Address: P.O. Box 1737, Davidson, NC 28036
Phone: (704) 892-2230 / (800) 768-0380
Director of Admissions: Robert Gardner
Multicultural Student Recruiter: Robert A. Douthit
1991–92 tuition: $13,680
Room and board: $4,160
Application deadline: Early decision: 11/15; regular decision: 2/1
Financial aid application deadline: 2/15
Non-white freshman admissions: Applicants for the class of '95: 249
  Accepted: 40%
  Accepted who enroll: 47%
  Applicants accepted who rank in top 10% of high school class: 42%
  In top 25%: 75%
  Median SAT: 500 V, 560 M
  Median ACT: 23.2
Full-time undergraduate enrollment: 1,555
  Men: 55%
  Women: 45%
Non-white students in
  1987–88: 7%
  1988–89: 9%
  1989–90: 10%
  1990–91: 9%
Students In-state: 47%
Top majors: 1. Economics 2. Psychology 3. Physics
Retention rate of non-white students: 86%
Scholarships exclusively for non-white students: Davidson Scholar Award:

STUDENT ENROLLMENT

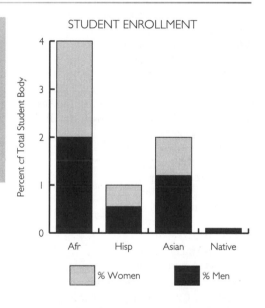

GEOGRAPHIC DISTRIBUTION OF STUDENTS

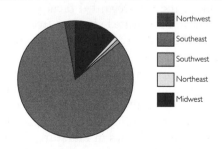

merit-based; $1,000–$5,000 per year; approximately ten awarded each year.

Duke Scholars Award: merit-based; $500–$3,000 per year; approximately five to ten awarded each year. Class of '85 Scholarship: merit-based; $1,000 per award; one awarded each year to a minority freshman.

Remediation programs: None

Academic support services: Tutoring is available in most academic subjects.

Ethnic studies programs: The college offers an interdisciplinary major in South Asian Studies, involving art, anthropology, classical languages, economics, history, political science, religion, and sociology. Twenty-one courses are offered in the major, in which seven faculty members teach.

Ethnic studies courses: Davidson offers more than seven courses in Latin American Studies, two courses in African-American Studies, and more than five courses in East Asian Studies.

Organizations for non-white students: Black Student Coalition

Notable non-white alumni: na

Tenured faculty: 97

Non-tenured faculty: 30

Student-faculty ratio: 12:1

Administrators: 166

 African-American: 4%

 Hispanic: 0

 Asian-American: 0

 Native American: 0

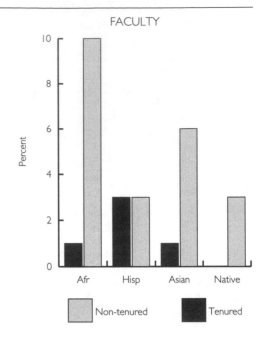

FACULTY

Percent

Non-tenured   Tenured

Recent non-white speakers on campus: Brenda H. Tapia (assistant chaplain, Davidson College); Dr. Jackie Looney (associate dean, Duke University Graduate School); Sonia Sanchez (poet); Elisabeth Mudime-Boyi (professor, Duke University); Mark Mathabane (author)

Davidson College is one of the South's most prestigious and academically rigorous institutions of higher learning. The 154-year-old college has the educational opportunities, the well-regarded faculty, and the facilities that are increasingly attracting bright and motivated students from other parts of the country.

But Davidson remains distinctly Southern and conservative. About 30 percent of the student body is from North Carolina, while the majority of the school's students are from other parts of the region. And the Honor Code, typical at many Southern colleges and universities, strictly enforces the school rules against "cheating" and "lying." Social life is dominated by an active Greek system.

Davidson requires that all of its students complete an extensive core curriculum that includes courses in literature, fine arts, religion and philosophy, natural science and math, and the social sciences. Students have the option of enrolling in the school's five-course humanities sequence that satisfies many of the core requirements. Students must also take a cultural diversity course that explores "societies or cultures which differ from that of the United States." Courses in Davidson's well-regarded South Asian Studies program can be used to satisfy the requirement.

Some of the college's best departments are economics, political science, and history. The sciences, particularly biology and chemistry, are strong. The school's Dean Rusk Program in International Studies enhances the school's already impressive opportunities in the area; more than a third of the students at Davidson study abroad in such countries as Spain, Mexico, India, and England. (The Rusk Program is named for Dean Rusk, a Davidson alum and Secretary of State during the Johnson and Kennedy administrations.) The school's "Black Literature" course is not well regarded by students, but its "Francophone Africa and the Caribbean" course is. "The professor, Lauren Yoder, is excellent," says a student.

Academics at Davidson are strenuous. Fortunately, one of Davidson's best assets is its accessible faculty. The president of the college, John Kuykendall, even teaches a popular religion course. "It's not unusual to call a professor at his or her home to ask for help, or even to go to their houses for class or dinner," says a student. "It's so easy to get help from them." Small class sizes, even in lower-level courses, are also the norm.

African-American and female students majoring in the sciences are able to take advantage of the school's participation in COSEN (Carolinas-Ohio Science Education Network), an organization of colleges that provides consortium-wide peer groups, faculty mentors, and research possibilities for students. "If it wasn't for the program, I know I wouldn't have stuck out my science major," says a student. "The opportunities for meeting with minority faculty at the other schools, and the female faculty at those schools, has been especially supportive."

The social outlets for the school's students of color leave something to be desired, according to students. Most of the school's social life takes place at Patterson Court, where all of the school's six predominantly white fraternities are located; in a recent year, only three African-American males were members of three different fraternities. Recently, the school's African-American student group, the Black Student Coalition (BSC), approached the student government and the administration with the possibility of establishing a historically black fraternity on campus. According to a student, "the idea was turned down because the administration and student government thought it would serve only to segregate the campus. They worried that all of our social life would take place at the fraternity and that we wouldn't mix with any of the other student clubs or fraternities on campus." Davidson has no sororities; rather, women join eating clubs, of which several African-American women are members.

A popular hangout for Davidson's African-American students is the Black Student Coalition House, which has a television and a meeting area for the Black Student Coalition's biweekly meetings. The house, open twenty-four hours a day, "is primarily a place where we can relax and be ourselves." For social activities, the BSC sponsors an annual balloon sale and a party for first-year students. The BSC has also sponsored socials with all of the fraternities. During the 1991–92 school year, students established a Black Women's Support Group, which meets once every two weeks.

Students report that there is little racial integration on campus. "Everyone eats at the Vail Commons on campus," says a student. "There's a corner table where all of the black students eat, and we get asked all the time by white students, 'Why don't you sit with us?' We want to ask them, 'Why don't you sit with us?'" The school's mixers, a social function designed to introduce first-year female and male students to one another, have been described as particularly uncomfortable for the school's relatively small class of first-year students of color. "At one of the events, I got fixed up with a white guy, and when he found out I was black he suddenly said he had to go study," says a first-year student.

Davidson is a sports-minded campus, particularly when it comes to intramurals. It's estimated that nearly 80 percent of the student body participates in at least one of the intramural activities, while varsity sports also enjoy high rates of participation. Basketball and soccer are the most popular. The Baker Sports Complex offers impressive facilities, especially for a school of Davidson's relatively small size.

For many of the school's students of color, social life takes place off campus. Most weekends, students will make the hour-and-a-half trek to North Carolina A & T, a predominantly black university in Greensboro. Davidson, North Carolina, has a small African-American population, but students say there is little interaction between the town and the college. Davidson is just twenty miles north of Charlotte.

While Davidson works to become a more nationally recognized college, the school continues to attract conservative students from affluent backgrounds, most often from the South. Deviations from the norm (i.e., the status quo) are the exception here, where an asymmetrical haircut is regarded as radical.

A Davidson degree is highly respected in the region, and is becoming increasingly so across the country. For students of color, earning that degree at this point in time will involve a challenge that involves more than just serious commitment to academics. "A lot of the minority students tell minority applicants who are visiting the campus to come here only if they don't mind not having a social life. Here, you're forced to be friends with other minority students whom you might not get along with simply because there are so few of us. But I came to Davidson because of its small size, internship possibilities, and academic reputation."

DUKE UNIVERSITY

Address: 2138 Campus Drive, Durham, NC 27706
Phone: (919) 684-3214
Director of Admissions: Harold Wingood
Multicultural Student Recruiter: Arnice Jones
1992–93 tuition: $15,700
Room and board: $5,243
Application deadline: 1/1
Financial aid application deadline: 3/1
Non-white freshman admissions: Applicants for the class of '95: na
  Accepted: na
  Applicants accepted who rank in top

10% of high school class: 89%
In top 25%: 96%
Median SAT: na
Median ACT: na
Full-time undergraduate enrollment: 6,000
  Men: 46.7%
  Women: 53%
Non-white students in
  1987–88: 18%
  1988–89: 20%
  1989–90: 22%
  1990–91: 22%
Students In-state: 15%

STUDENT ENROLLMENT

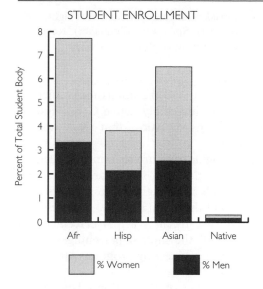

% Women   % Men

GEOGRAPHIC DISTRIBUTION OF STUDENTS

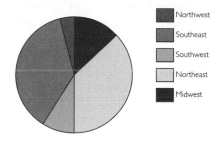

Northwest
Southeast
Southwest
Northeast
Midwest

Top majors: 1. Political Science
2. Economics 3. English

Retention rate of non-white students: 90%

Scholarships exclusively for non-white students: Reginaldo Howard Memorial Scholarship: mcrit-bascd; cach award is valued at $6,000; seven awarded each year; renewable; available to African-American applicants.

Remediation programs: None

Academic support services: Peer tutoring is available in all academic subjects. The Black Alumni Mentorship Program also provides academic support.

Ethnic studies programs: The university offers African-American Studies, with more than a dozen courses.

Ethnic studies courses: Duke offers more than 45 courses in Asian and African languages and literatures. Language study includes Arabic, Swahili, Chinese, Korean, and others. Courses are also offered in the economics and history of Japan, China, and Latin America.

Organizations for non-white students: Alpha Kappa Alpha, Alpha Phi Alpha, Delta Sigma Theta, Kappa Alpha Psi, Omega Psi Phi, Black Student Alliance, Dance Black, Modern Black Mass Choir, Duke Society of Black Engineers, Black Women's and Men's Support Groups, *Prometheus Black* (literary magazine), Karamu (theater group), Black Pre-health Organization, Students of the Caribbean, Spanish-American Latin Student Association

Notable non-white alumni: na

Tenured faculty: 887

Non-tenured faculty: 791

FACULTY

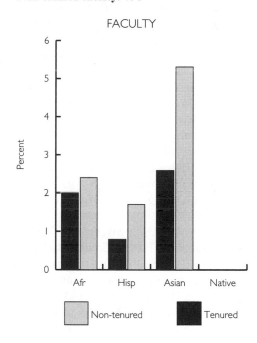

Non-tenured   Tenured

Student-faculty ratio: 12:1

Administrators: na
  African-American: 5%
  Hispanic: 1%
  Asian-American: 1%
  Native American: 0

Recent non-white speakers on campus: Maya Angelou (author and poet); Dr. Johnnetta Cole (president, Spelman College); Jesse Jackson (former U.S. presidential candidate and civil rights activist); Spike Lee (filmmaker); Rev. Al Sharpton (civil rights activist)

There is more to Duke than basketball (although the Duke admissions office no doubt appreciates the publicity on ESPN) and an incredibly active Greek system. There are also academic programs—and admissions statistics—that rival those at almost any of the prestigious Ivy League schools.

Duke students enroll in either the School of Engineering or the Trinity College of Arts and Letters. Students in the well-regarded engineering school aren't strangers to the liberal arts, as they are at many other schools. Although Duke engineers must enroll in at least five courses in the humanities and the social sciences, many elect to double-major in a program in Trinity College. In a recent year, 24 percent of the school's engineering students were women, one of the highest percentages in the country. The biomedical, electrical, and mechanical engineering programs are among the most popular.

Trinity College's English department boasts some of the nation's best-known literary theorists and has become increasingly popular as a result. The program in public policy studies rivals Georgetown's and Princeton's and is one of the top such undergraduate programs in the nation; it requires students to complete an off-campus internship in such places as the nation's capital. Math, history, chemistry, and art history are standouts. Marine biologists have access to Duke's laboratory on Pivers Island in addition to the university's 135-foot research vessel, the *Cape Hatteras*. The university also offers several interdisciplinary programs—such as the Asian and African languages and literature program and the program in film and video—for students who might otherwise feel confined studying in a single academic department.

The school's Afro-American Studies program is "rebuilding," say students, particularly since the recent departure of noted scholar Henry Louis Gates, Jr., to Harvard. But, says a student, "I am disturbed at how long it is taking to fully develop this program, even though African-American Studies courses are among the most popular on campus." According to one student, about five or six courses are offered in the area each semester. Recently, the university appointed George Wright, a former vice-provost at the University of Texas at Austin, to head the program.

To graduate, Trinity College students must complete an expository writing course, as well as courses in five of six areas: arts and literature, civilizations, foreign languages, natural sciences, quantitative reasoning, and social science. An alternative is Program II, which allows students, working closely with a faculty adviser, to design their own curriculum. Students must also complete "small-group learning experience" courses (seminars, tutorials, or independent study projects) during their first three years at the university.

When it comes to academic intensity, Duke has the reputation of being one of the more laid-back schools of its caliber. That has changed somewhat, however, with the increase in the number of required courses from 32 to 34. In addition to accessible faculty, the university offers a vast array of academic support services, from graduate school students—"They serve as big brothers and sisters and counselors"—to staff and alums. Caroline Lattimore, dean of minority affairs, is high on most people's list as a source of support. "Dean Lattimore is an incredible role model for minority students," says a junior. "She symbolizes scholarship, dedication, community awareness, and a special loving attitude toward everything she does." Students also feel comfortable turning to William Turner, professor at Duke's divinity school, C. Eric Lincoln, professor of religion, Martin Bryant, professor of psychology and sociology, and Leonard Beckum, vice-provost of the university. Vice-president for student affairs Janet Smith Dickerson is also said by students to be a dynamic force on campus.

Duke is one of the nation's elite institutions of higher education, but it is also one that remains largely segregated along racial lines, although students say the situation is improving somewhat. "Racial integration is better here than at most campuses in the South, but the natural separation of cultures does occur. The parties are beginning to show a good deal of mixing. This is due to some of the student groups on campus and projects such as SPECTRUM, whose sole purpose is race integration, and Students of the Caribbean, whose members vary from Asian to African." SPECTRUM, whose most recent co-presidents were Asian-American and African-American, recently opened its own residential theme house that includes students from various backgounds.

The separation of the races—particularly among African-American and white students—is most evident in the school's living situations. "The living units are not integrated, but not because of any conscious attempt to keep the races separated," says a student. "The majority of the African-American community prefers the privacy and social scene of central campus apartments." The separation is also evident in some favorite gathering spots on campus. "The Campus Inn bench, where white students congregate, and what we call the black bench, both on West Campus, are only twenty-five to thirty feet from one another," says a student, "yet there's miles of separation between them." The marked separation between the races, or, more specifically, the amount of self-segregation at the university, was the focus of a recent piece on *60 Minutes*.

Duke's cultural student groups "are very influential on campus because they keep life in perspective and sponsor plenty of programs," says a student. The Black Student Alliance (BSA) has become increasingly active in recent years, especially politically; during a recent year, the BSA staged demonstrations to demand the hiring of more faculty of color and against the university's refusal to cancel classes for Martin Luther King, Jr.'s Birthday.

But the group isn't without its social side. During a recent school year, it sponsored a step show as well as several informal get-togethers. The school's five traditionally black fraternities and sororities have parties and dances, as well as providing opportunities for community service. Some of the Greek organizations have sponsored forums on AIDS and the Gulf War, and have coordinated canned-food drives for countries in Africa. The members of Alpha Phi Alpha recently obtained their own residence facility located on West Campus, where the majority of Duke's predominantly white fraternities are located. It's the first time a black Greek organization has had such a facility on that part of campus. Many of the school's black student organizations meet in the Mary Lou Williams Cultural Center, located in the West Union Building.

Duke's African-American community is composed of a diverse group of students.

"My African-American friends are all different," says a senior. "They come from Brooklyn and North Carolina and Chicago, and some are rich and others aren't. It makes for an interesting mix of students."

The campus's Spanish-American Latin Student Association (SALSA) is primarily a "social" organization, according to a student member. "We get together mostly to speak Spanish and to listen to music," she says. Another member would like to see the organization become more active in coming years. "When I first got to Duke there would be at least fifty people at meetings," says a junior. "Now, not that many come, maybe twelve or fifteen."

The Bryant University Center, located on West Campus, is the hub of student activity at Duke. The center offers three theaters, a game room, two art galleries, television rooms—in short, almost everything the socially conscious undergrad could want. The university also sponsors several student musical groups—including a Jazz Ensemble and Chapel Choir—and theater groups—such as Hoof 'n' Horn—that regularly schedule performances. Duke also has two student film societies that have frequent screenings, all free of charge, and there's an art museum as well. And, of course, there are those athletic teams—especially the basketball team—that consistently draw national attention and long lines for tickets. Duke's campus is spectacularly beautiful—especially the Chapel on West Campus—and much of it is inviting for quiet walks.

Durham is a predominantly African-American community, and students report that town-gown relations between the campus's students of color and residents are "extensive." Students have the opportunity to interact with area residents through various tutoring programs and as volunteers with the Durham Housing Authority. "Many students get involved with tutoring programs for the children of the community and most students find local churches welcoming," says a student. Students comment, however, about the sometimes uneasy relations between Duke's African-American students and the relatively poor African-American residents of Durham, many of whom work in the university's food and custodial services.

Outside of community service, students can catch a game of the Durham Bulls, a minor league baseball team made famous by the Kevin Costner movie, and can take advantage of the cultural and social outlets of the Triangle Area, the primary center of culture and education between Washington, DC, and Atlanta that includes Greensboro and Chapel Hill. The area is also home to several large universities, among them the University of North Carolina and North Carolina Central, a predominantly black university.

Academics are rigorous, but, say students, worth all the effort. "I would recommend Duke to a prospective minority student. The university is best for the student who is looking for a challenge, academically and socially. Duke is one of the few predominantly white institutions where the administration actively listens to the concerns of its minority students. Duke is not a place that has extensive ethnic studies programs—Duke offers a little bit of everything. Duke is not perfect. It is a microcosm of the real world. I guarantee that the Gothic Wonderland is a roller-coaster ride that demands students who can settle down, buckle up, and take the initiative."

GUILFORD COLLEGE

Address: 5800 West Friendly Avenue, Greensboro, NC 27410
Phone: (919) 316-2100
Director of Admissions: Larry West
Multicultural Student Recruiter: James Williams
1991–92 tuition: $10,270
Room and board: $4,514
Application deadline: 3/1
Financial aid application deadline: 3/1

Non-white freshman admissions: Applicants for the class of '95: 189
Accepted: 56.6%
Accepted who enroll: 43%
Applicants accepted who rank in top 10% of high school class: 9%
In top 25%: 22%
Median SAT: 435 V, 480 M
Median ACT: na
Full-time undergraduate enrollment: 1,388
Men: 48.9%
Women: 51.1%

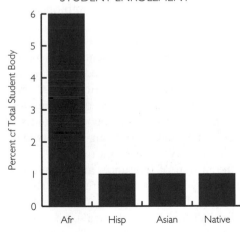

STUDENT ENROLLMENT

Non-white students in
1987–88: 7.1%
1988–89: 7.5%
1989–90: 7.9%
1990–91: 7.1%

Geographic distribution of students: na
Students In-state: 40%
Top majors: 1. Business and Management 2. Psychology 3. Justice and Policy Studies
Retention rate of non-white students: 70%
Scholarships exclusively for non-white students: Honors Scholarships: two half-tuition scholarships awarded each year; need- and merit-based
Remediation programs: na
Academic support services: The Academic Skills Center offers tutoring and other support services in a wide variety of areas.
Ethnic studies programs: The college offers a concentration in African-American Studies.
Ethnic studies courses: Guilford offers courses in various departments related to Africa, South America, and Asia.
Organizations for non-white students: African-American Cultural Society
Notable non-white alumni: Michael Lear Carr ('73, History; president, ML Enterprises, and former Boston Celtic basketball player); Stanley Scot Givens ('82, Biology; oncologist); Yolanda Leacraft ('80, Sociology; JVC Commission on Status of Women); Keith Miller ('82, Economics; vice president, Nations Bank); Kevin Taylor ('87, Accounting; assistant program development director, BET)
Tenured faculty: 63
Non-tenured faculty: 28
Student-faculty ratio: 14:1
Administrators: na
African-American: 7%
Hispanic: na
Asian-American: 1%
Native American: na
Recent non-white speakers on campus: Dr. Ben Hayford (visiting professor, University of Cape Coast, Ghana); Mary

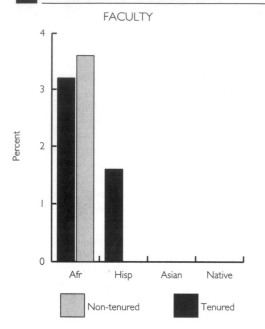

FACULTY

Chiltoskey (Cherokee storyteller); Stephen Curwood (producer of public radio environmental programs)

Close faculty-student interaction at Guilford College isn't the exception, it's the norm. "The president of the college, Bill Rogers, and I are friends, but it's not something I brag about, because a lot of the students here are friends with him," says a student. "His wife, Beverly, loves to bake, and they always have us over to their house for meetings or dinner. That's one of the best things about this school. You can get to know your professors, even the president." Guilford students also commonly refer to their professors by their first names.

In the Quaker tradition (the college was founded by Quakers in 1837), Guilford students are also heavily involved in the school's policymaking. Students sit on almost every governing board, and, as opposed to everything being ruled by majority, decisions are arrived at by consensus, even within student organizations. "At first I thought the process wouldn't allow for much individuality, but the discussions involved in arriving at different decisions open you up to other people's points of view, and they also make you a better listener. Nine times out of ten, students leave meetings where decisions were made feeling good," says a sophomore.

Also in keeping with Quaker tradition is the notion of tolerance, an attitude that is taken quite seriously at the college. "I feel very comfortable here, even though there aren't that many people of color on campus. But the majority of students are very open to race and gender issues, and we haven't had any real racial controversies in the two years I've been here," says a student. "There's also a very diverse student population here, even within the minority population, which helps make a lot of students feel comfortable. There are students who have a wide diversity of opinion, and come from various socioeconomic backgrounds and geographic areas."

Guilford is a liberal arts college, and to graduate, students must satisfy distributional requirements that include a foreign language and a course in intercultural studies "to encourage students to expand their horizons beyond the American-European tradition to the cultures of Asia, Africa, or Latin America." One of the courses that satisfy the intercultural studies requirement is "African History." "The professor, Adrienne Israel, is excellent." Additional intercultural studies courses are offered by the political science, religion, and art departments, among others.

Students rate highly the school's psychology, biology, justice and policy studies, and business programs. Guilford's democratic management program, the only one of its kind in the country, is "designed to prepare students for the cultural, economic, philosophical, and business aspects of working in employee-owned or -managed organizations."

The college's African-American Studies concentration includes five courses in five different departments. The program's "Racial and Ethnic Relations" course, offered by the sociology department, is popular with students, as is the course's professor, Joseph Graves.

While faculty-student interaction is one of the hallmarks of an education at Guilford, students also find each other effective sources of support. "If you're having a problem in a class and you need help, pretty much all you have to do to get help is talk to someone you know who had the class and did well. Almost never will a student turn you down."

Guilford's African-American Cultural Society has about 15 to 20 active members, who meet weekly in the Residence Life Office's lounge, located in Milner Hall. The group's biggest activity is its annual Cotillion. "This year we held the dance in order to start a scholarship fund for African-Americans to attend Guilford," says an organizer of the event. "We've named the scholarship in honor of Sarah T. Curwood, a Guilford alum. We had an excellent turnout of faculty and students, and two board of trustee members from New Jersey drove down just for the dinner." AACS members also sold tickets for the Cotillion at North Carolina A & T, a predominantly black university about ten minutes from Guilford. "That's the first time we've ever really sponsored anything formal with students from A & T," says a student.

The recently formed Sweet Diversions is a five-member group that performs spirituals and gospels. "The members didn't know each other before they came to campus; they come from nearly as many states as there are members, including North Carolina, West Virginia, New York, and Massachusetts. They're one of the best and most popular performing groups on campus," says a student.

Other active Guilford groups include Project Community, a student volunteer organization, and the school's varsity athletic teams, which have won several championships recently. The city of Greensboro offers a variety of activities of its own. The Greensboro Coliseum hosts sporting events, shows, and concerts, and the city's recently renovated Carolina Theatre has presented concerts by Wynton Marsalis and Spyro Gyra. Seven other colleges and universities are also located in the Greensboro area, among them Bennett, a historically black college for women. Students sometimes head to these schools, as well as others, for various social and cultural events.

A popular figure on campus is Joanna Iwata, director of student services. "We can always turn to her for help about anything to do with AACS," says a student. Iwata also helped originate Guilford's Leadership Enhancement, Advancement, and Development program, in which students are able to fine-tune their leadership skills by meeting with guest speakers and discussing readings. It is tough to get into the three-year-old program; in a recent year, 35 students applied for 12 spots. "But there are so many opportunities for leadership here that the students who don't get in aren't too disappointed."

Also popular on campus is Jimmy Williams, an admissions counselor, who is described as "nice and full of humor. He interacts with the students well. He helped start the phone-a-thons, where we call prospective Guilford students who are minorities and talk to them about Guilford and college in general. That program has been successful in getting many of the African-Americans who are here now to enroll at Guilford. In fact, I believe that this year's group of African-Americans is one of the brightest we've had since I've been here."

Students were disappointed when the administration did not cancel classes for this year's teach-in marking Martin Luther King, Jr.'s Birthday. The day featured a presentation by AACS, Sweet Diversions, and North Carolina A & T students who spoke about African history. The day ended with a candlelight vigil.

With the school's emphasis on academics and tolerance, a Guilford education can be rewarding in many ways. "I'm happy here because I'm comfortable," says a student. "You know how you hate to refer to your college as your home because that will only upset your parents? Well, that's the way I feel here because it's like a home, where everyone can relate like one big family. We don't have all the resources of a larger school, but the people here help you get whatever it is you need."

UNIVERSITY OF NORTH CAROLINA/CHAPEL HILL

Address: Chapel Hill, NC 27599
Phone: (919) 966-3621
Director of Admissions: Dr. James Walters
Multicultural Student Recruiter: Dr. Herbert
  L. Davis, Jr.
1991–92 tuition: $1,248 (in-state); $7,116
  (out-of-state)
Room and board: na
Application deadline: 1/15
Financial aid application deadline: 3/1
Non-white freshman admissions: Applicants
  for the class of '95: 2,465
  Accepted: 43%
  Accepted who enroll: 51.2%
  Applicants accepted who rank in top
  10% of high school class: 56%
  In top 25%: 87%
  Median SAT: 540 V, 547 M
  Median ACT: na
Full-time undergraduate enrollment: 14,346
  Men: 40.3%
  Women: 59.7%

Non-white students in
  1987–88: 13%
  1988–89: 13.7%

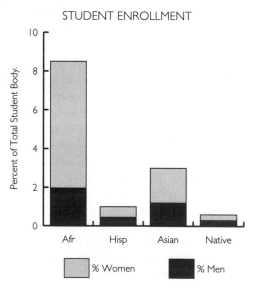

STUDENT ENROLLMENT

Percent of Total Student Body.

Afr   Hisp   Asian   Native

□ % Women   ■ % Men

1989–90: 14.6%
1990–91: 15.8%

GEOGRAPHIC DISTRIBUTION OF STUDENTS

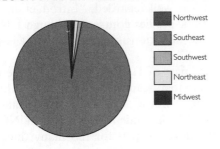

- Northwest
- Southeast
- Southwest
- Northeast
- Midwest

Students In-state: 83%

Top majors: 1. Biology 2. Business 3. Political Science

Retention rate of non-white students: 92%

Scholarships exclusively for non-white students: Pogue Scholarships: merit-based; $5,400 for each award; ten awarded each year. Minority Presence Scholarships: need-based; amount varies.

Remediation programs: None

Academic support services: The university offers departmental tutorial services; Scholastic Advancement Session, offered for minority students by the Office for Student Counseling; Academic Skills Enhancement Sessions; and a mentor program for minority students.

Ethnic studies programs: The university offers programs in African American Studies, East Asian Studies, and Latin American Studies.

Organizations for non-white students: Alpha Kappa Alpha, Kappa Alpha Psi, Phi Beta Sigma, Zeta Phi Beta, Alpha Phi Alpha, Omega Psi Phi, Delta Sigma Theta, Black Student Movement

Notable non-white alumni: na

Tenured faculty: 1,371

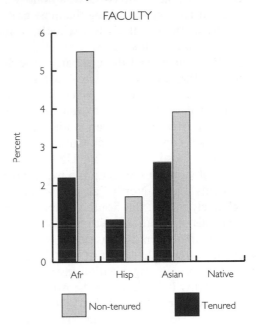

FACULTY

Non-tenured   Tenured

Non-tenured faculty: 874

Student-faculty ratio: 14:1

Administrators: 572
   African-American: 8.5%
   Hispanic: 1.4%
   Asian-American: 6.6%
   Native American: 0

Recent non-white speakers on campus: Spike Lee (filmmaker); Coretta Scott King (civil rights activist and widow of Martin Luther King, Jr.); Andrew Young (former UN ambassador and mayor of Atlanta)

Established in 1789—the year of George Washington's first inauguration—the University of North Carolina is America's oldest state university. With top-flight academics, a more than motivated student body, and a beautiful campus, it's no wonder that students from all over the country come to Chapel Hill.

Academics at UNC can be demanding. The school's strengths include the liberal arts, and in order to graduate, students must complete 14 required general education courses, including English composition, foreign language, math, philosophy, natural science, social science, and Western and non-Western history classes. The university offers 66 undergraduate degree-granting programs, and students say some of the best of them are sociology, political science, English, and classics. Other top-notch and popular programs are journalism and business administration, which also have competitive admissions. UNC's honors program is well regarded. "Introduction to African History" is among the most popular ethnic studies courses. Although UNC is one of the country's top schools, academic competition isn't as keen as it is at other well-known schools.

UNC has earned the nickname "the Southern part of Heaven," no doubt due in part to the school's 687-acre campus, one of the most beautiful in the country. But for the school's students of color, the nickname is not exactly apt. "We certainly don't call it that," says a student active in the Black Student Movement, UNC's primary African-American student group. "We have to fight for too many things, like a self-contained Black Cultural Center and a Black Studies department."

There's also the fact that UNC remains a largely segregated university. "This is most obvious in the campus's living situation," says a student. "Most of the white students live on North Campus, which is near all of the classrooms. Mid-campus is relatively mixed. But South Campus is where the majority of the black students live. And this segregation isn't only between black and white students. My best friend is Jewish, and when she was doing some research for an organization she's involved in, she discovered that most of UNC's Jewish students also live on South Campus."

One campus organization intent on raising the campus's awareness about issues of diversity is Students for the Advancement of Race Relations. "The group sponsors a multicultural week. Recently the group invited Sister Souljah to speak, which was interesting and drew a mixed crowd. But on a day-to-day basis, there is little bonding or even interaction between white and non-white students," says a sophomore.

Until recently, the BSM and much of the campus has seen little political activity, particularly when it comes to race awareness. But with the sudden death in 1991 of Sonja Haynes Stone, a popular African-American Studies professor, much of the campus became galvanized for action. "She touched not only the lives of the black students but also the lives of white students who took her classes and who knew her. She was a role model to all of us, and we want to keep her memory alive."

In fact, her memory is being kept alive through the kind of political activity—demonstrations, rallies, petitions—that, according to a student, "hasn't been seen since the days of the Vietnam protests." Along with the student government of '92 and the Campus Y, the BSM has issued a list of demands to the UNC board of trustees. "We wanted the Black Cultural Center to be renamed the Sonja Haynes Stone Black Cultural Center, which the trustees did. We're waiting on the rest to happen. We want an endowment for a professorship in her name, we want a freestanding BCC (the BCC is currently in the school's student union), we want African-American Studies to be turned into a department, and we want higher wages for the school's housekeepers."

With approval from the administration, students have been fundraising for a new Black Cultural Center. "So far, the fundraising is going pretty well," says a student. But students are discouraged by Chancellor Hardin's attitude about such a center. "He says he wants a BCC that's a forum and not a fortress. He likes the setup the way it is now. But the setup really isn't that great. Right below us, in the basement, is the Cabaret, which has events at least twice a week. The events there are so loud that it's like they're in the room with us, so having meetings on those nights gets to be difficult, and we have meetings in there almost every night."

Each year, the BCC hosts an open house for the campus community. "It's tremendously successful. At a recent open house, the majority of those who came were non-black."

The 1992–93 school year is the BSM's twenty-fifth anniversary on campus. To celebrate, "we'll be having a coronation ball, with a homecoming court, a casino night, and a reception for new students," says a BSM leader. "We've also started a Dorm Activation System, in which one BSM member in each dorm will be in charge of getting BSM information to all black students who live at his or her dorm. This is so we can become more unified."

BSM's weekly paper, *The Black Ink,* is a good source of information about the events going on on campus and in the area. Six to eight pages long, the paper is entirely student-generated. Says a student about the professionalism of the paper: *"The Black Ink* used to be the worst of all the papers, but in the last year it has turned around to become one of the finest pieces of journalism on campus. It hits lots of different issues and speaks with a strong voice."

In addition to its political activism, the BSM, with more than 300 active members, sponsors step shows and dances. The group meets weekly, on Wednesdays, in the Upendo Lounge in the Chase dining hall.

Chapel Hill is one of the country's best college towns. There are more than ten movie theaters in the Chapel Hill area, as well as all sorts of restaurants and clubs. Duke University and North Carolina State are within easy driving distance, and interaction among students from the different schools is frequent. But, as at many large universities, there's never a shortage of things to do on campus. The Carolina Union hosts various events, including first-run-movie nights. Attending varsity sports events, especially basketball games, is a must, and intramurals are also popular.

At the present time, a student reluctant to get politically involved may find attending UNC to be a lonely experience, as many of the school's African-American students are becoming increasingly active. Should you desire a top-flight education, mixed with some political activity, then you may find UNC rewarding. "I'm glad I came here, although I've had my ups and downs. But my experiences here have made me a stronger and more knowledgeable person. If you want to be happy here, my advice is to get involved."

NORTH CAROLINA STATE UNIVERSITY

Address: Box 7103, 112 Peele Hall, Raleigh, NC 27695-7103
Phone: (919) 515-2434
Director of Admissions: Dr. George R. Dixon
Multicultural Student Recruiter: na

1991–92 tuition: $1,254 (in-state); $7,122 (out-of-state)
Room and board: $3,150
Application deadline: 2/1
Financial aid application deadline: 3/1

Non-white freshman admissions: Applicants for the class of '95: 1,271
Accepted: 64%
Accepted who enroll: 57%
Applicants accepted who rank in top 10% of high school class: 37%
In top 25%: 74%
Median SAT: 425 V, 484 M
Median ACT: na
Full-time undergraduate enrollment: 17,967
Men: 62.8%
Women: 37.2%

STUDENT ENROLLMENT

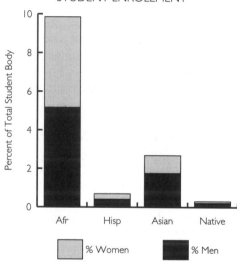

Non-white students in
1987–88: 16.8%
1988–89: 16.9%
1989–90: 16.8%
1990–91: 16.8%

GEOGRAPHIC DISTRIBUTION OF STUDENTS

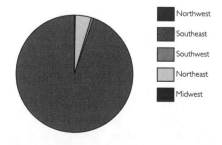

- Northwest
- Southeast
- Southwest
- Northeast
- Midwest

Students In-state: 66.8%

Top majors: 1. Electrical Engineering 2. Business Management 3. Computer Science
Retention rate of non-white students: 44%
Scholarships exclusively for non-white students: Mary McLeod Bethune: merit-based; average award is $1,000. College of Forest Resources Dean's Minority Scholarship: merit-based; $1,000 for each award. National Action Council for Minorities in Engineering: $500–$3,500 for underrepresented minority students; merit- and need-based. College of Textiles Dean's Minority Scholarship: merit-based; each award is valued at $1,000. Pulp & Paper Foundation Scholarship: $1,000; need-based; available to African-American students.
Remediation programs: Courses in "Developmental Reading," "Basic Algebra," and "Basic Skills and Concepts in Biology" are available.
Academic support services: A network of African-American coordinators, one in each of NCSU's nine colleges, develops, coordinates, and evaluates special programs to enhance the academic progress of African-American students. A one-credit course for minority first-year students is available to aid in adjustment to university life. A peer mentor program is also available.
Ethnic studies programs: The university offers African and African-American Studies minors.
Ethnic studies courses: na
Organizations for non-white students: African-American Design Student Association, Omega Psi Phi, African-American Science and Health Society, New Horizons Choir, African Students Association, National Technical Association, Alpha Kappa Alpha, Alpha Phi Alpha, Delta Sigma Theta, Phi Beta Sigma, Sigma Gamma Rho, Kappa Alpha Psi, Nigerian Student Association, Partners of Black Entrepreneurs, Black Repertory Theater, Black Student Board, Society of Black Physical and

Mathematical Scientists, African-American Heritage Society, NAACP, Dance Visions, Society of African-American Culture, National Association of Black Accountants, Zeta Phi Beta

Notable non-white alumni: Dr. Marcus L. Martin ('70; Pulp & Paper Science; director, Emergency Medicine Residency); Audrey Kates Bailey ('76, Communications; program developer, UNC Public TV); James Gwyn, Jr. ('70; pilot, American Airlines); Philip G. Freelon ('75, Architecture; architect); Dr. Paula Smith Sawyer ('79, Pre-medicine; clinical director)

Tenured faculty: 1,028

Non-tenured faculty: 434

Student-faculty ratio: 14:1

Administrators: 163

  African-American: 4%

  Hispanic: 0

  Asian-American: 1%

  Native American: <1%

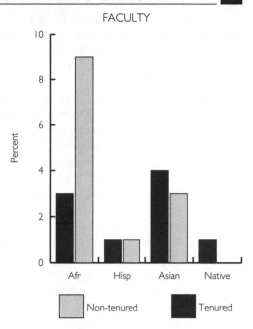

FACULTY

Recent non-white speakers on campus: Dr. Na'im Akbar (clinical psychologist); Christine Dardern (aerospace engineer); C. T. Vivian (race awareness consultant); Octavia Butler (science fiction author); David G. Du Bois (writer and professor, University of Massachusetts, and son of W. E. B. Du Bois)

North Carolina State University is not just your average oversized state university. Sure, there are the usual headaches of attending a school with more than 17,000 other students—large class sizes, a pain-in-the-neck registration system, to name just a few. But NC State's terrific academic programs, especially in technical fields, sets the 106-year-old university apart.

Established in 1887 as a land-grant institution, the university still offers top-notch programs in agriculture, among them poultry science, agronomy, and animal science. The university's School of Design is one of the foremost in the country. Design students are able to concentrate in such areas as architecture, environmental design, product design, and visual design. NC State's College of Engineering is also outstanding and offers 16 undergraduate programs, including aerospace, chemical, and computer. For students interested in working in textile design, NC State's College of Textiles is one of the best in the country, and graduates of the program are in high demand by employers. NC State is definitely a technical-oriented university, so don't attend school here if you're looking for noteworthy programs in liberal arts. One of the most popular programs in the school's College of Humanities and Social Science is business management.

Students rave about some of the school's African-American Studies courses, particularly "African-American History I & II," taught by Joanne Woodard. Students also praise "Interracial Communication," taught by Gail Hankins.

For academic assistance, students turn to the Academic Skills Program, located in Reynolds Coliseum, which most students say is effective. The Program of Academic Support Services, which helps find tutors for students, is respected. As NC State is a rather large institution, professors can be distant, but students praise their friendliness and accessibility once they're approached. Many of the large courses are broken into smaller group discussions which are led by teaching assistants.

The African-American Student Affairs Office provides additional support. The office coordinates a freshman orientation for incoming African-American students, as well as a peer mentor program. "Upperclass students are paired with new students according to major and interest, and it's one of the programs that really helped me succeed here as a freshman. It's kind of like a big brother/big sister program," reports a junior. Wanda Covington, the director of the office, is highly respected by students.

Students also have access to the programs at the African-American Culture Center, a new facility that opened on campus in the spring of 1991. "The center is really nice. The third floor has a library, offices for student groups, and conference rooms. The second floor has an art gallery with student art. Most of the black student groups have their meetings in the center, where there's also a small movie theater." In addition, the school's African-American student groups, particularly fraternities or sororities, sponsor parties and dances at the center on weekends. However, one student comments: "The center is now more office-oriented, and students don't tend to hang out there as much. Mostly, students hang out in the student center." Larry Campbell, the center's coordinator, is a well-regarded resource for students.

The Black Student Board (BBB), a part of the Union Activities Board, focuses much of its attention each year on coordinating NC State's Pan-African Festival, a weeklong event in April. "There are so many events as part of the week that's it's difficult to take advantage of them all," says a senior. "There are usually three or four guest lecturers, a concert, a banquet for students who've earned a 3.0 GPA or better, a talent show, and a picnic, and our gospel choir, with more than a hundred members, performs. It's basically a week where we can celebrate our culture and a time for all of us to get together." In a recent year, there were about 40 active BSB members.

With about 70 active members, the Society of African-American Culture, which works frequently with the BSB, "is more community-based," says a student. "They tutor in the Raleigh projects and in the area high schools. It's also a political voice. For example, last year the organization worked to get an African-American literature class to be one of the courses that could be used to fulfill a university-wide course requirement, and it worked. We got petitions signed and we had our meetings; it was a positive experience." The university's Black Repertory Theater—for novices and the more experienced—recently staged a production of *Ceremonies in Dark Old Men.*

NC State's largest black student group is the National Society of Black Engineers, which has nearly 200 members. Like the Society of African-American Culture, NSBE members are community-oriented, and also visit area high schools. The Society of Black Physical and Mathematical Scientists attracts a large and active membership. The school's eight traditionally black fraternities and sororities also work closely with the Raleigh community, by sponsoring food drives and tutoring programs. The women of Delta Sigma Theta built a house for a needy family with the volunteer group Habitat for Humanity and also coordinated a successful blood drive.

With all of these active organizations, NC State's African-American student population is close-knit. "We all pull together to help each other out. When we see each other on campus, we say hello to each other, and we all know that we're there for one another." One of the school's newer groups is Amandela, started by the men of the Omega Psi Phi fraternity, which provides peer support for its male members. As an alternative to the usual frat scene, a group of African-American men and women recently formed a coed fraternity, the Kemetic Benu Order.

NC State is located a mile west of Raleigh, North Carolina's state capital, but students say they don't feel as if they attend a city college, as the campus has several grassy areas and many trees. Raleigh is located just a half-hour drive from Chapel Hill and Durham, the homes of the University of North Carolina and Duke University, respectively. The area formed by the three universities is known as the Triangle, and there are more than enough local off-campus diversions to keep most students happy. The Big Four Day, which involves intramural competition against Duke, UNC, and Wake Forest University, brings out NC State's many diehard fans to cheer on their teams. One of the school's biggest assets, however, may not be location or academic programs, but the warmth of the students. "People aren't strangers on campus. Students are always saying hello to one another," observes a senior.

While NC State may be a large institution, students say the university provides the resources and a more than friendly student body that make it manageable. One student doesn't let the school's size intimidate him. "I chose NC State because of its reputation. I've taken outstanding courses and have had good professors who take a real interest in their students. It's a great place to grow and mingle with all kinds of people." Adds another student: "You're never lost in a crowd here, except maybe at football or basketball games."

WAKE FOREST UNIVERSITY

Address: Box 7305, Reynolds Station, Winston-Salem, NC 27109
Phone: (919) 759-5201
Director of Admissions: Bill Starling
Multicultural Student Recruiter: Juliet Jordan
1993–94 tuition: $13,000
Room and board: $4,330
Application deadline: 1/15
Financial aid application deadline: 3/15
Non-white freshman admissions: Applicants
  for the class of '95: na
  Accepted: na
  Accepted who enroll: na
  Applicants accepted who rank in top
  10% of high school class: na

Median SAT: na
Median ACT: na
Full-time undergraduate enrollment: 3,596
  Men: 51%
  Women: 49%
Non-white students in
  1987–88: 3.5%
  1988–89: 7.5%
  1989–90: 7.5%
  1990–91: 8.02%
Geographic distribution of students: na
Students In-state: 33%
Top majors: 1. English
  2. History
  3. Business

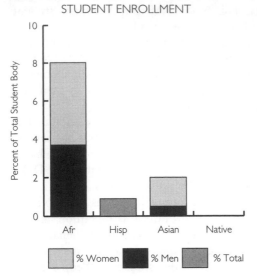

STUDENT ENROLLMENT

Percent of Total Student Body

■ % Women ■ % Men ■ % Total

Retention rate of non-white students: 92%
Scholarships exclusively for non-white students: Joseph G. Gordon Scholarship for African-American students: seven full-tuition scholarships awarded each year; need- and merit-based. Black American Scholarship Fund: merit-based; about 34 awarded each year; average amount is $4,958.
Remediation programs: None
Academic support services: The university's services include a writing lab and tutoring in most academic subjects.
Ethnic studies programs: None
Ethnic studies courses: "Sociology of the Black Experience," "Civil Rights: Slavery Seminar," "Black Writers," "Liberation Literature."

Organizations for non-white students: Alpha Kappa Alpha, Delta Sigma Theta, Alpha Phi Alpha, Black Student Alliance, Gospel Choir, Black Christian Fellowship
Notable non-white alumni: na
Tenured faculty: 195
Non-tenured faculty: 126

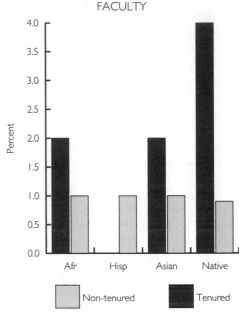

FACULTY

Percent

■ Non-tenured ■ Tenured

Student-faculty ratio: 12.5:1
Administrators: 63
  African-American: 5%
  Hispanic: 0
  Asian-American: 0
  Native American: 0
Recent non-white speakers on campus: Charlayne Hunter-Gault (news correspondent)

Wake Forest is one of the premier small liberal arts universities in the South, but with a twist: the 158-year-old university competes in the competitive athletic Atlantic Coast Conference, which includes such powerhouse teams as Duke University and Georgia Tech.

Top-flight academics, some of the most rigorous around, are what brings students to this highly regarded institution. (Since 1986, the university has graduated four Rhodes Scholars, the most of any school in the South.) Wake Forest's emphasis on the liberal arts is reflected in its core curriculum, which requires that students study a foreign language and complete studies in four other areas: literature and the arts;

history, religion, and philosophy; the social and behavioral sciences; and the natural sciences and math.

Students say that most departments at the university are strong, especially biology, economics, and English. The school's science department received an added boost with the recent completion of the Olin Physical Laboratory, said to be one of the best such facilities in the Southeast. Wake Forest's highly regarded School of Business and Accountancy offers the school's most popular majors. Students say the "Sociology of the Black Experience" and "Race and Ethnic Relations" courses are popular.

A highlight of a Wake Forest University education is close interaction with faculty members; one faculty star is Maya Angelou, a poet laureate of the United States and the author of numerous books, including *I Know Why the Caged Bird Sings.* "Her classes are great and demanding, when you can get into them," says a senior. In a recent year, as part of her "King and His Era" course, she invited Coretta Scott King to speak to her class.

Students add that other African-American faculty members are equally important in furthering the interests of students. Alton Pollard, an assistant professor of religion, recently earned the school's Excellence in Teaching Award. "Besides being an excellent faculty member, he's also a help to students outside of the classroom," says a student. "He's helped us with the Kwanzaa celebration, speaks at many functions on campus, and knows a lot about African-American history." Herman Eure, an associate professor of biology, "is always speaking at meetings and serving on committees. He and the other black faculty members are all working very hard for us. There's a lot of burnout among them, though, because they're called on to do so many things, either by us or by the administration."

Founded in 1835 by Baptists, Wake Forest still retains some of the conservative zeal of its founders. The Baptist Student Union is the most active religious student group on campus and has its own lounge for meetings. The Honor Code, which requires all students to report offenders, is strictly enforced, and punishment—such as dismissal from the university—is harsh. Most dorms are single-sex, and students are avowedly—and happily—Republican. "Most of the white students here are from upper-class backgrounds, attended private high schools, and have never interacted with a minority person before," comments a student. "They have their stereotypes to work through, and so do we. In order to do well here, you just have to know how to handle these situations." The university also remains a largely regional institution; more than 40 percent of the students are from North Carolina, and the majority of the others are from nearby states. "We have a hard time getting students from the North to come down here to school," says an administrator.

The Greek system is the predominant social force on Wake Forest's campus. Nearly half of the student body joins one or another of the campus's 13 national fraternities, seven local societies (for women), and three national sororities. The majority of the school's African-American students pledge one or another of the three historically black Greek organizations. "There are a couple of black students in the white fraternities, but with the resurgence of interest in traditionally black fraternities and sororities, especially at mostly white schools, the historically black Greek organizations here have also become more popular. The difference here and nationally, though, between our organizations and those that are mostly white is that ours are primarily service societies while theirs are mostly social."

Wake Forest's Black Student Alliance, with about 60 members, meets every Monday at the Black Student Alliance lounge in the school's Business Center. In addition to activities for Black History Month, the BSA sponsors Black Awareness Week, usually held during the fall semester. During a recent Black Awareness Week, members sponsored a poetry reading with Maya Angelou and various panel discussions. Some of the panels focused on the roles of African-American men and women in the '90s. At the beginning of each school year, the BSA has a cook-out to greet the freshmen. The BSA recently co-sponsored a reception for Wynton Marsalis, the trumpeter, after his performance on campus.

BSA members also seek to assist each other academically. "In addition to trying to educate the community and ourselves about African-American issues, we try to provide emotional and academic support for our members. If one of our members needs help in a class, we'll get someone to help him," says a biology major.

The Black Christian Fellowship, one of the school's many religious organizations, recently sponsored two revivals on campus and its gospel choir performs regularly.

The university is seeking to diversify its curriculum, faculty, and student body. A recently appointed Presidential Commission on Race Relations, made up of faculty, students, and administrators, suggested 33 areas in which the university needs to improve, one of which was getting the school to recruit more African-American males who are not on athletic scholarships. According to *The Chronicle of Higher Education,* during the 1990–91 school year 59 of the school's 111 African-American male students were athletes, and while the African-American enrollment accounted for 7 percent of the student population, 29 percent of its athletes were African-American. "When I came here [in 1983], the number of African-American students was tiny, and they were predominantly athletes," said Thomas Kearn, Jr., president of the university, in the *Chronicle* article. "We all agreed that this was a very bad thing and that we were failing in this responsibility."

Wake Forest's campus is beautiful and well manicured. Most student social life takes place at fraternity parties or at the Benson University Center, which opened in the fall of 1990 and offers a food court, a film theater, a game room, and study lounges. To unwind, the majority of Wake Forest students will participate in intramural activity or in the school's extracurricular clubs and organizations. Attending varsity athletic events, especially basketball, is also popular.

Winston-Salem (pop. 145,000) is located in the Piedmont Triad, a major center of technology that includes Greensboro and High Point, and students are able to take advantage of the cultural resources of the area, such as attending performances and concerts at nearby North Carolina School of the Arts. The city's museums and concert hall also offer off-campus cultural diversions.

About his years at Wake Forest, one senior says: "If a student chooses to attend school here, he or she will learn a lot more than Wake Forest University meant to teach them. The student will learn about racism and class discrimination. But the university has challenged me not to categorize people or to judge. It's its own miniature world here."

UNIVERSITY OF NORTH DAKOTA

Address: University Station, Grand Forks, ND 58202
Phone: (701) 777-2011
Director of Admissions: Dr. Monty Nielsen
Multicultural Student Recruiter: na
1993–94 tuition: $2,165 (in-state); $5,273 (out-of-state)
Room and board: $2,548
Application deadline: None
Financial aid application deadline: 3/15
Non-white freshman admissions: Applicants for the class of '94: 144
  Accepted: 94%
  Accepted who enroll: 95.6%
  Applicants accepted who rank in top 10% of high school class: 3%
  In top 25%: 28%
  Median SAT: na
  Median ACT: 20
Full-time undergraduate enrollment: 9,274
  Men: 54%
  Women: 46%
Non-white students in
  1987–88: 3.9%
  1988–89: 3.8%
  1989–90: 3.9%
  1990–91: 5.1%
Students In-state: 76.3%
Top majors: 1. Education 2. Nursing 3. Psychology
Retention rate of non-white students: 47%
Scholarships exclusively for non-white students: Native American Grant: need- and merit-based; $500 per award; 15 to

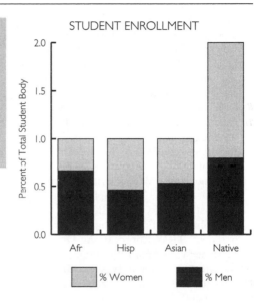

STUDENT ENROLLMENT

GEOGRAPHIC DISTRIBUTION OF STUDENTS

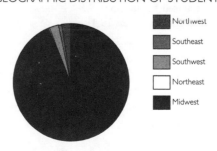

20 awarded each year. Black Student Tuition Waiver: need-based; five awarded each year.

Remediation programs: None

Academic support services: Tutoring in all academic subjects as well as for-credit courses in study skills and reading improvement. The university also offers programs in relieving test anxiety.

Ethnic studies programs: The university's Indian Studies program, established in 1977, offers more than 15 courses, including courses in American Indian languages. The program includes a major and minor. Tenured faculty: 3.

Ethnic studies courses: The university offers one course in African-American literature and courses in Asian and Latin American Studies.

Organizations for non-white students: American Native Student Association, Black Student Association, Chinese Student Association, Indian Association, Native American Cultural Center, Era Bell Thompson Cultural Center, Native American Aviation Association, Native Americans into Medicine, Seven Fires, American Indians AIDS Awareness Council

Notable non-white alumni: Fritz Pollard ('39, Education; '36 Olympic bronze medalist, track); General Bernard Randolph ('64, Engineering; former vice president, TRW Corporation); Dr. Marlene Ward ('66, Education; educator); Dr. Karen Swisher ('81, Education; professor, Arizona State University)

Tenured faculty: 287

Non-tenured faculty: 351

Student-faculty ratio: 19:1

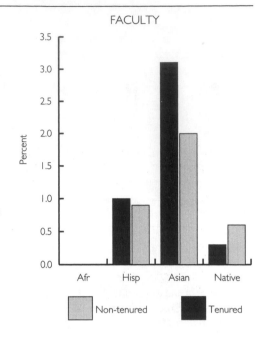

FACULTY

Administrators: 144
  African-American: 0
  Hispanic: 1.3%
  Asian-American: 0.6%
  Native American: 6.2%

Recent non-white speakers on campus: Wilma Mankiller (chief, Cherokee Tribe of Oklahoma); Ambrose Little Ghost (spiritual leader); Mike Her Many Horses (lecturer); Alvina Alberts (tribal elder); Sam Little Owl (teacher); Mario Praeda (director of Minority Student Programs, University of Minnesota/Crookston); Diedra McCalla (musician)

The University of North Dakota has two things going for it that state universities generally don't: an unusually friendly student body and close student-faculty interaction. "I transferred from a university in Canada and I was shocked at how nice everyone is here. The professors even know your first name. Where I came from, a professor probably didn't even know how many students were in his classroom."

UND also has a nationally recognized program in aviation. The program, which draws the school's largest out-of-state student enrollment, offers four different four-year programs with 50 courses, among them aviation administration, airport administration, airway science, and aeronautical studies. Occupational therapy and medical technology are solid and popular programs, as are the earth science and chemistry departments. Highly regarded in the region is UND's medical school, which works closely with Indians into Medicine, a university-sponsored support group established in 1973 that seeks to graduate more Native Americans into medical schools and into the health professions.

The university's Indian Studies program "does a pretty good job educating students about the Indian culture," says a recent graduate. Popular courses in the program are "Introduction to Indian Studies" and "History of the Three Affiliated Tribes," which explores the relations between the local Mandan, Hidatsa, and Arikara tribes. A "Race Relations" course has been effective, according to students, "in generating some pretty heated discussions about the issues of multiculturalism." Courses in African-American Studies "are exciting because they're mostly taught in seminar style, which is conducive to open discussion."

The Native American population is the largest group of students of color on campus. Approximately 30 Native American students are active in the school's University of North Dakota Indian Association (UNIDA). For more than twenty-five years, UNIDA has sponsored Time-Out Week, which features speakers and workshops, often about Native American education. "A lot of students and state residents come to the events. We publicize them for quite a while all over the state." UNIDA also sponsors the university's largest powwow, called Wochipi, a two-day affair usually held in Hyslop Sports Arena in April. Indians into Medicine sponsors a one-day powwow, usually held at the Civic Center in Grand Forks.

The American Native Student Association "is smaller than UNIDA but very active," says a student. "The group focuses on sobriety and family activities, where UNIDA is more college student-oriented." Recent ANSA events have included a masquerade powwow for Halloween and a potluck dinner at the Native American Cultural Center. "The office provides us with assistance when it comes to financial aid concerns and refers us to places for tutoring, as well as offering academic and personal tutoring. The center also serves as a meeting place for UNIDA and other Native American student groups," says a student. The director of the center, Leigh Jeanotte, "does a good job relating to students and helping us with any problems we may have." According to another student, "the American Indian population here is tight. We all know each other."

The Era Bell Thompson Cultural Center is a resource center for Asian-American, African-American, and Hispanic students, although much of the campus doesn't see it as such. "Most people here perceive the center as the Black Culture Center, which it isn't," says a student. "We're working to make it more accessible to a more diverse group of students."

The center has a multicultural library, office space for the Black Student Association, which has a computer, and living facilities for two "caretakers." "You have to apply for the position, and you're selected by the center's director and the dean of students." Toni Scott, who joined the center as director in the fall of 1992, has been a hit with students. "She helps us with everything, from getting tuition waivers to planning activities. She also knows administrators, which is a help when we need to get things accomplished." The center, which is open to students from 8 a.m. to 10 p.m., also has a TV, a stove, and a huge living room "where students can hang out and be comfortable. The center is like one big family. There's a regular group of students who come here."

Although there is no organized Hispanic student group, the center and the University Program Committee will be sponsoring UND's first National Hispanic Celebration, during September. "We're working to get the Hispanic students more organized, and we're hoping events like these will bring them out."

The Black Student Association, with about 12 active members, "has undergone some significant changes recently," says a BSA leader. "We changed our name—from Union to Association—because we wanted to sound less like a group meant only for black students." Some recent BSA events included movie nights, showings of Spike Lee films, and a popular cookout at Dayton's, a department store in Grand Forks. "We serve soul food with chicken, beans, and peach cobbler, all for free," says a student. The Era Bell Thompson Cultural Center and the BSA also sponsor a Black Writers Conference, offered to students for credit.

Growing in popularity each year is the University Program Committee-sponsored Hands Across Campus, "where the goal is to get a human chain going around campus in a show of unity." Students, faculty, and administrators participate in the event.

Near the Minnesota border, Grand Forks doesn't offer much in the way of entertainment, and can prove to be a culture shock for students coming from larger cities. But the majority of UND's students are from the area or from small towns throughout the state. The university also attracts students from towns just over the Minnesota border—Minnesota students pay only North Dakota in-state tuition prices through a special tuition reciprocity program—as well as from Canada.

UND sports and numerous other on-campus cultural events (held at the impressive Chester Fritz Auditorium) are enough to keep students on campus for much of the year.

The school's relative isolation and laid-back atmosphere did not prevent one senior from enjoying her four-year experience at UND. "This is a small campus in a small town, and it's not like there's a lot to do in town. But the students are incredibly friendly and helpful. It's refreshing, especially when you're used to the impersonal nature of a large city."

O H I O

ANTIOCH COLLEGE

Address: Yellow Springs, OH 45387
Phone: (513) 767-7331 / (800) 543-9436
(out-of-state)
Director of Admissions: Jimmy Williams
Multicultural Student Recruiter: Cheryl
Welch

1992–93 tuition: $14,038
Room and board: $4,263
Application deadline: Rolling admissions
Financial aid application deadline: 5/1

"My parents went to a college that had an alternative curriculum and a radical student body, and I knew I wanted to attend a similar type of school," says a communications major of his decision to attend Antioch College, one of the country's oldest "alternative" schools. Although the campus is not as radical as it was in the 1960s (and what campus is?), Antioch students take seriously—to some extent anyway—a statement read at every graduation ceremony: "Be ashamed to die until you have won some victory for humanity."

What makes Antioch "alternative," among other things, is its unique co-op program, a part of the college's curriculum since 1921. Antioch, which divides its academic year into quarters, requires its students to complete at least six co-ops. Students use their co-op jobs for résumé building and, says a student, "to grow. The jobs we get aren't slinging burgers at Wendy's or anything like that. During my co-ops, I've edited the school paper here at Antioch, worked in a clothes factory for the visually impaired, and worked for the Minority Activists Apprenticeship Program in Oakland, California. In fact, the co-op advisers who help place you definitely discourage you from doing a co-op in your own hometown. They believe you should get out and experience the world. Co-op forces many people to be on their own for the first time. It teaches you how to present yourself, how to do your own laundry, and how to search for an apartment."

Many students who choose to attend Antioch do so because of the co-op program, but it is not without its critics. "The program is very stressful on relationships, let alone friendships. My girlfriend and I haven't seen each other for nine months. We talk and write, but we're starting to ask each other if maybe we've outgrown the relationship. I imagine the counseling center here deals a lot with relationship problems like this." Winter quarter can also be a drag, say students, because the majority of students leave campus for their co-ops. In a recent year, only about 290 of the school's 700 students were on campus. "It gets tiring after a while seeing the same old faces every day while planning Black History Month activities. During last year's winter quarter, only about three African-American men were on campus. When I had two of the guys in my room, I realized we had enough to have a meeting of Men of African Descent," says a student. During a typical fall and spring quarter, about 500 students can be found on campus.

When not off campus or doing co-op work on campus, students are in class learning the good old liberal arts. Students say that they get a great deal of individual attention in the science programs and that psychology and the popular interdisciplinary communications major are also well regarded. As might be expected at a school with Antioch's progressive bent, the college offers programs in environmental and peace studies.

The college also initiated a unique cross-cultural program of study, which examines "in a systematic and integrated way the range and diversity of human sociocultural adaptations." As part of the program, students must complete a field experience and a co-op job. For six students in the program, their field experience took them to the Gullahs of South Carolina's Sea Islands and to rural Keysville, Georgia, to examine two distinct African-American cultures, a trip that was reported in *The New York Times*. At the end of the three-month program, students are expected to complete papers and offer oral presentations about their experiences.

Antioch students don't live in fear of grades. Instead, professors give written evaluations of course work. For pre-med majors, and anyone else who wants them, letter grades can be made available, upon request. Students also evaluate their professors' performances at the end of the semester and can recommend that a consistently ineffective and unpopular professor be dismissed.

Antioch has three cultural student groups, the most active of which is the Third World Alliance, an eighteen-year-old organization on campus that does not permit white students at its meetings. "We do have open meetings from time to time," says a student member, "but we decided it is best to have just Third World students attend meetings." During Black History Month, the group sponsored several dances. It also recently sponsored a "Ninety-Minute Jam Session." "We're in Yellow Springs, Ohio, where there aren't a lot of music stores or clubs, and we can sometimes lose touch with contemporary music, so we have the Jam Session," says a senior.

The recently formed student group Sisters of African Descent, which also doesn't have white students at its meetings, "was formed because the women of color on campus don't have the cohesion of some of the other groups. The women come from different backgrounds and religions and places in the country, so the group was formed by a student to bridge some of the differences." The group, which has about 25 members and serves to provide peer support, "is looking stronger."

Antioch has a Women's Center, but African-American women on campus have complained that the center is not responsive to their needs. "The black women were always having to explain what it means to be an African-American female in this country, and this attitude created strife," says a Third World Alliance leader. "But the center is now attempting to become more sensitive to the concerns of women of color." (By the way, men are not permitted at the Women's Center meetings.)

Despite the exclusivity of some of its student groups, "Antioch stresses community." Students refer to their professors by their first names and participate in major decision-making committees at the college, including faculty hiring and tenure, housing, and curriculum development. Every Tuesday night, faculty and students meet to discuss matters concerning the Antioch community.

Antioch is unique in American higher education for many reasons, including its small size—only 671 in 1990, according to the U.S. Department of Education. "We students have access to what goes on here, to everything from setting the social agenda to helping create new curriculum. The administration and the faculty make themselves open to us. I know that I can walk into the president's office and talk to him. You're not going to find that at Ohio State." In 1990, 0.4 percent of Antioch's students were Native American, 1.5 percent were Asian-American, 6.9 percent were African-American, and 2.5 percent were Hispanic. (The college admissions office declined to respond to our questionnaire requesting the most up-to-date statistics.)

When it comes to diversity of opinion, Antioch students cover the gamut, minus Young Republicans, that is. The typical Antioch student is liberal if not radical, and has a genuine interest in changing the world. Tie-dyed T-shirts are a fashion must at the college, the food cooperative is a happening place on campus, and the gay lifestyle is just another weave to the fabric of Antioch student life.

The town of Yellow Springs itself now has an alternative lifestyle community, most of whom are associated with the college or are Antioch grads who just didn't want to leave a good thing. There is little social distraction in town, save some health-food stores, several restaurants, and a used-book store. There are no fraternities or sororities at Antioch, nor are there any varsity sports teams.

Antioch is not for everyone. But for students interested in an alternative and progressive campus environment, you'll certainly find it here.

CASE WESTERN RESERVE UNIVERSITY

Address: Cleveland, OH 44106
Phone: (216) 368-4450 / (800) 362-8600
 (in-state); (800) 321-6984
Director of Admissions: Susan Dileno
Multicultural Student Recruiter: na

1992–93 tuition: $14,450
Room and board: $4,410
Application deadline: 3/1
Financial aid application deadline: 2/1

If there ever was a university with a split personality, Case Western Reserve University is it. CWRU is the result of a 1967 merger between Case Institute of Technology, an engineering school, and Western Reserve, a liberal arts school, and both, to a large extent, have maintained their own identities. A walk along Euclid Street, which cuts through the center of the university's campus and the city of Cleveland, illustrates the point: "I'm living on the south side [the Western Reserve side] of campus this semester, and this is the first time that I've ever seen most of these people. I had no idea they went to this school," says a mechanical engineering major.

CWRU is known for its outstanding and tough academics, and enjoys an excellent reputation with employers. First-year students enroll in Case Western Reserve, but after declaring a major they attend either Case Institute or Western Reserve. To graduate, all students must satisfy one of three core curriculums. The Case Core includes courses in math, chemistry, computing, physics, and the humanities and the social sciences. The Western Reserve Core includes courses in literature and the arts, history and culture, social and behavioral sciences, and science. The LAMBDA (Liberal Arts/Mathematics-Based Alternative) Core, offered by both schools, "provides the cultural and intellectual background necessary for effective participation in a society that is increasingly driven by technological imperatives." The LAMBDA Core includes courses in the sciences and mathematics, as well as courses in the humanities and the social sciences. All students must take a course in composition.

Among the best programs at Case Institute, which has received grants for study from NASA, are any of the engineering programs, especially mechanical and electrical engineering; aerospace engineering is said to be the program's toughest major. Math and physics, as well as macromolecular science, are strong, and pre-med majors—biology and chemistry especially—are also well regarded. The school's polymer science and its new concentration in medical anthropology are among the few such undergraduate programs in the country.

Among the strongest majors at Western Reserve are English, history, psychology, and art education and art history, which are linked to the Cleveland Museum of Art. The school's African-American and African history courses are taught regularly by Christopher Williams, a visiting professor from Kent State University. "His courses are excellent. He knows his history, and he's a nice person."

The school's Minority Scholars Program (MSP), primarily offered to first- and second-year students, is one of the most important—and effective—sources of academic support for minority students. Established in 1990, MSP provides a summer orientation program, as well as faculty mentors and peer support. "The freshmen have no idea how good they've got it with MSP. The program has tons of stuff," says a senior who didn't get to reap the benefits of the program. Margaret Boulding, an assistant dean of minority programs, is highly praised by students. "Without her, the minority engineering program here would cease to exist. She's someone we can go talk to. She also helps us get internships."

Academics at CWRU can be overwhelming, but students have been known to take advantage of some of the abundant cultural and social opportunities in the area. CWRU's campus is part of University Circle, Cleveland's cultural center, which includes the Cleveland Museum of Art, rated one of the country's finest, Severance Hall, home to the Cleveland Orchestra, and the Cleveland Museum of Natural History. On the more social side, some of the men find the dating scene at CWRU tough; the university's ratio of men to women is nearly two to one. "It's not too bad, though. We're located in downtown Cleveland, and there are lots of clubs and bars around for us to go to. There are also various other colleges, including the University of Akron and Cleveland State."

On campus, a hub of activity is Thwing Center, the university's student union, which is also the most culturally diverse place on campus. Thwing offers Charlie's Place, a restaurant with Pizza Hut pizza, a bookstore, and an art gallery. Numerous student organizations, among them the African-American Society and the Asian-American Association, have their offices in Thwing.

The African-American Society, with about 65 active members, meets regularly in Thwing Center to plan social and cultural activities. "The society goes wherever the members want it to go. My first two years as a member, we were primarily cultural, with speakers and movies and such. Now I'd say about 80 percent of our concentration is on social activities." By far the society's biggest bash is the annual Ebony Ball, usually held in the fall semester. In a recent year, the bash attracted more than 2,000 students, from all races and ethnicities.

For cultural activity, the Black History Month planning board, in conjunction with the society, has primary responsibility for planning events during February. Activities include screenings in Thwing Center of such films as *Eyes on the Prize* and various speakers. "The unity among the African-American students here is strongest after a dance, or after an event for Black History Month," comments a student.

Students looking for a party school won't be content at CWRU, but the hardworking engineer or liberal arts major will. The reward at the end of four years here is knowing that your degree will impress future employers. "CWRU really prepares you for the real world," says a student. "You have to solve real problems, to think for yourself. That's been one of the most valuable things I've learned."

KENYON COLLEGE

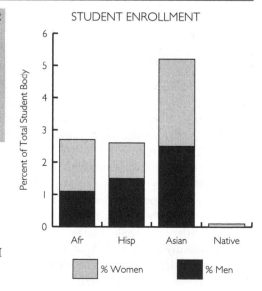

Address: Ransom Hall, Gambier, OH 43022
Phone: (614) 427-5776 / (800) 848-2468
Director of Admissions: John Anderson
Multicultural Student Recruiter: Matthew Davis
1993–94 tuition: $18,140
Room and board: $3,700
Application deadline: 2/15
Financial aid application deadline: 2/15
Non-white freshman admissions: Applicants for the class of '96: 282
   Accepted: 55.3%
   Accepted who enroll: 30.1%
   Applicants accepted who rank in top 10% of high school class: 38.2%
   In top 25%: 79.4%
   Median SAT range: 460–590 V, 510–650 M
   Median ACT range: 21–26
Full-time undergraduate enrollment: 1,488
   Men: 48.7%
   Women: 51.3%

STUDENT ENROLLMENT

Percent of Total Student Body

Afr   Hisp   Asian   Native

% Women   % Men

Non-white students in
1988–89: 5%
1989–90: 6%
1990–91: 7%
1991–92: 9%

GEOGRAPHIC DISTRIBUTION OF STUDENTS

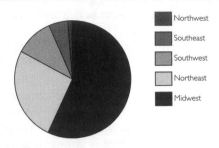

- Northwest
- Southeast
- Southwest
- Northeast
- Midwest

Students In-state: 36.4%
Top majors: 1. Biology 2. English
3. International Studies
Retention rate of non-white students: 95%
Scholarships exclusively for non-white students: Howard Hughes Scholarship: $1,000 merit-based award; available to African-American students majoring in the natural sciences. Black and Latino Merit Scholarships.
Remediation programs: None
Academic support services: Tutoring is offered in most academic subjects, as well as a writing center.
Ethnic studies programs: The college offers concentrations in Asian Studies, established in 1990, and in African and African-American Studies.
Ethnic studies courses: na
Organizations for non-white students: Adelante (a Latino student group), Black Student Union, Gambier Organization for Cultural Awareness, Asian Student Alliance, RAP
Notable non-white alumni: Alison Joseph (poet)
Tenured faculty: na
Non-tenured faculty: na
Student-faculty ratio: 11:1
Administrators: 120
African-American: 4.2%
Hispanic: <1%
Asian-American: <1%
Native American: 0
Recent non-white speakers on campus: Jesse Jackson (former U.S. presidential candidate and civil rights activist); Maya Angelou (author and poet); Dr. Na'im Akbar (clinical psychologist); Maxine Hong Kingston (author); Barbara Reynolds (columnist, *USA Today*); Christine Choy (filmmaker); Blandina Cardenas Ramirez (director, Minority Concerns, American Council on Education, U.S. Commissioner on Civil Rights)

Kenyon College is a friendly place to go to school. "Anytime you walk down Middle Path, you find yourself saying 'Hi' to somebody and stopping to talk with somebody else and just generally seeing lots of people you know," says a junior. "You always feel like there are people you can talk to here, about anything."

Kenyon is also an excellent liberal arts college. The 169-year-old school is renowned for its English department, which has graduated some of the twentieth century's more notable writers, including poet Robert Lowell and novelists E. L. Doctorow and Peter Taylor. English is by far the most popular major on campus. Two of the college's literary journals—*The Kenyon Review* and *Hika*—are internationally acclaimed. Students also praise the school's political science, history, and classics departments. The college curriculum includes the innovative Integrated Programs in Humane Studies, a two-year interdisciplinary concentration that allows students to study the "Human Predicament in History" by taking courses outside of their major. The college also recently instituted a synoptic major, in which students are able to create their own interdisciplinary major. A recent example of a student's synoptic major is "World Hunger," which included study in biology, economics, and sociology. Theater students have access to the well-equipped Bolton Theater. (Paul Newman is a Kenyon graduate.) The history department's "African History" and "African-American History" courses are praised by students.

Close student-faculty interaction epitomizes the college experience at Kenyon, which is fortunate, as the academic climate at such a small school can be intense. All professors, except visiting scholars, are required to live within a ten-mile radius of campus. It's common for students to have dinner with their professors—in their homes. Students and faculty also interact on the playing fields, in intramural competition. The school's Writing Center "is used a great deal and is very effective," according to a student.

The Black Student Union (BSU), which has about 15 active members, meets once a week in the BSU lounge, located in the Pierce Eating Lounge. The lounge has a small library, African and African-American art, and a mural painted by an African-American student. The BSU helps coordinate events for Black History Month. In 1992, the celebrations included a film series that focused on famous African-American historical figures. For Martin Luther King, Jr., Day, the college, with BSU involvement, sponsored a candlelight march and showed a filmed speech by King. Another cultural group, ASIA, founded primarily for Asian and Asian-American students, has not been active in recent years.

Mila Collins, dean of multicultural affairs, advises the BSU. "Mila is a very active adviser," says a sophomore. "But it's not like she treats her position as a job. It's a part of her personal life as well. It's like having a twenty-four-hour mom away from home." Adds another student: "Whenever we feel we can't get something done, we always say let's go to Mila. She can help us out."

Although Kenyon went coed in 1969, students claim the school is still male-oriented. As an example, students point to the number of fraternities versus the number of sororities. (Nearly half of Kenyon's men pledge fraternities.) "There are seven fraternities on campus and only one sorority [established in 1988], which many people consider kind of a joke," says a student. In a recent year, two African-American female students were members of the local sorority and four African-American men were members of a fraternity.

The fraternity scene dominates the social life at Kenyon, for Greeks and non-Greeks. The administration, some say, is pushing for a change in the Greek system; a recent study found that the fraternities on campus were sexist. But other on-campus extracurriculars abound. Particularly active is the staff of *The Collegian,* the campus daily newspaper. The Kenyon Film Society shows movies on campus a few times a week. Kenyon's Dramatic Club stages several productions each year, including annual fall and spring dance concerts. Musical groups, particularly two a cappella groups, are popular.

Gambier is indeed a small town, "many cornfields away from civilization," with not much more than a couple of stoplights and a mini-market. Mount Vernon, a predominantly white community a few miles from campus, is easily accessible, thanks to a free shuttle service that leaves campus several times a day. The town offers shopping opportunities not found in the more immediate community. When escaping the confines of a small-school environment becomes necessary, Columbus, home of the Buckeyes of Ohio State and other social and cultural sites, is just forty-five minutes away by car.

Although the college has reason to boast about its geographic diversity—less than a quarter of its students are from Ohio and more than 40 other states are represented—it has less reason to do so when it comes to racial and ethnic diversity. Despite recruiting efforts, Kenyon remains a rather homogeneous community of students in this regard. In addition, many of the school's students of color come from Ohio, most notably from the Cleveland area. There is also said to be little socioeconomic diversity within the student body; according to an English major, "many students here come from upper-middle-class backgrounds." Students are quick to add that their classmates are on the whole relatively tolerant of racial and cultural diversity.

The reasons to come to Kenyon include supportive faculty and top-notch academics. "The classes and the professors here are great," says a student. "I know I'm getting an outstanding education. But there are times, socially, when I wish I had gone elsewhere for college."

MIAMI UNIVERSITY

Address: Glos Admission Center, Oxford,
  OH 45056
Phone: (513) 529-2531 / (513) 529-5621
Director of Admissions: Dr. James S. McCoy
Multicultural Student Recruiter: Janice
  Edwards
1992–93 tuition: $4,096 (in-state); $8,686
  (out-of-state)
Room and board: $3,360
Application deadline: Early decision: 11/1
  Regular decision: 1/31
Financial aid application deadline: 2/15
Non-white freshman admissions: Applicants
  for the class of '97: 626
  Accepted: 84%
  Accepted who enroll: na
  Applicants accepted who rank in top
  10% of high school class: 33.9%
  In top 25%: 61.2%
  Median SAT range: 450–540 V, 490–560 M
  Median ACT range: 20–25
Full-time undergraduate enrollment: 14,374
  Men: 46.6%
  Women: 53.4%

Non-white students in
  1988–89: 3.8%
  1989–90: 4.3%
  1990–91: 4.7%
  1991–92: 4.9%

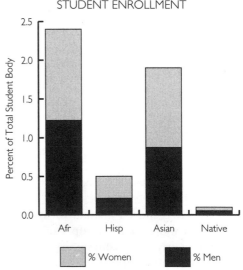

STUDENT ENROLLMENT

Percent of Total Student Body

Afr   Hisp   Asian   Native

% Women   % Men

GEOGRAPHIC DISTRIBUTION OF STUDENTS

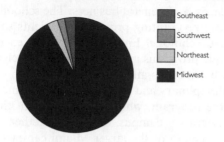

- ■ Southeast
- ▨ Southwest
- ▧ Northeast
- ■ Midwest

Students In-state: na

Top majors: 1. Psychology 2. Business 3. Accountancy

Retention rate of non-white students: 60%

Scholarships exclusively for non-white students: Black Student Achievement Grant: need-based; renewable. Black Scholars Program: merit-based; $1,600–$3,000 a year; renewable. Beatrice Scholars: merit-based; $5,000 for each award; available to entering African-American and Hispanic first-year students from the Chicago area; renewable. Albers Black Accountancy Scholarship: merit-based; $5,000 a year; available to African-American accounting majors; renewable.

Remediation programs: None

Academic support services: The Office of Minority Affairs provides a mentor program, as well as other academic support services. The Learning Assistance Center and the Writing Skills Center also provide academic support.

Ethnic studies programs: The university's Black World Studies, established in 1970, is interdisciplinary, involving literature, religion, history, geography, psychology, and political science.

Ethnic studies courses: The university's history and political science departments offer several courses in Asian and Latin American Studies.

Organizations for non-white students: Center for Black Culture and Learning, Alpha Kappa Alpha, Delta Sigma Theta, Alpha Phi Alpha, Kappa Alpha Psi, Honors Program Committee for Black Awareness, Black Student Action Association, Minority and Women's Professional Association, Miami University Gospel Singers, Asian-American Association

Notable non-white alumni: Randy Ayers (Education; head men's basketball coach, Ohio State University); Dr. William Burke (Education; director, Los Angeles marathon); Rita Dove (English; professor, University of Virginia, and 1987 winner of the Pulitzer Prize for poetry); Wayne Embry (Education; vice president and general manager, Cleveland Cavaliers NBA basketball team); Dr. Marilyn Hughes Gaston (Science; director, Bureau of Health Care Delivery and Assistance, U.S. Department of Health and Human Services); Dr. Lloyd Phillips (Chemistry; chief of thoracic surgery, Veterans Administration Medical Center, Dayton, OH)

Tenured faculty: na

Non-tenured faculty: na

Student-faculty ratio: 19:1

Administrators: na

Recent non-white speakers on campus: Maya Angelou (author and poet); Dr. Na'im Akbar (clinical psychologist); Tony Brown (host and producer, *Tony Brown's Journal*); Jacqueline Fleming (psychologist); Dr. Samuel D. Proctor (pastor, Abyssinian Baptist Church, New York City)

Named for the Native Americans who formerly inhabited the area, Miami University in Ohio has attracted recent attention as a "public Ivy." With quality academics, a beautiful campus setting, and supportive staff and faculty, Miami has become one of the Midwest's more respected public universities.

Most undergraduates study in one of the majors offered by Miami's School of

Business Administration. Marketing and accounting are the most popular; also offered are programs in finance, decision sciences, and general business. The school's College of Arts and Sciences has nearly 40 degree-granting programs. Students say the strongest departments in the college are psychology, English, political science, and history. The college also offers such unique programs as diplomacy and foreign affairs and aeronautics. Education is said to be rigorous and respected.

Miami's Western College Program is interdisciplinary and is characterized by small seminar-style class discussions. Students in the program, who usually represent the more liberal contingent of an otherwise conservative campus, also live together in residence halls on Western campus, a historic section of the larger Miami campus.

Students praise the school's Black World Studies major. "These courses are well taught and will give you a strong foundation to continue your education at the graduate level, but I would suggest that anyone entering this major and seeking to make it their life's work should supplement their course work by doing a number of independent studies to expand their knowledge," says a Black World Studies major. "Being at a university in dire need of cultural diversity has inspired me to learn more about my African-American culture," says another student. "For this reason I have declared BWS as my minor. Rodney Coates [the program director] is very enthusiastic about making the program successful." Another professor who expects a great deal of his students is Edgar Tidewell, who teaches "Black American Literature." "He has personally helped me with my writing style and challenged me to get the most out of what I read," says one student.

The Center for Black Culture and Learning, located in Bishop Hall, has a computer, a lounge area, a conference room, and a small library. According to one student, students are now "mounting an effort to supply the center with more works and artifacts that illuminate the culture and experiences of African people and people of African descent."

For support, students are able to turn to a variety of professors and staff members. Rosemary McCullough, coordinator of program development and minority affairs in the Center for Black Culture and Learning and adviser to the Black Student Action Association (BSAA), has practically attained cult status among students. "Dear to the students who know her as 'Mother Miami,' she works with minority students in getting them acclimated to the Miami environment," says a senior. Comments another student: "She supports all of the students and gets to know us on a personal level so she can offer complete support. I can't even begin to describe the countless things she has done for the minority student community. It's an unwritten law that if you need help, you go to Ms. McCullough." William Madison, a BSAA adviser and the director of special projects in Miami's School of Business Administration, is also supportive of students. "His door is always open for any student who has a problem or just wants to seek safe haven," says a student. "I have gotten to know him because of BSAA and he is always willing to offer support as well as advice on any project I am engaged in. We as students can sense that he really does believe in us and respects what we have to say."

The BSAA is a cohesive and active student organization. "The BSAA sponsors a Unity Fest each fall in which different vendors and cultural performers participate," says a student. "It is a campus-wide event. We also sponsor a Black Alumni/Ebony

Elegance homecoming weekend to which alumni are invited and several programs are planned for the weekend. The entire event culminates on Saturday night with a semiformal dance." The Miami University Gospel Singers (MUGS) sponsors annual fall and spring concerts, as well as a gospel festival in February, in which area colleges and universities participate. "Each year the event is sold out and is a big success," says a sophomore.

The university's four traditionally black fraternities and sororities are active and popular with students. "Most of the social activities in the black community run through the fraternities and sororities," reports a senior. They include parties, dances, and community service projects.

Despite the efforts of various student groups, the social scene here is dominated by the school's predominantly white Greek system, which accounts for nearly half of the student body. The university has earned the nickname Mother of Fraternities because it is where four national Greek organizations were founded. Much of the weekend partying takes place at the fraternities, and students say there is some tension between Greeks and non-Greeks. The sororities don't have residential houses; they have blocks of suites in some of the on-campus dorms.

For non-Greeks, or Greeks looking to party, Oxford has a few watering holes, as well as a couple of restaurants and movie theaters. The town, which basically consists of the college, is rural and predominantly white; other than the bar scene and some shopping, students say there is a dearth of interaction between students and town residents. Students who need a taste of urban life drive to Cincinnati, about forty-five minutes away.

Despite recruitment efforts, Miami remains a rather homogeneous institution, not only racially and culturally but also politically and socially. Most students are conservative and the Young Republican student group is by far more active than the school's Democratic club. What diversity of opinion there is at Miami can usually be found on the Western campus.

Miami is one of the Midwest's top-rated public schools, and regularly attracts large applicant pools. Students appreciate their school's academics as well as its support programs. "I would recommend this school to a prospective minority student who understands that Miami is an excellent school but needs to work on minority/majority relations," says a sociology major. "There are plenty of organizations to thrive in and anyone who is willing to dedicate themselves to promoting change will succeed." Adds another student: "Here, you don't have to struggle through your problems alone because there is always help for you."

OBERLIN COLLEGE

Address: Carnegie Building, 101 North Professor Street, Oberlin, OH 44074
Phone: (216) 775-8411 / (800) 622-OBIE
Director of Admissions: Thomas Hayden
Multicultural Student Recruiter: Dwight Hollins
1991–92 tuition: $16,375
Room and board: $5,155
Application deadline: 1/15
Financial aid application deadline: 2/1

Non-white freshman admissions: Applicants for the class of '95: 637
Accepted: 77.3%
Accepted who enroll: 26.8%
Applicants accepted who rank in top 10% of high school class: 44%
In top 25%: 64%
Median SAT: 540 V, 610 M
Median ACT: na
Full-time undergraduate enrollment: 2,801
Men: 46%
Women: 54%

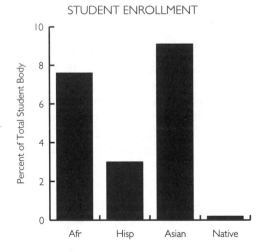

STUDENT ENROLLMENT

Percent of Total Student Body (y-axis, 0 to 10)

Afr   Hisp   Asian   Native

Non-white students in 1990–91: 19.6%
Geographic distribution of students: na
Students In-state: 16.5%
Top majors: na

Retention rate of non-white students: na
Scholarships exclusively for non-white students: None
Remediation programs: None
Academic support services: Oberlin offers tutoring in most academic subjects, as well as study skills courses.
Ethnic studies programs: Oberlin offers majors in Third World Studies, Black Studies, Latin American Studies, and East Asian Studies.
Organizations for non-white students: Abusua, Asian-American Alliance, Central American Task Force, La Unión de Estudiantes Latinos, Minority Students for Careers in Higher Education, Oberlin Asian Students in Science, Oberlin Black Science Students, Shanshi Student Committee (Asian interest group), Steps Toward Excellence Program (minority students interested in business careers), Voices for Christ (gospel music group)
Notable non-white alumni: Johnnetta Cole ('57; president, Spelman College); Jewel Stradford Lafontant ('43; former U.S. Deputy Solicitor General); Natalie Hinderas Monagas ('46; concert pianist); Gilbert Moses ('64; film producer and director, Emmy winner for *Roots*); Carl Rowan ('47; syndicated columnist); Niara Sudarkasa ('57; president, Lincoln University, PA); Jackie Vaughn III ('54; Michigan Senate president pro tem)
Tenured and non-tenured faculty: 241
Non-white faculty: 11%
Student-faculty ratio: 13:1
Administrators: na
Non-white: 12%
Recent non-white speakers on campus: Dr. Ivan Van Sertima (author); Hugh Masekela (South African trumpeter and composer); Rex Nettleford (professor and vice-chancellor, University of the West Indies)

At most college graduations, wearing a cap and gown, usually in black, is de rigueur for graduates. But not at Oberlin College, where each year many students donate the funds that would have gone to the cost of renting the cap and gown to a worthy cause decided upon by the seniors.

Such activity is not new to Oberlin. In fact, the school is famous for it. Students have only to turn to their school's founders for inspiration, particularly when it comes to issues of racial and ethnic tolerance and diversity. As Oberlin's original trustees stated, in 1835: "The education of the people of color is a matter of great interest and should be encouraged & sustained in this Institution." Not much later, circulars distributed in the area describing Oberlin said: "Youths are received as members, irrespective of color." In 1862, Oberlin graduated the country's first African-American female student, and by the turn of the century the college had graduated one-third of all African-American graduates of predominantly white institutions. In 1841, Oberlin was the first school in the country to graduate women.

Today, Oberlin is one of the country's top liberal arts colleges and still attracts—and graduates—a diverse student population. Oberlin's catalogue lists nearly 1,000 courses, a phenomenal amount considering the college's relatively small size. Across the board, Oberlin's academic programs are outstanding, especially Russian, English, East Asian Studies, and art history. The school's Allen Art Museum is superb, and is often ranked third behind Yale's and Harvard's museums. Oberlin's psychobiology, chemistry, and biology programs are equally recognized. In a recent *U.S. News & World Report* survey, Oberlin's science program was ranked first among national liberal arts colleges. Some of the school's more popular ethnic studies courses are "Black Arts Workshop," "Images of Asia," and "Borderlands History." Self-designed majors are also popular.

Oberlin has an internationally famous conservatory of music, which enrolls approximately 20 percent of the college's student body. The conservatory sponsors more than 350 performances a year—"from classical to jazz, rock to funk, bluegrass to blues"—and draws world-class artists to its concert halls.

To graduate, students must satisfy a cultural diversity requirement, but students complain that the requirement "has not altered the curriculum at all. It has merely relabeled it," says a student. "Instead of offering new courses which would focus on multiculturalism and racial issues, the administration and faculty have created a false sense of improvement. In addition, language courses like French and Spanish meet this requirement. Most students would meet this kind of requirement anyway."

While students say the academics at Oberlin are demanding, they are not competitive with one another for grades; in fact, they are each other's best support. The college sponsors various other support services that students say are quite effective, including peer tutors and "a diverse group of counselors, most of whom are highly qualified and able to serve the needs of minority students."

When not studying, Obies are often participating in one of the school's cultural student organizations, which are influential in campus politics. After listing the myriad activities sponsored by the groups—from forums and dances to speakers and community service projects—one student said: "These are only a few of the things that go on in the people of color communities. There is so much going on it is difficult to mention everything. Most of the multicultural activities are organized by the student organizations, whether it be social, political, or educational. Student organizations, essentially, bear the responsibility of being the educators about minority concerns."

The Asian-American Alliance, which sponsors a big sib/little sib mentoring program for members, is the umbrella organization for the Oberlin Korean Students Association, the Asian Women's Group, and SHAKTI, a South Asian student group. "Although the student organizations are very involved, the rate of Asian student participation is not as high as in recent years," comments a student. "There will always be a few active students. The organization is constantly reaching out to new students. The level of awareness regarding Asian-American issues at Oberlin, however, is higher than at most Midwestern schools and most colleges in general." The alliance, which meets weekly to "focus on topical issues for discussion," also sponsors a monthly speaker series, a biannual student conference, and a film series.

Abusua, the African-American student organization, "is so active that there is always something going on. There are numerous subgroups within Abusua which are fairly autonomous." Some of the activities sponsored by Abusua include a big brother/big sister program, an African Market, and a Friday lecture series. For interested students, the college also sponsors an Afrikan Heritage House and a Third World House, both residence hall facilities.

La Unión de Estudiantes Latinos, another student group, sponsors dance and theater performances, as well as a film series and band and other musical performances.

Despite the activity of these groups, students say there is little interaction among their members. "There is no coalition between communities of color, and there seems to be little understanding between the communities." Adds another student: "Cliques here tend to form along racial lines." The separateness of the groups was discussed in a recent *New Republic* magazine article.

The controversy surrounding "political correctness" has not bypassed Oberlin. "It's true Oberlin is very progressive and the liberal of liberals. You are always confronted with debate and discussion and forced to examine the issues with a critical eye. On the other hand, Obies can be overly critical. Some accuse Oberlin students of limiting freedom of thought and discussion and voicing 'PC.' Some students may be giving 'PC' opinions because they believe that is correct. However, I think most people at Oberlin do voice their own individual opinions. Critical thinking, the ability to voice my opinion and express my individual identity, is what I gained from my four years at Oberlin. As a result of this heightened level of social and political awareness at Oberlin, the environment is more conducive to open discussion about multiculturalism and minority concerns. This doesn't mean it's paradise but it's certainly closer than many other schools."

The students' biggest complaints—besides "attending college in the middle of nowhere"—are leveled at what they perceive to be a conservative administration. "I feel that although Oberlin students are progressive, the administration isn't or doesn't seem to be." Comments another student: "Most of the current administrators at Oberlin are coming from the conservative and hard-line control side. Consequently, they are less open to learning about what the concerns of students really are. Except for a few administrators in departments like Student Support Services, most really are ignorant about the issues facing minority students—issues like financial need, racism, feelings of isolation, lack of minority administrators and faculty members."

Oberlin's campus is also the site of a variety of other student activities. Says a student: "The exciting aspect about being at Oberlin is the opportunity to learn about so many issues. Every day there is at least one or two events going on. It's not a matter of what there is to do, but, rather, which event is the one you would most like to attend." The college regularly brings well-known lecturers and performance groups to campus each year; recently, the college hosted the Chinese Magic Revue, the Ishangi Dancers of Africa, and the Flying Karamazovs. Spontaneous fun, as opposed to campus-wide parties, is the rule here. Dorm parties or get-togethers are common, at which students participate in "long conversations about almost anything, from South Africa to 'Who am I?'"

The town of Oberlin (pop. 10,000) has a first-run movie theater and "no shortage of fast-food places." Less than an hour away by car, Cleveland, with its museums, clubs, and other universities such as Case Western Reserve and Cleveland State, allows students to escape the sometimes confining atmosphere of the college; the college sponsors shuttle buses into the city on Saturdays.

The academic and social challenges at Oberlin won't be for everyone. The college is certainly not typical, and neither are its students, which are the two reasons Obies would probably cite for choosing to attend college in Ohio in the first place. "What I like about Oberlin is that it encourages individualism and critical thinking," says a student. "It is a place that stands out. It's not like other liberal arts colleges, or like the Ivies. It has something more to offer—the opportunity to develop your own unique identity and sense of self, and there aren't any frats or sororities. You will be challenged. I can guarantee that."

OHIO STATE UNIVERSITY

Address: Third Floor, Lincoln Tower, 1800 Cannon Drive, Columbus, OH 43210
Phone: (614) 292-3980
Director of Admissions: Dr. James Mager
Multicultural Student Recruiter: Dr. Ruth Russell
1991–92 tuition: $2,568 (in-state); $7,608 (out-of-state)
Room and board: $3,900
Application deadline: 2/15
Financial aid application deadline: 3/1
Non-white freshman admissions: Applicants for the class of '94: 2,565
Accepted: 77.5%
Accepted who enroll: 31.4%
Applicants accepted who rank in top 10% of high school class: na

Median SAT: 404.9 V, 465.9 M
Median ACT: 19.5
Full-time undergraduate enrollment: 34,349
Men: 53.5%
Women: 46.5%
Non-white students in
1987–88: 8.18%
1988–89: 8.6%
1989–90: 9.12%
1990–91: 9.53%
Geographic distribution of students: na
Top majors: na
Retention rate of non-white students: 70%
Scholarships exclusively for non-white students: Excellence Scholarships: merit-based; full tuition. Prestigious Scholarships: merit-based. Distinction

STUDENT ENROLLMENT

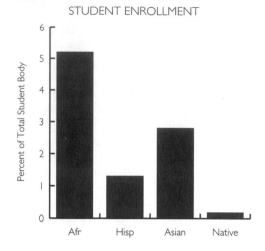

Percent of Total Student Body

Afr   Hisp   Asian   Native

Freshman Foundation Program. Tutoring is also available in most subjects, as are the services of the Academic Support Program, the Learning Skills Program, the Access Program, and the University Monitoring Program.

Ethnic studies programs: OSU offers programs in Black Studies, Asian Studies, and Hispanic Studies.

Organizations for non-white students: na

Notable non-white alumni: Archie Griffin (only two-time Heisman Award winner, assistant director of athletics, Ohio State); Faye Wattleton (former president, Planned Parenthood); Michael White (former Ohio state senator and mayor of Cleveland); I. Ray Miller (Ohio state representative); Otto Beatty (Ohio state representative)

Tenured faculty: na

Non-tenured faculty: na

Student-faculty ratio: 14:1

Administrators: na

Recent non-white speakers on campus: na

Scholarships: merit-based. Cover tuition, room and board, books and supplies, transportation, and other expenses.

Remediation programs: na

Academic support services: Academic and non-academic support services are available to students as part of the

With a student population that would rival that of many medium-sized cities, Ohio State University has the academic and social opportunities befitting one of the country's largest and most comprehensive institutions of higher learning.

Through its nineteen colleges and seven schools, OSU offers more than 200 different academic majors, many of which are among the best such programs in the nation. The College of Engineering has sixteen areas of study, ranging from aeronautical and astronautical engineering to welding engineering. The College of Business, which has the school's most popular majors, offers accounting, business administration, marketing, finance, and numerous other programs. Founded as a land-grant institution, OSU's College of Agriculture enjoys an international reputation, and the university's College of Veterinary Medicine is the largest in North America and ranks among the top four in the country. Programs ranging from education to Slavic languages are also highly regarded.

OSU's Black Studies department—one of the first such programs in the country—is outstanding, and is staffed by numerous highly respected scholars, such as Linda Myers, a psychology professor, Horace Newsum, an associate professor who recently headed the National Coalition of Black Studies, and William Nelson, a political science professor. The department, which offers instruction in five African languages, including Zulu, Yoruba, Hausa, and Swahili, lists such popular courses as "Economics of the Ghetto," "Racism and Sexism," and "Psychology of the African-American." The department's introductory course in Black Studies is also well regarded.

While OSU students study a wide diversity of subjects, they all have one thing in common: they must satisfy general education requirements by enrolling in courses such as math, writing, a foreign language, arts and humanities, natural science, and social science. Students must also complete a course entitled "Issues of the Contemporary World."

Professors in introductory courses mostly remain elusive, and students in such classes often learn from television monitors that line some of the school's large lecture halls. In upper-level courses, however, students say professors are a bit more available. Across the board, students praise their faculty for their academic smarts.

The Office of Minority Affairs provides numerous academic retention programs that win student praise, the most successful of which is its University Mentoring Program, which has also won national recognition. The program matches an undergraduate with an upperclassman as well as a professor or university staff member. The president of the university, E. Gordon Gee, also regularly serves as a mentor. Although students complain about the bureaucracy of the office, they are hopeful that the interim acting provost in charge, David Williams, a law school professor, will help cut through some of the red tape. Students also say the office's tutoring program is effective.

The Frank W. Hale Black Cultural Center, located on South Campus, is one of the most impressive such centers in the country, and has served as a model for other universities looking to develop their own similar resources. The center was named for a former vice-provost of minority affairs at the university, who still attends center functions. "The center is very popular," says a student. "We strive to maintain a familylike atmosphere here. We treat everyone who walks through our doors as family, even people who have never been in the center before. I think we've been very successful at doing that." The center, established on campus in 1989, has an impressive African and African-American art collection, an African/African-American Hall of Fame with photographs of prominent OSU graduates, a lounge with a big-screen TV, a kitchen, and study areas. Frank's Place, a sort of cabaret in which students and staff exhibit their talent, is also at the center. Students observe Kwanzaa and Malcolm X's birthday at the center.

The head of the center is Lawrence Williamson, "whose strength is his accessibility to students and his willingness to work with them." Williamson, an art historian, is primarily responsible for the center's art displays.

For many members of OSU's African-American community, campus life has been anything but laid-back. During the spring of 1992, in reaction to recent national and local incidents, students, faculty, and staff formed a new campus organization called Afrikans Committed to Improving Our Nation (ACTION), which issued a letter demanding that the university meet 22 points for improving the quality of life for the school's African-American students. The demands, sent to the university president, included a strengthening of the retention and scholarship opportunities for African-American students; the renaming of the school's Black Studies department as the Pan-African Studies department; the creation of a dorm that would serve as a cultural residence hall; a salary cap of $85,000 for all university personnel; a more diverse campus security force; and including a course in Black Studies in the school's general education requirements.

As of the fall of 1992, after a six-hour meeting with the president of the university at the Hale Center to discuss the demands, students have won numerous concessions. Students now have the option of living in the African/African-American Living/Learning Center, which currently houses more than 70 students. Students have also won funds to expand the Hale Center and a commitment to strengthen the African Development Fund, which will continue to finance certain already established retention programs.

Not all of the activities of the school's African-American students are political, although, according to a science major, "they do take up a lot of our time." The historically black Greek organizations "are into outreach programs in a big way" in the Columbus community, and they also coordinate parties and dances. Most active, perhaps, are the three residence hall associations—South Areas Black Student Association, Olentangy Black Student Association (which represents West Campus), and Black Association of North Campus Students—that make up the Tri-Black Student Association. Each of the organizations meets weekly to address campus concerns, and they host an annual fashion show, the Egyptian Madness Week, bowling parties, and a tour of historically black colleges.

The Hispanic student groups, according to members, are also working to establish a cultural center of their own, as well as to strengthen Latin American Studies and get a more diverse faculty and staff.

High Street, with its bars, restaurants, and other night spots, is definitely well traveled. The state capitol is only a few minutes away by car or via the city's easily accessible public transportation service. A new mall is located just a few minutes' drive from campus, as are numerous galleries, parks, movie theaters, and ethnic neighborhoods. Nearly 20 percent of the city of Columbus is African-American, and students have access to numerous off-campus cultural and political resources, including a chapter of the NAACP, the Coalition for Concerned Black Citizens, and an African Center.

OSU's campus is a hopping place every night of the week, but especially on the weekend that OSU takes on archrival University of Michigan in football. Numerous parties—to say the least—are staged around the event. There are more than 500 organizations to keep students busy, and varsity and intramural sports are a way of life for many. Sports facilities abound on this sports-crazed campus.

Size has a great deal to do with going to OSU. Students bemoan the fact that they feel sometimes like numbers, but they also see the advantage of going to a school rich in resources. "I've sometimes wished I'd gone to a smaller school to get more personal attention, but then I wouldn't have had access to all that I have," says a science major. "Coming here has made me a stronger person. I've come to know my culture more, and I've come to see that OSU is a microcosm of the larger society. If I can make it here, I know I can make it in the real world when I graduate."

OHIO WESLEYAN UNIVERSITY

Address: 61 South Sandusky Street, Delaware, OH 43015

Phone: (800) 862-0612 (in-state) / (800) 922-8953 (out-of-state)

Dean of Enrollment: Don Bishop

Multicultural Student Recruiter: Karen Fasheun

1991–92 tuition: $13,610

Room and board: $4,884

Application deadline: 3/1

Financial aid application deadline: 3/15

Non-white freshman admissions: Applicants for the class of '95: 165

Accepted: 80%

Accepted who enroll: 36%

Applicants accepted who rank in top 10% of high school class: 30%

In top 25%: 53%

Median SAT range: 400–500 V, 480–580 M

Median ACT range: 20–25

Full-time undergraduate enrollment: 1,992

Men: 50%

Women: 50%

GEOGRAPHIC DISTRIBUTION OF STUDENTS

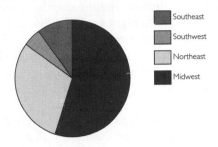

- Southeast
- Southwest
- Northeast
- Midwest

Non-white students in

1987–88: 6%

1988–89: 6%

1989–90: 6%

1990–91: 6.8%

Students In-state: 45%

Top majors: na

Retention rate of non-white students: 83%

Scholarships exclusively for non-white students: Multicultural Awards: merit-based; four full-tuition and ten half-tuition are awarded each year.

Remediation programs: None

Academic support services: The university provides tutoring in most academic subjects, a Writing Resource Center, and seminars in study skill development and time management.

Ethnic studies programs: The university's Black World Studies, which consists of five courses, is offered as a minor.

Ethnic studies courses: The history department offers a course in Asian Studies and three courses in Latin American Studies.

Organizations for non-white students: na

Notable non-white alumni: na

Tenured faculty: na

Non-tenured faculty: na

Student-faculty ratio: 14:1

Administrators: na

Recent non-white speakers on campus: na

STUDENT ENROLLMENT

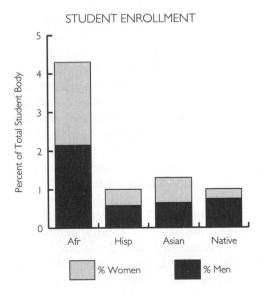

Percent of Total Student Body

Afr | Hisp | Asian | Native

% Women   % Men

David Warren is far from your typical university president. Within the first hundred days of his presidency in 1984, Ohio Wesleyan's new president decided the best way to get to know students, and understand their concerns, was to live with them. He stayed at 18 of the school's residences, including fraternities, dorms, and the Black Cultural House, asking students questions about life at OWU. Explaining his decision, President Warren said: "I want our young people to teach me about and trust me with their dreams and dreads; their hopes and expectations."

Personal attention from faculty and administrators is common at OWU, a small university with strengths in the liberal arts and pre-professional studies. "I had a professor meet me and some other students in the library the night before finals to help us get through some difficult material," says a junior. Students add, however, that the academic climate is, in the words of a senior, "relaxed and not overly competitive."

OWU's academic strengths have long been in pre-professional studies, including everything from pre-business and pre-veterinary studies to pre-physical therapy and pre-engineering. The school's Center for Economics and Business, established in 1985, brings speakers to campus and offers a course on entrepreneurship. Fine arts, with programs in graphic arts and plastic arts, and economics are among the school's more popular majors. The sciences, particularly biology and zoology, are also well regarded.

Students give high marks to the school's Black World Studies program. Harold Pinkston, an English and humanities professor who teaches courses in the program, is popular with students. "He was the first black professor to teach at Ohio Wesleyan," says a student. "He's a respected faculty member because he combines the theoretical with real-life experiences."

A unique and popular aspect of OWU's curriculum is the National Colloquium, which, according to President Warren, who instituted the program, is "a semester-long examination of an issue of central public importance and concern." A recent colloquium focus was "The Melting Pot Myth Meets Reality: Racism and American Life." Speakers, usually academics from other colleges, visit the campus each year to discuss issues connected with the colloquium topic. Students earn credit for the colloquium by taking a seminar or other courses that deal with the colloquium topic.

The Writing Resource Center is one of OWU's frequently used sources of academic support. "Even if you're an excellent writer, the center is a help," says a student. Students also turn to Kathryn Ogletree, director of the Office of Minority Student Affairs, for support. "She's a trained psychologist, and is very knowledgeable about how to deal with people. She's caring, and sometimes she's like a mother to some of the kids here. She's also very bright. She has contacts outside of the university, which helps us to bring prominent and interesting guests onto campus for lectures."

OWU has some impressive academic facilities, including the Beeghly Library, one of the largest libraries at a four-year private college in Ohio. The school's Chappelear Drama Center offers outstanding facilities for the school's theater and dance department. With 11 buildings listed in the National Register of Historic Places, OWU's 200-acre campus is spacious and beautiful. In 1992, the university celebrated its 150th anniversary, culminating in the completion of a successful five-year, $50 million capital fund campaign and the construction of the Hamilton-Williams Campus Center, which houses a pub and a food court.

Nearly 50 percent of OWU's students are members of national Greek-letter organizations. One of the school's fraternities is Alpha Phi Alpha, a historically black fraternity. For the past five years, the men of Alpha have earned the campus's community service award, and for two consecutive semesters recently, the fraternity had the highest GPA of any Greek organization on campus. In addition, 100 percent of the men (29 in all) who have pledged the Alpha chapter at OWU have graduated.

The Student Union on Black Awareness (SUBA) is the school's most active cultural student group. It meets once a week in "the Cave," a "gathering place for African-American student groups that is connected to Stuyvesant Hall, a dorm on campus," says a student. With the university, SUBA co-sponsored a series of speakers for Black History Month, primarily professors of economics and sociology from various colleges and universities, including Ohio State and West Virginia University.

Sisters United, an African-American student group, established on campus in 1970, has about 20 members, who meet biweekly. In addition to serving as emotional support, Sisters United helps sponsor the annual Black Cultural Festival, a daylong event that features student performances and an African-American banquet. The festival is offered as part of the school's Black History Month celebration.

OWU remains an overwhelmingly Greek-oriented school. More than half of its men and women join one of the Greek organizations, and fraternity parties provide much of the weekend social life. The school offers a variety of housing options, including Austin Manor, where students live side by side with retired alums and emeritus professors in an "intergenerational residential community," and language theme houses. Students are also sports enthusiasts; more than 85 percent of the men and 55 percent of the women are involved in some sort of organized sport activity, whether varsity or intramural competition. The men's soccer, basketball, and lacrosse teams consistently have winning seasons. Students report little activity on either end of the political spectrum on campus.

Delaware is lacking in the social and cultural departments, according to students, although the town does have a movie theater, a bookstore, and some restaurants, all within a five-minute walk of campus. Columbus, the state's capital and home to Ohio State University, is only twenty minutes away by car and offers access to a symphony, a multilevel mall, and numerous theater and other cultural opportunities. Cleveland and Cincinnati are both about an hour away.

Ohio Wesleyan's size fosters a sense of community and opportunity that can't be duplicated at many other institutions of higher learning. "Experiences here have prepared me for my future," says a student. "I've experienced a variety of things, academically and socially, that I wouldn't have at other, larger schools. This is a campus of leaders. For those who choose to get involved, there are many campus and community service activities in which to participate. I would do OWU all over again."

WITTENBERG UNIVERSITY

Address: P.O. Box 720, Springfield, OH
45501
Phone: (513) 327-6314 / (800) 677-7558
Director of Admissions: Ken Benne
Multicultural Student Recruiter: Keeon
Gregory
1992–93 tuition: $14,500
Room and board: $5,300
Application deadline: 3/15
Financial aid application deadline: 3/15
Non-white freshman admissions: Applicants
for the class of '95: 280
Accepted: 75%
Accepted who enroll: 45%
Applicants accepted who rank in top
10% of high school class: 40%
In top 25%: 65%
Median SAT: 440 V, 500 M
Median ACT: 21
Full-time undergraduate enrollment: 2,250
Men: 46%
Women: 54%

1989–90: 9%
1990–91: 8.7%
Geographic distribution of students
Midwest: 80%
Students In-state: 70%
Top majors: 1. Biology 2. Business
3. Pre-law
Retention rate of non-white students: na
**Scholarships exclusively for non-white
students:** Minority Achievement
Scholarships: amount of each award
varies from $1,000 to $6,000.
Remediation programs: None
Academic support services: The college
offers math and writing workshops.
Ethnic studies programs: The university
offers a major course of study in East
Asian Studies.
Ethnic studies courses: The university offers
three courses in African-American
Studies and two courses in American
minority studies.
Organizations for non-white students: Delta
Sigma Theta, Kappa Alpha Psi, Black

STUDENT ENROLLMENT

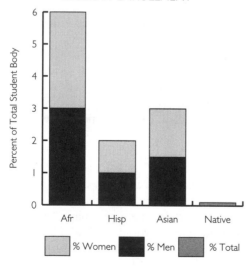

Non-white students in
1987–88: na
1988–89: 9.1%

FACULTY

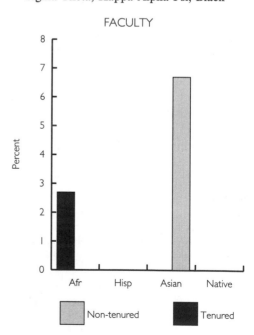

Culture House, Concerned Black
Students, Black Gospel Choir
Notable non-white alumni: Benjamin Hacker
(admiral, U.S. Navy); Rev. Sherman
Hicks (Lutheran bishop of Chicago
Metro Church); William Noble
(president, Noble & Noble Corp.); Janet
E. Jackson (municipal judge)
Tenured faculty: 111
Non-tenured faculty: 45
Student-faculty ratio: 13:1

Administrators: 99
African-American: 6%
Hispanic: 0
Asian-American: 1%
Native American: 0
Recent non-white speakers on campus:
Randall Robinson (executive director,
Trans-Africa); Spike Lee (filmmaker);
William Gray (director, United Negro
College Fund); Juan Williams (creator of
"Eyes on the Prize" PBS Series)

It's easy for a school to get lost in the crowd, especially in a state with so many fine four-year public and private colleges and universities. But Wittenberg University, with its commitment to the liberal arts and small class size, is distinctive.

Students say the school's standout departments include biology, chemistry, psychology, East Asian Studies, and education. Business administration, the school's most popular major, is said to be demanding, as is the computer science program. Students say professors are easily accessible and that academic competition is not overly intense.

In order to graduate, students must show a proficiency in writing, quantitative reasoning, and a foreign language. Students must also take a non-Western studies course, a requirement that can be satisfied with study abroad, and first-year students must take "Common Learning," a freshman seminar-style course taught by a students' adviser.

Academic assistance can be found at the Writer's Workshop, which one student said "gives you a chance to get ideas from peer tutors that you don't get from your professors. The service is really helpful."

The Multicultural Affairs Office provides a peer advising network for first-year students, who are paired with an upperclass student "who helps direct them to the school's different tutoring services. The mentors help the first-year students socially and academically." The Multicultural Affairs Office also creates programming to "open up cultures to other students and faculty." A recent event sponsored by the office was Cross Roads, an international food festival to which students contributed dishes from their respective cultures. International students also performed dances at the outdoor event, which took place near the school's main dining hall. The director of the office, John Young, is someone "we can go talk to whenever we need to. He's also knowledgeable about the black community and history. He teaches a 'Blacks in Politics' course, and he is able to help us create better events and activities," says a campus student organizer.

The Concerned Black Students (CBS) organization, which meets every other Wednesday in Krieg Hall, the music building on campus, also provides cultural awareness programming. The group, composed of about 50 members, brings speakers and movies to campus each semester. Recently, CBS brought to campus the stage production of *The Meeting,* a play about a fictional encounter between Malcolm X and Martin Luther King, Jr. The event drew a "nice-sized crowd," reports a campus leader. Wittenberg's Black Culture House "is used primarily for socializing and studying. Depending on the academic term and how busy everyone is, the house is frequently used by students. I'm not surprised to see twenty-five to thirty students there at a time." Although the house does not have living facilities, it does have a full kitchen, a living room, and a small library.

Wittenberg's African-American students also interact with students at other area colleges, such as Wright State and Central State, a predominantly black institution. Although Wittenberg does not officially recognize Alpha Kappa Alpha and Alpha Phi Alpha, two traditionally black Greek organizations, several interested students pledged these organizations at Wright State, about a twenty-minute drive from Springfield. Kappa Alpha Psi and Delta Sigma Theta, two other traditionally black organizations, have chapters on campus and have about three members each.

The area around Wittenberg boasts some beautiful countryside, but students say the town of Springfield (pop. 68,000) offers few social and cultural outlets. As many of Witt's students live in off-campus apartments furnished by the university, much of the social life takes place there, or in fraternity houses. For those with cars, Dayton is only a half hour away, while Columbus is just an hour northeast. Wittenberg's athletic teams—especially men's baseball and football—have given students something to cheer about; they are usually highly ranked in Division III competition. A popular event is the school's annual Festival of the Reformation service, held on campus in Weaver Chapel, a reminder of the school's Lutheran heritage. The Wittenberg Series brings noteworthy speakers and performance groups to campus each year. Recently they have included Nobel Prize winner Elie Wiesel and the Vusisizwe Players, who depict black South African life.

While Wittenberg has some good academic departments, two of the school's biggest draws are the warmth of its students and its small size. "I'm glad I came here," says a junior, "especially because of the school's reputation with employers. I also feel that I'm getting a good education, and I've been able to take on leadership roles here I wouldn't have had at a larger school." Adds a Wittenberg fan from the Big Apple: "If we were this friendly in New York City, we'd be arrested."

COLLEGE OF WOOSTER

Address: Galpin Hall, Wooster, OH 44691
Phone: (216) 263-2000 / (800) 877-9905
Director of Admissions: Hayden Schilling
Multicultural Student Recruiter: na
1993–94 tuition: $15,425
Room and board: $4,450
Application deadline: 2/15
Financial aid application deadline: 2/15

Non-white freshman admissions: Applicants for the class of '95: 136
Accepted: 71.3%
Accepted who enroll: 27%
Applicants accepted who rank in top 10% of high school class: 20%
In top 25%: 45%
Median SAT: 470 V, 480 M
Median ACT: 20

Full-time undergraduate enrollment: 1,850
  Men: 49%
  Women: 51%

STUDENT ENROLLMENT

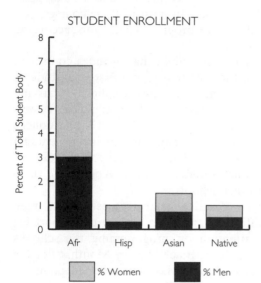

Percent of Total Student Body

% Women   % Men

Non-white students in
  1987–88: 8%
  1988–89: 8%
  1989–90: 8%
  1990–91: 9.3%
Students In-state: 46%
Top majors: 1. Engineering 2. Pre-law
  3. Pre-med
Retention rate of non-white students: 93%
**Scholarships exclusively for non-white
  students:** Clarence B. Allen Scholarship:
  merit-based; $10,000 per award; available

GEOGRAPHIC DISTRIBUTION OF STUDENTS

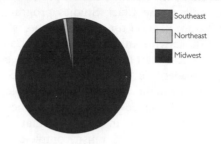

Southeast
Northeast
Midwest

to African-American students;
  renewable.
Remediation programs: None
Academic support services: The college has a
  Reading and Writing Center and a Math
  Assistance Center.
Ethnic studies programs: The college offers
  a major in Black Studies, which includes
  more than 25 courses.
Ethnic studies courses: na
Organizations for non-white students: Black
  Women's Organization, Black Student
  Association, Harambe House
  (African-American men's organization)
Notable non-white alumni: na
Tenured faculty: na
Non-tenured faculty: na
Student-faculty ratio: 11.5:1
Administrators: na
Recent non-white speakers on campus: Louis
  Stokes (U.S. representative from Ohio);
  John Lewis (U.S. representative from
  Georgia); Angela Davis (political
  activist); bell hooks (professor and activist)

If you think having the opportunity to work one-on-one with a faculty member (and not a teaching assistant) is something that only happens in graduate school, then you don't know about the College of Wooster. The college has long been known for its innovative Senior Independent Project, in which students work individually with one or another of the college's faculty members. The student chooses the subject he or she wants to study, and, near the end of the student's senior year, submits the project or thesis for approval. Some recent examples are a physics major's study of the way bones expand with changing temperature and a theater major's play about the Vietnam War.

The Woo, as students affectionately refer to their college, is solely an undergraduate institution devoted to the liberal arts and sciences, where close interaction with the faculty is the norm. Students praise the history, economics, and English departments, as well as the Black Studies program. According to a senior, "the Black Studies program is good for those students who don't know their history, and it's also good for those who know a great deal about their history. In most of these courses, you get to hear a lot of different perspectives." One of the program's highlights, according to a student, is "Introduction to Black Studies."

To graduate, students must complete a core curriculum that includes courses in the social sciences, the natural sciences, and the humanities, and first-year students must participate in seminars that introduce them to interdisciplinary learning. First-year students must complete a seminar course titled "Difference, Power, Discrimination: Perspectives on Race, Gender, Class and Culture." The college sponsors various joint-degree programs with other major universities, including engineering programs with Case Western Reserve University, the University of Michigan, and Washington University, in which students study at Wooster for three years followed by two years at one of the other schools.

The Black Student Association, with about 45 active members, meets once a week in a lounge in the student center. In addition to providing a place of support for students, the BSA focuses much of its attention on programming the school's Diversity Conference, held in February to celebrate Black History Month. "For the conference we like to invite speakers on black topics who have different points of view," says a campus leader about the weeklong event. "The speaker might be radical or he or she might be conservative. We do this because we recognize there is diversity of opinion within the African-American community." As part of the conference, the BSA schedules workshops, whose topics have focused on the relationships between African-American men and women and time management.

The BSA's adviser, Lenore Barnes-Wright, "is fantastic," says a business major. "She will do anything to see that we graduate from here. She works with us financially and academically. We always know we can talk to her if we have any problems." Barnes-Wright, who also serves as the school's director of the Office of Black Student Affairs, was instrumental in getting organized on campus the Peer Mentor program, in which upperclass students work closely with first-year students. Barnes-Wright "makes sure we all know where everything is on campus so that we can be effective mentors and communicate to the student anything he or she needs to know about the campus, socially or academically," says a senior.

The Men of Harambe, an African-American student group whose name means "We Build Together" in Swahili, hold meetings "every Tuesday night that are required of its members," says a leader of the organization. In a recent year, approximately 11 men were members of the group. While the BSA deals with campus events, the Men of Harambe focus, in the words of a member, "on topics relevant to today's diaspora." The group brings to campus each year a speaker to commemorate the death of Malcolm X. The group also sponsors a Kwanzaa celebration each December. The Men of Harambe's faculty adviser is Akwasi Osei, a professor of Black Studies and of political science. "We already respect Osei professionally because he is a successful member of the faculty," says one student. "We also like him because he always seeks to touch base with the students."

The Harambe House provides living space for up to 12 men. "The house is a permanently chartered residence facility," according to a resident; it has a kitchen and double and single rooms. "We try to arrange it so that half of the men in the house are upperclassmen and the other half are freshmen. This is so the upperclass students can act as mentors for the new students." There are no similar living arrangements for African-American women.

The Black Women's Organization also provides a source of peer support. In addition, the group sponsors various activities, including a Sadie Hawkins dance and workshops. About 17 women attend a typical BWO meeting. According to one student, Asian-American and Hispanic students "tend" to join the school's International Student Organization.

The students at Wooster tend to be more liberal than students at other area schools, and are somewhat politically active and aware. "During my first year, there were several marches and even a sit-in. Those made me aware of issues I hadn't thought about before," says a recent graduate. The College of Wooster has no fraternities or sororities, which usually serve to establish a hierarchy in a school's social life. The college does have clubs for men and sections for women, but students say they aren't exclusive the way Greek organizations can be.

Outside of club parties, social life at the Woo is fairly relaxed, but the college's more than 70 student organizations liven things up a bit. Groups include the musically, politically, or dramatically oriented, and are active and popular. The school's sports teams, especially football and men's and women's soccer teams, have fared well in recent years, as have the men's basketball and baseball teams. And any athletic competition against archrival Denison University draws crowds. Wooster's Scottish heritage is evident in the school's band, which wears kilts during performances.

The town of Wooster (pop. 22,000) doesn't offer many alternatives to on-campus social life, so students looking for off-campus excitement usually head to Akron, about an hour north, or to Columbus, about an hour and a half south.

Respected academics and opportunities for close interaction with faculty and staff are definite reasons to attend the Woo. One student says: "I knew I would strive to be successful wherever I went to college. But I've been able to get involved in a lot of activities here that I wouldn't have been able to at a larger university."

UNIVERSITY OF OKLAHOMA

Address: 1000 Asp Avenue, Norman, OK
  73019-0430
Phone: (405) 325-2251 / (800) 234-6868
Director of Admissions: Marc Borish
Multicultural Student Recruiter: na
1992–93 tuition: $1,768 (in-state); $4,959
  (out-of-state)
Room and board: $3,358
Application deadline: Rolling admissions
Financial aid application deadline: 3/1
Non-white freshman admissions: Applicants
  for the class of '96: 1,227
  Accepted: 92%
  Accepted who enroll: 57.8%
  Applicants accepted who rank in top
  10% of high school class: na
  Median SAT: na
  Median ACT: 23
Full-time undergraduate enrollment: 12,422
  Men: 55%
  Women: 45%
Non-white students in
  1987–88: 10.4%
  1988–89: 10.3%
  1989–90: 10.9%
  1990–91: 11.8%
Students In-state: 82%
Top majors: 1. Engineering 2. Business
  3. Journalism/Communications
Retention rate of non-white students: 79.6%
**Scholarships exclusively for non-white
  students:** The university offers more than
  50 merit- and need-based minority
  scholarships, including: Award of

Excellence: merit-based; renewable;
$1,500 each year; number of awards not
restricted; available to all minority
applicants. Honors Scholars: merit-based;
renewable; $1,000; number of awards
each year not limited. Margin of Quality
Minority Scholarship: merit- and
need-based; $1,000; renewable; five
awarded each year; recipient must be a
business major.
Remediation programs: Academic and
non-academic development programs are
offered through Project Threshold.

STUDENT ENROLLMENT

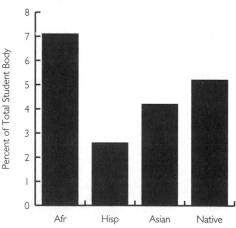

Academic support services: Minority Student Services, Freshman Orientations, Helping Hands University Achievement Class, Minority Internships, Peer Counseling Sessions, Study Skills Seminars, Time Management Workshops, Computer Labs, the Writing Center, Minority Engineering Programs.

Ethnic studies programs: The African and African-American Studies program, established in 1977, is interdisciplinary, involving courses in history, literature, sociology, psychology, and other areas. The Native American Studies program, established in 1977, is interdisciplinary, and includes courses in several departments. The Latin American Studies program offers courses from at least six departments. Asian Studies, offered as a major and minor, was established in 1952 and involves anthropology, geography, history, modern language, and three other departments.

Organizations for non-white students: American Indian Science and Engineering Society, American Indian Social Workers Association, American Indian Student Association, Alliance of Indigenous People, Asian-American Student Association, Black Business Students Association, Black Student Association, Hispanic-American Student Association, Society of African-American Men, National Society of Black Engineers, NAACP, National Society of Black Journalists, Society of Hispanic Professional Engineers, Heritage Enemble, Kappa Alpha Psi, Alpha Kappa Alpha, Alpha Phi Alpha, Delta Sigma Theta, Omega Psi Phi, Phi Beta Sigma, Sigma Gamma Rho, Zeta Phi Beta, and numerous others

Notable non-white alumni: Richard Arrington, Jr. (mayor, Birmingham, AL); J. C. Watts (corporation commissioner and first African-American elected to statewide office in Oklahoma); Agapito Mendozo (assistant to the vice-chancellor of academic affairs, University of Missouri/Kansas City)

Tenured faculty: 505

Non-tenured faculty: 343

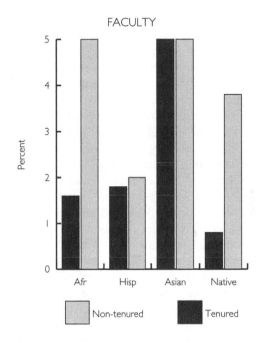

FACULTY

Student-faculty ratio: na

Administrators: na

Recent non-white speakers on campus: Julianne Malveaux (contributing editor, *Essence* magazine); Ken Kashiwahara (ABC News bureau chief, San Francisco); Nikki Giovanni (poet); W. Richard West (director, Smithsonian Institution's National Museum of the American Indian); Larry Echohawk (Idaho state attorney general); Rigoberta Menchu (winner of the 1992 Nobel Peace Prize)

For those in the know it comes as no surprise that the University of Oklahoma, a school with one of the finest petroleum engineering programs in the nation, includes among its list of famous alums the CEO of Exxon. Oklahoma has also had four recent recipients of Black Student Engineer of the Year awards, one of whom went on to become the first African-American woman ever to be chosen for the U.S. Navy's selective program in nuclear engineering.

While the university's list of alums may be impressive, equally impressive is Oklahoma's commitment to retaining and graduating its students of color. This is most evident in the school's recently restructured Office of Student Support Services, which has counselors who work with each of the school's four major ethnic groups: African-American, Native American, Hispanic-American, and Asian-American. "I don't know how I could have survived here if it hadn't been for that office," says an engineering major. Counselors offer financial aid advice, counsel, tutor, and even award scholarships. Larry Medina, the counselor in charge of Hispanic student services, is described by a senior as "someone who is like our dad."

The office has also recently established the Minority Intern Program, in which upperclass students work with freshman as they adjust to college. "We're kind of like a new student's retention mentor," says a student. "We each spend about three to five hours a week helping the students in whatever way we can, from finding them tutors to guiding them around campus. At the end of the year, the freshmen fill out evaluations about the program, and all of them rate it highly."

In fact, Oklahoma's retention programs have been so successful that the retention rate of the school's students of color equals that of the retention rate of the school's white students. "We had no idea that it was going so well—that is, not until the university president announced the news to us at a banquet that honored African-American students. We were all pretty shocked and charged up about that news." OU also leads the Big Eight in enrollment of students of color.

In addition to the support of the school's retention programs, students are also able to turn to various cultural organizations for peer support. With about 350 members, the Black Student Alliance is the largest and most active. At the beginning of each year, the BSA sponsors Show and Tell, a program geared to first-year students in which representatives from the school's 27 African-American student groups perform skits as a way to advertise their groups' functions. In 1992, as part of Oklahoma's homecoming festivities, the BSA sponsored its first Ebony Homecoming Queen. In addition, the BSA's Kwanzaa celebration and parties are popular. The BSA's most ambitious event is its annual Stompdown, a step show that attracts spectators and participants from around the region. During a recent Stompdown, 5,000 people watched as more than 19 groups performed.

But the event of which BSA members are perhaps most proud is its annual banquet, held at the end of the school year, in which members are honored for academic achievement and community service. "Not only does it draw a large BSA crowd, but something we're always impressed by is that the president of the university always comes, and so do the deans of the different undergraduate colleges, who give out awards. With so many awards, it can be a long afternoon, but I don't think there's anybody in the room who doesn't think it's worth it."

Also active on the Oklahoma campus are the school's predominantly black Greek organizations, who, according to one student, sponsor parties and dances almost every weekend. In contrast to other schools that have such large black Greek systems, students say Greek relations are good, thanks to the efforts of the school's National

Panhellenic Council, which consists of representatives of each of the organizations. All of the groups are committed to public service. Omega Psi Phi fraternity members, for example, regularly tutor at an area middle school, while Delta Sigma Theta members sponsor a mentor program for teenage girls and fundraising events for a local sickle-cell anemia chapter.

Relations between predominantly black and predominantly white Greek organizations are also better than at most schools. Black Greek organizations have representatives at Panhellenic/Interfraternity Council meetings, and a system is in place in which chapter members who attend events or parties sponsored by other chapters win points. The Greek chapter with the most points at the end of the term is honored as the chapter of the year. "The system definitely encourages the organizations to interact more," says a sorority sister. In addition, when the women of Delta Sigma Theta asked for help after their props for a carnival went up in flames during a storage facility fire, members of Kappa Delta, a predominantly white sorority, lent them theirs. "It turned out to be a really nice carnival," says a Delta.

The school's black cultural center was recently renamed the Henderson-Tolson Cultural Center, in honor of Oklahoma's first two African-American professors, Melvin Henderson, Jr., and George Tolson. "They are still on staff, and every once in a while they come back and talk to us about the history of the BSA and how far we've come." As of now, the center is used primarily as a meeting place for the school's black student organizations, but BSA leaders are looking to broaden its use in the near future. "We want to make it more of a cultural center with an art gallery and library," says a student. The center has TV and meeting rooms, and during finals it is open for twenty-four-hour-a-day studying.

Only seven years old, the Asian-American Student Association is the school's newest cultural organization. Its biggest event is the Asian-American Cultural Weekend, to which the group invites speakers, and it coordinates parties and art exhibitions. The association also sponsors two community service projects, including a program in which members adopt a needy child in the area. Recently the group established a policy of having two new staff and faculty advisers every two years, "so we can get the staff more involved," says a student. A recent adviser students speak highly of is Man Ho, a professor of social work.

One of the group's most successful events, however, was a party it co-sponsored with the Hispanic-American Student Association (HASA). "It was a Valentine's Day party. We had it because we felt that the minority groups don't do much together socially or politically."

HASA, with about 50 members, meets monthly in the Oklahoma Memorial Union to plan such events as Fiesta Calle (Street Party), held annually in the armory on campus, which features booths offering primarily Puerto Rican foods. Fifteen HASA members recently traveled to Chicago to attend the three-day National Hispanic Leadership Conference. HASA's most popular campus-wide event is its Mother of All Burrito Sales, the money from which goes to fund the trips to conferences.

Despite the efforts of HASA, membership in the organization remains low. "There are many Hispanic students here who don't want to identify with their culture, except when it comes to getting scholarship opportunities, which is the saddest reason of all," says a HASA leader. "Everyone who has come to meetings and events has really liked it. We do about four mailings a year to all of the Hispanic students on campus inviting them to events, and we leave it up to them at that point whether they'll participate. Larry Medina has created a HASA scholarship, which has generated ten new HASA members."

Oklahoma has the reputation of graduating more serious partiers than serious thinkers, but the school, just coming off a three-year probation imposed by the NCAA, is looking to polish its image. For starters, the university has two honors programs, as well as an honors house for students enrolled in the programs, which are available to the academically talented. Petroleum, geological, and nuclear engineering are some of the school's respected engineering programs, while political science, chemistry, and the fine arts rank with the best such programs in the state. Architecture and business also win high marks from students.

The school's minor program in African-American Studies is described by one student as "excellent." Courses in African-American and African history are popular. Students say that the school's Asian Studies program is small but respected.

While students at Oklahoma tend to be on the more conservative side of things politically, students of color are heartened by the recent turnout for the school's Martin Luther King Celebration, which drew, in the words of one student, "a tremendous number of white students" to the candlelight vigil. But students say relations between Oklahoma's Hispanic-Americans and African-Americans could be improved; members of the two groups rarely attend each other's events. Students praise the efforts of the university in attempting to foster a greater respect for Oklahoma's students of color. Following verbal harassment of Native American students two years ago by fraternity members, for example, the university adopted a racial harassment policy, with some prodding by student organizations.

Norman is known by African-American students as a "Sundown Town, because we feel we should be out of town by sundown," says a student. "Norman is certainly not as open-minded as the university is," adds the student. Students say most of their social life is centered on campus, or, for the adventurous, the drive to the Burger King in town or to Oklahoma City isn't out of the question.

Despite less than ideal town-gown relations, Oklahoma students of color are more than just content with their undergraduate experiences, thanks to a supportive administration and retention programs, and active student organizations. "I wouldn't have made a different college choice, and I recommend Oklahoma to any student looking to attend college," says a transplanted Texan. "There's a tremendous amount of closeness among the minority students here, which makes for a positive and friendly experience for all of us."

OKLAHOMA STATE UNIVERSITY

Address: Stillwater, OK 74078
Phone: (405) 744-6876
Director of Admissions: Dr. Robin H. Lacy
Multicultural Student Recruiter: na
1992–93 tuition: $1,620 (in-state); $4,620
(out-of-state)
Room and board: $3,070
Application deadline: Rolling admissions
Financial aid application deadline: 3/1

Non-white freshman admissions: Applicants
for the class of '95: 953
Accepted: 68%
Accepted who enroll: 56%
Applicants accepted who rank in top
10% of high school class: na
Median SAT: na
Median ACT: 23.8
Full-time undergraduate enrollment: 13,362
Men: 55%
Women: 45%

STUDENT ENROLLMENT

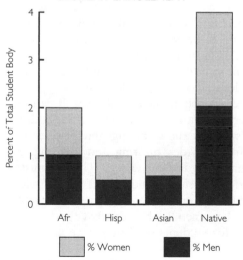

Percent of Total Student Body

Afr | Hisp | Asian | Native

% Women   % Men

Non-white students in
1987–88: 7.6%
1988–89: 8.2%
1989–90: 8.8%
1990–91: 9.2%

GEOGRAPHIC DISTRIBUTION OF STUDENTS

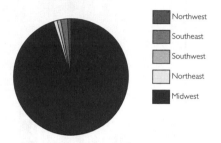

Northwest
Southeast
Southwest
Northeast
Midwest

Students In-state: na
Top majors: 1. Accounting 2. Electrical
Engineering 3. Electronics Technology
Retention rate of non-white students: 68%
**Scholarships exclusively for non-white
students:** Thurgood Marshall Award:
need- and merit-based; three awarded
each year; each award is valued at
$1,000. Black Faculty and Staff Award:
three awarded each year; amount of
award varies; need- and merit-based.
Remediation programs: Courses are
available in remedial reading and math.
Academic support services: The University
Assessment Center offers tutoring
services as well as courses in developing
study skills.
Ethnic studies programs: None
Ethnic studies courses: The university offers
four courses in East Asian Studies, as
well as Chinese- and Japanese-language
study. Two courses are offered in African
Studies, one in African-American
Studies, and two courses in Native
American Studies.
Organizations for non-white students:
National Association of Blacks in
Accounting, NAACP, Minority Women's
Association, Afro-American Student
Association, Burning Black Gospel
Choir, Black Business Student Asso-
ciation, Native American Student
Association, Hispanic Student Associ-
ation, African Student Organization,

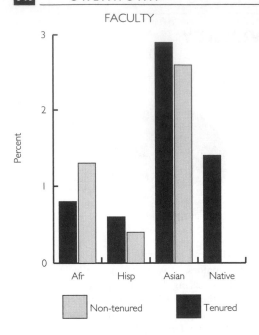

FACULTY

Percent

Afr   Hisp   Asian   Native

Non-tenured   Tenured

Afro-American Student Association, Korean Student Association, Latin American Student Association

Notable non-white alumni: na
Tenured faculty: 648
Non-tenured faculty: 235
Student-faculty ratio: 22:1
Administrators: 35
  African-American: 1.34%
  Hispanic: 5.7%
  Asian-American: 2.9%
  Native American: 8.6%
Recent non-white speakers on campus:
  Marsha Gillespie (former editor, *Essence* magazine); Wilma Mankiller (chief, Cherokee Tribe of Oklahoma); Reginald Wilson (senior scholar, American Council on Education); Jacqueline Fleming (psychologist); Atallah Shabazz (civil rights activist and daughter of Malcolm X)

Oklahoma State University is more than just the state's land-grant institution. Yes, agriculture is still one of the school's most popular and respected programs, but the university, founded in 1890, also offers programs in business, engineering, architecture, accounting, and veterinary medicine. But students interested in a more well-rounded liberal arts experience may want to head south on Highway 35 to the state's other large public university, as OSU is more preprofessionally geared.

Academics are not as rigorous as they are at some other schools, but the university's Minority Programs and Services Office, located in the student union, provides whatever support students need. "The office has helped me a great deal. It can take a lot of the responsibility for keeping me here. The atmosphere at the office is casual and very friendly, and there are always students there talking and just relaxing between classes," says a student. The office provides tutoring and advising, but students complain that the office is underfunded by the university. "The administration here doesn't really make the office a priority," says a student. Office counselors, all of whom are people of color, are available for each of the university's four major ethnic groups. "All of the counselors do a phenomenal job with what they're given by the administration. They're always there for students, and they have us as their priority."

The coordinator of the Minority Programs and Services Office is Dr. Howard Shipps, who is described by one student as "always accessible and willing to help us students out." While the office provides effective academic and personal counseling, one student sees yet another benefit. "As we're all under one roof, it gives members of the different cultural groups access to one another, and we get a chance to talk about issues and to learn about each other's events."

In January 1992, the university created the new position of vice president of multicultural affairs, and appointed Gregory Washington. "He's been pretty accessible so far, but it's going to take time before a position like that can make a true difference. But he's definitely on the right track. He also has a direct line to the president of the university." As part of a search committee, students were involved in selecting Washington for the position.

Cultural support groups are somewhat active on campus. The Afro-American Student Association, with about 120 members, is primarily a cultural group, according to students. "We try to create a cultural awareness on campus about African-American concerns and to provide a forum where students can discuss problems here at the university and in the country," says a student leader. The association recently hosted the fifteenth annual Big Eight Black Student Conference, held annually at different Big Eight campuses. The conference offered lectures and workshops, focusing on "Black Identity," "Black Male/Female Relationships," and such other topics as African-American religion and history. The association also hosts an annual soul food dinner, twice-yearly fashion shows, and a Miss Black OSU pageant, "one of our most popular events." Adds the student: "We also try to make our meetings more interesting and exciting by having skating and bowling parties."

Parties in the school's African-American community are most often hosted by the historically black Greek organizations. "Every weekend someone has a party going on, either at the student union or at one of their houses." (The men of Kappa Alpha Psi and the women of Delta Sigma Theta have residence facilities.) The historically black Greek organizations are also involved in the surrounding Stillwater community. Members of Kappa Alpha Psi participate in an adopt-a-child program that lasts throughout the school year, and members of Delta Sigma Theta recently coordinated a Say No to Drugs Games Day. The proceeds went to a nearby drug rehabilitation center.

The Hispanic Student Association, whose active membership varies from 20 to 50 students "depending on the event and the time of year," is primarily a social organization. "We have Christmas parties and Valentine's parties, and we have dances, both on and off campus, either at hotels or in ballrooms." The group also sponsors cultural events, including a recent art exhibit, classical guitar performances by area guitarists, and movie nights. In addition, the HSA plans activities for Hispanic Heritage Week, usually held in April. The event features speakers and workshops, one of which discussed perceptions of Columbus's discovery of America. Two popular faculty members who can be seen frequently at some of the larger HSA events are Dr. Cida Chase and Dr. Santiago Garcia, both from the Spanish department.

The Latin American Student Association is primarily for international students. "The line between the HSA and the LASA is kind of fuzzy because we sponsor many events together," says a campus leader.

Oklahoma State University's student body—most of whom come from small towns around the state—and administration are conservative. All dorms are single-sex, the Greek system is active and provides much of the campus's social life, Christian organizations are an important part of many a coed's daily life, and you'd be hard pressed to find a Young Democrat member while Republicans are plentiful. Like the university, Stillwater (pop. about 40,000) is conservative, and offers little in the way of a social life for students. Most undergraduates head home for weekends (hence the university's suitcase-school image) or make the drive to Oklahoma City or Tulsa—both about an hour from Stillwater—for off-campus excitement.

Many students appreciate the size and location of their college's town. "Stillwater residents are definitely supportive of the university, and we're very involved with one another. I like Stillwater because there are few distractions here and it's located an hour away from the two largest cities in the state—Tulsa and Oklahoma City."

Students appreciate OSU for its academics, its location, and, most of all, its Minority Programs and Services Office. "OSU is a fine school," says a student, "made even stronger because of that office's services and counselors."

O R E G O N

UNIVERSITY OF OREGON

Address: 240 Oregon Hall, Eugene, OR
  97402
Phone: (503) 346-3201 / (800) BE-A-DUCK
Director of Admissions: Jim Buch
Multicultural Student Recruiter: Mentha
  Hynes
1992–93 tuition: $2,721 (in-state); $7,851
  (out-of-state)
Room and board: $3,076
Application deadline: 3/1
Financial aid application deadline: 3/1
Non-white freshman admissions: Applicants
  for the class of '95: 798
  Accepted: 88.2%
  Accepted who enroll: 40.3%
  Applicants accepted who rank in top
  10% of high school class: 22.3%
  In top 25%: 56.6%
  Median SAT range: 430–550 V,
  460–600 M
  Median ACT range: 15–28
Full-time undergraduate enrollment: 12,274
  Men: 47.3%
  Women: 52.7%
Non-white students in
  1987–88: 6.9%
  1988–89: 7.9%
  1989–90: 8.6%
  1990–91: 9%
Students In-state: 60%
Top majors: 1. Business 2. Journalism
  3. Sociology
Retention rate of non-white students: na
Scholarships exclusively for non-white

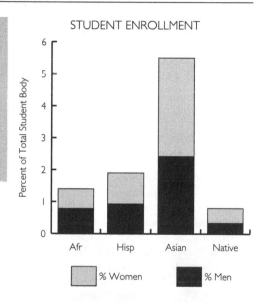

STUDENT ENROLLMENT

Percent of Total Student Body

% Women   % Men

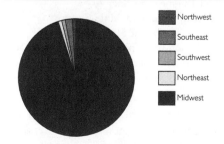

GEOGRAPHIC DISTRIBUTION OF STUDENTS

Northwest
Southeast
Southwest
Northeast
Midwest

students: Underrepresented Minorities
Achievement Scholarship: full tuition and
fees; 32 awarded each year; must be an

Oregon resident and a graduate of an Oregon high school and of African-American, Hispanic, or Native American descent; merit-based. Underrepresented Minority Achievement Scholarship for College Juniors: full tuition; 38 awarded each year; must be an Oregon resident and of African-American, Hispanic, or Native American descent. Jewel Hairston Bell Scholarship: $500 or more; one awarded each year to a student who has exhibited leadership in the "cause of diversity" at the university.

Remediation programs: None

Academic support services: The Educational Opportunities Program and the Academic Learning Services provide academic support services.

Ethnic studies programs: Oregon's Asian Studies program offers a major and a minor. Established in 1941, the program includes courses in anthropology, political science, religious studies, and sociology. The university's Folklore and Ethnic Studies program includes more than two dozen courses in African-American, Latin American, and Asian American studies.

Organizations for non-white students: Asian/Pacific American Student Union, Black Student Union, MECHA, Native American Student Union, Cross-Cultural Residence Hall, Alpha Kappa Alpha, Kappa Alpha Psi, Black Women of Achievement, American Indian Science and Engineering Society, African-American Male Support Group, Native Hawaiian Student Union

Notable non-white alumni: Ahmad Rashad (TV sportscaster); Richard Muñoz (clinical psychology professor, University

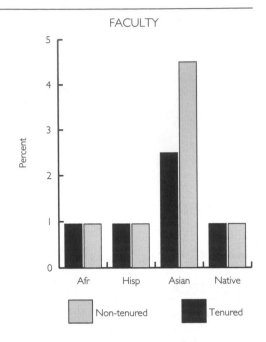

FACULTY

Percent

Afr   Hisp   Asian   Native

Non-tenured ▨   Tenured ■

of California/San Francisco); Harriet Adair (Kellogg Fellow); Paula Gunn Allen (author and UCLA professor)

Tenured faculty: 451

Non-tenured faculty: 155

Student-faculty ratio: 19:1

Administrators: 60

African-American: <1%

Hispanic: <1%

Asian-American: 0

Native American: <1%

Recent non-white speakers on campus: Atallah Shabazz (civil rights activist and daughter of Malcolm X); Cesar Chavez (labor leader and head of the United Farm Workers); Fatima Meer (South African author); Alanis Obomsawin (filmmaker)

The University of Oregon, one of the Pacific Northwest's better-regarded public institutions of higher learning, offers a wide array of academic and social opportunities.

Oregon is divided into seven colleges. The College of Business Administration (CBA), housed in impressive new facilities, has the most popular major programs, particularly finance and accounting. CBA students must satisfy more than half of their graduation requirements by taking courses in the College of Arts and Sciences. Within the College of Arts and Sciences, students say political science, journalism, and chemistry are tops. Other departments that win student praise are architecture, education, sociology, and international studies. The university's honors college is well regarded.

Oregon's academic and non-academic support systems win praise from students. "If I were a professor and could give the student support services here a grade for their interests in and commitment to minority students, I would give them an A," says a student. The Office of Multicultural Affairs (OMA) works especially closely with Oregon's students of color. "A lot of the staff at OMA really care about students," says a campus leader. "They make you feel as if you're not the only one on campus." Adds another undergraduate: "The counselors at OMA create an extremely aware environment when it comes to racial issues on campus." OMA offers academic advising, computer support, mentoring, and tutoring assistance. OMA's Retreat Weekend wins praise from students. OMA invites the incoming first-year minority students to campus to participate in workshops that introduce them to the academic and social aspects of life at Oregon. A junior says that the weekend has provided her with friends that have lasted her three years at school. "The program makes you feel as if you're a part of a family on campus," she says. Among the OMA staff members, students say that Jim Garcia is "a great help when it comes to seeking academic advice." Perhaps two of the support staff who are most sought after by students are Edwina Welch, an OMA academic adviser, and Mentha Hynes, an assistant director of admissions. "If it weren't for them," says a student, "there's no doubt I wouldn't be here today. They are both there whenever I need them, students can go to them as friends as well as for advice, and they genuinely care that we succeed."

Students find additional support in the school's four cultural student groups. The Black Student Union is "very active" on campus, report students. "The BSU has done a good job in making blacks feel more comfortable here," says a BSU member. For Black History Month, the BSU brings to campus various speakers and artists. In May, the BSU sponsors an annual Black Arts Festival, and during a recent year the group held a reception for first-year African-American students. The BSU also works with the admissions office to recruit more African-Americans. There is one traditionally black fraternity and one traditionally black sorority, which students say work closely with the BSU in planning activities.

MECHA, the school's Latino student group, is active in sponsoring activities around Cinco de Mayo and Day of the Dead. The group also sponsors a fall conference each year at which students and guest speakers address concerns of the Latino community. The Native American Student Union sponsors two annual powwows, which students say are well attended by students and faculty members. The powwows take place in the school's gym and offer a food festival and dance. Each of the cultural student groups has its own office, which are all located in Eugene Memorial Union and are provided with areas for meetings.

Adams Hall, the school's cross-cultural living center, is popular with students. More than 50 undergraduates, representing the school's various minority groups, live in the residence hall. The living unit sponsors workshops in study skills and cultural awareness. "Living in the hall helps a lot here in dealing with being a minority on a predominantly white campus," says a student.

As it rains a great deal in the city of Eugene, it makes sense that the university's mascot is the duck. But the weather doesn't dampen students' spirits. Students participate in a wide variety of activities and organizations. Jogging is the extracurricular sport of choice, while the school's varsity football, basketball, and track and field teams have enjoyed some recent successful seasons.

Oregon has traditionally attracted a bohemian student body, students who seem more of the iconoclastic '60s than the pragmatic '90s. There are plenty of granola types on campus, among whom tie-dyed T-shirts, torn jeans, and Birkenstocks are de rigueur. Just as prevalent—and obvious—are the more preppy members of the campus, who are usually involved in one or another of the school's predominantly white Greek organizations, which provide much of the Friday- and Saturday-night social activities. On the whole, Oregon students tend to be more liberal than conservative—gay and lesbian student groups are active on campus—and are deeply concerned about the environment. Conservation is a big issue here. The majority of the university's students hail from the state; about 20 percent come from California and other states in the region—and nearly a hundred foreign countries.

And who can blame them? The area around the city contains some of the most pristine countryside you'll find in the Northwest. Hiking, skiing, and fishing are popular off-campus activities. Two large parks are within walking distance of campus, as are a shopping center and several bars and restaurants. Portland is within easy driving distance of Eugene.

Oregon has some outstanding academic programs, and offers opportunities to meet students with diverse, and certainly vocal, perspectives. For a student from Los Angeles, there's one more reason to attend this school: "I like the atmosphere in Eugene. It's refreshing after the intensity of LA—and the air is so clean!"

REED COLLEGE

Address: Portland, OR 97202-8199
Phone: (503) 777-7511 / (800) 547-4750
Director of Admissions: Robert Mansueto
Multicultural Student Recruiter: Dr. Rudolph Jones
1993–94 tuition: $19,250
Room and board: $5,230
Application deadline: 2/1
Financial aid application deadline: 3/1
Non-white freshman admissions: Applicants for the class of '95: 417
  Accepted: 64%
  Accepted who enroll: 25%
  Applicants accepted who rank in top 10% of high school class: na
  Median SAT: na
  Median ACT: na

Full-time undergraduate enrollment: 1,203
  Men: 53%
  Women: 47%
Non-white students in
  1987–88: 11%
  1988–89: 10%
  1989–90: 10%
  1990–91: 8.4%
Geographic distribution of students: na
Top majors: 1. English 2. Biology 3. History
Retention rate of non-white students: 90%
Scholarships exclusively for non-white students: None
Remediation programs: None
Academic support services: The college offers a Writing Center and tutoring in most academic subjects.

STUDENT ENROLLMENT

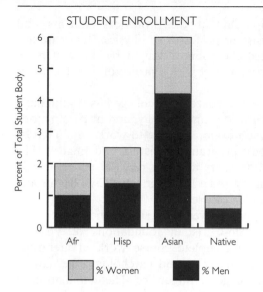

Percent of Total Student Body

Afr   Hisp   Asian   Native

% Women   % Men

Ethnic studies programs: None
Ethnic studies courses: The college offers more than eight Asian Studies courses, primarily focusing on history. The anthropology department offers two courses on Africa.
Organizations for non-white students: Black Student Union, Hispanic Club
Notable non-white alumni: na
Tenured faculty: na
Non-tenured faculty: na
Student-faculty ratio: 15:1
Administrators: na
Recent non-white speakers on campus: David DePriest (conductor, Oregon Symphony)

Reed College offers one of the most intense—and most respected—liberal arts educations in the country. And Reed students are more than up for the challenge; admissions standards at this 82-year-old school rival those at almost any of the best-known schools back East.

But there's an aspect to the Reed experience that sets it apart from almost any other school in the country: its student body, which has some of the most eclectic and individualistic students you'll find on any American college campus. At Reed, almost anything goes, although conservative Republicans will certainly feel out of place here. Liberal politics are in, as are tie-dyed T-shirts and torn jeans.

Which isn't to say Reedies, as Reed students affectionately refer to themselves, have a great deal of time on their hands to stage protests or to head to the nearby state capital to do some lobbying. Studies at Reed are demanding, and the disheveled look so common among many Reedies isn't due so much to all-night partying as to all-night studying. The studying has its rewards. The college has produced more Rhodes Scholars—30 in all—than any other liberal arts college in the country, and it has ranked first in all academic fields in the number of students who go on to earn their Ph.D.s.

Reed students expect a great deal of themselves academically, and pressure to do well is usually self-induced. There is little academic competition among students, no doubt fostered by the school's relaxed approach to the traditional grading system. Rather than earning a letter grade at the end of the term, students receive extensive written evaluations from professors. (Letter grades are recorded, but are available to students only upon request.) In addition, there is no dean's list or class ranking.

Students also have the benefit of working with faculty who genuinely want to see their students succeed, and over the course of the term, close relationships between students and professors usually develop. One of the professors students find particularly helpful is Mary James, an assistant professor of physics. There are few large lecture classes here; the typical Reed classroom is taught by the conference method, small classes of 10 to 20 students who meet with a professor who facilitates discussion.

Reed's academics are outstanding across the board. The college has traditionally been strong in the sciences, particularly chemistry and biology, and physics majors, after passing an Atomic Energy Commission exam, are able to work on a TRIGA nuclear reactor. Students also praise Reed's programs in history and English. The school's Eric V. Hauser Library (open 120 hours a week) recently underwent $7 million worth of renovations and has a gallery and a language lab. "Civil Rights and Liberties" is one of the school's more popular courses.

Reed requires all first-year students to take the yearlong Humanities 101 course, which focuses on the "classical and Judeo-Christian foundations of Western civilization." Students are also expected to complete course work in literature, philosophy, and the arts; history, the social sciences, and psychology; the natural sciences; and math, logic, or a foreign language or linguistics. The culmination of a student's years at Reed is the required senior thesis. Some recent thesis topics: "Verbal Aspects of Black English" and "Women as an Untapped Resource in Economic Development."

Despite Reed's liberal reputation, the campus is surprisingly racially and socio-economically homogenous. "Reed is 100 percent homogenized," complains a student. "Almost all students come from the same upper- and upper-middle class background, and because of this they often are out of touch with what it means to be a minority in this country."

Adds another student: "Most of the students gripe about [the enrollment of so few students of color at Reed] and many of us, due to the pressures of school and work and perhaps ignorance, are unconsciously apathetic toward changing this situation," says a student.

Students recently formed a Black Student Union and a Hispanic Club, but, according to one student, "because they're fairly new, they haven't yet thrown socials." The groups meet weekly, primarily for peer support.

There are no varsity sports at Reed, but students compete in numerous club sports, such as handball, rugby, and skiing, oftentimes against other schools in the Northwest. The school's Sports Center is one of the campus's most frequented spots.

Student organizations, however, are much more popular and often revolve around sociopolitical issues, such as Earth Day, the Environmental Coalition, and Abortion Rights Action. Says a student about the club life at Reed: "Some organizations such as Reed Out of Apartheid, the International Student Organization, the Community Service Project, and Amnesty International may focus on groups of minorities, such as Hispanic-Americans and African-Americans, and devote their time and effort toward changing the present system and helping minorities achieve a better life. It is hard for students, with the work load and the pressure at Reed, to form minority organizations or to keep them active. Reedies often see themselves as part of the larger community and not just as part of a minority. Overall, the fact that one is a minority seems to fall by the wayside as one is involved with sleeping, eating, going to conferences, labs, and lectures, studying, and all of the activities that most Reedies are involved in."

Portland has undergone a renaissance of sorts in recent years, and has won awards for its revitalized downtown. The city, which has a large Asian and Asian-American population, as well as smaller African-American and Hispanic communities, offers numerous theaters, a diverse array of restaurants, and the Portland Trail Blazers basketball team. Pioneer Courthouse Square is a popular downtown destination. However, according to one student, southeast Portland, the area immediately around the campus, is the site of a large number of hate crimes and white pride organizations in the city. Students add, however, that racist incidents in the area have rarely, if ever, affected Reed students.

Reed may not have enough students of color to provide a more familiar learning and social environment. But the student who chooses to come to school here will nonetheless be greeted by a supportive community of students and professors. "I would recommend my school to a prospective minority student as a place that *wants* to address his or her concern," says a student. "Reed is trying very hard to increase minority enrollment, but as with change, it is slow. I would recommend Reed to *anyone* who wants to pursue a rigorous academic education."

WILLAMETTE UNIVERSITY

Address: 900 State Street, Salem, OR 97301
Phone: (503) 370-6300
Director of Admissions: James M. Sumner
Multicultural Student Recruiter: na
1992–93 tuition and room and board: $17,350
Application deadline: 2/1
Financial aid application deadline: 2/1
Non-white freshman admissions: Applicants
for the class of '95: 163
Accepted: 87%
Accepted who enroll: 33%
Applicants accepted who rank in top
10% of high school class: 35%
In top 25%: 60%
Median SAT range: 450–580 V,
480–600 M
Median ACT range: 20–29
Full-time undergraduate enrollment: 1,659
Men: 45%
Women: 55%
Non-white students in
1988–89: 10%
1989–90: na
1990–91: 10%
1991–92: 12%

Students in-state: 50%
Top majors: 1. Psychology
2. Business/Economics 3. Political
Science
Retention rate of non-white students: na
**Scholarships exclusively for non-white
students:** Multicultural Achievement
Scholarships: 20 awarded each year;

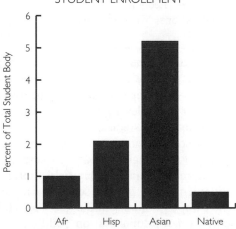

STUDENT ENROLLMENT

GEOGRAPHIC DISTRIBUTION OF STUDENTS

FACULTY

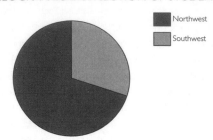

- Northwest
- Southwest

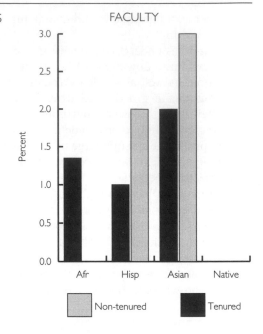

Non-tenured   Tenured

merit-based; each award valued at between $1,000 and $4,000.

Remediation programs: None

Academic support services: Tutoring is available in most academic subjects.

Ethnic studies programs: None

Ethnic studies courses: The university offers about seven courses in Japanese and Chinese Studies, involving history, political science, Japanese-language study, and art. The history department offers a course in African-American Studies; the political science department offers "Latin American Political Systems." Also offered is a "Minorities Seminar" and "World Views: Latin America."

Organizations for non-white students: Black Student Organization, American Indian Association, Hawaii Club, Unidos Por Fin

Notable non-white alumni: Augusto P. De La Torre (Economics; official, International Monetary Fund);

John West (Music; professional musician)

Tenured faculty: 74

Non-tenured faculty: 32

Student-faculty ratio: 13:1

Administrators: 83

African-American: 1 total

Hispanic: 1 total

Asian-American: 4 total

Native American: 1 total

Recent non-white speakers on campus:

Harry G. Britt (president, San Francisco Board of Supervisors); Nien Cheng (author); Giancarlo Esposito (actor)

Located across the street from the state capitol building in Salem, Willamette, founded in 1842, was the first university west of the Mississippi. Although the university primarily has regional appeal—nearly all of its students are from West Coast states—it provides rigorous and well-regarded programs in the liberal arts and pre-professional studies.

New construction and renovation have continued to upgrade Willamette's already beautiful, although compact, 57-acre campus. Most recently, the university opened the impressive Mark O. Hatfield Library, named for Oregon's senior senator and a Willamette alum, and the school's science center has undergone needed improvement. The campus's oldest building, Waller Hall, was rededicated in the fall of 1989 as the school's new administration building.

Political science is one of the university's top departments, and many majors take advantage of the internship possibilities at the state capitol building or at local government agencies. The school's well-regarded international studies program allows students to focus on one of four regions: Western European, Eastern European, East Asian, or Hispanic. Willamette's music department, with programs in performance and education, presents student and faculty recitals year-round. Languages, particularly French, are popular with students. The university also has small graduate schools of law and business.

Willamette enjoys a unique relationship with Tokyo International University ("our Japanese sister college"), which has an academic and residential building, completed in 1989, across the street from the campus. Willamette students have access to TIU's facilities and course offerings.

Due to its low undergraduate enrollment, Willamette students have the opportunity to work closely with their professors. Even large lecture classes have no more than 50 students, while the average class size is about 15. "Relationships with the faculty are very personal here, which is one of the reasons why I wanted to attend Willamette," says a student. "We have profs here who will take a student out to dinner."

The Office of Multicultural Affairs, located in the Putnam University Center, "always has tea, coffee, and goodies for anyone who just wants to stop by and relax," says an international studies major. The office, which hosts an international coffee hour every Thursday afternoon, also publishes a weekly newsletter that announces the events and activities sponsored by the school's cultural student groups. Joyce Greiner, director of the office, "is like a mom to many of us," adds the student. "She really cares for the students and she tries to get to know all of us. If you're in a weird mood for some reason, she'll sit you down and ask you what's wrong, and if she can't help you, she'll find someone on campus who can." Franklin Meyer, vice president for student affairs, whose office is near the Office of Multicultural Affairs, also works closely with students. "He's a very nice man," comments a student. "He's very approachable. Even if he's incredibly busy, he won't take a talk-to-me-later attitude. Students always come first for him, and he'll stop what he's doing to talk to any student."

The Unidos Pro Fin, with about "six or seven active members," focuses a lot of its energies on their annual weeklong celebration of Mexican Independence Day in September. Recently, the group brought onto campus guest speakers and sponsored panel discussions for area elementary and high school students. "The events get more and more successful each year," says a junior. As part of a fundraiser for a scholarship program, the group brought to campus Mexican dancers from the area. "More people from the community showed up than people from campus," says a student.

Each year in April, the various cultural student groups help sponsor an International Extravaganza, in which booths are set up around campus. During a recent year, a Latin band performed as part of the festivities. The Hawaii Club sponsors "a successful luau each year that is well attended."

Nearly 15 percent of Willamette's students are from foreign countries, which adds an international flavor to the campus. A popular residence on campus is the Willamette International Student House (WISH), a coed residence that can accommodate up to 37 students. "People who live in the house come from all over the world, including Bulgaria, Russia, Kuwait, Mexico, and, of course, America," says a student. "We're like a family here. It's a special place. We have our own cook, except on weekends, because she has those days off. Each weekday a table is set aside in the dining room for a particular language where only that language can be spoken, such as Chinese, Japanese, or French."

Willamette is a school that has been relatively free of blatant racist incidents, according to students, but there was an uproar on campus recently when a series of racist notes were left on an African-American student's dorm door. "The whole campus turned out on the plaza to demonstrate against the incidents," says a student. "The president and a lot of other administrators spoke about how they deplored the incidents and a lot of people wore rainbow ribbons symbolizing opposition to racism. Fliers were also put in everybody's mailbox that said something like 'I'm Against Racism.' It was amazing to see so many on campus turn out for the demonstration."

Although more than a third of the students belong to one or another of the school's five fraternities or three sororities, all of which are nationally affiliated, the Greek system does not dominate the social scene here. "The Greeks have their functions, but there is no tension between us," says a non-Greek. "There are some minority students in the Greek living units, not a lot, but there are some. But if a student doesn't want to be in a house, it's not because of race. It just comes down to the person and whether he or she wants to be a member of a Greek organization." Most weekend parties, however, take place in the fraternities, but students can also find alternatives to the Greek functions at the Bistro, a student-run coffeehouse, or at any of the other on-campus events—including two annual film series or clubs sponsored by the Associated Students of Willamette University, the school's student-programming board.

Salem offers a variety of off-campus opportunities, including Nordstrom Mall, more than ten cinemas within six blocks, and numerous restaurants. The city also has its own symphony and live theater. When students find Salem limiting, as many often do, they can travel to Portland and Eugene, the state's largest cities, both within an hour's drive of campus.

Although the university's enrollment of American-born students of color is tiny—particularly among African-Americans and Hispanics—Willamette's atmosphere is nonetheless, says a student, "warm and supportive of *all* students." The emphasis is hers, not ours.

PENNSYLVANIA

ALLEGHENY COLLEGE

Address: Meadville, PA 16335
Phone: (814) 332-4351 / (800) 521-5293
Director of Admissions: Gayle W. Pollock
Multicultural Student Recruiter: Jonathan
  Pittman
1991–92 tuition: $14,600
Room and board: $4,120
Application deadline: 2/15
Financial aid application deadline: 2/15

Non-white freshman admissions: Applicants
  for the class of '95: 239
  Accepted: 79.5%
  Accepted who enroll: 24.7%
  Applicants accepted who rank in top
  10% of high school class: 25%
  In top 25%: 65%
  Median SAT: na
  Median ACT: na
Full-time undergraduate enrollment: 1,850
  Men: 48%
  Women: 52%
Non-white students in
  1987–88: 5%
  1988–89: 6%
  1989–90: 6.4%
  1990–91: 6.7%
Geographic distribution of students: na
Students In-state: 23%
Top majors: 1. Biology
  2. Economics/Psychology 3. Political Science
Retention rate of non-white students:
  60%–70%
**Scholarships exclusively for non-white
  students:** None

Remediation programs: The college offers
  courses in basic writing and math, as well
  as the Educational Enhancement
  Program for at-risk students who do not
  meet usual admissions criteria.
  Participation in summer preparatory
  program, which includes special advising,
  counseling, and tutoring, is required.
Academic support services: Peer tutoring is
  offered in most academic subjects, and
  the school's Counseling Center provides
  study skills workshops. The school also
  offers a Reading Improvement Program,
  a Writing Center, and a Mathematics
  Improvement Program.

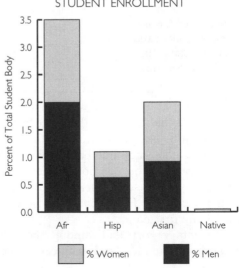

STUDENT ENROLLMENT

Ethnic studies programs: Allegheny offers a Black Studies minor, an interdisciplinary program that includes courses in the English, history, philosophy, political science, religion, and sociology/anthropology departments. The school also offers interdisciplinary programs in Latin American and Caribbean Studies.

Ethnic studies courses: The college's curriculum includes several courses in Asian Studies, as well as a course of study in Asian-American Literature.

Organizations for non-white students: Advancement of Black Culture, Phi Beta Sigma, Zeta Phi Beta, Multicultural Coalition, Unión Latina, Black Cultural Residence for Men, Black Cultural Residence for Women

Notable non-white alumni: Paul Ssemogerere (Political Science; minister for foreign affairs, Uganda); Robert A. Marchman (Political Science; director of enforcement, New York Stock Exchange); David F. Johnson (Chemistry; former chief, laboratory of analytical chemistry, NIH); Herbert Niles, Jr. (Pre-medicine; president, Medical Society for the District of Columbia); Richard O. Butcher (Pre-medicine; national board member, National Medical Association)

Tenured faculty: 75

Non-tenured faculty: 96

Student-faculty ratio: 11:1

Administrators: 102

African-American: 3%

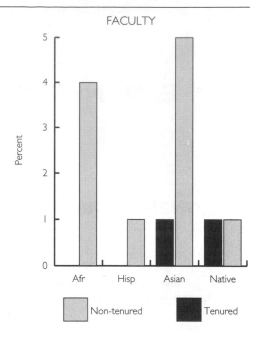

FACULTY

Hispanic: 2%

Asian-American: 2%

Native American: 0

Recent non-white speakers on campus: Derrick Bell (author); Katie Geneva Cannon (associate professor, Episcopal Divinity School); James A. Adams (chairperson, natural sciences department, University of Maryland at Eastern Shore); Constance Garcia-Barrio (author); William Willimon (professor of Christian ministry, Duke University); Nikki Giovanni (poet); Paule Marshall (author)

There's a joke about the weather in Meadville, Pennsylvania, Allegheny College's hometown, that goes something like this: "How do I get to Meadville?" The response: "Drive until you hit the rain and then look for the signs."

The weather may not be a selling point for Allegheny, situated on a beautiful 72-acre campus, but the possibilities for close interaction with faculty are. "I've got friends at a state school here in Pennsylvania where being one in the crowd is usual in many courses. Here, that's almost an impossibility, since all my professors know me by my first name."

Students report that among the school's best departments are psychology, English, economics, and political science, while chemistry and biology are also considered tops, as is evident from these programs' high enrollments. Nearly a third of the students major in one of these two areas. Allegheny students enjoy high placement records into medical and law schools. To graduate, students must complete general education requirements that include a freshman seminar that focuses on a single topic, such as "Humor" or "Political Theory," and courses in the humanities and the social and natural sciences. Seniors must also complete an independent project in their major, which usually involves an oral defense before faculty members.

Although the courses in the Black Studies program are not, according to students, taught by the school's best professors, Laura Quinn, an assistant professor of English, is well respected. "Although she's not black, she's one of those people who know a lot about African-American and Native American culture," says a student. "She also goes out of her way to help." Quinn's "Alternative Traditions to American Literature" course, which in a recent year focused on the works of Native Americans and African-Americans, has been well received by students.

For academic assistance, students are able to turn to the services of the Writing Center. "The tutors at the center are good at helping you to see your flaws," says a student. "They'll tell you that you can do better than that, and they'll point to what needs improving." Tutors in other departments are also helpful, report students.

Allegheny is primarily a residential campus, with most students staying put on weekends. The town of Meadville offers little social or cultural activity, so students rely mostly on what's available on campus. For many of the students at Allegheny, this means fraternity parties, as more than half of the student body joins one or another of the school's six fraternities or six sororities. "The Greek system is intense here. When a girl can't get into the sorority of her choice, she cries for nearly a semester. Then she'll make another attempt to get into the same sorority." The system is reasonably integrated. According to one student, in a recent year about 10 African-Americans, mostly men, were members of fraternities and sororities, as were two Hispanic students and several Asian-American students.

As an alternative to the Greek system, students take advantage of the activities at the Campus Center, which puts on Wednesday-night movies. For Black History Month, the center showed *Juice* and *Boyz 'N the Hood*. Intramural competition, especially between fraternities, and varsity sports are popular.

Unión Latina has about 15 active members and meets weekly. Much of the energy of Unión Latina focuses on the activities for Latin Cultural Week, an annual event held on campus. The week features speakers and convocations. Unión Latina was reorganized during the 1991–92 school year after some personal infighting among members. During a recent year, the members of Unión Latina's executive board included whites, Asians, African-Americans, and one Latin American student.

The Advancement of Black Culture, which has about 45 members, meets regularly in the Black Cultural Center in Murray Hall, which has a library. ABC sponsors an orientation program for new students, events for Black History Month, and an alumni weekend.

Recently, the school sponsored a Black Cultural Floor. In the spring of 1992, three

African-American students lived on the floor. Residents of the floor have sponsored movies, a panel discussion about racism on the campus, and a dinner with members of other theme houses "so we can all get to know each other better."

The student body at Allegheny is more homogeneous than most. One student describes the typical Allegheny student as "upper-middle-class, from a small town outside of a large city, where he or she has never interacted with students of color." For one student from a large city, the transition from high school to college in Meadville has at times been difficult, but, she says, "my experiences here have taught me to be a stronger person. I often miss not going to school with more minority students, and coming here has been a challenge, but I've gotten a good education and I've liked a lot of my professors."

BRYN MAWR COLLEGE

Women's college
Address: Ely House, Bryn Mawr, PA 19010
Phone: (215) 526-5152
Director of Admissions: Elizabeth Vermey
Multicultural Student Recruiter: na
1993–94 tuition: $17,135
Room and board: $6,450
Application deadline: Early decision: 11/15; regular decision: 1/15
Financial aid application deadline: Early decision: 11/15; regular decision: 1/15
Non-white freshman admissions: Applicants for the class of '97: 381
    Accepted: 51%
    Accepted who enroll: 36%
    Applicants accepted who rank in top 10% of high school class: 70%
    In top 25%: 89%
    Median SAT: na
    Median ACT: na
Full-time undergraduate enrollment: 1,200
Non-white students in
    1988–89: 22%
    1989–90: 24%
    1990–91: 24%
    1991–92: 22%
Geographic distribution of students: na
Top majors: 1. English 2. Political Science 3. Biology
Retention rate of non-white students: 85%
Scholarships exclusively for non-white students: None

Remediation programs: None
Academic support services: The college offers study skills tutoring and academic tutoring in most subjects.
Ethnic studies programs: The college offers majors in Africana and East Asian Studies, and students may supplement any major with concentrations in Hispanic and Hispanic-American Studies.
Ethnic studies courses: Bryn Mawr offers "Breaking the Silence: The Asian Experience in America," as well as courses in American ethnic and racial studies.
Organizations for non-white students: Asian Students Association, Hispanic Student

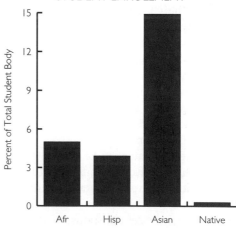

STUDENT ENROLLMENT

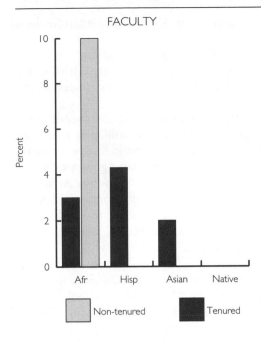

FACULTY

Percent

Non-tenured   Tenured

Afr   Hisp   Asian   Native

Association, COLOR, Minority Coalition, Sisterhood (African-American student association), South Asian Women, Perry House (African-American cultural center), Hispanic/Latina Cultural Center

Notable non-white alumnae: na

Tenured faculty: 92

Non-tenured faculty: 28

Student-faculty ratio: 9:1

Administrators: na

   African-American: 3%

   Hispanic: 1%

   Asian-American: 5%

   Native American: 1

Recent non-white speakers on campus:

   Jamaica Kincaid (author); Marian Wright Edelman (president, Children's Defense Fund); Gaiash Kibos (Native American chief); Wilson Goode (former mayor of Philadelphia)

Bryn Mawr does well what women's colleges do best: it graduates confident, intelligent women into the work force and into graduate schools. During the years 1986 to 1989, for example, *all* Bryn Mawr students who applied to law school were admitted, as were 93 percent of those who applied to medical school; and in a 1989 survey, the college ranked first in the country—ahead of Harvard and Yale—in the percentage of undergraduates who earned Ph.D.s in the social sciences, humanities, and languages during the years 1977 to 1986.

Bryn Mawr is a rigorous liberal arts college that attracts students from nearly every state in the nation and dozens of foreign countries. The school has excellent programs in the classics, English, and the sciences. Psychology, sociology, archaeology, art history, and Russian are also outstanding.

The college recently established an Africana Studies program, but, according to a student, "the word is not in yet about how effective it is, but we're excited it's here. There's been a high demand on campus for these courses for a while." "Stability and Change in Modern Africa" is one of the program's more popular courses. To graduate, students must complete distribution requirements in the humanities, math, the social sciences, and the laboratory sciences, and they must show a proficiency in a foreign language and in English composition.

Bryn Mawr enjoys a unique cooperative arrangement with Haverford College, located just 1.2 miles away or, as one student put it, "about fifteen minutes away on foot." A shuttle van that runs twice an hour also connects the campuses. Students on both campuses cross-register for courses and majors, live on either campus, and participate in co-sponsored extracurricular activities. Bryn Mawr students are also able to enroll in courses at the University of Pennsylvania, in Philadelphia, or

Swarthmore College, but they report that interaction with these schools is less frequent because of the distances to them.

Bryn Mawr professors have high expectations of their students, and students expect a lot of themselves. But students praise the close interaction they have with faculty. "The low student-to-faculty ratio they have here is one of the school's strongest suits," comments a student.

The college has several faculty and staff members who are especially supportive of students of color. Rhonda Hughes, a math professor, "is always willing to meet with you and help you, no matter which department you're majoring in," says a biology major. "She's put me in touch with several of her friends and colleagues around the country who are involved in areas I'm interested in pursuing." Alfonso Albana, a professor of physics and coordinator of the college's Minority Women in Science program, also works closely with students. Students also point to Christopher Ridenhour, an assistant director of admissions, and Joyce Miller, director of the Office for Institutional Diversity, as strong supporters.

For social outlets, students are able to take advantage of the activities and support provided by the school's cultural organizations. Hispanic Student Association (HSA), established on campus in 1988, has about 15 members. "The group is democratic and does whatever the members want it to do," observes a student leader. "We've sponsored speakers, parties with Hispanic groups at Haverford and Swarthmore colleges, and an annual film series." Once a week, HSA members participate in a tutoring program in conjunction with the Catholic Social Services agency in Philadelphia. Group members tutor Hispanic children on a one-to-one basis.

The Asian Students Association is, says a recent graduate, "a cultural organization that has a lot of potential as both a support group and a political force as needed. It's an opportunity to get Asian women to interact with each other as friends and then to realize their role as Asian women. We try to get them to feel stronger about their backgrounds and take pride in their culture. During the first semester, we sponsor Asian Awareness Month. We have movies, speakers, panel discussions, and [in a recent year] we had several events geared toward contemporary Japanese art, like Corky Lee's photography show."

Sisterhood, an African-American student group with about 30 active members, is made up of both African-American and international black students. For Black History Month, Sisterhood sponsors an annual panel discussion with professors and students. In a recent year, a panel discussion focused on the issue of affirmative action. "There was an excellent turnout for the discussion, which in large part was a response to an editorial in the bi-college [Bryn Mawr/Haverford] newspaper. The article was about how minority students shouldn't be accepted into the country's top schools because they lower standards." Sisterhood also helps sponsor a gospel choir concert each year in which groups from area churches and colleges perform, as well as a bazaar in which jewelry, books, and clothing are sold. Because the college begins its spring semester on Martin Luther King, Jr., Day each year, some Sisterhood members are petitioning the administration to seek alternatives.

Sisterhood meetings are usually held in the Perry House, a residence of interest to students of African descent. The house has a large living room, a kitchen, and a small library, as well as upstairs living quarters for seven students.

By far the most common extracurricular activity at Bryn Mawr is studying, and students say they are much "more uptight" about their studies than students at other schools. Weekend and late-night studying is the norm, and the school's social life usually consists of conversations with friends at the library or in the dorms. Ever since nearby Haverford went coed in 1970, the dating scene isn't what it used to be; the women on the campuses outnumber the men by almost three to one.

For parties, students will generally head off campus, either to Haverford or Philadelphia, which is about twenty minutes away by train—the station is two blocks from campus. Temple University and the University of Pennsylvania, both in Philadelphia, are host to a variety of parties and fraternity step shows that students frequently attend. Other opportunities in the city include the Philadelphia Museum of Art, the country's third largest, as well as a rich diversity of neighborhoods, restaurants, clubs, and theaters. The town of Bryn Mawr is primarily an affluent white residential community that offers little to students.

Intramural sports don't get much following at Bryn Mawr, although in recent years the school's varsity soccer, gymnastics, and swimming teams have gone to national championships.

Bryn Mawr has long attracted a liberal student body. Students are active pro-choicers and feminists, and gay and lesbian issues are in the forefront. But students say that within this liberal atmosphere there is also a great deal of diversity—from mainstream moderate to radical. While students don't always come here fans of single-sex education, they generally graduate as diehard loyalists, I'd-do-it-again types. "I like the fact that Bryn Mawr is all women, and I'd never trade that," says a chemistry major. "At a women's college you get—well, I wouldn't say special treatment, but it is, I guess. There's more focus on you, and you're appreciated for being a woman. It's not realistic, I know, because you won't be treated the same way out in the world, but it makes for better learning. You don't feel pressured like you would in a coed environment."

Bryn Mawr is a serious and intellectual place. And, for women, it does what it sets out to do. Says a recent graduate: "I don't know if it's the college experience in general or just Bryn Mawr, but when I call friends from home now, they tell me, 'You sound so confident and self-assured, very positive.' Bryn Mawr seems to be unique in that you find yourself talking about different things, with a different attitude."

BUCKNELL UNIVERSITY

Address: Lewisburg, PA 17837
Phone: (717) 524-1101
Director of Admissions: Mark D. Davies
Multicultural Student Recruiter: Terry Carter
1991–92 tuition: $15,550
Room and board: $3,825
Application deadline: 1/1
Financial aid application deadline: 2/1

Non-white freshman admissions: Applicants for the class of '94: 277
Accepted: 67%
Accepted who enroll: 17%
Applicants accepted who rank in top 10% of high school class: 48%
In top 25%: 90%

Median SAT: 480–620 V, 500–650 M
Median ACT: na
Full-time undergraduate enrollment: 3,350
  Men: 54%
  Women: 46%

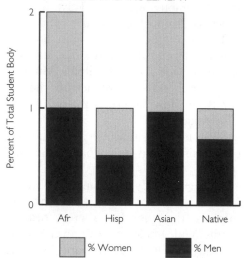

STUDENT ENROLLMENT

Non-white students in
  1987–88: 5%
  1988–89: 5%
  1989–90: 6%
  1990–91: 6%

GEOGRAPHIC DISTRIBUTION OF STUDENTS

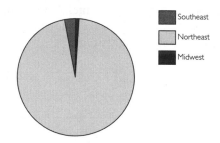

Southeast
Northeast
Midwest

Students In-state: na
Top majors: 1. Economics 2. Business
  Administration 3. Engineering
Retention rate of non-white students: 86%
**Scholarships exclusively for non-white
  students:** None

Remediation programs: None
Academic support services: The Writing
  Center and peer tutors are available.
Ethnic studies programs: The university
  offers an interdisciplinary Black Studies
  minor, involving the English, economics,
  history, geography, psychology, religion,
  and sociology departments.
Ethnic studies courses: na
Organizations for non-white students:
  African-American Culture Society,
  Cumbre (Hispanic society)
Notable non-white alumni: na
Tenured faculty: 180
Non-tenured faculty: 65

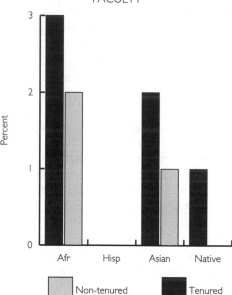

FACULTY

Student-faculty ratio: 14:1
Administrators: 80
  African-American: 4%
  Hispanic: 0
  Asian-American: 0
  Native American: 0
Recent non-white speakers on campus: Dick
  Gregory (political activist); Helen
  Walker-Hill (composer)

Bucknell University offers its largely career-conscious students top-notch programs in business administration and engineering, as well as in the liberal arts and sciences. Students attracted to Bucknell tend to be conservative and to come from the upper-middle-class suburbs of New England and the Middle Atlantic states.

Bucknell has long been known for its outstanding engineering programs, and for good reason. The school boasts six areas of engineering study (engineering sciences, chemical, civil, computer science, electrical, and mechanical) as well as state-of-the-art equipment in the recently renovated Charles A. Dana Engineering Building. With only about 600 majors enrolled in the engineering programs, students are also able to work closely with professors. Says a recent graduate of the programs' student-faculty interaction: "What I admire most about Bucknell is the relationships that students can develop with professors. I was genuinely surprised at how accessible the professors are to their students."

In the liberal arts, Bucknell is strongest in economics, psychology, English, international relations, and Japanese Studies and East Asian Studies. Management is one of the school's most competitive, and popular, programs. Bucknell's offerings in the fine arts—such as theater, music, and dance—were recently enhanced with the opening of the Weiss Center for the Performing Arts. The school's Black Studies minor is generally praised by students. According to a student minoring in the area: "Course selection is very good and the professors are very knowledgeable." "Blacks in Mass Media" is one of the program's more popular courses.

The school's African-American Culture Society offers a variety of activities to its 45 active student members. Society members usually meet in a lounge in the Student Forum. During Black History Month, the group sponsors speakers and a film series. In December, members also sponsor a Kwanzaa celebration. Bucknell is located close to Lycoming College, Bloomsburg State, Susquehanna, and Penn State, and interaction between the universities is frequent, particularly when it comes to planning cultural events.

To raise awareness of various cultures on campus, in 1986 Bucknell established the Multiculture Center. Meetings of the campus chapter of the NAACP are usually held in the center, which has a small library that contains information about graduate school fellowships. Alem Asres, director of the center, joined Bucknell's staff in September 1991. According to a student active in the African-American Culture Society, Asres has been meeting with students to discuss different aspects of campus life. Asres was successful in getting the campus community to recognize Martin Luther King, Jr., Day. He organized a reception in honor of Dr. King, which "consisted of a luncheon where faculty and administrators expressed their feelings about King." Speakers included African-American and white administrators and staff members.

Outside of the school's incredibly strong Greek system—fraternity parties are among Bucknell's biggest social events—students participate in a diverse array of clubs, from the Camera Club to the Cycling Club. Sports are also an important aspect of a typical Bucknell student's life, either as participant or as fan. Men's football and basketball enjoy a following, while women's field hockey and tennis events can also get competitive. Bucknell has an 18-hole golf course. The university's campus itself is worth mentioning; its 300 beautiful acres grace the edge of the Susquehanna River, the crew team's practice field.

The town of Lewisburg is, as students say, "three hours from everywhere." The town has a movie theater, stores for shopping, and a variety of restaurants, as well as a hand-dipped-ice-cream store that gets the thumbs-up from students. Bucknell is close enough for the energetic to make day trips to New York City, Philadelphia, and Washington, DC.

Like other liberal arts colleges and universities in central Pennsylvania, Bucknell is, in every sense of the word, a homogeneous place to go to school. The majority of students vote Republican, come from well-to-do families, and are happy in their fraternities and sororities. Students who see this as intimidating won't be content here. But for students who consider it a challenge, the rewards include a degree from one of the country's more respected institutions of higher education. "Bucknell is a lot of work, a lot of fun. My experience here has taught me to not give up on what I believe in and has given me direction. Bucknell has definitely been a learning experience for me."

CARNEGIE-MELLON UNIVERSITY

Address: Pittsburgh, PA 15213
Phone: (412) 268-2082
Director of Admissions: Michael Steidel
Multicultural Student Recruiter: Michael White

1992–93 tuition: $16,000
Room and board: $5,500
Application deadline: 2/1
Financial aid application deadline: 2/15

There isn't much that Carnegie-Mellon University students take as seriously as they do their academics, but the annual buggy race, part of Spring Carnival, the school's biggest extravaganza, comes in a close second. "With all of the demands placed on us academically here, the carnival is a must, and the buggy race is one of the weekend's high points," says a student.

For the buggy race many CMU organizations—from fraternities to cultural groups—create and race the most aerodynamic vehicles possible. "The engineers of each of the groups design the buggies, and the buggies get more sophisticated each year. I don't have any part in designing them, but they're amazing to watch in action," says a music major. And what's more, the event's biggest winner of late hasn't been one of the school's engineering societies, but SPIRIT, CMU's African-American student organization. "We're the team to beat," says a student. "We won in 1988, '89, and '91, and we're looking to win again."

As might be expected on a campus where there are enough engineers to sponsor such an event each year, CMU is a hot engineering school. If you can survive the engineering program here, job prospects are good. The school's chemical and electrical engineering programs are nationally recognized. CMU also boasts top programs on the other end of the academic spectrum; CMU's drama and music programs—two of the best such programs in the country—have graduated the likes of Ted Danson and Shari Belafonte. However, most of the other humanities programs are considered weaker, particularly foreign languages. Other strong CMU programs are architecture and biology. To graduate, all CMU students must take an entry-level writing course as well as a computer skills workshop. CMU is divided into six colleges; because of the requirements imposed by each college on its students, there is little interaction among students in these areas.

To say that CMU stresses computer literacy is nearly an understatement. Even beyond the required computer skills workshop, the university incorporates computers into almost every academic department. In a first-year philosophy course required of humanities majors, for example, students use computers for logic problems. The philosophy department even offers a major course of study in logic and computation and a Ph.D. program in computational linguistics.

CMU is regarded as one of the most academically demanding schools in the country. At many of the country's top universities, the hard part is getting in. At CMU, getting in *and* surviving its academic rigors can be tough, although students concede that the engineers and science majors have it the toughest. Students say that professors are accessible, but that the quality of teaching sometimes suffers due to some of the professors' emphasis on their own research.

The school's Carnegie-Mellon Action Project (CMAP), established in 1968 and located in Hamburg Hall, "does a good job in helping minority students get a handle on academics and offering emotional support," says a student. Gloria Hill, director of the program, "is accessible and willing to talk to students whenever she has a free moment. The office has non-white counselors who are helpful. Members of SPIRIT also offer tutoring services, primarily in math and physics.

SPIRIT, the school's most active cultural student group, "compensates for a lack of cultural activity on campus," says a student. "For Black History Month there is never a shortage of activities. We've had lawyers from around the area come and speak, as well as many other professionals. We've, of course, had parties. It's a very productive month for us." "But," adds the student, "we have had a hard time pulling the freshmen into the organization." SPIRIT also provides two successful tutoring programs for area children of elementary and high school age.

Although the majority of the school's African-American students hail from Philadelphia, Washington, DC, and Maryland, students also come from as far as California, Nigeria, and Trinidad. "This is a family, with a cause, as in coordinating events for Black History Month," says a student. Adds another student: "The African-American students here are pretty tight with one another. Basically, we know that we're all here for each other."

Because the enrollment of African-Americans at CMU is relatively small, SPIRIT networks with area African-American student unions, particularly at the University of Pittsburgh.

The university sponsors a living unit for African-American students called the SPIRIT House, which "has a great view of the intramural fields across the street," says a student. The coed house, which in a recent year had four men and five women, has a full kitchen, a fireplace, and a living room, "where some of the SPIRIT meetings take place." Students must apply to live in the house. "Out of the nine who live here now, all but three will be back next fall. We got enough applications to fill the spots, and we had to reject one person."

Although academics and on-campus activities absorb much of a CMU student's time, students do manage to get off campus now and then. Pittsburgh has undergone a rebirth in the past few years. The city, which has prominent African-American and Hispanic communities, is home to the Pittsburgh Pirates baseball team, and draws popular performers to the area. Students also visit restaurants, bars, and clubs in the area.

With CMU's academic diversity, there really isn't a typical CMU student. "There are some very open-minded people here, and I've never come across anyone who's been blatantly racist," comments a student. "The gay student group is probably one of the most active on campus these days. They took out a page in the campus newspaper called CMU-Out, where lots of students came out. The women's group is also very active."

There is one word, however, that can describe the majority of CMU students: pre-professional. There are few "lost" liberal arts students wondering about life and where it will lead them. Most CMU students are directed when it comes to their future careers, and they are hot job prospects. "I've had to grin and bear the academics. I'd always wanted to come to school here, but the idealized version of this place is certainly different than the reality. The professors and the students work on a professional level. They nurture you. It's intense, but when I get out in the real world, I know I'll be prepared."

DICKINSON COLLEGE

Address: P.O. Box 1773, Carlisle, PA 17013
Phone: (717) 245-1231
Director of Admissions: J. Larry Mench
Multicultural Student Recruiter: na
1993–94 tuition: $17,660
Room and board: $4,930
Application deadline: 3/1
Financial aid application deadline: 2/15
Non-white freshman admissions: Applicants
    for the class of '94: 259
    Accepted: 73%
    Accepted who enroll: 18%
    Applicants accepted who rank in top
    10% of high school class: 35%
    In top 25%: 65%
    Median SAT range: 470–590 V, 530–630 M
    Median ACT: na
Full-time undergraduate enrollment: 2,000
    Men: 47%
    Women: 53%

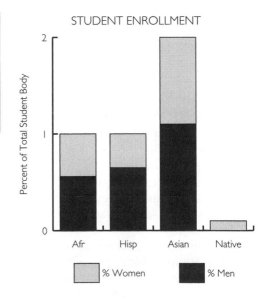

STUDENT ENROLLMENT

Percent of Total Student Body

Afr   Hisp   Asian   Native

% Women   % Men

GEOGRAPHIC DISTRIBUTION OF STUDENTS

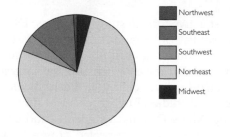

- ■ Northwest
- ■ Southeast
- ■ Southwest
- □ Northeast
- ■ Midwest

Organizations for non-white students: African-American Society, Latin American Club, East Asian Society, Multicultural House, African-American/West Indian Awareness Group, East Asian House

Notable non-white alumni: na

Tenured faculty: 94

Non-tenured faculty: 68

Non-white students in
  1987–88: 3%
  1988–89: 4%
  1989–90: 4%
  1990–91: 5%

Students In-state: 25%

Top majors: 1. Economics 2. Political Science 3. Psychology

Retention rate of non-white students: 79%

Scholarships exclusively for non-white students: None

Remediation programs: None

Academic support services: Peer tutoring is available in most academic subjects

Ethnic studies programs: The college offers a certificate program in Latin American Studies, which involves language study, economics, political science, and anthropology. The college also offers an East Asian Studies major, an interdisciplinary program involving history, music, religion, and political science. Instruction is available in the Chinese and Japanese languages.

Ethnic studies courses: Courses in African-American studies include "Race and Racism in America," "Afro-American History," and "The Black Experience." Five other courses, including "Comparative Race and Group Relations," focus on the American minority experience.

FACULTY

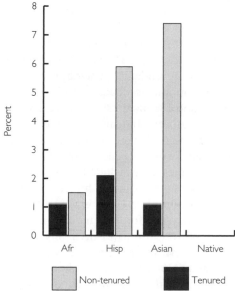

Non-tenured   Tenured

Student-faculty ratio: 11:1

Administrators: 73
  African-American: 2.8%
  Hispanic: 0
  Asian-American: 1.4%
  Native American: 0

Recent non-white speakers on campus: Sonia Sanchez (poet); Louise Bias (mother of former basketball star Len Bias); Ruby Olson (Haliua Sapom Tribe)

Dickinson College doesn't only provide its students with a quality liberal arts education, an active Greek system, and a variety of internship possibilities. The college, founded in 1773, before the signing of the Declaration of Independence, also ensures—with cross-cultural and foreign-language requirements—that students learn about the world beyond Carlisle, Pennsylvania.

Dickinson sponsors one of the country's most active foreign study programs. Each year more than a quarter of its student body studies off campus, in such locales as Italy, Japan, Russia, Spain, and Cameroon. In addition, almost all of the college's foreign-language programs are excellent. In fact, Dickinson graduates the largest number of language majors of any undergraduate private college in Pennsylvania. Dickinson's departments of policy and management studies, English, classical studies, history, economics, and biology are also strong. Many Dickinson students choose to double-major; a popular combination is the school's highly respected programs in political science and East Asian Studies. Dickinson's Latin American Studies program is said by one student to be "small but solid." The school's "African-American Novel" course has been well received by students.

Two East Asian Studies faculty members—Ann Hill, assistant professor of anthropology, and Harry Krebs, associate professor of East Asian Studies—are well regarded by students. "Their approaches are unique," says a student. "They encourage discussion and feedback." Professor Krebs has been the recipient of two awards at Dickinson for his outstanding teaching.

To graduate, students must take a freshman seminar, an interdisciplinary course that introduces students to liberal arts at the college. Each seminar focuses on a different topic, and students choose the one they'd like to study from a list of more than 30; recent topics have included "Playwrighting" and "Physics and Dance." Students must also take courses in the humanities, social sciences, and natural and mathematical sciences. To satisfy the cross-cultural studies requirement, students must show a proficiency in a foreign language and take a course in comparative civilizations.

Dickinson graduates definitely interest graduate school admissions offices. Over the past five years, 92 percent of its students applying to law school were accepted, 99 percent of its business school applicants were also accepted, as were 85 percent of its medical and dental school applicants. To help students gain work experience, Dickinson sponsors an active internship program during the academic year. About 150 students participated in the program in 1990. Some recent internships were with AT&T Communications, the Department of Justice, and Merrill Lynch.

Getting to know your professors at Dickinson is no problem, as most classes have no more than 20 students and are often taught in seminars; foreign-language professors can often be found at the foreign-language theme houses for lunch. For additional academic support, students take advantage of the school's peer tutoring services, which, according to one student, are "available in every subject, from Russian to calculus."

The school's three main cultural student groups—the African-American Society (AAS), the Latin American Club (LAC), and the East Asian Society—offer primarily peer support for members, although each sometimes sponsors guest lectures, movie nights, and other events. During a recent year, the AAS sponsored a basketball tournament that involved community residents. The Latin American Club recently sponsored Reggae Rhythms, a night of reggae music that featured a live band and dancing, and the East Asian Society sponsored a potluck dinner of East Asian dishes.

Dickinson's Office of Multicultural Affairs assists student groups in their programming. The office also publishes each year a student-written newsletter that focuses on local, national, and international topics. Career and graduate school information are also included in the newsletter. During the spring semester, the office, along with the cultural student groups, sponsors the Black Arts Festival/Multicultural Fair, a four-day event that features visiting lecturers and artists and displays. Recent performance groups have included the Peking Opera and the Asian-American Dance Theater.

The office's director, Pamela Blake, is "an excellent listener and adviser, not only on club matters but also on personal matters," says a student. Blake also advises the AAS, the LAC, and the Multicultural House, a student residence. For support, students also turn to Arturo Fox, a professor of Spanish. "He is aware of the lack of unity on campus among Hispanic students, and he gives me helpful suggestions and advice on personal as well as academic problems."

Dickinson offers an impressive amount of housing options to students. The majority of students live in the school's coed and single-sex dormitories. Each year, the resident advisers of the dorms are required to provide cultural programming to residents. Workshops involve speakers and role-playing sessions in which students pretend they're members of other ethnic or racial groups. Other housing options, for upperclass students, include the Multicultural House, an African-American/West Indian Awareness Group House, and an East Asian House. Residence in the houses is open to both white and non-white students who are active in sponsoring cultural events and activities during the school year. Last year, for example, the African-American/West Indian Awareness Group House and Latin American Club members sponsored a Black Cultural Festival, which presented art displays and speakers.

Most of Dickinson's social life, especially on the weekends, centers on its predominantly white Greek system. The Campus Activities Board, which is made up of numerous committees, seeks to provide alternatives to Greek life by sponsoring comedy nights, musicians, and other performers. Two film societies—Dickincinema and the Film Society—bring movies to campus on a regular basis. Popular on-campus student hangouts are Union Station, the Lumberyard, and the Kline Life/Sports Learning Center. The college brings a great deal of culture and political programming to campus through its lecture series, most notably the Public Affairs Symposium.

Carlisle, a predominantly white community of about 20,000 residents, has shopping malls, numerous pizza restaurants, and a movie theater complex. However, as most of the social life at school takes place on campus, students say they rarely venture into town. For a taste of urban life, students will sometimes travel to Harrisburg, about twenty miles away, or Baltimore, about a hundred miles away. Philadelphia and Washington, DC, are both about a two-and-a-half-hour drive from the school. Cars are a must for those looking to get off campus; there is little in the way of public transportation.

Dickinson has a great deal in common with some of its peer institutions in central and southern Pennsylvania. Students are relatively conservative, usually have a pre-professional bent, and there is little racial or cultural diversity among their student bodies. Attending school at Dickinson, according to one student, can at times be a lonely and frustrating experience, but, she adds, "it will definitely help you with your future, especially if you plan to become part of corporate America, a politician, or a doctor. Dickinson is a microcosm of those worlds."

FRANKLIN AND MARSHALL COLLEGE

Address: 637 College Avenue, Lancaster,
  PA 17604-3003
Phone: (717) 291-3951
Director of Admissions: Peter Van Buckirk
Multicultural Student Recruiter: Kathryn P.
  Blaisdell
1993–94 tuition: $19,675
Room and board: $3,980
Application deadline: 2/1
Financial aid application deadline: 2/1
Non-white freshman admissions: Applicants
  for the class of '95: 749
  Accepted: 43.6%
  Accepted who enroll: 29.1%
  Applicants accepted who rank in top
  10% of high school class: 47.4%
  In top 25%: 66.7%
  Median SAT: na
  Median ACT: na
Full-time undergraduate enrollment: 1,800
  Men: 55%
  Women: 45%

STUDENT ENROLLMENT

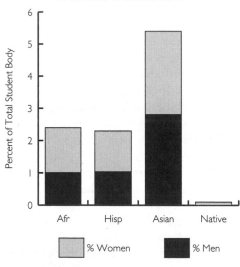

Non-white students in
  1987–88: na
  1988–89: na

1989–90: na
1990–91: 7.6%
1991–92: 14%

GEOGRAPHIC DISTRIBUTION OF STUDENTS

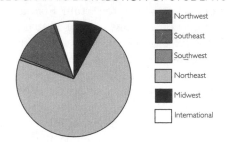

- Northwest
- Southeast
- Southwest
- Northeast
- Midwest
- International

Students In-state: 21%
Top majors: 1. Government 2. Biology
  3. Business
Retention rate of non-white students: 84%
**Scholarships exclusively for non-white
  students:** William Gray, Jr., Scholarship:
  need-based; lessens loan amount and
  work study; value depends on need.
  LULAC/F&M Scholarship: need-based;
  available to admitted students referred
  through League of United Latin
  American Citizens National Centers
Remediation programs: The Summer
  Program for Excellence is offered to
  selected incoming first-year students to
  introduce them to the school's academics.
Academic support services: The college
  offers tutoring in most academic subjects
  and a writing center.
Ethnic studies programs: The college offers
  a minor in Asian Studies, which includes
  about 25 courses.
Ethnic studies courses: F&M offers about
  six courses in Latin American Studies
  and about seven courses in African and
  African-American Studies.
Organizations for non-white students: Black
  Student Union, Association of Hispanic

Americans, Chinese Cultural Society, Asian Student Organization

Notable non-white alumni: William H. Gray III ('63, History; former U.S. representative, head of the United Negro College Fund)

Tenured faculty: 90

Non-tenured faculty: 73

Student-faculty ratio: 11:1

Administrators: 120

African-American: 4%

Hispanic: 2.5%

Asian-American: 0

Native American: 0

Recent non-white speakers on campus: Yolanda King (civil rights activist and daughter of Martin Luther King, Jr.); Atallah Shabazz (civil rights activist and daughter of Malcolm X); William Raspberry (urban affairs columnist, *Washington Post*); Bobby Seale (former Black Panther); William Cole (music educator)

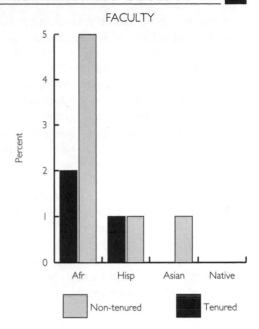

FACULTY

Non-tenured   Tenured

Question: What do Bates, Bowdoin, Union, Middlebury, and Franklin and Marshall colleges have in common, besides relatively small student populations and strong academics? Answer: Each has limited the use of the SAT. Now, F&M applicants who rank in the top 10 percent of their high school graduating classes have the option of submitting two samples of their writing instead of their SATs. "Our underlying assumption is that what is most important as a predictor of academic success is the work ethic and study skills, especially where there's been some rigor in the academic program," says Phyllis Leber, a chemistry professor and a member of the committee that proposed the option, in an article in the *Philadelphia Inquirer*.

Whatever criteria F&M's admissions office uses to admit students, one thing is certain: it consistently attracts a bright and motivated student body. For those looking to enter graduate school, take note: Franklin and Marshall consistently does well when it comes to sending students off to Ph.D. programs; by disciplines, F&M is first in geology and second in chemistry.

F&M students also tend to be relatively homogeneous, conservative, and laid-back when it comes to student activism. Observes a student: "The typical F&M student is basically out to get rich and to be in a fraternity or sorority. A recent program that focused on women's issues drew only about twenty women, for example, while a lip synch contest drew practically the entire student body." But, she adds, "there are people here who do want to change the world for the better, mostly geology majors who want to better the environment."

Students say F&M's top departments are chemistry, English, psychology, business, accounting, government, and geology, which is said to one of the best such departments in the country; math is considered to be weaker. To graduate, students must take nine College Studies courses: scientific inquiry, social analysis, art, foreign cultures, history, literature, and systems of knowledge and belief. There are also cross-registration possibilities with Gettysburg and Dickinson colleges.

Computers—in particular, Macintoshes—are a big deal at F&M. The college strongly recommends that students have their own computers, which it offers to students at a sizable discount. In a recent year, more than 70 percent of an entering class purchased a Macintosh when they got to campus. (Students also have free use of Mac computers at the school's Academic Center.)

One student says that although she and other students are frustrated by a lack of an African-American Studies program, she feels that some individual courses are strong, particularly the "African-American Literature" course, taught by Regina Jennings. "Jennings is doing special things with her classes, and she is fighting very hard to make African-American Studies a minor."

Academics can be tough at F&M, but professors are accessible for assistance. "During my freshman year, I was intimidated about visiting my professor, but I got over that after my first meeting with her. Recently I left a message on my religion professor's office phone machine, and she returned my phone call from Philadelphia, where she lives. That is the kind of attention you get here." Another source of academic—and emotional—support is Marion Coleman, director of multicultural student services, which provides tutoring. "She's our link to the administration, and the administration's link to us. She has an open office, and is always willing to talk to us, especially about academics."

The town of Lancaster, according to students, is quaint and rural. There is little to do off campus, "except maybe go to the mall." For off-campus diversions, students often head to parties at Millersville University, just a twenty-minute drive from campus. Students are able to pledge historically black fraternities or sororities at Millersville, but a student says "the interest in doing so has diminished recently." Philadelphia, with its rich variety of daytime and nighttime activities, is a little more than an hour away and is easily accessible by train. Baltimore, New York City, and Washington, DC, are each about a two-and-a-half-hour drive from campus.

Fraternity parties rule the weekend nightlife at F&M—although they are now no longer officially recognized by the college administration—but students report that few non-white students attend the parties. "Every once in a while we [minority students] will go to the parties, but since a lot of us don't drink, it can be intimidating since a lot of drinking goes on at the parties." In a recent year, about 10 non-white students were members of the school's Greek organizations.

There are other sources of entertainment for students, including the Black Cultural Center on campus. "The building is three stories tall, and we use it for meetings, parties, watching TV on the weekends, and studying. Although it has no living facilities, the house does have a living room, a full kitchen, and a dining room."

A primary activity of the Black Student Union, with about 20 active members, is its annual Black Cultural Arts Day festival, to which faculty, students, and alums are invited. "On a Friday, there will be a lecture by a visiting speaker. On Saturday, there's a dinner and dance. And on Sunday, there's a brunch. It's basically an opportunity for students to interact with alums and faculty in a relaxed way." The

BSU also recently sponsored a talent show, which received only a mild turnout.

A student describes the African-American community at F&M as "tight. We look out for each other. We do have our occasional disagreements, but we try to work them out. Sometimes it feels as if we're a family."

Although F&M's social life may not guarantee a twenty-four-hour-a-day good time, students are drawn to the school because of its strong academic programs and reputation. "I do have problems when I have to deal with such an apathetic student body, but the academics here are challenging, and there are plenty of activities in which to get involved."

GETTYSBURG COLLEGE

Address: Gettysburg, PA 17325
Phone: (717) 337-6100 / (800) 431-0803
Director of Admissions: Delwin Gustafson
Multicultural Student Recruiter: na

1992–93 tuition: $17,650
Room and board: $3,815
Application deadline: 2/15
Financial aid application: 2/1

Gettysburg College is rich in history. The great Civil War battle was fought on the edge of the campus, and Gettysburg students and faculty were among those in attendance in 1863 when Abraham Lincoln gave his famous address on the steps of what is now the school's administration building. It's no coincidence, then, that Gettysburg College is home to the well-regarded Civil War Institute, part of the school's equally well-regarded and popular history department.

Gettysburg's academic riches aren't confined to the history department. The school's English department, which publishes the highly respected *Gettysburg Review,* is one of the school's best, as are the natural sciences and political science departments. The management department—which allows students to concentrate in entrepreneurship, human resources, and accounting and finance is popular. Students majoring in the social sciences like the school's Washington Semester, a joint program with American University in DC that allows students to pursue internship possibilities in the capital. The required First Year Colloquy focuses on an interdisciplinary topic and is designed to strengthen students' reasoning, writing, and thinking skills. In addition to various distribution requirements, Gettysburg students must prove a proficiency in a foreign language to graduate.

Students say the school's African-American Studies program, offered as a minor course of study, is in a "building" phase, and was recently strengthened with the addition of an "African-American Literature" course. The program focuses on the study of people of Africa and the diaspora. According to students, among the program's more popular courses is "South African History and Change." The Consortium Exchange Program allows students to enroll in courses at Dickinson and Franklin and Marshall colleges.

With about 1,900 students enrolled, easy access to professors is a hallmark of a Gettysburg education. It's not uncommon for professors to put their home telephone numbers on their course syllabuses and invite students over to their homes for dinner and classes.

Although Gettysburg College may be educationally diverse, there is little diversity among its students. The college declined to participate in the guide, but from student leaders we learned that a recent first-year class had four African-American students. In total, during the academic year 1991–92 there were 38 non-white students enrolled at the college, about 25 of whom were African-American and six of whom were Latino. Exact figures for Asian-American students enrolled at the college could not be obtained. Most of the African-American students at Gettysburg are from the Philadelphia and Pittsburgh areas, while others hail from DC, New Jersey, New York City, and Alabama.

There is also little diversity among the school's white students. More than 60 percent of the students at Gettysburg are from Pennsylvania, New Jersey, or New York, and are conservative politically and socially. "There are those who are actively concerned about multicultural issues here on campus, but they're usually members of the Women's Rights group and GECO, the Gettysburg Environmental Concern Organization," observes a student.

The school's Intercultural Resource Center (IRC), in the words of a student, "is a home base for the school's minority students, a home away from home." The IRC has a computer lab and genealogical research materials "for all ethnic groups, with an emphasis on African-American families," as well as tutoring services. Although the IRC is open to all students, one student says it is most popular among African-American students. The IRC coordinates the unique Minority Youth Education Institute, which allows IRC-related students to interact with area high school students in workshops dealing with topics such as "African-American History" and "Discrimination."

The IRC is now "in a transitional period because there is no permanent dean in charge," says a student. A new dean should be in place, say students, beginning in the fall of '92. Frederick Douglass Opie, the interim acting dean of the IRC, and Brian Haynes, an assistant dean, are always available to students. "If one is not there the other almost always is. They're always realistic and encouraging," according to a student. Also helpful to students is Derrick Gondwe, an economics professor who teaches African-American Studies. He was one of the architects of the IRC and is currently an IRC advisory board member.

As is true at many other central and southern Pennsylvania colleges and universities, fraternities and sororities—to which about 60 percent of the students belong—are the dominant social force on the Gettysburg campus. The Greek units are homogeneous, although in a recent year four African-American students were involved in the fraternities. Intramural and varsity sports are popular, and the school has an impressive gymnasium.

For cultural activity, the Black Student Union, which has about 14 active members, sponsors a step show, as well as fashion and talent shows. Each year, the BSU holds a Round Table Discussion, in which prominent speakers engage students in what one student described as "active and challenging" question-and-answer sessions. A recent visitor was Lenora Fulani, head of the progressive New Alliance party. The discussions, according to a student leader, are usually attended mostly by African-

American students. "Recently an editorial in the school paper commented on the fact that too few whites attended the discussion."

Says a student about the Gettysburg African-American community: "When there's a major problem on campus, we're there for each other. The BSU is sometimes a home away from home for some of us, especially for those who come from twelve hours away to attend school here."

BSU members hold their weekly meetings in the BSU Room, located in Plank/Student Activities Center, which is provided with couches and a small library. The room is also popular with students for studying.

The town of Gettysburg doesn't offer much in terms of nightlife, although the park next to campus is great for jogging and playing Frisbee. Students needing a taste of city life are able to head to Harrisburg, thirty-six miles away, or Baltimore, just about an hour's drive from campus. For additional social activity, Gettysburg's BSU interacts with students at Hood and Mount St. Mary's colleges, two nearby women's colleges.

Like other prominent colleges in this part of Pennsylvania, when it comes to issues of diversity of just about any sort, Gettysburg is lagging. But for students willing to brave the challenges of such a homogeneous atmosphere, the rewards are there. "When the time comes for me to get a job, I'll be glad I came here, especially because of the education offered at Gettysburg and the reputation of the school," comments a junior. "I've been successful here. I'm on a lot of student boards, but that can sometimes get to be a bit much, because it feels as if I'm called on to speak for the entire African-American race. You just have to be disciplined, and know when to say no."

HAVERFORD COLLEGE

Address: 370 Lancaster Avenue, Haverford, PA 19041-1392

Phone: (215) 896-1350

Director of Admissions: Delsie Z. Phillips

Multicultural Student Recruiter: Pamela Turner

1993–94 tuition: $17,827

Room and board: $5,950

Application deadline: 1/15

Financial aid application deadline: 1/31

Non-white freshman admissions: Applicants for the class of '95: 451

Accepted: 40%

Accepted who enroll: 29%

Applicants accepted who rank in top 10% of high school class: 36%

In top 25%: 56%

Median SAT range: 500–650 V, 500–650 M

Median ACT: na

Full-time undergraduate enrollment: 1,147

Men: 56%

Women: 44%

Non-white students in

1988–89: 15.4%

1989–90: 17.8%

1990–91: 18%

1991–92: 19%

Geographic distribution of students: na

Top majors: 1. English 2. History 3. Biology

Retention rate of non-white students: 90%

Scholarships exclusively for non-white students: Ira Reid Scholarship: need-based; partly replaces loan and job expectation.

Remediation programs: None

Academic support services: The Minority Science Scholars Program and the

STUDENT ENROLLMENT

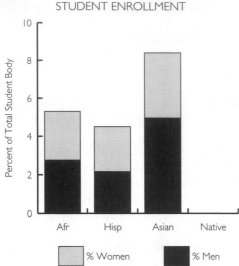

Percent of Total Student Body

□ % Women   ■ % Men

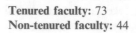

FACULTY

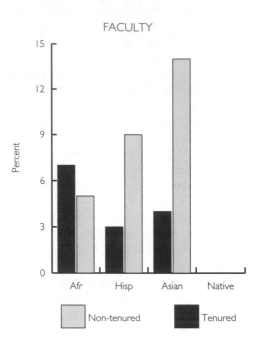

Percent

□ Non-tenured   ■ Tenured

Minority Humanities Scholars Program provide academic support services.

Ethnic studies programs: The college offers concentrations in Africana Studies, East Asian Studies, intercultural studies, and Latin American Studies.

Organizations for non-white students: Black Student League, Black Cultural Center, Latin American Student Organization, Asian Student Association, Asian Student House, La Casa (Latino theme house)

Notable non-white alumni: Juan Williams ('76, Philosophy; author); James Baker ('56, Political Science; Economic Assistant's Program director to the United Nations); James B. MacRae (acting administrator, Office of Information and Regulatory Affairs, Office of Management and Budget)

Student-faculty ratio: 11:1
Administrators: 113
   African-American: 8%
   Hispanic: 2%
   Asian-American: 2%
   Native American: 0
Recent non-white speakers on campus: June Jordan (poet); George Stallings (founder, African-American Catholic Church); Nomanda Ngubo (South African labor organizer); Cesar Chavez (labor leader and head of the United Farm Workers)

Evidence of Haverford's Quaker roots can be found in most aspects of campus life. Haverford students refer to their professors by their first names (and why not, many of them are their good friends), students are expected to adhere to the Honor Code, as it is adopted each year by the Student Association, and the campus has a relaxed—and friendly—feel to it that other schools of its caliber sometimes don't.

One of the best reasons to attend Haverford—besides getting up every day in one of the country's most beautiful college settings—is its outstanding faculty. Many of the professors are well-known scholars in their respective areas, and student-faculty interaction is close. "All of my friends who go to other schools are surprised at how well I get to know my professors, and I am equally surprised to find out how little they get to know theirs," says a philosophy major. "Whenever I see our dean on campus, which is often, we always say hello to one another."

Another reason to attend this small college is its outstanding and prestigious academics. The school boasts renowned departments of philosophy and English, and biology is said to be especially demanding. In recent years, all Haverford students who applied to medical school were accepted. One student, who plans to attend medical school, claims that the school's Minority Science Scholars Program "is one of the best programs on campus." The program is available to any minority student who signs up, and it provides peer tutoring, guidance from faculty, and opportunities for research. Haverford also has excellent programs in history, religion, music, and economics.

In order to graduate, students must complete a Social Justice course requirement, as well as distribution requirements in three divisions: the humanities and the social and natural sciences. Students must also show a proficiency in a foreign language and satisfy a physical education requirement.

Academic opportunities, although diverse for a school of Haverford's size, are significantly enhanced due to the college's close relationship and proximity to Bryn Mawr, a women's college located just 1.2 miles away. (Haverford was one of the last of the elite all-male colleges in the country to go coed; it did so in 1980.) In fact, the interaction between the two colleges is so extensive that students live at each other's college dorms and participate in various bi-college activities, including a jointly written newspaper. Students at the colleges also share course listings, and thousands of courses are cross-registered by students each year. However, the academic departments of the two colleges are not competitive; in fact, they're complementary. For example, Haverford students are able to take Italian and Russian at Bryn Mawr, languages not offered at Haverford, and Bryn Mawr students are able to take advantage of Haverford's strengths in philosophy and the sciences.

For those not up to the fifteen-minute walk to Bryn Mawr, there's always the shuttle van that leaves campus almost every half hour. Haverford students are also able to enroll in courses at Swarthmore and the University of Pennsylvania. "We definitely take fewer courses at Swarthmore than at Bryn Mawr, and we take even fewer courses at Penn," remarks a junior. "Even though Philadelphia [Penn's hometown] is only twenty minutes away by train, it's still a pain to get there."

Haverford's Black Student League (BSL), which has about 30 active members, recently sponsored, in the words of one student, "a candlelight vigil for those who have lost their lives on behalf of civil rights in this country. We didn't do too much advertising for the event; we did it mostly for ourselves. But because it was so successful we plan to advertise it more next year so we can get the entire campus involved. During the vigil, we walked around the campus and ended up at the dining center, where we read all the names of the individuals who lost their lives." For Black History Month each year, the group sponsors We Speak, an event in which "students and faculty of color read their own poems or poems and works of more famous African-Americans," says a student. "It's a forum for blacks to express their feelings about being black at Haverford and in this country. We do it mostly for the white audience and professors, so that they get a better sense of who we are. The event gets a good turnout each year from the administration, deans, and faculty."

A housing option for selected students is the Black Cultural Center, which was renamed in the spring of 1992 the Ira DeA. Reid House, in honor of Haverford's first African-American professor, who bequeathed the house to the college. In order to live in the house, which can accommodate up to four students, students must go through an application process in which they write a proposal stating what they plan to accomplish in the house in terms of cultural awareness. The decision about who eventually lives in the house rests with members of the multicultural affairs staff and previous house residents. The house has a small library and three bedrooms, and, according to one student, is in need of repair, but "we don't think the administration will be giving us any money anytime soon to upgrade it because the new student center [due to be completed in 1994] will include a multicultural student area." As a way to improve the quality of the living space in the house, students plan to begin contacting alums for donations. The center will make the Reid house more centrally located, as plans are now for the center to be built near the house.

During the 1992–93 school year, students formed the Latin American Student Organization because of differences with members of La Casa, a student group composed mostly of members from Latin American countries. "We had [economic] class differences with La Casa members," says a junior. "We found that they weren't sympathetic to and understanding of what it means to be Hispanic in America, especially since most of their members are from Latin America and will return to their countries after graduating. There was just a lack of communication between them and us." At this point, LASO, with about ten members, serves as a peer support group, although the group recently sponsored a forum on racism.

Despite the activities of the various cultural student groups and living units, students say Haverford can be too homogeneous and, for that reason, at times frustrating. "Even though Haverford is like a nirvana when it comes to academics, I don't want to give the impression that this place is all hunky-dory," says a student. "Although we don't get hit by glass bottles and slurs aren't yelled at us like at some other schools I could name, the racial tension is felt here on a more intellectual level. We get questions like 'Why do you all have to have a house?' and 'Why do you have to eat together in the dining center?' It can be frustrating here sometimes. People always want to talk about these things, but I get tired of explaining their prejudices to them. The students here really want to be good people, but it gets to be a burden having to be asked these kinds of questions all the time."

Haverford certainly isn't a party school. But Bryn Mawr and Haverford do co-sponsor several parties during the school year, as well as concerts and movies. More than 75 percent of the campus participates in intramural activities. The biggest party of the year is Haverfest, an outdoor event before finals in the spring that offers concerts, barbecues, and a variety of outdoor activities.

Attending such a small college can at times be confining. For urban nightlife and entertainment, students will take the easy twenty-minute SEPTA ride into Philadelphia, with its myriad of cultural opportunities, including museums, restaurants, concerts, and theaters. Bars and other night spots are also available. With Penn, Drexel, and Temple in the city, Philadelphia can be described as a college town.

Like students at other schools with a Quaker heritage, Haverford students are generally on the progressive side of the political spectrum. The school supports an active Bisexual, Gay, and Lesbian Alliance, which publishes its own newsletter, and students are active in community projects, among them a big brother/big sister program in Philadelphia. Most students, however, come from the eastern seaboard states and from upper-middle-class families.

Despite the school's relative lack of diversity, students find their professors and peers to be supportive. "When I came here as a freshman four years ago, I sensed the community spirit here right away. And now that I'm a senior, I can still feel it. Haverford is amazing in that way."

LAFAYETTE COLLEGE

Address: Easton, PA 18042
Phone: (215) 250-5100
Director of Admissions: G. Gary Ripple
Multicultural Student Recruiter: Marcus Amos

1992–93 tuition: $16,725
Room and board: $5,190
Application deadline: 2/1
Financial aid application deadline: 1/30

A popular T-shirt worn by Lafayette College students, especially at gridiron matches against archrival Lehigh University, reads: "Lehigh: Because We All Couldn't Get into Lafayette." Competition between the schools, in athletics and in admissions, is keen. Both schools offer top-notch engineering and science programs in beautiful campus settings. But when it comes to that annual football game against Lehigh—for which special cement goalposts and bleachers are erected—watch out! In 1992, post-game activities got so out of control that, well, let's just say Lafayette administrators must have been relieved the game was *not* held at home.

Like Lehigh, Lafayette enrolls a relatively small number of students of color. Although Lafayette's admissions office declined to participate in our guide, we were able to learn from student leaders that during the 1991–92 school year there were approximately 70 African-Americans and 30 Latinos enrolled at the college. According to the U.S. Department of Education, in 1990, 2.5 percent of the student body was Asian and 0.1 percent was American Indian.

Despite these figures, students say Lafayette is a friendly, if homogeneous place to go to school. Many of the students—who come from more than two dozen states and almost as many foreign countries—are conservative politically and often come from upper-middle-class backgrounds. The school's Greek system is huge, encompassing more than half of the student body. (There are no historically black Greek organizations at Lafayette.) But students say fraternities aren't the dominant social force they once were, due in large part to Pennsylvania's strict laws against underage drinking, laws the Lafayette administration takes seriously, and the creation recently of the school's College Center, its new student union, which serves as a meeting place for students and student groups.

Unusually close interaction with faculty is common at this 177-year-old school. Most professors live on or near campus, and a faculty member lives in each of the school's dorms. One of the school's most popular teachers is Arthur Gorman, a math professor. "Gormie, as we sometimes refer to him, comes to all of our ABC [Association of Black Collegians] meetings and helps with our activities. He's a real asset for us multicultural students."

Lafayette has long been known for its outstanding programs in mechanical, electrical, civil, and chemical engineering, and academic competition among engineers is keen. Biology, chemistry, economics, and business earn high marks from students, who also say the school's new interdisciplinary Black Studies minor is excellent, for both its breadth of study and its outstanding professors. "John McCartney is one of the school's more popular professors," comments a senior. "He teaches most of the Black Studies courses in the government and law department. He's always accessible." Rexford Ahene, an economics professor from Ghana, is also popular.

The most active of the school's cultural student groups is ABC, which has about 40 active members. According to students, ABC coordinates all of the programming for Black History Month. "Although we haven't done that much this year," says a student, ABC did help bring Angela Davis to campus in a recent year. ABC, which meets twice a month, also sponsors two programs for area young people, including Black Children Can, which mixes "fun and learning," and a tutoring service at the Shiloh Baptist Church in Easton. Lafayette's African-American students also publish a monthly newspaper titled *Aya,* the Ghanian word for fern.

ABC is now able to take advantage of new office space in the College Center. In a recent year, the center's four offices were used by the ABC, a woman's organization, the International Student Association, and Outreach, a student-volunteer service. The ABC office is equipped with a computer and a printer.

The college sponsors single-sex residence facilities for African-American students at the Black Cultural Center. "Each year it alternates sexes," says a student. Up to three students are able to live in the center, which has three single rooms, a living/meeting area, a full kitchen, and African art. The center, which had been located on campus since the 1970s, was moved across the street from campus on McCartney Street "to a nicer house." However, now that the house is technically located in the town of Easton and comes under town ordinances, the BCC has come under strict scrutiny from the local police department. In a recent year, local police officers raided a BCC party, telling everybody to leave the house because the music was too loud. After the students were able to return to the house, students demanded that the university address the treatment of those at the party by the police officers. "One of the administrators here was a friend of one of the officers, and he talked to him for us, and since then we've had no problems with the local police," says a student.

Members of ABC frequently interact with members of Lehigh's Black Student Union, and students from both schools attend events sponsored by either school. The majority of Lafayette's African-American students come from New Jersey, New York, and Pennsylvania.

The school's newest cultural student group, SALSA [Student Alliance of Latinos and South Americans], was formed because some students felt that the school's already existing Latin American Club addressed only international issues. Group members hope that the group will survive. SALSA, which as of now meets once every two weeks, borrowed its constitution and name from Lehigh, which has a similar organization.

To promote racial understanding on campus, the college sponsors periodical Racism Forums, usually attended by about 100 students. "They're not that successful because the students who should attend don't," says a student. "About half of the students who attend are white, and they're the same ones who come to the forums every time one is offered. At a recent forum they turned off the lights and asked anyone who felt like it to stand up and talk about race issues on campus."

Fraternities are an integral aspect of Lafayette's social life. In a recent year, four African-American men and one African-American woman were members of one or another of the school's fraternities or sororities. Students report that tension exists between the administration and the school's Greek faction. "The administration is trying to get rid of the fraternities," says a student. "It thinks the fraternities are taking up too much of the campus social life. There's very little for the independents to do other than go to the frat parties." One student reports that, although minorities feel comfortable at the parties, few go "because there's more drinking than dancing."

Easton, which has a large African-American population (and is the birthplace of boxer Larry Holmes), offers students few cultural and social opportunities save those for community service and fast-food dining. The school's Morris R. Williams Center for the Arts brings performers to campus. New York, Philadelphia, and Atlantic City are each about an hour-and-a-half drive away.

A Lafayette degree is an impressive credential. It has certainly caught the attention of graduate school admissions offices; in recent years, more than 90 percent of those who applied to medical and business schools were accepted.

Although the social life at the college may be lacking for those longing for big-city action, one student wouldn't have it any other way. "I've met people here who are great. Although the Greek life is dominant, I make sure I have a good time, even if I'm not in a sorority." Adds another student: "I know I'm getting a very, very, very good education."

LEHIGH UNIVERSITY

Address: Alumni Memorial Building #27, Bethlehem, PA 18015

Phone: (215) 758-3100

Director of Admissions: Patricia G. Boig

Multicultural Student Recruiter: na

1993–94 tuition: $17,750

Room and board: $5,500

Application deadline: 2/15

Financial aid application deadline: 1/31

Non-white freshman admissions: Applicants for the class of '95: 982
   Accepted: 62.9%
   Accepted who enroll: 21.5%
   Applicants accepted who rank in top 10% of high school class: 34%

   In top 25%: 74%
   Median SAT range: 440–550 V, 520–670 M
   Median ACT: na

Full-time undergraduate enrollment: 4,392
   Men: 63%
   Women: 37%

Non-white students in
   1987–88: 5%
   1988–89: 7%
   1989–90: 8%
   1990–91: 8.2%

Students In-state: 23%

Top majors: 1. Accounting 2. Electrical Engineering 3. Mechanical Engineering

Retention rate of non-white students: 75%

STUDENT ENROLLMENT

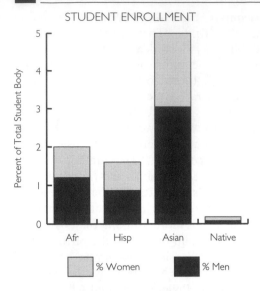

% Women   % Men

GEOGRAPHIC DISTRIBUTION OF STUDENTS

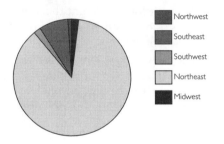

- Northwest
- Southeast
- Southwest
- Northeast
- Midwest

Scholarships exclusively for non-white students: None

Remediation programs: None

Academic support services: Challenge for Success provides non-academic and academic support for African-American and Hispanic students. Tutoring, mentoring, and peer counseling are also available.

Ethnic studies programs: The university offers a minor in Latin American Studies, an interdisciplinary program, involving courses in economics, history, government, international relations, and modern foreign languages. Lehigh also offers an East Asian Studies major and minor involving Japanese- and Chinese-language study, anthropology,

history, and international relations. A program of study can also be designed, with the assistance of a faculty adviser, in Afro-American Studies.

Ethnic studies courses: The university offers two courses in American race relations, "American Ethnic Groups" and "Race, Ethnicity, and Minorities."

Organizations for non-white students: Umoja (theme house for African-American and Hispanic students), Minority Programming Committee, Black Student Union, Genesis (gospel choir), SALSA, Omega Psi Phi, Association of Minority Business Students, National Society of Black Engineers, Kappa Alpha Psi, Society of Together Ebony Men

Notable non-white alumni: Ralph Albert Williams (Accounting; vice president, Citibank/Citicorp)

Tenured faculty: 306

Non-tenured faculty: 101

FACULTY

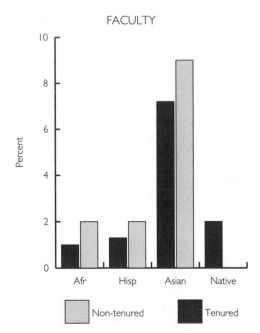

Non-tenured   Tenured

Student-faculty ratio: 14:1
Administrators: 337
  African-American: 4%
  Hispanic: 1%

Asian-American: 0

Native American: 0

Recent non-white speakers on campus: Irma Palabi Francis (artist); Dr. William Luis (director, Latin American Studies, SUNY/Binghamton); Dr. Gwendolyn Goldsby-Grant (psychologist and *Essence* magazine contributor); Chuck D (member of the rap group Public Enemy); Conrad Muhammed (National Youth Leader of the Nation of Islam)

Most students who graduate from Lehigh University will no doubt remember two things about their undergraduate years: the outstanding education they received and the football competition against Lafayette College, the oldest football rivalry in the country. One recent game was so intense that the presidents of the two colleges had to hold a press conference to explain the shenanigans of their students.

Recent graduates will also remember the marked strides the university has made since they first arrived on campus in diversifying the curriculum and the living options. The school's curriculum now includes Latin American and Afro-American Studies programs, and the Umoja House and the Latino House, which can accommodate more than a dozen students each, are recent additions to the campus's housing options. "The minority students and the organizations have the commitment of everyone from the president of the university on down," says a senior. "The president attends minority student recruiting weekends, and he comes to many of our activities. Lehigh has long been known as a conservative and homogeneous school, so we're having to overcome a bad rep in this area. But things have definitely improved with these programs."

One program that receives rave reviews from students is the Challenge for Success (CFS) program, which seeks to recruit and retain students—primarily Hispanics and African-Americans—through a six-week pre-orientation session. CFS, located in the university center, also has a peer counseling program. The director of CFS, Sharon Brown, "is everybody's friend. People stop by her office just to say hello." Says a student of her CFS experience: "The CFS summer program was a key factor in my transition from high school to college. The courses I took, as well as the college dorm experience, made it easier for me to adjust to Lehigh life in the fall. I was able to get to know the layout of the campus—where my classes would be, the libraries, the gym, etc. As a result, my anxiety about getting lost during the first week of classes was cured. I also stopped worrying because I made a lot of friends."

Largely through the efforts of Brown, the university recently instituted a Minority Connections program, in which students meet weekly in the CFS office for a rap session. "It's not like a club or anything. It's all done confidentially and provides a stable source of support for students," says a pre-med major who participates in the sessions.

Lehigh students are professionally oriented. The spirit of Lee Iacocca—an alum and benefactor—is strong here. The university is best known for its engineering programs, the most popular being electrical, mechanical, civil, and chemical engineering. The school's business program is well respected, and includes five different major programs; finance and accounting are the most popular. Among Lehigh's liberal arts programs, which students say are on the whole weaker when compared with their more technical counterparts, students praise government, English, and journalism. German students have the added benefit of the resources of German

House, a language theme house where students speak only German. Lehigh offers an accelerated six-year M.D. program with the Medical College of Pennsylvania in Philadelphia, which includes summer study at Lehigh.

Academics can be strenuous, but the school offers various resources, including tutoring services in every subject, that are easily available, and group study sessions are popular. Students report that professors are always willing to lend a hand. When classes get too large, sometimes into the hundreds in introductory courses, they hold small-class sessions once a week, in which a teaching assistant instructs and administers quizzes and tests. "With all of the academic support they offer here, there's no reason why you can't get good grades," says a student.

Lehigh's social life is, as is true at many other Pennsylvania colleges, dominated by the Greek life "on the hill." Nearly half of the student body belongs to the school's 29 fraternities and eight sororities. "There's always a party going on at one or more of the fraternities," says a student. Although only a small percentage of the school's non-white students join one or another of these organizations, students say they will still head to the hill for some of the fraternity parties. "But not all the minority students feel comfortable going to the hill for a party," says a student. "There are still those black students who will only hang with black students, and those Hispanics who will only hang with Hispanics." Adds another student: "You can take advantage of a lot here. It all depends on how flexible you are socially."

Intramurals are by far the most popular extracurricular activities on campus, especially between dorms and fraternities; more than 80 percent of the student body participates in at least one of the school's 40 intramural sports clubs. There are more than 100 student organizations in politics and student government and music and volunteerism, and the school's Stabler Arena, an athletic complex, offers a myriad of opportunities. Lehigh's 1,600-acre campus is one of the most beautiful around; half of the grounds are prepared as woodlands.

The Student Alliance for Latinos and South Americans (SALSA), with about 30 active members, was recently established on campus. SALSA members sponsored a trip to Philadelphia to participate in that city's Hispanic Heritage Month celebrations. "But mostly we do little things to bring us together, like pizza and domino parties. We don't have much money, so we go to the events that Hispanic students at nearby colleges sponsor so that we can learn from them. Hopefully, soon we will able to have the events that the organizations at Glassboro State and Rutgers/Camden have." (Both schools are located in southern New Jersey.)

Although Lehigh lacks a diverse student body, students say the small numbers bring them closer together. "At Lehigh, we Hispanics and African-Americans make up a small percentage of the population. But most of the time we're like a big happy family. There are those times when you are just having one of those days. You just don't know how to deal with the stress of two exams on the same day, or maybe you have a personal problem and need someone to talk to. At these times we are always there for each other."

At Lehigh—a school known for its engineering programs, which have traditionally attracted more men than women—a little more than a third of the students are women. Men looking to improve their dating chances will head to Philadelphia, about an hour and a half away, or to New York City, about a two-hour drive.

As the university's curriculum and student body grow increasingly more diverse, students say the school is becoming more comfortable for students of color. "I'm going to miss it a lot when I graduate because there's so much that is happening, and that has happened since I first came here. Lehigh has prepared me for the real world. Academics are tough; I can't believe how much I've pushed myself."

LINCOLN UNIVERSITY

Address: Lincoln Hall, Lincoln University, PA 19352

Phone: (215) 932-8300, ext. 206

Director of Admissions: Jimmy Arrington

Multicultural Student Recruiter: na

1991–92 tuition: $2,550 (in-state); $3,650 (out-of-state)

Room and board: $2,700

Application deadline: Rolling admissions

Financial aid application deadline: 3/1

Non-white freshman admissions: Applicants for the class of '95: 1,357

Accepted: 873

Accepted who enroll: 364

Applicants accepted who rank in top 10% of high school class: 9%

In top 25%: 34%

Median SAT: 360 V, 380 M

Median ACT: na

Full-time undergraduate enrollment: 1,211

Men: 42%

Women: 58%

Non-white students in

1987–88: 95%

1988–89: 96%

1989–90: 96%

1990–91: 95%

Geographic distribution of students: na

Students In-state: 46%

Top majors: 1. Business 2. Social Sciences 3. Public Affairs and Protective Services

Retention rate of non-white students: 85%

Scholarships exclusively for non-white students: None

Remediation programs: The university offers remedial programs in math, reading, and developing study skills.

Academic support services: Lincoln's Counseling Center provides tutoring and other academic support services.

Ethnic studies programs: na

Ethnic studies courses: Lincoln offers courses in African-American history, business, psychology, and sociology, as well as courses in Latin American Studies.

Organizations for non-white students: Alpha Phi Alpha, Phi Beta Sigma, Alpha Kappa Alpha, Zeta Phi Beta, Delta Sigma Theta, Kappa Alpha Psi, Omega Psi Phi

Notable non-white alumni: Thurgood Marshall ('30; first African-American Justice of the U.S. Supreme Court); Nnamdi Azikiwe ('30; first president of Nigeria); Hildrus A. Poindexter ('24; authority on tropical diseases); Langston

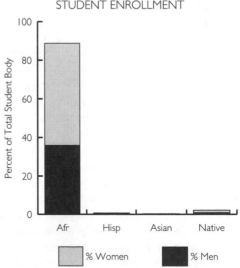

STUDENT ENROLLMENT

Percent of Total Student Body

% Women   % Men

FACULTY

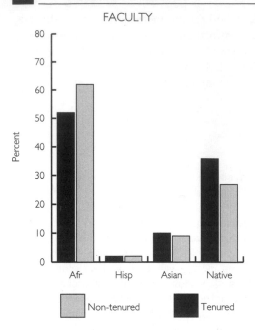

Hughes, ('29; poet) Edward Wilmot Blyden III ('48; educator and diplomat)
Tenured faculty: 42
Non-tenured faculty: 45
Student-faculty ratio: 10:1
Administrators: 81
  African-American: 80%
  Hispanic: 0
  Asian-American: 0
  Native American: 20%
Recent non-white speakers on campus:
  Chinua Achebe (author); Henry Louis Gates, Jr. (professor, Harvard University); Ruby Dee (actress); James Farmer (former director and founder of CORE)

Founded in 1854, Lincoln University is America's first historically black college. Although not as well known as some of the country's other historically black colleges and universities, Lincoln does offer, in the words of a student leader, "a sense of history and spirit that can't be found in most places."

Lincoln's list of graduates is indeed impressive and includes a long line of American civil rights leaders and artists—the late Supreme Court Justice Thurgood Marshall and poet Langston Hughes are Lincoln graduates—and many former and current African heads of government. The first president of Nigeria and the first president of Ghana, for example, graduated from Lincoln. Lincoln was founded to educate African men to return to Africa to be missionaries.

Today, the university offers programs in the liberal arts and teacher education. Students say that some of the school's best department's are English, political science, and communications. Foreign-language instruction, which includes Swahili and Japanese, are also said to be good. The history department, with only three professors, is said to be solid. The Lincoln Advanced Science and Engineering Reinforcement program provides academic and financial assistance.

With such a small student population, students say getting to know professors is relatively easy. Students also feel that being taught primarily by non-white professors has its advantages. "I'd say that about 80 percent of Lincoln's faculty is non-white, and I think the faculty sometimes feels more comfortable teaching at a predominantly black institution because they can be more honest and can discuss things they might not feel able to at a mostly white school," says a senior. "This makes us feel more secure with them, and we can relate to each other's experiences."

Students appreciate the opportunity to learn from an Afrocentric perspective, although certain programs have their detractors. "English is taught primarily from a Western point of view here," comments a humanities major. "You could take enough English courses here to satisfy a major yet still not have studied any African or African-American authors. This has caused certain students to complain and ask that more African poetry be integrated into the English curriculum. The history courses are also usually taught from the Western perspective, usually because of the textbook we use for class, but the professor may supplement the reading with his perspective."

Lincoln's campus is isolated, to put it mildly, but, says a student, "few students end up transferring because of our location." The school is forty-five miles from Philadelphia, "which can be a sort of a culture shock for many of the students since a majority of them come here from large cities." The campus is beautiful, with a combination of old and new architecture, and quiet, which, comments more than one student, is conducive to studying. Cheyney University of Pennsylvania, also a historically black institution, is just forty-five minutes away, and students say interaction with Cheyney students is frequent. Students also drive the twenty-five minutes for parties and other events at the University of Delaware.

For on-campus fun and excitement, fraternities—to which about 10 percent of the male students belong—sponsor cabarets, formal dances, and step shows. "Our fraternity parties are well known around the area," says a non-member. There are clubs for each active major, as well as various religious organizations, which sponsor their own activities. Each club at Lincoln has a week in which members are able to plan activities that raise the campus's awareness about their particular club's aims. Students can often be found hanging out at the Rec Room, located in the gymnasium.

"A sense of family exists between many of the students here," says a student, but, he adds, "it can get too cliquey sometimes. You pretty much hang out all four years with the friends you made freshman year."

Although the school sponsors a big brother/big sister program, students believe the campus could be doing more to interact with the community. "We need to take more of an active part in the community. We need to help out more in Lincoln Village, about a mile and a half from campus, which is poor and mostly black," asserts a student active in student government. "Next semester I think we'll start getting the student body more involved in that community, such as having students help fix up houses."

In conjunction with the Forerunners Institute, located in Philadelphia, Lincoln's student government association sponsored the first World Conference of African Students, which took place in Philadelphia's Sheraton Inn during the spring of 1992. More than 200 students attended the event, from schools as far as the University of the Bahamas and universities in Sierra Leone and South Africa. The three-day event featured forums and workshops that focused on self-awareness, racial consciousness, and choosing careers from a global perspective. "The event was so successful that plans are now to have another one next year," says a student who helped organize the event.

Lincoln may lack the cachet of some of the country's more elite black colleges, but the student who chooses to attend this school "surrounded by cornfields" won't be disappointed. He or she is virtually guaranteed a solid education, while learning with a somewhat diverse group of people—and in the midst of all that history. "I'm overwhelmingly glad I came to Lincoln. Since I came here, I've become more politically aware. I'm not so quick to label something as racist, since I'm more likely to try to understand all points of view. I've also come to appreciate the vast diversity among African-Americans."

Adds another student: "Lincoln is full of opportunities. You can really shine at Lincoln. At a small school such as this, you can make things happen."

MUHLENBERG COLLEGE

Address: 2400 Chew Street, Allentown, PA 18104
Phone: (215) 821-3200
Director of Admissions: Christopher Hooker-Haring
Multicultural Student Recruiter: Kenneth Roberts
1991–92 tuition: $15,115
Room and board: $4,260
Application deadline: 2/15
Financial aid application deadline: 2/15
Non-white freshman admissions: Applicants for the class of '95: 225
  Accepted: 76%
  Accepted who enroll: 19%
  Applicants accepted who rank in top 10% of high school class: na
  Median SAT: na
  Median ACT: na
Full-time undergraduate enrollment: 1,610
  Men: 45%
  Women: 55%
Non-white students in
  1987–88: 3%
  1988–89: 4%
  1989–90: 5%
  1990–91: 6.45%
Geographic distribution of students: na
Students In-state: 38.8%
Top majors: 1. Psychology 2. Sciences 3. Business
Retention rate of non-white students: 82%
Scholarships exclusively for non-white students: Commitment to Excellence: merit-based; $4,000 for each award; 20 awarded each year; renewable. Select Scholarship: need-based; $3,000 for each

award; two offered each year; renewable.
Remediation programs: None
Academic support services: The Office of Academic Support provides tutoring in most subjects, as well as courses in time management and study skills development.
Ethnic studies programs: None
Ethnic studies courses: The university's history department offers "Afro-American History" and two courses in East Asian Studies. The political science department offers about one course each in African, East Asian, and Latin American Studies.
Organizations for non-white students: Black Student Association, Culture Club, Gospel Choir, Hispanic Club

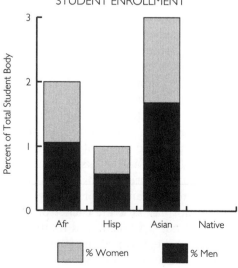

STUDENT ENROLLMENT

Percent of Total Student Body

Afr   Hisp   Asian   Native

% Women   % Men

Notable non-white alumni: Roma Theus ('69; lawyer)
Tenured faculty: na
Non-tenured faculty: na
Student-faculty ratio: 12:1
Administrators: na

Recent non-white speakers on campus: Wilson Goode (former mayor of Philadelphia); Dennis Raheem Watson (executive director, National Black Youth Leadership Council); Bill White (president, National Baseball League)

Like a handful of other liberal arts colleges in Pennsylvania, Muhlenberg College provides a solid education combined with an active Greek social life. Like students at these other Pennsylvania schools, Muhlenberg students tend to be conservative and pre-professionally oriented.

One of Muhlenberg's claims to fame is its outstanding pre-med programs, especially in chemistry and biology. The school, which sends a whopping 15 percent of a typical graduating class on to medical school, has excellent science facilities, including the Shankweiler Biology and Trumbower Science buildings. Business administration is the only major more popular than those in the sciences. Accounting, unusual for a liberal arts college, is also available. Reflecting the school's religious heritage—the school was founded in 1848 by Lutherans—students say the religion and philosophy departments are excellent. The education program is also strong, and art and drama students have access to the resources of the school's impressive Center for the Arts, designed by noted architect Philip Johnson. Students say the school's "African-American History" course is so popular that "it's hard to get into if you're not a history major."

Academics at Muhlenberg are competitive—especially among pre-med students—and, as students are required to complete 34 credits for graduation, demanding. To graduate, students must complete general academic requirements in two areas: Skills, which includes courses in writing, oral expression, reading, and a foreign language; and Perspectives, which includes courses in literature, the fine arts, religion and philosophy, human behavior and social institutions, history, physical and life sciences, and non-Western cultures.

Although students find the school's academics challenging, they also consider the school's support services—particularly the faculty—helpful. "There's almost no reason why a student can't succeed here, short of his or her total lack of effort," says a student. "I really believe Muhlenberg is into retaining all of its students." Students also say that Muhlenberg's Academic Support Services—which provides tutoring and study skills seminars—is effective. The director of the center, Priscilla Howard, "is phenomenal at her job," says a student. "Her interest in students is sincere, and she herself often works one on one with students." The director of the Minority Affairs Office, Edgar Berry, is "very concerned about his students, and sometimes students complain that he can be too paternalistic, but I think even these students wouldn't want him any other way," says a student.

While students have little to complain about when it comes to the quality of their academics, they do want a more diverse social life. "We're going through a phase here where everyone is complaining about the lack of social life, but the administration is very open and student-oriented and is listening to what the students want," says a student. A recent activity sponsored by the administration, says the student, was a keg party—yes, beer was served to those who could prove they were of legal drinking age (21)—after a basketball game.

Fraternity parties are popularly attended weekend functions, although students say they don't dominate the school's social life. Seegers Union, the campus student center, is also a place to be seen, especially at the student-run Red Door, a non-alcoholic bar that hosts live entertainment. The center also has a game room, student organization offices, and a snack bar.

The Black Student Association (BSA) recently reestablished itself on campus, after being absent from student affairs at Muhlenberg for more than twenty years. The BSA, which meets in Seegers Union, has about 20 active members. The BSA recently sponsored an essay contest in a fifth-grade class at a local elementary school. The topic of the essay assignment was "What Would I Change If I Were Martin Luther King, Jr.?" Future BSA plans are to adopt a local high school, where members will tutor.

The Culture Club, which focuses on international student themes, recently sponsored a Unity Ball, at which faculty and staff played against Culture Club members in either basketball, for men, or volleyball, for women.

Housing options have recently become more diverse, as students are now able to apply to live in Ujima Suite, a multicultural living unit located in Benfer Hall. In a recent year, living in the coed suite were four African-American students, one African student, and a white student. More than 15 people had applied to live in the suite, according to students, but it can only accommodate up to six students. Living assignments are decided by lottery.

Muhlenberg is within a few miles of several colleges, including Lehigh University, Lafayette College, and Moravian College, and there is a great deal of interaction among students socially and culturally. The college is also within easy walking distance of shops, restaurants, and watering holes, but other than these off-campus distractions, the city of Allentown (pop. 100,000) doesn't offer much in the form of entertainment.

Muhlenberg students are, on the whole, a homogeneous and conservative bunch. Many are from Pennsylvania and New Jersey, "but the campus seems to be getting more diverse, not just racially but also geographically," observes a student. Learning in such an atmosphere won't appeal to everyone, but for students looking for a respected and supportive learning environment, Muhlenberg has a great deal to offer. Says a student: "There are a lot of challenges here and a lot of opportunities to make a difference. And academically this place is fantastic."

UNIVERSITY OF PENNSYLVANIA

Address: Philadelphia, PA 19104
Phone: (215) 898-7507
Director of Admissions: Willis Stetson, Jr.
Multicultural Student Recruiter: Clarence Grant

1992–93 tuition: $16,838
Room and board: $6,330
Application deadline: 1/1
Financial aid application deadline: 2/15

When Benjamin Franklin founded the University of Pennsylvania more than 250 years ago, he wanted to establish an institution where learning would be "both useful and ornamental." Franklin would be proud of his school. The university's Wharton School of Business is certainly "useful"—and world-class—and the school's "ornamental" programs in the liberal arts and sciences have many a top-notch department.

The university is divided into four schools. The School of Nursing, the only such program in the Ivy League, has its own Center for Nursing Research. The School of Engineering and Applied Science, which enrolls about 1,400 undergraduates, offers eight different majors, such as bioengineering, chemical engineering, civil engineering systems, and electrical engineering. The College of Arts and Sciences offers a wide range of impressive courses of study; among the more noteworthy are Asian Studies, history, geology, anthropology, English, American Studies, and sociology. The Wharton School of Business offers concentrations in numerous areas, including accounting, finance, insurance, labor relations, marketing, and public policy and management.

Students praise the school's African-American Studies program for its wide range of courses, which cover anthropology, religion, politics, music, and history. "Black Politics in America," "Black Psychology," and "Black Intellectuals" are some of the program's more respected courses. Highly regarded faculty include Houston Baker, A. Leon Higginbotham, John Roberts, and Robert Wilson.

Students think the Latin American Studies program is getting stronger each year, although they are still frustrated about a decision the university made in the spring of 1992 to deny tenure to a popular professor in the program. In response to the tenure decision, students staged a demonstration on Locust Walk, a main drag through campus. A well-received course in the program is "The World That Columbus Made," taught by Nancy Farriss, a well-regarded history professor.

All Penn undergraduates must take courses in the humanities, mathematics, and the sciences. Students may enroll in courses at Haverford, Swarthmore, or Bryn Mawr, liberal arts colleges located just outside of Philadelphia. Qualified Penn students also have the ability to enroll in courses at any of the university's outstanding graduate school programs in law, business, arts and sciences, or nursing.

Even by Ivy League standards, the academic atmosphere at Penn is a pressure cooker. According to students, professors pile on the work. However, the university provides numerous academic support services to lessen the intensity, and students say professors are easily accessible. "Most classes are relatively small, usually no more than twenty-five students, although there are some larger lecture courses," says a student. "But the professors, even in the bigger classes, will take time out for students."

The Greenfield InterCultural Center, which houses the offices of the United Minorities Council and other cultural student groups, has an academic peer mentoring program that pairs upperclass students with freshmen, and provides computers and a library for student use. The director of the center, Rene Gonzalez, is especially supportive of students.

The W. E. B. Du Bois College House "is a mainstay for black housing on campus," says a marketing major, "and is becoming more popular with first-year students." The four-story residence, which in a recent year housed about 120 men and women, has kitchen facilities, a library, and a meeting room. The house sponsors several of its own functions during the school year, including educational and cultural workshops. One of the better-known such programs is the house's annual "Souls of Du Bois" conference, which focuses on issues in the African-American community.

The Black Student League (BSL), which meets twice a month at the Du Bois House, sponsors an annual talent show, Martin Luther King, Jr., Day forums, and a Kwanzaa dinner. The BSL also coordinates annual clothes drives and works closely with the West Philadelphia Community Center. Positive Images, an African-American student group, provides tutoring services to students at nearby junior high and high schools. The Black Wharton Undergraduate Association's biggest event is its annual forum, held in February, which brings corporate bigwigs to campus. "It has been billed as the premier undergraduate conference of its kind in the country," says a student organizer of the event.

MECHA, a Chicano student organization, "is like a little family. We have our problems, but I know I can depend on members for almost anything," says a student. The group, with about 35 active members, who are mostly Mexican-Americans from California and Texas, provides peer support for members by sponsoring various social functions, including study breaks. In addition, the group is beginning to work with the admissions office to help increase the Chicano presence on campus. MECHA receives a great deal of staff support from Olga Rubio, an assistant dean of counseling at the university, Thomas Leal, director of South Campus, and Rene Gonzalez. "They're all a big part of the group, by coming to our events and meetings," says a student.

The Chinese Students Association is one of the more active Asian student groups on campus; Students for Asian Affairs, also active, is one of the newer campus organizations. The groups sponsor workshops and social mixers, and are becoming more politically active as they attempt to get more of Penn's Asian and Asian-American students involved in issues relevant to their communities.

The United Minorities Council, comprised of representatives of nine of the school's cultural student groups, "seeks to bring students together to sensitize each other to the other groups' concerns, and to raise awareness on campus about the groups," says a UMC leader. A major function of the UMC is its annual Celebration of Culture festival, which features food booths, performers, and arts and crafts displays and sales. The UMC also sponsors lectures and forums during the school year.

Despite the work of the cultural student groups, and the recent increase in the number of students of color on campus, Penn has had its share of racist incidents in recent years. During the 1991–92 school year, for example, students dumped water from the windows of one of the school's high-rise undergraduate dorms onto other students who were demonstrating against the Rodney King verdict. Women pledging a Latina sorority also had items thrown at them from the same windows. In addition, students complain of racist slurs, campus police harassment (although students are hopeful this situation will improve with the appointment of a new commissioner), and offensive editorial cartoons in the campus newspaper. "The comfort level of attending school here is sometimes pretty low for students of color, which is why the cultural student groups are so important to many of us for support," says a student.

Students say there are three types of Penn students. "There are those who are attuned to concerns of racial diversity, and are very, very aware. There's another segment of the population who don't think students of color belong on 'their' campus. And then there are those who are apathetic, and haven't thought much about the issues either way."

The university's location in the center of Philadelphia is convenient, but students say crime is a problem in the area immediately surrounding the campus. Although the university's 260-acre campus is largely self-contained, it is only a short distance to numerous sites of historical interest, such as Independence Hall and the Liberty Bell, and to many cultural attractions, including the Afro-American Museum, the Academy of Music, and theaters, restaurants, clubs, and bars. The black-owned Know Thyself bookstore is located just a few blocks from campus. There's a large Hispanic population in the north side of the city, but students say there is little interaction between them and the campus. The Chinatown section of Philadelphia, with its shops and restaurants, is also a short distance from campus. The City of Brotherly Love is two hours from New York City and Washington, DC, both of which are easily accessible by train.

"I'd do it again," says a student about his decision to attend school at Penn, echoing the sentiments of many other undergraduates. Students praise their school for its location and the quality of its faculty and academics, although judgments about the quality of life for students of color aren't overwhelmingly enthusiastic. "I made the right decision to come to Penn. I'm earning an Ivy League education, and there's so much to do on and off campus," says the student. Adds another student: "There's a lot of work that needs to be done to make the campus more racially tolerant, and I've gotten angry and frustrated about the situation many times. Coming here has made me a stronger person emotionally and has gotten me more active in issues of cultural diversity and politics."

PENNSYLVANIA STATE UNIVERSITY

Address: University Park, PA 16802
Phone: (814) 865-5471
Director of Admissions: Anna Griswold
Multicultural Student Recruiter: Gary Kelsey

1992–93 tuition: $4,548 (in-state); $9,574 (out-of-state)
Room and board: $1,710
Application deadline: Rolling admissions
Financial aid application deadline: 2/15

Being one in the crowd takes on new meaning at Pennsylvania State University, a school where nearly 40,000 graduate and undergraduate students traverse the school's campus every day. State College, the town in which the university is actually based, is aptly named.

To make an undergraduate educational experience a bit more intimate, the university is divided into ten colleges, which cover almost every field imaginable, from arts and sciences and agriculture to engineering and business. The school's journalism, agriculture, and engineering programs are nationally recognized, and meteorology, accounting, astronomy, and chemistry are also ranked highly.

Among the school's best African-American Studies courses are "African-American Dance," "African-American History," and "African-American Literature," which emphasizes the contributions of women. The school's extensive main library contains a section on African-American works and each month devotes itself to a different theme. Recent themes have focused on prominent black athletes and women. Latin American history courses are also respected.

Penn State is one of the few public universities in the country with cultural diversity requirements, which were integrated into the curriculum beginning with the students who entered during the 1991–92 school year and "which can range from African-American Studies to women's studies," says a student. "There's the good and the bad to the requirement, and no way have all the kinks been ironed out of it yet. For example, the engineering majors, who already have more than their fair share of required courses, don't want to have to take yet another course, but the administration is working on accommodating all students in this regard."

The university offers an impressive array of sources of academic assistance for undergraduates. Most prominent is the Multicultural Resource Center. "Every minority student has a guidance counselor there, and the counselors do everything from having pizza parties to offering scholarship information," says a senior who used the services frequently during her first year. "The counselors also know all their students' grades. They are definitely hands-on. The office also oversees a sort of big brother/big sister program, in which older students take new students around campus, work with them during study sessions, and socialize with them. It's a formal program that helps a lot of students get through four years at Penn State." To assist students with course selection, each of the school's ten colleges has a Minority Counselor. The counselors also sponsor career fairs and provide internship and job advice.

On most college campuses, student activism hasn't reared its head since the late '60s or early '70s, but in the spring of 1989 many Penn State African-American students staged a sit-in at the university's Telecommunications Building that generated much media attention. The students, reacting to several racist incidents on campus, issued several demands to the university: that Black Studies be renamed African-American Studies (it was); that an African-American be named a university vice-provost (an African-American was appointed to the position of assistant vice president); that a cultural diversity course be required of all students (it is); that at least two of the school's student-sponsored concerts each year include African-American artists (Ray Charles was a recent performer); and that a new cultural center should be opened (plans are in the works for one to open in 1995).

Unfortunately, the Black Caucus has since experienced a significant decrease in student membership. "We went from 300 to 100 active members after the sit-in, especially after those who were most active graduated," says a student leader. "Some of the recent Black Caucus student administrations never really actively pushed to increase membership in the group. But with some of the stuff that's been going on around the country lately, students are calling the Black Caucus office all the time saying they want to get involved."

The Black Caucus, which serves as the umbrella group for the school's 35 African-American organizations, sponsors a plethora of social and cultural activity that would make any undergrad's head spin. "We have speakers, picnics, parties, a basketball league, and even our own homecoming celebrations," says a student.

An activity that generates a good deal of student interest is the group's Friday Forums. Each week's topic is set by Black Caucus committee members. "Everyone at the forum is allowed to talk, and we do it sort of like on *Oprah*. The forums are always really vocal, especially when it comes to discussing racism. But we've also talked about everything from the AIDS epidemic and political correctness to why we need to buy $125 sneakers. Sometimes we even role-play. One time we had the men and women at the meeting role-play the Anita Hill–Clarence Thomas scene; the men had to be Anita and the women had to be Clarence."

In 1992 the Black Caucus also sponsored its first homecoming festivities, which featured a float for the king and queen. "This was my favorite part of the year," says a student, "because everybody on campus got to see us in action. Behind the float we had dancers, and local car dealers loaned us cars to ride in. It was kind of scary for us to participate because it cost us so much money, but I think everyone thought it was more than worth it." The festivities, largely attended by alums, included a Friday-night dance, a Saturday-afternoon banquet, and Sunday discussion groups.

Predominantly black Greek organizations provide an alternative to Black Caucus activities, and representatives of each serve on the all-black National Panhellenic Council. One of the council's largest sponsored events is its annual step show, which, according to a student, is huge. Students not interested in joining Greek organizations are able to participate in what are called social fellowships, one each for men and women. "Mostly they provide peer support, but they also do charity work like canned food and clothing drives. The difference between us and the Greek organizations is that there's nothing secret about us." Predominantly black and white Greek organizations come together each year for Ebony and Ivory Week, which puts on movie nights, dances, and blood drives. "But that is one of the few times when they interact," says a student.

The Latino Caucus, with about 25 active members, meets once every two weeks and sponsors and co-sponsors various events, such as speakers and bowling parties. With the Caribbean Student Association, the group invited Laurence Prescott, a professor in the Spanish department, to speak about the cultures of the Caribbean. "That discussion is what got me more involved in the caucus and learning about my heritage," says a member. Members of the Latino Caucus and Kappa Alpha Psi, a predominantly black Greek organization, recently sponsored a dance party. "It was great because we got to teach the Kappas the salsa and other Latin dances."

Students were also successful recently in starting a Hispanic sorority, Sigma Iota Alpha, which has eight members.

State College, ninety miles west of Harrisburg, is a predominantly white community that offers few social outlets for students of color. The Lion's Den is one of the few town clubs frequented by African-American students, but, because of the state's drinking laws, it serves only those at least 21 years of age. Students warn that the area surrounding the town is home to various white supremacist groups.

Like the town in which it is located, Penn State remains overwhelmingly white. Despite the efforts of the admissions office, students of color account for only about 6 percent of the school's 20,000-plus undergraduates. Attending this school can be lonely, but if a student is able to make his or her way to any of the student clubs, especially those culturally relevant to his or her background, the transition from high school to college can be a bit easier. "Getting active in the Black Caucus was the best thing I did here," says a member.

For the student coming to Penn State, the first day will no doubt be a shock, as the university, in a word, is huge. There is never a shortage of activities, and the support services are there, but the student needs to take the initiative and hunt for them. A good starting point is the university's Student Fair, held at the beginning of each year to introduce first-year students to the various organizations at the university.

While finding a niche can seem overwhelming, for many students it's well worth the effort. Says a junior: "I'm really proud of my college choice. Penn State is not for everybody. There's a lot here that can be intimidating. But Penn State does help build an independent spirit in students, and I'm glad I'll be graduating into the real world with that spirit. It's definitely been an uplifting experience, especially feeling that I can hold my own with any other college graduate because of the quality of education I'm earning here."

SWARTHMORE COLLEGE

Address: 500 College Avenue, Swarthmore, PA 19081-1397
Phone: (215) 328-8300
Director of Admissions: Robert Barr, Jr.
Multicultural Student Recruiter: Gloria Thomas Walker
1991–92 tuition: $16,465
Room and board: $5,520
Application deadline: 2/1
Financial aid application deadline: 2/1

Non-white freshman admissions: Applicants for the class of '94: 671
Accepted: 35%
Accepted who enroll: 9%
Applicants accepted who rank in top 10% of high school class: na
In top 25%: 100%
Median SAT: na
Median ACT: na
Full-time undergraduate enrollment: 1,309

Men: 52%
Women: 48%
Non-white students in
1987–88: na
1988–89: 13.3%
1989–90: 15.2%
1990–91: 16.9%
Geographic distribution of students: na
Top majors: na
Retention rate of non-white students: na
Scholarships exclusively for non-white students: None
Remediation programs: The college offers a non-credit course that emphasizes reading and study skills development.
Academic support services: Tutoring is available in all academic subjects.
Ethnic studies programs: The Asian Studies program, which involves five tenured faculty members, was established in 1976.

STUDENT ENROLLMENT

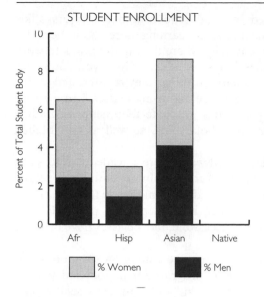

FACULTY

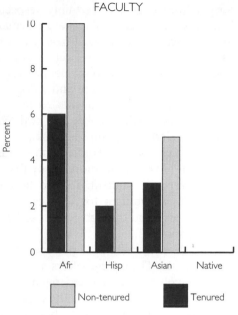

First-, second-, and third-year Chinese-language instruction is also offered. The interdisciplinary Black Studies program, which includes over 25 courses and involves four tenured faculty members, was established in 1969.

Ethnic studies courses: Swarthmore offers about four courses in Latin American Studies.

Organizations for non-white students: Swarthmore African-American Student Society, Swarthmore Asian Organization, Hispanic Organization for Latino Awareness

Notable non-white alumni: na

Tenured faculty: 105

Non-tenured faculty: 62

Student-faculty ratio: 9.5:1

Administrators: 35
African-American: 12%
Hispanic: 0
Asian-American: 3%
Native American: 0

Recent non-white speakers on campus: Dick Gregory (author and political activist); Cesar Chavez (labor leader and head of the United Farm Workers); Sandra Cisneros (author and poet); Le Xuan Khoa (philosophy professor, University of Saigon)

When Chris Edley, an African-American, was asked to accept the position of Michael Dukakis's presidential campaign adviser back in 1988, he could guess it was due to his experience as a Harvard Law professor as well as to his politics. But he also knew it was due to his ties to Swarthmore College, his and Dukakis's alma mater. "That's how I got the job," said Edley in an interview with the *Washington Post*. "Swarthmore graduates think that they're the best of the best. There's a strong institutional loyalty."

Edley may just be right. Swarthmore provides its students with one of the best and most demanding undergraduate programs in the country. The college is consistently ranked by the editors at *U.S. News & World Report* as one of the country's top three liberal arts colleges. And students don't just come to the college because they want to be assured of job or graduate school placement when they finish here, although a

Swarthmore degree is certainly respected by grad schools and employers alike. Students come because they have a genuine interest in learning more about the world around them. "I transferred from a large university where the big thing was to work as little as possible and still get good grades," says a student. "Here, you don't hear about grades much. You see people working hard on things they're interested in. It's easier for me to work here and I do, because I care about my classes." In a recent year, 23 Swarthmore students received prestigious graduate fellowships, including two Fulbright Scholarships and two Watson Scholarships, as well as five Mellon Minority Undergraduate Fellowships.

For many first-year students, the transition to Swarthmore's academic rigors can be tough. "I've studied more in my first semester here than in my entire high school career," reports a student. To ease the adjustment and to deemphasize the importance of grades, all courses for first-semester freshmen are taken on a pass/fail basis. Students also find their professors to be highly accessible; most classes have no more than 15 students.

English, economics, and political science are said to be among Swarthmore's best departments. The college offers a rigorous honors program for juniors and seniors, which involves tutorials and an oral exam at the end of a student's senior year. Swarthmore is also one of only a few undergraduate colleges in the country to have an engineering department, but unlike at other, larger schools, Swarthmore's engineering students have the opportunity to be exposed to the liberal arts. "An unusual aspect of the program is that even as an engineering major you can still get an excellent, well-rounded liberal arts education," says a recent graduate.

The college's Black Studies program, which requires students to enroll in at least five Black Studies courses and to complete a thesis, also gets high marks from students. "The program offers a wide variety of courses in a wide variety of disciplines. You can take Black Studies courses in the English, history, linguistics, and political science departments. This means that a typical Black Studies course may include students of various majors," says a student. "The History of African-American Peoples" is one of the area's more popular courses.

The Asian Studies program, however, gets less than stellar reviews from students. "The program is marginalized," states a student. "The Chinese-language courses are taught, for example, by non-tenured track professors, even though the program has been on campus for more than seven years." Members of the Swarthmore Asian Organization (SAO) are working to have more Asian-American Studies courses included in the college curriculum. Recently, SAO members were influential in getting the college to include an "Asian-American Literature" course in its curriculum. As of now, the course is scheduled to be offered on a temporary basis, but students hope it will become a permanent part of the department's curriculum.

At a school where academics are tough, to say the least, academic support services are, at times, a must. "There is a lot of academic support for students, from clinics to tutors to study groups," says a biology major. Students say the Black Cultural Center provides a great deal of support. The center has three computers for student use, a library containing books by and about African-Americans, and seminar rooms in which many of the Black Studies courses take place. The Black Cultural Center also serves as a social gathering place for students. Swarthmore African-American

Student Society (SASS) meetings are held at the center, and students are able to enjoy the center's living and TV rooms and use its kitchen facilities.

The Office of Minority Affairs is also located in the Black Cultural Center. The dean, Joe Mason, is "supportive not only of African-American students but also of Hispanic and Asian-American students," says a student. "He makes sure the administration does what it says it's going to do." One student comments that it was in large part due to Mason's efforts that the center was recently renovated. Alison Williams, an assistant professor of chemistry, is another professor highly regarded by students. "She's a role model because she's in the sciences," says a biology major. "She's also involved in supporting women of color on campus. Recently she helped organize support groups for women of color."

The various cultural student groups also provide support. In the past, the Swarthmore Asian Organization served primarily as a social organization for its members. The group recently sponsored a campus-wide party and a potluck dinner with members of Asian organizations at Haverford and Bryn Mawr colleges. Each year SAO sponsors Asian-American Month activities, usually in the spring semester, in which the group brings to campus various speakers and a film festival. In an effort to integrate the curriculum and faculty and staff, the purpose of SAO has become more political on campus, say students. SAO members also regularly attend East Coast Asian Union meetings and have attended a meeting at Cornell University about Asian-American Studies. The Swarthmore African-American Student Society and the Hispanic Organization for Latino Awareness (HALO) sponsor films, lectures, discussion groups, parties, and study groups.

Swarthmore has long been known for attracting a left-of-center student body. The students come from all over the country, although primarily from the Northeast. In addition, Swarthmore's reputation transcends oceans; more than 40 foreign countries—accounting for about 8 percent of the school's students—are represented in its student body.

Despite the college's liberal atmosphere, the campus hasn't been free of racist activity. A portrait of Malcolm X, after being removed anonymously from a wall in a main campus building, "was found slashed in a mock lynching" during the 1991–92 school year, says a student. "The students of color protested," says a student, "but the administration wasn't supportive. The incident made it a tough semester for many students of color."

Swarthmore is located within a thirty-five-minute drive of Bryn Mawr and Haverford colleges. A shuttle service regularly serves the campuses. Students are able to enroll in classes at the other two colleges, as well as at the University of Pennsylvania, and take advantage of some of the other schools' extracurricular programs. According to one student: "Students of color here at Swarthmore are more likely to go to the other campuses to take courses than are white students. There aren't that many students of color here, so it's important sometimes that we visit the other campuses."

Swarthmore College isn't exactly known for its nightlife. When students aren't studying, they feel they should be. But small room get-togethers are common, and the Tarble Social Center, renovated in 1986, has a snack bar and student lounges, popular destinations for the study-weary. At least once a week, the center hosts concerts, movies, and parties. According to students, the town of Swarthmore "is politically conservative and predominantly white." Students say they have little reason to venture into the community.

When the pressures of small-college life get too much, students will head by train into nearby Philadelphia; the SEPTA commuter station sits on the edge of campus. Philadelphia, one of the country's largest cities, is the home of many prominent universities, such as Temple and the University of Pennsylvania, and offers a rich variety of restaurants, bars, and cultural attractions. The Philadelphia Museum of Art, one of the country's finest, is a destination for some of the college's art classes.

Swarthmore attracts Ivy-quality students, but also students who don't want to be bothered with all of those schools' traditions and, by comparison, large enrollments and distant faculty. The Swarthmore experience is indeed intense, and four years here will be a challenge. Says a student: "Being a [student of color] at Swarthmore requires that you demand a lot of yourself. The best way I can describe this is 'mental toughness.' If one is to succeed at Swarthmore, one must have an inner strength."

TEMPLE UNIVERSITY

Address: Broad Street and Montgomery
   Avenue, Philadelphia, PA 19122
Phone: (215) 787-7200
Director of Admissions: Randy Miller
Multicultural Student Recruiter: Allen Beery
1991–92 tuition: $4,636 (in-state); $8,576
   (out-of-state)
Room and board: $4,681
Application deadline: 6/15
Financial aid application deadline: 5/1
Non-white freshman admissions: na
   Median SAT: na
   Median ACT: na
Full-time undergraduate enrollment: 15,651
   Men: 49%
   Women: 51%
Non-white students in
   1987–88: 22.5%
   1988–89: 23.4%
   1989–90: 24.8%
   1990–91: 26.6%
Geographic distribution of students: na
Top majors: na
Retention rate of non-white students: na
**Scholarships exclusively for non-white
   students:** None
Remediation programs: The Russell Conwell
   Center provides various remedial services.

Academic support services: Temple provides academic advising and tutoring.
Ethnic studies programs: Temple offers a program in African-American Studies.
Ethnic studies courses: The university offers various courses in Latin American Studies, including "Latin America Through Film and Fiction," "Oppression

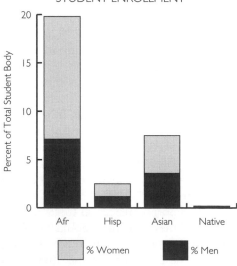

STUDENT ENROLLMENT

Percent of Total Student Body

Afr   Hisp   Asian   Native

% Women   % Men

and Omission in Latin American Literature," "Historical Continuity and Social Change in Latin America," and "Perspectives on Latin America."

Organizations for non-white students: Alpha Phi Alpha, Alpha Kappa Alpha, Omega Psi Phi, Delta Sigma Theta, Kappa Alpha Psi, Phi Beta Sigma, Sigma Gamma Rho, Zeta Phi Beta, Hispanic Student Association, Minority Pre-med Association, NAACP, African-American Student Union, Vietnamese Student Group, Caribbean Awareness Student Association, Temple Korean Student Association, Chinese Student Association, Korean Campus Crusade

Notable non-white alumni: Bill Cosby (comedian, actor, and civil rights activist)

Tenured faculty: 1,093

Non-tenured faculty: 254

Student-faculty ratio: 12:1

Administrators: 750

African-American: 19.5%
Hispanic: 0.9%
Asian-American: 2.1%
Native American: 0.7%

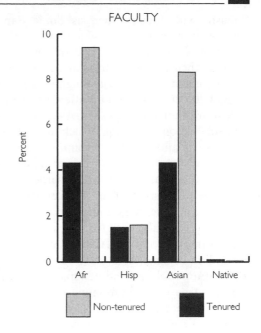

FACULTY

Recent non-white speakers on campus: Spike Lee (filmmaker); Maya Angelou (author and poet)

While students at most universities can only dream of having required core curriculums that include courses about race relations, Temple University students get the real thing. As of 1991, all Temple students must take "The Sociology of Race and Racism" as a part of the school's recently redesigned core curriculum. Such offerings in a core make sense at Temple, a school founded by a Baptist minister who wanted to make education available to individuals of all economic and racial backgrounds.

Temple also boasts the country's first and only Ph.D. program in African-American Studies, headed by Molefi K. Asante, a noted scholar. "Professor Asante is always in a good mood, and he's always willing to talk to students, even high school students who are interested in learning more about the program and about Temple."

The students also praise the program. "A lot of professors in the program push students to do well. Some students think courses in the program are going to be easy, but they soon find they're not. I took one class, and the professor didn't think our research writing was good enough, so he worked with all of us on our writing until it was." Adds the student: "Another positive aspect of the program is that a lot of graduate students teach the courses, and they're often younger and can relate to the students well. They sort of become our mentors."

Temple also offers other strong programs, particularly in the school's radio-television-film, business, communications, accounting, and journalism departments.

English, with faculty such as Sonia Sanchez, a highly acclaimed poet, is also considered strong.

Temple's writing center and tutoring services are helpful to students, but not as much as their fellow students are. "No one is afraid to ask other students for help," says a student. "I was struggling in the library with some work for a chemistry class, when a student saw me and offered to help. That sort of stuff goes on a lot."

A tremendous amount of networking also goes on within the African-American Student Union (AASU), which has about 30 active members. "It's mostly an educational and bonding group. At our weekly meetings we talk about different topics, mostly as ways to get our minds thinking about important issues," says a student. The group has sponsored programs about AIDS and interracial relationships, and it helps to sponsor an African Street Fair, a weeklong event held on campus, which features vendors and a concert.

Other groups also seek to bring students together. The recently formed Tribe Called 40, a support group for African-American men, "helps members stay in school. It's a bonding organization that's really been successful," says a student. *The Burning Torch* is a popularly read newspaper published periodically by members of Temple's African-American community.

But the Student Activities Center (SAC) "is where everybody hangs out. It's to the point that we're very possessive of what goes on in the center. If an organization other than the AASU or one of the other groups sponsors an event in SAC, we almost feel that we should be told about it. We feel like it's the only place where we can see African-American students, especially outside on SAC's patio on hot days."

Students also praise the high level of student camaraderie. "I've been to other schools, and even some historically black schools, and students there all seem cliquey. If I'm alone at SAC, I never feel that I can't talk to other people. Everyone here is very friendly. We also go to each other's off-campus houses a lot."

Temple's traditionally black Greek organizations are also active on campus, sponsoring numerous dances and parties throughout the school year. The Alpha Kappa Alpha sorority also recently sponsored a Man Auction—where the men served the women for a day—while the women of Delta Sigma Theta sponsored the African-American book festival, as well as its Delta Night at the Apollo and fashion shows.

Students frequent parties at area schools, most often at Cheyney and Lincoln universities, predominantly black schools. The men of Phi Beta Sigma fraternity are also closely aligned with the Sigmas at the University of Pennsylvania, as members of each pledge together and co-sponsor various events and parties.

Temple is primarily a commuter campus, which can make it difficult, despite the efforts of various student organizations, to sustain interest in student groups—or just friendships. Of the school's more than 15,000 undergraduates, only about 20 percent live on campus, and many of Temple's students also have part-time jobs. While Temple attracts students primarily from the surrounding area, there are students from all 50 states and more than 60 countries, making for a diverse student body. Temple has the largest African-American student population of any of the Pennsylvania state universities.

The city of Philadelphia offers an abundance of off-campus diversions—everything from restaurants and clubs to museums and concerts. The neighborhood in which

Temple is located isn't the greatest—the area is generally considered run-down—but students report that the school's campus security system is more than adequate.

Temple's motto is "Persevere and Conquer," and many who attend school here do just that. Temple is a solid academic institution that defies the myths of a typical commuter school. Says a student: "The community atmosphere and the friends I've been able to make are probably among my favorite reasons for going to school at Temple."

VILLANOVA UNIVERSITY

Address: Villanova, PA 19085
Phone: (215) 645-4000
Director of Admissions: Stephen Merritt
Multicultural Student Recruiter: Charles
  Wright

1992–93 tuition: Arts, and Commerce and
  Finance: $13,200; Nursing and Science:
  $13,590; Engineering: $13,870
Room and board: $5,870
Application deadline: 1/15
Financial aid application deadline: 3/15

Although Villanova University has yet to achieve the name recognition of other Catholic institutions such as Georgetown University and the University of Notre Dame, the 151-year-old university, located outside of Philadelphia, provides its mostly pre-professional students with a respectable education.

Villanova's College of Commerce and Finance, which offers programs in business administration, accounting, and economics, is popular with students. Students praise the college for its facilities—Bartley Hall, which houses the college, recently underwent renovations—and job and graduate school placement. Villanova's College of Liberal Arts and Sciences has strong programs in psychology and astronomy. Nursing and engineering, with major courses of study in chemical, civil, electrical, and mechanical engineering, are also recommended.

Students are able to major and minor in African-American Studies, a program students say is strong. One popular course is "Black Drama." Maghan Keita, a history professor in the program, is described by one student as "one of the strongest teachers we have here. He's constantly exposing 'Nova students to events, such as debates on multiculturalism." Interdisciplinary programs in Latin American Studies and ethnic studies are offered.

Although it is a midsize university, 'Nova's student-faculty relations are reportedly quite strong. Classes are usually small, so getting to know your professor isn't difficult. But students have complained that teachers too often rely on Catholic traditions rather than on getting their students to think critically and freely. One student suggests: "Don't even mention abortion around some of these professors."

For cultural diversity programming, Villanova's Black Cultural Society is the most active. With about 25 members, the BCS sponsors various activities for Black Culture Week, including speakers and an African cuisine night. The group recently held its first awards ceremony for its members, an event attended by faculty and staff as well as students. At the end of each year, the BCS also sponsors a picnic for members.

"BCS members support one another," says a student. This is most obvious in the organization's Mentor-Buddy Program, which attempts to pair an upperclass student with a first-year student, usually on the basis of majors. "You contact the freshman before the summer is over, and when you and he or she arrive on campus, you take them on a tour. I couldn't have gotten through the year without my mentor." Apathy can be a problem in the school's African-American community. "Half of the members of the BCS attend everything, but the other half come just every so often."

Novelette Emery, the BCS's staff adviser, "provides much-needed support, but gives guidance without running the show. She also brings area events to the attention of the BCS," says a student.

Villanova's newest cultural student group is the Asian Student Association, which has about 50 active members. Says a student about why he helped found the organization: "I wanted to provide a way for Asian students to bond. I never knew Asians on campus until I started the group. That was tragic. Now I think students feel freer to talk to other Asians, and maybe there will be less apathy toward our own race." According to the student, the group's primary focus is to provide social opportunities for members; most recently, the ASA won a coed volleyball championship on campus. The ASA has also begun to interact with Asian student groups at area colleges, such as Swarthmore and the University of Pennsylvania.

To promote multicultural awareness, the school's Campaign for Community sponsors a Diversity Awareness Day that has "workshops running from morning to afternoon on such subjects as Irish issues, religious studies, the mass media, and the United States from a Central American's perspective, as well as an international poetry reading." Twenty workshops were sponsored. The group's steering committee had 12 members, including an African-American and an Asian-American student. Its first activity in a recent year was to present a diversity skit, followed by group discussions, during freshman orientation.

Diversity of just about any sort is not one of Villanova's hallmarks, hence the school's nickname Vanillanova. "If you're a metalhead or into black leather jackets, you'll be persecuted. This place is very conservative and very Catholic." But another student adds: "I've met some of the brightest students I've ever known here at Villanova. A lot of the students are ignorant of cultural diversity, but it's because they were sheltered when they were growing up. They're not prejudiced. Just ignorant."

The university lacks a racially and ethnically diverse student body, to say the least. The university did not respond to our admissions survey, but we learned from students that of the university's approximately 11,000 undergraduate and graduate students, 200 are African-Americans. Among the school's undergraduate population of about 6,300 students, about 50 are of Asian descent and about 1 percent of the campus is of Hispanic descent. The majority of the students at Villanova attended private high schools, and 85 percent of the student body identifies itself as Catholic. The Catholic tone of the student body, as well as the school's large and active ROTC program, keeps the tenor of the school rather sedate and conservative.

Students who want a more diverse social life often find time, mostly on weekends, to take the twelve-mile train ride into the City of Brotherly Love, with its smorgasbord of cultural and social activities, particularly as the predominantly white community around campus offers few off-campus diversions for students of color. Villanova is a "dry" campus, so much of its social activity focuses on one of the bars that line Lancaster Avenue. Students also attend the frequent parties at off-campus apartments, in which about half of the student body lives.

Sports are popular—both for participants and for those content to sit back and watch. Villanova's basketball team is usually a top contender in the NCAA's Division I and its games get huge turnouts; football games are also well attended.

Apathy is one of the complaints students have about their peers, and the lack of diversity is another. But few complain about the quality of the education they're receiving at Villanova. "Villanova prepares you well educationally, and I've gotten really involved in clubs and other organizations. The location is relaxing, and it's not too far from Philadelphia, which is nice to get away to every once in a while. I like it here."

RHODE ISLAND

BROWN UNIVERSITY

Address: 45 Prospect Street, Providence, RI
02912
Phone: (401) 863-2378
Dean of Admissions and Financial Aid: Eric
Widmer
Multicultural Student Recruiter: Anthony
Canchola-Flores
1993–94 tuition: $19,156
Room and board: $5,612
Application deadline: Early action: 11/1;
regular decision 1/1
Financial aid application deadline: 2/1
Non-white freshman admissions: Applicants
for the class of '95: 3,338
Accepted: 26.9%
Accepted who enroll: 44.3%
Applicants accepted who rank in top
10% of high school class: 90%
In top 25%: 98%
Median SAT range: 560–670 V,
610–740 M
Median ACT range: 24–30
Full-time undergraduate enrollment: 5,671
Men: 51.8%
Women: 48.2%
Non-white students in
1987–88: 18.1%
1988–89: 18.8%
1989–90: 20.2%
1990–91: 22.1%
Students In-state: 3%
Top majors: 1. Biology 2. International
Relations 3. Engineering
Retention rate of non-white students: 91%

STUDENT ENROLLMENT

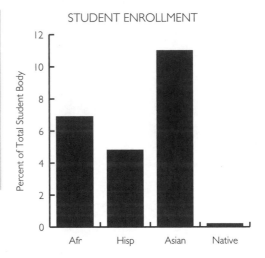

GEOGRAPHIC DISTRIBUTION OF STUDENTS

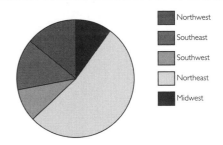

Northwest
Southeast
Southwest
Northeast
Midwest

**Scholarships exclusively for non-white
students:** na
Remediation programs: None
Academic support services: Tutoring is
available in most academic subjects.

Ethnic studies programs: Departments at Brown include Latin American Studies, South Asian Studies, Afro-American Studies, and Hispanic Studies.

Organizations for non-white students: African Students Association, Latin American Students Organization, Asian-American Students Association, Minority Peer Counselors, Bi-Racial Student Support Group, la Federación de Estudiantes puertorriqueños, Black Pre-med Society, Black Psychology Students Association, National Society of Black Engineers, Building Bridges: Asian Women Together, Cambodian Students Association, Native Americans at Brown, Chinese Students Associaton, Cultural Association of South Asians, Black Seniors Organization, Filipino Alliance at Brown, Organization of United African People, Hong Kong Students Association, South Asian Students Association, U.S.-Japan Society, Third World Pre-business Society, Third World Pre-law Society, Korean Students Association

Notable non-white alumni: Steve Jordan (professional football player, Minnesota Vikings); Inman Page (first African-American graduate of Brown and former president, Morehouse College); Ethel Tremaine-Robinson (founder, Alpha Kappa Alpha); Theodore Newman (retired chief justice, District of Columbia Court of Appeals); J. Saunders Redding (first African-American professor at an Ivy League university, Cornell)

Tenured faculty: 412

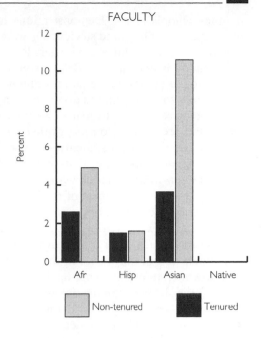

FACULTY

Non-tenured / Tenured

Non-tenured faculty: 123

Student-faculty ratio: 9:1

Administrators: 533
African-American: 5.8%
Hispanic: 1.3%
Asian-American: 1.3%
Native American: 0.0019%

Recent non-white speakers on campus: Bishop Desmond Tutu (Nobel Peace Prize winner and South African civil rights activist); Cesar Chavez (labor leader and head of the United Farm Workers); Dr. Louis Sullivan (former secretary, Health and Human Services); Frank Chin (playwright)

There are numerous reasons why Brown University, one of the eight members of the illustrious Ivy League, is one of the country's most popular and most selective schools. There are the university's outstanding academics—most of which are nationally recognized—and there is the school's lack of distribution requirements and of a core curriculum—standards at most other institutions. Then there is the school's location, between Boston and New York City, and, of course, there is Brown's stellar faculty.

But what makes Brown truly unique among universities of its caliber—and what encourages so many motivated and intelligent high school seniors to send their applications this way—is its student body, the Ivy League's most progressive and politically active. Students are aware of national and local issues in a way that students at other schools aren't. Demonstrations have been waged against the CIA for its on-campus recruiting, and suicide pills were stocked on campus, mostly as a symbolic gesture, in case of a nuclear disaster. Both events received national attention.

For many Brunonians (as Brown students are called), participating in meaningful protests or rallies is on an equal footing with academics, although the typical Brown student sees to it that studies don't get away from him or her. Students at Brown are also more accepting of diversity—whether of the racial, cultural, sexual, or religious sort—than are students on most other college campuses today. This is no doubt in part because the Brown student body itself is so diverse.

Says a student about her first-year living situation: "My freshman roommate was from a city in Latin America whose name I couldn't begin to pronounce, much less place on the globe. Members of my unit were from all over too—my neighbors were from France and New York, people down the hall hailed from Canada, Nebraska, Puerto Rico, Texas, Providence . . . you get the picture. Within weeks, we all found friendships in each other's company, not to mention a better sense of ourselves as individuals and of our places in the world."

Non-white students, no matter from where on the globe, are also made to feel a part of the Brown community—and in particular the university's multicultural community—early on, thanks to the Third World Transition Program, an 18-year-old program that introduces students to the academic and social life at the university. Students praise the four-day program. "At first, I thought TWTP only meant a few extra days to get to know people. But by the end of the program, TWTP and the term Third World came to represent pride, unity, and a special bonding that we as people of color share," says a senior. Adds another TWTP student: "TWTP is an eye opener! Not only does it contribute to making you a more conscious member of your own cultural background, but at the same time it is instrumental in creating a bond between peoples of different racial and cultural backgrounds. A perfect start to schooling at Brown."

TWTP is coordinated in part by 40 Minority Peer Counselors, upperclass students who serve as mentors to new students during their first year at Brown. "MPCs, who live with new students throughout the school year, are excellent sources of support," says a human biology major.

Once the TWTP program is over, however, students complain that there is less interaction between students of various cultures. "Except in crisis situations, there is not a great deal of Third World unity at Brown," comments a senior. "Unfortunately, it seems as if this trend will continue, specifically between blacks and Asians, perhaps mirroring national sentiment. Blacks are definitely less of a political force on this campus than they used to be, and black enrollment has been declining slightly while the opposite is true for Asians. In terms of minorities and whites, there is some integration, but many whites in particular tend to feel that it is not enough. I would estimate that about two-thirds of the black students tend to 'hang' black, whether at black parties or eating in the 'Little Africa' section of the cafeteria. White students are the main ones who have problems with the current situation." Adds another student: "The same black students who eat and party together tend to live together. The same applies to white students. Wriston Quad is known as a white area, while black students are centered on Pembroke campus."

A "crisis situation" which brought students of all backgrounds together was the recent takeover of a campus administration building, which resulted in the arrest of more than 250 students and considerable media attention. (We told you Brown is politically active.) Students were protesting the university's policy of not being need-blind in admissions, a policy due in part to the university's relatively low endowment, the lowest in the Ivy League.

In the fall of '91, students also united for a rally in favor of Brown's recently adopted hate-speech rule, which was challenged when a white male student yelled racist and homophobic epithets at other students. The student was found guilty of violating the campus regulation and was dismissed from school. According to a student participant, a student of color coalition stormed a meeting convened to discuss the case. "I want to point out that minority students' voices are heard by the administration, and usually something is done about our concerns," says a student. One administrator students have come to rely on is Armando Bengochea, an assistant dean of the college.

A popular spot on campus for students of color to meet and "just relax" is the centrally located Third World Center, which sponsors numerous cultural events, including an Asian-American Arts Festival, Black History Month activities, and Puerto Rican and Native American awareness weeks, just to name a few. The center, popular with students, has classrooms and conference rooms, lounges (complete with a TV and VCR), a modest library, and office space.

Any discussion of Brown that doesn't mention its unstructured—and some would say controversial—approach to education wouldn't be complete. In short, Brown has no graduation requirements, outside of your major, that is. Working with faculty advisers, students pick their own courses of study, without having to adhere to a prescribed curriculum.

Students do have the option of earning the more conventional letter grades (no pluses or minuses, though, and you can't earn lower than a C) or Satisfactory/No Credit. A student must decide which system of grading he or she prefers by the end of the fourth week of classes.

For some students, this sort of freedom can be a bit much. But for the majority of Brown students, it's a chance to grow and to act independently. "Because of the Brown curriculum, my dorm mates and I have all had the chance to explore different academic disciplines, with surprising and, I think, successful, results. My roommate switched from pure engineering to engineering/economics. I've had the freedom to figure out that, as much as I love science, I don't want to do medicine. I found comparative literature, which allows me to look at literary canons and my own life in entirely different ways. Even more importantly, although these decisions are my own, I haven't been alone in making them; faculty and deans and friends have been there to help."

Some of Brown's best and most popular programs are English, history, geology, computer science, religious studies, political science, and math. Engineering and pre-med programs—which allow qualified students to pursue an eight-year liberal arts and medical program at Brown and its medical center—also have their fans, as do self-designed programs of study.

Brown's Center for the Study of Race and Ethnicity in America supports the teaching and research of issues focusing on African-Americans, Asian-Americans, Latinos, and Native Americans. "My job is to help faculty. The center exists to serve departments, not compete with them," says Rhett Jones, the center's newly appointed director and professor (and co-founder) of Afro-American Studies. Jones is involved in more than just the center. In 1972, he helped organize the Sankore Society, Brown's organization of black faculty, administrators, and appointed personnel. He has also worked extensively in the world outside the Van Wickle gates, having helped to create the Black Studies Consortium of Rhode Island and served as a member of the Rhode Island Black Task Force of Higher Education.

The university's Afro-American Studies program receives cautious praise from students. "Ethnic studies at Brown is strong compared to other schools, judging from the conversations I've had with students at other Ivies. That's not saying much, though. Afro-American Studies is generally known for its unreliability, canceling courses which were in the official listing almost every semester because of lack of faculty to teach them. If one or two key professors resign or retire, there will be very little left in terms of Black Studies here." Courses that earn student respect are "Black Women Writers" and "Afro-Brazilians and the Brazilian Polity." On the other hand, students considered the program's "African History Until 1870" weak because, according to a student, "it offered the usual perspective on African history, which didn't go over well with many in the class who wanted more Afrocentrism."

Brown can gloat over its impressive graduate school placement record. Of those who apply to law school, 90 to 95 percent are accepted to one of their top three choices, and of those who apply to business school, nearly 100 percent are accepted. Brown also consistently ranks among the top five colleges in the nation in the percentage of applicants accepted to medical school.

Providence, the state capital and Brown's home, is just forty-five minutes from Boston and a little more than three hours from New York City, popular destinations for shoppers and party seekers. Providence isn't without its amenities, though. "Ethnic neighborhoods abound here. I never had a chance in Indiana to walk down the street to a Portuguese bakery to buy freshly baked sweet bread or to wander down a street and hear people speaking anything but English. Providence has very strong and active ethnic groups that bring a great deal of cultural diversity to the area, as well as great restaurants." The editors at *Newsweek* magazine recently ranked Providence, which has African-American and Portuguese communities, as one of the "ten hottest cities in America." However, students say "there have been a few run-ins between black students and the Providence cops, because young black males are always suspects" and are frequently stopped by police and asked for identification.

Brown is a school for the mature and the motivated, and it is also for the student interested in going to school with a diverse group of students. Writes a student: "I came to Brown because I read in a college guide that it was the ideal place for a black student to receive an Ivy League education without being subject to elitist attitudes. Brown has its share of problems, but I would still recommend it over other predominantly white schools of the same genre, as long as the student's family can afford the cost. From the president, Vartan Gregorian, on down, I think the administration is reasonably responsive to minority student input, especially if it is pushed."

PROVIDENCE COLLEGE

Address: Providence, RI 02918
Phone: (401) 865-2535
Director of Admissions: Michael Backer
Multicultural Student Recruiter: na

1992–93 tuition: $12,600
Room and board: $5,300
Application deadline: 2/1
Financial aid application deadline: 2/1

Providence College is a midsize school that's big on sports. More than 80 percent of the student body participates in athletic activities at the college, and the college fields 10 varsity athletic teams for men and 10 for women, all at competitive NCAA Division I levels. In recent years, the Friars have been ranked among the top 20 nationally in men's basketball, ice hockey, cross-country, and soccer, and in women's basketball, volleyball, ice hockey, and field hockey.

Although the typical Providence College student may not be as competitive on the academic field as he or she is on the athletic field, Providence College does offer a respectable education—with a strong Catholic bent. The college was founded in 1917 by the Preachers of the Province of St. Joseph, commonly referred to as the Dominicans. Today, the college remains under Catholic control and retains many of the characteristics of a religious institution, right down to its team nickname: the Friars. Church service is a popular activity among students, most of whom—nearly 90 percent—are Irish or Italian Catholic. Birth control counseling is not offered by health services; there is a Pro-Life but no Pro-Choice group on campus. And all dorms are single-sex, with strictly enforced visiting hours. (A student caught on the premises of an opposite-sex dorm after hours is fined.)

PC students study and play hard. Students say the school's strongest and most popular departments are in business administration, which allows students to concentrate in accounting, marketing, or finance. Philosophy and religion rank as two of the school's most respected programs, and education and English earn high marks from students. The college's Latin American Studies program is small but decent, say students. In addition to a core curriculum, students must satisfy two years' worth of Development of Western Civilization, an interdisciplinary program that examines chronologically some of the great works of Western thought, everything from the *Iliad* to the works of the French philosopher Jean-Paul Sartre.

PC faculty members are almost always easily accessible; it's not uncommon for professors to give out their home telephone numbers on the first day of class. A professor popular with students is Eric Hirsch, a sociologist, who is actively involved in the group Students Organized Against Racism and the Board of Multicultural Student Affairs. Robert Hamlin, director of the MLK Scholarship program, which seeks to bring more students of color onto campus, is also supportive of students.

More than 95 percent of the student body is white. (PC did not respond to our admissions questionnaire.) To help non-white students adjust to PC socially and academically, the college established, as a result of student protests and demands, the Office of Minority Student Affairs in 1988. "We're in and out of the office all of the time. It's almost like a train station," says a student. The dean of the office, Wilesse Comissiong, "knows what's going on, and she knows how to give us academic and social help. She's very involved with students, attends all the events, and tries to include all cultures in the office's programming." One of the office's more successful efforts is its Peer Mentor Program, which pairs upperclass students with first-year students to teach them the ropes of PC campus life.

The school's Board of Multicultural Student Affairs, a student organization, has about 60 active members, four of whom serve as board officers. In a recent year, the majority of board members—about 40—were African-American, while five were white, four were Asian, and about a dozen were Hispanic. In the fall of '91, the board was given new offices in Slavin Center, the school's student center; they have a small library. Despite its new quarters, the board "is not operating as it should be," according to a student active in the group. Board members blame the problem partly on lack of funding. "The student congress allocates money to each club. Last year we got $3,500. This year we got $3,000." According to the student, the Rugby Club was awarded $9,000 by the student congress. "We just don't understand that," comments the student. PC's Afro-American Society brings guest speakers to campus each semester, sponsors dances throughout the school year, and holds an annual candlelight vigil to commemorate the birthday of Martin Luther King, Jr.

Providence, the capital of Rhode Island, offers students numerous off-campus diversions—when athletics and academics aren't in the way—among them an orchestra, museums, and numerous ethnic restaurants. The city is also home to four other colleges, including Brown University and the Rhode Island School of Design. Students often attend parties and events at the other schools. Some fantastic beaches are also located just a half hour's drive from campus. At PC, students are active in any number of social service, religious, or special-interest groups. Students have the chance to get familiar with each of the groups' offerings at the school's annual Club Fair. A popular on-campus hangout is the Slavin Center, with an ice-cream parlor and pizza parlor, as is the school's impressive Peterson Recreation Center, opened in 1980.

Diversity of any sort is hard to find at Providence College, but, says a student, "the majority of PC students are becoming aware of the need for more diversity, and we have no problems with many of the white students here. Unfortunately, though, there are still those who just don't care."

UNIVERSITY OF RHODE ISLAND

Address: Kingston, RI 02881
Phone: (401) 792-9800
Director of Admissions: David Taggart
Multicultural Student Recruiter: na

1992–93 tuition: $2,874 (in-state); $9,308 (out-of-state)
Room and board: $5,050
Application deadline: 3/1
Financial aid application deadline: 2/15

At many schools, especially at a state university, the odds of seeing a college president on campus, or of seeing him or her at any student function other than at graduation, are small, to say the least. At the University of Rhode Island, however, Robert Carothers, the school's new president, is a familiar sight, and he attends student events, including those sponsored by cultural groups. "He's all for diversity on campus," says a student. Carothers won even more fans recently when he decided against having the school stage his inauguration, which would have cost thousands of dollars.

No less impressive to students at URI is the school's Special Programs for Talent Development—located on the second floor of the Taft Building—an academic and non-academic resource for economically disadvantaged students, as well as for African-Americans, Latinos, Asian-Americans, and Native Americans. "Talent Development is the main reason I would do URI all over again," says an English major. "TD is like one big family. If TD students are the young people of the family, then Leo Dimaio, TD's director, is definitely the father. This man puts his neck on the line for you. If he finds out you're not in class when you're supposed to be, it's not unlike him to go to the student's dorm room, wake him if he's missing a morning class, and get him to class. TD has turned out doctors, lawyers, and professional athletes. TD's office is open to anyone."

Edward Givens, Sharon Forleo, and Frank Forleo, academic advisers at TD, are also of tremendous support to students. "When I just want to sit and talk to someone, I know I can go there. Ed, Sharon, and Frank always listen to us, and we can talk about almost anything with them." John McCray, vice president of student development, provides additional support. "He gets things done for us. If I have a problem, I know he'll help me out. For instance, I knew I needed a job on campus to make ends meet. So I went to him for advice. By the end of the day, I had two phone calls from administrators on campus who said they had job openings in their departments. I know it was because of him that I got the offers. He also eats with students in the dining halls."

Although administration and faculty support is strong, students report that peer support is less so. "The only time the minority students ever really come together for anything here is when something negative happens, like when a racist remark is made by someone. Very few students really care. You see the same few students at all of the cultural awareness meetings. It's also very cliquey. You have the football players there. You have the basketball players there. And you have the cheerleaders over there. URI students, and not just the minority students, are apathetic. People basically don't care."

When students do care, some come together in the form of the Latin American Student Association (LASA), which has about 45 active members. "LASA is probably the most up-and-coming and visible multicultural student group on campus," says a student. "They sponsor a brunch called 'A Coming Together' with Latin American food, birthday parties for their members, and a conference on campus in which fourteen other colleges and universities participated. They're a very tight and active group." In addition, five URI students have affiliated with the Latin-oriented Lambda Psi Lambda fraternity at Brown University, located about thirty minutes from campus.

Uhuru Sasa, a Swahili term meaning "freedom now," has been on URI's campus for about twelve years. Although the organization has sponsored forums and parties for Black History Month, a student member claims the group, with about 15 to 20 active student members, is not unified enough to coordinate more events. "We also don't have the numbers of African-American students enrolled here to do more, but there's also a lot of tension among the black students that keeps us less active. It's mostly just a matter of personalities not mixing well. There's a lot of gossip and rivalry. Last year, we managed to have Spike Lee on campus, and a bunch of us, along with the president of the university, had dinner with him, and we told him about the problems Uhuru Sasa was having."

In an attempt to have more resources directed at URI's students of color, more than 200 students staged a sit-in at one of the school's administrative buildings in the fall of 1992. Students demanded an upgrading of the school's Multicultural Student Center and more counseling services. As a result of the sit-in, university president Robert Carothers agreed to include students of color in the planning of the new center, as well as to hire more minority academic counselors.

Although URI can't be described as a suitcase school, one report has it that nearly half of the student body leaves campus on weekends. Many in-staters return home, while others head into Boston, Providence, or Hartford, all easily accessible by car or train. (An Amtrak station is located near campus.) Rhode Island beaches are also close by. Aside from a couple of bars and restaurants, Kingston, a small, rural community, is a less popular off-campus destination for students.

When students do stay on campus, weekend entertainment is often provided by the school's fraternity parties. Intramurals are big here, and varsity sports, especially football and sailing, generate a great deal of school spirit. The student center, a popular place to be seen, has a restaurant and comfortable lounge space.

When it comes to academics, URI offers students solid educational opportunities. All first-year students enroll in University College. Students then apply to the college of their choice within the university. According to students, the most competitive—and most popular—programs are engineering, business, and education. Students are able to major in any one of nine different engineering programs, including computer engineering, electrical engineering, and ocean engineering. The College of Business Administration offers seven different majors, such as accounting and finance. The school's nursing and five-year pharmacy program are also well regarded. In the College of Arts and Sciences, students say the strongest departments are English, political science, and computer science. URI's School of Oceanography, with a campus on Narragansett Bay, is one of the best such programs in the country.

The university also has some rigorous distribution requirements that must be completed for graduation, including courses in English communication, literature and the fine arts, foreign language and culture, the natural and social sciences, and math. A plus of attending URI, one of the country's smaller public universities, is that close interaction with faculty is common. "I know a lot of the staff and faculty by their first names," says a junior.

URI is a midsize state university that offers impressive academic support services and a respectable education. "Students who want active student groups may want to go elsewhere, or come here and work to make what we have here more active. But at the same time, I know I'm getting a good education here, and it's a good place to work with professors."

FURMAN UNIVERSITY

Address: Greenville, SC 29613
Phone: (803) 294-2034
Director of Admissions: J. Carey Thompson
Multicultural Student Recruiter: na
1993–94 tuition: $12,480
Room and board: $3,952
Application deadline: 2/1
Financial aid application deadline: 2/1
Non-white freshman admissions: Applicants
for the class of '96: 119
Accepted: 62%
Accepted who enroll: 45%
Applicants accepted who rank in top
10% of high school class: 57%
In top 25%: 94%
Median SAT range: 480–580 V, 540–650 M
Median ACT: 24–28
Full-time undergraduate enrollment: 2,474
Men: 46%
Women: 54%
Non-white students in
1987–88: na
1988–89: na
1989–90: 4%
1990–91: 4%
Geographic distribution of students: na
Top majors: 1. Economics/Business
2. Biology 3. Political Science
Retention rate of non-white students: na
**Scholarships exclusively for non-white
students:** None
Remediation programs: None
Academic support services: Tutoring services
are available in all academic subjects.

Ethnic studies programs: None
Ethnic studies courses: The university offers
"Minority Politics" and a course in
African-American history. All students
are required to enroll one of 26
Asian/African Studies courses.
Organizations for non-white students:
Student League for Black Culture,
Brotherhood of the Sphinx, Furman
Gospel Ensemble
Notable non-white alumni: Dr. Angela
Franklin ('81; professor and dean,
Morehouse School of Medicine); Sarah
Reese ('71; opera singer, Metropolitan
Opera, New York); Dr. Denise Everett
('79; director, Child Sexual Abuse Team,
Wake Forest Medical Center); Stanford

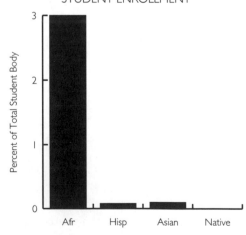

STUDENT ENROLLMENT

Percent of Total Student Body

Afr   Hisp   Asian   Native

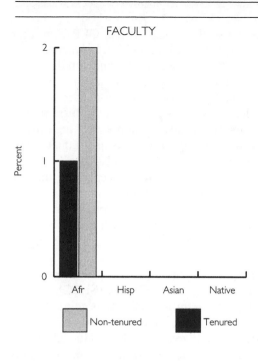

FACULTY

Non-tenured

Tenured

Jennings ('84; professional football player, Cincinnati Bengals)

Tenured faculty: 163

Non-tenured faculty: 74

Student-faculty ratio: 12:1

Administrators: 18

    African-American: 1%

    Hispanic: 0

    Asian-American: 0

    Native American: 0

Recent non-white speakers on campus: Jesse Jackson (former U.S. presidential candidate and civil rights activist); Dick Gregory (author and political activist); Theo Mitchell (politician); Randy Eddy (attorney)

After more than 160 years, Furman University and the conservative Southern Baptist Convention, which controlled it, have gone their separate ways. In a region where change doesn't come often, that's big news.

What hasn't changed, however, is Furman's commitment to undergraduate education. The university has excellent and popular programs in economics, business administration, and accounting. Among the school's humanities offerings, history, religion, and English are said to be outstanding. At Plyler Hall of Science, which houses the departments of geology, physics, mathematics, computer science, and psychology, sophisticated research facilities are available for undergraduate use. The school's unique urban studies program includes off-campus study opportunities in such cities as Washington, DC, and Philadelphia. Marian Stobel, who teaches the "Black Experience in America" course, is well regarded on campus. "She's extremely sensitive to the needs of minority students," says a student leader.

No one graduating from Furman can bypass the college's extensive liberal arts requirements, which include courses in eight different areas, ranging from English composition and the fine arts to physical education and the natural and social sciences. As part of the requirements, students must also take a course in Asian or African Studies. Students are able to choose from more than 25 courses to satisfy the requirement, which focuses on the region's literature, politics, philosophies, and religions. Among the courses are "African Traditional Religions," "Oriental Art History," and "Chinese Philosophy." Students say that one of the more popular courses in the program is "Peoples of Black Africa," a sociology course.

Furman students must also satisfy the Cultural Life Program (CLP) requirement to graduate. Before graduating, students must attend at least 36 CLP events, which consist of university-sponsored lectures and musical events. A recent CLP event that generated a great deal of campus-wide attention was a presentation on racism by a University of Georgia student group. "It was effective because Furman students got a chance to talk openly about racism and racial stereotypes," says a junior. "A lot of the comments were painfully honest and candid, but it was a much-needed forum."

Furman students, who take their academics seriously, frequently turn to the school's Office of Minority Student Affairs for academic support. The office's director, Artie Travis, "has a strong mind with strong ideas," says a student. "His door is always open." Bonnie Brown, an assistant in the office, also works closely with students. "She always gives students encouragement and advice," adds another student. "Both she and Artie show us that we can achieve something in life." In addition, students often turn to Judy Holmes, a business administration professor, Aaron Bell, a political science professor, and Cherie Maiden, a professor of modern languages. "These three professors are role models because they are highly intelligent and care a great deal for their students."

For the past several years, most of the cultural student groups at Furman have remained dormant, including the Student League for Black Culture (SLBC). "There are too few black students on campus to keep an organization like that going," states one student. The group has managed to sponsor some films, lectures, and forums dealing with the African-American experience. In a recent study conducted by the staff of *The Chronicle of Higher Education,* Furman was one of a few dozen schools in the country where the majority of its African-American male students were on athletic scholarships.

There is a somewhat active Greek system, although the university administration doesn't officially recognize Greek organizations. The school has small chapters of two historically black Greek organizations, Alpha Phi Alpha fraternity and Alpha Kappa Alpha sorority. An African-American student was recently elected to serve as president of the school's Interfraternity Council, which represents predominantly white and black Greek organizations. "His election will increase awareness and concern about black issues," observes a student. "It will also increase the input and influence that minority groups have on campus."

The school's Greek organizations are nominally integrated; during a recent year, two predominantly white fraternities each had one African-American member, and Alpha Phi Alpha had a white member. Says a student about the school's Greek system: "The fraternities and sororities are all open to anyone and a minority wouldn't be hindered from joining. The separation occurs nonetheless, mostly by personal choice." A student adds, however, that there is little interaction between the black and white Greek groups.

Students say the campus "could be more integrated," but, says a junior, "you wouldn't be made to feel uncomfortable at a party if you were the only minority. At all of the meals in the dining halls, black students sit at various tables with white friends. There is sometimes a 'black table,' but it isn't because they aren't comfortable elsewhere. It is a bonding time for them."

Relations between the school's African-American students and the African-American community in Greenville are described as tense by students. "The black members of the community think we black students are snobs," says a student. "We are not well liked by them. The members of Alpha Phi Alpha held a step show on campus that was well advertised throughout the area, but the response was very poor." Greenville, only five miles from campus, does provide a variety of off-campus diversions for students needing to escape the small-college atmosphere. Malls, movie theaters, restaurants, and clubs are within easy driving distance of campus. For a more diverse city life than what Greenville can provide, students will sometimes make the two-and-a-half-hour trek to Atlanta.

Furman remains a largely conservative school with a definite religious tone to campus life. All dorms are single-sex, and the men's and women's dorms are on opposite ends of campus. Visitation rules in the dorms are strictly enforced, and infractions are punished with fines and letters home. Furman is a dry campus, and the school's religious student groups—especially the Baptist Student Union and the Fellowship of Christian Athletes—are among the most active on campus. The student-run Social Activities Board works to bring films, speakers, and dances to campus each weekend, but students say campus-wide events don't generate a great deal of student interest.

Furman students remain largely conservative, politically and socially, with little room for deviation. The majority of the school's students come from upper-middle-class families and for the most part don't mind the school rules.

Says a senior of her four years at Furman: "I would recommend Furman to a minority student. The school has a lot of problems, but I feel now that more of them are being addressed. A minority student, however, needs to know what he or she will be facing here—a lack of a social life, not many role models. But there are many rewards—strong friendships among minority students, an excellent education, and a chance to take a stand in defense of their own race. Furman and the Furman experience will make a minority student a stronger person."

UNIVERSITY OF SOUTH CAROLINA

Address: Columbia, SC 29208
Phone: (803) 777-7700 / (800) 922-9755
  (in-state)
Director of Admissions: Terry Davis
Multicultural Student Recruiter: na

1992–93 tuition: $2,818 (in-state); $7,046
  (out-of-state)
Room and board: $3,218
Application deadline: Rolling admissions
Financial aid application deadline: 4/15

Just when things were looking up for the University of South Carolina—admissions standards were increasing, the endowment was enhanced—the university was hit with a scandal. *The Chronicle of Higher Education* sums up the incident in a recent article: "James B. Holderman, who as president of the University of South Carolina brought prestige but also shame to the institution he headed for 13 years, pleaded guilty last week to using his position to earn $25,000 in illegal compensation." Holderman retired, and the university "is bouncing back from this temporary setback," say students.

Carolina, a school known more for its parties than for its academics, has numerous standout departments, especially its nationally recognized programs in journalism and international business. Computer science and engineering, both housed in impressive new facilities, are excellent, as are Carolina's business and education programs. English, history, and geography are also good.

Students say the school's Afro-American Studies program could be better, but it does offer such popular courses as "African History" and "Psychology of the Black Experience." Ronald Atkinson, a history professor who teaches the "African History" course, was recently awarded an outstanding-teacher-of-the-year award.

As at most big universities, Carolina has large class sizes, especially in introductory-level courses, which are often taught by teaching assistants. But, with effort, students say relations can be established with professors.

African-American students are by far the largest minority population represented at the university. Of more than 25,000 students enrolled in 1990, 12.5 percent were African-American, while 0.1 percent were Native American, 1.5 percent were Asian, and 0.8 percent were Hispanic. (The university did not respond to our admissions questionnaire; the above figures were obtained from *The Chronicle of Higher Education*.)

Carolina enjoys an excellent retention rate for students of color, thanks in no small part to the efforts of the Minority Assistance Peer Program (MAPP). Usually about 50 upperclass students are assigned five or six first-year students "to be more than their counselors, to be their friends," says a MAPP counselor. "We like to think of MAPP as a team effort rather than as an organization because we all have the same goal: to see that minority students successfully graduate from the university. We take the new students on tours of the campus, take them to the career center, and get them familiar with key people."

One of those key people is Ralph Johnson, a coordinator in the Office of Minority Affairs. "He has his hands on everything and is easy to get along with," says a student. Johnson was responsible for getting MAPP off the ground, along with a student group called Students Educating and Empowering for Diversity (SEED). Established in the spring of 1990, SEED "is a group that facilitates discussion about racism and sexism," according to a SEED member. "We perform role-playing skits in the residence halls as a way to get people in touch with what they're thinking and what their peers are thinking. The group is growing each year, and it's incredibly diverse. There are Asians, blacks, and whites."

The Office of Minority Affairs, located in Russell House, helps students "with any problem we may have," says a student. "They're kind of like the liaison between the administration and the minority students."

Unfortunately, however, SEED is one of only a few places where students from different cultures and backgrounds mix. "At the beginning of the year, the university has an orientation program that includes a party, where whites and blacks mix. But after that, I guess most students tend to hang out with people that they're comfortable with. Few people cross the line, but no one is going to kill you if you do. The attitude here is: to each his own." However, students say some people do take advantage of the opportunities for interaction—in the classroom and in SEED. "There are all sorts of students here—from rich to poor, from conservative to liberal. Carolina opens your eyes to a lot. You learn about other people, and you can't help but interact with them."

The African-American community at Carolina, although diverse, "is pretty cohesive and tight, and it's made me realize that I didn't miss a whole lot by not going to a traditionally black college," says a student. "The African-American student population is fairly large at the university, which is one reason I decided to come here. There's a lot more to do here for African-Americans than just join fraternities or sororities." The Association of African-American Students (AAAS), with about 50 active members, holds weekly meetings. Each year, it sponsors Block Fest parties, in which a portion of the campus is sectioned off so that vendors can sell African garb, jewelry, and food. "It's basically a celebration of African-American culture," says a student. The AAAS also coordinates events for Black History Month, featuring speakers and forums. A recent forum posed the question "Do Blacks Segregate Themselves?" "That forum was very well attended, by blacks and whites. Every year there seems to be an editorial that asks why blacks have their own organizations and fraternities and sororities and why we sit together at meals, so we decided to have the forum. It went pretty well and was very civilized. Although there was no resolution about some of the differences, it was good because we got the dialogue going." Another popular AAAS event is its annual Miss Black USC Pageant, which, in the words of one student, "is almost like a beauty pageant but with talent involved."

The historically black Greek organizations "are incredibly active," says a student. The women of Delta Sigma Theta sorority sponsor an annual Stomp Fest, a step show which attracts participants and viewers from as far away as Georgia and Florida. The Deltas also sponsor a walk for hunger and work in an area homeless shelter. Most of the organizations' parties are held at the Russell House, the school's student union.

African-American students aren't strangers to campus politics and are regularly elected to positions on the Student Government Association; recently, African-American students served as the student body president and treasurer.

The city of Columbia (pop. 500,000) "is really more of a town, although it is the state capital," says a student, who adds that the city is relatively comfortable for non-white students. Columbia provides internship possibilities with area businesses and government agencies, as well as its share of cultural and social activities. MAPP students also interact with the community by sponsoring a tutoring program at the Brooklyn Baptist Church, located not far from campus.

The University of South Carolina, along with the region in which it is located, is rather conservative. Recent controversy centered on visitation hours at some of the dorms; the administration wasn't keen on the idea of having visitors of the opposite sex in single-sex dorms. The majority of the students here are also proud Republicans and more than likely from the state; about 80 percent of the students call South Carolina home, while students also hail from almost every other state in the country, as well as from several different foreign countries.

Students say they enjoy good relations with the administration, particularly Dennis Pruitt, dean of students and vice president of student affairs. "The administrators always have their doors open to students of color, and all students for that matter. Dean Pruitt listens to student concerns and he takes action."

Despite its recent troubles, Carolina isn't a school that will let scandal get in the way of its goal of becoming one of the South's top universities. For now, students are enjoying the feeling of attending an up-and-coming university. "I'm definitely glad I came here. I've enjoyed the people. I think my experiences here are unmatchable. I've learned a lot by being involved in SEED and MAPP, but more than that, I've been able to feel needed and I've been able to fit in."

WOFFORD COLLEGE

Address: 429 North Church Street, Spartanburg, SC 29303-3663
Phone: (803) 597-4000
Director of Admissions: Charles H. Gray
Multicultural Student Recruiter: E. Renee Peeler
1991–92 tuition: $9,790
Room and board: $4,150
Application deadline: 2/1
Financial aid application deadline: 3/1

Non-white freshman admissions: Applicants for the class of '95: 111
Accepted: 77%
Accepted who enroll: 36%
Applicants accepted who rank in top 10% of high school class: 35%
In top 25%: 77%
Median SAT range: 360–570 V, 390–600 M
Median ACT: na

Full-time undergraduate enrollment: 1,117
Men: 62%
Women: 38%

Non-white students in
1987–88: 9.1%
1988–89: 8.6%
1989–90: 9.8%
1990–91: 9.7%

Students In-state: 69%

Top majors: 1. Accounting 2. Psychology 3. Chemistry

Retention rate of non-white students: 90%

Scholarships exclusively for non-white students: Wofford Scholars Program: merit-based; three $5,000 scholarships are awarded each year.

Remediation programs: None

STUDENT ENROLLMENT

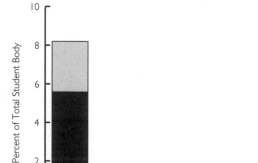

% Women   % Men

GEOGRAPHIC DISTRIBUTION OF STUDENTS

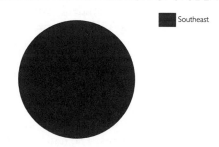
Southeast

Academic support services: The college provides tutoring in most academic subjects, as well as a writing lab.
Ethnic studies programs: None
Ethnic studies courses: The college offers a course in African-American history and a

course in African history. The Spanish department offers "The Hispanic World: Spanish in America," the Religion department "Asian Religions," and the Art department "Oriental Art."

Organizations for non-white students: Association of Afro-American Students, Alpha Kappa Alpha, Delta Sigma Theta, Kappa Alpha Psi, Omega Psi Phi, Gospel Choir

Notable non-white alumni: Douglas Jones ('69; first black Wofford graduate, product manager, Michelin); Dr. Donadrin L. Rice ('71, Psychology; associate professor of psychology, West Georgia College); Dr. Alvin Wells ('83, Biology; assistant professor and research fellow, University of South Florida); Joyce Payne Yette ('80, Economics/Government; attorney)

Tenured faculty: 44

Non-tenured faculty: 23

Student-faculty ratio: 15:1

Administrators: 55

　African-American: 6%
　Hispanic: 0
　Asian-American: 2%
　Native American: 0

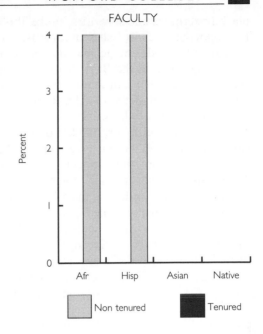

FACULTY

Recent non-white speakers on campus: Nikki Giovanni (poet); Walter Fauntroy (District of Columbia delegate to U.S. Congress); Michael Harper (poet)

Wofford has long been looked to as one of South Carolina's top liberal arts colleges, and was the first school in the state to be granted a Phi Beta Kappa charter, one of only five colleges in the Carolinas that can boast of such an honor. (Duke, Davidson, Furman, and Wake Forest are the others.)

Although solid academics have been available at Wofford for generations, diversity of just about any sort is a relatively new concept at the 138-year-old college. It wasn't until 1969 that the college graduated its first student of color—an African-American—and in the 1970s it graduated its first female. "You've got to remember, this is the South, where things are sometimes slow to change," says a senior. Adds another student: "It's what we call late integration."

Students report that Wofford's transition from an all-white and all-male institution has been "good," particularly in recent years. "The administration is always willing to listen to us and wants to know what we want or need," says a leader of the school's Association of Afro-American Students (AAAS). Students point to the school's first sponsored Diversity Week activities as a sign of Wofford's growing cultural awareness (although diversity for many members of Wofford's Greek organizations often means mingling with non-Greeks.) Activities during Diversity Week included a volleyball tournament, a panel discussion of racial problems on campus, and a Greek awareness day in which members of the school's fraternities, including the school's historically black fraternities and sororities, spoke about some of their organizations' traditions. In support of diversity issues on campus, many students wore gold-and-black ribbons.

Progress was also made recently when the AAAS got a meeting room on campus. "It's a big room in the Burwell Building, but we only get to use half of it," says a student. "The other half is used by the career services office. Our half, though, has African art, a cabinet with a VCR and TV, and many couches." AAAS, which has about 20 active members, meets regularly, usually on Wednesday evenings, and, in the words of a member, "seeks to promote the social and service aspects of the campus." Many AAAS members serve as big brothers to elementary school students at a nearby school and conduct voter registration drives, both on and off campus. AAAS also sponsors parties, "the kind where we just get to know each other." These events are well attended by the school's African-American students. To liven things up, students from all-female Converse College and University of South Carolina/Spartanburg are invited, and usually attend. A chapter of the NAACP is being established that will be located at University of South Carolina/Spartanburg and will include all of the area college students as members.

There is very little diversity among the African-American community on campus. "Most of the African-American males here are on athletic scholarships," says a student-athlete. "If my numbers are right, I think all fifty-five African-American men, with the exception of maybe four or five, play either football or basketball. In fact, because so many of AAAS members are on teams, we have to schedule our AAAS meetings around the games." All of the school's non-white students are from the Southeast.

A debate is beginning to take shape on campus about what to do with the vacant house on Fraternity/Sorority Court. Certain students hope to convert the house into a facility for one of the school's historically black Greek organizations. "Omega Psi Phi is the oldest black fraternity on campus, and they may have first dibs, but the Kappas [Alpha Psi] have the most members," says a student. Students are also considering whether to use the house as a meeting place for the AAAS. However, part of the controversy, says a student, focuses on how receptive the white students, particularly members of the all-white Greek organizations on the Court, are to having a historically black organization next door. (During a recent year, Pi Kappa Alpha fraternity, known as the jock frat on campus, was the only Greek organization on the Court that had African-American members.) Situated next to the vacant house is the Kappa Alpha fraternity, whose symbol is the Confederate flag.

Wofford's strength is in the liberal arts and sciences, and students say the school's pre-med program is excellent and rigorous. The typical Wofford student is pre-professional, which accounts for the popularity of the school's business and accounting programs. The school's computer and math departments were strengthened recently with the completion of the $5.5 million Olin Building.

Wofford's academic calendar includes Interim, a four-week period in January in which students are able to study independently, sometimes working on research with a professor, serve as interns, or take a course on campus. Recent on-campus courses taught by Wofford faculty have included "AIDS: Past, Present, and Future," "The VAX as an Electronic Forum," and "The FBI, Martin Luther King, and the Civil Rights Movement."

In terms of social life, in addition to that provided by the fraternities and sororities, Wofford's Campus Union sponsors events such as college-wide dances, concerts, and films. Religious groups are also active, particularly the Wesley Fellowship and the Baptist Student Union. Wofford's varsity sports teams, which compete against Division II schools, enjoy good reputations, especially in football and basketball.

Within walking distance of campus students are able to find shopping districts and numerous restaurants, and Memorial Auditorium, not affiliated with the college but located next to campus, features concerts, touring Broadway plays, and other attractions. Wofford is just sixty-five miles south of Charlotte, North Carolina.

Wofford College remains a largely conservative Southern school with a primarily regional appeal, but for students looking for a small-college experience and planning to stay close by after graduation, Wofford deserves close inspection. Says a recent graduate: "Wofford has broadened my perspective. You need to be able to talk about different subjects with different people on different levels. Wofford has definitely prepared me for that."

S O U T H   D A K O T A

UNIVERSITY OF SOUTH DAKOTA

Address: 414 East Clark Street, Vermillion, SD 57069

Phone: (605) 677-5434

Director of Admissions: David Lorenz

Multicultural Student Recruiter: Lily Redlightning

1993–94 tuition: $1,376 (in-state); $3,213 (out-of-state)

Room and board: $2,488

Application deadline: Rolling admissions

Financial aid application deadline: 2/15

Non-white freshman admissions: na
  Applicants for the class of '95: na
  Accepted: na
  Applicants accepted who rank in top 10% of high school class: na
  Median SAT: na
  Median ACT: na

Full-time undergraduate enrollment: 6,064
  Men: 47%
  Women: 53%

Non-white students in
  1987–88: 3.79%
  1988–89: 4.34%
  1989–90: 4.86%
  1990–91: 4.87%

Geographic distribution of students: na

Top majors: na

Retention rate of non-white students: na

Scholarships exclusively for non-white students: Rosebud Yellow Robe Scholarship: need-based; amount varies. Cato Valandra Endowed Scholarship: awarded to a junior or senior with 2.5 GPA or better; merit-based; award amount varies each year. Anita Van Dyke Eels Miller '88 Fund: need-based; amount varies. Claudia Maxine Henry Andrews Living Memorial Scholarship: need-based; amount varies each year. Essay Competition for American Indian Students: $1,000, $500, and $300 scholarships awarded each year.

Remediation programs: Office of Student Support Services provides tutoring, counseling, and advising to students with disabilities, first-generation college students, and low-income students.

Academic support services: Courses in career exploration, library resources, academic study skills; workshops at orientation on

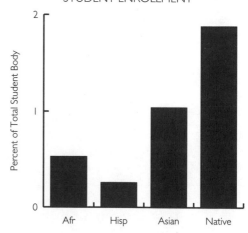

STUDENT ENROLLMENT

Percent of Total Student Body

Afr   Hisp   Asian   Native

study skills. Residence hall tutoring programs are also available through the Counseling Center.

Ethnic studies programs: An American Indian Studies minor, which includes more than 15 courses, is available as well as 9 courses in American Indian education.

Ethnic studies courses: na

Organizations for non-white students: Chinese Student Friendship Association, Students for Civil and Human Rights, Tiospaye Council (Native American organization)

Notable non-white alumni: Tillie Black Bear (former chairwoman, National Committee on Domestic Violence); Lionel Bordeaux (president, Sinte Gleska College, Rosebud, SD); Elizabeth Cook-Lynn (writer); Kevin Locke (dancer, musician, storyteller); Robert Penn (visual artist); Edward F. Parisian (Bureau of Indian Affairs)

Tenured faculty: na

Non-tenured faculty: na

Student-faculty ratio: 18:1

Administrators: na
  African-American: 1%
  Hispanic: 1%
  Asian-American: 0
  Native American: 6%

Recent non-white speakers on campus: B. F. Maiz (poet); James Farmer (former director and founder of CORE); Wilma

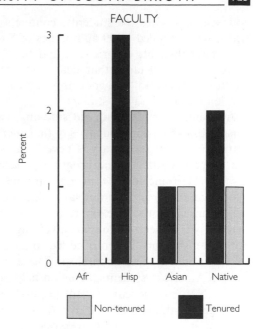

FACULTY

Mankiller (chief, Cherokee Tribe of Oklahoma); Shirley Chisholm (former U.S. representative and first African-American woman to run for president); Juane Quick-To-See Smith (artist); Yako Myers (Mohawk Indian, led anti-racism workshops); Faye Wattleton (former president, Planned Parenthood); Maya Angelou (poet and author)

With only about 5,000 undergraduates, the University of South Dakota is one of the nation's smallest publicly funded four-year universities. "The U," as it is commonly referred to by students, combines the best of a large liberal arts college with the advantages of a public institution.

The U has decent class sizes and a faculty that, according to one student, likes to teach. However, students do complain about the unevenness of some of the school's academic programs. The best departments, they say, include business, computer science, and education. The minor in American Indian Studies is said to be strong. One of the program's most popular teachers is Robert Bunge, an associate professor of modern languages. "He teaches Lakota language and dance, and a lot of Native American students go to him for advice because they know him from classes."

The Institute of American Indian Studies, located in Dakota Hall, "is an informational outlet," says a student. The institute, which provides tutoring and counseling services for students, conducts the American Indian Research Project, which has compiled 1,200 audiotapes of Sioux Indians and members of other tribes describing their life experiences, and the South Dakota Oral History Project, with more than 2,500 tapes that deal with the state's history. Leonard Bruguier, the institute's director, "is a good role model, is helpful, and is able to offer advice or just lend an ear," says a student.

Academics, or just plain old studying, isn't exactly first on many USD students' lists of things to do. Students say that there is little academic competition and that getting a seat at the library is never a hassle. But for those who need the support, the university offers some programs—particularly Trio—that have earned student respect. "Trio includes a tutoring component, Upward Bound, and a Talent Search, which works to recruit more Native American students to the U. The university even has counselors who live on reservations to do the recruiting." Also available is Wowokiya, a mentor program involving professors and incoming first-year Native American students. Recently added to the school's counseling system are the services of two minority peer counselors. These volunteer counselors, who themselves are Native American students, focus on helping other Native American students.

The Native American student population is the largest minority group at the U. A leader in the school's Native American student group, Tiospaye, describes the community as "one where everyone knows each other, and some of us are even related. But all of us share a community bond that makes going to school here more comfortable." The majority of the Native American students at USD are from the state; a few come from the surrounding states. "But no matter where they're from, they're always taken into the community as friends," adds the senior.

Tiospaye (the Lakota word means "extended family") has about 35 active members and "seeks to make the campus community culturally aware," says a student. Its largest event is the annual Native American Cultural Awareness Week celebration, usually held in April, which features speakers and workshops on reconciliation and racism, among other topics. "The week culminates in a two-day powwow that attracts spectators and tribes from all over the area," says a student. Tiospaye works closely with members of the Native American Law Students Association, a group associated with the university's law school.

Less active but still a voice on campus is the organization Students for Civil and Human Rights. "They focus mostly on civil rights issues, and recently invited a speaker for Martin Luther King, Jr., Day, and brought in speakers for Cultural Awareness Week." A recent president of the group was a Native American.

If you're imagining Vermillion to have been the sort of town where at the turn of the century not a whole lot happened save the occasional gunfight, you may not be too far wrong. The town may have done away with the gunfights, but it hasn't provided many alternatives. "To do almost anything you have to go to Sioux Falls and Yankton, towns in South Dakota, or Sioux City, Iowa, which is about forty-five miles away. That's where the malls are. The good thing about our location, though, is that we get more studying done." Vermillion is probably about the right size for many of the school's students, as many come from even smaller towns. "Some of the students here are from hick towns and they're the ones that can be closed-minded when it comes to diversity, but we really don't hang out with them," says a Tiospaye member. "With events like Cultural Awareness Week we let those people know we're here. On the whole, this is a pretty comfortable place for minority students, even though there aren't very many of us."

The U is the state's largest school, and includes the state's only graduate schools of law and medicine—two aspects of the university that encourage many to attend as undergraduates. But the best aspects of the university may be the friendliness of the student body and its relatively small size. USD, says a student, "is large enough to permit exposure to a lot of different ideas, yet small enough to keep me feeling comfortable. Everywhere I go I run into both people I know and people I don't know."

TENNESSEE

RHODES COLLEGE

Address: 2000 North Parkway, Memphis,
  TN 38112
Phone: (901) 726-3000 / (800) 844-5969
Director of Admissions: David Wottle
Multicultural Student Recruiter: Karen
  Conway
1993–94 tuition: $14,758
Room and board: $4,708
Application deadline: 2/1
Financial aid application deadline: 3/1
Non-white freshman admissions: Applicants
  for the class of '95: 261
  Accepted: 49%
  Accepted who enroll: 32%
  Applicants accepted who rank in top
  10% of high school class: 59%
  In top 25%: 91%
  Median SAT range: 530–640 V,
  550–670 M
  Median ACT range: 23–27
Full-time undergraduate enrollment: 1,363
  Men: 45%
  Women: 55%
Non-white students in
  1987–88: 7%
  1988–89: 7%
  1989–90: 7%
  1990–91: 8%
Students In-state: 58%
Top majors: 1. Biology 2. Psychology
  3. Business Administration
Retention rate of non-white students: 87%
**Scholarships exclusively for non-white
  students:** Dean's Scholarships:

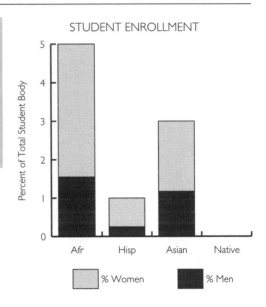

STUDENT ENROLLMENT

Percent of Total Student Body

□ % Women   ■ % Men

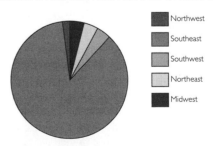

GEOGRAPHIC DISTRIBUTION OF STUDENTS

■ Northwest
■ Southeast
■ Southwest
□ Northeast
■ Midwest

merit-based; half to full tuition; five
awarded each year; available to

African-American students; may be renewed for three years.

Remediation programs: None

Academic support services: Tutoring in most academic subjects is available, as are the services of the Writing Center.

Ethnic studies programs: None

Ethnic studies courses: History courses include "Introduction to Afro-American History," "The Civil Rights Movement," "Native American History," and "The Intellectual History of African America." Anthropology and sociology: "Racial and Ethnic Minorities." English: "Black Writers in America." Music: "Black Music in America." Political Science: "Black Politics." International Studies: "Government and Politics of Africa," "Issues in African Politics," "Government and Politics of China," "Governments and Politics of Japan," "Government and Politics of Southeast Asia."

Organizations for non-white students: Black Student Association, Alpha Kappa Alpha, Kappa Alpha Psi, Delta Sigma Theta, All Students Interested in Asia

Notable non-white alumni: Vicki Gilmore Roman ('75, Economics; assistant treasurer, Coca-Cola); Juan Carlos Hrase ('72, Spanish; Paraguay's ambassador to Japan)

Tenured faculty: 49

Non-tenured faculty: 58

Student-faculty ratio: 12:1

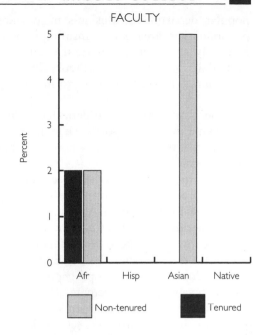

FACULTY

Percent

Non-tenured   Tenured

Afr   Hisp   Asian   Native

Administrators: 90

African-American: 6%

Hispanic. 0

Asian-American: 0

Native American: 0

Recent non-white speakers on campus: William Julius Wilson (sociology and public policy professor); D'Army Bailey (Circuit Court judge, Memphis); Carolyn Lambert (child advocacy coordinator of Black Children's Institute of Tennessee); Beatrice Berry (comedian)

Rhodes is a quality liberal arts college that is working to shake its image as a primarily Southern school and establish one that is decidedly more national. With strong academic programs, a healthy endowment, and close student-faculty interaction, the 135-year-old school has all of the elements to do just that.

Although Rhodes is located in midtown Memphis, don't assume you'll have to deal with urban congestion and tall buildings (although parking on and around campus can be a problem). Rhodes's campus is stunning and parklike, with manicured lawns and shrubs, and 13 buildings—many of which are built of stone with slate roofs—that are on the National Register of Historic Places.

The college offers an impressive array of academic programs, especially for a school of its size. Rhodes students are about as pre-professionally oriented as you'll find anywhere, and business administration remains one of the school's most popular departments. Business majors are able to take advantage of internship possibilities in area banks, insurance companies, and stock brokerages. Rhodes is especially strong in the natural sciences, particularly biology. Psychology is also praised by students. The school's international relations department, which gets high marks, provides avenues to internships with the CIA and the Department of State.

Rhodes students are athletically inclined. Nearly 20 percent of the students participate in varsity sports, while more than half compete on the intramural field. For the past three years, the school's football team has been ranked in the top twenty in Division III.

One of the school's newest student organizations is All Students Interested in Asia (ASIA). Recently, group members have sponsored activities for the Chinese New Year. The Black Student Association (BSA), according to one student, "isn't that active" because academics and the school's relatively low number of African-American students get in the way of planning activities. A BSA event that is popular and successful is its annual Gospel Extravaganza, held at a nearby church. Although Rhodes does not have a gospel choir, the BSA invites the gospel choirs of area colleges and high schools to participate. The event was created to establish scholarships for Rhodes's African-American students, and with the proceeds of a recent concert, the BSA was able to award three scholarships, totaling $1,200. According to one student, the event was a success, because of "the amazing turnout of support from the campus and the area community."

The BSA has its office in Tuthill Hall, but because numerous other groups have their meetings there, BSA members are hoping to move their organization to a building on campus that is less trafficked. The BSA's present office has a TV, stereo, couches, and a small library of textbooks. "A few students will use the office to hang out in, but it's primarily used for studying."

Students say that Karen Conway, the BSA's staff adviser, works diligently on the students' behalf. "She's a role model in that she's always willing to listen to you." Conway has also worked to organize the successful Let's Talk sessions, in which students meet "to talk about everything from sex and dating to people on campus." The weekly sessions, which meet in the social room at the Robinson Residence Hall, usually attract about 20 African-American students.

The campus also has two theme houses, one each for African-American male and female students. The houses, each of which accommodates about six students, are organized around certain themes. The Women of Culture House encourages residents to examine the diversity within the African-American female community. Living in the house are African-American women of various religions and backgrounds. Intercultural House residents focus on issues confronting African-American males. In order to live in the houses, students must apply to the college administration.

There is no shortage of off-campus entertainment. Overton Park is across the street from campus. For parties, African-American students at Rhodes will frequently head to nearby LeMoyne-Owen College, a historically black college, or to Memphis State or Christian Brothers College. There's also a great deal of cultural entertainment in Memphis, including an African-American ballet troupe and a theatrical company, which was founded by a Rhodes graduate. Bars and blues clubs are also part of the cultural makeup of the city.

Nearly a third of the students at Rhodes are native Tennesseans, while the majority come from other parts of the South. Other than some geographic diversity, however, there is little diversity of just about any sort on this small campus. Most of the students are from affluent suburbs throughout the South, and most are heading to careers in law, business, or medicine. The campus is also incredibly Greek; more than two-thirds of the students participate in one or another of the school's six fraternities or seven sororities, all of which are predominantly white. In addition, the majority of the African-American males on campus are athletes.

Rhodes claims: "Our ivy is in a league by itself." Whether or not the college's educational opportunities rival those of the Ivies matters little to one of Rhodes's students. "I'm glad I came to Rhodes for college," says the campus leader. "My personality came out a lot here."

UNIVERSITY OF TENNESSEE/KNOXVILLE

Address: 320 Student Services Building, Knoxville, TN 37996-0230
Phone: (615) 974-2184 / (800) 221-8657 (in-state)
Director of Admissions: Dr. Gordon Stanley
Multicultural Student Recruiter: na
1992–93 tuition: $1,898 (in-state); $5,498 (out-of-state)
Room and board: $3,066
Application deadline: 7/1
Financial aid application deadline: 2/14
Non-white freshman admissions: Applicants for the class of '95: 679
  Accepted: 67%
  Accepted who enroll: 33%
  Applicants accepted who rank in top 10% of high school class: 18.3%
  In top 25%: 30.6%
  Median SAT range: 370–510 V, 430–570 M
  Median ACT range: 19–24
Full-time undergraduate enrollment: 19,385
  Men: 51%
  Women: 49%
Non-white students in
  1987–88: 7.24%
  1988–89: 6.88%
  1989–90: 7.13%
  1990–91: 7.69%

Geographic distribution of students: na
Students In-state: 69.6%
Top majors: 1. Finance 2. Economics 3. Psychology
Retention rate of non-white students: 79.9%
Scholarships exclusively for non-white students: Tennessee's colleges of Engineering, Agricultural Sciences, Business Administration, Architecture,

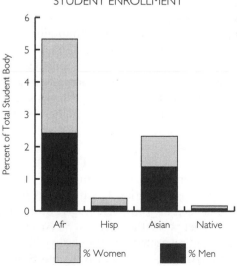

STUDENT ENROLLMENT

Percent of Total Student Body

Afr Hisp Asian Native

% Women   % Men

and Education offer full and partial awards.

Remediation programs: na

Academic support services: The university offers the Office of Minority Student Affairs' peer mentoring program, an English writing lab, various tutorial services, and the Educational Advancement Program.

Ethnic studies programs: Offered are interdisciplinary programs in Afro-American and Latin American Studies.

Ethnic studies courses: na

Organizations for non-white students: Black Cultural Center, Alpha Kappa Alpha, Delta Sigma Theta, Sigma Gamma Rho, Zeta Phi Beta, Alpha Phi Alpha, Omega Psi Phi, Phi Beta Sigma, Association of Black Communicators, Black Cultural Programming Committee, Black Law Student Association, Black Male Caucus, Love United Choir, NAACP

Notable non-white alumni: na

Tenured faculty: 780

Non-tenured faculty: 205

Student-faculty ratio: 17:1

Administrators: 1,072
  African-American: 7%
  Hispanic: 1.12%
  Asian-American: 3.92%
  Native American: 0.28%

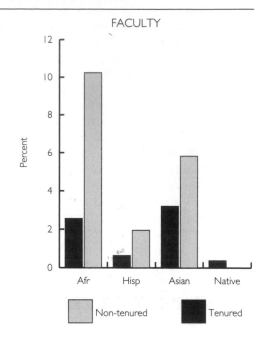

FACULTY

Recent non-white speakers on campus: Dr. Maulana Karenga (founder of the Kwanzaa celebration and chair of Black Studies at California State University); Li Lu (deputy student commander at Tiananmen Square); Carol Simpson (ABC news anchor)

Situated near the Smoky Mountains and having one of the country's largest basketball arenas, the University of Tennessee/Knoxville has never really been looked to as one of America's more sophisticated or respected universities. But with new facilities—including a $30 million library—several recently endowed faculty positions, and an upgrading of admissions standards, UT is looking to challenge other, more prominent institutions of higher learning as one of the country's major research universities.

Academic programs in such pre-professional areas as business and engineering rank among UT's best. Thanks to various programs and recruitment efforts, the enrollment of African-Americans in UT's College of Engineering, which provides co-op opportunities, has increased from 26 students in 1972 to 200 in 1989. Other areas such as journalism, agriculture, and architecture are also well respected.

Students see the university's African-American Studies program as being "beneficial and respected," particularly with such popular courses as "Major Black Writers" and "African-American Religious Studies." The program continues to grow at UT;

in the fall of '92, two new courses—one in literature and the other in religion—were added to the curriculum.

Despite the recent upgrading of the faculty, class sizes are still large, particularly in lower-division courses. Honors courses, however, are the exceptions, but they're reserved for select students with a 3.25 GPA. Students say upper-level courses almost guarantee you classes with smaller enrollments and individual attention from your professor.

At UT there are two places to be seen. The first is the University Center, with its bookstore, cafeteria, and movie theater. The second place—or first place depending on whom you're talking to—is the Black Cultural Center, on Volunteer Boulevard, a main strip through campus. "The center is very, very popular with students. It's like somebody's house," says a student leader. "You can go there and always see people studying or being tutored. As the main library has cut back on its hours, the center is open twenty-four hours a day for student use." Members of the National Society of Black Engineers, for example, conduct study nights at the center. "The center is kind of like UT's community center for African-American students," adds a student.

The center has study rooms, a library with textbooks that students can check out for the semester, office space for various student organizations, and the Office of Minority Student Affairs. The director of the office, Jane Redmond, is a favorite with students. "She's the glue that keeps us all together," comments a student. "She sits in on all of our meetings and always offers her assistance." The center also sponsors a mentor program in which graduate students and faculty members work with younger, usually first-year students. "The whole office really pushes for students to succeed," says a student. In addition to Redmond, popular center staff members include Arthur Baxter, who oversees the tutoring program, and Lydia Jones, who coordinates the mentor program.

One of the school's more active student groups to have an office in the Black Cultural Center is the Black Cultural Programming Committee, which coordinates much of the cultural awareness programming on campus. Recent such events have included an African dance troupe, a Kwanzaa celebration, and several prominent speakers. For Martin Luther King, Jr., Day, the group sponsored a week of events that culminated in a birthday party. "We basically try to be the missing link between the administration and the students, as the university, with all of its cultural activities, sponsors little for African-American students," says a student leader. "But we do get a lot of help when it comes to funding for our events, so it's kind of as if the administration relies on us to do this. The student government also tries to be supportive of our events and other cultural programming activities. For example, in the fall, we and the student government are sponsoring a month's worth of workshops and events about race relations on campus and in the country. The important thing for us is that we get a wide diversity of opinion for our panel discussions, including conservatives and liberals."

A student adds that the Black Cultural Programming Board does not seek to be a political organization. "Many of us are political, but we don't use the committee as a political voice. Within the black community here there is an array of political viewpoints, and we would never attempt to speak for all black students, so we try to represent all of the African-American students in our programs."

Students credit the center for the heightened level of race awareness on campus. "Because of the BCC, racism is less of an issue on campus than it had been in the past," says a student. "Dr. Redmond addresses these issues with the administration when they need addressing. We just don't let racist incidents go by." She adds: "I may not always feel at home here, but I know I belong here, especially because of the center and the National Society of Black Engineers. I feel that the gap between white students and myself is filled with the activities of the BCC and these other groups."

UT's predominantly black Greek organizations are active on campus, sponsoring community activities and parties. Each year, for example, members of Delta Sigma Theta sorority host a banquet in which they honor African-American students who have earned a 3.0 grade point average or better. In addition, every year a week is set aside for each of the school's black Greek organizations, in which attention is drawn to their community service projects, such as visiting area nursing homes. Each organization's week puts on a step show and culminates with a party. "The events during the weeks are very popular because it's important for the campus community at large to see not just the activities of the Black Cultural Center but also those of other black student groups," says a student.

UT is located in the city of Knoxville, which offers a wide diversity of off-campus activities. On the edge of campus is Cumberland Avenue, also known to students as the Strip because of its popular bars and clubs. Most popular with African-American students are Lucille's and Bullfrog's, jazz and reggae clubs located in Old City, a portion of Knoxville within easy reach of campus thanks to the city's trolley service. Also in the area are malls and restaurants. In addition, there are several black-owned businesses in the city, including restaurants, beauty salons, barbershops, and music stores. In fact, interaction with the African-American community in Knoxville is frequent, as many residents attend functions at the BCC.

Several recent racist incidents, in the form of graffiti, perpetrated anonymously by individuals claiming to be representing white supremacist groups, have taken place in Fort Sanders, a relatively integrated area popular with students living off campus. "Sometimes we do feel the weight of our race going to school here in Knoxville," says a student. But the student praises the reaction of the administration to the incidents. "We took the situation to the chancellor's office, and they were definitely sympathetic. They've instructed the campus security to begin heavily patrolling the area, and they made a statement condemning such actions. The administration definitely tries to be supportive of our issues." According to students, the incidents are still under investigation.

With enhanced educational opportunities and name recognition, UT is looking to the future, and so are its students. "As a black student, you'll have it hard anywhere you go, and you've got to want to make it yourself," says a recent graduate. "You can't expect others to do it for you. If they did, they'd be sheltering you. I think that this campus is pretty representative of all types of people. By going here, you have a pretty good idea of what it's going to be like out in the world." Adds a political science graduate: "UT had a good reputation when I first got here, but in the four years that I've been here it has moved forward. Things like the funding of a dozen chairs of excellence and the establishment of the distinguished scientists program have all been forward steps. I came at an exciting time."

VANDERBILT UNIVERSITY

Address: Nashville, TN 37212
Phone: (615) 322-2561
Director of Admissions: Neill Sanders
Multicultural Student Recruiter: Monica
   Ward

1992–93 tuition: $15,975
Room and board: $5,764
Application deadline: 1/15
Financial aid application deadline: 2/15

Vanderbilt University, with its rigorous academics and affluent and conservative student body, is one of the South's better-respected institutions of higher learning.

Vandies, as they commonly refer to themselves, choose to study in one or another of the school's four divisions: arts and science (by far the biggest undergraduate division), education and human development, engineering, and music. The well-regarded Peabody College, the education division, requires students to major in a liberal arts subject. The School of Engineering, the oldest and largest private engineering school in the South, offers majors in ten areas, including biomedical, chemical electrical, and environmental and water resources engineering. Vanderbilt has a five-year program with Fisk University, one of the oldest historically black colleges in the country, in which students are able to earn a science degree from Fisk and an engineering degree from Vanderbilt. (Carolyn Williams, an assistant dean for minority affairs and an associate professor, works closely with minority engineering students.) Among the arts and sciences, students rate highly the history, political science, economics, English, and psychology departments. Academic competition is keen on this largely pre-professional campus.

"Oriental Art" is one of the more popular courses in the school's small but respected East Asian Studies program. "The course taught me not only about art but also about the culture of the area," says a student. Milan Mihal, the course's professor, also advises the school's Asian Student Association (ASA). Students say the school's Japanese- and Chinese-language instruction calls for improvement. "My Japanese professor, who comes from UC/Berkeley, said that our third-year course is the equivalent of the first-year course at Berkeley," says a student. Members of Vanderbilt's ASA are working to get a Japanese-language hall established in one of the dorms.

The ASA was established at Vanderbilt in 1986 when, according to a member, "about 10 Asian students who were all friends decided to meet more formally. Currently there are about 150 students on our mailing list and about 30 or so who come to our meetings." ASA meetings are held in the Community Partnership House, which provides office space for the ASA and other student groups. The house, formerly a fraternity, has "computers, a lounge with a fireplace, and a huge basement for meetings," says a student. ASA members frequently go on road trips to meetings around the South. Recently, the ASA sponsored a trip to Atlanta to attend a Chinese Students Association Conference. The Asian New Year Festival, held annually on campus by the ASA, features a cultural dinner of Indian, Chinese, Japanese, and Thai food. During a recent year, the festivities included Filipino dancers, a Vietnamese fan dance, and a fashion show. According to a student, the event has become increasingly popular on campus. "In 1991, about 90 students and faculty came" to the festival, he says. "In 1992, we were expecting about 150, but about 200 showed up." The ASA recently sponsored a retreat for members in a state park in Tennessee, in which students discussed plans for the group. Members of the organization have also tutored area high school students in English.

African-American and other students are able to take advantage of the resources of the Black Student Alliance (BSA) and the Bishop Joseph Johnson Cultural Center. The center, established in 1984, serves as a meeting and study facility for students and maintains a test file. The center helps sponsor the Heritage Series, which consists of three symposiums per semester that feature scholars of African-American culture. With the chaplain's office, the center also sponsors a lecture series for Martin Luther King, Jr., Day. The director of the center, Ray Winbush, is well regarded by students. The BSA also sponsors parties and guest lectures.

A sense of wealth and affluence permeates much of Vanderbilt's campus social life. Parents of Vandy students are reportedly among the richest in the country, and the campus has an elite and pervasive Greek system, which is predominantly white; more than 40 percent of Vandy students are members of a fraternity or sorority. Getting into the right fraternity or sorority is so important to many students that some women have even been known to transfer to another college should they not get into the sorority of their choice. "It's amazing to see all the money and expensive cars and clothes most students have here," says a student. "It sometimes makes adjusting to the campus a bit more difficult, especially if you come from a humbler background."

Although Greek life is the undisputed activity of choice for many students, the school also sponsors other social outlets, including more than 200 student clubs. Young Life, a Christian student group, is one of the school's more popular non-Greek organizations, and the frequently used Madison Sarratt Student Center houses a game room, an art gallery, a cinema (which shows first-run films almost nightly), art studios, student organization offices, and lounges. The Student Recreation Center offers state-of-the art sports facilities, and attending varsity basketball and football games is popular on weekends. On most Fridays, Alumni Lawn, on the north side of campus, is the site of outdoor concerts.

According to the U.S. Department of Education, of the school's 9,161 students in 1990, 0.2 percent were Native American, 2.6 percent Asian, 4.7 percent African-American, and 0.9 percent Hispanic (Vanderbilt declined to respond to our admissions questionnaire). The school does not offer the racial or geographic diversity of some of the South's other prominent universities, such as Emory or Duke. Although only slightly more than 10 percent of the students are from Tennessee, the majority are from Southern suburbs.

For entertainment many students head into Nashville, with its wide assortment of bars, clubs, and restaurants. The city is best known for its country music, however, and students will often get tickets to the Grand Ole Opry. Nashville is also home to the Tennessee Performing Arts Center (the Sarratt Main Desk serves as a Ticketmaster outlet, handling ticket sales for many of Nashville's and the campus's cultural events), which hosts numerous productions each year.

Vanderbilt's traditional Southern atmosphere can prove stifling. But for one student, an education at Vanderbilt has strengthened him. He says: "A lot of people say they wouldn't have the courage to come here. But I say do it, if you get accepted. If you really want to find out what you are made of, then Vanderbilt is the place to come. They'll train you; they'll mold you. You'll bend them; they'll bend you. But in the end, you'll come out with a back of steel."

T E X A S

RICE UNIVERSITY

Address: Houston, TX 77251
Phone: (713) 527-4036 / (800) 527-OWLS
  (out-of-state)
Director of Admissions: Ron Moss
Multicultural Student Recruiter: Yolanda
  Lozano

1992–93 tuition: $8,500
Room and board: $5,200
Application deadline: 1/1
Financial aid application deadline: 2/15

Rice University is able to offer its students two things that few other schools can: one of the country's top educations and low tuition prices. In fact, Rice combines these qualities so effectively that in 1992 *Money* magazine ranked it as the country's best college buy for your education dollar.

What makes all of this possible is the university's endowment; at about $1 billion—or almost $250,000 per student—it's the fourth largest in the nation.

Students at Rice take their studies seriously. For generations, the university has been known for its outstanding programs in engineering and science, some of which rank among the best in the country. But in recent years, the university has successfully worked to enhance its offerings in the liberal arts, most notably English, fine arts, history, and political science. In fact, since 1988, Rice students have had to satisfy distributional course requirements that ensure they're exposed to areas other than that of their major. That means "humanities students are now required to take a two-semester foundation course to give them a solid grounding in the physical sciences and mathematics . . . [and] science and engineering majors take foundation courses to acquaint them with the ideas, literature, history and art our culture has produced." "African-American Literature," "History of Civil Rights," "Minorities in the Schooling Process," and "Race and Ethnic Relations" rank among the school's more popular ethnic studies classes.

"We spend a lot of our time being stressed out about our grades," says a student. "Students here are competitive academically, and all-nighters aren't uncommon, even when it's not finals." Although more than one student described the educational atmosphere at Rice as intense, the university has an impressive academic and non-academic support network that somewhat eases the tension.

To appreciate the network, you need first to understand the university's housing arrangements. When they arrive on campus, first-year students are assigned to live in one of eight residential colleges, where they will live for their four years at Rice. Each coed college, which accommodates about 220 students, is self-governing, has dining facilities, and ultimately develops its own personality. ("Weiss is the wildest. They have a party every year that everyone in Texas knows about.") Competition among the colleges—particularly in the form of intramurals—is heated, and students acquire a sense of loyalty to their respective colleges that almost outshines their loyalty to Rice.

In addition to providing much of the social life for students, the colleges also have built-in academic support networks. Each college comes with its own non-resident faculty members—about 20—who eat their lunches, every day, at the college, and who act as students' academic advisers. Each college also has two resident faculty or staff members. "If you need help with something, anything, you can ask your professor or adviser about it over lunch," says a student.

The Office of Multicultural Affairs (OMA), located in Rice Memorial Center, "is effective with its tutoring programs, especially for science and engineering majors," says a student. The office also sponsors a Minority Leadership Weekend for students "to discuss race relations on campus and to help us develop leadership skills." "I can walk into the office anytime and feel comfortable," says a senior. "OMA is our connection to the administration." About every two or three months, the office publishes a newsletter, edited by students, that contains scholarship information and editorials. The director of the office, Kathi Clack, is popular with students. "She's great. She helps us with programming events, and you can talk to her about anything."

Students are concerned, however, with the effects of the office's lack of funding. "When I was a freshman, we had African Heritage and Hispanic weeks. But the office is low on money, so we now have to condense the programs into a single week. We call it Unity Through Diversity Week, which takes place during the spring semester. As part of the week we have forums, show a movie, and have a party. It's a successful week. It's just too bad that's all it is, a week."

The Hispanic Association for the Cultural Enrichment of Rice (HACER) has about 20 members and meets twice a month, "usually for lunch at Sammy's," a café on campus. HACER tutors members of Rice's custodial staff in English, and goes to Cuban and Mexican restaurants in the area. Richard Tapia, a professor of mathematical sciences, Enrique Barrera, an assistant professor of mechanical engineering, and Angela Valenzuela, an assistant professor of sociology, are supportive of students and of HACER events. "They're great examples and easily accessible. Professor Barrera lives in Jones Hall [one of the residential colleges]. Even if you're having problems with a class or with a professor you can go to them for advice and they will almost always help you out."

The Black Student Union (BSU), with about 20 active members, sponsors "rap sessions where we talk about different topics, such as 'Black Female/Male Relationships' or 'Should Integration Occur at the Expense of Losing Our Culture?'" The group also invites speakers to campus, usually as part of Black History Month. Lucille Fultz, an assistant professor of English, is well regarded by students and regularly attends BSU events.

Despite the work of these groups, Rice doesn't have the cultural programming of other schools. "We're short on time and short on money," says a HACER member. "It's hard to get students to come to our events when studying is so key here." Adds another student: "Most students here are apathetic when it comes to issues of diversity, except when it comes to things like affirmative action. For every one student here who's for it, you'll have ten strongly against it. But most students are apolitical and are too busy to think about politics. Very few political views are expressed here. And sexism is a problem here. There's that engineering mentality here that's more macho than anything else. I don't date guys here because of that."

While academics take up much of a Rice student's time, they're still able to make room for some downright, all-out parties, the most popular of which is an annual bicycle relay race that includes a great deal of beer chugging. Both men and women, about a fifth of the school's students, participate. Although the school doesn't have one of the more successful football teams in the state—almost a sin in the eyes of many Texans—it does have one of its more successful marching bands, called the MOB (Marching Owl Band). Members wear gray felt caps and vests, and playing ability comes second to having a sense of humor for many of them; MOB is well known for its halftime antics, usually done at the expense of the other team's marching band. TGIF parties are also common at each of the colleges.

Students of color, however, say that few, if any, campus-wide activities suit their entertainment interests. So many will head to the parties and cultural events—when time allows—at one of the nearby schools, particularly the University of Houston and Texas Southern, a predominantly black university. Houston itself, the fourth-largest city in the country, provides additional cultural and social outlets, including numerous bars, clubs, and restaurants, as well as a symphony, ballet, and theater. The beach at Galveston Island, on the Gulf of Mexico, is only an hour away. Getting to most of these destinations requires a car, as not much public transportation services the area.

A popular bumper sticker you can see around Texas says, "I Must Be Smart, I Got Into Rice." As one of the country's most selective and rigorous institutions of higher learning, the driver just may be right. But when it comes to issues of diversity and multiculturalism, the university, in the words of a student, "needs a lot of uplifting." Adds another student: "I've had a positive experience here, especially academically. In terms of multicultural issues, Rice leaves something to be desired. I guess you can't have the best of both worlds."

SOUTHERN METHODIST UNIVERSITY

Address: Dallas, TX 75275
Phone: (214) 692-2058 / (800) 323-0672
  (out-of-state)
Director of Admissions: Andrew Bryant
Multicultural Student Recruiter: na

1992–93 tuition: $12,500
Room and board: $5,000
Application deadline: 1/15
Financial aid application deadline: 1/15

Cars—the prevalence of them and their price tags—have an amazing way of coming up in conversations about Southern Methodist University. "They're everywhere here. It's been estimated that three in four students have a car. And not just any car. They have BMWs. Mercedes-Benzes. And Jaguars. Every once in a while you'll see a Ford or a Chevy, but not too often."

Like students at other prominent Southern universities, SMU's predominantly white student body is affluent and conservative. Approximately half of the students hail from Texas, the school's Greek system is pervasive and elitist and provides much of the school's social life, and for many students partying often takes precedence over studying. What variety there is at SMU can be found among students enrolled in the school's theater and fine arts departments.

The university's admissions office did not respond to our questionnaire concerning student enrollment. According to student leaders, however, of the school's approximately 5,500 undergraduates in 1992, less than 4 percent were African-American, 6 percent were Hispanic, less than 1 percent were Native American. According to the U.S. Department of Education, in 1990 4.1 percent of the campus was Asian-American.

SMU's football team is one of the few college teams to have been suspended by the NCAA for violating certain rules, such as illegal payments to recruit athletes. (Cars and expensive watches weren't out of the ordinary.) And at a school where football athletes were gods on campus and generated much of the school's spirit, this certainly hurt. However, the Mustangs have since made a comeback, although as yet not on the scoreboard.

Ever since the suspension, which took place during the 1987 season, the university has placed more of a priority on academics, especially since the arrival on campus of the new president, A. Kenneth Pye, formerly of Duke University. One of the school's successes is its Learning Enhancement Center, which has "excellent tutoring programs" in almost every subject. The center is in Ownby Stadium (yes, the football stadium), because, says a student, "it's near the freshmen quad and its convenient location encourages students to use it." A part of the center's resources, but located in Clements Hall, is the Oracle, a not-for-credit program that "teaches you how to study and to succeed in school. They help you with time management, how to use a textbook, and how to take tests." Another student comments that the SMU faculty is generally accessible. "SMU has so much academic support. They really want you to succeed," she adds.

One of the school's best-regarded and most popular programs is its school of business, housed in impressive new facilities that has state-of-the-art computer equipment. Business students are able to take advantage of a 3-2 program with SMU's own graduate school of business administration, which has been ranked by *Business Week* magazine as one of the top 40 business schools in the country. Engineering is also popular. SMU's Meadows School of the Arts, housed in the Owens Arts Center, offers outstanding art facilities as well, including a museum with one of the largest collections of fifteenth- to twentieth-century Spanish art outside of Spain. Among the arts and sciences programs, students say history and political science are strong.

In order to graduate, students must satisfy distribution requirements as part of the Common Educational Experience. All first-year students enroll in Dedman College, the school's arts and sciences division. Business, engineering, applied science, and the arts majors then enter the relevant schools to complete their degree.

"Literature of Minorities" and "Black and White" are two of the university's more popular ethnic studies courses. "A lot of students here are into multicultural issues, and the 'Black and White' course lets students get their opinions out." Adds another student: "The course 'Mexican-American History: 1848 to the Present' is the best course I've taken. It filled in the voids left open by my high school education. The professor [John Chavez] is very knowledgeable."

The predominantly white Greek organizations, to which about half of the student body belongs, provide much of the social life on campus. Alpha Phi Lambda is a coed fraternity with a mostly Hispanic membership, but it does not yet provide residence facilities. "The members are looking into acquiring a house," says a student. "But not too many of the minority students at SMU choose to join a fraternity or sorority, except for those who are middle- or upper-class economically," reports an undergraduate.

With about 35 to 40 active members, SMU's College Hispanic American Student association (CHAS) sponsors an annual Hispanic Issues forum, a weeklong event that features panel discussions and a film series. Recent panels have focused on Hispanic voting in national and local elections and multiculturalism in the arts. Angel Loredo, CHAS's adviser, "is very good. He's Hispanic and the students relate to him easily. He keeps in touch with everybody, and if he isn't able to help us as a group or as individual students, he directs us to those on campus who can."

The university sponsors two organizations for African-American students, the Association of Black Students and the Black Awareness Committee, a part of the Program Council, the campus-wide student planning committee. The association, with about 40 to 50 active members, sponsors a Kwanzaa celebration, and, during Black History Month, various speakers and a film series. Recently, the organization sponsored floats in the school's homecoming day parades. During the year, the organization also sponsors weekly church services and an adopt-a-school program, in which members tutor students at Harrell Budd Elementary School. The association's adviser, Hazel Watts, who also serves as coordinator of African-American Student Services, "has a close connection with incoming students. She's easy to talk to. She tells us that we're here because we're achievers and scholars, that we're here to get an education, and that we have as much of a right to be here at SMU as anyone."

The Black Awareness Council sponsors a Harambe celebration and brings different performers to campus. Recently, the council sponsored a march as part of Martin Luther King, Jr.'s Birthday. The march, which, according to one student, involved about 40 to 50 people of various races, began at Bishop Boulevard and concluded at Dallas Hall, the school's oldest building, located in the center of the campus.

At the beginning of each school year, the university sponsors a mixer and a picnic for incoming first-year students of color that "provides a relaxed atmosphere before things get started, like classes and papers."

For non-Greeks, social life is what you make of it. "We're encouraged to do well here. With more than 140 student organizations to choose from, there's also a lot to do, and many chances to serve in leadership positions," says a student. The new Hughes-Trigg Center houses student organization offices, as well as a hair salon and a travel agency, and is a hub of activity. Meadows School of the Arts puts on more than 300 productions on campus each year. Sports of all kinds are popular at SMU. The Program Council and student government are also active. Dallas, the eighth-largest city in the country, is a rich source of entertainment, and offers a variety of clubs, bars, and restaurants, as well as the Dallas Cowboys and the city's symphony, opera, and museums.

For socializing, many students head off campus. "There are clubs with a Latino focus in the area, and, of course, movies, bowling, and many other activities. But this isn't just for Hispanic students. Most individuals will go off campus for social activity."

Going to school on such an affluent campus can be intimidating, especially for students from more humble backgrounds. As the university begins to place more emphasis on academics, it is also beginning to attract a more interesting student population. But, says a student, "in general, the minority student who chooses to come to school here has to go through a lot of pain to make it to graduation. But after the first two years, you start to find your place and make the most of it."

SOUTHWESTERN UNIVERSITY

Address: University at Maple, Georgetown, TX 78626

Phone: (512) 863-1200 / (800) 252-3166

Director of Admissions: John W. Lind

Multicultural Student Recruiter: na

1993–94 tuition: $11,000

Room and board: $4,484

Application deadline: 2/15

Financial aid application deadline: 3/1

Non-white freshman admissions: Applicants for the class of '95: 244

Accepted: 55%

Accepted who enroll: 37%

Applicants accepted who rank in top 10% of high school class: 59%

In top 25%: 91%

Median SAT range: 440–570 V, 510–650 M

Median ACT: na

Full-time undergraduate enrollment: 1,231

Men: 46%

Women: 54%

Non-white students in

1988–89: 12%

1989–90: 14%

1990–91: 15%

1991–92: 16%

Geographic distribution of students: na

Students In-state: 91%

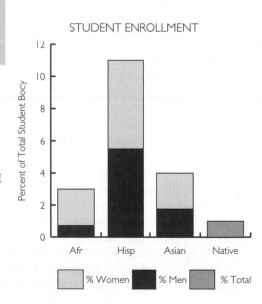

STUDENT ENROLLMENT

Percent of Total Student Body

% Women   % Men   % Total

Top majors: 1. Business 2. Psychology
     3. Biology
Retention rate of non-white students: 84%
Scholarships exclusively for non-white students: Presidential Scholars:
     merit-based; awarded to two
     African-American and Hispanic students
     each year; each award covers tuition;
     interview required.
Remediation programs: None
Academic support services: The Office of
     Assistant Dean for Academic Services
     offers workshops in developing study
     skills.
Ethnic studies programs: None
Ethnic studies courses: The university offers
     more than 12 Asian Studies courses in
     English, history, political science,
     religion, economics, and art. The
     university also offers courses in
     African-American and
     Mexican-American history.
Organizations for non-white students:
     EBONY (an African-American student
     group), Hispanic Awareness Society
Notable non-white alumni: Rev. Roberto
     Gomez (superintendent, Rio Grande
     Conference, United Methodist Church);
     Rev. Jose L. Palos (coordinator,
     Congregational Development, Rio
     Grande Conference, United Methodist
     Church); Ernesto Nieto (executive
     director, National Hispanic Institute)
Tenured faculty: 42
Non-tenured faculty: 30
Student-faculty ratio: 12:1

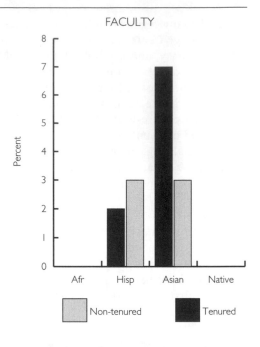

FACULTY

Non-tenured   Tenured

Administrators: 33
     African-American: 15%
     Hispanic: 3%
     Asian-American: 3%
     Native American: 0
Recent non-white speakers on campus: Paul
     Fuller (assistant professor, Knoxville
     College); Dumisani Kumalo (Winnie
     Mandela's brother); Samuel Proctor
     (visiting professor, Vanderbilt
     University); Tonia Cooke (news anchor);
     Deborah Wong (professor, University of
     Michigan)

Southwestern University has long been overshadowed by other colleges and universities in Texas, including the richer Trinity and the larger University of Texas. But in recent years, Southwestern, the state's oldest institution of higher education, is coming into its own as a respectable college recognized for the quality of its teaching and its commitment to the liberal arts and pre-professional studies.

This small college offers more than 30 degree-granting programs, an impressive amount for a school of its size. Some of the more popular programs are history, sociology, psychology, biology, and chemistry. Southwestern also offers majors in women's and international studies, and in child study and language development. The school's impressive new $6.5 million library, opened in 1988, houses the archives of the late U.S. senator John Tower, a Southwestern alum. The

"African-American History" course, offered every other year, is popular with students.

Faculty and staff are especially supportive of students, one of the pluses of attending a small school. Each semester, faculty members serve late-night breakfasts for all students during a study break from finals. Vincent Villa, a biology professor, "is a professor who cares so much for his students that you often see the lights in his office on long after all other faculty members have gone home," says a communications major. Adrianne Jones, an admissions officer, "is a large part of the reason minority students remain at Southwestern," reports an international studies major.

The school's cultural student groups—EBONY, an African-American student organization, and the Hispanic Awareness Society—are, says a student, "only influential to a small portion on this campus." Adds a Hispanic Awareness member: "I hate to say this but I think all the Hispanic Awareness group did this past year was organize Hispanic Awareness Week activities, which included food tasting and dancing. I hope to change the role this organization plays on campus, but it will be a tough job." Students point to a lack of student interest as the main reason for the absence of interest in cultural awareness.

A major exception, however, came during a recent open forum that brought to campus Dinesh d'Souza, the conservative author of *Illiberal Education,* who is opposed to race-based scholarships and who believes that multicultural curriculums are so political that they stifle discussion. The forum drew a large student turnout and a great deal of student and staff opinion. "Things like this debate are the signs of a healthy, thinking campus emerging from a comatose state," said a sophomore in a *New York Times* article about the forum.

The school's Multicultural Affairs Office helps promote "cultural awareness through films and seminars," according to a student. The director of the office, Gregory Washington, works closely with students.

Students say that "overall campus racial integration is good. The African-American students may have a tendency to group together socially and at dinner, but not to an exclusive degree. Asian and Hispanic students are completely integrated. Campus parties are open to and attended by all. The Greek system is typically not as integrated, but that is changing." Students point to the Kappa Alpha fraternity as the least integrated campus Greek organization. "They just pledged their first Asian student, and they've never pledged an African-American. Almost everyone here thinks they pledged the Asian student just because they wanted to look more integrated in the administration's eyes," says a student.

Georgetown is a predominantly white midsize town of about 25,000 residents that has small African-American and Hispanic communities. Students report little interaction between students and town residents, and, except for some beautiful countryside, the town is largely ignored by students looking for off-campus diversions. In fact, on weekends, the campus generally clears out, most students heading to Austin, about thirty minutes south, to the parties at the University of Texas and the nightlife of the state's capital. The city is such a popular destination that the Southwestern administration is planning to establish a shuttle service between Georgetown and Austin. "If they did that, it would be great," says a student, who often goes to parties at UT. Plans are in the works for the van to drop off and pick up students at various Austin locations, including a shopping mall and UT's library.

When not traveling for their social life, students can often be found at one of the school's five fraternities for parties. About 40 percent of the campus is Greek, but the Greeks don't dominate the social scene, according to students. "You never feel like you have to be a member of a fraternity or sorority to have a good time," says a student. "You're pretty much accepted on campus whether you're Greek or not." Mask & Wig, the school's drama society, produces four shows a year in the school's Alma Thomas Fine Arts Building. Homecoming, which is also popular, "features unusual entrants such as synchronized yuppies marching with briefcases and *Wall Street Journals.*"

Students say the reason to come to Southwestern isn't so much the level of cultural awareness as the quality of the school's education. "I would not recommend this school to a prospective minority student on the basis of its record of addressing minority concerns," says a student. "Southwestern is becoming aware, but has a long way to go before I would give it such a recommendation. I would recommend Southwestern on the basis of its being a challenging and academically stimulating school. A student who is basically in touch with his or her ethnicity and does not feel the need to be surrounded with organizations or programs specifically catering to his or her ethnic background would do well here. Relations are good between minority and non-minority students. Never have I been uncomfortable at Southwestern as an African-American female, which speaks loudly for the school. Southwestern is a wonderful place for anyone to live. You are not treated any particular way because of your ethnic background. You are treated however you cause yourself to be treated."

UNIVERSITY OF TEXAS/AUSTIN

Address: Austin, TX 78712-1159

Phone: (512) 471-7601

Director of Admissions: Shirley Binder

Multicultural Student Recruiter: Augustine Garza

1992–93 tuition: $1,240 (in-state); $4,830 (out-of-state)

Room and board: $3,920

Application deadline: 2/1

Financial aid application deadline: 4/1

Non-white freshman admissions: Applicants for the class of '96: 5,077

Accepted: 64%

Accepted who enroll: 52%

Applicants accepted who rank in top 10% of high school class: na

Median SAT: 521 V, 600 M

Median ACT: 25

Full-time undergraduate enrollment: 35,911

Men: 53%

Women: 47%

Non-white students in

1987–88: 17.8%

1988–89: 18.9%

1989–90: 19.9%

1990–91: 21%

Geographic distribution of students: na

Students In-state: 76%

Top majors: 1. Liberal Arts 2. Psychology 3. Pre-business

Retention rate of non-white students: na

Scholarships exclusively for non-white students: Texas Achievement Award: merit-based; available to first-year students who are Texas residents; 395 awarded in a recent year; each award is

STUDENT ENROLLMENT

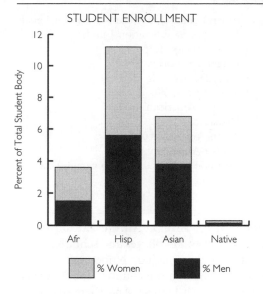

% Women   % Men

valued at $2,000. Texas Honors Achievement Award: merit-based; available to first-year students who are Texas residents; 332 awarded in a recent year; each award is valued at $5,000. State Scholarship for Ethnic Recruitment: need-based; available to first-year students who are Texas residents; 34 to 38 awarded each year; each award is worth approximately $1,000.

Remediation programs: None

Academic support services: UT/Austin offers Supplemental Instruction Programs, as well as peer tutoring and mentoring. The Engineering/Math/Science Equal Opportunities program also offers academic support.

Ethnic studies programs: UT/Austin offers a major in African and Afro-American Studies, an interdisciplinary program established in 1969. Tenured faculty: 2. UT/Austin's major and minor in Mexican-American Studies was established in 1970. Tenured faculty: 4. UT/Austin also offers majors in Oriental and African languages and literature. Tenured faculty: 14.

Organizations for non-white students: Alpha Kappa Alpha, Alpha Phi Alpha, Asian Culture Committee, Association of Latin American Students, Beta Chi (Blacks in Communication), Black Pre-law Association, Black Student Alliance, Caribbean Students Association, Delta Sigma Theta, Filipino Students Association, Hispanic Business Student Association, Hispanic Pre-law Association, Hong Kong Students Association, Innervisions Gospel Choir, Japanese Student Association, Kappa Alpha Psi, Korean Undergraduate Student Association, Mexican-American Association of Pharmacy Students, Mexican-American Student Leadership Council, Mexican Student Association, MECHA, Omega Psi Phi, Panamanian Students Association, Pi Sigma Pi, PRIDE, Sisterhood of Black Women, Texas Union Chicano Culture Committee, Texas Union African-American Culture Committee, Texas Union Asian Culture Committee, Zeta Beta Psi

Notable non-white alumni: Fernando Belaúnde Terry ('35, Architecture; former president of Peru), Earl Campbell ('79, special assistant, vice president for

FACULTY

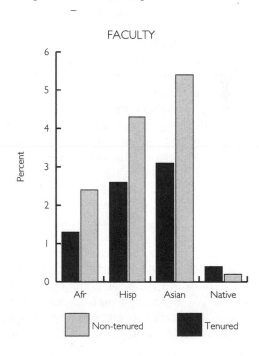

Non-tenured   Tenured

student affairs, University of Texas);
Barbara Smith Conrad ('59, Music;
mezzo-soprano, Metropolitan Opera,
New York City); Luis Flores-Arias ('23;
engineer, Mexico City, Mexico); Hector
Garcia ('36, '40; physician and founder,
American GI Forum of the United
States); Reynaldo Garza ('39; senior
circuit judge, U.S. Court of Appeals,
Fifth Circuit); Vilma Martinez ('64;
attorney and former president and
general counsel, Mexican-American Legal
Defense and Education Fund)
Tenured faculty: 1,356
Non-tenured faculty: 983
Student-faculty ratio: 20:1
Administrators: 396
  African-American: 3.5%
  Hispanic: 2.2%
  Asian-American: 0
  Native American: 0.02%
Recent non-white speakers on campus: na

Here are just some of the highlights at the University of Texas at Austin: The university offers more than 100 undergraduate degree programs in 11 colleges and schools (many of them excellent); its more than 2,300 faculty members include Nobel and Pulitzer Prize winners; the university's endowment is the richest in the country, topping even Harvard's; and its library system is the country's sixth largest. And there are more Texas Longhorns—more than 36,000—than there are people in most Texas towns.

Now here are some UT/Austin problems: Introductory-level class sizes are huge, sometimes numbering into the hundreds; professors are often inaccessible, particularly as many are involved in their own research; and getting into required courses can be difficult. (A new over-the-phone registration system instituted in 1990 has made that process more agreeable.)

UT/Austin's large size is a fact of life, one that elicits mixed reactions from students. "I wish I'd gone to a smaller school. Unless you need tutoring, there's absolutely no nurturing that goes on here," says an English major. Observes a senior: "The school is huge, but that means there are more opportunities and more people to meet."

Students rely heavily on the university's retention service programs—especially the Mapping a Plan for Success (MAPS)—when it comes to academic advice. The program, designed for students of color, provides peer advisers and referrals for tutoring. A mentor program that matches second-semester students with faculty members also "makes a difference," says a finance major. In addition, each year the Black Student Alliance (BSA) conducts an orientation program for incoming African-American students that introduces them to various organizations and programs available to them.

Joining one or more of the school's student organizations also helps to make life at UT/Austin less daunting. The BSA sponsors "various ongoing educational programs," says a BSA leader, including a speaker series. Students also attend area conferences and visit area junior high schools to talk with students about African and African-American history. The *Griot,* a prominent student-generated newspaper, commands a majority of BSA's funding. The paper, issued about twice a semester, "is a forum for the black community that includes articles about local and national issues. We go through other prominent black papers, such as the *Amsterdam News* out of New York City and Los Angeles' *Centennial* and include some of their articles."

For social activity, the school's traditionally black Greek organizations throw most of the parties and dances, scheduled most weekends, usually off campus at an area hotel or apartment complex. The organizations are also involved in the Austin community; members of Kappa Alpha Psi help coordinate an East Austin cleanup day. Zeta Phi Beta sorority and Alpha Phi Alpha fraternity are the only two Greek organizations that have houses; the Alphas' house is located on the ritzy, more expensive west campus.

The Asian Culture Committee's budget has been quadrupled within the last year. "Our budget increase has allowed us to invite some impressive people to campus, including Maxine Hong Kingston, the Asian Repertory Theater Company, and a dance troupe from New York City. We used to have dances to raise money, but now there isn't as much pressure to fundraise." The committee also sponsors Asian Day, conducted in the Texas Union, which features food, art, and other displays that reflect various Asian cultures, particularly those of China, Japan, and Korea.

In addition to some impressive academic support services, there are those famed Texas academics, which include some of the best programs in the nation—business administration, architecture, journalism, biology, accounting, engineering, and psychology among them. UT/Austin's African-American Studies program has some top-notch professors, such as John Warfield and Ted Gordon, as well as such popular courses as "The Black Male" and "Introduction to African-American History." The school's only Asian-American Studies class, "Chinese in the United States," is so popular that in a recent year only half the students who signed up for the course were able to attend.

To describe UT/Austin's student body is a little like describing the stars in a particular galaxy. Most are bright, with more than half finishing in the top 10 percent of their high school graduating classes, and, while more than three-quarters are from the Lone Star State, every state in the Union is represented, as are more than 100 foreign countries. "There are many political perspectives," says a student about his peers at UT/Austin, which, on the whole, is a slightly more progressive place than other schools in the state. "You have groups like Young Texas Democrats, Student Democrats, and Student Advocating Valid Education, a group that's against any sort of multicultural course requirement." Students find troubling, however, the number of Confederate generals and soldiers honored with statues that dot the campus greens.

Back in 1990, PRIDE (Proposed Reforms to Institute Diversity in Education) gathered students of all colors. "Basically, we issued a proposal to the university asking for more ethnic studies courses and a multicultural center, something that would be a sort of a home away from home for minority students," says a student organizer. But, he adds, "so far, nothing much has come of the proposals."

The Minority Information Center, located in the University Teaching Center, is well used. "It's pretty small, and it's in the basement of a building." The center has three computers, a test file, and scholarship information, as well as a small library "of Black Consciousness."

Austin, the state capital, is billed as one of the country's ideal college towns, but, comments a student, "most of the places, especially along Sixth Street, cater to white students. But the city is beautiful and clean. Right now there are organizations fighting to save the city's environment from corporations that are threatening to ruin the city's streams. The city is very political, and there are a lot of cowboy hats." For the school's African-American community, the Jamaica Racquet Club, a dance bar, and Catfish Station and the Elephant Room, both jazz clubs, are popular Austin destinations.

Some of the more popular on-campus extracurricular opportunities include movie nights and many other forms of entertainment at the Texas Union. Attending just about any athletic competition—especially against the University of Oklahoma—is a popular weekend activity; students can also head to one of the many concerts sponsored by the school's Performing Arts Center.

Surviving—indeed, thriving—at UT/Austin means getting involved. According to students, the UT experience should only make you wiser. "I've gotten used to going to school here, but the place certainly toughens you and your senses. It makes you look to your inner strength, parts of me I didn't know until I got here. But you also need to rely on others and turn to those places that will support you, because going to this school can be overwhelming."

TRINITY UNIVERSITY

Address: 715 Stadium Drive, San Antonio, TX 78212
Phone: (512) 736-7011
Director of Admissions: Sara Krause
Multicultural Student Recruiter: na
1991–92 tuition: $10,200
Room and board: $4,370
Application deadline: 2/1
Financial aid application deadline: 2/1
Non-white freshman admissions: Applicants for the class of '94: 517
  Accepted: 66%
  Accepted who enroll: 24%
  Applicants accepted who rank in top 10% of high school class: 90%
  In top 25%: 99%
  Median SAT: na
  Median ACT: na
Full-time undergraduate enrollment: 2,223
  Men: 48%
  Women: 52%
Non-white students in
  1987–88: 11.6%
  1988–89: 13.1%
  1989–90: 14.7%
  1990–91: 15.7%
Geographic distribution of students: na

Top majors: na
Retention rate of non-white students: 75%
Scholarships exclusively for non-white students: University Scholarship: a partial merit award for any incoming first-year student who has been recognized through either the National Achievement Program or the National Hispanic

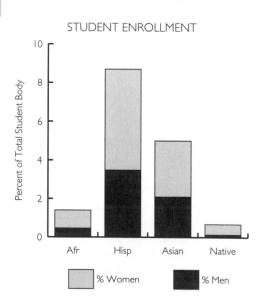

STUDENT ENROLLMENT

Scholarships Program. The number of the $2,000–$4,500 awards varies each year.

Remediation programs: None

Academic support services: Trinity offers tutoring in most academic subjects as well as the services of the Writing Center.

Ethnic studies programs: None

Ethnic studies courses: The university offers 4 courses in Latin American Studies and 10 courses in East Asian Studies.

Organizations for non-white students: Trinity Minority Student Network, Black Student Union, MECHA, Las ALAS (Association of Latin American Students), Board of Minority Interests and Diversity

Notable non-white alumni: na

Tenured faculty: 167

Non-tenured faculty: 67

Student-faculty ratio: 11:1

Administrators: 75

  African-American: 2%

  Hispanic: 4%

  Asian-American: 0

  Native American: 0

Recent non-white speakers on campus: Alex Haley (author); Oscar Arias (former Costa Rican president); Andrew Young (former UN ambassador and mayor of Atlanta); Dr. Julio Noboa Palanco (minorities researcher)

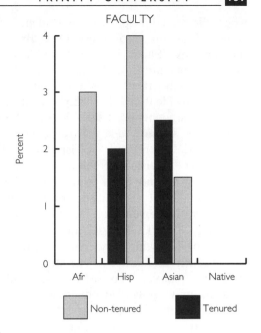

FACULTY

If you choose to go to Trinity, be sure not to hang a wet towel on your dormitory balcony. It's against school rules. Trinity has one of the newest and best-kept campuses in the Southwest, and the university wants to keep it that way. With strong academics and some outstanding faculty members, the 124-year-old university is also working to maintain its status as one of the best liberal arts universities in the West.

Trinity's students are primarily pre-professional, so it's no surprise that the school's department of business administration is the most popular—and most respected. Political science, economics, and philosophy are also excellent, and students praise the school's chemistry and biology departments.

Many of Trinity's departments are complemented by outstanding facilities. The Maddux Library contains more than 675,000 volumes, an impressive number for a relatively small school, and art and music students have the excellent resources of the Ruth Taylor Fine Arts Center. The Computing Center, open twenty-four hours a day, and the school' science laboratories are equally impressive.

One of the pluses in attending Trinity is the accessibility of professors; students are often on a first-name basis with them. One member of the business administration faculty who has gained the respect of Trinity students is William Burke III, who holds a law degree from Howard University. "He has been influential on this campus in talking to minority students and in helping them out when they need help," says a student. "He's an excellent teacher and he really cares." Students also praise Ollie Bryant, assistant dean of financial aid and scholarships. "She invited all of the black women on campus—there are twenty-two of us—to her home for lunch and all of us for the first time really got the chance to know each other," says a student.

A notable feature of Trinity's academic program is its Common Curriculum. First-year students must take the First-Year Seminar, based on an interdisciplinary theme. The seminar each year focuses on a different topic; past topics have included "Love and Death" and "Racism and Nationalism." The university is considering adding the "Racism and Nationalism" course to its permanent history department curriculum because of its popularity with students.

Students must also satisfy course requirements in Seven Fundamental Understandings: Understanding the Intellectual Heritage of Western Culture, Understanding Other Cultures, Understanding the Role of Values, Understanding the Nature of Knowing, Understanding the Physical World through Science, Understanding the Human Social Context, and Understanding Aesthetic Experience and Artistic Creativity. To satisfy the Understanding Other Cultures requirement, students may study "Introduction to Asian Art," "Islamic Traditions," or "Latin American Cultural Traditions." "African-American History," Trinity's only African-American Studies course, can also be taken to satisfy the requirement, but the university hasn't offered the course in recent years.

While students are impressed with their school's academic programs, many of Trinity's students of color are less than impressed with their school's social life and administration. "The administration just won't do anything to keep us here," says a student. "And when they ask us for some input, they don't pay any attention to what we have to say. They certainly aren't implementing anything we suggest." Students point to the university's failure, after several formal and informal requests, to hire a minority faculty adviser, create an ethnic studies minor of any kind, and to find office space for the school's student cultural organizations. Currently the groups meet in various dormitory lounges. "I finally had to transfer from Trinity because I got so tired of making these simple requests," says a former student.

Students also point to the school's poor retention of African-American students. Of the five African-Americans who were to be members of Trinity's class of '91, for example, only two remained to graduate, and of the two African-Americans who were to be juniors during a recent year, only one remained. "The administration likes to compare the school to places like Oberlin, Amherst, and Carleton. They even have this formal list of the schools they think we're similar to," says a student. "But in the area of minority issues we are light-years behind. The other schools have minority faculty advisers, offices for minority student organizations, and ethnic studies minors, but we don't."

The cultural student organizations on campus provide some support for the campus's students of color, but, according to one sophomore, "because they are still fairly young, most are still trying to establish themselves." The Black Student Union (BSU) sponsors activities for Black History Month. During a recent year, the groups brought a guest lecturer to campus and hosted screenings of such films as *Glory* and *A Soldier's Story*. In addition, the BSU has sponsored informal group sessions during which students and outside speakers discussed such issues as interracial dating and the Americas before the arrival of Columbus.

MECHA, a Hispanic student group, is active in community outreach services and acts primarily as a social organization for its members. Many MECHA members help tutor in the local middle school. Recently, MECHA sponsored a Social Fest, a party on campus in which students were treated to a band and Latin American food. According to one student, the party was a hit with the campus community. "We got to talk to Hispanic students about their culture and their concerns," says a student. "It was like a large outdoor classroom."

Other than the tutoring services provided by MECHA, there is little interaction between Trinity students and the San Antonio community, which has a sizable Hispanic population. "The school is totally isolated from the surrounding community," says a junior. "The community feels that Trinity is a country club for elite students."

The Coates Center Program Board sponsors many of the school's on-campus social programs, such as aerobics, parties, and dances. Varsity tennis, *the* sport at Trinity for years, underwent a recent major revamping; always a tough Division I competitor—the men's and women's teams had won six national championships—the university demoted it to Division III status. Football and basketball don't get much student following. The local fraternities and sororities are popular, but, according to students, aren't well integrated.

San Antonio, the country's ninth-largest city, is host to numerous fiestas, festivals, and parades each year, and has museums, a renowned symphony, and a zoo. St. Mary's Street, an area near campus, is popular with students for its restaurants and night spots. For parties, many of Trinity's students of color will head into town or attend one of the parties at nearby University of Texas at San Antonio. "One of the reasons I chose to attend Trinity was that I would be able to take advantage of the many cultural opportunities in San Antonio and at UT/San Antonio," says a junior.

During the past decade, Trinity has skyrocketed from an obscure, mostly regional school known for little but its country club image. With a healthy endowment—one of the country's largest in terms of per student spending—used to enhance academic offerings and facilities, it has gained attention as a more prominent national university. For now, however, many of Trinity's students of color are disgruntled with their college choice, but are also hopeful that with a more sympathetic administration their quality of life will improve. "I would recommend this school to a prospective minority student as a place that is attempting to address his or her concerns," says a student. "The university has focused on its current lack of diversity and is working toward improving in this area. New students coming here, it's hoped, will see numerous changes. These students can also be paramount in helping to facilitate these changes by becoming campus leaders and involved in minority student organizations."

UTAH

UNIVERSITY OF UTAH

Address: Salt Lake City, UT 84112
Phone: (801) 581-7281 / (801) 581-8761
Director of Admissions: Stayner Landward
Multicultural Student Recruiter: Gregory Abrams
1993–94 tuition: $1,879 (in-state); $6,376 (out-of-state)
Room and board: $5,175
Application deadline: 7/1
Financial aid application deadline: 2/15

Non-white freshman admissions: Applicants for the class of '94: na
Accepted: na
Accepted who enroll: na
Applicants accepted who rank in top 10% of high school class: na
Median SAT: 1,000 (math and verbal combined)
Median ACT: 21
Full-time undergraduate enrollment: 14,053
Men: 56.2%
Women: 43.8%
Non-white students in
1988–89: 5.2%
1989–90: 5.6%
1990–91: 5.5%
1991–92: 6.2%
Geographic distribution of students: na
Top majors: 1. Communication 2. Psychology 3. Political Science
Retention rate of non-white students: na
Scholarships exclusively for non-white students: All scholarships are merit-based: John A. Moran Scholarship, Meritorious

Minority Awards, Non-resident Meritorious Minority Award, Minority Achievement Awards, Minority Engineering Program Scholarship, Chicano Scholarship Fund
Remediation programs: na
Academic support services: na
Ethnic studies programs: Within the university's ethnic studies department, students are able to minor in any one of three areas: African-American, Chicano-American, or Native American Studies. The program, established in 1973, is interdisciplinary, involving history, sociology, theater,

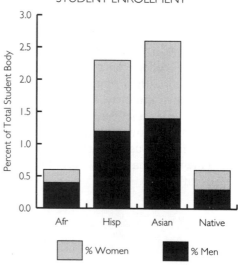

STUDENT ENROLLMENT

communication, English, and other departments. Faculty: 31.

Organizations for non-white students: African-American Student Union, Asian-American Association, Black Athletes Student Association, Chicano Student Association, Intertribal Student Association, Minority Engineering Science, Minority Law Caucus, Polynesian Student Association, Society of Hispanic Professional Engineers, Vietnamese Student Association, Japanese-American Student Association

Notable non-white alumni: Dr. Ronald G. Coleman ('66, Sociology; vice president for academic affairs and associate provost for diversity and faculty development, University of Utah); Dr. Ed Trujillo ('75, Chemical Engineering; professor, University of Utah); Sen Nishiyama ('31, English; journalist, Tokyo); Kathleen Spencer ('75, '77; Education; deputy commissioner, Financial Institutions, State of Utah); Gil Alvarez ('84; State Department of Social Services, Youth Corrections); Jimmy Gurule ('74, '80, English, JD; first Hispanic Assistant U.S. Attorney General); Tyrone Medley (circuit court judge)

Tenured faculty: 959
Non-tenured faculty: 440
Student-faculty ratio: 15:1
Administrators: 132
African-American: 0.01%
Hispanic: 0.02%

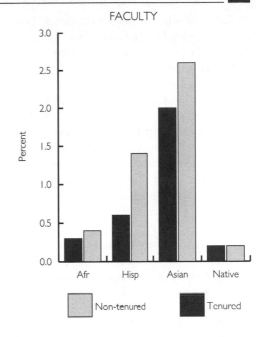

FACULTY

Asian-American: 0.02%
Native American: 0.01%

Recent non-white speakers on campus: Dr. Niara Sudarkasa (president, Lincoln University); Ronald M. Aramaki (Office of Minority Affairs, University of Michigan); Leanov Boulin Johnson (professor, Arizona State University); Roy Jefferson (former Washington Redskin football player and current businessman); Ishmael Reed (poet and author); Dr. James Diego Virgil (professor, UCLA); Spike Lee (filmmaker)

Something peculiar—from the conservative Mormon standpoint anyway—is happening in the state of Utah: it's becoming, although only slightly, a more diverse and progressive state. The state capital, Salt Lake City, now has an Italian-American mayor; Mormons, who once represented the majority of the state's residents, now account for less than half of Utah's population; and since 1991 people in the state twenty-one years of age and older can buy liquor by the drink. "We're not quite Greenwich Village, but we've gone from a small-town mentality to a much more cosmopolitan community with a far greater global perspective," says Salt Lake City's mayor in a *New York Times* article.

The University of Utah is undergoing a cultural renaissance of its own, on a scale similar to the state's. Recently, students elected their first African-American students to serve as student body presidents, both of whom were women; students of color are represented on the school's student senate; and students are working to get faculty approval of a cultural diversity course to be required of all Utah undergraduates.

Students say the school's best departments are in the sciences, notably biology and chemistry. Political science is also said to be quite good, as are the business and nursing programs. The most popular majors at the university are in business, the social sciences, and the humanities. The Honors program is said to be especially rigorous. Engineering—which has departments of bioengineering, chemical, civil, and electrical engineering, computer science, materials science and engineering, and mechanical engineering—is also popular with students.

The school's ethnic studies program is relatively strong, according to students, who point to such courses as "African-American Literature," "Educational Psychology," and "The Asian-American Experience." Among the popular professors in the program are Horuko Moriyasu, Bill Watkins, who is a former member of the Black Panthers, and Wilfred Smith, who also advises the school's African-American Student Union.

The Center for Ethnic Student Affairs, housed in the student union, provides a great deal of academic and non-academic counseling, and, according to a junior, "gets used a lot by students." But, he adds, "it would get used more if it wasn't in such a weird location. There are no signs, and to get to the center you have to go to the third floor by using stairs that are hard to find." The center provides office space for several of the school's cultural student groups. Augustin Trujillo, director of the center, and staff members Beverly Fenton, Kwoda Woods, and Karen Kwan-Smith, are especially supportive of students.

Utah is largely a commuter campus; in fact, more than 80 percent of its 13,000 students commute, and only 7 percent live in dorms—the rest live in fraternity or sorority houses. But students make time to participate in student groups, including organizations with a cultural focus. Utah's African-American Student Union is one of the school's more active student groups, and has recently coordinated several speakouts and open forums. The group, which meets twice a month and has about 25 active members, also recently brought area high school students to campus to participate in the union's School Daze program, in which they were introduced to professors, athletes, and college students. To raise money to aid some of those who suffered during the Los Angeles riots, the union hosted a Gospelfest on campus.

The Asian-American Association is Utah's newest student group; after starting with only 4 students in the summer of 1992, it now has more than 60. The group is focusing on activities for the school's first Asian-American Week, to be held in April. Plans include food booths, speakers, and entertainment. The group is also working to host events, such as movie nights, for Chinese New Year. Utah has long had student groups for individual cultures, such as Chinese and Polynesian clubs, but students say they haven't been strong because of their relatively small size. The association plans to work closely with the other Asian student organizations. The Chicano Student Association and the Intertribal Student Association also coordinate events, such as social mixers and lectures.

An event that is popular with the Salt Lake City and university communities is the school's annual Multicultural Week festival, held on centrally located Union Plaza, "where everyone hangs out and socializes." The festival, coordinated by the Multicultural Board of the Associated Students of the University of Utah, features food booths, local bands, and vendors.

The fact that the university is largely a commuter school contributes to a lack of school spirit, with the exception of the intense football rivalry with Brigham Young University. Varsity football and basketball games get good turnouts, as do the frequent weekend fraternity parties. Much of the socializing takes place at private dorm or off-campus parties. "You make a lot of your own fun here," says a student. The Pie, a local pizza joint, is a popular hangout, especially between and after classes, and a new athletic complex draws many student athletes.

Salt Lake City offers numerous multicultural resources, although the city, like the state, is predominantly white. The Asian-American Association works with the Asian Association of Utah, which has helped the student group arrange for speakers and other events. The local NAACP chapter is active, and has recently helped the African-American Student Union to coordinate political events and lectures. The famous Mormon Tabernacle Choir calls the city home, as does the Utah Jazz, a professional basketball team. Numerous productions are put on at the Pioneer Memorial Theater, and the Utah Symphony is internationally recognized. The campus is also located near some of the country's best skiing resorts, including Alta and Snowbird. The U.S. Olympic ski team annually practices nearby.

While it's hard to discuss the university without referring to the influence of the Mormon Church—according to one estimate, more than half of the university's students belong to the Church of Jesus Christ of Latter-day Saints—students say the social and political attitudes here are more moderate than conservative.

The university offers an attractive campus to its largely commuter student body. Utah also provides students with a respectable education, and a rather subdued social life. For some students, the combination is worth four years of their time. "The university is homogeneous to a fault, but there are many nice students here," says a sophomore. "I'm glad I came, especially to get away from the smog and other problems of growing up in a large city."

VERMONT

BENNINGTON COLLEGE

Address: Bennington, VT 05201
Phone: (802) 442-6349
Director of Admissions: Karen Parker
Multicultural Student Recruiter: Teri M. Donnelly
1991–92 tuition: $19,400
Room and board: $3,800
Application deadline: 3/1
Financial aid application deadline: 3/1
Non-white freshman admissions: Applicants for the class of '95: 56
   Accepted: 83%
   Accepted who enroll: 37%
   Applicants accepted who rank in top 10% of high school class: na
   Median SAT range: 480–610 V, 480–610 M
   Median ACT: na
Full-time undergraduate enrollment: 569
   Men: 41%
   Women: 59%
Non-white students in
   1987–88: na
   1988–89: 5.89%
   1989–90: na
   1990–91: 6.15%
Geographic distribution of students: na
Top majors: 1. Literature and Languages 2. Visual Arts 3. Social Sciences
Retention rate of non-white students: 89%
Scholarships exclusively for non-white students: None
Remediation programs: The college offers basic writing courses as well as tutoring for non-native speakers of English.

Academic support services: na
Ethnic studies programs: None
Ethnic studies courses: na
Organizations for non-white students: AHANA-PRISM (a multicultural student group organized to coordinate cultural programming)
Notable non-white alumni: Ulysses Dove (dancer/choreographer); Harry Sheppard (dancer/choreographer); Philomena Williamson (painter); Kay Murray (legal counsel, New York City Department of Juvenile Justice)
Tenured faculty: 46
Non-tenured faculty: 39

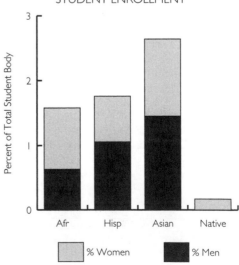

STUDENT ENROLLMENT

Percent of Total Student Body

Afr   Hisp   Asian   Native

% Women   % Men

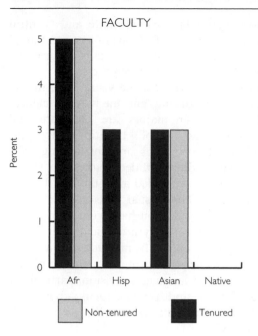

FACULTY

Percent

5
4
3
2
1
0

Afr   Hisp   Asian   Native

Non-tenured   Tenured

Student-faculty ratio: 8:1
Administrators: 61
　African-American: 0
　Hispanic: 0
　Asian-American: 0
　Native American: 0
Recent non-white speakers on campus:
　Judith Jamison (artistic director, Alvin
　Ailey American Dance Theater); Harvey
　Gantt (former mayor of Charlotte, NC,
　and unsuccessful candidate for the U.S.
　Senate in a race against Jesse Helms)

Bennington College is a small progressive school in rural Vermont where the students aren't so much political as artsy. Students don't organize demonstrations against the administration. They perform. Or they paint. Or they choreograph. Or they write.

At Bennington students welcome diversity. In fact, they crave it. Students come from more than 36 states and 17 foreign countries, but geographic diversity is hardly the most noticeable variety on campus. Bennington has always attracted the (self-proclaimed) iconoclast, the sexual adventurer, the hipster, the granola cruncher, and, of course, the artist (who is usually also one or more of the above). And there is a feeling here that Bennington students are less concerned with a student's race or ethnicity than with his or her creative output. "Students here very much respect sincerity of effort, regardless of what it is," says a recent graduate. "What qualifies as important is the kind of dedication that is put into it." Adds a senior literature and psychology major: "Bennington is a particular type of school that attracts certain types of people. I think I am one Asian out of ten, and one Korean out of three Korean students. This is not bad, though. We do not have the racial tension that exists in so many colleges, nor do I feel awkward about being a minority. Bennington seems very tolerant of people's differences."

Bennington's communal style of living helps students to avoid exclusivity. There are no fraternities or sororities, nor are there any private eating clubs, as there are at some of the other, more prominent liberal arts colleges in the Northeast. There are 15 student houses on campus, 12 of which are situated along the Commons area, and students are in charge of their house's governance. House rules are established at the beginning of each term, and weekly meetings, usually on Sunday evenings, are held to discuss other house issues. One student reports that the houses are "quite livable," and that each house contains a working fireplace, a kitchenette, and a central living room area. "The campus is set up so that you really feel part of a community," says a student. According to another student: "Everything is very racially integrated." All dorms and bathrooms are also completely integrated between the sexes.

Bennington's academic program includes seven divisions: the visual arts, music, literature and languages, the social sciences, dance, drama, and the natural sciences (which includes math). Among the most popular majors are literature and languages, visual arts, and the social sciences. The school's traditional strengths lie in the arts, and students say the visual arts programs are outstanding. The Center for Visual and Performing Arts (VAPA) allows students access to studio space on a twenty-four-hour basis, and has a gallery modeled after the fourth floor of the Whitney Museum in New York City. "The Visual Arts Center is an incredible space," says a recent graduate. "Not only do you have your own studio space, but everyone in visual arts, regardless of what they are studying, is under the same roof." The dance division receives high marks from students. In order to graduate, dance majors must organize and publicly perform at least three pieces. Bennington is also well known for its literature and languages division, particularly because of some of its more illustrious former and present faculty members, including Bernard Malamud. The student-run literary magazine, *Silo,* the campus's only publication, was awarded a prize in 1987.

Don't be too quick to assume that all Bennington students are either dancing or drawing. Some are studying the sciences as well as math. "I came here as a literature major," says a recent graduate, "until I took Betsy Sherman's biology class. It was just so much more exciting than any science I had ever taken in high school." Recent Bennington graduates have gone on to advanced study in biology, chemistry, and medicine at such top-notch places as Yale, Harvard, and Cornell.

Ethnic studies aren't exactly abundant at Bennington, but several of the courses offered win student praise. Chinese-language courses are offered, and students say the course's professor, Chichung Huang, is "full of wisdom and kindness." Phebe Chao, who teaches "Black America," a literature course, has also earned student respect. "She is one of the most inspiring teachers I have ever had," says a literature major. "From the endless line of students sitting in front of her office during class registration, I would say that she is well loved by her students." William Dixon, who teaches the "Black Music" course, is popular with students, and in 1976 *Jazz* magazine voted him musician of the year. One student reports that the Hispanic literature courses are "very good." AHANA-PRISM (African, Hispanic, Asian, Native American), a multicultural student group, has been meeting recently with faculty members in an attempt to have more multicultural courses included in the curriculum.

Whatever their majors, Bennington students are free to design their own course of study, with the assistance of a faculty adviser. Instead of final exams, students must write final papers. Instead of receiving letter grades at the end of a term, they receive extensive comments from their professors. This lack of an academic structure is in large part why many students chose to come to Bennington in the first place. Close faculty interaction is another draw.

A practical part of the Bennington education is the Field Work Term (FWT).

Between the fall and spring semesters, students have the opportunity to work full-time in careers of their own choosing. To assist students in their FWT job hunts, the Student Placement Office lists more than 1,100 positions each year. Recent FWTs have included a reporting internship at *Fortune* magazine, computer programming at AT&T, and archival assistantships at the Getty Center for the History of Art and Humanities in California.

For rest and relaxation, students can attend any number of student readings or productions. The school publishes a weekly calendar of such events, as well as scheduled speakers from off campus. Last year, Judith Jamison, artistic director of the Alvin Ailey American Dance Theater, and Harvey Gantt, who lost to Jesse Helms in a controversial North Carolina U.S. Senate race, spoke on campus. Students say attendance at the speakers' lectures was good.

The town of Bennington, about five miles from campus, has a couple of movie theaters and restaurants, but little else. New England countryside surrounds the campus and the town. About an hour away, Albany, New York, is the closest city, and Boston and New York City, both no more than four hours away, are also popular destinations.

If you're a football jock, don't bother attending school here. (No varsity sports are offered, and a proposed new athletic facility is meeting with student ambivalence.) But if you're free-spirited and creative—and want the seclusion of a rural environment and a small-college atmosphere then going to school near the Green Mountains of Vermont will prove to be a rewarding experience.

MIDDLEBURY COLLEGE

Address: Middlebury, VT 05753
Phone: (802) 388-3711
Director of Admissions: Geoffrey Smith
Multicultural Student Recruiters: James Thompson, Kathy Lindsey
1991–92 tuition: $21,200 (room and board included)
Application deadline: 1/15
Financial aid application deadline: 2/1
Non-white freshman admissions: Applicants for the class of '95: 352
  Accepted: 45%
  Accepted who enroll: 37.5%
  Applicants accepted who rank in top 10% of high school class: 39%
  In top 25%: na
  Median SAT range: 500–540 V, 530–610 M
  Median ACT: na
Full-time undergraduate enrollment: 2,000
  Men: 50%
  Women: 50%

Non-white students in
  1987–88: 4%
  1988–89: 5%
  1989–90: 6%
  1990–91: 10%
Students In-state: 1%
Top majors: 1. Political Science
  2. English/American Literature
  3. Psychology
Retention rate of non-white students: 80%
Scholarships exclusively for non-white students: None
Remediation programs: The Pre-enrollment Program provides entering first-year students with an introduction to the academic and non-academic support programs at the college.
Academic support services: The college provides peer tutoring in most academic subjects and a Writing Center.
Ethnic studies programs: The college offers

STUDENT ENROLLMENT

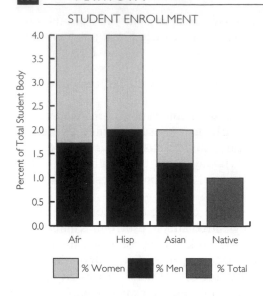

Percent of Total Student Body

| % Women | % Men | % Total |

GEOGRAPHIC DISTRIBUTION OF STUDENTS

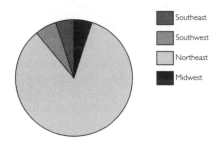

Southeast
Southwest
Northeast
Midwest

an East Asian Studies major, an interdisciplinary program involving political science, sociology/anthropology, history, religion, philosophy, as well as Japanese- and Chinese-language study.

Ethnic studies courses: The college offers eight courses in African and African-American Studies, three in Latin American Studies, two on American race relations, and "Native Peoples of North America."

Organizations for non-white students: African-American Alliance, Olé (Organización Latino Americana y Española), East Asian Cultural Club, Hispanic-American League, Latin American and Caribbean Alliance, Middlebury Asian Student Organization

Notable non-white alumni: Ronald H. Brown ('62; lawyer; national chairperson, Democratic Party; Secretary of Commerce)

Tenured faculty: na

Non-tenured faculty: na

Student-faculty ratio: 12:1

Administrators: na

Recent non-white speakers on campus: Kwame Toure (political activist)

Yes, Middlebury College offers an excellent liberal arts education, and the school's idyllic campus setting is the stuff of picture postcards. On most fronts, Middlebury's educational opportunities compete with the best of them. But on another, less cerebral front, the 193-year-old school has few, if any, rivals: its dining service includes all-you-can-eat Ben and Jerry's ice cream. (For the health-conscious, the dining halls also serve ice cream lower in cholesterol and fat.)

Middlebury is world-renowned for its 10 language programs, a phenomenal number considering the school's relatively small enrollment. Students from all over the world come to the campus in the summer to study in one of the school's "total immersion" language programs. Language study includes Chinese, Japanese, Russian, French, and Hebrew, and is complemented by extensive study-abroad opportunities. Nearly 40 percent of the student body studies abroad, in such places as France, Russia, and Italy. Students can put their language study to good use by majoring in the school's excellent international politics and economics interdisciplinary program. Middlebury also has outstanding English, political science, history, and biology departments.

Students at Middlebury enjoy close relations with their professors, especially since classes usually number no more than 20 students, and generally even fewer. Professors have been known to get involved in students' extracurricular activities and intramurals, and they often invite students to their homes for class and dinner. Especially supportive of the school's student of color community is John Walsh, Middlebury's chaplain. "He attends many of the cultural student groups' meetings and activities, and he's always trying to get the administration to get the campus to become more diverse racially and ethnically," says a student. One of the administrators students turn to and respect a great deal is James Thompson, an admissions counselor, who is also a Middlebury alum.

Middlebury is one of the few schools in the country to have the Winter Term schedule, which allows students to study on or off campus for the month of January. Students, who must complete four Winter Terms in order to graduate, also have the option of pursuing off-campus internship or research opportunities during the month. During a recent Winter Term, more than 100 courses were offered on campus, including "Women in Contemporary Chinese Literature" and "Race and Ethnicity: Cross-Cultural Perspectives." Courses in the humanities, the natural and social sciences, and a foreign language are also required for graduation.

Middlebury has never been known as a politically active campus, but all that changed during the spring semester of the 1991–92 school year, when students—in particular members of the African-American Alliance, the Middlebury Asian Student Organization (MASO), and the Latin American and Caribbean Alliance—staged a sit-in, lasting nearly three days, in front of the dean's office. Protesters demanded better recruitment of students, faculty, and staff of color, as well as a more diverse course curriculum. The event generated local press attention, and "it made the campus community more aware of our concerns," says a student. "Professors and students stopped and talked to us and asked us what it was we were seeking. Some students and professors even brought us food and drinks during the sit-in."

As a result of the sit-in, the administration agreed to hire for the 1992–93 school year a liaison to work as an intermediary between the student of color community and the administration.

"The liaison is scheduled to be here for the year, and we're not sure if there will be such a position after he leaves," says a student. "The administration is always telling us that it's impossible for them to hire a full-time staff person in charge of multicultural affairs because of the budget. Yet there is so much construction going on around campus that it makes us wonder why not. The school has brand-new racquetball courts, a new student center, and a new amphitheater that's still under construction. After a while we say, 'What is going on here?'"

In addition to the sit-in, the groups are active in raising the cultural awareness of the campus in other ways. The Middlebury Asian Student Organization, the campus's newest cultural student group, has about 15 to 20 active student members. The organization recently staged a Lunar Year celebration, and helps coordinate events with the school's East Asian Cultural Club. According to a student, MASO is spending most of its resources letting the campus know about its existence. "We're trying to make the campus aware of our organization," reports a sophomore. "Within the next two years, we hope to become more political, and not just social, by working to get the admissions office to recruit more Asian-American students to Middlebury." The East Asian Cultural Club primarily sponsors cultural programs about East Asia and is rarely, if ever, political, according to a student.

The Latin American and Caribbean Alliance works to coordinate programming for the school's Latin American Month, held during April. Olé, a Hispanic group whose members are mostly international students from Latin America, co-sponsors events with the Latin American and Caribbean Alliance during Latin American Month. One student reports, however, that "there is tension between the two groups. Olé members don't like to identify with the concerns and problems of the Hispanic-American community. They don't consider themselves American, so usually they separate themselves from us." For Black History Month, the African-American Alliance sponsors speakers, movies, and workshops.

The African-American and Hispanic-American Bicultural Center, located "on the edge of campus, between the campus and the town," is a relatively new and popular option to dorm living at Middlebury. The center, established on campus in the fall of '91, has residence facilities for up to 19 students, in "spacious and beautiful" single and double rooms. In the center, students have access to kitchen facilities, a living room, and a "small but growing library" of works relevant to the Hispanic-American and African-American communities. Students say that although there was initial concern that the center would only segregate the campus, they think it is becoming better known and more frequented. According to one student, professors use some of the center's first-floor office space during their office hours as a way to encourage more students to learn about the center, which hosts numerous lectures and other events.

The town of Middlebury (pop. 7,500) is, in a word, rural. The area around the campus is an outdoor person's dream; ski slopes (the college has its own ski center) are nearby and biking and jogging are popular activities over the area's country—and often hilly—roads. While there isn't a lot to do in town, except for a few watering holes, Boston and New York City are both within a few hours' drive. Burlington is about an hour away by car.

Sports are an important aspect of the lives of many Middlebury students. Men's varsity lacrosse, women's varsity swimming, and the school's ski teams are usually nationally ranked. The Fletcher Field House and the McCullough Gymnasium house some impressive athletic facilities. The Middlebury College Activities Board arranges for concerts, dances, films, and other social events on campus. The Undergraduate, with its dining area and game and TV rooms, is a frequented spot. And the college hosts numerous lectures, films, and dance and musical performances throughout the year.

Middlebury attracts students from all over the nation and from dozens of foreign countries. Despite the geographic diversity, Middlebury is one of the country's more racially homogeneous elite private colleges, no doubt a reflection of the fact that Vermont is one of the least racially diverse states in the country. "I would like to structure a Winter Term project where I would take a Middlebury class into the inner city," says a student. "So many of the students here are naive. Many of them, even the students of color, are from private high schools. It's not that they're not interested in cultural diversity. It's just that they've led such bubbled lives."

Sometimes this lack of cultural diversity can be trying for students. "We're pulled in so many different directions," says a student. "We have to do our studies, which can be rigorous here. And then we need to help incoming students of color adjust to the campus atmosphere. We try to serve as mentors for the freshmen. And then we sponsor cultural events for the campus, to try to raise their awareness. By the time we get to be juniors and seniors, we're usually exhausted."

There are more reasons to come to Middlebury than all-you-can-eat ice cream. There's the school's excellent academics, intimate learning environment, and, in the words of one student, "a better chance to get to know myself than if I'd gone to a larger, more urban school." She adds: "Coming to Middlebury has made me stronger. There have been times when I've literally packed my bags to leave, but I end up staying. The school has taught me how to survive. If I'd gone to a school with more students of color who are more organized and active, it would have been easier, but I wouldn't have learned as much. This is an elite atmosphere here. And I'm learning how to deal with it now, before I graduate into the 'real world.'"

UNIVERSITY OF VERMONT

Address: Clement House, Burlington, VT 05401
Phone: (802) 656-3370
Director of Admissions. Carol Cotman Hogan
Multicultural Student Recruiter: na
1991–92 tuition: $4,900 (in-state); $13,500 (out-of-state)
Room and board: $4,142
Application deadline: 2/1
Financial aid application deadline: 3/1
Non-white freshman admissions: Applicants for the class of '95: 398
Accepted: 89.5%
Accepted who enroll: 27.5%
Applicants accepted who rank in top 10% of high school class: na
Median SAT: 450 V, 540 M
Median ACT: na
Full-time undergraduate enrollment: 7,925
Men: 47.5%
Women: 52.5%
Non-white students in
1988–89: 4.6%
1989–90: 5.5%
1990–91: 5.8%
1991–92: 7.0%
Geographic distribution of students: na

Students In-state: 46%
Top majors: 1. Political Science 2. Business Administration 3. Psychology
Retention rate of non-white students: 87%
Scholarships exclusively for non-white students: The Henderson Scholarship: need-based; amount varies; approximately four awarded each year.
Remediation programs: None
Academic support services: Office of Special Student Services provides programs in

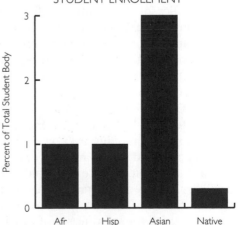

STUDENT ENROLLMENT

Percent of Total Student Body

Afr   Hisp   Asian   Native

tutoring and counseling, as does the Office of Multicultural Affairs.

Ethnic studies programs: None

Ethnic studies courses: "Race and Cultures," "African Studies."

Organizations for non-white students: Black Student Union, Asian-American Student Union, Alianza Latina, Native American Student Union

Notable non-white alumni: na

Tenured faculty: na

Non-tenured faculty: na

Student-faculty ratio: 16:1

Administrators: na
   African-American: 1%
   Hispanic: <1%
   Asian-American: 2%
   Native American: <1%

Recent non-white speakers on campus: Spike Lee (filmmaker); Peggy Brooks Bertram (poet); Gimbu Kali (professor, Northwestern University); Jamaica Kincaid (author)

In recent years, the University of Vermont has become increasingly known as one of the country's better-respected public universities, thanks to academic upgrading, generally good facilities, and a beautiful campus setting. Last year, only about half of the school's applicants were accepted, a statistic that admissions officers at even some of the country's better-known private schools would savor.

More recently, however, the 202-year-old university has come to be known for a spirit of political activism that has rarely been seen on this otherwise tranquil college campus. The protests all focus on the relative lack of cultural and racial diversity in the school's curriculum, faculty, and student body. A shanty town, called Diversity University, was built on the campus green—it was later burned down by counter-protesters—several student sit-ins were staged at the Waterman Building, the school's main administration building, in which several students and a faculty member were arrested, and petitions have made the rounds. After a year marked by such demonstrations and reports of what *The Chronicle of Higher Education* says was "an increasingly bleak financial picture" for UVM, George Davis, the university president, resigned. "It is apparent that support for my leadership is not sufficiently strong for me to carry on what I started," Davis said. Students had complained that Davis did not regularly attend meetings of the Cultural Diversity panel, a committee of students and administrators.

The Office of Multicultural Affairs (OMA), located in the Center for Cultural Pluralism on the Redstone Campus, provides much of the academic and non-academic support for the university's students of color. OMA is a "great place to hang out," says a student about the office, which has a lounge, a TV and VCR, and staff offices. OMA, which is frequently used by students, employs two part-time graduate students to serve as academic tutors. The school's cultural student organizations also meet at OMA. Students say that OMA director Rodney Patterson, who also serves as a pastor at a local church, works closely with students and student groups. The Center for Cultural Pluralism regularly brings speakers to campus.

Other staff and faculty members especially supportive of students of color include Richard Johnson, director of student activities, and Roxanne Lin, an English professor. "They are approachable as friends more than just as faculty," says a student. Students also turn to Laura Fishman, associate professor of sociology, and Lawrence McCrorey, professor of physiology and biophysics.

The university is divided into eight colleges. In the College of Arts and Sciences, the university's largest division, students say the history, economics, and political science departments are best, while the English department is also well regarded. The school's environmental science program is said to be outstanding. The School of Agriculture has a dairy farm, which produces ice cream for the school's cafeterias, and a research center. The recent completion of a new business education building, Kalkin, and the addition of several new faculty members have enhanced the business school's reputation. Business administration is the business school's most popular major, while students also praise the accounting and marketing information systems programs. Many business majors take advantage of the school's co-op program with IBM, which has offices in Burlington.

Students in several of UVM's undergraduate divisions are required to take the one-credit "Race and Cultures" course. Students primarily read periodical literature about various cultural and racial topics. As part of the course, students of color at the university lead class discussions. "Most of the students in the class hadn't interacted with minority students before, so we gave them a chance to ask us anything they wanted to about our cultures," says a student. "The discussions would get quite interesting." The College of Arts and Sciences does not require students to take the "Race and Cultures" course, but in the fall of 1991 the college created its own three-credit multicultural class requirement. Business school students are not required to take either course.

There are four cultural student organizations on campus, and students say they have become increasingly active in recent years. The Black Student Union, which meets biweekly, was established on campus about six years ago. For Black History Month, the group has offered an all-you-can-eat soul food dinner and invited African-American female poets to campus for readings of their works. The Alianza Latina, which was established three years ago, is primarily a social organization, according to student members, but has also brought prominent speakers to campus. The Asian-American Student Union, also primarily a social organization, screens films and prepares cultural foods for the school's annual Oktoberfest. The Native American Student Union sponsors activities as well.

An alternative to dorm life is the school's Living/Learning Center, which houses the majority of UVM's students of color. The center, which houses more than 500 students, coordinates over 30 programs each year that seek to raise students' awareness about almost any sort of diversity. Recent programs have included artistic performances, sign language workshops, and guest speakers.

UVM's relatively new student center is the site of a great deal of activity, including movie nights, as are the school's predominantly white Greek organizations. Students are also able to participate in numerous musical and drama clubs, as well as play on intramural sports teams. Varsity sports, especially hockey, skiing, and soccer, are popular, but due to heavy snows during the season, the school has no football team.

Burlington, a predominantly white community, is said to be an excellent college town, with many pubs, clubs, shopping opportunities, and restaurants. Montreal is only an hour and a half away, and Boston and New York City are 200 and 300 miles away, respectively.

Racial and cultural diversity are hard to come by at this state-supported university,

no doubt in large part because the state of Vermont is one of the least diverse in the country. But the university is geographically diverse. Although the majority of the students are from the Northeast and the Middle Atlantic states, others are from dozens of other states and foreign countries. Only little more than half of the students are from the state. Students are on the whole more liberal than conservative, and environmental issues generate a great deal of student attention.

With student prodding, UVM has begun to put racial and cultural issues on the front burner. Although students shy away from completely recommending their school to prospective applicants, they feel their four years here have only served to strengthen them. "I would recommend this university because of its potential," says a senior. "I find that on the whole this is a good school where the students get together and discuss the issues. I've found that there are many professors and staff members you can express your feelings to, so you don't feel alone. Also, I feel the university is patterned after American society, and if you can attend this school and make it, then it's possible to make it in the 'real world.'"

V I R G I N I A

HAMPDEN-SYDNEY COLLEGE

Men's college
Address: Box 667, Hampden-Sydney, VA
  23943
Phone: (804) 223-6120 / (800) 755-0733
Director of Admissions: Anita H. Garland
Multicultural Student Recruiter: M. Deane
  Cheatham III
1993–94 tuition: $12,576
Room and board: $4,398
Application deadline: 3/1
Financial aid application deadline: 3/1
Non-white freshman admissions: Applicants
  for the class of '96: 50
  Accepted: 58%
  Accepted who enroll: 35%
  Applicants accepted who rank in top
  10% of high school class: 10%
  In top 25%: 25%
  Median SAT range: 460–590 V,
  470–580 M
  Median ACT: na
Full-time undergraduate enrollment: 950
Non-white students in
  1988–89: 4%
  1989–90: 4%
  1990–91: 4%
  1991–92: 6%
Students In-state: 51%
Top majors: 1. Economics 2. History
  3. Political Science
Retention rate of non-white students: 70%
**Scholarships exclusively for non-white
  students:** None
Remediation programs: None

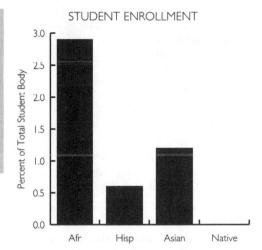

STUDENT ENROLLMENT

Percent of Total Student Body

Afr   Hisp   Asian   Native

GEOGRAPHIC DISTRIBUTION OF STUDENTS

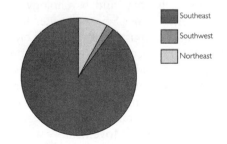

■ Southeast
▨ Southwest
□ Northeast

Academic support services: The college
  offers departmental tutoring, as well as
  peer academic advising, writing labs, and
  study skills seminars.

Ethnic studies programs: None

Ethnic studies courses: The English department offers "Introduction to African-American Literature," the history department offers "The Civil Rights Movement," "Black America," and "East Asia," the Spanish department offers "Latin American Prose and Poetry," and the religion department offers "World Religions." Also offered are "African Christianity" "Afro-American History," and "The Civil Rights Movement."

Organizations for non-white students: Brothers of Hampden-Sydney (black student organization)

Notable non-white alumni: Maurice Jones ('86; Truman and Rhodes Scholar)

Tenured faculty: 52

Non-tenured faculty: 38

Student-faculty ratio: 13:1

Administrators: 65

    African-American: 2%

    Hispanic: 0

    Asian-American: 0

    Native American: 0

Recent non-white speakers on campus: Nikki Giovanni (poet); James Gee (attorney); Shirley Chisholm (first African-American female presidential candidate); Juan Williams (author and columnist); Rodney Ruffin ('82; administrative law judge, Washington, DC)

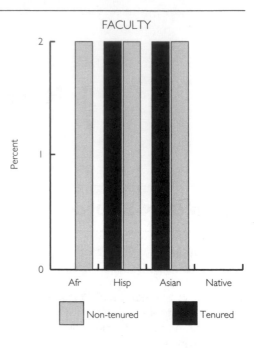

FACULTY

Non-tenured   Tenured

Hampden-Sydney, founded in 1776, is a traditional liberal arts college for men. The college's first board of trustees included illustrious members James Madison and Patrick ("Give me liberty or give me death") Henry, and many of its campus buildings have been designated as historic landmarks.

Classics, history, and psychology are among the school's best academic departments. The Gilmer Science Center houses impressive research facilities for students majoring in chemistry, physics, and biology, one of the school's more popular majors. Students are also able to concentrate in international studies, which involves an independent study project and a semester or year abroad. Although the school offers no pre-professional programs—it's strictly liberal arts here—many students double-major in economics and in another discipline. Some of the school's more popular cultural studies courses are "African Christianity," "Afro-American History," and "The Civil Rights Movement."

When students can't find what they want in the curriculum at Hampden-Sydney, they can enroll in courses at six nearby colleges: Hollins, Randolph-Macon, Randolph-Macon Woman's College, Sweet Briar, Mary Baldwin, and Washington and Lee.

To graduate, students are required to take seven courses in the humanities, four in the natural sciences, and three in the social sciences. Students must also take a year's worth of English composition and rhetoric, and study a foreign language—the school offers German, Russian, French, and Spanish—through the second-year level. Hampden-Sydney students abide by a strict honor system. Infractions—which can lead to failure in a course or dismissal from the college—cover everything from cheating on an exam to stealing.

The school's most effective academic support service, according to students, is the faculty advising system. Students and faculty develop extremely close relationships, and most introductory classes have fewer than 25 students; in upper-level courses, the number is much lower. As many professors live on campus, they are not strangers to campus-wide events or to the library. "Whenever I see my English professor on campus we stop and talk, sometimes about nothing in particular, sometimes about a problem I'm having in class," says a sophomore. "The professors here really want to help students."

One of the school's faculty members whom students find most helpful is Robert Rogers, dean of freshmen and a professor of religion. "Because he wears several hats within the Hampden-Sydney system, he provides the African-American students with many links to the administration and to other professors that they otherwise might not have," says a student. "He's also a good listener, and always takes time if a student needs to talk to him."

For peer support, African-American students at the college participate in the activities sponsored by the Brothers of Hampden-Sydney, the college's only cultural student group. "This is a totally voluntary and informal organization of the African-American students at Hampden-Sydney," says a student. "This group has been very active in sponsoring events such as film festivals, cultural awareness programs, lectures, as well as parties and dances. It is also a support group for the African-American students that allows them to discuss some of their problems and vent some of the frustrations that they may have."

According to a student, Hampden-Sydney's African-American students are a close-knit group. "As of now, Hampden-Sydney has only twenty-eight African-American students. Most of these students are very close to each other and form a very effective support group. For this reason, the African-American students, except in classroom situations, often choose to socialize with each other. This is not to say that these students are separatists or exclusionists, but they simply choose to spend their leisure time with people who share similar experiences."

Although this is an all-male school, there is enough activity on campus to keep students around during the week. More than a third of the students participate in varsity sports, while 80 percent are involved in intramurals. Other popular activities are student government, writing for the school newspaper, the *Tiger,* and performing in various musical groups. Hampden-Sydney is also very Greek. More than half of the student body pledges one or another of the 12 national fraternities on campus, and a great deal of the school's social life (i.e., parties) takes place on the Circle, where 11 of the 12 fraternity houses are located.

Presently, however, no minority students are members of the Greek system, which may account for some of the bad feelings between certain members of Greek organizations and the school's African-American community. Students point to a recent incident at a Kappa Alpha fraternity party. "Several minority students and members of the fraternity were involved," reports a student. "The students, who had gone to the fraternity house for a social gathering, were called derogatory names and nearly engaged in a physical confrontation. The administrative response was to reprimand the individual students involved but not the entire Kappa Alpha fraternity."

In 1990, students also issued a complaint against the Hampden-Sydney security force, because of an incident in which African-American students, an alum, and prospective students were harassed by an officer. "Because of this confrontation, a formal complaint was filed with the head of the department," says a student. "As a result, not only did the students receive written apologies, but the entire police force volunteered to attend a seminar that dealt with race relations."

Fortunately, Hampden-Sydney students are allowed to have cars on campus. Getting away from it all requires wheels, as the nearest town, Farmville, offers little but a coffee shop and a Hardee's. Students often road-trip to one of the area colleges—Hollins and Sweet Briar are popular destinations—or to the cities of Richmond, Lynchburg, and Charlottesville, all of which are around an hour's drive from campus.

Hampden-Sydney students, like their school, are conservative and traditional. The Young Republicans organization is an active student group on campus, and khakis are the pants of choice. More than half of the student body comes from Virginia, more specifically from the more affluent suburbs of Richmond, while most of the rest of the students are from other parts of the South.

The educational opportunities at Hampden-Sydney certainly weren't lost on Maurice Jones, class of '86, the school's first African-American Rhodes Scholar, who served as student body president during his senior year. Says Jones of his undergraduate years: "To me Hampden-Sydney was not a college: it was a community, a family. Everyone really cared for you. If you just showed that you were serious about getting an education, people would give you everything you needed."

HOLLINS COLLEGE

Women's college
Address: P.O. Box 9707, Roanoke, VA
  24020
Phone: (703) 362-6401 / (800) 456-9595
Director of Admissions: Anne B. Parry
Multicultural Student Recruiter: Cheryl R.
  Hilton
1991–92 tuition: $11,600
Room and board: $4,600
Application deadline: 2/15
Financial aid application deadline: 3/31
Non-white freshman admissions: Applicants
  for the class of '95: 39
  Accepted: 71.8%
  Accepted who enroll: 35.7%
  Applicants accepted who rank in top
  10% of high school class: 57%

In top 25%: 57%
Median SAT range: 410–460 V, 490–510 M
Median ACT: na
Full-time undergraduate enrollment: 788
Non-white students in
  1987–88: 2.4%
  1988–89: 2.1%
  1989–90: 2.2%
  1990–91: 4.4%
Students In-state: 42%
Top majors: 1. Economics 2. French
  3. Biology/Chemistry
Retention rate of non-white students: 89%
**Scholarships exclusively for non-white
  students:** King Endowed Scholarship:
  need-based; one $799 scholarship
  awarded each year.

STUDENT ENROLLMENT

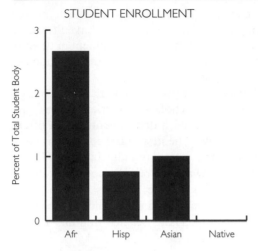

GEOGRAPHIC DISTRIBUTION OF STUDENTS

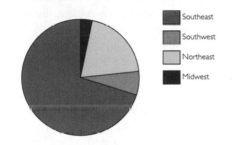

Southeast
Southwest
Northeast
Midwest

Remediation programs: None
Academic support services: The college
offers a Writing Center.
Ethnic studies programs: None
Ethnic studies courses: The history
department offers "Introduction to Latin
America," "Latin America Since
Independence," "Japan in the Modern
World," and "Traditional East Asia."
The English department offers
"African-American Literature."
Organizations for non-white students: Black
Student Association, Multicultural Club

Notable non-white alumnae: Cynthia Hale
('75, Music; pastor, Ray of Hope
Christian Church); Cecelia M. Long ('70,
German; general secretariat, United
Methodist Church); Patrice Taylor
Johnson (Sociology; Assistant Attorney
General)
Tenured faculty: 47
Non-tenured faculty: 30

FACULTY

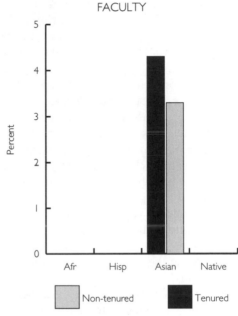

Non-tenured   Tenured

Student-faculty ratio: 10:1
Administrators: 77
   African-American: 1.3%
   Hispanic: 1.3%
   Asian-American: 0
   Native American: 0
Recent non-white speakers on campus: Linda
Brown Smith (civil rights activist); Cheryl
Brown Henderson (civil rights activist)

Hollins College is a small traditional liberal arts college for women located on the
outskirts of Roanoke, Virginia, "the business, medical, commercial, and entertainment center for southwestern Virginia," a fitting location, as these are the careers
many Hollins women plan to pursue—or marry into—upon graduation. Although
marrying a Washington and Lee fraternity man still remains a crowning achievement
for some Hollins women, the majority of them are career-oriented.

One of the school's outstanding characteristics is its small size, which means professors are easily accessible. "One thing about Hollins is that I haven't met a professor yet who would not take the time to talk with me about a problem or answer questions," says a recent graduate. "They are interested in the students as students, not only as potential majors in their particular fields."

Hollins's best departments are psychology and English, and it has well-known graduate school programs in both areas. Many noted scholars and writers have come to the school either to teach or to study. Hollins's English department, which offers a popular "African-American Literature" course, was the first in the country to have a writer-in-residence program, and it publishes the internationally famous *Hollins Critic,* which has featured works by E. L. Doctorow and Derek Walcott. More than half of the school's psychology majors pursue graduate degrees in the field. Pre-professional majors, particularly in computer science and economics, are becoming increasingly popular. The school's relatively new Dana Science Building is well equipped for chemistry, biology, and physics majors.

Hollins's Short Term adds variety to the college's academic schedule. Students spend four months on campus each semester, but during the month of January they are free to pursue on- or off-campus internships or research possibilities. Some of the more popular off-campus opportunities have taken students to CNN, IBM, ITT, and Merrill Lynch. To graduate, students must complete two courses in each of four areas: fine arts, humanities, natural sciences, and social sciences. Physical education courses and a first-year writing course are also required.

For academic support, students are able to turn to the Writing Center. The center's student tutors are "very accessible and helpful," says a student. "They will help you with almost any aspect of a writing assignment. It's also open late [until about 10 p.m. during the week], so you can have a tutor proofread an assignment before you hand it in."

Numerous staff and faculty members are especially supportive of Hollins students of color, particularly Jong Ra, a political science professor, and Bansi Karla, a chemistry professor. "Both of these professors are well known by students," comments a student. "Both live on campus and are involved with the students and faculty on personal levels." Cheryl Hilton, an admissions officer, and Jeanne Larsen, an associate professor of English, also work closely with students.

Like students at other colleges in Virginia, Hollins students are held to an Honor Code, in which they "pledge to conduct [themselves] in an honorable and trustworthy manner at Hollins College by not lying, stealing, or cheating." Students are to report any violators to an Honor Court, and punishment could be as severe as dismissal. The code is well received by students. "It's great attending a college where you know you don't have to worry about someone stealing your things," says a sophomore. With few exceptions, students are also able to schedule their own exams and test-taking locations.

Hollins's Black Student Association (BSA), which has about 15 active members, helps African-American students "deal with the problems that they have on a predominantly white campus." There was talk recently about the establishment of a BSA house, but, according to a BSA member, such a house "would do more harm than good. We felt that if we isolated twenty African-American people in a house on a white campus, either they or we would feel even more separated in campus life. Not only would we be minorities; we'd be minorities living off by ourselves." Recent BSA events have included a fashion show, a candlelight vigil on Martin Luther King, Jr., Day, and a talent show. BSA members also frequently attend events at the Harrison Museum of African-American Culture in Roanoke.

"We have a small but enthusiastic group of black women who attend Hollins," says a student. "Every February, for Black History Month, we sponsor several widely publicized activities and have a rally or two, and our events are widely supported and accepted by the Hollins community." Jerry Suarez, director of the school's office of special services and events, is the BSA's adviser. "She is really nice. She is always willing to talk to us. Her door is always open. She's very accessible, almost like a friend."

Much of Hollins's social activity doesn't take place on campus at all, but at any number of nearby colleges and universities, most notably Washington and Lee, Hampden-Sydney, and Virginia Tech. The fact that so many Hollins students leave campus on weekends to attend off-campus parties lends credence to its image as a suitcase school. One student estimates that more than half of the campus clears out on weekends.

Students do have on-campus extracurricular opportunities, however. Sports are popular, particularly with the completion of the school's new $7 million athletic complex, which has an impressive swimming pool and fitness facility. Riding is also popular with students; in 1991, Hollins hosted the Intercollegiate Horseriding Championship. Tinker Day is a favorite school tradition, in which the entire student body and faculty ascend Tinker Mountain for a day of picnicking and song.

Hollins attracts a conservative student body. But it is different from other women's colleges in that women's issues are hardly on the front burner. In fact, the school doesn't offer a women's studies program, and lesbians, usually a dynamic element at Northern women's schools, certainly aren't out of the closet here. "I think there's a difference between the Northern and Southern colleges," says a student. "In the Northern schools women are more outspoken than we are here about women's issues. At Hollins, I have yet to hear debate outside the classroom about abortion and women's rights."

But students praise the school for opening career doors. "I would not recommend Hollins as a place for a minority student to become attuned to herself as a minority woman," says a senior. "She would have to enter Hollins as an aware minority woman in order to preserve her identity. I do recommend Hollins as a place where a woman can become more aware of herself as a productive member of society."

RANDOLPH-MACON COLLEGE

Address: Ashland, VA 23005
Phone: (800) 888-1762
Director of Admissions: Jeffrey Papa
Multicultural Student Recruiter: Lisa Hill
1993–94 tuition: $12,105
Room and board: $4,750
Application deadline: 3/1
Financial aid application deadline: 3/1
Non-white freshman admissions: Applicants
   for the class of '97: 106
   Accepted: 57%
   Accepted who enroll: 25%
   Applicants accepted who rank in top
   10% of high school class: na
   Median SAT: na
   Median ACT: na
Full-time undergraduate enrollment: 1,118
   Men: 49%
   Women: 51%

STUDENT ENROLLMENT

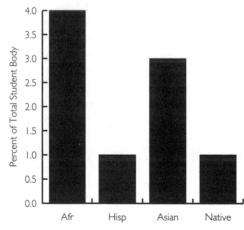

Non-white students in
   1988–89: 5%
   1989–90: 5%
   1990–91: 6%
   1991–92: 6%
Geographic distribution of students: na
Top majors: 1. Economics/Business
   2. Psychology
Retention rate of non-white students: na
**Scholarships exclusively for non-white
students:** Outstanding Black Student
Scholarship: need- and merit-based; each
award is valued from $5,000 to full
tuition; available to African-American
students.
Remediation programs: The college's RISE
program is designed to introduce
students to the school's academic and
social life.
Academic support services: Academic
support is provided by the Writing,
Math, and Learning Centers.
Ethnic studies programs: Asian Studies
minor.
Ethnic studies courses: The college's history
department offers "History of Africa."
The sociology department offers "Racial
and Cultural Minorities."
Organizations for non-white students: Black
Student Union, Multicultural Association
Notable non-white alumni: na
Tenured faculty: na
Non-tenured faculty: na
Student-faculty ratio: 11:1
Administrators: na
Recent non-white speakers on campus: Nikki
Giovanni (poet); Dorothy Gilla
(columnist, *Washington Post*); Lawrence
Wilder, Jr. (lawyer, son of Virginia
governor Douglas Wilder); Pie Minxin
(Ph.D. candidate, Harvard University)

Randolph-Macon College is one school that has never lost sight of the liberal arts.
For generations, the small college has also valued the personal approach to education.
   To ensure its graduates are exposed to subjects in the arts and sciences, students

must complete an extensive and rigorous core curriculum that includes courses in English composition, history, a foreign language, and physical education. It is one of the few schools in the country that requires students to take classes in math, laboratory sciences, and computer science.

To fulfill these requirements and for other study, students have access to impressive research facilities. The school's new McGraw-Page Library has a word-processing center and more than 240,000 volumes, an impressive amount for such a small school. The Copley Science Center provides outstanding facilities for students studying biology, chemistry, physics, computer science, and psychology. Students say some of the school's best-respected programs are psychology, education, and computer science. The sociology department's "Racial and Cultural Minorities" course wins praise from students, who say they'd like to see it offered more often.

Students say that their professors are among the school's best educational support networks and that many go out of their way to make sure their students are succeeding. It's not uncommon for a professor to call a student if he or she has been absent from class. Students find Charlotte Fitzgerald, a sociology professor and a coordinator of the school's women's studies program, especially helpful. "She is always aiming to open the minds of African-American students here," comments a student. "She urges us to learn more about ourselves and our culture. Then she encourages us to share our new knowledge in hopes of changing the racial imbalance on our campus."

For additional academic support, students go to the Writing Center. "The peer tutors are good there," says a psychology major. "They're usually upperclass students, and they give you advice about your paper. They can also tell you what they think the professor wants."

R-MC's RISE program is "an interdisciplinary study skills course designed to introduce students to academic standards" at the college. The program meets for two weeks, just before the beginning of school. For one student, participating in the RISE program was beneficial. "The program helped me a lot," she says. "It helped me with different sorts of skills I needed in school, especially time management."

The Black Student Union is "more disorganized this year than it has been in the past," says a student. The group, established on campus in the mid-1980s, has sponsored few recent activities. Anthony Keitt, the BSU's adviser and director of the Office of Minority Affairs, is helpful to students. "He serves as a positive role model, especially for black males," says a student. "He acts as a link between the administration and students of color." The Office of Minority Affairs helps coordinate cultural programming on campus, including events for Black History Month and leadership skills workshops.

According to one student, campus parties are racially diverse, although the dining situations are less so. "There are approximately forty black students enrolled here, the majority are white students, and a small minority are Asian and Hispanic students," says the student. "Everyone attends the campus parties because there isn't much social activity in general. In the dining hall, the fraternity and sorority people sit together, the white students sit together, and the black students sit together."

The Greek system is big at R-MC. About half of the men join one or another of the nine fraternities on campus, while less than a third of the women join a sorority.

Students report that the Greek houses are only reasonably well integrated; in a recent year about two African-American male students were members of a fraternity. While fraternity parties are popular weekend activities, students can also frequently be found at the school's Alphonso Payne, Jr., Student Center, which has a snack bar, offices for student government, and study and social lounges.

For additional social life, students will sometimes head off campus. "There's not much to do here on campus," comments a student, "so we will go to one of the local colleges," which include Virginia Commonwealth, the University of Richmond, and Virginia State, a predominantly black university. "Some colleges are a long distance to travel, but it's worth it." One student says she leaves campus "once every two weeks, depending on my course load." According to another student, having a car on campus is important if one is to have a social life. Washington, DC, about ninety miles north, is a popular destination. Students also travel to Richmond, about fifteen miles away, home to the Richmond Coliseum, which has hosted such performers as Patti LaBelle and Hammer. In the more immediate area, students find time on Sundays to go to some of the nearby churches that are predominantly African-American.

R-MC certainly has a long way to go to become a more racially and culturally diverse community of students and faculty. But the resources are here, particularly with supportive faculty and the Office of Minority Affairs, to help students succeed. "For a black student, R-MC can seem a difficult place, almost a foreign land, but that impression lasts only as long as you let it," says a recent graduate. "Unlike many places where you're down before you start, R-MC—through its staff, programs, and students—will give you a chance to be the best you can be."

RANDOLPH-MACON WOMAN'S COLLEGE

Women's college
Address: 2500 Rivermont Avenue,
  Lynchburg, VA 24503
Phone: (804) 947-8100 / (800) 745-7692
Director of Admissions: Jean Stewart
Multicultural Student Recruiter: Candace
  Foxx
1993–94 tuition: $13,200
Room and board: $5,780
Application deadline: 3/1
Financial aid application deadline: 3/1
Non-white freshman admissions: Applicants
  for the class of '97: 106
  Accepted: 57%
  Accepted who enroll: 25%
  Applicants accepted who rank in top
  10% of high school class: 22%
  In top 25%: 35%

Median SAT: 450 V, 460 M
  Median ACT range: 23–24
Full-time undergraduate enrollment: 1,118
Non-white students in
  1988–89: 4%
  1989–90: 5%
  1990–91: 5%
  1991–92: 8%
Students In-state: 40%
Top majors: 1. English 2. Economics
  3. Art
Retention rate of non-white students: na
**Scholarships exclusively for non-white
  students:** Robert A. and Martha Crocker
  Spivey Scholarship: merit-based; each
  award ranges from $2,500 to $5,000.
  Maureen Landis Honor Scholarship:
  merit-based; the $2,500 renewable award

STUDENT ENROLLMENT

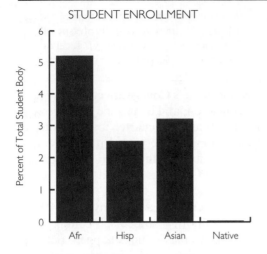

GEOGRAPHIC DISTRIBUTION OF STUDENTS

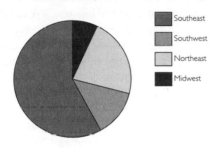

- Southeast
- Southwest
- Northeast
- Midwest

is given to an incoming first-year student each year.

Remediation programs: None

Academic support services: The school's Learning Resource Center offers computer assistance and study aids for note and test taking, listening, reading, memorization, goal setting, management, controlling stress, word processing, and speed reading. A Writing Lab with peer tutors and a faculty director is also available.

Ethnic studies programs: None

Ethnic studies courses: The college offers about ten courses in six departments devoted to ethnic and racial studies, including "American Indian Literature," "Masterpieces of Asian and African Art in Washington, DC, Museums," "Civil Rights," "American Folklore and Folklife," "Literature of Spanish-Speaking Minorities Living in the U.S.," "Contemporary Latin American Literature," and "African Women in the Twentieth Century."

Organizations for non-white students: Black Student Association, Pan-World Club

Notable non-white alumnae: Brenda Wilson ('72, English; independent media producer, formerly with National Public Radio); Rosalind Bradley-Coles ('78, Biology; writer, winner of *Ebony* magazine writing contest, 1989); Rev. Marcia Y. Riggs ('80, Religion; assistant professor, Drew University); Linda Gutierrez ('77, Sociology/Anthropology; president, Mexican-American Bar Association); Evanda Jefferson ('70, Chemistry; executive, Chevron USA)

Tenured faculty: 46

Non-tenured faculty: 44

FACULTY

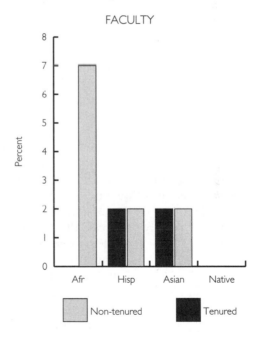

- Non-tenured
- Tenured

Student-faculty ratio: 9:1

Administrators: 83

  African-American: 6%

  Hispanic: 0

  Asian-American: 0

  Native American: 0

Recent non-white speakers on campus: Faye Wattleton (former president, Planned Parenthood); Gerald Early (author); Gloria Scott (president, Bennett College); Maxine Hong Kingston (author); Eleanor Holmes Norton (professor of law, Georgetown University); Jocelyn Elders (U.S. Surgeon General designate)

Randy-Mac, as the women of Randolph-Macon Woman's College affectionately refer to their school, offers an intimate liberal arts education, and its résumé is impressive. It was the first college for women in the South to receive a charter for a chapter of Phi Beta Kappa, the nation's leading collegiate honor society, and it was the first private women's college in the South to be accredited by the American Chemical Society. In a 1989 issue of *Southern Magazine,* R-MWC was selected as one of the 28 best liberal arts colleges in the South.

Unlike at many colleges and universities where bureaucracies thrive, R-MWC's administration "really, really cares about its minority students," comments a sophomore. "It may take a year or so for the office to make things happen, but they will happen. It also has something to do with the student body. In the recent past, you would have minority students here who would have just complained. But today, we complain and want things to change. And the administration will listen." A recent example, says a student, is the administration's much-lauded decision, after student urging, to enhance the peer support and interaction among the school's African-American students. "The administration is in the planning stages of putting together a retreat for all minority students on campus. The retreat will probably last from a Friday to a Sunday, during part of freshman orientation. The upperclass students will report a day before the new students, and we will have a chance to see each other and talk before we greet the first-year students." Representatives of the dean of students' office will also be present on the retreat. For the first time last year, the college, again after student urging, sponsored race sensitivity seminars for faculty, staff, and resident advisers.

To help ease the transition from home to college, R-MWC sponsors a Host Family program in which area families, some of which are African-American, are paired up with interested first-year students. If a student decides to participate, she is able to choose some of the qualities she desires in her host family. "The host family invites the student over for dinner and checks in on her if she wants them to. They will also send her little care packages, all as a way of making the new student feel comfortable coming to school here." First-year students of color at R-MWC are also able to pick the race of their roommate before they report to campus.

R-MWC is a liberal arts college and is known as one of the most academic women's schools in Virginia. Students give high marks to the English, biology, psychology, art, and economics departments, as well as to their school's communications and business programs. Students praise their faculty for their intelligence and their commitment to students.

Ethnic studies course offerings, however, are rather limited. "Let me put it to you this way. This is a women's college, and we just started a women's studies department here a few years ago. Very few of the women here have any idea why it's important to study women's issues or feminism, let alone race or ethnicity. So that might give you an idea of the priority the women here put on ethnic studies courses." The college does offer two courses in African-American Studies—"Civil Rights" and a literature course—as well as several "Latin American Civilization" courses, but students say these are offered only periodically. Over twenty-five years ago, however, R-MWC was one of the first liberal arts colleges in the South to offer students the chance to concentrate in Asian Studies.

As at many other Virginia colleges, the students at Randy-Mac are expected to follow a strict Honor Code, which allows students to self-schedule their exams and succeeds in developing a great deal of trust among students. The code also applies to social life, "but it's not followed as much as we do for the academics. If we see underage student drinking, we usually don't report it. We really feel strongly that cheating on an exam is wrong, and that it hurts everyone in a particular class because all of our grades will be affected."

Students say that "there is always someone at the Writing Lab to help out with your papers." Students also report that upperclass students offer social and academic support. The Learning Resource Center, the main source of academic support, "seeks students out who aren't doing too well after midterm or finals. They'll put a note in your mailbox telling you about their services, but it's up to the student to take them up on it."

The weekend social life at R-MWC doesn't happen at R-MWC at all, as "maybe 200 of the 700 or so women here are gone all weekend, and of those who didn't go away for the entire weekend, many go away for the day and come back late." Where do they all go? "Hampden-Sydney is our brother institution, and a lot of women will go there over the weekends, but for me that means going there and being insulted and being treated like meat," says a student. As many of the school's African-American students are from the state, many go home for the weekends, or stay on campus studying. The University of Virginia is within an hour's drive, and Washington, DC, is three hours away. "The key is to have a car." While there's not a heck of a lot to do in Lynchburg—thanks to Jerry Falwell and his Moral Majority—the area provides ample opportunity for skiing and just being in the great outdoors, as the college is located in the foothills of the Blue Ridge Mountains, which offer some of the most scenic territory in the region. Some of the school's dorm rooms have views of the mountains.

When students are on campus, the Programming Board brings various performers and events to campus. Recent events have included Cherokee Indian Dancers, various music recitals and lectures, as well as numerous films and plays. For a recent Black History Month celebration, students viewed *School Daze* and *Do the Right Thing*. R-MWC's Woman's Resource Center sponsors an annual speaker series; a recent panel discussion topic was "Women and Leadership: Lessons for the '90s."

The Black Student Association, which has about 40 members, "ideally meets once every two weeks, but it depends on what's going on." The BSA focuses on social activities, and recent events have included dance parties with a DJ and step shows. The BSA also interacts with other multicultural student groups at such nearby schools as Lynchburg College, Virginia Military Institute, and rival Sweet Briar College, also a women's college.

While not all Randy-Mac students are career-oriented, there are those who come to school here to reap the benefits of attending a quality liberal arts college for women.

"I chose R-MWC because I wanted a college where I would receive a well-rounded and first-rate education, and both of these requirements have been fulfilled," says a recent graduate. "Along with my strong academic program, I have had many leadership experiences and I feel confident in my preparedness for the future."

UNIVERSITY OF VIRGINIA

Address: Charlottesville, VA 22906-9011
Phone: (804) 982-3200
Director of Admissions: John A. Blackburn
Multicultural Student Recruiter: Michael A. Mallory
1993–94 tuition: $4,350 (in-state); $12,250 (out-of-state)
Room and board: $3,800
Application deadline: 1/2
Financial aid application deadline: 3/1

Non-white freshman admissions: Applicants for the class of '96: 2,904
Accepted: 45%
Accepted who enroll: 48%
Applicants accepted who rank in top 10% of high school class: 66%
In top 25%: 91%
Median SAT: 570 V, 640 M
Median ACT: na

Full-time undergraduate enrollment: 11,251
Men: 49%
Women: 51%

Non-white students in
1988–89: 16%
1989–90: 18%
1990–91: 19.1%
1991–92: 22%

Students In-state: 65%

Top majors: 1. English
2. History/Government 3. Rhetoric and Communications

Retention rate of non-white students: 85%

Scholarships exclusively for non-white students: Jerome Holland Scholarships: merit-based; $10,000 each year; renewable; approximately ten awarded each year to non-residents. University Achievement Awards: merit-based; full tuition; must be a Virginia resident; 50 awarded each year. Virginia Engineering

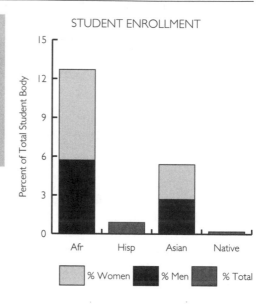

STUDENT ENROLLMENT

Percent of Total Student Body

% Women   % Men   % Total

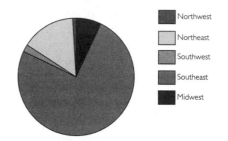

GEOGRAPHIC DISTRIBUTION OF STUDENTS

Northwest
Northeast
Southwest
Southeast
Midwest

Scholarship: merit-based; number awarded each year varies; value amount varies, but does not exceed $1,000; recipient must be a Virginia resident.

Remediation programs: None

Academic support services: Tutoring is available in most academic subjects.

Ethnic studies programs: The university offers programs in African-American and African Studies, Latin American Studies, and Asian Studies.

Organizations for non-white students: Black Student Alliance, Alpha Phi Alpha, Kappa Alpha Psi, Omega Psi Phi, Phi Beta Sigma, Black Greeks Organization, Alpha Kappa Alpha, Delta Sigma Theta, Zeta Phi Beta, Sigma Gamma Rho, Asian Student Union, Council of Black Student Leaders, La Sociedad Hispanica

Notable non-white alumni: na

Tenured faculty: 1,024

Non-tenured faculty: 676

Student-faculty ratio: 11:1

Administrators: 400

Recent non-white speakers on campus: Amiri Baraka (author and poet); Maya Angelou (author and poet); Rosa Parks (civil rights leader); Spike Lee (filmmaker)

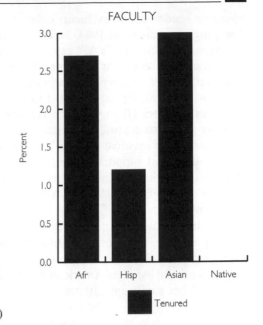

FACULTY

Tenured

The University of Virginia is one of the country's most respected public institutions of higher learning and, with its high-powered academics and top-notch faculty, attracts students from every state in the nation and dozens of foreign countries.

Some of the academic programs at the university rival those at many of the country's top schools. UVA's English department, which has on staff Pulitzer Prize-winning novelist Rita Dove, is nationally recognized. The university's McIntire School of Commerce competes with the Wharton School of Finance at the University of Pennsylvania for the title of the country's best undergraduate business school, and engineering and architecture are said to be especially competitive and rigorous. History, government, foreign affairs, and rhetoric and communications are also UVA standouts.

UVA's African-American and African Studies program, established in 1981, "could be stronger if they had a more diverse faculty teaching the courses," says a student. "The core courses necessary for completing the major are taught by faculty members who have not yet earned the title of professor but are still lecturers." Jeanne Toungara, a professor of African history, is one of the program's more respected members.

The Office of Afro-American Affairs, established in 1976, is an active and integral part of campus life for many of the school's African-American students. The office sponsors an annual award ceremony for African-American students and faculty, works with the African-American Parents' Advisory Association, and coordinates various orientation week activities for incoming students. The office has also established the Peer Adviser Program, in which upperclass students help introduce incoming students to the social and academic life at UVA. The student pairings are based on academic and extracurricular interests as well as on undergraduate schools. The program, started in 1984, "is an excellent way to help African-Americans adjust to school life here at UVA," says a student. "It reassures you that there is always somewhere you can turn for support that you may not be able to find elsewhere." The Nat Turner Library, which contains extensive research materials focusing on African-American topics, is part of the office. The office also coordinates events and activities for Black History Month; recently, it hosted an African-American film series and various lecturers and musicians. The associate dean of the office, Sylvia Terry, "is a warm and sensitive woman," says a student.

For additional support, students are able to turn to numerous faculty and staff members, including William Harris, professor in the school of architecture and former dean of the Office of African-American Affairs, and Greer Wilson, director of Newcomb Hall.

The Black Student Alliance (BSA), according to a student leader, "is one of the more proactive multicultural student organizations at the university. The BSA promotes cultural awareness by holding biweekly forums on various topics concerning the African and African-American communities and by inviting guests to campus to speak." After racist epithets were scrawled on a campus bus stop during a recent school year, the BSA "scheduled meetings with university officials and the student council, which resulted in the formation of a Thirteenth Standard of Conduct which states that any university student guilty of any type of racial harassment is subject to some degree of punishment," says a student.

In addition to the BSA, students are able to participate in numerous other African-American student groups, ranging from the religious and the professional to the literary and the historically black Greek organizations, which sponsor a variety of community service projects and social gatherings.

UVA is perhaps the most segregated university of any of the nation's premier schools. In the words of one student: "There is racial segregation on every aspect of university life, with the exception of the classrooms. The Hispanic students seem to 'blend in' with the larger university community. Asian and African-American students are marginalized by the larger society, although it appears as if they segregate themselves from white students. The segregation occurs in the dining halls, housing, parties, fraternities and sororities, and at football games, where there is even a section in the stadium where black students sit during games."

Students say the segregation is due in part to the heavy emphasis on Greek life at UVA, which, says one student, "breaks up a lot of the campus into smaller groups that rarely socialize." Adds another student about the tone of the campus: "The majority of the students are apathetic politically, and lack knowledge about any real racial or political issues. Among the ones that are knowledgeable, most are conservative. We have a conservative political magazine, *The Virginia Advocate,* but no liberal counterpart. There is a small, active and vocal group which focuses particularly on environmental, feminist, and gay and lesbian issues and holds rallies and other activities, but they usually don't have very good turnouts."

Charlottesville, a predominantly white community, has an African-American population, but according to one student "there is very little interaction among students of color and the Charlottesville community. However, some African-American students are involved in big sibling/little sibling and other mentoring programs in the Charlottesville public school and public housing systems." Students rarely head into town for socializing. When they need to get away, they might drive to Washington, DC, about two hours away, or to Richmond.

On-campus activities for the majority of the students centers on predominantly white fraternity parties. But the fraternities have been having a hard time of it lately. During a recent school year, federal authorities raided a fraternity house suspected of dealing drugs and few people were surprised that students were rounded up. The University Union sponsors a variety of social events, such as dances, movies, concerts, and other social gatherings, as alternatives to the Greek life. Approximately 85 percent of the students participate in varsity or intramural sporting events.

Attending UVA, one of the most conservative and traditional universities in the South, can be a trying experience, even for the most confident student of color. But prospective students should note that the university's student of color enrollment has increased significantly in recent years, making what could be an alienating experience less lonely. "If the minority applicant is interested in getting involved with minority issues, then he or she won't find much here," says a student. "But in academics and social activities among their own ethnic groups, there are plenty of options."

VIRGINIA MILITARY INSTITUTE

Men's college
Address: Lexington, VA 24450
Phone: (703) 464-7211
Director of Admissions: Don Troppol
Multicultural Student Recruiter: na
1991–92 tuition: $2,770 (in-state); $8,310 (out-of-state)
Room and board: $3,525
Application deadline: 4/1
Financial aid application deadline: 3/1
Non-white freshman admissions: Applicants for the class of '95: 103
  Accepted: 67%
  Accepted who enroll: 44%
  Applicants accepted who rank in top 10% of high school class: na
  In top 25%: 29%
  Median SAT: 452 V, 518 M
  Median ACT: na
Full-time undergraduate enrollment: 1,281
Non-white students in
  1987–88: 12.7%
  1988–89: 13%
  1989–90: 13.1%
  1990–91: 13.3%

Geographic distribution of students: na
Students In-state: 65%
Top majors: 1. Economics/Business 2. History 3. Mechanical Engineering
Retention rate of non-white students: 69%
Scholarships exclusively for non-white students: Du Pont Scholarship: merit-based; $4,100 awarded each year to

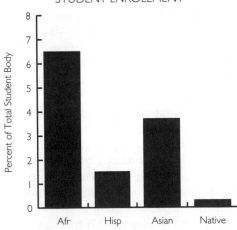

STUDENT ENROLLMENT

Percent of Total Student Body

Afr   Hisp   Asian   Native

a minority out-of-state applicant; one awarded per year. Virginia Undergraduate Student Financial Assistance Program: need-based; awarded to African-American applicants. Virginia Transfer Grant Program: merit-based; one $2,497 grant awarded each year to a transfer applicant.

Remediation programs: None

Academic support services: Study halls as well as tutorial assistance are available in most academic subjects.

Ethnic studies programs: None

Ethnic studies courses: None

Organizations for non-white students: PROMAJI (a multicultural student group)

Notable non-white alumni: na

Tenured faculty: 71

Non-tenured faculty: 45

Student-faculty ratio: 13:1

Administrators: 20

African-American: 10%

Hispanic: 0

Asian-American: 0

Native American: 0

Recent non-white speakers on campus: Lt. Gen. Julius Becton; Dennis Watson

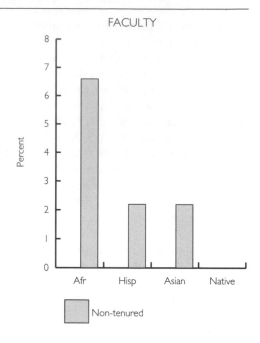

FACULTY

(executive director, National Black Youth Leadership Council); L. Douglas Wilder (Virginia governor); Gen. Colin Powell (Chairman, Joint Chiefs of Staff)

The Virginia Military Institute isn't for everyone, and it's certainly not for women. Or that's what a federal District Court judge ruled in 1991 when the Justice Department sued unsuccessfully to have the school admit women because it accepts state funds. "VMI truly marches to a different drummer," the judge said, "and I will permit it to do so." Says a student elated with the judge's decision: "The whole experience here is a *series* of experiences. If women came here, you'd still get a military education, but it wouldn't be VMI."

Just what is the VMI experience like? In a word: regimented. The VMI cadet's day starts with reveille at 0655 hours, and is followed by nonstop drills, classes, and other obligations until lights out at 2300 or, for seniors, 0100. Reporting on the federal government's case against VMI, *The New York Times* noted: "The regimen includes 12-mile marches with 70-pound packs, cleaning rifles and incessant demands for perfection in dress. Any violation of the honor code, which forbids lying, cheating, stealing, or tolerating those who do, is punishable by expulsion."

The VMI routine can be toughest on freshmen, known informally on campus as "rats." According to the *Times,* "as much as 10 percent of every freshman class leaves the school after about the first month of unrelenting harassment" by upperclass students, who, according to one cadet, "feel the need to verbally beat up on rats." To become a man at VMI means to pass breakout, in which first-year students are, according to the *Times* article, "forced into a blinding mud bath, [and] wrestle upperclassmen until they can crawl, clamber and tug each other up two steep hills. Once atop the hills, these first-year students are no longer 'rats,' whose faults in posture or uniform could doom them to verbal assaults and dozens of push-ups."

Among the most popular majors at VMI are economics and business and history. The school's engineering programs—which offer civil engineering, electrical engineering, and mechanical engineering—are also popular. Civil engineering, which has been a part of the institute's curriculum since it was founded in 1839, is one of the oldest such programs in the country. The school's international studies program is well regarded and admittance into the program is competitive. International studies majors are encouraged to study a foreign language. As might be expected, many of the courses at VMI have a military perspective, such as "The Literature of War," "American Military History," and "Revolution, Politics and Protest: Art as Propaganda in the 19th and 20th Centuries."

To graduate, VMI students must complete athletic and academic course work. Students are required to study chemistry, English, history, math, and computer science, as well as swimming, boxing, and wrestling. The reward for all of these physical and academic rigors? After participating in one of the school's ROTC programs—a requirement—cadets are offered commissions as officers in either the Air Force, Army, Marines, or Navy and are imbued with a strong sense of camaraderie and loyalty.

For academic support, cadets are offered supervised study halls, tutoring in all subjects, and faculty academic advising, all of which students say are effective. "Some of [the success of our advising system] is due to the fact that we treat all students exactly the same—same uniform, same meals, same barracks, same rooming conditions, same military and conduct regulations, same academic support," says Lamont Ferwell Toliver, assistant director of new cadet advising. "Our system is designed to be color-blind." For additional support, students have found Gregory Mixon, an assistant professor of history, and Lt. Gera Miles, an instructor in English, to be especially helpful.

The school breeds alumni loyalty. VMI's $86.7 million endowment, when broken down to per student spending, ranks first among public institutions of higher learning. The amount surpasses the endowments of such similarly sized and nationally prominent colleges as Haverford and Mills.

Students say there is little overt racism on campus. "Due to its small size, VMI is very racially integrated, and this includes all parties, the dining hall, and the barracks," says a student. PROMAJI is the school's only cultural student group. Each year it offers campus-wide programs on issues relating to culture, race, and African-American history, and group members are active in community outreach.

Cadets at VMI don't have much of a social life. First-year students get no off-campus privileges, and first-class cadets (seniors) are allowed to leave campus Saturday nights, but must be back in their barracks at 2200 hours. Whatever their skill level, VMI cadets participate in sports. The school fields more than 10 varsity teams and 12 club and intramural sports. Football and lacrosse are the school's most successful sports.

When students do leave campus, they often head to Washington and Lee University, located nearby, or to any of the women's schools in the area, including Mary Baldwin.

Students report that the city of Lexington "treats all cadets in a friendly manner, regardless of the cadet's racial heritage." VMI is just ninety miles north of Roanoke, and only a couple of hours' drive south of Baltimore and Washington, DC.

VMI typically attracts conservative young men, usually from the state, and certainly not with ideas contrary to the school's strict, some would say narrow, vision of how one should behave. "Due to the fact that VMI is an all-male military school, it's obviously not a place for everyone," says a student. "If a prospective student wants to receive the type of disciplined education that the school offers, I do recommend VMI. But if a prospective student wants to come to VMI and participate in demonstrations, and expect others to join him, I do not recommend VMI."

VIRGINIA POLYTECHNIC INSTITUTE AND STATE UNIVERSITY

Address: Blacksburg, VA 24061-0202
Phone: (703) 231-6267
Director of Admissions: David R. Bousquet
Multicultural Student Recruiter: Thomas Jenkins
1993–94 tuition: $3,300 (in-state); $9,168 (out-of-state)
Room and board: $3,016
Application deadline: 2/1
Financial aid application deadline: 2/15
Non-white freshman admissions: Applicants for the class of '95: 3,822
  Accepted: 64%
  Accepted who enroll: 25%
  Applicants accepted who rank in top 10% of high school class: 30%
  In top 25%: 63%
  Median SAT: 456 V, 554 M
  Median ACT: na
Full-time undergraduate enrollment: 18,690
  Men: 59%
  Women: 41%
Non-white students in
  1987–88: 8%
  1988–89: 8%
  1989–90: 9%
  1990–91: 13%
Geographic distribution of students: na
Students In-state: 75%
Top majors: 1. Biology 2. Engineering 3. Accounting
Retention rate of non-white students: na

Scholarships exclusively for non-white students: Powell Scholarship: merit-based; $2,000 awarded per scholarship. Academic Excellence Scholarship: merit-based; $2,000 awarded per scholarship.
Remediation programs: None
Academic support services: The university provides study skills help sessions and workshops in time management, textbook reading, test preparation, reducing test anxiety, and memory improvement. The sessions are designed

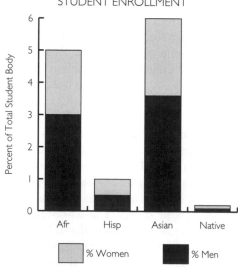

STUDENT ENROLLMENT

for both individuals and groups. The School's Student Transition Program, offered as a summer program for incoming first-year students, includes course work in English and math.

Ethnic studies programs: The university's Black Studies program, established in 1991, is interdisciplinary and is offered as a minor.

Organizations for non-white students: Alpha Phi Alpha, Kappa Alpha Psi, Omega Psi Phi, Phi Beta Sigma, Alpha Kappa Alpha, Delta Sigma Theta, Sigma Gamma Rho, Zeta Phi Beta, Black Student Alliance, Black Organizations Council, Asian-American Student Association, Indian Student Association, NAACP, Ujima Dance Theatre, and others

Notable non-white alumni: Dell Curry (Sociology; professional basketball player, Charlotte Hornets); Wayne Robinson (Business; former professional basketball player)

Tenured faculty: 1,489
Non-tenured faculty: 443
Student-faculty ratio: 17:1
Administrators: na

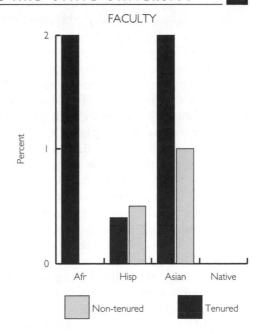

Recent non-white speakers on campus: Jacqueline Fleming (psychologist); Bish Sanyal (associate professor of urban and regional planning, MIT); Maya Angelou (author and poet)

As its name suggests, Virginia Tech is a school with strong programs in such fields as engineering and architecture. But before you write it off as too "techie" for your interests, you should note that the school has an award-winning theater company, a top-notch English program (prominent poet Nikki Giovanni is on staff here), and more than 400 different student organizations and clubs. *Money* magazine included it on its list of the top 100 schools that offer you the best education for the money.

Which isn't to say the school doesn't have outstanding programs in engineering. Most prominent among them is electrical, followed closely by chemical and computer engineering. The school's five-year architecture program is as demanding as it is well regarded; it offers off-campus study opportunities in Switzerland. The College of Business has gained in popularity lately, while the College of Agriculture and Life Sciences, as might be expected at a land-grant institution, is respected. Virginia Tech's aerospace and ocean engineering program is nationally known and helps students find jobs with NASA and the aerospace industry.

Courses in African-American history and literature are among the most popular in African-American Studies. Professor Virginia Fowler, who teaches the African-American literature course, is a favorite. In addition to being a powerful lecturer, Nikki Giovanni works with student organizations; during a recent year, she helped judge the winning essay for a writing contest sponsored by a historically black fraternity, Alpha Phi Alpha. "Minority Group Relations," offered by the sociology department, is also appreciated by students for its open classroom discussion format. The course's professor, Michael Hughes, is supportive of students. Students also praise the work of H. D. Flowers, head of Virginia Tech's African-American Studies Program, particularly for his efforts in the school's recent production of August Wilson's play *Fences;* Virginia Tech's production of the play earned it a spot as a finalist in the 1993 American College Theatre Festival competition.

Class enrollments, especially in entry-level courses, can be huge, and can be overwhelming to students used to high school class sizes. Learning by television monitor is also the rule for many such courses. But, once reached, professors are more than willing to lend a hand, according to students.

Virginia Tech's predominantly black Greek organizations provide much of the on-campus social life for the school's African-American community. In addition to almost weekly parties and dances, the Greek organizations sponsor various community service projects. "It's not like there's a whole lot to do off campus," says a student. "Blacksburg is a small, rural town." One student estimates that of the approximately 20,000 Blacksburg residents 500 are African-American. "Other than certain community service projects, such as tutoring, we don't interact with the area residents much," says a student.

The Black Student Alliance has been less than active in recent years. Says a BSA leader: "The Greek organizations have picked up where the BSA left off. The BSA, on the whole, fell down on a lot of its responsibilities. In this way, the campus has completely turned around in the four years I've been here."

The men of Alpha Phi Alpha, for example, sponsor an adopt-a-highway project, in which members are responsible for keeping a portion of Route 652 clean. In addition, the Alphas sponsored an Easter egg hunt for young people at a nearby church.

Although the BSA, with about 84 registered members, isn't as active as it has been in the past, it recently coordinated various programs, including a discussion and performance by Queen Latifah, a film series, and three annual informal dances. BSA members also attend statewide leadership conferences, held annually at the College of William and Mary. Kathy Cantrell, the BSA staff adviser, "has been a help to us with all of our programming," says a BSA leader. Virginia Tech's chapter of the NAACP is active, sponsoring speakers, conferences, and panel discussions.

Students report that Virginia Tech's African-American student community is close-knit. "The black students here are almost like a family. There's a tremendous amount of support for one another. We work with each other as tutors, or help each other find help, and we're there for each other as friends." A popular gathering spot for Virginia Tech's African-American students is the Black Cultural Center, established on campus in the fall of 1991. The center, located in the student union, includes an art gallery and meeting space for the school's African-American student organizations. The director of the center, Carol Crawford Smith, is well respected by students. Before coming to Virginia Tech, Crawford Smith was with the Dance Theatre of Harlem. Crawford Smith is also the adviser to the campus's Ujimma Dance Theatre.

Students add that the white students on campus are also generally supportive, and that there is little racial tension. Comments a senior: "The unrest among the black students isn't so much about overt racial stuff, but more about the lack of programming that is geared to African-American students. Everything is geared to white students, especially homecoming and concerts. We're not saying we want our own programs; we just want to be included more."

When it comes to interaction between the predominantly black and white Greek organizations, students say there is some activity. "The white fraternities might ask us to perform a step show at one of their events or to co-sponsor a party, or give donations to one of their philanthropies, or vice versa. It's hard sometimes to match up dates, but we definitely try."

Studies are first on almost everyone's list, but students do take part in intramural activity, which includes everything from softball, by far the most popular, to Ping-Pong. Popular spots on campus are the school's new student center, which has movie theaters, fast-food restaurants, and a bowling alley, and the War Memorial athletic complex.

Virginia Tech is not just for engineers. "I'm glad I came here because it's got that small-town environment where everyone seems to know you, yet you don't feel like you're on some small campus. There's a tremendous amount of support here, and the education I'm getting is terrific."

WASHINGTON AND LEE UNIVERSITY

Address: Lexington, VA 24450
Phone: (703) 463-8710
Director of Admissions: William M. Hartog
Multicultural Student Recruiter: Angelia V. Allen
1991–92 tuition: $11,575
Room and board: $4,000
Application deadline: 1/15
Financial aid application deadline: 2/1

Non-white freshman admissions: Applicants for the class of '95: 51 (African-American applicants only)
Accepted: 43%
Accepted who enroll: 50%
Applicants accepted who rank in top 10% of high school class: 21%
In top 25%: 88.9%
Median SAT: na
Median ACT: na
Full-time undergraduate enrollment: 1,602
Men: 62%
Women: 38%
Non-white students in 1987–91: na
Geographic distribution of students: na
Students In-state: 20%
Top majors: na

Retention rate of non-white students: 97%
Scholarships exclusively for non-white students: None
Remediation programs: None
Academic support services: Tutoring is available in most subjects.
Ethnic studies programs: None

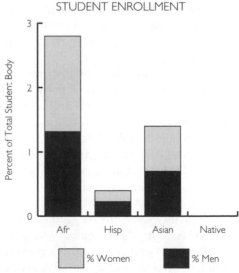

STUDENT ENROLLMENT

Percent of Total Student Body

Afr   Hisp   Asian   Native

% Women   % Men

Ethnic studies courses: "West-African History," "African-American Politics," topic courses in Asian and African history, "African-American Literature," and "Women in Black Literature" are offered.

Organizations for non-white students: Minority Student Association, Alpha Phi Alpha

Notable non-white alumni: William Hill ('74, '77; Superior Court Judge, Atlanta)

Tenured faculty: na

Non-tenured faculty: na

Student-faculty ratio: 11:1

Administrators: na

Recent non-white speakers on campus: Joe Clark (former high school principal and character for the film *Lean on Me*); Nikki Giovanni (poet); Louise Bias (mother of former basketball star Len Bias); Jesse Jackson (former U.S. presidential candidate and civil rights activist)

U.S. News & World Report ranks Washington and Lee University as one of the top 25 liberal arts colleges in the country, one of only two colleges in the South to be so honored. (Davidson College in North Carolina is the other.)

But if the editors of *U.S. News* had a category for tradition, and the students' pride in their school's tradition, W&L would leave most colleges and universities behind. The focus of much of this tradition is Robert E. Lee, the Civil War general, who later served for five years as W&L's president. Lee is buried on campus in Lee Chapel, a tourist attraction. (Picture postcards of his crypt are sold in the school's bookstore.) "The fact that a Civil War general is buried on campus wouldn't be so bad, but many of the students exalt his name and his ideals, which can be a little disconcerting to us minority students, as he did defend slavery. The white students here, especially the males, are always saying how privileged W&L students are to attend this school because of Lee and the traditions he left behind. There's an organization on campus, Katekon, whose objectives are to preserve the goals and spirit of Lee. It's one of the most selective and competitive clubs on campus." According to one student, to date there have been no students of color in the organization.

"This isn't to say that students here aren't tolerant. They're just conservative," adds a student. "The guys here dress in a certain way, usually khakis, yellow ties, and blazers, and so do the girls, usually in Laura Ashley dresses with little flowers on them."

The faculty and the administration are much more progressive-minded than the student body. Numerous faculty members and administrators attend activities sponsored by the Minority Student Association, including minority students' Parents Weekend. The administration, in the last three years, has begun honoring Martin Luther King, Jr.'s Birthday and Black History Month with various activities and events. And despite the majority of the white students' sentiments against having a historically black Greek organization on campus, the administration actively supported such an endeavor; since 1991 the university has had a chapter of the historically black fraternity Alpha Phi Alpha.

The faculty seems to be genuinely concerned that their students of color succeed in the classroom. "I remember one time when my philosophy professor came up to me after class and expressed his concern that he hadn't heard me speak up in class during a discussion of affirmative action. I was the only African-American in class.

He didn't know how to take my silence, and seemed to really care that I not feel uncomfortable. This kind of attitude by professors for their minority students is not the exception but the rule. I think most minority students at W&L would rate the faculty highly. The professors take extra pains to get to know their multicultural students."

Perhaps the staff member most supportive of W&L's students of color is Anece McCloud, an associate dean of students and adviser to the Minority Student Association. "Anece is very accessible and genuinely concerned about her students," says a junior. "She's supportive of us no matter what. Each year, she sponsors a barbecue cookout at her home for all the minority students at the school and the law school. Professors and administrators come, so it's a good icebreaker for students to get to know their professors. The event definitely makes new students feel more comfortable on campus and in the classroom."

The Greek system at W&L encompasses nearly the entire student body; 80 percent of the students join one or another of the school's 14 fraternities and 4 sororities. In a recent year, approximately four African-American male students were members of a fraternity, while one African-American woman was a member of a sorority. "Most of the fraternities are open-minded, and probably wouldn't mind having minorities as members and don't mind having us at their parties. But there are a few fraternities that minorities are told to be sure to stay away from, such as Kappa Alpha, Phi Delta Theta, and Sigma Alpha Epsilon. Every year, the KAs have an Old South Ball, where the members dress up in Confederate costumes and remember the good old days by making toasts to Dixie. Needless to say, the party rubs us a little the wrong way. The number of Confederate flags in the fraternity house alone can be a little intimidating." But, adds the student, "I want to make clear that there are members of these groups that don't always agree with their organizations. Even within KA [which was founded by Lee] there are some members who aren't like that."

An important outlet for the school's students of color is the Minority Student Association, which has about 26 active members. "Our group is not separatist," says a student. "We advertise all of our activities, and anyone is invited to attend. Anyone is able to join. It's important to us that other students join because we feel that integration is a two-way street. But right now, having an integrated group isn't as easy as we'd like. MSA is composed primarily of African-American students. It's not that the majority students here are racist or anything. It's more of an invisibility factor. The students here just don't try to understand you."

Some recent MSA events were a Parents' Weekend, a Christmas party for underprivileged children of the area, and tutorial projects for area students. The MSA also interacts frequently with the multicultural student group at the Virginia Military Institute, located "just a five-minute walk from campus." "But the group is primarily a source of emotional support for students, and seeks to project a positive image of minority students to the campus."

The MSA holds its meetings in Chavis House, on Lee Avenue on the edge of campus. The house provides residence facilities for up to four students, and has a small reading room, called the Maya Angelou Library, containing books and textbooks donated by students and faculty members. The library also has on file past tests and helpful hints about professors and classes to take and to avoid.

Although women were admitted to Washington and Lee in 1985, the campus still appears to be having trouble adjusting to being coed. "During this past year, there were a few sexual assault cases reported, but the general feeling is that there are probably a lot more than just those that are reported," says a student. "But the professors say the quality of academic work has definitely gone up since women have been on campus."

W&L's academics are challenging; weekend studying is often necessary. W&L, which has a small law school, has outstanding programs in history, journalism, and foreign languages. For the school's many pre-professionals, W&L's School of Commerce, Economics, and Politics offers excellent—and rigorous—programs. East Asian Studies and computer science enjoy good reputations, and the school's drama programs received a boost recently with the completion of a new multimillion-dollar performing arts center. Beginning in the fall of 1992, the school will offer an African-American literature course as part of its standard curriculum. "African-American Politics" and "Women in Black Literature" earn high marks from students. To graduate, W&L students must satisfy various distribution requirements, including English composition, math, literature, philosophy, religion, and history.

Although much has changed at W&L since Lee's tenure as president—women and students of color are now enrolled, for example—one can't but feel that there's still a great deal here that would make him proud. One undergraduate says: "There are times when I have wished I was anywhere else but here. But I've learned a lot about myself and others. I also know I've gotten an excellent education here."

COLLEGE OF WILLIAM AND MARY

Address: Williamsburg, VA 23185
Phone: (804) 221-3999
Director of Admissions: Virginia Carey
Multicultural Student Recruiter: Roxie
  Williams

1992–93 tuition: $4,048 (in-state); $11,428
  (out-of-state)
Room and board: $3,900
Application deadline: 1/15
Financial aid application deadline: 2/15

For many, the fact that the College of William and Mary, the nation's second-oldest university, is a public institution comes as a surprise. There's the school name (the university was named for King William and Queen Mary, who chartered the school back in 1693); there's the size of the school—about 5,000 undergraduates—which is about half the size of the other prominent public university in the state; and the fact that more than a third of its students come from outside of Virginia.

With top-flight academics, William and Mary is considered one of the country's public Ivies—schools that offer Ivy League educations at state-supported costs. The school's best departments are government and history, as well as economics, biology, and English. The school's international relations program enables students to concentrate in African, East Asian, or Latin American Studies. Business administration is well regarded and is the school's most popular major.

At William and Mary, professors are accessible and are committed to undergraduate teaching. "I think every professor I've had here gives us his or her home telephone number, in case we need help after office hours," comments a senior. (Try getting that kind of exposure at State U.) It's fortunate that professors are helpful because the academics here can be very challenging.

Students say the social and academic atmosphere have become more comfortable for students of color in recent years. "When I got here as a freshman, the fraternity brothers of Kappa Alpha would stage an Old South Ball, where they would honor the Old South by riding around campus on horses and wearing Confederate uniforms," remembers a senior. "That isn't done anymore, largely because of the protests of the black students. Also four years ago, the Black Student Organization and the Korean student group were the only cultural groups on campus. Now there are more than ten." The number of students of color has also grown significantly in recent years. In 1978, for example, the student body was little more than 2 percent African-American; today that figure is up to more than 6 percent. The college's admissions office declined to respond to our questionnaire, but according to the U.S. Department of Education, in 1990 about 3.1 percent of the campus was Asian, 1.1 percent was Hispanic, and 0.2 percent was Native American.

With about 100 active members, William and Mary's Black Student Organization (BSO), established on campus in 1971, is by far the school's most active cultural group. Each year, the BSO has a float in the school's homecoming parade, as well as a formal BSO Ball during homecoming weekend. The BSO sponsors a monthly film series and an annual dinner to welcome freshman. BSO officers also write letters to incoming African-American students before they arrive on campus. Students say that the school's student government association is getting more receptive to BSO activities. "When I first arrived here, we received only eight hundred dollars a year from the Board of Student Advisers; this year they gave us five thousand. It's kind of an affirmation of our purpose."

However, one BSO member says that "the BSO is not as active and tight as it has been in the past. I think it's due to the academics here, which can be demanding. But I also think it has to do with the overall apathetic attitude of the campus, and not just among African-American students." A recent incident involving the school's yearbook galvanized many of the African-American students on campus. "The yearbook included a picture of a student in blackface, and beneath the picture it said something like 'The Old South rises again.' The BSO wrote a letter that was printed in the school paper demanding an apology. We talked to the yearbook editor about the picture, and he said it was because they didn't have any other pictures available. That tells you how active the yearbook committee is. This year, we're taking over pictures to the yearbook office to ensure that something like this doesn't happen again."

The Office of Multicultural Affairs, which offers academic and non-academic assistance to students and student groups, "is too small for the BSO. We've definitely grown beyond them," says a student. "We've become financially independent. We also were the only group vying for the office's attention. Now there are so many more. Not as many black students go there as in the past. The ones who do go there usually participated in the office's summer orientation program. There's also good academic support on this campus, which means we don't have to go to the Office of Multicultural Affairs. We can go to the Office of Academic Support and the Study Skills Center for that kind of help."

The BSO certainly isn't the only group in which the school's African-American students participate. In 1992, the university nominated its first African-American Rhodes Scholar, and another African-American recently headed the Honor Council, which enforces the school's strict Honor Code. A recent student body president and a homecoming queen were also African-American.

In large part due to the support of the Office of Multicultural Affairs, William and Mary graduates an impressive 85 percent of its African-American students. For its successes, the university was featured in a 1988 *New York Times* article. Carol Hardy, associate dean of the office, is the driving force behind much of the school's success in retaining African-American students. "I'm an advocate," she says in the *New York Times* article. "They know that nothing is so bad that they can't tell me. . . . But the thing I give them more than anything else is that I believe in them. I believe they can learn, will learn, and do learn."

Although there appears to be much support for William and Mary's African-American students, little attention seems to be paid to its Hispanic and Asian-American students. A small group of students is attempting to get established a Hispanic student group to be called Organización de Latinos Unidos. "We have a Latin American Club, which meets once every two months, but they focus only on international issues. Many of its members are international students, and many will go back to their home countries. We're going to try to pattern our organization after the BSO. We have a brother/sister relationship with them."

With so much attention given to academics, William and Mary has never been described as a party school. Whatever parties there are most often take place at one of the school's 11 fraternity houses. Varsity football games get large turnouts, especially since the team has lately been having successful seasons. Intramurals are popular, and include everything from basketball to ultimate Frisbee. The school's new athletic complex is also well used.

Williamsburg, Virginia, is a tourist mecca, and the college's Ancient Campus sits on the edge of it. Other than its historic significance, Williamsburg offers little socially. One student adds that there is also little interaction between students of color and the local minority community.

There's a reason William and Mary has thrived for 300 years: its excellent academics and its ability to consistently attract a talented and motivated student body. "I've had a good time here. Whatever kind of experience you want in college, you can pretty much have it, whether it's only being with minority students, athletes, or being on student government."

WASHINGTON

UNIVERSITY OF PUGET SOUND

Address: 1500 North Warner Street,
Tacoma, WA 98416
Phone: (206) 756-3211
Director of Admissions: George H. Mills
Multicultural Student Recruiter: na
1993–94 tuition: $15,090
Room and board: $4,300
Application deadline: 3/1
Financial aid application deadline: 2/1
Non-white freshman admissions: Applicants
for the class of '95: 517
Accepted: 66.3%
Accepted who enroll: 34.1%
Applicants accepted who rank in top
10% of high school class: 31.2%
Median SAT: na
Median ACT: na
Full-time undergraduate enrollment: 2,822
Men: 42%
Women: 58%
Non-white students in
1988–89: 7%
1989–90: 8%
1990–91: 8%
1991–92: 10%
Students In-state: 64%
Top majors: 1. Business 2. English
3. Politics and Government
Retention rate of non-white students: 52%
**Scholarships exclusively for non-white
students:** Business and Public
Administration Diversity Scholarships:
merit-based; renewable; $500 to $2,500

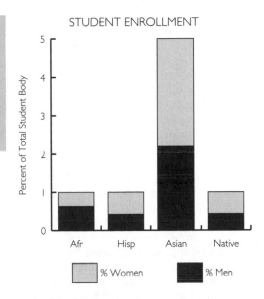

STUDENT ENROLLMENT

Percent of Total Student Body

Afr   Hisp   Asian   Native

% Women   % Men

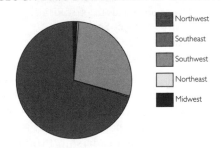

GEOGRAPHIC DISTRIBUTION OF STUDENTS

Northwest
Southeast
Southwest
Northeast
Midwest

per award; about eight awarded per year.
Business Leadership Minority Awards:

merit-based; $500 to $1,500 each year; renewable; five awarded each year. Great Teachers Minority Merit Award: merit-based; $1,000; renewable; one awarded each year; recipient must intend to pursue a teaching career.

Remediation programs: None

Academic support services: The university offers peer tutoring and courses in test reading, vocabulary development, math, and study strategies. There is also a Writing Center.

Ethnic studies programs: UPS offers East Asian Studies in which students study related topics on campus for a year, followed by a year's course of study and travel in various East Asian countries.

Ethnic studies courses: The university offers one course in African-American history and one course in Native American Studies. Also provided are Latin American and Hispanic Studies courses, offered by the Spanish department.

Organizations for non-white students: Black Student Union, Hui-O-Hawaii

Notable non-white alumni: Leslie Braxton (Communication/Theater Arts; pastor, Shiloh Baptist Church, Buffalo, NY); Banasree Mallick (Education; principal, Jennie Reed Elementary School, Tacoma); Gregory E. Jackson (English; deputy prosecutor, King County, Washington); Andrew Lofton (Education; Seattle budget director); Sam Chandler (English; assistant director, Tacoma Urban League); Thomas Dixon (director, Tacoma Urban League); Henry Jackson (assistant dean of students, University of Puget Sound)

Tenured faculty: 129

Non-tenured faculty: 131

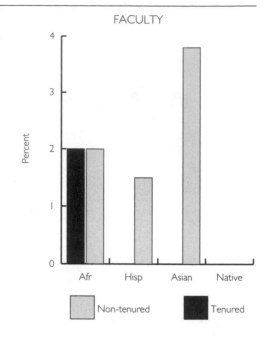

FACULTY

Non-tenured / Tenured

Student-faculty ratio: 13:1

Administrators: 130
  African-American: 1.5%
  Hispanic: 0.8%
  Asian-American: 3%
  Native American: 0

Recent non-white speakers on campus: Rev. Samuel B. McKinney (pastor, Mount Zion Baptist Church, Seattle); Claiborne Carson (editor and director, Martin Luther King, Jr., Papers Project); Dick Gregory (author and political activist); Joe Clark (former high school principal and character for the film *Lean on Me*); Barbara Christian (professor, University of California/Berkeley); Giancarlo Esposito (actor)

The University of Puget Sound is one of the better-respected liberal arts universities in the Pacific Northwest. The 105-year-old university, which has a small law school, attracts a student population that is largely conservative and pre-professional.

UPS's Business Leadership Program (BLP), available to a select few students on the basis of SAT scores and high school transcripts, is well regarded on campus. In addition to their business courses, students in the four-year program study the liberal arts and are paired with Tacoma or Seattle business executives who act as mentors.

The Pacific Rim Program, another respected and selective program on campus, allows students to spend a school year in Asia, traveling to more than 10 countries, including Japan, Thailand, Malaysia, and Vietnam. Once there, students study the host country's politics, art, economy, and religion. The program, open to students who have taken requisite language and cultures courses on campus and have survived the application process, is sponsored by the university's top-notch East Asian Studies program. Other strong departments at UPS are math, politics and government, religion, English, psychology, and biology.

To graduate, UPS students must satisfy core requirements that include courses in written and oral communications, math, history, humanities, natural world, society, fine arts, and comparative values. Courses for the comparative values requirement focus primarily on Western civilizations—with the exception of the course "Japan's Modern Century"—and include "Women and Social Change," "Critical Perspectives on Literature," and "European Peasants and their World."

One of the school's relatively few non-Western cultural studies classes is the popular "Intercultural Communications" course, offered by the communications department, which introduces students to interpersonal communications in such countries as Japan, China, and Austria.

UPS has an exceptionally nurturing faculty. "One of the reasons I came to school at UPS is the faculty, who care for students every bit as much as the admissions office says they do. They're truly dedicated." In particular, Henry Johnson, an assistant dean, "does a good job relating to the students and he listens. He also helps us with cultural events and he attends them." Recently, Johnson helped coordinate an intercultural communications workshop. Also especially supportive of UPS's students of color is George Roundy, director of academic and career advising services, Sharon Hamill, a psychology professor, and Susan Owen, a professor of communication and theater arts.

Hui-O-Hawaii, with more than 100 members, is UPS's largest and most active student club. Each year during Parents' Weekend, it sponsors a luau, featuring food and dancing, that is well attended by the UPS community. "I've felt great pride, as one of the Hui-O-Hawaii members, in organizing the annual campus luau," says a recent graduate. "We've involved students from all across the United States in a Hawaiian tradition that they probably wouldn't have discovered anywhere else." Hui-O-Hawaii, which meets every other week in the student union, also hosts a social gathering to welcome incoming students, and members recently ventured to a local elementary school to teach students traditional Hawaiian songs. While the focus of the group is on Hawaiian culture, it also includes other Asian traditions, such as Japanese-style tempura cooking. Serni Solidarios, the adviser to the group and director of student programs, "helps us with the really big programming events," says a student. "He's always there when we need him." The Black Student Union, with about 25 active members, sponsors a dance each year and brings guest speakers to campus.

Among the student organizations at UPS are the literary, special-interest, and religious groups. By far the most active are the school's 12 fraternities and sororities, which dominate much of the campus social scene and to which about a third of the university's students belong. Sports, particularly men's varsity football and women's varsity soccer, are popular. The school's Foolish Pleasures festival, during which well-known comedians come to campus and student-produced films are shown, is enthusiastically supported by the campus.

With such beautiful surroundings—Puget Sound is ten miles away, the Pacific Ocean is an hour-and-a-half drive from campus, and nearby mountains offer great downhill-skiing opportunities—it's no wonder many students are into the great outdoors. In fact, the university encourages students' closeness with nature. Each year, first-year students participate in the school's Prelude and Passages, a part of orientation in which students spend their first week of college hiking and swimming in and around Washington State's Hood Canal and, back on campus, participate in small-group discussions with professors.

Seattle, home to the mammoth University of Washington and sundry other off-campus diversions, is just an hour away. UPS is located in an upper-middle-class, predominantly white area of Tacoma known as the North Side. The South Side has African-American and Korean populations, but students say there is little interaction with them. The area around campus has a few bars, a shopping center, and movie theaters, which students say they feel comfortable visiting. Point Defiance Park is a three-mile jaunt from campus and is especially popular with students "when the sun shines," says a student. The park has a zoo and an aquarium.

Issues of multiculturalism are relatively late in blooming at UPS, but this isn't enough for students to dissuade prospective applicants from attending. Students like the intimate college education they're receiving on a campus that they say is friendly. "I've learned a lot about myself by coming to UPS," says a student. "Being a student here has been a very challenging, yet rewarding experience. I have taken a better look at my heritage and its meaning in my life since coming to this predominantly white setting. I believe it is up to students such as myself to educate other students about diversity, which is one reason I've stayed and why I encourage other multicultural students to attend."

UNIVERSITY OF WASHINGTON

Address: 1410 N.E. Campus Parkway, Seattle, WA 98195
Phone: (206) 543-9686
Director of Admissions: W. W. Washburn
Multicultural Student Recruiter: Enrique Morales
1991–92 tuition: $2,178 (in-state); $6,075 (out-of-state)
Room and board: $3,684
Application deadline: 2/1
Financial aid application deadline: 3/1

Non-white freshman admissions: Applicants for the class of '95: 2,433
Accepted: 71.8%
Accepted who enroll: 55%
Applicants accepted who rank in top 10% of high school class: 20%
In top 25%: 50%
Median SAT range: 400–460 V, 430–520 M
Median ACT range: 22–28
Full-time undergraduate enrollment: 23,053

STUDENT ENROLLMENT

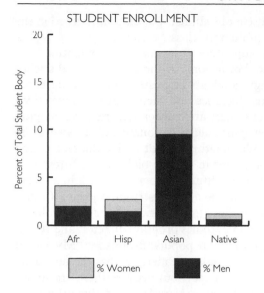

Percent of Total Student Body

Afr   Hisp   Asian   Native

% Women   % Men

GEOGRAPHIC DISTRIBUTION OF STUDENTS

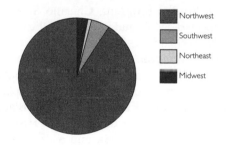

Northwest
Southwest
Northeast
Midwest

Men: 51%
Women: 49%
Non-white students in
1987–88: 22.6%
1988–89: 23.7%
1989–90: 24.9%
1990–91: 26.1%
Students In-state: 90%
Top majors: 1. Psychology 2. Sociology
3. English

Retention rate of non-white students: 85%
Scholarships exclusively for non-white students: Minority Affairs Freshman Merit Awards: merit-based; $1,000–$2,000 for each award; available to Washington State residents.
Remediation programs: na
Academic support services: The university offers academic tutoring in most subjects.
Ethnic studies programs: As part of the American ethnic studies department, students are able to major in either Afro-American, Asian-American, Chicano, or American Indian studies.
Organizations for non-white students: African Student Union, MECHA, Asian/Pacific Islander Student Union, Black Student Union, Native American Student Council, Association of Chinese Students and Scholars, Pacific Rim Student Association, Singapore Student Association, Chinese Social Betterment Society, Taiwan Study Society, Chinese Student Association, Taiwanese Student Association, Filipino Student Association, Thai Student Association, Hong Kong Student Association, Vietnamese Student Association, Hui-O-Hawaii, Hispanic Business Association, Japanese Student Association, Minority Student Health Science Organization, Khmer Student Association, Korean Student Association, Laotian Student Association, Society of Hispanic Professional Engineers
Notable non-white alumni: na
Tenured faculty: na
Non-tenured faculty: na
Student-faculty ratio: 12:1
Administrators: na
Recent non-white speakers on campus: na

Students who attend the University of Washington have the best of two worlds. Their school is one of the country's highly rated state-supported universities and it is located in Seattle, one of the country's most desirable cities.

"U Dub" students also take their studies seriously, and many are surprised at the high expectations of some of their professors. Students are more than able to handle the work, however; more than half of the school's student population finished in the top 10 percent of his or her high school graduating class.

Most of the school's academically competitive students find contentment in Washington's well-respected business school or in some of the school's noted science programs, including chemistry and zoology. Students interested in medical research are able to take advantage of some of the facilities and faculty at the university's medical school, nationally recognized for its heart and cancer research. Washington also has terrific programs in engineering, particularly aeronautical, as well as in international studies, math, and English. Washington doesn't let its unique location go to waste; the university offers noted programs in marine biology and forestry.

Washington's interdisciplinary Afro-American Studies program, which in a recent year had about 40 undergraduate majors, wins rave reviews from students. Course highlights include "Introduction to Black Studies" and "African-American Political Thought." Johnnella Butler, the American ethnic studies program director, and Albert Black and John Walter are three of the program's more popular professors. "My biggest complaint about the program, though," says a student leader, "is that the university catalogue lists dozens of fascinating courses each year, but because there are so few instructors in the program few classes are actually offered. And the ones that are offered are usually too crowded to get into because they are all extremely popular."

Students say Washington's American Indian Studies program, Chicano Studies, and Asian-American Studies are also well respected, while judgment is still out on the school's American ethnic studies major, established in 1985.

To raise the cultural awareness on campus, Washington has a unique system of hiring student commissioners to head up diversity programming. Each of the school's four principal cultural groups has its own student commissioners: African-American, Asian, Native American, and Chicano/Latino students. For example, the Black Students' Commission "helped sponsor something almost every day for Black History Month," says a student, including a talent show, a lecture series, and a discussion with Queen Latifah, a well-known rap star. During the school year, the commissioner helped coordinate a Kwanzaa program.

The American Indian Students' Commission helps coordinate an annual powwow and brings to campus various lecturers and organizes events for the school's annual Native American Awareness Week, which in a recent year included storytelling sessions, a drum group that performed on Red Square, a main campus area, and guest speakers.

Each of these commissioners works independently of the school's student of color organizations in planning activities, although the groups will often co-sponsor events. The Black Student Union, which meets once a week, is involved in the recruitment and retention of students, and is working to establish a tutoring program for younger children in the area.

The Native American Student Council "does a lot of work for so few active students," says a council member. "We sponsor retreats on reservations in the area, and we helped build a traditional longhouse of cedar on one of them. We're also politically active. When we played in the Rose Bowl, which had as its theme Columbus's discovery of America, we protested and made the local news. We protested in front of the school museum; it still displays Native American artifacts, which we want returned to their rightful places. Similar demonstrations were held by students at Michigan and UCLA."

The council also works with the commission to stage the annual powwow, which one student describes as "huge. It's estimated that 40,000 people attend the event throughout the weekend." The powwow is held on Sand Point naval base, located not far from campus.

One student describes the Native American community at the university as close-knit; about half the students are older than thirty. "Many of the American Indian students here are older and have families. About half of them are from Washington, about a third are from Alaska, and others are from Canada, Idaho, and Montana."

One large event sponsored recently by MECHA, the school's Hispanic student organization, was its Day of the Virgin Mary, which featured a program at the Ethnic Cultural Theater. "We packed the theater for the show," says an event organizer. "More than two hundred people showed up, and afterward we had a food festival across the street at the Ethnic Cultural Center."

Other active Hispanic student groups include the Hispanic Business Association and the Society of Hispanic Professional Engineers. "Having these groups active is refreshing. They've all become active fairly recently. Before, there was just MECHA, which most people perceived as activist, so it's nice to have some pre-professional organizations for students. Students in MECHA tend to be more liberal arts types." In part due to the efforts of these student groups, the university's Hispanic student enrollment has increased by nearly 30 percent in recent years, according to a student leader.

The Ethnic Cultural Center "is comfortable," in the words of one student, and provides a great deal of social and academic resources for students. The center has a TV room, a library, office space for student organizations, and, in each of the wings informally divided among the student groups, a mural with a scene that reflects a particular group's culture. But, according to students, the university plans to raze the current center by 1993 to make way for an expansion of athletic facilities. (The commissioners' offices are located on the second floor of the student center.) No site for a new cultural center has been planned. "That's our biggest question: 'Where is the new center going to be?'" says a senior. Another student is more hopeful: "I think whatever they build will definitely be an amazing facility." Students are also able to use the Ethnic Cultural Theater, until recently used by a local theater company.

Designed to provide academic and personal support, the Office of Minority Affairs receives mixed reviews from students, largely because of what students consider the office's ineffective staff leadership, which, students say, is responsive only to a select few students. As evidence, students point to the selection process of the office's Student Advisory Board. "Representatives of the board are supposed to represent the constituencies of the school's different cultural organizations, but the representatives are not elected by students. They are handpicked by the office staff; students don't have a say in the makeup of the board. Therefore the board is perceived to be pretty much non-functional."

During the 1991–92 school year, due to their frustration with the board, students formed the Ethnic Students Council, which represents each of the groups. The council members are elected. The group was active in getting the Ethnic Cultural Theater returned to student control.

Coalition building among the student groups has been increasing of late. "Usually the organizations get caught up in our own things, but we're working to rally support for an Ethnic Studies Requirement [ESR] and we want to be at all of the formal debates and discussions about the requirement." The five-credit requirement was rejected in late 1991 by Washington's faculty. Students are concerned that an alternative diversity requirement proposed by the faculty, called American Cultural-ism, "is a watered-down version of the ESR. Students have no say in the proposed requirement; it's entirely up to the faculty. The proposed requirement strays away from race awareness, and now looks to be just a comparative course that will include European-American perspectives. We want the requirement to focus on racism, prejudice, and race relations, but now we'll be focusing on the art of this culture and the history of that culture, while never really discussing issues of racism."

In the last decade, Seattle has become one of the country's fastest-growing and most popular cities. Bumper stickers plead with Californians to stay put and not move up north. But every year people from around the country pack up and move to Seattle, no doubt attracted by its laid-back atmosphere and the natural beauty of the countryside. Famed Mount Rainier can be seen from various spots on campus. The city has numerous ethnic populations as well as restaurants and other attractions. One student observes that "except for the Greek system, Washington students are pretty accepting of diversity." The university's gay and lesbian student organization is not only tolerated but influential in campus politics.

The University of Washington is one of the country's largest schools, and getting lost in the crowd is easy. But with its active and tightly knit student organizations, students are able to find their niche. "U Dub has been quite an experience, and I've enjoyed most of it. I've learned most from being involved on campus. If I hadn't been involved in organizations, I might have been lost at sea." And, given the university's location near the Pacific Ocean, the metaphor is more than apt.

WHITMAN COLLEGE

Address: Walla Walla, WA 99362
Phone: (509) 527-5176
Director of Admissions: Madeleine Eagon
Multicultural Student Recruiter: Craig Spriggs
1993–94 tuition: $15,650
Room and board: $4,790
Application deadline: 2/15, 12/1 early admission
Financial aid application deadline: 2/15
Non-white freshman admissions: Applicants for the class of '97: 197
  Accepted: 86%

Accepted who enroll: 46%
Applicants accepted who rank in top 10% of high school class: 30%
In top 25%: 70%
Median SAT range: 460–600 V, 520–640 M
Median ACT: na
Full-time undergraduate enrollment: 1,200
  Men: 48%
  Women: 52%
Non-white students in
  1988–89: 8.3%
  1989–90: 8%

STUDENT ENROLLMENT

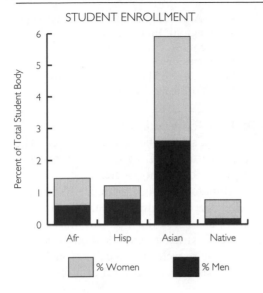

Percent of Total Student Body

Afr   Hisp   Asian   Native

☐ % Women   ■ % Men

GEOGRAPHIC DISTRIBUTION OF STUDENTS

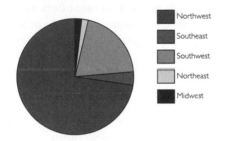

■ Northwest
■ Southeast
▨ Southwest
☐ Northeast
■ Midwest

1990–91: 9.3%
1991–92: 10%
1992–93: 14%

Students In-state: 40%

Top majors: 1. Biology 2. Sociology
3. History

Retention rate of non-white students: 70%

**Scholarships exclusively for non-white
students:** Diversity Scholarship:
need-based; each award ranges from
$4,500 to $17,000; 30 to 40 awarded each
year; renewable.

Remediation programs: None

Academic support services: The Study
Resource and Writing Centers provide
support, as do student tutors in most
academic subjects.

Ethnic studies programs: Japanese Studies
program

Ethnic studies courses: Offered are
"Minority Politics in America," "Race
and Ethnic Group Relations," and
"Background of Black Protest Rhetoric,"
as well as several courses in Asian and
Hispanic politics and history.

Organizations for non-white students:
Multi-Ethnic Student Organization,
Ohana (Hawaiian student group),
MECCA House (multi-ethnic theme
house), Asian Student Association,
Indo-Meztiso (Hispanic student group)

Notable non-white alumni: George Holifield
(Political Science; judge); Margaret
Murphy (Political Science; foreign service
officer)

Tenured faculty: 71

Non-tenured faculty: 20

FACULTY

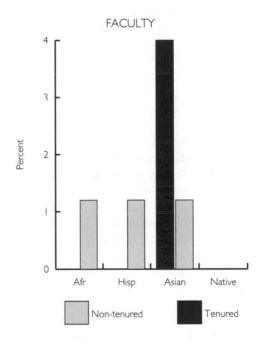

Percent

Afr   Hisp   Asian   Native

☐ Non-tenured   ■ Tenured

Student-faculty ratio: 11:1

Administrators: 87
African-American: 2%
Hispanic: 0
Asian-American: 1%
Native American: 0

Recent non-white speakers on campus: Dr. Charles King (president, Urban Crisis Center, Atlanta); Lillian Rayhol-Rose (consultant about race issues); Chery Chow (member, Seattle City Council); Shawn Wong (professor of Asian-American Studies, University of Washington); Brenda Jones (vice president, Security Pacific); William Wiley (senior vice president, Battelle Laboratories); Shirley Chisholm (former New York councilwoman)

Once you get past the wheat and onion fields of southeastern Washington, you'll arrive at Whitman College, one of the Northwest's top liberal arts colleges. The 134-year-old school is the state's only private institution of higher learning with a Phi Beta Kappa chapter, the country's most prestigious honor society.

Whitman College gives new meaning to an intimate learning experience. With only about 1,200 students—all undergraduates—class sizes are small, usually numbering no more than 15 students. "Professors encourage us to seek them out for assistance," says a student. "My English professor gave the class her home telephone number, and she said if we have any problems with class we're welcome to call her at home. My brother goes to a larger university, and he doesn't get that kind of attention at his school."

English, chemistry, psychology, and geology are said to be among Whitman's best-respected departments. The school's relatively new music building offers impressive facilities for music students. Students are also able to combine a course of study in environmental studies with one of various science majors, such as biology or chemistry. During the 1991–92 school year, the college offered its first "African-American History" course, but, according to one student, "it wasn't as interesting as students hoped. We would like to have read more books and texts with African-American perspectives."

First-year students are expected to complete a Freshmen Core, in which they select for a semester's study one of three topics: "The Origins of Modernism," "Great Works," or "Classical Greece." Students must also complete distribution requirements and a Senior Colloquium. Whitman students have high acceptance rates into medical, law, and business schools.

Whitman's Japanese Studies program is well regarded, and is complemented by the school's Tekisui-Juku, an on-campus residence facility in which students are expected to speak only Japanese. The house has a Japanese garden, and residents sponsor numerous Japanese cultural awareness events for themselves and the campus—ranging from a screening of *Ghostbusters II* that had Japanese subtitles to Japanese tea ceremonies. Professor Akira Takemoto, a Japanese-language instructor, works especially closely with house residents.

The college also sponsors other theme houses. The Chinese House, the school's smallest, with about five residents, focuses on developing Chinese-language skills. A native Chinese speaker lives in the house to help students with the language. Residents host various all-campus activities, such as celebrations for Lunar Festival and Chinese New Year. The MECCA (Multi-Ethnic Center for Cultural Awareness) House, which can accommodate up to nine residents, coordinates events for Black History Month and Asian Awareness Week. Residents also sponsor study skills workshops, AIDS awareness discussions, and film screenings. There are also theme houses for the study of French and German language and culture and Environmental and Fine Arts houses.

Ohana, a student group comprised mostly of Hawaiian students, is active on campus. "Whitman seems to have a large draw from Hawaii and parts of Oregon, Washington, and California that have sizable Asian populations," observes a biochemistry major. "These people have gotten together and formed the Ohana Club for Hawaiians, which serves as a support group. A lot of the Asian and Asian-American students like to go to the theme houses to hang out in a comfortable, familiar atmosphere. The houses and Ohana provide jumping-off points for people to discuss Asian culture and their concerns." African-American students are in the beginning stages of forming an on-campus Black Student Union.

Whitman is located in a rural—and remote—portion of the state. The predominantly white community of Walla Walla "isn't exactly the big city," as one student aptly noted. But the college offers a variety of activities—speakers, fraternity parties, organizational events—to keep most students busy. "Yes, Whitman is a small school in a fairly small town," says a recent graduate. "We don't pretend to offer a replica of big-city activities or nightlife. But that's okay, because what Whitman can offer is a new and expanded definition of evening or weekend activities. Contrary to what people might think, boredom at Whitman is rarely a problem."

Most of the social life at Whitman occurs in one of two places: at a fraternity house—their weekend parties are the center of weekend nightlife—or on the intramural field. Nearly 75 percent of the students participate in at least one intramural activity: indoor soccer, basketball, or softball, to name just a few. According to the college, nearly 20 percent of the students are also on a varsity team, such as Nordic ski racing, basketball, and baseball. (Don't go looking to join the school's football team; there isn't one.) Whitman's most successful team won't be found on the athletic fields, however; the school's speech and debate team is consistently ranked as one of the top such teams in the country. The college's theater program is also active, putting on at least a dozen productions each year.

About half of Whitman's students are from Washington, while the majority of the others are from various states in the West, most notably California and Oregon. Students come from more than 30 states in all, as well as nearly two dozen foreign countries. Despite the geographic diversity, Whitman remains a racially homogeneous institution. Students add, however, that the school's atmosphere is tolerant of almost any sort of diversity. "It appears that Whitman is a homogeneous community, and to some extent it is," says a politics major. "But for a minority student, myself included, there is no better way to get to know yourself than through a community where at first glance you may have felt excluded. This community has allowed me to put the racial issue into perspective. I've found that at Whitman it's the person who counts. The only one who stands in your way here is yourself."

WEST VIRGINIA

SHEPHERD COLLEGE

Address: Shepherdtown, WV 25443
Phone: (304) 876-2511 / (800) 344-5231
Director of Admissions: Karl L. Wolf
Multicultural Student Recruiter: Ernest
 Lyles and Geraldine Parkam
1992–93 tuition: $1,954 (in-state); $4,500
 (out-of-state)
Room and board: $3,500
Application deadline: 2/1
Financial aid application deadline: 3/1
Non-white freshman admissions: Applicants
 for the class of '94: 155
 Accepted: 80%
 Accepted who enroll: 66%
 Applicants accepted who rank in top
 10% of high school class: 15%
 Median SAT range: 500–600 V, 500–600 M
 Median ACT range: 26–30
Full-time undergraduate enrollment: 3,559
 Men: 40%
 Women: 60%
Non-white students in
 1988–89: 3.4%
 1989–90: 3.5%
 1990–91: 3.6%
 1991–92: 4.4%
Geographic distribution of students: na
Top majors: 1. Business Administration
 2. Education 3. Nursing
Retention rate of non-white students: na
**Scholarships exclusively for non-white
 students:** Minority Student Leadership
 Scholarships: merit-based; eight awarded

each year to in-state students; $1,100
each award; seven $3,000 awards given
each year to out-of-state students;
renewable. Storer Scholarships:
merit-based; two or three scholarships
awarded each year; renewable; $300–$400.
Remediation programs: Courses are offered
 in writing, math, and reading
 comprehension.
Academic support services: Courses are
 available in developing test-taking skills,
 reading comprehension, and time
 management.
Ethnic studies programs: None

STUDENT ENROLLMENT

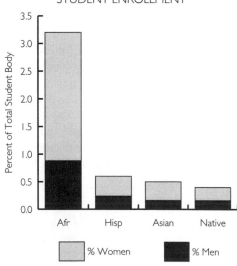

Ethnic studies courses: The college offers a course in Afro-American history, and in "American Ethnic Literature."

Organizations for non-white students: AHANA (African, Hispanic, Asian, and Native American) Student Organization

Notable non-white alumni: Robert Holmes (Political Science; director, Southern Center for Strategies in Public Policy, and member of the Georgia House of Representatives)

Tenured faculty: 70

Non-tenured faculty: 48

Student-faculty ratio: 18:1

Administrators: na
African-American: 4.3%
Hispanic: 2.1%
Asian-American: 0
Native American: 0

Recent non-white speakers on campus: Dr. Calvin Morris (associate professor, Howard University); Dr. William B. McClain (professor, Wesley Seminary); Marita Golden (author)

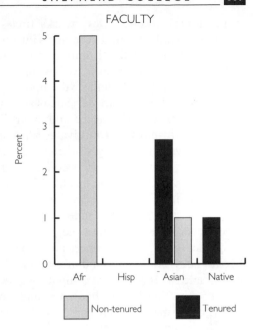

FACULTY

In many ways, Shepherd College resembles a midsize private institution of higher learning—relatively stiff admissions standards and a beautiful campus—but it isn't. Shepherd is a publicly funded college that often costs less for out-of-state students than public universities in their home states.

Shepherd is also a school that offers respectable academics. The 122-year-old college has more than 70 degree-granting programs, "everything from education, fine arts, and psychology to computer programming, marketing, and hotel-motel and restaurant management." The school's programs include the standard liberal arts fare as well as fashion merchandising, graphic design, and photography. Among the school's most respected programs are history, business, and English. Shepherd's recently completed Frank Creative Arts Center enhances its arts and drama program offerings. "Perspectives in Diversity," a sociology course, is well received by students. "The class discusses racial problems in the country and tries to think of solutions for them," says a student.

No matter what their majors, however, all Shepherd students are exposed to the liberal arts and must study art, music, English, speech, literature, math, economics, a foreign language, and science, as well as physical education. Class sizes are small—usually no more than 20 to 25 on the average—and students say their professors are accessible. "The teachers really help you," says a nursing major. "You're not just a number here."

For additional academic support, students are able to rely on a variety of faculty and staff. Particularly helpful is Reverend Ernest Lyles, the assistant dean of multicultural affairs. Lyles "works tirelessly with students, letting us know he is available to talk with and keeping us informed about activities for minority students," says a student, adding: "I think minority students are treated fairly at Shepherd but I would like more social activities and lectures geared toward us. With Reverend Lyles's efforts, I think things will improve." Momoud Darboe, a sociology professor, is also helpful. "He's an African who is influential with students of all ethnicities because he is a good teacher and smart," says a student. Joe Merz, a psychology professor, "inspires and motivates all students, and encourages self-determination and improvement among students." Students also say that Michael Riccards, the college president, "wants to become culturally aware and he wants his campus also to be culturally aware. He has let AHANA, a student cultural organization, put on several events, and we've appreciated that." Harry Young, the dean of student affairs, "supports us in all of our endeavors."

Students have also found the peer support available through AHANA (African, Hispanic, Asian, Native American) to be important. "We've sponsored Black History Month activities, such as a dance and a Showtime at Shepherd talent show, a gospel night, and a Jungle Fever night, where we had a discussion about interracial relationships. We've also had an ethnic fair that included entertainment that related to African-Americans, Hispanics, Asian-Americans, and Native Americans." Reverend Lyles advises AHANA.

Shepherdstown is the oldest town in the state, and Harpers Ferry, the site of John Brown's raid, is just a few miles down the road. As many of the school's students of color are from the area, students say town-gown relations are good. "The community is friendly and positive, and the area itself is diverse when it comes to ethnic groups." According to students, the town offers little in the way of off-campus diversions. But it does offer location: the college is a little more than an hour from Washington, DC, and Baltimore, and the cities are accessible by train or car. Students visit the cities to attend professional sporting events or to go to museums or concerts. The university's annual World Affairs Seminar brings impressive speakers to campus to discuss current events.

On campus, students are able to participate in a rich variety of activities, especially sports. The school's varsity football team has had several recent successful seasons, and the women's swimming team has sent members to national championships. The College Center, with its snack bar, pub, and bookstore, is the place to be seen on campus. "Whatever your special interest, you're likely to find a club of like-minded students to join," says a student. About 1,500 of the school's 3,700 students are part-time students who commute to campus from the area, but students say they're as involved in campus events as full-time resident students.

Scenery, strong academics, and a "friendly" student body are reasons to attend this public university. And there's another reason: the cost of tuition. Says a student: "My uncle is a Shepherd alumnus and several members of my family have taken classes here. When it came time to select a college, I chose Shepherd for its high academic standards and because the tuition is a good deal."

WEST VIRGINIA UNIVERSITY

Address: Morgantown, WV 26506-6009
Phone: (304) 293-2121 / (800) 344-9881
 (in-state)
Director of Admissions: Tammy Fayre
Multicultural Student Recruiter: na

1992–93 tuition: $1,850 (in-state); $5,018
 (out-of-state)
Room and board: $4,000
Application deadline: 3/1
Financial aid application deadline: 3/1

Don't be too quick to dismiss West Virginia University as a backwoods kind of school. Here are a few promising facts about the 128-year-old university: twenty-three WVU students have earned prestigious Rhodes Scholarships; nearly half the student body comes from out of state; several impressive new facilities have gone up on campus, including a new Engineering Research Building and a College of Business and Economics; and the university offers more than 176 degree-granting programs from the bachelor's through the doctoral level.

While WVU's achievements are impressive, the university is also committed to seeing that students of all academic backgrounds succeed at the university. In particular, WVU's PASS-Key (Personalized Academic Support Service) Program for African-American students orients incoming first-year students to campus social and academic life. Freshmen work with peer mentors and are introduced to the school's many academic support programs, including Reading and Writing Laboratories and the Mathematics Learning Center. "I believe that the PASS-Key Program is an essential part of the freshmen experience at WVU," says a student. "In addition to being a support system, the program also establishes a basis for future scholastic endeavor. As a PASS-Key mentor, I help new students, and I have grown from the experience."

As WVU is a land-grant institution, some of its best programs are in agriculture and engineering. Other pre-professional programs, such as pre-med and business, are also WVU strengths. The education, journalism, and nursing programs are well regarded and popular. WVU's African-American Studies program, said by students to be excellent, includes noteworthy courses in history and literature. The university's Honors Program offers qualified students small class sizes and housing on an honors floor in Arnold Hall.

Although WVU is a large university, students say professors are usually available and are more than willing to make time for students. One of the school's staff members who is particularly accessible to students is William Little, director of WVU's Center for Black Culture and Research. "He's helpful with everything, and always has an open-door policy," says a student. The center, which is a popular hangout with students, houses the school's African-American Studies program, as well as a library, computers for student use, and a lounge area. "The center is my home away from home, and the staff there definitely creates a family atmosphere." An additional staff member students turn to is Charles Blue, who oversees the emergency student loan fund. Colleen McMullen, an administrative assistant at the center, "works with us a lot, too," says a student. McMullen helps coordinate the center's annual Leadership Retreat, held at a nearby resort.

While such programs are impressive, the university's enrollment of minority students is less so. WVU's admissions office declined to participate in our guide, so enrollment statistics for students of color were obtained from a recent issue of *The Chronicle of Higher Education* that quoted the U.S. Department of Education's 1990 figures for non-white student enrollments at the nation's four-year schools. According to the listing, of WVU's more than 20,000 students 1.6 percent were Asian, 2.8 percent black, 0.6 percent Hispanic, and 0.1 percent Native American.

When not at the center, many of the school's African-American students are participating in Black Unity Organization (BUO) meetings and activities. "The unity among black students has improved since I've been on campus," says a senior. "Before, it was always Greeks doing their own thing, or BUO members doing their own thing, or people not involved in either. But now we seem to be working more together."

Working together, at least for the approximately 75 BUO members, means planning a variety of social and cultural events. The most ambitious event of the 1991–92 school year was the group's own homecoming king and queen ceremony. "To my knowledge, minorities have never been represented on the homecoming queen's court. There's an application fee, I think of thirty dollars, and then there's an interviewing process. But a minority candidate has never made it past the interview. They say the interview decision is based on academics, but we've nominated candidates who have done well academically, and they still don't make it through. So we decided to have our own pageant. Our nominees participated in the school-wide homecoming parade, but then we had our own ceremony and party in a room in the Mountainlair Plaza," the school's student union.

In addition to homecoming activities, the BUO sponsors an annual membership drive, a tailgate party before the first football game of the season as a way to greet new BUO members, and a community service project in which members participate in an adopt-a-child project. A well-received Masquerade Ball was held around Halloween time.

The BUO's *Minority Awareness Corner* monthly newspaper is distributed free to the campus. The publication is eagerly awaited, as it lists events and contains history and news sections. It also has a section devoted to a hot topic; a recent article was "Do Black Women Keep Black Men Down?" WVU's seven historically black Greek organizations—four fraternities and three sororities—see to it that they sponsor their fair share of parties and service projects.

Morgantown, WVU's hometown, has a small African-American community, but students say they feel uncomfortable when they walk into area stores, and, adds a student, "there's absolutely nothing for African-Americans to do socially downtown." But students say enough activity is scheduled on campus to satisfy them.

With some strong academics and a solid regional reputation, WVU can be a good college choice. Students wanting a more diverse campus community may have to look elsewhere, but for students who take advantage of PASS-Key and get involved in campus activities, four years at WVU can be a worthwhile experience. Says a political science major: "West Virginia University has turned out to be a good choice for me because it has provided me with the extracurricular and academic opportunities to achieve. Programs at the school attempt to make the campus environment a comfortable place for minority students. I would encourage any student seeking the opportunity to grow intellectually, academically, and culturally to consider attending WVU."

BELOIT COLLEGE

Address: 700 College Street, Beloit, WI
  53511
Phone: (608) 363-2500 / (800) 356-0751
Director of Admissions: Thomas Kreiser
Multicultural Student Recruiter: Bob
  Obrohta and Devon Wilson
1993–94 tuition: $15,430
Room and board: $3,520
Application deadline: 3/1
Financial aid application deadline: 4/1
Non-white freshman admissions: Applicants
  for the class of '96: 102
  Accepted: 83.3%
  Accepted who enroll: 27.1%
  Applicants accepted who rank in top
  10% of high school class: 9.5%
  In top 25%: 42.8%
  Median SAT: 532 V, 556 M
  Median ACT: 25
Full-time undergraduate enrollment: 1,087
  Men: 45%
  Women: 55%
Non-white students in
  1988–89: 7.1%
  1989–90: 8.2%
  1990–91: 6.7%
  1991–92: 8.2%
Students In-state: 34%
Top majors: 1. Psychology 2. Creative
  Writing 3. Economics and Management
Retention rate of non-white students: na
Scholarships exclusively for non-white
  students: Charles Winterwood

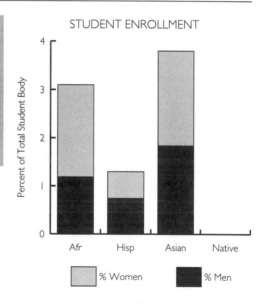

STUDENT ENROLLMENT

Percent of Total Student Body

Afr Hisp Asian Native

% Women   % Men

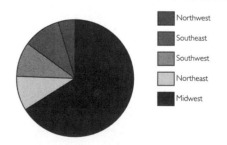

GEOGRAPHIC DISTRIBUTION OF STUDENTS

Northwest
Southeast
Southwest
Northeast
Midwest

Scholarship: need- and merit-based;
$3,000; renewable.

Remediation programs: None

Academic support services: The college has an Education Development Program and a Study Skills Center.

Ethnic studies programs: Beloit offers an Asian Studies minor, an interdisciplinary program involving language, history, anthropology, and politics. The college also offers an interdisciplinary minor in Latin American Studies.

Ethnic studies courses: na

Organizations for non-white students: Black Student Union

Notable non-white alumni: na

Tenured faculty: na

Non-tenured faculty: na

Student-faculty ratio: 12:1

Administrators: na

Recent non-white speakers on campus: Rev. Joseph Echols Lowery (director, Southern Christian Leadership Conference); Mary Carter Smith (storyteller); Marian Wright Edelman (director, Children's Defense Fund); Edward Perkins (director general of the Foreign Service and former ambassador to South Africa); Wilma Mankiller (chief, Cherokee Tribe of Oklahoma)

Beloit College was founded in 1846 by seven Yale College graduates to be the "Yale of the West." While Yale has since grown to become a major research university, Beloit has been content to remain a quality college committed to the liberal arts.

Beloit is unique among many of its peer institutions in the Midwest, as it has traditionally attracted a slightly left-of-center student body. "I teach 'Women in Politics,' and I've had students go to Washington twice in the last year to march at the White House," says Georgia Duersti-Lahti, an assistant professor of government. "A Madison [Wisconsin] newspaper just ran a photo of a whole group of Beloit students at a rally at the state capital. One of my students is in Seattle right now, working with the homeless. Who says students are apathetic? Not here!"

Students are drawn to Beloit for its innovative programs and commitment to the liberal arts. Unusual for a small liberal arts college, geology and anthropology are two of Beloit's standout departments, which allow for field research in nearby Indian burial grounds and make available the extensive materials of the school's Logan Museum of Anthropology. Chemistry, biology, psychology, and English are also well regarded. Beloit's museum studies program allows students to use the resources of the school's impressive Wright Museum of Art and Logan Museum. However, Beloit's only African-American Studies course, "African-American History," is considered weak by students.

To ensure a liberal arts foundation, Beloit requires students to satisfy distribution requirements in natural science and mathematics, social science, arts and humanities, and in interdisciplinary studies. Students are also required to take a two-part writing program, as well as the school's First Year Initiative, a seminar-style course designed to introduce freshmen to Beloit and to the liberal arts.

Students needing to supplement course work or looking for additional research materials are able to take advantage of the resources at the University of Wisconsin/Madison, an hour north on I-90. Students can cross-register at the university. The college also sponsors a program with American University in Washington, DC, which allows students to study political and governmental issues.

To assist non-white students with their studies, the college's Educational Development Program (EDP), established in 1974, provides them with tutoring, academic advising, and mediation with faculty and administration, among other services. "EDP helped me a lot in the beginning to get my bearings at college. Now it is really useful in broadening my scope and showing me where and how I can establish my ideas and goals," says a junior. Suzanne Bellrichard, director of the program, "is always there and she helps me deal with my problems. She is encouraging. She helps students get together for the Black Student Union," says a student. Charles Ellis, an EDP assistant, "is also always there for us." Ranjan Roy, a math and computer science professor, is active in the school's Asian community. "He is a role model for the Asian students. He invites them over to his house for social gatherings."

While Beloit students may be active, the school's African-American community has been less so—that is, until recently, with the formation during the 1991–92 school year of the Black Student Union (BSU). "The BSU has really been helpful here at Beloit. It gives me a voice, finally, and the opportunity to talk to other people who know where I'm coming from. The BSU has really united us black students on campus. We are more willing to talk to one another, share ideas, and now I can finally feel comfortable here. I don't need to call home or go home so much. The group has helped me realize that no matter where I am I can be me, and that I am not abnormal, or wrong if I don't conform. The BSU has helped me to realize that I can be home wherever I am." For now, BSU functions have included informal gatherings, as well as a gospelfest, several parties, a vigil to celebrate Martin Luther King, Jr.'s Birthday, and a Black History Month program. Many BSU members are active in the Beloit community, tutoring in local elementary and high schools.

BSU members also saw a resurgence of political activism among their ranks when the school's radio station, WBCR, canceled a gospel program popular with the city of Beloit's African-American community. "When the gospel show on the radio was canceled, the BSU fought to put it back on, and now hosts the show themselves. This was not so much because the students of the BSU are up listening to the radio at seven a.m. on Sunday, but because the community was. BSU students alternate and get up at six-thirty a.m. to get ready to do the show."

Students report varying levels of interaction between students of different cultures and races. "Beloit has few minorities to be racially integrated in the first place, but I would say that we really don't integrate too much. I think people sit with people they know. Most of the time, those people will be of the same race, whether it is white, black, or Asian. Our dorms are pretty mixed. The Greek houses are certainly not integrated. Each has a majority of one race, and black people are hardly ever in any of the frats or sororities on campus. The theme houses are not really that mixed either." Adds a sophomore: "As far as integration goes, Beloit is much better than other schools I've visited. Dining areas and dorms are pretty well integrated. At parties, there are no exclusions."

The city of Beloit, largely a blue-collar town that has seen better times economically, has a sizable African-American population. Many of Beloit's African-American students are from the area. "There are good relations between the African-American students at Beloit and the community because half of these students live in the community. Other African-American students, whenever possible, try to interact with the community as well," largely through the efforts of the BSU. Many of the college's African-American students from Beloit first learn of the school through its Help

Yourself Program, in which Beloit students participate as mentors, tutors, and teachers in area elementary schools. Brenda Atlas, director of the program, is a resource for students even after they enroll at Beloit. "She is the one who got me to come to school here, and she is always checking up on me to see how I am doing," says a student.

The city of Beloit doesn't offer much save some restaurants, mostly Italian, and some movie theaters, and the Wisconsin countryside isn't far from campus. Students who need a more active social life can head up to Wisconsin's ultimate college town, Madison, or to the nightlife of Chicago, just ninety miles away.

On campus, students have a say in how their school is run. Twelve students serve on the school's Academic Senate, which also includes the college president, the vice president for academic affairs, and several other administrators, and nearly 40 other students sit on the Community Senate, which focuses on student issues and includes the director of student activities. Fraternities and sororities, which aren't the let's-drink-until-we-get-sick variety found at most schools and which are only minimally integrated, are becoming increasingly popular. Men's varsity basketball has had some recent successful seasons, as have the women's soccer teams. Intramural sports are also popular. Beloit's new $6 million sports center should make almost any sports enthusiast's day.

Beloit doesn't look much like Yale, but it never really wanted to do so in the first place. Beloit is a school where a respected education can be had without the ivy and pressure of its founders' alma mater. "I would now recommend Beloit to students of color as an institution that may address their concerns because Beloit looks like it might be able to cater to some of the needs of minority students if it allows the BSU to grow. I might not have recommended Beloit to someone last year as an institution that would be able to address a black person's concerns. However, I would have suggested Beloit because it is a good institution that really challenges you and encourages people to test themselves and reach new heights. It is also filled with well-meaning, if not always helpful, people."

LAWRENCE UNIVERSITY

Address: P.O. Box 599, Appleton, WI 54912
Phone: (414) 832-6500 / (800) 227-0982
Director of Admissions: na
Multicultural Student Recruiter: Alan
  Wimes
1992–93 tuition: $15,342
Room and board: $3,429
Application deadline: 2/1
Financial aid application deadline: 3/1
Non-white freshman admissions: Applicants
  for the class of '96: 106
  Accepted: 74.5%

Accepted who enroll: 36.7%
Applicants accepted who rank in top
  10% of high school class: 40.5%
In top 25%: 55.7%
Median SAT range: 440–630 V, 480–640 M
Median ACT range: 22–27
Full-time undergraduate enrollment: 1,200
  Men: 49%
  Women: 51%
Non-white students in
  1987–88: 3.6%
  1988–89: 3.9%

STUDENT ENROLLMENT

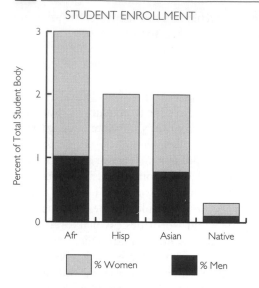

% Women *% Men*

1989–90: 5.5%
1990–91: 5.8%

Geographic distribution of students: na

Students In-state: 31%

Top majors: 1. English 2. Government
3. Psychology/Biology

Retention rate of non-white students: 88%

Scholarships exclusively for non-white students: Heritage Scholarships: merit-based; $2,500–$5,000 each; no specific number awarded each year. William Randolph Hearst Scholarship: amount of award varies; one awarded each year; need-based.

Remediation programs: None

Academic support services: Tutoring is available in most academic subjects, as well as the Writing Lab and workshops in study skills and time management.

Ethnic studies programs: East Asian languages, established in 1989.

Ethnic studies courses: na

Organizations for non-white students: Black Organization of Students, Students in Support of Asian Culture, Songhay (African-American theater)

Notable non-white alumni: Harold E. Jordan ('73; attorney); Joseph F. Patterson, Jr. ('69; vice president, Guardian Insurance); Michael J. Lofton ('76; concert singer, Metropolitan Opera); Shigeto Tsuru ('35; president, Village Shonan, Tokyo)

Tenured faculty: 77

Non-tenured faculty: 41

FACULTY

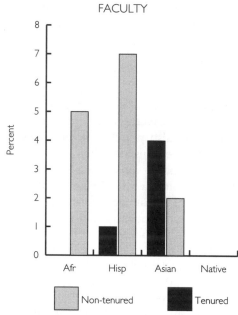

Non-tenured *Tenured*

Student-faculty ratio: 11:1

Administrators: 27

African-American: 10%
Hispanic: 3.7%
Asian-American: 3.7%
Native American: 0

Recent non-white speakers on campus: William Raspberry (urban affairs columnist, *Washington Post*); Claiborne Carson (editor and director, Martin Luther King, Jr., Papers Project); Javier Sanjinés (professor, University of Maryland)

With a population of only about 1,200 students, Lawrence is a small university that is committed to the liberal arts, facts that drew many of the students to the school in the first place. "One of the general reasons I like Lawrence is that the atmosphere

here is very personal and you are not lost in the crowd," says a first-year student. "Lawrence also has high academic standards and a strong curriculum. Even as a freshman, I enjoy having professors as instructors in classes that are small. I think things like this show the school's commitment to a good liberal arts education where the student is always the main concern."

Some of Lawrence's best departments are biology, political science, Slavic languages, chemistry, physics, and history. With the $6.8 million expansion in 1991 of the Music-Drama Center, the college has been able to upgrade its already respected offerings in these areas. Music students are able to earn bachelor of arts and bachelor of music degrees in the school's rigorous five-year degree program. The school's art programs were enhanced with the recent completion of the $5 million Wriston Art Center.

Students praise the university's Freshman Studies program as one of their school's curricular highlights. For the program, in seminar-style courses of no more than 15 students, first-year students study some of the great works of Western thought, including *Discoveries and Opinions of Galileo* and Homer's *Odyssey*. Students must also satisfy general education requirements centered on two themes: Language and Civilization—which includes courses in a foreign language, English literature, art, music or theater, and in history, philosophy, or religion—and Logic and Observation, which consists of courses in math and the social and the natural sciences.

The chance to pursue individual study opportunities is also a hallmark of a Lawrence education, and one that not many students pass up. In a recent year, 72 percent of the students took tutorials, 36 percent did independent study, and 8 percent undertook independent honors projects. According to students, interaction with professors is the school's most effective support network. The Writing Lab, equipped with computers, printers, and peer tutors, is also helpful.

The Black Organization of Students (BOS), which is open to all students on campus, "is very effective in the sense that, if nothing else, it provides students of color with a forum and an audience to hear and discuss whatever problems that the student might be having, be the problem academic, personal, or whatever." In recent years there have been about 15 to 20 active BOS members, and organization members have taken part in events such as a meeting of students representing various Black Student Unions across the state, which was held at the University of Wisconsin in Madison. The BOS also sponsors occasional parties, usually held at the Black Cultural Center, a freestanding house located on the northern edge of campus. The center also has a kitchen and a small library that contains works of African-American writers as well as textbooks.

Although about a third of the students join one or another of the school's five fraternities or three sororities, Greek life in no way dominates. Fraternities hold most of the school's weekend parties, but options such as movies at the Student Center are available. The university also plays host to a list of impressive speakers and performers each year. Lawrence can truly be described as a musical campus; more than 70 percent of the students participate in at least one of its 15 musical groups, which range from the Symphony Orchestra to a well-regarded Jazz Ensemble. Celebrate!, a popular outdoor arts festival, draws community residents to the campus each year.

Appleton (pop. 65,000), a predominantly white community, isn't a source of much entertainment for students, and there is little interaction between Appleton residents and Lawrence students. Usually, when students head off campus, they will make the trek to Madison or Milwaukee, both about two hours away by car; Chicago, a less popular destination, is about four hours away. But most students are content to stay close to home and take advantage of the wealth of activities and events sponsored regularly on campus.

Like most schools in Wisconsin, Lawrence has a relatively low enrollment of students of color, which no doubt reflects the state's demographics. Many of the students of color who do attend hail from either Chicago or Milwaukee. Says a student: "I'd say racial integration on campus is okay, but could definitely be improved. I have noticed in the short time I have been here that the minorities as well as the international students tend to form their own groups, but this is not done to the exclusion of others nor are they excluded by others. I think that this results from the fact that most of the international students come from the same high school or area, and most of the minority students come from the same high school or area. It's the people that come from the same high school who hang around together."

Students are attracted to Lawrence because of its strong tradition in the liberal arts and because of the sense of community fostered by its small size. "I would recommend Lawrence to anyone, whether or not they were a minority student," says a student. "However, I think minority students who are willing to explore and try new experiences will gain more than those who prefer to stay with what they already know. This is also the basic philosophy of a liberal arts education. From what I have experienced in my time here, minority and international students are treated by the school, the school community, and the outlying community just like any other students." Adds an art student: "I would recommend this school if the prospective student is looking for a place where he or she can grow mentally or intellectually and if he or she doesn't mind working hard. If they're looking for a little Morehouse or Party U., I'd look elsewhere."

MARQUETTE UNIVERSITY

Address: 1217 West Wisconsin Avenue, Milwaukee, WI 53233
Phone: (414) 222-6544
Director of Admissions: Leo B. Flynn
Multicultural Student Recruiter: Carlos Garces
1991–92 tuition: $9,540
Room and board: $3,900
Application deadline: Rolling admissions
Financial aid application deadline: 3/1
Non-white freshman admissions: Applicants

for the class of '95: 792
Accepted: 73%
Accepted who enroll: 34%
Applicants accepted who rank in top 10% of high school class: na
In top 25%: 31%
Median SAT: 430 V, 500 M
Median ACT: 25
Full-time undergraduate enrollment: 8,500
Men: 51%
Women: 49%

STUDENT ENROLLMENT

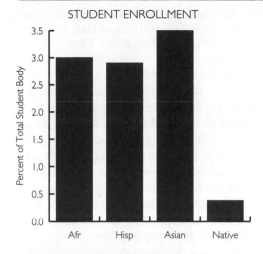

GEOGRAPHIC DISTRIBUTION OF STUDENTS

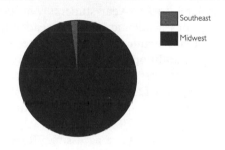

Non-white students in
1987–88: 11%
1988–89: 9.6%
1989–90: 9.9%
1990–91: 9.9%

Students In-state: 82%

Top majors: 1. Business Administration
2. Communication 3. Engineering

Retention rate of non-white students: na

Scholarships exclusively for non-white students: Minority Engineering Scholars: student must be accepted to the College of Engineering; merit portion is up to $4,000 and the need portion offers tuition assistance of up to $2,650.

Remediation programs: The university offers programs in English as a second language.

Academic support services: The university offers academic support services through the Freshman Frontier Program, the Educational Opportunity Program, and the Writing Lab.

Ethnic studies programs: Marquette offers a major in Latin American Studies and an interdisciplinary minor in Asian Studies.

Ethnic studies courses: Three courses in African and African-American Studies, "Native Peoples in North America," "Multicultural Literature," and courses offered through the Latin American and Asian Studies programs.

Organizations for non-white students: Alpha Kappa Alpha, Kappa Alpha Psi, MU Gospel Choir, Black Student Council, Raíces (Hispanic student group), Asian-American Student Association, American Indian Student Association, Multi-Cultural Center

Notable non-white alumni: Glen "Doc" Rivers (professional basketball player, New York Knicks); Ralph L. Metcalfe (former U.S. congressman and Olympic gold medal winner in track and field)

Tenured faculty: 312

Non-tenured faculty: 285

FACULTY

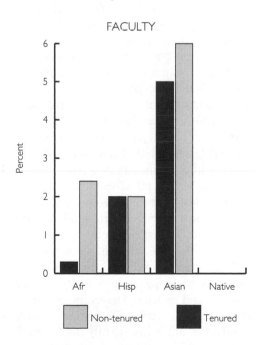

Student-faculty ratio: 15:1

Administrators: 436
   African-American: 5.7%
   Hispanic: 1.3%
   Asian-American: 1%
   Native American: 0.2%

Recent non-white speakers on campus: Jaime Escalante (educator); Dr. Rafael Venegas (consul general, Colombia); Dick Gregory (author and political activist); Rodney Grant (actor)

There are those who choose to attend Marquette, which enrolls sizable numbers of in-state and Chicago students, because it is close to home. But most students come here because of the university's commitment to the liberal arts in a Catholic context.

The 112-year-old university has nine different undergraduate divisions. The school's most popular courses are in the School of Business Administration, which offers majors in accounting, business economics, and business administration, as well as concentrations in numerous other areas, such as finance. Political science, philosophy, and religion are among the best departments in the College of Arts and Sciences. The journalism program is outstanding, as are the offerings in engineering.

Marquette has a variety of academic support services. Students say the Educational Opportunity Program is very effective in providing tutoring and advice about course selection. The Freshman Frontier Program, available to first-year students who do not meet regular admissions standards, also provides academic and non-academic support. As part of the program, students must attend a summer orientation before the beginning of their first year at the university. In addition, students must carry a reduced academic work load. The Writing Lab's student tutors assist students in almost every aspect of the writing process. "The Writing Lab has been very helpful to me," says a junior. "The student tutors offer good, sound advice, and I know they've also helped other students."

Although the university is midsize, students say professors are accessible. Rarely are they too busy for students, even when heavily involved in their own research. Priests live in many of the on-campus dorms, and many become friends and mentors of individual students.

Students are able to find non-academic support at the school's Multi-Cultural Center (MCC), established in 1972. "The MCC is our lifeblood," says a student. "It's the center of everything for Marquette's minority students." There are two deans in the MCC who advise students about non-academic matters and assist cultural student groups in coordinating and scheduling programs and activities. "The deans are one hundred percent effective in relating to students," says a student. The MCC, located in the school's student union, has a lounge and a multicultural library.

The most active cultural student group on campus is the Black Student Council (BSC), which focuses a great deal of its attention on events for Black History Month. Recently the BSC brought various civil rights activists to campus and sponsored an African-American dinner. In addition, the BSC sponsored a College Bowl, in which students participated in a contest based on their knowledge of African-American history and culture. The event, which took place in Weasler Auditorium, was well attended by students. On campus there is also a historically black fraternity, Kappa Alpha Psi, and a historically black sorority, Alpha Kappa Alpha, which work closely with the BSC in planning events and activities.

Other groups sponsor occasional, yet significant, events during the school year.

The American Indian Student Association, for example, sponsors an annual daylong powwow, in which tribes from around the state come to campus to participate in an arts and crafts sale and a dance contest. The day ends with a dinner. Raíces, Marquette's Hispanic student group, provides a social outlet for students and brings various speakers to campus.

All the groups have come together to demand that the university institute a cultural diversity course to be required of all students. The proposed course, as designed by the students, is to cover Asian-American, Native American, African-American, Hispanic, and European issues. Students aren't optimistic about the chances of its being added to the curriculum, however. "The administration, including the president of the university, is dead set against such a course," says a student. "But we're still going to try because we think it's important to make the campus more aware of multicultural issues."

Marquette is located near downtown Milwaukee, the home of the Brewers and the Bucks, professional baseball and basketball teams, respectively, and more bars than you can lift a mug to. Going into the city for nightlife—especially to nearby Wells Street with its myriad of bars—is common practice, but students also host their own dorm room parties.

Much of the on-campus activity is courtesy of the Associated Students of Marquette University (ASMU), which brings concerts, dances, and speakers to campus. With its indoor tennis courts, Universal weight room, and swimming pool, students have more than enough reason to unwind at the Helfaer Tennis Stadium and Recreation Center. The Warriors may not be as strong as when Al McGuire led the team to the NCAA Division I championship in 1977, but the basketball squad still draws crowds. WMUR, the university's radio station, and MUTV, its television station, provide impressive equipment for student use.

Students of color say there is not much diverse programming when it comes to campus-wide social events, but they point to the revitalized weekly Pub Nights as a sign of progress. Each week, different types of music are played, including rap, jazz, and Latino rhythms.

With its high crime rate, the neighborhood in which the university is located has never been anything to brag about, let alone travel into unescorted. The university is proposing to spend $20 million during the next several years refurbishing the area, including renovating housing, providing health-care services, and creating an alternative high school for at-risk students. "This is a neighborhood in crisis," says an assistant to Marquette's president, in a recent *New York Times* article about the proposed renovations. "We have to be the catalyst. If this whole west area is not saved as a good neighborhood then the city of Milwaukee has some major problems."

Although many of the students at Marquette are from the Wisconsin/Illinois area, the university also attracts students from every state in the Union and from more than 50 foreign countries. And, as a Jesuit institution, the university attracts a sizable Catholic student population.

Marquette may be in a city, but it is far from being a city university. More than three-quarters of its students live on campus, and there is a sense of community here—thanks in large part to a committed faculty—that isn't common among other, more urban universities. "The people I've met here have been great, and trying to get the multicultural course requirement instituted has been a learning experience. Although I may get frustrated with the administration sometimes, I feel I'm getting a good education."

RIPON COLLEGE

Address: 300 Seward Street, P.O. Box 248, Ripon, WI 54971
Phone: (800) 94-RIPON
Director of Admissions: Paul J. Weeks
Multicultural Student Recruiter: Tami Thronson
1993–94 tuition: $14,340
Room and board: $3,810
Application deadline: 3/15
Financial aid application deadline: 4/15
Non-white freshman admissions: Applicants for the class of '95: 66
Accepted: 70%
Accepted who enroll: 41%
Applicants accepted who rank in top 10% of high school class: 15%
In top 25%: 55%
Median SAT range: 400–510 V, 480–540 M
Median ACT range: 18–24
Full-time undergraduate enrollment: 838
Men: 50.3%
Women: 49.7%

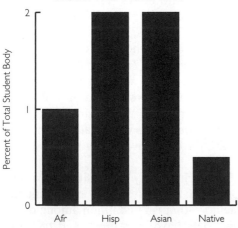

STUDENT ENROLLMENT

Percent of Total Student Body

Afr   Hisp   Asian   Native

Non-white students in
1988–89: 4%
1989–90: 4%
1990–91: 4%
1991–92: 5%
Geographic distribution of students: na
Students In-state: 40%
Top majors: 1. English 2. History 3. Politics and Government
Retention rate of non-white students: na
Scholarships exclusively for non-white students: None
Remediation programs: None
Academic support services: The Educational Development Program offers academic support.
Ethnic studies programs: The college offers a program in Latin American studies.
Ethnic studies courses: The college's history department offers three courses that focus on American minority themes
Organizations for non-white students: Multicultural Club
Notable non-white alumni: Al Jarreau ('62, Psychology; jazz singer); Loretta House Webster ('59, Biology; vice-chancellor, University of Wisconsin at Stevens Point); Jerry Waukau ('78, Anthropology/Economics; health administrator, Menominee Tribal Clinic); Daniel T. Mao ('73, History/Russian; director of marketing and operations, Asia, U.S. Summit); Dr. William C. Jordan ('69, History/Russian; professor of history, Princeton University)
Tenured faculty: na
Non-tenured faculty: na
Student-faculty ratio: 11:1
Administrators: na
Recent non-white speakers on campus: Dick Gregory (author and political activist)

With a little over 800 students and a student-to-faculty ratio of only 11 to 1, Ripon College can't help but provide its students with an intimate setting for their liberal arts educations. According to university statistics, the average class size at Ripon is 12 students and 80 percent of the classes have fewer than 20 students.

Ripon stresses the traditional liberal arts in its curriculum. To graduate, students must complete distribution requirements in behavioral science, fine arts, humanities, natural sciences, mathematics, a foreign language, and writing. Students claim that Ripon's best departments are history and the physical sciences, especially chemistry, while economics, politics and government, and anthropology also enjoy good reputations. "American Race Relations and Immigration," "Introduction to African History," and "Historians and South Africa" are described by one student as "excellent." Russell Blake, who teaches the "American Race Relations and Immigration" course, is described by a student as someone "I could be open with in class about anything that had to do with racial issues."

To help students keep up with their studies, the Educational Development Program offers both peer counseling and tutoring in all academic subjects. One student who has taken advantage of the program describes it as "quite effective." Adds another student: "Students who go to the program finish their classes with better grades." The program's director, Dan Khrin, who is also an adviser to the Multicultural Club on campus, is "active in getting information about the program out to students."

Ripon, like other schools in Wisconsin, has a relatively small student of color population. The Multicultural Club serves as a source of support for many of these students. One member says that the organization is "very influential and active" in organizing events and bringing speakers to campus. Recently it sponsored activities for Black History Month spread out over a three-day weekend. Events included a step show performed by members of Alpha Phi Alpha, a traditionally black fraternity from the University of Wisconsin/Oshkosh, as well as a talent show and a soul food dinner.

The club has three faculty advisers, including Dan Khrin; Dean Katahira, a chemistry professor; and Leslie Bessent, a history professor. Students describe these advisers as "supportive" and "helpful" in talking with students about personal problems and in getting events off the ground. Students also comment that Katahira serves as a role model for students on campus. "Katahira is very supportive of students, whether they're minority or Caucasian," observes a student. Recently, Katahira was involved in organizing Christmas Around the World, an event for which students and faculty provided food from various cultures.

For the first time in the college's history, the school will now have a Black Student Union (BSU). One of the African-American students instrumental in organizing the BSU says that the group's name generated a "great deal of controversy" on campus. "Students and faculty were concerned that we were going to be a group segregated from the rest of the campus," explains the student. "We had to go before the student senate at least three times before they would approve our name." As of this writing, the BSU does not have an office, nor does it have any activities planned. Professor Blake of the history department will be the BSU's faculty adviser. "He is open to all students of color. We are glad that he consented to be the adviser."

There are six fraternities, two sororities, and one coed fraternity active at Ripon, all of which are predominantly white. Much of the social life at Ripon centers on these organizations, and students of color say they've never been made to feel uncomfortable at any of their functions. Most of the fraternities and sororities are housed in student dormitories, and all members of Greek organizations eat with non-Greeks in Pickard Commons, the college dining hall. For such a small college, Ripon sponsors an impressive list of extracurricular clubs and activities: a big brother/big sister program, a Women's Educational Support Organization, and various musical groups, just to name a few.

The town of Ripon (pop. 17,000) is very much of the Midwest; it is a small town where the people are friendly and the streets are clean. Besides saying hello to passersby on the street, there's little to do. But Milwaukee and Madison, both of which are hubs of social and cultural activity, are only ninety minutes away, while Chicago, only three hours south, is also a popular destination for those who need big-city diversions.

Although Ripon has a small student of color population, one student says that the campus has changed since she started there four years ago. "Because of the work done by the Multicultural Club," says the recent graduate, "Ripon students are more aware of the issues facing minority citizens in this country."

UNIVERSITY OF WISCONSIN/MADISON

Address: 750 University Avenue, Madison, WI 53706
Phone: (608) 262-3961
Director of Admissions: Millard Storey
Multicultural Student Recruiter: Roxanne Allison
1992–93 tuition: $2,290 (in-state); $7,480 (out-of-state)
Room and board: $3,850
Application deadline: 2/1
Financial aid application deadline: 2/1
Non-white freshman admissions: Applicants for the class of '94: 1,487
Accepted: 70.7%
Accepted who enroll: 36%
Applicants accepted who rank in top 10% of high school class: 25%
In top 25%: 63%
Median SAT range: 408–535 V, 511–655 M
Median ACT range: 20–27
Full-time undergraduate enrollment: 25,043
Men: 50%
Women: 50%

Non-white students in
1988–89: 6.2%
1989–90: 6.7%
1990–91: 7.1%
1991–92: 7.1%
Geographic distribution of students: na
Students In-state: 71%
Top majors: 1. Electrical Engineering 2. Mechanical Engineering 3. Bacteriology
Retention rate of non-white students: 60%
Scholarships exclusively for non-white students: Chancellor Scholarship: available to underrepresented ethnic minorities; merit-based; available to state and out-of-state residents; amount for in-state recipients covers tuition and fees, while out-of-state recipients receive up to $4,500 annually.
Remediation programs: Developmental courses in reading and math are offered.
Academic support services: The university offers chemistry tutorials and tutoring in most other academic areas, as well as a

STUDENT ENROLLMENT

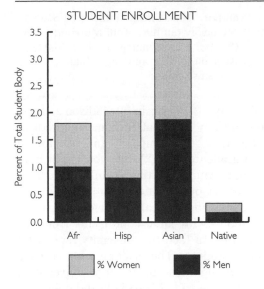

Percent of Total Student Body

% Women   % Men

writing lab and courses in developing study skills.

Ethnic studies programs: The university offers an Asian-American Studies major, established in 1970, involving more than 50 courses. Honors courses are available in the program. Faculty: 10. UW also has an African languages and literature department, the only such department in the country, as well as Afro American, Asian American, Asian, and Latin American Studies.

Ethnic studies courses: As part of a 3-credit ethnic studies course requirement, students are able to choose from 100 such courses.

Organizations for non-white students: Alpha Kappa Alpha, Alpha Phi Alpha, Delta Sigma Theta, Kappa Alpha Psi, Omega Psi Phi, Phi Beta Sigma, Zeta Phi Beta, American Indian Science and Engineering Society, Asian-American Student Union, Black Greek Panhellenic Council, Committee for the Study of the African Diaspora, La Colectiva Cultural de Aztlan, MECHA, Multi-Ethnic Business Student Society, Pacific Asian Women's Alliance, Unión Puertorriqueña, Black Engineering Society, Black Student Union, Womanist

Colectiva, Wunk-Sheek, Hmong Student Association

Notable non-white alumni: Robert Teague (Journalism; NBC commentator); Richard Lowe III (History; justice, New York Supreme Court); Sidney B. Williams (Chemical Engineering; patent director); Elzie L. Higginbottom (Agricultural Economics; president, East Lake Management)

FACULTY

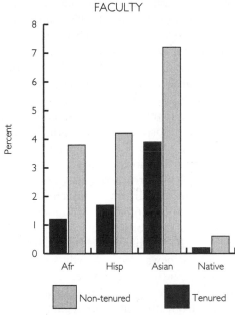

Percent

Non-tenured   Tenured

Tenured faculty: 1,770
Non-tenured faculty: 529
Student-faculty ratio: 12:1
Administrators: 505
  African-American: 4%
  Hispanic: 2.2%
  Asian-American: 0.8%
  Native American: 0.4%
Recent non-white speakers on campus: Dr. Betty Shabazz (widow of Malcolm X, director of communications and public relations, Medgar Evers College); Avery Brooks (actor, director, musician, professor of theater, Rutgers University); Cesar Chavez (labor leader and head of the United Farm Workers); Dr. Melvin

Peters (associate professor, Duke University); Faye Wattleton (former president, Planned Parenthood); Lola Lai Jong (poet and author); Kitty Tsui (poet and author); Audre Lord (poet and author); Nien Cheng (author); N. Scott Momaday (author); Toni Morrison (Pulitzer Prize-winning novelist); Maya Angelou (author and poet); Juan Williams (author)

There are as many opportunities at the University of Wisconsin in Madison as there are students on the Union terrace on just about any spring afternoon. Hundreds of students pack the terrace to appreciate the view, the company, and (we are in Wisconsin, after all) the beer. As one recent graduate says: "While you might have trouble finding an empty chair on the terrace, you won't find it difficult to take advantage of the university's academic and social opportunities."

The 144-year-old university is indeed huge, and geographically diverse. The college enrolls students from every state in the Union—with large contingents from the Northeast—and more than 125 foreign countries. In fact, the university ranks fifth among all U.S. universities in number of foreign students. This diversity adds a certain sophistication to the campus that is rare among most other large universities, particularly in the Midwest, and no doubt contributes to UW's socially and politically charged atmosphere. Along with Berkeley, UW was one of the most politically active campuses in the country during the 1960s. Today, as one student noted, there are still demonstrations going on somewhere on campus almost every day of the week, whether it's a pro-choice rally or a gay rights demonstration.

Students are drawn to the school for its incredible breadth and wealth of academic programs, some of which rank among the best in the country. The nationally recognized business school offers more than 10 majors, including marketing, accounting, and real estate. The journalism school is also top-notch, offering courses in public relations, broadcast news, and news-editorial. Among the school's programs in the liberal arts, history, math, sociology, economics, German, and political science are excellent. Biology, chemistry, and physics are first-rate. The engineering school also earns high marks from students. Recent campus additions include new engineering and computer science buildings. The school has an Ethnic Reading Area in the College Library.

Wisconsin's African Studies Program is one of the major centers in the country for study and research about Africa. In addition, the African Languages and Literature major is the only such program in the country. Harold Scheub, a professor in the program, "is really dynamic in class, even if there are more than 200 students in the room." The school's Afro-American Studies program is excellent, according to students, and the Asian-American Studies program, established in 1990 as a result of numerous student protests, is the only such program in the Midwest. Amy Ling, head of the program and a professor of English, is a favorite with students. Her course "Asian-American Women Writers" is popularly received. "Rather than lecture to us, Ling tries to get us to enter lively discussions about the material we read in class," says a student.

Don't expect to establish an easy rapport with professors in introductory courses. Classes can number in the hundreds, but upper-level courses can be more intimate, sometimes with as few as 20 or 30 students.

Social opportunities abound at this mega-university, and students say the cultural student groups are influential and active. "The minority organizations on this campus work very hard to make UW/Madison a great place to be," says a student. Recently, for example, the Asian-American Student Union organized the school's first Asian-American Week. The week was so popular that the group has expanded it to a month. The Black Student Union, MECHA, and La Colectiva Cultural de Aztlan, a Mexican-American student group, are also active on campus, sponsoring forums, guest lecturers, films, and parties. Wunk-Sheek, a Native American student group, sponsors an annual powwow.

Established in 1988, the Interim Multicultural Center (IMCC), located in the Memorial Union, is a popular place on campus for students. According to a senior, the IMCC provides "an excellent home for interested minority students. It is a place where I can be respected, where I can be different and still be appreciated. There is no other place better for minority students on campus. The offices of the five largest minority organizations are housed in one room of the IMCC. This is where I have had the most opportunity to interact with minority students. This is where I get all my education on multiculturalism and diversity." According to students, the IMCC is to get a permanent home at the Red Barn, a gymnasium and a national historic landmark on campus that will be converted into office space for student use. The plan to convert the building is under review by the advisory board to the state governor.

Students report that, for the most part, the campus has good relations with the Madison community. "For example, at the last Chicano dance I attended, the guests ranged from young children to the elderly of the area," says a student. "I know that the Chicano student organization, La Colectiva Cultural de Atzlan, and the community depend on each other for support. Similarly, the Hmong students are very connected with their community. A recent demonstration organized by our Hmong Student Association brought in hundreds of Hmong from all over the state." Adds another student: "The relations between minority students and the community are very close. Madison is still a very tolerant place for minorities."

Students also participate in a myriad of other social activities, ranging from intramurals and professional associations to political clubs and religious organizations. State Street is *the* scene on campus. The street is lined with vendors, preachers shouting their sermons, restaurants of all varieties, and bars galore. And any Badger football game, whether the team is losing or winning, is, in a word, wild.

Despite the campus's more open-minded atmosphere, it hasn't been without incidents of racism. Recently, two predominantly white fraternities—Phi Gamma Delta and Zeta Phi Beta—committed offenses that received local and national media attention and mobilized much of the campus. The Phi Gamma Delta fraternity's annual Fiji Island bash featured a caricature of a black man with a bone through his nose, and Zeta Phi Beta held a "slave auction." According to one student, the incidents had one positive side effect. "One of the greatest results of the incidents was the formation of the Minority Coalition, in which, for the first time, the various minority groups united to mobilize against such occurrences in the future." The formation of the coalition also started a dialogue among the groups that hadn't existed before the incidents.

Wisconsin's student publications, particularly the conservative *Badger Herald,* have also been the source of recent controversy. "The *Daily Cardinal,* a liberal-to-moderate publication, has consistently supported the issues of minority students," says a senior. "Their editorials often deal with minority or women's issues. But the *Herald* is very conservative, running editorials against affirmative action and against the efforts minority groups have made during the past years. Last year, the coalition even went so far as to boycott the paper, by not advertising in it and by refusing to speak to its reporters. This year the boycott was lifted, although I would dare to say that most minority student activists still choose not to speak with the *Herald,* myself included."

Like the state in which it is located, the University of Wisconsin, despite its geographic diversity, is a racially homogeneous institution. In 1988, as a way to encourage more students of color to enroll at the university, the administration instituted the Madison Plan, the goal of which was to double the number of non-white students on campus in five years. According to reports, the plan has been ineffective. Officials blame the poor performance on personnel turnover and state budget plans. "I feel it was the turnover and the hiring freeze [of admissions recruiters] that really cramped our style," said Akbar Ally, coordinator of the plan and special assistant to the vice-chancellor for academic affairs, in a *Chronicle of Higher Education* article.

But many students had long been critical of the plan. "From the very beginning, one of the big complaints about the Madison Plan was that it was full of rhetoric," says a former Asian-American student leader in the *Chronicle* article. "Lofty promises but little action or concrete suggestions." Students also complain they had little input in formulating the plan. Recently, however, the administration has sought student input on how to more effectively recruit students of color. "They decided to wait until failure was inevitable before turning to students," says a campus leader.

Despite some of the recent controversies on campus—and the school's relative homogeneity—students recommend UW to prospective minority applicants as much for its high-powered academics as for "the sensitivity of much of the student body to minority issues." Adds another student: "Madison is a good school with a strong national reputation. I've learned a great deal here, as much from the classroom as from my extracurricular activities. The IMCC has been one of the best classrooms, and I know many of the other students of color feel the same way. It's made the big-college experience more manageable."

WYOMING

UNIVERSITY OF WYOMING

Address: Laramie, WY 82071-3435
Phone: (307) 766-5160 / (800) 342-5996
Director of Admissions: Richard A. Davis
Multicultural Student Recruiter: Oliver
  Wilson
1993–94 tuition: $1,648 (in-state); $5,182
  (out-of-state)
Room and board: $3,341
Application deadline: 8/10
Financial aid application deadline: 3/1
Non-white freshman admissions: na
  Median SAT: na
  Median ACT: na
Full-time undergraduate enrollment: 8,156
  Men: 50%
  Women: 50%
Non-white students in
  1987–88: 5.59%
  1988–89: 6%
  1989–90: 6%
  1990–91: 6.8%
Geographic distribution of students: na
Top majors: na
Retention rate of non-white students: na
**Scholarships exclusively for non-white
  students:** na
Remediation programs: Remedial instruction
  is available in most academic subjects.
Academic support services: The university
  provides a Learning Center.
Ethnic studies programs: A minor course of
  study is available in Japanese Studies,
which includes courses in Japanese
language and literature.
Ethnic studies courses: The history
  department offers two courses in East
  Asian Studies, "History of Indians of the
  United States," and "Latin American
  Civilization." The political science and
  English departments also offer ethnic
  studies courses.
Organizations for non-white students:
  Association of Black Student Leaders,
  Hispanic Student Organization,
  Asian-American Student Association,

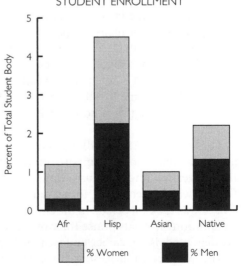

STUDENT ENROLLMENT

Keepers of the Fire (Native American
student group)
Notable non-white alumni: na
Tenured faculty: 393
Non-tenured faculty: 220

Student-faculty ratio: 19:1
Administrators: 94
Recent non-white speakers on campus: Don
Reed (comedian); Lettleton Altsone
(artist); Gregory Russell (artist)

The University of Wyoming, located at 7,200 feet above sea level in the Rocky
Mountains, is the only four-year university—public or private—in the state. State
residents are proud of their university, especially its football team. "People from all
over the state come in droves to watch the Cowboys play football," says a fan.

The university is divided into six undergraduate colleges: agriculture, arts and
sciences, commerce and industry, education, engineering, and health sciences. The
school's engineering program is top-notch and offers majors in agricultural, electrical,
and chemical engineering. Wyoming's petroleum engineering and geology programs
are among the best in the country. The commerce and industry division has three
departments: accounting, economics, and business. The music program is said to be
outstanding.

"Although we don't have many courses in cultural studies, the ones we do have
are really good," says a senior. Students point to such highly regarded courses as
"African Politics" and a course offered by the American Studies department called
"Cultural Diversity." "History of Indians of the United States," "Chicano Studies,"
and "Native American Studies" are also popular. Lewis Nkosi, a professor of
English and a noted South African author, teaches here. Colin Colloway, a history
professor whose specialty is Native American history, "is a real asset to the
university," says a student. "His classes are always so full that some people have
to sit on the floor."

With only a little more than 8,100 students, Wyoming is a relatively small state
university, which means gaining access to faculty isn't as difficult as it might be
at larger institutions. Students still complain, however, that introductory courses
can be huge, sometimes numbering more than 300 students. "But," adds a student,
"there are a lot of really supportive faculty and administrators." Three individuals
whom students often point to as supporters, especially of cultural activities, are
Terry Roark, the university's president, Albert Karnig, provost and vice president
for academic and student affairs, and James Hurst, associate provost for student
affairs. "They come to the Association of Black Student Leaders [ABSL] meetings
and events, and they know me by my first name," says a student active in the
ABSL.

The Minority Affairs Office, located in Knight Hall, offers tutoring in all academic
areas, as well as other support services, which students say are effective. Recently,
the university hired Adenay Coker to head its new African-American Education
Office, which, according to a student, "offers cultural and educational support."
Coker was the first person in the country to earn a Ph.D. in African-American Studies.
In addition, students praise the work of the Indian Education Office, which provides
academic advising, career counseling, and tutoring to students.

The Multicultural Resource Center (MRC), located in the Wyoming Union, is
primarily a social spot. The MRC has a small library of books by Native American,

African-American, Hispanic, and Asian-American authors and two computers. "We use the office to meet friends, to have meetings, to eat in, or just to relax between or after classes," says a student. The director of the office, Jason Thompson, "is very helpful in telling you how to go about getting something done and how to avoid the bureaucracy of the place," says a student leader.

The Association of Black Student Leaders sponsors several annual events, including a fashion show and a Gospel Extravaganza, both held during Black History Month. The group, with about 15 active members, also sponsors lectures and panel discussions throughout the school year. With the university, the ABSL is sponsoring a photo exhibit, "I Dream a World," which has been on national tour. Several of the ABSL's panel discussions are directed at including the African-American male athletes in campus life, "because often they come from larger cities and aren't used to the slower pace here, and they don't tend to get involved in clubs, so we try to help them out," says an ABSL leader.

MECHA, the Hispanic student organization, meets weekly and has about 15 members. The group's energies are mostly focused on coordinating events for Chicano Week, usually held during the fall semester. Recent events have included speakers, a performance by a Mexican dance group, a banquet, and a dance.

Each spring members of the Keepers of the Fire, a Native American student group, sponsor a powwow, which features dancing, singing, and arts and crafts displays by Native American area residents. According to members, the event is well attended by students, faculty, and Laramie residents.

The school's Ethnic Minority Council, which consists of members of the four cultural student organizations on campus, has become more vocal and active in recent years. The council serves as a liaison between Wyoming's students of color and the student government organization, which oversees budgeting for all campus groups. One student reports that because of the Ethnic Minority Council more money has been given to cultural student groups for events and speakers.

The predominant mood on campus, politically and socially, is conservative, according to students, and "there can sometimes be a problem with diversity issues here. But there are a lot of good things going on," says a student. "Last year [1991–92] two African-American students ran for the positions of student body president and vice president; they lost, but by very few votes. We all thought that was a good sign; it was a close race." Students of color on campus have had the most difficulty with the school's newspaper, *The Branding Iron.* "There's been outright racism in the paper. For instance, whenever there's a fight on campus involving black and white students, the black students are always blamed for it. Their names are plastered all over the paper, they print their ages, and the person, if he's black, is always identified as black, even if race isn't an issue. Things got really heated last year between the paper's editorial staff and the black students on campus, and even the administration got involved. This year, there's a new staff and we're hopeful that the paper's attitudes will change."

Some of the more heated battles between black and white students take place at the Drawbridge Club, across the street from campus. "Some of the cowboys from the area and the black students, especially athletes, will start fighting with little reason," says a student. But, adds the student, "the fights aren't always race-related.

The football team recently got into a fight with the baseball team, or they'll start because of personality conflicts." Despite the off-campus barroom brawls, students often describe the on-campus scene as friendly.

Laramie is a predominantly white community of about 26,000 residents; there is a small African-American community and a comparatively large Hispanic community in town. Residents frequently attend ABSL events, particularly the Gospel Extravaganza, and students attend services at some of the area's black churches. Recently, ABSL members visited a nearby elementary school, where they read folk tales to students, and conducted panel discussions at area junior high and high schools. Also in town is a Latin American Club, which is frequently visited by students. The town also offers several movie theaters, restaurants, and an ice-skating rink. The Whirl Inn and the Bridge are among the clubs and restaurants that are popular with African-American students.

What sets Laramie apart from other college towns is the surrounding countryside, which more than one student describes as "spectacular." "If you're into wide-open spaces, this is the place to come," says a student. "The air is clean, the mountains are only ten minutes from campus, and there's all sorts of opportunities nearby to fish, hunt, hike, and rock-climb." Laramie is also located near some cultural and social centers, such as Denver, Colorado, which is about two hours from campus. Cheyenne, only about forty-five minutes away by car, is home to an Air Force base and is the site of an annual Ebony Fashion Show. The university is an hour from Fort Collins, Colorado, the hometown of Colorado State University. "There's a big black student population at CSU," says a Wyoming student, "and a lot of students will go down there for the weekends for parties and to go to the clubs." Wyoming has a program with CSU in which students are able to study at one another's university for a semester or a year at in-state tuition prices.

For the student who hails from a large city, or even a medium-sized one, attending school at the University of Wyoming will probably be something of a culture shock. "But once the student gets over that, then this can be a really great place to go to school," says a student. "Yes, sitting in a class of three hundred students where you're one of three students of color can be a bit much. But that has its advantages, because you can really make a difference here, especially if you get involved in student organizations."

AMERICA'S PREDOMINANTLY BLACK COLLEGES AND UNIVERSITIES

Schools marked with an asterisk are members of the United Negro College Fund, which supplied the information contained in this list.

ALABAMA (12)

Alabama A & M University
Huntsville, AL 35762
(205) 859-7011

Alabama State University
Montgomery, AL 36195
(205) 872-4201

S. D. Bishop State Junior College
Mobile, AL 36690
(205) 690-6412

Concordia College
Selma, AL 36701
(205) 872-3053

Lawson State Community College
Birmingham, AL 35221
(205) 925-1666

Lomax-Hannon Junior College
Greenville, AL 36037
(205) 382-6605

*Miles College
Birmingham, AL 35208
(205) 923-2771

*Oakwood College
Huntsville, AL 35896
(205) 837-1630

Selma University
Selma, AL 36701
(205) 872-2533

*Stillman College
Tuscaloosa, AL 35403
(205) 349-4240

*Talladega College
Talladega, AL 35160
(205) 362-2752

Tuskegee University
Tuskegee, AL 36088
(205) 727-8011

ARKANSAS (4)

Arkansas Baptist College
Little Rock, AR 72202
(501) 372-6883

*Philander Smith College
Little Rock, AR 72202
(501) 375-3117

Shorter College
North Little Rock, AR 72114
(501) 374-6305

University of Arkansas/Pine Bluff
Pine Bluff, AR 71601
(501) 541-6500

DELAWARE (1)

Delaware State College
Dover, DE 19901
(302) 736-4901

DISTRICT OF COLUMBIA (2)

Howard University
Washington, DC 20059
(202) 806-2752

University of the District of Columbia
Washington, DC 20008
(202) 282-7550

FLORIDA (4)

*Bethune-Cookman College
Daytona Beach, FL 32015
(904) 255-1401

*Edward Waters College
Jacksonville, FL 32209
(904) 355-3030

Florida A & M University
Tallahassee, FL 32307
(904) 599-3225

*Florida Memorial College
Miami, FL 33054
(305) 625-4141

GEORGIA (10)

Albany State College
Albany, GA 31705
(912) 439-4095

*Clark Atlanta University
Atlanta, GA 30314
(404) 880-8000

The Fort Valley State College
Fort Valley, GA 31030
(912) 825-6315

*Interdenominational Theological Center
Atlanta, GA 30314
(404) 522-1772

*Morehouse College
Atlanta, GA 30314
(404) 681-2800

Morehouse School of Medicine
Atlanta, GA 30310
(404) 752-1500

*Morris Brown College
Atlanta, GA 30314
(404) 525-7831

*Paine College
Augusta, GA 30910
(404) 722-4471

Savannah State College
Savannah, GA 31404
(912) 356-2240

*Spelman College
Atlanta, GA 30314
(404) 681-3643

KENTUCKY (2)

Kentucky State University
Frankfort, KY 40601
(502) 564-2550

Simmons University Bible College
Louisville, KY 40210
(502) 776-1443

LOUISIANA (6)

*Dillard University
New Orleans, LA 70122
(504) 283-8822

Grambling State University
Grambling, LA 71245
(318) 247-6941

Southern University System
Baton Rouge, LA 70813
(504) 771-4680

Southern University/New Orleans
New Orleans, LA 70126
(504) 486-7411

Southern University/Shreveport
Shreveport, LA 71107
(318) 674-3300

*Xavier University of Louisiana
New Orleans, LA 70125
(504) 483-7577

MARYLAND (4)

Bowie State College
Bowie, MD 20715
(301) 464-3000

Coppin State College
Baltimore, MD 21216
(301) 383-4500

Morgan State University
Baltimore, MD 21239
(301) 444-3333

University of Maryland/Eastern Shore
Princess Anne, MD 21853
(301) 651-2200

MICHIGAN (1)

Shaw College at Detroit
Detroit, MI 48202
(313) 873-7920

MISSISSIPPI (11)

Alcorn State University
Loman, MS 39096
(601) 877-6100

Coahoma Junior College
Clarksdale, MS 38614
(601) 627-2571

Jackson State University
Jackson, MS 39217
(601) 968-2121

Mary Holmes College
West Point, MS 39773
(601) 494-6820

Mississippi Industrial College
Holly Spring, MS 38835
(601) 252-1750

Mississippi Valley State University
Itta Bena, MS 38941
(601) 254-9041

Natchez Junior College
Natchez, MS 39120
(601) 445-9702

Prestiss Normal and Industrial Institute
Prestiss, MS 39474
(601) 792-5175

*Rust College
Holly Springs, MS 38635
(601) 252-4661

*Tougaloo College
Tougaloo, MS 39174
(601) 956-4941

Utica Junior College
Utica, MS 39175
(601) 886-8085

MISSOURI (2)

Harris-Stowe State College
St. Louis, MO 63103
(314) 533-3366

Lincoln University
Jefferson City, MO 65101
(314) 751-2325

NORTH CAROLINA (11)

*Barber-Scotia College
Concord, NC 28025
(704) 786-5171

*Bennett College
Greensboro, NC 27402
(919) 273-4431

Elizabeth City State University
Elizabeth City, NC 27909
(919) 335-0551

Fayetteville State University
Fayetteville, NC 28301
(919) 486-1141

*Johnson C. Smith University
Charlotte, NC 28216
(704) 378-1000

*Livingstone College
Salisbury, NC 28144
(704) 633-7960

North Carolina A & T University
Greensboro, NC 27411
(919) 379-7500

North Carolina Central University
Durham, NC 27707
(919) 683-6100

*St. Augustine's College
Raleigh, NC 27611
(919) 828-4451

*Shaw University
Raleigh, NC 27611
(919) 755-4920

Winston-Salem State University
Winston-Salem, NC 27110
(919) 761-2011

OKLAHOMA (1)

Langston University
Langston, OK 73050
(405) 466-2231

PENNSYLVANIA (2)

Cheyney University
Cheyney, PA 19319
(215) 758-6332

Lincoln University
Lincoln University, PA 19352
(215) 932-8300

SOUTH CAROLINA (8)

Allen University
Columbia, SC 29204
(803) 254-4165

*Benedict College
Columbia, SC 29204
(803) 256-4220

*Claflin College
Orangeburg, SC 29115
(803) 256-2710

Clinton Junior College
Rock Hill, SC 29732
(803) 327-7402

Denmark Technical College
Denmark, SC 29042
(803) 793-3301

*Morris College
Sumter, SC 29150
(803) 775-9371

South Carolina State College
Orangeburg, SC 29115
(803) 536-7013

*Voorhees College
Denmark, SC 29042
(803) 793-3351

TENNESSEE (7)

*Fisk University
Nashville, TN 37203
(615) 329-8500

*Knoxville College
Knoxville, TN 37914
(615) 524-6514

*Lane College
Jackson, TN 38301
(901) 424-4600

*LeMoyne-Owen College
Memphis, TN 38126
(901) 774-9090

Meharry Medical College
Nashville, TN 37208
(615) 327-6111

Morristown College
Morristown, TN 37814
(615) 586-5282

Tennessee State University
Nashville, TN 37203
(615) 320-3432

TEXAS (9)

*Bishop College
Dallas, TX 75241
(214) 372-8000

*Huston-Tillotson College
Austin, TX 78702
(512) 476-7421

*Jarvis Christian College
Hawkins, TX 75765
(214) 769-2174

*Paul Quinn College
Waco, TX 76704
(817) 752-5891

Prairie View A & M University
Prairie View, TX 77445
(409) 857-3311

Southwestern Christian College
Terrell, TX 75160
(214) 563-3341

*Texas College
Tyler, TX 75703
(214) 593-8311

Texas Southern University
Houston, TX 77004
(713) 527-7036

*Wiley College
Marshall, TX 75670
(214) 938-8341

VIRGINIA (6)

Hampton Institute
Hampton, VA 23668
(804) 727-5231

Norfolk State University
Norfolk, VA 23504
(804) 623-8760

*St. Paul's College
Lawrenceville, VA 23868
(804) 848-4451

The Virginia Seminary and College
Lynchburg, VA 24501
(804) 528-5276

Virginia State University
Petersburg, VA 23803
(804) 520-6572

*Virginia Union University
Richmond, VA 23220
(804) 257-5600

WEST VIRGINIA (1)

West Virginia State College
Institute, WV 25112
(304) 766-3111

VIRGIN ISLANDS (1)

College of the Virgin Islands
St. Thomas, US VI 00801
(809) 774-9200